AN EARLY TOWN ON THE DEH LURAN PLAIN
EXCAVATIONS AT TEPE FARUKHABAD

Plate 1. Polychrome Decorated Jar (X063).

MEMOIRS OF THE MUSEUM OF ANTHROPOLOGY
UNIVERSITY OF MICHIGAN
NUMBER 13

AN EARLY TOWN ON THE DEH LURAN PLAIN
EXCAVATIONS AT TEPE FARUKHABAD

EDITED BY HENRY T. WRIGHT

With Contributions By:
Ellen Berger
Barbara Bohr
Antoinette B. Brown
Elizabeth Carter
Lawrence Cohen
Arthur S. Keene
Susan Kus
Anne Miller
Naomi Miller
Richard W. Redding
Margaret Schoeninger
Nancy Talbot
Henry T. Wright

ANN ARBOR
1981

© 1981 Regents of The University of Michigan
All rights reserved
Printed in the United States of America
ISBN 0-932206-87-5

TABLE OF CONTENTS

List of Figures ix

List of Tables xi

List of Appendix Tables xiii

List of Plates xv

Introduction (by Henry T. Wright)
    Research Design 1
    The Excavations at Farukhabad 4
    The Analysis 8
    The Plan of the Present Work 10

PART ONE: THE BAYAT AND FARUKH PHASES

    I. Stratigraphy and Structural Features of the Bayat and Farukh Phases 12
        Introduction 12
        Bayat and Farukh Phase Stratigraphy 12
        Bayat and Farukh Phase Features 17

    II. Ceramics of the Bayat and Farukh Phases 23
        Introduction 23
        Khazineh Red Ware 23
        Bayat Red Ware 23
        Burnished Black Ware 23
        Fine Black-on-Tan Ware 23
        Susiana Buff Ware 23

    III. Other Artifacts of the Bayat and Farukh Phases 43
        Chipped Stone Tools 43
        Heavy Stone Tools 47
        Bone Tools (by Richard W. Redding) 49
        Other Ceramic Artifacts 50
        Unbaked Clay Artifacts 53
        Bitumen Artifacts 53
        Woven and Tied Artifacts 53
        Fine Stone Artifacts 53
        Summary 54

    IV. The Distribution of Artifacts in the Bayat and Farukh Phases 55
        Introduction 55
        Stylistic Developments and Phase Subdivisions 57
        Activity Variation During the Farukh Phase 60

    V. A Summary of the Bayat and Farukh Phases 63

PART TWO: THE URUK, JEMDET NASR, AND EARLY DYNASTIC PHASES

VI. Stratigraphy and Structural Features of the Uruk, Jemdet Nasr,
and Early Dynastic Phases 71
   Introduction 71
   Uruk, Jemdet Nasr, and Early Dynastic Stratigraphy 71
   Uruk, Jemdet Nasr, and Early Dynastic Features 76

VII. Ceramics of the Uruk, Jemdet Nasr, and Early Dynastic Phases 91
   Introduction 91
   Sargarab Ware 91
   Uruk Ware 95
   Straw Tempered Ware (by Anne Miller) 126
   Gray Ware (by Barbara Bohr) 130
   Concluding Note 135

VIII. Other Artifacts of the Uruk, Jemdet Nasr, and Early Dynastic Phases 136
   Introduction 136
   Chipped Stone Tools 136
   Heavy Stone Tools 141
   Concrete Artifacts 149
   Bone Tools (by Richard W. Redding) 150
   Metal Artifacts 152
   Other Ceramic Artifacts 152
   Unbaked Clay Artifacts 156
   Bitumen Artifacts 157
   Woven Artifacts 157
   Fine Stone Artifacts (by Susan Kus) 158
   Shell Artifacts (by Nancy Talbot) 162
   Summary 163

IX. Artifact Distribution in the Uruk, Jemdet Nasr, and
Early Dynastic Phases 164
   Introduction 164
   Technical and Stylistic Developments and Phase Divisions 165
   Activity Variation During the Uruk and Jemdet Nasr Phases 174

X. A Summary of the Uruk, Jemdet Nasr, and Early Dynastic Phases 181
   The Early and Middle Uruk Phases 181
   The Late Uruk Phase 185
   The Jemdet Nasr Phases 188
   The Beginning of the Early Dynastic Phase 192
   Summary 194

PART THREE: THE ELAMITE AND LATER PHASES

XI. The Elamite Phases 196
   Elamite Stratigraphy 196
   Elamite Features 197
   Elamite Ceramics (by Elizabeth Carter) 200
   Chipped Stone Artifacts of the Elamite Phases 216
   Other Stone Artifacts of the Elamite Phases 216
   Other Artifacts of the Elamite Phases 216
   A Summary of the Simashki, Sukkalmahhu, and Transitional Phases at
      Tepe Farukhabad (by Elizabeth Carter) 218
   Summary and Conclusions 222

XII. Evidence of the Parthian and Sasanian Periods 224
    Introduction 224
    Ceramics of the Parthian and Sasanian Periods
        (by Lawrence Cohen) 224
    Other Artifacts of the Parthian and Sasanian Periods 226
    Summary 226

PART FOUR: PLANT AND ANIMAL USE
XIII. The Plant Remains (by Naomi Miller) 227
    Introduction 227
    Seeds 227
    Charcoal 231
    Distribution of Plant Remains Within the Site 231
    Discussion 232

XIV. The Faunal Remains (by Richard W. Redding) 233
    Introduction 233
    The Non-Mammalian Remains 234
    Class Mammalia: The Materials and Distribution 239
    Class Mammalia: Summary and Conclusions 253
    The Composition of the Mammalian Fauna 254
    Comments on the Environment at Tepe Farukhabad 257
    Human and Animal on the Deh Luran Plain: 4000 to 1500 BC 259

PART FIVE: CONCLUSIONS
XV. Fourth Millennium Deh Luran in the Nexus of Exchange 262
    Perspectives on Exchange 262
    The Nexus of Transport 264
    Production and Export on the Deh Luran Plain 265
    Imports to Farukhabad 272
    Changing Systems of Interregional Exchange 275
    Interregional Exchange and State and
        Urban Development 277
    Thoughts on Future Work 278

Bibliography 280

Appendices
    A. Provenience Units at Tepe Farukhabad 285
    B. Artifact Counts in Farukhabad Provenience Units 303
    C. Measured Ceramics 330
    D. Other Measured Artifacts 372
    E. Faunal Elements (by Richard W. Redding) 391
    F. Floral Elements (by Naomi Miller) 427
    G. Human Osteological Remains (by Margaret Schoeninger
        and Antoinette B. Brown) 431
    H. Radiocarbon Age Determinations 436
    I. Multi-Element Neutron Activation of Obsidian Samples from
        Tepe Farukhabad (by Arthur S. Keene) 438

LIST OF FIGURES

1. A map of Greater Mesopotamia 2
2. Flow chart of the initial working model 2
3. Contour map of Tepe Farukhabad 5
4. Northwest section of Excavation A 13
5. Southeast section of Excavation A 14
6. East southeast section of the lowest step in Excavation A 15
7. Upper portion of the southeast section of Excavation B 16
8. Lower portion of the southeast section of Excavation B 17
9. Bayat and Farukh phase buildings 20
10. Khazineh Red, Burnished Black, Bayat Red, and Fine Black-on-Tan Ware vessel rims 25
11. Earlier Susiana Ceramics 26
12. Susiana ware: vessel bases 27
13. Susiana ware: Narrow-based vessels with matching stand 28
14. Susiana ware: Narrow-based vessels and matching stand 29
15. Susiana ware: Band motifs on bowl rims 31
16. Susiana ware: Horizontal and vertical curved line motifs on bowl rims 32
17. Susiana ware: Dot motifs on bowl rims 34
18. Susiana ware: Sigma and slash motifs on bowl rims 35
19. Susiana ware: Step motifs on bowl rims 36
20. Susiana ware: Diamond motifs on bowl rims 37
21. Susiana ware: Other motifs on bowl rims 38
22. Susiana ware: Other motifs on bowl rims 39
23. Susiana ware: Basin rims 40
24. Susiana ware: Jars 42
25. Chipped stone tools: Microliths, piercing-reaming tools, and sickles 44
26. Chipped stone tools: Cutting-scraping tools 45
27. Chipped stone tools: Denticulates, notches, and other small tools 46
28. Chipped stone tools: Choppers 48
29. Miscellaneous artifacts of the Farukh Phase 52
30. Scatter plot of the metric attributes of vertical curved line motifs from Sabz and Farukhabad 60
31. Bayat phase settlement on the Deh Luran plain 67
32. Farukh phase settlement on the Deh Luran plain 68
33. Post-Farukh phase settlement on the Deh Luran plain 69
34. Northeast section of Excavation A 73
35. Southeast section of Excavation C 77
36. Uruk, Jemdet Nasr, and Early Dynastic small buildings 80
37. Jemdet Nasr large buildings in Excavation A 82
38. Uruk and Jemdet Nasr large buildings in Excavation B 85
39. Other Uruk features in Excavation B 89
40. Sargarab ware: Reconstructed vessels 92
41. Sargarab ware and related vessels: Bowls with beaded rims and hatched strips 94
42. Sargarab ware: Heavy basins and jars 96
43. Sargarab ware: Bowls and jars with rounded lips and bowls with flat lips 97
44. Sargarab ware: Jars with flattened lips and various jar parts 98
45. Uruk ware: Conical cups 100
46. Uruk ware: Round lip and incurved bowls 101
47. Uruk ware: Flat lip bowls 102
48. Uruk ware: Round lip jars of the Uruk phases 103
49. Uruk ware: Round lip jars of the Jemdet Nasr and later phases 104
50. Uruk ware: Expanded rim jars 106
51. Uruk ware: Flared expanded jar rims 107
52. Uruk ware: Low expanded and other jar rims 108
53. Uruk ware: Ledge rim jars 109
54. Uruk ware: Bottles and band rim jars 110
55. Uruk ware: Jar appendages and textured motifs 112
56. Uruk ware: Bases and monochrome decoration 113
57. Uruk ware: Black-on-red painted decoration 114
58. Uruk ware: Polychrome decoration 118
59. Uruk ware: Polychrome decoration 119

60.	Uruk ware: Polychrome decoration	120
61.	Uruk ware: Polychrome decoration	121
62.	Polychrome motif types and an example of a design statement	124
63.	Miscellaneous Uruk ware ceramics	127
64.	Histogram of beveled rim bowl volumes	129
65.	Gray ware jars and other forms	131
66.	Gray ware jars and handles	132
67.	Cross-plot of gray ware jar attributes	133
68.	Chipped stone tools: Microliths and piercing tools	137
69.	Chipped stone tools: Large drills and sickles	139
70.	Chipped stone tools: Endscrapers and truncate pieces	140
71.	Chipped stone tools: Retouched pieces and denticulate flakes and blades	141
72.	Chipped stone tools: Heavy tools	144
73.	Grinding slab wear patterns	145
74.	Attributes of perforated and partially perforated stones	148
75.	Bone, shell, metal, and unbaked clay artifacts	151
76.	Other ceramic artifacts	155
77.	Fine stone artifacts	161
78.	Early Uruk settlement pattern	183
79.	Middle Uruk settlement pattern	184
80.	Late Uruk settlement pattern	185
81.	Late Jemdet Nasr settlement pattern	191
82.	Early Dynastic settlement pattern	193
83.	The northeast section of Excavation B	198
84.	Simashki phase pottery	203
85.	Sukkalmahhu phase pottery	205
86.	Sukkalmahhu phase pottery	207
87.	Sukkalmahhu phase pottery	208
88.	Sukkalmahhu phase pottery from Farukhabad and Susa	210
89.	Transitional phase pottery	212
90.	Second millennium pottery	213
91.	Transitional phase pottery from Tepe Farukhabad compared to pottery from Larsa, Ur, and Nippur	215
92.	Sukkalmahhu phase settlement patterns	220
93.	Parthian and Sasanian ceramics	225
94.	Dimensions of carbonized barley	228
95.	Leguminous seeds	230
96.	Equid dentitions	244
97.	Measurements of the distal metapodials of sheep, goat, and gazelle	247
98.	Sources of materials transported to Tepe Farukhabad	276
99.	Graphical presentation of changing indicators of material preparation and use through time	277

LIST OF TABLES

1. Farukhabad excavation measurements (m) 7
2. Later phases at Tepe Farukhabad 8
3. Bayat and Farukh phase wall attributes 21
4. Metric attributes of Susiana bowls 41
5. Bayat and Farukh phase chipped stone tools by layer 47
6. Stratigraphic Distribution of Farukh and Bayat Spindle Whorls 51
7. Attributres of bitumen spheres 54
8. Stylistic features of Susiana ceramics from Farukhabad 56
9. Design proportions on Susiana ceramics from Farukhabad 58
10. Ceramic features of Tepe Sabz, Zone A, and Tepe Farukhabad, Excavation A, Layers 33-36 59
11. Correlations of excavated later Susiana deposits on the Deh Luran plain 59
12. Farukh phase artifact correlations 61
13. Farukh phase mean densities 62
14. Landscape types on the Deh Luran plain 64
15. Uruk, Jemdet Nasr, and Early Dynastic walls 83
16. Uruk and Jemdet Nasr ovens 86
17. Uruk and Jemdet Nasr bins 87
18. Uruk and Jemdet Nasr cement vats 87
19. Uruk and Jemdet Nasr postholes 88
20. Uruk and Jemdet Nasr hearths and pits 88
21. Metrical attributes of conical cup rims 99
22. Metrical attributes of round rim bowl rims 99
23. Metrical attributes of round rim jar rims 105
24. Stratigraphic distribution of side/shoulder polychrome motif combinations at Farukhabad 123
25. Polychrome design complexity 123
26. Metric attributes of flat bases 126
27. Variance of deviations from expected Beveled Rim bowl volumes through time 129
28. Attributes of grayware jar varieties 134
29. Stratigraphic distribution of grayware jar attributes 134
30. Sickle edge utilization 138
31. Uruk, Jemdet Nasr, and Early Dynastic chipped stone tools 142
32. Stratigraphic distribution of the rough stone tools 146
33. Stratigraphic distribution of the possible spindle whorls 154
34. Stratigraphic distribution of the stone vessel fragments 159
35. Ceramic wares in Excavation A, Layers 22-1 166
36. Ceramic wares in Excavation B, Layers 36-19 166
37. Layer correlation based on wares 167
38. Jar types in Excavation A, Layers 22-1 168
39. Jar types in Excavation B, Layers 36-20 170
40. Bowl types in Excavation A, Layers 22-1 170
41. Bowl types in Excavation B, Layers 36-19 172
42. Phase ascription of the layers 173
43. Middle Uruk artifact correlations 175
44. Middle Uruk mean densities per cubic meter 176
45. Late Uruk artifact correlations 177
46. Late Uruk mean densities per cubic meter 178
47. Early Jemdet Nasr phase artifact correlations 179
48. Early Jemdet Nasr phase mean densities per cubic meter 179
49. Late Jemdet Nasr phase artifact correlations 180
50. Late Jemdet Nasr phase mean densities per cubic meter 180
51. Late Uruk ceramic variation from several areas in lowland Mesopotamia 187
52. Distribution of Simashki phase pottery types 202
53. Farukhabad Layers 18-15 and Susa 202
54. Distribution of Sukkalmahhu phase pottery types 209
55. Farukhabad Layers 14-11B lower and Susa AXV and AXIV 209
56. Distribution of transitional phase pottery types 214
57. Elamite chipped stone artifacts 217
58. Twisted barley grains 228
59. Wheat:Barley ratio by phase 228
60. Dimensions of carbonized emmer wheat (N=6) 229

61. Samples with unusually high proportions of particular types of carbonized plant remains 231
62. Phases recognized at Tepe Farukhabad with associated excavation layers and volumes of the samples 234
63. A summary of the distribution of the elements of the class Osteichthyes (the fish) 236
64. A summary of the distribution of the elements of the class Reptila (the reptiles) 237
65. A summary of the distribution of the elements of the class Aves (the birds) 239
66. A summary of the distribution of the elements of the class Mammalia (the mammals) 241
67. Density ratios of the identifiable and the three categories of unidentifiable material for each phase 240
68. Unidentifiable to identifiable density ratios by phase 242
69. Density ratios for the major mammal groups by phase 243
70. Distal metapodials of *Ovis*, *Capra*, and *Gazella* recovered: measurements and identifications 246
71. Raw fusion data for the limb elements of the Sheep-Goat(-Gazelle) recovered 249
72. Scores of fusion for each element by phase 250
73. Measurements made on the elements of the genus *Bos* recovered 252
74. Gazelles, equids, cattle, sheep, and goats in the Farukh phase excavations 254
75. The computation of density ratios for the Bayat Phase at Tepe Sabz 256
76. The relative proportions of each ungulate to the other ungulates by phase for Farukhabad and the Bayat Phase at Tepe Sabz 258
77. Correlation matrix resulting from comparisons of each vertebrate group, hectares occupied on the Den Luran plain, and scored site size 260
78. Preparation and utilization of Medium Gray chert per cubic meter 268
79. Asphalt per cubic meter 269
80. Variables related to sheep and goat products 272
81. Variables related to the import of technical materials 274

LIST OF APPENDIX TABLES

A1.	Catalogue of Field Units	285
A2.	Characteristics of analytical units	299
B1.	Chipped stone artifacts of the Farukh and Bayat Phases	304
B2.	Chipped stone artifacts of the Uruk Phases	308
B3.	Chipped stone artifacts of the Jemdet Nasr and Early Dynastic Phases	310
B4.	Diagnostic ceramics of the Farukh and Bayat Phases	314
B5.	Diagnostic ceramics of the Uruk Phases	318
B6.	Diagnostic ceramics of the Jemdet Nasr and Early Dynastic Phases	322
B7.	Farukh and Bayat Phase body sherds	326
B8.	Uruk Body sherds	327
B9.	Jemdet Nasr and Early Dynastic body sherds	328
B10.	Occurrence of polychrome motifs	329
C1.	Attributes of Farukh and Bayat Phase ceramics	335
C2.	Attributes of Uruk, Jemdet Nasr, and Early Dynastic ceramics	348
C3.	Attributes of polychrome motifs	367
C4.	Attributes of straw tempered ceramics	369
C5.	Attributes of Grayware jars	370
C6.	Design statements for Uruk, Jemdet Nasr, and Early Dynastic painted jars	371
D1.	Attributes of blade and flake tools	373
D2.	Attributes of blade cores	380
D3.	Attributes of celts and related objects	382
D4.	Attributes of utilized pebbles	382
D5.	Attributes of grinding slabs and mortars	383
D6.	Attributes of beads	383
D7.	Attributes of spindle whorls	384
D8.	Attributes of perforated and partially perforated stones	385
D9.	Attributes of perforated and partially perforated sherds	385
D10.	Attributes of molded gypsum concrete objects	386
D11.	Attributes of ceramic troughs and cylinder drains	386
D12.	Attributes of stone vessels	387
D13.	Attributes of bone tools	387
D14.	Bitumen waste attributes	388
D15.	Attributes of finished bitumen artifacts	390
D16.	Attributes of woven mats, fabrics, and lashings	390
E1.	Elements of the Class Osteichthyes	391
E2.	Elements of the Class Reptilia	392
E3.	Elements of the Class Aves	393
E4.	Identifiable elements of the Class Mammalia	393
E5.	Weights of unidentifiable mammalian fragments	421
E6.	Distal medapodial measurements and identifications	425
E7.	Marine molluscs from Tepe Farukabad	426
F1.	Botanical samples	427
F2.	Carbonized remains from Tepe Farukhabad	428
F3.	Identified charcoal from Tepe Farukhabad	430
G1.	Tooth measurements from the Farukhabad burials	433
G2.	Strontium assays for human and animal bone	433
I1.	Obsidian artifacts	440
I2.	Trace elements used in the 1974 obsidian analyses	441
I3.	Quantitative change of the later Deh Luran obsidian industry	441
I4.	Parts per million determination for obsidian trace elements from geological sources and standards	441
I5.	Parts per million determination for obsidian trace elements from archaeological sites	442

LIST OF PLATES

1. Polychrome decorated jar .... Frontispiece
2. General views of Tepe Farukhabad 443
3. Farukh Phase structures 444
4. Uruk structures 445
5. Details of Uruk structures 446
6. Jemdet Nasr structures 447
7. Details of Jemdet Nasr structures 448
8. Farukh Phase vessels 449
9. Other Farukh Phase artifacts 450
10. Early and Middle Uruk ceramic vessels 451
11. Late Uruk and Jemdet Nasr ceramic vessels 452
12. Grinding tools and drain of the Uruk and Jemdet Nasr Phases 453
13. Celts and grinder of Uruk and later phases 454
14. Perforated stones 455
15. Concrete artifacts 456
16. Unbaked clay artifacts 457
17. Bitumen artifacts 458
18. Fine stone and bone items 459
19. Marine shell artifacts 460
20. Fine stone and ceramic items 461
21. Select mammalian elements 462

INTRODUCTION

This monograph deals with research on a small center of the fourth millennium B.C. in southwest Iran. In this initial chapter, the reasoning behind the research design, the standards used in fieldwork and analysis, and the organization of the rest of the monograph are presented.

In 1967, I completed a study of the agricultural economy of the town of Ur during the first part of the Early Dynastic Period. I felt that the understanding of the development of states and urban societies could best be improved by considering factors other than agriculture, such as interregional trade, intercity warfare and diplomacy, and central political organization (Wright 1969a: 122). The problem, therefore, was to choose which of these factors could best be approached with a small project using the methods at that time available. I considered and rejected the idea of a project using site survey methods to study a textually documented war of the Early Dynastic Period. The most reasonable plan seemed to be a study of the relations between interregional trade, competition, and the rise of town—centered settlement patterns. Data could be obtained from excavations in a town on a transport route between highlands and lowlands.

Kent Flannery and Frank Hole encouraged me to consider the Deh Luran Plain in southwestern Iran. This plain presented three immediate advantages. First, it was located between the highlands and the lowlands in a reasonable place for a trade route (Fig. 1). Second, it was a small, well—defined environmental unit within which one could hope to control the multiple factors affecting trade and competition. This would have been difficult to do on a larger, more open unit such as the central Khuzistan Plains around Susa. Third, the work of Hole, Flannery, Neely, and Helbaek on the earlier settlements of the Deh Luran Plain (1969) provided useful data on chronology, environment, population, and subsistence not available for other areas. One site, called Tepe Farukhabad or Fakhrabad, had first been noted by Gautier and Lampre of the French Mission in 1903 (1905:83). Here, Hole and Flannery found painted sherds of the Susiana tradition of the fifth millennium B.C. as well as beveled rim bowls of the succeeding fourth millennium. The latter appeared to be asscociated with massive building foundations of mud brick. Farukhabad seemed an ideal site for the study of trade, competition, and town development.

RESEARCH DESIGN

Consideration of the logically possible relations between trade, competition, and town growth in the light of what was known about Mesopotamia in general, and of the research opportunities present in Deh Luran, resulted in the working model presented in Figure 2. There was evidence of increasing population and decreasing land quality from the previous work on the plain (Hole et al., op. cit. :369-371). In my research proposal, I argued that the testing of specific hypotheses drawn from this model would elucidate the relations between land productivity, agricultural techniques, the collection, transformation, and distribution of materials and products, the administration of such activities, and competition between centers of such activities. I hoped to find archaeological indicators of the activities of interest in the form of subsistence remains and canal patterns, the remains of workshops and storehouses, and weapons and the remains of fortifications. The specific hypotheses to be tested were the following: 1) That competition over agricultural land, perhaps dictated by increasing population and decreasing land quality, required fortified towns and specialists in military organization; and 2) That increased participation in interregional exchange, whose growth was perhaps dictated by the increasing total population of greater Mesopotamia, required specialists in economic administration, both to organize local export production and to redistribute imports. Even if one or both of these hypotheses were rejected, I still hoped to clarify the relations among the various activities.

Examination of both air and ground photographs of Tepe Farukhabad indicated that the site

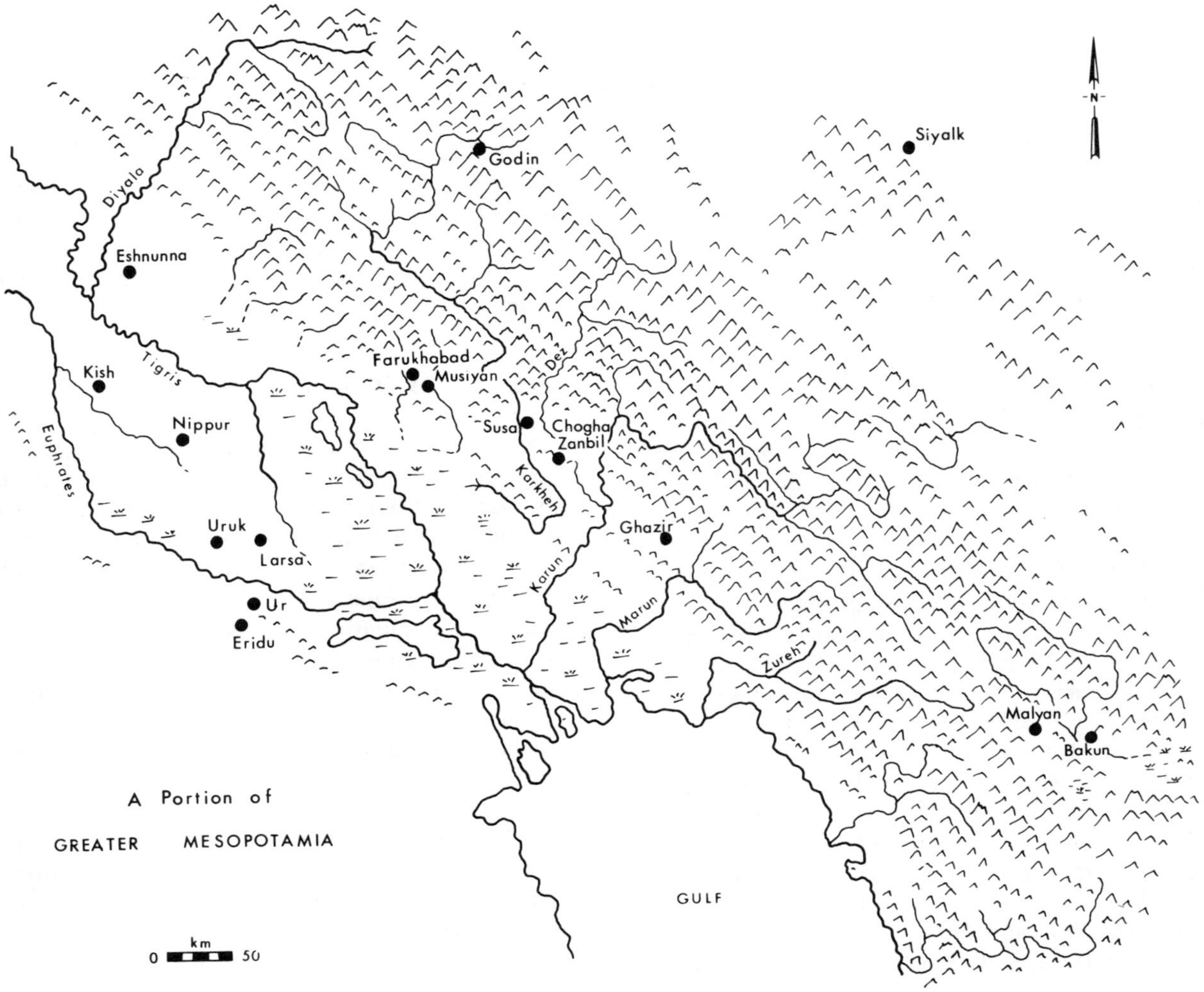

Fig. 1. A Map of Greater Mesopotamia.

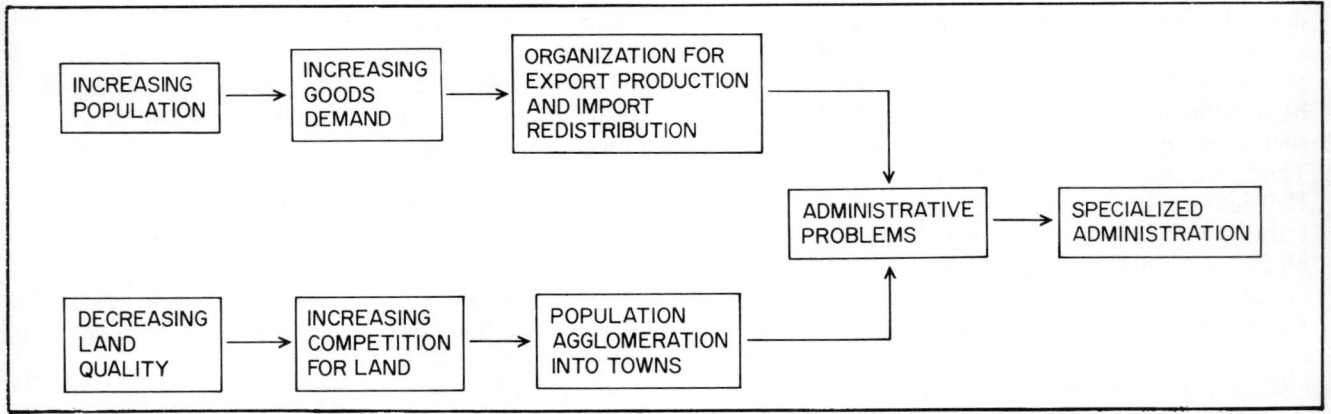

Fig. 2. Flow Chart of the Initial Working Model.

INTRODUCTION

had a small high central area with a surrounding lower flank. The mound had been cut deeply by the Mehmeh River. Previous descriptions seemed to indicate that the high central area was an earlier village mound, upon which had been placed the public buildings of the developing town, while the lower area was the housing of the later town. Assuming this to be the case, I composed the following field plan. At least two main excavations would be opened. One would be in the center of the river-cut face in order to provide a sequence of public buildings and associated debris. The other would be near the edge of the lower flank in order to transect any fortification walls and reveal a series of domestic buildings and associated debris. Changes in the relative quantities of traded materials would provide a measure of interregional trade, and their associations with the different kinds of architecture in the two excavations would provide an indication of the organization of this trade. From the excavations we would also derive a sequence of floral and faunal remains enabling us to assess changes in subsistence techniques, land quality, and availability of transport animals. If time permitted, two more stratigraphic excavations would be undertaken in order to expand the sample of excavated units. Finally, examination of nearby canal traces would produce associated ceramics and allow dating of the canals.

This plan was submitted to the National Science Foundation in September 1967 and was supported as N.S.F. Grant GS—138. I am deeply indebted to Dr. Richard Lieban and Mrs. Mary Green of the Foundation's Anthropology program for their help.

Before detailing the history of the excavations and the subsequent analysis, a brief preview of the revised research design, the one actually embodied in this monograph, would be helpful. There were several reasons for the revisions. First, little of the recovered data was useful in the consideration of conflict. As far as is known, massive town walls were rarely built before the third millennium B.C., and such modest walls and block houses as are known earlier would probably have been destroyed by erosion of the perimeter of such a steep mound as Farukhabad. Unequivocal weapons were virtually absent. Evidence of the violent destruction of buildings was not found. This leaves the evidence of settlement pattern in which the effects of conflict can be monitored only if other factors such as subsistence and exchange are correctly isolated and controlled. Second, far more could be learned about exchange than I ever would have thought possible. Relative increases in the quantities of imported materials did occur as predicted. However, since the Deh Luran Plain was not merely a way station, but produced a variety of useful resources of its own, the data on exports and imports proved more flexible than expected. For instance, there are in some cases—most outstandingly cherts—local low-quality resources which can be used as substitutes for imported finer materials. Estimates of the values of imported materials relative to local substitutes can be made with minimal assumptions, independent of variations due to the changing uses of tools made from the material. In another case, waste products from the local preparation of bitumen for export could be measured independently of finished objects so that export could be indirectly measured. With data such as these it was possible to redefine the independent variable, relative goods flow through a point in an exchange network, into separate import and export components. Third, a redefinition of the dependent variable was needed. My ultimate interest was in the development of societies with specialized administrative and political institutions, the classical problem of the origin of the state. Initially, the growth of towns was viewed as a component in this process and therefore as a kind of indicator variable. However, excavations at Farukhabad and elsewhere (Wright and Johnson 1975) produced direct evidence of the activities of administrators. Therefore it was possible to take the more satisfactory course of examining administrative development and town growth as two separate variables. I thus had three working propositions. One dealt with the mechanics of exchange, two dealt with the relation between exchange and other developments:

1) Increased participation in exchange networks begins with a local reorganization of production and an increase in export, rather than an initial increase in imports.

2) Increased production and export leads to increased administrative specialization and state formation.

3) Increased participation in systems of export and import leads to the growth of central towns.

Most of the analytical effort, however, was not directed toward the testing of such propositions. As usual, most of the effort was spent in controlling other variables, so that testing could be attempted. It was first necessary to build a local chronology so that contemporary excavation units and settlements could be correlated. After this, a tremendous amount of time was spent trying to describe and explain variation in material debris resulting from the performance of different activities within the community. Only when a beginning was made toward understanding such variation was it possible to consider the mechanics of exchange.

THE EXCAVATIONS AT FARUKHABAD

The excavation team began to arrive in Tehran early in February, 1968. We spent several weeks completing arrangements for an excavation permit. I am indebted to Prof. Ezatollah Negahban of Tehran University and Mr. David Stronach, Director of the British Institute of Persian Studies, for their advice on this matter. Through the kind offices of His Excellency Mr. M. Pahlbod, then Minister of Culture, and Mr. A. Pourmand, then Director of the Iran Archaeological Service, an excavation permit was granted. The detailed negotiations were handled by Mr. M. Khorramabadi, then Director of Excavations. Through the kindness of Prof. Robert McC. Adams we were able to borrow and repair a Landrover belonging to the University of Chicago's Oriental Institute. With the help of Dr. Robert Liimatainen, then Science Attache at the United States Embassy, we borrowed a surveyor's transit for mapping the site and excavations.

By late February the arrangements were complete and the team left for southwestern Iran. Dr. Robert Bettarel was Assistant Director and an excavation supervisor, Mr. Robert Gibbs was an excavation supervisor, and Mrs. Fran Wright was laboratory supervisor. Mr. Manouchehr Imani was the representative of the Archaeological Service. Mr. Nicholas Vester visited during the project and helped with the mapping and excavation. On March 2, 1968 a field camp was set up in the community of Deh Luran. Thirty local workmen were hired. A tent was rented as an equipment depot and shelter for the workers.

Tepe Farukhabad is a high mound of whitish color visible from throughout the central and northwestern Deh Luran Plain (32°35'N, 47°14'E, Pl. 2). The entire site is 190 m from northwest to southeast, and 140 m from northeast to southwest. The high central portion, excluding the lower terrace, is now 150 m from northwest to southeast, and 70 m from northeast to southwest. This central portion rises 30 m above the level of the present deeply incised Mehmeh floodplain, 25 m above the ancient flood plain, and only 20 m above sterile soil as determined by examination of the river-cut face (Fig. 3; Pl. 2). The only nearby habitations are a few semi-permanent tents to the north. At sunset, quiet except for the call of the jackal and the laughter of hyaenas, the site is impressive in its desolation.

The entrenched flood plain of the Mehmeh River covers areas west and south of the mound. In the past, river meanders have cut into the mound, eliminating perhaps 60 percent of its bulk. The original central mound was probably 200 m in diameter. Surface indications show that it grew more or less as I had suspected, but not at the period which I had expected. An initial sounding on the flanking terrace at the foot of what became Excavation C revealed several meters of Partho-Sasanian debris. While it is possible that earlier architecture underlies this terrace, there is no evidence of such in the eroded areas around its edge. I decided to concentrate on the remnant of the high central mound, the one remaining ha of the three ha early settlement. A permanent datum was provided by a concrete marker under a cairn emplaced years before by the oil company. The elevation of the marker was taken to be 162.8 m above sea level on the basis of a map prepared by the company. Since this map gave the elevation only to the nearest foot, this is an approximate metric equivalency.

The excavation units were laid out after an examination of the surface configuration of the site. The examination indicated three separate cuttings of the site by the river. The oldest episode cut the northwest end, leaving a steep slope now stabilized by grasses. The next episode cut away the entire southwest half of the mound. This left a steep slope which still-active gullies have cut into four major spurs. The most recent episode cut into the west corner between the two previous cuts, leaving a near vertical cliff in constant danger of collapse. The second stage of erosion had left a long transect through the heart of the settlement which could be excavated with relative ease and safety. Excavation debris could be dropped over

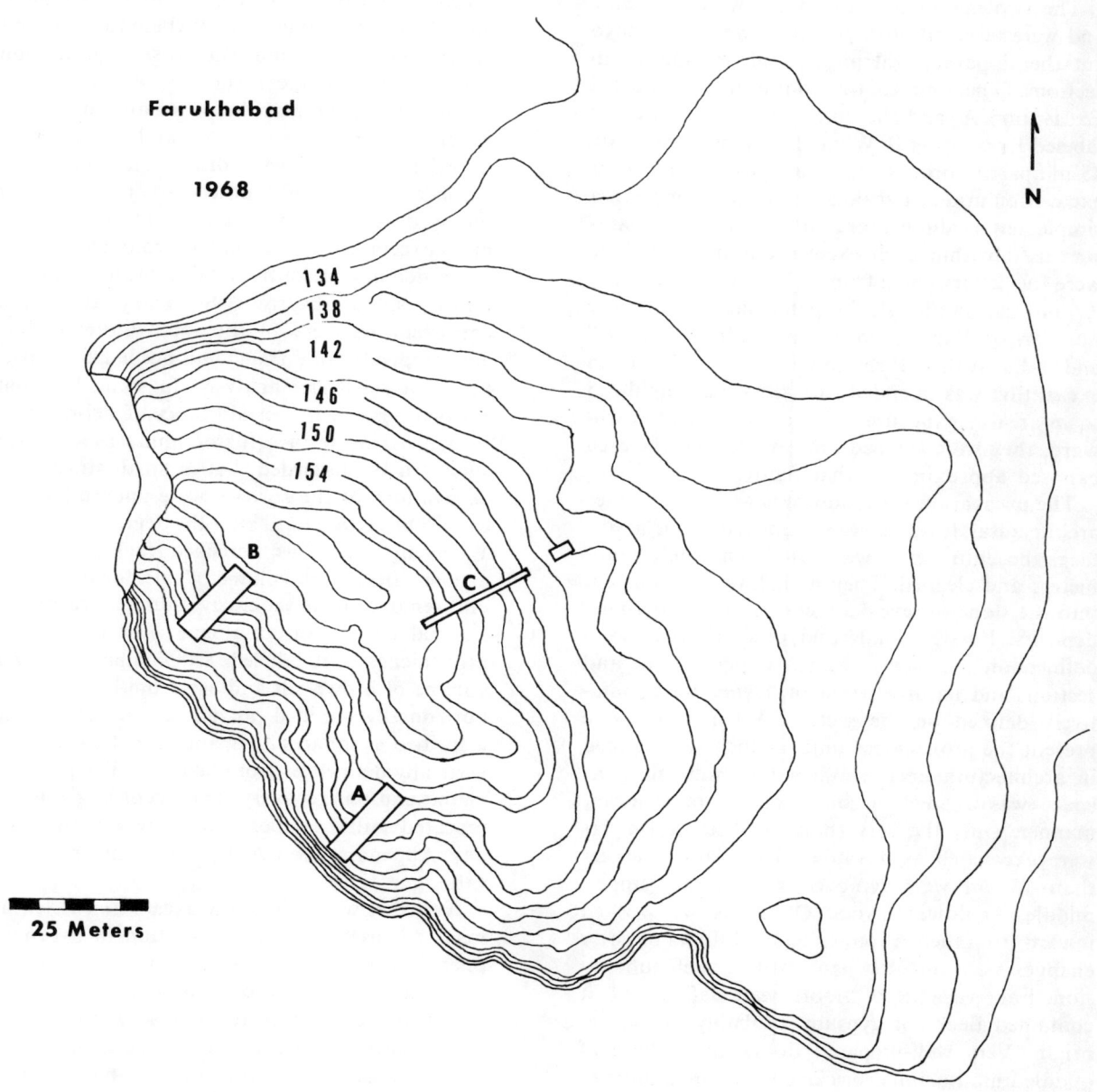

Fig. 3. Contour Map of Tepe Farukhabad. Contour interval equals 2 m.

the bank onto the present Mehmeh flood plain. I decided to place two major excavations on this slope, and two of the four spurs were randomly selected as locations for these excavations (Fig. 3). In retrospect, this method probably biased our sample in favor of large building because the spurs themselves are the areas more resistant to erosion, and thus probably areas with particularly massive stone and mud brick foundations. Because of this possible bias, I have not attempted to estimate statistical attributes of the total community such as percentage of ground devoted to large residences, or kilograms of chert discarded in a given period, much as I might like to do so.

The two main excavation units were 5 m wide and were oriented northeast-southwest in order to cut the slope at right angles and provide useful sections. The unit to the southeast was labeled Excavation A, and the unit to the northwest was labeled Excavation B. While these units are exactly 45 m apart in order to facilitate any future master excavation grid at Farukhabad, for our purposes a simple letter/number grid of one meter squares was used within each excavation. In each there were five letters going from 'A' on the northwest to 'E' on the southeast. Perpendicular there were numbers, in Excavation A running from '5' to '18' and in Excavation B running from '1' to '14'. Each excavation was intended to maintain a roughly 25 sq m area of exposure. As they proceeded downward, they were stepped outward so that the area exposed approximated that figure.

The excavation procedure was as follows. Once architectural features were removed from a surface, the entire area was cut down a few centimeters and cleaned. Then a shallow step was cut into the slope to reveal a section of the underlying deposits. Possible walls and other features were defined on the newly cleaned upper surface and section, and natural strata of 'layers' were tentatively defined on the section. When walls were present the provenience units or loci were defined in architectural terms. When they were not, the space was divided in some convenient arbitrary manner. Only the very thinnest of natural layers were excavated as a whole. Most layers thicker than 15 cm were removed in arbitrary upper, middle, or lower layers. Often, as we worked inward from the section, ephemeral floors or color changes were noted which justified such subdivision. Four varieties of 'floors' were defined. Most contained flecks of gypsum, probably of natural origin. Very well-prepared floors had a base of puddled mud or mud bricks covered by a layer of mud plaster. Ordinary floors had only a covering of mud plaster. Even simpler floors had only a very compact surface, without special base or layering. Finally, ephemeral floors had only a discontinuous compacted surface with or without special covering. In retrospect, an even more complex taxonomy of surfaces might have been useful in architectural and stratigraphic interpretation. In only one case was there a serious loss of stratigraphic control. This good fortune is attributable more to the relatively unweathered, multi-colored stratigraphy than to any special skill on our part. (The exceptional case occurred in the second millennium layers of Excavation B where the horizontal depositional stratigraphy was cross-cut by a sloping post-depositional green staining which may have resulted from the percolation of ancient sewage.) When mud brick wall stubs and other features were isolated, they were drawn on plans, photographed, numbered, otherwise recorded, and removed. All debris were screened through half cm mesh except material from the cleaning of sections, from demonstrated mud brick walls, and from known animal burrows. Screening allowed the consistent recovery of the small bitumen, bone, and chipped stone fragments needed for various kinds of statistical analysis. In some horizontal excavations, where certain types of debris can be recognized as terrace fill or mud brick collapse, such can be discarded, but in small stratigraphic excavations of the sort we were undertaking, one cannot be certain until after the deposit is removed. When in doubt, we screened the deposit. The artifacts from each volume of earth or provenience unit removed from the excavation were recorded in a serial excavation catalogue. For instance, the provenience unit labeled X485 might be from a volume of brown silt and ash from Excavation A, horizontally defined as a 2.5 by 2.0 m area identified as squares A, B, and half of C–12, 13 and vertically defined as from layer 25. The procedure of excavation, recovery, and recording might be repeated within each excavation several times each day. Appendix Table A–1 presents the provenience catalogue.

A further word about the excavation of features may be useful. Any association between soil phenomena and objects that was not routinely recorded in field notes, plans, or sections was designated as a 'feature' and serially numbered within each excavation. Features included pits, hearths, postholes, piles of stones or bones, burials, and mud brick wall stubs. The last, the most common type, were approached in the following way. Brick alignments were noted in scraping the excavation. These areas were isolated by removal of refuse or brick collapse from either side of their alignment down to the next possible floor. We then worked in from the side in hopes of finding brick faces or plaster. In many cases this was not possible and we cut into clean brick and mortar in hopes of finding the joints. If the feature still seemed to be a wall rather than a pattern of neatly fallen brick collapse, it was numbered, measured,

INTRODUCTION

and mapped. In order to provide final confirmation that a feature was a wall, we removed portions in order to examine the cross-section of the feature and to obtain whole bricks for measurements. There are two points in the excavation at which I think this procedure may have broken down. Both represent extremely weathered layers which were exposed to the elements for several centuries during abandonments of the mound. One is Excavation A, Layers 1 to 4; the other is Excavation B, Layer 37. Otherwise, though the field plans and sections occasionally leave something to be desired, I believe we have recorded the mud brick wall stubs adequately.

Our procedures revealed a number of features which pass all the tests for walls, but which only survive to a height of one or two brick courses. One would expect the debris of the upper walls to fill a room to a much higher level than this. Such wrecking to near floor level would only result when the debris of the destroyed building was hauled away and dumped elsewhere. The frequency of the practice at Farukhabad may result from the steep-sidedness of the mound, already at least ten m above the level of the plain by 4000 B.C. Constant filling around the edges would have been needed to level off the top of the mound, and building debris would have suited the purpose admirably.

During the course of the excavation various specialized samples were taken. Bags of earth were collected for water flotation to recover carbonized plant remains as well as tiny retouch flakes, rodent bones, and other items. Rectangular blocks of earth were cut out of the section for pollen analysis. Charcoal was collected in plastic bags for radiocarbon age determinations.

A third minor excavation was undertaken for a specific purpose and with modified procedures. This was a one m wide trench (termed Excavation C) transecting the northeast slope. It was undertaken during the last days of excavation in order to provide a section through the original outer perimeter of the central mound. First, the trench was stepped down the slope and the section was cleaned and recorded. Most of the recorded walls were those of small buildings. Perhaps because of erosion or quarrying of the mound perimeter for building materials by the Partho-Sasanian occupants, the only circumvallation discovered dates to the later second millennium B.C. Artifact samples for dating purposes were removed from some of the layers as exposed in the steps and the effort was closed. During the subsequent course of analysis, I often regretted being unable to expand our clearance of the small buildings in this area, but our resources were largely expended by then, and continuation was not possible.

A total of 1512 man-days, not counting the efforts of the supervisory staff, were spent at Farukhabad. While much of the excavation was done by the supervisors, several of the men of Deh Luran proved to be skilled excavators and most of them worked hard under difficult conditions of alternating rain and dust storms. It soon became apparent that we were underfinanced and short of supervisory staff; difficulties were compounded by vehicle breakdown, sudden changes of weather, and so on. Furthermore, the scarcity of food in Deh Luran, then separated from Andimeshk and Dezful by more than four hours of dusty track and two unpredictable river fords, made life even more difficult. The fact that Mrs. Wright, Dr. Bettarel, Mr. Gibbs, and Mr. Imani stayed with the project under these conditions until the very end is highly commendable. The fact that there were no major illnesses in the field is attributable to Mrs. Wright's careful attention to the preparation of meals in addition to her heavy burden of laboratory work.

The following table indicates the work done by the group.

Table 1: Farukhabad Excavation Measurements (m)

	A	B	C	Total
Top Elevation Above Sea Level	155.9	160.9	160.5	—
Bottom Elevation Above Sea Level	147.7	149.0	148.5	—
Total Depth	8.2	11.9	12.0	—
Width	5.0	5.0	1.0	—
Length	14.0	14.0	17.0	—
Average Exposed Floor area (m^2)	25.1	23.6	—	48.7
Excavated Volume (m^3)	206.0	290.0	24.0	520.0
Screened Volume (m^3)	102.8	143.8	—	246.6

With temperatures over 40°C, we left Farukhabad and Deh Luran on April 30th, 1968. I have returned three times in succeeding years. In 1969 I assisted James A. Neely in his intensive site survey of the Deh Luran Plain as a part of the second Rice University project under Frank Hole. In 1970, I returned to assist Richard Redding in the trapping of small mammals in the area. In 1973, I returned to repair the ditches and banks which protect the excavations from excessive rain damage.

Doubtless many readers will wish that larger exposures were made. Except for the above mentioned Excavation C, I disagree. From a practical point of view, a site like Farukhabad, cut in half by natural forces, is ideal for stratigraphic work such as ours, but not for extensive horizontal clearance. I would rather have several small stratigraphic excavations rather than one large one.

THE ANALYSIS

Since we were not certain that sherd samples shipped across the oceans would arrive safely in Michigan, we decided to undertake an extensive preliminary analysis in Iran. The goal was to record enough so that a useful report could be written even if by some chance the samples were lost. Mr. Imani made special arrangements with Mr. Nasser Bayani of the Kermanshah Office of the Ministry of Culture and Arts to set up a laboratory in that city. After returning Chicago's Landrover to Iraq, we began work in the laboratory. Several weeks were spent doing counts and drawings of the artifacts from all stratified provenience units, after which everything was taken to Tehran. Through the kindness of Mr. Pourmand, most of the stratified ceramics, stone tools, and animal bones were sent to the United States. They are now housed primarily at the University of Michigan Museum of Anthropology in Ann Arbor, The University Museum in Philadelphia, and Yale University in New Haven.

After this preliminary analysis, I felt obliged to make some decisions regarding terminology for artifacts and cultural units. For the artifact types, I have used simple verbal labels to facilitate memory and enliven the discussion. I have tried to follow the terminological precedents of my own previous publication (1969a), which I set after consultation with a number of scholars working in lowland Mesopotamia, and of the work of Hole, Flannery, and Neely (1969). The only new formal artifact names used in this volume are those for ceramic wares, such as Sargarab Ware and Uruk Ware. I have presented only verbal descriptions of these, as I believe more formal description should be proposed only after technological analysis. The fourth millennium B.C. in Greater Mesopotamia, with its rapidly changing ceramic technology, is certainly a fertile field for a person with such analytical interests. In the case of terminology for cultural units, I have followed a double standard. New local phases in the Greater Ubaid tradition have been given names based on sites or nearby modern communities, following the pattern set by Hole, Flannery, and Neely. These names are easy to remember and are distinguished by outstanding ceramic features easily learned and quickly noted during reconnaissance. Such phases probably define the remains of single societies. In the subsequent Protohistoric periods, however, stylistically well-defined local units are not easily perceived. Instead there are a series of broadly correlated local developments. I have opted for named phases with interregional applicability transcending the local differences which certainly exist. Such phases probably define time periods rather than social units, though this point is untested and will remain so until more accurate methods of dating are devised and applied throughout the area.

I would like to emphasize that I have no objection to broadly descriptive phase names such as 'Early Protoliterate'. However, such names are problem-specific. Given a concern with states as administrative systems, the term 'Protoliterate' is an excellent one. Given a concern with city growth, the term 'Protourban' might be more useful. Such problem-defining terminologies are not designed to isolate content-free temporal or social units for purposes of comparison by different scholars. Only such content-free terminologies require general agreement and uniform use.

Table 2: Later Phases at Tepe Farukhabad

			Layers	
		Exc. A	Exc. B	Exc. C
A	Partho-Sasanian	–	–	–
B1	Middle Elamite	–	–	–
B2	Transitional Elamite	–	1–11U	–
B3	Sukkalmahhu Elamite	–	11L–14	–
B4	Simaski Elamite	–	15–18	–
C	Early Dynastic	1–5	19–20	9–23
D1	Late Jemdet Nasr	6–12	21–23	24–26
D2	Early Jemdet Nasr	13–17	24–27	27–31
E1	Late Uruk	18–20	28–31	32–33
E2	Middle Uruk	21–22	32–34	–
E3	Early Uruk	–	35–36	–
F1	Late Farukh	23	37–39	–
F2	Middle Farukh	24–29	40–45	–
F3	Early Farukh	30–31	46–47	–
G	Bayat	33–36	–	–

INTRODUCTION

The series of phase names for Farukhabad, proposed in part during the preliminary analysis but continuously modified since, is presented in the following table. Letter designation follows the pattern of Hole, Flannery, and Neely

After returning to Ann Arbor, the samples were cleaned again and catalogued under the direction of Gibbs. I began a time-consuming analysis of the distribution of artifacts within the excavations as recorded in the counts made in Kermanshah, assisted by Gregory Alan Johnson and Ingrid Christensen. Though we learned a great deal about the use of computers, this work contributed little to this monograph since it soon became apparent that the typology devised in Kermanshah was too general. More than a year was spent constructing and statistically testing a new typology, preparing tables of measurements and counts, preparing illustrations, and checking field notes. Dozens of students in our laboratory course in museum techniques worked on these tasks, and many of them went on to do optional problem-oriented research on particular classes of artifacts. All completed papers dealing with these projects have been edited and are included here under the contributor's name.

The illustrations were prepared primarily by myself. Ellen Wilt and Margaret Van Bolt prepared several of the more difficult illustrations. The chipped stone was drawn according to the common conventions of Paleolithic archaeologists, the direction of flaking being indicated by convex lines concentric around the former position of the point of impact for each flake removal scar. The depth of shadow is indicated by the heaviness of these lines, with the light being conventionally above and to the left of the tool. I have retained this convention for the ceramic illustrations. The function of the shadow on the ceramics is to show the surface texture, particularly those marks which might indicate methods of manufacture. If we maintained the convention of putting the exterior view of the pot to the right and the section and interior view to the left, the shadow would be very heavy on both the interior and exterior of the vessel, obscuring features of interest. Therefore we have not followed the common practice, but have put the section and interior view to the right. In addition, we have tried to show asymmetries and errors in design when they occurred in hopes of conveying information on the methods of decorating pottery. We hope that these efforts will prove useful to the reader.

Large blocks of data were made available to interested specialists. Their contributions on the plants, animals, and later occupations have been included with minimal editing, and many of their conclusions have been cited in the various summary sections of the main body of the report. The descriptive sections of this main body were largely finished in the summer of 1970. Teaching and other responsibilities subsequently kept me from returning to the manuscript for several years.

During the course of analysis several preliminary papers have been published or otherwise circulated. The first was a brief note in *Iran*, Vol. VII (1968), composed immediately after our return from Kermanshah. Several errors in this report require correction. First, the reported height and length of the mound were too great. Second, the ascription of layers to phases differs slightly from that finally decided upon. Third, the correlation of the Deh Luran Phases with the Le Breton Susiana and Susa phases were incorrect, as discussed in the appropriate subsequent part of this monograph. Finally, the late building whose remains form the summit of the mound of Farukhabad is probably Parthian or Sasanian, not Early Islamic. Most of these errors were repeated in the "First Interim Report," a mimeographed document circulated to only a few individuals.

The third preliminary paper used the evidence of exports and imports from Farukhabad to consider a variety of propositions about exchange, state development, and town growth. This was presented at the American Anthropological Association meetings in New Orleans in the autumn of 1970. It was published in 1972, after much revision, as "A Consideration of Inter-regional Exchange in Greater Mesopotamia: 4000 to 3000 B.C." in "Social Exchange and Interaction," *Anthropological Papers* No. 46 of the University of Michigan Museum of Anthropology, edited by E. N. Wilmsen. The errors included in the first version of this paper, resulting primarily from the uncritical use of the data from the Kermanshah analysis, were repeated in the "Second Interim Report," another mimeographed document released to only a few people. These errors will not be detailed here. The published version of the 1970 paper was expanded in 1980 to form Chapter XV. The preceding chapters are essentially as they were written in 1974.

THE PLAN OF THE PRESENT WORK

This monograph has several purposes. First, it should make a contribution to the understanding of early exchange in Southwest Asia, and of the development of early states in general. Second, it should extend the culture historical sequence on the Deh Luran Plain from the end of the fifth millennium B.C., to which point the successive Rice University Projects under the direction of Frank Hole had taken it, up into the second millennium. The data used to achieve these purposes are presented in the appendixes so that the reader may reach his own conclusions regarding either aspect of the project. Hopefully these data, both the counts and measurements and the various illustrations, will be useful to other investigations commonly pursued but not emphasized in this work. Among these would be intra- and inter-regional stylistic comparison and sequence correlation.

The deposits cut by the excavations contained two obvious stratigraphic unconformities, marked by weathered horizons. The three divisions created by these unconformities contained very different cultural remains, and this has to some extent dictated the organization of this work. Thus, Part One is concerned with the Bayat and Farukh Phases, late manifestations of the Susiana Tradition. During the occupational hiatus after these two phases, as indicated by the weathering of Excavation A, layer 23 and Excavation B, layer 37, there is evidence at other sites on the Deh Luran Plain of at least two distinct cultural phases. These are discussed in the last pages of Part One. Part Two describes the deposits of the various Uruk and Jemdet Nasr Phases as well as a tentatively defined phase of the first part of the Early Dynastic Period. In the hiatus indicated by the weathering and erosion of Excavations B, Layer 19, and the weathering of Excavation A, Layers 1 to 4, the rest of the Early Dynastic Period and the Period of the Empire of Agade occurred. Part Three deals with the succeeding Elamite Phases and later times. Part Four presents information on plants and animals. Part Five offers some conclusions about inter-regional trade during the periods spanned by the first two parts.

Within the first two parts, a similar format is followed. First, the stratigraphy and features are presented. The feature data have been re-ordered and amplified from field records. For instance, once types of bins and hearths were isolated it was possible to find data on others not recognized and numbered in the field. These have been numbered and entered in the tables. In the second chapter, the ceramics are described with minimal use of statistics, because measurements of every example of each type from a 50 percent random sample of the provenience units are included in the appendixes. The third chapter covers chipped stone tools and other artifacts, and the fourth chapter is devoted to the distribution of artifact types in order to define cultural phases and to evaluate the different activities performed during these phases. This effort is included within the ceramic chapter in Part Three because the very limited horizontal exposure of the Elamite Layers precluded any kind of activity study. Fifth and finally, a summary chapter draws together the first four chapters of the section, the contributions of the ethno-zoologist and the ethno-botanist, and some of the survey data kindly made available by James Neely in order to provide a brief overview of what is known of the series of phases covered in that part.

In all parts, but particularly in Part One, an effort has been made to provide data comparable to that presented by Hole, Flannery, and Neely in the first Deh Luran report. This is not so, however, in the counting of sherds. My counts are always of vessels represented by a rimsherd or base or some such part. Two pieces from the rim of one vessel, with a few exceptions subsequently noted, are counted as one. This is done because some of the statistical manipulations used require that inter-dependency between observations be eliminated as much as possible. Beyond this, however, I found it most difficult to assign body sherds to specific bowl types in any duplicable manner. To mitigate this inconsistency I have presented some counts of the Tepe Sabz Bayat Phase material using the same standards used in this study of the Farukhabad material (Table 10).

In retrospect, there are many features of the analysis that I would like to revise. For instance, as a result of the work of Alain Le Brun (1971), Gregory Johnson (1973), and Helene Kantor on the Susiana Plain, it seems certain that the Uruk ceramic typology could be improved for purposes of both chronological study and studies of activities. Had I measured the entire ceramic sample, readers could re-classify all the ceramics in any way they chose. To take another example, studies of activity variation could have been improved if information on body sherds, chipped stone waste and scrap bone had been statistically analyzed. However, the number of artifacts and the number of provenience units from any single phase at Farukhabad is small. It seems better to wait until larger and more appropriate samples are available for analysis before undertaking such improvements in analysis and not to delay further the appearance of this report.

Elements of the final text not attributed to a particular author were prepared by Henry T. Wright, who has also taken the responsibility for the integration of all the elements. Parts of the text were critically examined by John Alden, Benjamin Fischler, Robert Henrikson, Gregory A. Johnson, Sander van der Leeuw, and Susan Pollock. The editing was done by David Victor with the assistance of Mary Coombs, Mary Hodge, Katherine Moore, and Carla Sinopoli. To these and to the many others who made useful suggestions and comments, the authors extend their sincere thanks.

PART ONE: THE BAYAT AND FARUKH PHASES

Chapter I

STRATIGRAPHY AND STRUCTURAL FEATURES OF THE BAYAT AND FARUKH PHASES

INTRODUCTION

Deposits of the Bayat Phase were removed from Excavation A, and deposits of the Farukh Phase were removed from both Excavations A and B. The stratigraphy of the deposits is well-defined, relatively horizontal, and broken by few intrusive cultural disturbances. The most common features are the unbaked mud brick walls of various kinds of buildings.

The stratigraphy of each excavation unit is discussed layer by layer from bottom to top, although layers were numbered from top to bottom. This reversal facilitates the presentation of interrelated depositional events. Then each type of feature is presented, and each building is discussed individually, the attributes of the building's walls being presented in Table 3.

BAYAT AND FARUKH PHASE STRATIGRAPHY

EXCAVATION A

Layer 37: Silt floors (.25 m in average thickness): The compact silt floors, with some ash, slant down and thicken from southwest to northeast inside the rooms of Feature 32, the wall stub of a small building (labeled 'a' on Fig. 6). The top of the layer is a roughly level, compact silt floor.

Layer 36: Silt and ash floors (.20 m): Southwest, or outside of Feature 32, this layer is green silt with a compact floor on top. Northeast, inside Feature 32, there are alternating layers of ashy silt and compact silt overlaid by a compact silt floor with some gypsum grit.

Layer 35: Brick debris (.20 m): Southwest or outside of Feature 32, there is a lens of ash, a pebble pavement, and a lens of green clay. Inside Feature 32 is a layer of silt and broken brick. The newly reconstructed Feature 32 has an interior partition (Figs. 6, 9a). The inside and outside deposits in this and the preceding two layers are dissimilar and unconnected; their correlation is based on relative altitude.

Layer 34: Silt, ash, and gypsum grit floors (.25 m): These floors occur at the same level both inside and outside of Feature 32. The uppermost floor has a few broken bricks embedded in it.

Layer 33: Silt and ash (.10 m): This is fill on top of the Layer 34 floors. It is capped by the brick packing of Layer 32.

Layer 32: Brick packing (.85 m): This is the foundation platform of Feature 30, a large building. Some of these bricks may be the dismantled upper walls of Feature 32. Because the bricks vary so greatly in size, however, there is no way to show this. The packing is capped by a layer of clean silt, perhaps mud mortar laid down to level off the platform top and to provide a base for floors.

Layer 31: Silt floors (.10 m): These are prepared floors constructed within the Feature 30 building.

Layer 30: Silt, gypsum grit, ash and brick (.20 m). Debris resulting from the deterioration of the building both within its rooms and in the alley outside of the rooms. In the east end of the alley there is an ash lens capping this layer. Otherwise the top is ill-defined.

Layer 29: Silt and broken brick (.90 m): This thick collapse deposit preserves the wall stubs of the large building of features 30 and 31 ('c' and 'e' on Figs. 4 and 5) to a height of more than a meter. Some gypsum grit occurs. Many flat oval limestone pebbles were found in the upper part of this debris, perhaps a result of the dismantling of the building. The top of Layer 29 is ill-defined.

Layer 28: Silt, gypsum grit, charcoal, and ash. (.25 m): Some lenses of ash occur in small pits cutting into Layer 29 and even into the top of Feature 31. The lenses show no continuity and there are no floors, suggesting that the area was used as a refuse dump.

Layer 27: Silt floors (.22 m): To the southeast this layer is a well-defined sequence of prepared floors becoming progressively thinner near the top. A single floor was arbitrarily chosen as the upper surface of this layer. To the northwest this floor is somewhat different: there are a few ash lenses and the upper surface of the layer is capped by an ash lens. Near the center of the excavation there is a concentration of flat oval pebbles.

Layer 26: Silt floors (.15 m): To the northeast these floors were ill defined and there is some ash in the fill between them. A building of unknown function (Feature 29, Fig. 4f) was built here during this period of deposition. To the southeast, in the uppermost five cm of Layer 27 and lowermost 10 cm of Layer 26, 16 successive compact prepared floors could be distinguished. To the southeast the top of this layer is greenish silt floor.

Layer 25: Silt with coarse gypsum grit (.22 m): This debris is from the deterioration of Feature 29 to the west and the construction and use of a probable storehouse to the east (Feature 28, Fig. 5g). Some clay of the type used for sealings occurs in this layer. The top of the layer is a compact gypsum grit floor to the southeast and an ash lens to the west.

Layer 24: Silt, gypsum grit, and floors (.15 m): There is no evidence of a structure in use at this time, but there are masses of fine clay fragments apparently scraped off containers during the process of sealing them (see Chapter IV, Pl. 16b). A storehouse must have been nearby. This layer is higher to the southwest, where it covers the wall stub of Feature 29, and slants down to the northeast.

Layer 23: Brown and green silt floors (.10 m): Lower Layer 23 has no outstanding features. It is capped by the brick packing of a platform (Feature 25, Fig. 4 h). To the east of the platform is a thin

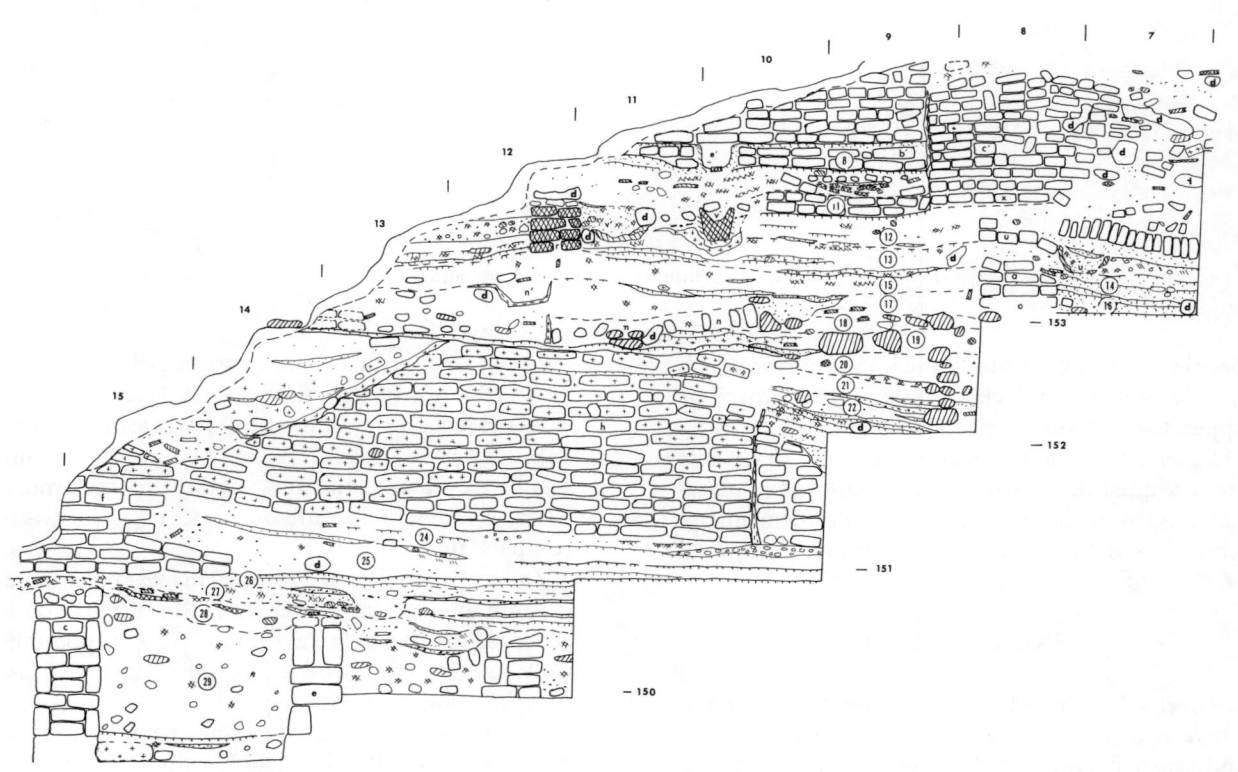

Fig. 4. Northwest Section of Excavation A.

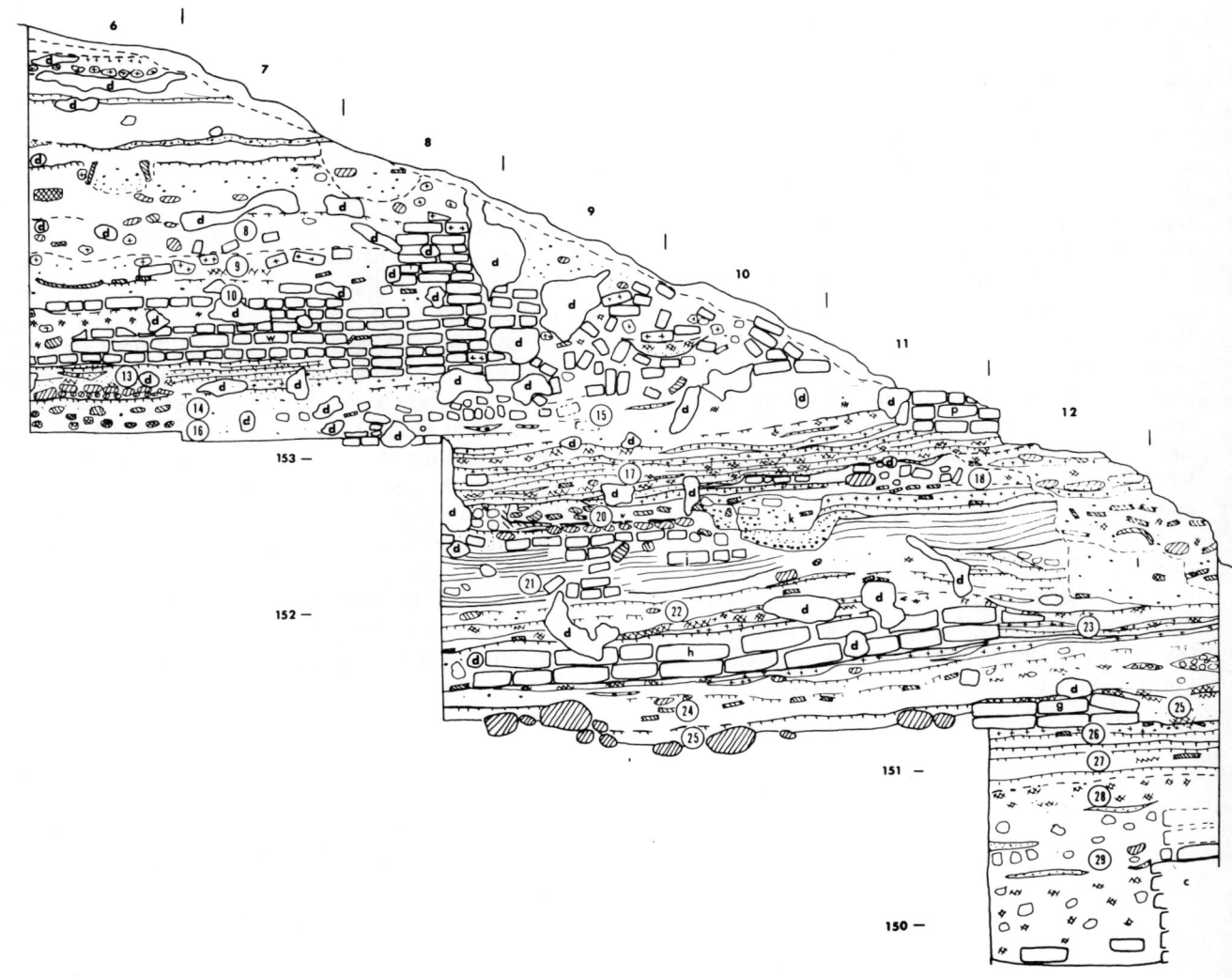

Fig. 5. Southeast Section of Excavation A.

flooring of brick visible in the section, over which is a deposit of green clay. These were removed as upper and middle Layer 23.

Layer 22: The lower portion of Layer 22 is a soft cross-bedded deposit probably composed of material eroded from the top of the platform mixed with Uruk debris. The upper portion is composed of silt and ash lenses of the later phase.

EXCAVATION B

Layer 47: Ash and silt with some floors (.28 m): There is a well-defined floor separating the lower and upper portions of this layer and an ephemeral floor at its top.

Layer 46: Silt, ash, and gypsum grit with some floors (.38 m): In the middle of the layer is a floor with evidence of burning and a scatter of lightly baked brick fragments. A wall footing runs from east to west across the north end of the very small 3.0 by 2.5 meter exposure of this level. The top is a compact floor.

Layer 45: Silt floors (.19 m): This layer has some gypsum grit in the lower two floors and some charcoal in the upper two floors. Several possible walls footings are founded in lower Layer 45. A compact floor caps the layer.

Layer 44: Silt and gypsum grit (.25 m): A complex of small rooms and walls (Feature 41, labeled 'a' on the section in Fig. 8) was founded on

STRATIGRAPHY OF THE BAYAT AND FARUKH PHASES

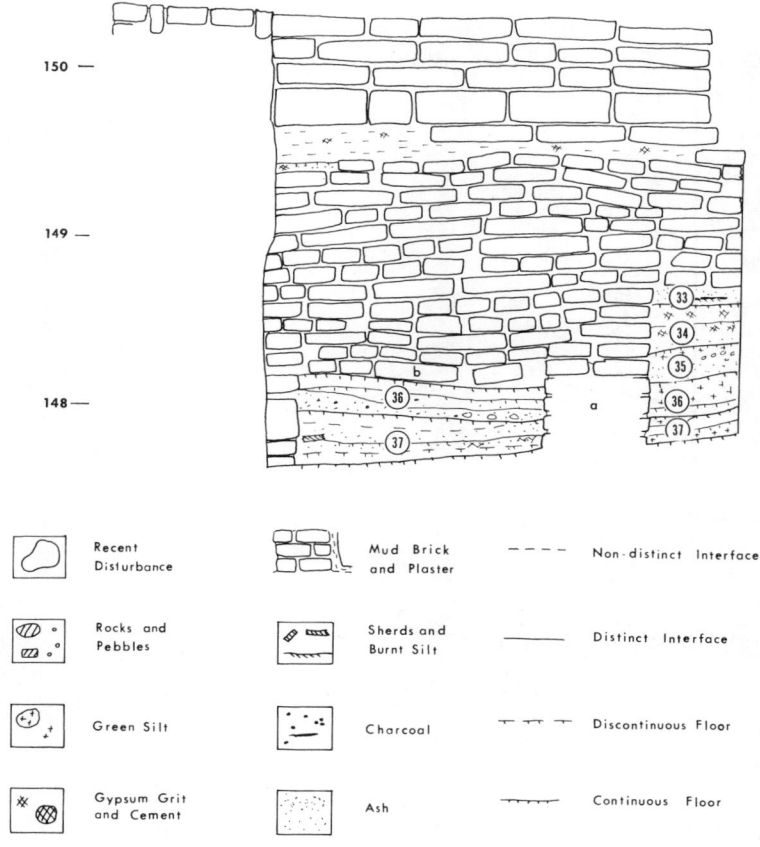

Fig. 6. East Southeast Section of the Lowest Step in Excavation A.

the middle of Layer 45, but was probably built in slight wall trenches cut from the top of Layer 45. Layer 44 is the fill of this complex. Variation in room fills is discussed in the subsequent description of Feature 41. The top of Layer 44 is a gypsum grit floor.

Layer 43: Silt, green silt, and gypsum grit floors (.30 m): These floors overlie the low mound of debris left by the room complex, parts of whose walls may still have been standing. There are broken brick fragments in the upper portion of the layer, probably resulting from the final leveling of Feature 41. The top is an ephemeral, compact floor.

Layer 42: Silt, ash, and gypsum grit (.25 m): To the southeast there are ephemeral floors with gypsum grit. To the northwest there is more ash in the deposit. Broken bricks and limestone cobbles are scattered throughout. A fragmentary wall stub was founded on middle layer 42. The top of this layer is a compact floor continuous to the southeast and ephemeral to the northwest.

Layer 41: Silt, gypsum grit, and broken brick (.25 m): Another building complex (Feature 40) was constructed on the top of Layer 42. This initial construction was disturbed at the point where it entered the section but a later reconstruction (Fig. 8b) is visible. The fill of these rooms contained cobbles and large blocks of orange and gray silt of a sort now seen eroding from the banks of the Mehmeh River. The purpose of these is unknown. The top of this layer is a compact floor.

Layer 40: Silt floors (.15 m): The Feature 40 complex is rebuilt. The floors and footings, sunk in a slight wall trench, are clearly visible in section. The top is a compact silt floor.

Layer 39: Silt, broken brick, and brick flooring, (.15 m): The brick flooring is visible in the north-

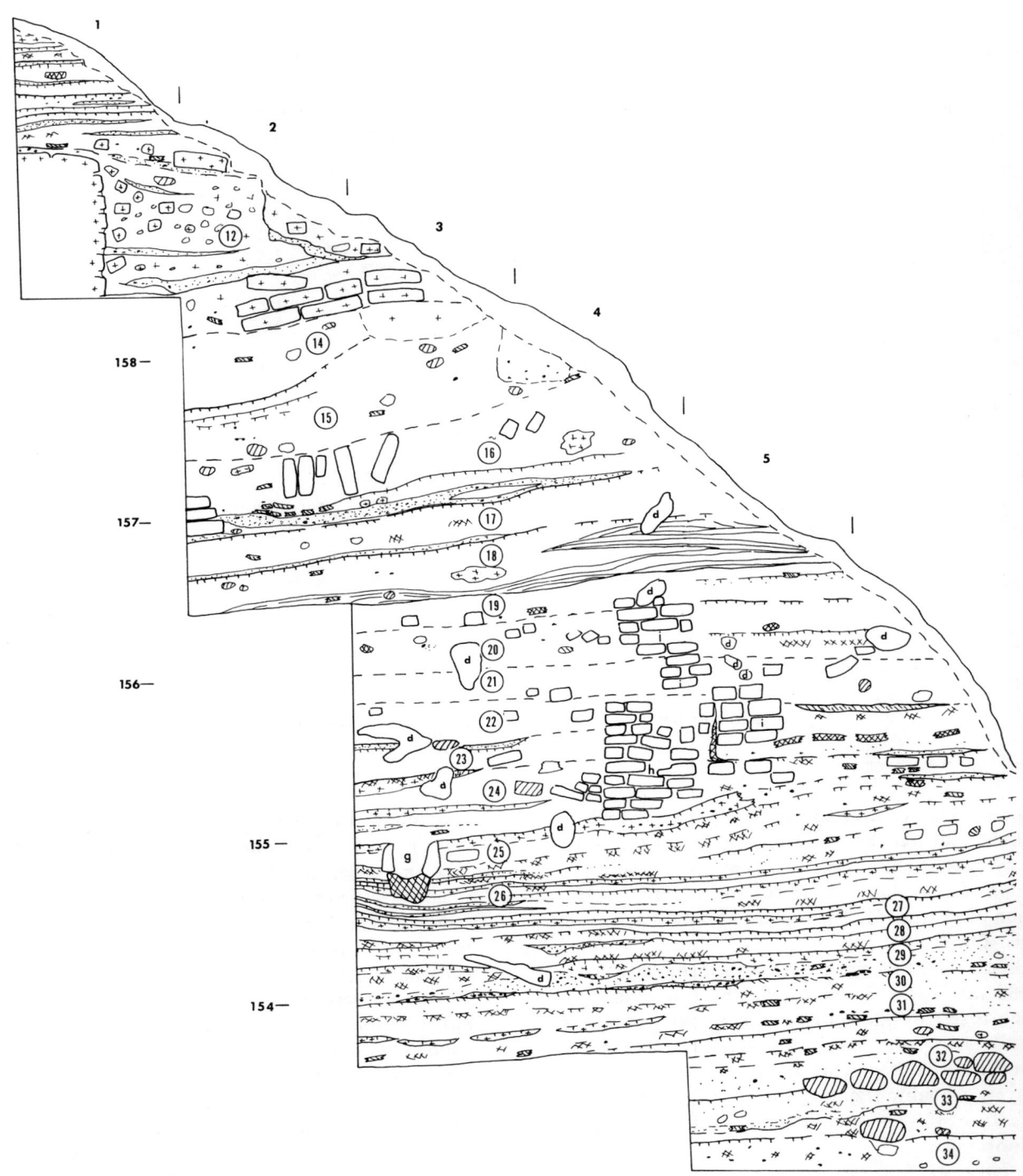

Fig. 7. Upper Portion of the Southeast Section of Excavation B.

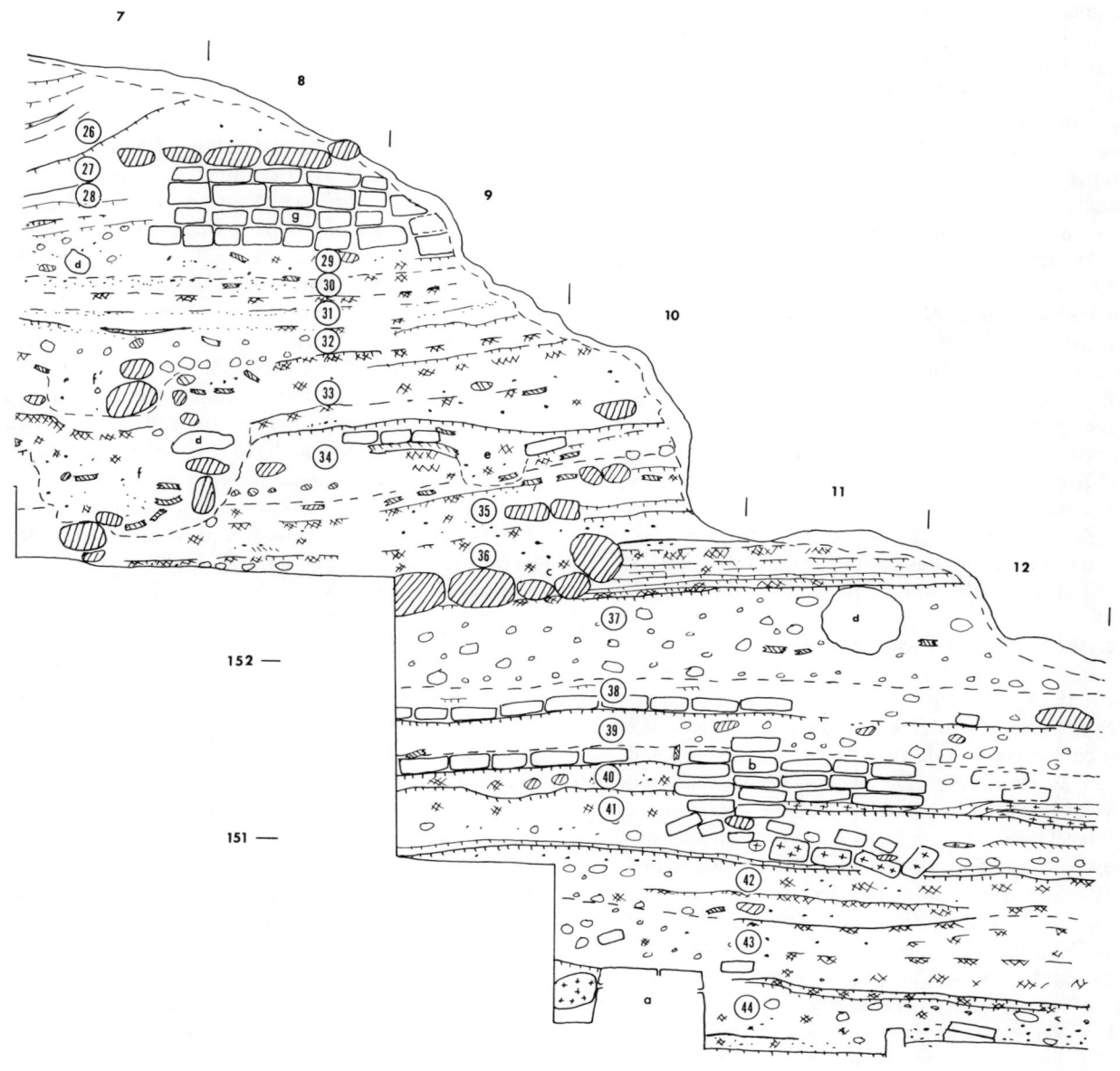

Fig. 8. Lower Portion of the Southeast Section of Excavation B.

east corner of the excavation but the structure to which it is related was not distinguished in plan. It may have been to the north or east. The top of this layer is ill-defined.

Layer 37: Silt and broken brick (.55 m): This homogeneous and virtually sterile building debris was much disturbed by rodents, probably because its upper surface was exposed for several centuries.

BAYAT AND FARUKH PHASE FEATURES

BUILDINGS

Most brick features are made of relatively large flat bricks between .29 and .65 m in length, .19 and .35 m in width, and .08 and .15 m in thickness.

Fragments of these large bricks are used extensively, but only in the case of Feature 40 in Excavation B is there definite evidence of a deliberately molded small brick. The bricks have only small amounts of crushed straw in the clay; some have no detectable straw. In a number of cases parallel vertical marks on the edges of the brick indicate removal of a mold; in one case parallel marks on the top of the brick indicate leveling of the clay mass and removal of the excess from the mold.

Bricklaying is usually haphazard. However, the care exhibited in the construction of the one well-preserved large building shows that skilled workmen could be organized when the need arose. Three patterns of bonding brick walls can be defined:

1) Stretcher bond: In this simplest pattern, the first course is laid end-to-end with the side or stretch of the brick visible. In the second course, the end of each brick is above the middle of a brick in the first. In the third course, the end of each brick is above the middle of a brick in the second. (e.g., the bricks are directly above those in the first course.) This is only useful for walls one brick-width thick, made primarily of whole bricks.

2) Stretcher-Header bond: In this pattern, the first course is laid side-to-side with the end or head of the brick visible. The second course has two rows of bricks end to end, so that the stretches are visible. The third row is like the first and so on. There are variants of this pattern for walls one brick-width thick made of fragments, for walls one brick-length thick, for walls one-and-one-half brick lengths thick, and for walls two or more brick lengths thick. This pattern is used frequently and often somewhat irregularly.

3) Stretcher-edge bond: The first course has bricks laid end-to-end with the stretch visible. Next, there are two bricks also laid end-to-end but on edge, exposing the flat top of bottom of the brick and raising the wall two courses. The fourth course is like the first (Feature 31, Fig. 4e). In a more complicated variant, the first course has two rows of stretchers. Next there are two courses of stretchers laid end-to-end on the center of the first course straddling the space between the two bricks. On either side of this is a row of bricks on edge (Feature 30, Fig. 4c, Fig. 3). The fourth course repeats the first and so on. An occasional header provides additional bonding. Although this bonding pattern should result in a relatively weak wall, there is no doubt that it was used in large, carefully designed buildings, both at Farukhabad and at Tepe Sabz (Hole, Flannery, and Neely, 1969:63: Fig. 15). Other attributes of building construction, for example corner bonding, plasters, and floors, will be detailed in the following paragraphs.

Small building (Excavation A, Feature 32, Layers 37–33, Fig. 9a): Portions of two small rooms and of an open space to the south of this building were exposed. In the earlier phase of construction very large bricks are used. The two rooms are 1.50 m from north to south but are of unknown length. In the later phase of construction, smaller bricks are used. There are indications of corner bonding in the partition at the east end of the east room (Fig. 6b). This room is only 1.50 by 2.10 m. Its entrance may have been in the northeast corner. Some walls show indications of mud plaster. There is a simple pilaster facing the open space. In the open space there is one area of durable pebble paving; otherwise the floors both inside and out are compacted silt, ashy silt, and gypsum grit. A polished black bowl had been smashed on the surface of the space. No other points of interest were noted.

Small building (Excavation B, Feature 41, Layer 44, Fig. 9b): Several rooms and hallways in the northwest corner of an extensive building complex were revealed in the excavation. A surrounding wall is laid in stretcher-edge bond. Immediately south of the north wall is a long narrow space (F,G) only .7 m wide. There were some large stones and a broken ceramic basin on the floor. East of the west wall is a somewhat wider space (C). This had been divided by a greenish brick partition to provide a room 2.00 by 1.40 m, on whose floor were a few sherds and an ash lens. Defined by these two spaces is a block of at least two rooms. To the west is a complete trapezoidal room (D) 2.40 m long, .90 m wide to the north, and 1.40 m wide to the south. This may have been entered from the room to the east. If so, the door was later blocked. Door-blocking is difficult to demonstrate when irregularly laid brickwork survives for only a few courses and lacks plaster. To the east is a room (E) 2.40 m long and more than 1.60 m wide. There are no features of note in these two rooms. All floors are of ashy silt.

During the time of upper Layer 44, a few alterations were made. Space C is again partitioned so that the south half of C is a very small room entered from the north. It is only 1.30 by 1.00

m. The west part of space F and the north half of C seem to form a small room 1.75 by 1.40 m. Room D may have been entered from this room through a door in its northwest corner. The hallway (G) and main rooms (D,E) remain the same. The floors of the outer hall and rooms are covered with ash and charcoal. The main inner rooms have compact gypsum grit and silt floors. The box-like arrangement of bricks at the northwest corner of room D has no floor or distinctive fill and is only one brick thick. Its significance is unknown.

Small building (Excavation B, Feature 40, Layer 41, Fig. 9c, Plate 3a): Layer 43 covers the wall stubs of Feature 41. A poorly preserved wall stub was found on the top of Layer 43. However, the feature 40 complex, founded on the top of Layer 42, does not utilize any of the old wall stubs as foundations. The rooms of this complex are north and west of the former structures and are only partially within the limits of the excavation.

A main wall made of very large bricks runs from east to west. This may be the north wall of a complex similar to Feature 41, described above. South of this wall is a large open space littered with brick fragments, pebbles, and large blocks of consolidated orange and gray silt from the Mehmeh flood plain. A two-meter long partition extends south into this space creating an alcove in the northwest corner. West of this alcove is a room of which one corner was exposed. The wall separating it from the large open space is constructed of very small bricks. The floor of this room has a compact puddled silt base. There is a large ash lens in this floor. To the north of the main wall is another large space with a silt and gypsum grit floor. The north and south spaces may have been courtyards connected by a gap visible in the east end of the main wall. In the north space, the corner of a room with a compact puddled clay floor was exposed, but the actual corner juncture of the walls is not preserved. Between the south wall of this room and the main wall is a narrow alley .80 m wide littered with pebbles and silt blocks. There are no evidences of wall plaster or of corner construction in this complex. In subsequent Layer 40, the possible gap in the main wall is filled. No plan of this later phase is available as a result of an excavation error.

Large building on platform (Excavation A, Features 30 and 31, Layers 32–29, Fig. 9d, Plate 3b): The small building, Feature 32, had been dismantled and packed with several layers of brick, perhaps from its own walls. Additional layers of larger brick bring this brick platform to a height of .85 m. This construction was more than 6.60 m from east to west and more than 5.00 m from north to south. The top is leveled with a layer of silt. On this is a well-built construction with walls laid in stretcher-edge bond. There is an outer wall (Feature 31) running from east to west. North of this is a smaller wall visible in the northwest section which was not further investigated. South of this is an alley or hall 1.30 m wide. The inner wall has a possible double pilaster facing this alley. This elaboration apparently proved weak and sometime after contruction a brick support .75 m in height was wedged in the alley between the inner and outer walls. There were no other features and virtually no refuse within this alley.

South of the inner wall, inside the building proper, there is a solid brick packing to the east and a hallway around an inner room to the west. A section of the hall shaped like to letter 'L' and a corner of the inner room were preserved. The north-south section of the hall east of the inner room is 1.15 m wide and the east-west section north of the inner room is 1.45 m wide. At the corner is a small pilaster. On the prepared silt floor of the east-west section were a large, conical cup, four small cups (two beside and two within the large cup) and a large cylindrical stand for the large cup. There were no other features or artifacts and very little refuse on the floors or in the fill of the hall. No features survive in the inner room.

This impressive building was dismantled and its rooms were filled with broken brick and flat pebbles. Perhaps the surviving complete bricks were taken elsewhere to build a new platform.

Wall stub (Excavation A, Feature 29, Layer 26, Fig. 9e): Only a small portion of this wall, running from north to south, was exposed. East of it is a large open space.

Building with Internal Stone Supports (Excavation A, Feature 28, Layer 25, Fig. 9e): One corner of the excavation revealed part of the east side of this building. The outer wall is made of broken bricks. Inside are parallel rows of rounded cobbles. The rows are about .40 m wide and separated by a space of about .55 m. The concentration of the type of clay used for sealings, as described in Chapter III, around and above this structure suggests that it was a store house.

Platform (Excavation A, Feature 25, Layers 23–22 Fig. 4h,i,5h): This platform was built by

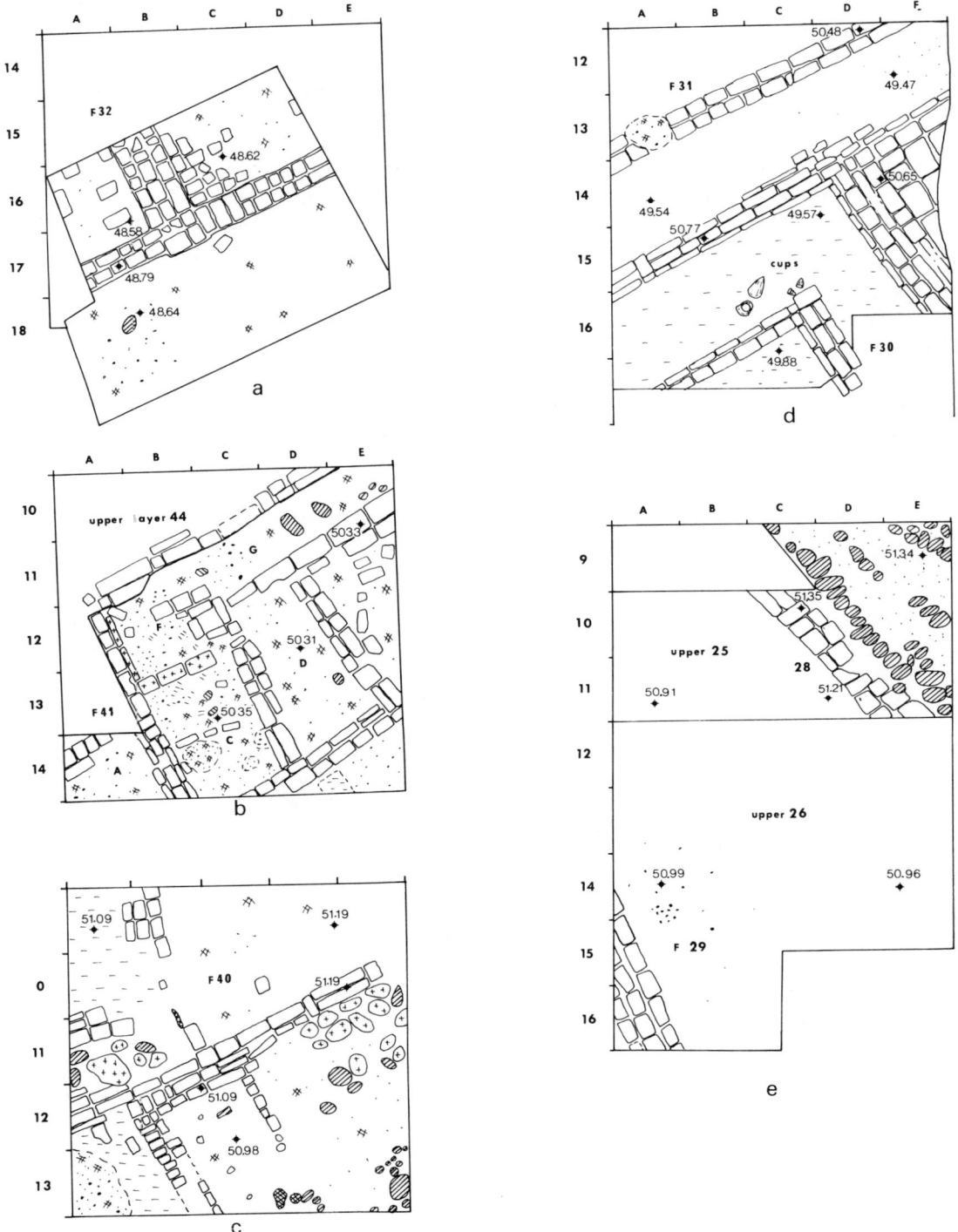

Fig. 9. Bayat and Farukh Phase Buildings. A. Excavation A, Feature 32: a small building. B. Excavation B, Feature 41: a small building; note the burned area on the floor. C. Excavation B, Feature 40: a small building, note the gypsum plaster; D. Excavation A, Features 30 and 31: the large building on a platform. E. Excavation A, Features 28 and 29: a possible granary and a wall stub.

STRATIGRAPHY OF THE BAYAT AND FARUKH PHASES

laying out three or more walls in stretcher bond and filling between them with broken brick until the area was level. Then ten layers of brick were piled up, raising the platform to a height of 1.32 m. The side is nearly vertical and has a definite mud plaster. This early platform is more than 5.70 m from north to south and more than 4.40 m from east to west. A later addition extends this to more than 6.90 by 5.70 m respectively. The floor and possible wall stub of a building once surmounting this platform (Fig. 4i) are visible in the northwest section. The top of this feature was eroded, cut into by later pits (Features 19 and 23) and stained green, probably from use of the pits as latrines. No plan of the possible building could be recovered.

SUMMARY OF THE BUILDINGS

The small building in Excavation A was not sufficiently uncovered to allow comparison with the others. The portions of two small buildings in Excavation B and of the large building on a platform in Excavation A are comparable in several respects. First, the walls face the cardinal points. Second, within the surrounding wall there is a long narrow hall or alley. Third, inside the alley are the rooms or blocks of rooms. Fourth, there is an absence of prepared hearths, bins, pits, or other features. The large building differs from the smaller ones in several respects. First, it is on a low platform. Second, it has two surrounding halls or alleys rather than one. Third its walls are carefully laid in an unusual bond and have elaborate pilasters. Fourth, its alleys and halls are relatively wide. Finally, the larger building is remarkably clean. Except for the set of cups, very little was found in it. The explanation of these similarities and differences will be considered after the analysis of artifact distributions is presented. In general, walled complexes of the sort represented by these buildings were widespread during the fifth millennium. For example similar structures are known from Tepe Gawra XV (Tobler 1950, plate XV) in northern Iraq: and Tall-i Iblis (Caldwell, 1968; Fig. 9) in eastern Iran.

Table 3: Bayat and Farukh Phase Wall Attributes

Ex.	Feature	Brick Sizes	Bond	Wall Thickness	Courses Surviving
A	F32 Lower	.55x.30m	irregular stretcher-header	E-W:.50m N-S:.60m	4+
A	F32 Upper	.35x.25x.10m	irregular stretcher-header	E-W:.40m N-S:.70m	5
B	F41	.30x.22m .40x.25m .55x.28m .65x.35m	irregular stretcher-header and stretcher-edge	outer:.45m inner:.40m	2
B	F40	.20x.11x.06m .32x.25m .45x.22m .50x.30x.10m	stretcher	E-W:.40m	3
A	F30, 31	.30x.19x.08m .30x.22x.10m .35x.25x.10m .29x.25x.09m .45x.25x.10m .50x.30x.15m	stretcher-edge	31:.45m 30 outer:.45m 30 inner E-W:.40m 30 inner N-S:.50m	11
A	F29	.32x.22x.10m	stretcher-header	.55	6
A	F28	.42x.28m	unknown	.55	1
A	F25	.32x.20m .45x.32m .48x.32m	unknown	unknown	0

The possible store house (Feature 28) in Excavation A is unusual. Otherwise similar structures in Tepe Gawra XVI, XVA, and XV (Ibid.) have interior supports of mud brick.

OTHER FEATURES

In Excavation A below Layer 37, the lowest layer excavated, a large circular oven or kiln could be seen eroding from the face of the mound. This would have been washed away in a season or two so it was cleaned and recorded. The floor of the feature was .90 m below the base of Layer 37. The complete construction would have been about 3 m in diameter. On its flat, fired plaster floor was .18 m of ash. Around and over the remains was a thick layer of mud brick fragments. Above this was a layer of compact silt floors which would have been labeled Layer 38 had it been excavated. This early oven is the largest known from the site.

Also in Excavation A are three small pits which were intrusive in Layers 28 and 29. One, 1.20 m deep and .40 m across, is visible on the southwest section in square A-13 (Fig. 4). Two others, 1.15 by .75 m and .85 by .60 m, both with ash and charcoal fills, are visible in plan in squares A, B-12, 13. These were not assigned feature numbers.

Concentrations of small oval flat pebbles were noted in Excavation A, Layer 29, square C-15, in the fill of the inner hall of the large building on a platform, and in Excavation B, Layer 38 lower, squares B, C-10. These are also unnumbered.

No other features were noted.

Chapter II
CERAMICS OF THE BAYAT AND FARUKH PHASES

INTRODUCTION

The ceramics of the Bayat and Farukh phase layers at Farukhabad present a relatively simple range of forms and a complicated variety of painted designs in contrast to the ceramics of the succeeding Uruk and Jemdet Nasr periods. In the following section the rare wares are described first, and the dominant Susiana Buff Ware is described last. Duplication of statements by Hole, Flannery, and Neely is kept to a minimum. The format is only slightly different from theirs, and the information should be comparable.

KHAZINEH RED WARE

Farukhabad examples of this ware contain quantities of crushed calcite, straw, crushed sherd, and sometimes, sand inclusions. The particles constitute 20 to 40 percent of the body; their median size is about one millimeter. The vessels are hand-built probably by lapping together rings of clay. They are usually fired to a red or brown color. Both black unoxidized cores and black smudges on the exterior occur. Surfaces are often roughly smoothed but brushed and pinched examples also occur (Fig. 10d,e)

The only form in this ware noted at Farukhabad is a medium-sized, hole-mouth globular jar. Two large examples are illustrated. One is from an alcove in a small building in Layer 40 of Excavation B (Fig. 10a) and is tempered with crushed sherds and limestone. Its rim diameter is 17.0 cm. The other, a lone example from a courtyard area in Layer 43 of Excavation B (Pl. 8b), is tempered with coarse sand. This essentially complete vessel has a volume of 18.0 liters, a maximum diameter of 34.8 cm, a height of 29.6 cm, and a rim diameter of 18.2 cm.

BAYAT RED WARE

The few Farukhabad examples of this ware have a compact paste with occasional and perhaps accidental inclusions of calcite and sand. Both body and slip are fired to a brick red color.

The only form noted is an open bowl (Fig. 10l-n) apparently shaped like those illustrated in Hole, Flannery, and Neely (1969 Fig. 67a). This ware, common at Tepe Sabz, is scarce at Farukhabad. It is not known whether this is a result of the differences in activities performed in the excavated areas of Tepe Sabz and Tepe Farukhabad or of stylistic differences between the two periods.

BURNISHED BLACK WARE

Few examples of this compact, reduced and highly burnished ceramic were found (Fig. 10i-k). As in the examples from Tepe Sabz (Ibid.: 168–69), there are mica inclusions in the clay. All examples are fragments of small open bowls. A reconstructed bowl with rim diameter of 23 cm is illustrated in Fig. 10i.

FINE BLACK-ON-TAN WARE

A few examples similar to those reported from Tepe Sabz (Ibid:167–68) are treated as Susiana Ware. One particularly well-preserved example is illustrated in Fig. 10o.

SUSIANA BUFF WARE

The numerous examples of this ware represented in the samples conform closely to the description presented by Hole, Flannery, and Neely (1969:

124-26). The clay is compact and well-cleaned. Quartz sand inclusions, probably a deliberate tempering, range from round to subangular, predominately the latter. A variety of unidentified minerals also occurs. Most vessels contain two to four percent fine sand grains. A few large jars and bowls have larger grains, while small bowls have little or no sand. Some fresh vertical breaks exhibit regular oblique lineations slanting from the outside of the vessel downward toward the inside of the vessel, an effect which may be produced by wheel-throwing. The ring bases found on some bowls are perhaps cut or tooled from otherwise flat bases of vessels inverted on a wheel. However, the surfaces of Susiana Ware vessels are scraped when stiff and often wet-smoothed as well; definite wheel traces are absent. Experimental work and technical analysis will be needed to demonstrate the techniques used to manufacture Susiana Buff Ware. Firing is well-controlled and colors vary from brick red to yellow-green, though most are a very light brown.

Hole, Flannery, and Neely have divided sherds of Susiana Ware into two types named in the binomial terminology of Americanists. They term these 'Susiana Buff' and 'Susiana Black-on-Buff'. Counts and weights of body sherds, divided into these classes, are given in Appendix Table B7. Counts of diagnostic sherds are given in Table B4. These data will enable the reader to compare the Farukhabad and Sabz samples in the quantitative manner used by Hole and Shaw (1967). Categories based on rim sherds and other diagnostic vessel parts are discussed below. Earlier Susiana sherds were brought up into Bayat and Farukh Phase levels by various earth-moving activities. Two represent the Chogha Mami Transitional Phase (Fig. 11a,b), one represents the Khazineh Phase (Fig. 11c) and two represent the Mehmeh Phase (Fig. 11d,e). Layers deposited in these, and perhaps other, phases doubtless constitute the yet unexcavated lowest five m of deposit at Farukhabad.

SMALL BOWLS

The overwhelming majority of our sherds are parts of small bowls of types 11 and 12 of Hole, Flannery, and Neely (1969:153-57). Below, I divide rims of these forms on the basis of design motifs and discuss variations in vessel size and shape associated with each motif. The measurements in the Appendixes permit the readers to reanalyze the bowls in terms of other typologies should they so choose.

First let us consider bowl bases. Measurements are in Appendix Table C1.

Wide Bowl Base (Fig. 12a,b): These bases are scraped to form, in one quarter of the cases, a gently rounded bottom, and in the rest a slightly flattened bottom defined by a slight carination. Only about one sixth are plain. The rest have one or more concentric painted bands around the base. These bases range from 0.3 to 0.7 cm in vessel side thickness, in contrast to large flat bases, discussed below.

Narrow Bowl Bases (Figs. 13a,b; 14a, b;): These bases are on nearly conical vessel bodies. A majority are scraped and then rounded (Fig. 13a) but some are shaved down as if with a knife,

---

Fig. 10. Khazineh Red, Burnished Black, Bayat Red, and Fine Black-on-Tan Ware Vessel Rims. (N.B.: The ceramic captions present inclusions, body color below the outer surface, paint color for the best preserved remnant, rim or neck diameter in cm, Excavation number, University of Michigan Museum of Anthropology catalogue number also used in the appendix tables, and Layer number. If the actual Munsell color code is given, the sherd is not recorded in an appendix table.) A. Hole mouth jar with nodes, crushed sherd and crushed calcite (limestone), body 5YR 7/4 (pink), diam.: 16; X649, 60629 (B40). B. Hole mouth jar rim, straw and calcite, body 2.5YR 6/6 (light red), diam.: ca. 15; X256, 60185 (A17,18). C. Same, crushed sherd, body 5YR 6/6 (reddish yellow), diam.: ca. 18; X615, 60615 (B40). D. Same with combing, crushed sherd, body 7.5 YR 6/6 (reddish yellow), diam.: ca. 15; X756, 60695 (B47). E. Same with oval impressions, crushed sherd, body 10YR 8/4 (very pale brown), diam.: ca. 24; X756, 60695 (B47). F. Same, crushed sherd, shell, hematite, straw, body 5YR 6/6 (reddish yellow), diam.: ca. 18; X648, 60626 (B40). G. Same, straw and calcite (similar to 60185 above), body 2.5 YR 5/6 (red), diam.: ca. 10; X533, 60553 (B34). H. Same, straw and calcite, body 7.5 YR 7/4 (pink), diam.: ca. 24; X493, 60263 (A27). I. Black burnished bowl, calcite and fine micaceous sand, body 10YR 5/1 (gray), surface 10YR 4/1 (dark gray), diam.: 24; X671 (A35). J. Black burnished bowl rim, calcite, body 10YR 4/1 (dark gray), burnished surface N 3/0 (very dark gray), diam.: 30; X726, 60673 (B44). K. Black burnished base, calcite body 2.5 YR 3/2 (very dark grayish brown), burnished surface N 3/0 (very dark gray), carination diam.: 12; X704, 60325 (A36). L. Bayat red bowl rim, calcite, body 2.5 YR 6/6 (light red), slip (?) 2.5 YR 6/4 (light reddish brown), diam.: 27; X607, 60293 (A29). M. Bayat red bowl rim, calcite body, 5YR 6/6 (reddish yellow), flaky slip 5YR 6/5 (light reddish brown), diam.: 27; X451 (A24). N. Bayat red bowl rim, calcite, body 2.5 YR 6/7 (light red) flaky slip 2.5 YR 5/6 (red), diam.: 23; X690, 60649 (B42). O. Fine black-on-tan vessel rim, no inclusions, body 7.5YR 7/5 (reddish yellow), paint 5YR 4/1 (dark gray), diam.: 24; X485, 60258 (A25).

CERAMICS OF THE BAYAT AND FARUKH PHASES

25

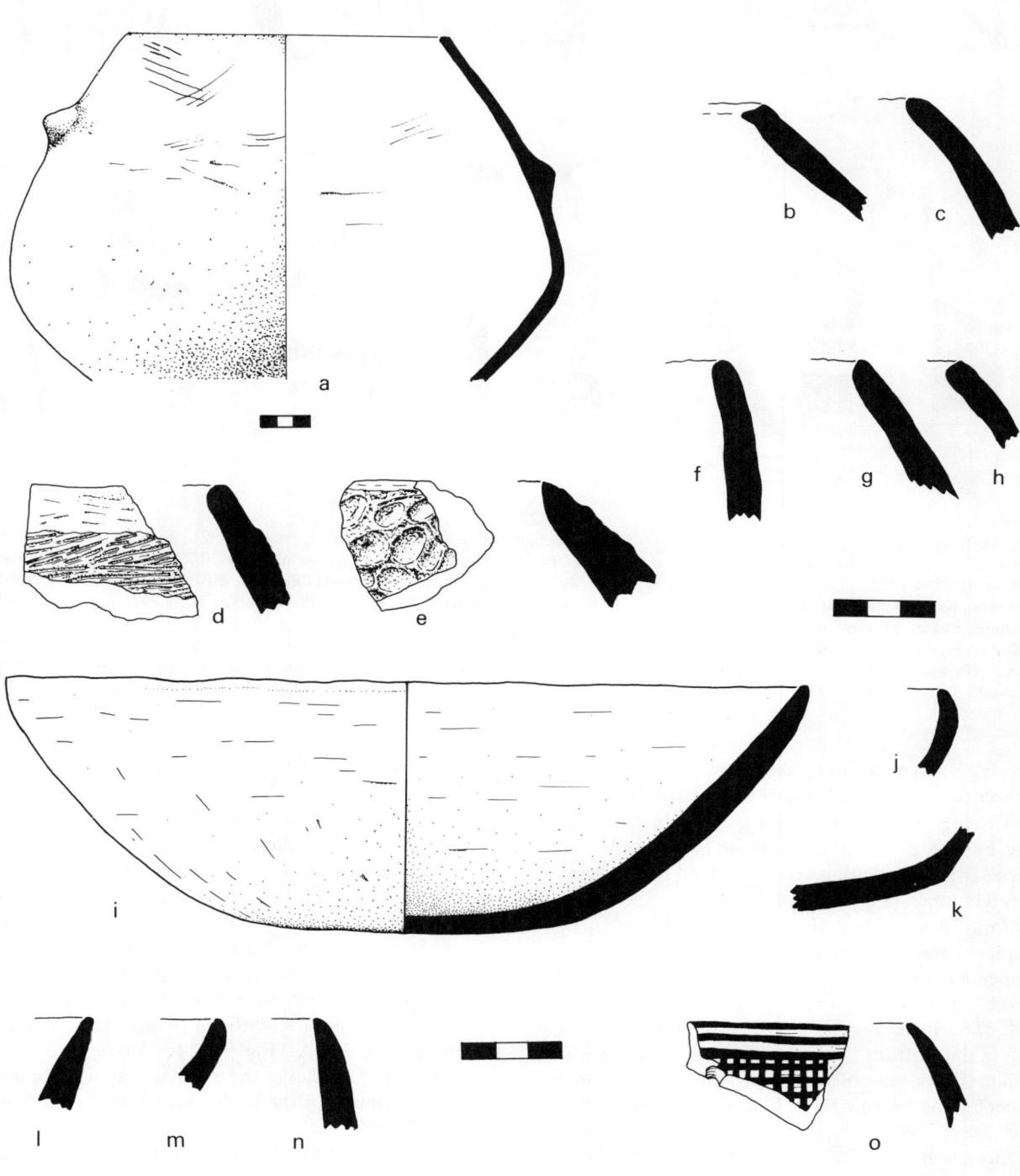

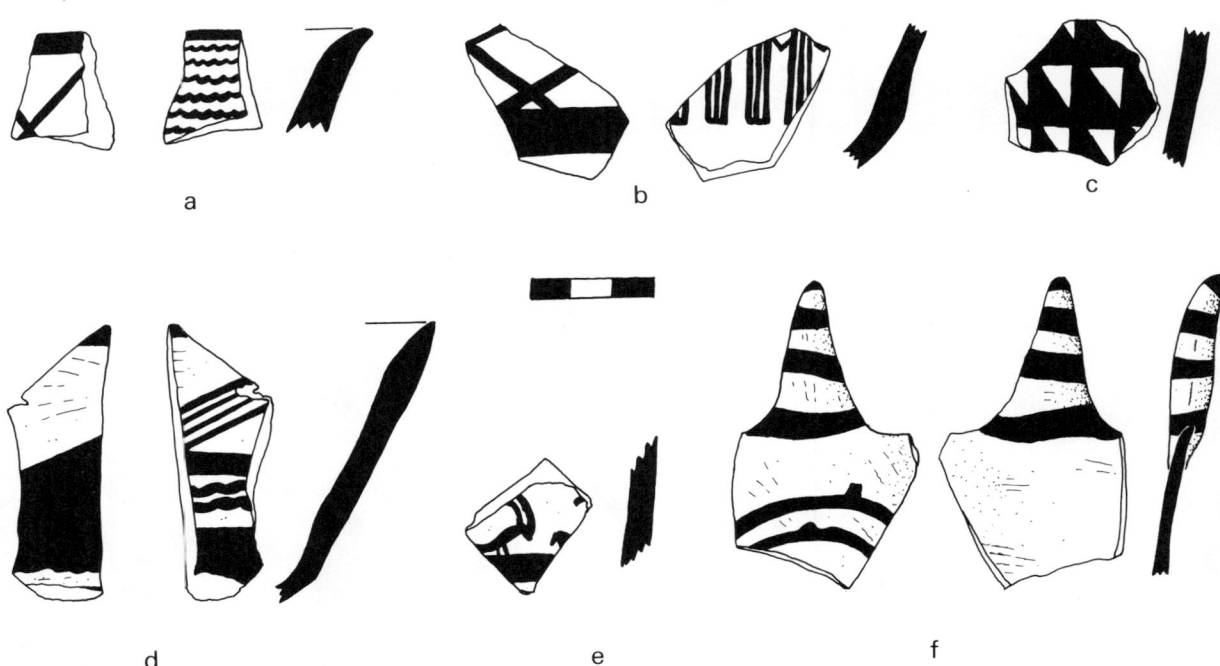

Fig. 11. Earlier Susiana Ceramics. A. Bowl rim, medium sand, body 2.5 Y 8/3 (white), paint damaged; X621 (B39) (cf. Hole 1977: Fig. 50a,b, Plate 34a-d,f, Chogha Mami Transitional Phase). B. Bowl carination fragment, fine sand, body 2.5Y 8/4 (pale yellow), paint damaged; X538, 60272 (A28) (cf. Hole 1977: Fig. 50f, Plate 34c,e,g, Chogha Mami Transitional Phase). C. Bowl sherd with exterior motif, fine sand, body 2.5Y 8/3 (white), paint 10YR3/1 (very dark gray); X443, 60241 (A24) (cf. Hole, Flannery, and Neely 1969: Fig. 61a, 62c, cf. Mehmeh Phase). D. Bowl rim and carination fragment, fine sand, body 2.5Y 7/4 (pale yellow), paint 10YR 3/1 (very dark gray); X585, 60291 (A30) (cf. Hole, Flannery, and Neely 1969: Fig. 56b, Fig. 57i-r, Khazineh Phase). E. Bowl sherd with interior motif, no visible inclusions, body 2.5 Y 8/2 (white), paint 10YR 4/1 (dark gray); X407, 60233 (A22) (cf. Hole, Flannery, and Neely 1969: Fig. 59b-m, Mehmeh Phase). F. Bowl rim with appendage, fine sand, body 2.5Y 8/3 (white), paint damaged; X547, 60281 (29).

leaving a small flat area on the base not subsequently rounded (Fig. 13b). As will be shown in Chapter V, this shaved base cup is restricted to the Farukh Phase. One example in the measured series is painted with a vertical curved line between straight lines (Fig. 14b).

Ring Bowl Bases (Fig. 12c, d;): There is no evidence that these bases were separately made and appended to the vessel. They seem to have been tooled from a flat base. The vessel base is usually flat. The inner face of the ring is gently concave while the bottom of the ring is quite concave and often shows possible scorings from turning on a wheel. This bottom is obliquely oriented so that the vessel would rest on the juncture between bottom and inner faces. The outer face is markedly concave, so that the juncture between the bottom and outer face forms an acute angle and is therefore often chipped and damaged during use. The rings range from 7 to 18 cm in diameter. Almost all examples have a band of paint on the outer face of the ring.

Plain Bowl Rims (Fig. 13a,b; 14a): These rims come from bell-shaped or hemispherical bowls with wide bases, as well as conical vessels with narrow bases, but there is no method available for differentiating rims of the two forms. A set of complete examples of the conical variety, including three small, and one large example associated with a cylindrical stand, were found on the floor of the large building on a platform (Features 30 and 31) in Excavation A (Fig. 13,14c; Plate 8c,d). No complete examples of the other variety were found. The diameters of the Plain Bowl Rims range from 6 to 28 cm.

Single Band Bowl Rims (Fig. 15a,b): These rims have one band of paint on the rim exterior. Some doubtless once had multiple bands or other motifs now broken off. Only rims one cm or longer could be measured on a diameter chart. From each

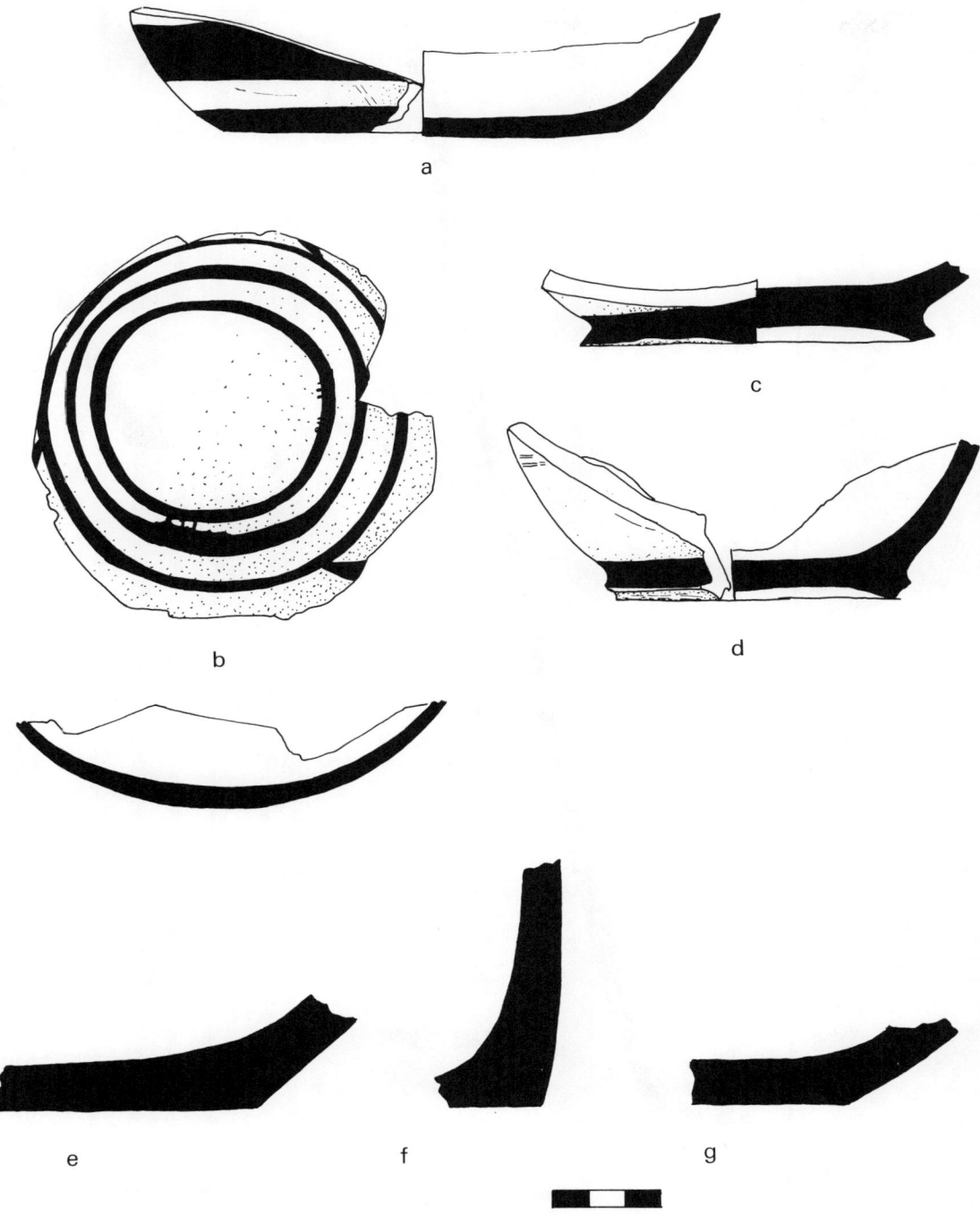

Fig. 12. Susiana Ware: Vessel Bases. A. Medium flat base, fine sand, body white, paint very dark gray; X31401 (B F10). B. Medium round base, fine sand, body pale olive, paint very dark gray; X695, 6065601 (B42). C. Ring base, fine sand, body white, paint dark gray, diam.: 10; X632, 6061501 (B39). D. Ring base, fine sand, body white, paint very dark grayish brown, ring diam.: 12; X751, 6069104 (B46). E. Heavy flat base, fine sand, body pink, diam.: 14; X752, 6069302 (B46). F. Heavy flat base, fine sand, body white, diam.: 13; X540, 6027401 (A28). G. Heavy flat base, fine sand, body pink, diam.: 12; X505, 6026801 (A F29).

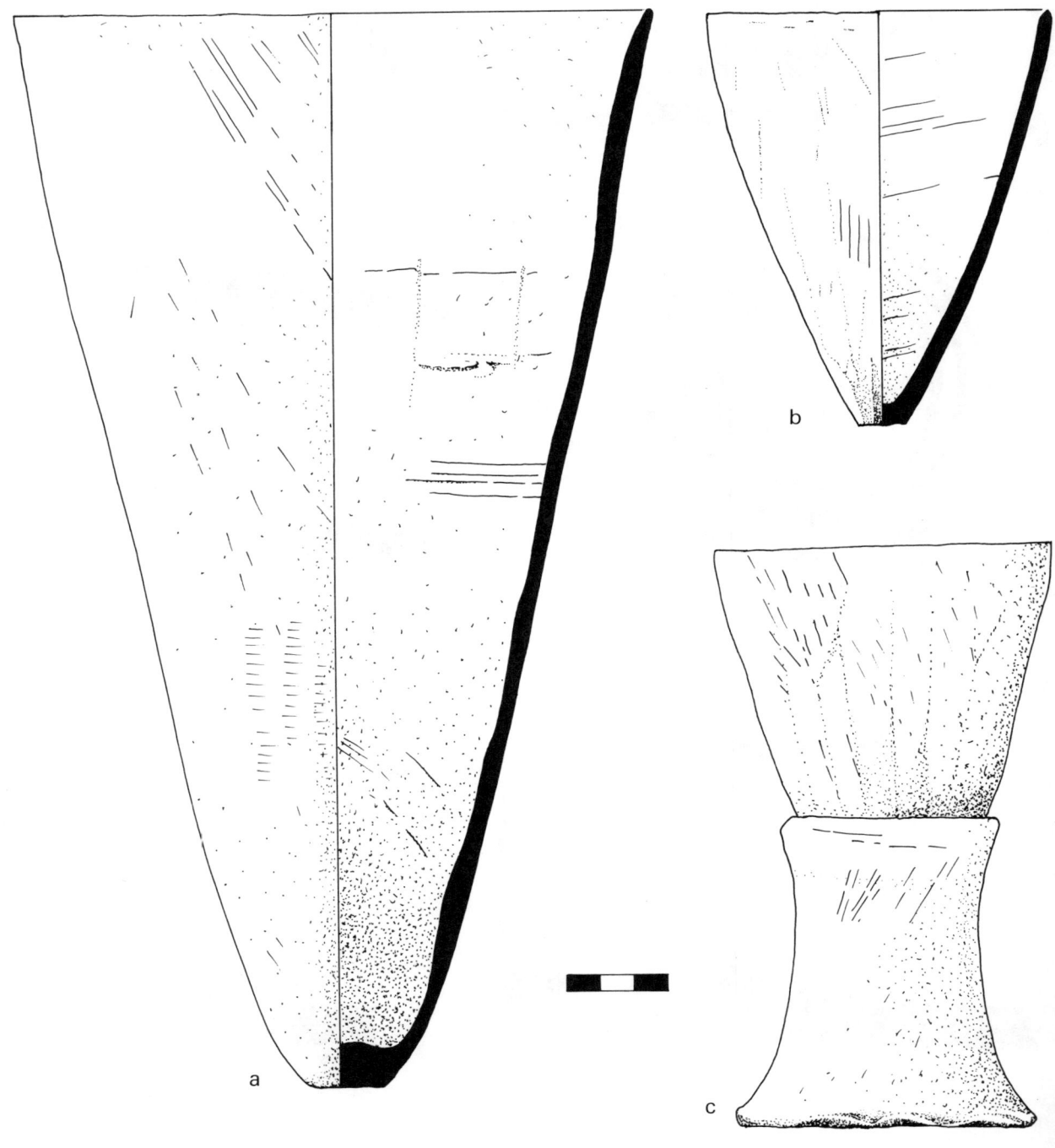

Fig. 13. Susiana Ware: Narrow-Based Vessels with Matching Stand. A. Large vessel, medium sand, body 7.5YR 8/3 (pinkish white), diam.: 19, height: 31.9; X609, 60787 (A31). B. Small vessel, medium sand, body 5Y 8/2 (white), diam.: 10, height: 11.9; X609, 6078901 (A31). C. Small vessel on stand, fine sand, body 2.5YR 6/4 (light red), upper diam.: 7, lower diam.: 9, height: 9.5; 6078901 (above) on X252, 60778 (A18).

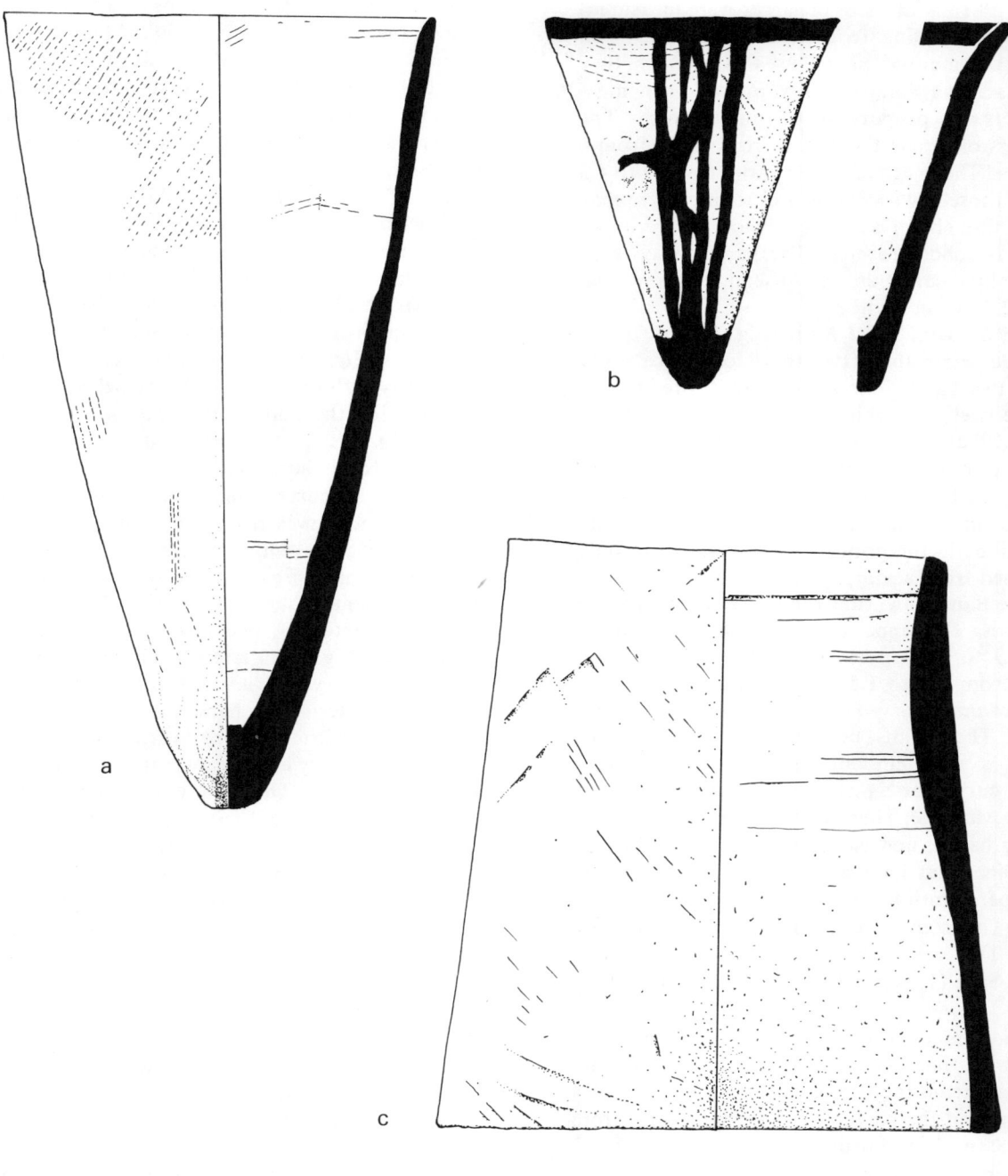

Fig. 14. Susiana Ware: Narrow-Based Vessels and Matching Stand. A. Large vessel, medium sand, body 2.5Y 8/2 (white), diam.: 11, height: 17.3; X491, 60784 (A26). B. Small vessel with vertical straight and curved line motif, fine sand, body 10YR 7/5 (very pale brown), paint 2.5YR 4/2 (weak red), diam.: 9, height: 11; X681 (B41). C. Large stand, matching vessel 60787 (Fig. 13a), medium sand, body 10YR 8/4 (very pale brown), upper diam.: 13, lower diam.: 16, height: 31.9; X609, 60787 (A31).

sample, all rims this size or larger were measured. If those attempting to compare their data with those in this monograph will use this criterion, they should achieve comparability in both rim measurements and proportions of rim categories. The diameters of Single Band Bowl rims range from 6 to 36 cm. The width of bands varies from .2 to 4.3 cm, but those few widths greater than two cm may best be thought of as vessels whose entire upper body was solidly painted. The paint always runs over the lip creating an interior band ranging from 0.2 to 2.7 cm in width.

Multiple Band Bowl Rims (Fig. 15c–h): In the measured series about two thirds of this category exhibit two bands, one sixth exhibit three bands, and one twelfth exhibit four or more bands. Note, however, that because of the above-mentioned one cm selection criterion, the proportions of different numbers of bands probably differs from the proportions on a series of whole vessels. The actual proportions in the population of vessels can only be learned from a sample of near-complete pieces. Multiple Band Bowl rims range in diameter from 8 to 38 cm. The uppermost exterior band ranges from 0.3 to 2.4 cm in width. The interior band ranges from 0.2 to 1.5 cm in width.

Horizontal Curved Line Bowl Rims (Fig. 16a–d): These rims usually have, from top to bottom, a wide circumferential band, a narrow band, a curved or zig-zag line, a narrow band and another wide one. There are variants with only two defining bands, and variants with more than one curved line. Rim diameters range from 12 to 34 cm. The upper exterior band width ranges from 0.2 to 1.5 cm. The interior band width ranges from 0.3 to 1.3 cm. This motif is common in the Bayat Phase at Tepe Sabz (Hole, Flannery, and Neely 1969:Fig. 62e, Pl. 29d,e).

Vertical Line Bowl Rims (Fig. 16e): This category of rim has one to four straight vertical lines extending from the rim band probably down to a band around the base. Rim diameters range from 12 to 28 cm. Exterior upper bands range from 0.3 to 1.4 cm. Interior rim bands vary from 0.3 to 0.6 cm. Examples are known from Bayat Phase layers at Tepe Sabz (Ibid.: Plate 29 h).

Vertical Curved Line Bowl Rims (Fig. 16f–h): This rim motif usually has four vertical straight lines with a vertical curved line in the middle between the second and third straight lines. The examples of this motif in the measured series were too few and too battered to accurately estimate ranges of diameters and rim band widths. This motif is characteristic of "Type 11a" from Tepe Sabz (Ibid.: 151–153, Fig. 60j, Plate 29b). It reaches its greatest popularity during the Bayat Phase. The examples found in Farukh Phase layers seem small and poorly drafted in comparison with earlier Bayat Phase examples, as will be discussed in Chapter V.

Dot Motif Bowl Rims (Fig. 17): These rims are distinguished by lines of free-standing ovoid dots. The more complete examples indicate that there are at least two motifs included in this category. One has pendant rectangles below the rim band and simple rows of dots between and below these rectangles (Fig. 17b–d). The other has one or more bold curved lines around the vessel with peaks approaching the upper rim band and lower base band (Fig. 17e–g); the lines of dots parallel both the bands and the curved lines. In at least some examples the curved line is not continuous but thins out and curves around in a small hook; there are small slashes within this hook. These hooks may represent vestigial animal bodies and the line may represent exaggerated horns. A similar element, without dots, occurs on a reconstructable small bowl (Fig. 22f, Plate 83). The rims of the dot motif category vary from 10 to 27 cm in diameter. The upper exterior rim band ranges from 0.2 to 0.7 cm, and the interior rim band varies from 0.3 to 0.7 cm in width. They are narrower than the rim bands on other bowls. There may be several distinct modes of dot size and spacing. It is possible that the larger dots are associated with the curved line variety. Larger samples would be needed to test this proposition. Dot motifs are not present on Bayat Phase bowls. The pendant rectangle variety is common in surface collections from the Ram Hormuz and Susiana plains, but the curved line variety seems to be distinctive to the Deh Luran plain.

Sigma Motif Bowl Rims (Fig. 18a–d): These rims are distinguished by a row of free-standing elements shaped like the Greek letter 'sigma' below the top band. Variants with an extra stroke (Fig. 18c) and with poor draftsmanship approaching an irregular curved line or even a slash (Fig. 18d) occur. Below this row are another band and additional, seldom preserved elements. Rim diameters vary from 12 to 42 cm. Both the uppermost exterior band and the interior band vary in width from 0.1 to 0.8 cm. The sigma element probably exists in the earlier Susiana design repertoire, but it first appears in quantity on bowl rims during the Farukh Phase.

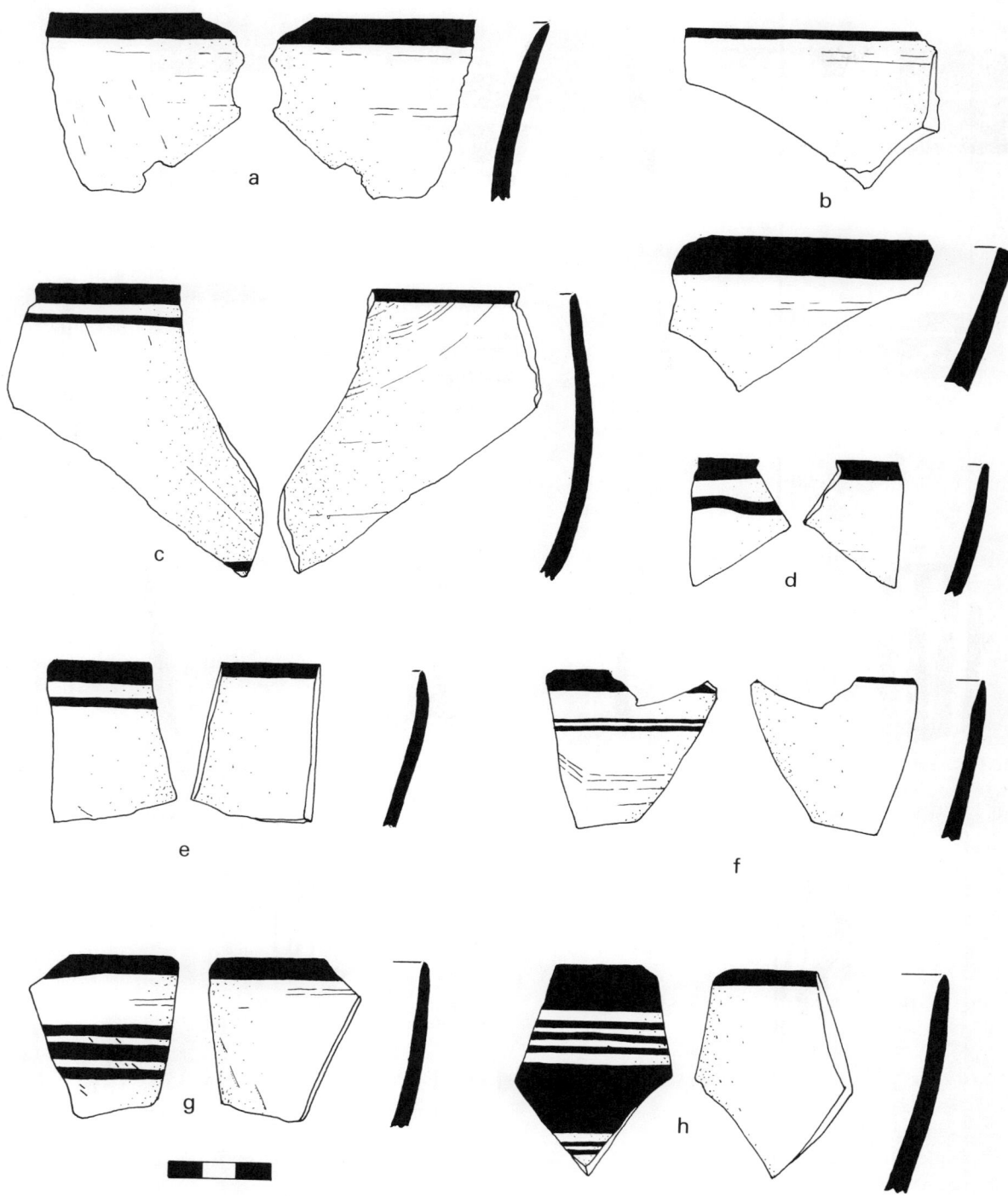

Fig. 15. Susiana Ware: Band Motifs on Bowl Rims. A. Fine sand, body light reddish brown, paint light red, diam.: 16; X446, 6024601 (A24). B. Fine sand and calcite, body pink, paint dusky red, diam.: 36; X736, 6068301 (B45). C. Fine sand, body very pale brown, paint very dark gray, diam.: 13; X485, 6025901 (A25). D. Fine sand, body white, paint very dark grayish brown, diam.: 16; C587, 6058301 (B36). E. Fine sand, body white, paint black, diam.: 16; X729, 6067501 (B45). F. Fine sand, body white, paint very dusky red, diam.: 16; X690, 6064901 (B42). G. Fine sand, body white, paint reddish black, diam.: 12; X485, 6025802 (A25). H. Fine sand, body white, paint dark gray, diam.: 17; X537, 6027002 (A28).

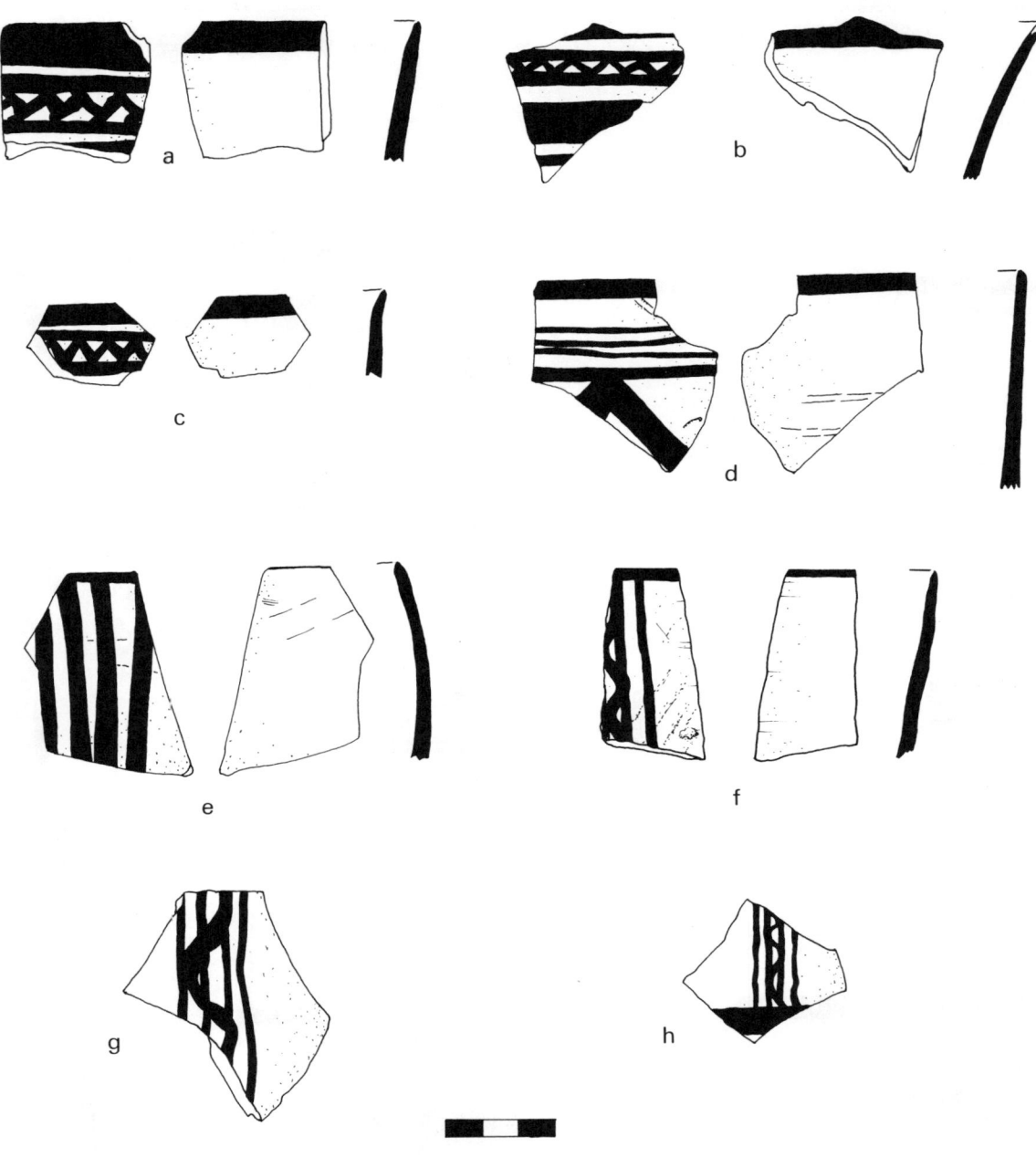

Fig. 16. Susiana Ware: Horizontal and Vertical Curved Line Motifs on Bowl Rims. A. Fine sand, body pale yellow, paint dark reddish brown, diam.: 22; X699, 6032301 (A36). B. Fine sand, body light gray, paint very dark gray, diam.: 30; X726, 6067301 (B44). C. Fine sand, body very pale brown, paint very dark gray, diam.: 16; X640, 6030301 (A31). D. Fine sand, body very pale brown, paint dusky red, diam.: 12; X645, 6062202 (B40). E. Medium sand, body pale yellow, paint dark olive gray, diam.: 21; X722, 6067101 (B44). F. Fine sand, body very pale brown, paint very dark gray, diam.: 22; X632, 6061501 (B40). G. Fine sand, body very pale brown, paint dark reddish brown; X645, 6062201 (B40). H. Fine sand, body white, paint dark gray; X686, 6064701 (B41).

Slash Motif Bowl Rims (Fig. 18e–f): These rims have rows of oblique slashes and other elements such as rectangles below the exterior rim bands. These slashes are usually free-standing. The rim diameters are large, varying from 22 to 45 cm. The rim shape seems similar to those of the Diamond Motif Bowl Rims described below. The upper exterior rim band ranges from 0.7 to 1.3 cm wide, while the inner rim band varies from 0.2 to 1.0 cm.

Step Motif Bowl Rims (Fig. 19): These rims are distinguished by a set of three or four elements between upper rim bands, always a wider band above a narrower one, and similar, but reversed, lower base bands. These elements descend from left to right. Each is a series of three or more connected scalene triangles with concave sides. A complete example with a Ring Base was found at nearby Tepe Musiyan (Gautier and Lampre 1905: 99, Fig. 151). However, several Wide Bowl Base fragments from Farukhabad are from bowls with step motifs. Rim diameters vary from 10 to 18 cm. Upper exterior rim bands vary from 0.3 to 1.6 cm. Interior rim bands vary from 0.2 to 0.7 cm. This motif seems to be distinctive to the Farukh Phase on the Deh Luran Plain.

Diamond Motif Bowl Rims (Fig. 20): On these rims there are usually three or more narrow bands immediately below the rim band. One finds, in cases where a substantial proportion of the rim is preserved, an equal number of small bands around the middle of the bowl's body. Two offset zig-zag lines between these sets of bands create alternating diamonds and opposed triangles. These are usually filled in with solid paint, oblique lines, or crosshatched lines. The rim diameters range from 18 to 34 cm. The upper exterior rim band ranges from 0.6 to 1.2 cm, and the interior band ranges from 0.2 to 1.0 cm in width. The diamond element is very common both in the earlier Deh Luran phases (Hole, Flannery, and Neely 1969:146, Fig. 55) and in fifth millennium ceramics throughout Greater Mesopotamia.

Other Bowl Rims (Fig. 21; 22; Plate 8e): In the measured series there were a number of bowl sherds with unique or rare designs. One is of Fine Black-on-Tan Ware (Fig. 21d). At least one has a motif often thought characteristic of Susa A (Fig. 22g). This sherd was in tertiary context in Uruk layers.

Comments on the Bowl Fragments: Six of the bowl types distinguished above are sufficiently numerous to allow statistical comparison of certain shared attributes as shown on Table 4.

With three exceptions the motifs occur on one bowl shape like Sabz "Type 11" (Ibid:155–57), usually with slightly out-turned sides and a diameter of about fifteen cm. The exceptions are 1) a plain conical form which constitutes a portion of the Plain Bowl rims and slightly lowers their rim angle; 2) a slightly smaller form with step motifs, and 3) a larger form like Sabz "Type 12" (Ibid.: 153–5) with Diamond Motifs and perhaps Slash, some Sigma, and some Horizontal Curved Band motifs.

Both rim bands on the Dot and Step Motif bowls are relatively narrow. The exterior rim bands on the bowls with Horizontal Curved Lines, Slash Motifs, and Diamond Motifs are all relatively wide.

It is possible that these bowls were either made for several different uses, each of which had a customary range of motifs, or were made by several different groups. The analysis of their association with other artifact types in the layers and features of Farukhabad, presented in Chapter V, seeks to clarify this problem.

LARGE VESSELS

In this category are placed all vessels other than small bowls.

Large Flat Bases (Figs. 12 e–g): These bases occur on both jars and large basins. Ranging in diameter from 10 to 36 cm, they are distinguished from Wide Bowl Bases by their thick sides, which range from 0.7 to 2.3 cm.

Large Basin Rims (Fig. 23): This category includes both the large basins, some oval (Ibid.: 127–29), and the "Bowl Type 15" (Ibid.:149–50) from Tepe Sabz. There are very few of the latter type (Fig. 23i). The sides are roughly scraped leaving both scratches and rows of parallel "chattermarks" perhaps created when a scraping tool is held against the turning vessel wall (Fig. 23b). The lips are usually flattened, but some are concave (Fig. 23e). The one reconstructed vessel has a definitely oval rim resulting from sagging or deliberate pulling after the vessel was formed (Fig. 23a). The diameters of the sample—measured with a circular diameter chart—range from 12 to 80 cm but the histogram of vessel diameters shows two modes, one at about 30 cm and one at about 50 cm. These probably represent the ends and sides of oval basin rims. The partially reconstructed example had a height of about 12 cm and a width

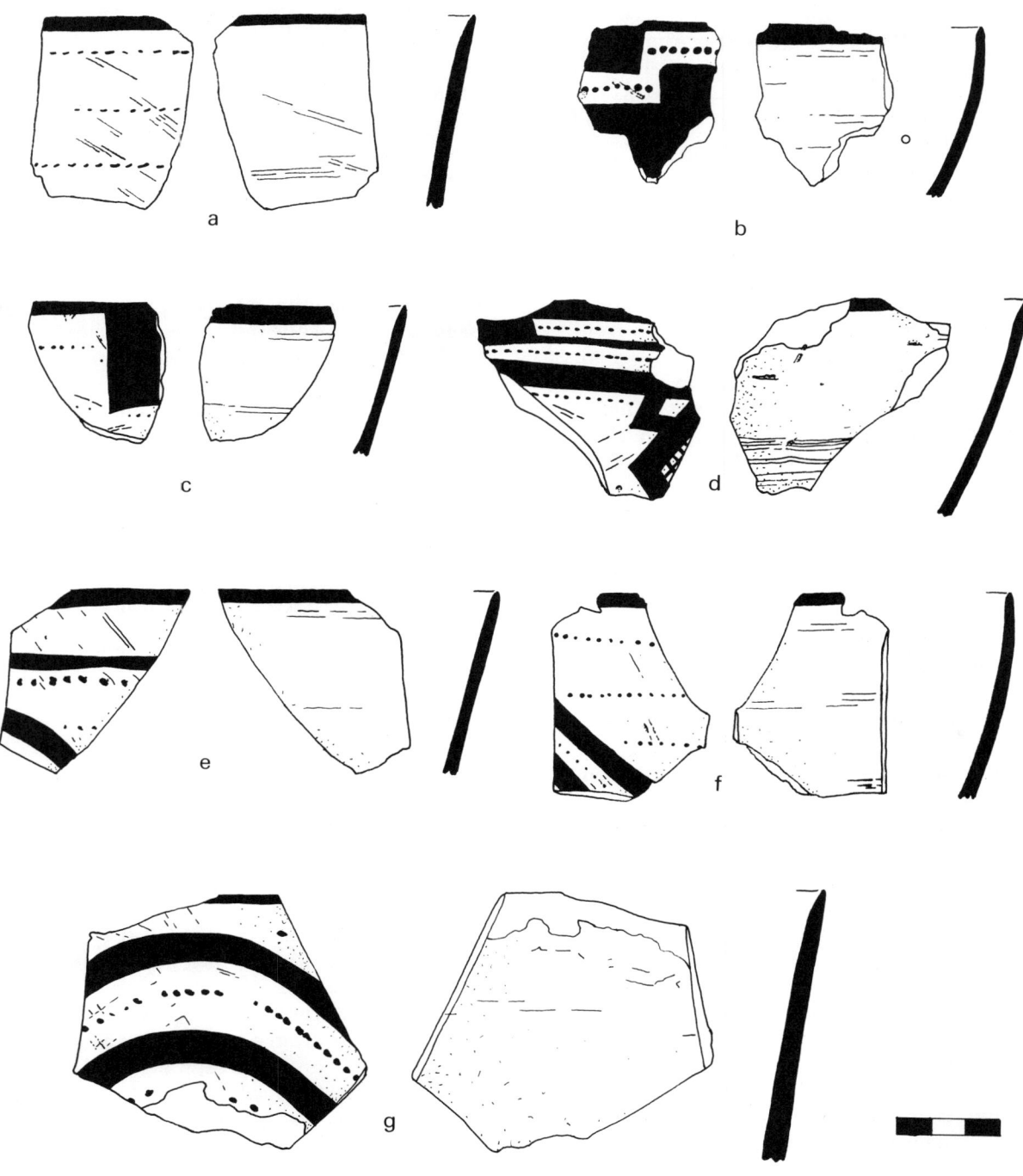

Fig. 17. Susiana Ware: Dot Motifs on Bowl Rims. A. Fine sand and limestone, body pink, paint very dark gray, diam.: 16; X722, 6067101 (B44). B. Fine sand, body white, paint very dark gray, diam.: 14; X752, 6069301 (B46). C. Fine sand, body very pale brown, paint dusky red, diam.: 12; X504, 6026601 (A27). D. Fine sand, body very pale brown, paint very dark gray, diam.: 13; X726, 6067301 (B44). E. Fine sand, body very pale brown, paint dusky red, diam.: 12; X648, 6062601 (B40). F. Fine sand, body white, paint very dark gray, diam.: 12; X537, 6027001 (A28). G. Fine sand, body very pale brown, paint very dark gray, diam.: 20; X729, 6066901 (B44).

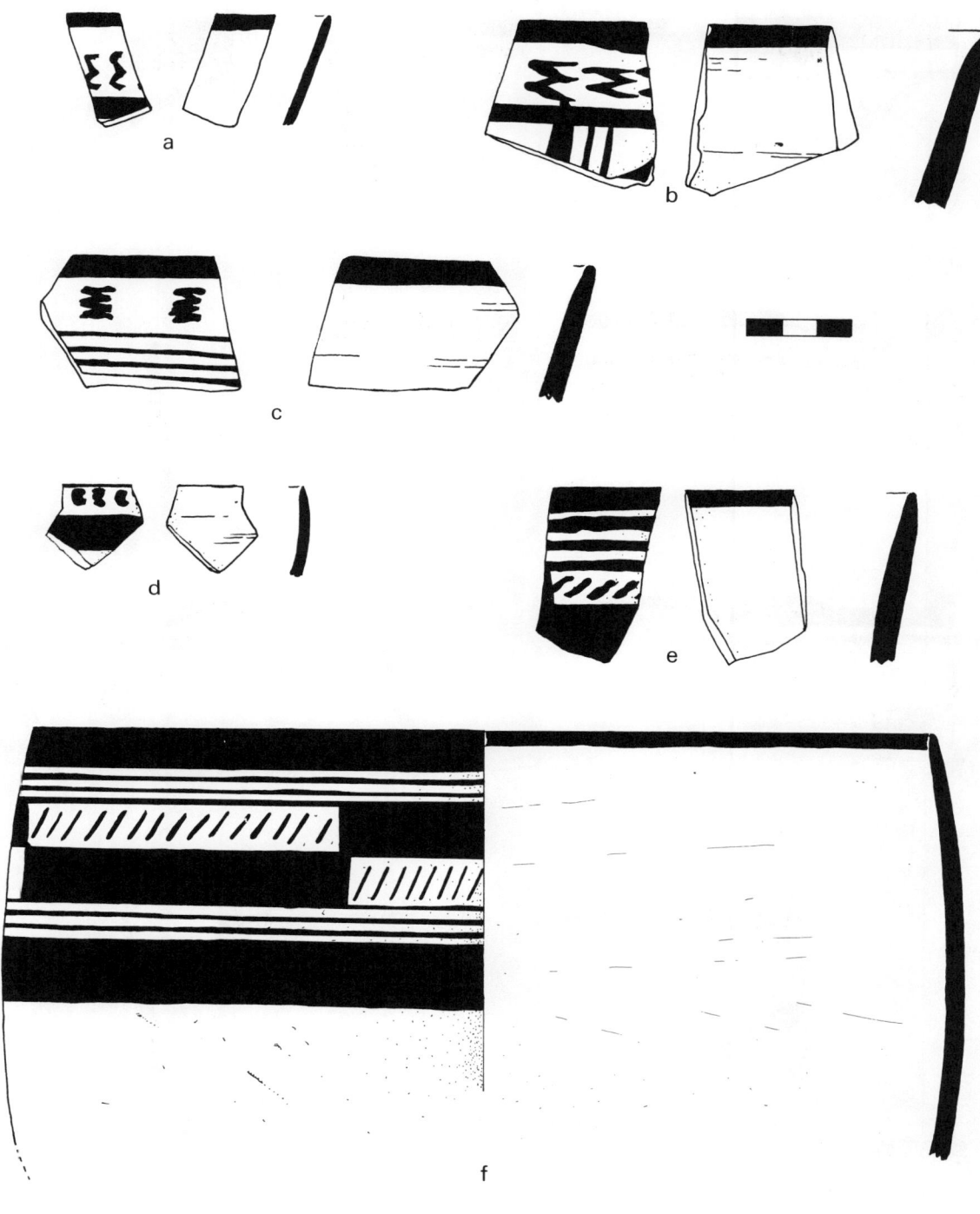

Fig. 18. Susiana Ware: Sigma and Slash Motifs on Bowl Rims. A. Fine sand, body very pale brown, paint very dusky red, diam.: 18, X638, 6030101 (A31). B. Fine sand, body pale yellow, paint very dark gray, diam.: 22; X440, 6023701 (A23). C. Fine sand, body very pale brown, paint very dark gray, diam.: 42; X721, 6066901 (B44). D. Fine sand, body pink, paint very dark gray, diam.: 7; X611, 6029701 (A). E. Fine sand, body white, paint dark gray, diam.: 22; X692, 6065201 (B42). F. Fine sand, body pink, paint very dusky red, diam.: 23; X493, 6026301 (A27).

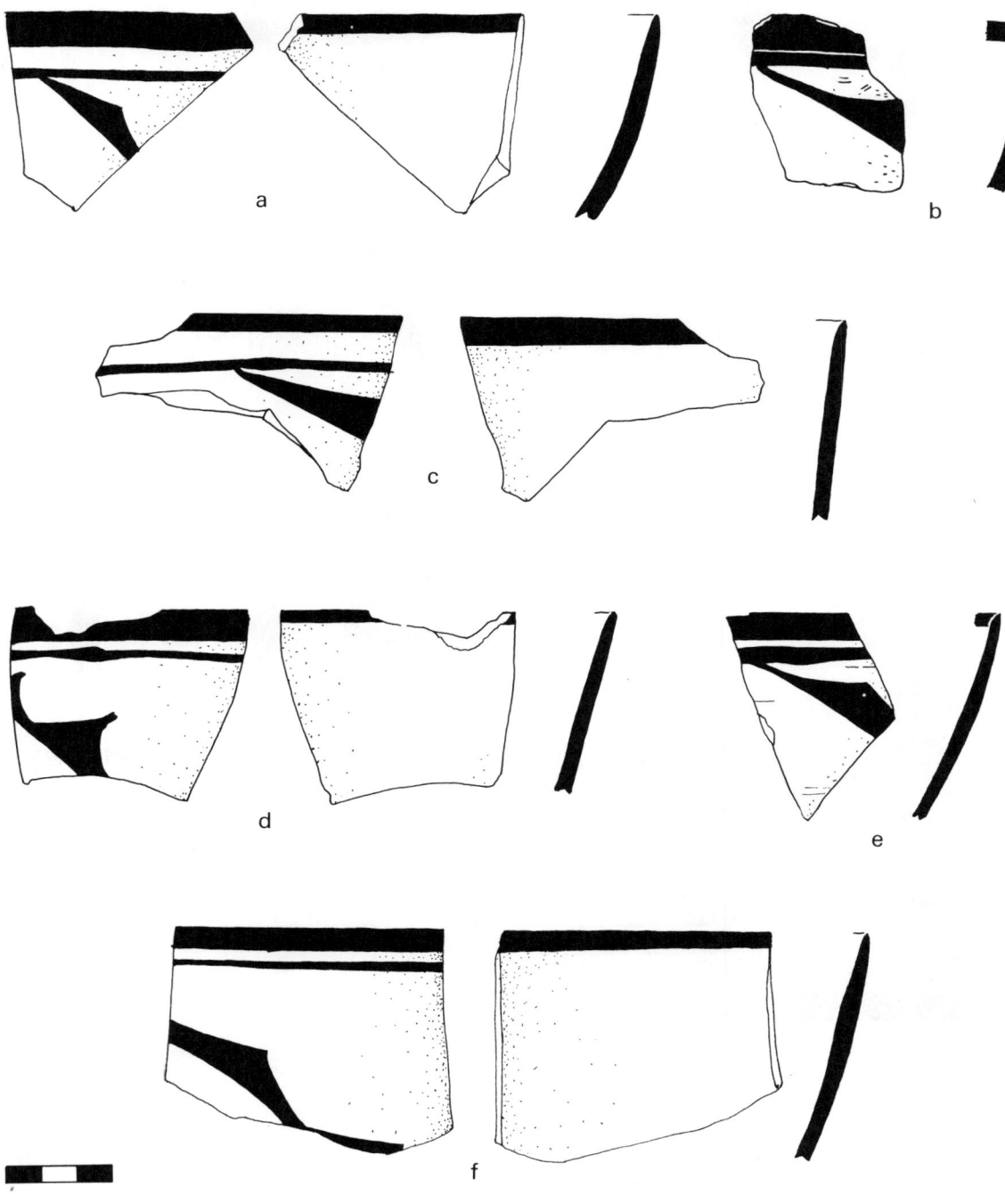

Fig. 19. Susiana Ware: Step Motifs on Bowl Rims. A. Fine sand, body pale yellow, paint brown, diam.: 14; X653, 6063301 (B41). B. Fine sand, body very pale brown, paint dark gray, diam.: 14; C611, 6029702 (A29). C. Fine sand, body pale yellow, paint very dusky red, diam.: 15; X486, 6026101 (A26). D. Fine sand, body white, paint very dark gray, diam.: 15; X743, 6068901 (B45). E. Fine sand, body very pale brown, paint very dark gray, diam.: 14; X611, 6029701 (A29). F. Fine sand, body pink, paint dark red, diam.: 14; X714, 6066401 (B44).

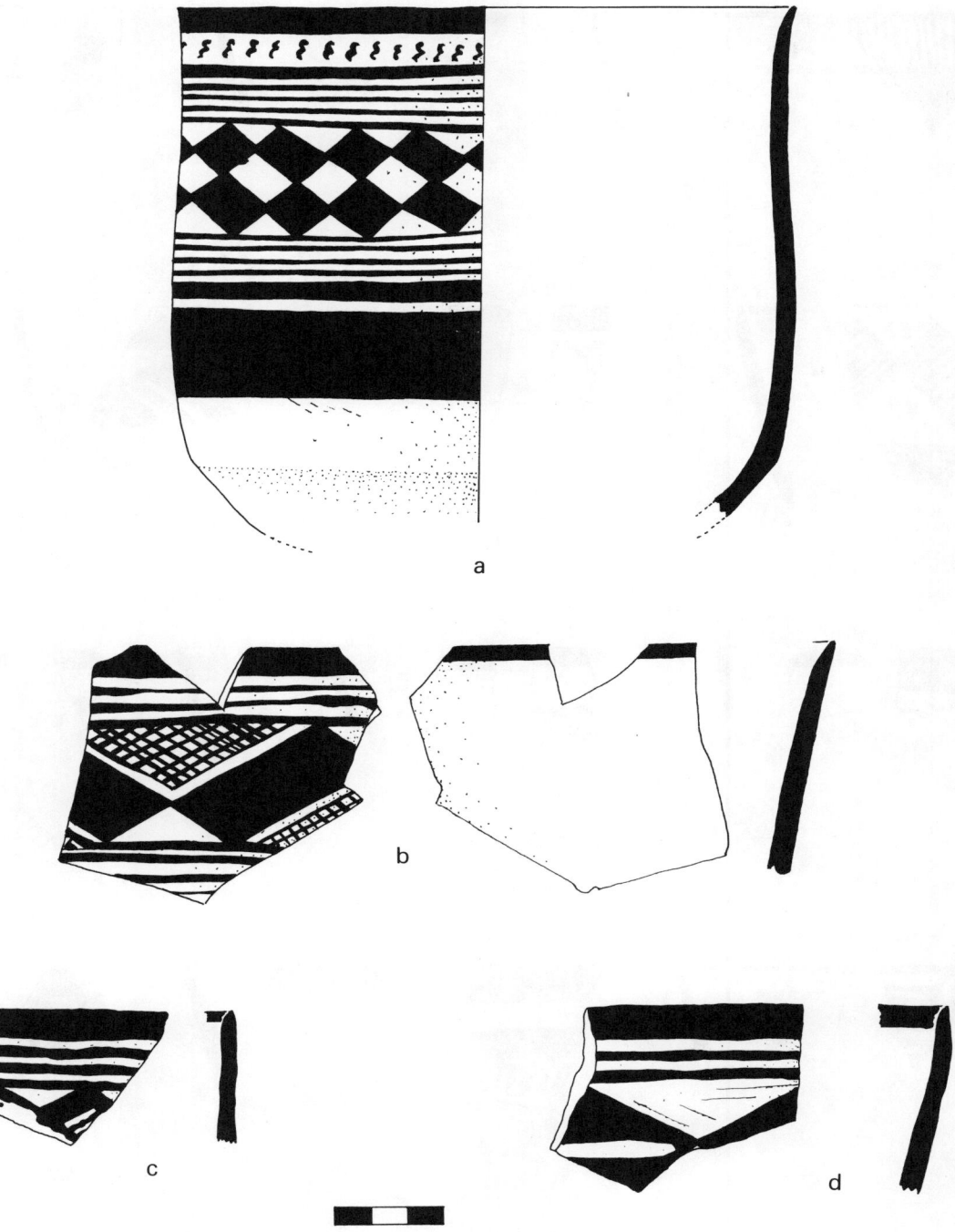

Fig. 20. Susiana Ware: Diamond Motifs on Bowl Rims. A. Bowl with sigma and diamond motifs, fine sand, body reddish yellow, paint very dark gray, diam.: 17; 6078001 (B40). B. Fine sand, body white, paint dark gray, diam.: 27, 6066403 (B44). C. Fine sand, body white, paint very dark gray, diam.: 18; 6066801 (B44). D. Fine sand, body pale yellow, paint dusky red, diam.: 31; 6069301 (B46).

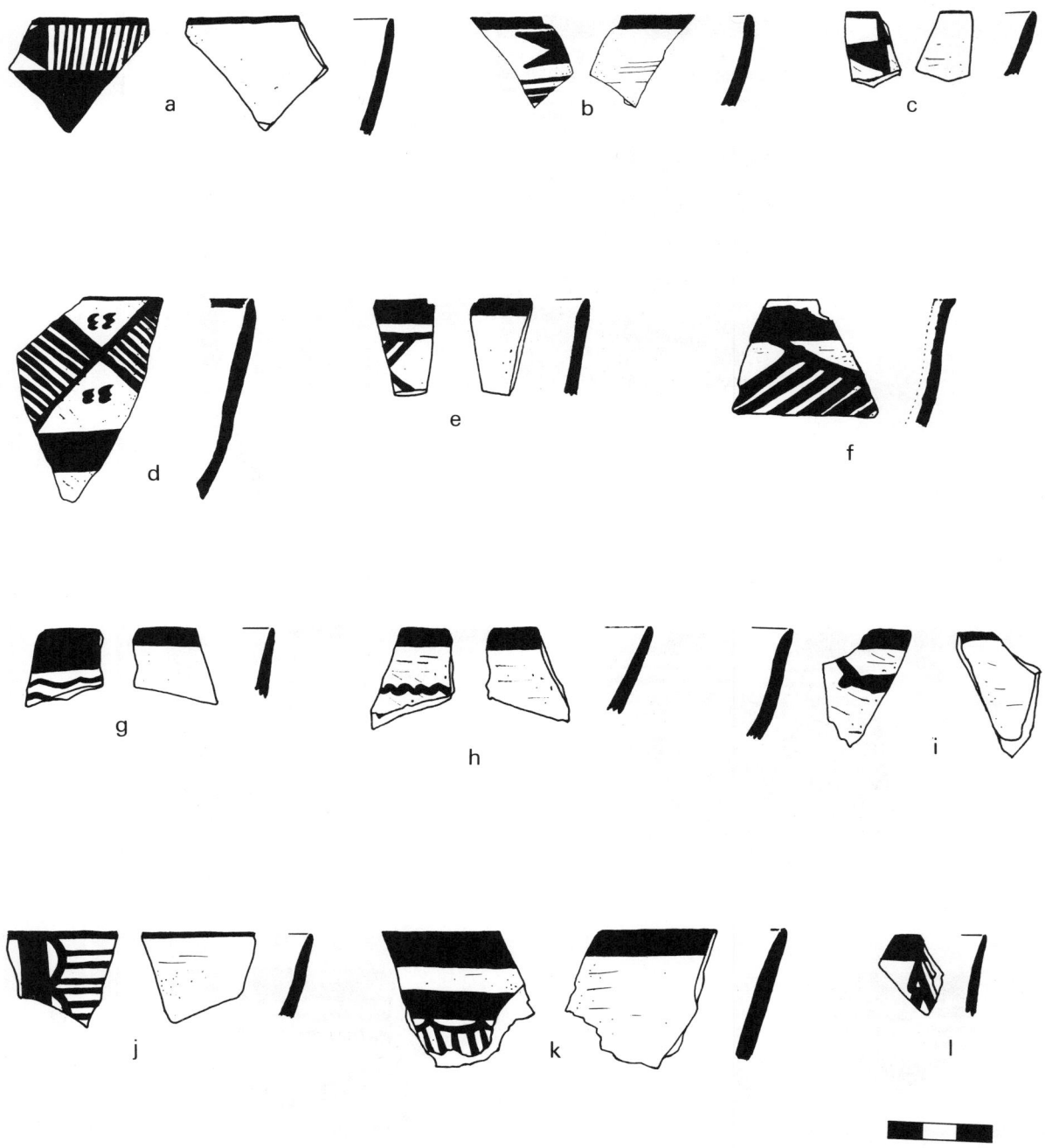

Fig. 21. Susiana Ware: Other Motifs on Bowl Rims. A. Fine sand, body white, paint very dusky red, diam.: 17; X752, 6069301 (B46). B. Fine sand, body very pale brown, paint black, diam.: 12; X635, 6062001 (B40). C. Fine sand, body very pale brown, paint black, diam.: 17; X486, 6026102 (A26). D. Cf. fine black-on-tan ware, fine sand, body light brown, paint dark gray, diam.: 11; X466, 6050501 (B32). E. Fine sand, body pink, paint dark reddish brown, diam.: 17; X729, 6067501 (B45). F. Fine sand, body light reddish brown, paint dark reddish brown, diam.: 27; X588, 6058701 (B36). G. Fine sand, body white, paint dark gray, diam.: 18; X420, 6048101 (B31,32). H. Fine sand, body light gray, paint very dark gray, diam.: 18; X484, 6025602 (A26). I. Fine sand, body white, paint dusky red, diam.: 14; X453, 6025201 (A26). J. Fine sand, body very pale brown, paint very dark gray, diam.: 14; X502, 6026401 (A27). K. Fine sand, body light gray, paint gray, diam.: 17; X486, 6026101 (A26). L. Fine sand, body very pale brown, paint dusky red, diam.: 10; X493, 6026301 (A27).

CERAMICS OF THE BAYAT AND FARUKH PHASES

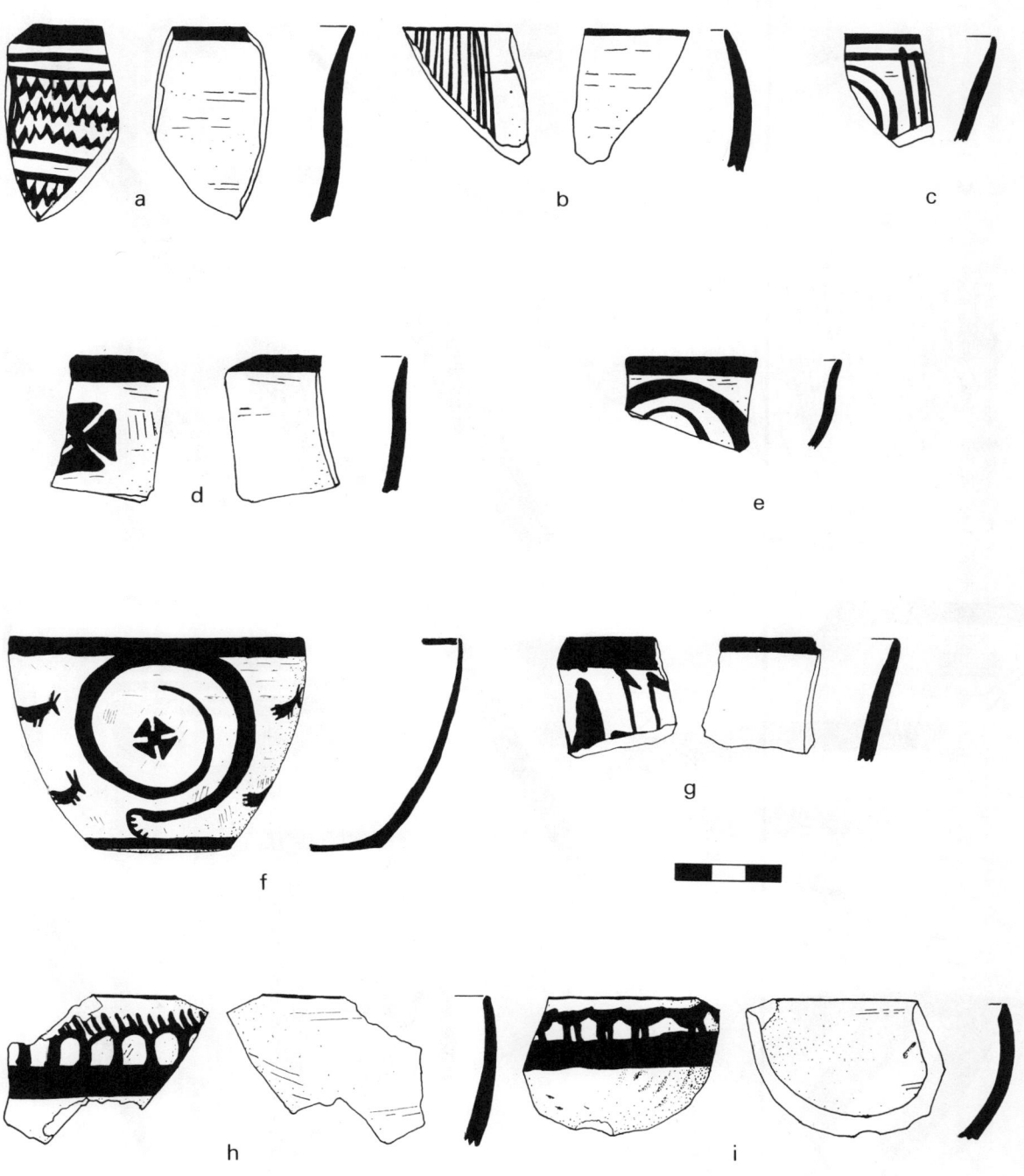

Fig. 22. Susiana Ware: Other Motifs on Bowl Rims. A. Fine sand, body white, paint dusky red, diam.: 14; X626, 6061303 (B39). B. Fine sand and limestone, body light reddish brown, paint dark reddish brown, diam.: 15; X708, 6066201 (B43). C. Fine sand, body pink, paint dark gray, diam.: 18; X369, 6045501 (B29). D. Fine sand, body pale yellow, paint dark gray, diam.: 17; X336, 6021701 (A21). E. Fine sand, body pale yellow, paint dark reddish brown, diam.: 9; X617, 6060501 (B39). F. Fine sand, body white, paint dark gray, diam.: 8; X449, 6024801 (A23). G. Fine sand, body white, paint dark gray, diam.: 13; X588, 6058702 (B36). H. Fine sand, body pale yellow, paint very dark gray, diam.: 11; X541, 6027701 (A28). I. Fine sand, body very pale brown, paint very dark gray, diam.: 8; X743, 6068901 (B45).

Fig. 23. Susiana Ware: Basin Rims. A. Fine sand, body pale yellow, diam.: 30; X739, 6068703 (B41). B. Fine sand, body pink, diam.: 42; X714, 6066408 (B44). C. Fine sand, body pale yellow, diam.: 55; X722, 6067101 (B44). D. Fine sand, body pale yellow, diam.: 45; X522, 6028502 (A29). E. Fine sand, body pale yellow, diam.: 40; C726, 6067304 (B44). F. Fine sand, body white, diam.: ca. 45; X752, 6069301 (B46). G. Basin rim with interior bands, fine sand, body 2.5Y 8/2 (white) paint 7.5YR 4/2 (dark brown), diam.: 30; X714, 60664 (B44). H. Large bowl rim with exterior motif, fine sand, body 5Y 8/3 (pale yellow), paint 10YR 4/2 (dark grayish brown), diam.: 30; X648, 60626 (B40). I. Basin rim with interior bands, fine sand, body 10YR 6/4 (light yellowish brown), paint 10YR 4/1 (dark gray), diam.: 27; X341, 61211 (A20–22). J. Basin rim with interior motif, fine sand, body 5Y 8/3 (pale yellow), paint 10YR 3/1 (very dark gray), diam.: ca. 40; X607, 60293 (A29).

Table 4: Metric Attributes of Susiana Bowls

	Rim diameter (cm)		Rim angle		Upper exterior band widths (cm)		Interior band widths (cm)	
	$\bar{x}$	s.d.	$\bar{x}$	s.d.	$\bar{x}$	s.d.	$\bar{x}$	s.d.
Plain N = 126	14.6	6.1	68°	10	—	—	—	—
Single Band N = 90	15.1	5.0	80°	12	.70	.66	.64	.36
Multiple Band N = 81	16.6	9.6	81°	7	.80	.39	.55	.23
Dot N = 26	15.3	4.2	83°	5	.41	.11	.40	.10
Step N = 23	13.6	2.0	87°	6	.30	.27	.46	.15
Diamond N = 14	24.9	5.6	80°	8	.89	.16	.51	.19

of about 35 cm, and a length of about 40 cm. The end had a diameter of 29 cm as measured on a circular chart and the side diameter of 48 cm.

A few examples have interior painting, some with wide horizontal (Fig. 23g) or oblique (Fig. 23i) bands and one (Fig. 23j) with a more complex motif.

High Jar Rims (Fig. 24a–f; Plate 8a): These jars had a globular or pear-shaped body and a relatively small neck. Rims are straight to everted; some lips are slightly thickened or flared. There is considerable variation in thickness and height of rim, but the measured series is too small to demonstrate whether or not distinct categories of rim form exist. Interior neck diameters vary from 8 to 38 cm. Thicknesses at the midpoint of the neck vary from 0.5 to 2.8 cm. Neck heights vary from 2.0 to more than 5.1 cm.

As in Bayat Phase Layers at Tepe Sabz, there are some unpainted examples and many examples painted with a thick coat of flaky dark paint (Hole, Flannery, and Neely: 153, Fig. 58e–j). There are also many examples with painted bands around the neck and shoulder. Some Farukhabad jars have pendant semi-circles and other elements below the shoulder bands.

Low Jar Rims (Fig. 24g–j): These few rims have necks less than two cm high. They range in interior neck diameter from 7 to 13 cm and in neck thickness from 0.5 to 0.7 cm. Observed neck heights range from 0.7 to 1.9 cm.

Most of these jars have elaborate painted motifs in bands and panels on the shoulder. A shattered shoulder lug or node from a small jar occurs. Elements observed on jar shoulders include checkerboard panels, solidly painted panels, free-standing zig-zag lines, and sigma motifs. This form is also known from earlier phases at Tepe Sabz (Ibid.:155, Fig. 58k–q) and at other fifth millennium sites in Greater Mesopotamia.

Fig. 24. Susiana Ware: Jars. A. High rim jar rim with solid paint, fine sand, body pink, paint very dark gray, diam.: 18; X722, 6067101 (B44). B. High rim jar rim with painted bands, fine sand and limestone, body light red, paint dark red, diam.: 17; X443, 6024101 (A24). C. High rim jar rim with solid paint, fine sand and limestone, body light red, paint dusky red, diam.: 20; X449, 6024801 (A23). D. High rim jar rim with solid paint, fine sand, body pale yellow, paint very dark gray, diam.: 27; X718, 6066801 (B44). E. High rim jar rim without paint, fine sand, body very pale brown, diam.: 18; X718, 6066802 (B44). F. High rim jar rim with solid paint, interior ledge variant, fine sand, body pale yellow, paint very dark grayish brown, diam.: 14; X635, 6062001 (B40). G. Low rim jar rim with solid paint, fine sand, body reddish yellow, paint dusky red, diam.: 17; X751, 6069101 (B46). H. Low rim jar rim, fine sand, body very pale brown, paint dark reddish brown, diam.: 10; X632, 6061501 (B40). I. Jar shoulder with node, medium sand, body 2.5Y 8/4 (pale yellow), paint 10YR 3/1 (very dark gray); X453, 60252 (A26). J. Low rim jar with nose lug, fine sand, body 10YR 7/3 (very pale brown), paint 10R 3/2 (dusky red), diam.: ca. 8; X744 (B46).

Chapter III
OTHER ARTIFACTS OF THE BAYAT AND FARUKH PHASES

CHIPPED STONE TOOLS

Dark Brown Chert, Medium Gray Chert, and Fine Red and Green Chert—all locally obtainable—were used for a majority of these tools. Non-local Fine White Chert, Fine Mottled Gray Chert, Fine Pink Chert, and other rare fine cherts were less frequent. Obsidian is very rare (see Appendix I). Variation in chert types will be discussed in the concluding chapter.

Dark Brown Chert usually occurs as flat pebbles. These are conveniently worked by using the top of the pebble as a ready-made platform, striking rough flakes or, rarely, short blades from one side. Medium Gray Chert occurs as large ovoid pebbles which can be split in halves or quarters, trimmed and used as blade cores. Non-local cherts were frequently brought in as prepared blade cores. Most blades and large flakes exhibit some irregular edge flaking or wear, but only a few show regular retouch or alteration.

Retouched tool types are defined below. The groups defined in Hole, Flannery, and Neely (1969) are followed closely wherever practical. Many of the tools are shown in Figures 25 to 28. Tools with edge retouch are oriented with the proximal or bulbar end up. Tools with end retouch are oriented with the presumed working edge up except in the cases of end scrapers, denticulate flakes and choppers. Measurements of tools are in Appendix Table D1.

MICROLITHS

Triangle (Fig. 25a): This microlith is made from a blade segment by retouching two opposed, oblique truncations until they meet at an approximate right angle. As only one triangle was found, it is impossible to show whether this is a form of trapezoidal projectile point related to those from more recent levels, or was a tool with some other use.

PIERCING-REAMING TOOLS

Drills (Fig. 25b–d, i): These have slightly convergent or, rarely, parallel sides and slightly rounded tips. Large examples occur (Fig. 25i). There is no visible evidence of rotary motion.

Pointed Pieces (Fig. 25f–h): These have rough, convergent retouch creating a blunt tip. Some have little retouch (Fig. 25f), while others have such extensive use that the point is blunt, and the tool might well be classed as a truncate piece (Fig. 25h).

SICKLE BLADES

Plain Sickles (Fig. 25 k,m): These are blades exhibiting a glossy sheen on the edge. The preferred material is Medium Gray Chert. Backing and end truncation are rare. Sometimes traces of bitumen mounting survive as discussed below (Fig. 25j, k, m). In most cases there is irregular flaking along the edge, made after or during use, which may represent an effort to resharpen the sickles. On only two of the 25 plain sickles were both edges utilized (Fig. 25m).

Denticulate Sickles (Fig. 25j, l): These differ from plain sickles only in the essentially complete edge retouch of the blade. In contrast to later examples the flaking is quite irregular. It is tempting to regard these as nothing but heavily resharpened plain blades. However, one example (Fig. 25j) had been first retouched and then mounted with bitumen, but not used. At least this example was deliberately notched before use.

CUTTING-SCRAPING TOOLS

End Scrapers (Fig. 26a, b): These are blades with converging retouch around one end creating a convex working edge. The three examples are very small and of fine, non-local cherts. These are attested only in certain layers of Excavation B.

Truncate Pieces (Fig. 26c–e): These have retouch from the inner face on one end of the flake. Those with both truncation and sickle sheen are classified as sickles. These Farukhabad examples tend to have an oblique concave truncation.

Retouched Blades and Blade Segments (Fig. 26j): These have fairly regular and usually shallow retouch on one or both edges. Plain blades (Fig. 26f, g, j) and blade segments (Fig. 26i) with limited signs of use are far more common. A segment is a

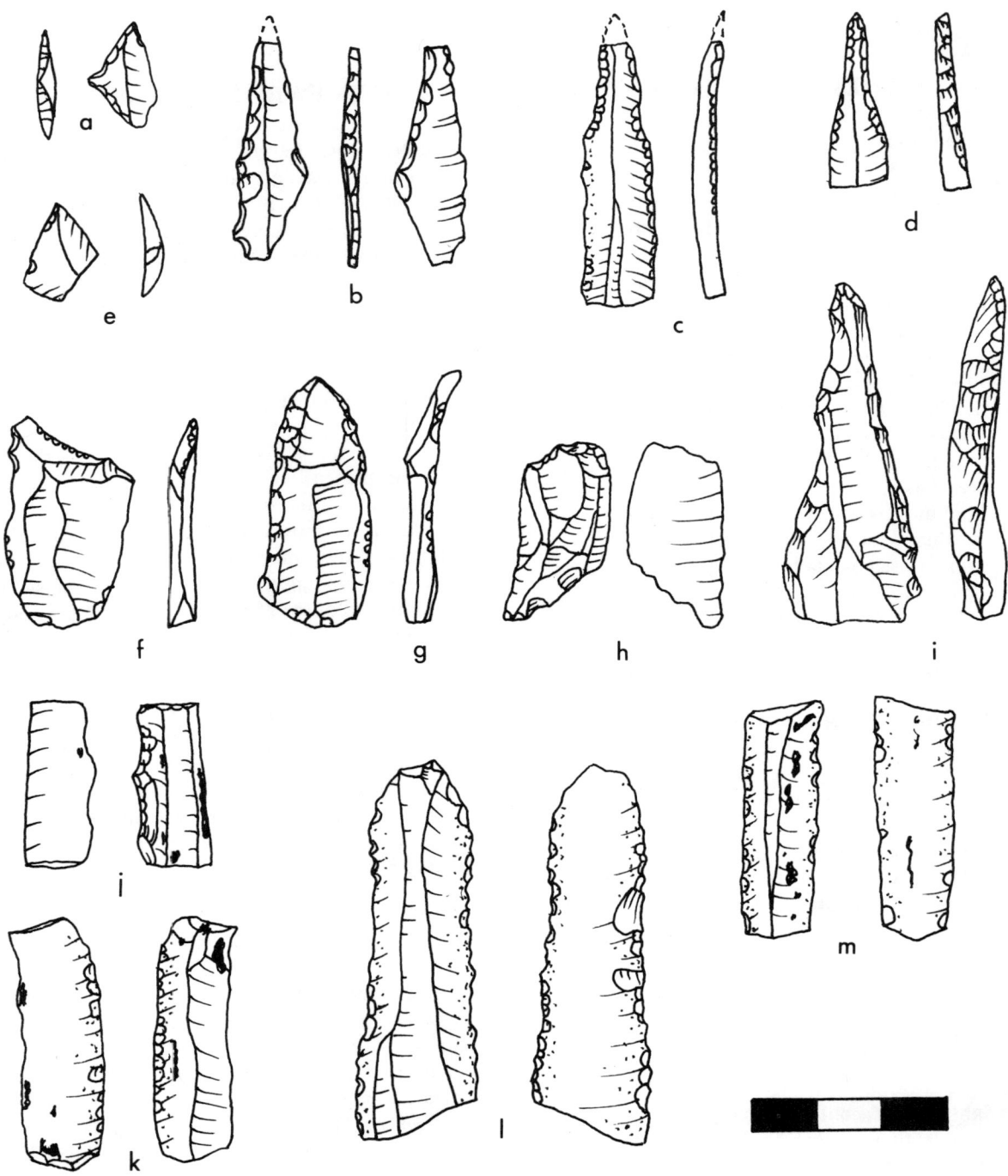

Fig. 25. Chipped Stone Tools: Microlith, Piercing-Reaming Tools, and Sickles. A. Triangular microlith, dark brown; X63208 (B40). B. Perforator, fine white; X49301 (A27). C. Perforator, coarse gray; X53801 (A28). D. Perforator, coarse gray; X48507 (A25). E. Pointed piece, fine white; X49309 (A27). F. Pointed piece, dark brown; X58303 (A29). G. Pointed piece, fine mottled gray; X58502 (A30). H. Pointed piece, fine mottled brown; X69901 (A36). I. Perforator, dark brown; X67601 (B41). J. Sickle blade, fine white; X75103 (B46). K. Sickle blade, coarse gray; X73901 (B45). L. Sickle blade, fine pink; X75101 (B46). M. Sickle blade, coarse gray; X75102 (B46).

OTHER ARTIFACTS OF THE BAYAT AND FARUKH PHASES

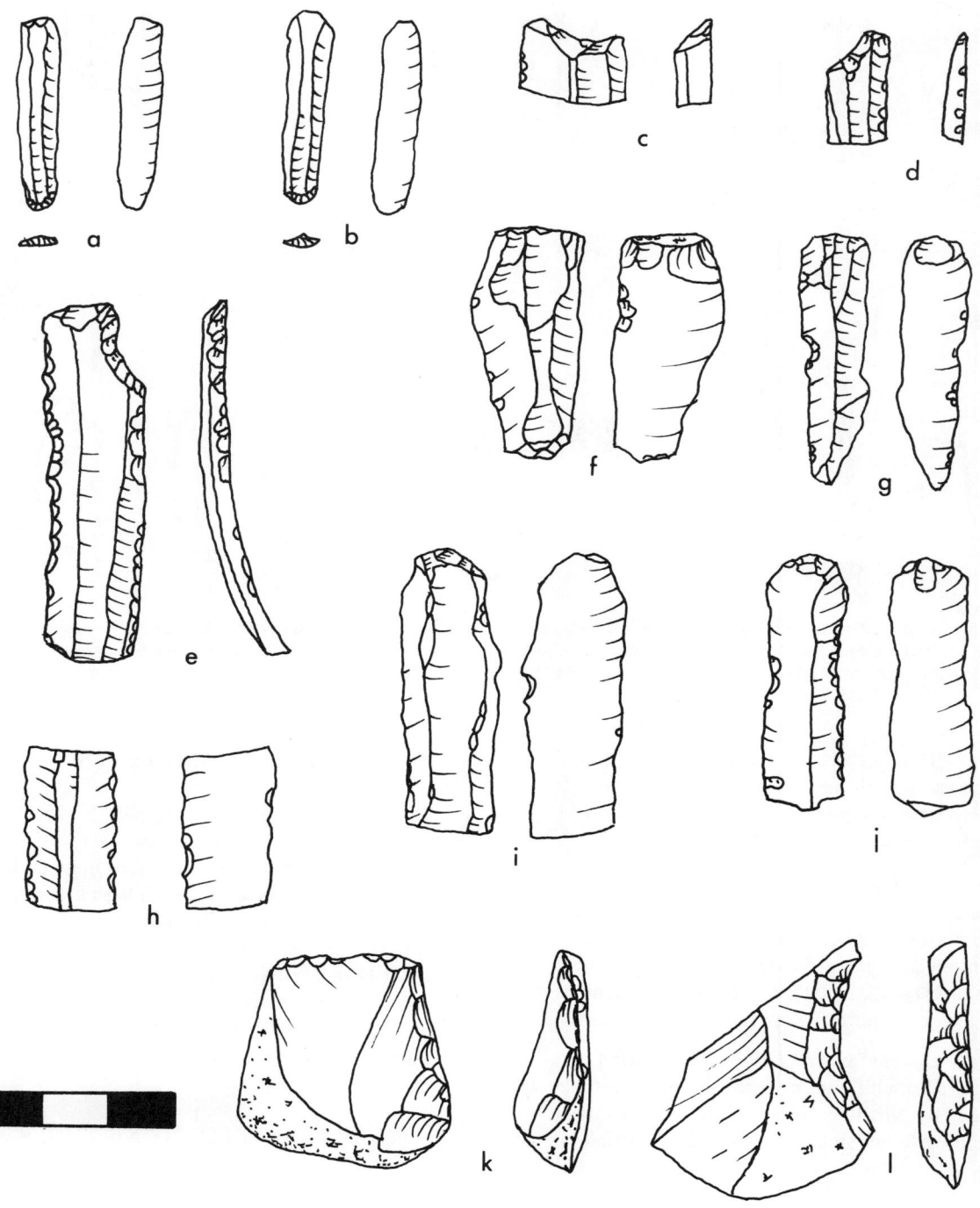

Fig. 26. Chipped Stone Tools: Cutting-Scraping Tools. A. Endscraper, translucent brown; X69005 (B42). B. Endscraper, translucent brown; X75207 (B46). C. Truncated piece, fine banded gray; X70401 (A36). D. Truncated piece, dark brown; X61401 (A31). E. Truncated piece, fine white; X67501 (B41). F. Blade, dark brown; X71401 (B44). G. Blade, dark brown; X58201 (A29). H. Blade segment, coarse gray; X50102 (A27). I. Blade, fine mottled gray; X74301 (B45). J. Retouched blade, coarse gray; X64902 (B47). K. Retouched flake, dark brown; X704 (A36). L. Retouched flake, coarse gray; X632 (B40).

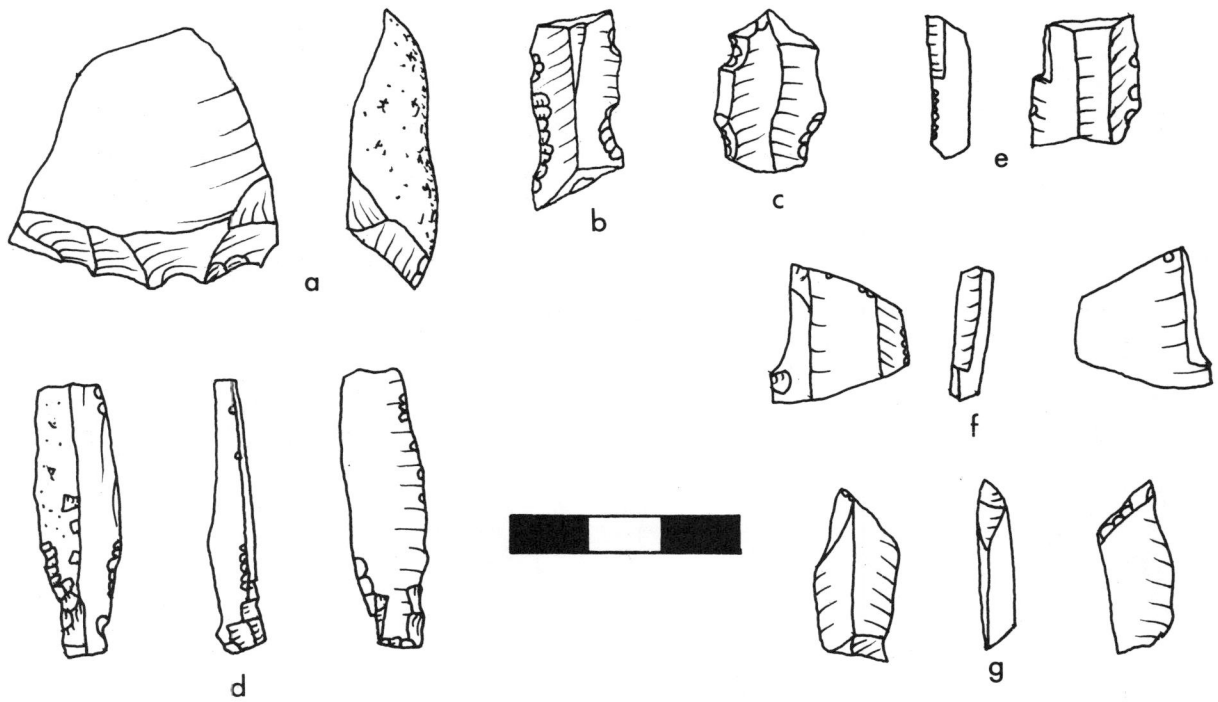

Fig. 27. Chipped Stone Tools: Denticulates, Notches, and Other Small Tools. A. Denticulate, dark brown; X486 (A26). B. Multiple notch, fine white; X69904 (A36). C. Multiple notch, fine mottled brown; X49306 (A27). D. Hafted piece, fine mottled brown; X69201 (B42). E. Possible burin, fine mottled brown; X45302 (A26). F. Possible burin, fine gray; X48405 (A26). G. Possible burin, fine gray; X44007 (A23).

medial or distal piece of a blade or any proximal piece whose length is less than three times its width. Proximal fragments longer than three times their width are classified as blades.

Retouched Flakes (Fig. 26k,l): These are flakes with even and usually shallow retouch. Extensive multiple retouch characteristic of side scrapers in other chipped stone industries is present though rare (Fig. 26l). Plain flakes with limited signs of use are more common than retouched flakes.

Denticulate Blades and Flakes (Fig. 27a): These have deep retouch flakes creating adjacent notches separated by small pointed teeth. Blades with denticulation and sickle sheen are classified as sickles.

Notched Blades and Flakes (Fig. 27b,c): These have one or more deep concave notches usually created by removal of more than one flake. If more than one notch is present they are separated by an unaltered flake edge.

OTHER SMALL TOOLS

Possible Hafted Piece (Fig. 27d): This thick convergent blade has both lateral retouch and small burin-like blows on the proximal end.

Possible Burins (Fig. 27e-g): These are made on small blade segments. On three, the blow was struck on a backed truncation on the end of the segment (Fig.27g). On three, the blow was struck on the snapped end of the blade segment (Fig. 27e,f). These are very small, and it is possible that they are an accidental result of some use pattern.

HEAVY CHIPPED STONE TOOLS

Choppers and chopping tools (Fig. 28a–d): These are made from locally available limestone pebbles. Some are barely retouched natural fragments (Fig. 28b), however most are made with a few blows on the end of a pebble in either one direction (Fig. 28c,d) or two (Fig. 28a).

OTHER ARTIFACTS OF THE BAYAT AND FARUKH PHASES

Table 5: Bayat and Farukh Chipped Stone Tools by Layer

	Drill	Pointed Piece	Sickle	End Scraper	Truncate Piece	Retouched Blade	Retouched Flake	Denticulate Blade	Denticulate Flake	Notched Blade	Notched Flake	Burin	Chopper Chopping Tool	Other	Totals
A23			2								1	1			4
A24			2		1										3
A25	1	1	2			1	2						1		8
A26						2	1					2			5
A27	1	2							1	1		1			6
A28		1	1			1			1			2			6
A29		1	1			1						2			5
A30-A31					1		1	2							4
A33	1				1	3	1		2						8
A34			1			1	1								3
A35	1														1
A36-		1	1		1		4		1						8
B37			1							1	1				3
B38						1			1						2
B39			5			3		1		1	1	1			12
B40	1		4			7	2		2	1	1			1 triangle	19
B41	1		2	1	1	8						2			15
B42			1	1		4	1							1 hafted piece	8
B43						2	2								4
B44			2						1	1	1	1			6
B45			1												1
B46			3	1		3			1			1			9
B47			1			2									3
Totals	6	6	30	3	4	34	18	2	9	6	6	11		2	

HEAVY STONE TOOLS

GRINDING TOOLS

Tools of this category were not particularly common. Four discoidal handstones or *manos* were found. There were fragments in Excavation A, Layer 25 (X447, X448) and Layer 26 (X455). An intact example from Excavation B, Layer 42, has a mean diameter of 10.7 cm and weighs 1.17 kg, and has a slight surface polish. A fourth example, also complete, was recovered from the same layer (X696). It has about the same diameter, (10.5 cm) and weight, (1.25 kg) but has heavy pecking on one surface forming a slight depression, and heavy polishing on the other surface.

There are no grinding slabs from Farukh and Bayat Phase layers.

OBLONG STONES (TABLE D4)

There are two oblong stones of the sort termed "Bitumen Stirrers" by Hole, Flannery, and Neely, (1969:192). One broken example, from Excava-

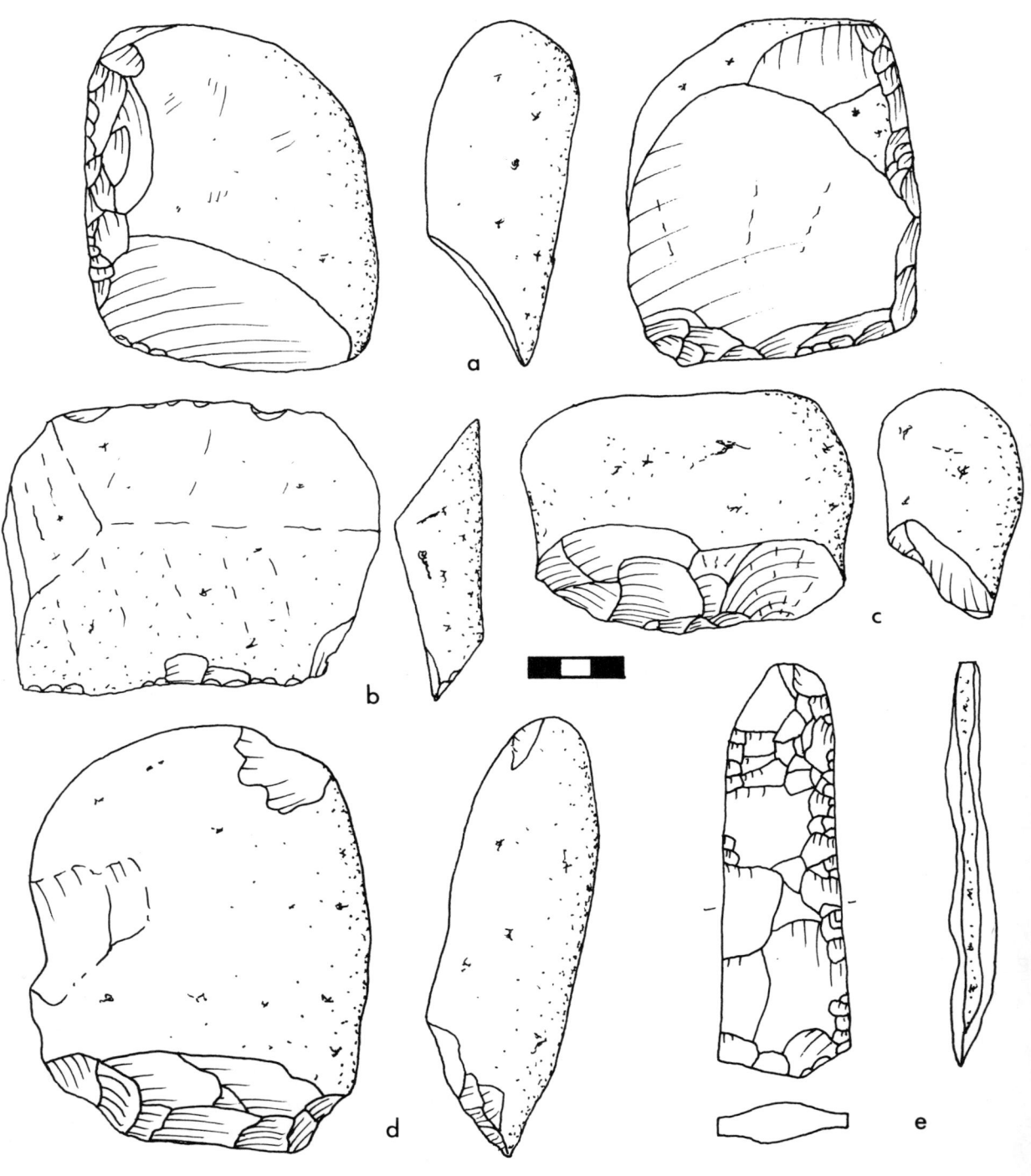

Fig. 28. Chipped Stone Tools: Choppers. A. Calcite chopper; X660 (A32). B. Calcite flake cleaver; X672 (A35). C. Calcite chopping tool; X493 (A27). D. Calcite chopping tool; X667 (A33). E. Calcite celt blank; X720 (B44).

tion A, Layer 36 (X704), shows no signs of use. The other, from Excavation B, Layer 40 (X632), shows some edge-battering and possible bitumen stains.

CELTS (TABLE D3)

A piece of flaked tabular calcite, 12.8 cm long, 3.8 cm wide and 1.1 cm thick, was found in Excavation B, Layer 44 upper (X720) (Fig. 28e). This could have been ground into either a celt or a chisel, but, though unbroken, it was never finished.

A finished calcite celt, from Excavation B, Layer 42, (X695, Fig.29a), shows "pot-lid" fractures indicating burning, overlain by flakes and scratches demonstrating reworking. This finished item is 14.9 cm long, 5.7 cm wide, and 1.6 cm thick suggesting that the above-described tabular piece was discarded because it was too narrow. Bitumen remnants show impressions of wood parallel to the long axis of the planar side, and lashings perpendicular to the long axis of the convex side; probably the tool was hafted like an adze or hoe on an 'L'-shaped handle. Because the celt is in Tehran, it has not been possible for an ethnobotanist to examine the wood impression and determine the species used.

A third artifact of this class from the same layer (X694, Fig. 29b) has two working ends, both chipped in use. It is 12.3 cm long, 8.7 cm wide, and 5.3 cm thick. The raw material is unidentified.

PERFORATED AND PARTIALLY PERFORATED STONES (TABLE D8)

These heavy stone artifacts present interesting interpretive problems. The four partially perforated stones range from 5.5 to 12.5 cm in diameter, 2.5 to 7.0 cm in thickness, and 0.11 to 2.15 kg in weight. All examples have depressions pecked on both sides which range in diameter from 1.8 to 3.5 cm. All are intact and none show signs of use on either the margin or the depression. The three fully perforated examples show slightly less variability, ranging from 7.8 to 12.9 cm in diameter, 4.0 to 6.0 cm in thickness, and 0.4 to 1.80 kg in estimated weight when unbroken. In two cases, the holes were created by conical depressions pecked from the two sides until they met. The depressions have mean diameters of 4.2 and 4.9 cm. Both stones are broken and show polish on the point of minimum diameter of the hole. The unperforated stones seem to be unfinished examples of this type of artifact. Note that, as one might expect with rejects, the unfinished items exhibit a wider range of variability in all attributes. That these two forms are closely related is suggested by the fact that they co-occur in adjacent layers of both Excavation A and B. Such stone tools could be interpreted as digging stick weights, net sinkers, or loom weights. These propositions will be formally considered in Chapter IX after presentation of a larger series of measured examples.

The third perforated stone has an overall polish on its nearly spherical surface. The hole is drilled rather than pecked. This may have been a characteristic Mesopotamian mace head, but its hole is not perfectly even and a handle would not have set well in it.

STONE VESSELS

A fragment of a cylindrical or barrel-shaped vessel of dark granite of the acidic type with much hornblende and few light minerals was recovered from an early layer (A36, X704). The vessel would have been 12.7 cm in diameter with walls about 1.1 cm thick. The exterior has rounded horizontal grooves each .35 cm wide and .13 cm deep and separated by .18 to .27 cm of uncut surface (Fig. 29c).

From later layers, there are several sherds of coarse sandstone about 1.6 cm thick (B44, room C; X722). These could have been part of a shallow vessel, but as it has very little curvature it could also be part of a small grinding slab or palette.

BONE TOOLS
by Richard W. Redding

There are three classes of bone tools from these periods, all of which were fashioned from large mammal bone.

Spatulate pieces (Table D13): All these fragmentary artifacts were cut from flat pieces of long bone or scapula. Several stages of manufacture and use, as well as several parts of the implement are represented, making description difficult. All seem to have been relatively long with cut, trimmed sides and with narrow convex working edges.

Among the possible unfinished pieces are a large scapular fragment with a obliquely ground side but no surviving working edge (B43, X707). In addition there is a small fragment of convex working edge similarly beveled with only a slight polish (B40, X635). More polished from use is a tool cut from a plate of large mammal long bone exhibiting beveled sides and a corner of a convex working edge, rounded and polished from use (B43,X709). From the same unit is a completely worked plate with extensive polish. One of the two narrow convex ends had been ground and scored shortly before disposal in an apparent effort at resharpening (B43, X709, Fig. 29e). This tool approaches one illustrated from the Bayat Phase of Tepe Sabz (Hole, Flannery, and Neely 1969:Fig. 93d). Finally, there is a heavily used piece with beveled working edge and extensive polish (B42, X694). This type of tool must have been used to work something soft. It would have been useful in scraping the fatty deposits from the insides of hides.

There is one scapular fragment with scratches but no definite working edge (B40, X630) and one with only a drilled biconical hole about .50 cm in diameter (A23, X449).

Needle or Awl: The rounded and polished tip of an awl or needle whose shaft is .46 by .23 cm was recovered. The material could be reptile rather than mammal bone (B47, X755).

Planed Articular Ends: Three fragments of large mammal bone have ground facets. One is from a scapula (B42, X690) and two are unidentifiable (B41, X677; B41, X675). These could be abraders for a substance such as wood or they could be the handle ends of spatulate tools. If so, it is surprising that they lack polish. Therefore, we favor the first interpretation.

OTHER CERAMIC ARTIFACTS

DRAINS

A sherd of a large slab construction without surviving rims was found in Excavation A, Layer 23 (X437). This may be a fragment of a troughshaped drain tile. It exhibits a right angle. The tiny remnants of the presumed base shows the imprint of a granular soil surface, and the interiors and the exterior of the side exhibit rough finger smoothing. The side averages 1.8 cm thick and was at least 14 cm high. The intact piece may have resembled the complete example of the Uruk Period (B31, X424, Fig. 76a) subsequently described in Part Two.

MULLER (FIG. 29f)

One of these widely known artifacts was found in Excavation A, Layer 25. Its head was 5.8 by 4.5 cm and it exhibited use-chipping around the edge and many unaligned scratches on its convex surface. Similar marginal chipping is visible on an illustrated example from Tepe Sabz termed a "bent ceramic nail" (Hole, Flannery, and Neely 1969: Fig.91).

SPINDLE WHORLS
(FIG. 29g–j, TABLE D7)

Three types of ceramic spindle whorls occur in the Farukh and Bayat Phases. All are deliberately formed rather than cut from sherds. Most are fired to intense reddish hues in contrast to later forms discussed in Chapter IX. All are of relatively light weight although there is much variation. The 18 ovoid examples from all phases range from 4.7 to 15.1 gm in weight. Weight correlates positively with hole diameter ($r = .44$). Since there is no necessary mechanical relation between these two attributes, the heavier whorls may have been intended for larger spindles and heavier weights of thread (Parsons 1972). In general, whorls are common in and around small buildings.

Concavo-convex whorls: There are no complete examples of this type termed "Chariot Wheel" whorls by Hole, Flannery, and Neely on the basis of a large sample from Tepe Sabz (1969:206; Fig. 89). These are relatively large in diameter and concavo-convex in section. Buff painted designs of an irregular sort sometimes occur on the convex, presumably upper, surface. Both are small fragments and may be extrusive from earlier layers.

Plain ovoid whorls: This is the predominant form of ceramic whorl in these phases. It is similar to the form called "ovoid-discoidal" by Hole, Flannery, and Neely (1969:206). Such whorls do not differ significantly in weight or diameter from the generally later notched form, but they may be thicker and have smaller holes.

Notched ovoid whorls: In contrast to the more numerous Uruk examples, the Farukh examples

Table 6: Stratigraphic Distribution of Farukh and Bayat Spindle Whorls

	Concavo-Convex	Plain Ovoid	Notched Ovoid	Totals
A24	1	–	–	1
A25	–	1	–	1
A35	–	1	–	1
A36	1	–	–	1
B39	1	1	–	2
B41	–	3	1	3
B42	–	–	1	1
B43	–	1	–	1
Totals	3	7	2	

have relatively long and widely-spaced notches. This difference in attributes supports the contention that these are not instrusive pieces.

PERFORATED SHERD

A very thin, plain Susiana sherd only 0.42 cm thick, was chipped into a rough disc with a mean diameter of 2.0 cm. It was found in Excavation A, Layer 26 (X484). A hole, 0.58 cm in diameter, was drilled through its center. At Tepe Sabz such sherds apparently served as blanks for small ceramic rings of unknown use (Hole, Flannery, and Neely 1969:Plate 36a-d).

CERAMIC WHEEL

A battered disc with hubs was found while cutting a step below Layer 40 in Excavation B. It was originally more than 8.8 cm in diameter. Its hubs were 2.87 cm from side to side and its hole was 1.40 cm in diameter (X629).

GRATE

Fragments of a heavily straw-tempered, soft-bodied object were found in Excavation A, Layer 26 (X486). It was fired to a greenish color (5Y 8/3). If the complete item was circular, the rim suggests a diameter of about 28 cm. It averages 1.8 cm thick on the edges but reaches a maximum of 3.2 cm toward its center. There are rough holes about 2.8 cm in diameter pushed through this disc, each about 2.8 cm from its neighbor. If evenly spaced, there would have been about 20 such holes. Fragments of a similar item were found in the layer below (A27, X493). When complete, it would have been about 30 cm in diameter, averaging 1.5 cm on the edge and reaching 3.7 cm toward the center. Its holes are about 3.2 cm in diameter and its color is reddish (1OYR 8/4). These are associated with the possible storage structure (Feature 26) and perhaps served to allow air circulation, while keeping larger pests out.

EXCISED SLAB (PLATE 9c)

A small fragment of a possible ceramic stamp or decorative tile was found in Excavation A while removing the mud brick fill of the later platform (Feature 25, X384). The clay body is similar to the coarser Susiana Wares used for jars, exhibiting coarse sand inclusions. To make this object, a slab about 1.8 cm thick was cut from wet clay, and lines were cut into one surface. The piece was then fired. Each excised line was trapezoidal in section, being about 0.4 cm deep, 0.3 cm wide at the bottom, and 0.7 cm wide at the top. The design is composed of multiple chevrons. Similar pieces from Djaffarabad on the Susiana Plain are thought to have been stamps (Dollfus 1971: 58, Fig. 23). They differ, however, from ours in being ovoid and convex, as one might expect of a stamp. Also, the Farukhabad example shows none of the surface or edge wear one would expect on a stamp.

CERAMIC FIGURINE (PLATE 9b)

Only one animal figurine was recovered from deposits of the earlier phases at Tepe Farukhabad. This was in Excavation A incorporated into the brick fill of the later eroded platform (Feature 25, X389). It is the hindquarters of a quadruped with short tail, made from Susiana Ware and fired to a greenish color (2.5Y 6/4). The legs, 5.06 cm high and 1.81 cm wide across the buttocks, are molded together as a single unit. There are long painted lines down the legs, along the two sides, and down the spine. Short oblique lines connect the side and spine line. Richard Redding notes that the spine of the representation rises to a rounded prominence just before the tail, a feature common in living members of the genus *Bos*. No local existing

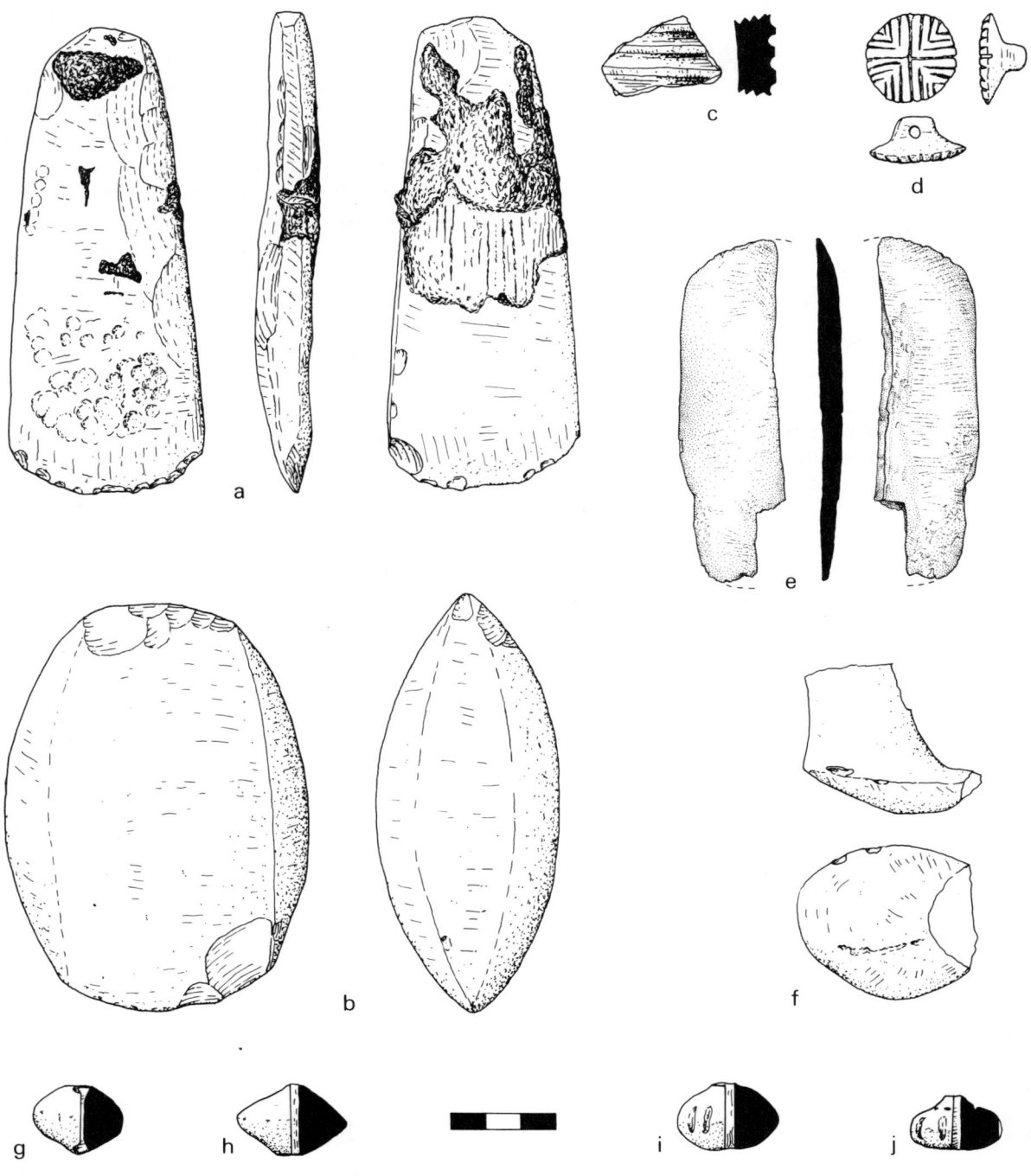

Fig. 29. Miscellaneous Artifacts of the Farukh Phase. A. Celt with bitumenous remnant, calcite; X695 (B42). B. Double-ended celt, material not identified; X694 (B42). C. Grooved cylindrical vessel sherd, granite; X704, 60325 (A36). D. Stamp seal, material not identified; X698 (B42). E. Spatulate object, large mammal bone; X709 (B43). F. Muller fragment, ceramic; X454 (A25). G. Plain ovoid spindle whorl, pale brown ceramic; X485 (A25). H. Plain ovoid spindle whorl, pink ceramic; X628 (B39). I. Notched ovoid spindle whorl, white ceramic, X659 (B41). J. Notched ovoid spindle whorl, very pale brown ceramic; X693 (B42).

species of *Bos,* however, are known to be striped; so, if the painted marks are any more than artistic license, they may well represent a kind of harness.

UNBAKED CLAY ARTIFACTS

The activity of sealing packages or containers of goods is probably attested in Excavation A, Layers 24 and 25, by the occurrence of masses of sealing clay (Plate 16b). Fifty kgm of pieces were weighed and examined in the field. Most are amorphous, but some have the ropy surface texture of discarded swipings or smoothings of very wet clay. There were a few fragments of ovoid or roughly hemispherical shaped lumps probably intended as stoppers or bale knot seals, but there were no broken finished pieces. This is unfortunate, but is to be expected, since there is no necessity that goods should be opened at the place where they are being sealed.

SMALL SPHERE

This object averages 1.31 cm in diameter and weighs 2.41 gm. It is from Excavation A, Layer 25 (X485). It is similar to the counters used in spherical bulla in later periods (Amiet 1972:64–70).

BITUMEN ARTIFACTS (Table 7, Table D15)

In spite of the vast quantities of bitumen brought from Ain Gir for processing at Farukhabad (See Chapter XV), very few artifacts of bitumen were found. In these phases there were only twelve shaped artifacts or parts of artifacts.

There were seven fragments of bitumen which covered matting and three fragments which covered lashing. These are discussed below. Such mats are useful as somewhat waterproof door or window covers; the only one found *in situ,* however, was lying on the floor on top of Layer 45 in Excavation B, perhaps within a brick structure.

There is one bitumen sickle mounting on which impressions indicate seating in a grooved wooden stock.

There are three bitumen spheres (Plate 17b). One has straw in the bitumen. These items range in diameter from 2.55 to 2.94 cm. The use of these items is unknown. Note that bitumen balls do not bounce.

There is one roughly conical object 5.2 cm high and 4.5 by 3.8 cm at its bottom. A hole through the top penetrating almost to the base shows the impressions of a reed. This base seems to have been melted (X745, B45, Plate 17e). This may be a part of a melted perforated ovoid. Such a form occurs in subsequent Uruk layers.

Most of these bitumen artifacts were found in Excavation B in and near the remains of small buildings.

WOVEN AND TIED ARTIFACTS
(Table D16)

Identification of the genera of reeds or rushes used in mat manufacture has not been attempted. Those used for these mats range in width from 1.5 to 2.0 cm. All are made in a two-over-two-under twill pattern. There are seven examples.

Three sets of bitumen fragments have lashing or possible basket impressions. Two have the cordmarks of heavy lashings, probably around bitumen patches on ceramic vessels. One has the cordmarks of light lashings over or around a set of wooden slats or carved panel. None of these were sufficiently well preserved to infer the shape of the complete lashing.

Among the many pieces of unbaked clay found in Excavation A, Layers 24 and 25, was one with the faint impression of a cloth with a texture like that of linen. The impressed surface was unfortunately destroyed during transport to the laboratory.

FINE STONE ARTIFACTS

BEADS (TABLE D6, PLATE 18e)

Two beads were found. One is a partially finished bead of calcite, probably a cave travertine (B41,X659). This will be further discussed with other unfinished calcite beads of the later phases. The other is a large glazed paste or faience bead, still with blue-green surface (A28, X540). This unique bead is from a well-stratified context; however, such beads are made today and I suspect it is intrusive. Further stratified examples from this period are needed.

ALABASTER RING FRAGMENT

An item that may be a segment of a ground alabaster ring occurred in Excavation B, Layer 41 (X681). If circular it was once about 11 cm in exterior diameter. It may, however, have been another form as it tapers slightly from 0.79 by 0.64 cm to 0.71 by 0.50 cm in the 1.90 cm segment surviving. A similarly tapered piece from the much earlier Ali Kosh Phase at Ali Kosh was thought by Hole to have been a pendant (Hole, Flannery, and Neely 1969:237 and Fig. 104c).

STONE BALLS (PLATE 9a)

Two very regular limestone spheres were found in Excavation B, Layer 41. The smaller (X680) was pecked into shape. It is 3.61 cm in diameter and 66 grams in weight. The larger (X675) was first pecked, then ground into final form. It is 4.88 cm in diameter and 151 gm in weight. The sizes of these balls fall within the ranges reported for balls from the Mehmeh and Bayat Phases at Tepe Sabz (Hole, Flannery, and Neely 1969:200). I have no suggestions as to the function of this class of artifact.

SEAL (FIG. 29d, PLATE 9d)

A button seal made from a fine gray slate or siltstone was found in Excavation B, Layer 42 (X698). It measures 2.5 by 2.7 cm across its oval face. The seal cutter first quartered the surface with two incised lines at right angles. In each quadrant he placed six incised lines forming a set of three nested chevrons not quite joined at the angle.

SUMMARY

Let us now consider a tentative classification by use, rather than material. Most non-ceramic artifacts were probably used in technical activities. Choppers and many of the chipped stone cutting tools were probably used in meat preparation; the sickles and grinding artifacts were probably used in the preparation of plant foods. The other scraping and cutting tools, the piercing and reaming tools, the celt or adze, and the spindle whorls were probably all used to manufacture various other artifacts. The bent nail and the perforated stones were also probably used in technical activities of some sort. Some artifacts were architectural elements. Among these are the sewer fragment, the grate, the reed mats, and perhaps the fragmentary lashings. Some artifacts were probably commonly used for personal adornment and social distinction. The linen-like cloth, the beads, and perhaps the alabaster ring fragment or pendant could have been so used. Other artifacts were probably used in the control of the movement and storage of goods. The seal, the evidence of sealings, and the possible macehead could be so considered. Finally there are a number of items whose use is difficult to demonstrate or even surmise. Among these are the stone and bitumen spheres, the excised ceramic slab, the animal figurine, and the perforated sherd.

Table 7: Bitumen Spheres

Number	Layer	Diameter	Weight
X628	B39 lower	4.46	66.7 g
X635	B40 upper	2.55	12.4 g
X745	B45 bottom	2.94	16.4 g

Chapter IV

THE DISTRIBUTION OF ARTIFACTS IN THE BAYAT AND FARUKH PHASES

INTRODUCTION

We expect a variety of behavior patterns to affect the distribution of artifacts in any archaeological site. First, the various tools used in one activity may be stored together or broken together. This creates positive correlations between the broken parts of a single artifact type and between the various parts of artifacts used together. At the same time, such behavior creates negative correlations between the broken artifacts used in spatially separate activities. Unfortunately artifacts are almost never dropped where they are used. The second set of patterns involves the collection of primary garbage and its deposition elsewhere as secondary garbage. Different cleaning methods, for instance the picking up of larger pieces as opposed to the sweeping up of smaller pieces, may lower positive correlations between use-associated artifacts or even between the bases and rims of a single vessel type. Even with a single method of cleaning and dumping, the inevitable mixing of garbage from different activity areas will lower correlations. Since secondary garbage is far more common than primary garbage, archaeologists who seek to extract behavorial information from their sites must deal with such mixed deposits. The third behavior pattern involves the re-excavation of secondary garbage and its tertiary use for mud brick or for architectural fill. The former usually contains only a few small artifacts, but the latter can contain quantities of hopelessly mixed material. Fortunately, such tertiary garbage seems to be rare at Farukhabad, and the few cases that were noted were easily recognized because they contained large quantities of sherds from widely separated time periods. Fourth, it is likely that the inhabitants of a settlement will change their technology because of new materials, new methods of manufacture, and new adaptive problems. New artifact types will have negative correlations with those they replaced if deposits from a long span of time are considered. Fifth and finally, as generations of artifact manufacturers come and go, artifact styles will change, because of both chance variations and deliberate manipulation in the transmission of techniques and of symbolic embellishment. Once again, if deposits from long spans of time are considered, there will be negative correlations between artifacts in new styles and those they replaced.

The excavations at Farukhabad were not designed to elucidate the full social and economic organization of fourth millennium Deh Luran communities. Nevertheless, it is important to gain some understanding of the factors outlined above, as best one can with the available samples, to provide a context for the several kinds of variables which are the central focus of this study. In particular, I will attempt to unravel the five sets of behavior patterns noted above in the following manner. First, strictly stylistic variables, (e.g. the variations in motifs painted on a particular vessel shape), will be examined to isolate sets of near-contemporary excavation units within which activity variation can be considered. These sets will be our cultural phases and subphases. Having defined such sets with stylistic criteria, I will next compare the criteria with those of the previously defined phases on the Deh Luran Plain. These criteria will be specific to particular vessel shapes, variations between which will be considered later in the study of activity variation. This should avoid the problems of circular reasoning in the construction of both chronological units and activity-related groups from the same series of artifact samples. Second, the pattern of correlations between common artifact shapes from excavated deposits of a limited chronological span will be considered in a series of steps. First, correlations resulting from the breakage of a single tool type will be eliminated after consideration of the evidence of recon-

Table 8: Stylistic Features of Susiana Ceramics from Farukhabad

	Bowl				Rim			Painted Motifs			
A23	4	9	8	—	—	—	—	—	—	—	2
A24–25	16	41	36	1	—	—	1	4	—	1	8
A26–27	24	25	32	2	1	—	—	10	—	2	2
A28–29	43	21	13	2	2	—	3	4	3	1	3
A30–31	11	—	—	—	1	1	1	—	—	—	—
A33–34	12	3	—	—	2	1	—	—	—	—	—
A35–36	22	8	2	—	—	—	—	—	—	—	—
B37–39	5	11	15	1	1	—	—	1	—	—	2
B40	21	26	27	2	3	3	1	8	3	2	8
B41	6	20	15	3	2	—	3	7	2	3	6
B42–43	11	19	28	4	2	—	—	7	9	4	10
B44–45	8	18	21	6	1	1	—	16	9	4	12
B46–47	27	15	20	—	2	3	2	3	—	3	7

Table 8: Stylistic Features of Susiana Ceramics from Farukhabad (con't)

	Painted Motifs			Bowl Base Form				Jar Neck Motifs			
				Wide	Narrow	Shaved	Ring				
A23	—	3	2	20	—	—	—	1	2	4	1
A24–25	—	2	—	59	1	2	6	5	2	5	1
A26–27	1	—	—	75	—	4	16	2	8	14	2
A28–29	—	—	3	31	6	6	3	—	1	2	1
A30–31	—	1	—	4	—	6	2	—	—	3	1
A33–34	—	—	—	4	1	—	1	—	—	1	1
A35–36	—	—	1	5	3	—	—	—	—	1	1
B37–39	1	2	2	28	2	2	6	4	1	4	—
B40	1	—	3	65	1	3	7	3	8	6	3
B41	3	1	—	31	3	3	7	—	10	1	—
B42–43	1	3	2	53	—	4	13	13	6	2	2
B44–45	2	2	2	27	2	5	2	2	6	11	1
B46–47	—	—	7	53	2	3	18	—	3	29	6

structable examples. Second, correlations resulting from disposal together will be isolated using the evidence of pieces of similar sizes and shapes. Third, the remaining correlations will be sorted to isolate those correlations which perhaps result from the use of items together in the same activity. Throughout this process, little attention will be paid to low correlations because of the attenuation problem resulting when, as is usually the case with the Farukhabad data, correlation coefficients are computed from variables with low counts (Cowgill, 1970). Fourth, the spatial distribution and feature association of each tool category will be examined to further elucidate the possible activity-related tool groups and the organization of activities. In Chapter VI, these inferences will be coordinated with others to produce a series of propositions about community organization during each phase.

STYLISTIC DEVELOPMENTS AND PHASE SUBDIVISIONS

The stratigraphic distributions of vessel parts in Excavations A and B are summarized in Table 8. Summary proportional computations derived from Table 8 are presented in Table 9. More detailed listings will be found in Appendix B. In the following discussion, I will compare changes in motifs on each vessel shape in the two separate stratigraphic columns, considering first the bowl motifs and then the jar motifs. As the design motifs on a single form can be considered a closed domain, the use of proportions is legitimate (Cowgill, 1968:3; Speth and Johnson 1976:48–49).

Plain bowl rims show a marked proportional decrease through time in Excavation A. Since these rims are found on both narrow- and wide-based forms, and the narrow-based forms vary as a result of different activities, as shown later in this chapter, this rim is not in any event useful for delimiting phases. Bowl rims with bands, almost all of which seem to be from wide-based forms, are more useful. Bowls with multiple bands comprise 42 to 63 percent of the bowl rims from all the layers in the two excavations, except for the four lowest layers of Excavation A. The small sample of bowl rims from these layers has only 16 percent rims with multiple bands.

Bowls with other more complicated rim motifs, almost all of which are also from wide-based forms, require extensive comment. Rims with combinations of vertical or horizontal curved and straight lines occur sporadically throughout both sequences. They are the only motifs occurring on the smaller wide-based bowl form in the four lowest layers of Excavation A. Rims with dot motifs are particularly common in Excavation A, Layers 24–29 and Excavation B, Layers 40–45. The varieties with the pendant rectangles and with the curved lines show no consistent stratigraphic trends. Rims with step motifs are common throughout except in the lowest four layers of excavation A. In the latest layers under consideration at this point, A 23 and B 37–39, when complex rim motifs in general, and dot motifs in particular, become rare, step motifs become proportionally the most common small bowl motif. Among the larger wide-based bowls, rims with sigma motifs show no consistent stratigraphic distribution. Those rims with slash motifs occur only in the middle layers of the two excavations. In contrast, those with diamond motifs occur throughout the sequence, but are proportionally more common in Layers A 28–29 and B 46–47. The only larger bowl rim with a complex motif from the lowest four layers of Excavation A exhibits a diamond motif as do several body sherds.

The only observed attribute of bowl bases which one may consider stylistic rather than technical is that of the vertical shaving of narrow bowl bases to a near point. The four lowest layers of Excavation A have only the round based forms. Shaved bases comprise a majority in Layers 31 to 24 in Excavation A and all layers of Excavation B. Because painted jar rims and bowl rims are virtually absent from Layers A 30-31, it is the shaved bases on the narrow bowls found on the floors of the Feature 30 building which lead me to group these layers with later layers rather than earlier layers.

The only observed stylistic attribute of jar necks is the degree of painting on the neck. Completely painted rims occur throughout the two sequences and this is the only variety attested in the six lowest layers of Excavation A. Rims with bands occur in Layers 29 to 23 of Excavation A and throughout Excavation B. Unpainted rims are attested above Layer 29 in Excavation A, and above Layer 45 in Excavation B.

The sequence of stylistic changes in the ceramics in the Susiana tradition at Farukhabad can be summarized as follows:

1) A phase with many small bowls, some plain and some with simple rim band or a few straight and curved lines, either horizontal or vertical; with a few medium-sized bowls with diamond motifs; and with high-necked jars with fully painted necks (A33–36).

2) A phase with plain, shaved base cups; with a wider variety of decorated bowls, most distinctively with dot and step motifs; and with jars with a variety of neck decoration. On the basis of bowl motifs, this phase can be tentatively subdivided into three subphases.

A) An early subphase with the first dot and step motifs on the smaller bowl forms, and with primarily diamond motifs on the larger forms (A 30–31, B 46–47).

Table 9: Design Proportions on Susiana Ceramics from Farukhabad

	Bowl Rims										Jar Necks		
	% Pln.	% Bnd.	Among Band % Mult. Band	% Other	Among Other* % ▲▼	% ⁞⁞	% ◣	% ᶝᶝᶝ	% \\\\	% ◇	% Pln.	% Bnd.	% Solid
A23	14	61	48	25	–	–	–	–	–	–	–	–	–
A24–25	14	72	48	14	0	31	50	12	0	0	42	16	42
A26–27	24	60	58	16	6	75	12	0	6	0	9	33	58
A28–29	44	37	42	19	10	42	15	0	0	15	–	–	–
A30–31	73	0	–	27							–	–	–
A33–36	66	25	16	9	–	–	–	–	–	–	–	–	–
B37–39	12	68	60	20	–	–	–	–	–	–	–	–	–
B40	19	51	53	30	9	40	25	0	3	9	17	47	35
B41	8	54	48	38	7	44	22	3	11	0	0	89	11
B42–43	11	51	63	38	5	52	26	7	2	5	61	28	11
B44–45	7	44	60	49	2	59	24	4	4	4	10	31	57
B46–47	30	40	58	30	7	22	25	0	0	25	0	10	90

* percentage not computed if ten rims or less

B) A middle subphase with many dot and step motifs and some sigma motifs on the smaller forms, and with the first slash motifs as well as continuing diamond motifs on the larger forms (A 24–29, B 40–45).

C) A late subphase with reduced quantities of complex motifs, the primary remaining ones being the step motif on the smaller bowls and the sigma motif on both larger and smaller bowls (A 23, B 37–39).

How do these units compare with those defined by Hole, Flannery, and Neely on the basis of the 1963 excavations at Tepe Sabz? Our first phase is unfortunately represented by only a few layers with low densities of artifacts. This small sample is most similar to those reported from their last phase, the Bayat Phase. The following table, based upon my examination of the rimsherds from the Tepe Sabz excavations now stored at Yale University, illustrates the relation between the two ceramic series. Absent from the Farukhabad rimsherd series is the vertical curved line motif, termed 'type 11a' by Hole, Flannery, and Neely (1969, 150–151). This motif, however, does occur on a body sherd. Also absent is the unpainted jar neck. This occurs later at Farukhabad, and its absence may reflect the very small number of jar neck fragments from the lowest layers of Excavation A. Present only at Farukhabad are bowl rims with multiple horizontal bands. They may be absent at Sabz because the

THE DISTRIBUTION OF ARTIFACTS IN THE BAYAT AND FARUKH PHASES

Table 10: Ceramic Features of Tepe Sabz, Zone A, and Tepe Farukhabad Excavation A, Layers 33–36

	Bowl Rims					Jar Rims		
Sabz	222	0	59	29	1	16	33	12
Farukhabad	11	2	2	0	1	0	2	2

layers at Farukhabad are slightly later. Nevertheless the two series are quite close, and I therefore tentatively assign Layers 33 to 36 in Excavation A to the later Bayat Phase.

If this is so, then our later phase must be more recent than any reported from Tepe Sabz. Indeed, it contains many elements not represented at Tepe Sabz in any of the defined phases. I term this new phase, immediately succeeding the Bayat Phase, the Farukh Phase. For purposes of subsequent discussion the layers in the two excavations at Farukhabad and the excavation at Tepe Sabz are taken to correlate in the following manner.

The Farukh Phase has very definite parallels in areas to the East of the Deh Luran Plain. The ceramic complex termed Susiana d on the Susiana Plain of Central Khuzistan (LeBreton 1957), is similar in having high proportions of bowls with dot motifs, sigma motifs, slash motifs, and diamond motifs as well as jars with a variety of neck painting. The Farukh Phase is distinctive in having quantities of the dot and curved line combination and in having the step motif. Doubtless there are other designs distinctive to what has been called Susiana d. Full comparison of the two complexes must await the recovery of new ceramic samples from the Susiana Plain. If this correlation with the Susiana Plain proves correct, then the previous correlation of Bayat and Susiana d (Hole, Flannery, and Neely 1969: 9, 370) cited in several works (Dollfus 1972: 76; and Johnson 1973:64) should be reconsidered. Bayat appears to be most similar to some portion of LeBreton's Susiana c, while Farukh is most similar to some portion of Susiana d. A Deh Luran equivalent of the Susa A ceramic complex, now well known from recent excavations at Djaffarabad (Dollfus 1971) and the Acropole of Susa (Le Brun 1971) has not yet been excavated. However, sherds similar to Susa A are known from the surface of Tepe Musiyan and sites east of Musiyan, as will be discussed in Chapter VI.

The fact that every defining feature of the Bayat phase occurs, at least to a limited extent, in deposits of the Farukh Phase raises a difficult problem in the interpretation of evidence from surface survey: how is one to differentiate a purely Farukh Phase site from a Farukh Phase site with underlying layers of the Bayat Phase? Are the few curved line motif sherds in such a collection Bayat Phase sherds from a lower level or are they Farukh Phase minor types? A solution to this problem can be suggested. Consider the vertical curved line motif 'Type IIa' of Hole, Flannery, and Neely, for which we have measured examples from deposits of the Bayat phase at Sabz and the Farukh phase at Farukhabad. The following graph (Fig. 30) compares the average width of the straight defining lines with the width of the curved central line. While examples with delicate lines occur in both phases, examples with heavy lines occur only in Bayat Phase deposits at Tepe Sabz. Even though the two sites are only a few km apart, it is still possible that the fine-line examples from Farukh layers at Farukhabad are extrusive from Bayat layers and that the difference is spatial, not temporal. However, should future study demonstrate more conclusively that the heavier bowls with the heavy painting are good indicators of Bayat Phase occupation on a site, then the surface surveyor's problem is solved.

Table 11: Correlations of Excavated Later Susiana Deposits on the Deh Luran Plain

		Farukhabad		Sabz
Farukh	F1	A23	B37–39	—
	F2	A24–29	B40–45	—
	F3	A30–31	B46–47	—
Bayat	G	A33–36	—	Zone A

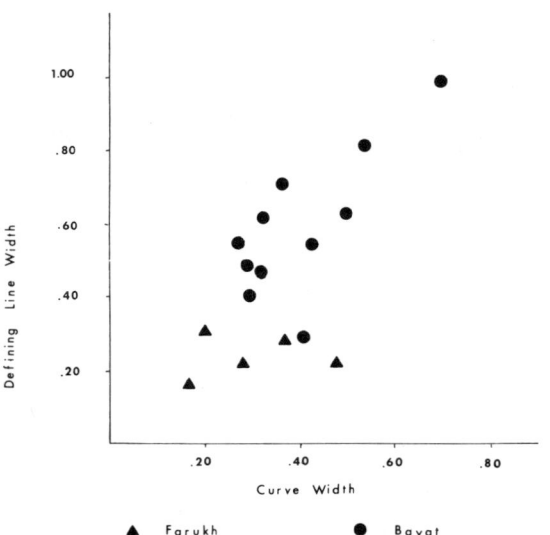

Fig. 30. Scatter Plot of the Metric Attributes of Vertical Curved Line Motifs from Sabz and Farukhabad.

ACTIVITY VARIATION DURING THE FARUKH PHASE

The Farukh Phase provenience units from excavations A and B can be combined to provide 52 artifact samples representing a single developing community (see Appendix Tables B1, B4). To monitor activity variation, we must statistically analyze these samples. Since the samples come from widely different volumes of excavated deposit, I have standardized the raw counts to counts per cubic meter. Further standardization through the use of percentages would distort the data because a section of an archaeological site is an open domain where classes of artifacts are often deposited at rates independent of each other, leading to varying densities. Were I to compute percentages, the count of each class of artifact would contribute to the total and that total would in turn influence the percentage assigned to every class in the sample. For example, if classes x and y had constant densities throughout the sampled site but class z had a varying density, the percentages of x and y would be negatively correlated with z and positively correlated with each other. The use of percentages would thus create artificial correlations. There are other means of standardizing artifact counts which would avoid this problem, such as class-to-class ratios, but their properties are not well understood.

Instead of further transforming the data set, I have adopted a statistic which minimizes the effect of any single provenience unit by considering only the rank order of each artifact density rather than the absolute density. This is a non-parametric measure of correlation called Spearman's rho which varies as does the familiar Pearson's product-moment correlation, from +1.00 for a strong positive relationship to −1.00 for a strong negative or inverse relationship (Siegel 1956: 202–213). In the Farukh Phase analysis of 52 provenience units any correlation greater than +.36 or less than −.36 is significant at the 99 percent confidence level. This means that if our samples are representative of the range of variation at the site and if, in fact, there was no relationship between the two variables, with repeated samplings of 52 units from the site, correlation coefficients greater than .36 would arise only 1 percent of the time by chance alone. Matters of significance aside, however, a correlation of .36 between two variables only accounts for about 10 percent of the variation in each variable. Therefore, I shall focus primarily on those correlations greater than .50, which account for more than 25 percent of the variation in each variable. When I want to test the association of an artifact with a single sub-phase, type of feature, or excavation unit, I will use the non-parametric Mann-Whitney U test, (Ibid.: 116–127) which is a rank-order based statistic for testing the significance of differing mean or modal tendencies.

The intercorrelations of all types present in at least half of the Farukh Phase provenience units is shown in Table 12. The matrix has been ordered by placing the positively correlated variables together on the margins and variables with low correlations far apart along the margins. This makes groupings of variables with high intercorrelations stand out.

The three highest intercorrelations doubtless result from the breakage of pottery vessels. Restorable examples indicate that high-necked jars have flat bases (+.62), basins also have flat bases (+.65) and bowls with band motifs characteristically have wide bases (+.64).

Other correlations probably result from use together in the same activity. All of the painted bowl rims show high intercorrelations (+.55, +.52, and +.51) which is to be expected since they are basically the same form differentiated by slight size variations and strictly decorative motif variations. Wide bowl bases correlate well with basin rims (+.61) and flat bases (+.52). The correlation of bowl rims with basin rims and flat bases are somewhat lower, perhaps because the tiny bowl rim sherds

Table 12: Farukh Phase Artifact Correlations

	Ring Bowl Base	Narrow Bowl Base	Plain Bowl Rim	Small Bowl Rim, Complex Motif	Large Bowl Rim, Complex Motif	Bowl With Band Motif	Wide Bowl Base	Flat Base	Basin Rim	High Neck Jar Rim	Chert Blade Segment
Ring Bowl Base	1.00										
Narrow Bowl Base	.12	1.00									
Plain Bowl Rim	.20	.27	1.00								
Small Bowl Rim, Complex Motif	.06	.27	.35	1.00							
Large Bowl Rim, Complex Motif	.21	.07	.22	**.55**	1.00						
Bowl With Band Motif	.03	.06	.22	**.52**	**.51**	1.00					
Wide Bowl Base	.23	.19	.36	**.40**	**.43**	**.64**	1.00				
Flat Base	.34	.21	.30	.28	**.41**	.35	**.52**	1.00			
Basin Rim	.07	.19	.30	.36	.37	**.47**	**.61**	**.65**	1.00		
High Neck Jar Rim	.41	.06	.37	.35	.34	**.43**	**.42**	**.62**	**.45**	1.00	
Chert Blade Segment	.14	.04	.34	.30	.17	.23	.22	.02	.09	.18	1.00

are cleaned up in a different manner than the larger bowl bases and basin fragments. Such hypotheses can best be tested when extensive horizontal excavations are undertaken, and the scattered pieces of single vessels can be mapped. In any event, there is reason to believe that the basins and the bowls were used together and to some extent their fragments were disposed of together. Finally there is a weak but significant correlation between high-necked jars and both basin rims (+.45), wide bowl bases (+.42), flat bases (+.41) and bowl rims with bands (+.43) suggesting that the jars were also used with the basins and bowls. Contrasting with this basin-bowl-jar group are narrow-based bowls with plain rims, and chert blade segments which do not correlate highly with any other variables.

During the Farukh Phase the area of the settlement exposed in Excavation B is covered with a succession of modest, insubstantial compounds while that exposed in Excavation A is covered by a succession of more elaborate constructions. The contrast of the gross artifact densities in these two areas of the site may contribute to an understanding of both this architectural contrast and the artifactual distributions discussed above. Table 13 presents the mean densities for a large number of variables some of which were not included in the previous correlation analysis because their occurrence is too irregular. Only one item proves to be significantly concentrated in one of the two excavations. This is the plain bowl rim which is three times more common in Excavation A than in Excavation B. The Mann-Whitney U Statistic is 147.5; the probability of this arising by chance

Table 13: Farukh Phase Mean Densities

	Exc. A	Exc. B	U	Significant?
Hole Mouth Jar	.46	.43	—	—
Narrow Bowl Base	.97	.87	289.0	no
Plain Bowl Rim	4.11	1.85	147.5	P=.986
Ring Bowl Base	1.03	1.85	290.0	no
Wide Bowl Base	10.05	6.67	235.0	no
Bowl Rim, Band Motif	11.36	6.99	759.5	no
Small Bowl Rim, Complex Motif	4.04	4.94	272.0	no
Large Bowl Rim, Complex Motif	1.23	.87	285.0	no
Flat Base	3.69	3.35	295.5	no
Basin Rim	4.99	4.28	285.0	no
High Neck Jar Rim	3.12	2.29	272.5	no
Low Neck Jar Rim	.27	.31	—	—
Drill	.06	.03	—	—
Pointed Piece	.14	.00	—	—
Sickle	.63	.68	—	—
Segment	1.72	2.17	268.0	no
Retouched Blade	.02	.24	—	—
Retouched Flake	.04	.11	—	—
Denticulate	.22	.11	—	—
Notch	.31	.21	—	—
Burin	.21	.07	—	—
Chopper	.25	.11	—	—
N=	17	35		

Note: Densities are expressed as mean artifacts per cubic meter. The Mann-Whitney U Test (Siegel 1956:116–127) is done for variables occurring in more than half the units.

alone is about three in one thousand (P=.0034). This statistical relation is elucidated by the find of a set of conical bowls with plain bowl rims and a cup stand on the otherwise clean floor of the larger platform building in Excavation A (F30–31, see Fig. 9d; Pl. 3b). Apparently these bowls were more commonly used in activities performed in or near these more elaborate structures, thus contributing to a higher density of plain bowl rims in the vicinity.

Now let us draw together the preceding observations, plus the observations of Redding regarding the fauna and the observations of Miller regarding the flora of the Farukh Phase into a coherent assessment of activity variation in this early town.

Chapter V

A SUMMARY OF THE BAYAT AND FARUKH PHASES

One of the functions of this monograph is to extend the sequence of cultural phases so ably set forth by Hole, Flannery, and Neely in 1969. In this chapter and in Chapter X, the interpretation of successive cultural developments between 4500 B.C and 2700 B.C. will be presented in summary form.

The environment of the plain has been described in the previously mentioned work, and reinterpreted by Michael Kirkby in a recent paper (1977). A brief summary will suffice. The plain is a shallow trough averaging 60 km long and 20 km wide. Its lowest point is about 120 m above sea level. It is bounded on the southwest by the Jebel Hamrin, a low range of hills formed from a much dissected anticline of sandstone, siltstone, and gypsum. This separates the plain from the vast alluvium of the Tigris and Euphrates rivers. The plain is bound on the northeast by a series of much more prominent anticlines which mark the beginning of the Zagros Mountains. The first of these is the Kuh-e Siah, an isolated arch of limestone rising to 1400 m above sea level. Behind this is an almost continuous scarp of younger sandstone and gypsum strata which defines the edge of a rolling surface largely above 1300 m. The Mehmeh River cuts through this cliff and enters the north corner of the plain. From there it runs southeast to the center of the plain, and turns sharply southwest, cutting across the Jebel in a narrow canyon. The Dawairij River runs around the east edge of the high country and enters the plain near the center. Here it turns sharply southeast and leaves the plain through the south corner. Kirkby's suggestion that the Dawairij once ran southwestward and joined the Mehmeh, but was diverted into its present course by canals, remains untested. For most of the plain's circumference the upper slopes are colluvial fans composed of angular sandstone and gypsum fragments eroded from the surrounding hills. These rocky slopes were cultivated during the first millennium A.D. (Neely 1974) and are today largely denuded of soil and vegetation except in the frequent small solution features along their lower periphery. In contrast, to the north and northeast near the points where the rivers break onto the plain, the upper slopes are composed of cherty gravels ultimately transported from the inner Zagros. These gravel slopes are difficult to cultivate for the most part, although every spring they carry an extensive grass cover. The lower slopes and alluvial fans of the rivers present the best opportunities for cultivation. Here the soil has a silty texture, and the runoff from rainfall and the flow of rivers and springs can easily be diverted into fields. These areas are also less prone to the accumulation of salts than the lower portions of the valley. These lower portions are of two distinct types. The first type is basins between the slopes and the river fans, which must certainly have existed since the time of the earliest known settlements (Helbaek 1969:390). These basins become swamps during the winter rains and saline wastes during the summer; they are covered with a dense growth of salt-loving herbs and shrubs. The second type of landscape in the lower area is the floors of the entrenched river valleys. These narrow bands along the rivers are covered with hummocks of sand and gravel from river flooding, and have numerous tamarisk and some poplar shrubs. Kirkby (1977:280–282) has argued that the entrenchment of the rivers occurred around 2000 B.C. Prior to this cycle of down-cutting, there were multiple channels shifting across the surface of the alluvial fans instead of a single entrenched channel. The distribution of Bayat Phase settlements on the Mehmeh alluvium (Fig. 31) suggests at least two channels, supporting Kirkby's proposition. Such raised multiple channels would lead to larger areas of high water table and easier irrigation opportunities than today and perhaps to a different distribution of tamarisk and poplar. Certainly these shrubs were present in the fourth millennium B.C. as indicated by charcoal from the excavated sites, but their distribution on the landscape may have been somewhat different.

Table 14: Landscape Types on the Deh Luran Plain

	sq. km	%
Rocky Slope	217	23
Gravelly Slope	259	28
Plain: Lower Slope	62	7
Alluvial Fan	229	24
Basins	80	8
River Flood Plain	94	10
Total	941	100

The dominance of the presently rare Indian gerbil among the rodent fauna at Ali Kosh, Tepe Sabz, and Farukhabad argues for a much broader area of soft moist soil than now exists, as we would expect with the rivers aggrading at plain level, rather than entrenched, and with concomitant widespread small-scale irrigation. It is likely that tamarisk and poplar were widely scattered along channel and canal banks and in low areas where run-off collected, rather than concentrated along river beds. The areas of each of the above outlined types of landscape today are presented in Table 14.

If the above discussion is correct, the plain would have had about 59 percent upper slopes and basins better suited for grazing, 7 percent lower slope equally suited for agriculture and grazing, and 34 percent alluvial fan and river flood plain better suited for irrigation agriculture. This is not an obligatory situation and doubtless under some conditions the slopes could be used for agriculture and the alluvial fans used for grazing. However, the proportions do indicate why the plain is today, and often was in the past, used primarily for grazing rather than plant cultivation.

The Deh Luran plain and its vicinity have a number of resources useful to craftsmen. These will be discussed further in Chapter XV but a brief introduction is warranted here. A black or dark brown chert occurs on the rocky slopes, and is concentrated in the gravels of the Mehmeh. A gray granular chert is found in the gravel slopes, particularly at the southeast end of the plain. Large limestone boulders used for grinding slabs and mortars, and gypsum boulders used for stone bowls are widespread. In addition to the tamarisk and poplar previously mentioned, there are substantial concentrations of oak on the ridges above 900 m to the northeast. All of these trees could be used as fuel, but poplar is preferable for roof beams and oak makes strong handles for tools.

Finally, on the northeast slope of the valley is a large bitumen seep. Bitumen is the univeral adhesive and waterproofing material of Greater Mesopotamia. In sum, Deh Luran is one of the areas closest to Central Sumer possessing quantities of stone, wood, and asphalt, However, only the last mentioned material is of a relatively high quality. Both the woods and the stones from Deh Luran are surpassed in quality by those from elsewhere, and the stones in particular serve as local substitutes to be used only when better material cannot be obtained from other areas. Nevertheless, except for metals, the area could be materially self-sufficient. This was never true of the alluvium of Mesopotamia proper, to the southwest.

Communities in the Susiana or greater Ubaid tradition had inhabited the plain for at least a millennium prior to the Bayat Phase. According to Neely's survey data, by the Bayat Phase there were about 21.0 ha of settlement on the plain. In the succeeding Farukh Phase, there were 19.0 ha. This difference is well within the range of uncertainty created by the difficulty of recognizing Bayat strata covered by Farukh strata from surface examination alone. For settlements in this size range a figure of 200 people per ha is often assumed (Adams 1965: 123–24; Johnson 1973:64–66). Such an assumption would imply about 3600 people on the plain during these phases. However, in the excavations at both Tepe Sabz and Tepe Farukhabad the fourth millennium layers exhibited periods of building regularly followed by periods of abandonment and use of the abandoned space as open courts. Unlike modern central Khuzistan villages, from which the above estimate is derived, more than half of these later Susiana communities would have been open space. A lower population estimate is thus indicated, but how much lower must remain unknown until more community plans and a better understanding of human living space requirements are available.

The subsistence resources and technology of these communities had changed little from the preceding centuries. Among the hunted animals, the onager and the gazelle remained dominant; among the herded animals the sheep, goat, and cattle were still dominant. At Tepe Sabz the only possible proportional change through time is the gradual increase in the proportion of sheep to goats. In the final Bayat phase layers from Sabz and in the combined Bayat and Farukh phases layers from Farukhabad, about one quarter of the animals consumed in the settlements were hunted onager and gazelle. Among the domestic animals about one eighth were cattle, with the remainder evenly divided between sheep and goats. It is difficult to be more exact as there was a demonstrably patterned variation in animal butchering within Farukhabad (see Chapter XIV, Table 74) which cannot have been properly sampled at either site. Among the few samples of domestic grain, wheat is predominant over barley. The only utilized wild plant food is the almond.

The domestic architecture of the Bayat and Farukh phases is represented by a sufficient number of partial plans from both sites so that a general pattern may be suggested. The basic unit is a compound with a surrounding wall. The sides of these structures face the cardinal points as do those of most excavated buildings of the fifth and fourth millennia B.C. in Deh Luran. Walls have shallow builders' trenches at best and stone footings are uncommon. Bricks are typically about .50 m long, and are laid in several patterns. Outer compound walls are characteristically thin, and neither possible gate (in Farukhabad BF 40 and in Sabz Zone A2) is well-preserved. Within the compound walls are both room blocks and open courtyards. Many of the attested rooms are very small. Doubtless the larger rooms were only partially exposed within our small excavations, and were therefore not measurable. Although the full dimensions of a single compound are in no case attested, they seem to have been fairly large and they may well have housed social units larger than the nuclear family. The evidence for social differentiation among domestic units will be considered shortly.

Food processing is directly attested by charred plant seed fragments and discarded bones. Sickles, though used in the fields, were often returned to the settlements for the replacement of lost or worn blades. Incoming grain could have been stored in either the building with internal supports (A F28) or in some of the very small rooms without evidence of doors. There is no evidence of grain grinding in the form of slabs or mortars at Farukhabad. This problem may be elucidated by the evidence from Tepe Sabz, where most Bayat Phase grinding slabs had been gathered up and placed with burials; perhaps this procedure was also followed at Farukhabad. The large circular oven in Excavation B would have been useful for baking bread and other things. The first step in animal food processing was the butchering of the animals killed in the hunt or selected from the herds. Sheep and goats were butchered in the settlements, doubtless with some of the ubiquitous larger blades and flakes. The animals were skinned and the lower limbs were cut off and discarded. The upper limbs and scapulae were cut from the rib cage, and lower limbs were cut from the pelvis. Some upper limb units, or perhaps whole carcasses, were roasted, but burned bone was not common and most meat must have been cut into smaller pieces and grilled or boiled. As all parts of the mammals larger than sheep and goats were present on the site they must have been killed there also, but the details of butchering and cooking are unknown. In general, there is little evidence of the actual cooking of food. Only the large but relatively rare Khazineh Redware jars exhibit the evidences of fire expectable from cooking. The complex of large high-necked jars, basins and small bowls of Susiana ware must have been used in other aspects of food preparation and serving.

Various forms of craft production are attested in and around the compounds. Local chert was extensively worked. There was some production of ceramics, and some type of fiber was spun into thread. Bitumen was processed for local use and export (see Chapter XV). Other activities are doubtless indicated by the presence of chert drills and pointed pieces, bone awls, possible baskets, perforated sherds, and so on. However, demonstration of the uses to which these artifacts were put awaits the study of larger samples from more extensive excavations. The only evidence of specialization within the community is the concentration of spindle whorls near the simpler structures at Farukhabad, a pattern which may well be due to chance. Furthermore, there exists no evidence of differences in the inferred activities between the communities of Farukhabad and Sabz.

The domestic units composing the community of Farukhabad are not equivalent. This is demonstrated first by the architecture. While their basic layout remains similar throughout, insofar as can be inferred from the small areas revealed, only the structures in Excavation A are on mud brick platforms. They have large walls with heavy plasters, and there is one probable case of a decorative pilaster. Probable storehouses are located near these elaborate buildings. On architectural grounds alone, it would seem that the occupants of this part of the settlement had access to more and better-skilled labor than did others. Second, while most ceramic vessels, artifacts, and other debris are similarly distributed around the buildings in both excavations, indicating that ordinary domestic functions were performed in both areas, there is one difference. Fragments of the plain conical cups are very common around the elaborate buildings of Excavation A, a point emphasized by the set found *in situ* in the hallway of the well-preserved building. Thus there is one kind of activity, perhaps, judging from the vessel shape, associated with the serving of liquids, that was more commonly performed around these platform buildings. Otherwise, the artifactual evidence indicates that the occupants of this part of the settlement were members of domestic units that led only slightly different lives from the other occupants of Farukhabad. Third, there are significant differences in the mammal remains around the elaborate as opposed to the simple buildings. In particular, the bones of the gazelle are more common near the larger building while the bones of equids and perhaps sheep and goats are more common near the smaller buildings (see Chapter XIV). Since, as was noted above, roasting was rare and meat may have been cut off the bone for preparation, this distribution of bones only indicates that those who butchered the animals were associated with different types of buildings. No doubt the meat was widely distributed. Given these inferences, the problem which remains is why the different species were favored by two different units. If the larger and putatively swifter equids had been butchered near the larger elaborate buildings, one could argue that larger, centrally co-ordinated hunting groups were needed. If hunted animals in general were near the elaborate structures one could argue that the hunt was the privilege of ranking groups. In both cases, however, the reverse pattern is found. Such possible arguments serve to emphasize how little is known about how equids were hunted, and indeed when they were first domesticated.

In any event, the domestic groups who lived in these two types of housing not only utilized different kinds of labor forces, they also controlled different classes of animals, for whatever reason.

That these contrasts recognized at Farukhabad are not a purely local phenomena is shown by the evidence from Tepe Sabz. The Zone A3 building (Hole, Flannery, and Neely 1969: Fig. 18), though not on a platform, has large and carefully constructed walls. The Bayat Phase layers here have high proportions of plain cup rims (Ibid.: Table 19). Finally, gazelle is more common than onager, and sheep and goat are relatively uncommon. Thus, in certain characteristics the area excavated at Sabz is much like the area exposed in Excavation A at Farukhabad. It seems reasonable to present for future testing the proposition that the inhabitants of the later Susiana communities were organized into ranked groups of some sort; such a state of affairs will be assumed for purposes of subsequent consideration of interregional exchange in the concluding chapter of this volume.

Now let us turn from the social organization of the community to the place of Farukhabad in the Deh Luran settlement system and to the changing social organization of the plain as a whole. During the later Susiana phases the data show much variation in settlement size and spacing (Neely, personal communication). Although full analysis of these data must await Neely's completion and final publication of his survey, I will make a few qualitative comments.

During the Bayat Phase there seem to have been two settlement size categories. There are three settlements ranging in size from about three to five ha, and 17 of less than one ha. These settlements occur in two or perhaps three clusters on the alluvial fans of three essentially permanent streams (Fig. 31). The largest cluster is on the Mehmeh alluvium, the next is on the Dawairij alluvium, and the third and last may be at the juncture of the Chikad and the Dawairij. Dominating the first cluster is Tepe Sabz (DL-31) and dominating the second is Tepe Musiyan (DL-20) of which only the south portion seems to have been occupied at this time. It is not clear whether Farukhabad (DL-32) is a subsidiary settlement or a small center co-dominant with Tepe Sabz during Bayat times.

In the succeeding Farukh Phase, for which there is better ceramic control, a number of interesting changes occur (Fig. 32):

1) There is drop in the number of settlements in the west, and several new ones appear in the east, thus balancing the distribution of population on the plain.
2) Musiyan emerges as the largest center on the plain, with Farukh Phase sherds being found on all portions of the site. Very near Musiyan are two small satellite communities. It is likely that this central community was not nucleated but was, as Hole, Flannery, and Neely have said, "an agglomeration of many smaller mounds" (Ibid.:65).

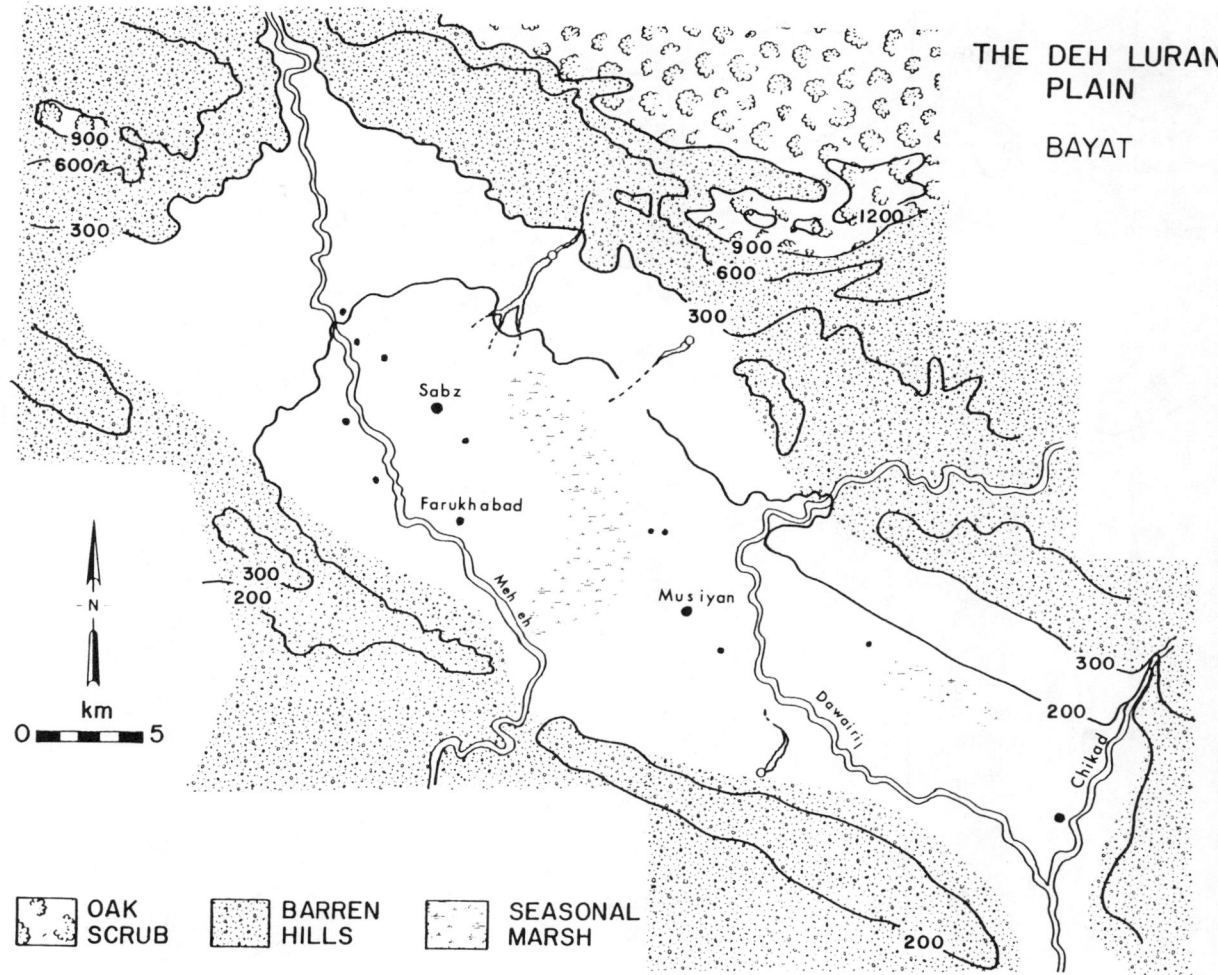

Fig. 31. Bayat Phase Settlement on the Deh Luran Plain.

3) Only Farukhabad to the west and perhaps site DL-87X to the east approach Musiyan in size. These may have become subsidiary centers. Apparently Farukhabad had ranking groups controlling labor and storage facilities.

4) Excavation on the smaller sites, however, may well reveal that ranking persons also resided at some of these as well as at the centers. Consider a few well-preserved smaller sites near Farukhabad. DL-247 is a surface level scatter of Farukh Phase artifacts. In contrast DL-286 is a low mound having a high eminence with Farukh Phase debris to one side on which a stamp seal, very similar to that from Farukhabad, was found. As in Hole's proposition regarding such sites on the Susiana Plain (Hole 1969:66–68), a site such as DL-286 may well have been the residence of a small, rural ranking group. If true, it is perhaps most useful, given the presently available data, to view Farukh Phase society as having settlements varying from a few very small ones without ranking figures through a greater number of larger settlements which often have ranking figures to a few even larger centers which always have ranking figures. Figure 32 shows that most of the sites on the west end of the plain

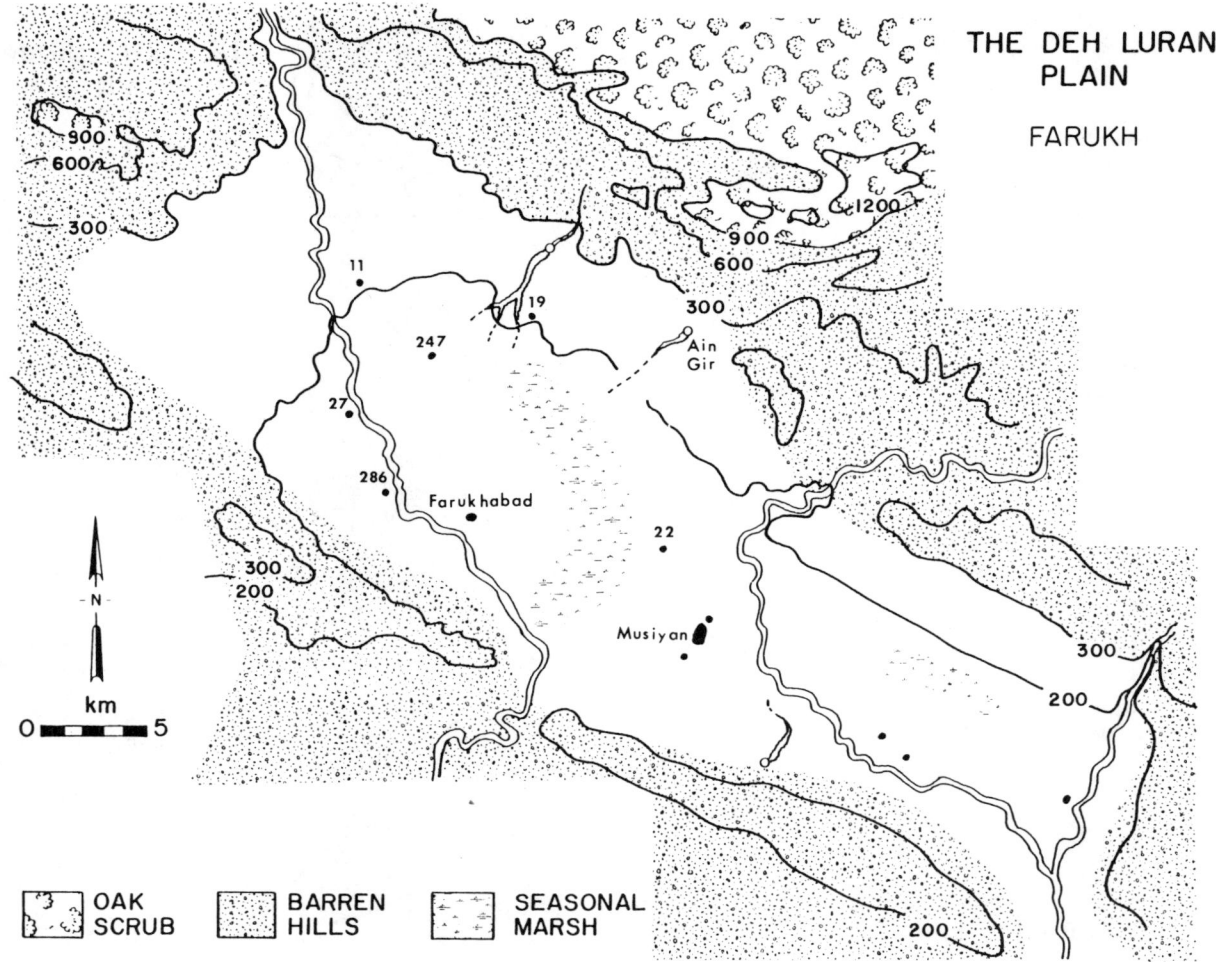

Fig. 32. Farukh Phase Settlement on the Deh Luran Plain.

could best communicate with Musiyan by way of Farukhabad. To further demonstrate that there is a hierarchical settlement organization would require additional classes of data.

In summary, by the late fourth millenium B.C. Deh Luran had developed a centralized network of communities whose complexity could only be guessed at ten years ago (Hole, Flannery, and Neely 1969:365). When representative samples of structures, debris, burials, and other features are recovered from all types of sites, the operation of this network will be elucidated in far greater detail than is now possible.

What were the broader relations of this developing society? A variety of relationships ranging from long-term, low-level ones such as the movement of individuals through kinship networks to brief, high-level relations involving the confrontation of entire societies must have existed. Given the present state of research, one can only outline some promising directions for future work.

A broad zone of similar ceramic motifs can result from some combinations of common heritage and ongoing relationships among potters. The similarities between the Bayat of Deh Luran, the later Susiana c of the Susiana Plain (LeBreton 1957:Fig. 4, 6), Eridu VIII and IX related communities in Southern Iraq, and Gawra XVII related

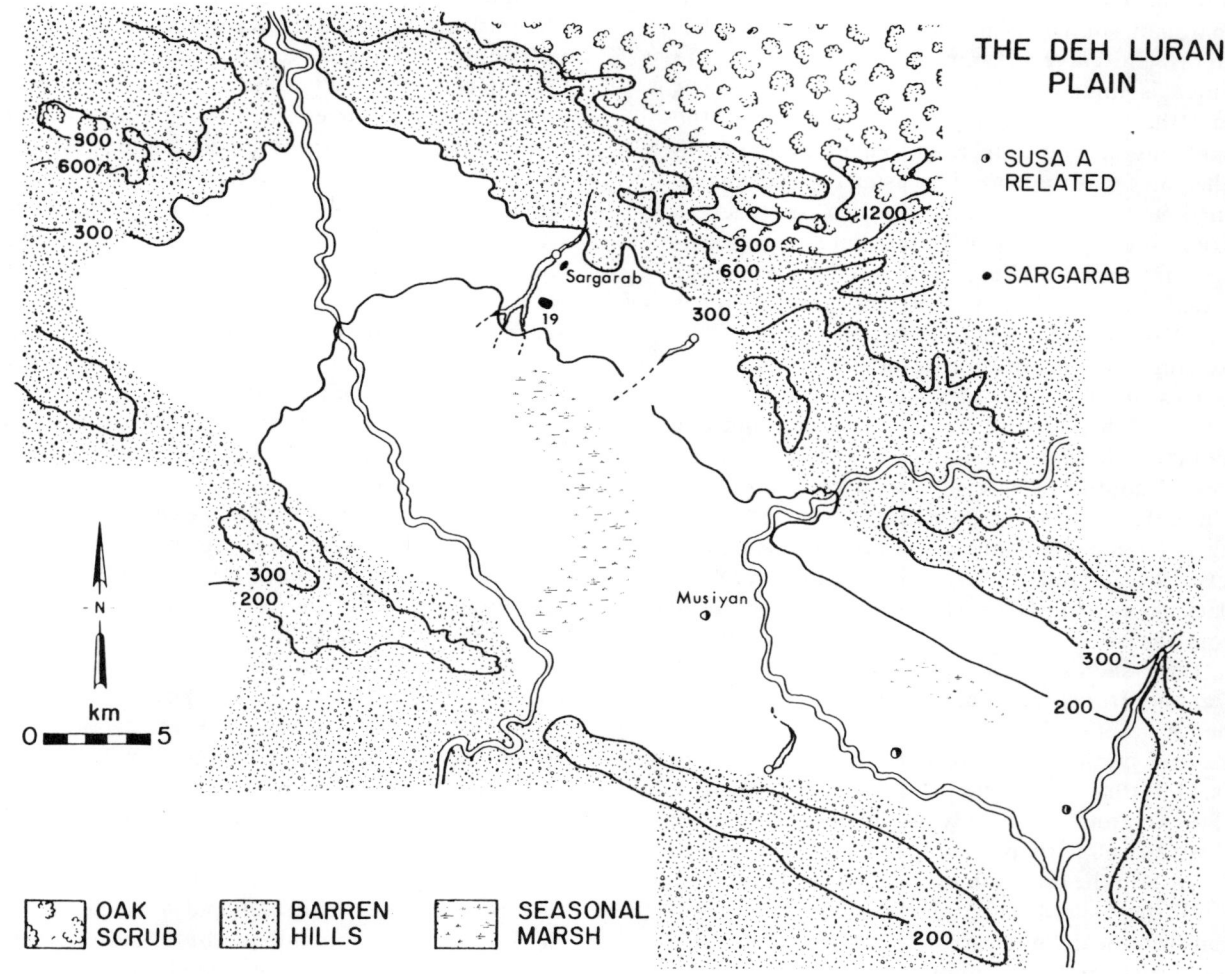

Fig. 33. Post-Farukh Phase Settlement on the Deh Luran Plain.

communities in Northern Iraq (Tobler 1950) are striking. This cannot result from common heritage alone since preceding manifestations contemporary with the Mehmeh Phase in Deh Luran seem to have been locally more distinctive. The similarities must therefore represent some kind of increased interaction throughout the lowlands. In contrast, the Farukh Phase is not similar to any known manifestation in Iraq, but is very close to Susiana d on the nearby Susiana Plain (LeBreton 1957:Fig. 7) and to such highland manifestations as Tall-i Bakun AIII (Langsdorf and McCown 1942). There seems to have been a shift in the zone of interaction such that southwestern Iran communicated less with the Tigris-Euphrates Plain, and entered into closer relations with the southern highlands of Iran. What types of interaction were involved and what might have caused such a shift are at present completely unknown.

Exchange networks can be defined by considering the types and sources of various raw materials. At this point only the existence of the network will be discussed; the structure and operation of such networks will be detailed in the final chapter. The primary surviving class of imported items from the Bayat and Farukh Phases is raw material for chipped stone artifacts. This includes a variety of finer cherts whose sources seem to be somewhere outside of southwestern Iran. The rare pieces of obsidian are more informative. Some of those from the Farukh Phase are from known Eastern Anatolian sources (Appendix I). The only other import is a carved granite bowl fragment whose source is unknown. There are no marine shells from the Gulf, no semi-precious stones from the highlands, and no copper, although we know from other sites that these were occasionally exchanged. One item that was certainly exported, as evidences of its processing are ubiquitous but finished artifacts are rare, is bitumen. In sum, an exchange system involving bitumen and fine grained stones may have existed, but the farther limits of the exchange system are poorly defined because the sources of chert are unknown.

Yet another type of broader relation, and one about which very little indeed is known, involves societal conflict. The evidence suggestive of conflict is the distribution of ceramics probably relating to an additional phase not yet documented by actual excavation. It is represented by a series of black-painted buffware sherds collected by Neely from the north end of Tepe Musiyan. The motifs on these sherds closely parallel those on Susa A Ceramics from the Susiana Plain. Among them are the 'X' motif, the line-dot motif, and the fine chevron motif. These are not known from either Farukh Phase ceramics or Susiana d ceramics. These ceramics occur only on the north portion of Musiyan and perhaps on one or two of the sites to the east, in the direction of the Susiana Plain (Fig. 33). If these sherds indicate a Post-Farukh occupation then the definite eastward shift coupled with a possible slight drop in population in Farukh Phase times is followed by a drastic eastward shift with abandonment of the western Deh Luran Plain and drastic drop in population in Post-Farukh times (Fig. 33). Note that this is not a uniform drop but rather an accelerating shift of population in the direction of Susa, the great center of the region.

Slightly later than these last communities of the Susiana tradition are two communities in the northwest end of the Deh Luran Plain (Wright, Neely, Johnson, and Speth 1975). One of these, Sargarab (DL-169), is on the upper slope near the passes that lead through the foothills and up the mountain scarps to the high flanks of Kabir Kuh. The settlement is on a terraced promontory accessible only through a narrow gate. The other, Chakali (DL-19), is a few km downstream near the juncture of the upper and lower slopes where spring waters can be easily spread out for purposes of small scale irrigation. These two small communities used ceramics showing no technical or stylistic relationship to the ceramics of the earlier communities discussed above. This Post-Farukh ware (discussed in the next section as "Sargarab Ware") shows definite affinities with highland ceramics. Without question a drastic change had occurred on the Deh Luran Plain.

Several possible conditions could explain the observed changes in settlements and ceramics. First, as suggested by Hole, Flannery, and Neely (1969:371), more than a millennium of irrigation agriculture with mineral-charged Mehmeh and Dawairij waters could have taken its toll, and the communities of the Deh Luran Plain could have been forced to move to other areas. The few remaining groups could have moved to the Sargarab area, and fallen into the network of a new group of potters. However, Kirkby (1977:272) argues that the near total salinization required to force abandonment of most of an area is not the pattern typical of the Deh Luran Plain. Second, the demographic changes could be a result of conflict between societies. It is unlikely that conflict between the small highland settlements and the Deh Luran communities would lead to drastic abandonment, but it is possible either that transhumant groups were involved—evening the balance of military forces—or that conflict between densely settled areas such as the Susiana Plain and the Tigris-Euphrates Plain made life on the intermediate Deh Luran Plain precarious. Unfortunately, there is no evidence which we may use for direct tests of propositions regarding conflict. Certainly, the evidence of fortifications and repeated destruction of settlements which we originally sought at Farukhabad has yet to be found in the excavation of any fifth millennium settlement in southwestern Iran.

PART TWO: THE URUK, JEMDET NASR, AND EARLY DYNASTIC PHASES

Chapter VI

STRATIGRAPHY AND STRUCTURAL FEATURES OF THE URUK, JEMDET NASR, AND EARLY DYNASTIC PHASES

INTRODUCTION

Deposits of these periods were found in all three excavations. The stratigraphy in these layers, in contrast to that in the earlier layers, is irregular, frequently broken, and difficult to trace. This may, in part, be a result of the many small intrusive features and of the different approach to architectural construction as discussed below.

Among the new types of features recorded in these layers are large pits, rectangular mud-lined bins, circular gypsum cement vats, hearths in shallow pits, and post holes. The attributes of buildings and other common types of features are presented in Tables 15 to 20. The letters following feature numbers will be found in the appropriate section drawings.

URUK, JEMDET NASR, AND EARLY DYNASTIC STRATIGRAPHY

EXCAVATION A

In this trench, Layers 22 and 21 are considered to be of the Middle Uruk Phase; 20 to 18 are Late Uruk; 17 to 13 are Early Jemdet Nasr; 12 to 6 are Late Jemdet Nasr and 5 to 1 are Early Dynastic.

Layer 21: Stratified silts (.26m): To the north and east of the eroded platform (Feature 25, Fig. 4h) are the floor deposits of a series of small Uruk walls (Features 20, Fig. 5j; 21; and 22) which form several small rooms and alcoves (Fig. 36c). The deposit is thicker and better stratified to the east showing two construction phases. A rough stone wall or footing running from north to south kept wash from the low mound of Feature 25 from damaging the structural complex. A hearth (Feature 24) and granary (Feature 26) penetrate the floors of these structures and the top of the platform. The top of the layer is a compact floor.

Layer 20: Green silt and gypsum grit floors (.20 m): This layer, to the north and east of the mound of the platform, brings the ground to a rough level. An elaborate oven-pit complex (Feature 17, Fig. 5k) and a nearby large pit filled with beveled rim bowls (Feature 19, Fig. 5l) were used. The top is a compact floor, well-defined to the southeast.

Layer 19: Silt floors and ash lenses (.15 m): This layer is restricted to the south and west portion of the unit. It includes the floor and fill of a structure whose stone footings cross the excavation (Feature 16, Fig. 4m). The top is ill-defined.

Layer 18: Silt and mud brick debris (.22 m): This layer is restricted to the southwest portion of the excavation. It is probably the collapsed debris of a small mud brick structure (Feature 15, Fig. 4n) whose north footing, though not clearly visible in either section drawing, runs across the excavation, but most of whose rooms have been eroded away (Fig. 36d). The top is a compact floor to the southeast.

Layer 17: Silt, green silt, and gypsum grit floors (.18 m): This occurs to the southwest, or outside, of the wall of Feature 12B (Fig. 4,5,34o). This layer thickens to the northeast where nine successive floors are visible. It thins and rises over the debris of Feature 15 to the southeast. On this low mound over Feature 15 is the corner of a brick footing noted only in section (Fig. 5p), but indicated on the plan (Fig. 37a). The top is a green silt floor.

Layer 16: Ash and silt floors (.15 m): This is northeast or inside, the wall stub of feature 12B. This wall stub and the one noted only in section

(Fig. 5p) were probably built at the time of upper Layer 17 and occupied in the time of Layer 16. The top of Layer 16 is an ephemeral floor.

Layer 15: Silt and gypsum grit (.15 m): This is further flooring, between the two wall stubs mentioned above. There is an alignment of stones running from Feature 12B southeast toward the other wall. These stones would limit slopewash from the northwest (Fig. 37a).

Layer 14: Ash silt and gypsum grit floors (.15 m): This layer is located within Feature 12B. There is no direct evidence for the correlation between layers 14 and 16 on the one hand and lower 13, 15, and 17 on the other.

Layer 13: Brown and green silt floors (.19 m): Lower and middle layers 13 are floors outside or southwest of the wall of reconstructed Feature 12A (Fig. 4q) and the new Feature 10C (Fig. 37b). Upper Layer 13 covers the wall stub of Feature 12A and could be traced across the entire excavation unit. It is the occupational surface associated with a building (Feature 1F) in the north corner of the excavation unit represented only by two wall stubs of gypsum cement brick. One is visible on the northwest section in Square 12 (Fig. 4r); the other is visible in the northeast section in Square B (Fig. 34s). A stone-lined hearth visible on the east section in Square 6 (Fig. 5t) was used at the time of Feature 12A.

Layer 12: Brick fragments, green silt, and ash lenses (.24 m): This is the occupational debris of a new structure which incorporates the shattered remains of the earlier gypsum cement building. Features 1E (Fig. 34u), 9B, and 10B (Fig. 5,34w) are walls of this large building with bin (Fig. 37c). Feature 11, a rectangular hearth or bin, is within them. There is a plaster lined posthole outside of the building (Fig. 4v). The top of this layer is poorly defined in most areas.

Layer 11: Brick packing (.16 m): The base of this layer is a refuse deposit of silt, gypsum grit, and charcoal, basically a continuation of Layer 12 depositional patterns. Above this are one or two layers of mud brick packing. A massive building incorporating Features 1D (Fig. 34x), 9A, and 10A (Fig. 34z) were constructed on earlier wall stubs at this time. The top is the uppermost fragmentary brick layer.

Layer 10: Silt, charcoal, and gypsum grit (.16 m): This is fill within the large building with brick packing. The top is a bituminous lens on the floor (perhaps a hearth in which bitumen was burned during processing) visible only near the northeast section (Fig. 34a′). Elsewhere the top is ill-defined and Layers 9 and 10 are combined.

Layer 9: Silt and brick fragments (.20 m): This is further fill during whose deposition the building deteriorated. The top is an ephemeral floor resulting from the compacting of brick fragments.

Layer 8: Brown silt, gypsum grit, and brick fragments (.18 m): In the passage between Features 10 and 1, there is a refuse fill as described above. Feature 8, a plaster vat, was situated in this passage (Fig. 37d). In the alcove northwest of Feature 9, Layer 8 was removed or never deposited and in its place are two layers of brick packing (Fig. 4b′). The top is a slightly compacted floor.

Layer 7: Silt, charcoal, and gypsum grit (.20 m): The brick packing noted above indicates reconstruction during Layer 7 times. Feature 1C (Fig. 4, 34c′) was constructed at this time and Feature 9A was probably modified. Another plaster vat (Feature 7) was probably used during the period of deposition of this layer. A possible posthole (Fig. 4e′) was southwest of the structure. Layer 7 is either the first fill of this reconstruction or the debris of reconstruction. The top of Layer 7 is a thick floor with traces of ash and a loose rush covering not distinguished in section.

Layer 6: Silt and brick fragments (.16 m): This is the last fill of the large structure. Though Feature 1 walls are later rebuilt, they are no longer very substantial. A small domed oven (Feature 6) was in use.

Layer 5: Silt and charcoal with complex floor (.30 m): Lower Layer 5 seems to cap Feature 1C. On top of it is a compact silt and gypsum grit floor overlain by thick scattered, ash lenses. Above these are further refloorings of green silt and of yellow silt. Features 3, 4, and 5 (Fig. 34f′), all plaster vats, were used at this time. Upper Layer 5 is capped by the ephemeral compact floor associated with the wall of Feature 1B (Fig. 34g′).

Layer 4: Silt and charcoal (.25 m): This is fill to the southeast of Feature 1B. Feature 2, a plaster vat northwest of Feature 1, may have been in use at this time. The top of this layer is a compact floor with loose rush covering, associated with the green brick wall of Feature 1B. There were isolated bricks lying on this floor.

Layer 3: Silt and green brick fragments (.22 m): Above this rush-covered floor is a layer of light brown silt, which is overlain by a layer of brick fragments representing the destruction of Feature

STRATIGRAPHY OF THE URUK, JEMDET NASR, AND EARLY DYNASTIC PHASES

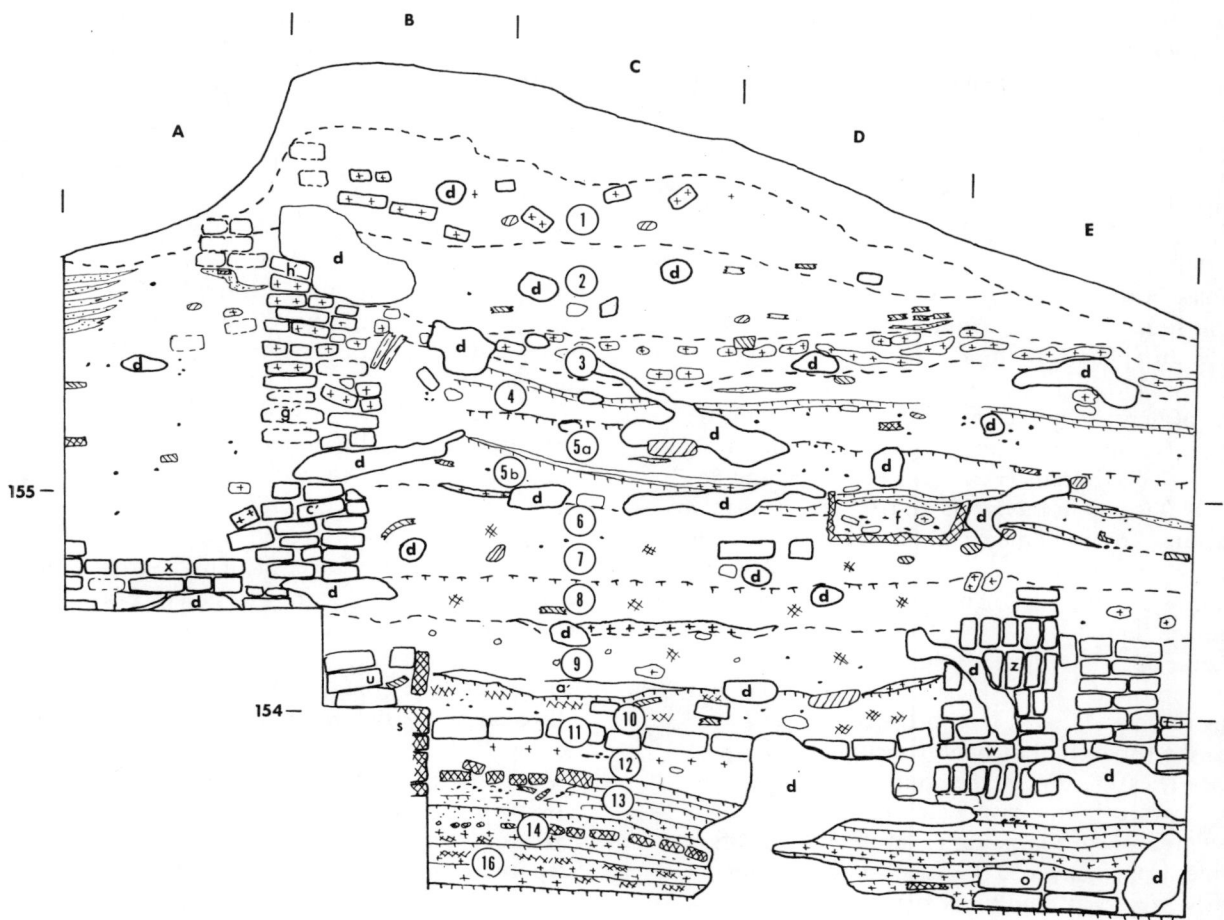

Fig. 34. Northeast Section of Excavation A.

1B. The top of this layer is an ephemeral floor associated with newly constructed Feature 1A (Fig. 34h', Fig. 36f).

Layer 2: Silt and charcoal (.42 m): This is a fill southeast of Feature 1A. Pebbles and areas of rush matting indicating ephemeral flooring were noted.

Layer 1: Silt with greenish brick fragments (.30 m): This is probably the destruction debris of Feature 1A. It is altered by soil weathering.

In summary, after the period of erosion following the Farukh phase, during which time the area was used only occasionally for pits and such, the area was covered with modest buildings. Thin discontinuous layers of debris were laid down. After the deposition of middle Layer 13, the area was cleared and a construction of gypsum cement was erected. For many years thereafter the area was covered with substantial structures leaving thick layers of refuse and brick collapse. After the deposition of Layer 6 the area was cleared and seems to have again been used for small structures.

EXCAVATION B

In this trench, Layers 36 to 35 are considered to be of the Early Uruk Phase; 34 to 32 are Middle Uruk; 31 to 28 are Late Uruk; 27 to 24 are Early Jemdet Nasr; 23 to 21 are Late Jemdet Nasr; and 20 to 19 are Early Dynastic.

Layer 36: Silt and gypsum grit (.38 m): Lower Layer 36 is a series of floors and fills associated with a structure with stone footing (Feature 37, Fig. 7c, 36a). South of the large room of this structure, an area perhaps part of another room largely destroyed by the erosion of the Mehmeh

River, there are six distinguishable floors on which were located a number of objects and features described later in this chapter. Areas north and east of this room were not excavated below the middle of Layer 36. Upper layer 36 is undifferentiated silt, ash, and gypsum grit, with brick fragments. The top of Layer 36 is an ephemeral floor.

Layer 35: Silt, gypsum grit, and charcoal (.28 m): There are only a few bricks and clusters of cobbles in this deposit. A pit oven (Feature 33) is cut in squares C–D–11 from upper Layer 35. The top is an ephemeral floor.

Layer 34: Silt, gypsum grit, and ash (.28 m): This layer of debris contains brick fragments, an alignment of stones, and an irregular area of brick flooring. The burials (Features 29, 34, 35, and 36, Fig. 39a) found in Layers 35 and 36 were probably excavated from middle or upper Layer 34. The pit of an infant burial is visible in the southeast section (Feature 29, Fig. 8e). The top of this layer is a compact floor.

Layer 33: Silt, gypsum grit, and ash: This complex deposit is .55 m thick to the southwest but thins to only .25 m to the northeast. Lower Layer 33 is the fill around a roughly rectangular heap of stones (Feature 28) in the south end of the unit. This feature is not visible in the sections but a contemporaneous large pit (Feature 30, Fig. 8f) is visible. Upper Layer 33 is an ashy deposit around a poorly preserved mud brick structure (Feature 26) and associated oven (Feature 27, Fig. 36b). This deposit slants down sharply in the north corner of the excavation, and as a consequence, this portion of upper Layer 33 was mixed during excavation with lower 33. The top layer of 33 is an ephemeral floor.

Layer 32: Silt floors and ash lenses: This layer is only .18 m thick to the southwest, above the heap of debris created by Features 26 and 28, but is .40 m thick to the northeast. There are only a few cobble concentrations and shallow depressions in this deposit. The top is a compact floor.

Layer 31: Silt floors (.22 m): Four floors are distinguishable to the northwest, but to the southeast these merge into one undifferentiated silt layer. A building of miniature bricks of which Features 22 and 23 form one wall and with which is associated a ceramic drain (Feature 24) and a small oven or hearth (Feature 25), was constructed on middle Layer 31 (Fig. 38a). Upper Layer 31 contains floors associated with this structure. The top of this layer is a compact floor.

Layer 30: Silt, gypsum grit, and ash floors (.15 m): These result from continued deposition inside and outside of the miniature brick building. There are no new features. The top is a compact floor overlaid by the ash lenses of Layer 29.

Layer 29: Silt floors and large ash lenses (.18 m): The large structure was apparently dismantled, since the floor of upper Layer 29 overlays the wall stub. On the open space two low circular mud brick platforms were laid (Features 20, Fig. 8g; and 21, Fig. 39b). Upper Layer 29 accumulated around these odd structures. The top of this layer is a compact floor.

Layer 28: Silt and ash lenses (.20 m): This is further accumulation around the circular features. A narrow north-south wall (Feature 19) is based on the top of Layer 29 but was probably constructed in a shallow trench during the time of deposition of upper Layer 28. This narrow wall is in approximately the same position as Feature 23. A continuation to the south (Feature 10E) was probably built at the same time above the stub of Feature 22. The compact floor at the top of Layer 28 would be the first floor constructed in conjunction with this wall.

Layer 27: Silt, green silt, and gypsum grit floors (.18 m): These are further floors laid down around Features 19 and 10E. The top is a compact, prepared floor of silt with gypsum grit.

Layer 26: Silt, gypsum grit, and ash floors: This layer is .12 m thick to the west (probably inside) of the Feature 10 and .24 m thick to the east of Feature 10. Several short additional wall segments were added to Feature 10D, creating rooms or alcoves to the east of it (Fig. 38b). In the alcove south of a gypsum brick addition (Feature 14) was a brick packing. The top of Layer 26 is a green silt floor.

Layer 25: Silt and gypsum grit floors (.22 m): Layer 25 accumulated in and around the rebuilt structure. A solid cobble pavement was laid in upper Layer 25 in the south room or alcove exposed in the excavation.

Layer 24: Silt and ephemeral floors: This layer is .30 m thick to the north, or outside, of Feature 10 but only .10 m thick inside Feature 10 over the cobble pavement. After Layer 25 was deposited the entire complex was rebuilt. Feature 19 was dismantled and the area northwest of Feature 10, which had been a room or court while middle Layer 31 to lower Layer 29 and while upper Layer 28 to Layer 25 were being deposited, became an open space as it had been in upper Layer 29 times. The new small rooms and alcoves southeast of Feature 10D were rebuilt on a larger scale as Feature 10C (Fig. 38c). On the court to the north of the building is a plaster-lined posthole (Feature 18, Fig. 8g′) and a few small brick alignments (Feature 17). In the southwest room a deep rectangular granary (Feature 15) was constructed probably from the top of Layer 24, though erosion obscures evidence of its final use. The top of Layer 24 was a compact silt and gypsum grit floor broken in many places.

Layer 23: Silt and ash (.30 m): This is a fill in and around Feature 10C (Fig. 8h) probably representing its deterioration. The interior of the building was plastered during this time. There is a compact floor at the top of this layer, perhaps associated with this restoration. A stone-footed brick wall (Feature 16) northwest of the Feature 10 building was constructed during the time of deposition of this layer.

Layer 22: Silt and brick fragments (.25 m): This is the last fill around restored Feature 10C. A rectangular mud-plastered bin was in use to the north of it. The outer wall of 10C was partially dismantled and the ill-defined scatter of bricks marking the top of this layer was laid down. Feature 10B (Fig. 8i, 38d) was constructed in upper Layer 22 times, apparently by partially dismantling the outer face of the old wall and packing a row of bricks against the inner plaster. Feature 16 was dismantled. Much of its footing was later destroyed by an Elamite pit. The top of this layer is ill-defined both within and north of Feature 10, but is an ash lens west of Feature 10.

Layer 21: Silt (.15 cm): This is fill within and around Feature 10B. There is a bin (Feature 12) and a plaster vat (Feature 13) north of the building. The top of the layer is marked by a scatter of vat fragments. Inside the building the top is an ephemeral compact floor.

Layer 20: Silt and brick fragments (.20 m): The previous depositional pattern continues. There is another scatter of vat fragments marking the top of lower Layer 20. After this was deposited, Feature 10B was demolished and Feature 10A (Fig. 8j) was constructed (Fig. 36e). Upper Layer 20 contains brick debris from this reconstruction. Its top is ill-defined outside of Feature 10A but is defined by a compact floor inside Feature 10A.

Layer 19: Silt (.15 m): This is fill outside of Feature 10A. There is only a compact floor within the feature. The top of Layer 19 is capped by the cross-bedded silts of lower Layer 18 indicating a long abandonment. Several points must be noted here. First, the correlation between what has been called Layers 24 to 19 inside and outside of Feature 10 makes reasonable architectural sense, but there is no direct proof of the correlation in the section. Second, a large Elamite pit cut down from Layer 18 into this deposit, eliminating small parts of Layers 23 and 24 and increasingly large parts of the higher layers. There was very little of Layer 19 *in situ*.

In summary, the eroded surface of the Farukh Phase mound was used alternately for small structures and open courts. The area was leveled at the time of Layer 32 and used as the site of an elaborate building during the time which Layers 31 and 30 were being deposited. This building was shifted away and the area was used as open space during Layer 29 and 28 times. It is then used for a very substantial building which, with successive rebuildings, became less and less impressive. At the same time the stratigraphy becomes less well-defined, particularly after the deposition of Layer 23.

EXCAVATION C

Excavation C is only one meter wide throughout most of its length. Most of the information on layers and features is embodied in the section shown on Figure 35. Feature numbers were not assigned here. Also, the assigned layer numbers are based on minimal evidence and are used here only for purposes of discussion. Additional excavation in this area would doubtless necessitate revisions. Layers 33 and 32 are of the Late Uruk Phase. Layers 31 to 24 comprise about two m of Jemdet Nasr debris from at least eight rebuildings of small structures. Layers 22 to 9 comprise about two m of floors and debris of the subsequent Early Dynastic Phase.

Layer 33: Brown silt, ash, and gypsum grit (.20 m): This layer, located southwest of a wall stub (labeled 'a' on Fig. 35) composed of two or more courses of two rows of headers, is probably an interior fill.

Layer 32: Brown silt, ash, and gypsum grit (.15 m): This layer lies southwest of a wall stub (Fig. 35b) composed of three courses each one row of headers, constructed on top of the Layer 33 stub.

At the base of this layer are broken bricks from this reconstruction and above it are bricks from its subsequent dismantling. The top of this layer is a compact floor.

Layer 31: Silt and gypsum grit floors (.25 m): These occur both northeast and southwest of a wall stub (Fig. 35c) composed of five courses of mud brick, each course except the lowest being composed of one row of headers and one of stretchers. The lowest, in contrast, is two rows of headers. It was founded on the middle of Layer 31. To the south there are probably interior floors with much ash. To the northeast are floors merging into broken brick from the destruction of the Layer 32 wall. The top of the layer is a compact floor outside the wall, and an ordinary mud plaster floor inside the wall.

Layer 30: Silt, gypsum grit, and broken brick (.45 m): This is probably a deposit of dismantled wall debris northeast of the Layer 31 wall. The correlation between Layer 30 and Layers 28 and 29 is unknown.

Layer 29: Silt, ash, and broken brick (.18 m): This layer lies above the floor plaster in the southwest or inside of the Layer 31 wall. Its top is a compact floor.

Layer 28: Silt and broken brick (.15 m): This lies above Layer 29. A small pit (Fig. 35d) dug from the top of Layer 28 penetrates into Layer 29. It contains small broken brick fragments and green silt. The top of the layer is an ephemeral compact floor.

Layer 27: Silt and gypsum grit floors (.18 m): A collapsed wall stub (Fig. 35e) is either the upper portion of the Layer 31 wall or, more likely, a flimsy wall associated with Layer 27. The top of this layer is a lens of silt.

Layer 26: Gypsum grit, silt, and ash floors (.15 m): These are the floors of a small room or passage defined by two wall stubs (Fig. 35f, g), each one header thick. The southerly stub is five courses high; the northerly stub is much rebuilt. The top of this layer is a compact ashy silt floor.

Layer 25: Silt with some ash (.18 m): This is further fill in the small room or passage. Its top is a compact silt floor.

Layer 24: Silt and broken brick (.35 m): Fill and destruction debris associated with a wall stub (Fig. 35h) one header thick and six courses high built roughly on top of the northerly Layer 26 wall. An ephemeral compact ash and silt floor separates the lower room fill from the upper broken brick. This layer is stained green. The top of this layer is defined by the base of a large pit.

Layer 23: Ash, charcoal, green silt, and small brick fragments (.50 m): This is the fill of a large intrusive pit cutting into the sequence of small structures below. There are charcoal lenses and ephemeral surfaces in the pit. The large shallow configuration of the pit suggests it was a borrow pit, while the green stain suggests subsequent use as a latrine. The top is a compact floor.

Layer 22: Ash and gypsum grit lenses (.20 m): This layer seals the pit. The top is a green silt lens.

Layer 21: Ash and gypsum grit lenses (.35 m): The top is a gypsum grit floor.

Layer 20: Silt and small brick fragments (.12 m)

Layer 19: Green and brown silt floors (.10 m).

Layer 18: Ash and silt (.15 m).

Layer 17: Green and brown silt floors (.10 m): Several large stones (Fig. 35i) in the section may mark a rough footing.

Layer 16: Ash and silt layers (.20 m).

Layer 15: Green silt layer (.10 m): Several large plaster vat fragments are in this layer.

Layer 14: Silt with ephemeral floors (.15 m).

Layer 13: Ash and compact silt floors (.12 m).

Layer 12: Ash and silt with some bricks (.55 m): This deposit is cut by a pit or terrace (Fig. 35j) in the lower portion of which are ash and silt floors. Too much of this is missing to hazard an interpretation. The top of Layer 12 is ill-defined.

Layer 11: Silt, ash, and gypsum grit (.15 m): The top layer is an ash lens.

Layer 10: Green silt and brick fragments. (.10 m) These bricks may be a badly damaged wall stub (Fig. 35k).

Layer 9: Silt, charcoal, and gypsum grit (.20 m): The top is an ephemeral floor.

Layer 8: Silt, ash, and broken brick (.55 m): The top is ill-defined.

Layer 7: Silt, ash, charcoal, and gypsum grit (.20 m): The top is ill-defined.

Layer 6: Silt and broken brick.

URUK, JEMDET NASR, AND EARLY DYNASTIC FEATURES

INTRODUCTION TO THE BUILDNGS

During these phases most bricks are relatively small. They are usually .21 to .30 m long, .10 to .18

STRATIGRAPHY OF THE URUK, JEMDET NASR, AND EARLY DYNASTIC PHASES

Fig. 35. Southeast Section of Excavation C.

m wide, and .06 to .10 m thick. They are usually rectangular in plan, either rectangular or parallelogram-shaped in longitudinal section, and either rectangular or trapezoidal in cross-section. Both finger smoothing and parallel vertical striae from molds are common on the sides of bricks. The tops sometimes have finger-marks and are sometimes slightly convex. These slightly convex surfaces often have faint facets, as if someone had attempted to flatten the convexity with pressure from a board. A rare characteristic of these bricks is a deep oblique groove in a corner of the upper surface. I have observed that such a groove is created by the brickmaker's wrist as he is trying to remove the mold from an adjacent brick.

There were several buildings with unusual bricks. A Late Uruk large building (Excavation B, Features 22 and 23) was made of bricks ranging from only .16 to .20 m long and .10 to .12 m wide. These tiny bricks were convex on sides, ends, and top. An Early Jemdet Nasr small building (Excavation A, Feature 12B) had a few large bricks of Farukh Phase size. Two successive small buildings of the Early Dynastic Phase (Excavation A, Features 1A and 1B) were constructed with markedly planoconvex bricks bearing a finger groove along the axis. Finally, there were two buildings with walls made of gypsum cement bricks (Excavation A, Feature 1F; Excavation B, Feature 14).

Neither stretcher nor stretcher-edge bonding are attested in these phases, perhaps because the bricks are too small. The most common bonding technique is stretcher-header, usually laid in a very irregular manner. Half-bricks and brick fragments are common. A new bonding pattern, header bonding, is used in the construction of some larger buildings. In this pattern, two or more rows of bricks are laid side-to-side in the first course; in the second course the same number of rows is laid side-to-side, but each brick straddles the gap between the two bricks below. The third course repeats the first, and so on. Cases in which a row is laid on edge, perhaps to level the wall, are rare. This bonding pattern is not strong but can be laid with a minimum of skill and supervision.

Plasters were noted on a number of walls, and shallow wall trenches with mud or stone footings occur.

SMALL BUILDINGS

Small Structure with Stone Footing (Excavation B, Feature 37, Layer 36 lower, Fig. 36a): One or two rooms of this structure were partly excavated. The more complete northern room is oriented east-west. The walls are footed with two rows of ovoid limestone cobbles. There is no trace of brickwork on these footings, though there are probable brick fragments in upper Layer 36 above the floors of the feature. The north room is 2.9 m wide and more than 5.0 m long. It has two successive prepared mud floors. On the lower floor is a small posthole with fired clay lining, two shallow hearths (one covered by the floor and probably slightly earlier), a beveled rim bowl and a loose, flat, baked brick of Farukh Phase type. On the upper floor is a similar posthole and a Fine Jar of Sargarab Ware. There is a possible gap in the footing on the south side of the room which may have been a door. The area south of this gap has six prepared clay floors and may have been another room in the structure. During excavation, the posthole and the absence of brick walls were taken as evidence that this footing was for a tent similar to the stone tent footings used by Luri herders today. However multiple floors, the possible presence of two rooms, and mud brick fragments in the fill all suggest a more substantial structure. Unfortunately the evidence is equivocal.

Small Building with Oven (Excavation B, Feature 26, Layer 33 upper, Fig. 36b): On the top of Layer 34 a low, roughly rectangular pile of boulders was laid. There is some poorly preserved brick northeast of this. On the top of Layer 33 upper is a somewhat better preserved construction. The top of the boulder pile forms a rough paving to a room or court which is more than 3.6 by 3.1 m. North of a very poorly laid brick wall is a mud and broken brick construction surrounding a large oval oven (Feature 27).

Small Building with Retaining Wall (Excavation A, Features 20 to 22, Layer 21 middle and upper, Fig. 36c): After the end of the Farukh Phase there was little use of the area of excavation A. Only long after the reoccupation of the Excavation B area were houses constructed there. Parts of three rooms of this first construction were exposed. A line of cobbles (Feature 18) separates the rooms from A, the erosional remnant of the last Farukh Phase platform. This special footing probably protected the building from excessive slope wash. The rooms are identified by letters. The northwest room (B) is 1.7 by more than 3.3 m. On its lower floor is a hearth (Feature 24) next to which is a beveled rim bowl. The northeast room (C) is more than 2.8 by 2.1 m. On both its lower and upper floors are large jar sherds. The south room (DE) is 3.4 by more than 2.2 m; there is an alcove in its northeast corner and a shattered jar on its upper floor. Probably contemporary with one of these floors was a rectangular mud slab bin (Feature 26). The relation is not certain because the top of this bin was obscured by an intrusive pit (Feature 19).

Small Stone Footed Structure (Excavation A, Feature 16, Layer 19, Fig. 4m): These stone footings are composed of one row of oval cobbles laid side-to-side. There is no evidence of brick construction on the footing. A large portion of one possible room and a small part of another were exposed. The larger room is more than 4.1 by 3.0 m and has a simple hearth around which are a few baked bricks.

Small Structure with Bins (Excavation A, Feature 15, Layer 18, Fig. 36d): The brick footings of the various reconstructions of this structure are .40 m southwest of and parallel to those of Feature 16. Apparently only the northeast wall and associated features survive, the rooms having been eroded away. Just inside of this poorly laid wall are two definite mud slab bins (Features 13 and 14) and a possible third attested only in section (Fig. 4n′) but restored on the plan. Each bin seems to be in an alcove. The two excavated bins were filled with loose silt, and charred barley and wheat.

Small Building (Excavation A, Feature 12B, Layers 14–17, Fig. 37a): This is the earliest attested stage of what was to grow into a large and well-planned building. Its thin, stone-footed wall runs from northwest to southeast. Northeast, or inside, of this wall is a smaller wall at an acute angle to the main wall. The critical juncture which might clarify this peculiarity is outside the limits of the excavation. Southwest of the main wall is an open space or passage in which there is a cobble retaining wall (perhaps associated with this feature or perhaps with a slightly later reconstruction) and a small hearth. South of the passage is a partially contemporary wall stub described next.

Wall Stub (Excavation A, Layer 15, Fig. 5p): This is attested only on the southeast section. It may be the northeast wall of a building parallel to that described above.

Small Building (Excavation A, Feature 12A, Layer 13 lower, Fig. 37b): This is a more substantial building located directly above Feature 12B. Small corners of two rooms were exposed. The southeast room has either a very thick wall or a bench or platform along its southwest wall and a pebble paved hearth on its floor.

Small Building (Excavation B, Feature 16, Layer 23, Fig. 38d): This building was erected north of the large building in this excavation as it was deteriorating; only a damaged corner was exposed. The east wall has a stone footing; its brickwork was destroyed by later pits. A small remnant of the south wall is in evidence on the northwest section. It is not clear whether the pits within are contemporary with, or slightly later than, this building.

Small Building (Excavation B, Feature 10A, Layer 20, Fig. 36e): This is the final construction phase of the large building with bin and posthole (Features 10C, 14 of this excavation). It is a small and shoddy replacement. Only the outer north wall and parts of two alcoves survive. Both inside and out there are many gypsum cement vat fragments not *in situ*.

Wall Stub (Excavation A, Features 1A and 1B, Layers 2-4, Fig. 36f): These poorly preserved scraps are above the large building (Features 1C, 9A) of this excavation, but they are at a different angle and are probably unrelated. There is perhaps a gypsum cement vat (Feature 2) west of the earlier stub. To the east is a reed covered floor. To the east of the later stub is a floor covered with reed matting. Both stubs are made of plano-convex brick, an important criterion of the Early Dynastic Period in alluvial Mesopotamia to the south.

LARGER BUILDINGS OF EXCAVATION A

Gypsum Brick Building (Excavation A, Feature 1F, Layer 13 upper, Figs. 4r, 34s): This building was thoroughly looted for reusable gypsum bricks. A tiny remnant of one wall running from northeast to southwest was incorporated into the wall of Feature 1E above. Likewise, a remnant of a wall running from northwest to southeast is visible in the northwest profile. The actual corner had been destroyed and could not be recorded in plan. Both inside and outside of these walls are two, perhaps three, prepared clay floors. There are no preserved associated features. It is difficult to say anything about this interesting construction. The greater part of it awaits future excavation.

Large Building with Bin (Excavation A, Features 1E, 9B, and 10B, Layer 12, Fig. 37c): The walls of this building are clear although the individual bricks are not easily isolated. The exposure includes the northwest, southwest, and southeast walls of a room 2.35 m wide and more than 4.0 m long. To the southwest is a possible mud slab lined bin. The clay seems to have been fired-reddened; it is possible that this was actually a rectangular hearth or oven, or that it was cut down and used as such late in its history. To the northeast are some cement vat fragments. Outside of this room is an alcove and a single row of bricks one course thick; just within this row is a plaster-lined posthole. Perhaps this represents a curb protecting a roofed porch or inset doorway outside of the building, rather than a small wall footing.

Large Building with Packed Brick Floor (Excavation A, Features 1D, 9A, and 10A, Layers 11-8, Fig. 37d): This building is on top of the wall stubs of that described above. The southwest wall (Feature 9A) is well-laid. The component walls are bonded into each other and the entire arrangement is plastered. The northwest wall (Feature 1D) is fairly well-laid, perhaps with pilasters, and plastered, but the southeast wall (Feature 10A) is a wretched piece of construction. The northeast section (Fig. 34) suggests that it is two walls side-by-side, with brick fragments forced into the crack between. Few traces of plaster are evident. There may have been an entrance or alley from the southwest between Features 9A and 10A, though no prepared door jamb was found. During Layer 11 times, after reconstruction, a layer of bricks, in some places two, was placed to level the floor. During Layer 8 times, a large gypsum plaster vat

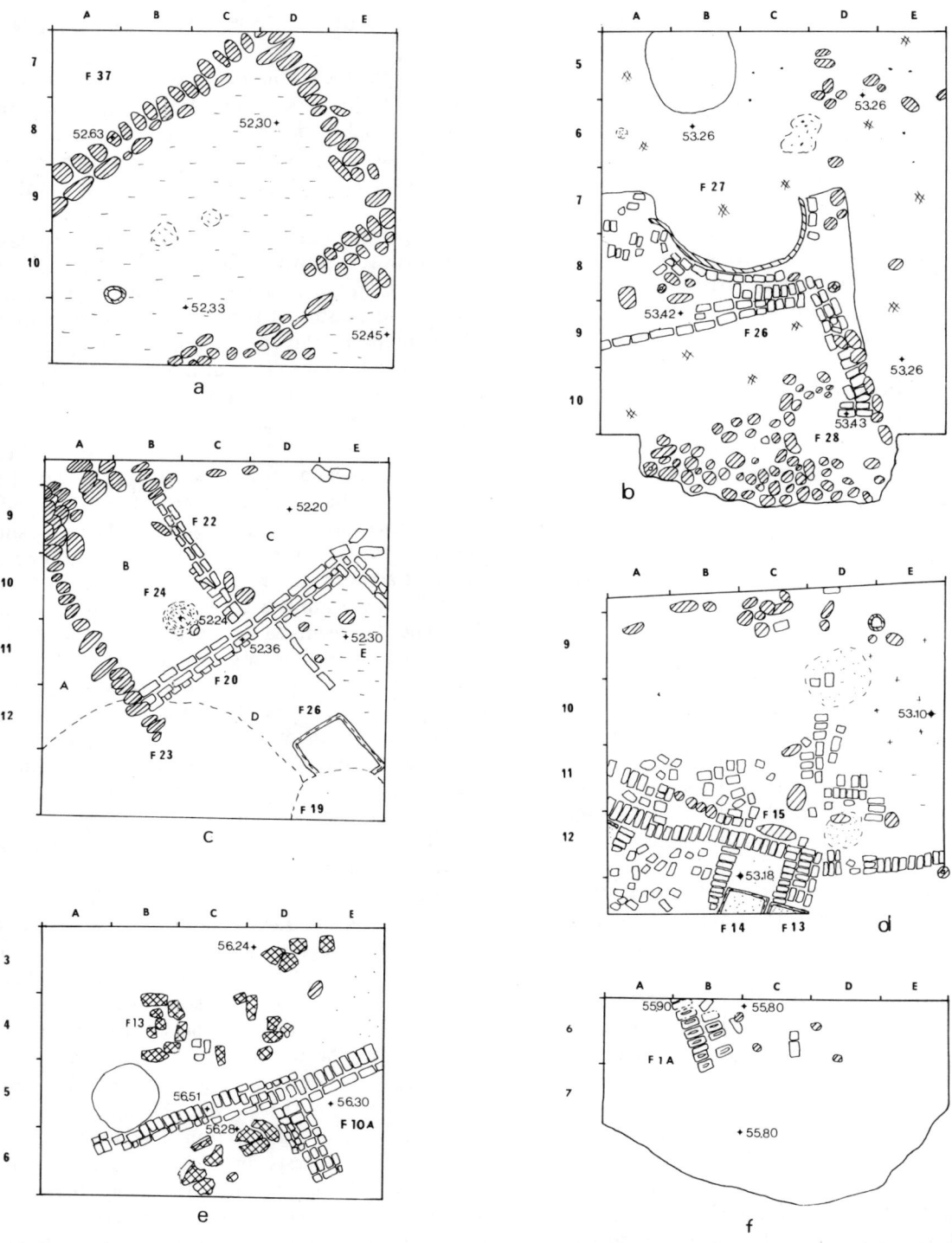

Fig. 36. Uruk, Jemdet Nasr, and Early Dynastic Small Buildings. A. Excavation B, Feature 37, a small structure with stone footing. Note the hearths and post hole. B. Excavation B, Feature 26, a small building. Note Feature 27, an oven, and Feature 28, a boulder pavement. The oval is Feature 6, an Elamite shaft. C. Excavation A, Feature 20-23, a small building with boulder retaining wall. Note Feature 26, a bin which has been restored from traces at a deeper level. One pit, Feature 23, is earlier than the building; the other pit, Feature 19, is later. D. Excavation A, Feature 15, a poorly preserved small structure. Note the two definite bins, Features 13 and 14, and fragment of a bin to the northwest. E. Excavation B, Feature 10A, a small building. Note the many gypsum cement vat fragments. F. Excavation A, Feature 1A, a small wall stub made of grooved plano-convex bricks.

(Feature 8) was placed inside the room or hall near the possible entrance. In addition, a posthole with a fired clay lining was placed in exactly the same position as the posthole associated with Feature 1E discussed above.

Large Building (Excavation A, Features 1C and 9A, Layers 7–6): This is a poorly laid and badly weathered reconstruction of the building below. Feature 10A probably continues in use as its southeast wall. There is one gypsum plaster vat (Feature 7) in the hall or room. This building is leveled on Layer 5 and becomes an open space. Features 2A and 1B are wall stubs of small buildings unrelated to this construction.

LARGER BUILDINGS OF EXCAVATION B

Large Building of Miniature Bricks (Excavation B, Features 22–23, Layers 31–30, Fig. 38a): This Late Uruk construction is the first major structure attested at Farukhabad after the end of the Farukh Phase. It is not completely certain, however, that it is the wall of a roofed building since no corner was found. Two segments of a single wall, running from north-northeast to south-southwest, are exposed. At the time of construction there was a small partition west of this main wall and a low curbing along part of its east face. Later, the west partition was removed and a possible buttress added to the east. In the large open space to the east there is one possible small oven. The floors to the west are prepared silt floors of the sort usually inside a building. If this is a large building, then one of its rooms was more than 4.6 by 1.9 m.

Large Structure (Excavation B, Features 10E and 19, Layers 28–27): The building of miniature bricks is leveled and the open space used for unknown activities evidenced by Features 20 and 21 (see "Other Features"). When these were abandoned the line of the main miniature brick wall is probably still evident from a low mound and some brick fragments. A single long, well-laid wall is built approximately along the line of the old wall. There are no clear adjoining walls or partitions of any sort. The only associated features are the eroding remnants of Features 20 and 21. This may be an enclosure wall rather than a building wall.

Large Building with Mud and Cement Brick Additions (Excavation B, Features 10D, 14, 19, Layers 26–25, Fig. 38B): Feature 19 is one brick thick, as it was before, but Feature 10E is thickened by the addition of a facing of mud bricks and brick fragments on its west side. A wall perpendicular to this runs west enclosing a possible room above that of the earlier miniature brick building. To the east of Feature 10D, a short parallel wall of shoddy brick is built on a packed mud footing. The short space between this and the main wall is filled with packed mud and brick fragments and covered with flat oval pebbles (Not shown on Fig. 38 b) as if for a door sill. This seems odd since it does not open on a well-defined room at this time. Somewhat later, in Layer 25 times, a gypsum brick addition (Feature 14), is added perpendicular to the west of the main wall. This addition is roughly contemporary with the gypsum brick building in Excavation A.

Large Building with Bin and Posthole (Excavation B, Features 10C and 14, Layers 24–22, Fig. 38c): Feature 19 is dismantled and the focus of the building shifts to the east. The step-like packing east of the main wall is faced on both sides with brick and filled with refuse. Courses of brick are laid above this and to the east providing a main north wall. The former north-south segment becomes the defining partition of an alcove within which were placed gypsum cement vats, now fragmentary. The former main north-south wall is reconstructed. The room within these massive walls is more than 4.3 by 3.6 m. Still attached to the west is the gypsum brick wall (Feature 14). This defines a small room within which a rectangular mud-plastered bin is later constructed (Feature 15). To the north is an apparently open space on which are two brick arrangements and a gypsum cement and mud-plaster lined posthole perhaps evidence of some kind of porch. In Layer 23 times, the interior of the large room receives a gypsum plaster. At this time a small building (Feature 16) is placed nearby.

Large Building (Excavation B, Feature 10B, Layers 22 upper and 21, Fig. 38d): The building is here subjected to a strange form of reconstruction. The outer facing of bricks is removed and an inner facing is added, covering the gypsum plaster. The building is thus slightly smaller but basically similar in plan. There is a rectangular mud slab bin in the space north of the building. Feature 10A, described above as a small building, is nothing more than the final reconstruction of this building on a yet more diminished scale.

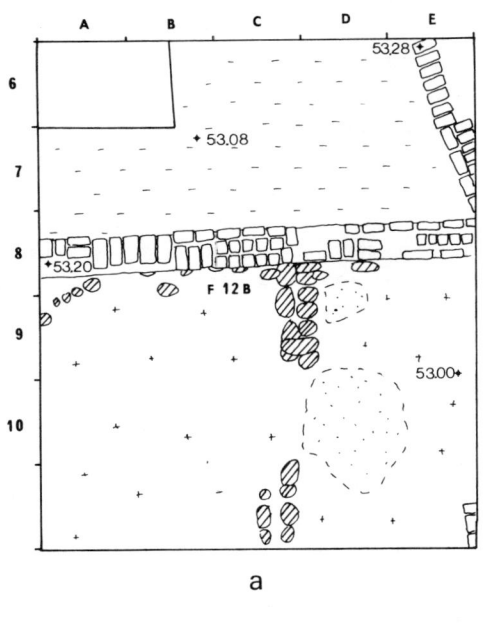
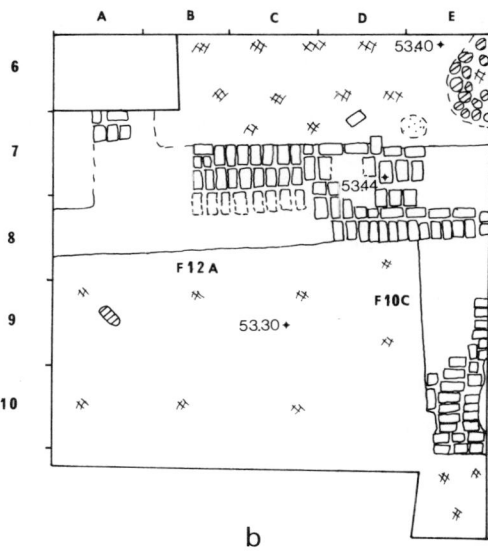
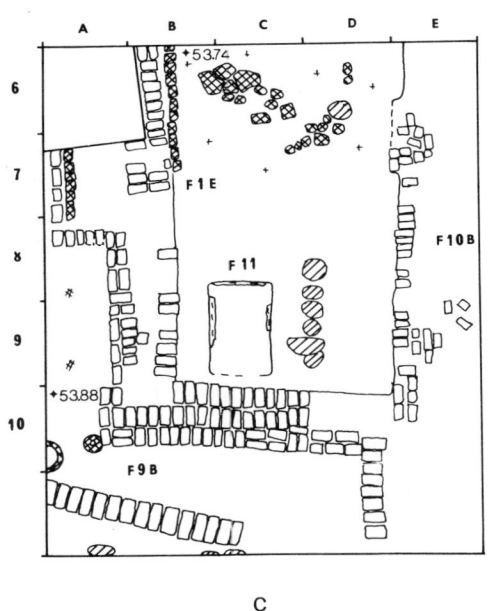
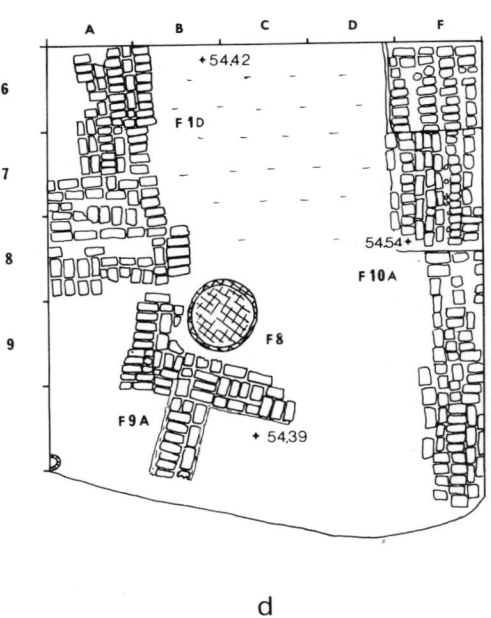

Fig. 37. Jemdet Nasr Large Buildings in Excavation A. A. Feature 12B at the level of Layers 16 and 17. Note the boulder retaining wall (which may in fact be related to higher feature 12A) and the wall stub at the lower right, reconstructed from evidence in the section. B. Feature 12A at the level of Layers 14 and 15. Note the stone paved hearth. C. Features 1E, 9B, and 10B at the level of Layer 12. The leftmost gypsum cement brick row is probably reutilized from a structure of level 13 represented in plan only by the in situ gypsum cement brick row to the right. Note the post hole with the gypsum plaster lining, the perforated gypsum cement item, the gypsum cement vat fragments, and the bin, Feature 11. D. Features 1D, 9A, and 10A at the level of Layer 8. Note the well-preserved gypsum cement vat.

STRATIGRAPHY OF THE URUK, JEMDET NASR, AND EARLY DYNASTIC PHASES

Table 15: Uruk, Jemdet Nasr, and Early Dynastic Walls

Exc.	Feature	Brick Sizes	Bond	Wall Thickness	Courses Surviving	Fig.
	Small Buildings					
B	F37	none	none	E-W:.55m N-S:.40m	0	8c, 36a
B	F26	.26x.14x.06m —x.13x.08m	stretcher-header	E-W:.40m N-S:.35m	2	36b
A	F20–22	20: .22x.11x.06m .23x.11x.07m .24x.13x.07m 22: .26x.17x.08m	stretcher-header	E-W:.30m N-S:.25m	2	5j, 36c
A	F16	none	none	.45m	0	4m
A	F15	.24x.12x.08m .27x.12x.08m	irregular stretcher-header	irregular	2	4n, 36d
A	—	.21x.12x.07m .35x.12m .35x.20m	unknown stretcher-header	.55	3	5p
A	F12A	.25x.13x.09m .26x.13x.08m .27x.13x.08m	irregular stretcher-header	.60	2	4q, 37b
B	F16	.30x.18x.10m	stretcher-header	.30	5	38d
B	F10A	.24x.12x.07m	irregular stretcher-header	.45	3	7j, 36e
	Large Buildings					
B	F22–23	22: .16x.10x.065m .18x.11x.055m .19x.11x.07m 23: .18x.12x.08m .19x.11x.07m .20x.12x.07m .20x.12x.07m	header	N-S:.80m E-W:.50m	5	38a
B	F10E–19	10E: .25x.13x.09m .26x.14x.07m	10E: stretcher-header 19: header	.30 .40	10E: 5 19: 4	38b
B	F10D–14	Main .23x.10m .30x.18m	irregular stretcher	.75	10	38b
		E-W .25x.10m	irregular stretcher-header	.65	5	
		N-S addition: .23x.11x.08m	irregular stretcher-header	.50	5	
		Step: .27x10m	mud and fragments	.80	—	
		Gypsum: .22x.13x.07m .23x.11x.06m	stretcher-header	.45	9	
B	F10C	N-S addition: .22x.12m .25x.14m	irregular	.50	3	7h, 38c
		E-W .21x.10x.07m	irregular stretcher-header	.80	3–4	
		N-S Main .23x.12x.07m .24x.11x.07m	irregular stretcher-header	.85	3	
B	F10B	.22x.12x.07m .23x.12x.07m	modified stretcher-header	N-S addition .40 E-W .45 N-S Main .75	6 4	7i, 38d
A	F1F	.21x.12x.08m .24x.14x.08m .26x.16x.09m	stretcher-header	.40	4	4r, 34s

Table 15: Continued.

Exc.	Feature	Brick Sizes	Bond	Wall Thickness	Courses Surviving	Fig.
A	F1E	.22x.10x.10m .25x.12x.10m	header	.90	6	5w,34u,w,37c
	F9B	.22x.13m .25x.12m	header	.70	2	
	F10B	.25x.12m .28x.15m	irregular	.85	3	
A	F1D	.23x.12x.07m .28x.13m	header	.95	7	34x,2,37z
	F9A	.22x.11x.07m	stretcher-header	.55,.45	7	
	F10A	.23x.12x.07m	irregular stretcher-header	.95	6	
	floor packing	.23x.13x.07m .24x.13x.07m .24x.13x.06m .23x.12x.07m				
A	F1C	.18x.10x.07m .20x.12x.07m .21x.14x.08m	stretcher-header	.60	5	34c′
A	9A	.18x.11x.07m .22x.12x.07m .28x.14x.10m	stretcher-header	.55	5	
A	F1B	.22x.15x.08m* .20x.12x.07m*	header	.50	6	34g′
A	F1A	.25x.15m* .23x.13m*	header	.60	5	34h′,36f

*plano-convex brick

SUMMARY OF THE BUILDINGS

Construction practices of these phases differ in number of respects from those of the Farukh and Bayat Phases. Brick sizes are smaller and bonding patterns are different. Stone or packed mud footings in slight wall trenches are more common and brick platforms under buildings are not attested. While interior floors are still of prepared mud, exterior floors frequently are not. These latter two construction practices contribute to the relative irregularity of the stratigraphy mentioned in the introduction.

Judging from the small portions we have exposed, buildings are composed only of adjacent rectangular rooms. There is no evidence of compound walls and alleys or halls around these room blocks as there was in the Farukh Phase. Though few complete rooms were found, even partial measurements of the rooms indicate that they were larger than Farukh Phase rooms.

"Simple" and "Elaborate" buildings of the Uruk, Jemdet Nasr, and Early Dynastic Phases are defined differently than were those of the earlier phases. The primary criterion is the thickness of the walls. Small buildings have thin and poorly laid walls; large buildings have thick walls, sometimes with special bonding, well-preserved plasters, and occasionally other embellishments. The Farukh Phase "Simple" and "Elaborate" buildings had walls of similar thickness and differed primarily in the presence of a platform and more careful bricklaying of the latter. Most buildings of the later phases had hearths, ovens, bins, and vats associated. Because of these associations and of the distribution of artifacts (see Chapter X), it seems likely that most had domestic functions.

OVENS

These are features, circular or oval in plan, with flat floors and vertical or converging baked mud walls. These possible ovens range in diameter from .40 to 1.95 m. Ovens of this type are found throughout the area today. When complete, they

STRATIGRAPHY OF THE URUK, JEMDET NASR, AND EARLY DYNASTIC PHASES

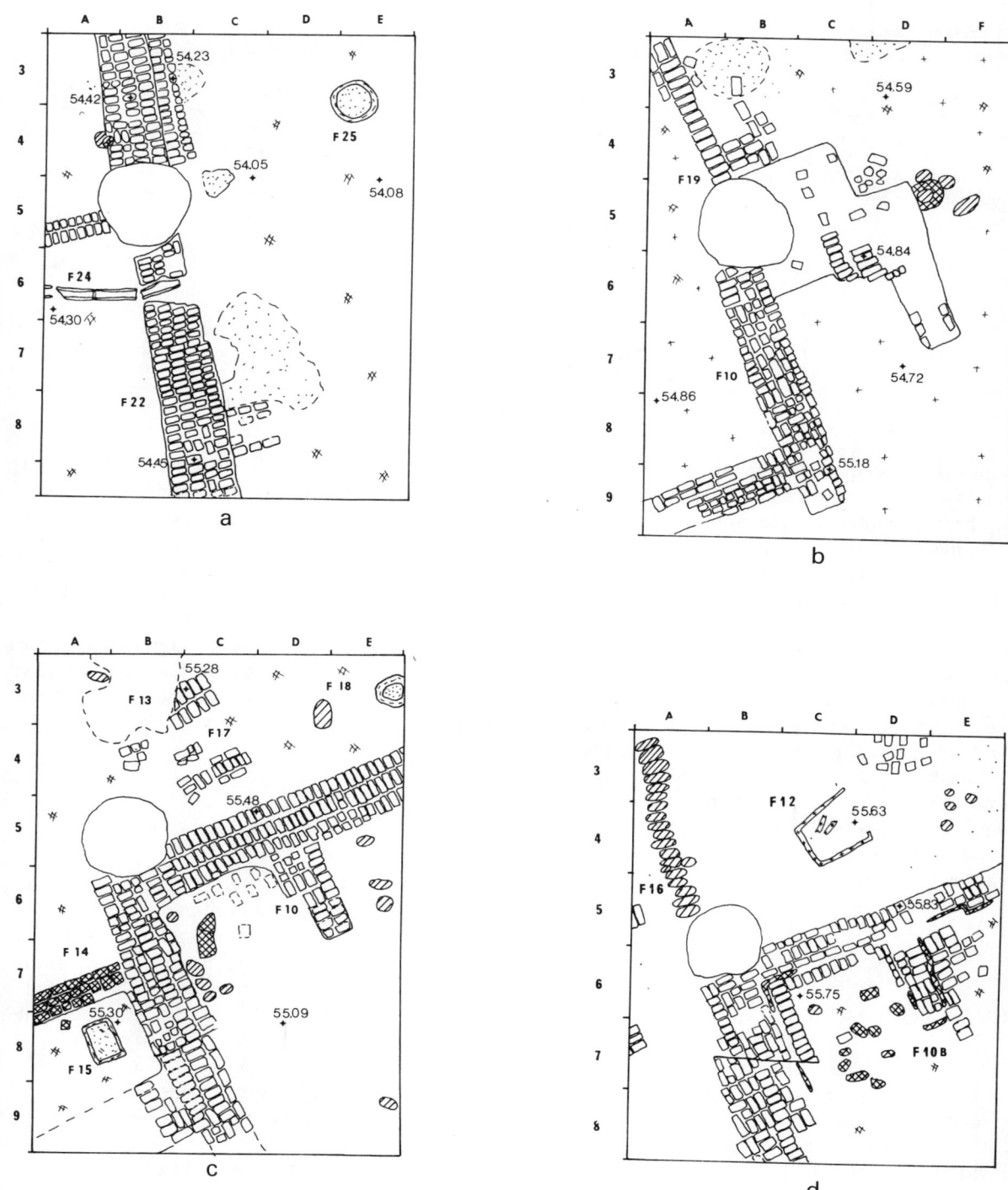

Fig. 38. Uruk and Jemdet Nasr Large Buildings in Excavation B. A. Features 22 and 23 at the level of Layer 30. Note the probable small oven, Feature 25, and ceramic drain, Feature 24. The oval is Feature 6, an Elamite shaft. B. Features 10D and 19 at the level of Layer 27. C. Features 10C and 14 at the level of Layer 24. Note the post hole, Feature 18; the small wall stubs, Feature 17; the gypsum cement brick wall addition, Feature 14; and the bin, Feature 13. D. Features 10B and 16 at the level of Layer 22. Note the gypsum plaster and the vat fragments on the floor; the bin, Feature 12; and the wall stub on the left, reconstructed from evidence in the section.

Table 16: Uruk and Jemdet Nasr Ovens

Ex.	Feature	Layer	Square	Base Length	Base Width	Depth	Floor	Fill	Fig.
B	F33	35	C,D–11,12	40(NW–SE)	.30	.20+	Flat Baked	Charcoal & silt	—
B	F27	33	B,C–7,8	1.95(NW–SE)	1.30	.70+	Flat Plaster	Ash & silt	36b
B	F25	31	C,D–3,4	.42(NW–SE)	.40	.10+	Flat Plaster	Ash layer	38a
A	F17	20	E–9,10	1.20(NE–SW)	—	.15+	Baked Plaster & Pebbles	Baked plaster & silt	5k
A	F6	6	D,E–6	.72(ENE–WSW)	.42	.20+	Flat Baked	Ash lenses	—

are roughly dome-shaped with openings at the top and side. In bread-making a small hot fire of twigs is set on the floor. When the sides are hot, flattened balls of unleavened dough are slapped against them and allowed to bake for about thirty seconds. Other foods can also be baked in these ovens.

The features classified as ovens vary greatly. Only two have the size and the well-baked floors characteristic of ovens today (Excavation A, features 17 and 6). The former has a small ash-filled pit near it (Fig. 5k). Two of the others are very small and may be large postholes or special hearths (Excavation B, Features 33 and 25). One does not have a clearly baked floor, perhaps because it was not long used or because it was seldom cleaned, thus insulating the floor with a layer of ash (Excavation B, Feature 27).

RECTANGULAR MUD SLAB BINS

Unlike ovens, these features are relatively uniform; however, they are without either ethnographic or archaeological parallels. The three deep and well-preserved examples were made in rectangular pits lined with unbaked rectangular slabs of clay. The top edge of each slab on the pit sides is rounded; the bottom is grooved and laps over the outer surface of the slab below. These bins probably extended above as well as below floor level. They range from .22 to .75 m below floor level but the full heights above floor level are unknown. They range in length from .80 to 1.02 m. One exceptional bin (Excavation A, Feature 11) has burnt plaster fragments within indicating reuse as a hearth or oven. Another (Excavation B, Feature 12) was unusual in being outside of a building.

The use of these bins is suggested by the fill of two of them (Excavation A, Features 13 and 14). Both contained quantities of carbonized barley and wheat. This is dispersed through a clean loose silt fill rather than burnt *in situ*. These bins may be granaries. If so, the grain must somehow have been removed, burnt, and swept back in the abandoned bin.

GYPSUM CEMENT VATS

These come into use after the beginning of the Jemdet Nasr Period and continue into the Early Dynastic Period. The few *in situ* examples are usually cylindrical in form. Fragments are common. These were apparently made by hand molding the cement for a few cm in height, letting it solidify, molding another layer, and so on. The two complete examples are .55 and 1.05 m high. One vat (Excavation A, Feature 2) was exceptional in that it had a deep concave base but no evidence of vertical sides.

The fill of the vats gives no indication of the uses to which the vats were put. Two have fine lenses of silt suggesting water deposition, but this is not an indication that they were designed to hold liquids or that they were effective at doing so. An experiment, such as filling a newly constructed vat with water, would be useful here. Vats occur both inside and outside of buildings.

STRATIGRAPHY OF THE URUK, JEMDET NASR, AND EARLY DYNASTIC PHASES

Table 17: Uruk and Jemdet Nasr Bins

Ex.	Feature	Layer	Square	Base Length	Base Width	Depth	Fill	Fig.
A	F26	21	D,E–12,13	1.02(N–S)	.95	.38	Silt and ash	36c
A	F13	18	C–13	–(NNE–SSW)	.55+	.75+	Silt and grain	36d
A	F14	18	B,C–13	.75+(NNE–SSW)	.80	.75+	Silt and grain	36d
A	F11	12	C–8,9	1.00(NE–SW)	.70	.25+	Ash and burnt plaster	37c
B	F15	24	A,B–8	.85(N–S)	.70	.78	Ash and charcoal	38c
B	F12	21	C,D–3,4	.80(E–W)	.60	.22+	Silt	38d

Table 18: Uruk and Jemdet Nasr Cement Vats

Ex.	Feature	Layer	Square	Base Length	Base Width	Depth	Bottom Shape	Fill	Fig.
A	F8	8	B,C–8,9	.85(NE–SW)	.80	1.05	Concave	Silt lenses, vat fragments	38c
A	F7	7	D–3	1.05	1.05	.15+	—	Silt, vat fragments	—
A	F5	5	D–5	.50+(NE–SW)	.50	.25+	Flat	Silt vat fragments	34f
A	F4	5	B,C–7,8	.60	.60	.15+	—	Silt, vat fragments	—
A	F3	5	B,C–8,9	.85(NW–SE)	.80	.55	Concave	Lensed silt, ash	—
A	F2	4	A–6,7	1.30(NE–SW)	—	.40+	Concave	Silt, vat fragments	—
B	F13	21	B–4	.90(E–W)	.70	—	—	Silt, vat fragments	36e

POSTHOLES

Frequent examination of floors failed to reveal any simple postholes; those found are more complicated. In all but one case (Excavation B, Feature 37), the hole has a molded gypsum cement base or cement vat fragment at its bottom. All but one (Excavation B, Feature 18) had also been fired *in situ* to a soft ceramic, but there is no evidence of charcoal in the fill of the hole. These seem to be permanent shallow postholes. Perhaps they are, at least in the later examples which are all just outside the walls of large buildings, seasonal porch or rack supports.

HEARTHS AND PITS

Hearths: These are shallow features with baked floors and no definable sides. The bases are usually concave and fill is often an ash lens. They range from .40 to .95 m in length. Ash lenses or burned areas on floors are not defined as hearths.

Pits: These are irregular and seldom as small as those noted in the earlier phases. In only one case (Excavation A, Feature 17) is the purpose of the pit clear. It served as an ash repository for an oven. All pits (including those used for burials, which are not considered here) were difficult to detect in plan.

BURIALS

Five burials (Fig. 39a) of the Middle Uruk period were found. The four in Excavation B, all probably originating from upper Layer 34 have no directly associated artifacts. One found eroding from the bank about 50 m northeast of Excavation B had a number of associations. Technical details of the osteology are presented in Appendix G.

Table 19: Uruk and Jemdet Nasr Postholes

Ex.	Feature	Layer	Square	Top Length	Top Width	Depth	Bottom Shape	Material	Fig.
B	F37	36	A–11,12	.18(NW–SE)	.12	.10+	—	Silt	36a
A	F34	11	A–9	.20(NE–SW)	—	.10+	Concave	Cement	4v
A	F35	8	A–9	.20(NE–SW)	—	.18	Concave	Vat frag.	4e'
B	F18	24	E–3	.25(NW–SE)	.20	.22	Concave	Cement	38c

Table 20: Uruk and Jemdet Nasr Hearths and Pits

Ex.	Feature	Layer	Square	Top Length	Top Width	Depth	Bottom	Fill	Fig.
Hearths									
B	38	37	D,E–9,10	.46(NW–SE)	.38	.28	Concave	Ash charcoal	—
B	37B	36	B–9,10	.40(NW–SE)	—	.06	Concave	Baked silt	36a
B	37C	36	B,C–9,10	.60(E–W)	—	.03	Concave	Silt	36a
A	F24	21	B,C–11	.80(NW–SE)	.60	.25	Concave	Ash and baked silt	36c
A	F40	17	D–9,10	.95(NW–SE)	.75	—	—	Ash	36d
A	F39	17	D–12	.70(NE–SW)	.65	.05	Concave	Ash	36d
A	F38	13	E–6	.95(NE–SW)	—	.12	Flat	Pebbles and ash	37b
A	F37	12	A–6,7	.36(NE–SW)	—	.19	Concave	Ash	4u'
A	F36	12	A–10	.42(NE–SW)	—	.16	Concave	Ash	4v'
Pits									
A	F23	22/23	A to D	3.45+(N–S)	3.10+	.60+	Concave	Ash, charcoal	36c
B	F45	32	C–9	.40	.40	.10	Concave	Green silt, sherds	—
B	F30	33	E–7,8	1.20(NE–SW)	—	.48	Concave	Silt	7f
B	F44	32	E–7	.64(NE–SW)	—	.34	Concave	Silt	7f'
A	F19	20	D,E–12,13	1.50(NE–SW)	—	.74+	Flat	Silt, sherds	5l
A	F17	20	E–10	.80(NE–SW)	—	.32	Concave	Ash, charcoal, silt	5k
B	F43	27	A–3,4,5	2.40(NE–SW)	—	.66	Concave	Ash, charcoal, silt lenses	—
B	F42	23	A–4	.61(NE–SW)	—	.58	Flat	Ash, charcoal, silt lenses	—

Infant Burial (Feature 29): The remains of this infant extended about five cm into the southeast section (Fig. 7e) on which the pit is clearly shown. Although it is poorly preserved, the fragments indicate that the body was on its right side with the spine oriented 40° east of north, the head slumped eastward and badly crushed, and the legs loosely flexed so that the distal end of the tibiae pointed about 55° east of north.

Child Burial (Feature 34): Much of this is in the northwest section. It is also poorly preserved. The body had slumped on its right side, bending the neck and leaving the skull upright facing approximately northeast. The spine is oriented approximately due east. A few fragments suggest the legs were loosely flexed but do not permit measurement.

Adult Burial (Feature 35): This individual extended into the southeast section but erosion had almost exposed it, so that it was easily cleaned and removed. The body lay on its left side facing

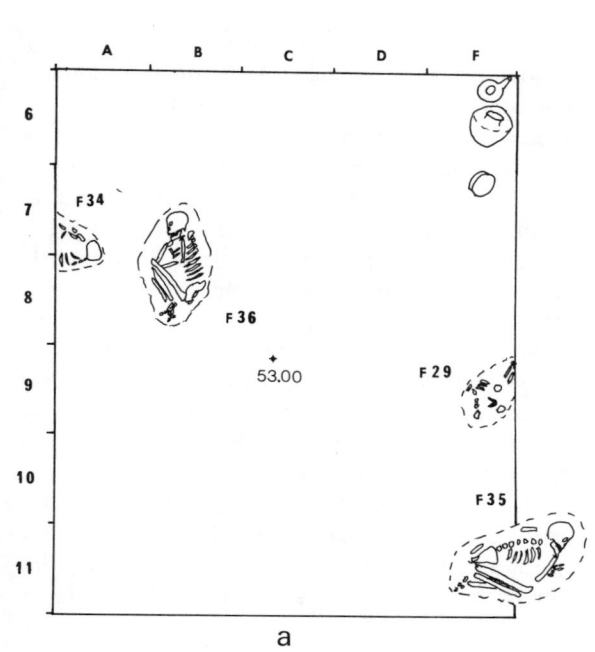
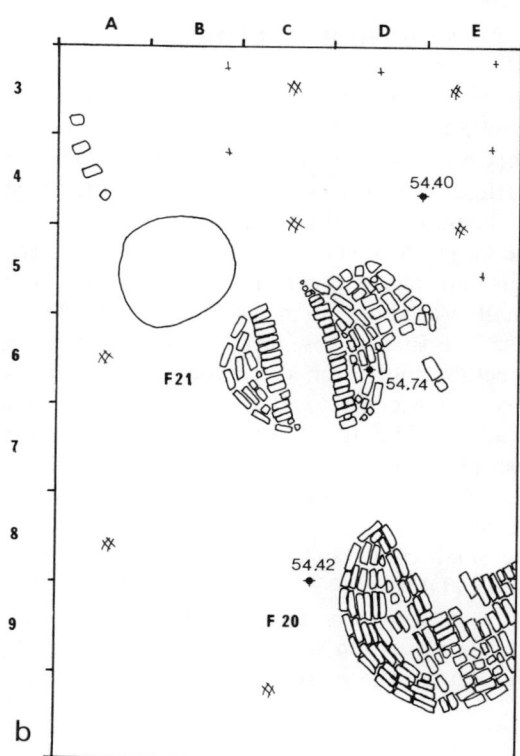

Fig. 39. Other Uruk features in Excavation B. A. Burials, Features 29, 34, 35, and 36, at the level of Layer 34. Note the vessel group on the upper right. B. The platforms, Features 20 and 21, at the level of Layer 29. The oval is Feature 6, the Elamite shaft.

approximately due south. The spine is oriented approximately 130° east of north. The right arm is loosely flexed with the distal end of the ulna pointing roughly east and the hand perhaps against the right side of the skull. The left arm was not mapped but the left hand is in front of the mandible, indicating tight flexure. The legs are very tightly flexed with the distal tibiae pointing 15° and 20° west of north. The right tibia and femur are parallel, suggesting some decomposition of the body prior to burial. This was identified in the field as a male.

Adult Burial (Feature 36): This individual lay on the right side, facing approximately 70° west of north. The spine is oriented about 10° east of north and the arms are only slightly bent with the hand under the knees. The legs are flexed with the distal end of the tibia pointing almost due south. There is no evidence of decomposition prior to burial. This was identified in the field as a female.

Adult Burial With Artifacts: These remains were damaged by erosion and the bone is poorly preserved. It probably lay on its back, but the skull and legs have slumped to the right. The spine is not preserved but must have been oriented toward the east. The skull faces approximately west. The right arm is bent at a 60° angle with its hand on the chest. The left arm was eroded away. The legs are flexed with the distal ends of the tibiae 100° west of north. At the knees of the corpse are a small black-on-red painted jar (Fig. 57a), three concrete bowls (Fig. 77g,h), one stone bowl (Fig. 77a), two small jars of alabaster (Fig. 77k,l), and a sandstone palette with hematite on one face. In the fill are an intact medium gray chert blade, a small pink limestone bead, a mussel shell, some carpals and long bone fragments of sheep or goat, and a long bone fragment from a large mammal. It is rumored that a second pottery vessel was removed from the burial prior to excavation.

It is notable that these burials show no uniformity of orientation or placement.

OTHER FEATURES

The most intriguing other features are two circular mud brick platforms in Layer 29, Excavation B. They are built of bricks ranging from .25 to .27 m in length, .12 to .13 m in width, and .07 to .08 m in thickness (Fig. 39b).

The larger, less well-preserved platform is missing its northeast quadrant (Feature 20), but originally was about 2.5 m in diameter and .42 m in height. The first of four brick courses is laid on edge below floor level; the second is laid flat. A third on-edge course and the fourth flat course were added. The alternation of flat and on-edge courses provides an effective bonding. A gap .75 m wide runs from north to south through the platform.

The small platform (Feature 21) is 1.70 m in diameter. Only two courses are preserved. The lower is laid on edge and the upper is laid flat. There is a gap .45 m wide, running from north to south through the platform, filled with soft dark silt. To the northeast of the platform is a small area of brick paving.

The uses to which these features were put is unknown. Solid circular platforms are known from other Mesopotamian sites, but none to my knowledge, exhibits a gap. The gap would allow access to the bottom of whatever rested on the feature. Perhaps a drain plug for a vat was there.

Another feature is a small area of mud brick paving (Feature 31) in Excavation B, Layer 34. It was a short distance above and northwest of a burial (Feature 35) and may have been related to it.

Also in the same layer was a large concentration of equid, bovid, and caprid bones (Feature 32) and a concentration of vessels buried intact. These may also have been related to the burials made at the time of deposition of the layer.

Finally, there were two roughly rectangular piles of cobbles, one in Excavation B, Layer 33 (Feature 28) and one in Excavation B, Layer 25. Both seem to be nothing more than architectural fill under or within rooms.

CHAPTER VII

CERAMICS OF THE URUK, JEMDET NASR AND EARLY DYNASTIC PHASES

INTRODUCTION

Throughout this long period, several wares—with very different combinations of clay body, throwing techniques, and firing technique—are important. These are presented more or less in the order in which they reach their height of popularity. In the beginning of this period, Sargarab Ware is dominant, but it is soon replaced by Uruk Ware. Less common, but certainly not rare, are those wares termed straw-tempered ware and gray ware. I have not given these special function wares proper names. Various rare wares also occur. Please note that certain ceramics sometimes termed "wares", such as "Uruk Red Wares" and "Jemdet Nasr Polychrome Ware" are viewed here as kinds of surface decoration found on a few forms of Sargarab or Uruk Ware. This is not to deny that there are true "Uruk Red Wares" elsewhere.

As in the Farukh and Bayat ceramic study (Chapter II), this discussion is intended to be introductory rather than definitive. Technical analyses and statistical studies of samples from a number of sites are needed.

SARGARAB WARE

This ware is tempered with a mixture of straw fragments and crushed calcareous mineral, both of which are usually destroyed in the firing process leaving holes in the clay body. There is much variation in the quantity of particles. Coarse Thickened Rim Bowls and Coarse Thickened Round Lip Jars have from 20 to 35 percent particles by volume, in all cases predominantly mineral. Incurved bowls have about 10 percent in most cases predominantly straw. Both Fine Jars and Expanded Rim Jars have two to ten percent inclusions with no obvious preference for straw or mineral. The coarser types of vessels are fired in a manner which produces frequent unoxidized cores and red surfaces. The finer types of vessels are frequently fully oxidized and range from light brown to greenish in color. This wide range in clay preparation and firing techniques deserves further detailed technical analysis. Vessel measurements are given in Appendix Table C2.

It was my first impression that all Sargarab vessels were wheel-thrown. Possibly some small round lip bowls and fine jars were thrown, judging by the oblique lineations on the clay body visible in vertical breaks, the surface striations and grooving, and vessel thickness symmetry. In contrast, basins and the round lip jars are certainly hand-built, but the techniques used for the most common shapes—incurved bowls and flared expanded rim jars—are not yet determinable. Some of the former appear to have hand-built lower bodies and wheel-finished upper bodies, suggesting a two-part construction. Clearly technical analysis is needed here too.

Except where noted, Sargarab Ware is characteristic of the Early and Middle Uruk layers at Tepe Farukhabad. It is similar to wares from Luristan (Young 1969: 4–6, Fig. 7,8; Wright, Neely, Johnson, and Speth 1975:131–133, Fig. 6).

Round Lip Bowls (Fig. 40e; 43b,c): These open forms range in rim diameter from 16 to 28 cm. The rims often curve slightly outwards. A complete example shown in Fig. 40e, has a height of 5.6 cm and a volume of .3 liters. It approaches Uruk Ware conical cups in shape.

Incurved Bowls (Fig. 41a,e,f): These small constricted forms usually have a distinct shoulder with sharply curved rims. Rim diameters range from 11 to 18 cm. Half the examples have a red slip.

Incurved Beaded Rim Bowls (Fig. 41b,g,h,i,l): These larger constricted forms curve gently inward. There is a marked exterior thickening with a definite break or angle at the juncture of the side and the thickening or "beading". Diameters range from 19 to 49 cm. About one tenth of the examples have a red slip. This particular Sargarab form does occur in Late Uruk layers and may have continued in use after the ware was no longer commonly made.

Incurved Beaded Rim Bowls with Impressed Strips (Fig. 41c,j,k,m): These have a rim form

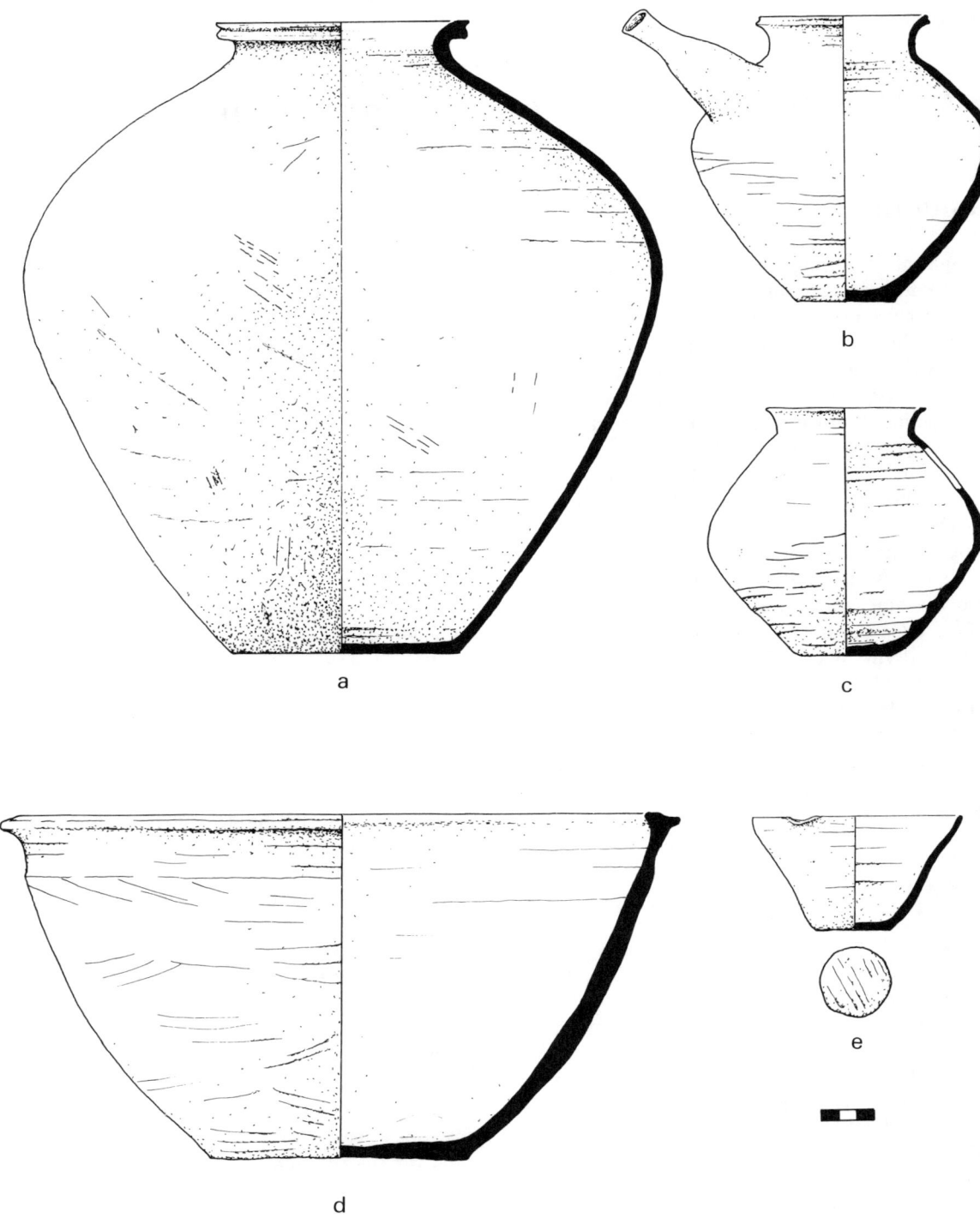

Fig. 40. Sargarab Ware: Reconstructed Vessels. A. Flared expanded rim jar, limestone and straw, body white, diam.: 14, body diam.: 35.0, height: 36.2; X574, 6078602 (B34). B. Flared expanded rim jar with spout, straw and limestone, body white to pale yellow, diam.: 9, body diam.: 16.8, height: 15.5; X574, 6078601 (B34). C. Round lip jar, straw, body white, diam.: 8, body diam.: 15.5, height: 13.7; X579, 6057802 (B34). D. Large ledge rim bowl, straw and limestone, body white, diam.: 41, height: 19.0; X336, 6021701 (A21). E. Round lip bowl or conical cup, limestone and straw, body very pale brown, diam.: 12, height: 5.6; X579, 6057801 (B34).

similar to the above described category. The beading is often heavier. There is a raised ridge or strip around the point of maximum diameter on which a series of oblique impressions has been made. Diameters range from 13 to 55 cm. Since there is no association between vessel size and presence of strips, the raised strip is not intended simply to strengthen a larger bowl. Half of the measured examples have a red slip.

There is one large example represented by two sherds in good context in Farukh Phase Layer 39 (60901, Fig. 41n). The body is straw and limestone tempered and distinctly red. The lip is horizontally flattened rather than beaded. The rim is not incurved. The raised strip is impressed with closely spaced oval finger impressions. This example is similar in shape to some Middle Uruk examples of Uruk Ware, and similar in type of impression to those from the site of Sargarab (Wright, Neely, Johnson, and Speth 1975, Fig. 7e).

Flat Lip Bowls (Fig. 43d,e): These bowls have nearly vertical rims and flattened horizontal or slightly oblique lips, sometimes with a slight ledge on the exterior. They range from 8 to 40 cm in diameter. Half have a red slip. Several have a black band around the lip.

Large Thickened Rim Basins (Fig. 42a,j–o): These large open bowls have flat bases, with flared sides and a heavy exterior beading on the rim. Heights range from five to ten cm. Diameters range from 44 to 72 cm. The body texture is very coarse. Most examples have burnished red slip.

Thickened Rim Round Lip Jars (Fig. 42b,e–i): These have flaring necks with rounded, relatively heavy rims. The body is coarse, as noted above, and the surfaces are roughly scraped. Neck diameters range from 8 to 15 cm. Nine-tenths of the vessels have a red slip. The form does not differ significantly in shape from Early and Middle Uruk examples of sand tempered Uruk Ware.

Round Lip Jars (Figs. 40c; 42d; 43k,l,n,o): These jars have finer tempering materials. The generally higher necks have slightly thickened rims. Neck diameters range from 7 to 13 cm. Only a quarter of the vessels are slipped.

Fine Jars (Fig. 43a,f–j, Plate 10d): These small, slightly restricted forms have necks which gradually become thinner and end in a thin rounded lip. The rims are slightly out-curved. Neck diameters range from 8 to 14 cm. There is one complete example (Fig. 43a, Plate 10d) with flat base, a height of 14.3 cm, maximum diameter of 13.9 cm, and a volume of 1.7 liters.

Flared Expanded Rim Jars (Fig. 40a–b; 44b–j, Plate 10a,b): These are distinguished by a high outcurved necks ranging in diameter from 5 to 17 cm. In nine-tenths of the measured cases, the lip of the expanded rim was concave in cross section. The flattened lips range from oblique to vertical, predominantly the latter, on which there is a slight overhang of the lip. There is often a slight concavity on the interior just inside the lip. There are two complete examples. One is small with a height of 15.5 cm, a maximum body diameter of 16.5 cm, a rim diameter of 8.5 cm, and a volume of 1.8 liters; it has a straight spout (Fig. 40b, Plate 10a). One is large and probably more typical of the sample as a whole, with a height of 35 cm, a maximum body diameter of 35 cm, and a volume of 17.4 liters (Fig. 40a, Plate 10b).

Some of these jars are covered with a red slip ranging from 7.5R 5/4 to 10.R 4/4 in the Munsell terminology (Fig. 44h,i). One has, in addition, black bands on the lip and neck. Another has oblique burnishing marks on the shoulder in the pattern of reserve slip wares (Delougaz 1952: Plate 171,39b). These red-slipped examples are predominantly Early Uruk in age.

High Expanded Band Rim Jar (Fig. 44a): These rims are similar to the above except that the neck has been compressed downward until the lip is almost resting on the jar shoulder. Neck diameters range from 11 to 20 cm, suggesting that these are generally larger jars than those described above. One of the jars has a finger impressed strip and a small node on its shoulder. This rim form is intermediate in shape between the Flared Expanded Rims described above and the later Uruk Ware Low Expanded Band Rims described below.

Other Jars (Fig. 43m): There is one rim from a jar with a high flared neck which has been bent over and flattened to form a ledge expanded rim.

Jar Parts (Fig. 44k–o): Cross-hatched incised panels, nose lugs, strap handles, and straight spouts were placed on vessels of Sargarab Ware: These are described below together with those of Uruk Ware since there are only a few of each.

Flat Bases (Fig. 40a–c; 43a): These range in diameter from 6 to 11 cm. One base has a red slip. The bottoms are scraped rather than tooled on a wheel. There is no known way of distinguishing bases of the different kinds of vessels defined above

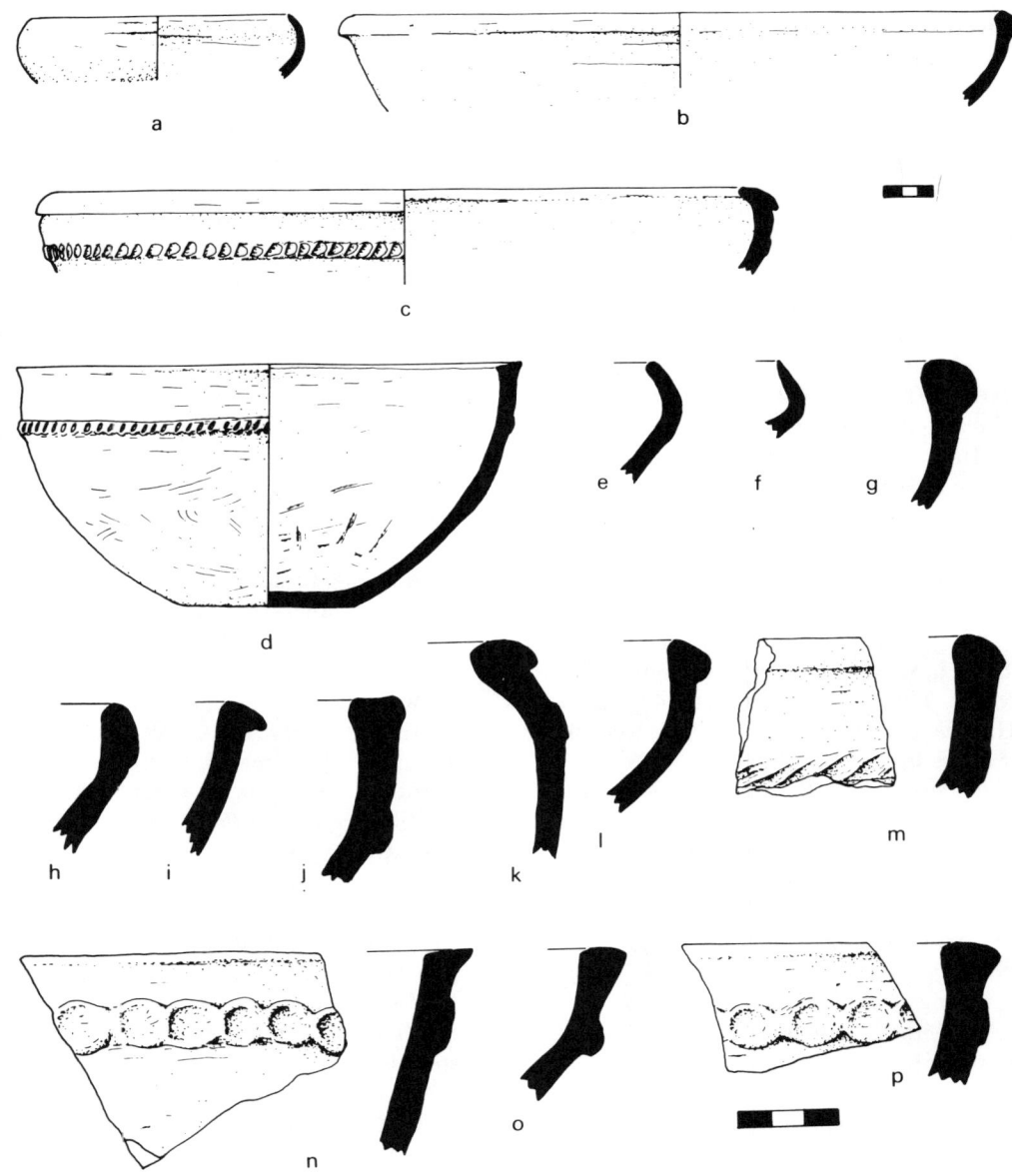

Fig. 41. Sargarab Ware and Related Vessels: Bowls with Beaded Rims and Hatched Strips. A. Incurved bowl, straw and limestone, body light gray, diam.: 16; X342, 6121301 (A F23). B. Incurved beaded rim bowl, straw and limestone, body pinkish gray, diam.: 40; X562, 6056301 (B35). C. Incurved beaded rim bowl with impressed strip, fine sand and straw, body light gray to pale yellow, diam.: 41; X515, 6053504 (B33). D. Uruk ware, incurved bowl with flattened lip, medium sand and straw, body pale yellow, slip dusky red, diam.: 29; X574, 6078601 (B35). E. Incurved bowl rim, straw and limestone, body reddish yellow, diam.: 18; X625, 6061101 (B39). F. Incurved bowl rim, limestone and straw, body very pale brown, diam.: 11, X34, 6121101 (A F19,23). G. Incurved beaded rim bowl, limestone and straw, body light red, diam.: 44; X515, 6053505 (B33). H. Same, straw and limestone, body pink, diam.: 31; X588, 6058703 (B36). I. Same, straw and limestone, body pale brown, diam.: 32; X427, 6048401 (B30). J. Incurved beaded rim bowl with impressed strip, straw and limestone, body olive yellow, diam.: 43; X336, 6021701 (A21). K. Same, straw and limestone, body light gray, diam.: 55; X342, 6121304 (A F23). L. Incurved beaded rim bowl, straw and limestone, body reddish yellow, diam.: 29; X342, 6121303 (A F23). M. Incurved beaded rim bowl with impressed strip, straw and limestone, body red, paint weak red, diam.: 40; X517, 6053901 (B33). N. Flattened lip bowl with impressed strip, limestone and straw, body reddish gray, diam.: 48; X602, 6060901 (B39). O. Uruk ware, incurved bowl with flattened lip, fine sand, body pink, diam.: 41; X514, 6053301 (B33). P. Uruk ware, incurved bowl with flattened lip, fine sand, body very pale brown, diam.: 39; X517, 6053903 (B33).

on the basis of rims. There is one ring base in the measured series.

URUK WARE

This ware contains quantities of sand in its clay body. It is likely that this results from deliberate tempering of the clay since bricks, drains and straw-tempered vessels seldom contain sand. However, the possibility that naturally sandy clays were deliberately selected cannot be eliminated without detailed technical analysis. The sand grains are sub-angular to round in shape. They are predominantly quartz minerals. Earlier Uruk Ware is frequently coarse and contains traces of straw and calcite like the related Sargarab Ware. Later in the Uruk Period, the rare coarse examples have crushed calcareous rock and small jasper pebbles in the paste. It is possible that these are not of local origin. All vessels are fired under well controlled conditions and reduced cores are rare.

Some Uruk Ware vessels show all the signs of wheel throwing, in both the internal fracture patterns and the surface markings. The exceptions are the large bowls and jars, the thickened round rim jars, and many of the small expanded rim jars, which are hand-built with rings or slabs. The major problem with these vessels is to determine whether successive improved types of rotating devices were used. As discussed below, at the very end of the Uruk period and later, conical cups have exclusively string-cut bases indicating that they are formed from a large lump of clay on a large wheel. However, finishing techniques have eliminated such diagnostic signs on larger vessels, and there is thus no standard criteria for dividing Uruk Ware into two wares, an early wheel-finished one and a later wheel-thrown one. This is the predominant ware used in the Late Uruk, Jemdet Nasr, and Early Dynastic periods. Vessel measurements are given in Appendix Table C3.

CUPS

This general category is distinguished by a conical or slightly bell-shaped body and a base often exhibiting the concentric oval marks made by cutting the pot off the wheel with a string. (Knife-cut bases are rare and usually earlier). Frequent asymmetry and excessive thinness of the base indicate the haste with which these vessels were manufactured. It is likely that the potter formed a series of small bowls from one large lump of clay on the wheel. American potters call this "throwing from the hump."

Conical Cup Rims (Fig. 45a,b,h–n): The rims of conical cups thin gradually to a rounded lip. Diameters range from 5 to 30 cm. Wheel scoring and grooving are particularly obvious. These rims grade into round bowl rims so that the categorization of a particular rim is sometimes difficult. The rims of the various base types described below are not distinguishable. Measurements of the rims of the successive phases are contrasted in Table 21.

The small Middle Uruk sample is relatively homogeneous, but variation becomes increasingly more complex through the Jemdet Nasr period. In Late Uruk times, more narrow, small-mouth examples increase mean rim angle. In Late Jemdet Nasr times both narrow and wide varieties become slightly larger.

Wide Conical Cup Bases (Fig. 45a–c): These bases range in diameter from 2.5 to 5.0 cm. Their bodies slope out at angles ranging from 42° to 75°. These occur in Late Uruk and throughout the Jemdet Nasr periods. The small number of Uruk conical cup bases relative to Uruk rims reflects the fact that what we have classified as conical cup rims from this period occur primarily on bases which are scraped or tooled rather than string-cut, and would therefore be classified as fine bases. Two complete examples of this early form with heights of 5.8 and 6.8 cm and volumes of .25 and .32 liters were found (Figs. 45a,b).

Constricted Conical Cup Bases (Fig. 45d,e): These bases range in diameter from 2.6 to 3.6 cm. Their bodies slope out at angles of 60° to 75°. They occur during the Jemdet Nasr period. One restorable cup has a height of 9.6 cm and a volume of .22 liters (Fig. 45e).

Conical Cups with Solid Feet (Fig. 45f,g): These bases range in diameter from 2.5 to 4.0 cm. The bases are in the form of small inverted cones both regular (Fig. 45f) and irregular (Fig. 45g). Above this base is a cylindrical stem. Above the stem the body flares out at angles of from 75° to 85°. Though no complete examples were found, the higher stemmed examples must have looked like wine glasses. It is not to be confused with the solid footed goblets manufactured in Lower Iraq during the Early Dynastic period which have basically conical forms (Delougaz 1952, p. 56–57, Plate 46;

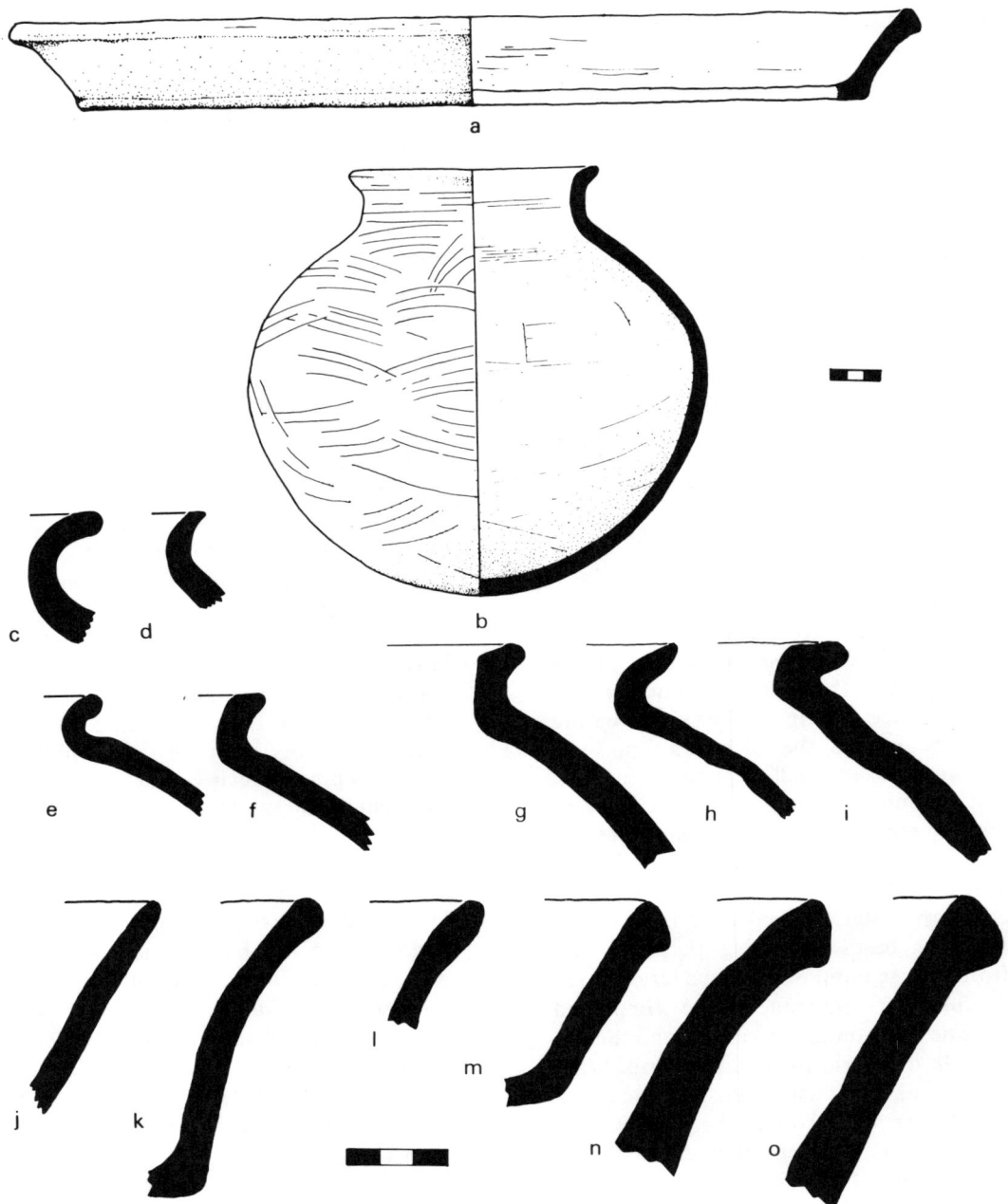

Fig. 42. Sargarab Ware: Heavy Basins and Jars. A. Thickened rim basin, limestone and straw, body brown, diam.: 57; X531, 6054901 (B34). B. Thickened rim round lip jar, fine sand and limestone, body light brownish gray, diam.: 17; X576, 6057501 (B36). C. Thickened rim round lip jar rim, coarse sand and limestone, body light yellowish brown, paint red to light red, diam.: 18; X573, 6057301 (B35). D. Round lip jar rim, fine sand and limestone, body pink to reddish yellow, diam.: 8; X566, 6056701 (B35). E. Thickened rim round lip jar rim, coarse sand, body light yellowish brown, paint weak red to red, diam.: 12; X573, 6057302 (B35). F. Same, coarse sand, body light brown, diam.: 14; X511, 6052601 (B33). G. Same, coarse sand, body white, diam.: 21; X299, 6020401 (A20). H. Same, coarse sand and limestone, body pink, diam.: 15; X462, 6049701 (B32). I. Same, coarse sand and limestone, body light gray to light brownish gray, diam.: 16; X284, 6040601 (B27). J. Thickened rim basin rim, straw and limestone, body dark reddish gray, diam.: ca. 20; X476, 6051401 (B33). K. Same, limestone and straw, body dark grayish brown, diam.: 48; X338, 6083301 (A F19). L. Same, limestone and straw, body dark gray to very dark gray, paint weak red, diam.: 60; X568, 6056902 (B35). M. Same, limestone and straw, body red, diam.: 37; X558, 6055901 (B34). N. Same, limestone and straw, body dark gray, paint red, diam.: 48; X568, 605690 (B35). O. Same, limestone and straw, body grayish brown, paint weak red, diam.: 72; X533, 6055301 (B34).

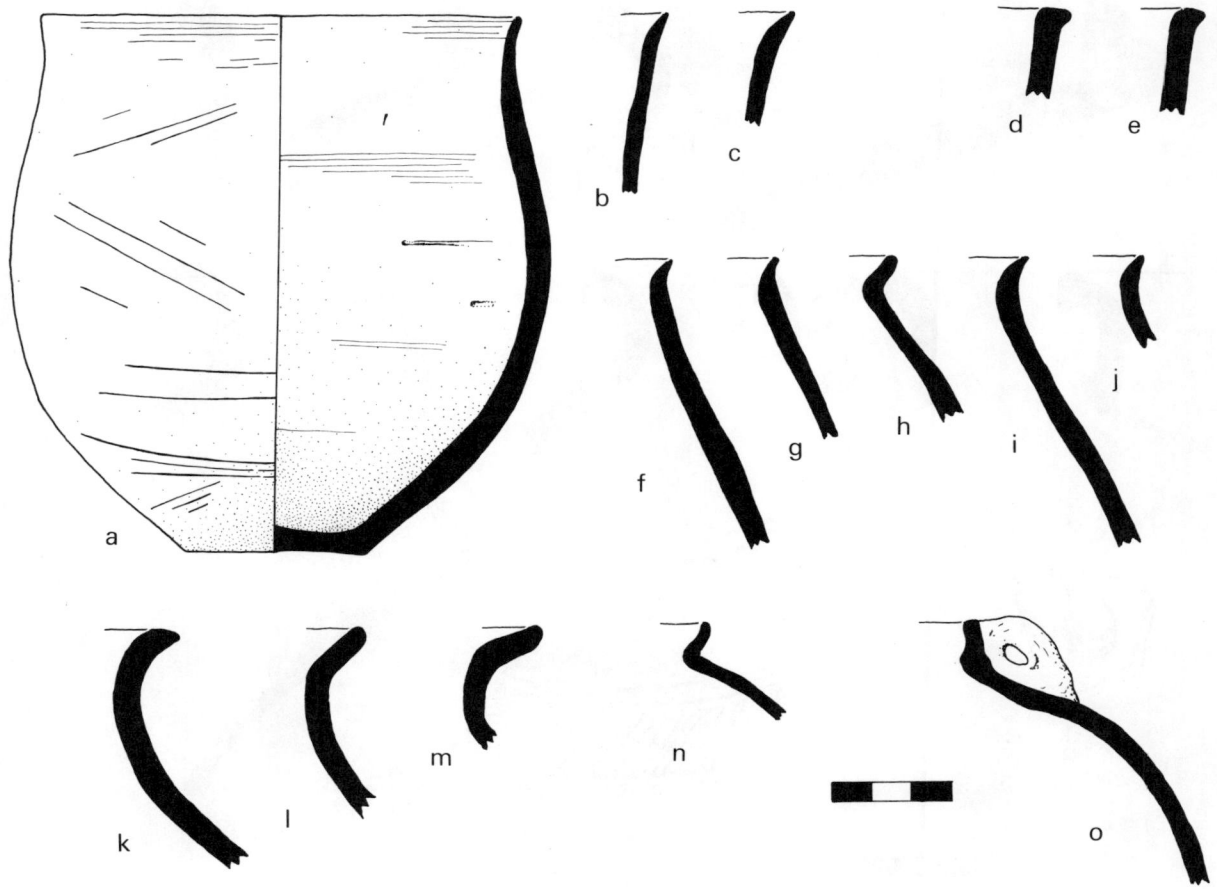

Fig. 43. Sargarab Ware: Bowls and Jars with Rounded Lips and Bowls with Flat Lips. A. Fine jar, straw and limestone, body light reddish brown, diam.: 12, height: 14.4; X588, 6058703 (B36). B. Round lip bowl rim, straw and limestone, body light reddish brown, diam.: 11; X515, 6053501 (B33). C. Same, limestone and straw, body pale yellow, diam.: 10; X517, 6053901 (B33). D. Flat lip bowl rim, straw and limestone, body light red, slip weak red, diam.: 26; X458, 6049501 (B32). E. Same, straw and limestone, body light reddish brown, slip weak red, rim top dark reddish gray, diam.: 30; X432, 6049301 (B31). F. Fine jar rim, limestone, body red, diam.: 11; X338, 6083301 (A F19). G. Same, limestone, body light reddish brown, diam.: 11; X560, 6056101 (B34). H. Same, straw, body pinkish gray, diam.: 11; X342, 6121301 (A F23). I. Same, straw and limestone, body light reddish brown, diam.: 9; X596, 6059201 (B36). J. Same, limestone, body light red, diam.: 11; X560, 6056106 (B34). K. Round lip jar rim, limestone, body reddish yellow, slip weak red, black burnished rim top, diam.: 11; X476, 60514 (B33). L. Same, limestone and straw, body pink, diam.: 11; X514, 6053301 (B33). M. Round lip jar variant, limestone and straw, body pale yellow, diam.: 11; X342, 6121307 (A F23). N. Round lip jar rim, limestone, body reddish yellow, slip weak red, diam.: 10; X600, 6059701 (B37). O. Same with small lug, straw and limestone, body reddish yellow, slip weak red, diam.: 10; X600, 6059702 (B37).

Wright 1969a: 63, Fig. 16d). The form is common in the Early Jemdet Nasr period, although it continues into the Early Dynastic Period.

BOWL RIMS

Round Lip Bowls (Fig. 46a–h): These bowls were hemispherical in form with sides straight or slightly incurved. The bodies are usually thicker than those of conical cups. The measurements of bowls from successive phases are contrasted in Table 22.

In each phase there are a majority of deep hemispherical examples and a minority of shallow plate-like examples. In the Uruk, bowls are generally larger and there are a number of very large round rim bowls, while in the Jemdet Nasr there

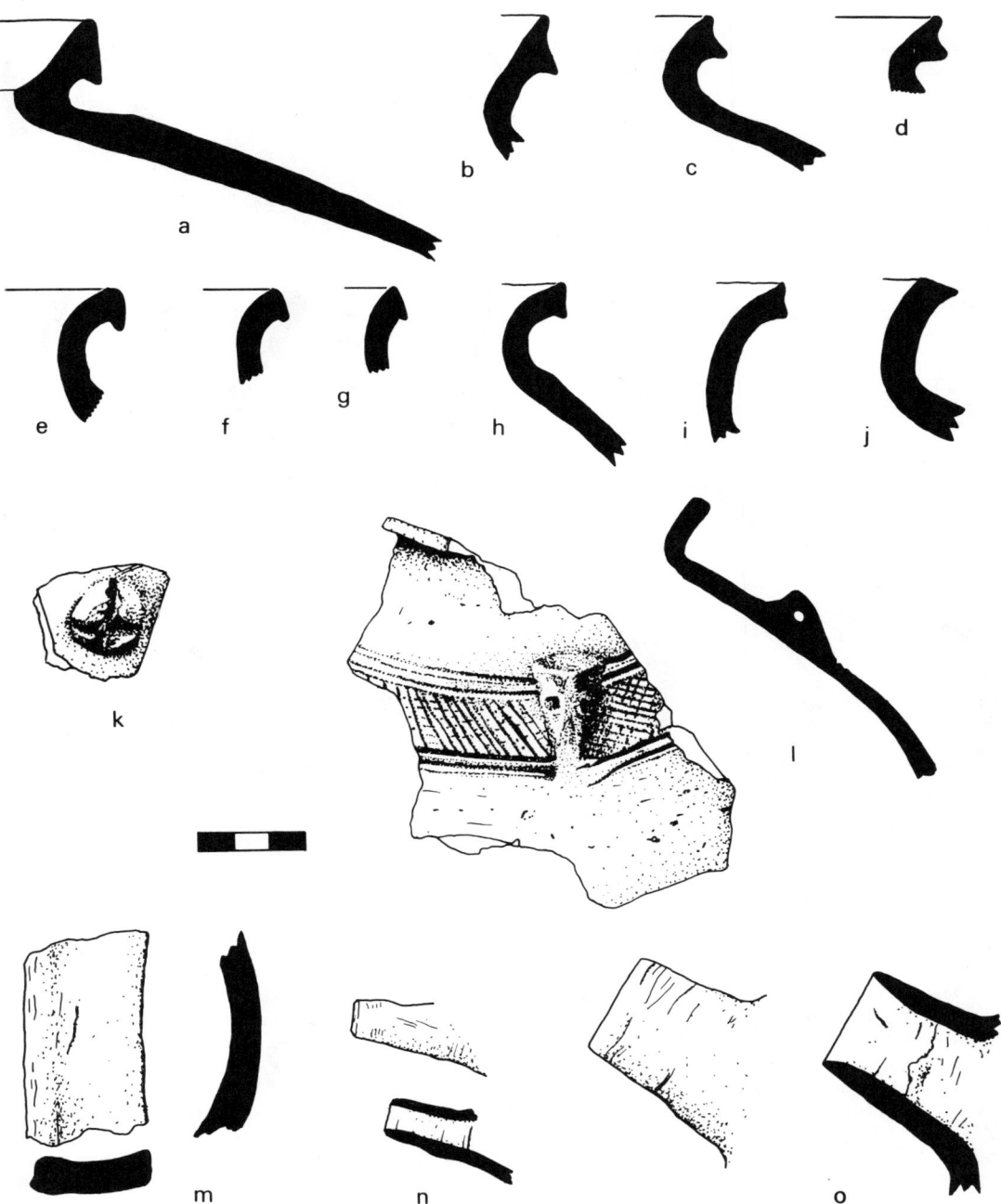

Fig. 44. Sargarab Ware: Jars with Flattened Lips and Various Jar Parts. A. High expanded band rim jar rim, limestone and straw, body light red, diam.: 25; X408, 6023401 (A F27). B. Flared expanded rim jar rim, fine sand, body very pale brown, diam.: 20; X515, 6053502 (B33). C. Same, straw and limestone, body light red, diam.: 13; X304, 6020901 (A21). D. Same, limestone, body light red, diam.: 14; X338, 6083301 (A F19). E. Same, limestone, body very pale brown, diam.: 19; X314, 6041401 (B F10). F. Same, limestone, body very pale brown, diam.: 14; X314, 6041402 (B F10). G. Same, straw and limestone, body red, diam.: 14; X587, 6058302 (B36). H. Same, straw and limestone, body gray, burnished slip dark red, diam.: 13; X462, 6049701 (B32). I. Same, straw and limestone, body light brownish gray, slip red, diam.: 15; X458, 6049501 (B32). J. Ledge rim jar, fine sand and straw, body very pale brown, diam.: 20; X476, 6051401 (B33). K. Node with incisions, straw and limestone, body light reddish brown; X408, 6023404 (A F27). L. Flared expanded jar rim with crosshatch incising and nose lug, straw, body very pale brown, diam.: 14; X233, 6082701 (A F19). M. Strap handle fragment, straw, body gray to light olive gray; X602, 60601 (B38). N. Spout, limestone, body pink; X515, 60535 (B33). O. Spout, limestone, body light red, slip red; X609, 60649 (B42).

CERAMICS OF THE URUK, JEMDET NASR, AND EARLY DYNASTIC PHASES

Table 21: Metrical Attributes of Conical Cup Rims

	Diameter (cm)		Rim Angle (degrees)		Body Thickness (cm)	
	$\bar{x}$	s.d.	$\bar{x}$	s.d.	$\bar{x}$	s.d.
Late Jemdet Nasr N=98	14.9	4.8	75	13	.42	.12
Early Jemdet Nasr N=30	11.9	3.9	75	11	.39	.12
Late Uruk N=32	12.6	3.6	72	11	.41	.10
Middle Uruk N=14	10.8	3.8	68	13	.42	.11

Table 22: Metrical Attributes of Round Rim Bowl Rims

	Diameter (cm)		Rim Angle (degrees)		Body Thickness (cm)	
	$\bar{x}$	s.d.	$\bar{x}$	s.d.	$\bar{x}$	s.d.
Late Jemdet Nasr N=17	17.0	6.8	73	16	.70	.14
Early Jemdet Nasr N=8	16.0	6.7	80	16	.66	.09
Uruk N=31	26.7	9.9	73	14	.74	.12

are a few very small examples and no large examples. The restricted fluted form (Fig. 46a) and the form with the slight exterior rim band (Fig. 46g), similar to certain stone bowls (Fig. 77), are unique.

Incurved Bowls (Fig. 46i,j): The two measured examples are small and markedly incurved. Each has a diameter of only 11 cm. The shape is similar to the larger Early Uruk Sargarab Ware form.

Incurved Bowl with Flat Lip (Fig. 41d,o,p, Plate 10e): This medium-sized form is not related to the above type. It is rather the Uruk Ware version of the Sargarab Ware Incurved Beaded Rim Bowl with hatched strip. However, the lips have a roughly horizontal flattening; marked incurving is rare. Diameters range from 32 to 58 cm. The hatched strips are often vertical rather than oblique, and finger impressions, rather than hatching with a sharp object, occur in about half the examples. This form occurs primarily in layers of the Middle Uruk period when Sargarab Ware is being replaced by Uruk Ware.

Flat Lip Bowls (Fig. 47 a,b,m-r, Plate 10 f,g): In these bowls, there is no expanding of the rim; the lip is merely flattened. They range in diameter from 14 to 50 cm. Some are similar to the simple round lip bowls in form but have flattened lips. A complete example is shown in Fig. 47a and Plate 10f. Its height is 10.9 cm; its volume is 2.4 liters. Others have rims of the distinctive carinate form with straight to slightly concave sides and oblique lip flattening. A complete example is shown in Fig. 47b and Plate 10g. Its height is 13.2 cm; its volume is 2.7 liters.

Beveled Lip Bowls (Fig. 47d,i-l): This large form usually occurs on a conical body. There is an oblique flattening of a thickened rim, like that of the true beveled rim bowl. However, the sandy, well-fired body precludes any confusion. Diameters range from 22 to 50 cm.

Ledge Rim Bowls (Fig. 47c,e-h): The available examples had large hemispherical bodies. The rim is similar to that of ledge rim jars as described below. Diameters range from 22 to 50 cm.

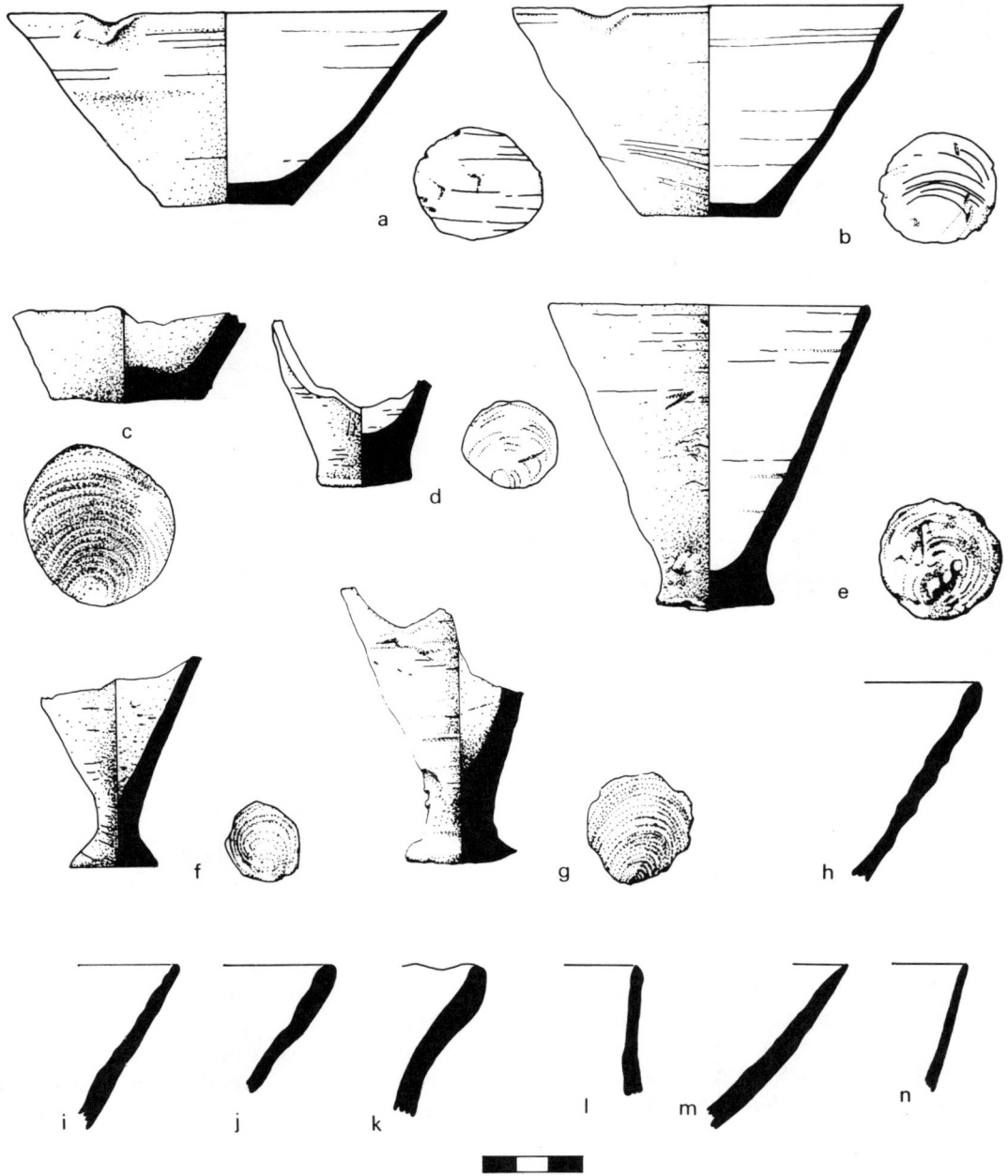

Fig. 45. Uruk Ware: Conical Cups. A. Conical cup with lip spout, fine sand, body light brownish gray to pale brown, diam.: 36, height: 5.8; X339, 6021901 (A21). B. Conical cup with lip spout, fine sand, body pink, diam.: 11.5, height: 6.8; X545, 6078301. C. Wide conical cup base, coarse sand, body white, base diam.: 14; X078, 6009401 (A6). D. Constricted conical cup base, fine sand, body pink, diam.: 3; X229, 6037003 (B23). E. Constricted conical cup, fine sand, body very pale brown, diam.: 9, height: 9.6; X217, 6017804 (A16). F. Solid-footed conical cup, fine sand, body light red, base diam.: 2; X296, 6019801 (A19). G. Solid-footed conical cup, fine sand, body pink, base diam.: 4; X311, 6041001 (B26). H. Conical cup rim, fine sand, body pinkish gray to pink, diam.: 15; C235, 6037501 (B24). I. Same, coarse sand, body very pale brown, diam.: 6; X304, 6020901 (A21). J. Same, coarse sand, body white, diam.: 17; X085, 6010613 (A7). K. Same, coarse sand, body very pale brown, diam.: 14; X102, 6012001 (A7). L. Same, fine sand, body light reddish brown, diam.: 10; X365, 6044601 (B28). M. Same, fine sand, body very pale brown, diam.: 11; X420, 6048101 (B31,32). N. Same, fine sand, body white, diam.: 6; X311, 6041002 (B26).

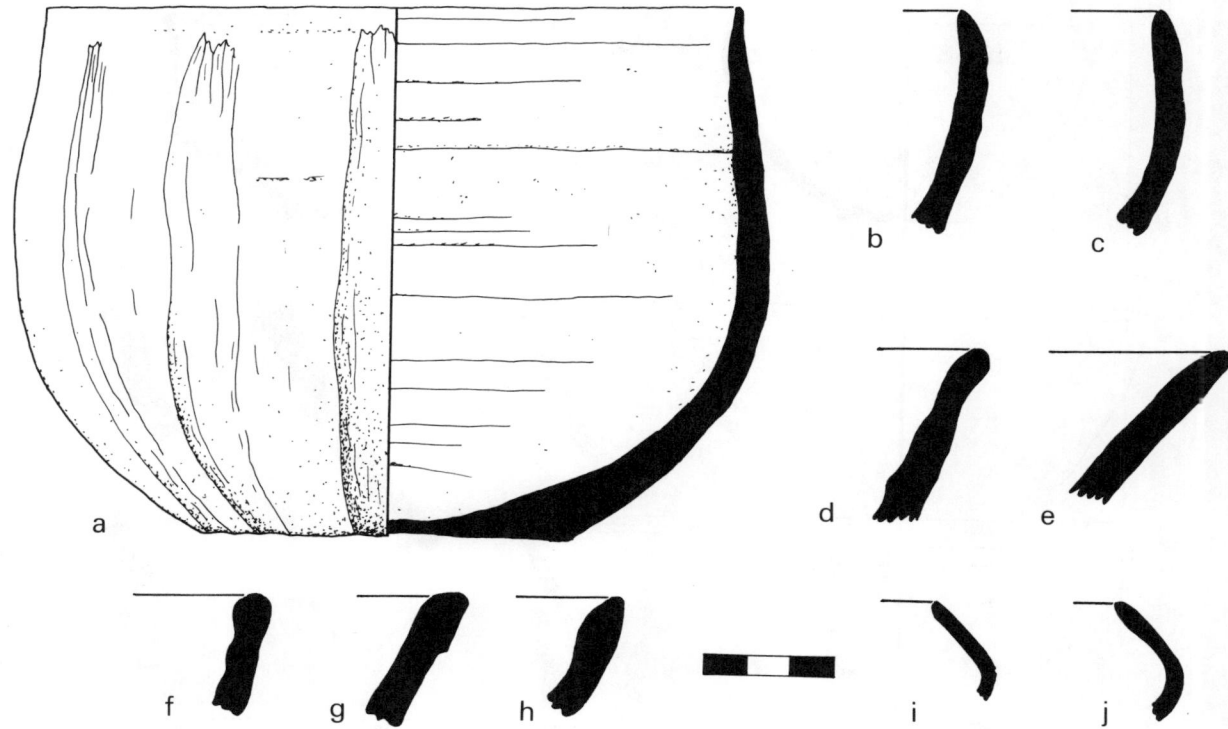

Fig. 46. Uruk Ware: Round Lip and Incurved Bowls. A. Round lip bowl with exterior fluting, fine sand, body pink, diam.: 16; X140, 6034002 (B F10). B. Round lip bowl rim, fine sand, body pink, diam.: 15; X244, 6038701 (B24). C. Same, fine sand, body very pale brown, diam.: 10; X217, 6017801 (A16). D. Same, fine sand, body very pale brown, diam.: 24; X176, 6035901 (B22). E. Same fine sand, body light reddish brown, diam.: 13; X429, 6048901 (B32). F. Same, fine sand, very pale brown, diam.: 18; X160, 6014801 (A13). G. Round lip bowl rim with exterior band, fine sand, body pink, diam.: 15; X244, 6038701 (B24). H. Round lip bowl rim with interior thickening fine sand, body pink, diam.: 11; X396, 6046201 (B30). I. Incurved bowl rim, coarse sand, body light red, diam.: 11; X282, 6040201 (B25). J. Same, fine sand, body very pale brown, diam.: 10; X120, 6013101 (A9,10).

JAR RIMS

Thickened Round Rim Jars (Fig. 42g,h,i): Most of these do not differ from the Sargarab form. The large examples usually have rough scraping on the body below the shoulder. Some examples of Late Uruk and Early Jemdet Nasr date are of fine textured clays containing small limestone and red chert pebbles rather than the usual range of coarse materials in the body. Some of these later examples have flattening on the inside of the rim. (Fig. 42i).

Round Lip Jars (Fig. 48,49): This simple form has a straight or slightly flared neck. The statistics show that the mean size changed little. Nevertheless one can detect considerable variation in shape through time. Flared thin varieties like the typical Sargarab round lip jar rim occur in the earlier Uruk (Fig. 48b,c,). Small straight (Fig. 48e,g,h) and thick flared (Fig. 48i,j) forms typify later Uruk. In the Jemdet Nasr, a thin high-necked variety develops (Fig. 49b,h-l). Here is a case where statistical studies of larger samples would surely allow us to isolate chronologically useful varieties.

Jars with Flattened Lips: The flattened jar rims of Uruk ware can be divided into two broad groups on the basis of a qualitative characteristic of the lip. In some cases the neck expands gradually until the flat lip is reached. These flared rims are probably created on the wheel by double and triple folding of the neck followed by a smoothing during rotation with decreasing pressure of the fingers. The resulting rim, frequently like an inverted triangle in cross-section, can then be pushed out, down, or up. A grooving of the flattened lip can result in an overhanging exterior ledge but such

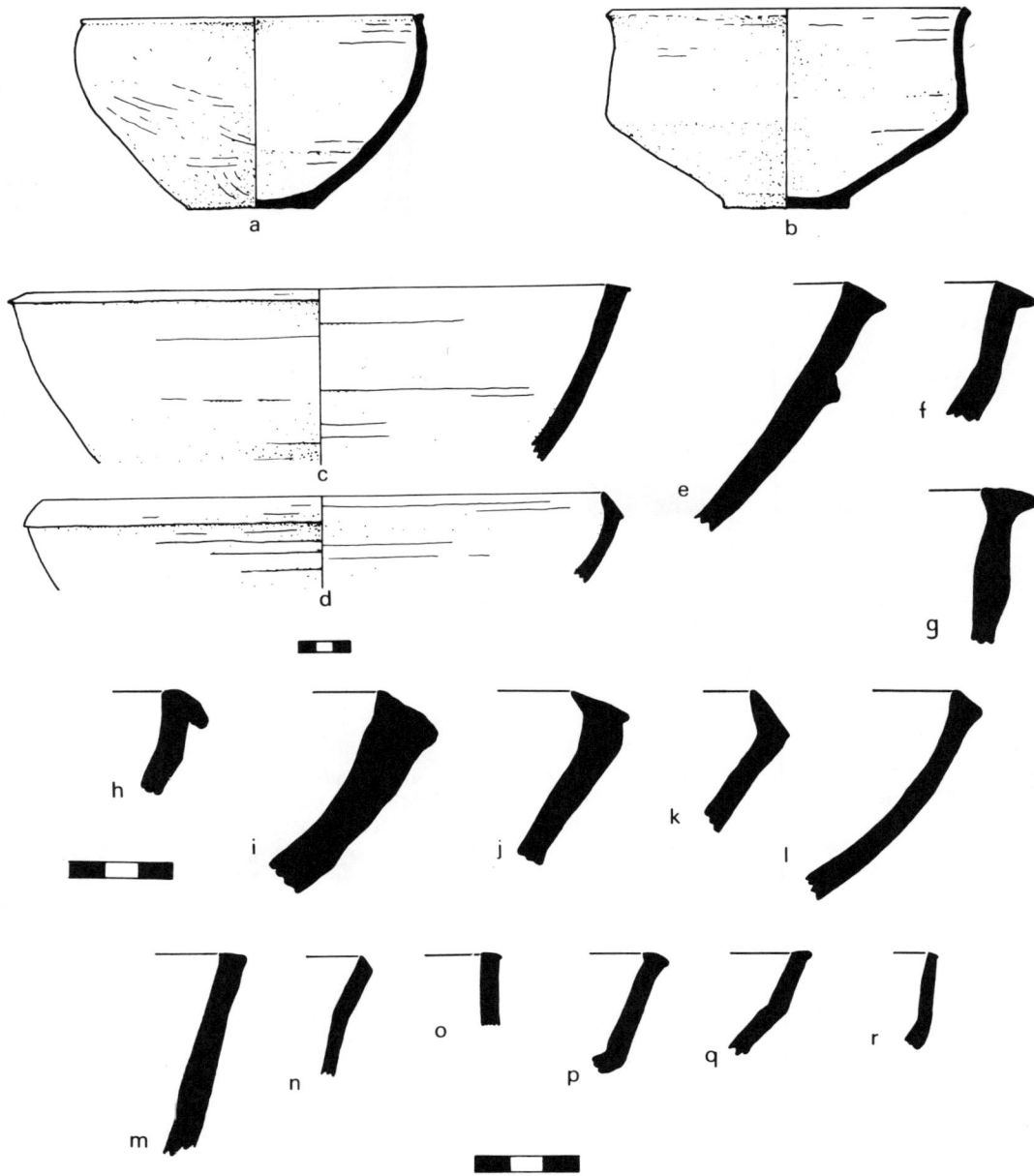

Fig. 47. Flat Lip Bowls. A. Flat lip bowl, fine sand, body pink to pinkish white, diam.: 22; X579, 6057802 (B34). B. Flat lip carinated bowl, fine sand, body white to pale yellow, diam.: 21; X579, 6057803 (B34). C. Ledge rim bowl rim, fine sand, body pink, diam.: 32; X306, 6083001 (A F19). D. Beveled lip bowl rim, fine sand, body pink, diam.: 42; X406, 6047101 (B31). E. Ledge rim bowl rim, fine sand, body pink, diam.: 34; X299, 6020401 (A20). F. Same, coarse sand, body pink, diam.: 45; X248, 6018009 (A17). G. Same, coarse sand, body white, diam.: 50; X396, 6046201 (B30). H. Same, fine sand, body pink, diam.: 31; X078, 6009401 (A6). I. Beveled lip bowl rim, fine sand, body pink, diam.: 41; X401, 6046401 (B30). J. Same, coarse sand, body pink, diam.: 33; X277, 6039501 (B25). K. Same, fine sand, body reddish yellow, diam.: 24; X401, 6046402 (B31). L. Same, coarse sand, body pink, diam.; 34; X299, 6020402 (A20). M. Flat lip bowl rim, fine sand, body pinkish gray, diam.: 37; X368, 6045201 (B29). N. Same, fine sand, body very pale brown, diam.: 20; X579, 6057801 (B33). O. Same, fine sand, body pale yellow, diam.: 15; X458, 6049502 (B32). P. Flat lip carinated bowl rim, fine sand, body pink, diam.: 30; X420, 6048101 (B31,32). Q. Same, fine sand, body pink, diam.: 24; X306, 6083001 (A F19). R. Same, fine sand, body pink, diam.: 11; X515, 6053504 (B33).

CERAMICS OF THE URUK, JEMDET NASR, AND EARLY DYNASTIC PHASES 103

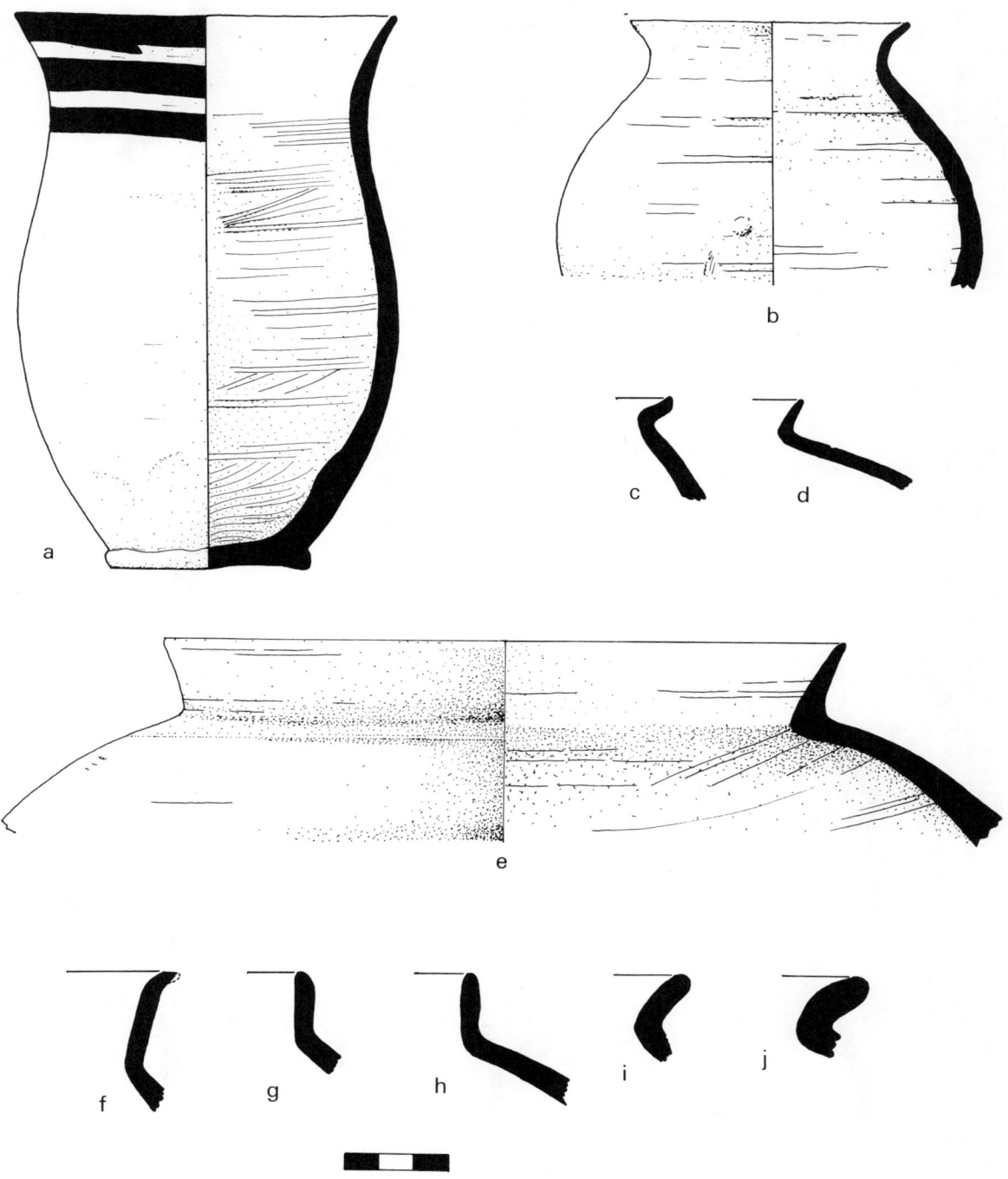

Fig. 48. Uruk Ware: Round Lip Jars of the Uruk Phases. A. Unusual round lip jar with painted bands and ring base, fine sand, body pink, paint very dark gray, diam.: 11, height: 16.5; X329 (A21). B. Round lip jar rim, fine sand, body pale yellow, diam.: 7; X481, 6051903 (B33). C. Same, fine sand, body white, diam.: 7; X468, 6050801 (B32). D. Same, fine sand, body white, diam.: 14; X404, 6046901 (B31). E. Same, fine sand, body very pale brown, diam.: 23; X396, 6046202 (B30). F. Same, fine sand, body pink, diam.: 10; X463, 6050001 (B32). G. Same, fine sand, body pink, diam.: 11; X462, 6049702 (B32). H. Same, fine sand, body very pale brown, diam.: 16; X462, 6049706 (B32). I. Same, coarse sand, body pink, diam.: 14; X368, 6045201 (B29). J. Same, fine sand and calcite, body pink, diam.: 19; X327, 6021201 (A21).

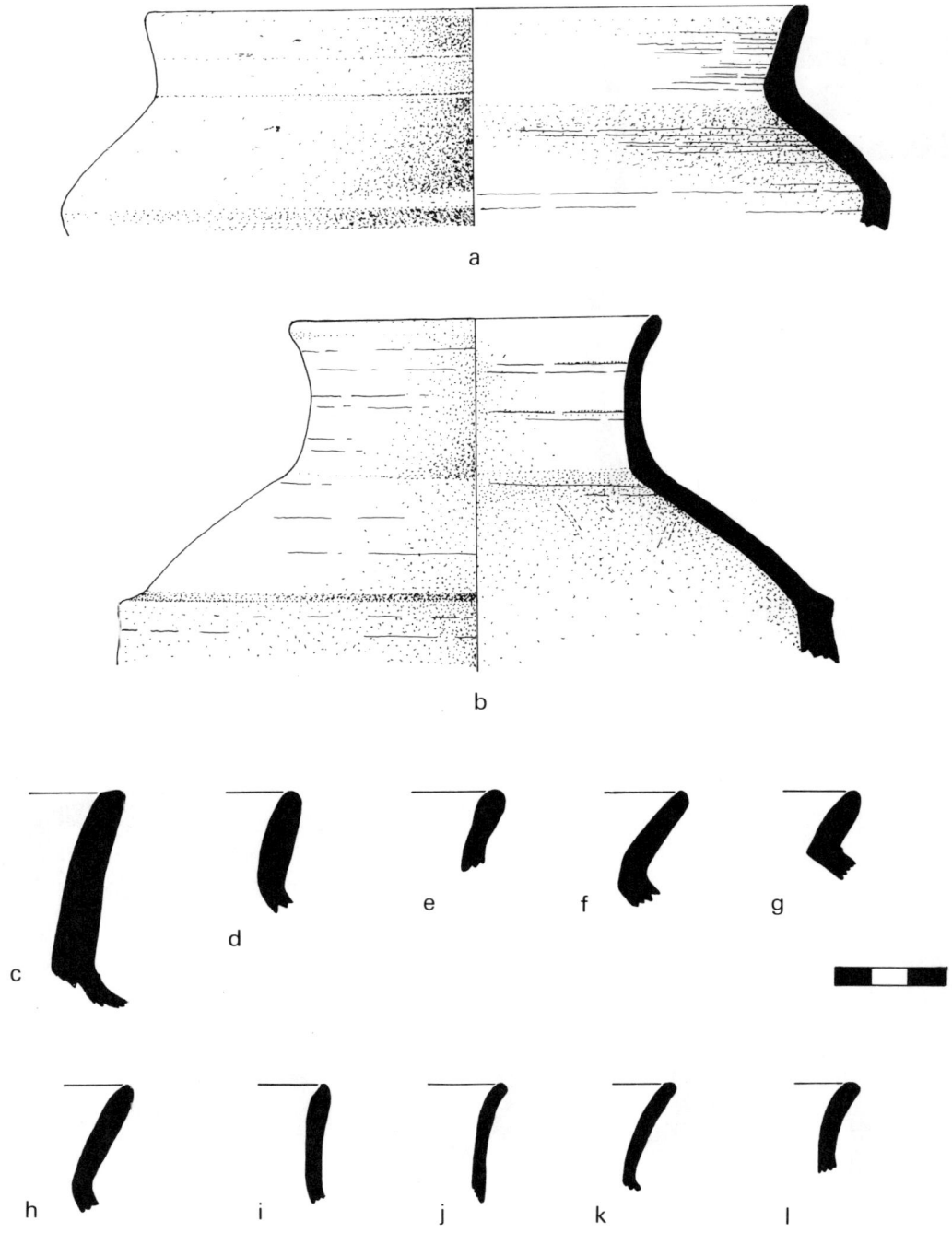

Fig. 49. Uruk Ware: Round Lip Jars of the Jemdet Nasr and Later Phases. A. Fine sand, body pink, diam.: 21; X167, 6035007 (B21). B. Fine sand, body pinkish gray, diam.: 12; X048, 6007905 (A3). C. Fine sand, body very pale brown, diam.: 21; X316, 6041702 (B27). D. Fine sand, body light reddish brown, diam.: 13; X101, 6011801 (A7). E. Coarse sand, body very pale brown, diam.: 13; X047, 6007702 (A3). F. Fine sand, body white, diam.: 19; X317, 6042002 (B27). G. Fine sand, body pink, diam.: 15; X316, 6041701 (B27). H. Fine sand, body very pale brown, diam.: 21; X228, 6036801 (B23). I. Fine sand, body white, diam.: 9; X078, 6009402 (A6). J. Fine sand, body pink, diam.: 11; X085, 6010601 (A7). K. Fine sand, body pink, diam.: 12; X085, 6010604 (A7). L. Fine sand, body pinkish white, slip reddish brown, diam.: 13; X060, 6008401 (A5).

CERAMICS OF THE URUK, JEMDET NASR, AND EARLY DYNASTIC PHASES

Table 23: Metrical Attributes of Round Rim Jar Rims

	Diameter (cm)		Rim Angle (degrees)		Neck Thickness (cm)		Neck Height (cm)	
	$\bar{x}$	s.d.	$\bar{x}$	s.d.	$\bar{x}$	s.d.	$\bar{x}$	s.d.
Late Jemdet Nasr N=29	13.6	4.0	61	15	.65	.23	2.05	.54
Early Jemdet Nasr N=12	14.8	4.8	47	18	.66	.19	2.01	1.14
Uruk N=39	15.9	11.4	66	17	.60	.22	1.85	.50

ledges are different in origin from those discussed below. This group is termed "Expanded Rims".

In other cases the neck is of roughly equal thickness from bottom to top and has a marked exterior ledge. Frequently there is a sharp break or quoin between ledge and neck. These are probably created on the wheel first by drawing up the clay from the shoulder-neck juncture with constant pressure, with at most a single folding of the neck. The resulting high rim is then pushed down with either a hand or tool held horizontally. The resulting rim, frequently like an inverted letter "L" in cross-section, can then be pushed down creating a band rim. This group is termed "Ledge Rims", and it includes "Bottles" and "Band Rim Jars" as well as "Ledge Rim Jars".

These technical interpretations are propositions which must be tested by analyzing cross-sections of both ancient and experimentally produced rims. It is possible that such analyses would indicate that these two qualitative groups are actually two poles of a continuum.

Small Expanded Rim Jars (Fig. 50a–f, Pl. 10c): These vessels are distinguished by vertical or slightly out-turned necks with a horizontal flat lip. They are frequently tempered with relatively coarse sand; they range in neck diameter from 9 to 20 cm, have shoulder grooving, and sometimes have strap handles (Fig. 50a, 55j, Pl. 10c) or horizontal twisted handles (Fig. 55k,l). One complete example with an almost spherical body is 13.3 cm high, 17.5 cm in maximum diameter, and 1.8 liters in volume (Fig. 50a).

Large Expanded Rim Jars (Fig. 50g–i): These vessels have out-turned necks and oblique lips. Their neck diameters range from 10 to 18 cm. The thicknesses suggest a relatively large vessel size.

Out-turned Expanded Rim Jars (Fig. 50 l–p): These vessels are distinguished by markedly out-turned, and therefore low, necks and a nearly horizontal flat lip. They approach true ledge rims but remain triangular in cross-section. Neck diameters range from 10 to 19 cm.

High Sloped Rim Jars (Fig. 50j–k): These few rims are distinguished by high, slightly expanded necks and a slight inward sloping flattening of the lip. One has a painted fugitive black band on the neck.

Flared Expanded Rim Jars (Fig. 51): These vessels are similar to the common Sargarab Ware form but are more variable. The necks curve or flare outward and the flat lips are oblique to vertical in orientation, more often the latter. Grooving of the lip occurs in almost half of the examples. Neck diameters range from 7 to 18 cm. Among the later examples at Farukhabad there may be two distinct varieties, one thicker with a low neck (Fig. 51k) approaching the low expanded band rims described below and one thinner with a high neck approaching the ledge rim form (Fig. 51 l–o).

Low Expanded Band Rim Jars (Fig. 52a–g): These vessels are similar to the Sargarab Ware High Expanded Band Rim Jars, but the necks have been pressed outward and downward to the point where there is often no neck remaining below the lip. The lips are vertical or even overhanging. Neck diameters range from 7 to 20 cm.

On one example there are small triangular punctations on the shoulder, on another there is a finger-impressed strip, and on several there is oblique reserved slip shoulder decoration. A miniature example has traces of black and red paint (Fig. 56o).

Other Expanded Rim Jars: There are three very heavy rims, large versions of the flared (Fig. 52i,j) and out-turned (Fig. 52h) types. There are two nearly identical rims with very low slightly out-

Fig. 50. Uruk Ware: Expanded Rim Jars. A. Small expanded rim jar with strap handle, coarse sand, body pink to pinkish gray, diam.: 11; X569, 6057101 (B35). B. Small expanded rim jar rim with shoulder grooving, coarse sand, body very pale brown, diam.: 11; X299, 6020402 (A20). C. Small expanded rim jar, coarse sand, body pink, diam.: 13; X293, 6019601 (A18). D. Same, fine sand, body pinkish gray, diam.: 22; X396, 6046205 (B30). E. Same, fine sand, body very pale brown, diam.: 22; X431, 6049101 (B32). F. Same with cross-hatch incising, fine sand, body reddish yellow, diam.: 11; X427, 6048402 (B30,31). G. Large expanded jar rim, coarse sand and limestone, body pink, slip dark red, diam.: 15; X562, 6056301 (B35). H. Same, fine sand, body white, diam.: 29; X373, 6045704 (B29). I. Same, fine sand and calcite, body white, diam.: 22; X560, 6056101 (B34). J. High sloped jar rim, coarse sand, body very pale brown, diam.: 16; X458, 6049501 (B32). K. Same, fine sand, body very pale brown, diam.: 12; X396, 6046201 (B30). L. Out-turned expanded jar rim, fine sand, body pinkish gray, diam.: 22; X396, 6046205 (B30). M. Same, fine sand, body white, diam.: 13; X292, 6019301 (A18). N. Same, coarse sand, body very pale brown, diam.: 18; X284, 6040601 (B27). O. Same, fine sand, body very pale brown, diam.: 17; X406, 6047101 (B31). P. Same, fine sand, body pinkish gray, diam.: 24; X367, 6045001 (B29).

CERAMICS OF THE URUK, JEMDET NASR, AND EARLY DYNASTIC PHASES 107

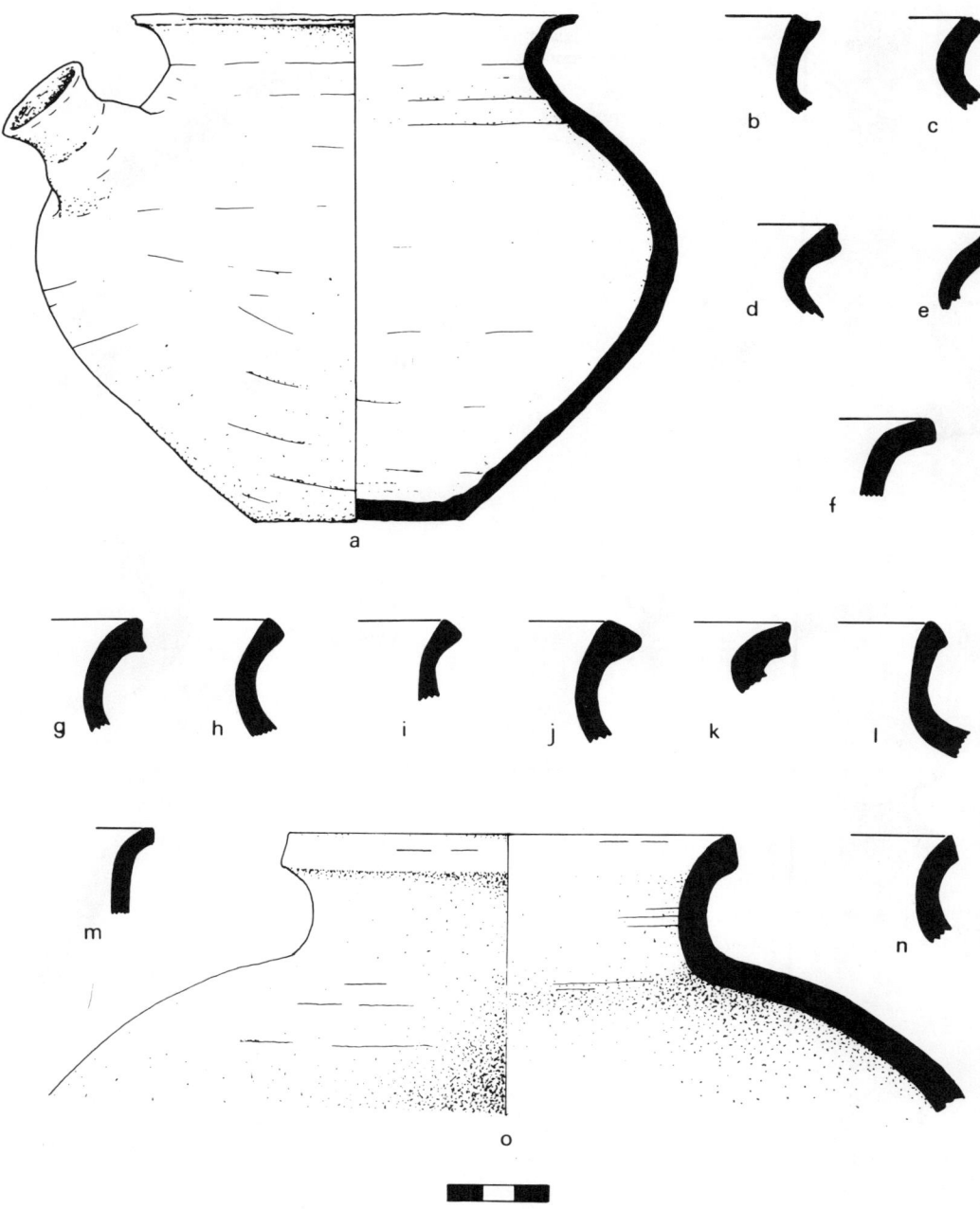

Fig. 51. Uruk Ware: Flared Expanded Jar Rims. A. Flared expanded rim jar with spout, medium sand, body pink, diam.: 13; X579, 60578 (B34). B. Flared expanded rim jar rim, calcite and coarse sand, body pink to pinkish gray, diam.: 14; X588, 6058701 (B36). C. Same, medium sand and calcite, body light brown, slip red, diam.: 10; X522, 6054301 (B34). D. Same, medium sand, body white, diam.: 12; X481, 6051902 (B33). E. Same, coarse sand, body light yellowish brown, diam.: 16; X476, 6051402 (B33). F. Same, fine sand, body very pale brown, diam.: 14; X432, 6049301 (B31). G. Same, coarse sand, body very pale brown, diam.: 14; X284, 6040603 (B27). H. Same, coarse sand, body white, diam.: 20; X313, 6041202 (B F18). I. Same, coarse sand, body white, diam.: 19; X313, 6041201 (B F18). J. Same, fine sand, body white, diam.: 16; X277, 6039501 (B25). K. Same, fine sand, body light gray, diam.: 15; X157, 6014301 (A13). L. Same, fine sand, body light reddish brown, diam.: 14; X047, 6007701 (A3). M. Same, fine sand, body white, diam.: 9; X298, 6077701 (B20). N. Same, fine sand, body light brown, diam.: 13; X272, 60392 (B F15). O. Same, fine sand, body pink to light brown, diam.: 12; X087, 6010301 (A7).

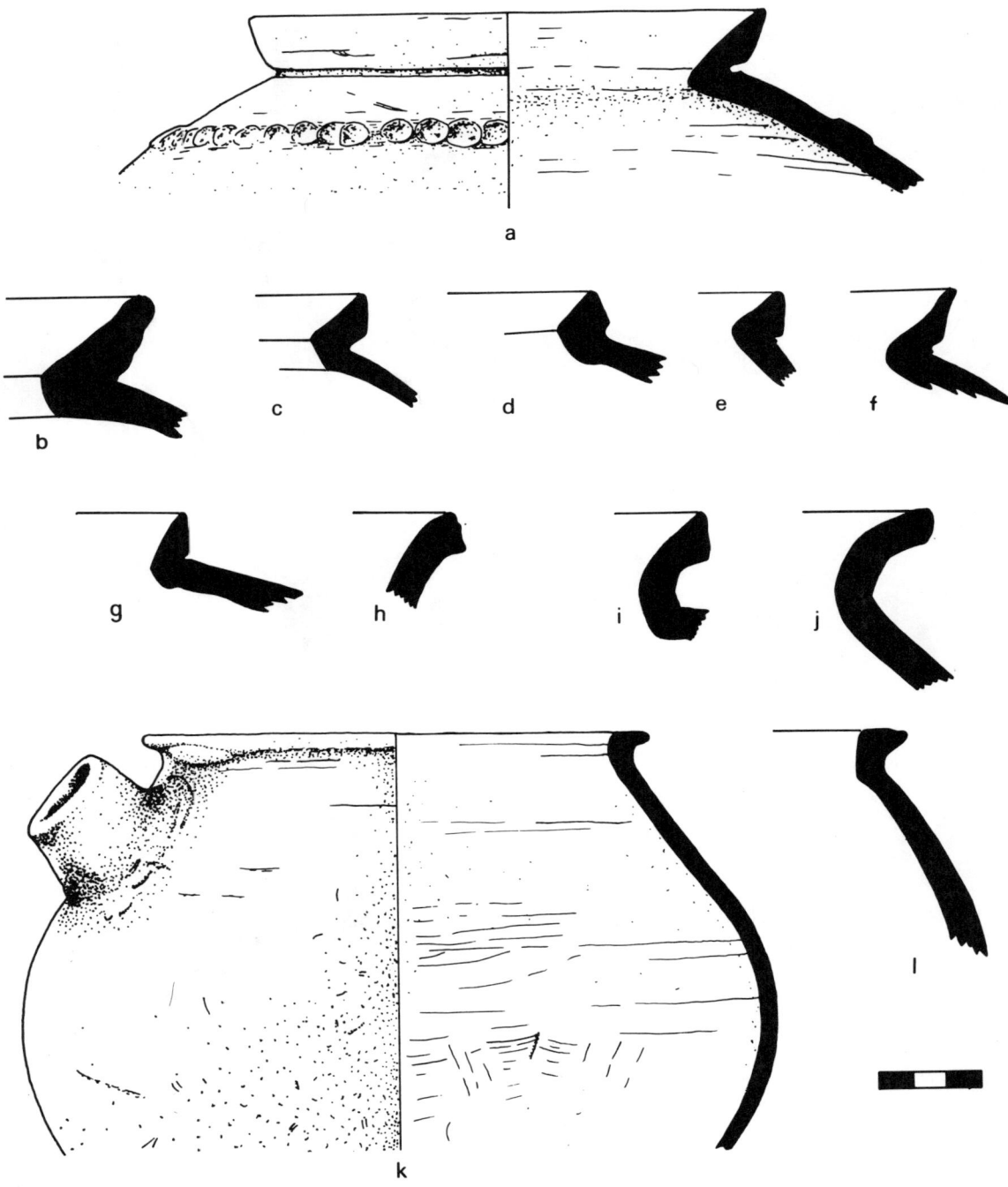

Fig. 52. Uruk Ware: Low Expanded and Other Jar Rims. A. Low expanded band rim jar rim, coarse sand and straw, body very pale brown, diam.: 14; X321, 6042401 (B28). B. Same, coarse sand, body pale yellow, diam.: 26; X338, 6083303 (A F19). C. Same, coarse sand, body pink, diam.: 16; X401, 6046301 (B30). D. Same, fine sand, body very pale brown, diam.: 12; X396, 6046203 (B30). E. Same, coarse sand, body pinkish white, diam.: 12; X295, 6020001 (A19). F. Same, coarse sand, body white, diam.: 14; X256, 6018501 (A17–19). G. Same, fine sand, body white, diam.: 13; X306, 6083001 (A F19). H. Other expanded rim jar, fine sand, body very pale brown, diam.: 19; X228, 6036801 (B23). I. Same, coarse sand and calcite, body very pale brown, diam.: 16; X531, 6054901 (B34). J. Same, calcite and fine sand, body pink, diam.: 14; X223, 6082702 (A20). K. Same, coarse sand and calcite, body white to pale yellow, diam.: 8; X579, 6057801 (B35). L. Same, fine sand, body white, diam.: 18; X458, 6049503 (B32).

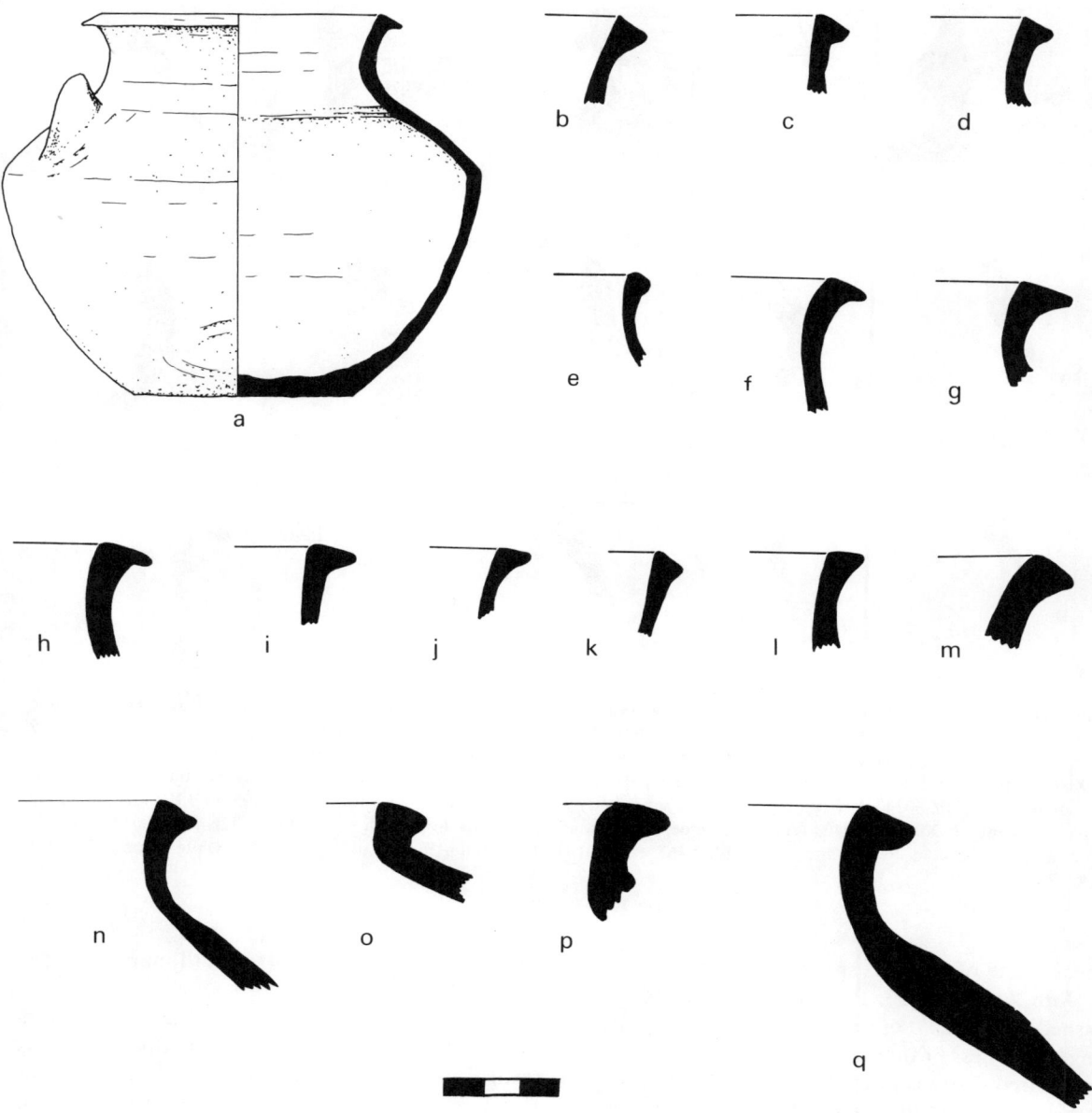

Fig. 53. Uruk Ware: Ledge Rim Jars. A. Miniature ledge rim jar with appendage, fine sand, body pink, diam.: 7; X272, 6039301 (B23). B. Ledge rim jar rim, fine sand, body very pale brown, diam.: 10; X217, 6017801 (A16). C. Same, fine sand, body very pale brown, diam.: 12; X240, 6038002 (B24). D. Same, coarse sand, body pink to pinkish gray, diam.: 12; X125, 6013302 (A11). E. Same, fine sand, body pink to pinkish white, diam.: 9; X235, 6037503 (B24). F. Same, fine sand, body light reddish brown, diam.: 13; X161, 6015001 (A13). G. Same, fine sand, body light gray, diam.: 13; X160, 6014801 (A13). H. Same, fine sand, body pink to light reddish brown, diam.: 14, X161, 6015002 (A13). I. Same, coarse sand, body very pale brown, diam.: 13; X373, 6045703 (B29). J. Same, fine sand, body very pale brown, diam.: 11; X173, 6035405 (B23). K. Same, fine sand, body white, diam.: 11; X104, 6012401 (A8). L. Same, fine sand, body white, diam.: 13; X176, 6035901 (B22). M. Same, fine sand, body white, diam.: 18; X043, 6007502 (A1–2). N. Same, coarse sand, body very pale brown, diam.: 13; X313, 6041203 (B F18). O. Same, fine sand, body white, diam.: 16; X403, 6046703 (B30). P. Same, fine sand, body pink, diam.: 22; X401, 6046401 (B30). Q. Same, coarse sand, body very pale brown, diam.: 16; X176, 6035902 (B22).

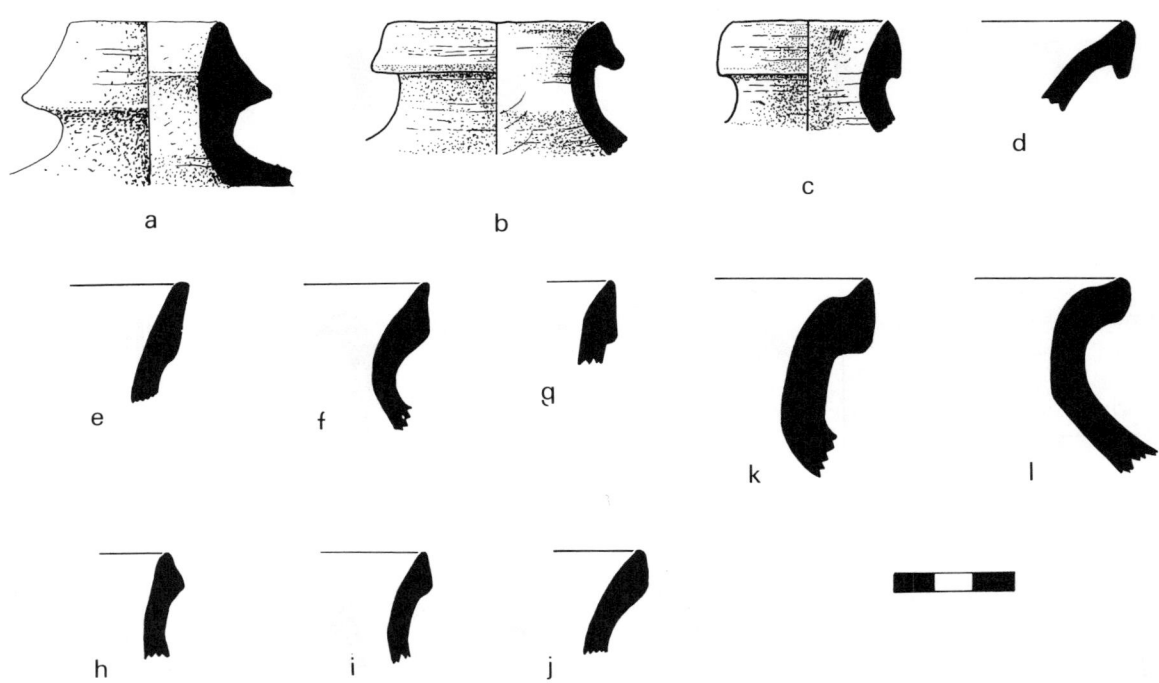

Fig. 54. Uruk Ware: Bottles and Band Rim Jars. A. Bottle, fine sand and limestone, body pink, diam.: 6; X396, 6046206 (B30). B. Same, fine sand and limestone, body pale yellow, diam.: 3; X588, 6055901 (B34). C. Same, fine sand and straw, body pale yellow, diam.: 3; X515, 6053503 (B33). D. Band rim jar rim, coarse sand, body very pale brown, diam.: 19; X324, 6043001 (B F15). E. Same, fine sand, body pink, diam.: 13; X087, 6010302 (A7). F. Same, fine sand, body very pale brown, diam.: 13; X229, 6037002 (B23). G. Same, fine sand, body very pale brown, diam.: 13; X140, 6034001 (B20). H. Same, fine sand, body very pale brown, diam.: 10; X272, 6039301 (B F15). I. Same, fine sand, body pink, diam.: 9; X060, 6008403 (A5,6). J. Same, coarse sand, body pink to pinkish white, diam.: 13; X196, 6017001 (A15). K. Lock rim jar rim, fine sand, body white, diam.: 17; X167, 6035001 (B21). L. Same, fine sand, body pinkish white, diam.: 12; X223, 6082701 (A F19).

turned necks, one of which is spouted (Fig. 52k,l).

Ledge Rim Jars (Fig. 53, Plate 11b): These are distinguished by necks of constant or slightly increasing thickness ranging from vertical to slightly outflared. Vessels range from 6 to 16 cm in neck diameter. The flat lips vary in thickness from horizontal to oblique in orientation. There may be a differentiation between thin and thick ledge forms in later Jemdet Nasr. The earliest example (Fig. 57) has painted black bands on the shoulder and lip. A complete miniature example is illustrated in Fig. 53a and Plate 11b. Its height is 10.0 cm; its maximum diameter is 12.0 cm and its volume is .6 liters.

Bottles (Fig. 54a–c): These are distinguished by very small neck diameters, ranging from two to six cm. Ledge and band rim variants exist. In other localities such forms occur on tall, narrow bodies which often have drooping spouts.

Band Rim Jars (Fig. 54d–j): These are distinguished by a relatively thick lip which is nearly vertical in orientation. In some terminologies such a rim is termed "collared". These were perhaps created by pressing a ledge rim down until it was flat against the neck. However it is possible that some of these were made by grooving the lower neck. These range in neck diameter from 7 to 27 cm.

Other Ledge Rims (Fig. 53o–q): There are three very heavy ledge rims.

Lock Rim Jars (Fig. 54k,l): There are some heavy band rim jars with marked grooves in the interior of the lip. This could guide the placement of a lid on the jar.

CERAMICS OF THE URUK, JEMDET NASR, AND EARLY DYNASTIC PHASES

OTHER JAR PARTS

The vessel groupings (which have been defined on the basis of rim form alone) in some cases have distinctive shoulder decorations, appendages such as handles and spouts, body forms, and bases. Ideally these should be included in the type descriptions; in most cases these associations are unknown, however, and they will remain unknown until larger numbers of complete or reconstructable vessels have been found. Meanwhile the jar parts must be described separately.

Impressed Strips (Figs. 52a, 55h): These elements are primarily from the juncture of jar bodies and shoulders. They were drawn up from the body of the vessel rather than applied after vessel construction. The impressions were made either with a finger or with a sharp object such as a stick. They vary considerably in size of strip, size of impression, and orientation of impression. There are general correlations between size of strip, size of impression, and thickness of jar body, but there are no definable categories of strip. Strips with closely spaced vertical finger impressions, which are typical of both Early Uruk bowls and a few Early Uruk Jars, are not included in this category. A rare variant with multiple impressed strips occurs (Fig. 55h).

Cross-Hatched Incised Bands (Fig. 50f, 55a,b): These are placed around the middle of the shoulder between two incised horizontal lines. The crossed series of oblique lines create a lattice of parallelograms. These bands are often associated with nose lugs and tend to occur on the larger varieties of expanded rim jar. The cross-hatched triangle is a late variant of this design (Fig. 55e, Plate 11c).

Black-on-Buff Painted Decoration: Horizontal straight and curved lines in dark paints occur on a variety of bowl and jar forms. A slightly incurved flat lip bowl has two pairs of straight lines (Fig. 56j), while a carinate flat lip bowl has both straight lines and curved lines (Fig. 56n). An ordinary ledge rim jar has straight lines on its shoulder (Fig. 56k), while a jar lacking a neck and with a variant ledge rim has straight and curved lines bordering a curved one (Fig. 56l). Two later jar rims, one a small ledge rim of bottle size (Fig. 56p) and one a flared flat lip (Fig. 56m) have closely spaced but poorly drafted straight and curved lines. Thus, monochrome decoration occurs on a wide variety of vessel shapes during a long period of time. It perhaps represents occasional experimentation rather than a continuing tradition.

Black-on-Red Painted Decoration: In the description of the Sargarab Ware vessels, I noted a number of jars and bowls with red slips and simple black painted bands. The techniques are applied to small jars of Uruk Ware as well. There is a restorable example from the burial found eroding between Excavations A and B (Fig. 57a), which is 12 cm high and 16 cm in maximum diameter. Its neck diameter is 5.0 cm, and there is a straight, slightly everted neck which probably had a round lip. A similar rim with neck diameter of only 1.3 cm (Fig. 57b) and a flared expanded rim with a neck diameter of 13.0 cm define the range of variation. The shoulders usually have appliqué elements; 70 percent have a small hatched strip near the neck, and half exhibit nose lugs. After the red slip is applied, concentric bands are painted in black on the shoulder, though in the smallest vessel these have been obliterated (Fig. 57b). Between these bands, a number of motifs are attested. Among these are curved lines (Fig. 57a), zig-zag lines (Fig. 57a), cross-hatch (Fig. 57i), arcs filled with grids (Fig. 57i–k), and triangles filled with grids (Fig. 57d) or lines (Fig. 57h). Between any two bands there is only one variety of motif, in contrast to the later polychrome jar shoulders. Nevertheless, these little jars certainly exhibit many of the features which came to distinguish the polychrome styles.

Polychrome Painted Decoration (Fig. 58–61, Plate 1): The relatively small excavations at Farukhabad produced a remarkably large series of polychrome sherds. These ceramics, closely related to the Jemdet Nasr and scarlet ware polychrome styles of Mesopotamia proper and the Diyala region (Delougaz 1952: pp.35–37, 48, 51, 60–72; Plates 7–15, 18, 33, 36, 52–62), will probably be of greater interest to some readers than other aspects of the Farukhabad data, so I will devote considerable space to their consideration.

The black and red painted jars of the Late Uruk and subsequent periods are a development distinct from earlier styles of ceramic painting. Their distinctiveness lies not in the use of several colors, which occasionally occurs on Susiana Ware vessels, or in their motifs, as most of these occur on earlier wares, but in the way in which the overall design of the vessel is composed. Most Bayat, Farukh, and earlier Uruk painted vessels are first divided into a set of bands one below the other. Each band is filled

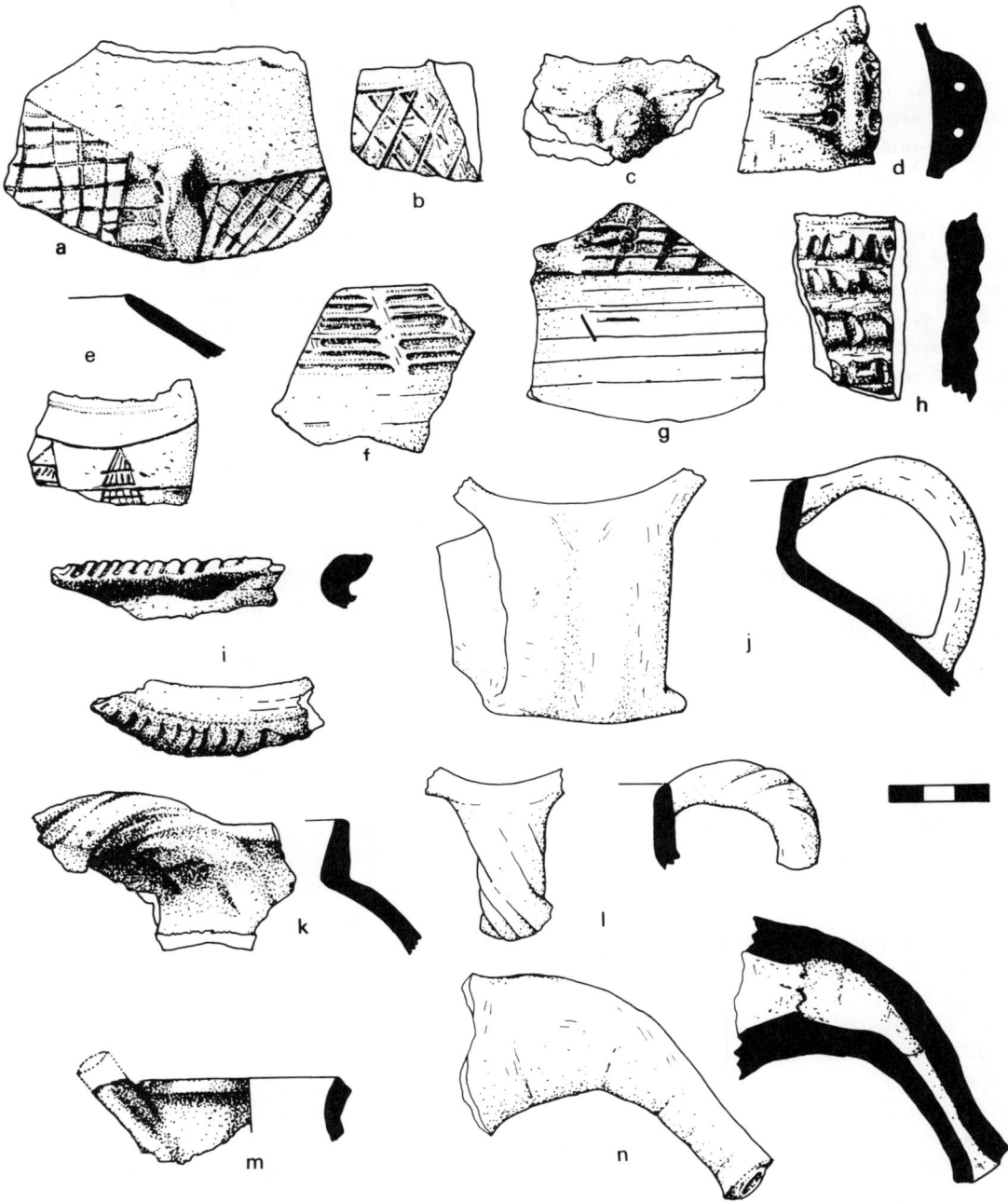

Fig. 55. Uruk Ware: Jar Appendages and Textured Motifs. A. Cross-hatch incised band with nose lug, fine sand, body yellow; X458, 6049501 (B32). B. Cross-hatch incised band, fine sand, body pinkish white; X403, 6046701 (B30). C. Node without perforation, fine sand, body pale yellow; X365, 60446 (B28). D. Nose lug with two perforations, fine sand and calcite, body pink; X217, 60178 (A16). E. Incised triangle, fine sand and calcite, body pink; X587, 60583 (B36). F. Incised grooves with oblique incisions, fine sand and calcite, body pink; X356, 6044001 (B F21). G. Incised grooves with oblique incisions, fine sand, body pink; X306, 6083001 (A19). H. Multiple impressed strip, fine sand and straw, body white; X645, 60622 (B40). I. Lip lug, fine sand and calcite, body light brown; X298, 60777 (A20). J. Strap handle on straight round lip jar, fine sand, body very pale brown, rim diam.: 13; X338, 6083301 (A F19). K. Horizontal twisted handle, limestone and coarse sand, body reddish yellow; X295, 60200 (A19). L. Twisted handle on straight round lip jar rim, fine sand, body reddish yellow, rim diam.: 8; X399 (B30). M. Attached spout, fine sand, body pink; X374, 60838 (A F19). N. Droop spout, fine sand, body light reddish brown; X588, 6058701 (B36).

CERAMICS OF THE URUK, JEMDET NASR, AND EARLY DYNASTIC PHASES

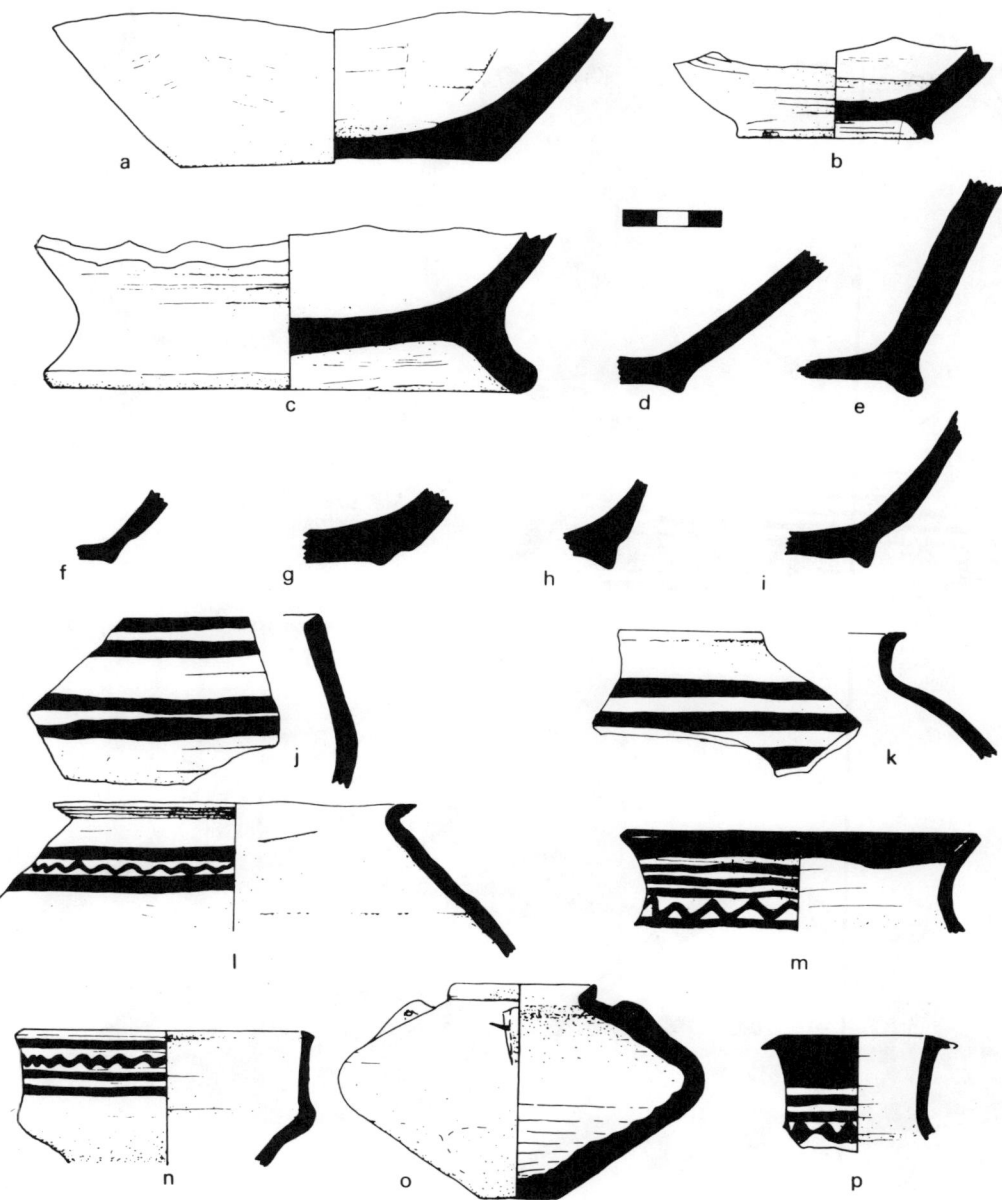

Fig. 56. Uruk Ware: Bases and Monochrome Decoration. A. Flat base, fine sand, straw and calcite, body pink to pinkish gray, slip red, base diam.: 10; X596, 6059201 (B36). B. Turned ring base, fine sand, body yellow, ring diam.: 6; X528, 60546 (B34). C. Same, fine sand, body light brown, ring diam.: 15; X048, 6007908 (A3). D. Same, fine sand, body pink, ring diam. 6; X359, 6044401 (B29). E. Same, fine sand, body pink, ring diam.: 11.5; X104, 6012401 (A8). F. Pinched ring base, fine sand, body white, ring diam.: 5; X047, 6007702 (A3). G. Same, fine sand, body pink to reddish yellow, ring diam.: 9.5; X048, 6007902 (A3). H. Same, fine sand, body very pale brown, ring diam.: 8; X040, 6007101 (A1,2). I. Same, calcite and fine sand, body reddish yellow, slip weak red, ring diam.: 12.5; X173, 6035401 (B23). J. Flat lip bowl with horizontal bands, fine sand, body 10YR 7/4 (very pale brown), paint 2.5Y 3/0 (very dark gray), diam.: 18; X433 (B31). K. Ledge rim jar with horizontal bands, fine sand, body 10YR 8/2 (white), paint 7.5YR 3/0, (very dark gray), diam.: 10; X514, 60533 (B33). L. Variant ledge rim jar with horizontal straight and curved lines, fine sand, body 7.5YR 8/4 (pink), paint 10YR 3/2 (very dark grayish brown) diam.: ca. 10; X338, 60833 (A20). M. Flared flat lip jar with horizontal straight and curved lines, fine sand, body 2.5Y 8/2 (white), paint 10YR 3/2 (very dark grayish brown), diam.: 9; X175 (B22). N. Carinate flat lip bowl with horizontal straight and curved lines, fine sand, body 5Y 8/2 (white), paint 5Y 5/3 (olive) diam.: 9; X531, 60559 (B34). O. Miniature low expanded band rim jar with nose lugs and traces of red and black painted design, fine sand, body 2.5Y 8.2 (white), paints damaged, diam.: 4.3; X467, 60785 (B32). P. Ledge rim jar with horizontal straight and curved lines, fine sand, body 2.5Y 8.3 (white), paint 2.5Y 3/1 (very dark gray), diam.: 3.4; X206 (B22).

Fig. 57. Uruk Ware: Black-on-Red Decoration. A. Round lip jar with nose lugs, straight and curved horizontal lines, fine sand, body 5YR 7/6 (reddish yellow), slip 2.5YR 6/7 (light red), paint weathered light gray, diam.: 5.3, shoulder diam.: 15.3, height: 13.0; X557, 60557 (B34). B. Round lip jar rim with nose lug, fine calcite, body 7.5YR 7/5 (pink), slip 5YR 6/6 (reddish yellow), diam.: 4.0, shoulder diam.: 7.0; X508, 60522 (B33). C. Fine jar variant with straight lines, fine calcite and straw, body 7.5YR 6/4 (light brown), slip 10R 4/3 (dusky red), paint weathered dark brown, diam.: 5.0, shoulder diam.: 9.6, height: 6.5; X567 (B35). D. Round lip jar with nose lugs, straight lines and triangles, fine sand, body 5YR 5/4 (reddish yellow), slip 10R 4/6 (red), paint 2.5 YR 3/0 (very dark gray), diam.: 6.0, shoulder diam.: 15.3, height: 10.9; X545 (Burial between Excavations A and B). E. Jar shoulder with nose lug, straight lines, fine calcite and sand, body 5YR 7/4 (pink), slip 10R 5/6 (red), paint 10R 4/1 (dark reddish gray), neck diam.: 7; X515, 60536 (B33). F. Round lip jar rim with nose lug, straight lines, fine sand, body 5YR 8/4 (pink), slip 7.5R 7/6 (light red), paint weathered gray, diam.: 7.0; X459 (B32). G. Jar shoulder with nose lug, straight lines and zig-zag variant, fine calcite, body 2.5Y 8/3 (white), slip 7.5R 4/6 (red), paint 5YR 3/1 (very dark gray), neck diam.: 4.5; X365, 60446 (B28). H. Jar shoulder with nose lug, straight lines and triangles, fine sand, body 5YR 5/4 (reddish brown), slip 7.5R 4/6 (red), paint 7.5YR 2/0 (black), neck diam.: 11; X370 (B29). I. Jar shoulder with straight lines, cross-hatch, and arcs; fine sand, body 2.5YR 6/6 (light red), slip 10R 4/5 (red), paint 5YR 4/1 (dark gray), neck diam.: 8.5; X481, 60519 (B33). J. Jar shoulder with grid, fine sand, body 10YR 4/3 (brown), slip 10R 5/6 (red), paint weathered, neck diam.: ca. 10; X429, 60489 (B32). K. Jar shoulder with cross-hatch, dots, and arcs; fine sand body 5YR 6/6 (reddish yellow), slip 7.5R 4/6 (red), paint 2.5YR 3/1 (very dark gray); X508, 60522 (B33).

with a motif which is repeated serially. The exceptions to this compositional approach are the small low-necked jars of the Farukh Phase on which the circumferential bands are sometimes broken vertically into segments each of which is filled with a different motif. (Fig. 24h–j). In contrast, the later Polychrome jars are divided horizontally creating bands, these are subdivided vertically creating 'segments', and these can be subdivided yet again to produce either horizontal or vertical 'plats'. Preferences for symmetries and for certain motif combinations are clear. In order to use the variations within and between local traditions of the Jemdet Nasr Style to elucidate social relations, we must first be able to clearly describe each one of the often complex motif combinations on a vessel. This cannot be done by simply listing motifs in the manner in which Farukh and Bayat ceramics were described. In this section, I will attempt to develop a set of symbols and rules which express the variations of polychrome design.

Since I am constructing a formalization on the basis of relatively few fragmentary polychrome jars, this effort will be necessarily simplified. It is important to note that an approach of the sort proposed below is a descriptive device. While ideally it would allow one to generate new polychrome jars acceptable to Jemdet Nasr painters, one does not know whether the painters actually used the particular "design grammar" proposed. This is, however, irrelevant to our present purpose, which is to rigorously assess variation within and between painted pottery samples. In some cases, there are two equally acceptable ways of symbolizing an aspect of the painting. For example, on Figure 62 the reader will note that motif B is merely a horizontal version of Motif A, as is also the case with D and C, K and J, and M and L. I could have created an operator which expressed the vertical versus the horizontal orientation of symbols. However, it seemed to me that there were already too many rules, and there were few enough motif symbols, so I chose to create more motifs. This arbitrary choice on my part will not affect the utility of the scheme in comparative studies as long as the same choice is consistently made.

The rules and basic terms of the formalization are as follows:

1) A description of a vessel involves three *statements* dealing with a) the neck, b) the shoulder, c) the side. Each statement deals with the *surface* of a truncated cone or distorted cylinder.

2) The surface is divided horizontally into one or more *bands*. In a descriptive statement, the bands are considered from top to bottom and the elements in each band are enclosed in parentheses. Within an undivided band, motifs can only be repeated horizontally. If two different motif elements are alternated within a band, one should begin with the most complex.

3) A band may be subdivided vertically into two or more *segments*. In a descriptive statement the elements in each segment are enclosed in parentheses. Within an undivided segment, motifs can only be repeated vertically. The most complex segment in a band is always considered first.

4) A segment may be sub-divided horizontally into two or more *plats*: a) If a plat contains only one motif, then in a descriptive statement, the motif symbol is enclosed in parentheses; b) if a plat contains vertically repeated motifs, then in a descriptive statement, these motifs are enclosed in oblique slashes thus: "/.../"; c) if a plat contains horizontally repeated motifs then in a descriptive statement, these motifs are enclosed in a set of sideways vs, the left with top facing right and the right with top facing left, thus: "<...>".

5) Any two surfaces, bands, segments, or plats may be separated by a *border* composed of straight lines of one or two colors. If one color is used for more than one successive line, then the border is considered to be a motif in a descriptive statement. Borders are expressed with a sequence of color codes separated by commas and not enclosed in parentheses.

6) In a statement, a *comma* is used to separate elements of similar magnitude such as color codes in borders as noted above, or successive alternated motifs in a band, segment, or plat.

7) In a descriptive statement a *motif* is symbolized by a capital letter, and its color or colors by "rd" for the light, usually red, paints, "bl" for the dark, usually black, plaints, and "rdbl" or "blrd" for a combination of the two. A variant motif is labeled with a *plus*.

8) In a descriptive statement, the fact that previous or subsequent motifs are broken off is indicated by a *dash*, "–" appropriately

enclosed in parentheses or other enclosing symbols.

9) In a descriptive statement, the fact that any element, whether it be a motif, a combination of motifs, a plat, a segment, or a band, is to be repeated until the end of the space indicated by an enclosing symbol, is symbolized by dots, ". . . ."

10) In a descriptive statement, if the vessel's design is attested to the base, the end of the vessel description is indicated by a *period*.

Eighteen motifs occur repeatedly on the neck, shoulder, and side of polychrome jars from Tepe Farukhabad. Measurements of some of those more commonly preserved are given in Table C3 in the Appendices. The occurrence of motifs in layers is given in Table 24.

A) *Vertical Straight Line* (Fig. 58a,c,e,k;60a,f; 61l,m): This is composed of parallel lines extending from an upper band to a lower band of the same color. These bands are described as part of the border. Some examples of this motif are slightly oblique rather than perfectly vertical. This occurs on all surfaces of the vessel: neck, shoulder, and side. It always stands alone on the neck, but is commonly alternated with Horizontal Opposed Triangles (M) on the shoulder and side. It may be either red or black; there is one example with both. It occurs in all periods of polychrome development.

B) *Horizontal Straight Lines* (Fig. 60a,e,f): This is composed of two or more parallel lines either as a horizontal fill in a segment or plat or as a circumferential band. It is found on necks and shoulders. On the latter it is sometimes alternated vertically in segments or plats with Vertical Opposed Triangles (L). This motif is more common in the later periods of polychrome development.

C) *Vertical Curved Lines* (Fig. 58): This contains a series of curved lines, usually out of phase rather than parallel. It occurs only on shoulders. Red examples are more common. The only black example is early, while the two alternated red and black examples, both very irregularly drafted (Fig. 58d), are relatively late.

D) *Horizontal Curved Lines* (Fig. 58b,g,h,i; 59d,61b,l): This contains a series of one or more circumferential curved lines usually out of phase. It occurs on necks, shoulders, and sides. It is usually red although black and combined examples occur. It is relatively late on necks, but it occurs throughout the polychrome development on shoulders and sides.

E) and F) *Isosceles Triangles* (Fig. 58g–k): This is composed of triangles with bases down repeated horizontally. The triangles have heavy defining black lines sometimes with additional parallel black lines outside of these (Fig. 58j). These triangles occur only on shoulders. Those with a solid fill are termed E; those with cross-hatch fill are termed F. A majority of the latter have black cross hatch; some have black lines one way and red lines the other (Fig. 58g,h). Triangle motifs are common early in the development.

G) *Diamonds* (Fig. 59b;61k): This is constructed by drafting a cross-hatch in a narrow segment or plat in such a way that the upper one quarter of each oblique line is not drawn in. The resulting series of vertically arranged diamonds is solidly filled in. This motif is known only on shoulders. It is either all black or black outlines with a red fill. It occurs early in the polychrome development.

H) *Arc and Ray* (Fig. 59c–i;61f): The arc is the critical element of this motif. In one case the arc is left open and rest of the band is filled in. In other cases the arc is filled in, but the rest of the plat is left untouched. In most cases, however, the arc is filled and there is at least one further arc parallel to the curve of the first from which small rays radiate. Sometimes there is a plain line and a rayed line (Fig. 59c,e) and sometimes there are two rayed lines (Fig. 59h). This motif occurs on shoulders and sides. It is usually black, though combined red and black examples occur. Arcs and rays occur through most of the polychrome development.

I) *Branch* (Fig. 59a,j–n;60a;61i): Composed of one, three, or five branches, each of which has narrow opposed leaves resembling a young date palm. Most occur on shoulders; one is on a side. A branch-like element is sometimes associated with the Caprid motif (R) as vegetation around the feet of the

CERAMICS OF THE URUK, JEMDET NASR, AND EARLY DYNASTIC PHASES

animal. The earliest example has a black stem and red leaves. The remainder are completely black. These occur late.

J) *Vertical Straight and Curved Lines* (Fig. 59c; 60a,c–f;61a): These are alternating straight and curved lines. The curved lines frequently have an amplitude exceeding the available space between straight lines, but are regularly drafted. Examples on shoulders are generally smaller than examples on sides. With only one exception the straight line is red and the curved line is black (in Table C6 the color of the straight line is given first; the color of the curved line is given second). This motif occurs throughout the development on shoulders, but occurs on sides only relatively late.

K) *Horizontal Straight and Curved Lines* (Fig. 60a,b,g): This occurs as alternating circumferential straight and curved lines. The drafting is often irregular; in some cases the curved line has been painted over twice. This motif is restricted to sides. In most cases the straight line is black and the curved line is red. It is intriguing that the vertical motif (J) has a color pattern which is the reverse of this horizontal motif. This is usually late.

L) *Vertical Opposed Triangles* (Fig. 59a;60a,d,e,f;61a,h): This is composed of two solidly filled isosceles triangles, the lower with point up and the upper with point down. The two triangles are necessarily of slightly different sizes because the sequences are on a conical surface; the measures given in Table C3 are means. This occurs only on shoulders. All examples are black. This motif occurs throughout the polychrome development, but seems most common in the middle.

M) *Horizontal Opposed Triangles* (Fig.58k; 60a,e,f;61l,m): These elements are similar to the above, and are also frequently asymmetrical. They occur on both shoulders and sides. Some early examples have one triangle filled with red and one with black; the rest are black. These also seem most common in the middle of the development.

N) *Grid* (Fig. 61a): This is composed of crossed vertical and horizontal straight lines; it must be in a rectangular segment or plat. Most are on shoulders but one is on a side. Both black and combined red and black examples are attested. This motif occurs late in the development of polychrome.

O) *Crosshatch* (Fig. 58a;60e;61b): This is composed of crossed oblique straight lines on a rectangular segment or plat. There are three examples on shoulders and one on a side. Two are black and two are combined. Most are late.

P) *Multiple Zig-Zag Lines* (Fig. 61d,e): Three more parallel zig-zag lines circumferentially in a band or horizontally in a plat constitute this rare motif. It is known only on shoulders. Most are black; one is red. Its occurrence is relatively late.

Q) *Alternated Oblique Lines* (Fig. 61c): This is composed of a series of vertical straight lines with parallel lines in between, first sloping one way, then the other. Most are on shoulders; one is on a side. All are black. This is relatively late.

R) *Caprid* (Fig. 60a;61i,k): This variable motif probably portrays a wild goat with large curving horns. Our examples are either fragmentary of poorly drafted. All are probably from shoulders. Black and combined color examples are attested. They occur throughout the long polychrome development.

Unique motifs are illustrated in Figures 59c; 61f,g,h,m.

Both rules and elements have now been minimally defined. Their use can be exemplified with the vessel shown in Figure 62, modified from an illustration of a complete vessel excavated by the Délégation en Perse in 1902 from nearby Tepe Aliabad (Gautier and Lampre 1905, Plate VII Facing page 140). The neck of this vessel has one band with a Curved Line (D) between two complex borders. Each bordering band had a black line, a red line, and a black line. This neck would be symbolized as:

1. bl,rd,bl (Dbl) bl,rd,bl

The shoulder is far more complicated. The upper limit of the shoulder is usually defined by a reverse carination. Otherwise it is defined by the tangent at 45 degrees. Therefore, the band of Vertical Lines (A) is on the shoulder. Below this is a band divided into segments every other one of which is divided

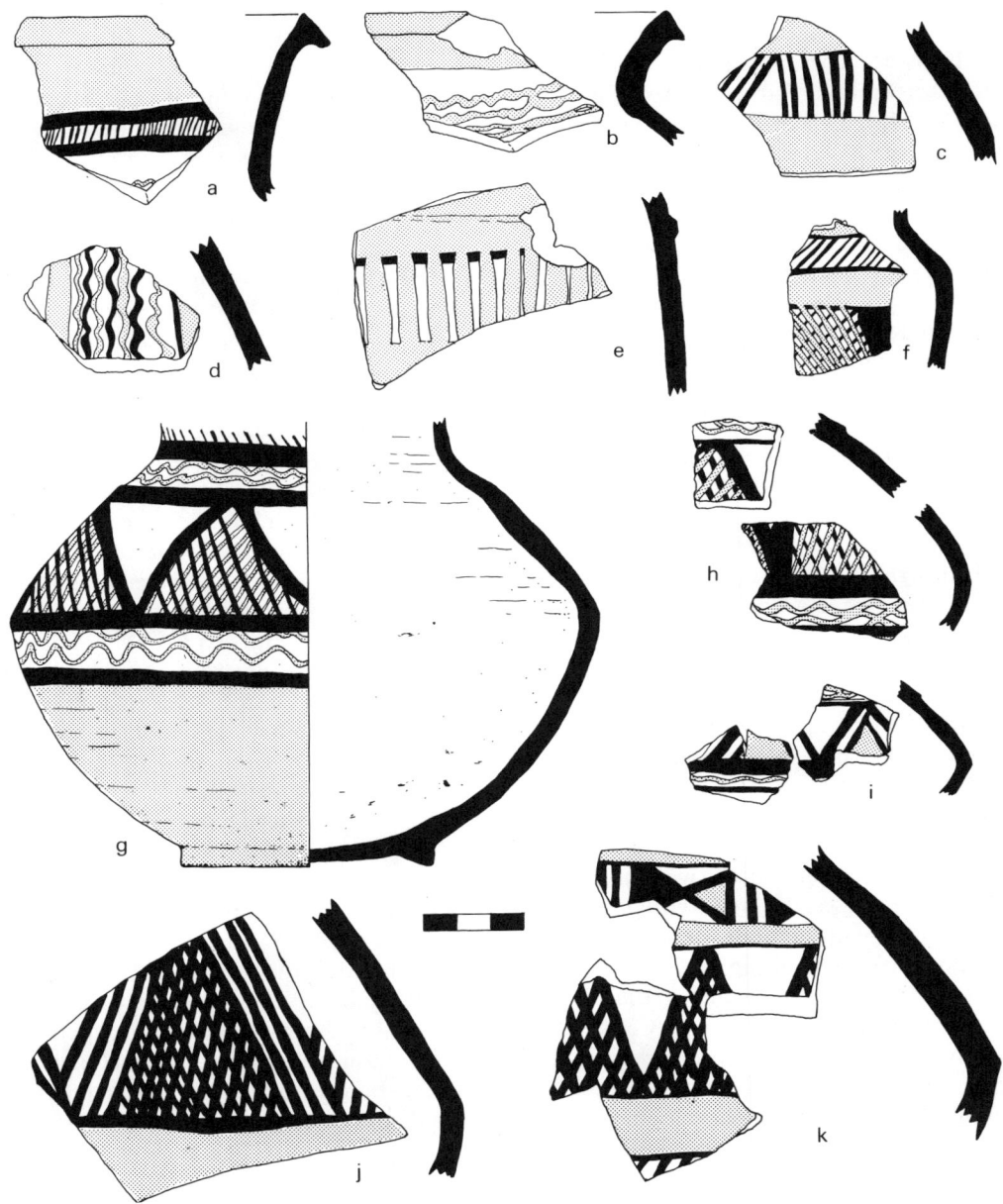

Fig. 58. Uruk Ware: Polychrome Decoration. A. Ledge rim jar rim with vertical straight lines, fine sand, body white, paints weak red and dark brown, diam.: 13; X141, 6034301 (B20). B. Ledge rim jar rim with horizontal curved lines, fine sand, body white, paint dark red, diam.: 14; X104, 6012401 (A8). C. Jar shoulder with vertical straight lines, fine sand, body 10YR 8/3 (very pale brown), paints 10R 5/4 (weak red) and 10YR 3/1 (very dark gray), shoulder diam.: 17; X062 (A5). D. Jar shoulder with vertical curved lines, fine sand, body 10YR 8/4 (very pale brown), paints 10R 6/6 (light red) and weathered gray; X119 (A9,10). E. Jar side with vertical straight lines, calcite, body 10YR 7/5 (very pale brown), paints 10R 4/5 (red) and 7.5YR 4/3 (brown), shoulder diam.: ca. 40; X078, 60094 (A6). F. Jar side and shoulder with oblique straight lines and cross-hatch, fine sand, body 5YR 7/4 (pink), paints 10R 5/5 (red) and 10YR 3/1 (very dark gray), shoulder diam.: 14; X102, 60120 (A7). G. Jar with triangles and horizontal curved lines, fine sand, body reddish yellow, surface white, paints light red and brown, shoulder diam.: 18; X319, 6042201 (B28). H. Jar shoulder with triangles and horizontal curved lines, fine calcite, body pinkish gray, paints 7.5R 5/6 (red) and very dark gray, shoulder diam.: 25; X306, 6080801 (A20). I. Jar shoulders with triangles and horizontal curved lines, no visible inclusions, body reddish yellow, paints weak red and reddish brown, shoulder diam.: 13; X338, 6083301 (A20). J. Jar shoulder with triangles, fine sand, body very pale brown, paints 7.5R 4/6 and dark reddish brown, shoulder diam.: 52; X15601 (A13). K. Jar shoulder with triangles and horizontal opposed triangles, fine sand, body very pale brown, paints 7.5R 5/6 (red) and dark gray, shoulder diam.: 28; X217, 6017801 (A16).

CERAMICS OF THE URUK, JEMDET NASR, AND EARLY DYNASTIC PHASES

Fig. 59. Uruk Ware: Polychrome Decoration. A. Jar shoulder with vertical opposed triangles and branches, fine sand, body 7.5YR 8/6 (pink), points 7.5R 5/6 (red), and 7.5YR 8/3 (very dark gray); X078, 60094 (A6). B. Jar shoulder with diamonds, fine sand, body 5YR 7/6 (reddish yellow), paints 10R 4/3 (weak red) and 10YR 3/3 (dark brown); X185, 60162 (A13). C. Jar shoulder with arc and rays, fine sand, body yellow brown, paints red and dark reddish brown; X17701 (B23). D. Jar shoulder and side with arch and horizontal curved lines, fine and calcite, body light brown, paints red and dusky red, shoulder diam.: 33; X160, 6014803 (A13). E. Jar shoulder with arcs and rays, fine sand, body white, paints red and dusky red, neck diam.: 13; X133, 6033601 (B20). F. Jar shoulder with arc and rays, fine sand, body light brown, paints weak red and dark gray, shoulder diam.: 25; X311, 60410 (B26). G. Jar side with arcs and rays, fine sand, body pink, paints red and dark red, shoulder diam.: 30; X14402 (B21). H. Jar side with arc and rays, fine sand, body white, paints weak red and reddish brown, shoulder diam.: 25; X26801 (B25). I. Jar side with arcs and rays, fine sand, body pink, paints weak red and reddish brown, shoulder diam.: 28; X244, 6038702 (B24). J. Jar shoulder with branch, fine sand, body 2.5Y 8/3 (white), paints 10R 4/5 (red) and 7.5YR 3/1 (very dark gray); X078, 60094 (A6). K. Jar shoulder with branch, fine sand, body 5YR 7/5 (pink), paint 10R 5/6 (red) and 5YR 3/2 (dark reddish brown), shoulder diam.: 33; X152 (A12). L. Jar shoulder with branches, fine sand, body 7.5YR 7/6 (reddish yellow), paints 10R 4/6 (red) and 5YR 4/1 (dark gray), shoulder diam.: ca. 33; X141, 60343 (B20). M. Jar shoulder with branch, fine sand, body 5YR 7/6 (reddish yellow), paints 2.5YR 4/5 (red) and 5YR 4/2 (dark reddish gray); X229, 60370 (B23). N. Jar shoulder with branches, fine sand, body 5YR 7/6 (reddish yellow), paints 10R 4/5 (red) and 5YR 4/2 (dark reddish gray), shoulder diam.: ca. 25; X126, 60135 (A11).

Fig. 60. Uruk Ware: Polychrome Decoration. A. Jar shoulder and side with straight and curved lines, straight lines, opposed triangle and branch, fine sand, body light red, paints red and dark reddish gray, shoulder diam.: 34; X17201 (B22,23). B. Jar side with straight and curved lines, fine sand and calcite, body pink, paints weak red and black, shoulder diam.: 40; X104, 60124 (A8). C. Jar shoulder and side with straight and curved lines and opposed triangles, fine sand, body white, paints red and black, shoulder diam.: 40; X232, 6037201 (B23). D. Jar shoulder with straight and curved lines and opposed triangles, fine sand, body pink, paints red and dusky red, neck diam.: 12; X21602 (A16). E. Jar shoulder with straight and curved lines, straight lines, opposed triangles and cross-hatch (section below and to left), fine sand, body very pale brown, paints red and dusky red, neck diam.: 20; X17101 (B22). F. Jar shoulder with straight and curved lines, straight lines and opposed triangles, fine sand, body white, paints red and dusky red, shoulder diam.: 48; X12101 (A10). G. Jar side with straight and curved lines, fine sand, body white, paints red and black, shoulder diam.: 43; X086, 6010801 (A6).

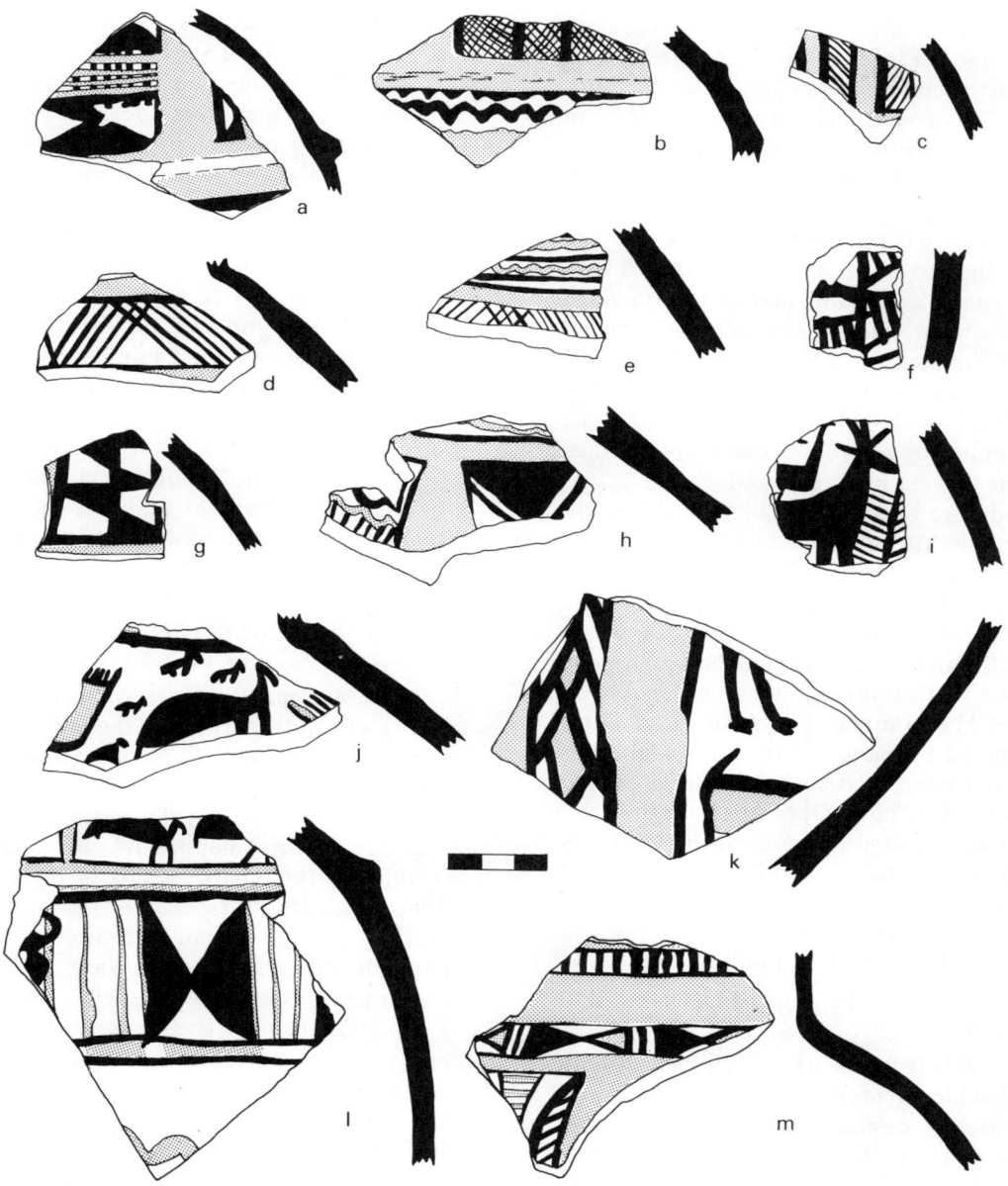

Fig. 61. Uruk Ware: Polychrome Decoration. A. Jar shoulder with grid, opposed triangles, fine sand, body 2.5Y 8/3 (white), paints 10R 5/6 (red) and 7.5YR 4/2 (brown), shoulder diam.: 36; X167, 60350 (B21). B. Jar shoulder with cross-hatch, horizontal curved lines, fine sand, body 10YR 7/5 (very pale brown), paints weathered, shoulder diam.: 44; X244, 60387 (B24). C. Jar shoulder with alternate obliques, fine sand, body 7.5YR 7/4 (pink), paints 10R 3/3 (dusky red) and 5YR 3/1 (very dark gray); X048, 60079 (A3). D. Jar shoulder with multiple zig-zags, fine sand, body 2.5Y 8/3 (white), paints weathered; X060, 60084 (A6). E. Jar shoulder with multiple zig-zags and horizontal straight and curved lines, coarse sand, body 10YR 7/5 (very pale brown), paints 10R 5/5 (weak red) and 5YR 3/1 (very dark gray); X048, 60079 (A3). F. Jar side with possible arc and ray variant, fine sand, body 7.5YR 7/6 (reddish yellow), paint 5YR 4/2 (dark reddish gray), shoulder diam.: ca. 19; X277, 60395 (B25). G. Jar shoulder with opposed triangle variant, fine sand, body 5YR 7/5 (pink), paints 10R 5/6 (red) and 5YR 3/1 (very dark gray); X078, 60094 (A6). H. Jar shoulder with opposed triangle variant, fine sand, body 5YR 7/5 (reddish yellow), paints 7.5R 4/7 (red) and weathered gray, X250 (A17). I. Jar shoulder with caprid and branch, fine sand, 10YR 8/4 (very pale brown) paint 5YR 3/0 (very dark gray); X068, 60091 (A5). J. Jar shoulder with animals, fine sand, 10YR 7/4 (very pale brown), paints 2.5 YR 4/8 (red) and 5YR 4/2 (dark reddish gray); X136, 60795 (B20). K. Jar shoulder with animals and diamonds, fine sand, body 2.5 YR 6/6 (light red), paints 10R 4/5 (red) and 5YR 4/3 (reddish brown); X306, 60830 (A20). L. Jar shoulder and side with animals, opposed triangles, and straight lines, fine sand, body 2.5Y 8/2 (white), paints 10R 5/4 (weak red) and 2.5YR 4/4 (reddish brown), shoulder diam.: 40; X118, 60127 (A9,10). M. Jar neck and shoulder with straight lines and opposed triangles, fine sand and calcite, body 7.5YR 7/4 (pink), paints 10R 4/6 (red) and weathered brown, neck diam.: 10; X164, 60153 (A13–15).

into plats. The undivided segment contains an elaborate example of a Branch Motif (I). Its symbol must therefore be modified with a plus, thus: "I+". The divided segment is separated from the undivided segment with a black line, a red fill, and a black line. The three plats are similarly separated from each other. The fact that black lines defining the left and right sides of the plats are broken by the red lines is not expressed in our code. The upper and lower plat of each divided segment are similar. Each has horizontal alternated Opposed Triangles (M) and Vertical Lines (A). The middle plat contains one motif only, the Multiple Zig-Zag Lines (P). The entire major shoulder band is delimited by a border of black and red lines. The shoulder would be symbolized as:

2. (Ard)bl,rd,bl((<Lbl,Abl,. . .>bl,rd,bl(Pbl) bl,rd,bl<Mbl,Abl,. . .)bl,rd,bl (I+bl) bl,rd, bl . . .) bl

The side is in most cases separated from the shoulder by a carination. In those few cases where it is not, all bands including and below the one touched by a vertical tangent are considered to be on the side. The example from Aliabad has three bands separated by black and red lines. The upper band has alternating Vertical Straight and Curved Lines (J) and Horizontal Opposed Triangles (M). These are not separated by borders; therefore this band contains alternating motifs, not segments. The lower two bands contain curved lines (D); that there is only one irregular line is not expressed in the statement. The side is symbolized as:

3. rd,bl (Jrdbl, Mbl,. . .)bl,rd,bl(Dbl)bl,rd,bl (Dbl) bl,rd

All the vessels from Farukhabad in which both side and shoulder were represented at least in part are symbolized in design statements in Table C6.

In order to assess the changes through time in side-shoulder motif combinations, Table 24 has been derived from the design statements. All possible combinations are entered (i.e. if two motifs occur on a shoulder and one on a side, the vessel is entered here twice; if two occur on each, the vessel is entered here four times). The small, diverse sample from Farukhabad required that some motifs be grouped. I have grouped Vertical and Horizontal Opposed Triangles (L and M), and all occurrences of Vertical Straight Lines (A) with Horizontal Opposed Triangle (M) or Horizontal Straight Lines (B) with Vertical Opposed Triangles have been noted only as L or M. Straight lines are recorded only when they stand alone. On the basis of this table, I suggest the following:

1) Shoulder surfaces with Vertical Straight Line Motifs (A), Isoceles Triangle Motifs (E,F), or Opposed Triangle Motifs (L,M) in combination with side surfaces with Horizontal Curved Line Motifs (D) occur early in the polychrome sequence.
2) Shoulder surfaces with Vertical Straight Line motifs (A), Vertical Straight and Curved Line motifs (J), or Opposed Triangle motifs (L,M) occur in combination with side surfaces with Horizontal Straight and Curved Line motifs (K) or Opposed Triangle motifs (M) in the middle of the development.
3) Shoulder surfaces with Grid motif (N), Alternating Oblique Line motifs (Q) or Vertical Straight and Curved Line motifs occur in combination with side surfaces with Vertical Straight and Curved Line motifs (J) in the later portion of the polychrome development.

There are no well-defined stages, though the early and middle portions of the polychrome development are of generally the late Uruk and Jemdet Nasr Periods, while the later portion is of the beginning of the early Dynastic Period. If this sequence of combinations is confirmed by future work, then the relative dating of the vessels from Tepe Aliabad by Delougaz (1952: 139) is only partially correct. Delougaz argued, on the basis of parallels with the "Scarlet Ware" of the Diyala, that these vessels are of the Early Dynastic I Period. Of the illustrated vessels from the French excavations, one exhibits Vertical Straight Lines and cross-hatched Isosceles Triangles on the shoulder and Horizontal Curved Lines on the side (Gautier and Lampre 1905: Fig. 282). It is probably a relatively early polychrome product. Two other vessels are likewise probably early (ibid., Figs. 283, 284). On the other hand, one vessel has Alternated Oblique Lines on the shoulder and Vertical Straight and Curved Lines on the side (ibid., Fig. 286). It is probably a relatively late polychrome product. One other vessel, that used in the above example (Fig. 62), is probably also late (Ibid.: Plate VII). Only one of the six illustrated vessels is of indeterminate age (Ibid.: Fig. 285).

Specific motif combinations aside, this formalization allows certain general trends in polychrome development to be expressed on a relative scale. For instance, are designs becoming more complex? Consider the following table (Table 25).

CERAMICS OF THE URUK, JEMDET NASR, AND EARLY DYNASTIC PHASES

Table 24: Stratigraphic Distribution of Side/Shoulder Polychrome Motif Combinations At Farukhabad

Major Motif on Side	EF	H	A	J,K	L,M	N,P	Other
D	A9,10(X11902) A9,10(X11903) A20(X30601) A20(X33801) B24(X31301)	A8(X10403) A13(X16003) B23(X19801)		A9,10(X11902) A9,10(X11903) A10(X12101) B23(X22902)	A10(X12101) A12(X15201) B23(X22901)		I:A12(X15201)
H							D:B21(X14401)
A			A8(X10407) A13(X16401)	B22(X17201) B23(X23201)	A13(X16401)		R:A17(X25101)
L,M			A8(X10407)	B22(X17201) B23(X23201)	B22(X17201)	A5(X06301)	
K				B21(X16704)	B21(X16704)	B21(X16704)	
J						A5(X06301)	
Other				O:A8(X10410)			R:A5(X08101)

Table 25: Polychrome Design Complexity

	Number of vessels	Mean motifs/ shoulder	Mean number of subdivisions
Excavation A, Layer 1–5	3	3.0	2.0
Excavation A, Layers 8–11	5	2.0	2.2
Excavation A, Layers 12–16	4	1.5	1.5
Excavation A, Layer 20	2	1.5	1.0

1. bl,rd,bl(Dbl)bl,rd,bl

2. (Ard)bl,rd,bl((<L bl,Abl,..>bl,rd,bl(Pbl)bl,rd,bl<Mbl,Abl,...>)bl,rd,bl

   (I+bl)bl,rd,bl...)bl,

3. rd,bl(Jrd bl,Mbl,...)bl,rd,bl(Dbl)bl,rd,bl(Dbl)bl,rd

Fig. 62. Polychrome Motif Types and an Example of a Design Statement.

If by complexity one means number of elements, this can be measured by the mean number of motifs per shoulder. The table seems to indicate an increase beginning in Late Jemdet Nasr. If by complexity one means the degree of involution of the composition, this can be measured by the mean number of subdivisions. Here also there seems to be an increase; however, this ceases in Late Jemdet Nasr. Doubtless other features usually subjectively evaluated can be similarly stated. Of course, my samples are small and likely to be skewed by differing degrees of vessel breakage. Nevertheless, this illustrates a use to which the design statements can be put.

The local polychrome tradition of the Deh Luran Plain, as evidenced by ceramics from Tepe Musiyan, Tepe Aliabad, and Tepe Farukhabad, is distinct from other local developments. While this is not the place for a full comparative study, a reemphasis of certain points, also made by Delougaz, is in order. One motif is used for major segments and plats only in the Deh Luran area as far as we know. This is the Arc and Ray Motif. The Caprid Motif is common on the Diyala to the West, and the Branch Motif may be common on the Susiana to the East. If these can be shown to be explicit political or ethnic symbols, like the "Lion and Sun" which was the symbol of imperial Iran, such distributions may prove to be most informative in the future. Some peripheral elements are also distinctive to Deh Luran as far as we know. These are the Curved Line and the Straight and Curved Line motifs.

In summary, I have attempted to treat the polychrome jar surfaces as statements in a "grammar of design". I have suggested a set of elements and a series of rules by which these elements can be arranged. The small sample from Farukhabad prevents a full presentation of the utility of the approach.

Nose Lugs (Fig. 44l;55a,c,d): Small lumps of clay are applied to the jar shoulder rather than being built up from the body. These are high and rounded near the neck and become gradually lower and narrower farther from the neck. The higher end is punctured with a small stick or splinter creating a hole tangent to the neck. There are usually four such lugs symmetrically placed on the shoulder of the jar. The small hole sizes and frequently weak bonding of lug to shoulder preclude the use of these lugs in suspension of the vessel; use of the lugs to lightly lash down a top or stopper seems a more likely procedure. Nose lugs are attested on small expanded rim jars with cross-hatch incised band of both Uruk and Sargarab Ware from Uruk layers (Fig. 44l,55a).

Variant forms include a regular nose lug without perforations (Fig. 53a), a lug with two perforations placed horizontally on a round bowl rim (Fig. 55d), and a round node without perforation (Fig. 55c).

Incised Grooves (Fig. 55f;g): This form of decoration is created by holding a sharp-edged tool against the shoulder of the vessel and turning the vessel on the wheel. Up to twelve such lines occur. In almost half of the examples, a series of oblique incisions radiating from the neck is placed on top of the grooves. This variation is called "Groove and Slash". These patterns are attested on small vessels with spherical bodies and small expanded rims. Most examples are from late Uruk and the earliest Jemdet Nasr Layers.

Strap Handles (Fig. 50a; 55j): These handles are made from wide, relatively thin strips of clay which are rounded on the edges and sometimes have one or two shallow grooves in the middle. The handles are attached to the lip and shoulder and rise in a gently curve allowing enough room to insert the four fingers of one's hand inside the loop. Rare associated features are a series of short grooves perpendicular to the lip at the juncture of handle and rim and a thickened lip lug opposite the juncture of handle and rim with similar short grooves (Fig. 55j). These handles also are attested only on vessels with globular bodies and small expanded rims. They occur in Uruk and early Jemdet Nasr layers.

Twisted Handles (Fig. 55k,l): This type of handle is rare in our series. Fragments of twisted vertical loop handles, perhaps like the strap handles described above, occur only in the Late Uruk period. Examples of twisted horizontal handles attached to the rims of vessels with globular bodies and small expanded rims also occur (Fig. 55k).

Straight Spouts (Fig. 44n,o; 52k): These vary considerably in length and diameter. The sample is too small to allow the definition of varieties of straight spouts; however long straight spouts are dominant in the Early Uruk period. Shorter examples occur in all periods. They are attested on Flared Expanded Rim Jars of Sargarab Ware and Ledge Rim Jars of Uruk Ware. In one interesting variant, from Excavation A, Feature 19, a pit of the Uruk period (X838), the spout is attached to the neck and lip of the jar (Fig. 55m).

Droop Spouts (Fig. 55n): This category of spout

Table 26: Metric Attributes of Flat Bases

	Diameter (cm)		Side angle (degrees)		Side thickness (cm)	
	$\bar{x}$	s.d.	$\bar{x}$	s.d.	$\bar{x}$	s.d.
Late Jemdet Nasr N=17	10.0	3.2	41	10	.77	.18
Early Jemdet Nasr N=20	12.0	5.0	44	8	.93	.20
Late Uruk N=44	9.1	5.4	43	8	1.02	.34
Middle Uruk N=36	8.1	3.3	41	7	.82	.28

shows little variation. The spout is conical with a large base and small end. It is curved downward and there is often a slight thickening of the lip of the spout.

BASES

Flat Bases (Fig. 50a; 51a; 56a): Flat bases are usually made by inverting the vessel and scraping the base to the desired thinness. Wheel scorings are thus obliterated on the exterior. Summary statistics are presented in Table 26.

In the Middle Uruk there is one small thin form of base. In the Late Uruk, there is a distinct small base, perhaps from bottles and smaller jars, and a distinct medium sized base, creating a bimodal curve of base diameter distribution. In the early Jemdet Nasr only the medium-sized form is attested.

Fine Flat Bases: These bases are smaller, thinner and more regular than those described above. Seldom scraped, they are either tooled on the turning wheel or cut off with a sharp-edged tool. They range in diameter from two to four cm. These are probably the bases of very small jars (Fig. 53a), of medium sized jars with narrow bodies, or of conical cups (Fig. 45a,b).

Turned Ring Bases (Fig. 56b–e): There are two types of turned ring base. The low variety is formed by inverting the vessel and tooling the heavy base on the wheel, leaving a circular ridge of clay around an otherwise rounded bottom; the high variety is made separately on the wheel and attached to an otherwise flat or rounded base.

Turned ring bases range from .4 to 2.2 cm in diameter. The one example in Sargarab Ware is high and well-made. A peculiarity attested on several later Jemdet Nasr polychrome jars is that the round bottom apparently projected below the low ring. Such vessels could not stand unsupported on a relatively hard and level floor.

Pinched Ring Base (Fig. 56f–i): This type of footed base is formed by pinching the edge of a flat base between thumb and forefinger, leaving a rough circular ridge of clay. Actual fingerprints are usually obscured by smoothing, but small depressions are visible. These bases range in diameter from 4 to 12 cm.

Miscellaneous Uruk Ware Ceramics: A number of vessel parts do not fit into any of the above categories. However, they may well prove to have useful parallels at other sites. There are a variety of bowls, several with textured decoration (Fig. 63a–h); there are several jars (Fig. 63i,k,m–p). Two fragments of possible fruit-stands with triangular cut-outs and other embellishments are also shown (Fig. 63j,l).

STRAW TEMPERED WARE
by Anne Miller

This ware was tempered with small quantities of straw fragments, and few examples contain sand in the clay body. The core of the sherds is sometimes unoxidized. The surfaces are usually red or orange, but occasionally buff or green colors occur. Vessel measurements are given in Appendix Table C4.

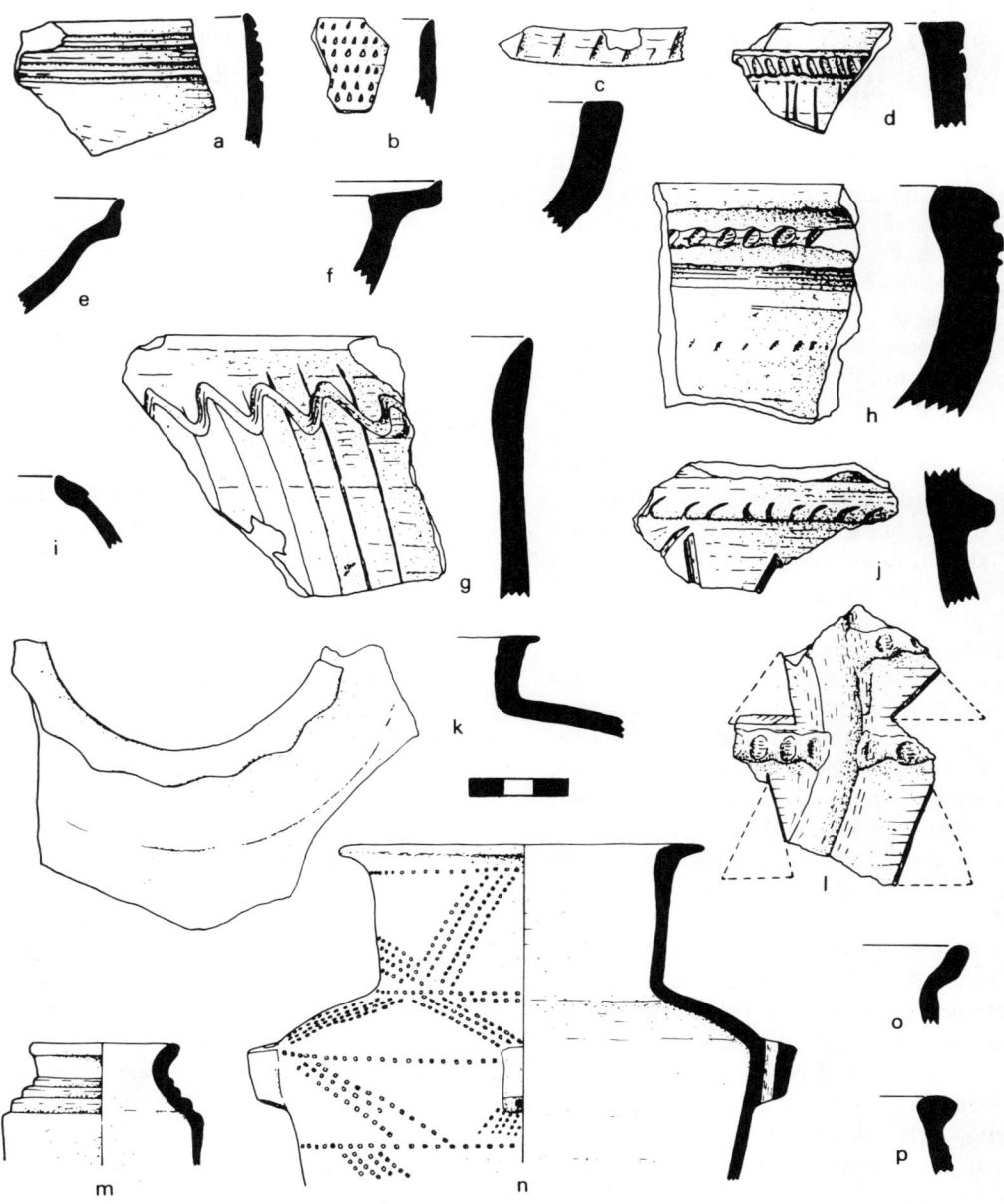

Fig. 63. Miscellaneous Uruk Ware Ceramics. A. Round lip bowl with horizontal grooves, fine sand, body 10YR 8/3 (very pale brown), diam.: 17; X125, 60133 (A11). B. Round lip bowl with triangular punctates, fine sand, body 7.5YR 7/5 (reddish yellow), diam.: 7; X427, 60484 (B30–31). C. Flat lip bowl with lip hatching, medium sand and calcite, body 5YR 7/4 (pink), diam.: 30; X463, 60500 (B32). D. Flat lip bowl with hatch strip and vertical incisions, fine sand, body 2.5Y 8/3 (white), diam.: 18; X295, 60200 (A19). E. Braced conical cup rim, fine sand, 5YR 5/5 (reddish brown), diam.: 26; X160, 60148 (A13). F. Bowl with lock rim, coarse sand, body 10YR 8/3 (very pale brown), diam.: ca. 36; X412, 60479 (B31). G. Large round lip bowl with horizontal curved line and vertical incisions, fine sand, body 10YR 7/4 (very pale brown), diam.: 24; X369, 60455 (B29). H. Heavy incurved bowl with grooves and hatched strip, coarse sand, calcite and straw, body 5YR 6/5 (light reddish brown), diam.: ca. 50; X368, 60452 (B29). I. Miniature neckless ledge rim jar, fine sand and calcite, body 7.5YR 7/5 (reddish yellow), diam.: 7; X289, 60190 (A18). J. Fruit stand fragment with hatched strip and triangular cutouts, fine sand and calcite, body 2.5YR 8/4 (pale yellow), exterior diam.: ca. 16; X226, 60365 (B23). K. Ledge rim jar with indented lip, fine sand, body 7.5YR 7/4 (pink), diam.: 11; X338 (A20). L. Fruit stand fragment with triangular cutouts, hatched strip, and vertical curved appliqué, fine sand, body 5Y 8/2 (white), paint splashed on vertical appliqué (not represented) 10R 5/6 (red) exterior diam.: 17; X119 (A9–10). M. Miniature round lip jar with grooved shoulder, fine sand, body 2.5Y 8/2 (white), diam.: 3; X534 (B33). N. Ledge rim jar with plaster filled dentate impressions and vertically perforated lugs, fine sand, body 5Y 6/1 (gray), diam.: 8; X061, 064 (A5). O. Thickened round lip vessel rim on cylindrical body, fine sand, body 7.5YR 6/5 (light brown), diam.: 14; X227, 60395 (B25). P. Thickened round lip vessel rim on grooved cylindrical body, fine sand, body 10YR 6/2 (light brownish gray), diam.: 26; X519, 60541 (B33).

BEVELED RIM BOWLS
(PLATE 11e,f, TABLE C4)

The beveled rim bowl is always made from an ordinary brick clay, tempered with crushed straw or chaff. The form is roughly conical. The exterior is rough and cracked, and the interior and the oblique lip are wet-smoothed. These bowls typically are five or six cm high and 18 or 19 cm in diameter, but there is a large shallow variety ranging up to 24 cm in diameter, and there is one miniature bowl only 4.0 cm high and 7.5 cm in diameter. The large deep form attested in Susa Acropole I, Level 17 (LeBrun 1971: Fig. 47) is not known from Farukhabad, and the tapered rim prototypic form known to the east (Johnson 1973:54, Plate Ib) is so rare that we consider it to be an accidental variant.

Substantial proportions of beveled rim bowls are characteristic of ceramic assemblanges of Uruk times throughout Mesopotamia, as has been known for more than thirty years. These bowls have been used as chronological horizon markers since the key synthesis of Delougaz (1952). However, the questions about the manufacture and use of these distinctive vessels raised by Delougaz have not been pursued until recently. Nissen (1970) presented the hypothesis that the bowls were mass-produced for use as ration bowls for the daily grain rations so frequently mentioned in the archaic texts. If this is true, then one could predict that the bowls would occur in a one unit volume, a two unit volume, and perhaps other divisions or multiples of one unit. There should be little variation from these standardized sizes. Let us consider this prediction utilizing the beveled rim bowls from Farukhabad. First, however, let us consider the method of manufacture.

A silty clay tempered with crushed straw, the same material used for mud bricks, is used for beveled rim bowls. All of the bowls have a spiral pattern in the clay of the base, suggesting the clay mass was first rolled or twisted. In 11 percent of the cases, the exterior of the base-side junctcure has deep vertical cracks suggesting that the relatively dry mass was forced outward by pressure at one point. Finger or knuckle marks are evident in the interior bottoms of 87 percent of the vessels, indicating that this pressure was exerted with a clenched fist. The exterior, both bottom and sides, is extremely rough. In latex impressions of these exteriors, chaff, roots, brick fragments, and plant stems were noted. This suggests that sometimes the mass was placed in a mold dug into the ground and forced out with the fist until it met the confines of the earth mold. The insides of the bowl and the beveled lip are wet-smoothed. Semi-liquid clay has dripped down the inside in all cases. This could be done with a rigid wet hand by holding the fingers on the inside and the thumb on the lip. The formed bowl could then be allowed to dry in the ground.

One possible manufacturing procedure was used in 1971 and produced perfect bowls. First clay was mixed, but not well cleaned or water-sorted. Holes were made in the ground, with an old bowl of the desired size; double handfuls of clay were flattened into slabs and then rolled into balls. A ball was placed in each hole in the ground. The potter than punched each one with a fist and pressed it against the sides of the hole. The potter then wet one hand and ran it rapidly around the inside of each mold, smoothing the insides and beveling the rim (by the time the last clay balls were reached, they were partially dry, resulting in cracking). The bowl was allowed to dry slowly in its earth mold before it was stacked for firing. Other methods are possible, and should be tested.

After firing, the cores of the bowls are frequently unoxidized. Most surfaces are red but some are fired to a gray-green color.

Detailed studies of the stratified measured bowls from Farukhabad have failed to reveal any significant trend through time in any single attribute. This failure may result from the fact that most Late Uruk bowls are from one large pit (Excavation A, Feature 19), while most Early and Middle Uruk examples are from ordinary layers of refuse.

Now let us turn to the problem of bowl volume. The bowls vary from a single miniature bowl with a rim diameter of only eight cm to an example 23 cm in average diameter. Only twenty are sufficiently complete to make a direct measurement of volume. In this group, actual volume correlates very higly with average interior diameter and interior height as one might expect with a vessel shaped like a truncated cone (Multiple correlation coefficient = .96). A regression analysis indicates that the best predictor of volume is: Log of Volume = 2.065 (log of diameter) + .807 (log of height) − .864 where natural logarithms are used. The predicted volume usually differs slightly from the measured volume. It is interesting to note that through time the amount of such variation seems to increase.

This increase should be independent of the

CERAMICS OF THE URUK, JEMDET NASR, AND EARLY DYNASTIC PHASES

Table 27: Variance of Deviations from Expected Beveled Rim Bowl Volumes through Time

	Layers	N	Mean Predicted Volume	Mean Deviation	Variance= $\Sigma(\text{Deviation}^2)$ / N	Variance/ Mean
Late Uruk	AF19	11	904	52	2908	3.22
Middle Uruk	B32–B34	6	618	34	1392	2.25
Early Uruk	B35–B36	3	516	18	403	.78

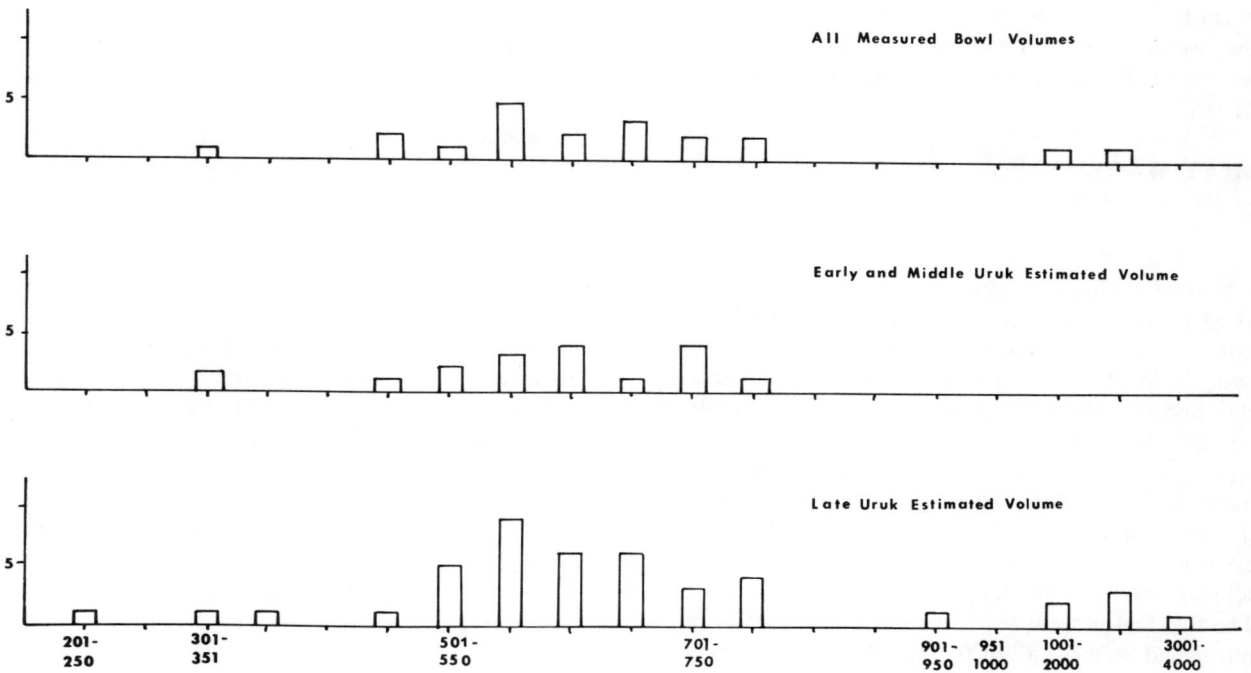

Fig. 64. Histogram of Beveled Rim Bowl Volumes.

unique occurrence of very large bowls in the Late Uruk sample. It may indicate that bowls are becoming less regular in shape during the Uruk Period.

On Figure 64, the measured volumes are presented. Most of these fall between 400 and 800 cc in volume, a considerable range. The most common volume is about 600 cc. The large bowls are 1850 and 2250 cc. This could result from the mixture of several different measurement systems. To control for change in metrology through time, the predicted volumes for Late Uruk as opposed to Early and Middle Uruk are presented. This does not reduce the range of variation within either the small or large bowl categories. It does indicate that the Late Uruk large bowls have roughly four times the volume of contemporary small bowls, but this conforms to no known ration system. From these data one must conclude that at Farukhabad beveled rim bowl volume does not support the ration bowl hypothesis as formulated.

This has several possible consequences. Perhaps there were ration systems in Deh Luran but the measuring was done with a ladle rather than with the bowl itself. Perhaps there were no standardized ration systems because the communities involved were so small, but the bowls were mass-produced for domestic uses anyway.

The problem of beveled rim bowl use will be further pursued in Chapter X.

SHALLOW PLATES

These tiny wheelmade objects could be stands or lids rather than vessels. They range in diameter from 8.0 to 12.0 cm. All are about 3.0 cm high. These are known only from the Uruk Phases.

OTHER STRAW TEMPERED VESSELS

Sherds are known which must have come from wheel-finished straw tempered jars and bowls, but few well-preserved rims are available. Also, a heavy rim of a large, shallow tray was noted (X374, AF19).

GRAY WARE[1]
by Barbara Bohr

Vessels of this ware characteristically contain 10 to 25 percent calcareous materials, either crushed calcite or crushed mussel shell or a mixture of the two. Crushed chert is a minor constituent of some clay bodies. (Those few gray wheel-finished sherds not of this local gray ware will be discussed separately later). The vessels were certainly built from rings or slabs of clay rather than being thrown on a wheel or made in a mold. The asymmetry of the vessels, the absence of grooves or scoring, and the breakage pattern all show this. The finished vessels were scraped and a third were burnished. Almost all of the vessels are in the form of jars. All vessels were fired in a reducing atmosphere and most have gray surfaces and cores, though some have gray-brown or even tan surfaces.

This ware first appears at Farukhabad during the Late Uruk. It may indeed be a local development of the Heavy Round Rim Jars of the earlier Uruk ware. It remains important until the site is abandoned during the Early Dynastic Period.

GRAY WARE JARS
(FIG. 65a,b, 66, PLATE 11a, TABLE C5)

These vessels have spherical bodies with round bases. They range in neck diameter from 9.0 to 19.0 cm. The two complete vessels are 31.0 and 32.0 cm high (Fig. 65 a,b). Many of the jars had small loop handles (Fig. 66o-q). A few of these larger vessels had spouts, indicating the pouring of liquids.

The Gray Ware Jars have several seemingly stylistic features. Some of the vessels have lightly burnished surfaces, and on a few of these the burnishing streaks are crossed, forming a distinctive pattern (Fig. 65a). Burnishing is more common in the earlier Gray Ware Jars. Shell tempering in contrast occurs only in later Gray Ware Jars. Yet another stylistic attribute involves rim form. Cross plotting of the measurements of rim height and rim angle indicates that there are two, perhaps three, clusterings of jars in a space defined by these two rim attributes (Fig. 67). There is a low out-turned form (A), a form of medium height with only slight out-turning (B), and a few jars with high, almost vertical necks (C). The first two groups are sufficiently large to warrant further discussion. The low necked form seems to have been somewhat smaller and to have had somewhat browner surface colors (Table 28). These slightly differences cannot readily be linked to manufacturing technique or to the possible uses of the vessels, nor do they show the consistent change through time that one would expect in simple style drift, such as we see in surface treatment and temper (Table 29). These subtle varieties seem to represent micro-traditions continuing through time. If they indeed represent shop or family traditions, one might expect an association with architectural units; however, there is no such association. We must conclude that there is no clear explanation of this variability at present. The recovery of dated samples from other Deh Luran sites will probably clarify this problem.

OTHER GRAY WARE VESSELS AND VESSEL PARTS

Several variant jars were found. One straw and limestone tempered example has a heavy expanded rim and rounded lip. Its neck diameter is 13 cm (Fig. 65g). A similar example has a thickening or lug with finger marks. Its neck diameter is 13 cm (Fig. 65e). Both are burnished. A limestone tempered jar handle is much larger than ordinary (Fig. 65i).

Gray Ware was sometimes used for forms other than jars. There is a small shell and limestone

---

[1]Much of this is extended and revised from a longer paper by Ms. Bohr entitled "Gray Ware Jars from Tepe Farukhabad", written in 1968 and on file in the records of the University of Michigan Museum of Anthropology.

CERAMICS OF THE URUK, JEMDET NASR, AND EARLY DYNASTIC PHASES

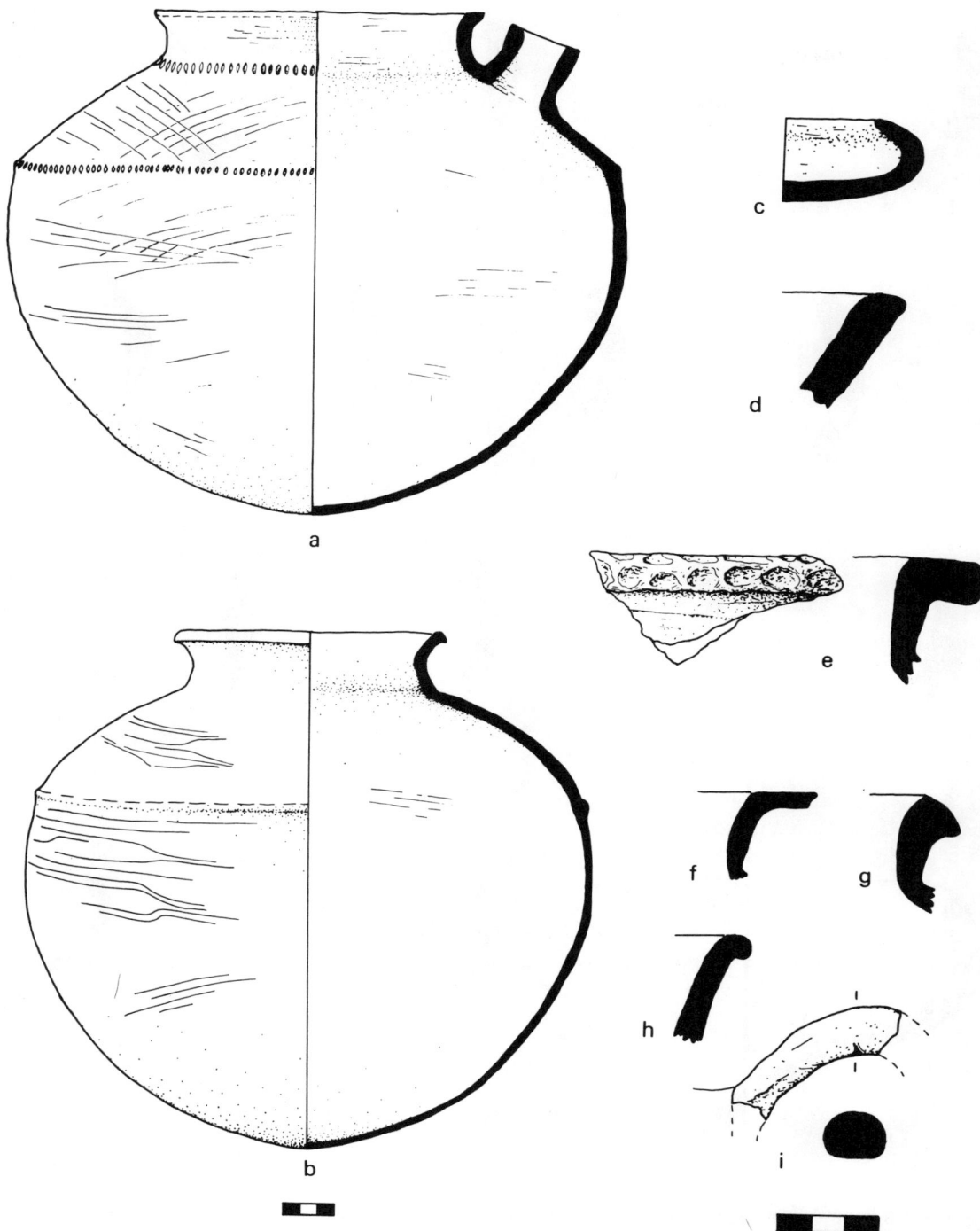

Fig. 65. Gray Ware Jars and Other Forms. A. Jar with spout, shell, body light brownish gray, diam.: 18, height: 31.3; X272, 60392 (B F15). B. Jar, shell and calcite, body gray, diam.: 16; X068, 60091 (A6). C. Incurved bowl rim, shell, body gray, diam.: 7; X167, 6035001 (B20). D. Flat lip bowl rim, calcite, body dark gray, diam.: 34; X226, 6036502 (B23). E. Lug with finger marks on jar rim, shell and straw, body dark gray, diam.: 13; X468, 6050801 (B32). F. Ledge-expanded jar rim on reduced Sargarab ware, calcite and straw, body yellowish red, slip weak red to red, diam.: 12; X568, 6056901 (B35). G. Heavy expanded rim jar rim, straw and shell, body light brownish gray, diam.: 17, X468, 6050802 (B32). H. Beaded lip bowl rim on reduced Sargarab ware, calcite and straw, body light red, diam.: 15; X587, 6058301 (B36). I. Loop handle, straw and calcite, body gray; X476, 6051401 (B33).

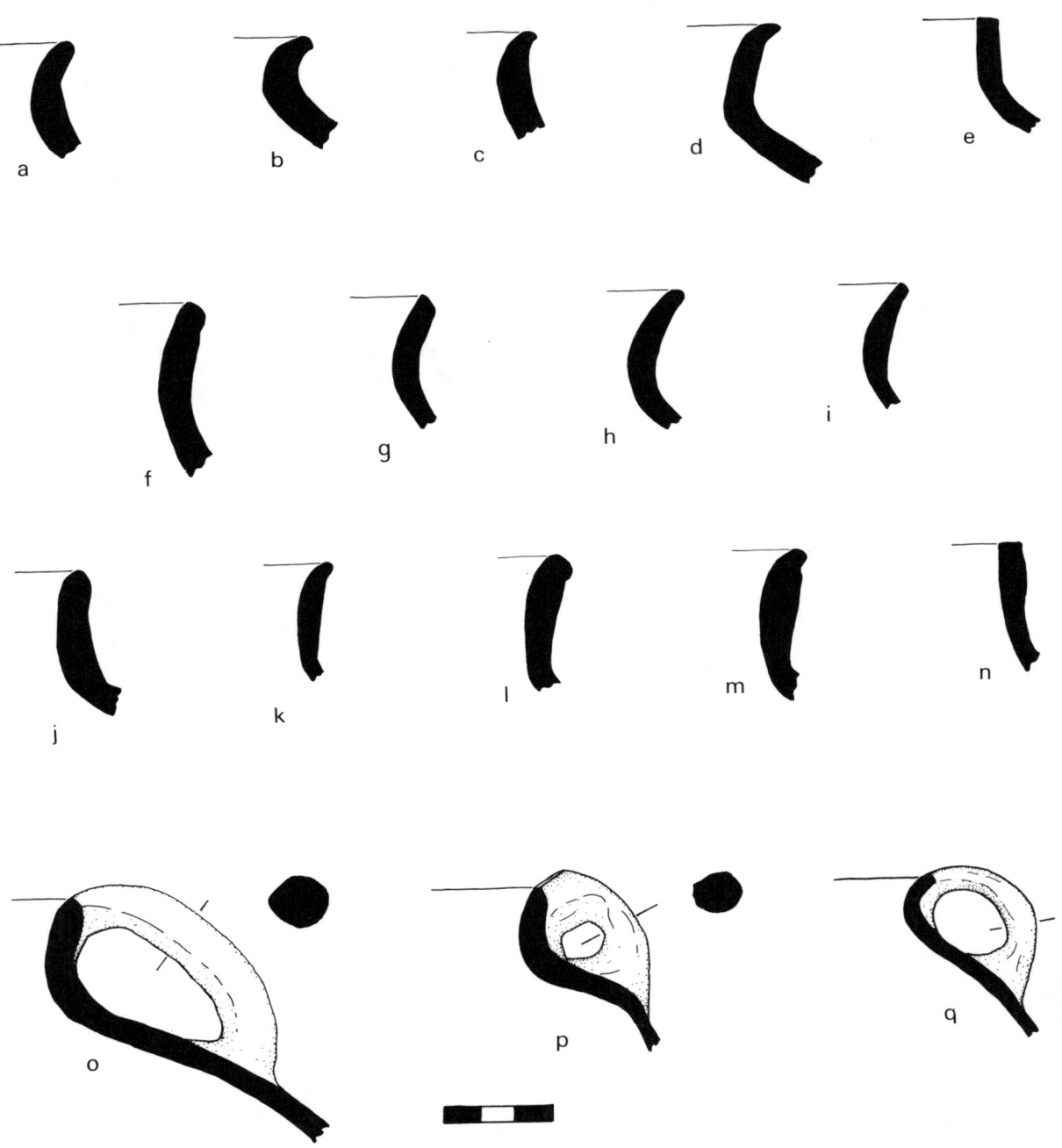

Fig. 66. Gray Ware Jars and Handles. A. Jar rim, form variant A, calcite and shell, body gray, diam.: 16; X194, 6016801 (A14). B. Same, calcite, body light brownish gray, diam.: 21; X060, 6008401 (A5, 6). C. Same, calcite, body light brownish gray, diam.: 14; X040, 6007104 (A1,2). D. Same, calcite, body light gray to gray, diam.: 15; X102, 6012002 (A7). E. Same, calcite and shell, body light gray to gray, diam.: 17; X104, 6012401 (A8). F. Jar rim, form variant B, calcite and chert, body light gray, diam.: 19; X217, 6017803 (A16). G. Same, coarse sand and calcite, body gray, diam.: 14; X034, 6033401 (B11). H. Same, shell and calcite, body light gray, diam.: 20; X086, 6010801 (A6). I. Same, calcite and chert, body reddish brown, diam.: 16; X102, 6012001 (A7). J. Jar rim, form variant C, straw and calcite, body dark gray, diam.: 21; X313, 6041202 (B F18). K. Same, shell, body light brown, diam.: 14; X086, 6010802 (A6). L. Same, calcite, body gray, diam.: 19; X196, 6017001 (A15). M. Same, calcite and shell, body gray, diam.: 19; X217, 6017801 (A16). N. Same, shell, body light brownish gray, diam.: 16; X078, 6009402 (A6). O. Jar rim with small loop handle, calcite and shell, body pale brown, diam.: 16; X313, 6041201 (B F18). P. Same, calcite, body light gray, diam.: 13; X217, 6017802 (A16). Q. Same, calcite, body light brownish gray, diam.: 12; X284, 6040601 (B27).

CERAMICS OF THE URUK, JEMDET NASR, AND EARLY DYNASTIC PHASES

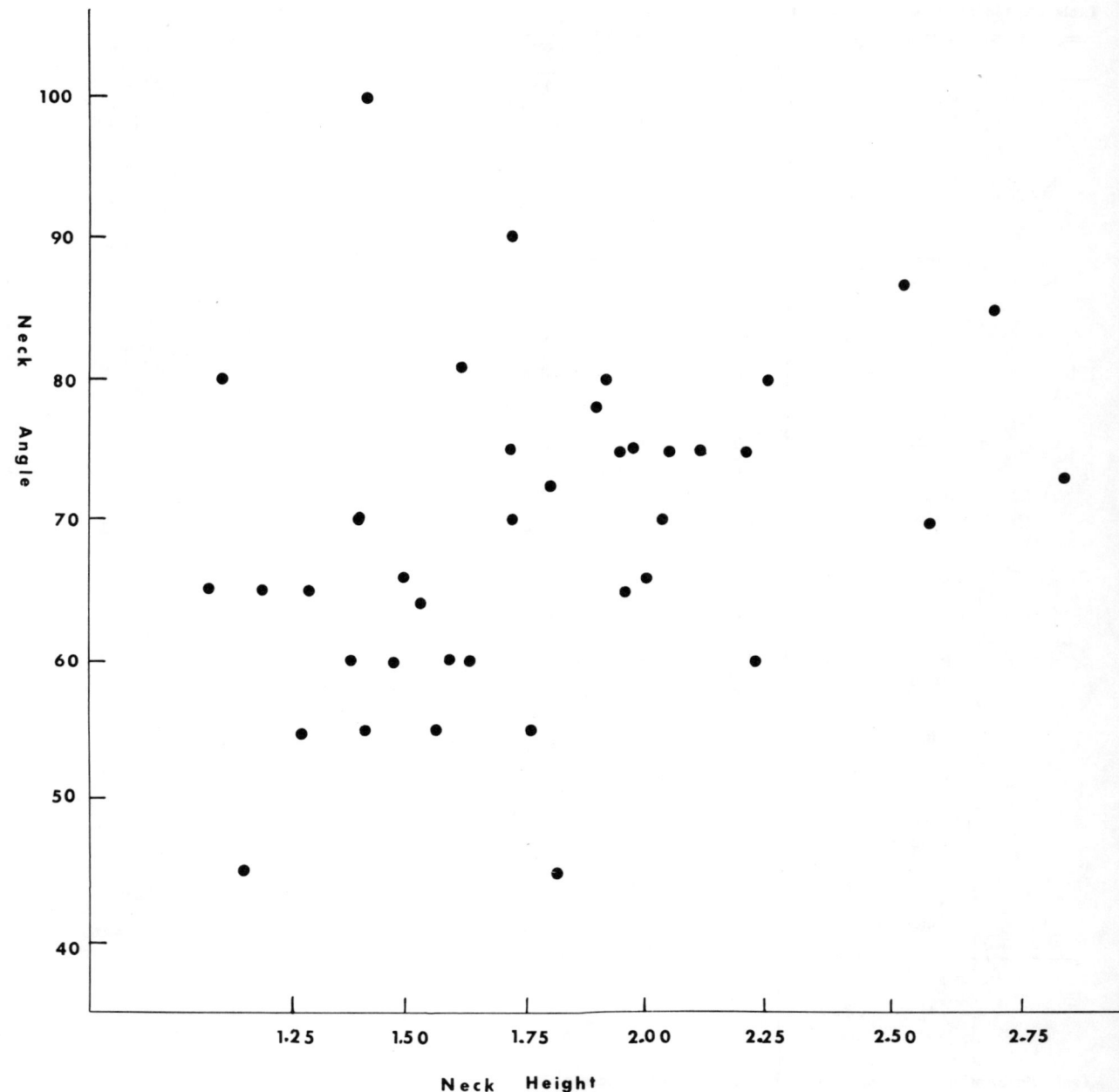

Fig. 67. Cross-Plot of Gray Ware Jar Attributes Showing the Three Possible Varieties.

tempered incurved bowl 7.0 cm in diameter (Fig. 65c). In addition there is a much larger flat lip bowl with a calcite tempering material (Fig. 65d). It is about 35 cm in diameter and burnished on both surfaces. A small hemispherical bowl with limestone temper is not illustrated. It is 10.5 cm in diameter. The lip is flat and there are three raised strips around the outside, each hatched with vertical incisions.

OTHER GRAY WARES

The ceramics described above are a local development of handmade reduced fired gray wares.

Table 28: Attributes of Grayware Jar Varieties

	Type	X̄	s.d.	Range
Paste Hue	A	19.13	1.94	5YR–2.54
	B	19.42	1.81	5YR–2.54
	C	19.58	1.02	7.5YR–10YR
Paste Value	A	5.83	0.78	4–7
	B	5.85	1.07	3–7
	C	5.50	0.55	5–6
Paste Chroma	A	1.96	0.98	1–4
	B	1.77	0.72	1–3
	C	2.17	1.17	1–4
Surface Hue	A	18.91	2.24	2.5YR–10YR
	B	20.61	1.62	10YR–2.5YR
	C	20.00	0.00	10YR–10YR
Surface Value	A	4.91	1.31	2–7
	B	5.23	0.83	3–6
	C	5.17	0.75	4–6
Surface Chroma	A	1.43	0.99	0–4
	B	1.31	0.63	0–2
	C	1.50	0.84	1–3
Neck Diameter	A	12.26	2.51	8–18
	B	14.61	3.07	9–19
	C	14.67	2.16	11–17
Rim Thickness	A	0.57	0.96	.39–.74
	B	0.59	0.11	.42–.74
	C	0.71	0.14	.51–.85
Rim Form Index	A	55.09	17.56	20–90
	B	107.54	10.21	90–140
	C	177.33	23.38	140–207
Rim Diameter	A	14.74	3.78	10–21
	B	17.15	3.31	12–22
	C	17.17	2.14	14–19
Shoulder Thickness	A	0.66	0.15	.46–1.00
	B	0.63	0.18	.33–.95
	C	0.68	0.12	.44–.80

Table 29: Stratigraphic Distribution of Grayware Jar Attributes

	Variety A	Variety B	Variety C
Early Dynastic	5	2	—
Late Jemdet Nasr	10	6	3
Early Jemdet Nasr	7	4	5

They are not reported from other contemporary sites, though one suspects they were indeed present. The "Uruk Graywares" of alluvial Mesopotamia are wheel finished in the forms well known in Uruk or Sargarab Wares. These seem to be ordinary vessels fired in a reducing atmosphere. A few such vessels are known from Farukhabad.

There is one jar with an expanded rim which has been forced over like a ledge (Fig. 65f). Johnson (1973: 55, pl. IIIk) has termed these "Ledge Expanded Jars". This example has a Sargarab Ware body with a light straw tempering. Wheel scoring is clear and there is a wavy burnishing pattern around the neck, which is 11 cm in diameter.

There is a probable bowl rim with a beaded or rounded lip of a similar Sargarab body (Fig. 65h). Both surfaces are lightly burnished but wheel-scoring is clear on the exterior. There is a bituminous stain on the interior. The diameter is about 15 cm.

Finally there is a ledge rim jar with an ordinary sandy Uruk Ware body. The neck diameter is 8.0 cm. The outer surface and lip are decorated with multiple bands and zig-zags of dentate markings filled with gypsum plaster (Fig. 63n).

In summary, the technique of reducing a vessel in the kiln to achieve a gray body color was used for a long period at Farukhabad. It appears on many clay bodies and forms but was most commonly used for rough hand-made jars.

CONCLUDING NOTE

This ends what must necessarily be only a preliminary introduction to the middle and later fourth millennium ceramics from Tepe Farukhabad. A more definitive study would begin with an analysis of production techniques, before turning to formal statistical studies of stylistic variation. To do such a study would require larger samples from a number of sites. Perhaps the very incompleteness of this chapter will inspire others to undertake such research. Let us now consider artifacts other than vessels of fired clay.

Chapter VIII

OTHER ARTIFACTS OF THE URUK, JEMDET NASR, AND EARLY DYNASTIC PHASES

INTRODUCTION

There is an increased diversity of non-ceramic artifact types during the Uruk to Early Dynastic periods. This results from both the greater volume of material excavated and the greater use of new raw materials and new techniques of fashioning such materials. When the material is fashioned into artifacts standardized throughout these periods, our discussion is in terms of types. When there are few items or there is little standardization, the discussion is in terms of individual items by period.

CHIPPED STONE TOOLS

These tools are made from the same types of raw materials and are worked in the same manner as those of the preceeding phases. The drawings follow the same conventions used for the illustrations of Chapter III except that the presumed working edges of the large drills are oriented downward. In this section comments will be restricted to definitions of additional characteristics of previously defined tool types.

MICROLITHS

Trapezoids (Fig. 64a–f; Table D1): These are narrow blade segments which have backing on one or both ends creating a trapezoidal shape. One example has backing on only one end (Fig. 68f). These may have been used, as were mounted European and Egyptian examples, as projectile tips. They occur from Late Uruk times onward.

PIERCING-REAMING TOOLS

Drills (Fig. 68g–k; Table D1): These are generally small, in contrast to earlier examples, and several are made on small flakes rather than blades (Fig. 68g,k). There are signs of rotary wear on several examples. Diameters range from 0.20 to 0.69 cm.

Pointed Pieces (Fig. 68l). These are similar to those discussed by Hole, Flannery, and Neely (1969:78–79).

Reamers (Fig. 68m): These blade tools have heavy retouch on both sides of the blade creating a long, narrow parallel-sided form similar to the "limace" of Paleolithic industries. Unlike the tips of drills, their tips are rounded and blunt.

Large Drills (Fig. 69a,b): Most of these tools are made from large flakes or fragments of medium Gray Chert. These are reduced on the edges with massive unifacial or bifacial flaking until a long piece, rhomboidal in section, remains. Use of the tool leaves the sharp edges battered and scratched. On some examples, there is clear evidence of rotary motion on the tip, while on others there is evidence of a bituminous hafting adhesive. Use as a large drill best explains both features. Such a drill would be ideal for cutting the holes in perforated stones. It is also possible that these were chisel bits or threshing-sled runners of the Anatolian type, but the wear pattern is not concordant with such possibilities.

PLAIN SICKLES (FIG. 69d–e)

Denticulate Sickles (Fig. 69f–i; Table D1): The earlier Uruk examples are similar to those of the preceding Farukh Phase and in most cases may be only resharpened plain sickles. Beginning in Late

OTHER ARTIFACTS: URUK, JEMDET NASR, AND EARLY DYNASTIC PHASES

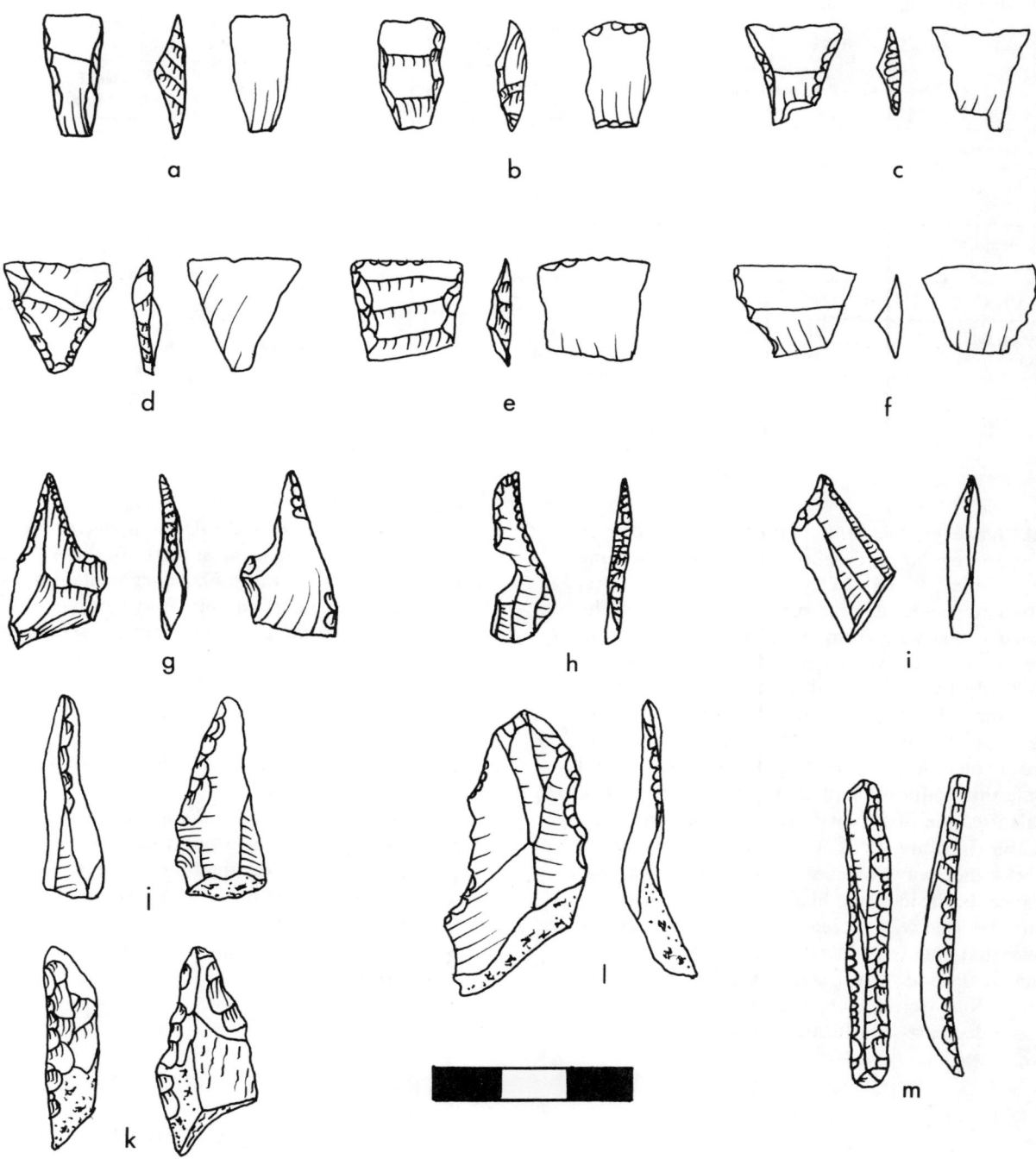

Fig. 68. Chipped Stone Tools: Microliths and Piercing Tools. A. Trapezoid, fine gray; X40401 (B31). B. Trapezoid, fine gray; X25407 (A17–18). C. Trapezoid, fine translucent brown; X04401 (A2). D. Trapezoid, dark brown; X21303 (A15). E. Trapezoid, dark brown; X06801 (A5). F. Trapezoid, coarse gray; X64003 (B23). G. Perforator, dark brown; X04003 (A1). H. Perforator, fine mottled gray; X29801 (A20). I. Perforator, coarse gray, X46604 (B32). J. Perforator, coarse gray; X40701 (A22). K. Perforator, dark brown; X28402 (A27). L. Pointed piece, fine translucent pink; X46602 (B32). M. Reamer, dark brown; X12602 (A11).

Table 30: Sickle Edge Utilization

	Plain Sickles		Denticulate Sickles	
	One Edge Used	Two Edges Used	One Edge Used	Two Edges Used
Early Dynastic	1	0	7	1
Late Jemdet Nasr	3	1	17	20
Early Jemdet Nasr	3	1	4	3
Late Uruk	1	2	2	1
Early and Middle Uruk	18	4	4	—
Farukh-Bayat	26	3	3	1

Uruk, however, the denticulations become deeper and more regular, and denticulated blades become more common. By Early Jemdet Nasr times, denticulate sickles are the predominant form. The denticulations vary from small to large and from closely-spaced to widely-spaced; a detailed statistical study by T. Douglas Price indicates only a wide range of variation rather than several distinct types of denticulation. Denticulation should increae the amount of cutting a blade can do and should thus reduce the number of blades expended. This raises the possibility that chert became more valuable in Late Uruk times. If so, one would expect other ways of economizing on chert. For instance, both sides of a blade rather than only one should be used with increasing frequency. Table 30 shows that this is in fact the case until the Early Dynastic Period. Until large samples from post-Jemdet Nasr settlements are available, however, the late decrease in utilization cannot be assessed.

CUTTING AND SCRAPING TOOLS (TABLE D1)

End scrapers (Fig. 70a,b): These are larger than earlier examples, though still rather small.

Truncate Pieces (Fig. 70c–f): These few examples show much variation. Both convex and concave working edges occur. One is sufficiently rough that it might well be classified as a pointed piece (Fig. 70f).

Retouched Blades and Blade Segments (Fig. 71a,b): Detailed statistical studies of these plain and retouched blades and blade segments did not indicate any significant changes in size or morphology through time or any significant clusterings of retouch attributes with blade form attributes.

RETOUCHED FLAKES AND BLADES

Denticulate Blades and Blade Segments (Fig. 71c,f): One example has a point on one end (Fig. 71c). Note that the denticulations on these are much too steep to provide an adequate sickle edge.

Denticulate Flakes (Fig. 71e,d).

Notched Blades and Blade Segments.

Notched Flakes.

HEAVY CHIPPED STONE TOOLS

Choppers and Chopping Tools (Fig. 72a,b,c): Choppers and chopping tools seem smaller than those of earlier phases. Large limestone flakes used as cleavers occur.

Hoes (Fig. 72d,e): These two examples are surprisingly late. One is of calcite and the other is of a sandstone or quartzite. The former is battered; the latter is relatively fresh. Whether these were actually used in digging and hoeing is not known.

OTHER ARTIFACTS: URUK, JEMDET NASR, AND EARLY DYNASTIC PHASES

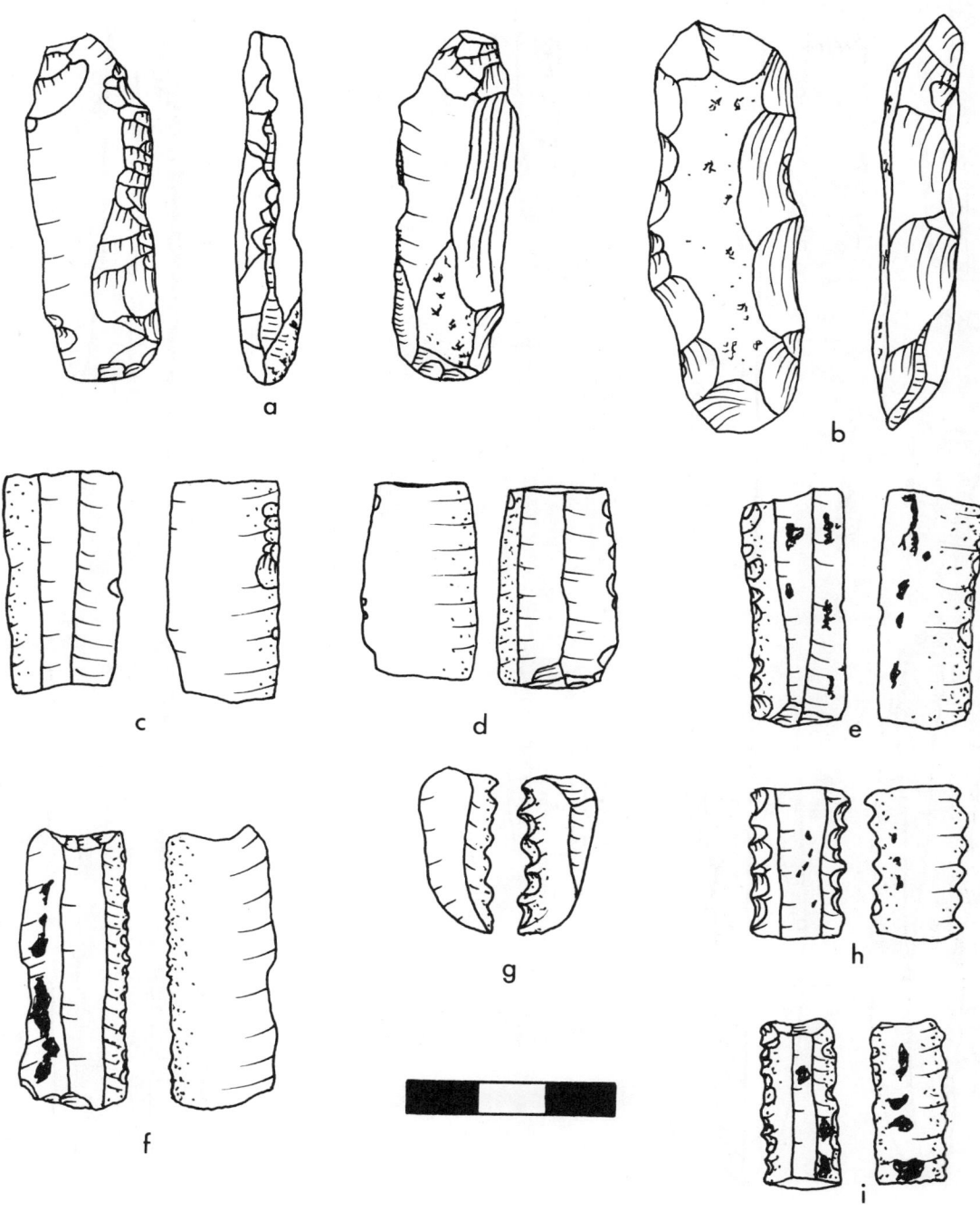

Fig. 69. Chipped Stone Tools: Large Drills and Sickles. A. Large drill, fine green; X432 (B31). B. Large drill, coarse gray; X462 (B32). C. Sickle blade, coarse gray; X51102 (B33). D. Sickle blade, coarse gray; X11811 (A9–10). E. Sickle blade, coarse gray; X51103 (B33). F. Denticulate sickle blade, coarse gray; X12005 (A9–10). G. Denticulate sickle blade, fine banded brown; X04301 (A2). H. Denticulate sickle blade, coarse gray; X20808 (A12–13). I. Denticulate sickle blade, coarse gray; X12604 (A11).

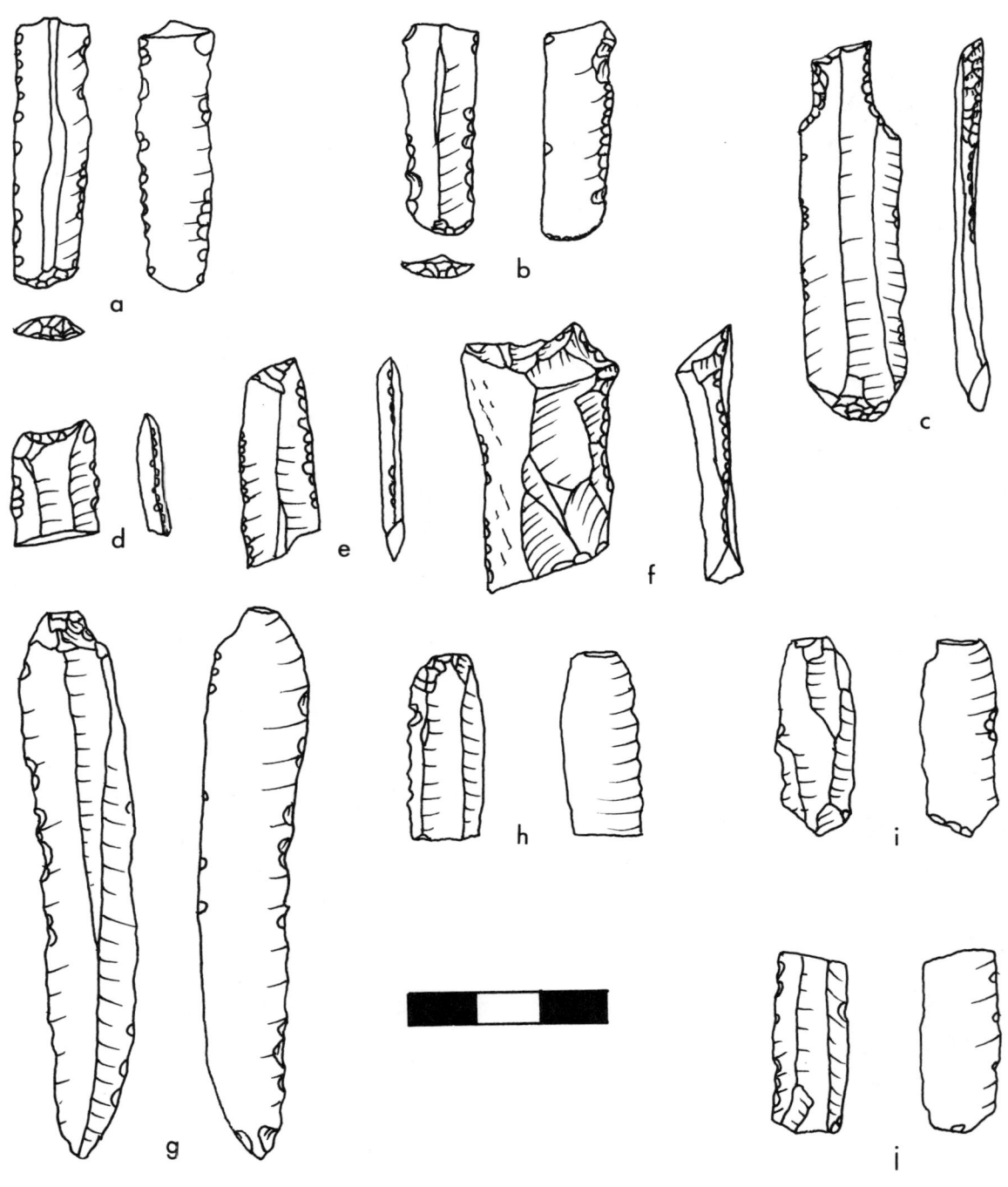

Fig. 70. Chipped Stone Tools: Endscrapers and Truncate Pieces. A. Endscraper, fine mottled gray; X46803 (B32). B. Endscraper, fine brown; X12503 (A8). C. Truncate piece, dark brown; X57902 (B35). D. Truncate piece, fine brown; X31901 (B28). E. Truncate piece, dark brown; X48101 (B33). F. Truncate and pointed piece, dark brown; X25604 (A17–19). G. Blade, coarse gray; X55801 (B34). H. Blade, dark brown; X56602 (B35). I. Blade segment, coarse gray; X10401 (A8). J. Blade segment, fine pink; X08701 (A7).

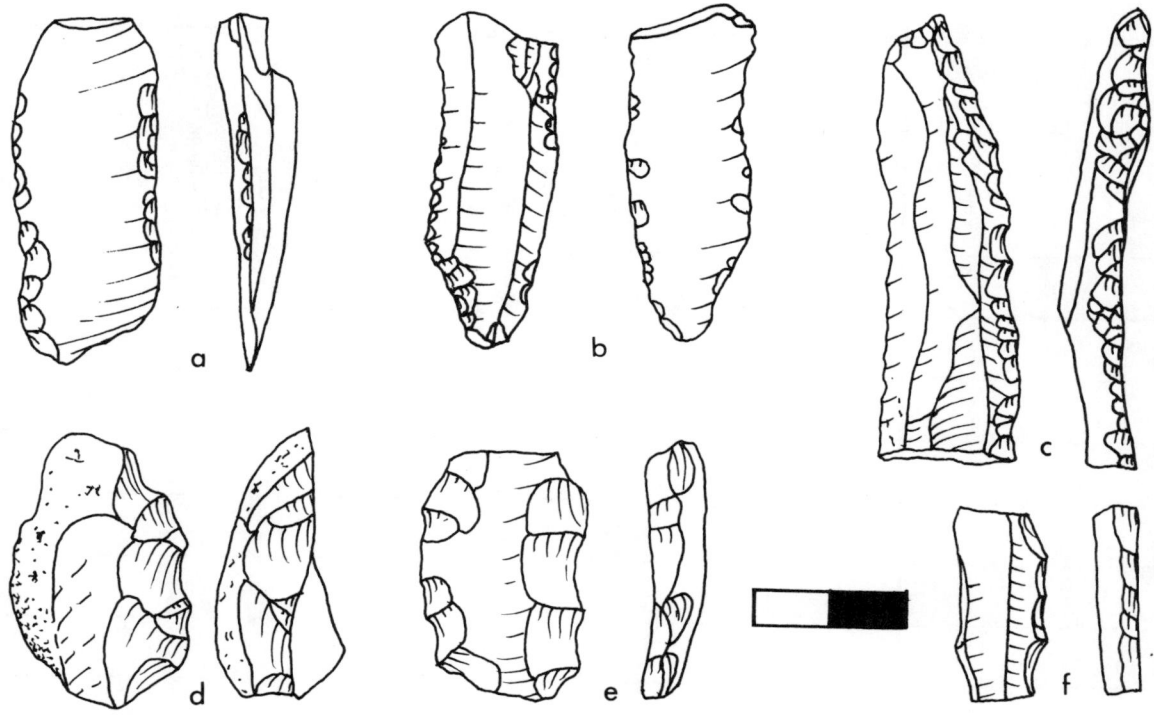

Fig. 71. Chipped Stone Tools: Retouched Pieces and Denticulate Flakes and Blades. A. Retouched blade, burnt; X24802 (A17). B. Retouched blade, fine banded brown; X41203 (B32). C. Denticulate blade, fine gray; X29803 (A20). D. Denticulate flake, dark brown; X298 (A20). E. Denticulate flake, coarse gray; X515 (B33). F. Denticulate blade, fine banded gray; X31703 (B27).

HEAVY STONE TOOLS

GRINDING SLABS AND MORTARS
(TABLE D5, PLATE 12)
by Ellen Berger

Descriptive information is available on ten complete and seven fragmentary grinding slabs and one fragmentary mortar. Two fragments have inadequate provenience information, because they were damaged in a flooding of our work space early in the excavation season.

The slabs are made from calcite (e.g. limestone), vesicular basalt, or conglomerate. Calcite boulders are easily obtained from the nearby Mehmeh River. Basalt, however, does not occur locally. It could have been imported by boat from the Middle Euphrates or Upper Tigris to the west, or by donkey from the Van or Urmia areas on the plateau to the northwest. Vesicular basalt is used for grinding tools in Mesopotamia from Jemdet Nasr times at least until Sasanian times. The conglomerate is like that of the Bakhtiari Formation north of the Susiana Plain. More exact knowledge of the sources of these stones is needed.

The slabs can be divided into four categories on the basis of the shape of the upper or grinding surface following Hole, Flannery, and Neely (1969: 171-181):

1) *Flat slabs*: These have flat or slightly convex uncurved surfaces (Plate 12c).
2) *Flat slabs with mortar*: These otherwise flat slabs have a small hemispherical concavity in the middle of the slab.
3) *Saddle slab*: These have concave surfaces with a marked curvature along the length of the slab (Plate 12b,e).
4) *Basin slabs*: These have a slightly concave grinding surface with a surrounding, raised rim (Plate 12d).

Table 31: Uruk, Jemdet Nasr, and Early Dynastic Chipped Stone Tools

	Trapezoid	Drill	Pointed Piece	Plain Sickle	Denticulate Sickle	Endscraper	Truncate Piece	Retouched Blade	Retouched Flake	Denticulate Blade	Denticulate Flake	Notched Blade	Notched Flake	Chopper-Chopping Tool	Hoe	Other
A1–2	1	1			4											
A3				1	1				2		4					
A5	1				1						2		1	1		1 burin (?)
A6					3						1					
A7				1	2						1		2			
A8					2	1		1								
A9–10		1		3	10				2							
A11					3		1									1 reamer
A12								2		1		1				
A13		1						3	6		1	1				
A14–15	1							4			2					
A16–17					1			2	5				2			1 burin (?)
A18		1							1				1			
A19					2				1							
A20		1			1			3	2	1	1		1			
A21					2			4			2		1			

OTHER ARTIFACTS: URUK, JEMDET NASR, AND EARLY DYNASTIC PHASES

Table 31: Uruk, Jemdet Nasr, and Early Dynastic Chipped Stone Tools (Con't)

	Trapezoid	Drill	Pointed Piece	Plain Sickle	Denticulate Sickle	Endscraper	Truncate Piece	Retouched Blade	Retouched Flake	Denticulate Blade	Denticulate Flake	Notched Blade	Notched Flake	Chopper-Chopping Tool	Hoe	Other
B20					2			4			3	1	1			
B21					3				1							
B22					14				1		1					
B23	1				3								1			
B24					1				1				1			
B25				2							1		2			
B26				1	2	1			1				1	2		
B27		1	1						2	1	1		2			
B28				1			1	1			2		1			
B29				1		1		3	2		2	1				
B30					1				3		1		1		1	
B31	1	1						4	3		1		1	2		1 large drill
B32		1	1	2		1	1	1		1			1	2		10 large drills
B33				2	2		1	2	4		2				1	
B34		1		4	3	1	2	3	1		1					1 reamer
B35				4				2	1							
B36		1		9				3	1		1	1		1		

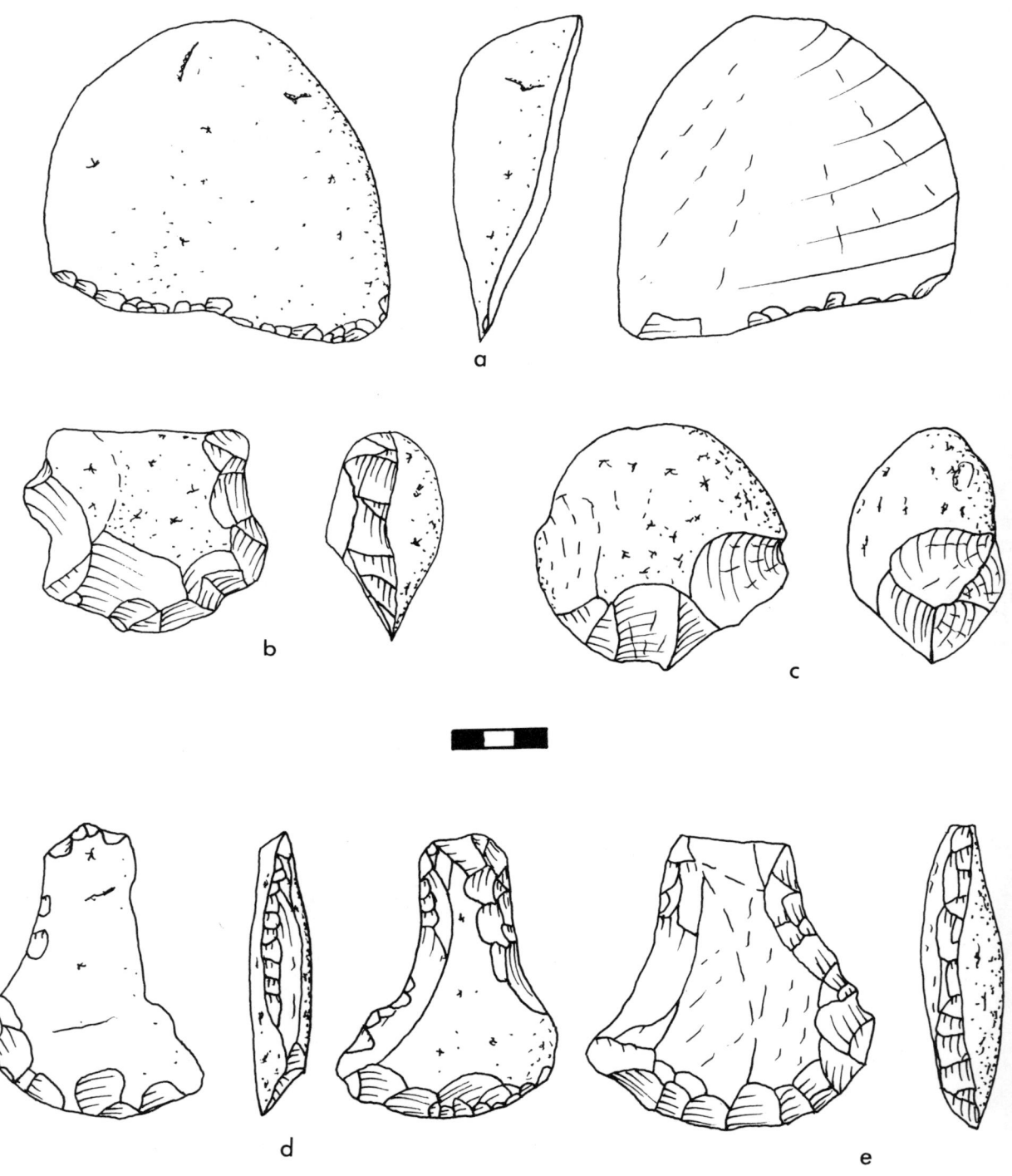

Fig. 72. Chipped Stone Tools: Heavy Tools. A. Calcite flake cleaver; X348 (B28). B. Calcite chopping tool; X432 (B31). C. Calcite chopper; X223 (A F19). D. Calcite hoe; X396 (B30). E. Sandstone hoe; X517 (B33).

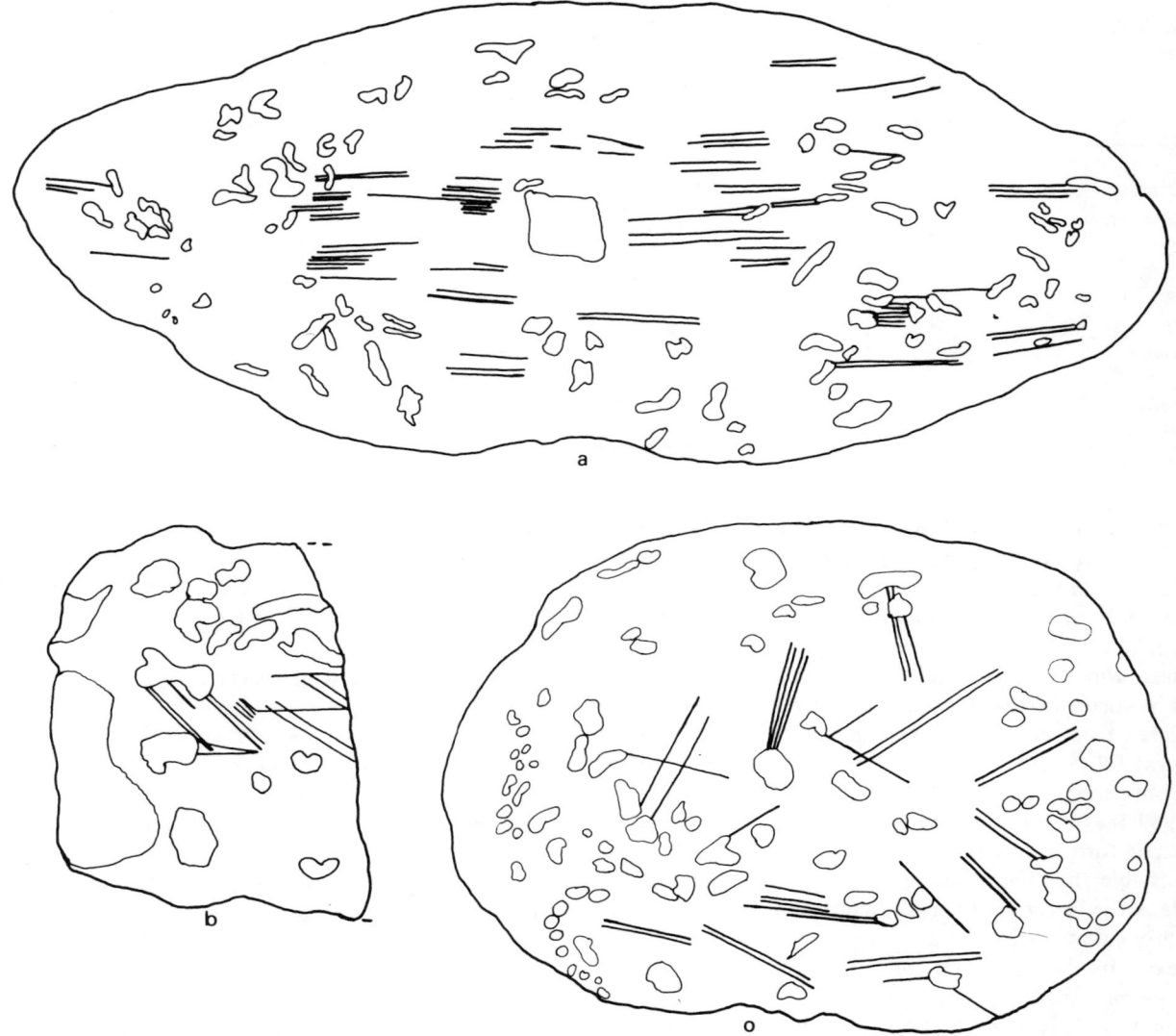

Fig. 73. Grinding Slab Wear Patterns: A. Saddle slab, calcite; X596 (B36). B. Flat slab, calcite; X314 (AF10). C. Flat slab, basalt; X127 (A9).

While mortars and flat slabs with mortars represent distinct activities, there is a possibility that saddle and basin slabs are only worn examples of flat slabs. This possibility is unlikely, however, since most flat slabs are thinner than the maximum height of the basin and saddle slabs, indicating that the latter were made deliberately from a much thicker piece of raw material rather than from flat slabs.

On a number of the slabs it is possible to detect marks resulting from use. Two flat slabs, one basalt and one calcite, exhibit scratches at all angles (Fig. 73c), which may indicate a roughly rotary motion. Two saddle slabs, one basalt and one calcite, exhibit scratches parallel with the long axis of the slab (Fig. 73b), which indicates a back-and-forth motion. One mortar of calcite exhibits a polish. This may result from the use of a pestle made of soft substance such as wood. Thus, usage marks indicate that at least three of the shape categories of slab and mortar were used in different ways. Furthermore, since the calcite and basalt examples of each shape exhibit similar scratches, there is no reason to argue that basalt artifacts had different uses from calcite artifacts.

The distribution of the different types of slabs is

Table 32: Stratigraphic Distribution of the Rough Stone Tools

	Flat Slab	Saddle Slab	Basin	Mortar	Partially Perforated Stone	Perforated Stone
Early Dynastic	—	—	—	—	—	—
Late Jemdet Nasr	2	1	—	—	2	2
Early Jemdet Nasr	—	2	1	2	1	2
Late Uruk	1	1	—	—	1	1
Middle Uruk	2	—	2	1	1	4
Early Uruk	—	1	—	—	—	1

The distribution of the different types of slabs is provocative. Flat slabs with mortars and basin slabs occur together in both Uruk and Jemdet Nasr contexts in piles of boulders near buildings. Only calcite examples are known. It is possible that these two were used together in a particular activity. It is also possible that they were repeatedly collected from earlier deposits and used as architectural fill. Saddle-mortar combinations are known from earlier Tepe Sabz (Hole, Flannery, and Neely 1969:181). On the other hand, flat and saddle slabs occur throughout the Farukhabad sequence. It is possible that flat slabs are the upper and saddle slabs the lower member of the grinding apparatus. Only calcite examples are known from Uruk contexts. In later contexts, only basalt examples are known. Since there is no evidence of changing function, it is likely that basalt and conglomerate, very durable materials, were used when economic conditions permitted their procurement.

PALETTES

Three small abrading stones were found in Middle and Late Uruk deposits. The largest is a rough rectangular piece of calcite 13.6 by 11.9 by 3.3 cm with an oval cavity 9.7 by 5.5 cm on one face. It weighs 940 gms. The rounded cavity is polished, and there are traces of red ocher and perhaps yellow ocher in and around it (B34, X579, Plate 12f). In a Middle Uruk burial found eroding between Excavation A and B, there was a roughly rectangular piece of gray sandstone worked to a convex form on all faces. It is 12.6 by 9.3 by 3.0 cm and weighs about 620 gms. It has a slight concavity on one face (X545). Another small gray sandstone rectangle measures only 7.6 by 6.0 by 1.5 cm and weighs 127 gms. There are possible traces of red and yellow ocher (B32, X466).

HAND STONES

The early inhabitants of Tepe Farukhabad could easily collect calcite pebbles from the bed of the nearby Mehmeh River. Many lacking modification and many with only a few scratches, similar to those paving the alleys of many older communities in Southern Iran, were counted, weighed and discarded during our excavation (Tables B1, B2, and B3). Only a few were utilized sufficiently to show the more diagnostic pecking or polish (Table D4). These usually were round and flat pebbles ranging from 8 to 13 cm in diameter and .35 to 1.30 kg in weight. Most were battered from use as hammers, and some were slightly polished from use in grinding.

OBLONG STONES (PLATE 12g)

Fifteen calcite pebbles were long and cylindrical and many of these showed signs of use (Table D4). The eleven intact stones ranged between 12 and 27 cm in length, and .30 and 2.60 kg in weight. Among the 15 oblong stones four were battered on one end, three were battered on the edge, four were polished, one had indications of bitumen adhesive in its hafting. None had bitumen stains. Perhaps these handy items were used for a different range of activities than in earlier periods.

OTHER ARTIFACTS: URUK, JEMDET NASR, AND EARLY DYNASTIC PHASES

CELTS AND RELATED TOOLS
(TABLE D3, PLATE 13b)

Two earlier Uruk calcite celts are similar to the Farukh Phase example and to examples from Tepe Sabz (Ibid:189). All three Farukhabad celts have slightly convex edges and narrow butts. One Uruk piece was neatly finished, but its blade was broken off and its butt shattered, perhaps in the final stages of manufacture (B33, X511). The other Uruk piece was retouched and worked around the butt and sides with bitumen traces in these retouch scars. The bit is convex and symmetrical in section with usage chips and heavy scoring superimposed over the abrasion from sharpening. The poll is plano-convex in section, suggesting that in spite of its symmetrical bit, the piece was mounted horizontally as an adze rather than vertically as an axe (B34, X579, Plate 13b).

A finished calcite celt fell out of Jemdet Nasr levels in the section of Excavation C after the close of fieldwork. This has a longer, narrower shape than the pieces described above and had been extensively retouched along the edges after use and just prior to disposal. The bit has not been retouched and is symmetrical and slightly polished and chipped from use. The poll is also symmetrical. There are traces of bitumen on the butt and poll but not enough to establish how the artifact was mounted.

All of these instruments were made from relatively soft calcite and their working edges are chipped or scored and polished. It is possible that these were hoe blades rather than adzes for cutting. A detailed study of a larger sample is needed.

Also from Jemdet Nasr deposits is a curious wedge made from a flat calcite pebble, two faces of which have been planed to form an angle of 30 degrees. The butt is battered and the edge is abraded, showing that the tool was indeed hammered into something as a wedge would be. There is also a small pecked depression in one face (B23, X299).

PERFORATED AND PARTIALLY PERFORATED STONES
(TABLE D8, PLATE 13)

A large series of these modified circular or oval flat pebbles were found in the late fourth millenium deposits. Figure 74 shows some metric attributes of both these and earlier pieces. As in the earlier occurrences, the partially and fully perforated stones seem to occur in the same or closely related layers. The former are pieces with pecked depressions on one or both faces which do not meet to form a hole. There is no other wear in the depression or on the surface around the depression. The unperforated stones range from 11.0 to 20.0 cm in diameter, 4.5 to 8.4 cm in thickness and .80 to 2.90 kgs in weight when complete. Th depressions range from a negligble diameter up to 5.5 cm. These are thus generally larger and heavier than the earlier partially-perforated stones. In contrast to the earlier examples, several are broken in half, apparently in the course of manufacture. The fully-perforated stones range from 6.8 to 19.0 cm in diameter, 2.7 to 6.3 cm in thickness, and .21 to 2.1 kgs in weight. They are more variable in size than earlier perforated stones and are generally smaller than contemporary partially perforated stones. If the latter are unfinished pieces, then only the larger pieces tended to be unsatisfactory or to break during manufacture. As in Farukh times, there is one specimen with a drilled hole and traces of surface polish (A11,X125). It is one of the few such artifacts of gypsum rather than calcite. It was probably a mace head. The remaining fully-perforated pieces have biconical holes, all but one of which are pecked. There are possible size modes of 0.4, 1.2, and 2.0 kgs. Their depressions range from 3.0 to 6.1 cm in average diameter. Thus, as with the two earlier pieces of this variety, the depressions tend to be larger than those of the partially perforated examples, supporting the idea that the latter are unfinished pieces. Only five of the eleven pieces of this variety exhibit definite polish at the point of maximum constriction of the hole and only three have been smashed into segments as were the earlier examples. In contrast to the earlier set, two-thirds are unbroken and one fifth exhibit no signs of use. In summary, the later examples of these artifacts are similar to the earlier in material, manufacturing technique, and range of size. They contrast, however, in that there are attempts to make very large pieces, most of which broke or were rejected, and that only a few of the finished pieces were battered to fragments at the end of their useful life; indeed only half of them are heavily used.

This leaves us with the question of the uses to which the perforated stones were put. Some possibilities can be rejected immediately: 1) They

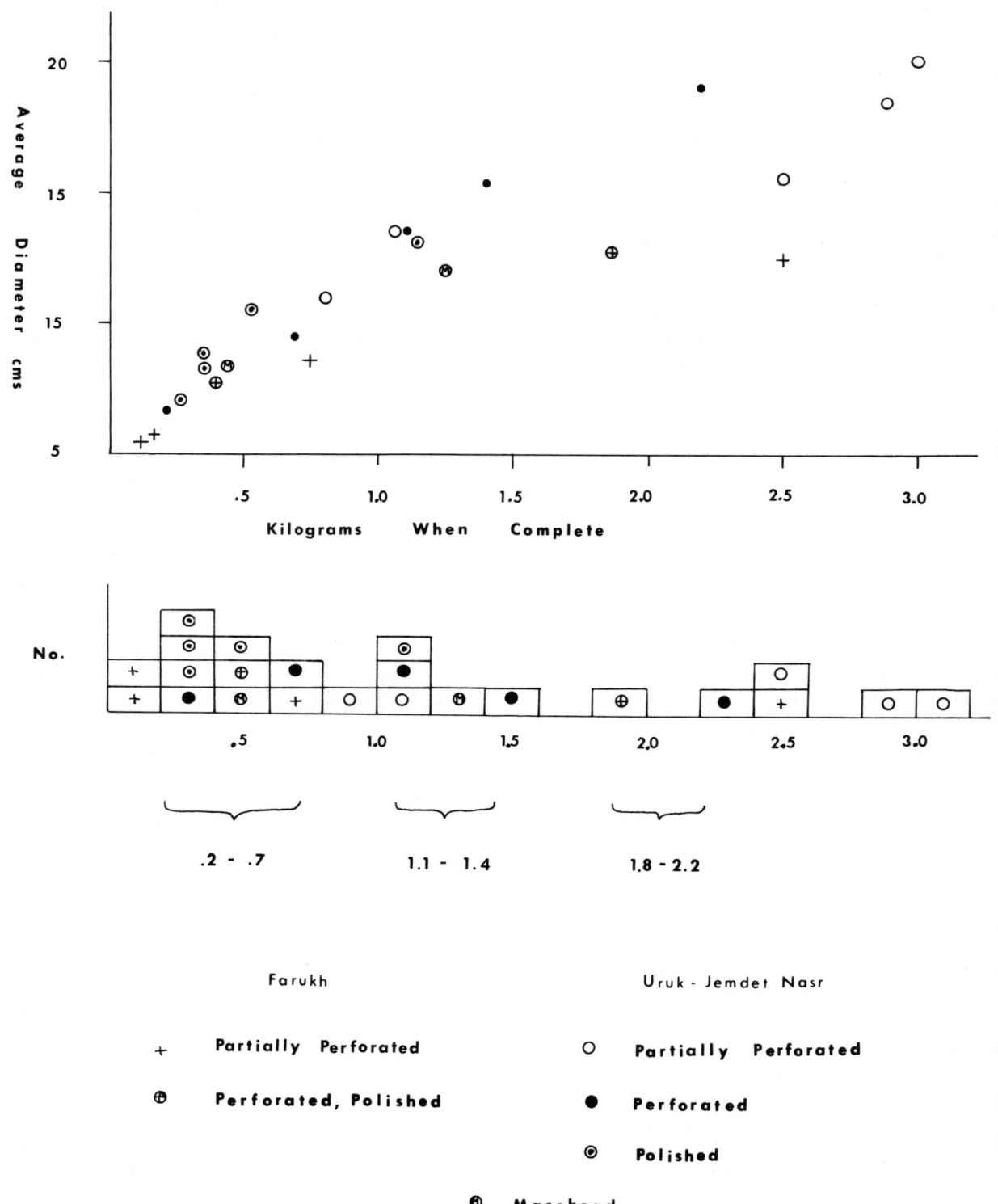

Fig. 74. Attributes of Perforated and Partially Perforated Stones.

OTHER ARTIFACTS: URUK, JEMDET NASR, AND EARLY DYNASTIC PHASES

cannot be net sinkers since fish were never important at Farukhabad and the incidence of stones does not co-vary with the incidence of fish bone. 2) It is unlikely that the flat pieces with the biconical holes were mace heads, since the two thicker pieces with nearly cylindrical holes indicate that perfectly reasonable mace-heads were made throughout the periods under consideration. In addition, some of the stones are rather heavy for such a use. 3) Use as a digging stick weight would seem to require that the stone be tightly fixed, precluding the development of a polish. However, abrasion against wood and fine silt eventually might create such a wear. Another problem with this possibility is that on seals, fourth millenium farmers are usually portrayed as using multiple part wooden-weighted digging sticks of the type familiar from Egypt (Amiet 1961: Plate 16; 276). Why should the Deh Luran Plain be unique? 4) Use as loom weights should create the observed polish in the holes and might explain why there seem to be several discrete size categories of finished perforated stones. There are possible representations of fourth millenium looms, but they do not show circular perforated elements (Amiet 1961: Plate 16; 275). 5) Perhaps there is a yet unknown use involving abrasion by a soft material.

In short, a few of these artifacts are probably mace heads, and the majority could be loom weights. This ambiguity could be quickly resolved if perforated stones were found in primary contexts; however, it is more likely that better understanding will come only after we study the relative incidence of the artifacts at many sites.

POSSIBLE DRILL REST (FIG. 77n)

An oblong marble pebble from a Middle Uruk layer (B34,X555) has pits in the top and bottom. The pebble is 5.53 cm long, 3.00 cm wide, and 2.05 cm high; it weighs 68.9 gms. The conical pits exhibit rotary scoring and are 2.05 cm in diameter and 1.14 cm deep. While the size and convenient form suggest that this was a rest for the top of a bow drill, there is in fact no way to eliminate the possibility that this is an unfinished perforated stone of unusual shape.

PAINTED STONE OVOID

A very regular egg-shaped pebble of grey quartzite has a unique painted design. The pebble is 9.60 by 6.10 by 5.42 cm and weighs 443 gms. One side has been pecked, perhaps to even out an irregularity. The other side has eight large dots of red ocher arranged in an oval. Each is roughly .9 cm in diameter and .5 cm from its neighbors. The paint is fugitive and survived only because the painted side was lying downward in an Early Uruk Layer (B36 lower, X594). This artifact was found on Easter.

CONCRETE ARTIFACTS

Objects made of a concrete, manufactured by burning gypsum or calcite and combining the mixture of ash and cement with water and a small amount of sand, first appear at the end of the Uruk Period. This material is used in a diversity of ways. Concrete objects other than bricks, vats, and small vessels are discussed below.

DISCS AND OVOIDS
(TABLE D10, PLATE 15b)

Both perforated and unperforated discs of various sizes were used. The two unperforated circular discs are nine and 11 cm in diameter and weigh 150 and 170 gms. Each was molded with the fingers on a packed mud surface. They would serve well as jar covers or as supports for pots during manufacture, but there are no signs of use or wear to confirm such contentions. One large oval disc, smoothed rather than finger-molded, is thick and heavy—weighing 1400 gms—and would not have made a good cover.

The perforated discs are manufactured either by cutting them from other objects or by molding them. The cut examples range in diameter from 6 to 12 cm and in weight from 30 to 160 gms. All, including the one unfinished partially perforated example, exhibit edge battering, which may occur during manufacture rather than during use. The other examples are roughly molded with the fingers in three cases and carefully smoothed in one case. The molded examples range from 14 to 19 cm in diameter and from 480 to 860 gms in weight; they have no wear in the perforation. The smooth example is thicker and heavier, weighing 1700 gms and has striations running through the hole as if from a cord. This example compares well with some of the perforated stones described previously and may have had the same use.

HEMISPHERES

These two objects are actually parabolic in cross-section because of an additional patch of plaster on the top. It seems likely that these were formed, as were the discs, by piling concrete on the ground around a stake. In both examples the hole from the stake was partially plugged at the base with a small addition of cement. The smaller hemisphere has a small oblique hole from its side to the medial hole, which is almost completely blocked from the outside and visible only because of a fracture. If this was a technical device to improve drying, one would expect a similar oblique hole on the larger hemisphere; the other is intact, however, and no such characteristic is detectable. The occurrence of these objects next to the entrance of the elaborate buildings in Excavation A suggests that they were holders for a light pole, perhaps supporting an awning or ornamental streamer but there is no way of confirming this proposition.

VESSELS (PLATE 15a)

The large vats, manufactured by coil-building and perhaps used as storage bins, were discussed previously as features. Small concrete vessels are considered with the fine stone vessels they so cleverly duplicate.

BONE TOOLS
by Richard W. Redding

SEAL (FIG. 75l, PLATE 18c)

From a Middle Uruk context, there is a stamp seal cut from a small piece of large mammal bone. It is in the form of a squatting human figure with large buttocks and with a tight flexing of the knees and elbows. Two incisions mark the neck. The head is featureless except for a drilled hole representing an eye. The figure is 1.91 cm from knee to back, 3.0 cm from buttock to head and .63 cm thick. There is a horizontal biconical perforation from the knee to the spine. The back has an oblique incised cross-hatch design. Each incision is .06 cm wide, and they are spaced .27 to .36 cm apart (B35,X567).

AWLS

There are awl fragments from the Middle and Late Uruk. One has a sharp tip with a shaft .86 cm in diameter (A21 lower, X337). The other's tip is shattered, but the shaft is .62 by .47 cm (B30,X339. A sheep or goat ulna from the Early Jemdet Nasr Period was probably the hilt of a similar awl (A13 upper X162). A short needle 3.89 cm long with a drilled hole .25 cm in diameter and a shaft .60 by .27 cm was found in Late Jemdet Nasr Layers (A9-10,X118 Fig. 75m).

SCRAPERS

There are two intact large scrapers also from the Late Jemdet Nasr Phase. One is made from an equid metapodial distal end and shaft. It was obliquely split, perhaps by twisting (Sadek-Kooros 1973), then beveled by transverse grinding on the sides and the outside of the split end to achieve a concave working edge. The tool is completely polished from contact with soft materials (A7, X087). The other example is from a fragment of the proximal end of the shaft of a large mammal tibia. It has a beveled convex working edge (A7,X085, Fig. 75a). There are three similar but lighter tools from roughly contemporary layers. In one case an intact sheep or goat tibia was broken by twisting, and the distal end was beveled by transverse grinding. It was then used with a gouging motion, creating a heavy polish (A8, X104, Fig. 75b). An example missing the working end was made from the distal portion of the shaft of a sheep or goat tibia. It shows a light polish on the surviving end, perhaps from rubbing against the hand (A6,X078). A barely used example is made from the proximal metatarsal of a sheep or goat. The bone had been broken by twisting and used a few times, leaving a few chips and a slight polish on the working end (C23,X750). In short, we have a class of tools used with a gouging motion on soft

OTHER ARTIFACTS: URUK, JEMDET NASR, AND EARLY DYNASTIC PHASES

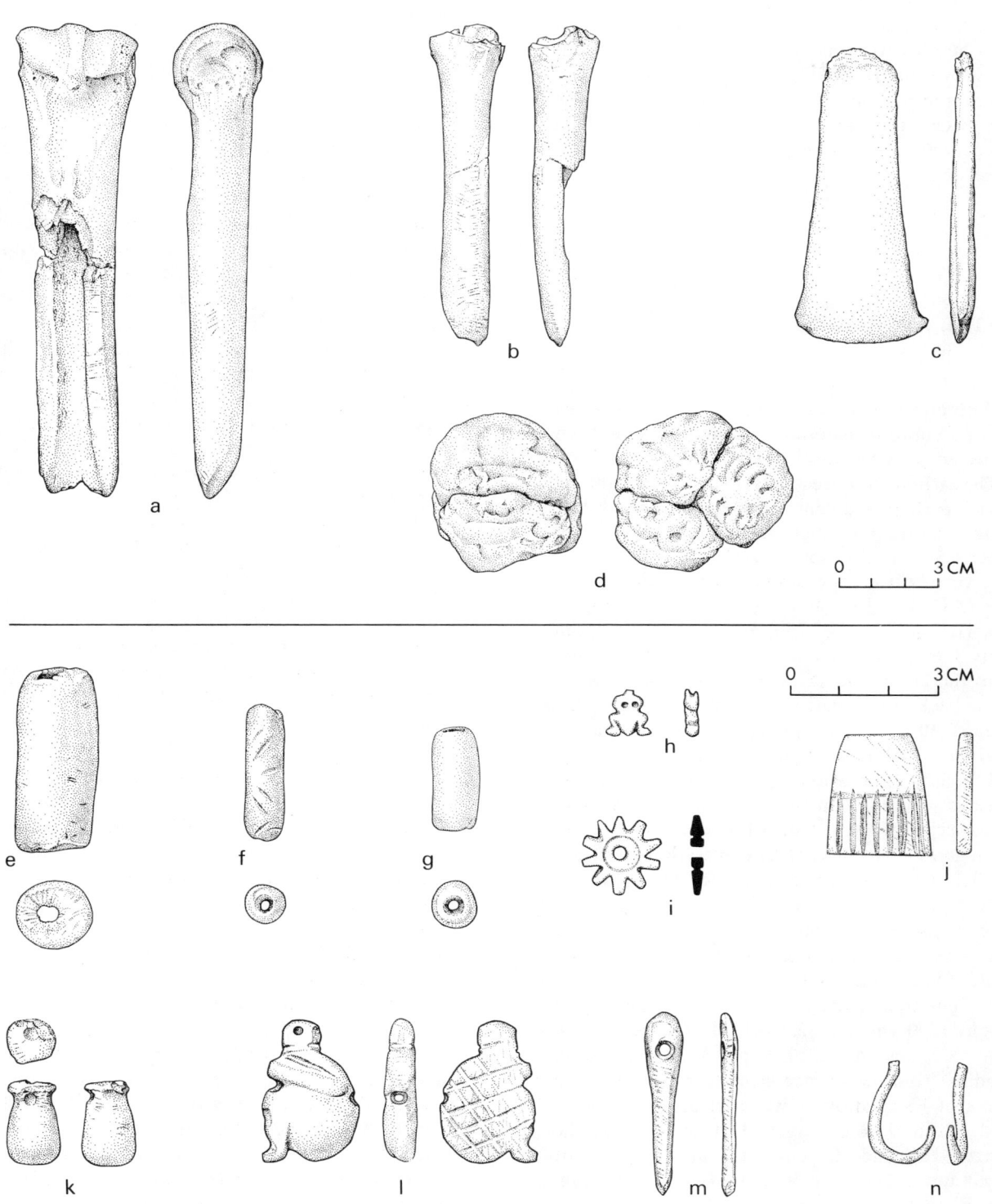

Fig. 75. Bone, Shell, Metal, and Unbaked Clay Artifacts. A. Beveled equid metapodial; X085 (A7). B. Beveled sheep or goat tibia; X104 (A8). C. Celt, cuprous metal; X010 (surface). D. Spherical bulla with seal impressions; X556 (B34). E. Unfinished shell bead; X225 (B23). F. Shell bead with incisions; X235 (B23). G. Shell bead; X103 (A8). H. Shell inlay element; X469 (B32). I. Shell ornament; X069 (A6). J. Shell inlay element; X469 (B32). K. Shell pendant; X130 (B20). L. Bone anthropomorphic stamp seal; X567 (B35). M. Bone awl with eye; X118 (A9–10). N. Fishhook, cuprous metal; X315 (B27).

materials. These vary from 7 to 15 cm in length and have beveled working ends varying from .9 to 2.4 cm in width. In contrast to the Farukh Phase pieces, the beveling is always on the outside. The edge seems too narrow to serve as a useful hide scraper. We are at a loss to suggest other uses for these items.

METAL ARTIFACTS

With one exception noted below, all metal items are of a cuprous material. They have not yet been subjected to a technical analysis.

The earliest recovered metal items are two oblong pieces, perhaps segments of pins from the Middle Uruk. One weighs 2.2 gms (B33 upper, X477); the other 1.5 gms (B33 lower, X515).

A very corroded, crumpled sheet weighing 5.1 gms (A13–14,X191) and a fish-hook weighing .7 gms (B27,X315, Fig. 75n) were recovered from Early Jemdet Nasr levels. Only the haft is missing from the latter. The distance from its barbless tip to the back of the shaft is 1.42 cm. The shaft at the point is .30 by .23 cm. It must have been for rather small fish, if indeed such were its intended prey.

The only Late Jemdet Nasr item is a twisted piece of wire, thought to be lead when excavated. However, Prof. A.A. Gordus of The University of Michigan Department of Chemistry bombarded a small fragment with neutrons and identified it as almost pure silver. It weighs .2 gms (A7,X087).

From the Early Dynastic Period, there are three possible slag pieces, each a mixture of copper oxide, ferrous oxide, limonite, and other constituents not immediately indentifiable. The largest weighs 1300 gms (A1–2,X141). Two others weigh only 18.6 gms (A5,X080) and 1.0 gm (A5,X060). Eroding from the surface near the Early Dynastic layers of Excavation A was a small celt or adze blade. It is 9.38 cm long, 3.84 cm wide at the flanged bit, and .68 cm thick at the point of maximum thickness. It weighs 94 gms (X010, Fig. 75c, Plate 13a).

Cuprous metals are thus attested at Farukhabad in the Middle Uruk Period, but evidence of metal working on the site does not appear until the Early Dynastic period.

OTHER CERAMIC ARTIFACTS

CERAMIC SLAG

This material is not common in the areas excavated, but enough was recovered to indicate that ceramics were being made at Farukhabad during certain periods.

From the Early Uruk we have two fragments of a spill of molten ceramic on a mud floor or on kiln walling weighing 130 gms, (B36,X576) and a similar spill on some fragments of mud brick weighing 188 gms (B36,X590).

From the Middle Uruk there is only a small vesicular mass weighing 3 gms (A21,X330).

From the Late Uruk there is a fused mass of beveled rim bowls weighing 292 gms. At least three bowls, two apparently nested, are visible (A19–20, X295). There is also a mass of ceramic slag weighing 86 gms (B31,X410).

In Early Jemdet Nasr context there is a dripped form of ceramic slag, somewhat like a stalactite, weighing 34 gms (A15,X213).

In general, ceramic slag is found near smaller buildings. In Late Jemdet Nasr times, when smaller buildings are no longer present on the summit of the mound, there is no slag in the samples. The activity presumably moved either to the site's periphery or to another site.

DRAINS (FIG. 76, PLATE 12h)

Both open or trough drains, similar to the Farukh Phase examples, and cylindrical drains occur. Drains range in age from Middle Uruk to Early Jemdet Nasr, but they are most common during the Late Uruk.

The trough drains have chaff-tempered bodies like those of bricks. Each is composed of three slabs forming a base and two sides. The basal slab was laid on an irregular ground surface often strewn with straw. The bottoms are usually slightly convex, ranging from 1.3 to 1.9 cm in thickness. The sides slant inward and range from 1.6 to 2.2 cm in thickness and 9.0 to more than 13 cm in height; the rims are roughly flattened. The one complete example (B31, F24, X424, Plate 12h, Fig. 76a) was found *in situ* leading through a gap at the base of a wall (BF23). It is 61 cm long and 24 cm wide. Each side curves downward at either end to meet the base. One other such curved piece was found (B27, X316).

OTHER ARTIFACTS: URUK, JEMDET NASR, AND EARLY DYNASTIC PHASES

The one definite cylindrical drain was *in situ* leading into the above mentioned trough (B31, F24, X424, Fig. 76b). It is 63 cm long and 20 cm in diameter. It has a coarse sand and straw temper. Two other fragments could be parts of cylindrical vessels, but as they are sand tempered, coarsely scraped, and roughly the same diameter as the *in situ* example, they are most reasonably interpreted as drains. One has a well-made ledge rim (AF19, X223).

CLAY SICKLES (FIG. 76)

Three definite fully vitrified clay sickle fragments and one possible fragment were recovered. The thickened tip of one sickle blade has a parallelogram-shaped section measuring 2.76 x 1.1 cm at a point 4 cm from its tip. The body is green (5Y 6/4) and quite sandy. There is a trace of red ocher on the blade. The working edge is crumbled but not retouched (B31, X426). From the same Middle Uruk layer there is a midsection of the blade of a sickle 6.41 by 1.15 cm at the widest point. The body is greenish (5Y 7/5) but no sandier than ordinary Uruk Ware. The blade is beveled and slightly retouched, leaving denticulations about .71 cm wide and .09 cm deep (X471, Fig. 76d). The slightly later handle of a clay sickle is roughly 2.75 cm in diameter with a blunt convex end. The body is tan rather than green (10YR 7/4). It is slightly flattened on one side so that it best fits the right hand. This piece is in a Late Uruk context (A19, X296). The dubious fragment may also be part of a handle. It is roughly parallelogram-shaped in cross section and measures 2.91 by 2.58 cm. In contrast to the other fragments, it is relatively soft and is tan is color (10YR 8/4). There is a stripe of red-brown paint down one side. This could be part of a large figurine. It is Early Jemdet Nasr in age (A9–10, X120). In summary, these curious artifacts appear in Middle and Late Uruk times even at Farukhabad, a site very near chert sources ideal for sickle blades.

CERAMIC SPINDLE WHORLS
(FIG. 76e–i, TABLE D7)

Ovoid whorls of the sort made in Farukh Phase times continued to be made, although most are darker and greener than earlier examples.

Plain ovoid whorls: One example recorded is from a Middle Uruk layer in Excavation B. It is well within the range of variation of Farukh Phase examples and may be extrusive (Fig. 76e). A large thin example of Jemdet Nasr age is unique (Fig. 76i).

Notched ovoid whorls: As noted in the discussion of Farukh-Bayat artifacts, these are similar in size to the generally earlier plain form. The small sample available shows much variation in notch size, spacing, and angle (Fig. 76f–h). Most examples are from Early and Middle Uruk deposits, but there are two examples from Jemdet Nasr deposits which fall within the range of variation of earlier examples and which are both from deposits with quantities of Uruk and Farukh sherds. They may be extrusive.

PERFORATED SHERD DISCS
(FIG. 76m, TABLE D9)

One thin Susiana Bowl sherd similar to the previously discussed Farukh Phase examples was found in a Middle Uruk layer. It is larger than those in earlier contexts. Since there is only one, it may well be extrusive (B32, X458).

A homogeneous group of four examples was found in Jemdet Nasr layers. These range in diameter from 3.4 to 4.4 cm in weight from 7.3 to 30.3 gms. It is important to note that the largest and heaviest example is unfinished but unbroken, so it may have been rejected because it was too large. The holes show nondescript abrasion. These have the same range of weights as do the molded spindle whorls and since they become more common as the molded whorls become less so (Table 33), they may have taken over the function of the molded whorls.

CHIPPED SHERD DISCS

The larger of these two items is made from the greenish (5Y 7/4) hard-fired base of a Susiana Ware Khazineh Phase bowl (cf, Hole, Flannery, and Neely 1969: Fig. 56b). The flaking is fresh. The smaller disc is made from a Sargarab Ware sherd (7.5Y 8/5) and it is battered around the edges. Such objects can be used as vessel lids, but since these are in one case carefully sharpened and in the other well-used, they might have been useful scraping tools. Both are from the same Middle Uruk layer (B33, X478, X524).

MINIATURE CERAMIC VESSEL (FIG. 76l)

This tiny bowl is only 2.45 cm in diameter and 1.48 cm high. The base is flat and the walls curve slightly inward. It seems to have been modeled around the finger tip. The body has no temper (10YR 7/3) (B20-21, X138).

ROLLED RIM RING (FIG. 76n)

This curious artifact has a hard-fired green (5Y 6/2) body. It was originally 9.1 cm in diameter and 1.87 cm high. The rim of the upper, or larger, opening was rolled inward to thicken the rim but when leather hard it was cut square. The lower, or smaller, opening has a rim which tapers to a sharp edge. This was further modified after firing by retouch on the inside and abrasion on the outside. This abrasion was created by setting the object on a flat surface such as a palette and gently rotating it. The item is from an Early Uruk layer (B36, X588). Similar items are reported from an Early Dynastic site in Southern Iraq (Wright, 1969a:73, Fig. 21d) and from Amouq Phase G levels in Turkey (Braidwood and Braidwood 1960: Fig. 212:5). A thorough search of the literature would doubtless reveal other cases. These have recently been found in association with kiln debris at Tal-i Kureh in the Kur River basin of Fars, and their excavator suggests their use in the scraping of still-soft ceramics (Alden 1979:87-88).

CERAMIC CONE (FIG. 76c)

One definite cone of the sort used to decorate building walls was made of Uruk Ware (10Y 7/4). Its head is 2.43 cm in diameter and it is 6.13 cm long. The head of this relatively small cone is unmodified and unpainted. The sides exhibit striations parallel to the long axis, presumably from the manufacturing process. There are small flakes driven along the axis from both the head and the sharp end, as if the object had actually been hammered into something (B30, X398). Fragments of cones are very difficult to distinguish from fragments of goblet stems. However, the latter

Table 33: Stratigraphic Distribution of the Possible Spindle Whorls

	CERAMIC			STONE
	Plain Ovoid	Notched Ovoid	Perforated Sherd	Disc
Early Dynastic	—	—	—	—
Late Jemdet Nasr	—	—	4	—
Early Jemdet Nasr	—	2	—	—
Late Uruk	—	—	—	—
Middle Uruk	1	3	—	3
Early Uruk	—	3	—	4

generally have detectable concentric thickenings resulting from the action of the potter's wheel.

CERAMIC BEADS (FIG. 76j,k, TABLE D6)

There are two kinds of ceramic beads. There are five relatively large cylindrical beads with large holes, two of which are burnished, perhaps from use, all from Middle Uruk Layers. Two were found on a small mud brick paving (Feature 31) directly over a burial (Feature 35). There are also two small ovoid ceramic beads with bitumen coatings from Late Jemdet Nasr layers.

ANIMAL FIGURINES

Two fragments apparently represent the hind quarters of bovids. One is lightly baked to a gray-brown color (7.5YR 5/2-7/4) with a short tail that curves out and downward. The legs are formed together and abbreviated, being only 2.76 cm long and 1.29 cm wide across the buttocks. The surfaces are rough and unpainted. For the reasons cited in the discussion of the Farukh Phase figurine in Chapter IV, this is considered to represent a bovid (B33, X511). Another tiny fragment, hardly baked

OTHER ARTIFACTS: URUK, JEMDET NASR, AND EARLY DYNASTIC PHASES

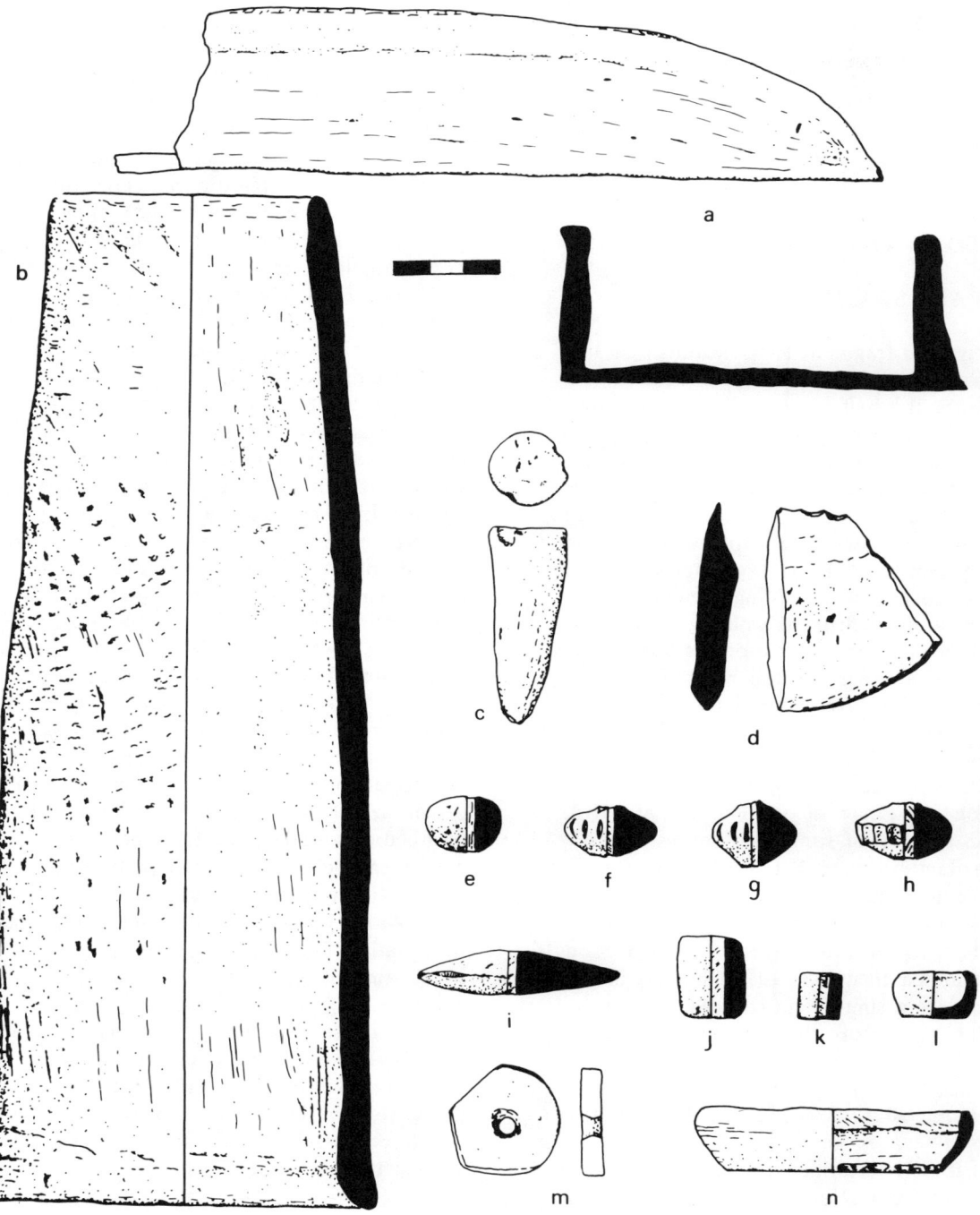

Fig. 76. Other Ceramic Artifacts. A. Trough drain, straw, brown ceramic; X424 (B31). B. Cylindrical drain, straw and calcite, very pale brown ceramic; X424 (B31). C. Wall cone, very pale brown ceramic; X398 (B30). D. Fragment of sickle blade, pale yellow ceramic (note edge retouch); X471 (B31). E. Plain ovoid spindle whorl, pink ceramic; X481 (B33). F. Notched ovoid spindle whorl, white ceramic; X213 (A15). G. Notched ovoid spindle whorl, white ceramic, X476 (B33). H. Notched ovoid spindle whorl, white ceramic; X529 (B34). I. Large disc whorl; 5Y 8/3 (pale yellow) ceramic, max. diam.: 6.25, thickness: 1.33, minimum hole diam.: 0.40, weight: 34.4; X175 (B22). J. Cylindrical bead, pink (7.5YR 7/3) ceramic; X529 (B34). K. Cylindrical bead, pink (7.5YR 7/4) ceramic; X528 (B34). L. Miniature vessel, very pale brown ceramic; X138 (B20–21). M. Perforated sherd disc, pale yellow ceramic; X229 (B23). N. Rolled rim ring, light olive gray ceramic; X588 (B36).

at all (10YR 7/4), is not measurable. There are several fingernail impressions in its flanks, so at first I thought it might be a tablet fragment. However it is modeled exactly like the above described piece. It is from a Late Jemdet Nasr locus (C24, X759).

UNBAKED CLAY ARTIFACTS

BALE SEALING (PLATE 16a)

A lightly-fired fragment of the sealing of a bale of skins was found. On the reverse is the imprint of fine hairs about a half cm long, like the hair on a gazelle, wild goat, or wild sheep. The string holding the skins together has a loose S-twist with strands 1.5 cm thick, an overall thickness of about .24 cm, and a twist period of about .55 cm. The surviving lower left hand corner of the sealing exhibits on its obverse the imprint of the lowest register of a cylinder seal over a series of fingerprints. The seal shows a row of quadrupeds walking from left to right. The head of one animal on the left and the hind legs of another on the right are visible. Similar impressions are well-known at both Susa (cf. Amiet 1972:Pls. 6–10—particularly Nos. 514–6 and 540–4) and Warka (cf. Amiet 1961:Pl. 10, Nos. 181, 185). This sealing fragment was found in Excavation A, Layer 20 (X299), a Late Uruk deposit in an area of simple residences.

This artifact indicates that small bales of goods packaged under the authority of the holder of a cylinder seal of a common genre were opened at Farukhabad. Its location suggests that these goods were distributed to individuals of modest means; however, since a single item can easily be moved about, this is no more than a suggestion.

SPHERICAL BULLA (FIG. 75d, PLATE 16e)

One of these interesting administrative artifacts was found in Excavation B, Layer 34, in an ashy feature probably intrusive from Layer 33, a Middle Uruk layer (X556). It is made of a tan, silty clay (10YR 8/4). Neutron activation analysis indicates the clay is local to Deh Luran (James Blackman, p.c.). It is roughly egg-shaped, with its longest dimension about 5.4 cm. Perpendicular to this, it is 5.2 by 4.4 cm. Its walls are about 1.5 cm thick and the interior cavity is about 2.0 cm in diameter. The surviving pieces constitute about 90 percent of the original bulla, which when intact would have weighed about 115 gms without its counters in the cavity. Within the cavity the imprint of at least one small tetrahedral counter about .85 cm on a side is clear. The bulla was broken in antiquity by a blow on the small end, creating three crescentic pieces. This blow obscured the imprinted number symbols, but at least three, perhaps five, small, deep circular to rectanguloid vertical imprints are visible. Each is .32 by .32 cm. These numbers apparently represent tens on the Susa Bullae (Amiet 1972: Pl. 66; No.520 exhibits nine of the next smallest unit), so the bulla records at least 30 items.

On the exterior of the finished bulla, at least three seals were impressed, one of which is unequivocal, the imprint of a stamp seal perhaps an oval, with a representation of a scorpion. The tail and front claws are not clear, but the body is definite. (cf. Amiet 1972:Pl. 4, 460; Pl.41, 460). The second imprint is of a rectangular stamp seal, 2.63 by 1.38 cm, with an arrangement of dots, perhaps representing two animals back-to-back (cf. Amiet 1972:Pl. 57, 400–407; Pl. 58, 408–413). The last are several imprints of a braided design or guilloche (cf. Amiet 1972: Pl. 6, 483–488). These could be snakes or animal tails or necks. Such designs seem to be characteristic of cylinder seals, but there is no way to tell in this case exactly what they represent.

The size of the bulla, the association with small tetrahedral counters, and the types of impressions closely parallel examples from Susa. As no comparable Middle Uruk material has been reported from Warka or other sites, the similarity is not yet informative. For this study the most important implication of this artifact is that a relatively large shipment of goods or animals was sent to Farukhabad under the authority of at least three sealbearers, two using ordinary stamp seals and one using a more unusual seal. Furthermore, there seems to have been an authority at Farukhabad which received the goods and checked the counters against the delivered items.

JAR STOPPERS (PLATE 16c)

One object with the imprint of a vessel rim and two which may have been formed for a similar use were recovered. All were of unbaked tan silty clay.

The earliest example was once of conical form which would have fitted into an everted neck, straight rim jar with a rim diameter of 9.5 cm, a rim angle of 60 degrees, and a neck height of 3.85 cm. When complete it would have weighed about 500 gm, but is was damaged during removal. The clay mass seems to have been rounded off in the jar neck and then shaved flat. There was no seal impression. This item was found in Excavation B, Layer 37—the mixed, eroded surface of the Farukh Phase mound. I attribute it to the Early Uruk because it would fit more easily into Early Uruk vessel forms and because it is difficult to conceive how a Farukh Phase unbaked clay artifact could have survived so close to the ground surface for the several centuries which elapsed between the Farukh and Early Uruk occupations. Neutron Activation Analysis indicates the clay of this stopper is unique and may not be local to the Deh Luran area (James Blackman, p.c.).

The definite stopper is a small oval form about 3.8 cm in diameter and 2.25 cm thick. It was twisted into the neck of a small vessel with a rim diameter slightly greater than 3.5 cm and an inner neck diameter of about 2.7 cm. It fits the mouth of several of our Late Uruk bottles exactly. The clay apparently contained a small twig which rotted away, leaving an impression on the underside of the stopper about .5 cm in diameter. The top of the stopper was shaved off and its roughly convex surface had some faint hand imprints, but there was no seal imprint. This artifact was found at the contact zone between an Early Uruk pit (Excavation A, Feature 23) and a Late Uruk Pit filled with beveled rim bowls (Excavation A, Feature 19) (X306,338,374). It is attributable to the Late Uruk period when bottles were common.

A large plano-convex mud form, circular in plan, bears no evidence of a vessel imprint, and may not have been intended as a stopper. It is 10.5 cm in diameter, 4.4 cm thick, and weighs 474 gms. Its clay contains several large pebbles. There are no imprints of interest. This artifact was in an Early Jemdet Nasr deposit (A13,X155).

OVOIDS (PLATE 16d)

There are two egg-shaped clay pieces, of the form usually termed 'sling missiles', from the Late Uruk Period. An example from the Beveled Rim Bowl Pit (A20, X338) weighed about 38 gms when intact and is 4.35 cm long and 2.97 cm in diameter. The other weighed about 34 gms when intact and is 2.71 cm in diameter. The small end is shattered, and the precise length is therefore unknown (B28, X349). These are close to the mean weight reported for unequivocal sling missiles of Hellenistic date (Korfmann 1973: 39–41).

BITUMEN ARTIFACTS (Table D15)

In these phases there are 24 shaped artifacts of bitumen. Fifteen are bitumen-covered matting fragments. The weave of the matting is discussed below.

There are many traces of bitumen on sickle blades, but only four mountings are well-preserved (Plate 17a). In three Jemdet Nasr and later cases, the blades are held against the flat surface of a wooden stock rather than mounted in a groove in the stock. In one Uruk example the blades are held in a groove, as in the earlier Farukh Phase example.

Three perforated ovoids are present, all in Middle Uruk layers (Plate 17d,e). These objects resemble a cigar, but are oval in cross-section. They range from 5 to 35 gms in weight. In two cases, the hole exhibits the imprint of a reed. The use of these objects is unknown. One lump of bitumen was used to seal lashing around a fabric wrapping or bag, discussed below. It lacks an actual seal impression. It was from the late Uruk pit filled with beveled rim bowls (A20, F19, X338).

Finally, there are several fragments of shaped lumps of bitumen from Late Jemdet Nasr layers. These forms are one means of packaging bitumen for storage or transport (Wright 1969: 58–60).

WOVEN ARTIFACTS (Table D16)

The reeds or rushes used for mats range from .4 to 1.8 cm in width. There seems to be a more common wide variety ranging from .9 to 1.8 cm and a less common narrow variety ranging from .4 to .7 cm in width. The latter was used only in Late Jemdet Nasr and Early Dynastic times. In one case the two types were used on the same mat, the narrower rush perhaps forming a border. All well-preserved fragments had a two-over-two-under twill pattern. There are nineteen examples. A bitumen sealing has the imprint of a flat-weave fabric with heavy warp and fine weft, similar to that used today in southwest Iran to make saddle-bags and floor coverings (X338).

On a gypsum cement fragment from Layer 29 of Excavation B there is a poor impression of a heavy, loosely woven cloth with a texture like that of coarse linen.

FINE STONE ARTIFACTS
by Susan Kus

BEADS AND PENDANTS
(FIG. 77s–x, TABLE D6)

There are two kinds of lapis lazuli beads. Most are small cylindrical beads of various lengths of Late Jemdet Nasr and Early Dynastic age. There is one larger and longer bead which is parallelogram-shaped in cross-section (A2, X044, Fig. 77w). It is Early Dynastic in age. This bead and one other still exhibit the parallel striations created during the manufacturing process. The rest have a dull polish probably resulting from use. Also, there is a conical pendant of this material. It is 1.32 cm in base diameter, 83 cm high, and weighs 1.82 gms (A6, X086, Fig. 77v).

The carnelian beads are of two types. There are two small short cylindrical disc beads. There is one longer ovoid bead (A12, X151, Fig. 77u). All have a dull polish. These are Late Uruk and Early Jemdet Nasr in age.

There is one large agate bead. An agate pebble was only partially worked, creating opposed convex polished surfaces, while having the edges rough (A12, X153, Fig. 77s).

Another large bead, unfortunately documented only in field laboratory records, may be of chlorite (B32, X467, Fig. 77t).

The two glazed paste (frit) beads are dissimilar in shape. One is a small rough ovoid. The other is a long ovoid with a spiral groove running around its surface from one end to the other (B20, X141, Fig. 77x). Both are a very pale green in color and from Jemdet Nasr contexts.

The two calcite beads from these later phases and the previously mentioned Farukh Phase bead deserve detailed discussion since they probably represent different steps in bead manufacture (Plate 18d–f). One, a rough limestone cylinder with striations on all faces and a hemispherical pit on one face (A7, X087), could have been intended as a miniature stone vessel rather than as a bead. Another is a smaller rough cylinder with two pits on opposed faces which meet creating a tiny hole (B41, X659). Finally, there is a finished disc bead of polished pink marble (B33, X511). The process of manufacture involved the grinding of a rough cylinder, the drilling of the hole from two sides, and finally, a further grinding and polishing. This series demonstrates that beads were manufactured from softer stones at Farukhabad. It is notable that the finished Middle Uruk example at first glance resembles carnelian.

STONE BOWLS (FIG. 77a–j)[2]

Vessels were made from calcite, gypsum, or a fine gray-green concrete. Most of these stones are of coarse-grained varieties which could be locally obtained, though there is one of a harder translucent green alabaster known from Haft Gel in Eastern Khuzestan (A6, X069). A hemispherical rotary borer of quartzite was found in an Early Uruk layer (B36, X595, Plate 13c). It measures 6.2 cm in diameter and neatly fits into a gypsum ring base from the same layer. During this period stone bowls were certainly cut at Farukhabad, and the practice doubtless continued. The concrete bowls were probably made in a mold, though careful smoothing has obliterated any evidence of this. This concrete can be distinguished from a fine sandstone only by means of a microscopic examination.

There are two major types of bowls. One has incurved sides, approaching a hemispherical shape (Fig. 77f–j). The rim usually has an exterior band and the calcite examples are sometimes polished. Diameters range from 9 to 28 cm, and side angles range from 55 to 90 degrees. The other type has conical sides, with a rim which is always simply tapered to a round lip (Fig. 77a–d). Diameters range from 8 to 18 cm, and side angles range from 45 to 75 degrees. There are several flat bases and one ring base, but the association between rims and bases is unknown. There is no association between form or material of the bowl and any measured attribute.

Table 34 shows that the hemispherical bowls are generally earlier. The one Jemdet Nasr example

---

[2] This is condensed and revised from a longer paper by Kus on file at the Museum of Anthropology. The minerals were identified with the help of Carol Dell and the concrete was identified by Paul Goldberg, then at the University of Michigan Department of Geology.

OTHER ARTIFACTS: URUK, JEMDET NASR, AND EARLY DYNASTIC PHASES

Table 34: Stratigraphic Distribution of the Stone Vessel Fragments

	Hemispherical Bowls			Conical Bowls		Other Vessels		
	Gyps.	Calc.	Conc.	Gyps.	Calc.	Gyps.	Calc.	Conc.
Early Dynastic	—	—	—	1	1	—	—	—
Late Jemdet Nasr	1	—	—	2	—	2	—	—
Early Jemdet Nasr	—	—	—	—	—	1	—	1
Late Uruk	—	1	—	2	—	2	1	—
Middle Uruk	1	4	2	1	1	2	—	1
Early Uruk	—	—	—	—	—	1	—	—

	HM	CN	Other		GYP	CAL	CON
ED–JN	1	4	4	ED–JN	7	1	1
Uruk	8	4	7	Uruk	9	7	3

has a grooved flat rim rather than the raised band of the earlier examples. Conical bowls continue into later periods. During the earlier periods, calcite and concrete are more commonly used. The one sherd of concrete from the Jemdet Nasr period was reused as an abrader and is probably extrusive.

OTHER FINE STONE VESSELS

Several unique fine stone vessels were recovered. A rimsherd of a calcite ledge rim jar was in a Late Uruk context (A19–20, X300, Fig. 77e). Its neck is 8.6 cm in diameter and .93 cm thick. The surface is smooth.

A tiny gypsum vessel was cut in a rough block, 1.90 cm high and trapezoidal in plan, 2.43 by 2.39 cm. The side edges of the block were slightly beveled, creating an octagonal shape, and a conoidal depression 1.9 cm in diameter and 1.44 cm deep was cut in the top (A6, X086, Fig. 77m).

A small jar was 1.80 cm high and 3.01 by 3.12 cm in plan. However, there was a low neck 2.19 cm in diameter and .45 cm high with thickened rim and rounded lip. A depression was hollowed 1.66 cm into the block. This little jar was in a Middle Uruk burial found between the two excavations along with two of the concrete bowls (X545, Fig. 77l).

Also in this burial was a larger calcite jar with ledge rim. It is 6.20 cm in diameter and 5.72 cm high. The neck is 3.55 cm in diameter and .60 cm high. The interior is hollowed to a depth of 3.8 cm apparently by gouging out a drilled hole (X545, Fig. 77k).

STONE DISCOIDAL SPINDLE WHORLS (FIG. 77r, PLATE 20c, TABLES 33, D7)

Six well-made whorls exhibit drilled biconical holes, in some cases with a wear like a gentle grinding rather than a polish. Estimated weights when intact of the presently available specimens range from 30.0 to 39.0 gms, though one unweighed piece was certainly somewhat heavier (X569). Holes range from .64 to 1.18 cm. there is one contemporary, very similar, ceramic whorl included on the same table. This group contrasts with the contemporary "notched ovoid whorls" described previously, which range in weights from 5.6 to 15.1 gms and in hole diameter from .46 to .75 cm. It is likely that these whorls were used to make a heavier weight of thread than the smaller ones (Parsons 1972:67).

EYE AMULET (FIG. 77o, PLATE 18b)

This calcite artifact is 2.05 cm high and, at the base, 1.60 by .76 cm (X173, B22). It weighs 4.25 gms, and probably weighed 4.40 gms when intact. The object was finished by grinding, but wear through handling has obscured all but a few scratches. The holes were drilled from two directions with a parallel-sides drill .26 cm in diameter. The break on the right is abraded and slightly polished. The intact hole shows slight polish on the upper margins, suggesting suspension by a cord. This Late Jemdet Nasr example is similar to other contemporary pieces (Mallowan 1947:33–35; Perkins 1949:191–192).

POSSIBLE WEIGHT (PLATE 20a)

There is a small ovoid pebble of calcite, one end of which has been ground flat. Such objects may have been weights. This Late Uruk example (B29, X368) is 3.99 cm long and weighs 62.0 gms. It conforms to no reported system of weights.

FIGURINE ELEMENT
(FIG. 77q, PLATE 18a)

A portion of a tiny carved gypsum artifact was recovered from a Late Jemdet Nasr context (A11, X126). The intact piece apparently had two conical elements, each of which had a curled tip, meeting at a base to form a "V". Each had several circumferential incisions around the curved conical element. Each element was 1.45 cm high and .65 by .47 cm at its base. If intact, the piece would have measured about 2.3 cm from tip to tip. There is a small hole .22 cm in diameter, drilled through the presumed vertical axis of symmetry from two directions. Richard Redding suggests that this is a representation of wild sheep horns in which the horns, which are in life curved back, are shown curved to the sides in order to convey their distinctive shape in a head-on view. If this suggestion is correct, this piece could have been part of a tiny, multiple-part high relief.

BEVELED DISC (FIG. 77p)

A gray stone disc with beveled edges was found in Early Jemdet Nasr layers (B24, X243). It is 2.44 cm in diameter, .46 cm thick, and has a center hole .42 cm in diameter. On the larger face there are three hemispherical pits each .43 cm in diameter and each having a trace of bitumen in its bottom. Certainly something was mounted in these pits, perhaps shell or fine stone pieces, perhaps forming an item of jewelry.

FLANGED CYLINDER (PLATE 20b)

This item, of an unidentified hard green rock, was found in a Late Jemdet Nasr layer. One end was flanged, and both ends were slightly convex. The flanged end is 2.50 cm in diameter and the plain end is 2.17 cm in diameter. The artifact is 1.71 cm thick and weighs 15.7 gms (A6, X084). This may have been an ear ornament. The recovery of such items in place in graves would confirm this.

CUT ALABASTER PIECES

These artifacts were found in Late Jemdet Nasr and Early Dynatic deposits. One is an oval alabaster pebble which has been ground flat on both faces. It is 3.27 by 2.36 by .82 cm and weighs only 8.6 gms (A5, X063). The other is a six-sided form of which two opposed faces are rough and the other four are ground flat. It is 2.25 by 1.84 by 1.79 cm and weighs 12.1 gms (A6, X078).

MISCELLANEOUS MINERAL FRAGMENTS

Two small crystals of yellow translucent gypsum found in an Early Uruk layer weigh 3.8 gms total (B36, X587). A piece of transparent mica from an Early Dynastic deposit weighs only 1.2 gms (B19, X129).

GROUND HEMATITE

A roughly triangular fragment of hematite was ground on one flat face and one side of the triangle, in both cases leaving a slightly convex surface. The object is 1.27 cm across the base, 1.50 cm high, and .63 cm thick (A17–18, X256).

GLASS BRACELET

While clearing an Early Uruk pit (AF23) cut into a Farukh Phase platform (AF25), a piece of glass bracelet was recovered (X383). It is of layered light and dark green glass with small nodes around its outer perimeter every 1.7 cm. The diameter of the intact bracelet would have been about 7.0 cm; it is .50 cm thick. Such artifacts are characteristic of recent nomad camps. As the pit was close to the present eroding surface of the mound, the piece is doubtless intrusive.

OTHER ARTIFACTS: URUK, JEMDET NASR, AND EARLY DYNASTIC PHASES

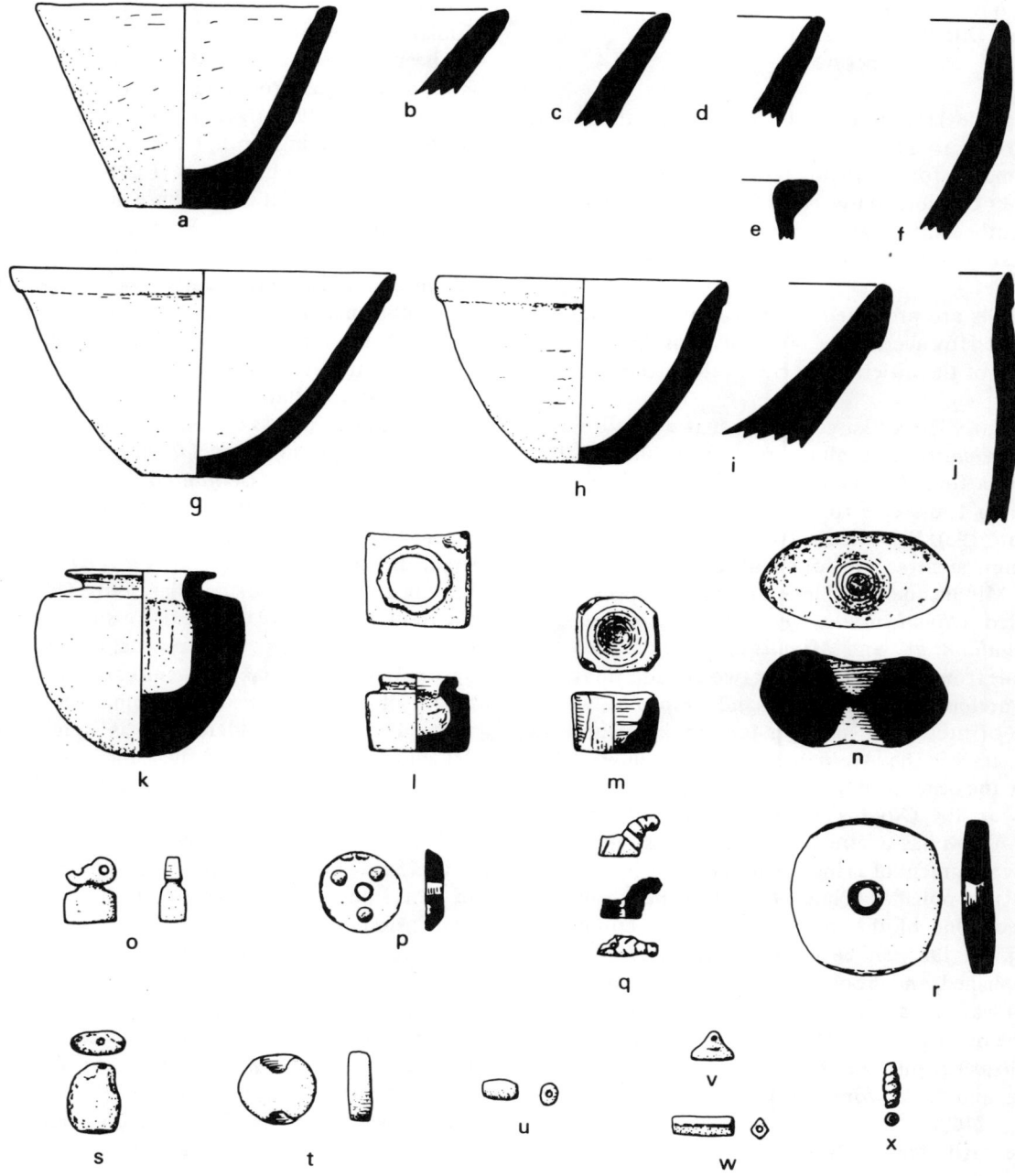

Fig. 77. Fine Stone Artifacts. A. Conical bowl, gypsum, diam.: 9.1; X545 (burial between Excavations A and B). B. Conical bowl rim, gypsum, diam.: 12.5; X060 (A5). C. Conical bowl rim, calcite, diam.: 17.0; X108 (B17). D. Conical bowl rim, gypsum, diam.: 13.5; X063 (A5). E. Ledge rim jar rim, calcite, neck diam.: 8.6; X300 (A19–20). F. Hemispherical bowl rim, gypsum, diam.: 17.0; X306 (A20). G. Hemispherical bowl with band rim, concrete, diam.: 15.0; X545 (burial between Excavations A and B). H. Hemispherical bowl with band rim, concrete, diam.: 8.6; X545 (same). I. Hemispherical banded bowl rim, calcite, diam.: 26.0; X517 (B33). J. Hemispherical banded bowl rim, calcite, diam.: 15.0; X531 (B34). K. Small jar, gypsum, neck diam.: 2.7; X545 (burial between Excavations A and B). L. Small jar, gypsum, neck diam.: 1.5; X545 (same). M. Small octagonal vessel, gypsum; X086 (A6). N. Possible drill rest, calcite; X555 (B34). O. Eye amulet, calcite; X173 (B22). P. Beveled disc, calcite; X243 (B24). Q. Figurine element, gypsum; X126 (A11). R. Spindle whorl, calcite; X596 (B36). S. Bead, agate; X153 (B36). T. Bead, chlorite (?); X467 (B32). U. Bead, carnelian; X151 (A12). V. Conical pendant, lapis lazuli; X086 (A6). W. Bead, lapis lazuli; X044 (A3). X. Bead with spiral groove, faience; X141 (B20).

SHELL ARTIFACTS
by Nancy Talbot[3]

During the later fourth millennium sea shells were brought to Farukhabad in increasing numbers, primarily for the manufacture of ornaments. The closest possible source is the Gulf, now 370 km to the southeast, though perhaps somewhat closer in the past. The Mediterranean is another possible source.

The shells are presented in taxonomic order in Table E7. However, here we will consider the utilization of the different species in the successive phases.

In the Early Uruk Phase only one marine shell, a *Conus tesselatus*, a mollusc preferring shallow waters, was found. It had been cut in half horizontally, or transverse to the aperture and main axis (Plate 19e). Repeated cuttings would produce small rings, such as are found in later phases.

In the Middle and Late Uruk Phases, five species were noted: *Oliva ispidula, Nerita albicilla, Conus sp., Dentalium sp.,* and *Mytilus sp.* They are all obtainable from the Gulf: the first two are intertidal species preferring rocks and sand respectively; *Mytilus*, or mother-of-pearl, is today taken from deep waters off the Arabian shore; *Dentalium* is found on the beaches of the Gulf. Various modifications occur; the *Oliva* is beach-worn and ground out; the *Nerita* has a similar hole; *Conus* is represented by a segment of a ring cut horizontally from a half shell and polished (Plate 19e); the *Dentalium* is unworked. One of the possible *Mytilus* sections (Fig. 75j, Pl. 19a) has been cut into a trapezoidal shape, polished, and grooved on the wider end (B32, X469). It was perhaps a piece of inlay representing a skirt. The other possible *Mytilus* section (Fig. 75h) was perhaps cut into the shape of a human head or of a frog, and drilled for suspension. It is .95 to .86 cm (B32, X469).

In the early Jemdet Nasr Phase, three species occur: *Engina medicaria, Strigatella literata,* and *Dentalium sp.* The first prefers rocky bottoms of unknown depths; the second prefers shallow sandy or muddy bottoms. In spite of our limited information on the habitat of these molluscs, it seems likely that all were easily obtainable. Modifications are similar to those noted earlier: the top of the *Engina* has been snapped and ground and the side has been ground through, providing two holes for suspension; the top of the *Strigatella* had been snapped but not ground, leaving a rough hole; the *Dentalium* is slightly ground on both ends (Plate 19h).

In the late Jemdet Nasr Phase, seven forms are identifiable: *Cypraea sp., Engina medicaria, Liochoncha sulcotina, Conus tesselatus, Dentalium, Mytilus,* and *Thais mancinella*. The first two prefer rocky bottoms; the third and seventh prefer shallow sandy or muddy bottoms; the fifth prefers deep water. Modifications are as before: the two *Engina* are beachworn (Plate 19g). They have been ground through at two points on the side providing several holes for suspension; the *Liochoncha* and *Conus* are unworked, the *Dentalium* is similar to the previous example of the same genus; the possible *Mytilus* section (Fig. 75i, Plate 19f) is cut into a small drilled ten-pointed star; the *Thais* has been heavily ground on one side (Plate 19b). The edges of the resulting hole are too weak for suspension (it is possible that in this case the powder of the shell was desired). Not identifiable to genus are four large cut pieces of *columella* perhaps from a large conch shell. Three are cylinders: one is longitudinally drilled (Fig. 75e), one is drilled and polished (Fig. 75g) and one is longitudinally drilled, incised and polished (Fig. 75f), perhaps for use as a cylinder seal. One is part of an unfinished pendant or labret (Fig. 75k). Thus of the twelve items of marine shell in this phase, five are perforated, allowing suspension.

There is one fragment of a ring cut from a *Conus* shell in subsequent Early Dynastic levels.

Three marine shell items—a similar ring, a *Thais* ground in the fashion described above, and a fragment of *Cardium*—were found in Elamite layers. The first and third are weathered, and the second was near a large pit intrusive into Jemdet Nasr levels. All may be extrusive from earlier deposits.

Several points can be made regarding these molluscs. First, there is an increase in the number of molluscs imported in the Late Uruk. Second, while some genera such as *Conus* and *Mytilus* are used during the course of many phases, others are known for only a limited period of time. This could be a result of the small number of shells available for study, or it could reflect changing sources. The latter possibility cannot be checked until better information on the habitat and distribution of

---

[3] I thank Dr. Henry Van der Schalie and Mr. Shikuei Wu of the University of Michigan Museum of Zoology for their help in identifying these molluscs.

modern molluscs on the Gulf is available. Third, while most of the attested species were probably obtainable from beaches, *Mytilus* could be obtained and imported only with some difficulty. Archaeological information from the ancient shellfisheries is needed.

SUMMARY

Let us consider these artifacts together, ignoring for purposes of this summary the fact that they are from very different periods. To what uses were these artifacts put? The fishhook, sling missiles, and trapezoids could have been used to obtain fish, wild fowl, and wild animals, and some of the perforated stones could have been used as sinkers or mace heads. The sickles, both chert and clay, were doubtless used to harvest grains and perhaps other plants. The choppers and many of the flake and blade tools could have been used in butchering, though evidence for this in the form of cuts on bones is rare. The slabs and hand stones would serve to prepare grains. Many artifacts must have been used in household and craft activities. Among these were the whorls and discs, drills, perforators, bone awls, and scrapers (both stone and bone). All of these must have been used variously on hides, fabrics, and wood. A diversity of items associated with costume, and therefore with social differentiation, were found. Little can be said about possible palettes for pigment, ear ornaments and other jewelry, and copper pins, other than that they were present. The beads are of a wide range of materials, from common clay and calcite to semi-precious carnelian and lapis lazuli, suggesting the presence of differing wealth. Innovations in architectural items are associated with such differences. The ceramic wall cone and shell inlay, doubtless embellished the exterior and interior of special buildings or their furnishings. The drains, continuing from earlier phases, seem to occur in areas of both simple and elaborate housing. Finally, there is a small but important group of artifacts used in the administration of the movement of goods. There are seals of bone and shell for authorizing the storage or transfer of goods, a possible weight for measuring goods, jar and bale sealings, and a messenger bulla recording the transfer of a shipment of goods to Farukhabad. As before, there are objects of unknown use such as the bitumen ovoids, a painted stone ovoid, concrete discs, figurines, and pieces of mineral.

Chapter IX

ARTIFACT DISTRIBUTION IN THE URUK, JEMDET NASR, AND EARLY DYNASTIC PHASES

INTRODUCTION

The distributional analyses of artifacts of these phases present new problems not faced in the previous study of Farukh-Bayat artifact distribution. In those earlier phases ceramic wares and vessel forms changed slowly if at all, while painted decoration exhibited clear stylistic variation. In the Uruk, Jemdet Nasr, and Early Dynastic Phases, the ceramics upon which we must base our phase definitions and relative chronology change in a very different and, for the archaeologist, less convenient manner.

First, there are frequent technological changes throughout these later phases: new wares appear, and previously rare shapes are produced. Second, entire categories of vessel shape appear or disappear. Similar changes occur throughout lowland Greater Mesopotamia. This could be because domestic activities are changing, because the availability or efficiency of ceramic material relative to leather or metal is changing, or for other, unknown, reasons. Third, these ceramics exhibit little decoration. While changes in such painted, incised, or appliqué decoration as exists are probably purely stylistic, changes in rim, body, or base shape could as easily result from changing uses as from changes in style. Finally, because there are so many distinct wares and shapes, the proportion of any one attribute combination in the ceramic inventory is very small, and, as a result, these samples are even more difficult to deal with than those from earlier phases. In an effort to build a useful relative chronology without introducing circularities into the subsequent study of activity variation, I will proceed as follows.

First, I will deal with technical changes within shape categories. Since the potter was obliged to use only one technique of clay preparation, of clay forming, and of firing on each vessel, each shape category can be treated as a closed domain, and the use of proportions is therefore legitimate.

Second, I will deal with changes in both actual decorative elements and in minor shapes of features within broader shape categories. Only if it can be argued that such a feature represents a differentiation within an existing shape category can the feature be considered stylistic rather than a result of changing use.

Third, while these two classes of changes will allow close correlation of the separate Farukhabad excavations, the division into phases must take into consideration the fact that very similar changes were occuring throughout Greater Mesopotamia. Greater weight will be given to demonstrably general changes.

Once the phases are established, I will proceed with a phase-by-phase analysis of activity variation in the same manner as in Chapter V. In no single case, however, will adequate sample sizes be available, even for the very simple statistical approach previously used. Nevertheless, I believe the effort will provide some controls for the subsequent consideration of traded materials and will help to guide future research directed specifically at the problems of economic and social organization.

Parenthetically, it is notable that the chronological study indicates that the stratigraphic quality of the two excavations is quite different. Excavation B has a thick sequence of Uruk Layers, while for this time Excavation A, which is higher because of the Farukh Phase platform buildings, has layers which are thin and badly eroded. On the other hand, Excavation A has a thick sequence of Jemdet Nasr deposits, while in Excavation B the Late Jemdet Nasr and Early Dynastic layers are badly damaged by pits. This illustrates why multiple excavations are always to be preferred as a basis for developmental statements.

DISTRIBUTION: URUK, JEMDET NASR, AND EARLY DYNASTIC PHASES

TECHNICAL AND STYLISTIC DEVELOPMENTS AND PHASE DIVISIONS

The four very different technical developments of interest to us here will be discussed in approximate chronological order. A data summary is presented on Tables 35 and 36.

The dominant ceramic ware in the earlier layers is the straw and limestone tempered Sargarab Ware; that of the later layers is the sand tempered Uruk Ware. There is no known technical superiority of one ware over another, and wares very much like both Uruk and Sargarab Wares were made in various later periods in both highlands and lowlands. The change is local to the Deh Luran Plain, but it is useful in correlating the separate excavations at Farukhabad. Medium sized jars and bowls in the four lowest layers of Excavation B are more than 70 percent Sargarab Ware, while the succeeding two are about 40 percent; afterwards the ware becomes minor. Comparable forms in the lowest three layers of Excavation A, excluding Feature 23, are about 40 percent Sargarab Ware, after which time the ware becomes minor. This indicates that Excavation B Layers 36–33 lower are older than any layers in Excavation A; and that B33 upper-32 are contemporary with A22–21.

Coarse Grayware jars appear in the later layers in both excavations. While Uruk and Sargarab Ware vessels were sometimes fired in a reducing atmosphere (in the former case producing what is sometimes called "Uruk Gray Ware"), this Grayware differs from the dominant wares in several other respects. It is tempered with crushed calcareous material, is handmade, and has surfaces often roughly burnished. It is possible that this ware is a technical development of specialization from Sargarab Ware since the larger thickened round rim jar, which frequently has a predominantly calcareous temper, survives later than other Sargarab forms and disappears shortly before the similarly formed Grayware jars appear. This ware also seems to be a local development not reported in adjacent areas. Grayware jars appear in Excavation B, Layer 24 and Excavation A, Layers 16–17. They occur in varying quantities thereafter. One change evident in gray wares is the introduction of pure mussel shell tempering as a supplement to calcite and chert tempering in Excavation B, Layer 20, and Excavation A, Layer 5.

Beveled rim bowls have a complex distribution probably resulting from changing production techniques and uses through time. These crude bowls are replaced everywhere throughout Mesopotamia by conical cups made on a fast wheel. We can control for variations in use by considering all small bowls, i.e., beveled rim bowls and conical cups together, as a closed domain and looking at the proportion of beveled rim bowls within this category. If the change to conical cups was indeed a result of the introduction of a larger and faster wheel into existing workshops, we can expect such a change to spread rapidly throughout the closely related workshops of lowland Mesopotamia. This technical change will be useful in defining phase boundaries. Beveled rim bowls comprise about 90 percent of the small bowls until Excavation B, Layer 27 and Excavation A, Layer 16–17. They drop steadily until, in Excavation B, Layer 23 and Excavation A, Layer 12, they drop below 20 percent and disappear. The beveled rim bowl sherds in the higher levels of Excavation B probably reflect the use of tertiary debris in building construction and the digging of pits.

In summary, from the evidence of technical changes alone, one could correlate the two excavations as shown in Table 37.

Does the evidence of possible stylistic change confirm or amplify this arrangement? There are nine changes of interest: four involving jar form, four involving surface decoration and appendages on jars, and one involving conical cup form. A data summary is presented in Tables 38 to 41.

The low expanded band rim jar seems to develop from the early flared expanded rim jar via the intermediate form represented at Farukhabad by the Sargarab ware high expanded band rim jar (Fig. 44a). The low form first appears in Excavation B, Layer 34. Cross hatch incising in a concentric band, a decorative device common on jar shoulders of both this and other types, first appears in the immediately succeeding layer. Both forms occur in Excavation A, Layer 21. Since there is virtually nothing in Layer 22, their absence there implies little.

The bottle, a narrow-necked, long-bodied form known throughout Mesopotamia, first appears in Excavation B, Layer 31 upper, and in Excavation A, Layer 21, becoming common in Layer 20. Droop or bent spouts, commonly attached to such

Table 35: Ceramic Wares in Excavation A, Layers 22–1

	Small Bowl Rims			Medium Bowl Rims			Medium Jar Rims					Combined Prop Sarg
	Straw BRB	Uruk Concup	Prop BRB	Sarg	Uruk	Prop Sarg	Sarg	Prop Sarg	Uruk	Gray	Prop Gray	
1–2	0	16	.00	0	1	.00	0	.00	24	7	.22	.00
3–4	0	3	.00	0	3	.00	0	.00	18	2	.10	.00
5	0	14	.00	0	2	.00	0	.00	23	7	.23	.00
6–7	0	28	.00	0	9	.00	0	.00	22	1	.04	.00
8	0	24	.00	0	4	.00	0	.00	14	0	.00	.00
9–10	0	45	.00	0	16	.00	0	.00	16	2	.11	.00
11–12	8	35	.18	0	9	.00	2	.06	30	1	.03	.02
13	43	24	.64	0	5	.00	0	.00	16	2	.11	.00
14–15	20	8	.71	0	5	.00	0	—	2	2	—	.00
16–17	52	16	.76	0	12	.00	0	.00	8	6	.42	.00
18	54	3	.94	0	5	.00	1	.20	4	0	.00	.10
19	51	5	.91	0	7	.00	1	.01	14	0	.00	.05
20	125	4	.96	0	7	.00	5	.31	11	0	.00	.21
21u	86	12	.88	1	1	—	5	.33	10	0	.00	.35
21m	18	1	.95	0	2	—	4	.57	3	0	.00	.44
21l–22	44	5	.89	3	6	.66	5	.62	3	0	.00	.47
F23	36	2		27	2		23	1.00	0	0	.00	.96

Table 36: Ceramic Wares in Excavation B, Layers 36–19

	Small Bowl Rims			Medium Bowl Rims			Jar Rims					Combined Prop Sarg
	Straw BRB	Uruk Concup	Prop BRB	Sarg	Uruk	Prop Sarg	Sarg	Prop Sarg	Uruk	Gray	Prop Gray	
19												
20–21	11	38	.22	0	21	.00	0	.00	35	10	.22	.00
22–23	14	63	.18	0	11	.00	0	.00	36	3	.08	.00
24	21	22	.48	0	3	.00	0	.00	10	2	.16	.00
25–26	31	22	.58	1	5	.16	0	.00	15	3	.20	.00
27	37	10	.78	0	0	.00	0	.00	10	1	.10	.00
28	29	3	.90	0	5	.00	0	.00	5	1	.20	.00
29u	93	13	.87	1	13	.07	20	.11	14	1	.05	.10
29l	77	5	.93	0	19	.00	0	.00	14	0	.00	.00
30	434	14	.96	2	29	.06	1	.02	43	0	.00	.05
31	761	22*	.97	3	22	.12	3	.06	45	0	.00	.08
32	395	10	.97	10	15	.40	13	.30	32[30]	0	.00	.34
33u	51	7	.87	2	5	.28	10	.43	13	0	.00	.45
33l	100	3	.97	24	13	.64	24	.82	5	0	.00	.73
34	100	4	.96	7	4	.63	16	.66	8	0	.00	.70
35	43	0	1.00	17	4	.80	15	.71	6	0	.00	.76
36	22	0	1.00	17	6	.73	22	.88	3	0	.00	.81

DISTRIBUTION: URUK, JEMDET NASR, AND EARLY DYNASTIC PHASES

Table 37: Layer Correlations Based on Wares

A	B
1–5	20
6–12	21–23
13–17	24–27
18–20	28–31
21–22	32–33 upper
	33 lower–36

bottles, appear in Excavation B, Layer 32, becoming common in Layer 31, and in Excavation A, Layer 20. While in a general sense, a bottle is just another type of small, spouted jar, there is no exact functional equivalent among the earlier spouted jars. One therefore cannot attribute its sudden occurrence throughout Lowland Mesopotamia to stylistic development within a use category, and one must reckon with the possibility that its appearance in any particular excavation may be a function of activity variation.

A contemporary and definitely stylistic development is the use of vertical twisted handles on small round-bodied round rim jars. Strap handles were used at the time of the earliest Uruk layers of Farukhabad, but the substitution of a twisted piece of clay is attested first in Excavation B, Layer 31. The late occurrence of twisted handles, correlative with bottles and droop spouts, is widely attested in lowland Greater Mesopotamia (Johnson: 1973:29ff).

Contemporary but rare stylistic features also widely attested at this time are cross-hatch triangles and groove and oblique incised jar shoulders (Johnson 1973:57–58).

Conial cup rims appear consistently in Excavation B, Layer 34 and above and throughout Excavation A. The earlier cups must have had fine bases, since the characteristic string cut bases are rare at first. Fine solid-footed conical cups appear in Excavation B, Layer 29 upper and Excavation A, Layer 19. They occur consistently until B23 and A9, after which they become less frequent. This seems to be a local development and at present is only useful for relating sites on the Deh Luran Plain.

Finally, there are correlated changes in jar rims in the later part of the sequence. A distinct thin high-necked variety of round rim jar appears in Excavation A, Layer 13 and Excavation B, Layer 24. A high-necked band rim jar, perhaps differentiated from the flared expanded rim jar, appears in Excavation A, Layer 13 and Excavation B, Layer 25, though it does not become common until Layer 23. It is not known whether these are local changes or whether they also occur elsewhere. The complicated changes in our sample of polychrome ceramics have alrady been presented and need not be reiterated here.

Given the above discussions, the sequence of mid-fourth to early third millennium layers from the main excavations at Farukhabad can be grouped and assigned to a Pan-Mesopotamian Phase System as shown in Table 42.

Now let us consider the total ceramic complex of each phase, and discuss its broader connections. First, however, we must consider the antecedents of the Early Uruk Phase on the Deh Luran Plain. As noted in the previous stratigraphic discussions, Layers A22 and B37 were disturbed and weathered. Obviously there was a depositional break, but at the time of excavation many Farukh Phase sherds were noted in the immediately succeeding layers and we thought that there might have been only a short break during a gradual shift from Susiana to Sargarab ceramics. Two discoveries eliminated this misconception. First, as discussed in Chapter 6, Neely found Susa A-related sherds on Musiyan and sites to the east. There is, therefore, a post-Farukh Phase with ceramics in the Susiana tradition. Second, Neely and I have investigated a site called Sargarab which lacks Susiana ceramics but has quantities of ceramics prototypic of the Early Uruk of Farukhabad (Wright, Neely, Johnson, and Speth 1975). Thus, there were at least two phases between the Farukh and Early Uruk Phases and the break in occupation must have lasted for several centuries.

A consideration of the ceramics from the surface of Sargarab will provide a useful introduction to this sequence: almost all of these ceramics are of the straw and crushed calcareous rock tempered Sargarab Ware. The major open forms are a small fine bowl with tapered curved rim, a medium-sized hemispherical bowl with beaded or beveled lip, and a medium-sized incurved bowl often with an applied thumb-impressed clay strip below the rim. The major restricted forms are a fine jar like those from Farukhabad and a medium-sized jar with flared neck, expanded rim, and rounded lip. Several oval nose lugs and a straight spout may have

Table 38: Jar Types in Excavation A, Layers 22-1

Layer	Gray sh/cal	Uruk Jar Rims round		Uruk Jar Rims expanded				Uruk Jar Rims flat				Sargarab Jar Rims			
		fn	oth	sm	lg	out	flr	low	ldg	bnd	lck	bot	fn	rnd	flr	thk
1–2	3/4	3	7				7		3	4						
3–4	1/1	7	5				3		1	2						
5	2/5	5	7	1			5		2	3						
6		6	3				1			2						
7	1	3	3				3		1	1						
8		4	2				3			5						
9–10	2		6				2		3	5						
11		2	4	1		1	4		2	6						
12	1	1					2		5	1	1				2	
13	2	2	3			2	3		4	2						
14–15	2						1		1							
16–17	6	fl rd	1	2				1	4							
18			1	3									1			
19			5	1	2		1	1	2			2	1			
20		1	2				1	2				5		3	1	1
21u		3	1	3				1	1			1	3	2		
21m			1			2							1	1	1	1
21l				1									1	1		
22					1		1							1	1	1
23													12	4	3	4

been appendages on jars. Red and cream slipping, sometimes with simple black painted designs, occurs on a few of the jars.

The Early Uruk Phase at Farukhabad also has a dominance of Sargarab Ware but there are a number of differences in vessel shape: fine bowls are replaced by small round lip bowls, hemispherical beaded lip bowls decline, and incurved beaded lip bowls become dominant. Oval rather than round impressions are more common on the raised strips on these bowls. Fine jars duplicate those at Sargarab, but flared neck jars are differentiated into a heavier variety with thickened round rim and finer varieties with simple round lip or expanded grooved lip. These finer jars have nose lugs and straight spouts and often have red slips and painted black bands. Up to 25 percent of the medium sized jars and bowls were made from Uruk Ware. Smaller globular jars with straight, round or flat rims with strap handles and ledge rim jars occur in this new ware. Medium-sized flat lip, beveled lip, and ledge rim bowls, the first of which is also attested in red-slipped Sargarab Ware, occur. Finally, the true beveled rim bowl is common in these layers. In summary, there are stylistic changes within Sargarab Ware which facilitate the correlation of ceramic samples from the Deh Luran Plain. In addition, there is a marked increase in new jar and bowl forms in Uruk Ware, as well as the introduction of the beveled rim bowl, which facilitates broader correlation.

The Sargarab Phase is one of a number of distinct local complexes which have been termed "Terminal Ubaid" in a recent paper (Wright, Neely, Johnson, and Speth 1975). Its closest technical and stylistic relationship are with Inner Luristan. The Early Uruk Phase at Farukhabad apparently

Table 38 (continued)

Layer	Other Uruk Jar Parts									Sargarab		
	h-s	grv	g&s	x-h	lug	s-h	t-h	spt	dr-s	h-s	lug	spt
1–2	5											
3–4	4											
5	3	1						1				
6	6											
7	2											
8	2							2				
9–10	4							5				
11	7											
12												
13	1	2				1						
14–15								1				
16–17	1	1										
18				1	2	1		1				
19						1	1	1	2			
20		1	1		2	1		1	1			
21u					1					1		
21m					1	1	1	1				
21l					1							
22											1	
23												2

represents a continuation of this highland-derived ceramic tradition with the addition of some characteristically Uruk vessel types. Since it lacks various widespread Early Uruk forms, such as the tapered rim or prototypic beveled rim bowl and the neckless ledge-rim jar (Johnson 1973:54–55), it is possible that only the latest portion of the Early Uruk Period is represented at Farukhabad. Under the best circumstances, the correlation of Farukhabad with other Early Uruk sequences would be difficult. Since no other local Early Uruk sequence is complete, and none of them are published in quantitative form, certainty is impossible. At present, a correlation with Warka-Eanna XIII or XII (VanHaller 1932) and with Susa Acrople I: 22 or 23 (Le Brun 1971) seems reasonable. Further work may require a taxonomic revision of the Early Uruk on the Deh Luran Plain.

During the Middle Uruk Phase at Farukhabad, all Sargarab jar and bowl types continue without consistent change in form or in ratio to each other. However, Uruk Ware vessels become more frequent and several new forms develop. Low expanded band rim jars appear. Cross-hatch incised bands are widely applied to jar shoulders. Long straight spouts are replaced by small conical forms. Beveled rim bowls increase greatly in quantity and conical cups, probably the fine sinuous-sided form, appear.

The Late Uruk Phase has a heavy dominance of Uruk Ware vessels. Sargarab Ware is used only for a few specialized forms. Uruk Ware jars include high proportions of small globular vessels with rounded or flattened rims and strap handles, now sometimes twisted, high proportions of low expanded band rim jars, some ledge rim jars, and some bottles with droop spouts. The use of flared expanded rim jars declines. Uruk Ware bowls

Table 39: Jar Types in Excavation B, Layers 36-20

Layer	Gray sh/cal	Uruk Jar Rims											Sargarab Jar Rims			
		round			expanded				flat							
		fn	oth	sm	lg	out	flr	low	ldg	bnd	lck	bot	fn	rnd	flr	thk
20	1/2	3	6				4	1	1	2						
21	7	3	6			2			4	2	1					
22	1	8				3			4	2						
23	2	3	2	2	1	4			3	3	1					
24	2	1	1			3			4			1				
25	2					3			3	1	1					
26	1					3			2		2					
27	1	fl	5			1	2		2							
28	1	rd	1	1				1		1	1					
29u	1		4	2		1		3	2			2				2
29l		1	3	2		1		2	1			4				
30			15	3	1	3	2	10	2		1	6				1
31		2	15	8		1	7	6	1			5				3
32		4	9	3	2		8	4	2				4	3	2	4
33u		2	1	3			4	1	2				3	3	1	3
33l			2			1		1	1				5	2	7	10
34		1		2			4	1					5	2	1	8
35		1	3	2									2	2	3	7
36				1			1		1				4	6	8	4

Table 40: Bowl Types in Excavation A, Layers 22-1

Layer	Straw Ware	Uruk Ware Rims							Sargarab Ware Rims						
	BRB	cup	rnd	flt	bvl	ldg	inc	inc bdd	cup	rnd	flt	inc	inc bdd	inc bdd h-s	bsn
1-2		16	1												
3-4		3			3										
5		14	2												
6		16	5		1	1									
7		12	1			1									
8		24	4												
9-10		45	9		4	1	2								
11	2	27	4	2	1		2								
12	6	8													
13	43	24	2		1	1	1								
14-15	20	8	5												
16-17	52	16	7	2	1	1	1								
18	54	3	3		1	1									
19	51	5	1		1 inc.										
20	125	4	1		1	1									
21u	86	12	1										1		
21m	18	1	1		1										
21l	27	2	1								1		1	1	
22	17	3													
F23	36	2	1				2		8	1		5	8	5	

DISTRIBUTION: URUK, JEMDET NASR, AND EARLY DYNASTIC PHASES

Table 39 (continued)

Layer	Other Uruk Jar Parts									Sargarab	
	h-s	grv	g&s	x-h	lug	s-h	t-h	spt	dr-s	h-s	lug
20	7										
21	4							1			
22	1										
23	1		1								
24					1						
25	1			1							
26								1			
27		1		1					2		
28		1	1					1			
29u	1		2	2	1	2	1v	2	4		
29l					1	1		2	3		
30	1+2	2	2	3	1	2	1v	1	1		
31	3+	1			5	3	1v 1h	5		2	5
32	2	1	1	4	4	7		2	1		
33u				2	3			1			1
33l				3	1			2			
34	1					2				1	1
35						1		2		1	1
36	2				2	1				1	2

Table 40: (continued)

Layer	Uruk Ware Cup Bases			Uruk Ware Other Bases					Sargarab Bases
	wid	cnst	sld	flt	fn	pnch ring	trn rng	trn fn	flt
1–2	5		1	3		6			
3–4				4		5	4		
5	1	1		8		3	5		
6	3		1	8		2	5		
7	2	1					5		
8	1	3		2	1	1			
9–10	6	4	1	2	1				
11	4	1	1	3			1		
12				2					
13	2		1	8	1				
14–15	1	1	3	9		1			
16–17			2	8		1			
18				5	1			1	
19			3	8	1				
20				3	2			1	
21u				4	3				
21m				7					1
21l				3			2		2
22									1
F23				1				1	4

Table 41: Bowl Types in Excavation B, Layers 36–19

Layer	Straw Ware BRB	Uruk Ware Rims							Sargarab Ware Rims						
		cup	rnd	flt	bvl	ldg	inc	inc bdd	cup	rnd	flt	inc	inc bdd	inc bdd h-s	bsn
20	5	11	2												
21	6	27	17	1			1								
22	3	24	3			1									
23	11	39	5		1	1									
24	21	22	1	1		1									
25	23	9	2		1										
26	8	13	2										1		
27	37	10													
28	29	3	2	1	2										
29u	93	13	9		2	2							1		
29l	77	5	12	1	2	2	1	1					2		
30	432	14	23	1	3	1	1						3		
31	761	21	9	5	6	1		1	1				5		2
32	395	10	6	6	3					1	2	2	2		3
33u	51	7	2			1		2							1
33l	100	3	3	6				4	5		2	11	6		4
34	100	4		2				2	1	1		5			5
35	43		1			1		2	2	1	1	4	2		
36	22		1	4	1				2	3	3	8	1		

include high proportions of round rim bowls, and consistent occurences of flat, beveled, and ledge rim bowls. Beveled rim bowls remain common, but true conical cups, string-cut from a large mass of clay, occur.

The Late Uruk Phase at Farukhabad is similar to other sites. It shares many features with Warka-Eanna VII to IV and Susa Acropole 19 to 17. Among these are twisted handles, cross-hatch triangles, grooved and oblique shoulder decorations, bottles, and droop spouts. The preceeding Middle Uruk Phase, like the Early Uruk, has many local features, but by interpolation, it probably correlates with the Warka-Eanna XI to VII, and Susa Acropole I: 21 to 20. While the first three widespread Late Uruk elements are single modes with reasonable prototypes in one or more local Middle Uruk sequences, the last two represent one distinct vessel form which seems to appear everywhere at about the same time. There are three possible explanations:

1) There is an as yet unrecognized prototype, and the bottle represents an ordinary stylistic development among the many closely related lowland Mesopotamian Uruk shops.

2) The form is widely spread because it is directly used in a previously uncommon activity. For instance, the bottle is a very sturdy vessel, and may have been used to hold liquids during journeys. With an increase in journeys, it would became widespread.

3) The form is widespread because it indirectly facilitates a new activity. Perhaps a liquid commodity is being traded in quantity for the first time.

If either the second or third explanation is correct, then some of the bottles from any Uruk center should be imports from other centers. This implication could someday be tested with mineralogical or trace-element analysis.

The early Jemdet Nasr pottery assemblege is, in many respects, a simplified version of the Late Uruk assemblage. Beveled rim bowls decline in frequency as do Uruk Ware medium bowls with rim modifications, leaving conical cups and medium round rim bowls. The fine solid footed conical cup is particularly common at this time. Among the Uruk Ware jars the ledge rim jar and a

DISTRIBUTION: URUK, JEMDET NASR, AND EARLY DYNASTIC PHASES

Table 41: (continued)

Layer	Uruk Ware Cup Bases			Uruk Ware Other Bases					Sargarab Bases
	wid	cnst	sld	flt	fn	pnch ring	trn rng	trn fne	flt
20	5	1	1	3			2		
21	1	1		1		1	1		
22		3							2
23	2	2	8	5	2		1		
24			4	4	1	1			
25	1		3	4	1		2		
26			3	5	1		1		
27	1		3	3	2				
28				8	1				1
29u			5	14	1		1	1	
29l	3			8	3				
30	1			14	6				
31	3			30	8				
32	1			18	6				4
33u				12	4			1	5
33l				12	3				6
34				16	2			2	4
35				4					8
36		1		7					9

Table 42: Phase Ascription of the Layers

Phase Name	Excavation A	Excavation B
Early Dynastic	1–5	19–20
Late Jemdet Nasr	6–12	21–23
Early Jemdet Nasr	13–17	24–27
Late Uruk	18–20	28–31
Middle Uruk	21–22	32–34
Early Uruk	—	35–36

version of the flared expanded rim jar are most common. Ring bases, including both high, wheel-turned and low, pinched examples, are common. Other Late Uruk jar rims, appendages and decorative motifs occur so rarely that they may well be extrusive earlier sherds. Found in the latest Uruk Layers and in the Early Jemdet Nasr layers are jars decorated in the early polychrome style with an emphasis on simple cross-hatched triangles on the shoulder and simple horizontal curved line motifs on the body. In addition, hand-made gray ware first becomes common in this phase.

The Late Jemdet Nasr Phase has the same range of conical cups and bowls as the preceding phase. Jars, however, show several changes. A fine high round rim jar differentiates from the ordinary low round rim jars; a band rim jar appears, perhaps a differentiation from the flared expanded rim jar. Ledge rim jars continue. Raised strips decorated with narrow oblique hatching become common on jar shoulders. The early polychrome style disapears in the middle of this phase, and the middle polychrome style, with an emphasis on alternate vertical curved and straight lines or simple straight lines on the shoulder and horizontal curved and straight lines on the body, becomes dominant. Grayware continues.

In the Early Dynastic period there seems to be a dominance of the wide-based conical cups. Medium jars and bowls do not change in shape, but they seem to be heavier and coarser. Only the late polychrome style with complex designs emphaizing grids and oblique lines on the shoulder along with alternate vertical curved and straight lines on shoulder and side is attested. Hand made gray wares become even more frequent, and the shell tempered variety appears.

It is difficult to correlate these three phases with those in other areas. The polychrome and the handmade gray ware are local developments not easily linked with those elsewhere. The changes in jar rims are distinctive, but they cannot be easily compared to Susa to the east, which participates in a totally different craft tradition at this time, Warka to the south, where Jemdet Nasr stratigraphies are incomplete (Nissen 1970), or the Diyala to the west, where no large samples of jar rims are described. The problem is compounded by the circumstance, similar to that noted in the Warka region by Nissen (1969; Adams and Nissen 1972), that Early Jemdet Nasr is similar to Late Uruk while Late Jemdet Nasr is similar to Early Dynastic, making the recognition of these phases difficult in surface collections from the Deh Luran Plain itself. For correlative purposes, we are left with the decline to insignificance of the beveled rim bowl and very general relationships between polychrome styles. On these grounds Early Jemdet Nasr would be equivalent to Protoliterate c on the Diyala, and Late Jemdet Nasr would be equivalent to Protoliterate d. By default, our Early Dynastic layers would be equivalent to Early Dynastic I or even later. For purposes of the subsequent discussion of settlement patterns the Jemdet Nasr phases will be considered as a unit.

ACTIVITY VARIATION DURING THE URUK AND JEMDET NASR PHASES

Insofar as it is possible, given the small number of provenience units from each phase, I will apply the same type of analysis that I used for the Farukh Phase to these later phases. First, the matrix of rank correlations between common artifact densities will be examined. Then the association of tools with different types of features and different excavation units will be considered and tested with the Mann-Whitney U-statistic or the Kruskal-Wallace H-statistic.

The Early Uruk Phase does not contain enough provenience units to undertake this type of analysis. However, the Middle Uruk Phase presents enough material to make an attempt. Table 43 presents the correlations of those items occurring in more than half of the 21 provenience units. Any coeffiecient greater than +.58 or less than −.58 is significant at the 99 percent confidence level. Any coefficient greater than +.44 or less than −.44 is significant at the 95 percent confidence level.

There are few correlations of significance and very few above .50. Generally, uniform low correlations will occur when only one basic type of activity area is being sampled. In the previously considered Farukh Phase units there were units with much domestic refuse including jar, basin, and bowl fragments and units with less domestic refuse, creating a pattern of positive correlations between the major domestic artifacts. In contrast, the excavated Middle Uruk layers, which with the exception of B32 seem to be sheet refuse in and around small simple structures have roughly equivalent densities of artifacts. The one reasonably high positive correlation is that of +.53 between round rim jars and flared expanded rim jars. Since these two types are separated primarily by the attribute of lip form, it is possible that these are simply stylistic variants within a single use category.

Layers A21U, A21M, and B33U are definitely associated with structures and can be contrasted with the other layers. B32U probably represents the time at which the area of Excavation B was cleared off for use as an administrative complex (as architecturally attested in overlying Layer B31) but its exclusion does not affect the outcome as presented in Table 44, which shows that there are no statistically significant differences between sheet refuse and refuse associated with structures.

In summary, our analyses of Middle Uruk debris in the two excavations provides evidence only of an undifferentiated domestic artifact complex. This is not surprising since the simple architecture, burials, and other features do not suggest much social or economic complexity. Doubtless more extensive sampling or better context would enable one to break this generalized artifact series down into activity specific groups used for cooking, eating, storage, and so on.

The series of sixteen Late Uruk provenience units is small but provocative. The correlations are generally positive, because of the very low densities of artifacts in certain layers. However, many high correlations stand out (Table 45). There are some correlations that probably arise because the parts of a single vessel are deposited together. Thus many conical cups probably had fine bases (+.51). Smaller round rim jars also had fine bases (+.75), while larger ones had flat bases (+.58), and some had spouts (+.46) and handles (+.57). Small expanded rim jars had flat bases (+.50) and spouts (+.62). Bottles had fine bases (+.52). On the other hand, some bottles certainly had spouts but the correlation is not high (+.34), probably because bottles are relatively uncommon and most spouts are associated with the other jars. Likewise, some round and flat rim bowls might have flat or fine

Table 43: Middle Uruk Artifact Correlations

95% = .44
99% = .58

	Fine Jar	Flat Base	Beaded Rim Bowl	Conical Cup	Small Ex Jar	Flrd Ex Jar	Rnd Lip Jar	BRB	Segment	Fine Base	Coarse Jar	Sickle
Fine Jar	1.00											
Flat Base	.00	1.00										
Beaded Rim Bowl	.04	.42	1.00									
Conical Cup Rim	.12	.36	.38	1.00								
Small Expanded Jar	.24	−.02	−.11	.36	1.00							
Flared Expanded Jar	−.34	.04	−.10	−.04	−.27	1.00						
Round Lip Jar	−.32	.21	.00	.23	.06	.53	1.00					
Beveled Rim Bowl	−.22	.25	.25	.37	.32	.35	.44	1.00				
Segment	.00	.06	.01	−.21	.15	−.04	.20	.42	1.00			
Fine Base	.08	.04	−.10	.00	.15	.08	.20	.15	.19	1.00		
Coarse Jar	.16	.16	.29	−.17	−.24	−.15	.27	−.10	−.31	−.06	1.00	
Sickle	−.01	−.05	.17	−.51	−.36	.10	−.23	−.18	.09	.02	.36	1.00

bases, but the correlations are all low (+.30 or less), and the larger low expanded band rim jars would have flat bases, but the correlation is low (+.22). This last may be explained by the high correlation between flat and fine bases (+.72) which could result from either an inadequate base typology or from a gathering up of bases for disposal together.

Putting these essentially trivial correlations aside, one is left with a number of more interesting ones. These can be separated into two groups. One is centered on round lip bowls. It includes the flat lip bowl (+.51), the ledge rim jar (+.71), and the low expanded band rim jar (+.57). The other is centered on the round rim jar. It includes the bottle (+.64) and the small expanded jar (+.58). The beveled rim bowl and the conical cup show middling correlations with both groups and with each other. Examination of the actual distributions show that the

Table 44: Middle Uruk Mean Densities Per Cubic Meter

	Structures	Sheet Refuse	U	P
Beveled Rim Bowl	23.30	22.97	50.5	Not Sig.
Conical Cup	2.30	.98	30.0	p = .90
Coarse Bowl	.41	.25	—	—
Round Lip Bowl	.36	.79	41.5	Not Sig.
Flat Lip Bowl	.14	.68	—	—
Beaded Rim Bowl	.77	1.65	38.5	Not Sig.
Round Lip Jar	1.79	.78	33.0	Not Sig.
Small Expanded Jar	.71	.35	44.0	Not Sig.
Flared Expanded Jar	1.42	.83	35.0	Not Sig.
Ledge Rim Jar	.41	.17	—	—
Low Expanded Jar	.26	.27	—	—
Coarse Jar	.53	1.02	43.0	Not Sig.
Fine Jar	.78	.63	45.5	Not Sig.
Nose Lug	.51	.25	—	—
Handle	.59	.41	—	—
Spout	.30	.45	33.0	Not Sig.
Flat Base	4.10	2.40	34.5	Not Sig.
Fine Base	1.26	.45	37.0	Not Sig.
Sickle	.30	.51	—	—
Ret. Blade	.27	.21	—	—
Ret. Flake	.14	.22	—	—
Segment	1.24	1.54	51.0	Not Sig.
Denticulate	.41	.25	—	—
	N=8	N=13		

NB: See Table 13. Tests are not attempted on types occurring in less than half the samples.

two groups can be adjacent areas of the same layer. This implies use in close proximity. One group contains a medium bowl and jars, complete examples of which tend not to have spouts or handles. The other group contains the smaller jars which often do have spouts and handles. Small bowls associate with both groups. The possibility that two closely related activities such as dry versus liquid food processing or serving can be isolated and mapped vis-a-vis architecture and other features should be pursued in further research.

Finally, there remain several correlations which I cannot explain, some of which are intriguing indeed. There is a significant correlation between spouts and chert blade segments (+.64). There are significant correlations between round lip bowls and round lip jars (+.55) and between flat lip bowls and small expanded jars (+.63) which also have flat lips. Perhaps the latter two represent stylistic associations crosscutting use groupings.

Now let us consider associations with features (Table 46). Two provenience units in Excavation A are associated with small buildings and five provenience units in Excavation B are definitely associated with large buildings. Also in Excavation B, four provenience units are associated with the circular brick platforms. Examination of Table 46 indicates that the simple structures of A19 and A18 have generally low artifact densities. The elaborate building of B31 and 30 has generally high densities, particularly of beveled rim bowls. The area around the platforms in B29 has relatively high densities of conical cup bases, spouts, bottles, and stone tools. This supports the proposition, based on structural considerations, that these platforms supported vats of liquid. In summary, the small series of Late Uruk provenience units come primarily from an area of the site devoted to special constructions, in contrast to the Middle Uruk samples which come from an area of small buildings with probable domestic functions and from areas of refuse probably associated with such buildings. Because of the more varied contextual associations, it was possible to suggest activity-related vessel groups and to suggest associations of some vessel shapes with types of features.

In the Early Jemdet Nasr Phase we have several definite small and large structures. Unfortunately only a small number of provenience units, with low densities in each unit, are available. For this last reason, the correlation coefficients tend to be low and unimpressive (see Table 47).

The correlations between flat bases and flared expanded jars (+.53) and ledge rim jars (+.47) probably result from parts of single vessels being deposited together. The correlation between flat

Table 45: Late Uruk Phase Artifact Correlations

99% = .67
95% = .45

	Low Ex Jar	Conical Cup	Ledge Rim Jar	Rnd Lip Bowl	Flat Lip Bowl	Fine Base	Flat Base	Segment	Spout	Sm Ex Jar	Rnd Lip Jar	Handle	Bottle	BRB
Low Ex	1.00													
Conical Cup	.37	1.00												
Ledge Rim Jar	.47	.53	1.00											
Round Lip Bowl	.57	.43	.71	1.00										
Flat Lip Bowl	.33	.33	.10	.51	1.00									
Fine Base	.51	.51	.26	.30	.10	1.00								
Flat Base	.22	.57	.25	.20	.23	.72	1.00							
Segment	−.08	.33	.02	.04	.31	.04	.31	1.00						
Spout	.03	.44	.30	.26	.28	.40	.71	.14	1.00					
Sm Ex Jar	.24	.64	.24	.43	.63	.42	.50	.41	.62	1.00				
Rnd Lip Jar	.48	.48	.37	.55	.23	.75	.58	.03	.46	.58	1.00			
Handle	.42	.24	.33	.38	.14	.31	.35	−.20	.15	.13	.57	1.00		
Bottle	.14	.33	.54	.42	−.01	.52	.43	.03	.34	.34	.64	.57	1.00	
BRB	.42	.34	.05	.28	.42	.46	.53	.06	.12	.31	.57	.47	.31	1.00

bases and bevel rim bowls (+.59) results from very high densities in four unrelated provenience units rather than a general relation between the densities in all units. This pattern of concentration suggests that these two rather bulky artifact fragments are being picked up and piled in localities out from underfoot, but that they are otherwise unrelated. In contrast, the correlation between flat bases and conical cup rims (+.58) reflects a general relation between densities in all units. Furthermore, the large base fragments and tiny cup rims should not be agglomerated by any single garbage collecting method. The correlation probably results from the use and breakage of cups and jars together and can be explained in the following way. Cups are broken with both ledge rim and flared expanded jars, both of which often have flat bases. Since these two jar types are uncorrelated (−.11), the correlation of cup rims with each jar type is lowered by the effect of the other (+.34 and +.35). The correlation between round and flat lip bowls (+.49) probably results from the fact that they are stylistic variants of one form with a single range of uses. Solid footed cup bases are independent of, or negatively related to, everything except notched chert tools. Thus, on the basis of the correlation matrix, one can recognize a loosely related group of jars and cups, perhaps subdivisible into a flared expanded rim jar with conical cup subgroup, a ledge rim jar with conical cup subgroup, and a group of medium-sized bowls. Solid footed cup bases and, to a limited extent, notched chert tools

Table 46: Late Uruk Mean Densities Per Cubic Meter

	Simple Structures	Elaborate Structures	Platforms	H	P(H)
Beveled Rim Bowl	24.23	107.81	41.83	9.31	p = .99
Conical Cup Rim	1.53	2.90	4.05	2.95	Not Sig.
Conical Cup Base	.57	.20	1.82	6.12	p = .95
Round Lip Bowl	.57	2.41	3.90	4.29	Not Sig.
Flat Lip Bowl	.47	1.68	1.37	2.84	Not Sig.
Band Lip Bowl	.67	.54	.80	—	—
Round Lip Jar	.37	2.29	2.32	3.91	Not Sig.
Small Expanded Jar	.20	.80	1.03	2.72	Not Sig.
Flared Expanded Jar	.37	.64	.00	—	—
Low Expanded Jar	.37	1.22	.80	1.82	Not Sig.
Ledge Rim Jar	.37	.54	1.15	3.16	Not Sig.
Bottles	.73	.92	1.67	1.82	Not Sig.
Handle	.07	.77	.82	2.41	Not Sig.
Spout	.73	.87	2.60	4.51	p = .90
Flat Base	2.20	3.78	4.98	1.78	Not Sig.
Fine Base	.47	.95	1.02	.16	Not Sig.
Segment	1.50	1.50	4.32	5.34	p = .93
Denticulate	.16	.36	.55	—	—
Sickle	.43	.17	.03	—	—
N =	3	9	4		

NB: The fourth column presents the Kruskal-Wallace Non-Parametric One-Way Analysis of Variance Statistic (H) (Siegel 1956:184–192)

tend to occur in provenience units other than those with high densities of either bowls or jars.

Now let us consider the contrast between the larger elaborate buildings in Excavation B and the smaller, simpler buildings in Excavation A, as presented in Table 48. Several significant differences extend and elucidate the artifact groupings suggested by Table 47. Round lip bowls and, to a lesser and non-significant extent, flat lip bowls tend to concentrate in the simpler buildings. In contrast, solid cup bases tend to concentrate in the larger buildings. The jars and other cups are uniformly distributed. In general, the larger buildings are cleaner. The distribution of beveled rim bowls is probably distorted by garbage disposal patterns and, in any event, is not significantly associated with either building type. In summary, while certain aspects of the domestic vessel complex are used in all sampled areas of the Early Jemdet Nasr community, solid footed cups tend to be used by the occupants of the more elaborate buildings, and medium sized bowls tend to be used by the occupants of the simpler buildings. Activities involving simple retouched chert tools are conducted primarily near the simple structures.

From the Late Jemdet Nasr layers, there are more provenience units, but almost all of them are associated with elaborate residential buildings, and all have low artifact densities. We can expect little contrast and few high correlations with such a sample, and inspection of the matrix in Table 49 shows that this is indeed the case. The only positive correlation of note is one between conical cup bases and band rim jar rims (+.44). This may represent a slight tendency for such cup and jar forms to be used together, since the two are not parts of the same vessel form and are usually not reprsented by pieces of similar shape and size that would be collected together and dumped in the same place.

With these Late Jemdet Nasr data, two contemporary architecturally similar but spatially separate building complexes can be compared for the first time. Table 50 shows that the artifact densities are remarkably close. All of the differences could be easily due to chance. In summary, the Late Jemdet Nasr elaborate residences have one generalized artifact complex which does not show any evidence of internal subgroupings.

The Early Dynastic samples are not adequate for this type of analysis. Now let us draw the artifactual, distributional, faunal, and botanical data into a synthesis of the late fourth millennium communities of the Deh Luran Plain.

Table 47: Early Jemdet Nasr Phase Artifact Correlations

	Solid Cup Base	Dent-Notch	Segment	Flared Expanded Jar	Ledge Rim Jar	Conical Cup Rim	Flat Base	Beveled Rim Bowl	Round Lip Bowl	Flat Lip Bowl	Grayware Jar
Solid Cup Base	1.00										
Dent-Notch	.48	1.00									
Segment	.01	.09	1.00								
Flared Expanded Jar	.00	.26	.32	1.00							
Ledge Rim Jar	−.08	.34	−.24	−.11	1.00						
Conical Cup Rim	−.27	−.05	−.09	.34	.35	1.00					
Flat Base	−.26	.27	.08	.53	.47	.58	1.00				
Beveled Rim Bowl	−.25	.35	.09	.34	.17	.37	.59	1.00			
Round Lip Bowl	−.36	−.10	.16	.23	.07	−.26	.23	.30	1.00		
Flat Lip Bowl	−.57	−.09	.11	.26	.04	.16	.28	.40	.49	1.00	
Grayware Jar	−.49	−.11	−.01	.26	−.03	.20	.08	.31	.09	.33	1.00

.95 = .48
.99 = .62

Table 48: Early Jemdet Nasr Phase Mean Densities Per Cubic Meter

	Ex A Small	Ex B Large	U	P
Beveled Rim Bowl	10.54	7.75	24.5	not sig.
Conical Cup Rim	3.85	3.82	—	—
Wide Cup Base	.32	.15	—	—
Constricted Cup Base	.15	.05	—	—
Solid Cup Base	.31	1.01	11.0	p=.99
Round Lip Bowl	1.37	.35	13.5	p=.95
Flat Lip Bowl	.80	.17	22.0	not sig.
Round Lip Jar	.34	.61	35.0	not sig.
Flared Expanded Jar	1.17	.91	—	—
Ledge Rim Jar	1.18	.90	—	—
Band Rim Jar	.26	.07	—	—
Spout	.10	.45	—	—
Flat Base	1.91	1.56	38.5	not sig.

Table 48: Continued

	Ex A Small	Ex B Large	U	P
Ring Base	.32	.31	—	—
Grayware Jar	.95	.27	20.0	not sig.
Segment	1.75	1.17	—	—
Sickle	.62	.42	—	—
Retouched Piece	1.24	.17	3.0	p=.99
Denticulate-Notch	.43	.84	23.0	not sig.
N=	8	10		

NB: See Table 13

Table 49: Late Jemdet Nasr Phase Artifact Correlations

	Ledge Rim Jar	Flared Rim Jar	Round Lip Jar	Band Rim Jar	Wide Base	Conical Cup	Round Lip Bowl	Segments	Flat Base	Sickles
Ledge Rim Jar	1.00									
Flared Rim Jar	.26	1.00								
Round Lip Jar	.22	.15	1.00							
Band Rim Jar	−.14	.15	.31	1.00						
Wide Base	−.11	−.21	.28	.44	1.00					
Conical Cup	.15	−.08	.30	.14	.30	1.00				
Round Lip Bowl	.21	.01	.39	.06	.24	.33	1.00			
Segments	.02	.29	.29	.33	−.12	.13	.29	1.00		
Flat Base	−.43	.03	.36	.28	.06	−.05	−.05	.34	1.00	
Sickles	−.44	.03	.25	.33	−.02	.05	.00	.24	.35	1.00

95% = .41
99% = .54

Table 50: Late Jemdet Nasr Phase Mean Densities Per Cubic Meter

	Ex A	Ex B	U	P
Conical Cup Rim	7.21	8.05	—	—
Wide Cup Base	.79	.28	43.0	not sig.
Constricted Cup Base	.44	.44	—	—
Solid Cup Base	.20	.50	—	—
Round Lip Bowl	1.25	2.40	57.5	not sig.
Flat Lip Bowl	.54	.38	—	—
Round Rim Jar	1.78	2.03	—	—
Expanded Rim Jar	1.05	.98	—	—
Ledge Rim Jar	.91	.91	—	—
Band Rim Jar	.77	.65	—	—
Spout	.25	.11	—	—
Flat Base	1.01	1.03	—	—
Ring Base	.79	.34	43.0	not sig.
Grayware Jar	.18	.97	43.0	not sig.
Segment	.82	1.02	—	—
Sickle	1.16	1.72	—	—
Retouched Piece	.21	.20	—	—
Denticulate	.08	.07	—	—
Notch	.17	.19	—	—
N=	15	9		

NB: See Table 13

Chapter X

A SUMMARY OF THE URUK, JEMDET NASR, AND EARLY DYNASTIC PHASES

THE EARLY AND MIDDLE URUK PHASES

As we noted in the closing pages of Chapter V, the Deh Luran Plain was sparsely populated during the Susa A and Sargarab Phases. Farukhabad itself was abandoned and the fields around it must have fallen into disuse. This does not mean, however, that a ground cover of grasses and shrubs would have again flourished, since the area around Farukhabad may have been grazed by domestic animals. If so, much of its surface would have been as bare as it is today. Only further paleoethnobotanical work can elucidate this point. In any case, during the Early Uruk Period, Farukhabad was resettled, most likely by communities related to the two communities of the preceding Sargarab Phase (See Chapter V). The entire plain witnessed a marked rise from the Sargarab settlement area of about 1.4 ha, indicating a population of about 300, to an Early Uruk settlement area of 9.3 ha, indicating a population of about 1800 or less (given the considerations previously discussed in regards to Bayat and Farukh Phase housing densities). During Middle Uruk times these figures rose only slightly to about 9.6 ha indicating a population of about 2000 or less.

The new occupants, who arrived during the Early Uruk periods, apparently hunted onager and gazelle, though it is possible that some of the equids in our sample from Farukhabad are domesticated animals. About one quarter of the animals in our bone sample were presumably hunted and these are primarily equids. The new settlers brought with them domestic cattle, goats, and probably sheep. About one animal out of six is a cow during the Early Uruk, but this drops to one out of 13 during the Middle Uruk. During the Middle Uruk, the remainder are evenly divided between sheep and goats as in the Farukh Phase. Most of these sheep and goats were kept until the age of one, but only half (presumably the females) survived past the age of three. This approaches the optimal slaughtering procedure to obtain the amount of meat from a herd. There are no Early Uruk plant remains. During Middle Uruk times, there is evidence that domestic barley was predominant over wheat, the reverse of the Farukh and earlier crop ratio.

The Middle Uruk is one of the few periods when there is any direct information on the human population. The sample is not large enough to make definite statements about the demographic organization, stature, or pathologies of the Middle Uruk inhabitants, but chemical studies of bone strontium indicate a fairly high animal protein intake (See Appendix G). It would be interesting to have a contrasting sample from a period of higher population density and lower animal consumption, such as from preceding Farukh time or succeeding Jemdet Nasr times.

The domestic units of the new inhabitants covered only part of the mound. Early Uruk structures were uncovered in only one layer of one excavation. This particular example has the sides, rather than the corners as in earlier periods, facing the cardinal points. The walls are founded on stone footings and the one measurable room covers more than 15 sq m, far larger than any attested Farukh or Bayat room. Its ceiling is apparently supported by a central post, and there is a small hearth in the room. Other hearths, possibly a small oven, and a large shallow pit are attested in open areas not covered by structures. Structures shifted around the mound throughout Middle Uruk times, but the same basic approach to construction as before is in evidence. Walls face the cardinal points and all are based upon stone footings. They are built with small bricks averaging only 25 to 13 by seven cm, in contrast to the large mud bricks of the Farukh Phase. The measurable rooms are smaller than in the Early Uruk example and there is no evidence of internal supports. Hearths and pits occur as before. New features include a very large oven and a rectangular, below floor, mud-slab lined bin, perhaps a household granary. In general, the buildings seem to have been fairly large and they may well have housed extended families.

There is both direct and indirect evidence of food preparation around these areas. Sickle blades for harvesting and slabs for grinding grains are ubiquitous. Choppers and large utilized flakes and blades, all probably used in butchering, are also present. There is a general increase in the density of waste bone on the site indicating that more meat was being eaten than in the earlier Farukh Phase community. The bone fragments suggest that the final stage of preparation in these phases involved the pounding of the meat—bone and all—followed by boiling. Such could have been done in the relatively common thickened round rim jars, which do show evidence of fire. Shape alone suggests that the flared expanded rim jars were used in storage and the smaller bowls and jars were used in serving, but a statistical study of Middle Uruk vessel part distributions provides no support for such propositions.

Various discrete craft activities are implied by the artifacts found in the Early and Middle Uruk settlement. In Early Uruk layers there is evidence of ceramic production, stone tool manufacture, bitumen working, and spinning as in the earlier communities. In Middle Uruk times, the addition of a new craft may be indicated by the presence of a drill rest, large drill bits concentrated in one area, and new forms of perforated stones.

Within the community at Farukhabad there is no evidence of social differentiation in either the buildings or the artifacts and food waste around the buildings. However, there are other possible sources of information on social differentiation, including items of personal adornment such as local clay and limestone beads which predominate during both the Early and Middle Uruk. The continuity in bead preference suggests no great increase in wealth in any segment of the community. The few burials provide invaluable information, unfortunately not paralleled in other fourth millennium phases at the site. Most individuals, old and young, male and female, lack goods or evidence of special funeral preparation. However, one person is buried with a number of possible cosmetic and food preparation artifacts. While differentiation of adults indicates only achieved and not necessarily ascribed rank differences (Saxe 1970), some social units in the Middle Uruk settlement had certainly accumulated greater wealth than others. The authority to use the administrative artifacts discussed below may have rested in such families. On the other hand, it is quite possible, given our limited exposure, that architecturally differentiated domestic units and other special buildings indicating more formal rank differences existed elsewhere on the mound. Certainly the pieces of marine shell inlay from the later Middle Uruk layers in Excavation B suggest that elaborate buildings, such as are attested in the Late Uruk, were already being built and furnished by the end of the Middle Uruk.

Whatever the social organization of the populace at Farukhabad, there unquestionably were political authorities in the settlement. The occurrence of simple seals coupled with the receipt of spherical messenger bulla indicates that shipments of goods were arriving at or being stored at Farukhabad, and that they could be counted and approved by a local authority. Such authority will be discussed in conjunction with the consideration of valley-wide settlement organization and broader relations which follows.

As previously detailed (Figure 33) the two Sargarab communities were located on the northwest piedmont of the plain near a permanent spring. During Early Uruk times there is a shift of settlement south onto the alluvial plain of the Mehmeh and the Dawairij, though the east portion of the plain remains little inhabited. The dominant settlement is a small center of about five ha (DL-292) (Figure 78). This briefly occupied site which has been virtually leveled by erosion, exhibits many stone footings and the stone lining of a small canal running down one edge of the site. In contrast to this are a number of small communities all of about one ha, one of which is Farukhabad (DL-20). During the succeeding Middle Uruk period (Figure 79), the total settled area remains at about the same magnitude but some former settlements are abandoned, among them the small center, and new ones are founded to the east. With these shifts Farukhabad becomes a centrally located settlement, in a mediating position between several smaller settlements. Perhaps the change to such a position was associated with the rise of authority figures at Middle Uruk Farukhabad.

The broader relations of the Early and Middle Uruk communities can, as before, only be suggested. While the technical antecedents of the Sargarab Ware ceramics are to be found in the

A SUMMARY OF THE URUK, JEMDET NASR, AND EARLY DYNASTIC PHASES

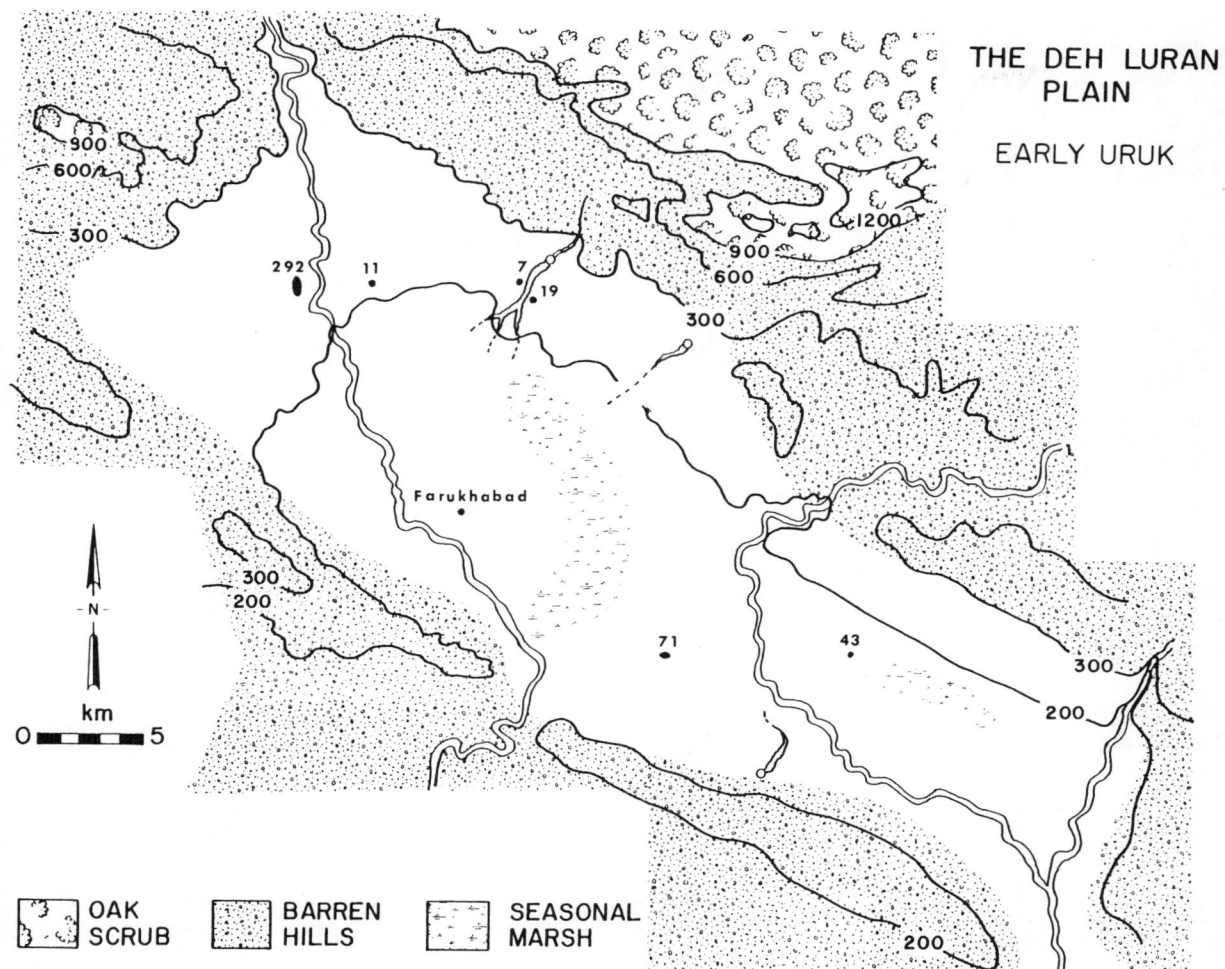

Fig. 78. Early Uruk Settlement Pattern.

Central Zagros (Wright, Neely, Johnson, and Speth 1975), little more can be said since the vessels exhibit few stylistic embellishments which could be compared with those of other areas. In contrast, increasing proportions of the vessels are of Uruk Ware, particularly small, straight neck jars with round or flat lips, or ledge rims. During the Middle Uruk, nose lugs and cross-hatch incising become common on these jars and new forms such as fine sinuous-sided cups appear. We do not know enough about Early and Middle Uruk ceramics in Iraq to say whether there is more interaction with the Susa area or the Uruk area, but certainly there are slowly increasing relations with some other areas of the lowlands. Whether this involves

exchange of vessels or the visits of itinerant potters cannot yet be determined. The stylistic elements of the seal impressions on the messenger bulla are similarly uninformative. All three impressions are similar to those known from Susa. Perhaps they would also prove similar to contemporary Middle Uruk Impressions from Warka; however, such seals and sealings have not yet been reported.

The evidence for long-range or interregional movement of goods and materials is similar to that for the Farukh Phase. Fine cherts are obtained from elsewhere, along with obsidian from the northwest. Most significant are a few pieces of copper and marine shell whose sources are most likely in the Eastern highlands of Iran and the Gulf

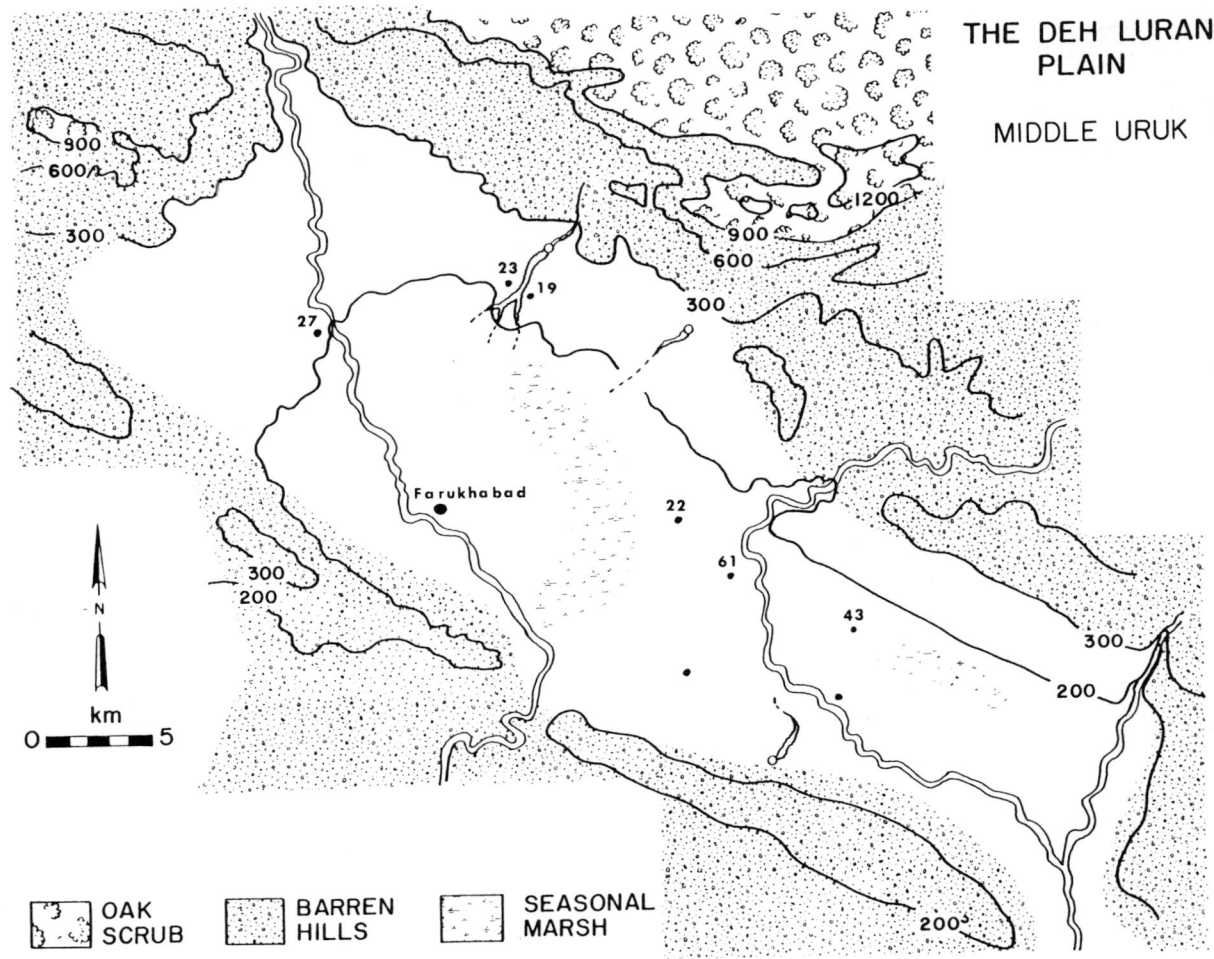

Fig. 79. Middle Uruk Settlement Pattern.

area respectively. This is evidence, albeit tenuous, for a shift in trade contacts toward the east. Bitumen remains the only documented export.

An indirect argument for a lessening of societal conflict can be made. During the Early and Middle Uruk phases there is a shift to more exposed localities than those on the Piedmont, and there is a shift into the formerly abandoned eastern end of the plain. Settlements are usually very small and the entire settled population of the plain does not exceed 2,000 people. It is unlikely that such small, exposed communities could have survived if there had been a serious military threat.

In short, the first two Uruk phases saw a repopulation of the western Deh Luran Plain under peaceful conditions. The community at Farukhabad grew from a small village covering only a portion of the mound to a larger centrally located settlement with local authorities who could receive and check goods from others. While most craft goods continue the local tradition established in Sargarab times, there was increasing interaction with other lowland Uruk centers, perhaps with the burgeoning society centered around Susa to the southeast (Johnson 1973). There was, as well, an appearance of raw material types coming from the east. These phases of gradual local development contrast strongly with the next phase.

A SUMMARY OF THE URUK, JEMDET NASR, AND EARLY DYNASTIC PHASES

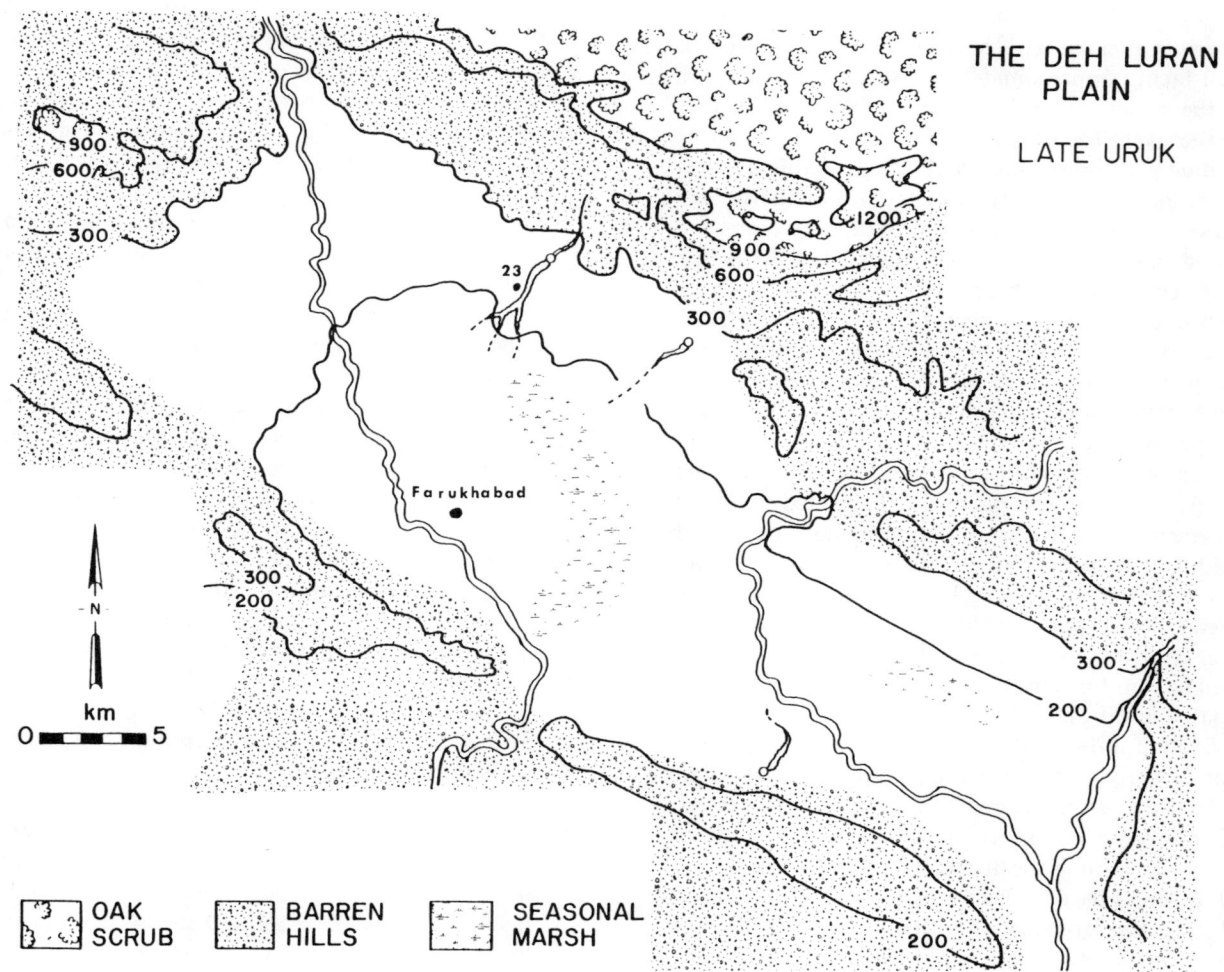

Fig. 80. Late Uruk Settlement Pattern.

THE LATE URUK PHASE

Only two settlements, covering 3.3 ha, are occupied during this phase. Most of the 600 people are concentrated at Farukhabad, the rest are at Chagha Sefid (Fig. 80). The same types of mammals are hunted and herded as before. The basic proportion of wild game seems to shift, with onager becoming more common, but the sample size is rather small. The overall density of the bones of wild game decreases while the density of domestic animals remains constant, indicating that less effort is being expended in hunting. The domestic forms remain the same with goats most common, sheep almost as common, and cattle in small proportion. Only two thirds of the sheep and goats reach the age of one year, indicating that many of the lambs are being killed before growth begins to level off. Perhaps this inefficient butchering strategy was forced on the Late Uruk inhabitants by a restriction of their access to summer pasture. The single Late Uruk botanical sample has more barley seeds than wheat, similar to those of the Middle Uruk.

Late Uruk domestic units are represented by only two successive structures in Excavation A. The earlier unit (Layer 19) has walls facing the cardinal points as in the Early and Middle Uruk. There are stone footings, but no traces of mud bricks remain. The best-preserved room covers 12 sq m and has a small hearth defined by baked brick fragments. The later structure (in Layer 18) is very poorly preserved with only an irregular mud-brick wall facing approximately northeast. The interior of the structure has been completely eroded away by the river. The only surviving features are a series of mud-slab lined bins which are probably domestic granaries similar to those found in the earlier periods. Around these small structures there are low densities of jars, bowls, and other artifacts.

In contrast to these simple buildings which continue previous architectural patterns, other Late Uruk exposures have features or characteristics that are new and probably not domestic. First, below the possible domestic buildings described above is a layer without buildings containing a large oven with a pebble-lined floor, a small pit to receive the ashes, and a large pit packed with beveled rim bowl fragments. Below this are the previously described Middle Uruk small structures similar to the Late Uruk structures above. These features may have been in a courtyard in the midst of a portion of the site covered by simple domestic buildings. The artifacts on this court seem similar to those around small buildings.

Second, most of the surfaces revealed in Excavation B were open courts during the Late Uruk, but in several layers the southeast edge of a large structure with corners pointing to the cardinal points is within the limits of the excavation. Its walls, composed of very small bricks about 18 by 11 by 7 cm, are relatively thick. These enclosed a space, probably a room judging by its well-prepared and well-preserved floor that was certainly considerably larger than the nine sq m actually exposed in the excavation. During one phase of use, a drain of ceramic cylinders and troughs was placed under the floor and through the wall out into the court to the southeast. There was a small oven or circular hearth in this court. Around this relatively imposing construction were high densities of jars and bowls, particularly beveled rim bowls. Whether this building housed a domestic unit or was for other activities cannot be established without more evidence from its interiors; unfortunately most of these have been eroded away and those that remain are very deep under later deposits.

Third, after this building was moved to the north or west, circular mud brick platforms were built on the court. Around these platforms are high densities of spouts, bottles, and small cups, indicating the dispensing of liquids around this locality.

Thus, Late Uruk Farukhabad in contrast to the earlier Uruk communities, was markedly differentiated. To the east we have evidence of simple domestic buildings and courtyards in which some special activities were performed. To the west we have evidences of elaborate structures, not necessarily domestic, with nearby courtyards in which quite different activities were performed.

The same technology for food procurement and preparation is present as before. Certainly most of the meat consumed was from domestic animals. The pounding and boiling of bone and meat together continues. The basic crafts of stone working, spinning and weaving, and potting continue in and near smaller houses. Beveled rim bowls are made, perhaps near the unusual oven and large pit amidst the simple domestic buildings. On the other hand, in contrast to the Farukh Phase pattern, bitumen waste is concentrated around the more elaborate building. This suggests that export production was being centralized around whatever institution was housed in that building.

The evidence of architectural and associated activity differentiation provides little evidence of the social organization within the community. The excavations reveal no certain elaborate residences and no burials. The absence of the latter is not surprising given that the top of the mound was probably covered with buildings and had relatively little unused open space. Even the appearance of ornaments made of previously unattested materials such as carnelian and dentalium shell is equivocal. There is little evidence of social restriction on these materials during this period.

There is, however, evidence of a variety of administrative activities. Sealed goods, both bottles and bales, were opened on the site. In addition, some of the artifacts suggest distributional activities. For instance, the marked concentration of beveled rim bowls near the elaborate building might be taken as such, even though the bowls from Farukhabad apparently do not conform to standardized sizes (Johnson, 1973: 129–39). The presence of a possible weight also suggests that the transfer of some type of commodity was carefully checked. However, none of these acitivites necessitate figures of high rank, nor does their presence indicate more than one level of decision-making hierarchy at Farukhabad itself.

One can hardly speak of valley-wide societal organization when there are only two isolated little settlements situated upon the most precipitous mounds on the plain. The evidence from Farukh-

A SUMMARY OF THE URUK, JEMDET NASR, AND EARLY DYNASTIC PHASES

Table 51: Late Uruk Ceramic Variation from Several Areas in Lowland Mesopotamia

		N	X̄	S.D.	Significant?
Strap Handles					
Width:	All Areas :	104	3.70	.88	No
	Warka Area:	16	3.53	.98	
	Farukhabad:	12	3.74	.93	
	Susa Area :	76	3.72	.86	
Thickness:	All Areas :	104	1.00	.22	No
	Warka Area:	16	.99	.20	
	Farukhabad:	12	.99	.33	
	Susa Area :	76	1.01	.21	
Cross-hatch Incised Bands					
Shoulder Thickness:	All Areas :	72	.82	.14	$p=.996$
	Warka Area:	10	.80	.12	
	Farukhabad:	11	.70	.13	
	Susa Area :	51	.86	.12	
Diagonal Line Width:	All Areas :	71	.08	.03	No
	Warka Area:	9	.07	.03	
	Farukhabad:	11	.10	.05	
	Susa Area :	51	.08	.03	
Diagonal Line Intersection:	All Areas :	72	77	19	$p=.985$
	Warka Area:	10	66	12	
	Farukhabad:	11	93	23	
	Susa Area :	51	76	18	
Bottle Necks					
Rim Diameter:	All Areas :	37	5.08	.72	No
	Warka Area:	14	5.21	.59	
	Farukhabad:	11	4.91	.83	
	Susa Area :	12	5.08	.79	
Inner Rim Angle:	All Areas :	37	72	11	No
	Warka Area:	14	75	7	
	Farukhabad:	11	68	16	
	Susa Area :	12	70	8	
Rim Top Angle:	All Areas :	37	153	23	No
	Warka Area:	14	147	29	
	Farukhabad:	11	155	18	
	Susa Area :	12	159	19	
Rim Height:	All Areas :	37	1.47	.60	No
	Warka Area:	14	1.55	.46	
	Farukhabad:	11	1.11	.58	
	Susa Area :	12	1.66	.70	
Space Height:	All Areas :	33	1.22	.50	$p=.99$
	Warka Area:	11	1.55	.46	
	Farukhabad:	11	1.37	.42	
	Susa Area :	11	1.01	.26	

N.B.: The samples used from the Warka region are those collected by Adams and Nissen (1972) in 1966 now curated at the Oriental Institute; those from the Susa region are those collected by G.A. Johnson (1973) in 1970-71. The significance test used is the Kruskal-Wallace non-parametric one-way analysis of variance (Seigel 1956:184-93). The difference in shoulder thickness of cross-hatch incised bands probably results from the presence of more small sherds in the screened Farukhabad samples, as opposed to the surface-collected Warka and Susa Region samples. The differences in space height (height of neck below the rim) of bottles and diagonal line intersection of cross-hatch incised bands are apparently significant regional differences, however minor.

abad necessarily has meaning only in terms of broader relations beyond the Deh Luran Plain itself. As before, let us first consider the stylistic affinities of the artifacts—particularly the ceramics. Except for the beveled rim bowls, almost all the vessels are of what we have termed Uruk Ware, and almost all are indistinguishable from the Late Uruk ceramics found at Susa, Warka, and other areas. Comparative statistics on a few distinctive types are given in Table 51. Without doubt there were very close relations between all the Late Uruk workshops of lowland Greater Mesopotamia. To what extent artifacts such as Uruk Ware vessels were actually imported is not demonstrable. The sudden appearance of a few clay sickles which elsewhere have a long history (Adams and Nissen 1972: 208-9), suggests something of the sort, since only a commissariat uninformed about the local abundance of chert would provide clay sickles to Deh Luran.

In this period, the movement of long-range goods shows little change. The occurrence of carnelian confirms the increasing eastward contacts inferred for the earlier Uruk phases, but (as will be detailed later) there is a further decline in both import and export.

The location of the two sites on very high mounds suggests unsettled conditions. Fortunately, actual intersocietal conflict can be inferred from evidence elsewhere, since the little settlement on the Deh Luran plain provides none except for a possible "sling missile" of unbaked clay. Johnson has presented settlement pattern evidence from the Susiana Plain to the east indicating a steady drop in population during the Late Uruk Period (1973: 143-6). A possible border area appears between the east and west halves of the plain (Ibid: Fig. 32), but by the end of the period the sites on the east half, including Chogha Mish, seem to have been abandoned. At Susa itself the latest Uruk buildings are leveled and buildings of a different scale and plan, containing different ceramics and texts with logographic signs, are built. At about the same time as this reconstruction, a number of new settlements—most composed of several small adjacent mounds—are founded, often near one of the abandoned—and more compact—Uruk settlements. Certainly major changes are taking place on the Susiana Plain, perhaps involving the movement of the first Elamite-speaking groups from the east into central Khuzestan. In contrast to this decline, Adams and Nissen's data from the Warka area to the south suggests a rise in population and settlement complexity during the Late Uruk (1972: 11-12). There is widespread representational evidence of homicide (Amiet 1961:312), siege, and captives (Amiet 1961:251). These pieces of evidence are in fact compatible with several sociopolitical interpretations, the detailing of which is not relevant to this work. It is apparent that the period was one in which established Middle Uruk polities were disintegrating and new ones were growing. Deh Luran, as a relatively small enclave between such units, was probably not a safe place for villagers, and those not directly concerned with the guarding of routes or borders or the policing of relations with transhumants would have moved away.

In summary, the small Middle Uruk settlement enclave withered away. During the Late Uruk period there were few occupants on the Deh Luran Plain. Within the small isolated outpost at Farukhabad a variety of differentiated activities were carried out. The extensive hunting and prudent management of domestic animals evidenced in the previous period declined. Both the remaining local subsistence activities and such crafts as bitumen preparation were probably carried out under the direction of a small administrative staff. Other crafts, such as the production of beveled rim bowls, may have remained in the domestic sphere. Only further work will show to what extent certain craft items came from outside the settlement, in part, presumably, in exchange for the processed bitumen.

THE JEMDET NASR PHASES

The economic and social recovery of the Deh Luran Plain during the Early and Late Jemdet Nasr Phases is not well documented because of difficulties in differentiating Early from Late Jemdet Nasr ceramics in the surface collections. Certainly most of the plain was reoccupied by Late Jemdet Nasr times, since large settlements are found on both of the earlier branches of the Mehmeh, in the area watered by the Sargarab stream near the present irrigated fields of the town of Deh Luran, and near the Dawairij in areas which would be most productive if watered by canals from that river. The presence of the Indian gerbil indicates year-round moist soil conditions with a heavy vegetation cover. Poplars grew along

A SUMMARY OF THE URUK, JEMDET NASR, AND EARLY DYNASTIC PHASES

the watercourses and aquatic birds and animals of the riverine thickets were brought to Farukhabad. There are thus many indications that this was a lush period, whether from better water management or increased rainfall or river flow.

Settlement area rose from about three ha to an area of about 30 ha by Late Jemdet Nasr times indicating at least 6000 people on the plain. Since the housing was dense during the Jemdet Nasr Phases at Farukhabad, a population estimate based upon a figure of 200 people per ha may be low. Much of the population increment results from the rise of a large, centrally located town at Musiyan, to which Farukhabad was probably subsidiary.

The same types of animals are hunted and herded as before, and density of hunted animals remains low. The onager is again only slightly more common than gazelle, a return to the pattern of the Early and Middle Uruk. Fish are common, particularly in Late Jemdet Nasr times, though their dietary contribution must have been small and at least some of them must have been brought from outside the area. The density of domestic animal bones increases, with goats in the majority, sheep a close second, and cows very rare as before. Domestic pigs may occur for the first time. The pattern of killing sheep and goats in intermediate between those of the Middle and Late Uruk with three-fourths of the animals surviving past one year of age, and half—presumably the females—surviving past three years. Among the domestic grains, barley continues to predominate over wheat. Almonds are also attested, as they were in Farukh Phase times.

In contrast to the preceding phases, Jemdet Nasr architecture shows much continuity through time, and many small changes leading to gradual transformations of the buildings in the main excavations throughout the Jemdet Nasr Phases, rather than isolated constructions being frequently abandoned and replaced as in the Uruk Phases. The easterly structure in Excavation A apparently begins as a building with rather thick walls and a rather large inner room or—less likely because of the well-prepared floor—a courtyard. The corners point to the cardinal points. These walls are rebuilt with a greater thickness and then are rebuilt again, expanding the room to the southwest. Definite hearths and bins indicate domestic activities. Subsequently, at the beginning of Late Jemdet Nasr times, the expanded southwest wall is removed and the walls to the southeast and northwest of it are rebuilt on a massive scale, though with shoddy techniques. This leaves an extrance hall or alley, which continues with various modifications until the end of the period. This building thus begins modestly but becomes more and more elaborate throughout its architectural history.

On the other hand, the westerly structure in Excavation B is built on the lines of the large Late Uruk building, through some time after its abandonment. Its walls face the cardinal points. The building is massive at its inception during the Early Jemdet Nasr Phase hearths and bins indicating a domestic function occur. During Late Jemdet Nasr times this westerly building becomes less massive and less carefully constructed with each successive rebuilding. Thus at this time, there were also two large elaborate constructions on the summit of the mound, each partially revealed in our rather small excavations. These two contrasting architectual histories indicate that on the summit of the mound of Farukhabad there were a number of residences of established domestic units whose prosperity, as indicated by their ability to construct substantial homes, gradually increased and decreased.

Regardless of size, the successive buildings were constructed in essentially the same fashion. The footings are set in shallow trenches sometimes with a mud mortar or packing but without stone footings. The walls are built of medium-sized bricks measuring about 23 by 13 by 7 cms. The bricklaying is sometimes competent, particularly in the smaller walls, but is usually irregular. Groups of unskilled and largely unsupervised workers may have been used for much of the work on these buildings. Floors are often carefully prepared, and both mud and gypsum wall plasters occur. The measurable rooms of these buildings are often substantial; they range in size from six to more than 20 sq m.

These buildings on the top of the mound must be compared to the small buildings revealed in section near the foot of the mound in Excavation C. These have thin walls and no surviving plasters and the one measurable room dimension was very small. This is probably our only evidence of the poorest and smallest domestic units of Jemdet Nasr times. It is notable that these walls also exhibit the continuity of rebuilding found on the top of the mound.

The densely packed Jemdet Nasr settlement was kept relatively clean, and most of our samples are associated with substantial buildings at the height of their prosperity, so an analysis of the correlations between technological items indicates little about variation in domestic activities in these buildings.

Some of the grain coming into these buildings was placed in small sub-floor granaries like those from previous periods. This type of granary disappears at the beginning of Late Jemdet Nasr times. Cylindrical plaster "vats" may have then served the same purpose. Charred seeds occur widely in these periods as do the grinding slabs and ovens probably used to prepare cereal products. Animals are butchered on the site as before; the Uruk practice of pounding the meat and bone together is not in evidence, however. Another difference that may well result from changes in food preparation and serving habits is a shift from a generally even ratio of jars to bowls during the Uruk to a ratio of more than two jars for every bowl during the Jemdet Nasr and Early Dynastic Phases. Caution must be exercised, since these changes could result from the use of wood or metal bowls rather than from actual change in the proportions of vessels used.

Most of the craft activities previously pursued continue. The lack of evidence of pottery production could be a result of the removal of such activities to the flanks of the mound. Whorls are rare, suggesting that spinning declined; however, the possibility that the wooden whorls, similar to these in use today, were introduced cannot be eliminated. Stone tool manufacture and bitumen preparation certainly continue, the latter definitely concentrated around the more substantial buildings. There are a number of odd tools suggesting other crafts, but evidence for these is not definitive.

How were several types of domestic units and craft activities organized in the community of Jemdet Nasr Farukhabad? There are several classes of evidence pertinent to this point:

1) There is some evidence of differing domestic activities in the substantial as opposed to the less substantial buildings on the summit of the mound. The solid footed goblet is more common around the more elaborate constructions. As in the Farukh Phase, the more prosperous families must have engaged in slightly differnt patterns of food serving, perhaps more frequent serving of liquids to guests. Note that polychrome jars do not seem to have been more common in the prosperous units. This pottery must have been accessible to everyone although our samples are, unfortunately, not large enough to establish whether a better quality of polychrome was found in more prosperous units.

2) While control over the types of basic foods does not seem to differ as it does in the Farukh Phase, the remains of exotic foods such as aquatic birds and marine fish, seem to be concentrated near the more substantial residences. One suspects that even with the larger samples from around the simple residences there would be little evidence of such exotic foods.

3) While some exotic materials such as marine shell and carnelian occur around unpretentious buildings, lapis lazuli and metals are attested only near the substantial buildings during Jemdet Nasr times. Such a pattern is provocative, but the tiny sample of such exotic materials precludes certainty.

In brief, as the families in these more substantial buildings reached heights of prosperity (indicated by the massiveness of their residences), they controlled certain crafts, had access to exotic foods and to certain valuable exotic materials, and they served food in different ways, perhaps indicating the greater burden of hospitality that is usually placed upon the more prominent families in the Near East.

There is little evidence of the administrative arrangements for the settlement of Farukhabad during the Jemdet Nasr Phase. One possible cylinder seal cut from marine shell was found near a Late Jemdet Nasr elaborate building. The absence of unbaked clay items which would provide a more detailed evidence of such activities may result from our own failures in recovery procedures during the first weeks of excavation.

Now let us look at the Plain as a whole. As was noted above, the Deh Luran Plain was dominated by the relatively substantial large town of Tepe Musiyan. How this came to be will not be known until Musiyan itself has been more fully investigated. There were small Uruk settlements to the north and south of the large mound, but intensive investigation by Neely has not revealed one diagnostic Uruk sherd on Musiyan itself; there is not one beveled rim bowl in the collections, suggesting that even Early Jemdet Nasr occupations must be minimal. Nevertheless, by Late Jemdet Nasr times, the entire surface of the abandoned Farukh Phase mound seems to have been occupied. Some of the

A SUMMARY OF THE URUK, JEMDET NASR, AND EARLY DYNASTIC PHASES

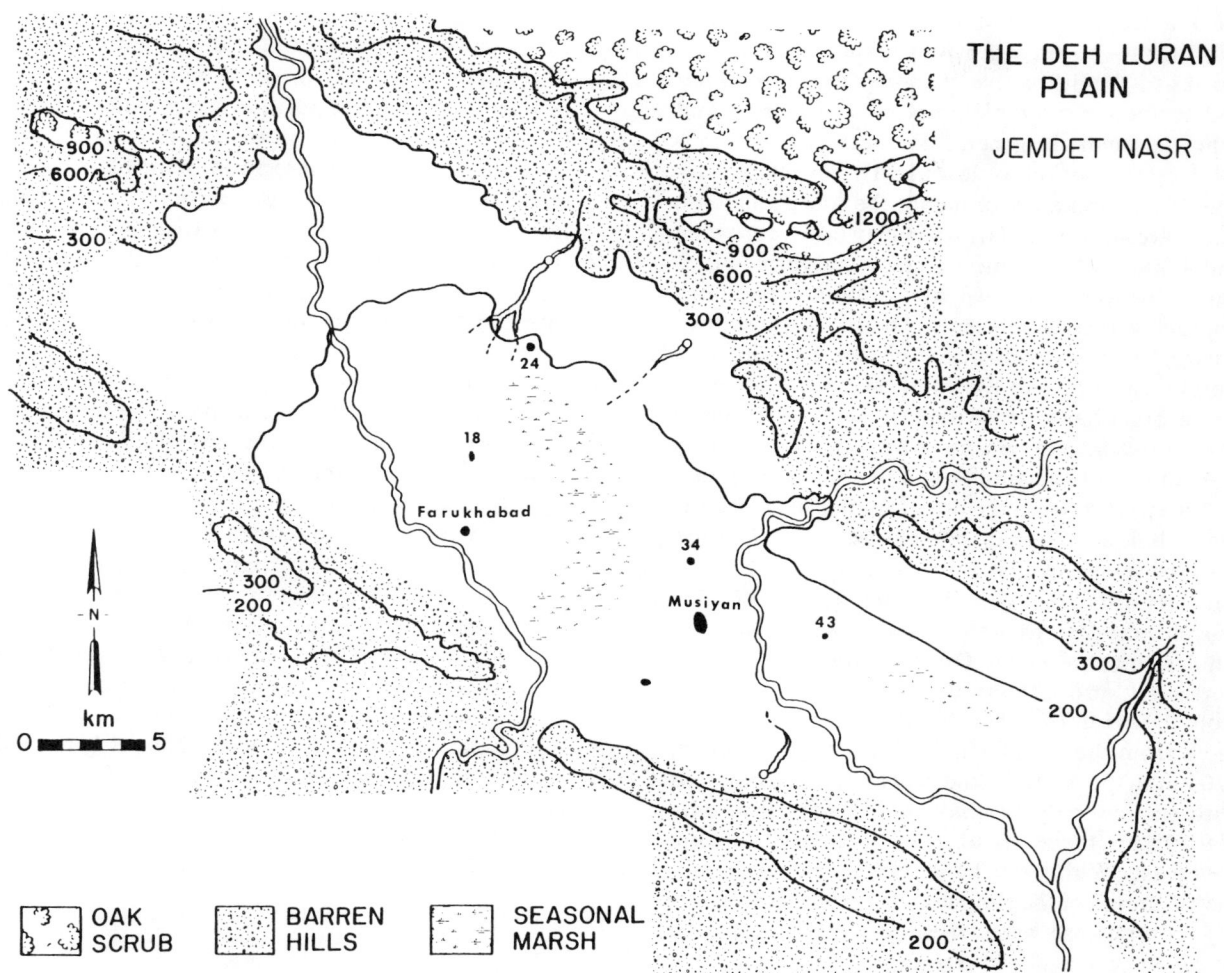

Fig. 81. Late Jemdet Nasr Settlement Pattern.

walls still visible in the sections of the 1902 soundings are massive. The looted tombs recorded on a nearby small mound in 1902 are similarly impressive (Gautier and Lampre 1905:75–80). While a twenty-fold increase in the population of the valley in three or four centuries is not biologically impossible, it seems unlikely. Some drawing of population from other areas to Deh Luran in general and to Musiyan in particular seems likely. The various settlements subsidiary to Musiyan on the plain are quite varied in their surface morphology and features. Tepe Bowla (DL-24), near the present town of Deh Luran, is similar in both area and shape to Farukhabad, and it has traces of a workshop for the manufacture of stone blade tools and repair of sickles. It also has a clay cone which suggests an elaborate building was present. In contrast, Tepe Sabz East (DL-18) is a slightly smaller oblong mound probably paralleling a former watercourse. It has no striking surface concentrations or features, and may well have been a simple village. Since it is close to but smaller than Farukhabad, it was probably under its control. The Late Jemdet Nasr settlement map (Fig. 81) reveals that Musiyan itself dominates several smaller settlements in a similar fashion. Thus there are three levels of settlement hierarchy, and probably at least two levels of decision-making hierarchy. Direct knowledge of decision-making organization on the plain, however, will only be possible when administrative artifacts are available from several settlements.

The broader relations of Deh Luran society in

the Jemdet Nasr period are perhaps better known than those of any previously discussed period thanks to the distinctive character of the ceramics and to the considerable amount of imported and exported items. In general, the pottery is a technical development out of lowland Uruk pottery, as is that of Mesopotamia proper to the south and west. There are strong similarities in clay body, throwing and building techniques, shapes and firing techniques between the two areas. While the shops producing Grayware seem to be local, those producing Uruk Ware must have continued to interact closely with those to the south and west. There is, on the other hand, little similarity with the ceramics of the Susiana Plain in clay body and firing technique and the similarities in form are general and may result from the use of similar manufacturing techniques. Perhaps the closest similarities are with the vessels from the tombs of highland Posht-e Kuh reported by Van den Berghe (1968). The polychrome designs of the Deh Luran jars also seem similar to those of the Diyala Plain 240 km westnorthwest across the foothills of the Posht-i Kuh from Deh Luran. There is also a similarity with those from the site of Jemdet Nasr itself in Akkad, 220 km to the west. On the other hand, the parallels with the few polychrome vessels from Susa, only 100 km to the east, and Tall-i Ghazir 245 km southeast (Whitcomb 1972), are restricted to geometric motifs of the simplest sort. Another interesting contrast between these assemblages is the common occurrence of certain of the more complex central motifs in only one of these areas. These may prove to be local ethnic or political symbols of some sort. Clearly this interesting class of ceramics would repay a detailed comparative study. For our purposes, it is sufficient to say that there is a definite border between Deh Luran and the Susiana, both technical and stylistic, while the former is in close interaction with Mesopotamia proper.

Some of this interaction must have been related to exchange. Various commodities such as fine cherts and stone for vessels continue to be imported. New minor imports such as marine fish, probably dried, and various items of adornment, also appear. In addition, heavy commodities like pieces of basalt and increasingly large quantities of metal appear. The basalt may come from Syria or south-central Anatolia and lapis lazuli definitely comes from northeastern Afghanistan, thus illustrating the tremendous geographical span of Deh Luran's exchange relationships. Much larger quantities of bitumen are processed, presumably for export. Certainly much of the stability of the community of Farukhabad during these periods must have resulted from its ideal position as a middleman and, for some commodities, as an exporter.

Some intimation of insecurity in the plain comes from the fact that there are fewer small settlements than in the Farukh and earlier Uruk Phases. Yet there is little evidence of conflict other than another isolated "sling missile", so we may presume that any threat involved only minor raiding. Such conditions were to prove shortlived.

In summary, in these periods there is unprecedented population growth with an accompanying quantitative expansion of the agricultural and craft production arrangements. Farukhabad, the outpost, develops once again into a small center, but it is soon dwarfed by the burgeoning central town of Musiyan. Deh Luran is perhaps one of several small urban systems around the foothills of Posht-e Kuh, in close contact with the groups that left the tombs in Posht-e Kuh (Van den Berghe, *op. cit.*). Relations with the Proto-Elamite communities of the Susiana were not close, but there is no real evidence in this period, which Braidwood has justly termed that of "the first internationalism" (Braidwood and Braidwood 1960: 517), of continuing conflict or barriers to exchange, whatever the relations may have been at the end of the Uruk Period.

THE BEGINNING OF THE EARLY DYNASTIC PHASE

Farukhabad can provide little more than a brief introduction to this long and complex period. Massive river erosion and intrusive pits limit our knowledge of the Early Dynastic occupation. On the Plain as a whole, about 23 ha of settlement were occupied which indicates a population of about 4500 inhabitants at the beginning of the period. However, though we know that smaller settlements were being abandoned, we do not know the situation at Musiyan. Possibly the people of the smaller settlements were crowding into more defensible town (Fig. 82).

The major observed change in subsistence is an increase in the proportion of the presumably domesticated pig. Hilzenhiemer's study of the fauna from third millennium sites on the Diyala (1941) indicates that this trend is not purely local. We lack plant remains from this period.

A SUMMARY OF THE URUK, JEMDET NASR, AND EARLY DYNASTIC PHASES

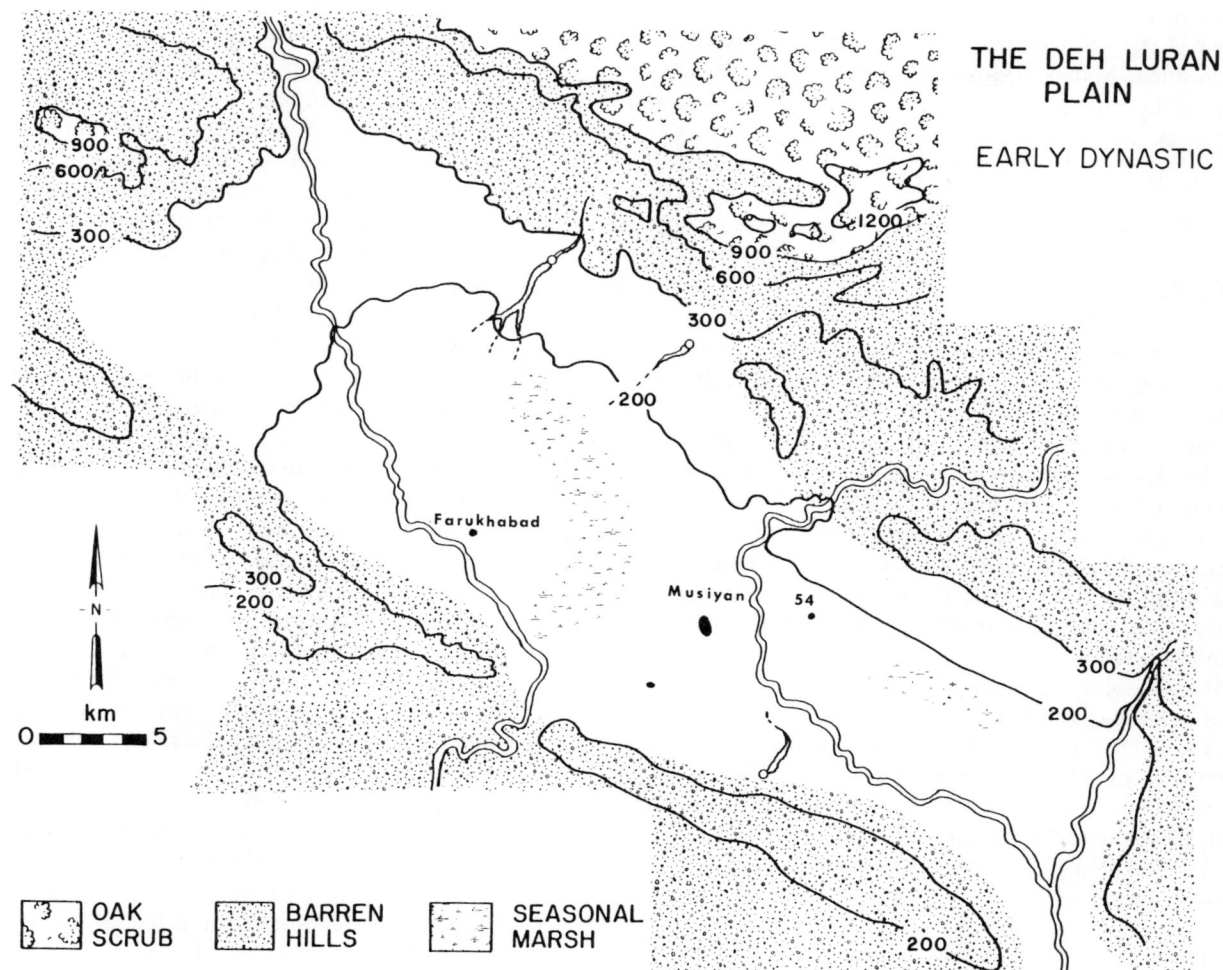

Fig. 82. Early Dynastic Settlement Pattern.

Domestic units are represented by fragments of buildings, which are simple thin-walled constructions in all three excavations. The building in excavation A to the west is made of plano-convex bricks and may have been more elaborate. However, it is badly eroded. In addition to the evidences of the usual craft activities around this building, there is a large piece of metal slag indicating that a cuprous metal is being refined in some way at Farukhabad. A concentration of bone scrapers on a courtyard floor in this area suggests hide working of some sort. Several lapis lazuli items occur in these same layers. A more prosperous family which controlled these new activities may have resided nearby. On the other hand, there was also a lapis item in the undistinguished remains of a small building in Excavation B, so it is equally possible that lapis had become a widespread commodity at this time. In any event, the level of construction at Farukhabad suggests depressed conditions during this period.

On the plain as a whole there are fewer communities. It may be during this period that the visible town walls of Musiyan are built. It could not have been much later since they are in places completely overridden by late third milennium refuse.

Though trade and exchange continue, and though there are generic similarities with the ceramics of both Mesopotamia proper and the

Susiana, there seems to have been increasing insecurity. Eventually, almost all the small sites were abandoned, and it is possible that only Musiyan remained, protected—to some extent—behind its ramparts.

SUMMARY

In Chapter V and in this chapter, we have summarized the history of the Deh Luran Plain between about 4400 B.C. and 2600 B.C. During this time, one cultural and ecological pattern—that of the Ubaid or developed ranked societies—reached its height and drew to a close. Another—that of the Uruk and Jemdet Nasr or early states—began, reached its peak, and declined. In broad terms, the Early Dynastic Period was transitional between the first states and the early empires which followed them.

At this point the reader may derive some value from a comparison of the peaks of these two cycles on the Deh Luran Plain, itself a marginal or provincial locality during both of these great florescences. Let us contrast some of what has been inferred of the economic and social organization of the Farukh Phase with that that the Late Jemdet Nasr Phase.

1) The two community systems had similar types of subsistence resources, though there were slight differences in strategy. The same hunting pattern was pursued, but there was a difference in the utilization of domestic sheep and goats, perhaps the result of differing emphases on food and fiber production during the two phases. Both systems involved the irrigation of extensive areas in order to grow grain, but apparently wheat predominated earlier and barley later. The later diversity of animal foods may have been necessitated by the fact that the population was greater than during the earlier florescence.

2) The two systems had three levels of settlement hierarchy and about the same number of settlements, but the Jemdet Nasr Phase settlements differ in two key respects. First, they are generally larger and must have been internally more complex and difficult to administer. Second, while all Farukh settlements except the very smallest seem to have been structurally similar, differentiated by size alone, the Late Jemdet Nasr settlements would seem to have been structurally differentiated. The central town and the intermediate centers were probably similar, but the smaller settlements lack the features characteristic of the centers as far as one can judge from surface evidence. Obviously, this last point is a proposition which must be tested with further excavation.

3) Within the one sampled intermediate-sized center which was used during the peaks of both of the community systems, there is evidence of two ranked classes of domestic units distinguised by residences of differing elaborateness. In both cases the higher-ranking units have domestic technologies similar to those of the other units except for inordinate quantities of smaller drinking vessels. Here the similarities between the two periods end. While the Farukh Phase units have differential access to types of mammals depending on their class, a situation involving sumptuary rules which need not imply differing access to amounts of food, the Late Jemdet Nasr units of high rank seem to monopolize certain kinds of food-stuffs, such as birds, a situation of differential access to quantity. Furthermore, there may be certain types of exotic raw materials which only the higher ranking or more properous units have access to. Finally, while there is little evidence that units have any specialized control of productive activities during the Farukh Phase, such is definitely the case later. The best evidence of control of a productive activity by the higher-ranking units involves bitumen, a commodity which is definitely leaving the plain, presumably in exchange for wealth from outside the plain. In short, several lines of evidence indicate that class organization had become exploitative by Jemdet Nasr times.

4) It would be ideal if this comparison could be concluded with a statement about the actual political organizations. However, our sole direct evidence of this is a single seal in each of the two phases. While the excavation was not designed to produce

A SUMMARY OF THE URUK, JEMDET NASR, AND EARLY DYNASTIC PHASES

such evidence, one would still prefer to have it. While we can plausibly assume that the administrative specialization evidenced during the Uruk Period continued and developed during the Jemdet Nasr, and the Jemdet Nasr administrative organization was as complex as that of contemporary societies to the east, west, and south, such assumptions are poor substitutes for the evidence that can and will someday be recovered with further fieldwork in Deh Luran. This issue will be taken up again in Chapter XV, when we turn to the problems of long-range exchange and state formation.

We now turn to the various reoccupations of Farukhabad during the period from 2200 B.C. to A.D. 200.

PART THREE: THE ELAMITE AND LATER PHASES

Chapter XI

THE ELAMITE PHASES

ELAMITE STRATIGRAPHY

Eighteen layers of Elamite debris were defined in Excavation B. An Elamite feature was exposed in Excavation C. In the following section the stratigraphy of Excavation B is described, beginning with the oldest and proceeding to the youngest. All are visible on Fig. 83.

Layer 18: Silt lenses (.18 m): To the southeast there are soft, stratified silt lenses with small charcoal fragments. To the northwest a large irregular pit penetrated down into Layer 22. This pit contains a burial (Feature 11), and is capped by the floor forming the bottom of Layer 17.

Layer 17: Silt floors, brick debris, and ash (.18m): This layer contains a complex sequence of architectural debris. Lower Layer 17 is composed of a floor and a fill. The floor is of compact silt and gypsum grit to the northwest of the wall of a building (Feature 9); above this, but pinching out to the east of the wall, is a layer of silt, broken brick, and ash lenses. Above this layer is the gypsum grit floor marking the beginning of upper Layer 17. This floor is to the north of the wall of another building whose wall runs east-west (Feature 8). To the south of this later wall is an ash covered floor. Over both this ash and the wall stub, thus covering the easternmost two meters of the excavation, is a layer of silt, probably deteriorated brick, capped by another ash lens.

Layer 16: Silt, brick debris, and ephemeral floors (.50m): Construction continues. A small portion of a wall stub is visible in the east corner of the excavation (Fig.7k) though this was not noted in excavation. There is a silt floor around this fragment of wall. Over this are scattered ash lenses and broken bricks in a layer of silt. Apparently these small early Elamite structures of Layers 17 and 16 shifted northeastwards out of the area excavated. In upper Layer 16 to the northwest are a few lenses of soft finely stratified silt like Layer 18. This may indicate local abandonment at this time. A large ash lens marks the top of Layer 16. A burial (Feature 8) penetrates into the layer from above.

Layer 15: Silt, brick debris, and ephemeral floors (.80 m): This layer slants down to the north from a construction fragment to the south largely destroyed by erosion (see Fig 7). A few bricks mapped on the eroded edge of the excavation are all that remains of this structure. This layer and the one above certainly should have been subdivided.

Layer 14: Silt and broken bricks (.20 m): A layer largely destroyed by the digging of a large pit to the northwest. It is likely that the rampart (Feature 4) was built on the top of Layer 14. We could not conclusively show this without cutting out part of the rampart, which we were not prepared to do since we could not do justice to this interesting structure in the time available. The large pit of succeeding Layer 13 may have been a borrow pit for fill or brick material for this rampart. A well or drain (Feature 6) cut through Layer 14 and more than 4.80 m down past Layer 32. It originated somewhere above layer 14. A group of vessels and bones, some human, were found in the highest surviving layers of this shaft.

Layer 13: Green silt and ash (.70 m): This is the lower fill of the large pit cutting through Layer 14 and down into Layer 16. The sequence of debris begins with a layer of silt and small brick fragments. Next there is a layer of gypsum grit, then a layer of silt, and finally a layer of large charcoal fragments with ash and broken brick interfingering toward the rampart with silt layers.

Layer 12: Green silt and ash lenses (.40 m): This is the upper fill of the large pit, and continues up and over the rampart. The layer is composed of

THE ELAMITE PHASES

alternating layers of ash, and silt with many brick fragments. These appear to be from the deterioration of the rampart wall. This rampart, Layers 12, 13, and parts of 14, 15, 16, 17, and 18 are stained green. The green stain cements the silts together to a rock-like consistency. James Knudstad, formerly architect of the University of Chicago's Oriental Institute, examined color slides of this green induration, and notes that in the climate of Mesopotamia, sewage forms such a deposit as it percolates through the ground. It is likely that this area of our excavation was used as a urinal during the time of Layers 12 and 13.

Layer 11: Ash and silt lenses (.60 m): This is a complex in the west portion of the unit. Lower Layer 11 has more gypsum grit and silt. Upper Layer 11 has more ash and burnt mud plaster fragments. This change in deposition accompanies the building of a structure (Feature 1) and related smaller walls not visible on the section, (Feature 5). To the north west of Feature 1, a plastered oven (Feature 3) was built.

Layer 10: Ash and silt lenses (.28 m): The building of another wall (Feature 2) parallel to Feature 1 defines the beginning of this layer. Ashy lenses predominate; silty lenses are rare.

Layer 9: Ash (.31 m): This layer is northwest of the new wall.

Layer 8: Compact silt floors, ash lenses and broken brick (.22 m): This layer is south of the Feature 1 wall. It is contemporary with the thick layers of ash north of the wall forming Layers 11 upper, 10, and 9. Its thinness provides an index of the short time period of the use of the oven.

Layer 7: Ash and silt lenses (.16 m): This layer marks the final deterioration of the wall and oven complex of Layers 11 upper to 9. The uppermost ash lens caps the stub of Feature 1, but the stub of Feature 2 still protrudes above the ground.

Layer 6: Lenses of silt, broken brick, and ash (.14 m): These seal the wall stubs. The uppermost silt lens completely covers them, though a hummock marked their location.

Layer 5: Pebble pavement (.08 m): This is restricted to the middle of the excavated area. Contemporary with this, a flimsy wall was built over the stub of Feature 2 and northwest of the pavement.

Layer 4: Compact silt floor and ash lens (.12 m): These overlie a pavement to the southeast of the wall.

Layer 3: Compact floor and ash lens (.08 m): These are southwest of the wall and indicate a major re-utilization of the building of which the flimsy wall was doubtless a part.

Layer 2: Series of compact floors (.10 m): There are no ash lenses.

Layer 1: Silt and broken brick (.15 m): Perhaps these are from the destruction of the structure represented by the wall and floors of Layers 3 and 2.

ELAMITE FEATURES

PITS

Large Shallow Pit (Layer 18): A quadrant of this irregular pit was excavated. It measures at least 3.5 m from northeast to southwest, and at least 2.0 m from northwest to southeast. A burial (Feature 11) described below is included in the pit fill. The pit was .65 m deep and cuts into the top of Layer 22. it is filled with a thick layer of silt and gypsum grit.

Large Deep Pit (Layer 13): A quadrant of this pit, perhaps a borrow pit for the construction of the rampart (Feature 4), was excavated. This quadrant is 1.0 m from northeast to southwest and 2.5 m from northwest to southeast. It is 1.3 m deep, and cuts into the top of Layer 16. Its fill is described above under the heading of Layer 13. The mandible of a true horse (*E. caballus*) was found here.

Shaft (Feature 6, Layer 14 or higher): This deep pit, in plan an irregular oval about 1.2 m in length was followed downward for 4.8 m. The fill was a soft brown silt. It contained a variety of debris from all occupational periods. Vessels and a fragmentary burial high in the shaft, described below, suggest that this feature originated from upper Layer 11 or perhaps higher, though the top of the feature was eroded away. We cannot say whether this was a well, a drain, or some other construction, without penetrating to its original bottom.

BURIALS

Extended Burial (Feature 11, Layer 18): The pelvis and legs of this individual remain in the unexcavated section. The upper body was supine

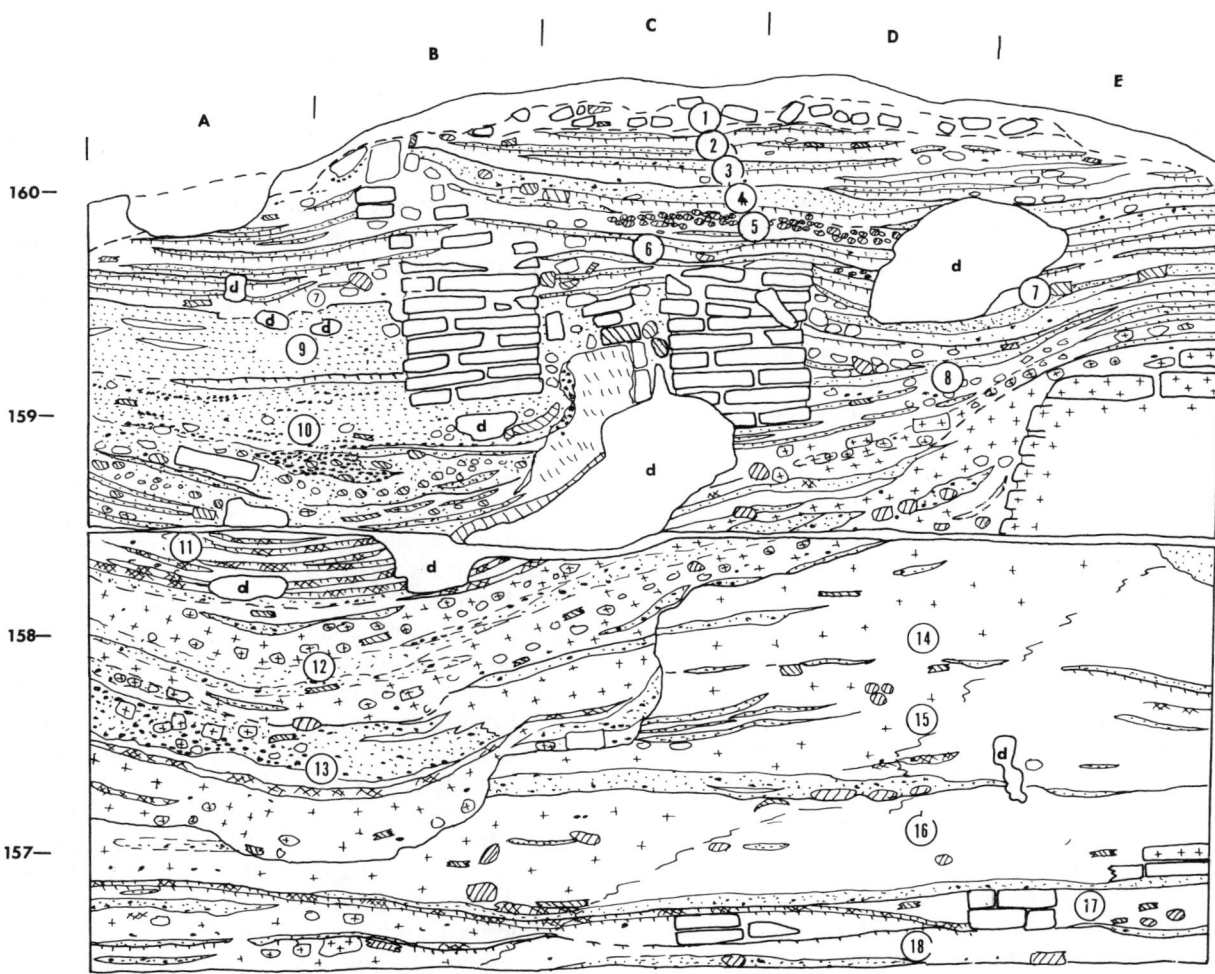

Fig. 83. The Northeast Section of Excavation B.

with arms flexed and crossed. The skull pointed southeast and the face southwest. No associated objects were noted. This dates to the earlier Simashki Elamite Phase.

Flexed Burial (Feature 7, Layer 15 or higher): Above this burial were the imprints of reed matting and a medium necked jar with flat-topped rim. The body was on its right side with the right knee and elbow tightly flexed, the left knee and elbow slightly flexed; the skull points northwest and faces southwest. A decayed asphalt soaked object, perhaps a small bowl, was found immediately behind the skull. A copper object, perhaps an ear ornament, was nearby. This dates to the Sukkalmahhu Elamite Phase.

Fragmentary Burial (Feature 6, Layer 14 or higher): Near the top of the shaft were found some human skull fragments, some bones of *Bos*, seven cobbles, and four fragmentary button base goblets. These date to Transitional Elamite Phase.

BRICK CONSTRUCTIONS

Wall Stub (Feature 9, Layer 17 lower): This wall is oriented N 45° E and runs completely across the excavation. The south portion is of four courses of simply bonded stretchers measuring .29 x .19 x .07 m. There are bricks on edge on either side of this wall, bringing it to a width of about .40 m. The north portion has two courses of brick,

THE ELAMITE PHASES

some larger, laid flat. It may have been a door jamb. On the interior floor to the northwest was a partially perforated stone, perhaps a door socket.

Wall Stub (Feature 8, Layer 17 upper): This wall is oriented N 80° E and runs from the east terminating abruptly in the middle of the excavated area. It is constructed with two courses of simply bonded square bricks .38 x .38 x .08 m. The interior floor is to the north of the wall.

Wall Fragment (Layer 16): A small exposure of a brick wall similar to that below. It is oriented approximately N 20° W. Note that these three successive structures seem to have shifted north and east and to have rotated counter-clockwise.

Construction Fragment (Layer 15): An eroded set of bricks laid flat. One measures .37 x .35 x .09 m. This may be a paving rather than a wall stub. In any event, judging by the slope of the layer it is probably related to a large structure to the southwest removed by erosion.

Wall Stub Complex (Layer 11 upper): The main wall (Feature 1) .60 m wide, is oriented N 70° E and runs through the excavation. There are ten surviving courses visible in the section. There are two sizes of bricks: a square type measuring .35 x .35 x .08 m and a rectangular type half that size. The bonding along the length of the wall is in a simple stretcher pattern. The bonding across the width of the wall is unusual. In the first course there are whole bricks to the south and half bricks to the north. In the second course there are half bricks to the south and whole bricks to the north. The third course is like the first; the fourth is like the second, and so on. Initially there was a doorway in this wall allowing access to the small interior rooms to the north, but this was blocked when these rooms were removed and the oven (Feature 3) was built. These interior partitions (Feature 5) are fragmentary. Where preserved, they seem to be of rectangular brick alone, and simply bonded. After construction of the oven, Upper layer 11 was deposited inside the structure.

Wall Stub (Feature 2, Layer 10): This is a wall constructed with bricks similar to those of Feature 1 and bonded in the same unusual manner. It is parallel to the earlier wall, and there is a .75 m space between the two walls in which the oven remains are located. Whether Feature 1 was in ruins at the time of Feature 2 is not known.

Wall Stub (Layer 5): This fragmentary construction, .40 m in width, probably runs N 40° E. The bricks are about .30 x .15 x .08 m. There is a pebble pavement southeast of this wall, suggesting the buildings exterior was on this side but this is not certain.

Rampart (Feature 4, Layer 13/14): The above described constructions are probably all parts of buildings and compunds. This feature is a massive rampart or terrace facing. There are two exposures. The one in Excavation B faces southwest. It is based at 158.4 m above sea level or slightly lower and survives for seven courses to a height of 159.3 m. The bricks are simply bonded. They range from .23 to .48 m in length, from .12 to .20 m in width, and from .12 to .14 m in thickness. The exposure in Excavation C faces north-northeast. It is based at 158.2 m above sea level or perhaps slightly lower and survives for twelve courses to a height of 160.0 m. The bricks are simply bonded. They range from .30 to .42 m in length, .20 to .24 m in width and .12 to .14 m in thickness. This rampart was at least 2.4 m in thickness. Further work is required to show the exact relation between these two exposures; however, their similarity suggests that between the two periods of Elamite small house construction there was a period when the summit of the mound was surrounded by a revetment.

OTHER FEATURES

Rectangular Oven (Feature 3, Layer 11 Upper): This small oven is a rectangular compartment .75 x 1.00 m inside the building bounded by Feature 1. The roof curve indicates a .70 m height. It has been almost completely emptied by rodents seeking a den: even its plaster had been much damaged. It is likely that the ash of Layers 11 upper to 9 came from this oven or similar ovens. There was no artifactual evidence of what was heated in this oven.

SUMMARY OF THE ELAMITE DEPOSITS

The Elamite occupations begin with the deposition of refuse and digging of pits on the eroded surface of the Early Dynastic mound, leaving Layer 18. A series of small houses are built on the area excavated during the time of Layers 17 and 16. Such construction may have continued nearby during the time of Layer 15 but there is little evidence of it. Layer 15 is the last containing ceramics of the Simashki Elamite Phase, which extends from 2100 to 1900 B.C., however, the basic depositional pattern continues. There is a definite change in depositional pattern after Layer 14. Pits are dug and a large rampart is built, traceable both in excavations B and C; Layers 12 and 13 are deposits around this deteriorating rampart. Lower Layer 11 is perhaps such a deposit also. This layer is the last containing ceramics of the Sukkalmahhu Elamite Phase which dates from sometime between 1900 to 1600 B.C. There is a distinct hiatus in ceramic development between upper 11 and lower 11. Next a complex of walls and an oven is constructed and an unknown activity occurs, leaving the ash of Layers upper 11, 10, and 9. Layer 8 includes material slightly before and contemporary with this oven episode. Layers 7 and 6 are refuse accumulating around the deteriorating complex. Layers 5 to 1 are the fill and floor of a small building put above the remains of the oven complex and the rampart. Layers 11 upper to 1 contain ceramics of the Transitional Elamite Phase which dates from sometime between 1600 and 1300 B.C.

ELAMITE CERAMICS
by Elizabeth Carter

INTRODUCTION TO THE ELAMITE CERAMICS[1]

Deposits of a second millennium B.C. date were found only in Excavation B (Layers 18-1) at Tepe Farukhabad. The sample, although small, is of value since it is part of the much longer ceramic sequence identified at Farukhabad. Furthermore, the ceramics can readily be compared to the better known sequences from both central Khuzestan to the east and Mesopotamia to the west. The sample studied included all rims, bases, and diagnostic parts from all well-stratified units. The majority of the body sherds were counted and discarded in the field. The size of the sample as well as the secondary nature of this study precluded any functional analysis, and what follows is primarily a descriptive presentation of the material. Accordingly an attempt has been made to accurately illustrate as much of the material as possible. Three main phases of ceramic development were identified at Farukhabad which correspond to the Simashki (ca. 2100-1900 B.C.) Sukkalmahhu (ca. 1900-1600 B.C.) and Transitional (ca. 1600-1300 B.C.) Phases of central Khuzestan (Carter 1971). The terminology—Simashki, Sukkalmahhu and Transitional Phases—used for central Khuzestan has been retained and used in reference to the ceramics from Farukhabad. This usage in no way implies that we have direct evidence of political control of the Deh Luran Plain by the rulers of the central area. It simply means that the ceramic assemblage recovered is so close to that know from central Khuzestan that new terminology would be superfluous.

SIMASHKI PHASE (ca. 2100-1900 B.C.) EXCAVATION B—LAYERS 18-15

The available stratigraphic and ceramic evidence from Excavation B at Farukhabad indicates that there is a gap in the excavated sequence which can be dated to the period between at least 2600 and 2100 B.C. (cf. Stève and Gasche 1971: 59-85 and Carter 1974: 219 for a discussion of the ceramics characteristic of this period). Apparently the Simashki phase occupation began with the deposition of refuse and some pit digging on the eroded surface of the Early Dynastic mound. Many of the sherds recovered from Layers 17-18 of known Early Dynastic and Jemdet Nasr types were worn in much the same way that sherds collected from the present-day surface of a mound are worn. The ceramic assemblage from Layers 18-15, though mixed, offers a *terminus post quem* for the slightly later and well-stratified layers identified in the excavation. Further expansion on this horizon will be necessary if a definitive study of Simashki phase ceramics of Farukhabad is to be done.

Simashki Phase pottery: Simashki Phase wares could be divided into the following five types:
1) Fine buff ware which is a compact, well-fired, buff-slipped buff ware ranging in color from a red-buff with a cream slip to a green-buff with a green-buff slip. It is similar to the Sukkalmahhu Phase fine ware and like it was used for high-necked jars and goblets.

---

[1] This study of the second millennium B.C. pottery from Tepe Farukhabad was originally included in my Ph.D. dissertation (Carter, 1971). Despite changes in the original format and the inclusion of newly published comparative material, the typology proposed at that time has not been revised.

2) Non-compact buff wares have a high proportion of straw temper which is burned out during the firing. Vessels in this ware are almost always buff to green-buff with a slip in the same color. This ware was used for jars and goblets which are shouldered and tend to be thin walled and unusually light.

3) Gritty buff ware is a buff slipped, brown-buff, green-buff, or buff ware with a fairly heavy grit temper clearly visible in the paste. Easily distinguished from the predominantly straw or sand tempered common wares of the second millennium B.C., this ware is the common ware of the third millennium B.C. in Khuzestan. At Susa it disappears in Ville Royal AXV (ca. 1900 B.C.) while at Farukhabad it is not found in Layers 14–1, but is known from Jemdet Nasr through Simashki phase layers.

4) Standard to medium-coarse ware, in contrast, is impossible to distinguish from the buff wares of all the phases of second and third millennium B.C. date. A straw and grit-tempered, buff-slipped, buff ware; it was used for ribbed jars such as Fig. 90h. A single sherd of this ware was decorated in a grid pattern in light pink paint and several sherds of standard buff ware decorated with geometric designs with a pinkish to dark red paint were also found. No standard third millennium monochrome painted wares were recovered although several polychrome painted sherds of this ware appeared to be extrusive into these layers.

5) Coarse buff ware is a heavily straw and grit tempered buff-slipped buff ware. Several examples appear to have had more grit than straw temper and are similar to the somewhat finer gritty-buff wares (type 3 above).

Simashki Phase rim and base types were divided into the following seven categories:

1) Small to medium cups and bowls in gritty-buff ware were divided into two sub-types: a) simple cups and bowls with slightly sinuous or rounded sides (Fig. 84c,d); b) small to medium dishes or bowls with an upright-indented band rim (Fig. 84a, b). A single example of a deep bowl with a carinated lower body was also found (Fig. 84e) and may date to an earlier period (cf. Stève and Gasche 1971: Plate 19:9).

2) Small to medium necked jars were divided into the following sub-types: a) fine ware, high-necked jars which often have a grooved rim (Fig. 84i,j); b) small to medium gritty-ware jar necks such as the example shown in Fig. 84l. The sample contained very few sherds of this type that were complete enough to decide vessel shape. In addition to the band rim example illustrated; direct, cut, and tapered rims were also included in the group. The absence of complete vessels precludes a more precise definition of the type. It is included here because it was found in association with other Simashki phase types and is possibly contemporary with them, although parallels with other Farukhabad material suggests that this group may also date to an earlier period. c) Non-compact ware jar necks and shoulders which came from vessels similar to that shown in Fig. 90g.

3) Medium to large necked, standard buff ware jars were divided into the following sub-types: a) open jars with grooved or corrugated necks (Fig. 84f,h); b) high-necked jars with exterior beveled band rims—the jar necks were either plain or corrugated (Fig. 84k,m).

4) Medium to large neckless jars with strongly out-turned rims which were either plain or grooved.

5) Large neckless jars or vats were divided into the following sub-types: a) closed forms which were either ridged or plain (Fig. 90e,f,h); b) open forms or vats with exterior beveled rims (Fig. 84g and 86j). These were made in standard to medium-coarse buff ware and are essentially the same type of storage vessels as those of the Sukkalmahhu Phase.

6) Small to medium flat, stump or disc bases were found in both gritty and standard buff ware. Medium stump or disc bases usually carried the spiral traces of the wheel on the lower body (Fig. 84o). The button base is found (four fragmentary examples) for the first time in these layers but only later does it become a common type.

7. Ring bases could be divided into the following sub-types: a) medium to large low ring bases in medium-coarse buff ware; b) medium to large high ring bases in standard to medium-coarse buff ware (cf. Sukkalmahhu Phase, type 11b).

Simashki Phase Dating: The occupation found in Layers 18–15 is dated to the period from ca. 2100 to 1900 B.C. This date range is based on the stratigraphic position of the levels and the pottery parallels that are summarized in Tables 52 and 53.

While there are some generalized parallels with Susa AXV, the closest and most specific parallels

Table 52: Distribution of Simashki Phase Pottery Types*

Layer	1a	1b	2a	2b	2c	3a	3b	4	5a	5b	6	7a	7b
B15			1	1	1				2½		1		
B15-16				2	1		1		3	1	1		1
B16E	1		1	2	4			2	3½		3	1	1
B17E					3			1			1	1	1
B17W		2	1⅓		1	1	2				1		1
B16-17		1	1	1	2		1				2	2	1
B18uE	2	2	2		6	2		2			7	2	
B18uW	2	1	1	1	1	1		6	1	2		1	1
B18lE					4								
B18lW	3		⅓	1	5	2		1	1	2	1	3	1
BF7	1		1						1				
B13-17 mixed				2							2		
B15-17 mixed			1					1			1	2	
B18-20 mixed	1	2	⅓	3	1	2	1	6	1	1	1	4	
Total	10	8	10	13	29	8	5	19	13	6	21	15	7
Percent within class	8	7	8	11	24	7	4	16	11	5	49	35	16
Totals					121 Rims						43 Bases		

*Fractions represent several sherds from a single vessel found in different layers.

Table 53: Farukhabad Layers 18-15 and Susa

FARUKHABAD	SUSA AXV	SUSA BVI-VII	ACROPOLE
Fig. 84a		Ghirshman 1968a Fig. 14	Stève and Gasche 1971 Pl. 2:5
Fig. 84b		*Ibid.* 11 bis	*Ibid.* Pl. 3:5
Fig. 84j			*Ibid.* Pl. 3:8
Fig. 84f	Carter 1971 Fig. 14:9		
Fig. 90f	*Ibid.* Fig. 15:7,8 (type of ware and decoration only)		*Ibid.* Pl. 3:6 (type of ware and decoration only)
Fig. 90h	*Ibid.* Fig. 15:9		

are with Ville Royale BVI and the material recovered from wells on the Acropole that are dated to the Ur III period (Stève and Gasche 1971: 45-57). Likewise the material from levels 3-4 of the 1972-1973 sounding in the Ville Royale (Carter 1974) appears to offer fairly close parallels to the Farukhabad 18-15 assemblage. Specific types found at Farukhabad and useful for dating are the upright-indented band rim bowl and the high-necked jar with a groved rim. In Mesopotamia the upright-indented band rim bowl is a common pottery form from the Akkadian to Larsa period. At Nippur it was found as late as the Old Babylonian period, but the concentration occurred in the late Ur III and early Larsa levels (McCown and Haines 1968 Plate 82: 19, 20,23 [type 8B] and Table II). These distinctive vessels are common in Ville Royale BVI at Susa but by the time of Ville Royale AXV have disappeared. At Farukhabad this type comprised 7 percent of the total assemblage of rims in layers 18-15 but was unknown in Layers 14-1. Also restricted to Layers 18-15 at Farukhabad is the high-necked jar with a grooved rim (8 percent of rims). Like the upright-indented band rim bowl this form has a long history in Mesopotamia. It has been found at various Meso-

THE ELAMITE PHASES

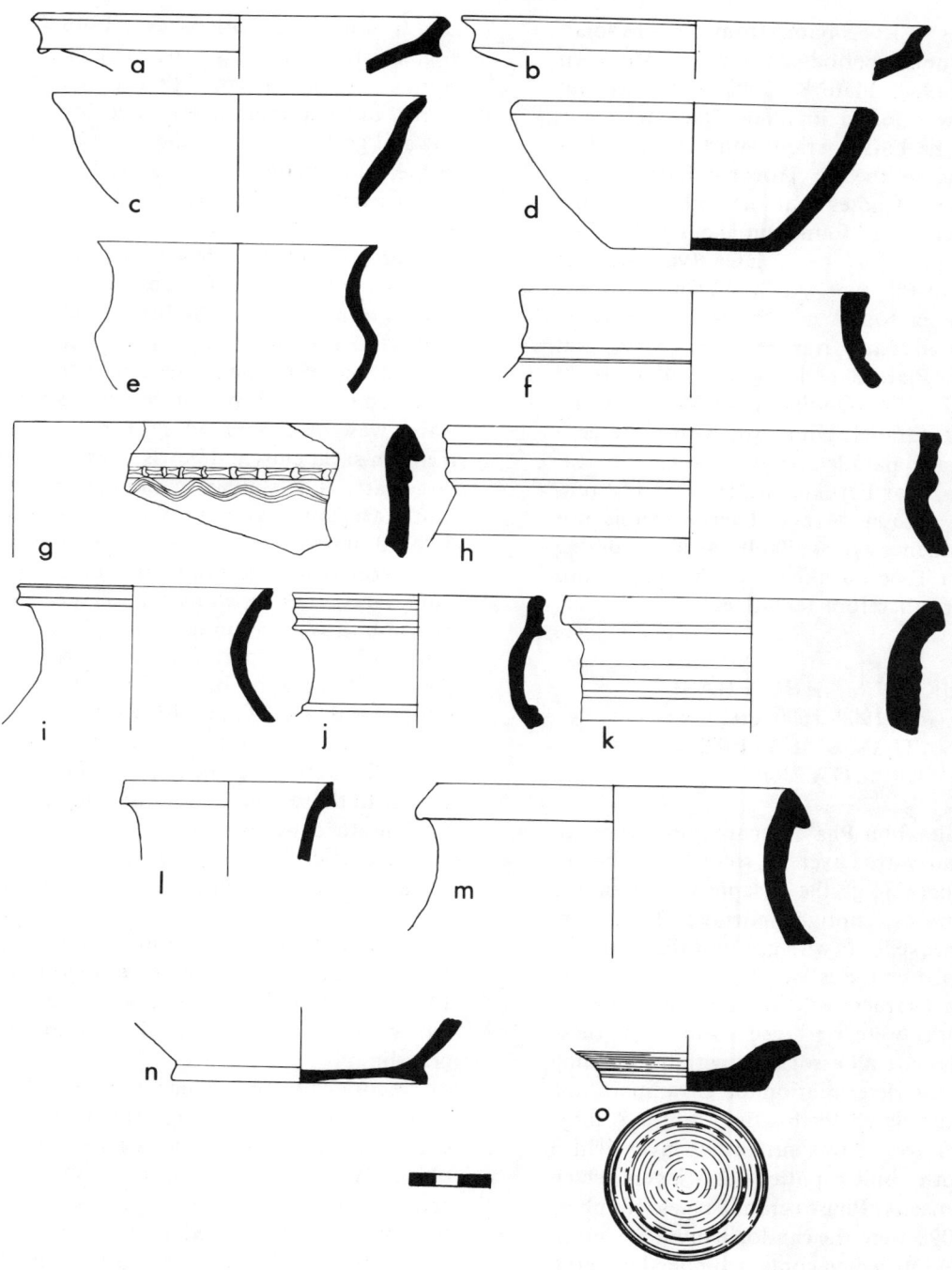

Fig. 84. Simashki Phase Pottery. A. Standard brown ware, pink buff slip, grit temper; X114 (B18). B. Standard red brown ware, pink buff slip, grit temper; X095 (B16–17). C. Standard brown ware, cream slip, grit temper; X098 (B13–17). D. Standard red brown ware, wet smoothed, grit temper, interior and exterior scraping; X112 (B18). E. Standard brown ware, brown buff slip, grit temper; X107 (B13–17). F. Standard green buff ware, green buff slip; X107 (B16–17). G. Medium coarse green buff ware, green buff slip, straw temper, combed decoration; X098 (B13–17). H. Standard pink buff ware, cream slip, grit temper; X113(B19). I. Standard green buff ware, green buff slip; X114 (B18). J. Standard red brown ware, possibly wet smoothed, grit temper; X109, X112, X113 (B17–19). K. Standard green buff ware, green buff slip, grit temper, perhaps overfired; X114 (B18). L. Overfired green black ware; grit temper; X100 (B16). M. Standard green buff ware, green buff slip, medium straw temper; X110 (B15–17). N. Standard brown ware, cream slip, grit temper; X113 (B19). O. Standard brown cored red ware, interior scraping, traces of wheel visible; X109 (B17).

potamian sites in levels dated from the Akkadian to Old Babylonian period. At Nippur (McCown and Haines, 1968: Plate 84 3,4 [Type 14a] and Table II) it was found in levels dated from the Akkadian to the Larsa period with the concentration occurring in the Ur III-early Larsa levels. Gibson (1971:163) notes that the elaborate triple grooving (such as is found on the Farukhabad examples) appears to be a later (viz. Ur III) development of this type. At Susa as at Farukhabad the type is found in association with the upright-indented band rim bowl (cf. Stève and Gasche 1971: Plate 3 and unpublished material from the 1972-1973 sounding in the Ville Royale). These specific parallels combined with more generalized ceramic parallels suggest a date of ca. 2100-1900 B.C. for Farukhabad 18-15. Unfortunately neither carbon 14 age determinations nor epigraphic evidence are available for use in dating these levels at Tepe Farukhabad. The suggestions made here are therefore tentative.

SUKKALMAHHU PHASE
(ca. 1900-1600 B.C.)
EXCAVATION B—LAYERS 14-11B
(LOWER)

The Sukkalmahhu Phase occupation is thought to have begun with Layer 14 since a number of ceramic changes (e.g. the disappearance of the gritty-buff wares, upright-indented band rim bowls, high-necked jars with grooved rims; and the appearance of numerous variant forms of button based vessels characteristic of the Sukkalmahhu Phase at Susa) were observed. Moreover, these layers (14-11B) are all associated with the building and subsequent deterioration of a rampart, the major structure dated to this time range. A large pit dug from Layer 13 was intrusive in layers which contained both similar pottery and layers which contained Simashki Phase ceramic types. Numbers X094 and X098 were the catalogue numbers given to these sherd lots which contained mixed material from Layers 16-13. When possible the material from these lots was assigned to either the Sukkalmahhu or Simashki Phase groups.

Sukkalmahhu Phase pottery (Table 54): Sukkalmahhu Phase wares could be divided into the following six types:

1) Fine buff ware is a highly fired, compact, buff, brown, or pink ware with a white or cream-colored slip. In some cases both paste and slip were fired to a greenish color. This ware is thicker and more compact than the later Transitional Phase fine wares, but like them it was used for high-necked jars and goblets. Most of the fine ware body sherds in the sample come from grooved, corrugated, or stepped jar shoulders such as those shown in Fig. 85g-i.

2) Standard buff ware has more straw temper than the fine ware. It has the same color range as the fine ware but tends to be brown-buff rather than pink. The slip, which is light in color, is thickly applied, but often the spaces left by the burned out chaff temper are visible on the vessel surfaces. This ware was used commonly for both small to medium-sized cups and bowls as well as medium to large jars. It is similar to the common standard buff ware found at Susa Ville Royal XV-XIV.

3) Medium-coarse to coarse buff ware contained both more straw and grit temper than the standard buff wares. It is generally buff-slipped, brown, or brown-buff ware although examples of green-buff ware with a green-buff slip and red-buff ware with a red-buff slip were found. The body sherds in the sample of this ware were either ridged or decorated with an applied cable ornament (perhaps plain examples were discarded in the field) and were similar to those found in Transitional Phase layers.

4) Smoothed wares similar to those described as characteristic for the Transitional Phase were found in limited numbers in Sukkalmahhu Phase layers.

5) Gray wares similar to those known from Susa Ville Royale AXV-XIV were found in Layers 14-11B at Farukhabad. The ware is gritty brown-red ware with a smoothed or burnished dark grayslip.

6) Decorated wares are uncommon in the Farukhabad assemblage except for sherds with bands of cable ornament. Two sherds decorated with a thin black paint characteristic of Larsa-Old Babylonian ceramics were found. A single sherd of standard buff ware with combed and incised decoration similar to those known in the Simashki Phase was found.

Sukkalmahhu Phase rim and base types could be classified as follows:

1) Small to medium cups and bowls with rounded bodies of medium depth and with slightly thickened rims could be sub-divided on the basis of rim shape: a) vessels with a rounded or rounded

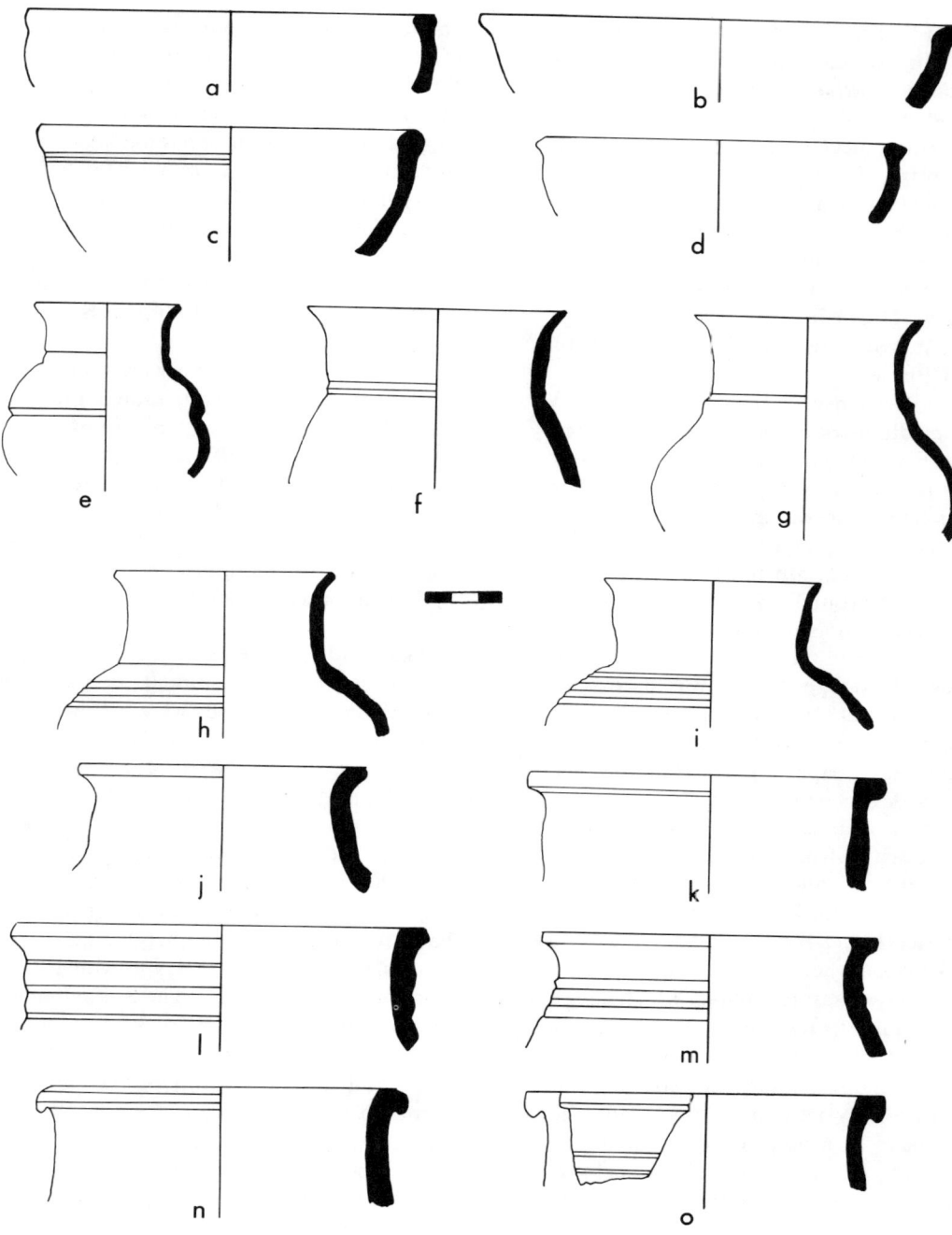

Fig. 85. Sukkalmahhu Phase Pottery. A. Standard green buff ware, green buff slip, medium straw temper; X057 (B12). B. Standard green buff ware, green buff slip, medium straw temper; X057 (B12). C. Standard green buff ware, green buff slip, medium straw temper, discolored; X057 (B12). D. Standard brown buff ware, cream slip, discolored; X057 (B12). E. Standard brown buff ware, cream slip, medium straw temper, discolored; X037 (B12). F. Medium coarse, friable, brown buff ware, pinkish buff slip, straw temper; X052 (B12). G. Standard brown ware, cream slip, straw temper, discolored; X072 (B13). H. Standard pink buff ware, white slip, medium straw temper; X072 (B13). I. Standard brown ware, cream slip, medium straw temper, discolored, X077 (B15–16). J. Standard buff ware, buff slip; X077 (B15–16). K. Standard brown buff ware, cream slip, medium straw temper, discolored; X052 (B12). L. Standard pink buff ware, cream slip, medium straw temper, ridges coated with "bitumen"; X094 (B13–16). M. Standard pink ware, cream slip, rim irregular and of a slightly coarser ware, medium straw temper; X053 (B11–13). N. Coarse brown ware, reddish brown slip, heavy straw temper, exfoliating; X053 (B11–13). O. Standard pink buff ware, cream slip, medium straw temper, discolored; X052 (B12).

flattened rim (Fig. 85a,c); b) vessels with a slightly overhanging rim which may be flattened, in-beveled or out-beveled (Fig. 85b,d). They were found in standard buff ware only.

2) Small to medium necked jars or goblets include all the fine ware rim sherds found in Layers 14–11B. To judge by the number of rim sherds and button and disc bases there seems to have been a rather varied series of high-necked jars and goblets. All of the more complete rim-plus-shoulder sherds are shown (Fig. 85e–i). The waisted jar (Fig. 85e) is from a mixed locus and perhaps belongs to the Simashki Phase.

3) Medium to large necked jars were found in standard to medium-coarse buff ware and were divided into two sub-types on the basis of rim shape a) Flat-topped rims: these jars' necks differ from those of type 2 (above) in size, ware and rim type. The rims, instead of being slightly everted and rounded or tapered, are thickened and overhanging and may be rounded (Fig. 85j–o), slightly beveled (Fig. 85a,c), or squared (Fig. 85f). They may have been trimmed on the top with a straight edge. Although this type of rim was used with several types of jar necks, the incompleteness of the sample prevents us from making a division on any other basis than rim shape. Figures 85j,k and 86a illustrate jar necks which are sinuous in profile and which come from unshouldered high-necked jars. Figures 85l–m are also from unshouldered jars but have corrugated necks and are similar to vessels found in the Transitional Phase (Fig. 89j) and the Simashki Phase (Fig. 84k). Fig. 85n,o illustrate vessels with a groove where the rim joins the vessel wall. Fig. 86e,f show examples of jars which have a small ridge which marks the join of the neck to the body of the vessel; b) Exterior band rims: they are of the same ware and fall in the same size range as type 3a jar necks. They are much less common and appear not to have been used for shouldered jars. Fig. 86b shows the unusual type; Fig. 86d belongs to the same general group but is slightly sinuous in profile.

4) Medium to large vats or neckless jars. In general vessels belonging to this group were larger than the necked jars; since many were coated with asphalt, they were possibly used as storage vessels. These range from standard to coarse ware and were most commonly made in medium-coarse ware. Fig. 86g,h illustrates the lower limit of the range while Fig. 86n,o shows the largest vessels of this type. In the middle layers the more open jar or vat forms were common. Only two sherds of the closed type similar to Fig. 90e,h were found. As in the case of the necked jars two sub-types were distinguished on the basis of rim shape: a) flat-topped rims which are rectangular or trapezoidal in section (Fig. 86g,i.k.l); and b) exterior beveled rims that are roughly triangular in section (Fig. 86h,j). This distinction is not quite as clear in this class of vessels as in the necked jars. Fig. 86m,n illustrates intermediate examples between the two groups. These are also found in Simashki Phase layers (Fig. 86i,j).

5) Smoothed ware jar rims were similar to those to be described for the Transitional Phase and like them were divided into two groups.

6) Gray ware jar rims similar to those found in Susa Ville Royale AXIII–XV were found in Layers 14–11B at Farukhabad (cf. Carter 1971:Fig. 15:4).

7) Flat string cut bases in standard to medium-coarse ware were found (Fig. 87q).

8) Button bases are an increasingly common base type: they are 34 percent of the bases in the Sukkalmahhu Phase assemblage and 53 percent in the subsequent Transitional Phase assemblage. The following sub-types were distinguished in the Sukkalmahhu Phase assemblage: a) Small button or knoblike bases, two to four cm in diameter, were found in fine to standard buff ware. Fig. 87 a–e illustrates the range of variation within the type. b) Medium to wide button bases, similar to type 3b of the Transitional Phase, but they generally do not have the moulding at the join of the base to the body (Fig. 87f–h,j–l,n–p). A single example (Fig. 87i) of the type with the moulding was found in Layer 12B. The Sukkalmahhu Phase group range in size from four to eight cm. A number of the bases had a fine spiral line made by the wheel on the bottom of the base (a feature common in central Khuzestan as well). Another feature of some of these base sherds from the Sukkalmahhu Phase is a small dab of heavily straw-tempered clay which was placed in the bottom of the vessel (Fig. 87l,n,p).

9) Medium to wide stump bases were found in the Sukkalmahhu Phase layers but were not as common as in the Simashki Phase. They usually carry the spiral traces of the wheel on the lower body and the base (Fig. 87m). They are commonly made in standard buff ware.

10) Disc bases are flatter and wider than button bases. They were made in standard to medium-coarse buff ware. In Sukkalmahhu Phase layers

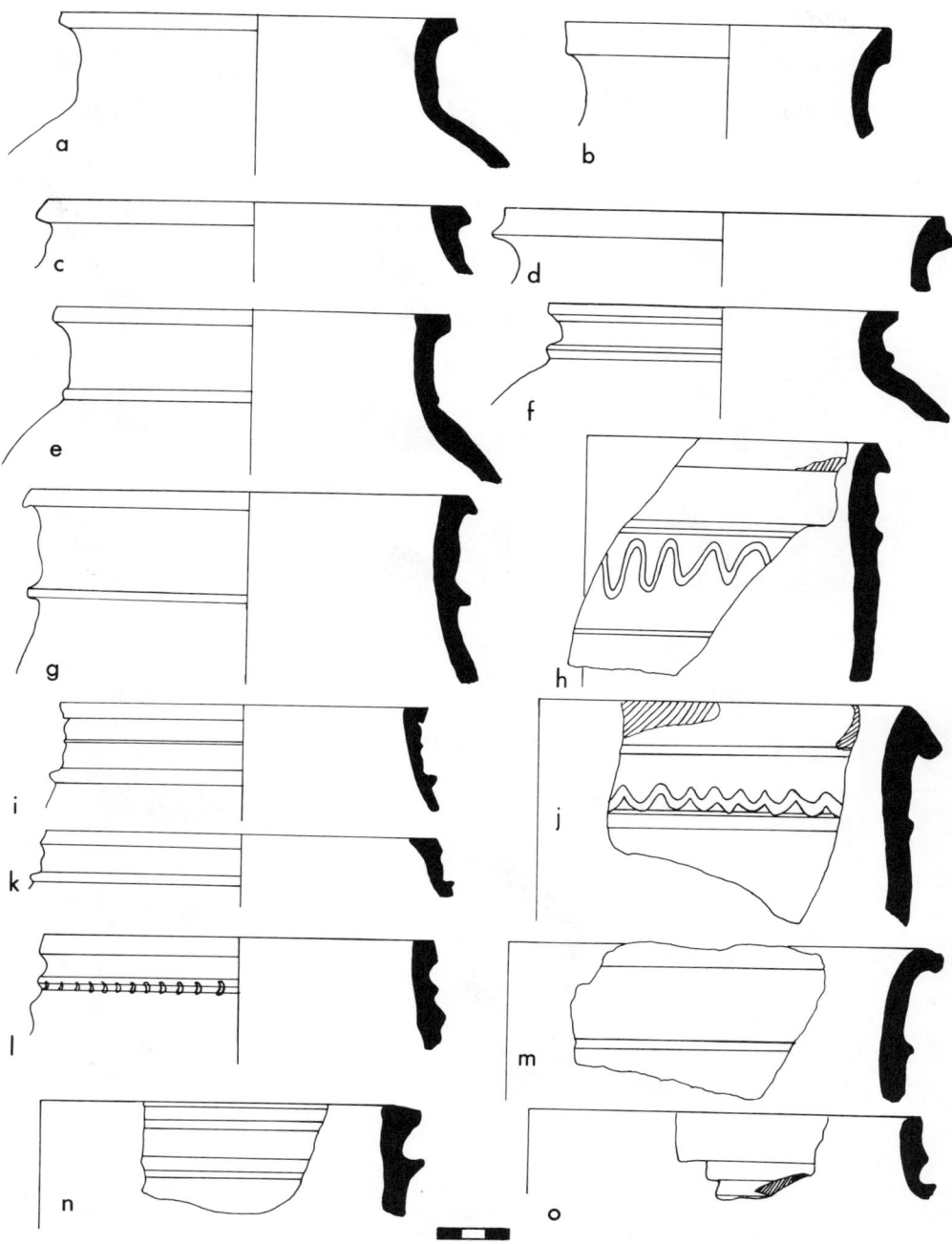

Fig. 86. Sukkalmahhu Phase Pottery. A. Standard brown ware, cream slip carelessly applied, medium straw temper; X055 (B11–12). B. Standard brown buff ware, discolored whitish slip, medium straw temper; X053 (B11–13). C. Standard brown buff ware, discolored whitish slip, medium straw temper; X098 (B13–17). D. Standard pinkish brown ware, discolored whitish slip, medium straw temper; X056 (B14). E. Standard fine buff ware, buff slip, partially discolored; X094, X076 (B15–16). F. Standard fine buff ware, pinkish buff slip, core as well as surface discolored; X053 (B11–13). G. Standard fine brown buff ware, buff slip, core as well as surface discolored; X055 (B11–12). H. Standard pink ware, cream slip; X054 (B11). I. Standard buff ware, buff slip, discolored, X094 (B13–16). J. Standard buff ware, buff slip, straw temper; X072 (B13). K. Standard buff ware, buff slip, medium straw temper; X037 (B12). L. Standard green buff ware, green buff slip, medium straw temper; X053, X058 (B11–13). M. Standard green buff ware, green buff slip, medium straw temper; X053 (B11–13). N. Standard buff ware, buff slip, straw temper; X072 (B13). O. Standard pink ware, cream slip; X053 (B11–13).

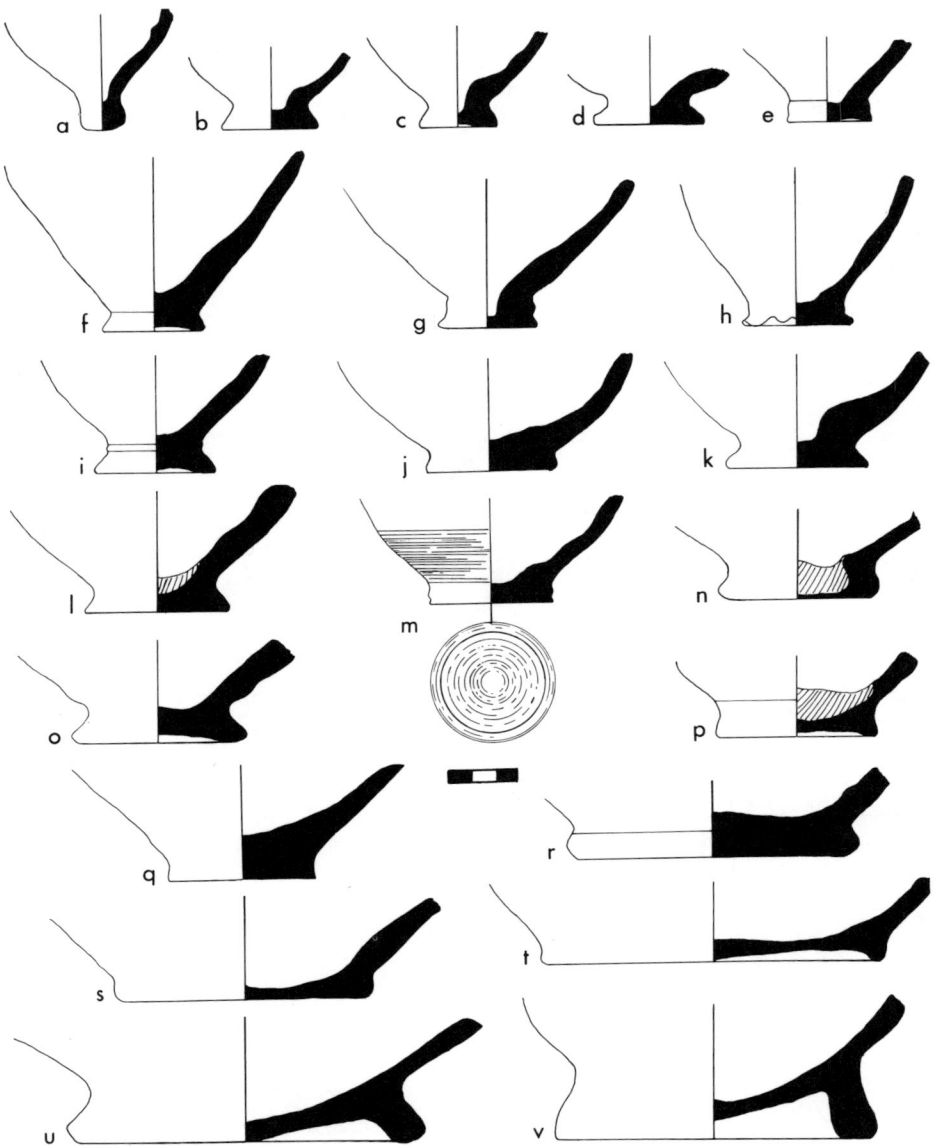

Fig. 87. Sukkalmahhu Phase Pottery. A. Standard brown buff ware, pinkish cream slip, discolored; X072 (B13). B. Standard pink buff ware, pinkish cream clip, fine line spiral base; X057 (B12). C. Standard brown buff ware, light slip, discolored; X058 (B12). D. Standard buff ware, light slip, discolored; X055 (B11–12). E. Standard pink buff ware, cream slip; X053 (B11–13). F. Standard brown ware, white slip, interior and exterior surfaces coated with bitumen; X098 (B13–17). G. Standard brown buff ware, buff slip, medium straw temper; X072 (B13). H. Standard brown ware, cream slip, fine line spiral base, edge of base retouched; X094 (B13–16). I. Standard brown buff ware, pink cream slip, medium straw temper; X052 (B12). J. Standard buff ware, fire blackened, medium straw temper; X058 (B12). K. Standard brown buff ware, white slip, medium straw temper; X037 (B12). L. Standard buff ware, buff slip, medium straw temper; X053 (B11–13). M. Standard pink buff ware, white slip, wheel scored base and lower body; X058 (B12). N. Standard buff ware, buff slip, bottom of interior filled with a dab of clay mixed with straw; X053 (B11–13). O. Standard buff ware, buff slip, bottom of interior filled with a dab of clay mixed with straw; X053 (B11–13). P. Standard buff ware, white slip, bottom of interior filled with a dab of clay mixed with straw; X072 (B13). Q. Standard brown buff ware, cream slip, discolored, string cut base; X058 (B12). R. Standard green buff ware, green buff slip, medium straw temper; X052 (B12). S. Standard brown red ware, cream slip, medium straw temper; X076 (B15–16). T. Standard green buff ware, friable, green buff slip, heavy straw temper; X076 (B15–16). U. Standard compact pink ware, cream slip, bottom reinforced by a bitumen coating inside and out; X074 (B15–16). V. Standard brown buff ware, cream slip, medium straw temper in ware used for the vessel body, the ring appears to have been added later and made of a clay which had a heavy straw temper; X072 (B13).

THE ELAMITE PHASES

Table 54: Distribution of Sukkalmahhu Phase Pottery Types

Layer	1a	1b	2	3a	3b	4a	4b	5a	5b	6	7	8a	8b	9	10	11a	11b
B1l1	2	1	1		1	1			2			1	1	2			
B12uE	2	4	7	9	1		2	2	2			1	5	6		1	2
B12uW	5	5	9	8½			2	5	4		2	4	3	2			2
B12lE	1	3	6½	10		4	4	2	1½		1	2	2	5	3		5
B12lW	2		1	7		1	4		2				3	3			
B13	1	1	2	5	2	4	1		½			1	1	2		2	3½
B14		1	1	1		1			½	1							1
BF7		1	1				1	1			2		1				
Mixed 11–13	5	3	9½	24½	5	3	5	1½	2		2	2	5	4	3	1	1½
Mixed 13–16	1		2			2	1					1	3	1			1
Mixed 13–17		1	4	2	1	2	1		2	1	8	1	1	4	1		
Total	19	20	44	67	10	18	21	12	16	2	16	13	24	29	7	4	16
Percent within class	8	9	20	30	4	8	9	5	7	1	15	12	22	27	6	4	15
Totals	229 Rims										109 Bases						

they range from 8–16 cm in diameter (Fig. 87r,s). As is evident from the illustrations and type descriptions, button, stump, and disc bases are more or less part of the same general type and are often difficult to distinguish from one another.

11) Ring bases were found in all the layers and in the Sukkalmahhu Phase layers they could be divided into the following sub-types: (a) low ridge-like ring bases in standard buff ware (Fig. 87t); (b) medium (Fig. 87u) to high (Fig. 87v) ring bases in standard to medium-coarse buff ware. On some of the ring base sherds the ring is made of coarse buff ware. On some of the ring base sherds the ring is made of coarse or medium-coarse buff ware while the body is in standard buff ware.

Sukkalmahhu Phase Dating: The ceramic assemblage recovered from Layers 14–11B at Tepe Farukhabad is dated from 1900–1600 B.C. on the basis of its resemblance to the assemblage known from Sukkalmahhu Phase levels at Susa. Fig. 88 illustrates some of these parallels: the rest are summarized in Table 55.

Two pieces of evidence suggest a gap in the Farukhabad sequence between the Sukkalmahhu and the following Transitional Phase: 1) the major construction of this earlier phase, the rampart, was allowed to fall into disrepair; and 2) the closest parallels to the Farukhabad assemblage were with the earliest of the Sukkalmahhu Phase levels known at Susa (Ville Royale BV and AXV); parallels with later levels are few. Generally speaking, these layers at Farukhabad are well-dated, but the problem of their specific time range and their relationship to the following Transitional Phase remains unsolved. It seems likely that layers 14–11B at Farukhabad date to the earlier part of the Sukkalmahhu Phase, but neither the Susa sequence nor the Farukhabad evidence is precise or complete enough to offer any more than the general date range of 1900–1600 B.C.

TRANSITIONAL PHASE (ca. 1600-1300 B.C.) EXCAVATION B—LAYERS 11 UPPER-1

At least two and possibly three building phases were identified in Layers 11 Upper to 1. The pottery recovered from these layers at Farukhabad

Table 55: Farukhabad Layers 14–11B and Susa AXV–AXIV

FARUKHABAD	SUSA AXV	SUSA AXIV
Fig. 85b	Carter, 1971: Fig. 14:1	Carter, 1971: Fig. 12:1
Fig. 85f		Ghirshman & Stève 1966: Fig. 24 (N5768)
Fig. 86m–n		Carter, 1971: Fig. 13:8
Grayware jar rim—not illustrated	Carter, 1971: Fig. 15:4	

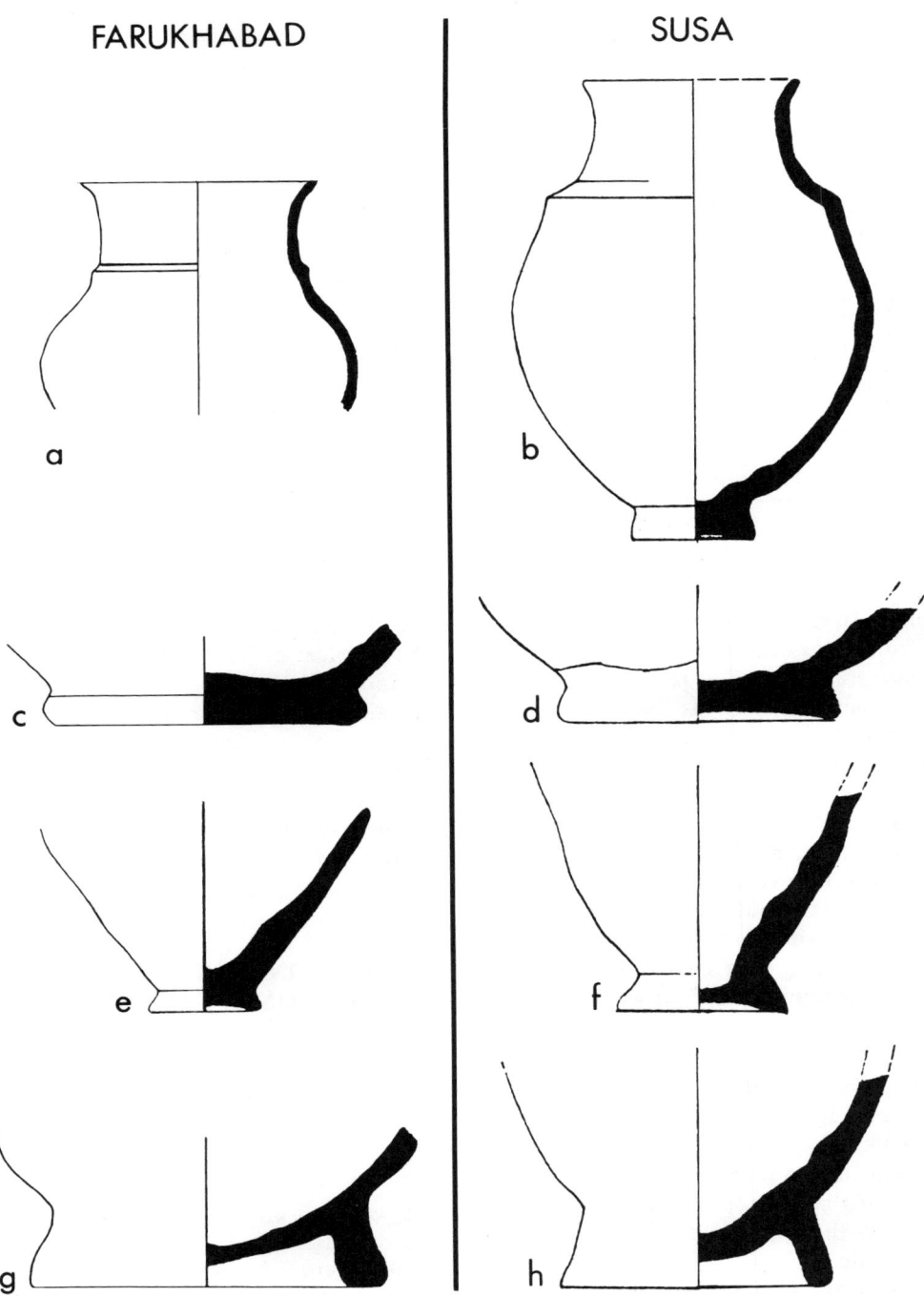

Fig. 88. Sukkalmahhu Phase Pottery from Farukhabad and Susa (all Susa pieces are in the study collections at Shush Museum). A. Fine brown buff ware, buff slip, core as well as surface discolored; X055 (Farukhabad B11–12, XIXth–XVIIIth centuries B.C.). B. Fine red buff ware, cream slip; S1135 = GS 6039 (Suse Ville Royale A XV, XIXth–XVIIIth centuries B.C.). C. Standard green buff ware, green buff slip, medium straw temper; X052 (Farukhabad B12, XIXth–XVIIIth centuries B.C.). D. Standard buff ware, buff slip, medium straw temper; s1124 (Suse Ville Royale A XV, XIXth–XVIIIth centuries B.C.). E. Standard brown ware, buff slip, medium straw temper, surfaces coated with bitumen; X098 (Farukhabad B13–17, XIXth–XVIIIth centuries B.C.). F. Standard red ware, cream slip; S1132 (Suse Ville Royale A XV, XIXth–XVIIIth centuries B.C.). G. Standard brown buff ware, cream slip, medium straw temper; the ring is made of a more heavily straw tempered clay; X072 (Farukhabad B13, XIXth–XVIIIth centuries B.C.). H. Red ware, buff slip, straw and grit temper; S1122 (Suse Ville Royale A XV, XIXth–XVIIIth centuries B.C.).

appeared to comprise a single unit and shared certain similarities with the central Khuzestan Transitional Phase assemblage. These similarities are enough for the moment to warrant retaining the term, but the nearly one to one parallelism of the Sukkalmahhu Phase ceramics found in Layers 14–11 lower with contemporary pottery from Susa is not duplicated. There are also a number of close parallels with ceramic forms known from Kassite Mesopotamia, which are not found in the central Khuzestan Transitional Phase assemblage. Furthermore, the term Transitional Phase is perhaps a misnomer when applied to the Farukhabad sequence or the Deh Luran Plain since a ceramic assemblage similar to that found in central Khuzestan from the following Middle Elamite Phase (ca. 1300–1000 B.C.) has yet to be identified either in excavated materials or in surface collections (Carter 1971)[1]. Nevertheless, lack of better evidence and a desire not to further complicate an already complex terminology led to the use of the term 'Transitional Phase' to describe the assemblage from these layers at Farukhabad. Future work will determine if the present choice made on the basis of limited evidence is correct.

Transitional Phase Pottery (see Table 56): Transitional Phase wares could be divided into the following types:

1) Fine buff ware, between 0.3 – 0.6 cm thick, is a non-compact grit and chaff tempered buff-slipped, buff ware. It is generally green but can be brown, pink or yellow-buff. Usually surface and paste are the same color. In the sample studied, fine ware was found to be used only for goblet and jar shoulders, necks and rims.

2) Standard buff ware is a buff-slipped buff ware which is heavier and more compact than the fine buff ware. It occurred in the same color variations as the fine buff ware. Several standard buff ware sherds were covered with a thin red wash. A single sherd has painted band (X018). It is possibly a spout fragment.

3) Medium-coarse buff ware is a heavily chaff tempered, buff-slipped buff ware which is almost always fired to a green color. The sherds in the sample of this type were generally decorated with an applied cable ornament or with ridges. They are probably from storage vessels, although no complete examples of vessels of this type were found. The ring-base sherds found in these layers are also all of this type of ware, except for one ring base sherd indicating the presence of heavy-coarse ware in the assemblage.

4) Smoothed ware is a low-fired friable ware characterized by a micaceous rock temper (possibly coarse sand) which is visible in the paste. The ware is often black cored and is gray-brown to brown-buff to red-orange in color. Both exterior and interior surfaces are well smoothed, sometimes taking on a burnish. In several cases tool marks were visible on the surfaces. Most of the rims are fire blackened and some appear to have been coated with asphalt. This ware was used for low necked or neckless jars and was first found in the Sukkalmahhu Phase layers. Unknown in central Khuzestan, this may be a local Deh Luran Plain ware.

Transitional Phase rim and base types were divided into the following categories:

1) Small to medium buff ware cups and bowls could be divided into two sub-types on the basis of rim shape: a) Straight or slightly rounded cups and bowls (Fig. 89a). b) Bowls of the same basic type but with a slightly overhanging rim which is usually flattened (Fig. 89b,c).

2) Small to medium-sized, buff ware jar or goblet necks and rims are probably from vessels similar to Fig. 89c. The variations in neck profile and rim shape are shown in Fig. 89d–f.

3) Medium to large standard buff-ware jars could be divided into four sub-types: a) Medium to high-necked jars with flat-topped rims. Similar to type 3a, Sukkalmahhu Phase, all the examples found in the Transitional Phase come from much smaller vessels (Fig. 89j); b) Medium high-necked jars with rounded, grooved or slightly indented rims (Fig. 89g–i). This type of rim was found only in the upper layers, and may be slightly later in date; c) Medium neckless jars formed a mixed group. All examples of the type are illustrated (Fig. 89k–l).

4) Smoothed ware low-necked or neckless jars with thick rounded, out-beveled or in-beveled rims could be divided into two sub-types: a) small to medium, brown to red-orange vessels (Fig. 89m); and b) medium to large gray-brown, brown, or buff examples (Fig. 89n,o).

5) Flat string-cut, standard buff-ware bases (Fig. 89x).

---

[1] There is no indication of a late second millennium B.C. occupation at Farukhabad outside of two pots found on the surface: Fig. 90b (cf. Ghirshman, 1964: Fig. 24), and Fig. 90d (cf. Ghirshman, 1968b: Pl. XCIX, G.T.–Z 1132, Tombe Construit 3).

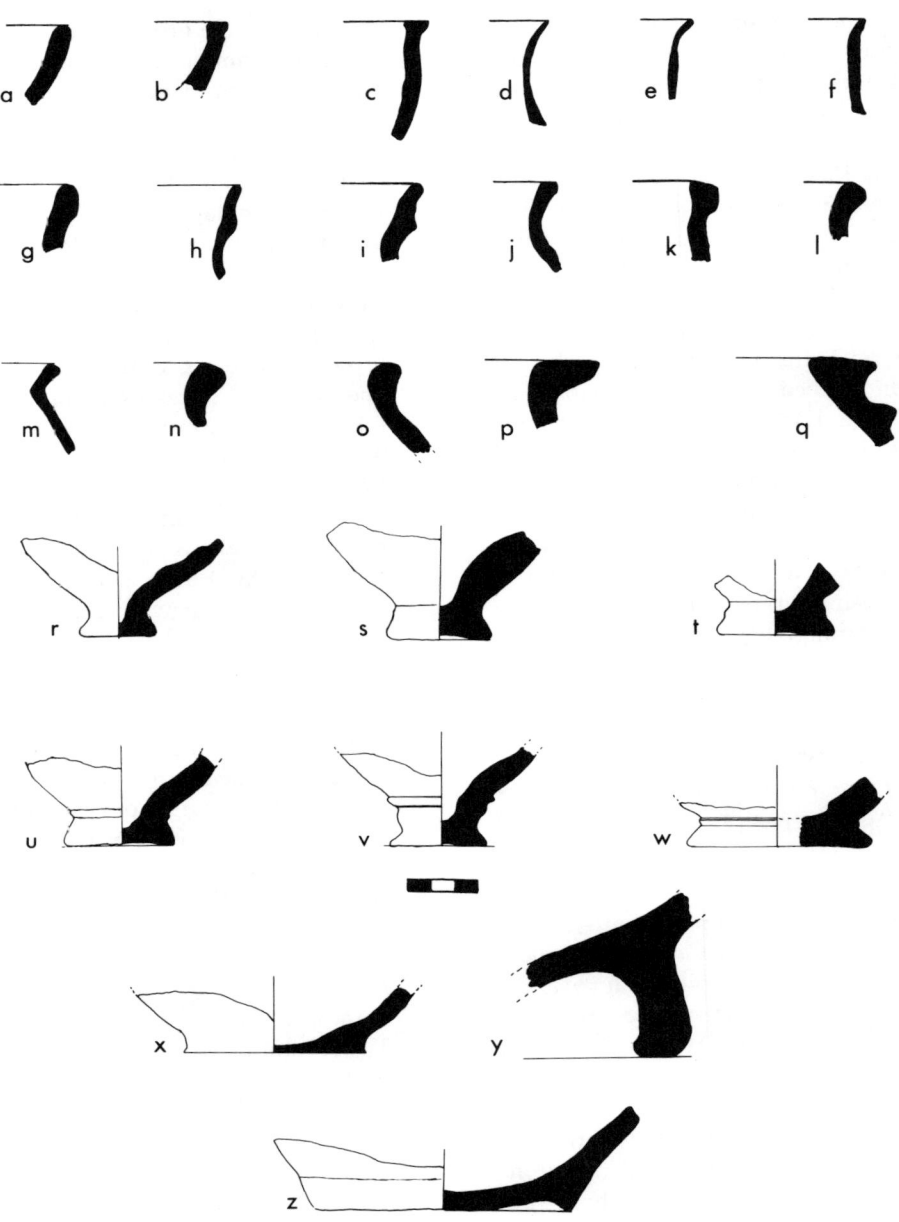

Fig. 89. Transitional Phase Pottery. A. Standard brown buff ware, pink-cream slip, diam.: 20; X030 (B11). B. Standard green buff ware, green buff slip, diam.: 21; X005 (B1–3). C. Standard brown buff ware, cream slip, diam.: 21; X026 (B10). D. Fine green buff ware, green buff slip, diam.: ?; X022 (B8). E. Fine green buff ware, green buff slip, diam.: 11; X017 (B7). F. Fine green buff ware, green buff slip, diam.: 8; X012 (B6). G. Standard green buff ware, green buff slip, diam.: 15.5; X007 (B4). H. Standard pink-brown buff ware, buff slip, diam.: 14.5; X005 (B1–3). I. Standard green buff ware, green buff slip, diam.: 14.5; X005 (B1–3). J. Standard buff, overfired, diam.: 15; X021 (B8). K. Standard buff ware, buff slip, diam.: 23; X009 (B4). L. Standard buff ware, buff slip, diam.: 20; X009 (B4). M. Smoothed gray cored brown-pink ware, traces buff slip, rim blackened, diam.: 17; X008 (B4). N. Smoothed gray cored brown buff ware, buff slip, diam.: 18; X018 (B7). O. Smoothed gray buff ware, buff slip, rim blackened, diam.: 17; X028 (B11). P. Medium coarse green buff ware, green buff slip, diam.: 26; X017 (B7). Q. Medium coarse green buff ware, green buff slip, diam.: 32; X012 (B6). R. Standard green buff ware, green buff slip; X018 (B7). S. Standard brown buff ware, pink-cream slip; X007 (B4). T. Standard brown buff ware, pink-cream slip; X025, X026 (B10). U. Standard brown red ware, buff slip, red wash; X005 (B1–3). V. Standard brown buff ware, buff slip; X027 (B8). W. Medium coarse green buff ware, green buff slip; X026 (B10). X. Medium coarse brown buff ware, buff slip; X017 (B7). Y. Coarse green buff ware, green buff slip, diam.: 30; X005 (B1–3). Z. Medium coarse green buff ware, green buff slip; X023 (B9).

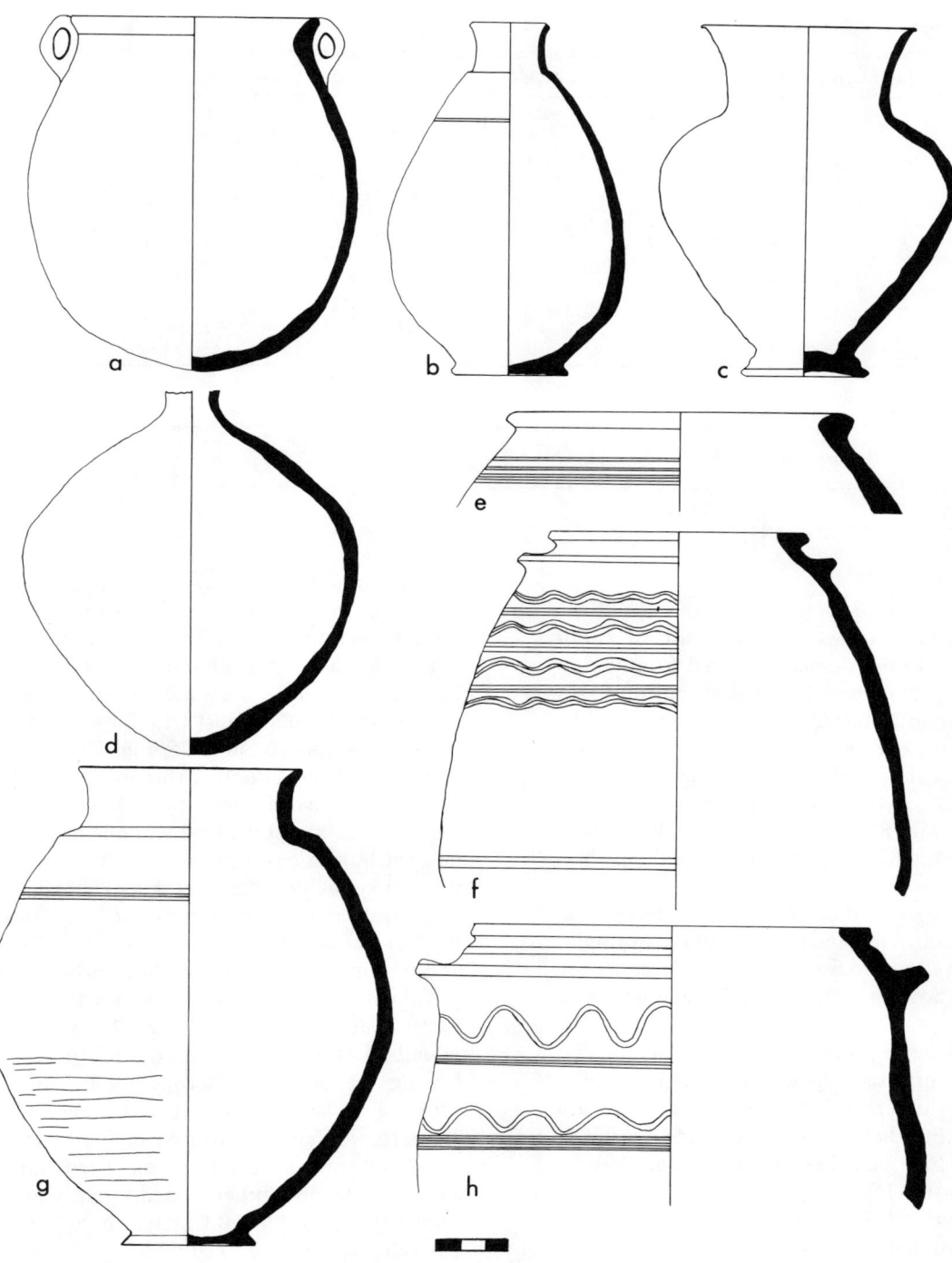

Fig. 90. Second Millennium Pottery. A. Smoothed, gray-cored brown buff ware, exterior buff slip, interior gray slip, micaceous temper; badly discolored; X057 (B12). B. Standard brown buff ware, buff slip, straw and black and white rock temper; X010 (surface). C. Fine green buff ware, green buff slip; X059 (BF16). D. Standard buff ware, buff slip, smoothed, badly exfoliating; X010 (surface). E. Medium coarse green buff ware, green buff slip, straw and grit temper; X097 (B15). F. Standard red orange ware, cream slip, combed decoration; X074, X077, X097 (B15-16). G. Standard green buff ware, green buff slip, medium straw temper, wheel scoring on lower body; X111 (B18). H. Medium coarse buff ware, buff slip, portion just below rib appears to have been coated with "bitumen" and tied with a rope, shallowly incised decoration; X097 (B15).

214 AN EARLY TOWN ON THE DEH LURAN PLAIN

Table 56: Distribution of Transitional Phase Pottery Types

Layer	1a	1b	2	3a	3b	3c	3d	4a	4b	5	6a	6b	7	8a	8b	8c
B1–3		2	7		4			1	1	1		4	1			1
B4			2	1	2	2		1			1	1				
B6W		2	1				1					1	1			
B6E	1	1	1								3		1			
B7W		3	4		3	1		2	2	2	1	1	2		2	
B7E	1	1			2	1					1	2	4			
B8E	3	6	14	1	1			1			1	1	2	1	1	1
B9W	1		3						1			1		1		
B10W		1	6	1				1	1	1		½				
B11u	1		2	1				2			1	1	1			
BF3	1	3	8	1	3		1	2	3			4½	2		3	
BF6			4		2						2				1	
Totals	8	19	52	6	17	4	2	9	9	8	12	18	8	2	7	2
Percent within class	6	15	41	5	13	3	2	7	7	14	21	32	14	4	12	4
Totals	126 Rims								57 Bases							

6) Standard buff-ware button bases could be divided into two groups: a) small plain or knoblike examples whose diameter ranged from two to four cm (Fig. 89r); and b) medium button bases four to six cm in diameter. Fig. 89s–v illustrates the main types. In over half of the sample there is a small ridge at the juncture of the base to the body of the vessel, or the vessel foot was sinuous in profile (e.g. Fig. 89t–v). There was only a single example of this base type found in Sukkalmahhu Phase layers.

7) Disc bases were found both with a ridge (Fig. 89w) and plain. While the majority of the examples were out-beveled, two were slightly undercut. They were found both in standard and medium-coarse buff ware.

8) Medium-coarse ware ring bases could be divided into three sub-types: a) low ring bases (Fig. 89z); b) medium ring bases—none of which are shown here, but they are one half to one quarter as high as the high ring base shown in Fig. 89y; c) high ring bases (Fig. 89y).

Transitional Phase Dating: The Transitional Phase at Farukhabad is dated from ca. 1600–1300 B.C. on the basis of pottery parallels with Susa, Haft Tepe and various Mesopotamian sites. The pottery parallels with Mesopotamia are illustrated by Fig. 91. These vessels are also similar to those known from Haft Tepe and Susa AXIII–AXI (cf. Carter 1971: Fig. 11). Unfortunately few of the forms from Transitional Phase layers are specific enough to be useful for precise dating or comparison. The button base jar or goblet, the most popular ceramic form, is also common earlier. Only the small ridge or moulding on the button bases appears to be a distinctive feature of vessels of this type found in post Old Babylonian context in Mesopotamia (Baqir 1945: Fig. 1). Recent work at Nippur seems to confirm this observation (Judith Franke, personal communication). As noted above, the ridge or moulding and sinuous profile distinguished button bases of these layers from those of the Sukkalmahhu Phase at Farukhabad.

Several small objects from these layers including the head of an Elamite female figurine (Plate 20f) and a humped bull (Plate 20d) perhaps support this date. However, there is also a figurine from Layer 6 at Farukhabad (Plate 20e) which closely resembles those from third millennium Ville Royale BV and the Acropole (cf. Ghirshman, 1968a; Fig. 19; and Stève and Gasche, 1971: Pl. 1:10). (Note that the position of the hands in the Susa examples differs from the Farukhabad examples). The only other evidence that would contradict the 1600–1300 B.C. date range proposed is a parallel of the smoothed ware jars (Type 4) with those found at Godin Tepe in Period II levels (ca. 750 B.C.) (Young 1969: Fig. 43: 1, 6, 7, 9, and p. 32). Nevertheless the majority of the parallels as well as the stratigraphic position of the material indicate a Transitional Phase date. Presently a date of closer to 1600 B.C. than to 1300 B.C. seems probable but until there is more material from

THE ELAMITE PHASES

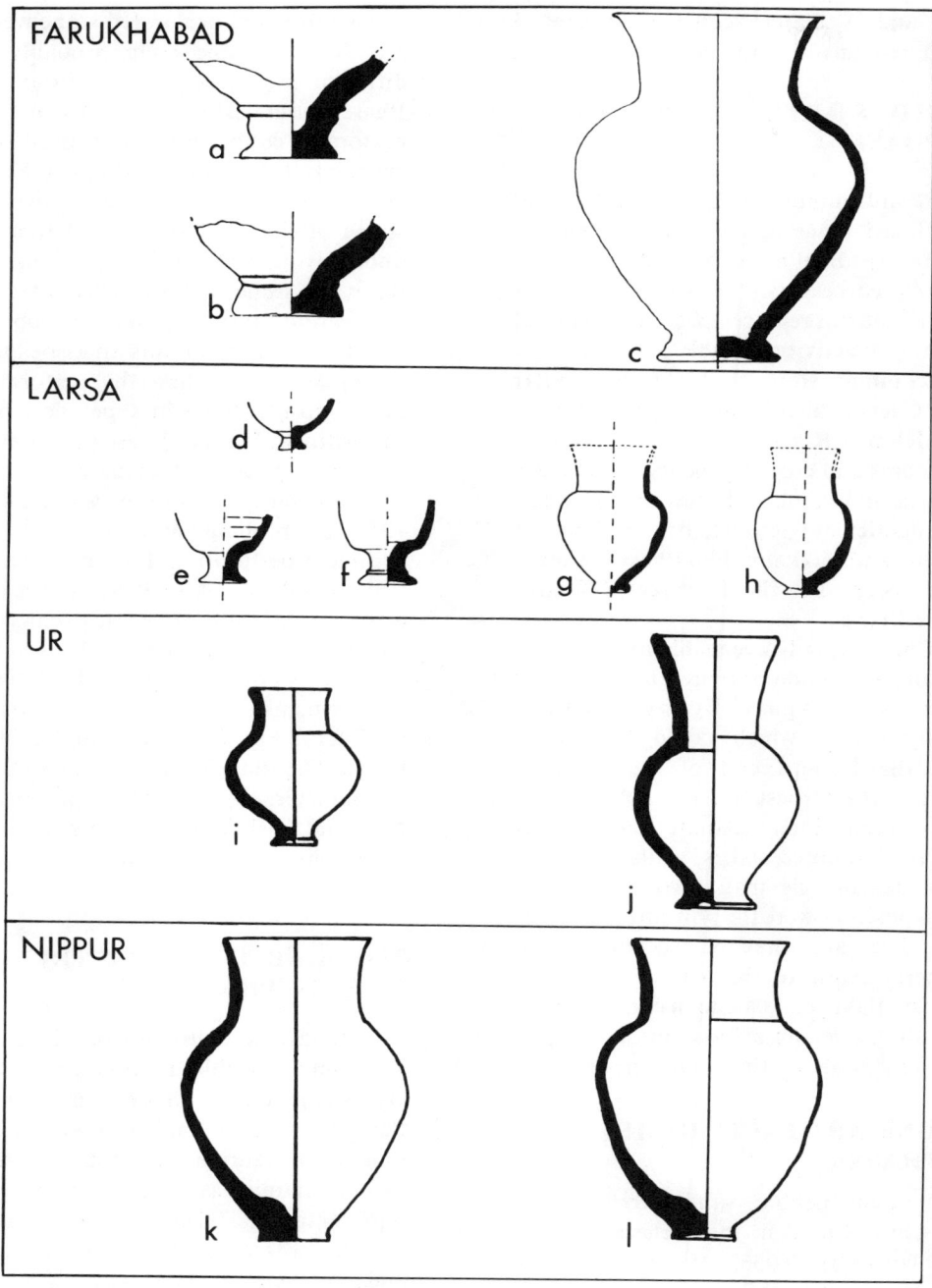

Fig. 91. Transitional Phase Pottery from Tepe Farukhabad Compared to Pottery from Larsa, Ur, and Nippur. A. Standard brown buff ware, buff slip, red wash; X005 (Farukhabad B1-3, XIIIth-XVIth centuries B.C.). B. Standard brown buff ware, buff slip; X021 (Farukhabad B8, XIIIth-XVIth centuries B.C.). C. Fine green buff ware, green buff slip; X057 (Farukhabad BF6, XIIIth-XVIth centuries B.C.). D. L573 Larsa Fouille Stratigraphique -2.50 m, Kassite (Syria XLV, Fig. 14:19, 1/5). E. L575 Larsa Fouille Stratigraphique -.50 m, Kassite (*ibid.*, Fig. 14:16, 1/5). F. L572 Larsa Fouille Stratigraphique -1.20 m, Kassite (*ibid.*, Fig. 14:10, 1/5). G. Larsa Fouille Stratigraphique -2.40 m, Kassite (*ibid.*, Fig. 14:17, 1/5). H. Larsa Fouille Stratigraphique -2.50 m, Kassite (*ibid.*, Fig. 14:19, 1/5). I. Ur KG/86, Kassite (Ur Excavations VIII, Pl. 43:86, 1/5). J. Ur KG/9, 16, 28, 47, Kassite (*ibid.*, Pl. 43:87, 2/5). K. "Usual ware, usually buff slip"; 2P433 Nippur TA 115 VI, Kassite-Assyrian (Nippur I, Pl. 98:1, Type 45a, 2/5). L. "Usual ware, usually buff slipped"; 3P143 Nippur TA VIII, Kassite-Assyrian (*ibid.*, Pl. 98:3, Type 45a, 2/5).

CHIPPED STONE ARTIFACTS OF THE ELAMITE PHASE

The second millennium occupants of Farukhabad made flaked stone artifacts less frequently and with more expedient materials and techniques than did their predecessors. Nevertheless, even at this date, metal had not replaced chert as a material for various cutting activities (Table 57).

The most common stone by far is the tabular Dark Brown Chert available on the gravel bars of the nearby Mehmeh River. All three phases produced rough cores and core fragments, many plain flakes both large and small, and a few rough blades. Flakes with denticulate retouch occurred in the earlier Simashki and Sukkalmahhu Phases. A small backed blade occurred in the more recent Transitional Elamite Phase.

Fine Red Chert, equally accessible in the river's bed though not so common, is represented by a few larger plain flakes in each phase. By way of contrast, Medium Gray Chert, which could have been obtained on the Eastern end of the plain, is common only in the earliest Simashki Phase, and absent in the Transitional Elamite Phase. It is possible that the few cores, flakes, blade segments, and sickle blades of this material are extrusive from earlier deposits as were the polychrome sherds noted above. The same may be true of the few objects of cherts exotic to the plain.

There is waste flakage of calcite in every Elamite Phase. A small cleaver on a flake and a chipped disc are the only tools of this rough material.

OTHER STONE ARTIFACTS OF THE ELAMITE PHASES

An oblong calcite pebble, similar to those of earlier phases, was found in the earliest Sukkalmahhu Phase layer (B14,X056,). It is 13.5 cm long with an oval cross section 3.7 by 1.6 cm. There is no definite evidence of use.

In a slightly higher Sukkalmahhu Phase layer (B12,X057), four burned pieces of a vesicular basalt grinding slab were found. Since such slabs were commonly used in the Late Jemdet Nasr and Early Dynastic periods but are otherwise unattested in Elamite layers, it is possible that these pieces were found on the surface of the mound and re-utilized.

Two forms of perforated stone were found; they are dissimilar and were probably put to quite different uses. Fixed in the floor of a Simashki Phase room (B18,X111), was an oval partially-perforated cobble 24 cm long and 16 cm wide and 5 cm thick. It had a conical hole 6.5 cm in diameter at the top and 5.0 cm deep. Given the size and shape of the hole, this would function well as a door pivot. Unfortunately, though placed in a floor, the stone was between a later well-shaft and the section, and there was no opportunity to see whether or not there was an associated door jamb. A similarly large partially perforated stone was found upside down in a pebble pavement of the Transitional Elamite Phase (B5). Certainly it was a re-utilized piece. Unfortunately we have no record of its attributes. In contrast is a small circular stone 12.8 cm in diameter and 3.6 cm thick with a complete perforation 1.6 cm in diameter. This is from a Sukkalmahhu Phase Layer (B12,X057). It is in the range of the medium-sized, fully perforated stones discussed in Chapter 9. As in the case of the earlier examples, we cannot be certain of its uses.

Fragments of two stone bowls, one a rim (B17,X108 Fig. 77c) were found in Simashki Phase layers. The rim is from a conical calcite bowl 18 cm in diameter, of the type common in the Jemdet Nasr and Early Dynastic periods. As the Simashki Phase pits brought up earlier sherds, it is likely that this piece is also extrusive.

OTHER ARTIFACTS OF THE ELAMITE PHASES

There are no figurines from the Simashki Phase. The only possible figurine from Sukkalmahhu layers is a roughly modeled piece which might be the head of an animal (B11,X029). By contrast, a number of figurine fragments were found in Transitional Elamite layers. Four are mold-made female representations. There were two sets of bare feet: one badly weathered from mixed context (X026) and one well-preserved with visible garment hem and six toes on each foot from Excavation B, Layer 10 (X024). There is one nude female figurine torso (B6,X013, Plate 20e), discussed above. There is one head with possible ear ornaments and headdress (X020, B7 Plate 20f) whose parallels are mentioned in the preceding discussion of Transitional Phase ceramics. Contrasting with these mold-made artifacts is a hand-modeled cow figurine with horns and a humped back (B6,X012)

THE ELAMITE PHASES

Table 57a: Elamite Chipped Stone Artifacts

Layer	Dark Brown Chert				Medium Gray Chert			Other	Limestone		
	Cores-Frags.	Lg. Flks.	Sm. Flks.	Other	Cores-Frags.	Lg. Flks.	Sm. Flks.	Other	Frags.	Sm. Flks.	Lg. Flks.
B15	1	3	2								
B15–16	2	1	5								
B16–17	3	10	8	1	1R	3				1	1
B17E	9	7	15	2 Bld.	2 1B		6	1 Fn. Rd. Lg. Flk. 1 Md. Gr. Sm. Flk. 1 Burn. Seg.	3		
B17W		3	7			1					
B18uE	3	6	12		3 1R	4	4	1 Fn. Rd. Lg. Flk. 1 Fn. Rd. Frag.	1	3	1
B18lE	5	6	18			1		1 Fn. Rd. Sm. Flk.		8	1
B18lW	1 1R	5	13			2		1 Bld. 1 Fn. Rd. Lg. Flk. 1 Fn. Rd. Frag.			1
Simashki Total	24	41	80		5	11	10		4	12	4

Table 57b: Elamite Chipped Stone Artifacts

Layer	Dark Brown Chert				Medium Gray Chert			Other	Limestone		
	Cores-Frags.	Lg. Flks.	Sm. Flks.	Other	Cores-Frags.	Lg. Flks.	Sm. Flks.	Other	Frags.	Sm. Flks.	Lg. Flks.
B11l		2	5	4				1 Fn. Gr. Sm. Flk.	1	1	
B12uE			3	4	1 Bld.		1		1	4	3
B12lE		6	5	9	2 Bld. 1 Dent.		1	1 Fn. Rd. Dent.		1	5
B12uW		1	5	3				1 Fn. W. Lg. Flk.	1		1
B12lW		3	1	1	1 Dent.		1 Ret				1
1B13	2	3	5			1		1 Fn. Rd. Lg. Flk.			
B14			1								1
B12–13		1	2	4				1 Fn. Rd. Lg. Flk.	1		1
Sukkalmahhu Total		15	25	30		1	3	1		4	6	12

Table 57c: Elamite Chipped Stone Artifacts

Layer	Dark Brown Chert				Medium Gray Chert			Other	Limestone		
	Cores-Frags.	Lg. Flks.	Sm. Flks.	Other	Cores-Frags.	Lg. Flks.	Sm. Flks.	Other	Frags.	Sm. Flks.	Lg. Flks.
B4	3	6	4					1 Fn.Rd.Lg.Flk.	2	2	
B7W	4	7	7	1 Ret. Sm.Flk					2	7	
B8E	5	3	10	2 Bld. Segs.				1 Fn. Gr. Ret. Triangle	1	1	
B9W		1	1	1 Bld.						1	
B10W	3	3	3					1 Fn. Rd. Lg. Flk.		1	
B11u	1R 1	1		1 Bld.							
BF3	1								2	2	
BF6		1	1	1 Bld.							
Transitional Total	17	22	25		0	0	0		7	14	0

which most certainly represents a *Bos* of the Indian type. The body is a red-brown ceramic with sand inclusions (7.5YR 7/5). From the nose tip to the back of its skull, the representation measures 3.1 cm. From horn tip to tip, it measures 4.1 cm (B6,X012). Parallels are noted above and this figurine is further discussed in Chapter XIV by Redding (Plate 20d).

There were three fragments of cuprous metal. One survives only as a completely corroded sheeting around a circular plano-convex clay core. The core is about 1.2 cm in diameter and .4 cm thick although the original object must have been larger. This fragment was found near the skull of a Sukkalmahhu Phase burial (BF7,X096) intrusive into Simashki Phase layers, and could have been part of an ear ornament, hair ornament, or hat. The other two items were small corroded lumps found together in Transitional Phase layers (B8, X021).These pieces weigh .65 and 4.90 gm respectively.

A SUMMARY OF THE SIMASHKI, SUKKALMAHHU, AND TRANSITIONAL PHASES AT TEPE FARUKHABAD
by Elizabeth Carter

The limited exposure and the few finds from the Elamite levels at Farukhabad do not permit a fruitful statistical study of artifact associations. Consequently we will turn directly to summary interpretations of the Elamite material based on such exposures as are available and on the settlement survey of the Deh Luran Plain.

THE SIMASHKI PHASE ca. 2100–1900 B.C.

Sometime around 2600 B.C. Tepe Farukhabad was abandoned or so ephemerally settled that the excavations and intensive surface pick-ups have failed to find any trace of the occupation. Indeed, Tepe Musiyan and a small village to the west (Tepe Bowla, DL-24) appear to have been the only permanent settlements on the plain during the last half of the third millennium B.C. Shortly before or after 2000 B.C., Farukhabad appears to have been re-occupied and several small villages in the area were resettled. The four known Simashki Phase sites cover a total of 23.5 ha suggesting a population of about 4700 people. Slightly more than half of this population was living about 14 km southeast of Farukhabad not far from the Dawairij River at Musiyan. The rest of the population was divided among three small villages: Farukhabad, Tepe Tenal Ramon (DL-27), and Tepe Bowla (DL-24), which all lay to the northwest of Musiyan. Tepe Farukhabad can very probably be taken as representative of the smaller Simashki Phase settlements on the Deh Luran Plain.

The limited exposure at Farukhabad revealed fragments of neatly constructed mud-brick buildings of a rather insubstantial character. A single burial with no associated gifts adds little to our knowledge of the period.

The ceramic assemblage consisted of unpainted, wheel-turned vessels made with some skill and in the same style as those found in the larger, richer towns of Mesopotamia and the Susiana. However, no definite preference for Mesopotamian or Elamite ceramic styles could be established. The populace still used chert for various cutting activities, and the rich metal technology attested to in the Susa burials of this period perhaps did not reach Farukhabad. Likewise one of the most beautiful and characteristic Simashki Phase crafts—the carving of elaborate asphalt vessels—is unknown at Farukhabad or Musiyan. A logical source of raw material would appear to have been the Deh Luran Plain, yet little evidence of asphalt waste and no finished products have been recovered from Simashki Phase contexts.

The absence of any written documents (tablets, inscribed bricks, cylinder seals or sealings) preclude speculation on the actual administration of the settlement of Farukhabad. The French excavators of Musiyan also rather disappointedly note that they did not find any epigraphic materials (Gautier and Lampre 1905). Thus, neither the great kings of Ur nor the Susian rulers of the Simashki Dynasty seem to have left a lasting mark in the Deh Luran Plain.

The artifacts and animal remains from Simashki Phase Farukhabad suggest an economy based on cereal farming and animal husbandry. Seemingly the small community at Farukhabad had a subsistence pattern little different from that of the preceding Late Jemdet Nasr settlement. The major food animals included goats, sheep, and some cows. Gazelle and equid were probably hunted. The ratio of hunted food animals to domestic food animals remains unknown since it is not always possible to distinguish wild from domestic equid remains. In any case, hunting does not seem to have contributed significantly to the Farukhabad economy of the early second millennium B.C.

While it is possible, perhaps even likely, that more substantial houses with grander furnishings are yet to be found at Farukhabad, to date the Simashki Phase finds from Farukhabad suggest a simple village of limited resources.

THE SUKKALMAHHU PHASE
ca. 1900–1600 B.C.

All the sites occupied in the Simashki Phase continued to be occupied in the succeeding Sukkalmahhu Phase. However, by the end of the Sukkalmahhu Phase there had been some major changes in settlement patterns on the Deh Luran Plain (Fig. 92). Tepe Musiyan was abandoned as was the village of Tepe Bowla (DL-24). At some point, two new settlements were founded: Tepe Goughan (DL-34) three kilometers north of Musiyan, and Tepe Patak (DL-35) east of the Dawairij River in the previously unoccupied southwestern section of the plain. Farukhabad and Tepe Tenel Ramon (DL-27) continued to be occupied throughout the Sukkalmahhu and following Transitional Phases. The enduring, if unspectacular, nature of these settlements may be due to their location on the Mehmeh which permitted easy access to water for irrigation and allowed them to control or at least observe traffic moving in and out of the plain along the river route (Carter 1971: 198–99). Since we have reason to believe the settlements are not contemporary, we cannot estimate Sukkalmahhu population.

Early in the Sukkalmahhu Phase a large mud-brick rampart or terrace was constructed on top of the large mound at Tepe Farukhabad. Portions of what now seem to be the same large structure were recovered in both Excavations B and C. If these remains are part of the same large construction, then an area 30 m wide and at least 55 m long was enclosed. The rampart or terrace stood at least 24 m above the level of the plain and offered an unparalleled vantage point over the relatively level and sparsely settled Deh Luran region.

Suggestions of a similar approximately contemporary construction have been recorded at Chogha Mish (Delougaz 1967: 147–8) in Central Khuzestan. At Musiyan a similar construction may have existed. The French report (Gautier and Lampre 1905: 65–70) that in the area north of their camp, on the summit of the mound, they uncovered a series of buildings and a platform of mud brick. They believed that the buildings were built on the platform. Surface collections and a careful reading of the site report suggest that the mud-brick platform and its associated buildings date to the late third or early second millennium B.C. The buildings on the summit of Farukhabad would have been easily visible from Musiyan and vice versa.

Unfortunately the only features associated with the Farukhabad terrace/rampart are a large pit and a flexed burial situated outside the face of the structure on the southwest shoulder of the eroded mound. Thus, in spite of the larger volume of Sukkalmahhu Phase deposits removed and the recovery of twice as many ceramics as from the preceding phase, no primary deposits of the Sukkalmahhu Phase have been excavated at Farukhabad. The evidence for the activities in the settlement, therefore, must necessarily be that of the artifacts alone, rather than that of context and associations. The lone burial contained a single pot, a decayed asphalt object, and a copper/bronze bangle of questionable association. The pit produced numerous pot sherds, a few rough flakes, and denticulate stone tools; no other artifacts of Sukkalmahhu Phase date were found.

The Sukkalmahhu Phase ceramic assemblage, like the earlier Simashki Phase assemblage, consisted primarily of well-made, buff-ware vessels. Unlike the Simashki Phase pottery where there was about one bowl to every jar, in the Sukkalmahhu Phase Farukhabad assemblage there were twice as many jars as bowls. The most explicit parallels are with Susiana ceramics from Ville Royale BV and AXV at Susa which suggest a date closer to 1900 B.C. than to 1600 B.C. for the Farukhabad assemblage.

These stylistic affinities also provide the only evidence useful in assessing the relationship between the Deh Luran settlements and those of Greater Mesopotamia during the early second millennium B.C. A number of general parallels exist between Larsa-Old Babylonian pottery and Sukkalmahhu Phase ceramics known from the Deh Luran region. The most explicit parallels, however, are with early Sukkalmahhu Phase Susiana pottery, and include a number of specifically Elamite ceramic traits (e.g. gray ware, painted flask). While there is no necessary link between

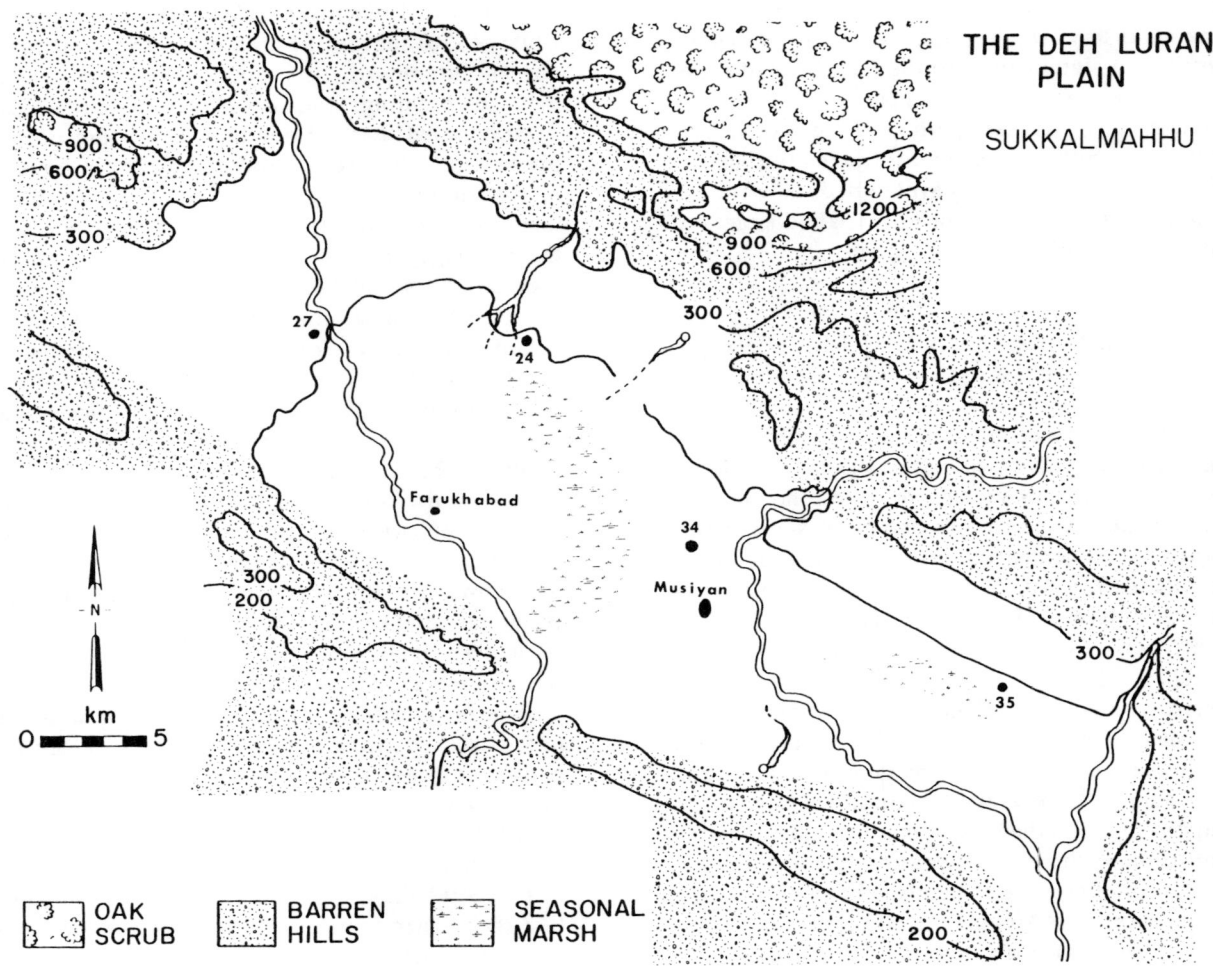

Fig. 92. Sukkalmahhu Phase Settlement Patterns.

shared craft traditions and political ties, the similar ceramic styles between Susiana and Deh Luran in this period may reflect a close relationship. The Sukkalmahhu Phase in Susiana was a period of growth and prosperity. This stands in contrast to the Deh Luran region where there appears to have been an irregular decline during the second millennium from a peak period of development (the early third millennium B.C.) when the settlements of the Deh Luran region seemed at least equal in size and originality to those of Susiana.

Faunal remains from the Sukkalmahhu Phase levels suggest a change in the village economy. The range of hunted animals and the amounts and kill pattern of sheep and goats remained the same. However there was a tremendous increase in the use of domestic cattle. Whether the increase is due to the nature of the deposit or whether there was a general change in the diet remains uncertain. Nevertheless, the percentage of cattle in the Sukkalmahhu Phase is unprecedented in the history of Farukhabad. Also found in the same deposit were the remains of a domestic horse, an uncommon animal in early second millennium B.C. Near Eastern contexts.

The nature of the architecture suggests a specialized settlement, perhaps a small fort or guard-post overlooking a river crossing. This proposition possibly explains the high proportion of cattle in the diet, if we assume that such a settlement would have been provisioned from Musiyan or another larger center. The presence of a domestic horse is likewise explicable in such an installation. Indeed, it is easy to imagine signals flashed between Musiyan and Farukhabad at a time of general unrest along the foothill road linking the Susiana and the Mesopotamian plain.

Obviously this is a highly speculative interpretation; nevertheless, it is possible that Farukhabad's specific function in the settlement system changed from that of a small village farming community during the Simashki Phase to an observation post along the Mehmeh during the Sukkalmahhu Phase.

At present there is no direct documentation of economic or administrative relations among the settlements, only the less eloquent archaeological evidence. The settlement pattern indicates that Farukhabad and the contemporary small settlements of the Deh Luran region remained subsidiary to the Susiana during the time of the Sukkalmahhu (1900–1600 B.C.).

TRANSITIONAL PHASE ca. 1600–1300 B.C.

The major changes in settlement patterns that began in the Sukkalmahhu Phase were fully realized in the Transitional Phase. Tepe Goughan (DL-34) replaced Musiyan as the center of settlement on the Deh Luran Plain growing to a size of at least 15 ha. External political factors, ease of communications, and access to a more reliable water source may have led to the establishment and growth of this new center on the Deh Luran Plain. Tepe Patak (DL-35) in the previously unsettled southeast quadrant of the plain reached its peak second millennium size of five ha. Tenel Ramon (DL-27) and Farukhabad on the banks of the Mehmeh remained as small villages on the western edge of the settled area. The total area occupied covered about 25 ha indicating a population of about 5000 inhabitants.

At Farukhabad, the rampart of the preceding Sukkalmahhu Phase fell into disrepair and there may have been a hiatus in occupation on the summit of the mound. Parts of two relatively substantial structures were built at right angles to the old revetment face. A rectangular oven whose use created quantities of ash was built between the buildings. These constructions were replaced by less substantial walls associated with a series of earthen floors and a pebble pavement. Although the rampart was no longer in use people living on top of the mound still had a commanding view of the traffic moving across the plain. No further building is attested on this part of the site. Farukhabad was abandoned sometime in the Transitional Phase and not resettled until Parthian times. Aside from the fragmentary architecture, a single burial of undistinguished character was dug from Transitional Phase levels.

Transitional Phase ceramics, like those of the preceding Elamite phases, are unpainted, wheel-turned, buff-wares. The same range and proportion of container forms (two jars to every bowl) is present as in the preceding phase. Parallels between the ceramics from Farukhabad Transitional Phase levels and Kassite Mesopotamia exist, but very few of the most common indicators of the Kassite Period found on Mesopotamian sites have been found in Deh Luran (e.g. the Kassite "chalice"). There are also definite similarities between Haft Tepe ceramics and Farukhabad Transitional Phase pottery styles, but the truly explicit parallels of the preceding phase are missing. Thus the ceramics of this period seem to have a distinctly local character. One can only speculate that this and other contemporary regional cultural developments noted elsewhere in Khuzestan (Carter 1971) are a reflection of the rise of various local rulers after the end of the Dynasty of the Sukkalmahhu and before the rise of the kings of the Middle Elamite Dynasty.

Several distinctly Elamite terra-cotta figurine fragments from these levels point to the continuance of Elamite household ritual, but the ceramics of the period suggest that craft relations with Nippur and Larsa were just as strong as those with the Susiana plain.

The faunal remains show that Simashki Phase patterns of animal utilization were resumed. The heavy dependence on cattle suggested by the Sukkalmahhu Phase animal bones may have been a temporary phenomenon linked to the seemingly specialized function of the settlement. Plant remains likewise suggest a simple farming community of no special distinction.

FARUKHABAD AND THE DEH LURAN PLAIN DURING THE LAST CENTURIES OF THE SECOND MILLENNIUM B.C.

Tepe Farukhabad and all other contemporary settlements on the Deh Luran Plain were very probably abandoned sometime during the Transitional Phase. The evidence rests on our knowledge of the ceramic assemblage for the Middle Elamite Phase (ca. 1300–1000 B.C.), which is based on excavated pottery from Susa and Chogha Zanbil (Carter 1971) in central Khuzestan. There is no excavated material from the Deh Luran Plain dated independently to this time range, and only a few surface finds are known which resemble dated types found in central Khuzestan. Thus it is possible (but in our opinion unlikely) that the late second millennium pottery found in the Deh Luran region cannot be identified on the basis of the central Khuzestan material. In any case the widespread, characteristic Elamite goblet form found in central and eastern Khuzestan, Luristan, and Fars has not been found in the Deh Luran Plain.[1]

Dating the abandonment of the Deh Luran region with precision is not possible. The ceramic parallels suggest a date sometime between 1500 and 1300 B.C. It does not seem unreasonable to suggest that lack of permanent settlement in the Deh Luran region is perhaps the direct result of the campaigns of the Middle Elamite rulers and their Babylonian enemies along the foothill road. A second and possibly no less important factor, the intrusion of the Iron I culture in Luristan, ca. 1300–1250 B.C. (Young 1967), may also have had disastrous consequences for the Elamite settlements of the Deh Luran plain.

SUMMARY AND CONCLUSIONS

Tepe Farukhabad was resettled sometime late in the third millennium after a period of abandonment that had lasted several hundred years. It remained a small settlement of limited resources and little distinction throughout much of the second millennium B.C.

The rampart or terrace constructed on top of the mound early in the millennium was by far the most substantial Elamite structure found. It seems likely to us that Farukhabad was a small look-out post or fort during the time of the early Sukkalmahhu (ca. 1900–1700 B.C.).

The recovery of a fairly complete ceramic sequence from Farukhabad spanning the period from ca. 2100–1500 B.C. provides evidence useful in assessing the broader cultural relations of the Deh Luran region with Greater Mesopotamia. The patterns of stylistic change seen in Elamite ceramics from the second millennium Susiana and Deh Luran are extremely close. The Middle Elamite ceramic assemblage of central Khuzestan (ca. 1300–1000 B.C.), however, has not been identified in Deh Luran.

The Simashki Phase pottery from Farukhabad was too limited to compare in any more than a general way to contemporary assemblages from the Susiana or Mesopotamia. The most explicit stylistic comparisons were between Susiana and Farukhabad Sukkalmahhu Phase pottery types. The rapid growth in Susiana during the first centuries of the second millennium and the contemporary decline of the Deh Luran region suggest that Musiyan and its satellite villages such as Farukhabad were subject to the rulers of the Susiana. The ceramics offer some indirect support to this hypothesis. The Transitional Phase pottery from Farukhabad is more original, although it shares certain links with Kassite Mesopotamian and central Khuzestan assemblages. The growth of Goughan and Patak during this time (ca. 1600–1300 B.C.) points to a brief period of renewed development on the Deh Luran Plain. Again, the ceramic evidence provided some support for this interpretation. Finally, Khuzestan Middle Elamite Phase ceramics (ca. 1300–1000 B.C.) were not found in the Deh Luran Plain; thus it appears that the region was deserted by 1300 B.C.

The only class of small finds of interest from Farukhabad were several terra-cotta figurine fragments from Transitional Phase levels. These indicate a preference for Elamite household ritual and perhaps a cultural orientation more Elamite than Mesopotamian.

The floral and faunal remains from Farukhabad indicate a simple village farming community, growing cereals and raising sheep, goats and cattle. Hunting never appears to have been very important to the economy. The only anomaly seems to be the large percentage of domestic cattle eaten in the Sukkalmahhu Phase. This pattern may reflect the specialized function of the settlement as a small fort or look-out post, hypothesized on the basis of the architectural remains.

The changes observed at Farukhabad from the early third millennium B.C. through the early second millennium B.C. reflect larger changes that

---

[1] Examples of this type are known from Bushire (Pezard 1914: Pl. 6:6) Malyan (Sumner 1974: Fig. 13a) sites in the Zohreh Valley (Oriental Institute Study Collection), Ram Hormuz plain (Carter 1971:55;14,15), and in Luristan (Thrane 1970: Fig. 31 lower righthand corner).

were taking place in the region. Early in the third millennium, Musiyan was, with the possible exception of Susa, the largest settlement in Khuzestan. The finds from Musiyan, Aliabad, and Farukhabad bear witness to an original culture with a fairly diverse economy that flourished in the region at this time.

At Musiyan, Gautier and Lampre (1905: 66–70) reported that mud-brick buildings associated with plain wares (probably of Simashki or Sukkalmahhu Phase date) replaced earlier constructions of baked-brick associated with pottery described as painted on a coarser fabric than the prehistoric wares (probably late Jemdet Nasr or Early Dynastic Phase types). The general impression gained by the French excavators of Musiyan was one of progressive decline and eventual abandonment in Elamite times (Ibid.:70–71). The site was abandoned as we see it during the Sukkalmahhu Phase. At Farukhabad the brief hiatus in occupation between the Sukkalmahhu and Transitional Phases was perhaps linked to the abandonment of Musiyan during the Sukkalmahhu Phase.

These impressions of local decay are re-enforced by the observation that the population of the region declined in the early second millennium B.C. from a highpoint reached early in the third millennium (Carter 1971: 240–2). The waning fortunes of the Deh Luran region may have been due to the change in river level which apparently took place during the early second millennium B.C. (Kirkby 1977: 282). More intriguing are the possibilities of political and economic factors outside the region: the rapid growth of permanent settlement in central Khuzestan could have drained the Deh Luran region of its population. It also seems possible that the region and other small pocket valleys on the western border of Elam were those most drastically affected by the conflicts between the Babylonians and the Elamites.

Bu 1600 B.C, Goughan (DL-34) had been established as the center of settlement on the plain; Tepe Patak (DL-35) had grown to a respectable size of five ha, and Farukhabad, which had been abandoned briefly late in the Sukkalmahhu Phase was resettled. Thus the pattern of decline observed earlier was reversed, if only for a short time. The brief but rather rapid development (ca. 1600–1300 B.C.) of the region was possibly the result of a decline in the authority of the later Sukkalmahhu. The desertion of the region in the last centuries of the millennium perhaps can be blamed on the wars between the great powers of the day, although the intrusion of the Iron I culture in Luristan (Young 1967) may also have had some effect on the Elamite settlements of the Deh Luran region.

The limited number of settlements on the Deh Luran plain during the second millennium precluded any widespread exploitation of the agricultural resources of the region. The size and location of Musiyan and Goughan, however, suggest that canal irrigation of some sort was practised. The Deh Luran plain was one of the small valleys at the edge of the mountains which offered good grazing land and a lower density of settled population than was found in either the Susiana or Mesopotamia. Limited textual evidence suggests that tribal groups could have shared the area with the settled population during the second millennium B.C. (Brinkman 1968; Kupper 1957). Furthermore, recent research has shown that second millennium settlement patterns were not very different from those of the present day (Carter 1971) and that the modern restricted area of farming is correlated with the considerable use of the Deh Luran plain for winter wet-season sheep and goat grazing (Kirkby 1977). It is possible that a similar situation existed in the second millennium. This, in turn, suggests a change from the situation observed in the fifth and possibly early third millennium.

Life in the Deh Luran region during the second millennium B.C. must have been influenced by a number of factors—access to water and productive soil; local and regional politics and trade; relations between nomadic and settled groups. The excavations at Farukhabad and the study of the region have led to the enumeration of these factors and the formulation of a number of possible explanations of the changes that took place during the period. Future research will perhaps allow us to estimate the extent to which these factors were operative in shaping the history of the region and to determine the utility of the various propositions generated by the work in the Deh Luran Plain.

Chapter XII

EVIDENCE OF THE PARTHIAN AND SASANIAN PERIODS

INTRODUCTION

The lower or northwest extension of Excavation C is on the Lower Terrace of Farukhabad. This was cleared early in the season by cleaning and enlarging a recent looters pit into a 2.2 by 1.5 m excavation. This disturbance had mixed deposits down to a depth of 1.8 m. Below this a single arbitrary layer .10 m thick was carefully removed. As this material proved to be Parthian or Sasanian and thus not in any way related to the objectives of our work, we did not continue in this area. However, a description of the ceramics and other artifacts recovered may well be of use to others, and so we present it here.

In this brief clearance, only one cultural feature was noted. On the cleaned lower surface of the excavation was a line of rectangular mud bricks laid end-to-end and running from northwest to southwest.

The surface distribution of the distinctive handmade red wares and glazed bowl sherds covered the entire lower terrace of the mound. In addition two glazed bowl sherds were found on the summit of the mound in association with the cobble foundations which cap the site. It is likely that this structure, also noted by Gautier and Lampre (1905: 84), was built in this period. As it is very eroded, it might be difficult to demonstrate this dating even with excavation.

CERAMICS OF THE PARTHIAN AND SASANIAN PERIODS
by Lawrence Cohen

In the lower extension of Excavation C, sherds of both handmade and wheelmade vessels were found. Unfortunately, because the sample is small, no form is well represented.

Only one handmade ware is represented. This poorly-fired thick pottery usually has a dark core and a red-brown surface. Its temper—large particles of crushed calcite—constitutes 10 to 20 percent of the clay body. Smoothing marks are visible on the outer neck and body, and on the inner neck. The interior surface is rough with deep striations possibly caused by scraping and dragging temper particles across the soft clay surface.

This ware is used mainly for medium to large jars. One such jar (Fig. 93a) has a simple flared neck. Another (Fig. 93b) has a similar flared neck with lip flattening. The third jar form (Fig. 93c) has a prominent ridge circling the interior neck-body juncture. There is one other form in the sample (Fig. 93d): a medium-sized ledge rim vessel, perhaps a bowl. Having been fired in a completely reducing atmosphere, the clay body is dark gray-brown throughout. The handmade jars resemble Early Sasanian types 304 to 310 from the Susiana Plain (Wenke 1976: Fig. 8). However, handmade forms may be local to each valley, and such very general parallels are therefore suspect.

Three wheelmade wares are present; one is glazed and two are unglazed. Unlike the handmade ware, all have been fired in a completely oxidizing environment.

The glazed wheelmade ware contains fine sand particles. However, the sand may only be a natural inclusion in the clay rather than a temper added by the potter, for it is present in only small quantities at best. The body ranges from very pale yellow to very pale brown in color. In the well-preserved cases the glaze is olive green, but when oxidized it becomes a chalky white coating.

In this small sample the glazed wheelmade ware is represented by two variants of the medium-sized bowl, and tooled disc base. One bowl (Fig.93e) has a carinated rim with a thickened, rounded lip. The other (Fig. 93f) has a straight rim and an outcurved lip with an interior groove. It is possible that the groove was made to receive the bowl's lid. The badly weathered base contains a higher proportion of fine sand than do the bowls, comprising about 20 percent by volume. In this case, the sand was probably added as a temper. The two bowl rims are quite distinctive, approaching types 428

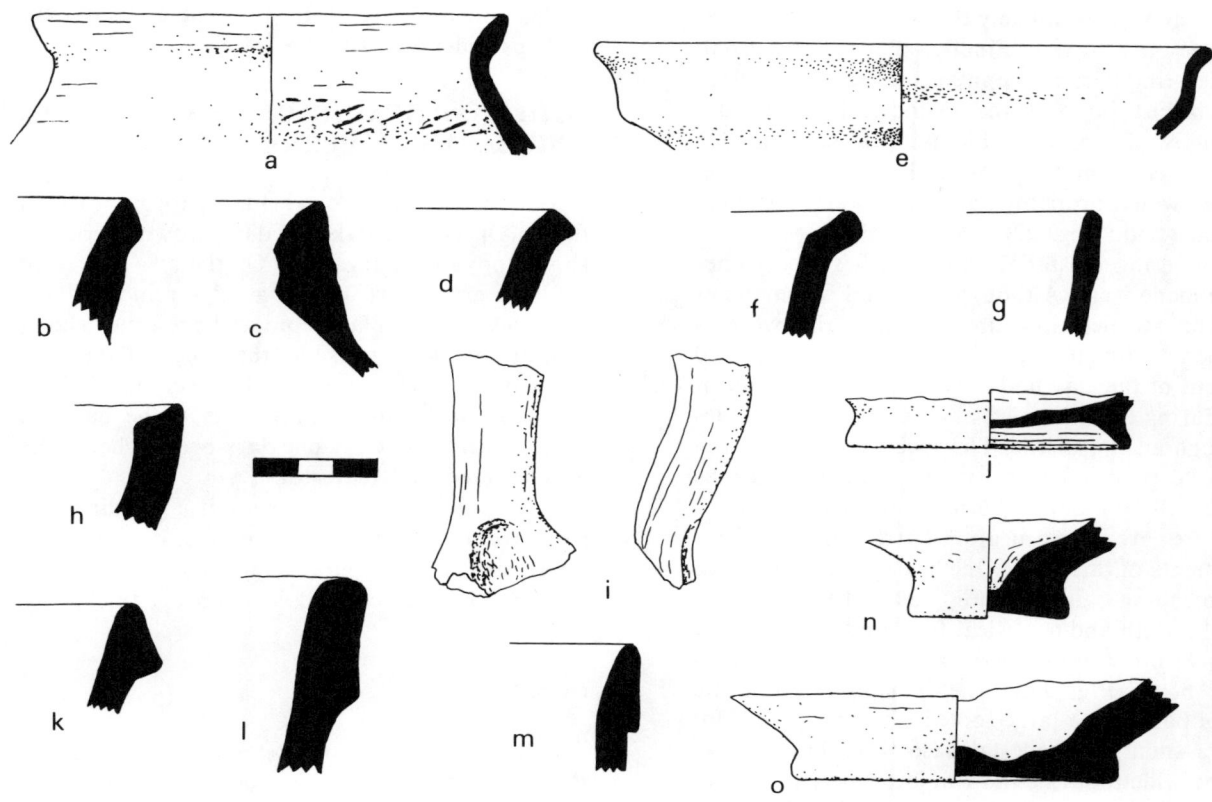

Fig. 93. Parthian and Sasanian Ceramics. A. Calcite, body 5YR 6/6 (reddish yellow), diam.: 23; X038, 60700. B. Calcite, body 2.5YR 6/8 (light red), diam.: 25; X038, 60700. C. Calcite, body 5YR 7/6 (reddish yellow), diam.: 24; X038, 60700. D. Calcite, body 10YR 4/1 (dark gray), diam.: 25; X038, 60700. E. None, body 2.5Y 8/4 (pale yellow), diam.: 31; X039, 60703. F. Sand, body 5Y 6/3 (pale olive), diam.: 35; X0747, 60707. G. None, body 10YR 6/3 (pale brown), diam.: 11, X039, 60703. H. Sand, body 5Y 7/3 (pale yellow), diam.: 43; X039, 60703. I. Sand, body 5Y 8/3 (pale yellow); X039, 60703. J. Sand, body 10YR 6/2 (light brownish gray), diam.: 7; X0747, 60707. K. Straw and sand, body 5Y 8/3 (pale yellow), diam.: 30; X039, 60703. L. Straw and sand, body 5Y 8/3 (pale yellow), diam.: 35; X038, 60700. M. Straw and sand, body 5Y 8/4 (pale yellow), diam.: 13; X039, 60703. N. Straw, body 5YR 7/4 (pink), diam.: 4; X039, 60703. O. Straw, body 2.5Y 8/0 (white), diam.: 8; X039, 60703.

(Wenke 1976: Fig. 10) and 329 (Wenke 1976: Fig. 8) from the Susiana Plain. A late Parthian or Early Sasanian date is indicated (Ibid: Fig 22).

Fine sand is the tempering material used in one of the two unglazed wheelmade wares. The sand usually comprises 20 percent of the body, but in some vessels only negligible amounts are present suggesting accidental inclusion. The bodies range from light brown to pale yellow in color. Fine wheelmade striations are often present on both surfaces of the rims and bases. Several types of fragments are represented: cup, basin and jar rims, handles; applied decorations; and bases.

Two small conical cup rims are present. One (Fig. 93g) is untempered, and has a rounded lip and slight thickening on an otherwise straight rim. The other contains fine sand and has a slightly beveled lip on its tapering rim. Another form in this ware is a heavy basin with straight sides and flat lip (Fig. 93h). There is also a medium-sized jar rim which is difficult to evaluate because the exterior is covered with a tenacious coating of cement. Among the vessel appendages are two handles, both with large amounts of included sand. One is the lower part of a cylindrical curved handle attached to the shoulder of a jar with one deep finger impression (Fig. 93i). The other is a small fragment of a strap handle. Also there is a very thick body sherd of a vessel almost one m in diameter with a heavy appliqué strip with oblique impressions. It is unlikely that this large vessel was thrown on a wheel. Finally, there is one small applied-ring base that contains no sand (Fig. 93j). The basin rim and the cylindrical handle are distinctive forms resembling types 300 and 336 respectively from the Susiana Plain (Wenke 1976: Fig. 8) which probably date to the Early Sasanian Period (Ibid.: Fig. 22).

Tempering material distinguishes the other wheelmade ware. Although fine sand is sometimes present as inclusions in the clay, the ware is tempered with straw particles constituting up to 10 percent of the clay body. The straw temper, burnt out during the firing, left abundant small flat holes throughout the sherds. The specimens range from white to pink in color. Fine wheelmade striations are usually present on both surfaces of the vessels.

There are two medium-sized band rim jar fragments of this ware. One has a wide mouth and a protruding band rim (Fig. 93k). The other has a small mouth and a vertical flat band rim or collar (Fig. 93 m). A large vessel with a similar rim may be a bowl (Fig. 93l). The remaining diagnostic vessel parts are a large tooled disc base (Fig. 93o) and a small flat pedestal base (Fig. 93n).

The wide mouth band rim jar closely resembles Type 431 of the Susiana Plain (Wenke 1976: Fig.10). This type is considered to be Terminal Parthian in date (Ibid.: Fig. 22). However, the small mouthed band rim jar, the disc base, and the pedestal base approach Transitional Elamite forms from Farukhabad (See Chapter XI, Fig. 89:9, 89:23, and 89:13 respectively). These, then were perhaps redeposited earlier pieces.

OTHER ARTIFACTS OF THE PARTHIAN AND SASANIAN PERIODS

The only chipped stone artifacts are a few rough flakes. Of the four flakes of dark brown chert, one shows possible utilization. Of the two flakes of medium gray chert, one is a ridge removal flake probably from a blade core and the other shows utilization. It is possible that these flakes are extrusive from earlier levels. However, if such were the case, we would expect them to be battered rather than fresh. Only one dark brown chert flake is weathered and battered.

Finally there is one fragment of a grinding slab made from Bakhtiari Conglomerate. Its upper and lower surfaces are parallel, its edge is perpendicular to the surface, and it is 4.5 cm thick.

SUMMARY

Late in the Parthian or early in the Sasanian Period, Farukhabad was once again occupied. There was a large masonry-founded structure on the top of the mound, and a concentration of structures around the base of the mound. The place of this settlement in the network of later settlements on the plain will be discussed by Neely in a later publication.

PART FOUR: PLANT AND ANIMAL USE

Chapter XIII

THE PLANT REMAINS

By Naomi F. Miller

INTRODUCTION

Tepe Farukhabad is located on the Mehmeh River (32° 35′N, 47° 14′E) at an elevation of about 140 m. Dry-farming is possible in this region, though irrigation has been known since the mid-sixth millennium (Helbaek 1969).

Botanical material was obtained by the flotation of soil samples of measured volume from selected locations, including oven fill, inside and outside surfaces, a granary, pot contents, ash lenses and post hole fill (Table F1). The samples were presorted in order to separate dirt particles and rootlets from ancient charred botanical remains. The identification of the remains is based on modern comparative material, some ancient comparative material from other Iranian sites kindly identified by Dr. Willem van Zeist, expertise obtained while working in Dr. van Zeist's laboratory at the Biologisch-Archaeologisch Instituut, Groningen, in the fall of 1975 and published seed illustrations (Brouwer and Stählin 1975, Beijerinck 1947, van Zeist and Heeres 1973, and others). The author, however, takes full responsibility for the identifications and analysis presented here.

As the quantity of material recovered was relatively small, seed counts alone, rather than percentages are provided.

SEEDS

BORAGINACEAE

Several samples contain boraginaceous seeds. On the basis of general shape, "warty" surface texture and two basal protrusions, the identification of *Lithospermum arvense*, a field weed is likely (cf. Brouwer and Stählin 1975). Unfortunately, a few obviously modern examples were found in one of the samples (X269B), in addition to one gray/black seed, probably carbonized in antiquity. Samples X520B and X732B each contain one gray/black seed of this species, also probably ancient.

GRAMINEAE

The grasses in the Farukhabad samples represent both cultivated wheat and barley as well as weedy genera.

Aegilops: The large seeded goat-faced grass was represented by one seed and one glume base in the Jemdet Nasr deposits.

Avena: One wild oat seed was observed in a late Jemdet Nasr context.

Hordeum: Barley grains are present in the samples, as is one internode. Most samples contain very few grains, however. With small samples it is not always possible to determine whether two-row or six-row barley is present. The former has only straight grains, but each spikelet of six-row barley contains one straight central seed and two asymmetrical lateral ones. As this observer tends to underestimate the number of twisted grains from known modern examples of barley, the fact that 44 percent of the barley grains are recorded as twisted supports the view that primarily six-row barley, *Hordeum vulgare*, was grown (Table 58).

Although total numbers are quite small, barley appears throughout the sequence, generally increasing in importance compared to wheat (Table 59).

One sample provided 15 measurable carbonized barley grains. Their dimensions are described in Fig. 94.

	AV. LENGTH (L) MM	AV. WIDTH (W) MM	AV. THICKNESS (T) MM	L/W	T/W
x̄	5.44	2.75	2.23	2.04	1.24
S.D.	.58	.42	.37	.32	.11
RANGE	4.6-7.0	2.0-3.6	1.5-2.9	1.63-2.75	1.08-1.40

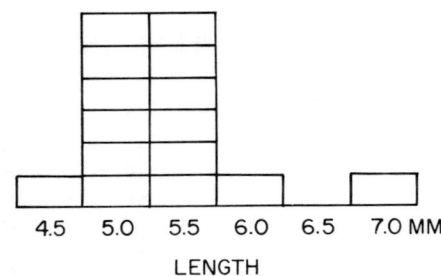

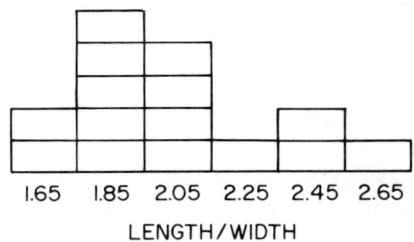
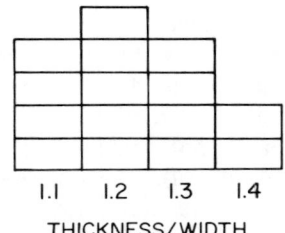

Fig. 94. Dimensions of Carbonized Barley.

Table 58: Twisted Barley Grains

Sample	# Twisted	Total
X036A	1	1
X222A	15	37
X286A	1	1
X665A	1	1
X269B	1	1
X732B	0	2
	19	43

Table 59: Wheat:Barley Ratio by Phase

Phase	Wheat	Barley	Wheat:Barley
Bayat	0	1	0
Farukh	5	2	2.50
Middle Uruk	2	4.5	0.44
Late Uruk	1	4.5	0.22
Early Jemdet Nasr	8.5	47	0.18
Late Jemdet Nasr	0	0	—
Early Dynastic	0	0	—
Elamite	0	0	—

cf. *Lolium*: Two seeds perhaps of rye grass were found in a Farukh Phase deposit.

cf. *Phalaris*: The identification of the one seed of canary grass from a Middle Uruk floor is uncertain due to the lack of comparative material.

Triticum: Wheat appears in the form of grains and spikelet forks. Most of the grains are definitely emmer (*Triticum dicoccum*, Table 60). There is one probable grain of einkorn (*T. monococcum*) in sample X732B which measures 4.8 mm in length, 2.0 mm in width, and 2.3 mm in thickness.

Although both glume bases are sometimes still attached to each other, frequently only one half of the spikelet fork is present. In appendix Tables F1 and F3, "minimum numbers" of spikelet forks have been computed by combining pairs of spikelet fork halves. The samples containing the highest densities of *Triticum* spikelet forks are apparently from outside locations, oven X474B, surfaces X665A and X269B, and granary X222A. Spikelet forks are a product of grain threshing. They may

THE PLANT REMAINS

Table 60: Dimensions of Carbonized Emmer Wheat (N=6)

	Av. Length(L) mm	Av. Width(W) mm	Av. Thickness(T) mm	L/W	T/W
$\bar{X}$	4.9	2.3	2.1	.465	.912
SD	0.57	0.27	0.34	.06	.07
Range	4.0–5.4	1.9–2.7	1.5–2.5	.39–.54	.87–1.05

represent a component of incompletely cleaned grain, or the carbonized residue of straw used as fuel. In any case, their numbers cannot be directly compared to seed remains, or even barley internodes, because their rate of preservation seems disproportionately high.

LEGUMINOSAE

The members of the Leguminosae represented at Farukhabad are all wild or weedy genera. In the absence of sufficient comparative material, it was necessary to rely primarily on illustrations for the identifications of the legumes. Thus, with some exceptions, the designations are not definitive. Helbaek (1969) has distinguished several broad classes of legumes on the basis of morphology: "oblong-reniform" *Medicago*, "blunt oval-rounded", *Trifolium* and *Melilotus* (Ibid.: 410) "flat, squarish, rhombic" *Astragalus*, and "slender cylindrical" *Trigonella* (*Ibid.*: 398).

cf. *Astragalus*: A total of six seeds were tentatively identified as *Astragalus* (Fig. 95a,b). Four measurable seeds have lengths of 1.2 to 1.5 mm.

cf. *Coronilla*: Five *Coronilla* seeds appear in one Early Jemdet Nasr sample. These are relatively long (1.6–2.8 mm) and narrow (0.6–1.4 mm) cylindrical seeds.

Hippocrepis: This distinctive horseshoe shaped seed appears in one Early Jemdet Nasr sample (Fig. 95c).

Medicago: This is the most numerous and ubiquitous seed in the Farukhabad samples. It is identified by its reniform shape, which is in most cases quite clear. Average length of the measurable seeds is 1.96 mm, with a range of 1.2 to 2.9 mm (N=22) (Fig. 95d–f).

cf. *Melilotus*: This genus has been distinguished (somewhat subjectively) from *Trifolium*; illustrations show its seeds to be proportionately narrower (Fig.95g).

cf. *Trifolium*: Clover appears periodically in small quantities in the samples. Measurable seeds vary from 0.7 to 2.1 mm in length, with a mean of 1.38 mm (N=17) (Fig. 95h).

Trigonella: This appears periodically in small quantities in the samples (Fig. 95i,j).

Although there is no identification to specific level of wild and weedy legumes, *Medicago*, *Melilotus*, *Coronilla* and perhaps *Trifolium* and *Trigonella* probably represent field weeds. The *Astragalus* and *Hippocrepis* in samples of Farukh-Bayat and Jemdet Nasr age are probably plants of the steppe (cf. Townsend 1974).

In general, the richest samples owe their high seed densities to the presence of legumes (Table 61). However, there is no correlation between functional area and presence of leguminous seeds. There are inside and outside surfaces which have them in relatively large quantities, as well as those which do not. The ubiquity of legumes, both weedy and of the steppe, can perhaps be explained by the possible role of these plants as fodder, and the subsequent use of animal dung for fuel.

MALVACEAE

One seed of *Malva*, probably representing a weed, appears in sample X665A.

PLANTAGINACEAE

Three *Plantago* seeds, presumably from fields, are present.

RANUNCULACEAE

One eroded seed of cf. *Adonis* was found; it probably represents a field weed.

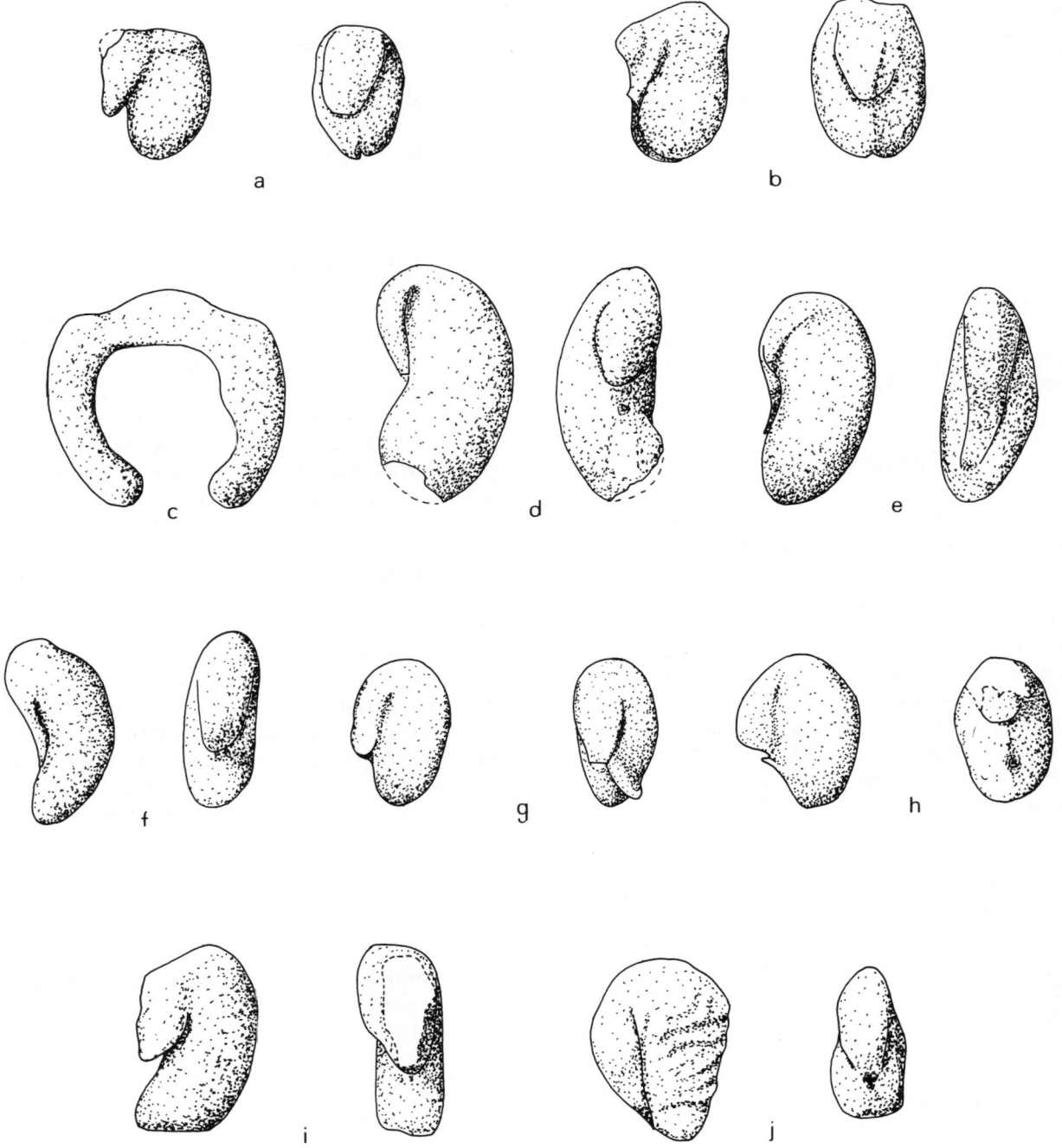

Fig. 95. Leguminous Seeds. A. cf. *Astragalus*, X702 II/A. B. cf. *Astragalus*, X702, II/A. C. *Hippocrepis*, X219A. D. *Medicago*, X665A. E. *Medicago*, X665A. F. *Medicago*, X332A. G. cf. *Meliotus*, X702 II/A. H. cf. *Trifolium*, X665A. I. *Trigonella*, X269B. J. *Trigonella*, X332A. Scale is 50 × natural size.

THE PLANT REMAINS

Table 61: Samples with Unusually High Proportions of Particular Types of Carbonized Plant Remains

Area Type	Phase	Sample	Seeds	Cereals	Glume Bases	Legumes	Pistachios
Inside Floors	Bayat	X702A	x			x	
	Middle Uruk	X332A	x			x	
	Early Jemdet Nasr	X220A					x
Outside Floors	Bayat	X665A	x		x	x	
	Early Jemdet Nasr	X269B	x		x	x	
Outside Oven	Middle Uruk	X474B			x		
Outside Granary	Early Jemdet Nasr	X222A	x	x	x		

RUBIACEAE

Galium, whose spherical seed has a circular hole at the attachment to the stem, appears in one sample. It probably represents a field weed.

ROSACEAE

A number of nutshells have been tentatively identified as almond (*Amygdalus*), on the basis of relative thickness (c. 1.5 mm, range 1.0–1.9 mm), and reticulate cross-section at 50X magnification. Most of the fragments have a smooth surface, like *Amygdalus scoparia* spach. Pistachio nuts also have a smooth surface, but wild *Pistacia eurycarpa* is thinner on average (0.5 mm) and has a fine-grained cross-section. A few fragments show two characteristics of almond, longitudinal shallow furrows on the outer surface and lacunae in cross section.

CHARCOAL

Several samples of charcoal from Farukhhabad were submitted for identification (Table F3). The following genera were noted:

Tamarix: Tamarisk is a common lowland tree, generally growing along streams and in areas of high water table. Many species are also quite salt tolerant.

Populus: Poplar grows commonly along streams, and is also frequently grown for use as roof beams.

Lycium: *Lycium*, a solanaceous shrub, forms part of the lowland riverine vegetation of Khuzestan; it is also found at higher elevations (Pabot 1960).

Quercus: Oak is the dominant tree of the Zagrosian forest, extending from northern Iran to Fars province. In Khuzestan, oak is found at evevations as low as 800 m(Pabot 1960), or about 20 km from Farukhabad.

Prunus: Almond grows commonly in the Zagros mountains, especially in the south and at lower elevations. In Khuzestan, it would not have appeared at elevations lower than 300 m (Pabot 1960), or about 18 km from Farukhabad.

It is not surprising that the most common wood in these samples is tamarisk, which is plentiful and locally available. The most distant types, oak and almond, comprise a very small proportion of the total amount of charcoal.

DISTRIBUTION OF PLANT REMAINS WITHIN THE SITE

Carbonized material was in most cases sparsely distributed within the sampled areas. Nevertheless, a few areas stand out as being relatively rich in botanical remains of various sorts (Table 61, F2).

An explanation of the spatial distribution of glume bases and legumes has already been alluded to, and can be illustrated with an ethnographic case. In highland Fars on the Marv Dasht, dung is frequently used for heating rooms as well as for cooking in outside hearths; inside cooking is today done primarily on a small kerosene stove. Straw is regularly used as the fuel for bread-making. A large quantity is put next to the hearth so that the rapidly burning fire can be fed constantly. Bread-making almost invariably takes place outdoors, due to the danger of using straw fuel inside in this manner. If these modern practices were the same as ancient ones, and if the presence of legumes does in fact result from the burning of dung as fuel, one would expect the observed distribution of material; glume bases would be found in outside contexts and leguminous seeds would be found both within and outside of structures, as is the case.

DISCUSSION

At a more general level, it can be seen that the patterns of plant utilization established in early times (Helbaek 1969) continued into the fourth millennium. In particular, the number of different species present in the human environment seems to remain relatively stable. Helbaek reported 31 genera from 18 families, compared to 20 from 8 at Tepe Farukhabad. This is not surprising, since his sampling was broader both temporally and spatially. For both studies, the bulk of the genera consists of various Gramineae and Leguminosae. In particular, cultivated cereals and small seeded legumes account for a major portion of the variety of the material.

The only definitely identified cultigens at Tepe Farukhabad are cereals. A few other cultigens occur in relatively small quantities in samples from the earlier phases on the Deh Luran plain, and their absence here is probably a function of sample size. Be that as it may, the three cereals are six-row barley, emmer wheat and einkorn wheat. The apparent predominance of barley can probably be attributed to its salt-resistant qualities and its lower water requirement. Helbaek noted a shift favoring barley cultivation of nearby Tepe Sabz, abandoned at about the time of the earliest samples from Tepe Farukhabad. He suggests that the abandonment of Sabz might have been due to the detrimental soil salinizing effects of irrigation. The similar increase in the importance of barley at Tepe Farukhabad, may result from similar agricultural practices and consequent local soil deterioration.

Small seeded legumes are numerically the most common group in the assemblage. The legumes are all uncultivated genera. The absence of lentils seems to represent a pattern continuing from the fifth into the fourth millennium. Although contemporary sites to the southwest, on the Susiana Plain, do have lentils (Jaffarabad, Sharafabad, KS 27; Miller 1978), the only significant occurrence on the Deh Luran plain is in a Mehmeh Phase sample from Musiyan (Helbaek 1969), somewhat older than the Bayat Phase.

The most common tree product represented in the samples by charcoal or fruit is tamarisk, which could have grown very close to the site. In contrast, nut shell fragments and wood charcoal from forest species form a very small percentage of the carbonized remains, despite the fact that a pistachio-almond steppe-forest may have been only 20 km from Tepe Farukhabad. Thus, there is little evidence for extensive utilization of forest resources.

Chapter XIV

THE FAUNAL REMAINS

By Richard W. Redding

INTRODUCTION

When I was invited by Henry Wright to examine the faunal remains from his excavations at Tepe Farukhabad, I accepted because the material presented a unique opportunity to examine several aspects of human exploitation of vertebrate resources. In particular, I was able to examine changes in patterns of utilization of faunal resources, methods of handling and preparing parts of butchered vertebrates, and relations of faunal elements and the fauna to cultural contexts. The extraction of information on these and other aspects of the utilization of fauna was made possible by techniques used in the recovery of material of Tepe Farukhabad.

These techniques have been described in Chapter I. Only a brief summary of those aspects that most facilitated the analysis of the faunal material is presented here. First, all of the primary cultural deposits at Farukhabad were dry screened in a 0.5 cm mesh. Screened faunal samples included most elements from small vertebrates and the small fragments of elements of larger vertebrates. The smaller elements of rodents and small fish may have been lost. These screened samples contained faunal remains that were not biased, with the possible exception of under representation of small fish, in terms of size of element or degree of fragmentation. Second, all of the material recovered during excavation was retained; there was no pre-sorting of the material before it reached the faunal analyst. Samples were not biased by the excavators' concepts of what was identifiable. This made possible the study of fragmentation of bone and its relationship to handling and preparation of meat. Third, the volume excavated was recorded for each unit at Farukhabad. This made possible direct comparisons of faunal complexes between deposits.

I would like to thank Gerald Smith for help in the identification of the fish material. Robert Storer and Emmet Hooper, curators of birds and mammals respectively, at the Museum of Zoology of the University of Michigan allowed me access to the collections under their care. I would also like to thank the following people for their advice and critical examination of the manuscript: J.A. Dorr, K.V. Flannery, D.M. Lay, J. Wheeler, and H. Wright.

METHODS UTILIZED IN THE ANALYSIS

Each element was identified to the lowest taxonomic level possible given its surviving characteristics. There is controversy over the utility of many characters for differentiating between similar species. Wherever I have made an identification based on a controversial character I have so stated and discussed the validity of the character. All of the identifications, with the exception of the fish remains, were done by the author.

For the purpose of the analysis, the excavation units were grouped according to cultural phases defined by the excavator. The six phase groupings utilized in this analysis are, from oldest to youngest, Farukh-Bayat, Early Uruk, Middle Uruk, Late Uruk, Jemdet Nasr, and Elamite. Presented in Table 62 is a list by phase of the excavation units composing each and the volume excavated in the sampling of each.

The number of minimum individuals has been calculated for each species by excavation unit. The minimum individual figure is based on the maximally represented element. For example, if the most frequently occurring element in an excavation unit for a species is a left unfused distal tibia and there are three of these, then the number of minumum individuals of that species for that unit is three. This technique requires the fewest assumptions and subjective decisions.

Table 62: Phases Recognized at Tepe Farukhabad with Associated Excavation Layers and Volumes of the Samples

Phase Groupings	Volume in m³	Phases Included	Excavation A: Layers	Excavation A: Volume	Excavation B: Layers	Excavation B: Volume
Elamite	26.3	Elamite	—	—	1–18	26.3
Jemdet Nasr	77.5	Early Dynastic	1–5	10.6	19–20	4.1
		Late Jemdet Nasr	6–12	20.0	21–23	12.8
		Early Jemdet Nasr	13–17	13.9	24–27	16.1
Late Uruk	29.0	Late Uruk	18–20	9.5	28–31	19.5
Middle Uruk	29.8	Middle Uruk	21–22	6.8	32–34	23.0
Early Uruk	12.4	Early Uruk	Feature 23	1.2	35–36	11.2
Farukh-Bayat	83.1	Farukh	23–31	25.9	37–47	43.3
		Bayat	33–36	13.9	—	—

A ratio of either the number or weight of the material recovered to the volume excavated has been employed to make certain observations. This ratio is referred to in this paper as the density ratio. It was proposed as a technique of faunal analysis by Willey and McGimsey (1954:44) and subsequently by Ziegler (1973:10–12). The density ratio has been used in this paper to examine differences between phases in utilization of different vertebrates, differences in occurrence of elements, and differences in treatment of mammalian material between phases. A more traditional method for making such comparisons utilizes the number of minimum individuals or raw counts of elements for each phase. Changes in both are presumed to indicate changes in utilization or treatment between phases or sites. However, the use of counts or minimum individuals does not eliminate variability due to differences between phases or sites in the volume excavated.

Four major assumptions are involved in making statements about the differences in utilization of vertebrate resources between phases or sites based on density ratios: 1) The sample for each phase/site contains similar types of activity areas. This is not always the case, but it can be controlled and such differences must be considered in the analysis of the Farukhabad fauna; 2) The sample excavated from each type of deposit in each phase is representative; 3) The rate of depostion of sediment in each type of deposit is the same between phases/sites; 4) Each type of element (e.g., distal humerus) for each vertebrate has the same probability of being deposited, recovered, and identified in each successive phase or between sites.

THE NON-MAMMALIAN REMAINS

CLASS CHONDRICHTHYES (SHARKS AND RAYS)

An unusual find from Tepe Farukhabad was two elements from a member of the Order Batoidea. A ray, possibly of the genus *Myliobatis*, is represented by two tessellate dentary plates. Both were recovered from a Late Uruk excavation unit B30 upper.

The Deh Luran Plain is approximately 270 km from the mouth of the Shatt-el-Arab on the Persian Gulf where the ray *Myliobatis aquila* is found at present (Khalaf 1961:13). This does not necessarily imply that a ray, or a portion of one, was traded or carried this distance to the Deh Luran Plain. Khalaf notes that at least three species of sharks ascend to the Tigris River as far as Baghdad and, even though species of the genus Myliobatis are not known to enter fresh water, members of other families of rays do so (Garmen 1913:415–27). It is possible that the ray may have come from the Tigris River which is only 75 km from Farukhabad. However, in the succeeding phase, the Jemdet Nasr, marine fish were being brought into the area from the Persian Gulf and/or the Shatt-el-Arab.

CLASS OSTEICHTHYES (BONY FISH): THE MATERIAL

Identification of fish remains from southwestern Iran to species or genus is difficult as there is little comparative material available. Hence, identifications of fish remains from Farukhabad were made, with one exception, only to family. A list of elements recovered and their stratigraphic associations is provided in the appendices. The distribution of elements by species by phase is presented in Table 63.

Eighty-four elements were recovered from the excavations at Farukhabad that could be assigned to this class. Most of these elements were fragments of spines, which further reduced the possibility of species designation. Of the 84 elements, seven were identified as representing the family Pomadasyidae, the grunters, and three as the family Cyprinidae, the minnows and carp.

Two of the cyprinid elements may represent the genus *Barbus*, the barbels, which is represented by numerous species in Asia. It is quite common in rivers and marshes and is also found in the Shatt-et-Arab (Khalaf 1961: 27-33). Fish of this genus are sold in the Bazaar at Ahwaz and are to be found occasionally in the city of Dezful. During late March and early April people stand along the highway between Ahwaz and Andimeshk, paralleling the Karkeh River, holding up strings of fresh barbels offering them for sale to travelers. These fish must be more accessible during this time of the year, possibly because they are breeding. Several of these fish were purchased from roadside vendors and the females were found to contain egg masses. Barbels may also be found in irrigation canals. When canals are periodically drained for cleaning the barbels are collected. Khalaf considers most members of this genus to be very good food fish.

A single serrated dorsal spine is assigned to the genus *Varicorhinus*. There is no common name for this genus but they are similar to barbels which resemble carp. Members of this genus are restricted to the upper regions and tributaries of the main rivers in the area (Khalaf 1961:33-34). Several specimens of this genus were procured in a small stream northeast of the city of Dezful (elevation 152 m), at an elevation of about 490 m. This stream is intermittent in its lower reaches on the Susiana Plain south of Dezful.

The family *Pomadasyidae*, the grunters, consists of marine fish. They are known to occur in the Persian Gulf and the Shatt-el-Arab (Blegvad 1944:121-27; Khalaf 1961:82-84). Blegvad notes that fish of this family are common throughout the gulf and in the harbor at Bushire. He claims that they are an excellent food fish and that members of the genus *Plectorhynchus* could be found in abundance in the bazaars of the coastal cities. The fish of this family have not been reported from any fresh water localities. The identification of this family is based mainly on the presence of several sets of pharyngeal arch fragments and premaxillae.

CLASS OSTEICHTHYES: THE DISTRIBUTION

The 84 elements are not equally distributed in all of the phases. The Farukh-Bayat units contain only one element and have a ratio of elements recovered to volume excavated (in cubic meters) of 0.01. The Early Uruk units contain two fish elements and have a density ratio of 0.16. Middle and Late Uruk units account for 4 and 14 elements respectively, resulting in ratios of elements recovered to cubic meters excavated of 0.13 and 0.48. One of the elements from the Late Uruk is a serrated spine assigned to the genus *Varicorhinus*. The majority of the fish material, 60 elements, is from Jemdet Nasr units. In this phase the density ratio is 0.77. The Jemdet Nasr material includes all seven elements of the marine family Pomadasyidae, as well as both of the elements identifiable as a cyprinid, probably *Barbus*. The Elamite levels contain three fish elements and have a density ratio of 0.11.

CLASS OSTEICHTYES: SUMMARY AND CONCLUSIONS

The data on habits and distribution presented above does not pertain to the two rivers on the Deh Luran Plain, the Dawairij and the Mehmeh. The Mehmeh River flows, at present, just southwest of Tepe Farukhabad, having, at some time in the past, eroded away a large portion of the site. Flannery (in Hole, Flannery, and Neely 1969:327), states that only the hardiest species of fish can live in these two rivers year round because of the low summer water levels and the accompanying high salinity. These observations may not be used in conjunction with the archaelogical data to draw inferences on the possibility of local availability of certain species of fish during the time periods represented in the excavation. It is not known whether these conditions were prevalent in the past on the Dawairij and Mehmeh. It should be expected that the regimes of these rivers have

Table 63: A Summary of the Distribution of the Elements of the Class Osteichthyes (the fish)

Element	Farukh-Bayat	Early Uruk	Middle Uruk	Late Uruk	Jemdet Nasr	Elamite
Cyprinidae						
cf. *Barbus*	—	—	—	—	2	0
varicorhinus	—	—	—	1	—	—
Pomadasyidae	—	—	—	—	6	—
Unidentified	1	2	4	13	52	3

probably changed with successive modifications of the drainage by human activities.

The barbels, such as *Barbus*, might have been obtained locally year round in the Mehmeh and the Dawairij Rivers. If summer conditions were unfavorable, they could have entered the two rivers during the rainy season when conditions were more favorable, possibly coming into shallow areas to breed during March and April. Members of the genus *Varicorhinus* could have been obtained in perennial streams in the mountains behind the Deh Luran Plain similar to those behind the city of Dezful. The members of the family Pomadasyidae could only have been obtained from the area of the Persian Gulf. The material representing this family is restricted to Jemdet Nasr levels. Possibly members of this family were transported to the site only during this phase.

The density ratios seem to indicate an increased utilization of fish resources through time. This trend continues through the Jemdet Nasr when marine fish were imported and then utilization of fish decreases in the Elamite levels. There were no butchering marks on any of the fish remains and only two spines exhibited any evidence of having been affected by fire. Fish were undoubtedly utilized as a food resource and were a portion of the diet in every phase.

CLASS REPTILIA (THE REPTILES): THE MATERIAL

The Class Reptilia is represented by 60 elements or fragments of elements. Forty-five of these were identifiable to the level of the family and 41 of these were further identifiable and represent one lizard and two turtles. Reptiles, particularly lizards, in the area are burrowers, hence, the information potential of this group is reduced due to the difficulty of distinguishing intrusive material. A complete list of the material recovered by excavation unit is presented in the appendices. A summary by phase is provided in Table 64.

Mauromys caspica: At least two individuals were identified on the basis of two carapace fragments. *M. caspica*, the Caspian Terrapin, is found in fresh water bodies throughout Iran. On the Deh Luran Plain it is restricted at present to freshwater springs (Hole, Flannery, and Neely 1969:325). On the Susiana Plain, the Caspian Terrapin is extremely common in irrigation canals and in ponded waters. They spend hours sunning themselves in groups of up to 20.

Trionyx euphraticus: The soft-shelled turtle is represented by 38 carapace fragments and a single limb bone. These may well be from a single individual and may be intrusive. Soft-shelled turtles are inhabitants of rivers, lakes, and marshes and prefer to burrow in soft mud bottoms (Carr 1952:411). *T. euphraticus* can be obtained from either the Dez or Karkeh Rivers on the Susiana Plain. They probably also inhibit the Dawairij and Mehmeh. They are rarely observed in irrigation canals.

Agamidae: There are four elements recovered that could be assigned to this family. Three of these elements are mandibles that display the acrodont condition characteristic of the agamids, while the fourth is an ilium. This family is composed of several genera of lizards, one of which, *Uromastix*, is known from the Deh Luran Plain. Sites on the Deh Luran Plain are frequently burrowed by members of this genus as well as the desert monitor lizard, *Varanus griseus*, family Varanidae (Hole, Flannery, and Neely 1969:325). I

THE FAUNAL REMAINS

Table 64: A Summary of the Distribution of the Elements of the Class Reptilia at Tepe Farukhabad

Element	Farukh-Bayat	Early Uruk	Middle Uruk	Late Uruk	Jemdet Nasr	Elamite
Mauromys caspica	—	—	—	—	—	2*
Trionix euphraticus	—	—	—	—	—	4
Agamidae	—	—	—	—	3*	1
Unidentified	2	2*	7**	—	1	—

* one element not intrusive
** six elements not intrusive

have removed a living specimen of the latter from its burrow 50 cm below the surface of an archaeological site on the Susiana Plain.

Unidentifiable Material: The remaining reptilian material consisted of nine vertebrae, a large articular, and a humerus, all from lizards, as well as four plastron/carapace fragments from unidentified turtles.

CLASS REPTILIA: THE DISTRIBUTION

Much, if not all, of the material representing this class may have been intrusive. The tests used to discern intrusive material were 1) the similarity in discoloration between the reptilian material and other elements from the same excavation unit that were not intrusive, 2) the proximity of burrows noted on the profiles and floorplans, and 3) the depth of the material from the present surface of the site. Using only the last criterion all but five of the reptilian elements could be considered intrusive were recovered within one of the surface. The material representing the soft-shelled turtle was found near the surface in proximity to a large burrow. This material was much lighter in coloration than other material from the same unit. Since the Mehmeh River is quite close to the site, this turtle may be considered to be intrusive, owing its presence on the site to post-mortem transport.

That material not considered to have been intrusive consists of nine elements. One represents an unidentifiable lizard from the Early Uruk and six others represent unidentifiable lizards from the Middle Uruk. A single agamid mandible was recovered from the Jemdet Nasr and a single carapace fragment from the Elamite represents a Caspian terrapin.

CLASS REPTILIA: SUMMARY AND CONCLUSIONS

The reptilian material from Tepe Farukhabad appears to have been mostly intrusive. Little information is provided by this group. The nonintrusive material consists of one fragment of turtle carapace and several lizard elements. None of the reptilian material exhibited any evidence of butchering or burning and this combined with the scarcity of material, suggests that reptiles played little or no part in the diet of the inhabitants during any phase.

CLASS AVES (THE BIRDS): THE MATERIAL

The avifauna from Tepe Farukhabad consists of 20 elements of which 12 were identifiable at least to the level of the family. The identifiable material represents at least nine species of birds, six of which are aquatic. In the following discussion all range and habitat data are taken from Allouse (1953), Vaurie (1965), or from my observations during a nine month period from September 1970 to May 1971. A summary of species represented by phase is provided in Table 65. A complete list of elements and their provenience can be found in the Appendices.

Phalacrocorax carbo: The cormorant is represented by a single element. Allouse describes the cormorant as a common winter visitor throughout Iraq. The cormorant prefers shallow waters along sea coasts, lakes, rivers and swamps. We first observed cormorants on the Susiana Plain in late November; they left the area by the end of March. They spent nights on a gravel island in the middle of the Dez River and would move out to irrigation canals early in the morning to feed. They were quite easy to surprise and shoot when feeding in the canals. I observed no cormorants on the Deh Luran Plain although suitable habitats were available; however, I spent only one day on the plain during the months when cormorants might have been there.

Egretta garzetta: The little egret is represented by a single element. Allouse considers the egret a common summer inhabitant in Iraq and notes that it is a passage migrant in April. We observed the little egret as well as the great white egret, *Egretta alba*, constantly from September through May, the entire length of our stay on the Susiana Plain. They were the most common large water fowl observed in the area. They remain in the area year round feeding in irrigated fields, irrigation canals, and rivers.

Threskiornithidae: This family is represented by two elements; a left coracoid and a right, first phalanx from the second pectoral digit. Both elements resemble those of the genus *Platelea*. The members of this genus, the spoonbills, inhabit open marshes, shallow lakes, and mud and sand flats near rivers. They are known to breed in northern Iran and Iraq. They winter on Lake Famus southwest of Shiraz (Lay, personal communication). We observed no members of this family in southwestern Iran.

Anatidae: Two elements recovered could be assigned to this family, which consists of the ducks and geese, many different species of which can be observed in the area. The most common ducks in the area are the mallards, *Anas platyrhynchos*, and the teal, *Anas crecca*. Ducks first appeard on the Susiana Plain in late November but were not common until January. By the end of March they had left the area. At night, ducks were concentrated along the major rivers, but just before sunrise they flew out to irrigated fields, irrigation canals and areas of ponded water whey they fed. One or two hours before sunset they could be observed returning to the rivers.

Falco sp.: An unidentified falcon is represented by a single element. Several species of falcons occur at present in southwestern Iran.

Gallinula chloropus: The moorhen is represented by a single element. This species is found in Iran and Iraq at present. It is sedentary, inhabiting aquatic vegetation along still and slowly moving bodies of fresh water, we observed this bird several times on the Susiana Plain along field drainage systems, backwater river channels, and ponds. It can be easily approached and prefers to run for cover rather than fly.

Larus sp.: An unidentified gull is represented by a single element. This genus is world-wide and the species occurs in varied habitats. The common gull and the herring gull *L. argentatus* and *L. canus* respectively were observed along the Dez river from late January through February.

Columba sp.: The pigeons and doves are represented by two elements. This genus is cosmopolitan and commensal with humans. The rock dove, *C. livia*, was observed frequently on both the Susiana and Deh Luran Plains.

Passeriformes: The songbirds are represented by a single element.

CLASS AVES: THE DISTRIBUTION

Farukh-Bayat: The birds are represented by one element in this phase. This is the element identified as being from a cormorant. The density ratio for this phase is 0.01.

Early Uruk: The Early Uruk units excavated contained no avifauna.

Middle Uruk: The avifauna of this phase consist of one unidentifiable element and two identifiable elements, representing a gull and a passerine. The density ratio for the Middle Uruk is 0.10.

Late Uruk: Like the Middle Uruk, this phase contained two unidentifiable and two identifiable elements. The identifiable elements of this phase represent a moorhen and one of the two doves/pigeons. The density ratio for this phase 0.14.

Jemdet Nasr: In addition to three unidentifiable elements, the Jemdet Nasr contained four identifiable elements. These include, the element identified as being from an egret, both elements from the family Anatidae, and one of the elements representing the spoonbills. The density ratio for this phase is 0.90.

Elamite: The birds recovered from the Elamite excavation untis are the falcon, one of the two doves/pigeons and the other spoonbill. In addition to these three identifiable elements, the Elamite units contained two unidentifiable elements. The spoonbill and the falcon and one of the unidentifiable elements were recovered from levels that lay outside what appears to have been a citadel wall. The density ratio for this phase is 0.19.

THE FAUNAL REMAINS

Table 65: A Summary of the Distribution of the Elements of the Class Aves at Tepe Farukhabad

Element	Farukh-Bayat	Early Uruk	Middle Uruk	Late Uruk	Jemdet Nasr	Elamite
Phalacrocorax carbo	1	—	—	—	—	—
Egretta garzetta	—	—	—	—	1	—
Threskiornithidae	—	—	—	—	1	1
Anatidae	—	—	—	—	2	—
Falco sp.	—	—	—	—	—	1
Gallinula Chloropus	—	—	—	1	—	—
Larus sp.	—	—	1	—	—	—
Columba	—	—	—	1	—	1
Passeriformes	—	—	1	—	—	—
Unidentified	—	—	1	2	3	2

CLASS AVES: SUMMARY AND CONCLUSIONS

Birds were probably utilized as a resource through the sequence at Tepe Farukhabad. The absence of avifauna from the Early Uruk may be due to the small volume of material excavated from this phase.

Although the associations of the birds in the Jemdet Nasr and the Middle and Late Uruk phases demonstrate nearly equal density ratios, the birds of the Jemdet Nasr are the largest and have the most attractive plumage and most meat, while those of the Middle and Late Uruk are smaller and more drab. The Middle and Late Uruk birds were in association with small structures while those of the Jemdet Nasr were found in association with large substantial structures which may have been elaborate residence. All but one, the egret, of the Jemdet Nasr birds are winter visitors and all are water birds. All but one of the Middle and Late Uruk birds are residents. Two of the four birds in both these phases, the gull and dove/pigeon, will inhabit human settlements.

There is no evidence that any of the birds were eaten. None of the bones exhibited evidence of butchering or burning. The birds may have been kept for eggs or plumage, or as pets, instead of having been exploited for meat. As noted above the doves/pigeons and gull will inhabit human settlements and may have died naturally. This is also true of many passerines.

Considering the egret as a resident, half of the identifiable bird remains are from migrants. Seventy-five percent of all the identifiable material comes from aquatic birds. Habitats exist at present on the Deh Luran Plain for all of the birds identified, and, except for the spoonbill and cormorant, all have been recently observed on the Deh Luran Plain.

CLASS MAMMALIA: THE MATERIALS AND DISTRIBUTION

THE IDENTIFIABLE VS. THE UNIDENTIFIABLE MATERIAL

The mammalian material was examined by excavation unit and initially divided into two categories; possibly identifiable and unidentifiable. Material of the first category was examined, identified, or else added to the material in the unidentifiable category. A summary of the mammals represented by the identifiable material listed by phase is presented in Table 66. A complete list of all identifiable mammalian elements by excavation unit is provided in the appendices.

The unidentifiable material was sorted into three categories and the weights of each recorded. One category consists of rib fragments, unidentifiable limb fragments, and skull fragments. This category has a total weight of 23,906 gm. A second category contains vertebrae and vertebrae fragments, only atlases and axes having been identified. Based only on size, all of the vertebral material represents sheep, goats and gazelles. The total weight of this category is 1,507 gm. Tooth fragments form a third category which has a total weight of 1,482 gm. Any tooth that was not complete enough to exhibit the characters of an upper or a lower and a right or a left was weighed as a tooth fragment. Almost all of the tooth

Table 66: A Summary of the Distribution of the Farukhabad Mammalian Material Number of Elements and (Minimum Individuals) by Phase

Mammal	Elamite	Jemdet Nasr	Late Uruk	Middle Uruk	Early Uruk	Farukh-Bayat
Hyaena hyaena	2(1)	—	—	—	—	—
Felis sp.	—	1(1)	—	—	—	—
Vulpes vulpes	2(1)	7(5)	—	3(3)	—	3(1)
Canis ssp.	7(4)	—	—	8(1)	2(1)	11(4)
Equus spp.	46(11)	21(12)	12(7)	39(6)	27(4)	17(9)
Sus scrofa	5(4)	31(9)	—	—	—	—
Dama d. mesopotamica	—	—	—	2(1)	—	—
Ovis	7(4)	25(14)	7(3)	6(5)	—	6(5)
Capra	12(7)	38(17)	8(5)	6(5)	2(2)	6(5)
Ovis-Capra-Gazella	225(26)	668(62)	179(16)	157(15)	62(7)	309(44)
Gazella	4(2)	13(8)	1(1)	7(4)	2(2)	14(6)
Bos taurus	55(5)	13(10)	5(1)	4(2)	3(2)	10(8)
Mus musculus	—	5(3)	—	—	—	—
Tatera indica	—	4(2)	2(2)	—	—	10(6)

fragments, with the exception of some of those from 20 excavation units, are from sheep, goats, and gazelles. These 20 units contain teeth fragments from cattle and/or equids as well. These occurrences are noted in the presentation of the weights of the three categories by excavation unit in the appendices.

The method described above has several shortcomings. A great deal of potential information is lost because of the rather gross categories into which the unidentifiable material was sorted for weighing. Ideally, one should break down each of the above categories into size ranges representing small, medium, and large mammals. Furthermore, the first category should have been broken up into its component parts: limb fragments, skull fragments, and rib fragments.

Further difficulties arose because the identifiable material was not weighed. Since counts of unidentifiable material are unsatisfactory, a comparison of unidentifiable and identifiable material on the basis of weights by size would be preferable. Unfortunately, we have counts of identifiable material by excavation unit and weights of unidentifiable material by excavation unit. A rough comparison of identifiable and unidentifiable material can be accomplished using the density ratio, as long as the comparison is restricted to a comparison of trends without examining absolute differences. The density ratios computed for each phase for identified limb and skull elements, for identified teeth, and for all three categories of unidentifiable material by phase are provided in Table 67. The density ratio for the identifiable material is the result of the division of the number of elements by cubic meters excavated, while the ratios of unidentifiable categories result from the division of the weight by cubic meters excavated.

Examination of Table 67 reveals that changes in densities occurred through time. The significance of these changes must be understood in terms of the processes and activities producing them.

An increase in the density of identifiable limb and skull elements could indicate two things: more bones are being deposited and/or identifiable portions of the bones are subject to decreased fracturing. The same is true of an increase in identifiable teeth. Since all vertebrae, except the atlas and the axis, were weighed as vertebral fragments, an increase in the density of vertebral material indicates an increase in the number of vertebrae present (the possibility that a large increase in the density of vertebral fragments is a reflection of an increase in the occurrence of vertebrae of large mammals has been rejected). An increase in the density of either unidentifiable teeth fragments or unidentifiable limb, skull, and rib fragments may indicate either an increase in total bones or an increase in the fragmentation of the available material. Thus the meanings of these changes for all the density ratios seems to be either increased or decreased occurrence, increased or decreased fragmentation, or a combination of these factors. It is possible to detect those cases in which a difference between two phases in density

Table 67: Density Ratios of the Identifiable and the Three Categories of Unidentifiable Material for Each Phase

	Ident. Material		Unident. Material		
Phase	Limb-Skull bones/m³	Teeth bones/m³	Vert. Frags. gm/m³	Teeth Frags. gm/m³	Limb-Skull frags. gm/m³
Elamite	7.9	5.3	10.9	15.3	220.0
Jemdet Nasr	7.2	3.3	6.7	3.2	66.4
Late Uruk	4.9	2.5	5.7	8.9	105.9
Middle Uruk	4.9	2.8	15.1	7.9	140.7
Early Uruk	5.3	2.5	0.9	4.0	148.9
Farukh-Bayat	2.0	2.4	0.9	3.4	46.5

ratio for a given category is due to increased/decreased fragmentation. A ratio of the unidentifiable to identifiable density ratio for limb and skull and for teeth for each phase is presented in Table 68. Changes in these ratios between phases reflect the effects of fragmentation. If these ratios are similar for a given category for two phases then the differences in the density ratios should be indicative of differences in the occurrence of material. Let us now consider Tables 67 and 68.

Three relative levels of fragmentation are apparent in the ratios of unidentifiable to identifiable limb and skull elements in Table 68. The Elamite, Middle Uruk, and Early Uruk have the highest levels of fragmentation. The Late Uruk and Farukh-Bayat have levels of fragmentation only slightly lower. The Jemdet Nasr has a very low level of fragmentation. The fragmentation of teeth follows the pattern described above for limb and skull elements, except that fragmentation of teeth is lowest in the Jemdet Nasr.

Several possible processes might account for changes in the level of fragmentation of bone: the processes of time, soil, and water; and the activities of the excavator. Water percolating through the site with a high concentration of calcium and sodium cations and CO_3 and SO_4 anions can promote growth of calcium carbonate and gypsum crystals in the cracks of bones. Growth of these crystals can fragment bone or render it so fragile that it fragments upon excavation. Crystal formation is particularly destructive of teeth. This process in semi-arid environments acts primarily on bone in the upper levels of a site. It can not account for the pattern of fragmentation observed at Farukhabad. Soil pH may also affect the state of fragmentation of bones but should be constant within a site. Somewhat related to both of the factors discussed above is soil types and their distribution within the site. In the Near East, within any one site, the soil type is fairly uniform from a geological perspective. Some fragmentation results from the process of excavation but this should be constant with any one excavator and any one site and could not account for the observed fragmentation.

The major post-depositional destructive forces acting on bone can be disregarded as causes of the pattern of fragmentation. This leaves two possible explanations for the observed differences. The first of these is the treatment of the bone by the inhabitants of the site. Meat may either be left on the bone or removed for preparation. In either case limb bones will be broken for the removal of marrow/fat and the skull broken for the removal of the brain. Removal of bones from meat before or after cooking, and simply breaking them in half to obtain the marrow/fat (Hole, Flannery, and Neely, 1969:291) will produce fewer fragments than smashing them. An extreme example of the latter occurs when meat containing bone is beaten with a rock or mortar and pestle, smashing the bones within the meat (Butzer 1964:427; Gould 1969:18; Lubbock 1864:416). The Lapps break the bones within the meat and then boil the result, allowing the marrow/fat to permeate the meat (Lubbock 1864:416). Quick burial or the discarding of bones directly into garbage pits will result in less fragmentation because of reduced exposure to wetting/drying and heating/cooling. Dogs and other vertebrates kept within the settlement can be a source of fragmentation of bone. Dogs are present at Farukhabad but no elements exhibited evidence of carnivore gnawing. It is unlikely that the observed differences in fragmentation among phases is the result of different densities of carnivores.

A second possible explanation for the observed

Table 68: Unidentifiable to Identifiable Density Ratios by Phase

	Elamite	Jemdet Nasr	Late Uruk	Middle Uruk	Early Uruk	Farukh-Bayat
Limb-Skull & Rib	27.8	9.2	21.6	28.7	28.1	23.2
Teeth	2.9	1.0	3.6	2.8	1.9	1.4

differences is dissimilarities in the cultural contexts of the samples excavated for each phase. The Jemdet Nasr excavation units do not include any pit features. The Elamite and all of the Uruk phases include samples of pits. The Farukh-Bayat phase more closely resembles the Jemdet Nasr in features sampled but has a ratio of unidentifiable to identifiable limb and skull material which falls in with the Elamite and Uruk phases. Further, according to the argument presented previously, one would expect greater levels of fragmentation in the absence of pit features. Fragmentation in the Jemdet Nasr is comparatively very low.

In summary, differences among phases in degree of fragmentation of limb and skull elements exist. In particular, this is noteable with the comparatively very low fragmentation in the Jemdet Nasr. These differences are probably due to distinct techinques for preparation of meat and/or dissimilar sampling of the phases. From the available data it appears that the former is more important than the latter; however, a sample of Jemdet Nasr material from pits is needed.

Taking into consideration the depressed level of fragmentation of the Jemdet Nasr, Table 67 may be examined for relative changes in occurrence of different categories of material. The density ratios for unidentifiable limb, skull, and ribs is low in the Farukh-Bayat and very high in the Elamite. The density ratios is low in the Farukh-Bayat and very high in the Elamite. The density ratios for the Uruk phases form an intermediate group. This variablility is probably due to differences among the phases in the types of deposits sampled. A large amount of the Elamite volume was removed from pit features. Very little of the Farukh-Bayat material was excavated from pits. A similar argument can be employed to account for the differences among density ratios observed in the unidentifiable teeth, identifiable teeth, and identifiable limb and skull categories. A similar argument could be utilized for the vertebral fragments category except for two anomalies. The occurrence of vertebral fragments in Early Uruk is much lower than expected and much higher than expected in the Middle Uruk.

ORDER CARNIVORA (THE CARNIVORES)

Hyaena hyaena: A right ulna and radius of a striped hyaena were recovered from an Elamite unit. Flannery, notes that the hyaena is not uncommon on the Deh Luran Plain at present. A single element from a hyaena was recovered from the Ali Kosh phase at Ali Kosh. Because only one element was recovered, although the hyaena is apparently common in the area, Flannery suggested that this species was not part of the diet (Hole, Flannery and Neely 1969:317). The same interpretation can be applied at Farukhabad. Neither of the two elements from Farukhabad exhibit any evidence of buring or butchering.

Felis sp. A small cat is represented by a scapula recovered from a Jemdet Nasr excavation unit. The scapula is too small for the jungle cat, *F. chaus*, and probably represents a wild cat, *F. catus* (see Lay 1967:215). There is no evidence that the animal was eaten.

Vulpes sp.: The 15 elements or fragments of elements that could be assigned to this genus represent at least 10 individuals. The red fox, *V. vulpes*, occurs at present on the Deh Luran Plain and was apparently eaten at Ali Kosh and Tepe Sabz (Hole, Flannery, and Neely 1969:314). Hatt (1959:38) quotes Reed in noting that the red fox is eaten during the winter in Kurdistan (northeastern Iraq). Although there are no butchering marks on any of the elements from Farukhabad and only one, a proximal femur, exhibits evidence of having been affected by fire, it will be assumed that foxes were utilized by the inhabitants. They may have been eaten and, possibly, utilized for their pelts. Since the fox would have been captured away from the site, if they had been utilized exclusively for thier pelts, we would expect to find in the site only elements of the manis and pes, which is not in fact the case. The distribution of elements and

THE FAUNAL REMAINS

Table 69: Density Ratios for the Major Mammal Groups by Phase

Mammal	Elamite	Jemdet Nasr	Late Uruk	Middle Uruk	Early Uruk	Farukh-Bayat
Canis spp.	0.27	0.00	0.00	0.27	0.16	0.13
Equus spp.	1.75	0.27	0.41	1.31	2.18	0.20
Ovis	0.19	0.22	0.14	0.20	0.00	0.06
Capra	0.15	0.35	0.17	0.10	0.08	0.02
O-C-(G)	8.56	8.61	6.17	5.27	5.00	3.72
Gazella	0.15	0.17	0.03	0.23	0.16	0.17
Bos	2.09	0.17	0.17	0.13	0.24	0.12
Sus	0.19	0.40	0.00	0.00	0.00	0.00

number of minimum individuals by phase is provided in Table 66.

Canis aureus: The jackal is considered in this report because material representing this species is absent. None of the material identified as *Canis* sp. fell within the size range of the jackal. Flannery (Hole, Flannery, and Neely 1969:314) notes that the jackal was absent from Ali Kosh and Tepe Guran, and Reed (1961:36) notes that no jackal remains were recovered at Jarmo. Flannery suggests that the absence of jackal remains from the sites on the Deh Luran Plain is indicative of some factor of human selection. Foxes are present in the sites on the plain while the jackal, which is at present the most common large, wild mammal on the plain, is absent. Since the jackal can be frequently observed during the daylight hours, Flannery's suggestion that the bias is because of the strictly nocturnal habits of the jackal as opposed to the partially diurnal habits of the fox is incorrect. Whatever the reason, it is evident that there was selection of foxes over jackals at Farukhabad.

Canis spp. The difficulty in distinguishing elements of the domestic dog. *C. familiaris*, from those of the small Near Eastern wolf, *C. lupus pallipes*, has been discussed by several authors (Reed 1961; Clutton-Brock 1962; Lawrence 1967). Lawrence suggests two criteria for distinguishing mandibles and maxillae of dogs and wolves, both related to the shortening of the muzzle found in some domestic dogs. One is the crowding of teeth, particulary in the mandible, so that overlapping or skewing of teeth occurs. The other is the shortening of the mandibular tooth row so that the posterior teeth bend up along the anterior edge of the coronoid process. The lower second and particularly the lower third molar appear to be rooted in this anterior edge. Using these criteria, two mandibles and a maxilla can be considered to come from the dog, *C. familiaris*. Two of the elements, one mandible and the maxilla, are from one unit in B11-12 and are identifiable as dog. This unit is not a screened sample and the analysis does not include other material from this unit. A right mandible from a screened unit retains fragments of most of its teeth. Its tooth row is so crowded anteriorly that the alveolae of the second premolar are continuous with those of the first and third premolars. The second premolar is also skewed and the posterior tooth row bends up sharply after the first molar (Plate 21a). The other mandible exhibits crowding. In the maxilla, the second premolar overlaps the third. All three of these elements are not as large as those of a greyhound and compare well with German shepherd. All material identified as *C. familiaris* is from Elamite units.

There are 24 other elements, including fragments of two additional mandibles and one maxilla, that could not be identified definitely as either wolf or dog. These are recorded as *Canis* spp. The number of elements and minimum individuals by phase is presented in Table 66. The density ratios for the material identified as *Canis* spp. are provided in Table 69. None of the canid material exhibited any evidence of burning or butchering.

ORDER PERISSODACTYLA
(THE ODD-TOED UNGULATES)

Equus sp.: The members of this genus known to occur or to have occurred in southwestern Iran are the ass, *E. asinus*, the half ass, *E. hemionus*, and the horse, *E. caballus*. The two subgenera of zebras have been eliminated from consideration since there is no evidence of their having been in the area.

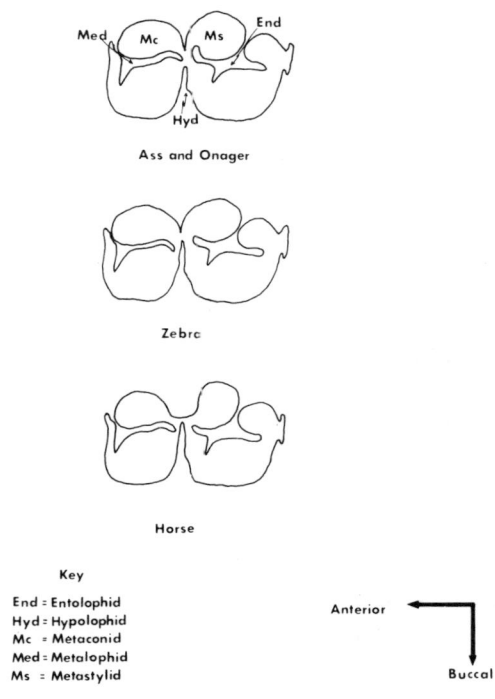

Figure 96. Equid dentitions.

In this genus the skeletal elements of each species are so similar that unless one recovers complete or nearly complete skulls or skeletons, it is almost impossible to identify them. Hilzheimer (1941:9–14) has proposed an index for separating complete metacarpals that appears to be reliable; unfortunately, no complete metacarpals were recovered from Farukhabad. The usual method of separating subgenera and even species of equids involves the use of numerous tooth characters. The utility of many of these characters as tools of identification is questionable (Groves and Mazak 1967). Groves and Mazak conclude that some of the criteria are reliable; those related to the lower teeth seem to be the most meaningful. Experience suggests that at least two of the characters described by Groves and Mazak for the lower teeth are valid for separating mandibles of the horse from those of the ass and half ass. The teeth used must be permanent and should be either the fourth premolar or a first or second molar. Examples with more than one tooth associated with a mandible are best. The two characters considered reliable are: the shape of the trough between the metaconid and the metastylid, and the size of the hypolophid (Fig. 96).

The only occurrence of equid material that satisfied all of these restrictions is a set of mandibles from an immature individual from an Elamite excavation unit. The fourth premolars are not yet erupted and the third premolar is only slightly worn. Using the ages of eruption provided by Silver (1963:291), this animal would have been about three years old; using the ages of eruption provided by Sisson and Grossman (1953:405), it would have been three and one half. The third molars are missing from both mandibles. All of the molars and the permanent premolars have a broad, u-shaped though between the metaconid and the metastylid. This is typical of the horse as opposed to the v-shaped though typical of the ass and half ass. The hypolophid extends up and between the entolophid and the metalophid, a condition also typical of the horse. In the ass and half ass, the hypolophid does not extend up between the entolophid and the metalophid. If these two criteria are reliable, then these two mandibles (Plate 21b,c) represent the horse, *E. caballus*. One of the lower incisors associated with these mandibles has an area of unusual wear on the labial surface (Plate 21e) which may be the result of the presence of a lip ring.

The 162 equid elements are scattered and represent at least 49 individuals (Table 66). There appears to be a concentration of equid material in the Early Uruk (Table 69).

In all but the Elamite phase, the equids are probably the half ass. The half ass was certainly available locally. There is no evidence of butchering or burning on any of the equid material. The half ass was probably hunted and utilized as a source of meat and hides. We can not exclude the possibility they may have been kept for labor. The horse was not available locally and must have been imported as a domesticate. Its introduction into the area complicates the interpretation of the Elamite equid material.

ORDER ARTIODACTYLA
(THE EVEN-TOED UNGULATES)

Sus scrofa: The pig is represented by 36 elements from at least 13 individuals. The best criterion of domestication for pigs is the reduction of the third molar (Hole, Flannery, and Neely 1969:309-11). Only one lower third molar was recovered and it is too fragmentary to measure. Whether the pigs from this site were domestic, wild, or a mixture of the two is uncertain.

Elements identified as *S. scrofa* were recovered only from Jemdet Nasr and Elamite excavation units (Table 66). Of the 31 pig elements from the Jemdet Nasr phase grouping, 25 are, in fact, from the few Early Dynastic I units which for the purpose of this study have been included in the Jemdet Nasr. The remaining 6 Jemdet Nasr pig elements are from the latest Jemdet Nasr units.

None of the pig elements exhibited evidence of butchering and only one, a mandible fragment, has been affected by fire. The pig was probably a part of the diet of the inhabitants of Farukhabad in the latest phases. The wild pig is common in Iran inhabiting gardens, riverine thickets, and any place where there is sufficient food and cover.

Dama dama mesopotamica: The Persian fallow deer is represented by a right distal tibia and a left radius, both from a mature individual. These two elements were recovered from a Middle Uruk excavation unit. This animal at one time was found throughout the Near East on forested hills, in mountain ranges, and riverine forests. It is nearly extinct at present (Harrison 1968:368); only a few individuals are known to exist in the tamarisk and poplar forests along the Dez and Karkeh Rivers.

There is no evidence that the animal was butchered or cooked. This combined with the rarity of elements might suggest that the fallow deer, like the hyaena, was not eaten. The fallow deer, in contrast to the hyaena, was probably rarely seen by the inhabitants of the area. It was probably not systematically hunted, but was killed, if possible, whenever encountered.

OVIS, CAPRA, AND GAZELLA

The skeletons of all three of these animals, the sheep, the goat, and the gazelle, are similar and it is difficult to identify individual elements. Separating elements of gazelles from those of sheep and goats is easier than separating sheep from goat material. At the time I did the identification of the Farukhabad material (1969-70), I felt comfortable with only five elements for separating sheep from goat. These were the petrous-temporal, horn core, calcaneum, distal metapodial, and the third phalanx. The criteria for separating all of these are discussed in Boessneck, Müller, and Teichert, (1964). At present, 1979, I utilize nearly all of the criteria delineated by Boessneck et al. except for some on tarsals and carpals, a few limb articulations, and the phalanges. I no longer feel that the third phalanx is reliable and, although they are identified in the appendices, they have not been utilized in sheep/goat calculations. The elements identified as sheep or as goat are utilized in this report to estimate the sheep/goat ratio. Hence, it is important to utilize only these elements that are reliable. Elements that could not be identified as sheep or as goat were classified as sheep-goat.

Almost any gazelle limb element can be distinguished from that of a sheep or goat. There are minor structural differences and gazelle limb elements tend to be longer and lighter. However, only those elements listed above as distinctive for sheep and goats and some limb elements that were obviously lighter, especially the first phalanx, were identified as gazelle. This means that the category of bones identified as sheep-goat, *Ovis-Capra*, probably include some gazelle limb elements as well as all of the gazelle teeth recovered.

There were 1764 elements or fragments of elements that could be classified as sheep, goat, or gazelle. Of these, 51 (representing at least 31 individuals) could be identified as sheep. Another 72 elements (representing at least 43 individuals) are goats and 41 elements (representing a minimum of 23 individuals) are gazelles. The remaining 1,600 elements could be identified only as *Ovis-Capra(-Gazella)*. The distribution of these elements by phase is presented in Table 66. Table 69 provides the density ratios of sheep, goat, and gazelle material. Measurements made on distal metapodials are presented in Table 70. A graph of these measurements by phase and species is provided (Fig. 97).

Ovis aries and Ovis orientalis: There is an abundance of sheep material, including cranial elements, while horn cores are virtually absent. Although female wild sheep, *O. orientalis*, sometimes lack horns (Harrison 1968:341), the absence of sheep horn cores from the excavations at Farukhabad would seem to indicate a largely hornless and hence largely female, domestic population (there exists the possibility that cores were selectively removed from the area). This contention is further sup-

Table 70: Distal Metapodials of *Ovis, Capra* and *Gazella* Recovered: Measurements and Identifications

Phase	Excavation Unit	Inner Spool (mm)	Outer Spool (mm)	$\frac{\text{Inner}}{\text{Outer}} \times 100$	Genus
Elamite	B 6	15.88	8.86	55.79	*Capra*
		16.35	8.80	53.82	
	B 7 F. 3	15.55	9.54	61.55	*Capra*
	B 11 upper	15.35	10.07	65.60	*Ovis*
	B 12 upper	16.27	9.00	55.32	*Capra*
		15.70	8.84	56.30	*Capra*
	B 18	15.20	8.35	54.93	*Capra*
		15.04	7.67	50.99	
E.D.I.	A 3 all	16.65	11.05	66.37	*Ovis*
	A 5 e	16.25	11.78	72.49	*Gazella*
		16.00	11.50	71.87	*Gazella*
	B 20 n	16.11	10.10	62.69	*Capra*
		14.88	8.20	55.11	
		14.43	9.52	65.97	*Ovis*
Jemdet-Nasr	A 7 n	17.82	10.05	59.76	*Capra*
		15.98	9.12	57.07	*Capra*
		15.94	9.60	60.23	*Capra*
	A 8 s	13.76	7.78	57.27	*Capra*
		14.19	8.17	57.58	
	A 8 below F. 8	15.04	10.14	67.42	*Ovis*
		15.82	10.73	67.83	
	A 9 & 10 sw	15.41	10.34	67.10	*Ovis*
	A 11 center	15.45	10.74	69.51	*Ovis*
		14.55	9.74	66.94	
	A 11 sw	14.00	8.80	62.86	*Capra*
	A 12 n	15.55	10.00	64.31	*Ovis*
		14.82	9.25	62.41	
		13.75	9.26	70.18	*Gazella*
		13.69	9.48	69.24	
	A 17 south	16.19	11.86	73.25	*Gazella*
	B 21 south	14.75	8.56	58.03	*Capra*
	B 22 lower n	14.78	8.70	58.86	*Capra*
		14.52	8.76	60.33	
		15.16	8.70	57.39	*Capra*
	B 24 F. 18	14.50	8.46	58.34	*Capra*
		14.62	8.07	55.19	
	B 24 upper n	15.64	10.60	67.77	*Ovis*
		15.77	10.44	66.20	*Ovis*
		15.05	10.58	70.30	*Gazella*
	B 24 s	14.20	10.33	72.75	*Gazella*
	B 27 w	15.15	9.40	62.05	*Capra*
Late Uruk	A 21 s	16.80	9.28	55.24	*Capra*
	B 30 w	15.27	8.82	57.76	*Capra*
Middle Uruk	B 32 lower n	15.09	9.11	60.37	Unident.
		14.65	9.40	64.16	Unident.
Early Uruk	B 36 lower	14.60	8.10	55.48	*Capra*
		15.20	9.50	62.50	
	B 36 upper nw	14.10	10.10	71.63	*Gazella*
		15.10	10.80	71.52	
Farukh-Bayat	A 22 F. 24	17.92	10.35	57.76	*Capra*
	A 34 all	15.37	10.64	67.64	*Ovis*
		14.93	10.10	67.65	
		15.44	10.77	69.75	*Ovis*
		16.19	11.31	69.86	
	B 37 all	19.25	11.36	59.01	*Capra*
	B 40 upper e	15.99	10.76	67.29	*Ovis*
	B 47 se	13.62	8.02	58.88	*Capra*

THE FAUNAL REMAINS

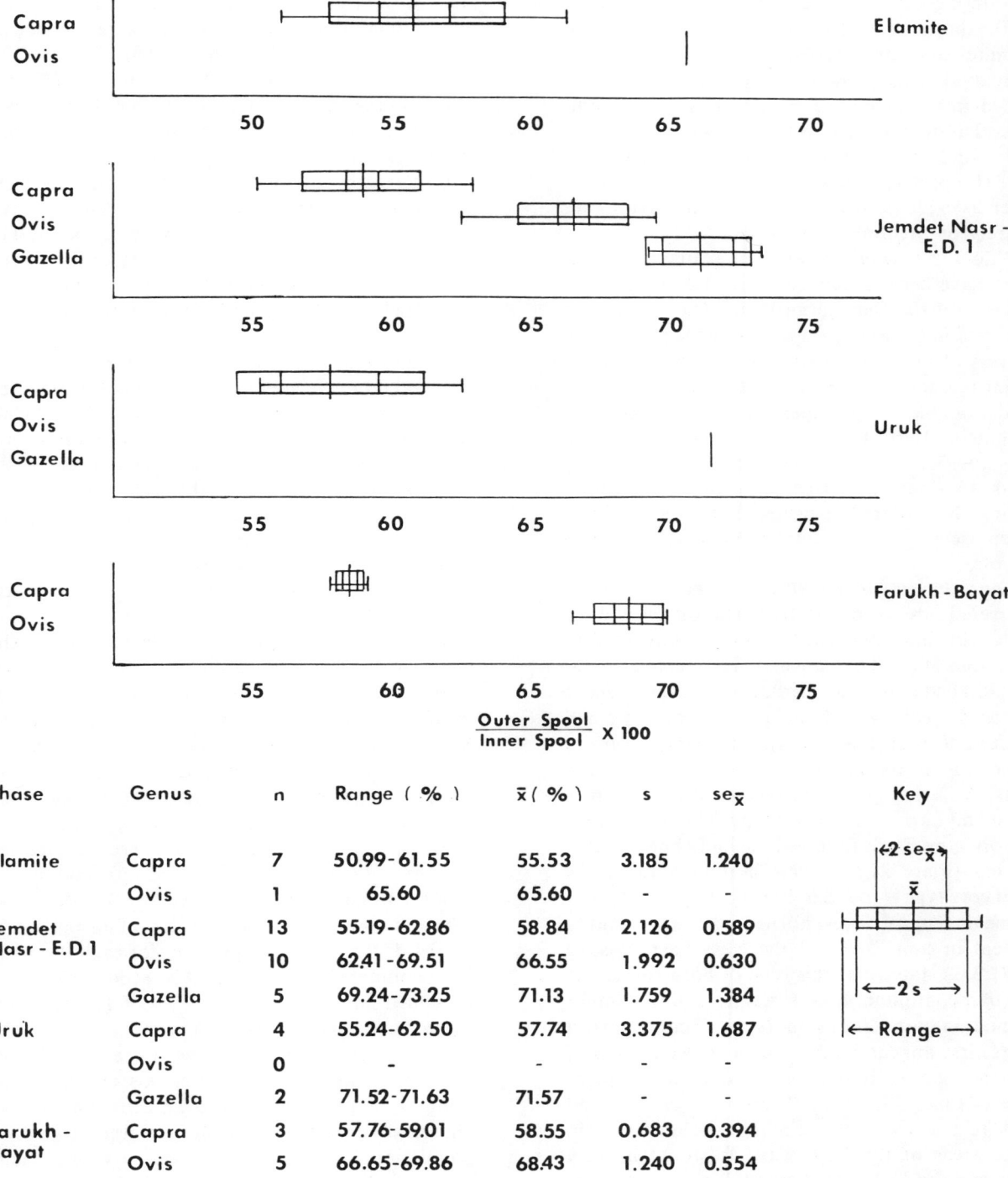

Figure 97. Measurements of the distal metapodials of sheep, goats, and gazelle.

ported by the two horn cores that were recovered. One of these, from a Farukh-Bayat unit, must be from a domestic individual, since it has a definite keel on the anterior edge that extends to the base of the horn core. The second core is from an Elamite unit and probably represents a wild individual. This horn core, although broken, was keeled posteriorly. The Farukh-Bayat core indicates that domestic sheep were present in this early phase and, although the Elamite core is from a wild sheep, it is from a late phase and cannot be taken as evidence that the sheep of this phase were entirely or predominately wild.

Wild sheep would have been available locally. They have been hunted recently in a rolling area just east of the Deh Luran Plain. They have been observed in fall and spring crossing the plain in the process of moving out to or back from the Jebel Hamrin, a low ridge west of the Deh Luran Plain.

Identifiable sheep elements were recovered from all but the Early Uruk phase (Tables 66 and 69). The absence of sheep elements from the Early Uruk does not imply that sheep were not utilized during this phase, but rather that no identifiable sheep remains were recovered from a small sample.

Capra hircus hircus: All of the goat horn cores recovered are medially flattened or twisted or both. This indicates that the goats at Farukhabad are domestic. The horn cores recovered at Farukhabad can be divided into two types. One is flattened medially and has a comparatively small amount of twist (Plate 21e,f). This scimitar type of horn core is found only in Elamite excavation units. All living goats observed on the Deh Luran Plain had horn cores of this type. The second type of horn core is not flattened medially but is highly twisted (Plate 21g,h). This homonymous screw horn core type is found in Farukh-Bayat and Early Dynastic I units. Screw horned goats are found at present in some areas of the Near East. Epstein (1971:277) states that this type of horn forms one end of a continuum from screw horned to scimitar horned in populations in Israel. Screw horned goats first appear in the fourth millennium B.C. and they gradually became the dominant type of goat (Zeuner 1963:140). There has been a trend back to goats with the scimitar type horn core in some areas of the Near East. It would be very interesting to know what breed characteristics are associated with scimitar versus screw horned goats. Changes through time and/or space of horn core type are to be understood in terms of changes in strategies of utilization of goats which are based on differences in ecology, physiology, production, and/or reproduction between the two types of goats. Identifiable goat elements were recovered from all phases (Tables 66 and 69).

Gazella subgutturosa: On the basis of horn cores, all the gazelle elements are from the goitered gazelle, *G. subgutturosa*. This gazelle is common on the Deh Luran Plain at present only because it is protected by law. We observed several groups of five to six individuals during two one-day trips. One of the reasons for the heavy predation on the gazelle in the area is the high quality of the meat. Elements and minimum individuals by phase are presented in Table 66 and density ratios in Table 69.

Ovis-Capra(-Gazella): There are 1,600 elements that could only be identified as sheep or goat or, in a few cases, possibly gazelle. This number illustrates how strongly sheep and goats predominate in the fauna of Farukhabad. The number of elements specifically identifiable as sheep or goat is only an indicator of the changing ratio of sheep to goats through the phases. These 1,600 sheep-goat (-gazelle) elements provide us with information on the butchering techniques used on sheep and goats and their life expectancy.

The sample of various limb elements for each phase is not large enough, except perhaps in the Jemdet Nasr, to allow the construction of survivorship curves as done for Ali Kosh and Tepe Sabz (Hole, Flannery and Neely 1969:285). A list of each type of element by phase and by fusion is presented in Table 71. Table 72 codes each element for fusion and presents the score by phase. The order of elements in the table has been altered to present them in order of fusion with coding as follows: fused bones were scored as 1.0, unfused as 0.0, and elements in the process of fusing were scored as 0.5. The average score for each element was computed and it is this score which is presented in Table 72. All ages of fusion were taken from Silver (1963:286).

Several observations can be made from these two tables. No discernible order exists in the small samples of the Farukh-Bayat and the three Uruk phases. If animals are being removed from the population, with fewer animals surviving each successive year, then one would expect that the scores in a phase should decrease as the age of fusion increases. This is the case in the Jemdet

THE FAUNAL REMAINS

Table 71: Raw Fusion Data for the Limb Elements of the Sheep-Goat(-Gazelle) Recovered at Tepe Farukhabad

Element	Elamite	Jemdet Nasr	Late Uruk	Middle Uruk	Early Uruk	Farukh-Bayat
Second Phalanx	0u 2f 0i 2in	4u 16f 1i 13in	3u 6f 0i 2in	1u 7f 0i 0in	0u 2f 0i 0in	0u 9f 0i 1in
First Phalanx	3u 2f 0i 9in	14u 44f 0i 25in	4u 6f 0i 4in	0u 13f 0i 5in	0u 5f 0i 1in	3u 9f 0i 13in
Prox. Tibia	1u 1f 2i 0in	4u 5f 1i 2in	0u 0f 0i 0in	1u 0f 0i 0in	0u 1f 0i 0in	0u 1f 0i 1in
Dist. Tibia	1u 2f 0i 2in	5u 10f 0i 1in	2u 4f 0i 0in	2u 4f 1i 0in	0u 3f 0i 0in	2u 2f 0i 0in
Prox. Femur	4u 1f 0i 2in	13u 3f 0i 1in	1u 1f 0i 0in	4u 0f 0i 1in	1u 2f 0i 0in	2u 4f 0i 0in
Dist. Femur	3u 4f 0i 0in	13u 2f 0i 3in	1u 1f 0i 0in	3u 2f 0i 2in	0u 0f 0i 1in	1u 1f 0i 0in
Prox. Radius	0u 6f 0i 0in	0u 17f 0i 1in	0u 1f 0i 0in	0u 6f 0i 0in	0u 2f 0i 0in	0u 5f 0i 0in
Dist. Radius	1u 1f 0i 1in	7u 4f 0i 3in	1u 1f 0i 0in	0u 0f 0i 0in	0u 1f 0i 0in	0u 2f 0i 0in
Prox. Humerus	2u 0f 0i 0in	4u 4f 2i 0in	0u 0f 0i 0in	0u 1f 0i 0in	0u 0f 0i 0in	0u 1f 0i 0in
Dist. Humerus	0u 6f 1i 5in	8u 22f 1i 10in	0u 4f 0i 6in	2u 6f 1i 3in	1u 1f 0i 2in	1u 5f 0i 4in

Dist.: Distal
Prox.: Proximal
u: unfused
f: fused
i: in process of fusing
in: indeterminate

Nasr and Elamite with minor exceptions. In the Elamite and Jemdet Nasr, there is little attrition until the age of about 13 months. The mortality rate, usualy between 5 and 20 percent, of lambs in their first six months is not detected, possibly because the deaths take place away from the site.

Between the ages of 13 and 16 months, 20 to 30 percent of the animals are cropped. After this age there is little attrition in the population and 50 to 60 percent of the sheep and goats survive beyond the age of 42 months.

One element that does not support this pattern

Table 72: Scores of Fusion for Each Element by Phase: Elements Arranged in Order of Fusion*

Element	Age of Fusion in Months	Elamite	Jemdet Nasr	Late Uruk	Middle Uruk	Uruk	Farukh-Bayat
Prox. Humerus	36–42	0.00	0.50	n.d.	1.00	1.00	1.00
Dist. Femur	36–42	0.57	0.13	0.50	0.64	n.d.	0.50
Prox. Tibia	36–42	0.66	0.55	n.d.	0.00	1.00	1.00
Dist. Radius	36	0.50	0.36	0.50	n.d.	n.d.	1.00
Prox. Femur	30–36	0.20	0.18	0.50	0.00	0.66	0.66
Dist. Tibia	18–24	0.67	0.66	0.66	0.64	1.00	0.50
First Phalanx	13–16	0.40	0.75	0.60	1.00	1.00	0.75
Second Phalanx	13–16	1.00	0.78	0.66	0.87	1.00	1.00
Dist Humerus	10	0.93	0.72	1.00	0.72	0.50	0.83
Prox. Radius	10	1.00	1.00	1.00	1.00	1.00	1.00

Prox.: Proximal   Dist.: Distal   n.d.: no data
*Ages and hence the order, from Silver, 1963

in the Elamite phase is the proximal femur. The majority of femurs are unfused and this results in an anomaly in the series of scores. Since there are only five proximal femurs in the Elamite sample, the high ratio of unfused to fused may be due to sampling error. It may also be due to some bias in the selection of unfused proximal femurs. The score for the proximal femurs in the Jemdet Nasr is also at variance with that of the other elements. In this phase the low score is supported by a similar score for the distal femur. Since the samples are large for both elements, 16 proximal femurs and 15 distal femurs, the anomaly in the Jemdet Nasr is due to the recovery of an abnormally high number of femurs from young animals. This indicates that femurs from immature sheep and goats were being selectively brought into the site or into the area of the site sampled. Two other elements exhibited anomalies. Data available for the distal humerus and proximal radius from Farukhabad suggest that the ages of fusion provided by Silver do not apply to domestic sheep and goats in southwestern Iran during these phases. According to Silver, these two elements fuse at the same age. From Table 71, it is apparent that all of the proximal radii are fused, while several of the distal humerii are not. The fact that this remains true for all phases decreases the possibility that this observation is due to sampling. It appears that in this area during these phases, the proximal radius was fusing prior to the distal humerus. In a study of age of fusing, Todd and Todd (1938) suggest that the proximal radius fuses at six months, two months before the fusion of the distal humerus. Todd and Todd's study is based on modern domestic sheep while Silver's study is based on semi-wild hill sheep. It is possible that this variance in age of fusion is due to differences in nutrition.

There are other problems with the data on fusion than those defined above. Sheep and goat elements are combined, hence the apparent age structure may represent an average of the survivorship of sheep and goats. There is no reason to expect that sheep and goats are managed in an identical fashion. The samples for each phase represents survivorship averaged over several years. Management strategies may be expected to vary over time and lamb mortality is quite variable. However, it is fair to emphasize that in the later phases at Farukhabad, for which we have larger samples, there is a larger than expected number of animals surviving beyond three years. The percentage surviving beyond three years, 50 to 60 percent, is more than might be predicted assuming that females were being kept for milk and most males slaughtered as juveniles. It appears that males were being retained in higher percentages in the herds than they are at present (1:10 to 1:50).

Elements of sheep-goat(-gazelle) are the only ones exhibiting evidence of butchering. Two astragalii have several cut marks on the anterior face, across the condyles. This is where they would occur if the butcher had missed in an attempt to separate the lower pelvic limb joint between the tarsals and the metatarsal and cut above the proper point. Only two femur fragments exhibit cutting marks. Butchering marks on the head of each are probably the result of separating the femur from the acetabulum. No pelvis was recovered intact. Most of the breaks are at the acetabulum and do not appear to be recent. The pelves may have been broken in attempting to separate the femur from the acetabulum. An ulna has several marks just below the olecranon, the point where one would cut in an attempt to sever the triceps (*Triceps brachii*), the deep flexor (*Flexor digitalis profundus*), and the middle flexor of the carpus (*Flexor carpi ulnaris*), to separate the ulna from the humerus. A radius shows cut marks under the medial lip of the proximal articulation, on the radial tuberosity at the insertion of the *Biceps brachii*. This mark represents an attempt to separate the radius from the humerus. Almost all of the distal humerii have marks but about only 17 of these are clearly the result of butchering activities. The majority of marks occur on the medial epicondyle near the origin of the middle flexor of the carpus (*F. carpi ulnaris*), and a branch of the medial flexor of the carpus (*F. carpi radialis*) and also where the lateral ligament (*Lig. collaterale ulnare*) attaches. These cuts were probably also made in an attempt to separate the ulna and the radius from the humerus.

The butchering technique for sheep-goat (-gazelle) at Farukhabad generally resembles that described for sheep-goat from Ali Kosh and Tepe Sabz (Hole, Flannery, and Neely 1969:288–291). The animal was skinned and the tail vertebrae were evidently carried away with the hide as none were encountered in the material from Farukhabad. The method for disjointing the head is unknown as none of the atlases and axes recovered exhibited butchering marks. Teeth and phalanges are quite common, so it may be assumed that butchering was done on the site. The metatarsals were disjointed, probably with the phalanges attached, as indicated by the marks on the astragalii. The distal portion of the pectoral limb, the metacarpal, and phalanges, can be separated easily without leaving any marks. Whether the metapodials were discarded, as suggested for Ali Kosh and Tepe Sabz (Hole, Flannery, and Neely 1969:290), is unknown. No metapodials were found intact, perhaps because they contain a large plug of marrow or fat.

The humerus was separated from the radius and ulna but it is unclear whether the scapula was separated from the humerus. No scapulae were recovered intact. The identifiable scapular material consists of fragments of complete glenoid fossae. Scapulae were evidently badly broken but whether this was due to butchering, preparation, or forces acting after they were discarded is unknown. The scapula is delicate and easily broken. There is no evidence that the tibia was separated from the femur but this can be accomplished without leaving any marks. The femur was separated from the pelvis by any means possible as blade marks were observed on femur heads and pelves appear to have been broken in butchering. In general, limb elements were broken for removal of marrow and fat. Complete limb elements, with the exception of one radius, were not recovered. Retouch on the ends of broken limb elements, as described by Flannery (Hole, Flannery, and Neely, 1969:291), was not observed. The sample of elements with butchering marks is quite small and no differences in technique between phases can be detected. The distal humerus was the element most frequently exhibiting butchering marks and examples were recovered from all phases.

Only ten sheep-goat(-gazelle) elements out of 1,600 exhibit evidence of having been affected by fire. These include two phalanges, two tarsii, two metapodial fragments, one proximal femur head, one distal humerus fragment, and two horn core fragments. The fire damage exhibited by these elements possibly results from roasting portions of meat on limb segments. If a hind limb were roasted with the metatarsal removed at its joint with the tibia, then the distal tibia, the tarsals and proximal femur would have no meat to protect them from the effects of the fire and would be burned. If the metatarsals and phalanges were left on them, all of these elements would be affected by fire. Humerii were separated from antebrachium. If it were then roasted, the distal end of the humerus would be exposed to the fire and burnt. The small number of burned elements indicates, however, that roasting on the bone was probably not the commonly used method of cooking meat. Alternative methods of cooking meat include roasting of meat after it has been removed from the bones and boiling either on the bone or after removal. Boiling of meat containing smashed bones versus removal of meat from bones to be cooked would explain the difference in fragmentation between the Elamite, Uruk and Farukh-Bayat phases and the Jemdet Nasr phase.

Bos taurus: Ninety elements recovered from Farukhabad could be assigned to this genus. The

Table 73: Measurements Made on the Elements of the Genus *Bos* Recovered

Phase	Excavation Unit	Element	Max. Height (mm)	Max. Length (mm)
Elamite	B 11 lower	Humerus	54.25*	—
	B 11 and 12	Dist. Metapodial	55.65*	—
		Dist. Metapodial	51.53*	—
		Dist. Metapodial	64.84*	—
		First Phalanx	33.24	64.67
		First Phalanx	38.70	61.15
		First Phalanx	27.59	63.25
		First Phalanx	u.m.	63.34
		Second Phalanx	28.76	41.35
		Third Phalanx	24.74	62.56
		Third Phalanx	27.38	66.09
		Third Phalanx	u.m.	69.19
		Third Phalanx	27.20	67.40
Farukh-Bayat	A 26 north	M_3	—	40.83

* : Read Max. Width for these elements
u.m.: unmeasurable
— : measurement not taken

possibility that the genus *Bison* occurred in the area has been rejected (Hole, Flannery, and Neely 1969:298). The criterion for differentiating wild and domestic cattle, *B. primigenius* and *B. taurus*, is a decrease in size of several skeletal elements. Only twelve of the *Bos* elements recovered are diagnostic and complete enough to be measured (see Table 73). Eleven of these 12 elements are from Elamite units. All of the Elamite elements are from domestic individuals. They compare well with those of the British Neolithic (Jewell 1963: 80–91). They variously fall in the range of the material from Tepe Sabz or Ras al Amiya (Hole, Flannery, and Neely 1969:305–306). One distal humerus measured only 54.2 mm in width which is comparable only to some Roman material (Jewell 1963:84) and is smaller than that of a recent domestic cow from Luristan, Iran (Hole, Flannery, and Neely 1969:305). These elements imply only that cattle of the latest phase were domestic. Fortunately, the other measurable element is from the earliest phases, the Farukh-Bayat, and is from a domestic individual. The element is an M_3 that is comparable to those of the European Neolithic (Degerbol 1963:70). Because the earliest and latest phases each contained elements from domestic individuals, all the cattle represented by elements recovered from all phases are probably domestic. The sample of measurable elements is too small to determine a ratio of males to females.

All of the elements recovered were fused except for two distal radii and the proximal humerus. These epiphyses both fuse between 42 and 48 months of age (Silver 1963:285).

The number of elements and minimum individuals by phase is provided in Table 66. The density of cattle is nearly constant in the first five phases at Farukhabad. In the Elamite the density of cattle elements is much higher (Table 69). Whether this increase is important can only be determined by examining the relationships of density ratios of cattle to those of other mammals in each phase.

None of the cattle elements exhibit evidence of butchering or of having been affected by fire. Nevertheless, cattle were probably utilized as a food resource as well as a source of hides and possibly labor.

ORDER RODENTIA (THE RODENTS)

Only mandibles, maxillae, and isolated teeth were examined during the analysis of the material of this order. There are three reasons for this: 1) the lack of post-cranial comparative material; 2) the indistinctiveness of post-cranial material; 3) the difficulty in distinguishing intrusive from non-intrusive material. Only two of the three criteria used in distinguishing intrusive from non-intrusive reptiles are useful in sorting out intrusive rodents. The criterion that cannot be used is the depth of the material within the site, since rodents are not restricted to the upper one m but will burrow quite deeply. Relative discoloration and association with known burrows are two criteria that can be used. A list of elements considered non-intrusive and their provenience is provided in the appendices.

Mus musculus: Five mandibles, containing varying numbers of teeth, represent the house mouse. *M. musculus* is quite common at present on the Susiana and Deh Luran Plains but is restricted to areas of human habitation and areas of lush vegetation. A mandible of the extinct ancestor of the house mouse has been recovered from a discarded bitumen lump from a Jemdet Nasr level. The lump was removed during the Jemdet Nasr period from an asphalt seep on the Deh Luran Plain which must have been collecting material since at least the Late Pleistocene.

All of the material identified as *M. musculus* was recovered from Jemdet Nasr units. The material was excavated from within mud-lined rectangular pits that have been interpreted as storage bins.

Tatera indica: The Indian gerbil is represented at Farukhabad by 16 mandibles, maxillae, and isolated teeth. We did not observe this animal on the Deh Luran Plain; however, our search was superficial. The Indian gerbil prefers moist soils with stands of grasses. I have trapped this animal in southwestern Iran only in irrigated fields, garden complexes, or degraded forests along the Dez and Karkeh Rivers. The drier areas of the plains in southwestern Iran are dominated by Sundevall's jird, *Meriones crassus*.

T. indica was recovered from only three of the five phases defined for this report (see the appendices). The Early Uruk units contained no rodent material, possibly the result of the small sample. The Elamite units contained elements identifiable as *T. indica* but all of them were judged intrusive. Some of these may not have been intrusive but, as the Elamite units were riddled with rodent burrows, no occurrence was very far from a burrow.

A SPECIAL NOTE ON MAMMAL ASSOCIATIONS

One interesting aspect of the distribution of the ungulates in the Farukh phase units deserves note. From an examination of Table 74, it is apparent that there is a difference in the number of gazelles and equids in th two excavations. This apparent difference was tested using a chi-square, with Yates correction, on the number of minimum individuals of ungulates by excavation. The result is statistically significant, suggesting that the occurrence of gazelles and equids in each excavation is not random. There is bias in the occurrence of one or the other animals in each excavation. A test using the number of elements recovered produced similar results.

Excavation A contains the remains of large structures built on prepared platforms. The structures of excavation B are small and without prepared platforms. It would seem that the inhabitants of large structures had preferential access to gazelles while rarely utilizing equids, and that the inhabitants of small structures utilized equids and had little access to gazelles. It has been noted above that gazelle meat is of high quality and is prized at present. The evidence from the Farukh phase suggests that in that phase at Farukhabad it was butchered primarily by high status individuals. Note that the other large ungulate, the cow, is almost equally distributed between the two excavations while both the sheep and goat were recovered only from units of excavation B.

CLASS MAMMALIA: SUMMARY AND CONCLUSIONS

Several trends in the utilization of different mammals are observable. Some of these have already been mentioned in the discussions of individual mammal taxa. Here, the primary emphasis will be placed on changes in utilization of taxa relative to each other.

The reader should keep in mind that such comparisons depend upon the assumption that the samples of faunal materials represent the full range of activities in each successive community. For the Farukh-Bayat and Late Uruk phases debris from both large and small buildings was sampled. In the Early and Middle Uruk units there is no evidence of large buildings, and the Jemdet Nasr units contain little evidence of small buildings. In addition, the Late Uruk deposits contain unique, probably non-residential, features. Unfortunately, the faunal samples are seldom large enough to control for such variation, so one must proceed with caution.

Table 74: Gazelles, Equids, Cattle, Sheep, and Goats in the Farukh Phase Excavations

	I by minimum indvs.		II by number of elements	
	Exc. A	Exc. B	Exc. A	Exc. B
Gazella subgutturosa	6	1	13	1
Equus spp.	2	7	5	12
Bos taurus	4	3	4	4
Ovis aries	0	3	0	3
Capra hircus hircus	0	5	0	6

Chi-sqaure, with Yates Correction, Test on Minimum Individuals of Gazelles and Equids by Excavation

	Exc. A	Exc. B	Total
Gazelle	6	1	7
Equid	2	7	9
Total	8	8	16

Observed O	Expected E	Expected (Yates) E(Y)	O–E(Y)	[O–E(Y)]²	[O–E(Y)]²/E(Y)
6	3.5	4.0	2	4	1.00
2	4.5	4.0	2	4	1.00
1	3.5	3.0	2	4	1.33
7	4.5	5.0	2	4	.80
					4.13*

THE COMPOSITION OF THE MAMMALIAN FAUNA

All but two of the wild mammals identified at Farukhabad could be found at present on the Deh Luran Plain. Both the red fox and the hyaena are quite common. The wolf is present although it is rarely observed. There is no recent record of the wildcat for the Deh Luran Plain; however, suitable habitat is available and it is probably present. The wild sheep is still hunted in the area. The Deh Luran Plain is one of the last areas in the Khuzestan area in which the gazelle is common. The half ass was undoubtedly an inhabitant of the area but is absent from the recent fauna. Similarly, the Persian fallow deer was apparently an inhabitant of the area but is no longer to be observed on the plain. The Indian gerbil is probably an inhabitant of the more lush areas of the plain, possibly being restricted at present to irrigated fields around the village of Musiyan. The house mouse is certainly present on the plain.

Conspicuous in their absence are numerous mammals known to occur or to have occurred on the plain or in the surrounding mountains. Hole, Flannery, and Neely (1969:262–3) recovered all of the animals listed above, except the fallow deer, from Ali Kosh and Tepe Sabz plus seven additional ones. Two of these, the beech marten and weasel, are represented by only a single individual and their absence from Farukhabad may be the result of an insufficient sample size. Another mammal not recorded at Farukhabad that occurs at Ali Kosh and Tepe Sabz is the long-eared hedgehog. The hedgehog is a shy, nocturnal animal and its presence at Ali Kosh and Tepe Sabz might be surprising were it not for the fact that hedgehogs are eaten at present in Kurdistan and are considered quite good (Flannery, personal communication). They are the prey of the fox and wildcat and could owe their occurrence at these sites to post-mortem transport. Two other taxa recorded at Ali Kosh and Tepe Sabz are Sundevall's jird and the bandicoot rat, *Nesokia indica*. Sundevall's jird inhabits drier areas than does the Indian gerbil and, interestingly Sundevall's jird is restricted, for the most part, to late levels of Ali Kosh just prior to the abandonment of this site. It is in these late levels of Ali Kosh that Helbaek (see Hole, Flannery, and Neely 1969:320) finds a tremendous increase in seeds of prosopis, a plant that he considers to have increased because of human corruption of hydrological and edaphic conditions. The bandicoot rat prefers moist ground that has a heavy plant cover. It appears to be restricted to stream, river and irrigation canal associations (Lay 1965:190). The bandicoot rat is represented at Ali Kosh by only two elements and its absence at Farukhabad may be the result of an insufficient sample. The wild goat, recorded at Ali Kosh, is absent from Farukhabad. Presumably it was present in the rugged areas near the Deh Luran Plain as it is still found on the Jebel Hamrin and in the Zagros Mountains behind Deh Luran (Hole, Flannery, and Neely 1969:266). Two other mammals present on the Deh Luran Plain, but not recovered from Ali Kosh, Tepe Sabz, or Farukhabad, are the jackal and the hare. The jackal has already been discussed. The hare, *Lepus capensis*, is certainly present on the plain and must be considered as a food source. Its absence is difficult to explain.

The wild forms from which each of the domestic taxa recorded at Farukhabad, with the exception of the horse, were derived are known to occur or have occurred in the area. Both wild goats and sheep are inhabitants of areas on or around the Deh Luran Plain. The progenitor of domestic cattle, *Bos primigenius*, was present on the plain. It was heavily utilized as a resource until the Sabz phase at Tepe Sabz (Hole, Flannery, and Neely 1969:303). It was not recovered from Farukhabad and it is not known when it became extinct in the area.

Since the wild ancestors of all of the three ungulates mentioned above are or were found in the area, we cannot be sure whether or not the domestic forms were introduced from outside the area. It is possible that they were but it is also possible that local wild populations were the source of the domestic populations or at least may have contributed to the gene pool. The horse certainly represents an introduction into the local fauna. The situation of the pig on the plain is an enigma. It is included in a discussion of domestic taxa, yet there is little osteological evidence that is was domestic in the area. As noted above, the wild pig is common on the Deh Luran Plain. Elements of the pig were uncommon in the material from Ali Kosh and Tepe Sabz. A single measurable element, a tooth, proved to be from a domestic individual. Because of the rarity of pig elements, Flannery suspects that the domestic individual was brought into the area and domestic pigs were not kept on the plain (Hole, Flannery, and Neely 1969:311). Pig material was recovered at Farukhabad only from the late units of the Jemdet Nasr and the Elamite Phase. Their appearance late in the sequence in quantity suggests that pigs were an introduced domesticate at Farukhabad.

COMPOSITION OF THE MAMMALIAN FAUNA IN EACH PHASE AND CHANGES BETWEEN PHASES

Presented below for each phase is a brief description of the composition of the mammal fauna preceded by a comparison of the composition of that phase to that of the antecedent phase. The comparison of the composition between phases is summarized from Table 69, while the composition of each phase is summarized from Table 76. Since the Farukh-Bayat Phases at Farukhabad are not preceded in the sample by another phase, no comparison of the Farukh-Bayat to an antecedent phase is provided. A comparison of the Farukh-Bayat at Farukhabad to the Bayat at Tepe Sabz is provided. The Bayat phase material from Tepe Sabz is summarized in Table 75.

The sheep-goat ratio provided in Table 76 is based on the sheep and goat elements identified exclusive of third phalanges and horn cores. As mentioned above, I no longer feel comfortable with identifications of third phalanges. Horn cores are excluded because goat horn cores are twice as likely to occur as are sheep horn cores since both sexes in goats have horns while only male sheep have horns.

The relative proportions of ungulates for each phase presented in Table 76 are proportions of counts of elements. Cattle, sheep, goats and gazelles have the same number of elements, so for these animals the proportion should reflect relative occurrence at the site. Equids have fewer elements and pigs more than the above taxa; for both of these the proportion must be compensated for this difference in number of elements. Cattle and equids are much larger than sheep and goats which are larger than the gazelle. Several workers have developed conversion factors for sheep, goats, and cattle. Depending on which estimate is used, one

Table 75: The Computation of the Density Ratios for the Bayat Phase at Tepe Sabz

	Counts of Elements by Mammal						
	Ovis-Capra	Gazella	Equus	Bos	Sus	Ovis	Capra
Bayat A1	16	10	4	5	3	2	1
A2	30	15	1	9	—	—	1
A3	62	16	8	5	1	2	6
	118	41	13	19	4	4	8

Estimated Volume Excavated

Bayat A1	15.75 m³
A2	18.75
A3	18.00
	52.50 m³

	Estimated Density Ratios						
	Ovis-Capra	Gazella	Equus	Bos	Sus	Ovis	Capra
Bayat A1	1.01	.63	.25	.82	*	*	*
A2	1.60	.80	.02	.48	*	*	*
A3	3.44	.88	.44	.28	*	*	*
	2.25	.78	.25	.36	.08	.09	.15

—: absent
* : not calculated

cow is worth six to twelve sheep or goats. These estimates are based on the weights of the animals and reflect only their use for meat. It is difficult to produce a conversion factor that considers multiple use. As a guide in the following discussion a conversion factor of 8:1 for sheep-goats to cattle will be utilized. The 8:1 factor will also be used for sheep-goats to equids. The factor is 1:1 for sheep to goats. Hence, in the following discussion, if eight sheep-goat elements were recovered for every cattle element, then it will be concluded that sheep-goats and cattle were of equal importance in the diet. If 64 sheep-goat elements were recovered for every cattle element then sheep-goats were eight times as important as were cattle.

Farukh-Bayat: During the Farukh-Bayat phases at Farukhabad, there is heavy dependence on sheep and goats. Members of these two species were twice as important as equids and four times as important as cattle. Sheep were utilized more than twice as frequently as were goats. Equids were more important than were cattle. Gazelle provided a minor component of the diet. Other mammals recovered from these phases include the fox and elements of the *Canis* spp. group. The canid material of the Bayat phase at Tepe Sabz has been referred to the species *C. familiaris,* the dog. This was done on the basis of osteological criterion as well as cultural context (Hole, Flannery, and Neely 1969:311–14). None of the canid material from the Farukh-Bayat at Farukhabad provided the necessary information to ascertain whether it was or was not dog. Also present in the area during these phases is the Indian gerbil. We have grouped the Farukh and Bayat phases together in this report for analysis. A comparison of the Farukhabad data with that from the Bayat phase at Tepe Sabz is valuable. We have been able to calculate the density ratios for the Bayat phase at Tepe Sabz for all ungulates as the authors have published the necessary raw data. Counts of elements recovered for each type of ungulate were obtained from tables in the fauna chapter (Hole, Flannery, and Neely 1969:262–330). The volume of the Bayat phase deposits was calculated from section drawings and the step-trench plan (Hole, Flannery, and Neely 1969:52 and 54). The densities obtained are provided in Table 75.

If the composition of the mammal fauna of the Bayat phase at Tepe Sabz was similar to that of the Farukh-Bayat phases at Farukhabad, we would expect, because of the differences in excavation technique, that the densities would be less at Sabz for all mammals. At Tepe Sabz all deposits were screened, including brick wall and brick collapse. At Farukhabad neither of these types of deposits were screened. Since bones are not normally recovered from walls and collapse, the amount of excavated screened deposit resulting in the recovery of a given number of bones would be greater at Tepe Sabz than at Farukhabad.

The composition of the mammal fauna in the Bayat phase at Tepe Sabz is not similar to that of the Faruk-Bayat phases at Farukhabad. The density of sheep-goat elements at Tepe Sabz is slightly more than half of that at Farukhabad while the density of elements of other ungulates is larger than at Tepe Sabz (Table 69 and 75). Equids are as important as sheep-goats, and cattle are more important than sheep-goats at Tepe Sabz. There is much greater reliance on cattle and equids at Tepe Sabz than at Farukhabad. The sheep-goat ratio at Tepe Sabz is similar to that for Farukhabad.

Early Uruk: In comparison to the Farukh-Bayat phases at Farukhabad there is an increase in density of sheep-goat elements. There is an increase in the density of both equid and cattle elements. Gazelle elements are recovered at the same level.

In the Early Uruk, sheep and goats are the predominately utilized mammal but are not the most important. Equids are clearly more important, in terms of diet, than sheep and goats. Sheep-goat are two-and-one-half times as important as cattle. Gazelle is a minor part of the diet. From the densities of identifiable sheep and goat it might appear that sheep were not utilized. However, the sample of elements used to calculate the sheep-goat ratio is one, a goat. Only one other mammal taxa was recorded from this phase, *Canis* spp. It is not known whether these elements represent the dog or the wolf.

Middle Uruk: In comparison to the Early Uruk, there is a decrease in the density of cattle and equid elements; all others increase. Equids are still more important than sheep-goats in this phase as only four sheep-goat elements were recovered for every equid element. Sheep-goats are five times more important than cattle. Sheep are utilized twice as frequently as are goats. Gazelles remain a minor component of the diet. Other mammals recorded for this phase include the fox, the dog or wolf, and the fallow deer.

Late Uruk: There is a major change in composition of the mammal fauna between the Middle and Late Uruk phases. The densities of equids, gazelle, and sheep drop while those of cattle, goats, and sheep-goats rise. For the first time cattle material occurs more frequently than gazelle. Sheep-goats are more important than both equids and cattle. Equids are two-and-one-half times as important as cattle. Sheep and goats are utilized with about the same frequency. Gazelle is exploited, relative to other taxa, at its lowest level in this phase. No canid material was recovered from this phase. The only other mammal represented in the sample is the Indian gerbil.

Jemdet Nasr: In comparison to the Late Uruk there is a decrease in the density of equids. The density of cattle elements remain the same while all other densities increase. Part of this increase may be due to decreased fragmentation. Pig material makes its first appearance in this phase. In this phase sheep-goats are more important, compared to other taxa, than in any other phase. Sheep-goats are four times as important as equids and six-and-one-half times as important as cattle. Equids are still more important than cattle. Pigs are more important than gazelles. Goats are one-and-a-half times as frequent as are sheep. Other mammals exploited in this phase are the fox and cat. The Indian gerbil and house mouse occur in the Jemdet Nasr but are probably not utilized.

Elamite: From the Jemdet Nasr to the Elamite, there is an increase in the occurrence of equid and cattle elements; all others decrease. There is a return to the greater reliance on equids that was last noted in the Middle Uruk. However, the horse makes its appearance in this phase and the equid material may represent a labor source rather than a food source. Cattle are of greater importance than sheep and goats and for the first time exceed equids in number of elements and probably importance. Sheep and goats are utilized in about equal frequency. Pigs and gazelles form a minor component of the diet. Dogs and possibly the wolf were recovered from the excavations. One other mammal was recovered, the hyaena, but it was probably not exploited.

COMMENTS ON THE ENVIRONMENT AT TEPE FARUKHABAD

The fauna recovered from Farukhabad is not sufficiently diverse enough to provide the informa-

Table 76: The Relative Proportions of Each Ungulate to the Other Ungulates by Phase for Farukhabad and the Bayat Phase at Tepe Sabz

Tepe Sabz
The Bayat Phase

Ovis-Capra	9.0:1	22.9:1	6.2:1		
Equus	—	1:1.3	1:1.4		Ident.*Ovis*:Ident.*Capra*
Gazella	—	—	2.2:1		3.0:1
	Equus	*Gazella*	*Bos*		

Tepe Farukhabad
The Farukh-Bayat Phase

Ovis-Capra	18.2:1	22.1:1	30.9:1		
Equus	—	1.2:1	1.7:1		Ident.*Ovis*:Ident.*Capra*
Gazella	—	—	1.4:1		2.5:1
	Equus	*Gazella*	*Bos*		

The Early Uruk Phase

Ovis-Capra	2.3:1	31.0:1	20.7:1		
Equus	—	13.5:1	9.0:1		Ident.*Ovis*:Ident.*Capra*
Gazella	—	—	1.1:5		0.1
	Equus	*Gazella*	*Bos*		

The Middle Uruk Phase

Ovis-Capra	4.0:1	22.4:1	39.2:1		
Equus	—	5.6:1	9.7:1		Ident.*Ovis*:Ident.*Capra*
Gazella	—	—	1.7:1		2:1
	Equus	*Gazella*	*Bos*		

The Late Uruk Phase

Ovis-Capra	15.0:1	179.0:1	35.8:1		
Equus	—	12.0:1	2.4:1		Ident.*Ovis*:Ident.*Capra*
Gazella	—	—	1:5.0		1:1.2
	Equus	*Gazella*	*Bos*		

The Jemdet Nasr Phases

Ovis-Capra	31.8:1	51.4:1	51.4:1	21.5:1		
Equus	—	1.6:1	1.6:1	1:1.5		Ident.*Ovis*:Ident.*Capra*
Gazella	—	—	1:1	1:2.4		1:1.6
Bos	—	—	—	1:2.4		
	Equus	*Gazella*	*Bos*	*Sus*		

The Elamite Phases

Ovis-Capra	4.8:1	56.2:1	4.1:1	45.0:1		
Equus	—	11.5:1	1.1:2	9.2:1		Ident.*Ovis*:Ident.*Capra*
Gazella	—	—	1.13:7	1:1.2		1.2:1
Bos	—	—	—	11.0:1		
	Equus	*Gazella*	*Bos*	*Sus*		

tion necessary to reconstruct the environment around the site during the occupation. However, some of the vertebrates, particularly the rodents, do provide some data.

The fish provide little data on the environment. We do not know if any were obtained locally, and some clearly were not. Import is a possibility even with the species that did or do occur locally. If we assume that all of the birds recovered had been obtained locally, there is no reason to hypothesize any change in the environment on the plain in order to account for their presence.

The rodent fauna from Farukhabad provides evidence that there has been a change in the environment around the site. The house mouse provides no information since it occupies varying habitats and occurs almost everywhere with humans. The Indian gerbil is at present restricted to areas of moist soil with dense stands of grasses. The area around Farukhabad at present does not fit this description. It is dry, although the Mehmeh River cuts quite close to the site, and the vegetation on the river side of the site consists of dense tamarisk stands broken by clearings with a loamy soil. The vegetation on the other side of th site consists of scattered annuals on a clayey soil. The Baluchistan gerbil, *Gerbillus nanus*, is found at present around the site. This would suggest that the area around Farukhabad from the Bayat through at least the Jemdet Nasr phase was characterized by a moist soil and a better vegetation cover. On the Susiana Plain there is a close relationship between the Indian gerbil and irrigated fields. Quite possibly the site was surrounded by irrigated fields during its occupation.

HUMAN AND ANIMAL ON THE DEH LURAN PLAIN: 4000 to 1500 B.C.

In this section the relation between the density of human occupation and the utilization of different vertebrates will be examined. Initially, a general statement on patterns of utilization of vertebrates at Farukhabad will be made; this will be followed by a description of the pattern of utilization for each phase along with a brief note on the occupation on the Deh Luran Plain during that phase.

During this time span, 4000 to 1500 B.C., the inhabitants of Farukhabad exploited sheep and goats as the major vertebrate resource. In some phases equids were as important or more important than sheep and goats. This is assuming that sheep, goats, and equids were utilized only as meat sources. It also assumes that the equid material in all phases but the Elamite represents the wild half ass. Cattle were utilized in all phases but were only as important as sheep and goats in the Elamite. Gazelle hunting in all phases was a minor contributor to the diet. Other mammals were utilized neither consistently nor systematically. The non-mammalian vertebrates were primarily aquatic and were exploited with increasing frequency through the sequence. They apparently never became a major resource.

Farukh-Bayat: During these phases human population was high relative to the other phases. Farukhabad, like Tepe Sabz, was one of several small centers. Tepe Sabz was evidently abandoned during the Bayat phase.

In this phase there was heavy dependence on domestic sheep and goats. Equids were more important than cattle and both were less important than sheep and goats. Sheep were utilized more frequently than goats. Non-mammalian vertebrates were exploited at a very low level. The inhabitants of large structures at the site, at least during the Farukh Phase, had preferential access to gazelle, and perhaps other vertebrates.

Early Uruk: Tepe Farukhabad was abandoned after the Farukh Phase and there was no occupation on the site during the succeeding Susa A and Sagarab phases. During these phases human population on the plain was very low. In the succeeding Early Uruk phase, human population on the plain rose but still must be considered to have been relatively low. Farukhabad was reoccupied as a village or possibly only as a temporary nomadic settlement.

During the Early Uruk, domestic sheep and goats were still the most commonly utilized vertebrate but the half ass was more important. The sheep to goat ratio is based on a very small sample.

Middle Uruk: During this phase human population on the plain was low to medium. Farukhabad was a village throughout most of this phase but by the later portion had become the only small center on the plain. The composition of the fauna in this phase resembles that of the Early Uruk. There was a reduction in the importance of cattle. Sheep were utilized twice as frequently as were goats. Fish and birds were utilized at very low levels.

Late Uruk: During this phase human popu-

Table 77: Correlation Matrix Resulting from Comparisons of Each Vertebrate Group, Hectares Occupied on the Deh Luran Plain, and Scored Site Size

Size	1.00										
Ha	0.33	1.00									
Equid	−0.83*	−0.21	1.00								
Ovis	0.50	0.42	−0.28	1.00							
Capra	0.62	0.51	−0.31	0.66	1.00						
O–C–(G)	0.17	0.58	0.04	0.71	0.83*	1.00					
Gazella	0.05	0.40	0.28	0.11	−0.15	−0.13	1.00				
Bos	−0.56	0.38	0.45	0.28	0.03	0.58	−0.03	1.00			
Sus	0.49	0.85*	−0.23	0.61	0.88*	0.85*	0.13	0.27	1.00		
Fish	0.71	0.26	−0.47	0.47	0.93**	0.60	−0.27	−0.27	0.69	1.00	
Bird	−0.04	0.13	−0.21	0.76	0.41	0.72	0.66	0.66	0.33	0.22	1.00
	Size	Ha	Equid	*Ovis*	*Capra*	O–C–(G)	*Gazella*	*Bos*	*Sus*	Fish	Bird

N = 6   D.F. = 4
* Coefficient at .95 = .81 (Significant)
** Coefficient at .99 = .92 (Highly Significant)

lation on the plain was very low and Farukhabad was the only small center. There is a clear decrease in use of hunted resources, equid, and gazelle, and an increase in the use of domestic sheep and goats. Sheep and goats were utilized at nearly the same frequency. The utilization of fish increased greatly and we have the first evidence of transport in vertebrate resources: a ray was brought into the area.

Jemdet Nasr: During the Jemdet Nasr human population on the Deh Luran Plain was relatively high and continued to increase so that it was very high in the Late Jemdet Nasr. Tepe Farukhabad was one of several centers during the Early Jemdet Nasr, and in the Late Jemdet Nasr it was a center subsidiary to the central town of Musiyan.

The Jemdet Nasr fauna resembles that of the Late Uruk. There is a further increase in the importance of sheep and goats over equids and cattle. Goats were utilized one-and-one-half times as frequently as sheep. This is the only phase for which there is good evidence of preference for goats over sheep. Pigs appeared late in this phase. Fish utilization was at its highest level and marine fish were being brought into the area from the Persian Gulf. There was selective utilization of large birds with luxuriant plumage in and around larger buildings.

Elamite: Only earlier Elamite units were excavated at Farukhabad, representing, in terms of the sequence of the Susiana Plain, the Simashki, the Sukkalmahhu and the Transitional phases of the Elamite period (Carter 1971:225–26). Four sites are known to have been occupied on the Deh Luran Plain during these early phases. Farukhabad was the third largest of the four sites. The human population of the plain was medium to high during the early portion of the Elamite phase.

In this phase sheep and goats were the most commonly utilized vertebrate but were exceeded in importance by equids, and, for the first time at Farukhabad, domestic cattle. The high level of equid utilization may reflect the introduction of the domestic horse. Utilization of pigs continued. Sheep and goats were utilized in nearly equal proportions. Utilization of fish decreased while use of birds increased slightly.

CORRELATION OF SITE SIZE AND OCCUPATION DENSITY

Table 77 presents a correlation of ha occupied on the plain and site size to densities for the vertebrates at Farukhabad. We have not used the population in the correlation as it is derived from the number of ha occupied. Site size for Farukhabad is scored as 1, 2, or 3, based on a small, medium, or large area of occupation. Equid densities correlate negatively (p = .05) with site size. The pig correlates with the density of occupation on the plain (p = .05). This is not unexpected as pigs thrive on land disturbed by humans. If we assume that the denser the human population, the more land utilized, then there will be more land available to pigs.

APPARENT RELATIONS BETWEEN VERTEBRATES

Correlation coefficients included in Table 77 describe the relationship of the density ratio of each vertebrate to that of every other vertebrate. Three of these are significant ($p \leq .05$) and one highly significant ($p \leq .01$). The accuracy of these relations can certainly be questioned on the basis of sample size alone; however, these will be examined and possible explanations for them suggested. These relationships should be explored in future studies.

One significant relation is between goats (*Capra*) and sheep-goat(-gazelle) material. The increase in density of either one was accompanied by an increase in the other. One possible explanation is that an increase in the use of sheep and goats is accompanied by a shift to increased reliance on goats. Another possible explanation is an increase in number of sheep-goat elements increases the probability of goat elements being identified. However, if this is true, there should also be a correlation between sheep and sheep-goat elements. This correlation is not significant. Pig densities correlate significantly with both goat and sheep-goat densities. The explanation for these relationships is probably tied into increasing human population and the increased reliance on sheep and goats with increasing population.

Probably the most tantalizing relationship is the highly significant correlation between the density of fish and goat elements. We will offer no explanation for this relationship but merely note it here and suggest it as an area for further study. It may represent a previously unnoted interconnection in the ecosystem on the plain.

PART FIVE: CONCLUSIONS

Chapter XV

FOURTH MILLENIUM DEH LURAN IN THE NEXUS OF EXCHANGE

by Henry T. Wright

PERSPECTIVES ON EXCHANGE

The purpose of this chapter is not to present, or even introduce, a theory of exchange among the last and most complex of the pre-state societies and the first and simplest states. This work is concerned with aspects of exchange as only a few of the many variables in the broader development of whole cultural systems. Nevertheless, to present Deh Luran as a case history relevant to the evaluation of our conceptions of broader developments, I shall begin with some general statements about exchange. If these are a contribution towards general formalizations about exchange systems of a certain sort, so much the better.

My concern is exclusively with exchange between, rather than within, polities or communities such that the terms of exchange are not implied within existing social or political units—for example families, lineage systems, markets, manorial estates, etc.—but must be negotiated anew with every perceived change in conditions. That which is exchanged can, and usually does, include some mixture of material goods, social personnel, and symbolic understandings. Sometimes it is the generation of understandings—ongoing alliances—which takes precedence over goods and personnel. Sometimes it is the movement of personnel or goods—often thought to be demographically or technologically necessary—which takes precedence over understandings. The former precedence is thought to be typical of egalitarian societies (Sahlins 1972:277ff), while the latter is thought to typify developed national states. However, for those societies at stages of development between these two ideal types, assumptions of precedence would seem ill-advised and, in any event, unnecessary to this discussion.

There are two classes of conditions which compel exchange between polities. First, geological and climatic processes have created great resource disparities on the surface of the planet. While most communities with simple technologies are potentially self-sufficient within their territories, there are many items in nearby territories which a given community lacks, at least some of which would make life easier, more pleasant, or more secure. With increasing technological complexity, local self-sufficiency becomes impossible and exchange for or appropriation of rare items becomes necessary for cultural maintenance. Second, no community can count on the future. Natural calamity can strike the most self-sufficient of communities and any community with more than one neighbor perceives that some are potentially more useful and/or reliable than others. In any case, whether one gives in exchange for other goods or gives to cement useful alliances, one will give that which is valued by the recipient.

If movement of goods, personnel and messages is to occur, it should—if there is to be any future continuity of movement—be a reciprocal and more or less balanced movement; that is, it must be an "exchange". However, before either party can be assured that balance is a potential if not an actuality, there must be some shared theory of valuation. General purpose moneys are exceptional in the universe of ethnographically known valuations. The set of items valued against each other is typically limited, one community sometimes having several exclusive and/or overlapping envalued sets. Likewise, the many types of metric for valuation are all less precise than the exact relative scales of modern moneys. It is interesting to note that a system of valuation using an absolute value scale, based on labor or whatever, has yet to evolve, though such have been used in conceptual baselines for the assessment of other scales.

Given the necessity of exchange, a range of

possible items to exchange, and a theory of valuation, exchange between a few communities is simple. Regulation of the production and transport of items is inherent in the negotiation of the exchange. When, however, enough polities are involved, some are connected only indirectly with others and items move via middlemen through linear or network arrangements. Indeed, producers may lack information about those who will receive their products, and vice versa. Some means is needed to regulate production throughout the network. To speak of regulatory devices, mechanisms, or institutions, however, would in many cases be to misplace concreteness. To be sure, regulatory activity is sometimes vested in defined institutions or effected by particular administrative practices. However, exchange regulation can be an activity dispersed throughout the system of activities, as in control of production by the setting of prices as a result of the actions of many sellers and buyers in a traditional market system. Whatever its form, regulation will have the effect of changing the volume of items moved or the values of specific items relative to those of other items, and thus the volume moved.

Given this basic discussion of the components of any exchange system—a related set of polities, items to be exchanged, a means of valuing items, and a means for regulating either the value or the movement of items and thus relations between polities—one can now turn to the archaeologist's task of explicating past exchange systems. At the outset, one must admit that none of these components can be directly observed. Even those material items which survive in the archaeological record cannot be "proven" to have been items exchanged from one polity to another. One can only demonstrate reciprocal movement given assumptions about material sources. Our knowledge of the socio-political components which participate in exchange depend on a multitude of archaeological data and assumptions, many discussed or alluded to in the previous fourteen chapters. Our knowledge of exchange value and of the regulation of exchange must be extracted from the evidence of the distribution of transported goods in space and—inferentially—time. It is convenient to consider such extraction first from imports, then from exports.

Imports, particularly material goods found far from their sources, are usually the first perceived evidence of exchange, and they might seem the most tractable source of information on exchange as a system. However, the occurrence of an import implies nothing about its value or the regulation of its value and movement. Changes through time in the quantity of an import in comparable deposits, need only indicate that more was given out for this import, not that there was any change of valuation. One provocative approach to the problem is to consider the absolute amount of the import at different sites in different social relations to the source (Renfrew, Dixon, and Cann 1969). To do this, one needs some estimate of absolute quantity discarded from a number of comparably sampled nodes in an exchange network. Another provocative approach is to consider imports which it can be argued were exchanged against each other (Winters 1968). In such cases, changes through time in absolute ratio at a single node can be assumed to indicate changes in value. In dealing with a single node in an exchange network, I have found it most convenient to consider imports for which there are local substitutes (Wright 1972). Increase in the value of that import, other demands being equal, would result in decreased use of the imported material and greater reliance on the substitute. Regulation of the import would be indicated by changes through time in volume and in value and the relation between these changes and those in other imports and exports. This approach has the advantage of limiting the effect of the differential sampling of activities through time, since substitute-to-import ratios are constructed only with tools of one functional class. A limitation of the approach is that it can only be used with relatively common, durable imports; one cannot make reliable ratios between rare occurrences.

Exports present an entirely different analytical problem. We may suspect that some items are exported because they appear at distant sites far from their material's source or sources. When only a source or production center is known, one can demonstrate export by showing that more items were produced at a site than were locally consumed. With a product whose waste by-products are durable the assessment of changing export volume is straightforward. One could estimate the waste discarded per unit produced and subtract that accounted for by discarded items, in cases where the item is standardized and discard is in ordinary domestic contexts. Alternatively, one could consider the changing ratio of waste to finished tools as an indirect indicator of effort expended on export. Beyond this, direct assessment of the changing value of exports at the locus of production seems impossible. Regulation of export production would be indicated indirectly by its changing social, specifically architectural, contexts in the site and the site's context in the local settlement system. In addition, regulation would affect the change through time in volume in relation to changes in other exports and imports.

Having introduced some concepts relevant to exchange between polities and some archaeological methods useful in assessing them, we can now consider the Deh Luran case. First, the position of Deh Luran in the regional structure will be described. Second, possible exports will be presented, with particular emphasis on the extraction, processing, and disposition of major exports. Third, imports will by similarly presented, and fourth, the systemic relations between import and export volumes and values will be discussed. Fifth, the relations between transformations in exchange and other cultural transformations will be examined. Sixth, and finally, future lines of research will be suggested.

THE NEXUS OF TRANSPORT

The isolation of the Deh Luran Plain has been noted in Chapters I and VI. From the point of view of the fourth millennium Deh Lurani, the difficulties of reaching other places were greater than today. The plain lies close to the juncture of four great regions, each region being composed of a diversity of small areas one day's travel or less in radius, centered on one or more agriculturally productive and densely populated areas. To the north and northeast is mountainous Luristan. One day's journey on foot takes the traveler to one of the higher valleys of Posht-e Kuh ("behind the mountain," from the perspective of one on the Iranian Plateau). In another three or four days, one can cross the valley of the Saimarreh and reach one of the larger inner valleys of Pish-e Kuh or inner Luristan (Goff 1971). To the northwest, departing Deh Luran by way of Farukhabad and crossing barren foothills for two days, one reaches the Mehran Plain, a marginal area of the Diyala Region, the northernmost part of the Mesopotamian alluvium. The center of this region, the Lower Diyala Floodplain, is another two or three days of travel from one small plain to the next. To the southeast, one traverses easily from Deh Luran to the Plain of Abbas and thence to the Karkheh River, crossing it at the edge of the great Susiana Plain of Central Khuzestan in about two days. It is the ease of this passage to the southeast, as opposed to that of the barren foothills to the northeast, that accounts for the persistant association of Deh Luran with Khuzestan rather than with another region. To the southwest, over the Jebel Hamrin, the Tigris, and (during the fourth millennium) an extension of the freshwater marshes, lay the Lower Mesopotamian Alluvium. Historically, however, few came by this direct route. It was more common to go north into the Diyala borderlands and approach Deh Luran by way of Mehran, a journey of four or more days. Lower Mesopotamia was unlike any of the component regions of Greater Mesopotamia in several respects. At its center lay not one but five or more adjacent areas of ramified river channels, all with opportunities for productive irrigation agriculture. However, these well-endowed areas were subject to sudden changes of river course, and as a consequence their configurations and the major loci of population were constantly changing. The approximate travel times suggested here are those for a person on foot based on 19th century accounts. Travel with loaded donkeys, almost certainly in use by the end of the fourth millennium, would be at the same rate, but the possible load would be increased by a factor of four or more. Travel with herds of sheep or goats would take twice as long at best.

If travel from Deh Luran to the nearby centers was difficult, travel to the sources of some of the items exchanged throughout Mesopotamia was far more time-consuming. Obsidian from Lake Van had to twist through the most precipitous ridges of the Zagros or the Anti-Taurus, a trip of 18 days at the least. Lapis lazuli from Badakhshan in Afghanistan had to cross some of the most arid basins of the Iranian Plateau as well as the Southern Zagros, a trip of no less than 60 days. It is unlikely that a single agent made the entire journey, and in the case of lapis, it is known that initial working of the material took place at highland centers (e.g. Tosi and Piperno 1973). However, the actual number of middlemen involved in the movement of any item at any period is unknown. Fortunately, for purposes of this study, it is not particularly important.

The important point for the consideration of

Deh Luran as a single node in the developing exchange network is that the most reliable land routes between southern Alluvial Mesopotamia and the Susiana (and thus Southern Iran beyond) cross the Deh Luran Plain. Any movement of items between highland and lowlands via Khuzestan is likely to pass this way. Unfortunately for archaeologists, we cannot assume that some fixed percentage of all items in transit was exacted by the Deh Luranis and randomly scattered across their settlements. We can assume, however, that Deh Luranis were able to obtain items in exchange at current relative values and rates. Also, we can assume that the Deh Luran communities, small though they were, had a sufficiently visible and useful position on the transport routes that large polities in the centers of the adjacent regions would seriously entertain relations of allegiance or alliance with them. The next consideration is that of what Deh Luran could offer in exchange for desired items and as evidence of close relations with other polities.

PRODUCTION AND EXPORT ON THE DEH LURAN PLAIN

There are a limited number of items which can be produced by a small population in a marginal valley of the Zagros foothills. Of these, only a few were demonstrably exported in quantity.

In the realm of inanimate materials, the most common are clays; however, the finished products—ceramics—are not easily transported overland and would not be more desirable than those made of clays elsewhere. One would expect Deh Luran ceramic vessels to be transported only when they were filled with an otherwise valuable product or endowed by their crafters with unique symbolic character. Examples of the latter—the export of unique Deh Luran painted ceramics—have yet to be reported elsewhere; for the present, one can assume that the ceramic shops at Farukhabad and other Deh Luran sites produced vessels mostly for local use.

Sedimentary rocks such as sandstone, conglomerate, calcite, and gypsum commonly occur in outcrops and river gravels around the plain. The first three are useful for grinding and cutting tools, but are not very durable. Overland transport would hardly seem worth the effort. The third and fourth were carved into vessels and were reduced to cements, but these were minor crafts which produced poor renditions of the fine alabaster and travertine vessels produced elsewhere.

Weathered from Zagros limestones and deposited in various loci on the plain were several kinds of chert. A small chert core, when reduced to blades, provides a large number of cutting tools. Thus, overland transport of a load of cores would be broadly useful. In addition, some of the regions near Deh Luran lack cherts, and their inhabitants would welcome such products. Certainly, the production of chert cores must be considered as potentially production export. Likewise, seeping to the surface of the plain from sedimentary strata is an impressive supply of asphalt. This versatile adhesive and waterproofing material can be cleaned and packed for transport, and is rare elsewhere. It too is a likely export.

Finally, among the inanimate materials are metamorphic and igneous rocks used for ores, pigments, jewelry, etc. These are rare in Deh Luran. There are no ores accessible to Bronze Age smiths. Harder semi-precious stones would occur rarely if at all in the gravelly alluvium. Such chance finds could not constitute regular exports.

In the realm of gathered living materials, though the mountain forests were close, there is little indication of the use of woods or other forest products at Farukhabad itself, and it is unlikely that any significant quantity was forwarded on. The primary wood in use at Farukhabad was tamarisk, common in riverine areas everywhere in Greater Mesopotamia. While the few bone tools may indicate limited local weaving of rush mats, export is unlikely since rushes are widely available. The wild fauna—fish, fowl, and mammal—of Deh Luran were limited in several ways. Aquatic niches were not common after the seventh millennium (Hole, Flannery, and Neely 1969) and after three millennia of hunting and of grazing by domestic animals, wild mammals were probably rare.

In the realm of farm products, the most visible would be cultivated plants. However, the range actually grown in Deh Luran was narrow. Only wheat and barley were common, as they were everywhere. It is unlikely that the limited and unreliable fields of Deh Luran would have provided a steady export. In addition, because of their bulk, grains would be difficult to transport overland.

Domestic animals were, in recent times, a prime export of the Deh Luran area. Sheep and goats in particular can gain some sustenance from most areas of the plain and can be kept in the mountains during the summer. The herds can transport themselves to other areas on their own feet, and many of their by-products—in particular hides, fiber, and dried milk products—are light and easily transported. Thus, the possibility that the considerable production of sheep and goats in Deh Luran (see Chapter XIV) was for export must be considered.

Finally, one must note a final possible export: the fourth millennium Deh Lurani themselves or their labor. However, except for the Jemdet Nasr Period, population remained low, and mass movement of laborers or of labor-intensive craft products could not have been sustained. Even in the Jemdet Nasr Phases, population did not approach the numbers employable and sustainable on the plain with wheat and barley cultivation and herding.

In sum, the preceding consideration of the plain's potentials indicates that exports of ceramics, sedimentary stone artifacts, woods, mats, grains, laborers, and labor-intensive craft products would all have been limited because of some combination of relatively poor supply quality, supply irregularity, transport cost, or relatively greater supply elsewhere. In contrast, cherts, asphalt, and sheep-goat products have to be considered as potentially important exports. Examination of the by-products of their production should allow a demonstration of their actual importance.

CHERTS

Three cherts are commonly found on the Deh Luran Plain, though only one seems to have been exported. Least common, though ubiquitous in gravels throughout the plain, are the Fine Red and Green Cherts. These have a silty texture, approaching glassy when heat-treated. Even thin flakes and blades transmit no light. Nodules are relatively rare, usually no more than eight cm in length and frequently flawed. Both rough and blade cores were made. Flakes and blades of this material wear easily and are presumably relatively soft compared to other cherts. Regretably, no durability experiments have been attempted with Khuzestan cherts. The Red and Green Cherts occur throughout the Central Zagros, and concentrations of large tabular pieces are found along the Inner Zagros. Quarry areas have been observed near Kermanshah, Khorramabad, and Neriz (James Blackman, p.c.). It is likely that finds of such chert near Farukhabad were used locally rather than transported.

Common in the gravels of the Mehmeh River, a few meters from Tepe Farukhabad, is fine Dark Brown Chert (7.5 YR 4/1–2). It occurs in neither the Pleistocene colluvial gravels nor the Dawairij River gravels to the east; its occurrence to the west is unknown, because our surveys of chert sources have not been extended toward Mehran. This Dark Brown Chert has a slightly silty texture, approaching smooth when heat treated. Only the thinnest flakes transmit light. Dark Brown Chert occurs as small tabular fragments never more than six cm thick. Blades must be struck lengthwise on the tabular pieces, and only a few can be removed from a given core. It is no surprise that this material is used primarily for rough flake cores. Like the Fine Red and Green Cherts, tools of this material wear easily. At present no sources of this chert are known outside of the Mehmeh valley. The only evidence that it has been transported are a few possible pieces from the northern Susiana, including some excavated from Uruk deposits at Tepe Sharafabad. It seems likely that, in spite of the ease with which pieces can be gathered, their inconvenient shape and the poor durability of tools made from the material made this chert a poor candidate for export.

Medium Gray Chert nodules are found in Pleistocene colluvial gravels between modern Deh Luran and modern Andimeshk, but the major concentration seems to be between the Chikad River on the eastern end of the Deh Luran Plain and the Karkheh River on the western edge of the Susiana Plain. The color varies from dark gray (10 YR 4/1) to red (2.5 YR 4/2), but tan (10 YR 6/3) and gray (10 YR 6/1) are most common. Small black discolorations occur, particularly in the easternmost sources. The texture varies from that of course sand to that of fine sand. Heating to 300° C for eight hours does not improve the texture, but it brings out a redder color. Thinner flakes are translucent. Medium Gray Cherts occur in ovoid nodules commonly measuring up to 15 cm in length. When broken into halves or quarters, an ideal preform for a blade core can be produced. Tools of this relatively granular material seem to have been durable, and they were the preferred chert for sickle blades throughout the outer zone of the Central Zagros during the fifth to third millennia B.C. In areas of these regions which lack cherts (other than a scatter of Fine Red and Green Chert), Medium Gray Chert was commonly obtained; even areas with other usable chert sources imported much of this chert. Thus, the production of Medium Gray Chert cores at Farukhabad must be examined to determine whether Deh Luran was exporting this stone, or whether, in contrast, it was communities in other places such as the Susiana (or those near yet unlocated bedrock sources) that made it available.

In order to produce a transportable core, Medium Gray Chert nodule halves and quarters must be trimmed on the sides. This produces both blocky fragments and larger flakes, usually with cortex remnant. These by-products are thus potential indicators of chert core manufacture. The number per cubic meter of fragments and flakes longer than two cm are presented in the fifth and sixth columns of Table 78. Weight per cubic meter would have been a more appropriate measure, but I did not realize this until after the samples had been divided. The fragments usually would have been discarded immediately and may thus be concentrated near work places, but many of the flakes would have been used as expedient cutting tools and be more widely scattered. Most of the Medium Gray Chert used at Farukhabad was in the form of blade segments (apparently general purpose cutting tools) and sickle blades. Their densities are given in the sixth and seventh columns of Table 78. However, while blade segments can be expected to be widely scattered in the settlement, sickles are liable to be discarded in fields as well as to be returned and discarded in limited areas where heated bitumen is available as mastic. As noted in Chapters IV and IX, sickles show a unique distributional pattern uncorrelated with others, and this is reflected in Table 78. For this reason, the ratio of fragments and large flakes to segments alone, is used as an index of production for export. With these data, we can now consider chert export through time.

In the Farukh Phase, the number of waste pieces per tool is relatively low. This does not mean that there was no export at this period, for there are almost two pieces discarded for every one used. However, in the absence of experiments showing the absolute amount of waste and tools produced by the stages of core-working, total export cannot be assessed, and we must be content with relative indications of export. It is interesting to note that while tools are evenly distributed, manufacturing debris is concentrated near the more elaborate domestic unit. After the period of desertion, during the Early Uruk Phase there is an increase in both the density of tools and of waste products. The number of waste pieces per tool remains about the same as it was, indicating no change in Medium Grey Chert export effort.

During the succeeding Middle Uruk Phase, overall tool density returns to more or less Farukh Phase levels, overall production remains at increased Early Uruk levels. This results in an overall doubling of the index of chert export. Production waste is about the same in the two simple domestic units sampled, but one has remarkably few tools, inflating the export index. During the Late Uruk Phase, overall production triples over that of the Middle Uruk but tool discard rises only slightly. Specific figures for architecturally associated debris show that densities are low near simple domestic structures, but waste density is very high around both the elaborate nondomestic building and around the circular mud brick platforms. Around the former building there are few tools and the highest recorded index of chert export occurs, while around the latter platforms there are quite a few tools and the index is high but not unprecedented. Thus the initial Middle Uruk increase in export is followed by further Late Uruk increase and concentration of export production around a special building.

During the Early Jemdet Nasr Phase, overall production waste density is halved, though tool use drops only slightly in the sampled areas, so the amount exported seems to be at the same relative level as during Middle Uruk. There seems to be no particular association between complexity of the domestic architecture sampled and the associated waste density or export index. Note that had we sampled a non-domestic building, such as that of the Late Uruk, overall densities might have been much higher. During the Late Jemdet Nasr and Early Dynastic Phases, there is a slight drop in waste density and in segment use, but a marked increase in sickle densities. I intepret this as a maintenance of Early Jemdet Nasr export levels, with an as yet unexplained increase in home repair of sickles, though the possibilities that chert export has declined or become centered in the newly re-emerged center at Musiyan cannot be rejected.

Table 78: Preparation and Utilization of Medium Gray Chert per Cubic Meter

		m³	Frags.	Large Flks.	Blade Segs.	Sickles	Frags. + Flakes Segs.
Early Dynastic Total: 15.70 (A5–1, B20–19)			.68	1.42	.34	.54	5.40
S?	A5–1	10.60	.66	1.13	.09	.56	19.00
S	B70–19	4.10	.73	2.19	.97	.48	3.00
Late JN Total: 32.95 (A12–6, B23–21)			.78	1.03	.33	1.09	5.48
E	A12–11	5.94	.00	1.01	.16	.50	6.00
E	A10–6	14.37	.48	.62	.20	.97	5.33
E	B23–21	12.64	1.42	1.02	.31	1.26	7.75
Early JN Total: 30.77 (A17–13, B27–24)			1.14	2.05	.52	.26	6.13
S	A17–14	8.14	1.44	1.47	.85	.12	3.43
S	A13L–M	3.60	.83	1.38	1.27	.00	8.00
E	A13U	2.15	.93	2.79	.46	.00	8.00
E	B26–24	13.81	.72	1.59	.43	.50	5.33
Late Uruk Total: 29.95 (A20–18, B31–28)			2.34	4.67	.90	.13	7.78
S	A19–18	6.00	1.00	.50	.33	.33	9.00
E	B31U–30	7.75	3.61	3.74	.25	.12	28.50
P	B29–28	8.80	2.15	6.25	1.13	1.13	7.40
Middle Uruk Total: 29.80 (A21, B34–32)			.93	1.77	.53	.36	5.09
S	A21	4.85	1.03	1.64	1.03	.41	2.60
S	B33U	3.40	.58	2.05	.00	.29	—
Early Uruk Total: 11.20 (B36–35)			1.60	1.60	1.16	.98	2.75
S	B36	3.20	3.75	4.06	2.50	2.50	1.92
Farukh Total: 74.98 (A31–23, B47–37)			.68	1.09	.73	.31	2.42
S	B41	5.40	.00	.92	1.48	.00	.63
S	B44	4.10	.00	.25	.73	.48	.33
E	A27–24	14.47	1.03	1.65	.82	.27	3.25

In short, the transformation in export production of chert at Farukhabad seems to have occurred during the Middle Uruk Phase when export doubled. Production for export seems to have reached a peak during the Late Uruk, then decreased slightly during the Jemdet Nasr and Early Dynastic Periods. The apparent peak of export during Late Uruk may result from chance sampling of more non-domestic, craft-oriented buildings during this phase, and the apparent drop in export production during Late Jemdet Nasr may be a statistical artifact of changed tool discard patterns; however the dramatic increase between Early and Late Uruk periods seems significant.

BITUMEN

The still active bitumen seep of Ain Gir is only 12 m north-northwest of Farukhabad. Here about ten liters of liquid asphalt floats to the surface of a pool of water each day and is carried out into a small valley where layer after layer hardens (Marschner, Duffy, and Wright 1978:98). No other active sources are reported in the area, but we cannot be sure that there were not other once-active sources where there are now only layers of rock asphalt, particularly on the Jebel Hamrin

Table 79: Asphalt per Cubic Meter

	Grams of Asphalt Waste	Grams of Utilized Asphalt	Assoc/ m^3	Utilized/ m^3	Ratio
Early Dynastic Total	794	15	50	1	50
S A 5–1	510	15	48		
S B 20–19	284	0	69		
Late Jemdet Nasr Total	6890	414	209	13	16
E A 12–11	98	0	16		
E A 10–6	2589	398	180		
E B 23–21	4203	16	333		
Early Jemdet Nasr Total	1112	16	36	1	36
S A 17–14	231	4	28		
S A 13L–M	25	0	7		
E A 13U	66	0	28		
E B 26–24	790	10	58		
Late Uruk Total	1344	16	58	1	58
S A 19–18	35	0	6		
E B 31U–30	491	0	73		
P B 29–28	477	10	54		
Middle Uruk Total	340	120	11	4	3
S A 21	71	4	15		
S B 334	44	0	11		
Early Uruk Total	467	0	41	0	—
S B 36	318	0	50		
Farukh Total	2191	362	29	5	6
S B 41	223	69	34		
S B 44	15	0	4		
E A 27–24	231	0	16		

where survey is at present impossible. Some nearby source was active more than 10,000 years ago, since the mandible of the Upper Pleistocene rodent, a *Mus* of Lagadda type, was found in a lump of hardened seepage. Rock asphalt was transported from sources such as Ain Gir to Farukhabad where it was either transported uncleaned or melted, cleaned, and transported, perhaps as shaped lumps. A few known asphalt pieces have more than 40 percent bitumen, a far greater amount than is known from any hardened source sample, suggesting that the purer liquid bitumen was sometimes used as well (Ibid.: 108). The evidence of asphalt preparation at archaeological sites is in the form of discarded dark brown angular chunks and melted flat pieces. Weathered Khuzestan asphalts from archaeological sites usually contain 16 to 32 percent bitumen, the rest being minerals of which up to half is quartz sand (Ibid.: Tables III, IV). All bitumens analyzed had between 5.2 and 6.2 percent sulphur of which the excess 34 S isotopes constituted from -7.7 percent to -8.9 percent. These sulphur attributes serve to distinguish the Khuzestan bitumens from Iraqi samples (Ibid.: 107). Deh Luran asphalts, both archaeological and modern source samples, can be approximately distinguished from central Khuzestan asphalts by the light color of the minerals and by the fact that they contain more than 40 percent very fine minerals (Ibid.: Fig. 5). Conclusive distinctions will be possible when gas chromatographic methods are extensively utilized (Marschner, personal communication). Given the mineral criteria cited above, we can say that one of the two Middle Uruk samples from Sharafabad on the Susiana Plain was probably from Deh Luran, but the other Uruk sample and the seven earlier samples from Sharafabad and other sites were from sources closer to the Susiana such as Masjud-i Suleiman. Apparently Deh Luran was not a major supplier for the Susiana (Ibid.:110). The Diyala to the northwest also had its own sources. By default, this suggests that some of the supply exported could have gone into the mountains of Luristan but that most would have gone to the large population centers of the lower alluvium to the south and southwest. Unfortunately most of the few recently analyzed Iraqui asphalts do not come from the parts of the alluvium most accessible to Deh Luran, and it is not surprising that we cannot document a single export from Deh Luran to Iraq (Marschner and Wright 1978: Table V).

In contrast to the many by-products of asphalt packaging are the relatively few pieces utilized as a water-proofing or cement as detailed in Chapters IV and IX. Most of the recorded utilized asphalt was mat impressed pieces, which must have resulted from the water proofing of architectural elements and furnishings. Examination of Table 79, shows that the occurrence of such utilized pieces was sporadic; perhaps this results from their limited use and also the ease with which they can be crushed to tiny pieces unless in a more protected depositional context (in contrast to the extremely durable chert tools).

The total recorded weight of asphalt by-products and of utilized pieces is given for phases and for architectural units with more than two cubic meters of screened debris (see third and fourth columns of Table 79). The waste by-products per cubic meter, in the fifth column, provides an index of total production most of which must have been for export given the few uses for asphalt in Deh Luran. The utilized pieces per cubic meter and the ratio of utilized to waste quantities are given for phase totals in the last two columns. With these data we can consider asphalt export through time.

In the Farukh Phase, absolute asphalt production is relatively low but much is utilized locally, resulting in a ratio of six gm of waste to every gram definitely used. There is no marked association of asphalt production with either simple or elaborate buildings. In Early Uruk, production is somewhat higher, but no utilized pieces were found in the small sample and a ratio cannot be computed. In the succeeding Middle Uruk Phase, production drops but much asphalt is used locally, giving a ratio of three gm of waste to every gram definitely used. The Middle Uruk Phase seems to have been a nadir of asphalt production for export from Farukhabad, though (as was noted before) this is one portion of the fourth millennium for which export of Deh Luran asphalt can be documented.

During the Late Uruk Phase, production increased to a relatively high level, particularly around the elaborate building of this phase. In contrast, local usage is hardly documented, so the ratio is a relatively high 58 gm of waste to every gram definitely used. Apparently expanded export production was centered around the elaborate building. In the succeeding Early Jemdet Nasr Phase, production drops but usage remains low and export remains relatively high. There is a tendency for elaborate domestic buildings to have more evidence of production near them than simpler ones. In the Late Jemdet Nasr Phase, overall asphalt waste density increased dramatically, as does the incidence of utilized pieces. However, it is possible that these high discard densities are characteristic only of the elaborate residences which dominate the excavation sample. Still the ratio of waste to utilized weight indicates relatively substantial production for export. Finally, in the Early Dynastic Phase, absolute production and local utilization drop back to Late Uruk levels, with a ratio of 50 gm of waste to every gram used. However, it is possible that these lower densities are characteristic of the simple residences in our available sample.

In brief, the evidence shows that there is an earlier period encompassing the Farukh to Middle Uruk Phases in which production is relatively low and export is minimal. Then there is a period encompassing the Late Uruk, Jemdet Nasr, and Early Dynastic Phases in which production is two to six times that indicated earlier and export relative to local consumption is three to ten times that indicated earlier.

SHEEP-GOAT PRODUCTS

This third class of likely exports of the fourth millennium is the most difficult to assess. Nevertheless, there are indications of changes in herding strategy and in production technology which can best be explained in terms of changing export of domestic animal products.

The age distributions of the sheep and goats indicates that earlier, during Bayat and Farukh Phase times, less than half the animals were allowed to survive past three years, probably because almost all males were killed for their meat as growth slowed. Later, however, during Jemdet Nasr times, more than half survived beyond the age of three, indicating that some males not useful in reproduction were being kept. Redding (personal communication) suggests that this indicates an interest in products other than meat or milk, for example wool or hair. Precisely when this shift occurred is not clear.

Another shift in animal management involves a changing preference for goats as shown in the second column of Table 80. In Farukh to Middle Uruk times, there was one goat for every sheep. During Late Uruk and Jemdet Nasr times, there were more than one goat for each sheep. A shift to specialized goat hair production would give the Deh Luran area an exchangeable product which would contrast with the wool fiber products thought to originate in alluvial Mesopotamia.

Is there any indication of changing approaches to sheep or goat fiber in the recovered elements of technology? Table 80 summarizes the incidence of items possible related to such fiber. Spindle whorls are at present used by women in the house or tent to make thread for their own use or for petty exchange and we assume that this was also the situation in protohistoric times. The density per cubic meter of all whorls not thought to be extrusive are given by phase. In Farukh, Late Uruk, and Jemdet Nasr times, when Farukhabad was a small center, few whorls were discarded. Most of these were found in simpler domestic buildings. In Middle Uruk times, when the site was just becoming a center, and in Early Uruk times when it was apparently only a village, the density of discarded whorls was high. Thus, whorl density may indicate part-time thread production and indirectly the socioeconomic position of settlement, but it indicates little about the mass processing of fiber and thread into exportable cloth.

Perforated stones were interpreted, by elimination of other possibilities, as loom weights in Chapter VIII. The densities of such stones and related items contrast strikingly with those of whorls. The possible weights were uncommon in Farukh times. By Early Uruk, they have increased in density and by Middle Uruk, their density has tripled. This is the period when large drill bit concentrations indicate the stones were being perforated around small structures in Excavation B. During Late Uruk, there were few possible loom weights. It is worth noting that this is the period in which a single bale seal with hide impression was found; it is possible that during this period of external control, bales of hides and fibers were shipped to some place with more labor for cloth production. It is also notable that no spindle whorls were found in Late Uruk deposits suggesting that production of thread decreased as much as cloth. Perhaps cloth was even imported during this period. During Jemdet Nasr times, weight density suddenly returns to its previous high level. In short, earlier in the Uruk Period production triples. After a Late Uruk collapse of production, it rises back to this former high level. In closing, it must be emphasized that it is simple production and not export that is documented here; there is at present no way to factor out local consumption and derive an indication of fiber product export.

SUMMARY

The overall picture of major production for export can be summarized as follows. At the small Farukh Phase center, there was some local production of Medium Gray Chert and asphalt, the latter, at least, almost certainly largely for export. Chert production was concentrated around elaborate buildings, but asphalt working was dispersed throughout the settlement. This pattern of production also appears to occur during Early Uruk times, but in Middle Uruk times, as Farukhabad again grew into a small center, there was a doubling of chert export and indications of increased weaving of fiber, presumably mostly wool from herds being managed primarily for meat production, perhaps for export or perhaps for local use. In Late Uruk, when Farukhabad became an outpost for an outside power, chert increased further, asphalt production for export showed a marked increase, and—while local weaving decreased—there was a new emphasis on goat production, perhaps for fiber. Much production seems to have centered on an elaborate non-domestic building. During Jemdet Nasr and Early Dynastic times, when Farukhabad was a small center subsidiary to the central town of Musiyan, chert export decreased slightly but remained at a steady high level, asphalt production and export

Table 80: Variables Related to Sheep and Goat Products

	Ovis: Capra	Spindle Whorls		Perforated Stones	
		No.	No./m³	No.	No./m³
Jemdet Nasr	1:1.50	4	.09	9	.14
Late Uruk	1:1.15	0	0	2	.07
Middle Uruk	1:1.00	6	.20	5	.17
Early Uruk	—	7	.62	1	.09
Farukh	1:1.00	9	.12	4	.05

fluctuated at a high level, and there was a definite emphasis on goat herding for their fiber with accompanying indications of a local weaving industry at a steady high level. Evidence of chert production occurs throughout the settlement, but asphalt production is concentrated around elaborate residences. This assessment of export, though imprecise, probably covers all possible exports; it seems unlikely that any major production for exchange has been missed.

IMPORTS TO FARUKHABAD

An import to a given settlement by definition leaves no by-products of its own manufacture there. If the artifact is not itself durable, there is no way to assess its place in exchange. Thus items of cloth, leather, or wood—which rarely leave traces in southwestern Iran—cannot be assessed. Even those items which are durable, in particular those which have specific uses or those that are socially valued, may be deposited only in limited contexts on the site. In contrast to the preceding consideration of exports, one cannot claim to have assessed all significant imports; one must be content to analyze a few aspects of import. In the following pages, both materials for technical items—including exotic cherts, volcanic stones, and metals—and material for social display—including items of marine shell and semiprecious stone—will be assessed.

EXOTIC CHERTS AND OBSIDIANS

The location and characterization of chert sources in southwest Asia is just beginning. In the future, with comprehensive sampling and chemical source characterization, precise ascription of archaeological cherts to sources will be as certain as ascription of obsidian now is. For the present, however, we must rely on approximate visual characterizations. On this basis, five groups of cherts occuring repeatedly at Farukhabad can be termed exotic and three of these can be ascribed to source areas.

Fine White and Pink Cherts: Usually these are mottled cherts with a fine-textured matrix and large mottles with texture approximating fine silt. Homogeneous and banded variants occur. The pinkish pieces (10R 6/3) appear to be heat-treated examples of the whitish material (N8). One piece of the white material was found in a sample of cherts from the Chikad River on the southeast margin of the Deh Luran Plain, and because of this occurrence, all fine white cherts were termed "local" in a preliminary study (Wright 1972: Table 1). While the major source may be somewhere in western Khuzestan or Posht-e Kuh, it is apparently not on the plain, and this chert is here considered "exotic". Both blade cores and rough cores were brought to Farukhabad and used throughout the sequence.

Fine Translucent Brown and Tan Chert: This chert is usually homogeneous or broad-layered (7.5 YR4/3). It occurs in small nodules on the terraces of the Middle Karun area, particularly in the Andaka plain northeast of Lali in eastern Khuzestan. There are bedrock sources near Shahr-i kurd (Alan Zagarell, personal communication). Blade cores were brought to Farukhabad and used earlier in the Farukhabad sequence.

Fine Mottled Gray Cherts: These excellent cherts usually have fine mottles, but homogeneous and banded varieties occur (10 YR 5/1). All are characterized by a blue-gray patina when weathered. No sources are known, but this chert is the predominate kind on Uruk, Jemdet Nasr, and Early Dynastic sites along the Euphrates channels, and the closest similar chert known to me is a darker and browner chert from the Jebel Bishri in Syria. It is possible that this chert is obtainable from the Middle Eurphrates or upper Tigris areas. Both blade cores and rough cores were brought to Farukhabad and used throughout the sequence.

Fine Banded Brown Cherts: These excellent cherts have regular lighter tan and darker brown layers. Color varies from brown (7.5 YR 5/4) to yellow (10 YR 5/6). My only source sample is from near Rutba on the modern Syria-Iraq border, from whence wadis doubtless carried pebbles northeastwards toward the Euphrates. The cherts from the

Early 'Ubaid site of Ras al Amiyah are predominately Fine Banded Brown Chert, and it occurs in later sites along the Euphrates channels. It is likely that the few Farukhabad examples were obtained from sources in the desert south of the Euphrates. It was used later in the Farukhabad sequence.

Fine Mottled and Banded Red Cherts: These have a glassy texture and bold mottling or banding and are often flawed (10 YR 5/4). The flawed quality suggests a source within Khuzestan near Deh Luran, but no source is known. This type of chert was used earlier in our sequence.

Obsidian: Like the exotic cherts, this glass-like volcanic material was used primarily for blade manufacture. All of the pieces recovered from Farukhabad are from sources near Lake Van in eastern Anatolia. All were used earlier in the Farukhabad sequence.

In the following analysis, increased scarcity relative to a local substitute is assumed to indicate increased value, because other possible causes of scarcity seem less likely. For example, all the imports with the partial exception of the fine mottled and banded red cherts flake and wear equally well, so it is unlikely that technical preference affects frequency. Also, with the exception of obsidian, all of the imports apparently come from nearby accessible regions, so periodic political closure is unlikely to have created scarcity.

The occurrence of exotic cherts is detailed in Appendix Tables B1–3, and some of the particular data relevant to this discussion are presented in Table 81. The third to seventh columns present imported chert blades and blade segments per cubic meter, an indicator of absolute import, assuming no change through time in disposal practices. The eighth to twelfth columns present the ratio of each exotic chert to local cherts, an inverse indicator of change in the value of each chert. The thirteenth column is the sum of these and represents change in aggregate value of all imported chert. We can now consider chert import to Farukhabad during the successive phases.

During the Farukh Phase, many chert cores were obtained from both other parts of Khuzestan to the east and the areas, probably to the west, which produced the Fine Gray Cherts. During the later Early Uruk Phase, it seems that the same source areas were used and that their values were maintained. The sole exception was the Fine White and Pink Cherts which became absolutely rarer (though overall chert used increased in the portions of the site sampled) and hence relatively more valuable.

During Middle Uruk, widespread change occurred. Total chert used decreased, and most exotics became rarer (e.g., more valuable). Fine Mottled Red cherts of unknown origin and the Fine Translucent Tan and Brown Cherts from the east were never to be significant again. However, Fine Banded Brown Cherts from the Southern Desert make their first consistent appearance. Only the Fine Gray Cherts maintain their value. However, in the succeeding Late Uruk, these too become rare and during both the Late Uruk and Early Jemdet Nasr periods, exotic cherts are only occasionally obtained.

This decline in chert import and deduced rise in the value of chert occurs in periods of increasing exports, as previously noted, so the decline cannot be explained in terms of decreasing exchange: there must have been an incremental increase in the value of these materials. However, the Late Jemdet Nasr decrease in deduced chert value occurs during a time of overall increasing exports, and the possibility that relative values remained constant while a greater quantity was obtained as a result of increased export must be considered after other exports have been discussed.

OTHER TECHNICAL MATERIALS

Materials other than cherts are sporadic in occurrence and of unspecified origin. They are considered only briefly in this monograph.

Vesicular basalt is found only in the later Jemdet Nasr and Early Dynastic deposits. It must be distinguished from a more massive but surficially pitted andesite, which is found locally in the form of small pebbles (W.R. Farrand, personal communication). Vesicular Basalt is found in Iranian Seistan, east and south-central Anatolia, the Jordan Graben, the Syrian Desert, and the Hejaz. The heavy pieces used as grinding slabs of Farukhabad would be difficult to move overland and one suspects sources near the Middle Euphrate or Upper Tigris were exploited, with river transport facilitating movement. Unfortunately, these are two areas from which I have no samples, so source identification would be premature. Whatever the

Table 81: Variables Related to the Import of Technical Materials

	Chipped Stone												Other Materials	
	Pieces per Cubic Meter						Exotic Pieces per Local Piece					Total Exotics per Local Piece	Basalt	Cuprous Metal
	Local	FW–P	FG	FTB–T	FBB	FM–BR	FW–P	FG	FTB–T	FBB	FM–BR			
Late Jemdet Nasr	.63	.12	.15	—	.03	—	.19	.23	—	.05	—	.47	4	—
Early Jemdet Nasr	3.47	.23	.10	—	.03	.03	.07	.03	—	.01	.01	.12	—	2
Late Uruk	2.97	.34	.07	.13	.03	—	.11	.02	.04	.01	—	.18	—	—
Middle Uruk	2.55	.27	.27	—	.03	.03	.11	.11	—	.01	.01	.24	—	2
Early Uruk	3.66	.18	.45	.36	—	.18	.05	.12	.10	—	.05	.32	—	—
Farukh	1.92	.47	.19	.23	—	.11	.24	.10	.12	—	.06	.52	—	—

source, the sudden pervasive use of basalt grinding slabs suggests that the commodity had become available because of either expansion of the exchange network, or acquisition of a large transport animal such as the donkey, or possibly because of introduction of new techniques of quarrying and working the slabs.

Objects of copper and cuprous alloys were only rarely discarded at Farukhabad. Probably most broken pieces were returned to the crucibles of local workshops or traveling smiths. Though there is no direct indication of a local shop prior to the occurrence of three pieces of metal slag in the Early Dynastic Period, such activity would have been local and need not have scattered debris very broadly. The occurrence of tools and tool fragments from Middle Uruk times onward shows that metal was imported, but the likelihood of extensive re-use precludes an assessment of the relative quantities involve. Two likely sources of copper for fourth millennium Deh Luran are south central Anatolia near Maden and Central Iran near Anarak or Kerman (Tylecote 1970), but there are other possible sources and there are as yet no reliable methods for distinguishing their products, particularly given the problem of the blending of different coppers during recyling.

MARINE SHELL

These were the most common durable display material used at Farukhabad, but their aggregate distribution should be used with due caution. We do not know why some molluscs, particularly *Conus*, were used throughout the sequence, while others were used only sporadically. We know that some had uses doubtless spatially restricted within communities, such as the use of *Mytilus* or "mother-of-pearl" for inlay, while others were perhaps from limited areas of the Gulf only occasionally participating in the network of interregional exchange. Nevertheless, it is interesting to note that the total pieces of marine shell per cubic meter is fairly constant after its appearance during the Early Uruk Period, except for an increase during the Late Jemdet Nasr Phase. This is not likely to be an effect of the bias of our Late Jemdet Nasr samples toward more elaborate architecture, since there is no association of shell with either simple or elaborate buildings during the Early Jemdet Nasr Phase. The presence of more than three times as much marine shell as before or after probably indicates either increased accessibility due to decreased value or increased export from Deh Luran.

SEMI-PRECIOUS STONE

Lapis lazuli, presumably from Badakhshan in North Afghanistan, and carnelian, which has many possible sources on the Iranian Plateau, are the only semi-precious stones found repeatedly. They have limited distributions at Farukhabad. Carnelian was recovered from Late Uruk to Late Jemdet Nasr deposits, while lapis was recovered in Late Jemdet Nasr and Early Dynastic Layers. These parallel the occurrences of the stones in southern Mesopotamia (Herrmann 1960). Given the few occurrences at Farukhabad, it seems prudent to make little comment about the absence of carnelian from Early Dynastic deposits and of lapis from Late Uruk and Early Jemdet Nasr deposits. It is striking that lapis lazuli, certainly the rarer material of the two, seems to become more common in the period when Farukhabad ceased to be the center of the Deh Luran Plain, and became a subsidiary of Musiyan. It is possible that lapis was undergoing a decline in relative value at the very time it became available to the Deh Luran communities, or, alternatively, that Musiyan's increased political importance facilitated increased access.

CHANGING SYSTEMS OF INTERREGIONAL EXCHANGE

During the period under consideration, extending from the late fifth to the early third millennium, one pattern of exchange declines, there is a long and complex period of adjustment, and another pattern of exchange emerges. The quantitative data relevant to these changes extracted from Tables 78–81, are presented graphically in Figure 99.

The Farukh Phase inhabitants, both prestigious and common, were processing small quantities of asphalts from the nearby bitumen spring, much of it probably for exchange. In contrast, Medium Gray Chert from the other end of the plain was mostly processed near the elaborate buildings associated with prestigious persons who perhaps had a special standing at Musiyan and communities closer to the chert source. There is no indication of a major weaving industry. In return for their exports, the inhabitants of Farukhabad must have received a range of goods, but the only ones that can be documented are exotic cherts and obsidian. Cherts came from eastern Khuzestan, probably by way of the Susiana, and from unknown sources to the west. Obsidian came from far Anatolia in very small quantities. Households in the excavated areas received about the same quantities of the different cherts. This suggests that the households did not have separate exchange relationships, but rather that they received imported cherts from a common pool or store (Winter and Pires-Ferreira 1976). Relative to later times, these cherts are readily accessible and have a low value relative to local cherts. When we turn to the modest Early Uruk community, with craft goods and architecture very different from those of the Farukh Phase, we find that the production of asphalt, Medium Gray Chert, and probably cloth is little different from that before. Also, the same types of exotic chert and obsidian are obtained, and most of them maintain their value relative to local stone. The only changes of note are the drop in the value of Fine White and Pink Chert and the appearance of marine shell. Thus, the Deh Luranis were participating in a long-lived and stable system of interregional exchange, probably regulated by persons of high rank. Precisely how this regulation was carried out and how the exchange system operated during the long period between the Farukh Phase and the Early Uruk Phase are subjects for future research.

The Middle Uruk inhabitants of the emerging small center of Farukhabad participated in a rapidly changing system. The relative value of all cherts except the Fine Gray increased. New and presumably costly commodities such as metals were being obtained. It is not surprising that the production of Medium Gray Chert was increased and that there is some indication of the increased weaving of local wool. Unfortunately our excavation sampled only modest housing and we have little evidence of social context of this apparent response to changing conditions. During the Late Uruk Period, however, the situation is clearer. Farukhabad is the only center on the plain, a tiny outpost of some larger polity. The value of imported chert relative to local substitutes is uniformly high. Other craft goods, perhaps even ceramics, are transported to Deh Luran. In return, there is a further increase in Medium Gray Chert export, and marked increase in asphalt production, both centered on an area of elaborate

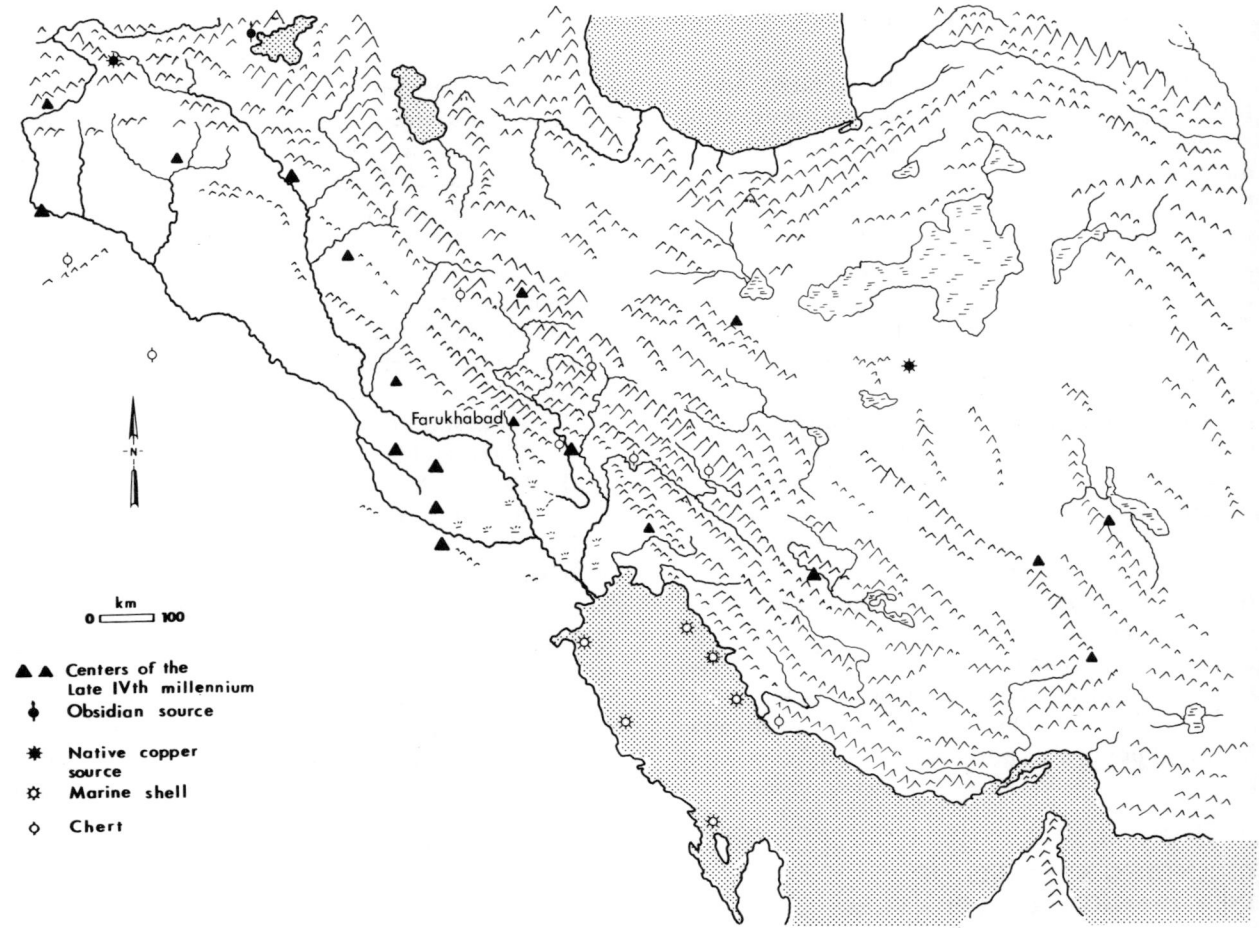

Figure 98. Sources of materials transported to Tepe Farukhabad.

probably non-domestic architecture and special features. There is a shift to goats, but a decline in evidence of local weaving, suggesting that the goat hair was shipped for final processing elsewhere. In short, the final result of a long period of increasing values—probably in response to the increasing demands of the great Uruk centers to the east and south—and of local efforts to increase production, is a reorganization of production, probably under the direct control of administrators from outside the plain. The evidence of Farukhabad is no longer of exchange between polities, but of the exploitation of a depopulated marginal area by a political center elsewhere.

During the Jemdet Nasr Period, the Late Uruk centers of Uruk and Susa decline and other centers arise. In this time of shifting control, Deh Luran has a period of growth and prosperity unparalleled in its history. The town of Musiyan grows quickly to a population of several thousand, and Farukhabad becomes one of its subsidiaries. Local crafts appear, among them apparently a revived local weaving industry, presumably emphasizing goat hair products. Medium Gray Chert export remains at a constant high level through both Early and Late Jemdet Nasr Phases. In contrast, asphalt production shows a decline from Late Uruk, followed by a marked increase during the Late Jemdet Nasr Phase. Imports, which had remained at their depressed Late Uruk level during the earlier phase show a correlated increase during the later phase. Chert value appears to decrease by a factor of four, but this is probably only a simple result of increased export. Even marine shell, whose value had remained constant since the Early Uruk Phase shows an increase in availability. Basalt and lapis lazuli appear in quantity. The locus of this increasing exchange is clear. Asphalt

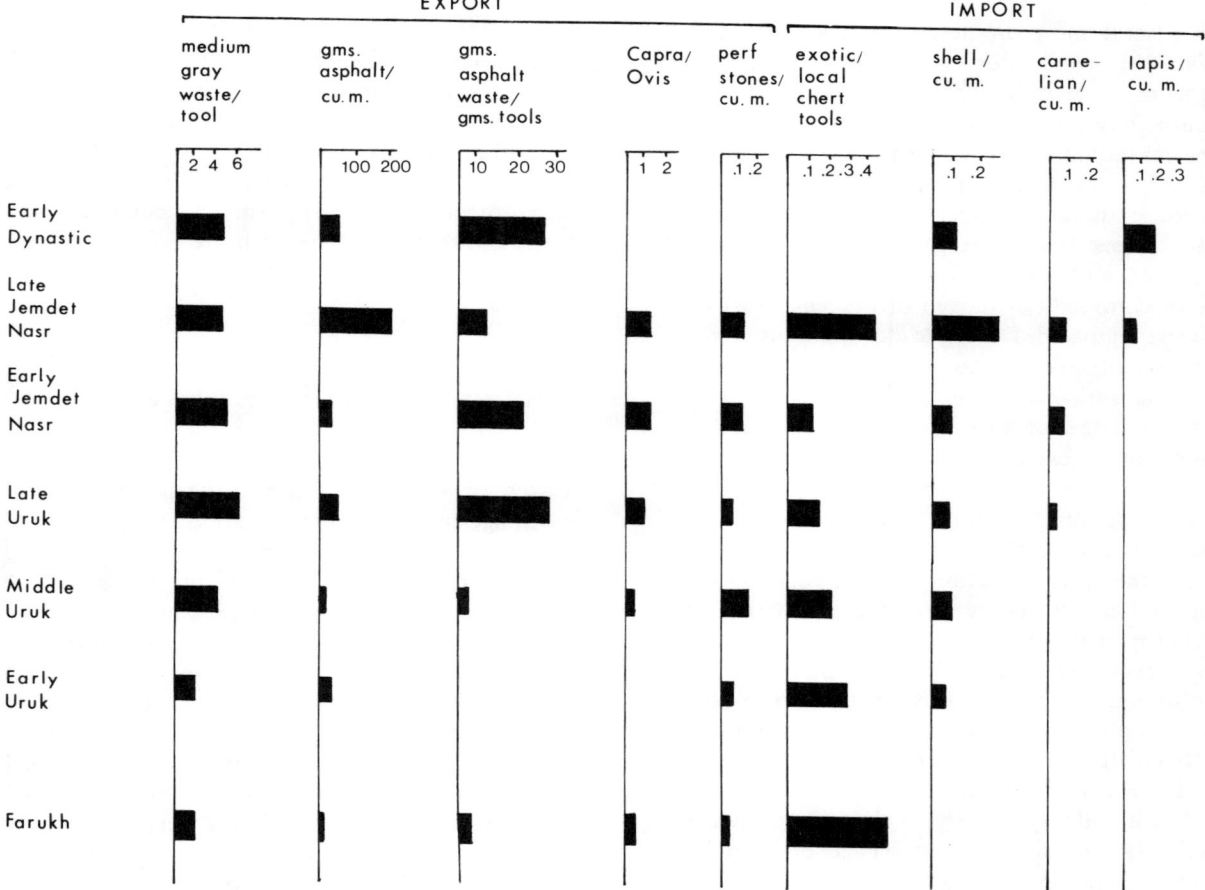

Figure 99. Graphical presentation of changing indicators of material preparation and use through time.

production is centered in elaborate residences and production in such residences shows an eightfold increase, while production in simple residences shows only a threefold increase. Imports are not uniformly distributed; some houses have more Fine Gray Chert while others have more Fine White and Pink Cherts. Thus, different families within the same community have built different exchange arrangements, and they profit differentially from their efforts. This contrasts with what is known of the earlier Farukh Phase system. While less stable, the later system may have been more responsive to changing conditions.

The Early Dynastic evidence seems to indicate a continuation of the Late Jemdet Nasr exchange pattern. However, erosion of the remains and our relatively small samples combine to prevent reliable assessment of chert use and animal manage-ment. A fair assessment of this period will not be possible until there is further excavation at Musiyan.

INTERREGIONAL EXCHANGE AND STATE AND URBAN DEVELOPMENT

A number of recent papers have argued that states, defined as sociopolitical entities with internally and externally specialized administrative activities, first emerged sometime during the Early Uruk Period in both central Khuzestan (Johnson 1973; Wright and Johnson 1975) and the southern alluvium of Mesopotamia proper (Johnson 1979). I continue to support this definition on the grounds that it subsumes most other classical definitions but has the advantage of being both more general and more precise, and I continue to support this explication of Mesopotamian state emergence since it best conforms with available evidence, however, spotty such may be.

The preceding section argued that interregional exchange as evidenced in Deh Luran—which is near the boundary between these two regions in whose centers states emerged—continued during this period with little evidence of change in the types of commodities moved or the way in which they were regulated. During Middle and Late Uruk when established states were growing and competing with each other, various efforts were made to re-organize Deh Luran's production and participation in exchange. It is only during Jemdet Nasr times that a new arrangment, capable of greatly expanding imports and exports, is in evidence at Farukhabad.

Thus, the transformation of inter-regional exchange seems to follow that transformation in control organization termed the origin of the state. If the Farukhabad data provide a correct assessment of exchange, then one cannot argue that increasing production for export is an explanation of initial state emergence in Greater Mesopotamia.

I have previously defined urban economies as those with fully specialized productive activities (Wright 1969a:1–2). The emergence of such an economy, could, in contrast to state emergence, be gradual. It is thus difficult to speak of the "first emergence of urban economies," defined as above or otherwise. Fourth millennium Deh Luran does provide an interesting case study, however. It appears clear that Farukh Phase productive activities were performed in all communities. During the Uruk Period, craft techniques change and new productive specialties are added, but all are performed at Farukhabad, in many cases by families with demonstrable agricultural involvements. During Jemdet Nasr times, some craft activities either do not occur or Farukhabad or occur only on the margins of the community. Other communities which are apparently purely agricultural have emerged. Also, the large central town of Musiyan has developed. These points indicate further increase in production specialization. The long-term pattern of increase correlates well with increased production for export as outlined in the previous discussion. Certainly the proposition that inter-regional trade and urban development are mutually interrelated requires further investigation, and the hypothesis that increased participation in interregional exchange leads to the growth of central towns cannot be rejected. In areas farther from Central Mesopotamia than Deh Luran, which were not previously brought under the direct control of existing states, such urban development may well have been linked to secondary state development. Such propositions should be formally developed and tested in other areas (Alden 1979).

THOUGHTS ON FUTURE WORK

Where might subsequent problem-oriented research be directed, regarding both interregional exchange in the ancient Near East in general and cultural developments during the late fourth to early third millennia in Deh Luran in particular?

To elucidate interregional exchange in general, both better theoretical constructs and more field research are needed. The first concern is best left for treatment in another type of paper. The second concern will require several types of excavation. First, it would be useful to repeat the Farukhabad research design—though with the improved sampling approaches and recovery techniques possible today—at other nodes in the network of transport. Such data, coupled with more precise identification of the sources of imports, would allow the study of changes in value through space as well as time (cf. Renfrew 1977). Second, if we are to understand the way in which exports and imports were regulated, we must seek data from contexts which allow the inference of year-to-year variation in production, consumption, and values. This will require a focus on rapidly deposited debris near material sources, workshops, storage areas, and domestic units. Large refuse filled pits seem to provide the best opportunities to recover such data (Wright, Miller, and Redding 1980). Third, another way to approach the problems of value and regulation, at least for third millennium participants in the exchange network, will be the study of the few archives which deal with such problems. Apparently many of the texts recently found at Tell Mardikh—ancient Ebla—do record traded commodities. The complete publication of such material will be a tremendous contribution.

While Deh Luran may not be the most extensively investigated component area of Greater Mesopotamia, it is with the appearance of this monograph, one of the most thoroughly documented. However, our knowledge of the sequence of environments, subsistence practices, settlement patterns, craft items and so on between 8000 B.C. and 1500 B.C. only sets the stage for new kinds of studies. In particular, we need a better understanding of sociopolitical organization. This will require excavations of a type not yet attempted in Deh Luran—extensive horizontal clearance—on both the smallest village sites and on the large center of Musiyan. Farukhabad itself is not appropriate for such work, but it too will someday require further excavation, if the Mehmeh does not completely destroy it, if only to use improved techniques to expand our small samples and further challenge the conclusions reached in the present work.

BIBLIOGRAPHY

Adams, Robert McC.
  1962   Agriculture and Urban Life in Southwestern Iran. Science 136:109–122.
  1965   Land Behind Baghdad: A History of Settlement in the Diyala Plains. University of Chicago Press. Chicago.
Adams, Robert McC. and Nissen, Hans J.
  1972   The Uruk Countryside. University of Chicago Press. Chicago.
Alden, John R.
  1979   Regional Economic Organization in Banesh Period Iran. University Microfilms. Ann Arbor.
Allouse, Bashir E.
  1953   The Avifauna of Iraq. Iraq Natural History Museum Publication 3. Al-Tafayyud Press. Baghdad.
Amiet, Pierre
  1961   La Glyptique Mesopotamiènne. Archaique. Éditions du Centre National de la Récherche Scientifique. Geuthner. Paris.
  1972   La Glyptique Sasienne. Mémoires de la Délégation Archéologique Française en Iran 43. Geuthner. Paris.
Baqir, Taha
  1945   Iraq Government Excavations at 'Aqar Quf: Second Interim Report, 1943–1944. Iraq (supplement).
Beijerink, W.
  1947   Zadenatlas der Nederlandische Flora. H. Veenman en Zonen. Wageningen.
Berghe, Louis van den
  1968   La Necropole de Bani Sarmah. Archeologia 24:53–68.
Blegvad, K.
  1944   Fishes of the Iranian Gulf. Danish Scientific Investigations in Iran, Part III. Einar Musksgaard. Copenhagen.
Boessneck, J., Muller, H. H., and Teichert, M.
  1964   Osteologische Unterscheidungsmerkmale Zwischen Schaf (*Ovis aries* Linne) und Ziege (*Capra hircus* Linne). Kuhn-Archiv, Bd. 78:1-2.
Bohr, Barbara
  1968   Grayware Jars from Tepe Farukhabad. Mimeographed paper in the files of the University of Michigan Museum of Anthropology. Ann Arbor.
Braidwood, Robert J. and Braidwood, Linda
  1960   Excavations of the Plain of Antioch I. Oriental Institute Publications 61. University of Chicago. Chicago.
Brinkman, John A.
  1968   A Political History of Post-Kassite Babylonia, 1158–722 B.C. Analecta Orientalia 43. Pontificum Institutum Biblicum. Rome.
Brouwer, Wather and Stählin, Adolf
  1975   Handbuch der Samenkunde. DLG-Verlag. Frankfurt-am-Main.
Butzer, Karl
  1964   Environment and Archaeology: An Introduction to Pleistocene Geography. Aldine. Chicago.
Caldwell, Joseph R.
  1967   Investigations at Tal-i Iblis. Illinois State Museum Preliminary Reports No. 9. Springfield.
Cameron, George
  1936   The History of Early Iran. University of Chicago Press. Chicago.
Carr, A.
  1952   Handbook of Turtles: The Turtles of the United States, Canada, and Baja California. Comstock Publishers Association. New York.
Carter, Elizabeth
  1971   Elam in the Second Millennium B.C.: The Archaeological Evidence. Unpublished doctoral dissertation. Dept. of Near Eastern Languages and Civilizations, University of Chicago. Chicago.
Carter, Elizabeth and Stolper, Matthew W.
  1976   Middle Elamite Malyan. Expedition 18:2:33–42.
Clutton-Brock, Juliet
  1962   Near Eastern Canids and the Affinities of the Natufian Dogs. Zeitschrift fur Tierzuchtung und Zuchtungsbiologische 76:2/3:326-333.
Cowgill, George
  1968   Counts, Ratios, and Percentages: Problems in Quantifying Archaeological Data. Unpublished manuscript on file at Brandeis University, Dept. of Anthropology. Waltham, Mass.
  1970   Some Sampling and Reliability Problems in Archaeology. *In*: Archéologie et Calculateurs, J.-C. Gardin and Mario Borillo, eds. Paris: Centre de la Récherche Scientifique, pp. 161–176.

BIBLIOGRAPHY

Delougaz, P.P.
   1952   Pottery of the Diyala. Oriental Institute Publication 63. University of Chicago. Chicago.
   1967   Chogha Mish. Iran 5:147–149.

Degerbøl, M.
   1963   Prehistoric Cattle in Denmark and Adjacent Areas. *In*: Man and Cattle: Proceedings of a Symposium on Domestication. A.E. Mourant and F.E. Zeuner, eds. Royal Anthropological Institute of Great Britain and Ireland, Occasional Paper 18:69–79.

Dollfus, Geneviève
   1973   Les Fouilles à Djaffarabad de 1969 à 1971. Cahiers de la Délégation Archéologique Française en Iran 1:17–162. Geuthner. Paris.
   1975   La Sixième Campagne de Fouilles à Jaefarābād, Xuzestan. Proceedings of the Third Annual Symposium on Archaeological Research in Iran: 13–22. Iranian Centre for Archaeological Research. Tehran.

Epstein, A.
   1971   The Origin of the Domestic Animals of Africa II. Africana Publishing Corporation. New York.

Gasche, Hermann
   1973   La Potterie Élamite du Deuxième Millènnaire A.C. Mémoires de la Délégation en Iran 47. Geuthner. Paris.

Garman, S.
   1913   The Plagiostoma (Sharks, Skates, and Rays). Memoirs of the Museums of Comparative Zoology at Harvard College 36. Harvard University Press. Cambridge.

Gautier, J.-E. and Lampre, G.
   1905   Fouilles de Moussian. Mémoires de la Délégation en Perse 8:59–149. Leroux. Paris.

Ghirshman, Roman
   1964   Suse. Campagne de Fouilles 1962–1963. Arts Asiatiques 10:3–20.
   1965   Suse du Temps des Sukkalmah. Campagne de Fouilles 1963–1964. Arts Asiatiques 11:3–21.
   1966   Tchogha Zanbil (Dur Untash) I:La Ziggurat. Mémoires de la Délégation en Iran 39. Geuthner. Paris.
   1967   Suse, Campagne de l'hiver 1965–1966. Arts Asiatiques 15:3–28.
   1968a   Tchogha Zanbil (Dur Untash) II: Temenos, Temples, Palais, Tombes. Mémoires de la Délégation en Iran 40. Geuthner. Paris.
   1968b   Suse au Tournant du IIIe au IIe Millénnaire avant notre ère, Travaux de la Délégation Archéologique en Iran—Hiver 1966–1967, Rapport Préliminaire. Arts Asiatiques 17:3–44.

Ghirshman, Roman and Stève, M.-J.
   1966   Suse, Campagne de l'hiver 1965-66. Arts Asiatiques 13:3–32.

Gibson, McGuire
   1973   The City and Area of Kish. Field Research Projects. Coconut Grove (Miami).

Goff, Clare
   1971   Luristan Before the Iron Age. Iran 11:131–152.

Gould, Richard
   1969   Yiwara: Foragers of the Australian Desert. Charles Scribners and Sons. New York.

Gremliza, F.G.L.
   1962   The Ecology of Endemic Diseases in the Dez Irrigation Pilot Area. Development and Resources Corporation. New York.

Groves, C.P. and Mazak, V.
   1967   On Some Taxonomic Problems of Asiatic Wild Asses: With Description of a New Subspecies. Zeitschrift für Saugertierkunde 32:6: 321–355.

Haller, A. von
   1932   Die Keramik der archaischen Schichten von Uruk. *In*: Vierter vorläufiger Bericht über die von der Notgemeinschaft der Deutschen Wissenschaft in Uruk unternommen Ausgrabungen. Abhandlungen der Preussischen Akademie der Wissenschaft: Philosophisch-Historische Klasse 6: 38–42. Berlin.

Harrison, D.L.
   1968   The Mammals of Arabia II: Carnivora, Artiodactyla and Hyracoidae. Ernst Benn. London.

Hatt, Robert L.
   1959   The Mammals of Iraq. Miscellaneous Publications of the Museum of Zoology 106. University of Michigan. Ann Arbor.

Helbaek, Hans
   1969   Plant Collecting, Dry Farming and Irrigation in Prehistoric Deh Luran. *In*: Hole, Flannery and Neely 1969.

Hermann, Georgina
   1968   Lapis Lazuli—The Early Phases of its Trade. Iraq 30:21–56.

Hilzenheimer, Max
   1941   Animal Remains from Tell Asmar. Studies in Ancient Oriental Civilization 20. The Oriental Institute, Chicago. University of Chicago. Chicago.

Hole, Frank, ed.
   1969   Preliminary Reports of the Rice University Project in Iran, 1968–69. Department of Anthropology mimeograph. Rice University. Houston.

Hole, Frank, Flannery, Kent V., and Neely, James A.
    1969   Prehistory and Human Ecology of the Deh Luran Plain: An Early Village Sequence from Khuzistan, Iran. Memoir 1. Museum of Anthropology, University of Michigan. Ann Arbor.

Hole, Frank and Shaw, Mary
    1967   Computer Analysis of Chronological Seriation. Rice University Studies 53:3. Houston.

Jacobsen, Thorkild and Adams, Robert
    1958   Salt and Silt in Ancient Mesopotamian Agriculture. Science 128:1251–1258.

Jewell, P.
    1963   Cattle from British Archaeological Sites. In: Man and Cattle: Proceedings of a Symposium on Domestication, A.E. Mourant and F.E. Zeuner, eds. Royal Anthropological Institute of Great Britain and Ireland. Occasional Paper 18: 80–100.

Johnson, Gregory A.
    1973   Local Exchange and Early State Development in Southwestern Iran. Anthropological Papers 51. Museum of Anthropology, University of Michigan. Ann Arbor.
    1979   The Changing Organization of Uruk Administration on the Susiana Plain. Presented at symposium entitled Archaeological Perspectives on Iran: From Prehistory to the Islamic Conquest at the School of American Research at Santa Fe, New Mexico.

Khalaf, Kamal T.
    1961   The Marine and Freshwater Fishes of Iraq. Ar-Rabitta Press. Baghdad.

Kirkby, Michael
    1977   Land and Water Resources of the Deh Luran and Khuzistan Plains. in: Studies in the Archaeological History of the Deh Luran Plain, by Frank Hole. Memoir 9, Museum of Anthropology, University of Michigan, Ann Arbor.

Korfmann, Manfred
    1973   The Sling as a Weapon. Scientific American 229:4:34–51.

Kupper, Jean-Robert
    1957   Les Nomades en Mésopotamie au Temps des Rois de Mari. Bibliothèque de la Faculté de Philosophie et Lettres de L'Université de Lièges, Fascicule 142. Société d' Edition. Paris.

Kus, Susan M.
    1969   Protoliterate Stone Bowls from Tepe Farukhabad. Mimeographed paper in the files of the University of Michigan Museum of Anthropology. Ann Arbor.

Langsdorf, Alexander and McCown, Donald
    1942   Tall-i Bakun A. Oriental Institute Publications 54. The University of Chicago Press. Chicago.

Lawrence, Barbara
    1969   Early Domestic Dogs. Zeitschrift fur Saugertierkunde 32:44–59.

Lay, Douglas M.
    1967   A Study of the Mammals of Iran Resulting from the Street Expedition of 1962–1963. Fieldiana:Zoology 54. The Field Museum of Natural History. Chicago.

Le Breton, Louis
    1957   The Early Periods of Susa: Mesopotamian Relations. Iraq 19:79–124.

Le Brun, Alain
    1971   Récherches Stratigraphiques à l'Acropole de Suse (1969–1971). Cahiers de la Délégation Archéologique Française en Iran 1:163–214. Geuthner. Paris.

Lubbock, J.
    1864   Cave Men. Natural History Review 4:407–428.

Mallowan, Max E.L.
    1947   Excavations at Brak and Chagar Bazar. Iraq. 9:1–259.

Marschner, Robert F., Duffy, Leo, and Wright, Henry T.
    1978   Asphalts from Ancient Townsites in Southwestern Iran. Paléorient 4:97–112.

Marschner, Robert F. and Wright, Henry T.
    1978   Asphalts from Middle Eastern Archaeological Sites. Advances in Chemistry Series 171:150–171.

McCown, Donald E. and Haines, Richard C.
    1967   Nippur I: The Temple of Enlil, Scribal Quarter, and Soundings. Oriental Institute Publications 78. The Unviersity of Chicago Press. Chicago.

Miller, Naomi
    1978   Preliminary Report on the Botanical Remains from Tepe Djaffarabad, 1967–74 Campaigns. Cahiers de la Délégation Archéologique Française en Iran 7:49–53.

Neely, James A.
    1969   Preliminary Report on the Archaeological Survey of the Deh Luran Region, 1968–1969. Preliminary Reports of the Rice University Project in Iran, 1968–1969. Department of Anthropology, Rice University. Houston.
    1974   Sassanian and Early Islamic Water Control and Irrigation Systems on the Deh Luran Plain. In: Irrigation's Impact on Society, Theodore E. Downing and McGuire Gibson, eds. Anthropological Papers 25, University of Arizona. Tucson.

Nissen, Hans J.
    1970   Grabung in den Quadraten K/L XII in Uruk Warka. Baghdader Mitteilungen 5:101–191.

BIBLIOGRAPHY

Negahban, Ezzatollah
    1967   Haft Tepe. Iran 5:140–141.
    1968   Haft Tepe. Iran 6:161.
    1969   Haft Tepe. Iran 7:173–177.

Parsons, Mary H.
    1972   Spindle Whorls from the Teotihuacan Valley, Mexico. *In*: Miscellaneous Studies in Mexican Prehistory, Jeffrey Parsons, ed. Anthropological Papers 45. Museum of Anthropology, University of Michigan. Ann Arbor.

Perkins, Anne L.
    1949   The Comparative Archaeology of Early Mesopotamia. Studies in Ancient Oriental Civilization 25. The Oriental Institute. The University of Chicago. Chicago.

Pézard, Maurice
    1914   Mission a Bender-Bouchir. Mémoires de la Mission Archéologique en Perse 15. Leroux. Paris.

Reed, Charles A.
    1961   Osteological Evidence for Prehistoric Domestication in Southwest Asia. Zeitschrift fur Tierzuchtung und Zuchtungsbiologie 76: 1: 31–38.

Renfrew, Colin and Dixon, John
    1977   Obsidian in West Asia: A Review. *In*: Problems in Economic and Social Archaeology, G. Sieveking, I. H. Longworth, and K. E. Wilson, eds. Duckworth. London.

Renfrew, Colin, Dixon, John, and Cann, J.R.
    1968   Further Analyses of Near Eastern Obsidians. Proceedings of the Prehistoric Society 34: 319–331.

Sadek-Kooros, Hind
    1972   Primitive Bone Fracturing: A Method of Research. American Antiquity 37:3:369–382.

Saxe, Arthur A.
    1970   Social Dimensions of Mortuary Practice. University Microfilms. Ann Arbor.

Sahlins, Marshall
    1972   Stone Age Economics. Aldine. Chicago.

Schacht, Robert M.
    1973   Population and Economic Organization in Early Historic Southwestern Iran. University Microfilms. Ann Arbor.
    1975   A Preliminary Report on the Excavations at Tepe Sharafabad, 1971. The Journal of Field Archaeology 2:307–329.

Siegel, Sidney
    1956   Non-parametric Statistics. McGraw-Hill. New York.

Silver, I. A.
    1970   The Aging of Domestic Animals. *In*: Science and Archaeology, Don Brothwell and Eric Higgs, eds. Basic Books. New York.

Sisson, S. and Grossman, J. M.
    1953   The Anatomy of the Domestic Animals (fourth edition). W. B. Saunders. Philadelphia.

Speth, John and Johnson, Gregory A.
    1976   Problems in the Use of Correlation for the Investigation of Tool Kits and Activity Areas. *In*: Cultural Change and Continuity, Charles E. Cleland, ed. Academic Press. New York.

Stève, M.-J. and Gasche, Hermann
    1973   L'Acropole de Suse. Mémoires de la Délégation Archéologique Française en Iran 46. Geuthner. Paris.

Sumner, William M.
    1972   Cultural Development in the Kur River Basin, Iran: An Archeological Analysis of Settlement Patterns. University Microfilms. Ann Arbor.
    1974   Excavations at Tall-i Malyan 1971–72. Iran 12:155–180.
    1976   Excavations at Tall-i Malyan (Anshan)1974. Iran 14:103–115.

Tchernov, Eitan
    1968   The Succession of Rodent Faunas During the Upper Pleistocene of Israel. Verlag Paul Paley. Hamburg.

Thrane, Henrik
    1970   Tepe Guran and the Luristan Bronzes. Archaeology 23:27–35.

Tobler, Arthur J.
    1950   Excavations at Tepe Gawra II. Museum Monographs. The University Museum, University of Pennsylvania. Philadelphia.

Todd, T. W. and Todd, A. W.
    1938   The Epiphyseal Union Pattern of the Ungulates with a Note on Cirenia. American Journal of Anatomy 63: 1: 1–36.

Tosi, Maurizio and Piperno, Marcello
    1973   Lithic Technology Behind the Ancient Lapis Lazuli Trade. Expedition 16: 1: 15–23.

Townsend, C. C.
    1974   Leguminales. *In*: The Flora of Iraq 3, C. C. Townsend and Even Guest, eds. Ministry of Agriculture and Agrarian Reform. Baghdad.

Tylecote, R. F.
    1970   Early Metallurgy in the Near East. Metals and Materials 4:285–293.

Vaurie, C.
    1965   The Birds of the Paleoarctic Fauna: A Systemic Reference (Non-passeriforms). H.F. and G. Wither. London.

Wenke, Robert J.
    1976   Imperial Investments and Agricultural Developments in Parthian and Sasanian Khuzestan: 150 B.C. to A.D. 640. Mesopotamia 10–11:31–221.

Whitcomb, Donald S.
    1972   The Proto-elamite Period at Tall-i Ghazir, Iran. Unpublished M.A. Thesis on file at the Department of Anthropology, University of Georgia, Athens.

Willey, Gordon R. and McGimsey, Charles R.
    1954   The Monagrillo Culture of Panama. Papers of the Peabody Museum of American Archaeology and Ethnology 49: 2: 1–158.

Winter, Marcus C. and Pires-Ferreira, Jane Wheeler
    1977   The Distribution of Obsidian among Two Oaxacan Villages. *In*: The Early Mesoamerican Village, Kent V. Flannery, ed. Academic Press. New York.

Winters, Howard D.
    1968   Value Systems and Trade Cycles of the Late Archaic in the Midwest. *In*: New Perspectives in Archeology, S.R. and L.R. Binford, eds, Aldine. Chicago.

Wright, Henry T.
    1968   Farukhabad. Iran 7: 172–173.
    1969a   The Administration of Rural Production in an Early Mesopotamian Town. Anthropological Papers 38. Museum of Anthropology, University of Michigan. Ann Arbor.
    1969b   Archaeological Survey in the Areas of Ram Hormuz, Shushtar, and Gotvand. Mimeographed paper in the files of the University of Michigan Museum of Anthropology. Ann Arbor.
    1972   A Consideration of Interregional Exchange in Greater Mesopotamia, 4000–3000 B.C. *In*: Social Exchange and Interaction. Edwin Wilmsen, ed. Anthropological Paper 46. Museum of Anthropology, University of Michigan. Ann Arbor.

Wright, Henry T., ed.
    1979   Archaeological Investigations in Northeastern Xuzestan, 1976. Technical Report 10. Museum of Anthropology, University of Michigan, Ann Arbor.

Wright, Henry T. and Johnson, Gregory A.
    1975   Population Exchange and Early State Formation in Southwestern Iran. American Anthropologist 77:267–287.

Wright, Henry T., Miller, Naomi, and Redding, Richard
    1980   Time and Process in an Uruk Rural Center. *In*: L'Archéologie de L'Iraq du Debut de L'Époque Néolithique à 333 Avant Notre Ère. M.-T. Barrelet, ed. Éditions du Centre National de la Récherche Scientifique. Paris.

Wright, Henry T., Neely, James A., Johnson, Gregory A., and Speth, John D.
    1975   Early Fourth Millennium Developments in Southwestern Iran. Iran 13: 129–147.

Young, T. Cuyler, Jr.
    1967   The Iranian Migrations into the Zagros. Iran 5:11–34.
    1969   Excavations at Godin Tepe: First Progress Report. Occasional Paper 17. Royal Ontario Museum. Toronto.

Zeist, Willem van, and Heeres, J.A.H.
    1973   Paleobotanical Studies of Deir 'Allā, Jordan. Paléorient 1: 21–37.

Ziegler, A.C.
    1973   Inference from Prehistoric Faunal Remains. Addison-Wesley Module in Anthropology 43.

Zohary, Michael
    1963   On the Geobotanical Structure of Iran. Bulletin of the Research Council of Israel: Botany 11D. supplement.

Zeuner, F.E.
    1963   A History of the Domesticated Animals. Hutchinson. London.

APPENDIX A

PROVENIENCE UNITS AT TEPE FARUKHABAD

The following two tables are included to facilitate further research with the samples recovered from Tepe Farukhabad. They enable the reader to know which excavation provenience units were included in various analyses and where these samples are stored today.

Table A1 is a summary of the actual field catalogue. The left-hand column is the four digit excavation number, marked on every diagnostic artifact. Throughout the preceding text such numbers are abbreviated to three digits and preceded by the letter 'X'. The middle column specifies the location from which the sample was removed, using the square and layer designations specified in the first chapter. The right-hand column indicates where the sample is located today. Six-digit numbers beginning with '60' are University of Michigan Museum of Anthropology catalogue numbers. Typically there are more than one, the first identifying the chipped stone items, the second identifying ceramics, and the other identifying less common materials. The letters 'P','Y', and 'C' designate samples sent to the University Museum in Philadelphia, Yale University, and the University of Chicago Oriental Institute respectively. The letter 'O' designates samples remaining in Teheran or, in a few cases, divided as type samples. Various soil, bone, and carbonized vegetation samples have been retained in Ann Arbor.

Table A2 specifies the aggregated analytical units used in much of the preceding analysis. The square designations are necessarily approximate. The excavation numbers are presented without an initial letter 'X'. Area, thickness, and volume estimates were made from field notes after the excavation. Measurement in the field is desirable.

Table A1: Provenience Units at Tepe Farukhabad

Field Catalogue Number	Unit Location: Description	Permanent Catalogue Number
0001	Excavation A: sherds scraped from Upper ¼	O
0002	Excavation A: sherds scraped from Middle, Upper ¼	O
0003	Excavation B: sherds scraped from Upper ¼	O
0004	Excavation B: sherds scraped from Middle, Upper ¼	O
0005	Excavation B: squares A-1 to E-1, layer 1-3 screen	C
0006	Excavation B: square B-1, layer 4	C
0007	Excavation B: square C-1, layer 4	C
0008	Excavation B: square D-1, layer 4	C
0009	Excavation B: square E-1, layer 4	C
0010	General surface material	60793
0011	Excavation B: square A-1 (half), layer 6	C
0012	Excavation B: square B-1, layer 6	C
0013	Excavation B: square C-1, layer 6	C
0014	Excavation B: square D-1, layer 6	C
0015	Excavation B: square E-1, layer 6	C
0016	Excavation B: square A-1, layer 7	60326,327
0017	Excavation B: square B-1, layer 7	C
0018	Excavation B: square C-1, layer 7	C
0019	Excavation B: square D-1, layer 7	60328,329
0020	Excavation B: square E-1, layer 7	C
0021	Excavation B: squares D-1, D-2, layer 8	C
0022	Excavation B: squares E-1, E-2, layer 8	C
0023	Excavation B: squares A-1, A-2, layer 9, gray ash lens	C
0024	Excavation B: squares A-1, A-2, layer 10, gray ash lens	C
0025	Excavation B: squares B-1, B-2, layer 10, gray ash lens with bricks	C

Table A1: Continued

Field Catalogue Number	Unit Location: Description	Permanent Catalogue Number
0026	Excavation B: squares B-1, B-2, some layer 7, Feature 3	C
0027	Excavation B: squares E-1, E-2, layer 12, gray brown silt layers	60330,696
0028	Excavation B: square A-1, Upper layer 11	C
0029	Excavation B: squares B-1, C-1, Upper layer 11	60331,332
0030	Excavation B: square D-1, layer 11	C
0031	Excavation B: squares A-2.5 to 3.5, to E-2.5 to 3.5, shovel, layers 11, 12	C
0032	Excavation B: square A-2, ½ A-3, layer 11A	C
0033	Excavation B: square A-1, layer 11A	C
0034	Excavation B: square B-2, ½ B-3, layer 11A	60333,334
0035	Excavation B: square B-1, layer 11A	60335,336,812,813
0036	Excavation B: squares C-2, ½ C-3, layer 11A	C
0037	Excavation B: squares D-1, D-2, D-3, layer 12	C
0038	Excavation C: surface to −1.70 m, perhaps disturbed debris around well or hut	60699,700,701
0039	Excavation C: −1.70 m to −1.80 m below south end	60702,703
0040	Excavation A: squares B-6, B-7, above 155.8 m	60070,071
0041	Excavation A: squares C-6, C-7, above 155.8 m	P
0042	Excavation A: squares A-6, A-7, above 155.8 m	60072,073
0043	Excavation A: squares A-6, A-7, B-6, B-7, 155.8 m to 155.58 m	60074,075
0044	Excavation A: squares C-6, C-7, D-6, D-7, 155.8 m to 155.58 m	60825, P
0045	Excavation A: squares A-8, E-8, B-9, C-9, D-9, scrapings below 155.6 m	P
0046	Excavation A: squares B-8, C-8, D-8, 155.30 m–155.6 m, layer + 3	P
0047	Excavation A: squares AB 6, 7, 155.30 m–155.6 m, layer + 3	60076,077
0048	Excavation A: squares D-6, 7, E-6, layer + 3	60078,079,726
0049	Excavation A: squares A-8, B-8, 155.0 m–155.3 m, layer 5	60080,081,082
0050	Excavation A: squares C-8, D-8, 155.0 m–155.3 m, layer 5	Y
0051	Excavation B: A, B-1, 2, ½ 3, Upper layer 11B	60337,338,814,815
0052	Excavation B: D, E-1, 2, ½ 3, Lower layer 12	C
0053	Excavation B: squares A-3 to E-3, layers 11B 12, 13, all pick and shovel	C
0054	Excavation B: squares A-2, B-2, Lower layer 11B	C
0055	Excavation B: squares C-2, D-2, Lower layer 11B, and layer 12	C
0056	Excavation B: square E-2, layer 14, ash lens in front of wall	C
0057	Excavation B: squares A, B, ½ C-2, C-3, Middle layer 12	60809
0058	Excavation B: squares ½ C-2, C-3, D-2, D-3, E-3, Lower layer 12, pick and shovel	C
0059	Excavation B: Feature 6, layer 12, 13, intrusive, heavily disturbed	C
0060	Excavation A: squares A-7, B-7, layer 5 some layer 6, from E-7, 8	60083,084,085,086,087
0061	Excavation A: squares C-7, D-7, layer 5	P
0062	Excavation A: squares C-6, ½ D-6, layer 5A.	Y
0063	Excavation A: squares ½ D-6, E-6, layer 5A.	Y
0064	Excavation A: squares ½ B-6, C-6, ½ D-6, layer 5B, Feature 1	Y
0065	Excavation A: squares ½ D-6, E-6, layer 5B	60088,089
0066	Excavation A: squares C-6, layer 5B, flotation sample 25 × 25 × 8 cm	O
0067	Excavation A: square E-6, layer 5B	O
0068	Excavation A: squares A-6, layer 5, west of wall Feature 2	60090,091,092
0069	Excavation A: squares C, D, E-8, 9, ½ 10, layer 6	P
0070	Excavation B: squares A-4 to E-4, layers 12 to 15, shovel	C
0071	Excavation B: square C-1, layer 6, flotation of ash lens	C
0072	Excavation B: squares A-2, A-3, B-2, B-3, layer 13, same 12—large pit filled with ash and brick layers	C
0073	Excavation B: squares C-2, C-3, D-2, D-3, E-2, E-3, layer 12, 15, green clay and some ash, pick and shovel	C
0074	Excavation B: squares A-4 to E-4, layer 15, pick and shovel	C
0075	Excavation B: squares A-2, A-3, layer 15 ±	C
0076	Excavation B: squares B, C, D-2, 3, layer 15 to 16, pick and shovel	C
0077	Excavation B: squares E-2, E-3, layer 15 to 16	C
0078	Excavation A: squares A, B-8, 9, ½ 10, layer 6	60093,094,095,096,097
0079	Excavation A: square E-7 layer 6, large pot and contents	P
0080	Excavation A: squares C, D, E-6, 7, layer 6	60098,099,100,101
0081	Excavation A: squares A, B-10, Feature 3, plaster vat	60102,103,104
0082	Excavation A: square D-6, Feature 5, plaster vat	P
0083	Excavation A: squares B, ½ C-½ 9, ½ 10, ½ C, D-½ 9, layer 7	O

APPENDIX A

Table A1: Continued

Field Catalogue Number	Unit Location: Description	Permanent Catalogue Number
0084	Excavation A: squares ½ B, C-8, 9, layer 7	Y
0085	Excavation A: squares D, ½ E-8, 9, layer 7	60105,106,727
0086	Excavation A: squares A, B-6, 7, layer 6	60107,108,109,110
0087	Excavation A: squares B, C-6, 7, layer 7	60111,112,113, 114,810
0088	Excavation A: squares D-6, D-7, layer 7	60728,729,Y
0089	Excavation A: squares A, B-6, 7, 8, 9, layer 7, cleaning around Feature 1	60730
0090	Excavation A: Feature 5, flotation sample from base of plaster vat, 25 x 15 x 10 cm	O
0091	Excavation A: square D-2, layer 6, oven	60115,116
0092	Excavation A: Feature 6, oven, flotation sample	O
0093	Excavation A: squares ½ B, C, layer 11B	P
0094	Excavation B: squares A-2, A-3 to E-2, E-3, layer 13 to 16, 156.25 m to 156.50 m, pick and shovel	C
0095	Excavation B: squares A-5 to E-5, 155.56 to 155.25, layers 16, 17, pick and shovel	C
0096	Excavation B: Feature 7 Burial, square A-3, 156.1	C
0097	Excavation B: squares D, E-2, ½ 3, layer 15, 156.1 to 156.25	C
0098	Excavation B: squares A, B-2, 3, layers 13, 16, 17, pick and shovel	C
0099	Excavation B: squares D, E-½ 3, 4, layer 16, top 17	C
0100	Excavation B: squares D, E-2, ½ 3, layer 16, 156.01 m to 156.44 m	C
0101	Excavation A: squares B, C-9, Feature 8	60117,118,731
0102	Excavation A: squares A, B-6, 7, 8, 9; cleaning Feature 10, pick and shovel of layer 7	60119,120,121, 732
0103	Excavation A: squares ½ C, D, E, layers 8, 9, ½ 10	60733
0104	Excavation A: squares C, D, ½ E-6, 7, layer 8	60123,124,125, 735,736,737
0105	Excavation A: squares B, C, D-½ 10, 11, layers 10, 11, pick and shovel	O
0106	Excavation B: squares A-6 to E-6, 155.20 m to 155.56 m, layer 18	C
0107	Excavation B: squares A, B-2, 3, 4, layer 16, pick and shovel	C
0108	Excavation B: squares D-2, layer 17, triangular area northwest of Feature 8, wall	C
0109	Excavation B: squares A, B-2, 3, 4, layer 17, west of Feature 9, wall	C
0110	Excavation B: squares C-2 to C-6, "stratigraphic control," layers 15 to 17, pick and shovel	C
0111	Excavation B: squares A, B-2 to 6, Upper layer 18,	60339,340,816,817
0112	Excavation B: squares A, B, ½ C-2 to 6, Lower layer 18	C
0113	Excavation B: squares A, B, ½ C, Upper layer 19	C
0114	Excavation B: squares ½ C, D, E-2 to 6, Upper layer 18	C
0115	Excavation B: squares ½ C, D, E-2 to 6, Lower layer 18	C
0116	Excavation B: squares ½ C, D, E-2 to 5, Upper layer 19	C
0117	Excavation B: squares D, E-6, layer 19, south or in front of wall, Feature 10	C
0118	Excavation B: squares ½ C, D, E-10, ½ 11, layers 9, 10	60126,127,128,129
0119	Excavation A: squares ½ C, D, E-8, 9, layers 9, 10	Y
0120	Excavation A: squares B, C, D-6, 7, layers 9, 10	60130,131
0121	Excavation A: squares A, ½ B-9, 10, ½ 11, layer 10, south of Feature 1D, and west of Feature 9, walls between floors	60738,Y
0122	Excavation A: squares C-6, east, layer 10, flotation 20 x 20 x 6 cm	O
0123	Excavation A: squares C-6, west, layer 10, flotation, 20 x 20 x 6 cm	O
0124	Excavation A: squares ½ C, D, E-10, 11, layer 11	Y
0125	Excavation A: squares A, B, ½ C, 10, 11, layer 11	60132,133,739
0126	Excavation A: squares B, C, D-9, 8, layer 11	60134,135,136
0127	Excavation A: square A-9, layer 9, corner of Feature 9, large, buff crenelated, ring base	60740,P
0128	Excavation A: square B-9, scrapings below vat of Feature 8	P
0129	Excavation B: squares A, B, ½ C, 3, 4, 5, 6, layer 19, contains material from bricks of Feature 10 wall, otherwise same as 0113	60341,342,343, 344,345,818,819, 820,821,822,823
0130	Excavation B: squares ½ C, D, E-3, 4, 5, 6, Upper layer 20	O
0131	Excavation B: squares ½ C, D, E-3, 4, Lower layer 20, broken brick and debris north of Feature 10	60824,P
0132	Excavation B: squares ½ C, D, E-5, 6, Lower layer 20, debris in two rooms south of Feature 10, wall	P
0133	Excavation B: squares A, B ½ C-6, Lower layer 20, south of Feature 10, wall	60335,336
0134	Excavation B: squares A, B, ½ C-3, 4, 5, Lower layer 20, north of Feature 10, minus Feature 6, and Feature 11	O

Table A1: Continued

Field Catalogue Number	Unit Location: Description	Permanent Catalogue Number
0135	Excavation B: squares Feature 11, burial	60337,338
0136	Excavation B: squares A-8 to E-8, Lower layer 20, pick and shovel	60795
0137	Excavation B: squares A-8 to E-8, layer 21, pick and shovel	O
0138	Excavation B: squares AB-3 to 6, Lower layer 20, including some Upper 21, Feature 6, Feature 11, etc. fill	O
0139	Excavation B: squares B, ½ C-3 to 5, Lower layer 20, north of Feature 10	P
0140	Excavation B: squares A, B, ½ C-6, 7, Lower layer 20, south of Feature 10	60339,340,341
0141	Excavation B: squares ½ C, ½ D-6, 7, Lower level 20, south of Feature 10	60342,343,344
0142	Excavation B: squares ½ D, E-6, 7, Lower layer 20, south of Feature 10, east	P
0143	Excavation B: squares ½ C, D, E-3 to 5, Upper layer 21, north of Feature 10	60345,346
0144	Excavation B: square A-7, Upper layer 21, south-west of Feature 10, walls	P
0145	Excavation B: squares B-7 to D-7, Upper layer 21, south of Feature 10, walls	60347,348
0146	Excavation B: squares E-7, Upper layer 21, south-east of Feature 10, walls	O
0147	Excavation B: squares A-3 to A-6, pit from above layer 20	O
0148	Excavation A: squares B, C, D-6, 7, layer 11	60741,Y
0149	Excavation A: square A-9, layers 10, 11	60137,138
0150	Excavation A: squares B, C, D-6, 7, 8, scrapings from brick floor, on top of layer 11	O
0151	Excavation A: square A-9, layer 12	60139,140,141,734
0152	Excavation A: squares ½ C, D, E-l0, 11, layer 12	60742,Y
0153	Excavation A: squares ½ C, ½ D-8, 9, layer 12	Y
0154	Excavation A: squares ½ B, C, ½ D-6, 7, layer 12	Y
0155	Excavation A: squares A, ½ B, to ½ E-13, pick and shovel	60804
0156	Excavation A: squares A, B ½ C-10, ½ 11, layer 13	60743,P
0157	Excavation A: squares ½ C, D, E-10, ½ 11, Upper layer 13	60142, 143
0158	Excavation A: squares A–½ 9, 10, layer 13 (includes some 0156)	60144,145,146
0159	Excavation A: scrapings from taking down bricks of Feature 10	O
0160	Excavation A: squares ½ B, C, ½ D-8 to 9, Upper layer 13	60147,148
0161	Excavation A: squares ½ B, C, ½ D-6 to 7, Upper layer 13	60149,150,151
0162	Excavation A: Feature 11, square oven(?), Upper layer 13	P
0163	Excavation A: flotation sample, square B-10, Upper layer 13, 20 x 20 x 10 cm	O
0164	Excavation A: squares A, B, ½ C-10 to 11, some Lower layer 13 and Upper layer 15	60152,153,154,744
0165	Excavation B: squares A-9 to E-9, layer 22 ±, pick and shovel	O
0166	Excavation B: squares A, ½ B-3, 4, 5, ash pit from above 20, some layer 21	60745
0167	Excavation B: squares ½ C, D-3, 4, 5, Lower layer 21	60349,350
0168	Excavation B: squares B, ½ C-3, 4, 5, Lower layer 21	P
0169	Excavation B: squares E-6, 7, south-east of Feature 10, Lower layer 21	60351,352
0170	Excavation B: squares B, C-6, 7, south Feature 10; Lower layer 21	P
0171	Excavation B: squares A-3, 4, 5 to E-3, 4, 5, Upper layer 22	Y
0172	Excavation B: squares E-7, 8, south-east Feature 10, layer 22 and top 23	P
0173	Excavation B: squares A-7, 8, ½ B-7, 8, south-west Feature 10, layer 22 and top 23	60353,354,355, 356,357
0174	Excavation B: square C—north of Feature 10, mud platform from mid 20 to base 21	O
0175	Excavation B: squares A, B ½, C-3, 4, 5, Lower layer 22 north of Feature 10B	P
0176	Excavation B: ½ C, D, E-3, 4, 5, Lower layer 22-same	60358,359,746
0177	Excavation B: squares A-3 to A-5, layer 23	O
0178	Excavation A: Feature 11; flotation sample, 20 x 20 x 10 cm	O
0179	Excavation A: squares A ½, B-7, layer 12, under Feature 10	60155, 156
0180	Excavation A: squares ½ C, D, E-11, 12, Lower and Middle layer 13	P
0181	Excavation A: squares ½ D, G-10, Upper layer 13, under part of Feature 10	O
0182	Excavation A: squares ½ D, E-6, 7, Upper layer 13, under Feature 10	O
0183	Excavation A: squares A, B. ½ C-10, Lower and Middle layer 13	60157,158
0184	Excavation A: squares A, B, ½ C-½ 8, 9, Middle layer 13	60159,160
0185	Excavation A: squares A, B-½ 6 to ½ 8, 9, Lower layer 13	60161,162
0186	Excavation A: squares ½ C, D-10, Middle and Lower layer 13	P
0187	Excavation A: squares ½ C, D-8, 9, Middle layer 13	P
0188	Excavation A: squares ½ C, D-8, 9, Lower layer 13	60163, 164
0189	Excavation A: squares A, ½ B-7, Upper layer 13 and some Lower layer 12	O
0190	Excavation A: squares ½ B, C, D, E-6, 7, scraping on top of wall of Feature 12	O
0191	Excavation A: squares ½ D, E-8, 9, 10, scrapings on top of wall of Feature 10	60805
0192	Excavation A: squares ½ B, ½ C-6,½ 7, Upper layer 14 north of Feature 12	60165,166

APPENDIX A

Table A1: Continued

Field Catalogue Number	Unit Location: Description	Permanent Catalogue Number
0193	Excavation A: squares ½ C, D, E, 6–½ 7, same	Y
0194	Excavation A: squares ½ B, ½ C–6,½ 7, Lower layer 14, north of Feature 12	60167,168
0195	Excavation A: squares ½ C, D, E–6, ½ 7, same	Y
0196	Excavation A: squares ½ C, D, E–11, 12, layer 15	60169,170
0197	Excavation B: squares D, E–3, 4, ½ 5, Upper layer 23	Y
0198	Excavation B: squares A, B-3, 4, ½ 5, Upper layer 23	Y
0199	Excavation B: squares A, B, ½ C–3, 4, Middle layer 23, green floor	O
0200	Excavation B: squares ½ C, D, E–3, 4, Middle layer 23, green floor	Y
0201	Excavation B: square C-4, Feature 12, mud-plastered bin	O
0202	Excavation B: squares B, C, D–5, 8, Lower layer 22, above plastered floor in room south of Feature 10B	60360,361
0203	Excavation B: squares B, C, D–5-8, Lower layer 22, below plastered floor in room south of Feature 10B	60747,Y
0204	Excavation B: square A-8, layer 23±, south of wall of Feature 13	Y
0205	Excavation B: square A–6, 7, layer 23, north of wall of Feature 13	O
0206	Excavation B: square E-5, 6, 7, Lower layer 22, in room southeast of Feature 10 B	60748
0207	Excavation B: squares B, C, D-6, 7, 8, scraped from mud brick of Feature 10 B as it was destroyed	60749,750
0208	Excavation A: squares A, B-7, layers 12 and 13, block south of Feature 1 D and over west Feature 12	61221
0209	Excavation A: squares E-7, 8, Upper layer 13, between Features 10 B and and 10 C	P
0210	Excavation A: squares C, D, E–7, Lower layer 13, under wall of Feature 12 A	P
0211	Excavation A: square E-11, layer 15	P
0212	Excavation A: squares A, B, ½ C-10, layer 15	P
0213	Excavation A: ½ C, D,½ E-10, layer 15	60171,172,173,174
0214	Excavation A: squares A, B, ½ C-7, 8, layer 15	P
0215	Excavation A: squares ½ C, D, E-7, 8, layer 15	60175,176
0216	Excavation A: squares ½ A, B, C–½ 6, 7, layer 16 between Feature 1 D block and Feature 12 B wall to south	Y
0217	Excavation A: squares D, ½ E-6, ½ 7, layer 16, north of Feature 12 wall	60177,178
0218	Excavation A: square B-7, top layer 16, flotation sample 25 x 25 x 5 cm	O
0219	Excavation A: square C-6, top layer 16, flotation sample	O
0220	Excavation A: square A-6, layers 14 and 16 (mostly 16), flotation sample 20 x 20 x 15? cm	O
0221	Excavation A: squares A, B, C-13, layers 17 and below, pick and shovel	O
0222	Excavation A: square C-13, from square clay lined pit, carbonized grain, to float	O
0223	Excavation A: squares D, E-12, from pit filled with bevel rim bowls, pick and shovel	60826,827,828
0224	Excavation B: squares A, B. ½ C–3, 4, Lower layer 23 except 0225	60362,363
0225	Excavation B: squares B-3, 4, disturbance in Lower 23 around plaster vat fragments Feature 13	Y
0226	Excavation B: squares ½ C, D, E-3, 4, Lower layer 23, north of Feature 10	60364,365
0227	Excavation B: squares A, ½ B-8, 9, Lower layer 23, south of Feature 13, southwest Feature 10 C	60366
0228	Excavation B: squares C, D-6, 7, Middle layer 23, south Feature 10 C	60367,368
0229	Excavation B: square E-6, 7, Middle layer 23, southwest Feature 10 C	60369,370,371,751
0230	Excavation B: squares B, C-9, Lower layer 23, south Feature 10 C	Y
0231	Excavation B: squares A-10 to E-10, .50m cut step, layer 24 and below, pick and shovel	O
0232	Excavation B: square A-8, Feature 15, Lower layer 23, clay lined square oven cut into top 24	60372,373,752
0233	Excavation B: Feature 15 southwest corner, flotation 15 x 15 x 18 cm	O
0234	Excavation B: Feature 15 northeast corner, flotation 15 x 15 x 15 cm	O
0235	Excavation B: squares ½ C, D, E-3, 4, Upper layer 24, north Feature 10 C	60374, 375, 811
0236	Excavation B: square E-8, Lower layer 23, south of small wall on plan Lower 23	Y
0237	Excavation B: square E-6, 7, Lower layer 23, north of above and southeast of Feature 10 C	Y
0238	Excavation B: squares C, D-6, 7, 8, Lower layer 23, south Feature 10 C	60376,377
0239	Excavation B: square A-8, layer 24, around Feature 15, south of Feature 13 wall and southwest Feature 10 C	60378

Table A1: Continued

Field Catalogue Number	Unit Location: Description	Permanent Catalogue Number
0240	Excavation B: squares A-6, ½ 7, layer 24, west of Feature 10 C	60379,380,381
0241	Excavation B: squares C, D-6, 7, Upper layer 24, south of Feature 10 C completely south of alcove section	P
0242	Excavation B: squares C, D-6, 7, layer 24, south of Feature 10 C but north of above in alcove	P
0243	Excavation B: squares E-6, 7, Upper layer 24, southeast of Feature 10 C	60382,383,384,385
0244	Excavation B: squares A, B, ½ C, Upper layer 24, north of Feature 10 C and Feature 6, some of Feature 14 disturbance	60386,387
0245	Excavation B: squares A-6, 7, Lower layer 23, west of Feature 10 C, north of Feature 14	P
0246	Excavation B: squares A, B, ½ C-3, 4, ½ 5, Lower layer 24, north of Feature 10 C, and Feature 6	P
0247	Excavation B: squares ½ C, D, E-3, 4, Lower layer 24, north of Feature 10 C	P
0248	Excavation A: squares A, B, ½ C-11, 12, ½ 13, layer 17	60179,180
0249	Excavation A: squares ½ C, D, E-11, 12, layer 17	P
0250	Excavation A: squares A, B, ½ C-9, 10, layer 17	P
0251	Excavation A: squares ½ C, D, E-9, 10, layer 17	P
0252	Excavation A: squares A, ½ B-12, layer 18, inside brick rectangle	60778, Y
0253	Excavation A: squares A, B, ½ C-10, 11, layer 18, broken brick	Y
0254	Excavation A: squares ½ C, D, E-10, 11, Lower layer 17 and Upper 18 except ash lens–lens and debris around the top of walls	60181,182,183
0255	Excavation A: squares A, B, ½ C-8, 9, Feature 12, layer 18	Y
0256	Excavation A: squares ½ C, D, E-8, 9 to wall of Feature 12, Lower layer 17, floors and ash lens, dipping down to the East, includes 18, and Upper 19	60184,185,186,187
0257	Excavation A: squares D-11, 12, flotation (2 samples 20 x 20 x 10 cm), layer 17, ash lens on sheet	O
0258	Excavation A: square, flotation; irregular sample from under 0257, at bottom of the lens	O
0259	Excavation A: square D-11, flotation, layer 17, irregular ash lens	O
0260	Excavation A: wall scrapings above layer 18	O
0261	Excavation A: square A, B, ½ C-8, 9, layer 19	60188,189
0262	Excavation A: square D-12, layer 17, screened sample from ash lens	P
0263	Excavation B: square A, B-6, 5, well under Feature 6, pick and shovel	O
0264	Excavation B: squares A-7, ½ 8, south of Feature 14, 10 cm of layer 24, and Feature 15 mixed, large sherds from Feature 15	O
0265	Excavation B: squares B, C, D-7, 8, in and on top of boulder floor, outside alcove of Feature 10	60388,389
0266	Excavation B: squares A, B, ½ C, E-5 to 8, layer 25, east of Feature 10	60390,391
0267	Excavation B: squares A, B, ½ C-3 to 5 (to wall of Feature 6), Upper layer 25	Y
0268	Excavation B: squares ½ C, D, E-3 to 4, Upper layer 25	O
0269	Excavation B: square B-4, layer 25, flotation 25 x 25 x 10 cm	O
0270	Excavation B: square C-3, layer 25, flotation, 20 x 20 x 10 cm	O
0271	Excavation B: squares B, C, D-6, 7, layer 25, in and at level of boulder floor of 0265, but inside alcove of Feature 10	Y
0272	Excavation B: squares A-8, Feature 15, lower contents	60392, 393
0273	Excavation B: Feature 15, flotation (Upper) 20 x 20 x 15 cm	O
0274	Excavation B: Feature 15, flotation (Lower) 30 x 20 x 10 cm	O
0275	Excavation B: squares B, C, D-6, 7, layer 25, inside alcove of Feature 10 C	O
0276	Excavation B: squares C, D, E-3, 4, layer 25	Y
0277	Excavation B: squares A-3 to 7, layer 25	60394,395,396
0278	Excavation B: squares ½ C, D-3, 4, 5, Upper layer 26, ash bed east of wall	60397,398
0279	Excavation B: squares ½ C, D, E-3, 4, Upper layer 26	Y
0280	Excavation B: squares A-6, 7, Lower layer 25	60399,400
0281	Excavation B: squares E-5, 6, layer 25	Y
0282	Excavation B: squares A-8, 9, around Feature 15, in south west alcove over brick floor at the level of Lower layer 25	60401,402,753
0283	Excavation B: squares E-5, 6, base 25, top 26, east of Feature 10 C	60403,404
0284	Excavation B: squares B, C, D, E-7, 8, layer 27, south of Feature 10 C alcove	60405,406,407,408
0285	Excavation B: squares B, C, D-5, 6, layer 27, inside Feature 10 C south alcove	Y
0286	Excavation A: Feature 13, grain pit, upper flotation, 18 x 15 x 25 cm	O
0287	Excavation A: Feature 13, grain pit, lower sample, 25 x 10 x 20 cm	O
0288	Excavation A: Feature 13, screened, fill	O
0289	Excavation A: Feature 14, B, C, 12-13, grain pit, screened, fill	60190,191

APPENDIX A

Table A1: Continued

Field Catalogue Number	Unit Location: Description	Permanent Catalogue Number
0290	Excavation A: Feature 14, flotation sample 25 x 25 x 5 cm under slabs in the plan	O
0291	Excavation A: squares D-9, 10, ash in lower 17, flotation 20 x 20 x 7 cm	O
0292	Excavation A: squares A, B, ½ C-9, 10, ½ 11, layer 18 brick debris and fallen wall	60192,193,194
0293	Excavation A: squares ½ C, D, E-½ 9, 10 to wall layer 18	60195,196
0294	Excavation A: squares A, B, ½ C-10, ½ 11, Upper layer 19, ash from oven (see 0256)	P
0295	Excavation A: squares A, B, ½ C-10, ½ 11, Lower layer 19, brown silt, over floor of top 20	60199,200
0296	Excavation A: squares ½ C, D, E-½ 8, 9, Lower layer 19	60197,198
0297	Excavation A: squares ½ C, D, E-½ 10, 11, ½ 12, Lower layer 19	P
0298	Excavation A: squares A, B, ½ C, between walls of Feature 12, and Feature 15, layer 20, brown silt	60776,777
0299	Excavation A: squares ½ C, D, E, between walls, layer 20	60201,202,203, 204,754, P
0300	Excavation A: squares A, ½ B-12, 13, layers 19, 20	O
0301	Excavation A: squares D, E-12, layer 20, over bevel rim bowl pit	P
0302	Excavation A: squares A, B, ½ C-11, 12, ½ 13, Upper layer 21	60205,206,207
0303	Excavation A: ½ C, D, E-11, 12, ½ 13, Upper layer 21	P
0304	Excavation A: squares A, B, ½ C-½ 8, 9, 10, Upper layer 21	60208, 209
0305	Excavation A: squares ½ C, D, E-½ 8, 9, 10, Upper layer 21	P
0306	Excavation A: Feature 19, Upper, screened	60807,808,829, 830,831
0307	Excavation A: Feature 19, Upper, flotation - no volume	O
0308	Excavation B: squares A-3 to 7, layer 26, west of Feature 19 wall	Y
0309	Excavation B: squares A, B, C-3, 4, layer 26, ash area east of Feature 10 wall	Y,60755,840
0310	Excavation B: square B-3, layer 26, flotation, 20 x 20x 10	0
0311	Excavation B: squares D, E-3, 4, layer 26, north Feature 10	60409,410
0312	Excavation B: squares E-½ 4, 5, 6, layer 26, east Feature 10	Y
0313	Excavation B: square E-3, inside Feature 18 - post hole?	60411,412
0314	Excavation B: wall cleaning of Feature 10	60413,414,415
0315	Excavation B: squares part A-3, 4, 5, 6, 7, layer 27, room west Feature 18, 10	Y
0316	Excavation B; squares A, B-3, 4, layer 27, east Feature 19	60416,417,418
0317	Excavation B: square C, D-3, 4, layer 27	60419,420
0318	Excavation B: squares E-3, 4, layer 27 and top 28	Y
0319	Excavation B: squares E-5, 6, layer 28 to green floor	60421,422
0320	Excavation B: squares A-7, 8, Lower layer 26 and layer 27	Y
0321	Excavation B: squares C-7, 8, layer 28	60423,424
0322	Excavation B: squares D-7, 8, layer 28	60425,426
0323	Excavation B: squares E-7, 8, layer 28	60427,428
0324	Excavation B: square A-7, Feature 15 Lower	60429,430,431
0325	Excavation B: square A-½ 9 to E-½ 9	O
0326	Excavation A: room A, Middle layer 21, top Feature 25	60210,211, 212
0327	Excavation A: room B, Middle layer 21, lower, mixed	O
0328	Excavation A: room C, Middle layer 21	60756, Y
0329	Excavation A: room D, Middle layer 21	Y
0330	Excavation A: room E, Middle layer 21	60213,214,215
0331	Excavation A: squares A, B-13, level of layer 21, ash pit	O
0332	Excavation A: square E-10, top layer 21, flotation of ash lens - hearth: 25 x 25 x 5 cm	O
0333	Excavation A: same as above, flotation, 50 x 10 x 10	O
0334	Excavation A: square 9-E, Upper layer 21, hearth	P
0336	Excavation A: room C, Lower layer 21	60216,217
0337	Excavation A: room D, Lower layer 21	P
0338	Excavation A: Feature 19, bevel rim bowl pit	60832,833
0339	Excavation A: room E, Lower layer 21	60218,219
0340	Excavation A: room B; top 22	Y
0341	Excavation A: Feature 23 and part Feature 19, large pit	61211,212
0342	Excavation A: Feature 23, large pit	61213,214, Y
0343	Excavation A: Feature 23, large pit, flotation sample 20 x 10 x 10	O
0344	Excavation A: room B, flotation samples, hearth, 10 x 10 x 5	O

Table A1: Continued

Field Catalogue Number	Unit Location: Description	Permanent Catalogue Number
0345	Excavation A: room B, other material, hearth	O
0346	Excavation A: Feature 19 north, Middle levels	60834,835,836
0347	Excavation B: squares A-3, 4, under Feature 19 wall top 28	60432,433
0348	Excavation B: squares C-3, 4, layer 28	60434,435, Y
0349	Excavation B: square C-3, layer 28, ash pit area	60436,437,438
0350	Excavation B: squares D, E-3, layer 28	Y
0351	Excavation B: squares D-4, ½ 5, layer 28	Y
0352	Excavation B: squares E-4, 5, 6, layer 28	Y
0353	Excavation B: squares A-6, 7, 8, layer 28	Y
0354	Excavation B: under Feature 10, layer 28	Y
0355	Excavation B: squares A-6, 7, layer 28, ash lens	Y
0356	Excavation B: Feature 21, rectangle inside	60439,440
0357	Excavation B: square A, B-3, 4, Upper layer 29	P
0358	Excavation B: A-5, 6, Upper layer 29	60441,442
0359	Excavation B: A-7, 8, Upper layer 29	60443,444
0360	Excavation B: A-½ 9, 10 to E-½ 9, 10, half meter cut step pick and shovel, below 0325	O
0361	Excavation B: well under Feature 6, pick and shovel	O
0362	Excavation B: C, D E-3, 4, Upper layer 29	P
0363	Excavation B: B-½ 5, 6, 7, 8, Upper layer 29, except Feature 22	P
0364	Excavation B: C-5, D-5, E-5, 6, Upper layer 29 around Feature 21	60757,Y
0365	Excavation B: C-7, 8, 9, D, E-½ 7, 8, 9, Upper layer 29 cleaning around Feature 20, 21	60445,456
0366	Excavation B: cleaning top Feature 20	60447,448
0367	Excavation B: A-3, 4, 5, Lower layer 29, west Feature 23	60449,450
0368	Excavation B: B-3, 4, 5, ½ C-3, 4, 5, Lower layer 29, east Feature 23	60451,452,453
0369	Excavation B: squares A, B-6, 7, 8, Lower layer 29	60454,455
0370	Excavation B: squares ½ C-3, 4, D-3, 4, 5, 6, Lower layer 29	P
0371	Excavation B: square A-9, pit cut into top 30, Feature 24	O
0372	Excavation B: square A-6, level of Lower layer 29, jube contents south of Feature 23, E-W segment; Feature 24	O
0373	Excavation B: square ½ C-3, 4, D-3, 4, 5, E-3, 4, 5, 6, more Lower 29	60456,457
0374	Excavation A: Feature 19 Lower, bevel rim bowl pit	60837,838,839
0375	Excavation A: Lower Feature 23, 20 x 20 x 5; flotation sample	O
0376	Excavation A: A, B, ½ C-12, 13, Feature 25, brick fill	O
0377	Excavation A: ½ C, D, E-12, 13, Feature 25, brick fill	O
0378	Excavation A: squares C-10, 11, top Feature 25 and layer 22	60220,221
0379	Excavation A: squares A, B-8, 9, layer 22 and top Feature 25 bricks	60222,223
0380	Excavation A: squares ½ C, D, E-8, 9, layer 22	Y
0381	Excavation A: square ½ C, D, E-8, 9, Lower 22 and top Feature 25 bricks	P
0382	Excavation A: ½ C, D, E-10, 11, layer 22	Y
0383	Excavation A: ½ C, D, E-10, 11, top Feature 25 bricks.	60224,225,226
0384	Excavation A: general cleaning of Feature 25 bricks	P
0385	Excavation A: squares ½ C, D, E-12, 13, Feature 25 bricks around Feature 23 pit and Feature 19 pit	60227,228
0386	Excavation A: square 13-E; ash pit below Feature 19 in rectangular hole in Feature 25 - Feature 26	60229,230
0387	Excavation A: hearth in C-11, Lower layer 22, Feature 24	60231
0388	Excavation A: same, flotation	O
0389	Excavation A: step cut 50 cm deep, below Feature 25	O
0390	Excavation A: square A, B, ½ C-13, Lower Feature 23, cut into Feature 25	Y
0391	Excavation B: layer 29, under Feature 20	P
0392	Excavation B: Upper layer 29, under Feature 21	Y
0393	Excavation B: Lower layer 29, under Feature 21	Y
0394	Excavation B: squares A-3, 4, Upper layer 30, west Feature 23	60458,459,460,697
0395	Excavation B: squares B-3, 4, Upper layer 30, east Feature 23	61215,216
0396	Excavation B: squares D, C, E-3, 4, Upper layer 30	60461,462,758
0397	Excavation B: squares A, ½ B-6, 9, layer 30, west Feature 22	61217,218
0398	Excavation B: squares C, D, E-5, 6, Upper layer 30	61219,220
0399	Excavation B: squares C, D, part E-7, 8, 9, layer 30, east Feature 22	P
0400	Excavation B: squares A-10 to E-10, layers 33–35±, 50 cm (to Boulder pavement) pick and shovel	O
0401	Excavation B: squares A-3, 4, 5, Lower layer 30, stone and gypsum floor west of Feature 23	60463,464

APPENDIX A

Table A1: Continued

Field Catalogue Number	Unit Location: Description	Permanent Catalogue Number
0402	Excavation B: square ½ B, C-3, 4, 5, Middle layer 30 wedge	P
0403	Excavation B: squares D, E, same	60465,466,467
0404	Excavation B: squares A, B-7, 8, 9, layer 31A; west Feature 22 pedestal	60468,469
0405	Excavation B: squares C, D, E-8, 9, Upper layer 21, east Feature 22 pedestal	P
0406	Excavation B: squares C, D, E-6, 7, same	60470,471
0407	Excavation A: square C-9, layer 22, Feature 24 hearth & oven over Feature 25	60232,233
0408	Excavation A: contents of Features 27: a mud plaster-lined pit in Feature 25 platform	60234
0409	Excavation A: part squares E-10, 11, layer 23, wedge shaped volume 0 to 8 cm below green silt	P
0410	Excavation B: square A 3–5, west Feature 23, between two gypsum plaster floors	60472,473,474, 475
0411	Excavation B: squares C, D-3, 4, ½ 5, Lower layer 31	60476,477
0412	Excavation B: squares E-3, 4, ½ 5, lower layer 31	60478,479
0413	Excavation B: squares C, D-½ 5, 6, ½ 7, Lower layer 31	Y
0414	Excavation B: squares E-½ 5, 6, 7, Lower layer 31	Y
0415	Excavation B: squares C, D-6, 7, layer 31, irregular ash deposit—see sheet	Y
0416	Excavation B: squares C, D, E-½ 7, 8, 9, Lower layer 31	Y
0417	Excavation B: square A-6, jube Lower layer 30 and Upper layer 31, pedestal under Feature 24	O
0418	Excavation B: well under Feature 6, pick and shovel	O
0419	Excavation B: squares C-7, 8, 9, Middle layer 31, discolored soil west of Feature 22 pedestal	Y
0420	Excavation B: squares ½ C, D, E, Lower layer 31 and Upper layer 32, east of Feature 22 pedestal	60480,481,482
0421	Excavation B: squares A-3, 4, 5, below gypsum floor, west of Feature 23	O
0422	Excavation B: squares B, C-3, 4, 5, Upper layer 31	O
0423	Excavation B: squares D, E-3, 4, 5, Upper layer 31	P
0424	Excavation B: square A-6, Feature 24, jube tiles	60759
0425	Excavation B: squares A, B-5, 6, west Feature 22 pedestal and under Feature 22 pedestal	P
0426	Excavation B: squares A, B, ½ C-8, 9, layer 31 B?	60483,484,485
0427	Excavation B: under Feature 22, layers 30, Upper 31	60483,484,485
0428	Excavation B: C, D,-6, 7, upper layer 32; ash deposit	60486,487
0429	Excavation B: C, ½ D, Upper layer 32, pt 6 above and around 0430	60488,489
0430	Excavation B: square C-6, Upper layer 32, bevel rim bowl concentration	O
0431	Excavation B: squares D, E-½ 6, 5, Upper layer 32	60490,491
0432	Excavation B: squares A, B, 1/3 C-5, 6, layer 31 C	60492,493
0433	Excavation B: squares A, B, ½ C-7, 8, layer 31 C	P
0434	Excavation B: squares A, B, 2/3 C-8, 9, layer 31 C	P
0435	Excavation B: Feature 6 well, pick and shovel	O
0436	Excavation B: Feature 25, Lower 31, flotation and charcoal	O
0437	Excavation A: squares ½ C, D, E-pt 8, 9, loose brick piling and refuse fill over layer 23—Feature 25	60235,Y
0438	Excavation A: squares D, E-10, Upper layer 23, 5 cm	P
0439	Excavation A: squares D, E-10, Middle layer 23, 5 cm	O
0440	Excavation A: squares D, E-10, 11, Lower layer 23, wedge shaped	60236,237
0441	Excavation A: squares D, E-10, 11, Upper layer 24, 5 cm	60238,239,P
0442	Excavation A: squares A, B-11, pt 10, layer 24	P
0443	Excavation A: squares A, B-12, 13, layer 24, a long brick	60240,241
0444	Excavation A: squares C, D, E-12, 13, layer 24 to plaster floor	Y
0445	Excavation A: square pt B, pt C-10, 11, Lower Feature 25 and Upper layer 23, between two walls charcoal floors and above	60242,243,244
0446	Excavation A: squares A, B-12, 13, Lower layer 24, to ash lens	60245,246
0447	Excavation A: squares A, B, ½ C-14, 15, pt 16, layer 25	P
0448	Excavation A: squares ½ C, D, E-14, 15, layers 25 and 26	P
0449	Excavation A: square pt C, D, E-9, Upper layer 23, under 0437	60247,248
0450	Excavation A: same, Lower layer 23 (Note: 0449 and 0450 combined under 0449)	O
0451	Excavation A: same, layer 24	60760,P
0452	Excavation A: square A-9, triangular area, layer 24	60249,250
0453	Excavation A: squares A, B, ½ C-14, 15, Upper layer 26	60251,252
0454	Excavation A: squares ½ C, D, E-12, 13, layer 25	Y

Table A1: Continued

Field Catalogue Number	Unit Location: Description	Permanent Catalogue Number
0455	Excavation A: square ½ C, D, E-13, 14, Lower layer 26	60253,254
0456	Excavation A: layers 18 to 24, wall cleaning	O
0457	Excavation B: squares A, B, ½ C-9, ½ 10, Upper layer 32	O
0458	Excavation B: squares ½ C, D, E-9, ½ 10, Upper layer 32	60494,495
0459	Excavation B: squares A, B, ½ C-7, 8, Upper layer 32	P
0460	Excavation B: squares ½ C, D, E-7, 8, Upper layer 32	P
0461	Excavation B: squares A, B. ½ C-5, 6, Upper layer 32	60797,Y
0462	Excavation B: squares ½ C, D, E-5, 6, Upper layer 32	60496,497,498
0463	Excavation B: square E-8, Upper layer 32, refuse concentration, 26 fragments sealing clay discarded	60499,500,501
0464	Excavation B: squares A, B, ½ C-9, ½ 10, Lower layer 32	O
0465	Excavation B: squares ½ C, D, E-9, ½ 10, Lower layer 32	60502,503
0466	Excavation B: squares A, B. ½ C-7, 8, Lower layer 32	60504,505,506
0467	Excavation B: squares ½ C, D, E-7, 8, Lower layer 32	60785,P
0468	Excavation B: squares A, B, ½ C-5, 6, Lower layer 32 except Feature 6	60507,508,509
0469	Excavation B: squares ½ C, D, E-5, 6, Lower layer 32 except ash	60803, P
0470	Excavation B: square E-5, Lower layer 32, ash and rock concentration	P
0471	Excavation B: square A-5, south ½, Lower layer 31 and layer 32, under wall segment	60510,511,512,Y
0472	Excavation B: squares A-11, E-11, step through 34, 35, pick and shovel	O
0473	Excavation B: square C-10, Upper layer 33, inside Feature 26, flotation 20 x 20 x 10 cm	O
0474	Excavation B: square C-10, same	O
0475	Excavation B: square A-10, layer 33, small ash pit cut into layer 33	Y
0476	Excavation B: squares A, B, C-pt 9, 10, Upper layer 33, ash fill inside Feature 26	60513,514,761, 800
0477	Excavation B: squares D, E-8, 9, 10, Upper layer 33, broken brick east of Feature 26	60802,P
0478	Excavation B: squares A, B, ½ C-7, 8, pt 9 to wall of Feature 26 except "oven", Upper layer 33	60515,516,517
0479	Excavation B: squares B, C-7, 8, Upper layer 33, inside oval of Feature 27 "oven"	Y
0480	Excavation B: squares ½ C, D, E-7, 8, Upper layer 33	Y
0481	Excavation B: squares A, B, ½ C-5, 6, Upper layer 33	60518,519,520
0482	Excavation B: squares ½ C, D, E-5, 6, Upper layer 33	Y
0483	Excavation B: wall cleanings	
0484	Excavation A: squares A, B, ½ C-14, 15, Lower layer 26	60255,256
0485	Excavation A: squares A, B, ½ C-12, 13, layer 25	60257,258,259
0486	Excavation A: squares A, B, ½ C-12, 13, layer 26	60260,261
0487	Excavation A: squares ½ C, D, E-12, 13, layer 25	Y
0488	Excavation A: squares ½ C, D, E-12, 13, layer 26	P
0489	Excavation A: squares A 10-11, Middle layer 24	P
0490	Excavation A: squares B-10, 11, C ½ 10, 11, D-11, Middle layer 24, solid jar sealings	O
0491	Excavation A: squares A, B, ½ C-½ 17, ½ C, D, E-16, cut step below layer 26, 50 cm, pick and shovel	60784
0492	Excavation A: squares ½ C, D, E-8, 9, 10, Lower layer 24, triangular area inside or north east of Feature 28 wall	P
0493	Excavation A: squares A, B, ½ C-14, 15, part 16, layer 27	60262
0494	Excavation A: squares ½ C, D, E-15, layer 27	60806, P
0495	Excavation A: square E-14, layer 27 above brick, flotaton 20 x 20 x 4 cm	O
0496	Excavation A: squares A, B-15, layer 27, 25 x 25 x 5 cm flotation	O
0497	Excavation A: squares A, B-15, layer 27, flotation 30 x 15 x 5 cm	O
0498	Excavation A: squares A, B-14, layer 27, flotation 30 x 30 x 5 cm	O
0499	Excavation A: squares A, B-14, layer 27, flotation 30 x 30 x 5 cm	O
0500	Excavation A: squares A, ¼ B-12, 13, layer 27	Y
0501	Excavation A: squares ¾ B, ½ C-12, 13 layer 27	O
0502	Excavation A: squares ½ C, ¾ D-12, 13, layer 27	60264
0503	Excavation A: squares ¼ D, E-12, 13, layer 27	Y
0504	Excavation A: mixture of 0500 to 0503, layer 27	60265,266
0505	Excavation A: removing Feature 29	60267,268
0506	Excavation A: squares A, B, ½ C-14, 15, layer 28, southeast of Feature 30.	P
0507	Excavation A: squares ½ C, D, E-14, 15 , layer 28, southeast of Feature 30	P
0508	Excavation B: under oval Feature 27, in squares A, B, ½ C, Middle layer 33	60521,522
0509	Excavation B: squares A, B, ½ C-7, 8 except 0508 Upper middle 33	P

APPENDIX A

Table A1: Continued

Field Catalogue Number	Unit Location: Description	Permanent Catalogue Number
0510	Excavation B: squares A, B, ½ C-9, 10 Middle layer 33?	60523,524
0511	Excavation B: squares ½ C, D, E-8, 9, ½ 10 Middle layer 33?	60525,526,527,528, 529,762,763
0512	Excavation B: squares A, B, C-½ 9, Feature 26, north wall, brick, Middle layer 33	60530,531
0513	Excavation B: squares D-9, 10, Feature 26, east wall, brick, Middle layer 33	O
0514	Excavation B: squares A, B, ½ C-5, 6, Lower layer 33	60532,533
0515	Excavation B: squares ½ C, D, E-5, 6, Lower layer 33	60534,535,536,537, 698
0516	Excavation B: squares A, B, ½ C-7, 8, Lower layer 33	Y
0517	Excavation B: squares ½ C, D, E-7, 8, Lower layer 33, except brick	60538,539
0518	Excavation B: squares A, B, ½ C-9, 10, Lower layer 33	60764,Y
0519	Excavation B: squares ½ C, D, E-9, 10, Lower layer 33	60540,541
0520	Excavation B: squares C-6 flotation, Lower layer 33, 20 x 20 x 13 cm	O
0521	Excavation B: squares A to D-½ 10, 0-25 cm below Feature 28	O
0522	Excavation B: squares A to D-½ 10, 25-50 cm below Feature 28 (?)	60542,543
0523	Excavation B: Feature 6, well at level of layer 34 screened	60544
0524	Excavation B: cleaning rocks of Feature 28	60765, Y
0525	Excavation B: squares A-9, 10, Lower level 33	Y
0526	Excavation B; squares B, C, D-9, 10, Lower layer 33	Y
0527	Excavation B: squares E-9, 10, Lower level 33	Y
0528	Excavation B: squares A, B, ½ C-5, 6, top layer 34	60545,546,547
0529	Excavation B: squares ½ C, D, E-5, 6, top layer 34	Y
0530	Excavation B: squares A, B, ½ C-7, 8, top layer 34	Y
0531	Excavation B: squares ½ C, D, E-7, 8, top layer 34	60548,549,550, 551
0532	Excavation B: squares A, B, ½ C-9, 10, top layer 34	Y
0533	Excavation B: squares ½ C, D, E-9, 10, top layer 34	60552,553,554 555
0534	Excavation B: square E-8, Upper layer 34, Feature 30, concentration of sherds in rocks	60766, Y
0535	Excavation A: squares A, B, ½ C-14, 15, northwest of wall of Feature 30, Upper layer 28	Y
0536	Excavation A: squares A, ¼ B-12, 13, Upper layer 28	Y
0537	Excavation A: squares ¾ B, ½ C-12, 13, Upper layer 28	60269,270
0538	Excavation A: squares ½ C, ¾ D-12, 13, Upper layer 28	60271,272
0539	Excavation A: squares ¼ D, E-12, 13, Upper layer 28 northwest of Feature 30	Y
0540	Excavation A: A, B, ½ C, square C-14, pt 15, Lower layer 28, northwest of wall of Feature 30	60273,274,275
0541	Excavation A: A, ¼ B-12, 13, Lower layer 28	60276,277
0542	Excavation A: squares ¾ B, ½ C-12, 13, Lower layer 28	60278,279
0543	Excavation A: squares ½ C, D, E-12, pt 13, Lower layer 28, north of Feature 10	O
0544	Excavation A: squares-cut steps 50 cm, layer 29 and below	O
0545	Excavation A: between trenches A, B, burial ± layer 32	60767,782,783,796
0546	Excavation A: alley between walls of Features 30, 31, 20 cm, Upper 29, west half	P
0547	Excavation A: alley between walls of Features 30, 31, east half, 20 cm, Upper 29	60280,281
0548	Excavation A: alley between walls of Features 30, 31, west half, 30 cm, Lower 29	P
0549	Excavation A: alley between walls of Features 30, 31, east half, 30 cm, Lower 29	P
0550	Excavation A: corner of room in square 17, 20 cm	60282,283
0551	Excavation A: corner of room in square 17, 20 cm	P
0552	Excavation A: 'L'-shaped volume in C, D, E-16, 10 cm, Upper 29	60284,285
0553	Excavation B: cleaning floor of top Lower layer 34	O
0554	Excavation B: A-11 to E-11 cut step, 50 cm below layer 33	O
0555	Excavation B: squares A, B, ½ C-5, 6, Lower layer 34	P
0556	Excavation B: squares ½ C, D, E-5, 6, Lower layer 34	P
0557	Excavation B: squares A, B, ½ C-7, 8, Lower layer 34	60556,557
0558	Excavation B: squares ½ C, D, E-7, 8, Lower layer 34	60558,559
0559	Excavation B: squares A, B, ½ C-9, 10, Lower layer 34	P
0560	Excavation B: squares ½ C, D, E-9, 10, Lower layer 34 except Feature 30, 31	60560,561
0561	Excavation B: squares A, ½ C-7, 8, Upper layer 35	P
0562	Excavation B: squares ½ C, D, E-7, 8, Upper 35	60562,563
0563	Excavation B: squares C, D-10, Middle and Lower layer 34, Feature 32, animal bones	O
0564	Excavation B: squares ½ C, D, E-8, 9, 10, bricks of Features 31 in Lower layer 34	P

Table A1: Continued

Field Catalogue Number	Unit Location: Description	Permanent Catalogue Number
0565	Excavation B: under Features 29, 30, Lower layer 34	60564,565
0566	Excavation B: squares A, B, ½ C-9, 10, 10 cm, Upper layer 35	60566,567
0567	Excavation B: squares ½ C, D, E-9, 10, Upper layer 35, room	P
0568	Excavation B: squares ½ C, D, E-9, 10, 20 cm, Upper layer 35	60568,659
0569	Excavation B: squares ½ C, D. E-11, 15 cm, all layer 35	60570,571
0570	Excavation B: square C-11, layer 35, contents of oven, Feature 33	O
0571	Excavation B: squares A, B, ½ C-7, 8, Lower layer 35	P
0572	Excavation B: squares ½ C, D, E-7, 8, Lower layer 35	Y
0573	Excavation B: squares A, B, ½ C-9, 10, Lower layer 35	60572,573,574
0574	Excavation B: squares ½ C, D, E-9, 10, Lower layer 33	60799,P
0575	Excavation B: squares ½ A, B, ½C-11, all layer 36	Y
0576	Excavation B: squares ½ C, D, E-11, all layer 36	60575,576,Y
0577	Excavation B: square A-6, Lower layer 35, Feature 34 burial	O
0578	Excavation B: square E-10, layer 34, Feature 35 burial	O
0579	Excavation B: square E-6, layer 34, pot group	60577,578,579, 580,581,768,786
0580	Excavation A: 'L'-shaped room, 40 cm of broken brick, Upper 29, 95 stones	P
0581	Excavation A: south room corner to brick pavement, Lower layer 29, 28 stones	P
0582	Excavation A: step below layer 29 south of Feature 30	60286,287
0583	Excavation A: 'L'-shaped room, Middle layer 29, 25 cm, same, 32 stones	60288,289
0584	Excavation A: west half alley between Features 30, 31, Lowest layer 29	P
0585	Excavation A: east half alley between Feature 30, 31, brown & gray granular fill, layer 30	60290,291
0586	Excavation A: east half, 10 cm, below layer 30	P
0587	Excavation B: squares A, B, ½ C-9, 10, Upper layer 36	60582,583,584,585
0588	Excavation B: squares ½ C, D, E-9, 10, Upper layer 36	60586,587,588
0589	Excavation B: squares A, B, ½ C-7, 8, Upper layer 36	P
0590	Excavation B: squares ½ C, D, E-7, 8, Upper layer 36	P
0591	Excavation B: squares B-7, 8, Feature 36, burial	O
0592	Excavation B: square E-11, Feature 35, burial	O
0593	Excavation B: squares A, B, ½ C-11, Lower layer 36 and Upper layer 37	60589,590
0594	Excavation B: north corner Feature 37 room, Lower layer 36	60769,Y
0595	Excavation B: squares A, B, ½ C-9, 10, Lower layer 36	60801,Y
0596	Excavation B: squares ½ C, D, E-9, 10, Lower layer 36	60591,592,593, 594,770
0597	Excavation B: squares ½ C, D, E-11, Lower layer 36	Y
0598	Excavation B: squares A, B, ½ C-11, Lower layer 37	P
0599	Excavation B: squares ½ C, D, E-11, all layer 37	O
0600	Excavation B: squares A, B, ½ C-9, 10, all layer 37	60596,597,598,599
0601	Excavation B: squares ½ C, D, E-9, 10, all layer 37	P
0602	Excavation B: squares A to E-11, layer 38, pick	60600,601
0603	Excavation B: squares ½ C, D, E-9, 10, all layer 38, screen, (squares A, B, ½ C-layer 38-sterile)	P
0604	Excavation B: squares A to E-12, layer 39?, cut step	O
0605	Excavation B: Feature 38, oven in D-9; top layer 38 yielded carbon	O
0606	Excavation A: cut to south of Features 30, 31, below layer 29, screened	Y
0607	Excavation A: 'L'-shaped room, Lower layer 29 to floor, 14 flatstones	60292,293
0608	Excavation A: cleaning false pedestals in west half alley between Feature 30, 31, layer 29, 13 stones	60294,295
0609	Excavation A: pot concentration, floor of 'L'-shaped room	60779,787,789
0610	Excavation A: south corner room, 10 cm, below brick pavement	Y
0611	Excavation A: triangular section behind north wall, 10 cm level	60296,297
0612	Excavation A: triangular section behind north wall, 10 cm level	Y
0613	Excavation A: triangular section behind north wall, 20 cm level, 21 flat stones	O
0614	Excavation A: 'L'-shaped room, 10 cm level below floor	60298,299
0615	Excavation A: cleaning step to 50 cm below brick pavement	O
0616	Excavation B: squares ½ C, D, E-9, 10, layer 38	60602,603
0617	Excavation B: squares ½ C, D, E-11, 12, top 39, (S to N: 5 to 10 cm)	60604,605
0618	Excavation B: squares A, B, ½ C-11, 12, top layer 39, (S to N: 5 to 10 cm)	O
0619	Excavation B: squares A, B, ½ C-9, 10, top layer 39, (S to N: 5 to 10 cm)	60606,607
0620	Excavation B: squares ½ C, D, E-9, 10-top layer 39	60608,609
0621	Excavation B: squares ½ C, D, E-11, 12, Middle layer 39, 10 cm, not screened, pick samples	Y
0622	Excavation B: squares A, B, ½ C-11, 12, Middle layer 39, 10 cm	Y
0623	Excavation B: squares ½ C, D, E-9, 10, Middle layer 39, pick	Y

APPENDIX A

Table A1: Continued

Field Catalogue Number	Unit Location: Description	Permanent Catalogue Number
0624	Excavation B: squares A, B, ½ C-9, 10, Middle layer 39, 10 cm	Y
0625	Excavation B: squares A, B, ½ C-11, 12, Lower layer 39	60610,611
0626	Excavation B: squares ½ C, D, E-11, 12, Lower layer 39	60612,613
0627	Excavation B: squares A, B, ½ C-9, 10, Lower layer 39	Y
0628	Excavation B: squares ½ C, D, E-9, 10, Lower layer 39	Y
0629	Excavation B: squares: 50 cm step at end of trench	O
0630	Excavation B: squares A, B, ½ C-13, top layer 40	P
0631	Excavation B: squares ½ C, D, E-13, top layer 40	60780,P
0632	Excavation B: squares A, B, ½ C-11, 12, top layer 40	60614,615
0633	Excavation B: squares ½ C, D, E-11, 12, top layer 40	Y
0634	Excavation B: squares A, B, ½ C-9, 10, top layer 40	60616,617,618
0635	Excavation B: squares ½ C, D, E-9, 10, top layer 40	60619,620
0636	Excavation B: step at end of trench, 50 cm	O
0637	Excavation A: deposit beneath 2nd brick pavement in south corner room, Lower layer 31	Y
0638	Excavation A: 'L'-shaped room, down to brick pavement level as in 0637, Lower layer 31	60300,301,P
0639	Excavation A: 50 cm cut in step	O
0640	Excavation A: west room below floor, layer 31	60302,303
0641	Excavation A: rodent skeleton in interior E-W wall of Feature 30	O
0642	No description	
0643	Excavation B: squares A, B, ½ C-13, Lower layer 40	P
0644	Excavation B: squares ½ C, D, E-13, Lower layer 40	P
0645	Excavation B: squares A, B, ½ C-11, 12, Lower layer 40	60621,622
0646	Excavation B: squares ½ C, D, E-11, 12, Lower layer 40	P
0647	Excavation B: squares A, B, ½ C-9, 10, Lower layer 40	60623,624
0648	Excavation B: squares ½ C, D, E-9, 10, Lower layer 40	60625,626,627,628
0649	Excavation B: squares D-9, Lower layer 40, large jar	60629
0650	Excavation B: squares A, B, ½ C-13, Upper layer 41	60630
0651	Excavation B: squares ½ C, D, E-13, Upper layer 41	60631
0652	Excavation B: squares A, B, ½ C-11, 12, Upper layer 41	Y
0653	Excavation B: squares ½ C, D, E-11, 12, Upper layer 41	60632,633
0654	Excavation B: squares A-14 to E-14, layers 42, 43, 44, 50 cm cut step, screen	O
0655	Excavation B: squares A-10, 11 to E-10, 11, Upper layer 41, cleaning to Feature 40-walls	Y
0656	Excavation B: squares A, B, ½ C-13, Middle layer 41	Y
0657	Excavation B: squares ½ C, D, E-13, Middle layer 41	60634,Y
0658	Excavation B: squares A, B, ½ C-11, 12, Middle layer 41 except Feature 40	Y
0659	Excavation B: squares ½ C, D, E-11, 12, Middle layer 41 except Feature 40	60635,636,637,638
0660	Excavation A: inside Feature 30, layer 32, packed brick, pick and shovel sample	60304,305,306
0661	Excavation A: same, southwest Feature 32 walls, 220 x 160 cm, layer 33, floor and burned debris, 15 cm thick	Y
0662	Excavation A: same, southeast Feature 32 walls, layer 33, floor and underlying burned debris; 210 x 165 cm, 10 cm thick	Y
0663	Excavation A: same, northwest Feature 32 walls, layer 33, 260 x 160 cm, 15 cm thick, broken brick	Y
0664	Excavation A: same, northeast Feature 32 walls, layer 33, 120 x 160 cm ± 15 cm thick, broken brick	60307,308
0665	Excavation A: square B-18, Lower layer 33, 30 x 30 x 5 cm, flotation	O
0666	Excavation A: square D-17, Lower layer 33, 35 x 35 x 3 cm, flotation	O
0667	Excavation A: area inside Feature 30, southwest of Feature 32 walls, broken brick below green floor, 220 x 160 cm, 70 cm thick	60309,310,771
0668	Excavation A: same, southeast Feature 32, 210 x 165 x 20 cm, broken brick	Y
0669	Excavation A: same, northwest Feature 32 walls, layer 34 under 0663, 70 x 75 x 20 cm (north half pick), brick packing	60311,312,313
0670	Excavation A: same, northeast Feature 32 walls, layer 34 under 0664, 210 x 85 x 20 cm (north half pick), brick packing	60314,315
0671	Excavation A: same, southwest Feature 32 walls under 0667, layer 35, 225 x 210 cm, green floor, pebble floor discarded, broken brick	O
0672	Excavation A: same, southeast Feature 32 walls, layer 35 under 0662, 210 x 215 x 15 cm	60316,317
0673	Excavation A: same, under and northwest of Feature 32 wall, layer 35, 100 x 190 x 20 cm, broken brick	60318,319

Table A1: Continued

Field Catalogue Number	Unit Location: Description	Permanent Catalogue Number
0674	Excavation A: same, under and northeast of Feature 32 wall, layer 35, 180 x 100 x 20 cm, broken brick	60320,321
0675	Excavation B: squares A, B, ½ C-9, 10, pt 11, Upper layer 41	60639,640
0676	Excavation B: squares ½ C, D, E-9, 10, Upper layer 41	60641,P
0677	Excavation B: squares A, B, ½ C-13, Lower layer 41	P
0678	Excavation B: squares ½ C, D, E-13, Lower layer 41	P
0679	Excavation B: squares A, B, ½ C-11, 12, Lower layer 41	Y
0680	Excavation B: squares ½ C, D, E-11, 12, Lower layer 41	60642,643
0681	Excavation B: squares A, B, ½ C-9, 10, Middle layer 41	P
0682	Excavation B: squares ½ C, D, E-9, 10, Middle layer 41	P
0683	Excavation B: squares A, B-11, 12, Lower layer 41, ash lens	60644,645
0684	Excavation B: squares A-15 to E-13, layers 44 to 46±, 50 cm cut step, screen	O
0685	Excavation B: squares A, B, ½ C-9, 10, Lower layer 41	P
0686	Excavation B: squares ½ C, D, E-9, 10, Lower layer 41	60646,647,P
0687	Excavation B: squares A, B, ½ C-13, Upper layer 42, 15 cm	P
0688	Excavation B: squares ½ C, D, E-13, Upper layer 42, 15 cm	P
0689	Excavation B: removing Feature 40, Upper-Middle layer 41	O
0690	Excavation B: squares A, B, ½ C-11, 12, Upper layer 42	60648,649
0691	Excavation B: squares ½ C, D, E-11, 12, Upper layer 42	60650
0692	Excavation B: squares A, B, ½ C-9, 10, Upper layer 42, 10 cm	60651,652
0693	Excavation B: squares ½ C, D, E-9, 10, Upper layer 42, 10 cm	Y
0694	Excavation B: squares E, D-13, shallow pit into layer 42	60653,654
0695	Excavation B: squares A, B, ½ C-12, 13, Lower layer 42	60655,656
0696	Excavation B: squares ½ C, D, E-12, 13, Lower layer 42	60772,Y
0697	Excavation B: squares A, B, ½ C-10, 11, Lower layer 42	60657,658
0698	Excavation B: squares ½ C, D, E-10, 11, Lower layer 42	P
0699	Excavation A: southwest of Feature 32, layer 36, 200 x 230 x 25 cm, brickfill—red floor	60322,323
0700	Excavation A: southeast of Feature 32, layer 36, same 0699, 200 x 175 x 25 cm	P
0701	Excavation A: north one m wide strip north of Feature 32, layer 35, pick, brick (broken)	P
0702	Excavation A: northeast corner inside Feature 32, Upper layer 36, flotation	O
0703	Excavation A: north—inside rooms of Feature 32, Upper layer 36, pick, brick fill	O
0704	Excavation A: northeast Feature 32, layer 36—many floors, 160 x 170 x 40 cm	60324,325
0705	Excavation A: northwest Feature 32, layer 36, same, 150 x 120 x 35 cm	Y
0706	Excavation B: squares A, B, ½ C-12, 13, layer 43 to floor, green in C, D, E-12, 13, gatch elsewhere	60659,660
0707	Excavation B: squares ½ C, D, E-12, 13, layer 43	Y
0708	Excavation B: squares A, B, ½ C-10, 11, layer 43	60661,662
0709	Excavation B: squares ½ C, D, E-10, 11, layer 43	Y
0710	Excavation B: square D-13, layer 43, painted jar	O
0711	Excavation B: square D-12, layer 43, red jar	60781,788
0712	Excavation B: square D-10, Upper layer 43, 30 x 30 x 10 cm, flotation	O
0713	Excavation B: squares C, D-13, Lower layer 43, lens not removed earlier	O
0714	Excavation B: squares ½ C, D, E-12, 13, Upper layer 44	60663,664
0715	Excavation B: squares ½ C. D, E-12, 13, Upper layer 44	P
0716	Excavation B: square C-13, Upper layer 44, 10 x 150 x 5 cm, flotation	O
0717	Excavation B: squares A, B, ½ C-10, 11, Upper layer 44	60665,666
0718	Excavation B: squares ½ C, D, E-10, 11, Upper layer 44	60667,668
0719	Excavation B: squares A-15 to E-15, 50 cm below layer 46, cut step, screened	61222,223
0720	Excavation B: midwest room A, Lower layer 44	P
0721	Excavation B: southeast room B, Lower layer 44	60669
0722	Excavation B: mid-center room C, Lower layer 44	60670,671,672,698
0723	Excavation B: mid-center room D, Lower layer 44	P
0724	Excavation B: mideast room E, Lower layer 44	P
0725	Excavation B: triangular area northwest of room A, Lower layer 44	P
0726	Excavation B: room G: 'east half' (northeast and north center), Lower layer 44	60673
0727	Excavation B: square B-14, room C, Lower layer 44, 25 x 10 x 25 cm deep, flotation	O
0728	Excavation B: square E-14, lower layer 44, 25 x 10 x 25 cm deep, flotation, room B	O
0729	Excavation B: squares A-14, 13, 12, top layer 45, below room A	60674,675
0730	Excavation B: squares C, B-14, 13, top layer 45, below room C	60676,677,773

APPENDIX A

Table A1: Continued

Field Catalogue Number	Unit Location: Description	Permanent Catalogue Number
0731	Excavation B: square C-13, top layer 45, 20 x 20 x 10 cm, flotation	O
0732	Excavation B: square A-13, top layer 45, 20 x 20 x 10 cm, flotation	O
0733	Excavation B: squares D-14, 13, ½ 12, top layer 45, below room D	Y
0734	Excavation B: squares D, C-14, top layer 45, south room C	60678,679,774
0735	Excavation B: squares A, B-13, 12, top layer 45, below room F	60680,681
0736	Excavation B: squares C, D, E-11, 10, top layer 45, below room G	60682,683
0737	Excavation B: squares E, D-13, 12, top layer 45, below room B	P
0738	Excavation B: squares E, D-13, 12, top layer 45, below room E	60684,685
0739	Excavation B: below west wall of Feature 41	60686,687
0740	Excavation B: squares A, B, ½ C-15, 14, 13, bottom layer 45	O
0741	Excavation B: squares ½ C, D, E-13, 14, 15 except room D, bottom layer 45	O
0742	Excavation B: square C-13, bottom layer 45 x 30 x 20 cm, flotation	O
0743	Excavation B: squares D-14, 13, 12, bottom layer 45, below room D	60688,689
0744	Excavation B: squares A, B, ½ C, top layer 46	Y
0745	Excavation B: squares ½ C, D, E-11, 10, bottom layer 45, below room G	Y
0746	Excavation C: step 6, vol: 100 x 110 x 70 cm	60704,705
0747	Excavation C: step 8, vol: 90 x 55 x 55 cm	60706,707
0748	Excavation C: step 8, vol: 90 x 55 x 55 x cm, below Feature 71	60708,709
0749	Excavation C: step, top layer 12	60710,711
0750	Excavation C: charcoal fill of pit, vol: 100 x 90 x 50 cm	60712,713,775
0751	Excavation B: squares A, B, C-13, 12, 11, top layer 46	60690,691
0752	Excavation B: squares A, B, ½ C-½ 15, 14, lower layer 46	60692,693
0753	Excavation B: squares A-15 to E-15, layer 48 +	O
0754	Excavation B: squares A, B, ½ 13, 12, 11, Lower layer 46	P
0755	Excavation B: squares A, B, ½ C-14, ½ 15, all layer 47	P
0756	Excavation B: squares A, B, ½ C-13, 12, 11, all layer 47	60694,695
0757	Excavation B: squares A, B, ½ C, 15, 14, layer 47, 20 x 20 x 10 cm, flotation	O
0758	Excavation B: squares E, D-13, 12, Lower layer 45, below room E	P
0759	Excavation C: step 12, 2nd floor, below pit	60714,715,716
0760	Excavation C: step 13, 1st floor	60717,718
0761	Excavation C: step 13, 2nd floor	60719,720
0762	Excavation C: step 14, 1st floor	60721,722,794
0763	Excavation C: step 14, 2nd floor	60723,724,725
0764	Excavation C: room D, bottom layer 45	P

Table A2. Tepe Farukhabad 1968: Characteristics of the Analytical Units

Layer	Squares	Excavation Numbers	Average Thickness x Area (m)	Volume (m3)
Excavation A:				
Above 155.8, all	A,B,C-6,7	040,041,042	.40 x 6	2.40
155.6-155.8, all	A,B,C,D-6,7	043,044,045	.20 x 8	1.60
Layer 3±, all	A to E-6,7; B,C,D-8	046,047,048	.20 x 12	2.40
Layer 5 W	A-6,A,B-7,8	049,060,068	.35 x 5	1.75
Layer 5 E	C,D,E-6; C,D-7,8	050,061-065	.35 x 7	2.45
Layer 6 N	½B to E-6,7	079,080,086	.18 x 7	1.26
Layer 6 S	½B to E-8,9,½10	069,078	.18 x 9	1.62
Layer 7 N	B to E-6,7	087,088	.20 x 8	1.60
Layer 7 S	C to E-8,½10	083,084,085	.25 x 7	1.75
Layer 8 N	C to ½E-6,7	104	.18 x 5	.90
Layer 8 S	½C to E-8,9,10	103,93	.18 x 8	1.44
Layer 9,10 N	B,C,D-6,7	120	.35 x 6	2.10
Layer 9,10 SE	½C,D,E-8,9,10,½11	118,119	.30 x 8.75	2.60
Layer 9,10 SW	A-9,10	121	.30 x 3.75	1.10
Layer 11 N	½B,C,D	148,150	.20 x 5	1.00
Layer 11 C	C,D-8,9	126	.20 x 4	.80
Layer 11 SW	A,B,½C-10,11	125	.15 x 5	.75
Layer 11 SE	½C,D,E-10,11	124	.15 x 5	.75
Layer 12 N	½B,C,D-6,7; ½C,½D-8,9	153,154,179	.24 x 6	1.44
Layer 12 S	½C,D,E-10,11	152	.24 x 5	1.20
Layer 13u S	A to E-10,½11	156,157	.10 x 7.50	.75

Table A2: Continued

Layer	Squares	Excavation Numbers	Average Thickness x Area (m)	Volume (m3)
Layer 13u N	A,½B-7; ½B to E-6,7,8; ½B,C,D-9	160,161,189,209,181, 182	.10 x 14	1.40
Layer 13 all	Middle-center	180,183-188,210	.19 x 19	3.61
Layer 14 all	½B to E-6,½7	192-195	.15 x 5.25	.80
Layer 15 all	A to E-½8,9,10; ½ C,D,E-11,12	196,211-215	.15 x 16.50	2.50
Layer 16 all	½B,C,D-½6,½7	216,217	.15 x 4.50	.70
Layer 17 S	A to E-11,12+	248,249,262	.18 x 11	1.98
Layer 17 N	A to E-½8,9,10	250,251	.18 x 12	2.16
Layer 18 N	A to E-½8,9,10; A,B,½C-½11; A,½B-12	252,253,255,293	.22 x 15	3.30
Layer 19 all	A to E-½8,9,10,½11; ½C,D,E-½11,½12	261,295,297	.15 x 18	2.70
Layer 20	A to E-½8,9,10,11,½12	298,299,301	.20 x 22	4.40
Layer 21u S	A to E-11,12,½13	302,303	.10 x 12.50	1.20
Layer 21u N	A to E-½8,9,10	304,305	.10 x 12.50	1.20
Layer 21m	Rooms B,C	327,328	.10 x 9.0	.90
Layer 21m	Rooms D,E	329,330	.10 x 6.0	.60
Layer 21l	Rooms C,D,E	336,337,339	.10 x 9.50	.95
Layer 22 all	½C,D,E-8,9,10,11	380,382,340	.20 x 10.0	2.00
Layer 23 all	B-10,11; C,D,E-9,10	438-440,445,449,450	.10 x 7.0	.70
Layer 24u SW	A,B-10,11,12,13; C,D,E-12,13	442-444	.15 x 14.0	1.00
Layer 24u NE	C,D,E-9; D,E-10,11	441,451	.15 x 7.0	.50
Layer 24l SW	A,B-10,11,12,13; C-½10,11; D-11	448,489,490	.15 x 10.0	.70
Layer 24l NE	C,D,E-9; D,E-10,11	492	.15 x 6.0	.55
Layer 25 N	A to E-12,13	485,487	.22 x 10.0	2.20
Layer 25 S	A to E-12,13; A,B,½C, pt 15	447,448	.22 x 12.0	2.62
Layer 26 N	A to E-12; A,B,½C-13	486,488	.15 x 7.50	1.00
Layer 26 S	½C,D,E-13; A to E-14; A,B,½C-15	453,455,484	.15 x 10.0	1.50
Layer 27 N	A to E-12,13	500-504	.22 x 10.0	2.20
Layer 27 S	A to E-14,15	493,494	.22 x 10.0	2.20
Layer 28 NW	A to E-13,14; A,B,C-14	535-543	.25 x 12.0	3.00
Layer 28 SE	½A,½B-15; C,D-½14,15; E-½15	506,507	.25 x 5	1.25
Layer 29	NW hall	546-549	.90 x 7	6.30
Layer 29u	L-room,corner room inside Feature 30	550-552	.45 x 5	2.25
Layer 29l	L-room, corner room	580,581,583,606,607	.45 x 5	2.25
Layer 29± NW	A,B-12; C,D-½12	611-613	.40 x 3	1.20
Layers 30-31 inside F30	L-room, corner room	609,610,614,637,638, 640	.30 x 5	1.50
Layer 33 all	see plan	661-664	.10 x 17	1.70
Layer 34 all	see plan	667-670	.25 x 18	3.00
Layer 35 all	see plan	671-674	.20 x 20	4.00
Layer 36 SE F 32	see plan	699,700	.20 x 8	1.60
Layer 36 inside F 32	see plan	701-704	.25 x 6	1.50
Layer 36 outside F 32	see plan	705		
Excavation B				
Layer 20u&l N	A to E-3,4; A,B-5	131,139	.20 x 9.5	1.9
Layer 20u&l SW	A,B,½C-6,7	133,140	.20 x 5	1.0
Layer 20u&l SE	½C,D,E-½5,6,7	132,141,142	.20 x 6	1.2
Layer 21u&l N	½B,C,D,E-3,4	143,167,168	.15 x 7	1.4
Layer 21u&l S	E-5; C,D,E-6; A to E-7	144-146,169,170	.15 x 7	1.4
Layer 22u N	A to E-3,4,5	171	.12 x 11	1.32
Layer 22l N	A to E-3,4,5	175-176	.12 x 11	1.32
Layer 22u&l S	½C-6,7; D,E-6,7,8	172,202,203,206	.25 x 6	1.50
Layer 23u&m N	A to E-3,4,½5-Feature 6	197-200	.20 x 11	2.20
Layer 23l N	A to E-3,4,½5 except Feature 6,225	224,226	.10 x 9	.9
Layer 23u&m S	A-8;C,D,E-6,7	204,228,229	.20 x 7	1.40
Layer 23l S	D,C,E-9; C,D-6,7,8	230,236-238	.10 x 12	1.20
Layer 24u N	A,B,½C-3,4,5; ½C,D,E-3,4	235,240,244	.15 x 14	2.1
Layer 24l N	A,B,½C-,3,4,5; ½C,D,E-3,4	245-247	.15 x14	2.1
Layer 24 S	E-6; C,D,E-7; C,D-8	241-243	.20 x 5	1.0
Layer 25u N	A,B,½C-3,4,½5; ½C,D,E-3,4	267,268	.11 x 12	1.43
Layer 25l N	A,B,½C-3,4,½5; ½C,D,E-3,4	276,277	.11 x 14	1.43

APPENDIX A

Table A2. Continued

Layer	Squares	Excavation Numbers	Average Thickness x Area (m)	Volume (m3)
Layers 25-27 S	E-5,6; D,E-7,8	265,266,271,281	.30 x 7	2.1
Layer 26 NE	½A to E-3,4; E-5,6	278,289,283,309	.25 x 9	2.25
Layer 26 W	A-½3,4,5,6; A,½B-7,8	308,320	.20 x 7	1.4
Layer 27 NE	½A to E-3,4	316-318	.18 x 7	1.26
Layer 27 W	A-½3,4,5,6; A,½B-7	315	.18 x 6	1.08
Layer 27 S			.18 x 4	.72
Layer 28 N		319,347,348,350-352	.20 x 10.5	2.1
Layer 28 S		321-323,353-355	.2 x 10.5	2.1
Layer 29u N	A to E-3,4,5; A-6;E-6	357,358,362,364,392	.11 x 17	1.90
Layer 29u S	A,B-6,7,8; ½C-7,8,9; D,E-½7,8,9	359,363,365,391	.11 x 10	1.20
Layer 29l W	A-3 to 8; ½B-6,7,8	367,369	.07 x 8	.6
Layer 29l E	½B to E-3,4,5; ½C,D,E-6	368,370,373,393	.07 x 12	.9
Layer 30 W	A-3 to 9; ½B,½C-6 to 9	394,397,401,427	.15 x 13	1.9
Layer 30 NE	½B to E-3 to 6	395,396,398,402,403	.15 x 13	1.9
Layer 30 SE	½C,D,E-7,8,9	399	.15 x 7	1.05
Layer 31u N	A to E-3,4,5 except Feature 23	410,422,423,425	.10 x 13	1.3
Layer 31u S	A to E-6 to 9 except Feature 23	404-406,426	.10 x 16	1.6
Layer 31l N	A-3,4,5; ½B,C,D,E-3 to ½7	411-415	.10 x 16	1.6
Layer 31l S	A,½B-6 to 9; ½C,D,E-½7,8,9	416,420,432-434	.10 x 14	1.4
Layer 32u N	A to E-5,6 except B-5	461,462,431	.20 x 13	2.60
Layer 32u S	A to E-7,8,9,½10	457-460,463	.15 x 17	2.55
Layer 32l N	A to E-5,6 except B-5	468,469	.2 x 9	1.8
Layer 32l S	A to E-7,8,9,½10	464-467	.2 x 17	3.4
Layer 33u N	A to E-5,6	481,482	.1 x 9	.9
Layer 33u&m Center	A to E-7, pt 8 except Feature 27	480,508,509	.2 x 5	1.0
Layer 33u&m SE	½D,E-8,9,10	477,511	.2 x 4	.8
Layer 33u&m SW	A,B,C,½D-½9,10	476,510	.2 x 6	1.2
Layer 33l N	A to E-5,6	514,515	.15 x 9	1.35
Layer 33l S	A to E-7,8,9,10	561-519,525-527	.15 x 20	3.0
Layer 34u N	A to E-5,6	528-529	.15 x 9	1.35
Layer 34u Center	A to E-7,8	530,531	.15 x 10	1.5
Layer 34u S	A to E-9,10	532,533	.15 x 10	1.5
Layer 34l N	A to E-5,6	555,556	.10 x 9	.9
Layer 34l Center	A to E-7,8	557,558	.15 x 9	1.5
Layer 34l S	A to E-9,10	559,560,565	.20 x 10	4.0
Layer 35u all	A to E-7 to 10	561,562,566,567	.20 x 20	4.0
Layer 35l all	A to E-7 to 10	571-574	.20 x 20	4.0
Layer 36l all	pt C,D-7; pt B,C,D-8; A to E-9,10,11	594-597	.20 x 16	3.2
Layer 37 all	A to E-9,10,11	598-601	.15 x 15	2.25
Layer 38 E	½C,D,E-9,10	603,616	.40 x 5	2.0
Layer 39u E	½C,D,E-9 to 12	617,620	.08 x 10	.80
Layer 39u W	A,B,½C-9 to 12	618,619	.08 x 10	.80
Layer 39m E	½C,D,E-9 to 12	621,623	.08 x 10	.80
Layer 39m W	A,B,½C-9 to 12	622,624	.08 x 10	.80
Layer 39l E	½C,D,E-9 to 12	626,628	.08 x 10	.80
Layer 39l W	A,B,½C-9 to 12	625,627	.08 x 10	.80
Layer 40u E	½C,D,E-9 to 13	631,633,635	.075x 12.5	.93
Layer 40u W	A,B,½C-9 to 13	630,632,634	.075x 12.5	.93
Layer 40l E	½C,D,E-9 to 13	644,646,648	.075x 12.5	.93
Layer 40l W	A,B,½C-9 to 13	643,645,647	.75 x 12.5	.93
Layer 41u NW	A to E-9,10; A,B,½C-11,12	652,655,675,676	.08 x 15	1.20
Layer 41u SE	½B,C,D-11,12; A to E-13	650,651,653	.08 x 10	.80
Layer 41m NW	A to E-9,10; A,B,½C-11,12	658,681,682	.08 x 15	1.20
Layer 41m SE	½B,C,D-11,12; A to E-13	656,657,659	.08 x 10	.80
Layer 41l NW	A to E-9,10; A,B,C-11,12	679,683,685,686	.08 x 15	1.20
Layer 41l SE	½C,D,E-11,12; A to E-13	677,678,680	.10 x 15	1.0
Layer 42u NW	A to E-9,10; A,B,½C-11,12	690,692,693	.10 x 10	1.0
Layer 42u SE	½C,D,E-11,12; A to E-13	687,688,691	.10 x 15	1.5
Layer 42l N	A to E-10,11	697,698	.10 x 10	1.0
Layer 42l S	A to E-12,13	695,696	.10 x 10	1.0
Layer 43 N	A to E-10,11	708,709	.30 x 10	3.0
Layer 43 S	A to E-12,13	707,713	.30 x 10	3.0
Layer 44u N	A to E-10,11	717,718	.15 x 10	1.5
Layer 44u S	A to E-12,13	714,715	.15 x 10	1.5
Layer 44l N				

Table A2. Tepe Farukhabad 1968: Characteristics of the Analytical Units

Layer	Squares	Excavation Numbers	Average Thickness x Area (m)	Volume (m3)
Layer 44l SW	Rooms A,C	720,722	.10 x 5	.5
Layer 44l SE	Rooms B,D,E	721,723,724	.10 x 6	.6
Layer 45u N	Rooms F,G	735,736	.10 x 6	.6
Layer 45u SW	Rooms A,C+	729,730,734,739	.10 x 6	.6
Layer 45u SE	Rooms B,D,E	733,737,738	.10 x 6	.6
Layer 45l N	Rooms F,G	745	.10 x 6	.6
Layer 45l SW	Rooms A, C+	740	.10 x 6	.6
Layer 45l SE	Rooms B,D,E	743,758,764	.10 x 6	.6
Layer 46u SW	A,B,½C-pt.11 to ½15	744,751	.15 x 9.5	1.4
Layer 46l SW	A,B,½C-pt.11 to ½15	752,754	.25 x 9.5	2.4
Layer 47 all SW	A,B,½C pt.11 to ½15	755,756	.28 x 9.5	2.7

APPENDIX B

ARTIFACT COUNTS IN FARUKHABAD PROVENIENCE UNITS

The following pages present the proveniences of artifactual material in each analytical unit. In Tables B1-3, chipped stone items and stone debris counts are tabulated. Local dark brown chert and medium textured gray chert are distinguished from other fine cherts. Among these others are fine red and green (R), mottled red (MR), gray (G), banded gray (BG), mottled gray (MG), coarse gray (CG), fine pink (P), mottled pink (MP), fine white (W), mottled white (MW), fine tan (T), mottled tan (MT), banded brown (BB), and translucent tan (TT) or brown (TB). Within these chert categories, various morphological types are specified. Rough cores (R), blade cores (B) and various core rejuvenation flakes (Rj) occur. Fragments or blocky pieces are not otherwise specified. Some large or small flakes and blades or blade segments may be lightly retouched (Rt). Other more heavily retouched artifacts are designated as notches (NCH), denticulates (DNT), perforators (PRF), pointed pieces (PtP), drills (DR), large drills (LG.DR), truncated pieces (TRN), end scrapers (ES), side scrapers (SS), burins (BRN), trapezoids (TRP), or microliths (MCR). Blade segments with sickle polish may have smooth unretouched edges, either one (S1) or two (S2), or denticulate edges, either one (D1) or two (D2). Throughout the chart, the cut-off point between large and small flakes is 1.5 cm. If the designation Rt (retouched) is followed by a colon ':', the number of retouched pieces is given by the number following the colon. However, an entry such as 'Rt, 5 ' indicates that there is one retouched item and 5 unretouched pieces. Finally, the right-hand column records a range of items, primarily hammerstones (HM), perforated stone (PS), choppers (CH) and handstones (HS).

In Tables B4-6, counts of vessels represented by rims, bases, and other classes of diagnostic parts are presented. The categories are presented in the order of discussion in Chapters III and VIII. The wing list is a summary of the abbreviations used in these tables.

Bowl Rims:
  incs/str—incision or strip
  incs—incised
  crvd—curved
  inc—incurved
  bvl—bevelled

Jar Rims and Parts:
  crse thk—coarse thick
  strp hnd—strap handle
  st—straight
  drp—droop
  spt—spout
  b-r shld—black on red shoulder
  poly shld—polychrome shoulder
  hor tw—horizontal twist
  sl—with slash
  tis—thumb impressed strip
  rs—reserve slip
  at—attached
  ldg—ledge
  exp—expanded
  flrd—flared
  rnd—round
  bnd—band
  h-s—hatched strip
  p-s—plain strip
  nkls—neckless
  ls—lip spout

Bases:
  ff—fine flat
  fr—fine ring
  rg—ring
  nrw—narrow

General:
  sm—small
  lg—large
  pl—plain
  pt—painted
  fn—fine
  hvy—heavy
  min—miniature
  S—shell
  L—limestone
  pnc—punctate
  bdd—beaded
  htch—hatched

Other:
  sh plt—shallow plate
  drn—drain
  grywr—grayware
  tr—trough
  cyl stnd—cylindrical stand
  pol—polished
  blk—black
  bot—bottle

  shvd—shaved
  cons—constricted
  sld—solid
  flt—flat

Painted examples on ordinarily unpainted forms are noted (pt).

In Tables B7-9, data on discarded body sherds, not otherwise utilized in this monograph, are presented. Both counts and weights in grams as recorded in the field are presented so that questions of degree of breakage of sherds in different kinds of deposits can be pursued.

Table B10 presents the occurrence of motifs on polychrome jar sherds by layer. If a sherd has two motifs, it is entered in the appropriate two columns. If a motif occurs several times on the sherds of a single vessel, it is counted only once. This listing supplements the more specific but less copious information on design organization recorded on Table C12.

304

Table B1: Chipped Stone Artifacts from Farukhabad: Farukh and Bayat Phases

	Dark Brown Chert							Medium Gray Chert							
	Core	Frag	Lg Flk	Sm Flk	Bld	Bld Seg	Other	Core	Frag	Lg Flk	Sm Flk	Bld	Bld Seg	Sickles	Other
A22		9	10	15	2		TRP		1	1	Rt,1				
A23	R,Rj	4	1	12					1		4			S1,D1	NCH
A24U SW	R	5	3	7	1			2R,2Rj	2	4	1			S1	
A24U NE		2		1					1			2			
A24L SW			1	3	1				3		3			S1	
A24L SE	2R	3	5	3					2					S1	
A25N		1	5	12					3	4	2			S1	PRF 2DNT
A25S	2R		2	12					1	1					
A26N				6	1				2	2	1				
A26S	4R	4	4	20			SS	R,Rj	1		4	1	7		
A27N		8	6	8	1				2	6	2	2	2		
A27S	R,2Rj	5	3	13				2R	1	3	3		3		2NCH
A28NE		3	5	29	3		DNT		2	3	1	1	1	S1	PRF
A28SE		5	4	8	1				2	2		2	1		
A29NW	R	4		28	2	1			1		5	Rt,1		S1	
A29U-lc		2	2	2						2					
A29L-lc	R	12	13	64	10	2	PtP	B	1		4	1	2		
A31-F30	B,R	6	5	26	2	1 2Rt	2DNT TRN	R		Rt	2		Rt		
A33		3	Rt,12	10					1	3					PRF
A34	2R	4	9	Rt,29	6	2				1	3	Rt,4		S2	
A35	R,B	6	8	18		1	DNT	R			1		1		
A36SE	3R	9	27	95	6	1		Rj		7	5	3	1		
A36-F32	2B,4R	12	3Rt,15	47	2					1	3		2	S1	
B36L	2R	9	10	16	6		DNT	2R		7	5	7			
B37	2R	7	6	19				B	3	7	8	1	2	D1	NCH BRN
B38E		1	3	7				R	2		3		3		
B39U E			1	Rt,6					1	1	1		1	2S1	DNT NCH
B39U W		3	Rt	3					1						
B39M E	R		1						1						
B39M W		1	6	2					1		1			S2	
B39L E		1	.5	12	1			3B	1	Rt,3	3		2		
B39L W	1	1	3	2				R		1			1	S1	
B40U E	1	2	1	2	1		S1	3R,B	2	6	8	2Rt	3		
B40U W	B	2	3	4	1	1	DNT MCR	R	6	Rt,3	3		Rt,4	S1	DNT NCH

APPENDIX B

Table B1: Continued

			Other Fine Chert					Calcite					
	Core	Frag	Lg Flk	Sm Flk	Bld	Bld Seg	Other	Frag	Sm Flk	Lg Flk	Peb	Crk Peb	Other
A22				BG	MG			6	9	2	1		
A23				W,2BP, BR,R,B, MB			BRN:MP DNT:BG	3	4	2	1	1	
A24U SW		R		R	TB,TW	T		5	8	2	2		
A24U NE					W	Rt:W		1	2	4	4	4	HM,HS
A24L SW		R		G	W			6	3	4			
A24L NE		R,MG			W	BT		1	4	3			
A25N		MP	MT	R,BG,G Rt:MR	2R MG		Sl:BG	1	9	3			
A25S		R		R	2W			5	13	3	2	1	3HS,CH
A26N		R	W Rt:MG					4	4			2	
A26S	Rj	R	MG		2W, TB BR	2BG,W BP	BRN:G BRN:MG	3	3	7	2	1	HS
A27N				MP	2W,G, MG			2	2	3	2	1	
A27S	B:MG Rj:BG Rj:BP		T	3BP,MG brnt	3W,T 4BP		PRF:W	4	5	4		3	CH
A28NE		3W		MG	W	R,W		4	1	3	3	1	CH
A28SE					W,P				4	3	4		CH
A29NW		B						1		1			
A29U-lc				R					1	3			
A29L-lc	B:BB	R		R,P	2W,P, T,MR	T		2	3	6	2		
A31-F30			BR	MP					2	1			
A33		MG		G,BY	3W brnt				2				
A34		2BG	4BG	2BG brnt	3BG	MG			4	2			CH,PS
A35			brnt		W, brnt			1	1		7	1	
A36SE		R,G	2R	2R,W,G, MG,P	BR	TB	TRN:MT NCH:W	1	2	2	1		
A36-F32		Rt,W	R	G	MG		PtP:MB	2	2	1	1	1	
B36L					2TB			2	2	1		3	CH,PS
B37					MR			3	3	6	1		PS
B38E						Rt:MG	NCH:W		1				
B39U E					MG		Sl:brnt	2	7				
B39U W	R:MG			2R				1	5		1		
B39M E	R:R							1	1	3			CH
B39M W		BR			MR,P		BRN:W	1	1				
B39L E			1			BP	NCH:P		1	2	1		
B39L W						TB	Sl:MR	1	3	3			
B40U E	R:W B:MB				TB,MP	Rt:BR, W	NCH:BG		8	1	1		
B40U W		R	2R		MG			1	9				

Table B1: Continued

		Dark Brown Chert						Medium Gray Chert						
	Core	Frag	Lg Flk	Sm Flk	Bld	Bld Seg	Other	Core	Frag	Lg Flk	Sm Flk	Bld	Bld Seg	Sickles	Other
B40L E		1	4	25				1	3	9			4	2Sl	PRF
B40L W		2	Rt,1	13	Rt	1			5		4	1			
B41U NW		3		8			TRN/ NCH PRF		2				Rt		
B41U SE				4											
B41M NW		4		5		1			2	2					
B41M SE				3									1		
B41L NW	Rj	2	2	6	Rt						1	4Rt,1			
B41L SE	R	4	1	1						1	2				
B41L NE				1									1		
B42U NW	R	4	2	14					1		3	Rt,3		Sl	
B42U SE		3		6				R,2B		3	5		1		
B42L N		2	3	3	2Rt,1				1	1	1		1	Sl	
B42L S	R	1	2	6	1			2R							
B43N	3R,Rj	4	2	15	2			B		2Rt,3	5		2Rt,2		
B43S		2	1	8					2		1	1			
B44U N			8	9		1	NCH						2	Sl	
B44U S	R	1		8	3	1	NCH								
B44L SW		1	1	2		1				1				Sl	
B44L SE		2		2										Dl?	
B44L N				1									1		
B45U N				3	1									Sl	
B45U SW		5	1	4						2	3			Sl	
B45U SE				1								1			
B45L N		2													
B45L SE		1			1								1		
B45L SW				1	4				1		1				
B46U SW		6	3	9				B,Rj	1		3	1	1	Dl,Sl	NCH
B46L SW		1	4	4	1	Rt,1				4	3	2Rt,2			
B47L SW	Rj		5	8						4	2	2Rt,2	2	Sl	
FEATURES															
AF25 Plat	4R	6	8	35	6				3	9	5		2		

APPENDIX B

Table B1: Continued

			Other Fine Chert						Calcite				
	Core	Frag	Lg Flk	Sm Flk	Bld	Bld Seg	Other	Frag	Sm Flk	Lg Flk	Peb	Crk Peb	Other
B40L E			R	W		Rt:W, 2R,W, Rt:MP, BP,T, brnt		4	11	5	2		
B40L W						Rt:W,W, MG, MT		1	2			1	
B41U NW			W		brnt		ES:BG	1	1	2			
B41U SE						Rt:BG BP			1				
B41M NW				R		2W							CH
B41M SE						Rt:MB			2				
B41L NW					W		S1:MT		2	3	1		
B41L SE				MG	Rt:MR MG		D2:R			1			CH
B41L NE									1				
B42U NW		R			TT	T	ES:TT HF:MG	2	3		2		2CH
B42U SE				G				1		2			
B42L N	R:BG			BP	Rt:MG R,brnt					Rt			
B42L S				2R,B	BP							1	
B43N				2R,MR		W,P		4	1	1			
B43S					brnt			3				1	
B44U N	B:R			brnt	T	MG,BP		1	2				
B44U S		W			MT		BRN:W		1				
B44L SW						W							
B44L SE	R:W	R									1		CH
B44L N			BP										
B45U N									1	1	1		
B45U SW					MR	G							
B45U SE				1									
B45L N													
B45L SE				R,MB	MB				1				
B45L SW					W,MP								
B46U SW		MB, brnt	R,G	MR, B, TB	BG,MP	W,MB, MR	D2:BP	2	1				
B46L SW	Rj:brnt	2W	5MG	2MG,TT	MR,W, MP	2MG,BP	ES:TB	1		2	1		CH
B47L SW			MG	2W, brnt	2brnt, TB,W	W		4	1				
FEATURES													
AF25 Plat	B:CG	R	MG,R	R,G	R,W,MG		S1:R	4	22	11	2	2	

Table B2: Chipped Stone Artifacts from Tepe Farukhabad: Uruk Phases

	Dark Brown Chert							Medium Gray Chert							
	Core	Frag	Lg Flk	Sm Flk	Bld	Bld Seg	Other	Core	Frag	Lg Flk	Sm Flk	Bld	Bld Seg	Sickles	Other
A18N	5R	13	Rt,13	49	5	1	NCH PRF		3	8	7		1		
A19	6R	13	22	39		2		R	3	4	10		1	S2,D1	
A20	6R	14	21	2Rt,90		6	DNT		6	5	11	2	3Rt,1		NCH
A21U S		4	8	18	2	1		B		1	2		2Rt	S1	
A21U N	R	3	12	19				R	1	2	9	2	Rt		
A21M BC		5	11	35	6		NCH		1	3	3			D2	DNT
A21M DE		3	1	7		1			1	1			1		
A21L		9	3	28		5		B	2	1	4	2	1		
B28N	5R	13	8	23			2DNT		2	5	16	1	1		NCH
B28S	2R	7	10	24	1					5	5		2		
B29U N	3R	14	20	56	Rt,2			R,B	9	22	31	Rt,6	6		
B29U S	2R	11	16	49		2		2R	5	4	2	1	1		
B29L W	B		3	12	2				1		4		2	S1	
B29L E	5R	14	17	46	3	1	2DNT	3R,Rj	2	19	25	1	3		
B30W		8	8	Rt:12	2	1		Rj	4	1	6	1			
B30NE	R,Rj	23	8	22	4		DNT NCH	3R,3B	3	Rt,17	9	5			
B30SE		17	8	41			DNT		15	5	11			D1	
B31U N	Rj	2	Rt,4	22	1				5	Rt,3	3	1	Rt		
B31U S	2R	4	5	10		1		R	1	1	3		1		
B31L N	2R,B	19	Rt,38	42	3			2R	8	36	12	4	1		
B31L S	3R	19	16	33	4		PICK?	R,2Rj	3	3	Rt,5		Rt:3		DNT PRF
B32U N	5R	7	3	24	3		PRF, CH	R	3	4	7				DNT 8LG.DR
B32U S	B	10	4	45	1	2		R	6	10	5		2		2NCH
B32L N	R	9	11	22	2			B	4	5	6	Rt	Rt,1	S1	
B32L S		3	6	29	1	3	S1			3	1	1	2		LG.DR
B33U N		3	5	11	1		TRNC								DNT SS
B33U C			3							3					
B33U SE	R	3	3		1					1			2	D1	
B33U SW	Rj		1	2				R	2	3	2	1			
B33L N		7	2R,4	11	Rt				1	2		3		S1	DNT
B33L S	R	4	14	Rt,16	2	6		B,R	1	7	6		Rt,2	S1	
B34U N		2	3	8	Rt			Rj			1		1	S1	
B34U C	R	3	7	9				R		1	1	1		D1	brnt
B34U S	R,Rj	3	4	14	1		DNT 2NCH		4	3	1				ES LIMACE
B34L N	R	2		4	1		PRF						1		
B34L C		2	7	Rt,12	Rt	1	DNT 2NCH	B	1	2	1		1	S1	

APPENDIX B

Table B2: Chipped Stone Artifacts from Tepe Farukhabad: Uruk Phases

	Other Fine Chert							Calcite				
	Core	Frag	Lg Flk	Sm Flk	Bld	Bld Seg	Other	Frag	Sm Flk	Lg Flk	Peb	Crk Peb	Other
A18N	R:R	3R	R	4R,P,B,G	BB,R	R,W,TP		16	17	16	4		
A19	R:G	Brnt	G	2R				14	18	Rt,11		2	
A20	B:MP	R		R,G	BG	Rt:MG, MT,R	PRF: MG DNT:G	19	28	9	1	10	Diorite flk
A21U S				2R		R		2	18	3			
A21U N				R,MG				4	1	8			
A21M BC		R		G,MB	Rt:MG			8	7	4	2		
A21M DE								1	2				
A21L				2G		MR		6	7	1	4	6	
B28N					R,W		TRN:TT Sl:R		2	2		1	
B28S		P,W		MB	BP,P	Rt:MT, BG,W,BP			3	1			HS
B29U N		2R,B		R		R		4	11	4	2	2	HS
B29U S		R		R			NCH: MP ES:B	6	4	2Rt,5	1		
B29L W	B:W			2R	MT			1	7			3	
B29L E		2R	3R Rt:R			TB,Rt: MP,MR/ W*		6	9	5			
B30W		T						4	3	4		1	CH:R
B30NE				R	B	TG		8	9	Rt:3	1	1	
B30SE								9					
B31U N			?	?		BW**		4	2	1			
B31U S							TRP:?	3	3	1			
B31L N						Rt:Brnt	NCH:R	5	2	11		1	CH
B31L S				2R,MG	TG,W	2Brnt		11	14	14			CH
B32U N			MG	R	BB/R†		Lg.DR: BG	8	13	4	1	1	
B32U S			R,MG	R,MR	MP			3	6	3	1	2	CH
B32L N		4R	MG	R,MG		R	ES:MP	2	3	6	1		
B32L S		R		2R	R,MP MR	BW	R,W	PRF: MR	6	3	1		1	Notched Pebble
B33U N			2R,G		2R,MG			2	1	3			
B33U C			R					1	2	2			
B33U SE						G			2	1			Granite Sphere
B33U SW		R			BG,MP Cryst			1	1				2HS
B33L N	Rj:W	R	R		2G			2	2	1			Hematite
B33L S	B:MG	R,MG BB		MG,G,R Rt:BB		W,P		8	4	8	3	1	HS
B34U N				W	MG		DNT:R D1:R	1	5	3			
B34U C		Brnt		R	Rt:R,W	Rt:T			3				
B34U S					Rt:?			3	4	4			
B34L N				MG,R		MR							
B34L C			R	R	R				4	2	2		

Table B2: Continued

	Dark Brown Chert							Medium Gray Chert							
	Core	Frag	Lg Flk	Sm Flk	Bld	Bld Seg	Other	Core	Frag	Lg Flk	Sm Flk	Bld	Bld Seg	Sickles	Other
B34L S		3	6	13		1		R	1	1	1			S1,S2	
B35U	R	7	7	14	2	Rt,1		R	3	2	4	2		S1	
B35L	4R	2	1	Rt,16	Rt,3			R	3	3	3			S2,S1	
B36U	2R,Rj	7	13	58	6	1	PRF	R,Rj	7	10	Rt,8		3Rt,6	2S2,6S1	
B36L	2R	9	5	16	4	1	DNT	R,B,Rj	5	3	1	Rt,2	4		NCH
FEATURES															
AF19 pit		1	2	4											LG.DR
BF45 pit															
BF20 base							2NCH			2					
BF21 base		1	Rt,2	8		1	NCH			1	1				
AF26 bin	R	2	1	8						1					
AF27 bin															
AF23 pit	4R	9	18	47	5		DNT		1	17	9	10	Rt	2D1	PRF
AF24 hrth				2			DNT	Rj			1				PRF
AF-hrth	R	5	2	9				R		1	1		2Rt		
BF27 oven			1	3			NCH						1		
BF31 paving	R	2	6	1						3	1				

Table B3: Chipped Stone Artifacts from Tepe Farukhabad: Jemdet Nasr and Early Dynastic Phases

	Dark Brown Chert							Medium Gray Chert							
	Core	Frag	Lg Flk	Sm Flk	Bld	Bld Seg	Other	Core	Frag	Lg Flk	Sm Flk	Bld	Bld Seg	Sickles	Other
A1	2R	4	13	18	2		PRF		2	4				D2,D1	
A2	1R	5	5	13					2	2	1			D1	
A3-4	2R	Rt,4	6	30	1		4DNT		2	Rt,2	1	2	1	D1,S1	
A5W	2R,Rj	6	5	24	2		TRP			1	3	1		D1	NCH
A5E		14	9	20	1		2DNT	1	2	2					
A6N	R	9	5	6		1			2	2	2				
A6S		22	12	26		Rt,2	DNT		2		1			3D1	
A7N	2R	2	5	7			DNT 2NCH			1				S1	
A7S	3R	14	25	22	3			R	2	1	3				
A8N	2R	3	17	10		1						1	1		
A8S		2	5	17	1				1				Rt,1	D1	
A9-10N	R	4	6	6										D1	
A9-10SE	R	1	8	15			D2			3		2		5D2, 2D1,S2	
A9-10SW	R	3	6	6			PRF SS	R		Rt,3		2	1		

APPENDIX B

Table B2: Continued

			Other Fine Chert						Calcite				
	Core	Frag	Lg Flk	Sm Flk	Bld	Bld Seg	Other	Frag	Sm Flk	Lg Flk	Peb	Crk Peb	Other
B34L S				Purple		Rt:W	D1:Brnt	1	7	2	1		Bitumen covered pebble,lg
B35U				R		MR	Sl:MP	2	5	4	3		
B35L		BP	R	TB		BR		2	7	2			
B36U	B:MG	2R,W MG	R	3R,W MG	MB	Rt:MB	Rt:MG, 2MG, W,MB	5	13	3			
B36L			W,R			MP,MG		1	1	3		4	CH
FEATURES													
AF19 pit								6				1	CH frag
B45 pit													
BF20 base													
BF21 base			2R					1	1				
AF26 bin				R	T	T		3	2	1			
AF27 bin													
AF23 pit		BB		2R	R,W,BG			1	11	10			Celt Blank
AF24 hrth													
AF—hrth								1	1				
BF27 oven			2									1	
BF31 paving						2BP,W		1	1	Rt,1			

*mottled red and white
**banded white
†banded brown and red

Table B3: Continued

			Other Fine Chert						Calcite				
	Core	Frag	Lg Flk	Sm Flk	Bld	Bld Seg	Other	Frag	Sm Flk	Lg Flk	Peb	Crk Peb	Other
A1				W,2Brnt				7		2			
A2							D1:BB		6				
A3-4				MG				6	4	1	2		
A5W	R:G Rj:BR		G	R			BRN:MB	2	2				CH
A5E			BB					2					
A6N	R:R		G	R,MR			D1:BR	4	1	1			
A6S	R:R	R	2R	R	MP	3R		2	1			2	
A7N		W,MR, MG			MP		D1:BB D2:BB		4	2			HS
A7S	R:R	W,P,R	R		G				1	3			
A8N			R				D2:BB	Rt					
A8S													
A9-10N													
A9-10SE							D1:R D1:MB						
A9-10SW							Sl:MG Sl:BB	1	1			1	

Table B3: Continued

	Dark Brown Chert							Medium Gray Chert							
	Core	Frag	Lg Flk	Sm Flk	Bld	Bld Seg	Other	Core	Frag	Lg Flk	Sm Flk	Bld	Bld Seg	Sickles	Other
A11N		4	2	20										D1	TRN
A11C			3	2		1	PtP			2	1			D2	
A11SW			5	6	1										
A11SE		6	3	16	1					2	2	Rt	Rt	D2	NCH
A12N	R	2	9	8	1		DNT			1					
A12S		1	3	3	1					1					
A13U S		11	23	48		2Rt,2			2	4	1		1		
A13U N	2R	4	Rt,15	15		2				2	2				
A13ML	R	15	30	2Rt,86	1	1	PRF		3	5	4		1		NCH DNT
A14	2R	2	6	11	Rt			R	1	1	2				
A15	R	15	21	84	4		2DNT TRP	R	2	1	4		3Rt,2		
A16		3	Rt,4	11	1	R				2	1				NCH
A17S	2R	8	11	49	Rt,1				5	2	2	1	1	D2	NCH
A17N	R	6	2Rt,19	51	5				4	Rt,5	8	2	1		
B20N		7	12	41	1		SS		2	5	7		Rt,1		
B20SW	2R	5	2	10		1	DNT			2	2	1	Rt,1		
B20SE	R	2	6	28	1		DNT NCH		1	2	4			2D1	DNT
B21N		10	3	32					5	1	3	1	1	D1	
B21S	R	5	8	6	1				2	2	4	1	1	DC1	
B22U N		1	4	12			DNT,D1				1		1	3D1	
B22L N			3	9					1		2		1		
B22S		4	3	6	1				1	3	1	1		8D2,D1	
B23U N		2	3	13					1	1	3				
B23L N		6	13	37				B	3	3				2D2	TRP
B23U S	3R	4	1	16	1				2	1	1	1			
B23L S		2	8	17					3	2				D1	
B24U N	2R	9	7	22	1		NCH			6	3			2D1	
B24L N	R	7	17	29						1	1		1		
B24S	R	3	10	21		1			2	2					
B25U N		6	8	18	1	2	NCH		2	2	2		2	S1,S2	NCH
B25L N	2R	7	7	72	3	1	DNT			3	4				
B25-26S	7R	20	64	Rt,204	8	4	NCH DNT	R	4	1	19	5	2	S1	
B26NE	4R	17	27	61	5	1	SS NCH		2	7	11	1	1	S1,D1	
B26W		9	6	10	4										
B27NE	R	Rt,9	10	27	1		NCH		4	3	3		1		
B27W	R	1	3	14	1					1					
B27S	11R	28	65	105	9		PRF NCH	B,R	4	14	35				DNT
C9-10		9	1	12			NCH	R			4				
C11-12		3		2											
C23U	R	4	4	6						2					

APPENDIX B

Table B3: Continued

	Other Fine Chert							Calcite				
	Core	Frag	Lg Flk	Sm Flk	Bld	Bld Seg	Other	Frag	Sm Flk	Lg Flk	Peb	Crk Peb	Other
A11N		R				W	D2:BB	2	2	4			
A11C						W							
A11SW			R,G				ES:TB	1		2			
A11SE			R	R					1				
A12N		R		R,W						1			
A12S		R		2R									
A13U S		R						3	2	Rt	1	2	
A13U N						Rt:W		2	5	3			
A13ML				R		Rt:MR		8	24	2Rt,6	2		
A14								6		1	2		
A15		R,Rt		2R	W	2MG		5	21	3		2	
A16								2	3	Rt		5	
A17S		2Brnt	W,MR	2R,G,MG 3Brnt				9	6	1		1	
A17N				MG	R		BRN:MT	5	10	2	2		
B20N				2R					6	1		1	CH
B20SW						G		1	3	1		2	
B20SE		R		2R		Rt:R		1	1	Rt,4			
B21N							D1:BB	1	1	Rt,4			
B21S		W							1	1	3		Congl. Frag
B22U N								1	3	2			
B22L N						Rt:BB, MP,MG					2		
B22S		MG,MP	R				D2:BR	2					Slab Frag
B23U N			MG	R	P	MG			3				
B23L N				MR,G		BG,MG		3	7	1	4		
B23U S							NCH:R	2	3				
B23L S		BG						4	2	1	1	1	
B24U N		R		R		MG		6	2	1		1	
B24L N				R,MP		Brnt		2	9	6			
B24S			R,MG					3	7	3	1		
B25U N		2R						4	5	2	2		
B25L N		R		MG				1	11	1	2	1	
B25-26S				R	W			11	12	5		1	
B26NE		BG,BP		R,B,MB	G,BG	R	D1:B	10	11	1	4	2	
B26W				R			ES:MG		3				2CH
B27NE		Cryst	G		MR		DNT:MG	3	11	2			
B27W									Rt,2	1			
B27S	R:R	R	R	R	R			12	14	1	4	1	
C9-10													
C11-12													
C23U													

Table B3: Continued

	Dark Brown Chert						Medium Gray Chert							
	Core	Frag	Lg Flk	Sm Flk	Bld	Bld Seg	Other	Core	Frag	Lg Flk	Sm Flk	Bld	Bld Seg	Sickles	Other
C23L	2R	5	1	1											
C24													1		
C28-29	2R		1	4			NCH			1					
C29,31		1	1												
C32		1	2	5	1										
C33		5		6						1	1				
AF3 vat		2	4							1					
AF5 vat				2											
AF8 vat	R		2	1						2	1				
BF13 vat															
AF11 bin		2		6								1			
AF14 bin			2	9		Rt		Rj	1	2	2				
BF15 bin				3					1						
BF18 post?	R	2	Rt,1	2											
AF6 oven			2	2						2					
AF17 oven				1											

Table B4: Ceramics from Tepe Farukhabad: Farukh and Bayat Phases

			Susiana Ware											
	Khazineh jar rim	Bayat Ware bowl rim		Bowl Bases				sm hvy bowl	Deep Bowl Rims					
Layer			cyl stnd	wide	nrw	shvd	ring		pl	one band	two+ bnds	horiz crvd	vert line	vert crvd	dot
A22					1				4	2					
A23				20					4	9	8		1		
A24U SW	2			14		1		2	2	7	6		1	1	1
A24U NE		1	1	4					1	1	4				
A24L SW				6			1		1	6	7				1
A24L NE			2	6			1	1		13	4				
A25N	1	1	1	18	1		1	1	6	8	9	1	1		5
A25S	3			11		1	3		5	6	7				2
A26N				20		1	3		5	9	10		1		3
A26S				18			2		3	6	4	1			2
A27N	3	1		22		2	7	pt	11	4	13		2		4
A27S	3	1	1	15		1	4		5	6	7		2		4
A28NE	1			18		1	1	pt	12	14	10		1	2	4
A28SE	1			3			1		8	1	2		1		
A29NW				2					1	1	1			1	
A29U-1,C						2	1		3						
A29L-1,C		1		5	6	3			19	5	2		2		
A31-F30		1		4		5	2		11			1	1	1	
A33				2			1		5	2					
A34				2	1				7	1		2			
A35				1	1				6	1					
A36SE	1			1	1		1		10	5		1			
A36-F32				2	1				6	2	2				
B35U				3					1			1			
B35L				1	1					2	1				
B36U					1	1	3		1		1				
B36L				3			1	1	2	2	2				
B37				6	2	1	2		1	2	3	2			
B38E											2				

APPENDIX B

Table B3: Continued

	Other Fine Chert							Calcite					
	Core	Frag	Lg Flk	Sm Flk	Bld	Bld Seg	Other	Frag	Sm Flk	Lg Flk	Peb	Crk Peb	Other
C23L							2D:MG						
C24						Rt:Brnt				1			
C28,29													
C29-31													
C32									1				
C33		R											
AF3 vat										1			
AF5 vat													
AF8 vat				G									
BF13 vat													
AF11 bin													
AF14 bin		T				MP		1		2			
BF15 bin						MG				2			
BF18 post?													
AF6 oven													
AF17 oven										1			

Table B4: Continued

| | Susiana Ware | | | | | | | | | | | | | Other |
| | Deep Bowl Rims | | | | | | | | Jar Rims | | | | | |
Layer	dot/crvd	dot/rect	sigma	slash	step	diamond	other motif	flat base	high plain	high band	high solid	low	basin rim	
A22							1		1					
A23			3		2	2		5	1	2	4	1	pt,3	
A24U SW					3			6		3	1		pt,4	
A24U NE					1			1		2			pt,5	
A24L SW					4		1	1	2		2		pt	
A24L NE		1	1		2			3			1		5	
A25N		1						8	3	1	2	2	2pt,5	
A25S			1		2		1	8	3		2	1	pt,9	
A26N		1	2		1	1	1	10	1	2	3		2pt,11	
A26S					1		3	2			2		pt,5	
A27N			3	1	3		2	8		4	6	1	2pt, 10	Susiana spt
A27S		2			1	1	2	4	1	2	3	1	5	
A28NE	2	1		1	3	1	1	7		1	1	1	pt,8	6 drain frags
A28SE	1				1			2			1		3	
A29NW													2	chaff bowl
A29U-1,C								1					2	
A29L-1,C				1	1			5					6	perf slab
A31-F30			1								3	1	1	
A33								1				1	pt,1	
A34						1		1			1		4	polished blk bowl; chaff bowl
A35					1			2					1	pol blk bowl
A36SE								3					1	pol blk bowl
A36-F32							1	3			1	1	6	
B35U			1		1			1						
B35L						2	1	1		4			2pt,3	
B36U			1					2					9	
B36L			1				1	3		1	2	1	8	
B37								5	1					
B38E					1			2		1				

Table B4: Continued

Layer	Khazineh jar rim	Bayat Ware bowl rim	Susiana Ware											
			\multicolumn{4}{c}{Bowl Bases}	sm hvy bowl	\multicolumn{6}{c}{Deep Bowl Rims}	
			cyl stnd	wide	nrw	shvd	ring		pl	one band	two+ bnds	horiz crvd	vert line	vert crvd	dot
B39U E	1			2					1	2	2				
B39U W				1								1			
B39M E				5							2				
B39M W				3					1	1	3				
B39L E		1		7		1	3		2	2	1				
B39L W				6			1			4	6				
B40U E	2		1	24	1	1	2		5	2	9				2
B40U W	2			12		1	4		4	14	11	1		1	1
B40L E	2		2	19			1	9	8	8		1		4	
B40L W				10		1			3	2	7	1	2		1
B41U NW				3			1			5	2	1			1
B41U SE	1			10	2					2	5			1	1
B41M NW	1			5		1	1		3	3	6	1		1	4
B41M SE				7						2	1				
B41L NW				3			3		3	6	1				
B41L SE				2		2	2			1	2			1	1
B41L NE				1	1					1	1				
B42U NW	1			20		1	1		4	6	9	2			1
B42U SE				6			2			5	2				
B42L N				10		1	3			2	8				
B42L S	1			8		1	3		1	3	3				4
B43N				6		1	2		5	1	10				
B43S	1			3			2		1	2					2
B44U N	1			6		1			2	5	7				
B44U S	1			3					4	5	11				5
B44L SW	1			2						3	2		1		3
B44L SE		1		5	1	1					3	1			1
B44L N				1			1								2
B45U N				2						1	1				
B45U SW		1		4	1	1			1	2	2				1
B45U SE				2		1				1	4				2
B45L N											3				1
B45L SE				1							1				2
B45L SW				1		1	1	pt	1	1					
B46U SW				15			8	2	5	4	7			1	1
B46L SW		1		21	1	3	3		16	6	7	1	2		2
B47SW	2			17	1		7		6	5	6	1	1	1	
FEATURES:															
AF25 plat	1			11					5	3	3		3	1	
AF30 plat				1					1						
AF30 alley									2	3					
BF45 pit			2	3			7		1						

APPENDIX B

Table B4: Continued

Layer	Susiana Ware													Other
	Deep Bowl Rims							Jar Rims						
	dot/ crvd	dot/ rect	sigma	slash	step	dia- mond	other motif	flat base	high plain	high band	high solid	low	basin rim	
B39U E					1		1	5	1				3	
B39U W											2		1	
B39M E								1			1		2	
B39M W	1		1				1						3	
B39L E					1		2	6	1				6	1 drain frag
B39L W					1	2		2	1	1	1		1	1 chaff bowl
B40U E	1				3	1	3	7		3	2	1	8	int ledge jar
B40U W					2			2		2		1	7	pol blk bowl base
B40L E	2	1		1	2	2	1	12	2	2	3	2	7	Susiana lug
B40L W		1			1		1	1	1	1	1		2	drain frag
B41U NW				1			1	3					2	
B41U SE	2	1	1		1			2				pt	pt,1	
B41M NW		1		1	1					1			3	drain frag
B41M SE								1					4	
B41L NW				1						4				
B41L SE		1			3					1			2	
B41L NE														
B42U NW	3	1		1	5			5	2				7	chaff bowl
B42U SE	1		1		1			7		1	3		3	
B42L N	1		1					5	1	2			7	
B42L S			1			1	1	5			2		4	
B43N	3	2			4		1	7		2			3	
B43S	1	1				1		1	1	2	1		1	
B44U N	1			1	1			1	1	2			6	
B44U S	5	2		2	3	5	1	4		2	3		10	drain frag
B44L SW	3	1				1					1		4	
B44L SE	1		2		2		2	1					4	
B44L N		1				1		5		2	1	1	3	
B45U N													2	
B45U SW					4		1	5	1		1		pt,6	Bayat red jar neck
B45U SE								2			1		3	
B45L N													2	
B45L SE					1		1	1			2		3	
B45L SW					2			3			2		4	
B46U SW					4	2	2	9		1	6	2	10	
B46L SW		2			3	3	3	16		1	12	2	2pt,13	pol gray bowl
B47SW		1				2	3	19		1	11	2	pt,8	pol blk bowl; 2 high ring bases
FEATURES:														
AF25 plat								1	1	3			13	
AF30 plat									1				2	
AF30 alley								1						
BF pit					1			4	4	1			13	

Table B4: Continued

Extrusive and Intrusive Materials:
A24U SW: 1 Sefid sherd, 1 Sabz sherd, 1 Khazineh sherd
A25N: 1 Uruk pinched ring base
A27N: 1 Elamite sherd?, 11 Uruk flared round rim jars, 1 BRB
A29NW hall: 1 Sefid sherd
A29L corner rooms: 1 Sefid, 1 Khazineh, 1 Mehmeh sherd, 1 BRB
A34: 1 Sefid sherd
A36: 1 Sefid sherd
B38E: 3 Uruk rims
B39U E: 1 Sargarab base, 1 Sargarab bowl with hatched strip
B39M E: 1 Sefid rim, 1 Uruk? round rim bowl
B39L E: 1 BRB, 1 Khazineh
B39L W: 1 Sargarab incised bowl
B40U W: BRB, Mehmeh bowl rim
B41M NW: Mehmeh bowl rim
B42U NW: 1 Sargarab spout
B42L S: 1 Sefid rim
B43S: Uruk strap handle, 1 Uruk flared expanded jar rim
B46L SW: BRB

Table B5: Ceramics from Tepe Farukhabad: Uruk Phases

Layer	Straw Ware BRB	Uruk Ware													
		Conical cups			Bowl rims					Jar rims					
		wide	sld	rim	rnd	flt	ldg	bvl	incs/str	rnd	flrd rnd	sm exp	out exp	low exp	flrd exp	ldg
A18N	54			3	3	incs	lg	lg		1		3				
A19	lg,50		3	5	2	lg		incs		min,4		1		2	2 lg,1	2
A20	125			4	1		1	1		2	1			2	1	
A21U S	69			10							pt	2				pt
A21U N	17			2	1					1	2p	1		1		
A21M BC	8			1	1			1		1			1			
A21M DE	10												1			
A21L	27			2	1							1				
A22	17			3											lg,1	
B28N	9			1	1			2				1				
B28S	20		5	2	1	1								imp		
B29U N	37		4	4	8		2	2		2		1	1	2st		1
B29U S	56		1	9	1					4		1				1
B29L W	28	2		2	4			1	1	1		1	1			
B29L E	49	1		3	8	1	2	incs		2	1	1		2	3 lg	1
B30W	101	1		6	5			2		2		2	1	2		
B30NE	129			3	12		1	incs		lg,10		1	1	6	1	1
B30SE	202			5	6	1 htch				2			1	2	lg	1
B31U N	159			5	2	2		1 htch		min,6	3		3		1	
B31U S	156	2		3	3	1pt		4		min,1		1	1	2		
B31L N	208				2			2	1	4	1	1				
B31L S	238			13	2	2pt	1	4		2	1	3		1	6	
B32U N	196			5	4	1				3	2	1			2	lg pt
B32U S	95			1	2	pt,1		1			2	1		1	2	1
B32L	min,34			1		1 htch		2		3		pt,1		3	1	
B32L S	70			2		pt,2				pt,2					lg,1	
B33U N	26			2					1	2		2			2	2
B33U C	14			3	1							1				
B33U SE	37			1		3 lg	1			1				1	1	
B33U SW				1					1							
B33L N	39			2	2	pt,1		2								pt
B33L S	61			3	1	pt,3				2	2			1		
B34U N	3			1				1						1		
B34U C	38			1											2	
B34U S	20			2		pt					pt			1		
B34L N	7															
B34L C	22					min,pt						pt			1	
B34L S	10											1				
B35U	11									2pt,1					lg,1	
B35L	32			1		lg	1		2	1	1	lg,2pt				
B36U	16					4		1				1				1
B36L	3			1											1	
B37	1															
AF19 pit				14	2		2			1				1 rs	2 lg	1
BF45 pit	42									1					1	
BF20 base					2											
BF21 base				1												
AF26 bin				1												
AF27 bin																
AF23 pit	36			2	1				2							
AF24 hrth	3													1		
BF27 oven	26				1	2										
BF31 paving	12				pt							1				

APPENDIX B

Table B5: Continued

Layer	Uruk Ware											Other
	Jar rims				Jar parts					Bases		
	bot	crse thk	h-s	X htch	hor incs	nse lug	strp hnd	st spt	drp spt	b-r shld	flt	oth	
A18N				1	pl	2	1	1		1	5	ff	cyl drn, pnc shld
A19	2		pn			1			2		8	ff	straw strp hnd
A20	5	1			sl,pl	2	1	1	1		3	2ff,fr	straw sh plt
A21U S	1			1		hor tw					3	ff	straw hvy base
A21U N	lg											2ff	cyl drn, grywr ldg rim jar
A21M B				1		1					6		straw sm bowl
A21M DE							1				1	2fr	
A21L				1							pt,2		
A22		1						2					
B28N					pl						2		poly shld
B28S					sl			1			6	ff	bnd, lock rim jars, grywr jar
B29U N		2	pl,pn	2	pl		1	1	1	1	4		grywr jar, cyl drn, straw hvy jar rim
B29U S	2				sl	2pl,1	hw,1	1	3		10	fr,ff	1 tr drn, straw sh plt, 2 straw flt bases, 3 colanders
B29L W	1							1			1		lg inc bowl
B29L E	3					1	1	2	2	1	7	3ff	cyl drn, tr drn, rect lug
B30W	2			1	2pl		1				3	ff	straw sm bowl, straw flt base, sm pnc bowl
B30NE	2		1	1	2sl		1	1	1		7	4ff,2fr	hi exp jar rim, straw hvy bowl rim
B30SE	2	1									4	ff,fr	lock rim jar
B31U N	2		2	1			1		1	1	5	2ff	
B31U S			1	1		2pt	3		2		4	ff	
B31L N	3					hor tw, tw,1			2		8	ff	lock rim bowl, straw lg ldg rim bowl
B31L S		4	2,tis	3	pl	1		2	2		13	4ff	hi exp jar rim, tr drn, colander
B32U N	1	1	1	1		1	1	1			6	ff	clay sickle frag
B32U S				1	sl	3	4		1		2		hi exp jar, nkls low jar rim, lg crse bowl rim
B32L N		2		2	pl		2			1	2	3ff	straw flrd exp jar, lg crse bowl rim
B32L S		1	1				pt,1			1	8	2ff	straw flrd exp jar, cyl drn
B33U N				2		3				2	3	pt,rg	hole mouth jar, monochrome shld, hi exp jar rim, tr drn
B33U C					htch					2	6	3ff	band rim bowl
B33U SE							1				3	ff	
B33U SW	1												
B33L N		3		2			1		1		4	2ff	grywr crse bowl, lg crse jar
B33L S			1		1		2				8	ff	tr drn
B34U N											1	ff,fr	sm loop hnd, bdd inc bowl
B34U C											2	fr	cyl drn
B34U S		1					2				8		2 sm straw plts
B34L N			1								1		
B34L C											2	ff	
B34L S											2		1 straw sm plt
B35U				1						2	4		
B35L		2						1	2		pt,2		tr drn, overfired bowl rim
B36U			pt,1			2	pt	1	1	1			ring
B36L							1				1		drn
B37													
AF19 pit			1		sl	1	2	at			7	5ff,fr	2 lg crse bowls, nkls ldg jar, pt tr drn
BF45 pit													cyl drn
BF20 base	1				sl						1		
BF21 base											1		
AF26 bin						1					1		
AF27 bin							1						
AF23 pit											1	rg	
AF24 hrth													
BF27 oven			1		pl								nkls ldg rim jar
BF31 paving				1							2	ff	

Table B5: Continued

Layer	Sargarab Ware																	Other
	Bowl Rim						Jar Rim						Jar Parts				Bases	
	rnd	flt	inc	bdd	bdd st	hvy	fine	flrd rnd	flrd exp	low exp	ldg	crse	h-s	X htch	nse lug	strp hnd	st spt	flt	oth
A18N						2	1												
A19								1											
A20							2		pt										rnd lip jar
A21U S			1				2		1					1				1	
A21U N							1		1										sm exp jar
A21M BC							1					1							
A21M DE								1	pt									2	
A21L	1		1	1			1	min										1	
A22				1				1	1						1			1	
B28N																		1	
B28S																			
B29U N		1								1									
B29U S																			
B29L W																			
B29l E																			
B30W				1				1											
B30NE				1															
B30SE				pt															
B31U N																			
B31U S																			
B31L N																			
B31L S	11sp			3															
B32U N	1	2		pt,2			1		pt										
B32U S		pt					pt	3	pt		1						1	2	
B32L N				1			pt,1					1							
B32L S			1	pt		1											1	pt,1	
B33U N							1										1	1	
B33U C							1											2	
B33U SE				2		2		1				1						2pt	st rnd rim jar
B33U SW						1	2pt	1										1	
B33L N	1			5	pt,1		1	2	pt,2		1	3					1		
B33L S	4		2	pt,5	2pt,1	1	pt,3		pt,2	1		2pt,2			1	1		6	rg hi exp jar rim
B34U N	pt			1			1											1	
B34U C				1		2													
B34U S				2	1	2	1	2				4							
B34L N																		1	
B34L C		1					2					2					1		
B34L S				pt		1	1	1	1			1			1			2	bnd rim bowl
B35U	1	pt	1	3		2	1	1	2			2						pt,7	
B35L	1			1	2	3	pt	1	1		1	2pt,1							
B36U		1	pt,1	6	1		pt,1	3	pt,4			4		1	1	2		6	inc bowl w/ htch strip
B36L	2	2		2			1	2	1								1	pt,2	
B37				1	1		1												
AF19 pit			1				1		2					1			1		
BF45 pit																			
BF20 base																			
BF21 base																			
AF26 bin											1								
AF27 bin							1						1 hs					2	
AF23 pit	8	1	6	8	pt,4		12	4	min,2			4				1	2	4	
AF24 hrth								1										1	
BF27 oven																			
BF31 paving	1		1	5				pt				3						2	1 st rnd lip jar, 1 bnd bowl

APPENDIX B

Table B5: Continued

Extrusive and intrusive material:

A18N:	Farukh-Bayat bowl rim with band, plain bowl rim
A19:	Sabz "pot" base, 2 Farukh-Bayat bowl rims, 2 high neck jar rims, wide bowl base, large basin rim, flat base, 2 Farukh shaved cup bases
A20:	Khazineh "Hajji Muhamed" bowl base, Sabz "pot" base, 4 Farukh-Bayat bowl rims, wide base, 2 high jar necks, basin rim, 2 Farukh shaved cup bases
A21U S:	Farukh-Bayat pl bowl rim, pt high neck jar, wide bowl base, Farukh shaved base
A21Uu N:	2 Khazineh bowl rims, 2 Farukh-Bayat ring bowl bases, Farukh high neck jar with bands
A21M BC:	Farukh-Bayat plain bowl rim, wide bowl base, cyl stand
A21M DE:	Farukh-Bayat basin rim
A21L:	Farukh-Bayat basin rim, ring base, bowl rim
B28N:	Farukh-Bayat ring round base, basin rim
B28S:	3 Farukh-Bayat bowl rims, 1 high neck jar rim
B29U N:	Farukh-Bayat painted bowl rim, ring base, Farukh shaved base
B29U S:	2 Farukh-Bayat painted bowl rims, wide bowl base, 2 high jar necks
B29L N:	Farukh-Bayat basin rim
B29L E:	Farukh-Bayat narrow bowl base, wide bowl base, 2 basin rims, Khazineh Ware hole mouth jar rim, painted bowl rim
B30W:	Farukh-Bayat painted bowl rim, basin rim, high neck jar rim
B30NE:	3 Farukh-Bayat painted bowl rims, 3 narrow bowl bases, flat base, basin rim
B30SE:	Farukh-Bayat painted bowl rim, 2 painted bowl bases
B31U N:	Farukh-Bayat painted bowl rim, basin rim
B31U S:	Elamite cup base, Farukh-Bayat painted bowl rim, wide bowl base, Khazineh Redware large bowl
B31L S:	Farukh-Bayat painted bowl rim, 2 wide bowl bases, 2 painted high jar necks, 2 basin rims, Farukh high jar neck with bands, 3 Bayat red bowl rims, Khazineh red hole mouth jar rim
B32U N:	Farukh-Bayat painted bowl rim, narrow bowl base, high neck jar rim, Farukh shaved base
B32U S:	Farukh-Bayat painted bowl rim, 2 ring bowl bases, high jar neck, 2 basin rims
B32L N:	2 Farukh-Bayat plain bowl rims, painted bowl rim
B32L S:	4 Farukh-Bayat painted bowl rim, 2 wide bowl bases, ring bowl base, high neck jar rim, basin rim
B33U N:	Farukh-Bayat painted bowl rim, narrow bowl base, high neck jar rim, basin rim
B33U C:	Farukh-Bayat painted bowl rim, low neck jar rim
B32U SE:	Farukh-Bayat narrow bowl base
B33L N:	Farukh-Bayat painted bowl rim, flat base
B33L S:	7 Farukh-Bayat painted bowl rims, 3 ring bowl bases, narrow bowl base, 2 basins, Bayat red bowl rim
B34U N:	3 Farukh-Bayat painted bowl rims, 2 narrow bowl bases, 1 Khazineh red hole mouth rim
B34U C:	Mehmeh painted bowl rim, Farukh-Bayat painted high neck jar, Farukh shaved cup base
B34U S:	3 Farukh-Bayat painted bowl rims, 2 wide bowl bases, 1 ring bowl base
B34L N:	Farukh-Bayat painted bowl rim, 2 wide bowl bases, 1 ring bowl base
B34L C:	Farukh-Bayat wide bowl base, narrow bowl base, basin rim
B34L S:	2 Farukh-Bayat painted bowl rims, 1 high jar rim, 2 flat bases, hole mouth rim
B35U:	6 Farukh-Bayat painted bowl rims, 1 high neck jar rim, 2 wide bowl bases, 2 basin rims, 1 Khazineh red hole mouth rim
B35L:	3 Farukh-Bayat painted bowl rims, narrow bowl base, Khazineh red hole mouth rim
AF19:	Farukh-Bayat plain bowl rim, painted bowl rim, large flat base
AF26:	Farukh-Bayat painted bowl rim
AF27:	Farukh-Bayat large flat base
AF23:	3 Susiana cylindrical stand fragments, 2 Farukh shaved base cups, 2 basin rims
AF24:	1 Susiana cylindrical stand fragment, 1 Farukh-Bayat basin rim
BF27:	2 Farukh-Bayat painted bowl rims
BF31:	5 Farukh-Bayat painted bowl rims, 1 Khazineh red hole mouth

Table B6: Ceramics from Tepe Farukhabad: Jemdet Nasr and Early Dynastic Phases

Layer	Straw Ware brb	Gray Ware jar	Conical Cup				Bowl Rims					Uruk Ware Jar Rims								
			wide	cons	sld	rim	rnd	flt	ldg	bvl	inc	rnd fn	rnd oth	sm exp	out exp	lo exp	flrd exp	ldg	bnd	lock
A1		2,2L				9						2	1				4	2	3	
A2		S,2L	5		1	7	1					1	6				3	1	1	
A3-4		S,L				3				3		7	5				3	1	2	
A5W		S,2L	1			7	3					3	3	1			2	1	2	
A5E		S,3L		1		7	2					2	4				3	1	1	
A6N					1	5	2					3								
A6S			3		ls	11	3		1	1		3	3				pt,1		2	
A7N						6							1				pt,1			
A7S		L	2	1		6	1		1			3	2				1		1	
A8N				1		3	4					3					2	2		
A8S			1	2	3s	21						1	2				1	2pt,1		
A9-10N			1			14	1			1	1	1					1	4		
A9-10SE		L	4	3	1	31	incs,8		1	4	1		7				pt,1	pt,3	4	
A9-10SW		L	1	1	1		14					1		1			1		1	
A11N			1			4					1	2	3	1	1		2		4	
A11C			1		1	1	incs,1	1											2	
A11SW			2	1		18	incs,3	1					1					1		
A11SE	2				ls	4				1	1						pt,2	pt,1		
A12 N	6	L				5						1						pt,1		
A12S					2s	3											2	2	1	
A13U S	11	L				3	1		1					2	2		pt,2		1	
A13U N	11	L	2			9	1			1			1	1					pt,3	
A13ML	21	L			1	12						1	2				1	1	1	
A14	10	L	1	1		4	1											1		
A15	10	2L			3	4	4										1			
A16	15	2L				3	3	1		1			1		1		3			
A17S	22	L			1	7	3	1	1				1					1	1	
A17N	15	3L			1	6	1			1				pt			1			
B20N	4	L	2		1	5							1				pt,1	1	1	
B20SW			2			5	1					1	1			1				
B20SE	1	S,L	1	1		1	1					2	4				pt,2			
B21N	3	3L		1	16		5	1				2	6				1	1	1	
B21S	3	4L	1			11	11					1	2				1	2pt,1	1	
B22U N	2					6		1				6					1		1	
B22L N	1	L		3	2s	12	3					2					pt,2	3	1	
B22S						6												pt min		
B23U N	1	L				13	1					1					1	pt		1
B23L N	6				2	12	1						1				pt		pt	
B23U S	1		1	2	2	9							1	1			1	pt,2	2	1
B23L S	3	L	1		4	5	3		1	1		2	1				1			
B24U N	5				3	8	1	1					1					2		
B24L N	14	L		2s	9							1					2	1		
B24S	2	L			1	5											1	1		
B25U N	10				2	3	1										1	3		
B25L N	13	2L	1		1	6	1			1				1			2		1	1
B25-26S	16			1	2	6	1					1		1			1			
B26NE	7	L			2	11	1										pt,1	1		2
B26W	1				s,1	2	1										1	1		
B27NE	14	L	1		s,2	5							3				1			
B27W	3					1														

APPENDIX B

Table B6: Continued

Layer	Uruk Ware												Other
		Jar Parts							Bases				
	h-s	p-s	hor incs	nse lug	strp hnd	st spt	drp spt	poly shld	flt	fine flt	pnch ring	trn ring	
A1	2							5	3		3		large flared jar
A2	3							3			3		
A3-4	4							1	4		5	4	
A5W	2			1					4		1		
A5E	3		1		1	1		5	6		2	4	dent gray ware, ledge rim jar stand
A6N	2	1						2	2		1	1	
A6S	4								6		1	4	
A7N	1	1						3				1	
A7S	1	1										4	
A8N	1	1							1			2	
A8S	1					2		4	1	1	1pt		plain lug stand
A9-10N	1								2				
A9-10SE	3					4		2	1	1			droop spout cut stand
A9-10SW	1					1		2	1				2 stands
A11N	4	3						1	2				
A11C	1								1				
A11SW	2												2 stands
A11SE											pt		
A12N									1				lock rim jar
A12S								2	1				
A13U S									3	1			sm inc bowl, str shld bowl
A13U N	1		2pl		1				2				strap handle with hatches
A13ML								3					
A14									2		1		
A15					1	1		1	7				
A16				1	1			3	3		1		sm inc bowl
A17S			pl						2				
A17N	1							6	3				
B20N	1	1						3			1		stand fragment
B20SW	1								2				
B20SE	5	1							1			1	lip spout
B21N	3	1				1			1		2	1	lock rim jar, sm inc bowl
B21S	1							2					trough spout
B22U N								2	2				stand fragment, lip spout
B22L N								1					
B22S	1							2		1			
B33U N	pnc							2	1			2	pt bottle
B23L N									1	2		1	
B23U S	1								1				
B23L S			lpl?					2					large exp jar, large flat bowl
B24U N									2				drain fragment, bnd rim bowl
B24L N								2	1	1			cut stand, sm inc bowl
B24S			lpl?						1		1		1 bottle
B25U N								1	2	1			
B25L N	1								2			2	x-hatch shld
B25-26S				1	2								
B26NE									1	3	1		
B26W					1			1	1	1		1	
B27NE				1									hvy jar, x-hatch shld
B27W									1				

Table B6: Continued

Layer	Straw Ware brb	Gray Ware jar	Uruk Ware Conical Cup				Bowl Rims					Jar Rims								
			wide	cons	sld	rim	rnd	flt	ldg	bvl	inc	rnd fn	rnd oth	sm exp	out exp	lo exp	flrd exp	ldg	bnd	lock
B27S	20				1	4							1		1		1	2		
C9-10		S	1										1							
C11-12													1							
C23U	1	S,L	5			1						2	3						2	1
C23L		S		1		1							3				1		2	
C24					1								1							
C28-29	5												1							
C29,31	3	L				1					1									
C32	10																			
C33	8				1											1				
AF3 vat												1								
AF5 vat			1		s	3		1		1		2					1		1	
AF8 vat			1			1				1			1							
BF13 vat							1											pt	1	
AF11 bin	3																	1		
AF14 bin	3		1			4	1						1							
BF15 bin			1			2											2	1		
BF18 post?																	2	1		
BF6 oven				1																
AF17 oven	8			1		1	incs													

APPENDIX B

Table B6: Continued

Layer	h-s	p-s	hor incs	nse lug	strp hnd	st spt	drp spt	poly shld	flt	fine flt	pnch ring	trn ring	Other
B27S			1pl				2		2	2			hvy jar
C9-10	1							3	2			1	
C11-12													
C23U	1							1	2		pt,3		
C23L	1											3	
C24								1					
C28-29									1				
C29,31								1	1			1	
C32			2pl										
C33								1					1 r-b shld
AF3 vat													
AF5 vat									1				
AF8 vat													
BF13 vat												1	
AF11 bin								1					1 x-hatch, grate
AF14 bin													nkls ldg jar, heavy jar
BF15 bin									1				
BF18 post?									1				
AF6 oven													
AF17 oven													

Extrusive and Intrusive Material:

A1:	Elamite jar rim; Farukh-Bayat high neck jar rim
A3-4:	Elamite jar rim; Farukh-Bayat basin rim, Farukh-Bayat bowl rim
A5E:	Elamite rim
A8N:	Farukh-Bayat ring base
A12N:	Sargarab flared expanded jar
A12S:	Sargarab flared expanded jar; Susiana basin rim
A13U S:	Susiana cylindrical stand fragment
A13U N:	Farukh-Bayat narrow bowl base, Farukh-Bayat bowl rim
A13M L:	Farukh-Bayat ring base, wide base
A15:	Farukh-Bayat ring base, basin rim, 2 bowl rims; Mehmeh red-red jar rim
A16:	Farukh-Bayat high neck jar, painted bowl rim
A17S:	2 Farukh-Bayat high neck jar rims, Farukh-Bayat ring base
A17N:	Farukh shaved base; Farukh-Bayat wide bowl base, painted bowl rim
B20SW:	Elamite ledge rim bowl
B20SE:	Simaski bowl
B22U N:	Elamite large basin rim
B23U N:	Farukh-Bayat wide bowl base
B23U S:	Farukh-Bayat basin rim
B23L S:	Farukh-Bayat ring base
B24U N:	Farukh-Bayat plain bowl rim
B24U S:	Farukh-Bayat basin rim, 2 painted bowl rims
B25U N:	Farukh-Bayat plain bowl rim, narrow base
B25L N:	Susiana narrow bowl base
B25-26S:	3 Farukh-Bayat painted bowl rims, 2 Farukh-Bayat plain bowl rims, Farukh-Bayat high neck jar rim
B26NE:	Farukh-Bayat painted bowl rim, wide bowl base; Sargarab beaded bowl rim
B27NE:	Farukh-Bayat ring base, 2 narrow bases; Sargarab incurved bowl; Uruk ware incurved bowl with hatch strip
B27W:	Farukh-Bayat painted bowl rim
B27S:	3 Farukh-Bayat painted bowl rims; 1 Sefid bowl rim
AF14:	Farukh-Bayat bowl rim

Table B7: Farukh and Bayat Phase Body Sherds

Unit	Buff Thick Ct.	Wgt.	Buff Medium Ct.	Wgt.	Thin Ct.	Wgt.	Painted Buff Ct.	Wgt.	Coarse Grit Ct.	Wgt.	Coarse Chaff Ct.	Wgt.	Other Ct.	Wgt.
A23	59	1790	184	1205	50	190	196	1095			3	65		
A24U SW	69	2055	260	1655	14	20	161	1100			2	100	1	—*
A24U NE	80	1945	196	675	2		72	615						
A24L SW	102	2690	353	2345	70	125	136	860	9	160				
A24L NE	50	1635	131	1245	4		72	505						
A25N	77	1945	210	1815	31	50	116	625						
A25S	42	1210	151	1250	6	5	51	310						
A26N	115	2295	408	3300	147	260	184	985			4	—	2	
A26S	80	2550	315	2310	60	85	197	1115						
A27N	164	5825	476	4837	126	240	236	1825	5	90	12	290		
A27S	108	3420	317	3120	71	85	166	1160	42	630	32	680		
A28NW	154	5510	378	2900	120	235	186	955	1		29	570		
A28SE	58	1700	118	855	56	70	62	490			14	375		
A29	14	300	41	305	32	100	15	80			9	95	1	—
A29U	13	1240	33	185	29	85	5	65						
A29L	41	2965	178	1760	153	381	47	445	1	530	26	277	1	
A29± NW	30	632	48	220	20	30	17	105			10	65		
A30-31 inside F30	56	2055	160	1490	54	100	33	228	8	55	33	415		
A33 all	4	100	51	501	48	82	19	110			16	50	1	30
A34 all	9	340	53	455	65	115	17	250			1	5		
A35 all	16	400	46	525	52	162	14	60	7	370	4	60		
A36SE F32	27	725	89	780	114	310	30	285			2	210		
A36 inside F32	22	985	35	515	33	100	14	120			20	—	1	—
A36 outside F32	53	1310	80	605	57	100	26	380			1	110	3	15
B36L all	62	1960	191	1995	41	150	45	385	31	380	22	285		
B37 all	47	1155	179	1420	47	95	59	375	10	190				
B38E	18	335	59	432	13	20	6	25			1	10		
B39U E	51	940	96	545	29	45	16	50			1	50		
B39U W	23	630	61	475	22	60	31	205						
B39M E	30	1165	24	290	1	—	15	240	20	200				
B39M W	17	310	53	400	16	46	37	330	2	195	2	40		
B39L E	71	3320	138	1295	21	75	36	290	4	110	1	65		
B39L W	20	410	85	770	21	45	45	340	8	80	2	40		
B40U E	106	4310	228	1995	26	50	130	1750	1	10	1	10		
B40U W	76	2340	173	1695	34	100	114	890	7	50			1	15
B40L E	144	4705	279	2260	45	105	155	1325	20	260	7	235		
B40L W	62	1675	153	1160	54	150	100	560	15	230	5	60		
B41U NW	14	400	80	585	23	30	114	390						
B41U SE	38	1375	110	985	11	50	57	410			3	50	2	—
B41M NW	49	2205	95	1170	20	70	46	450	2	10	1	55		
B41M SE	17	510	37	295	7	10	22	145			1	10		
B41L NW	19	630	32	310	12	41	19	185			1	30		
B41L SE	25	600	20	180	6	10	17	305	4	60				
B42U NW	82	3315	241	2325	46	160	158	855			1	30		
B42U SE	54	2935	103	1115	22	63	35	370						
B42L N	61	2075	100	1010	28	100	54	365	2	100	7	250		
B42L S	53	2460	105	1195	22	55	54	540	4	295	1	130		
B43N	109	3315	150	1795	51	105	93	1450			2	170		
B43S	23	925	57	680	28	30	27	230			1	160		
B44U N	66	3005	119	1385	38	165	70	950			2	230	1	—
B44U S	96	7295	123	2165	49	195	189	1790			1	140		
B44L SW	9	400	34	490	9	40	34	220	6	110	1	100		
B44L SE	92	4645	108	1515	12	70	49	540			2	90	1	—
B45U N	22	650	33	305	3	5	10	240			2	60		
B45U SW	19	1205	19	320	10	65	21	220			2	580	1	—
B45U SE	19	885	35	405	1	10	22	245			3	885		
B45L N	11	560	14	425	1	—	7	70			1	90		
B45L SW	16	640	25	315	7	40	29	340			1	150		
B45L SE	10	815	23	290	4	15	7	40						
B46U SW	92	3805	247	2625	30	107	142	1545					1	30
B46L SW	201	6880	350	3825	79	370	194	1080			10	155		
B47 all SW	119	5710	292	4825	60	180	61	705			8	585		
AF25 pit	66	2023	366	2930	51	130	88	740	13	80	74	695		
BF45 pit	36	2460	89	1465	3	5	12	475						

*hyphen indicates weights less than 5 gm

APPENDIX B

Table B8: Uruk Body Sherds

Unit	Thick Ct.	Thick Wgt.	Buff Medium Ct.	Buff Medium Wgt.	Thin Ct.	Thin Wgt.	Painted Buff Ct.	Painted Buff Wgt.	Coarse Grit Ct.	Coarse Grit Wgt.	Beveled Rim Bowl Ct.	Beveled Rim Bowl Wgt.	Other Ct.	Other Wgt.	
A18N	44	2480	341	3060	37	40	28	155	7	68	143	1950	1		G
A19 all	33	1841	491	5690	27	35	24	280	15	153	127	2750	6	83	G
A20	71	3610	691	7825	116	353	52	535	1	—	445	6880	1	3	G
A21U S	24	1620	256	2392	31	34	23	252	7	80	131	1760			
A21U N	12	490	122	1025	24	24	23	220			10	215			
A21M Rooms B,C	14	460	219	2770	47	135	30	110	10	60	19	250	1	—	G
A21M Rooms D,E			97	2337	14	30	14	135	4	3	90	595	2	85	
A21L	31	820	185	1570	42	50	21	270	15	70	98	1140	4	40	
A22 all	7	190	103	670	39	46	20	172	20	455	61	625			
B28N	10	480	173	1481	6	5	8	68	9	70	29	505	3	15	G
B28S	24	830	185	2352	8	10	16	80	7	90	40	800	2	—	G
B29U N	111	3727	507	5655	43	90	9	200	3	30	81	1200			
B29U S	75	3440	510	5920	32	70	21	235	4	162	156	3165	3	10	
B29L W	9	550	146	1460	24	85	7	45			66	630			
B29L E	130	5682	474	6705	15	40	13	190			152	3370	2	25	
B30W	45	2340	301	3717	5	25	13	235			271	4705			
B30NE	39	3075	850	10615	4	10	21	245	10	165	317	5800			
B30SE	62	2570	407	5470			4	40			635	9305			
B31U N	43	1770	432	4155	19	40	8	150			924	9600			
B31U S	57	2427	327	3070			21	285	2	75	675	12155			
B31L N	42	2355	303	3555	5	—	5	25			535	8035			
B31L S	107	4500	433	5290	25	60	41	360	51	685	636	10405	6	70	G
B32U N	36	1335	427	5260	11	27	28	205	1	12	819	8010	6	95	G
B32U S	76	2575	509	4960	38	60	54	473	17	130	257	2635	7	90	G
B32L N	10	360	350	3840	24	105	30	205	28	160	29	410	60	980	
B32L S	36	1810	252	3305	6	25	30	300			141	2360	2	10	G
B33U N	17	565	174	1360	36	60	28	290	37	485	54	655	3	25	G
B33U&M Center	7	230	136	1785	31	100	22	190	18	280	35	375	1	—	G
B33U&M SE	19	835	155	1275	44	160	28	290	27	335	53	590	8	110	
B33U&M SW	28	775	83	785	1	—	16	130	1	15	21	255	1	—	G
B33L N	24	1435	243	3000	13	40	30	335	2	—	43	640	9	135	
B33L S	95	4696	540	5925	30	55	66	725	88	1880	87	1375	33	400	
B34U N	15	585	110	1295	14	65	12	185	16	275	22	285	3	30	G
B34U Center	20	870	132	1705	25	65	23	300	4	130	54	830	1	40	
B34U S	76	1250	149	2650	11	25	25	185			9	210			
B34L N	4	70	16	320	2	—	8	95							
AF19 pit	21	1600	213	3447	5	20	27	500	18	555	424	8000			
AF23 pit	72	4130	766	9535	31	100	51	830	6	115	57	595			
AF24 hearth	4	155	17	150			6	25			9	170			
AF26 bin	9	175	37	350	1						47	360			
AF27 bin	9	390	38	600											
BF45 pit			4	65							78	1240	11	430	
BF20 base	10	360	46	710	2	20	1	—			29	475			
BF21 base	2	70	54	610	8	40									
BF27 oven	3	55	67	685	2		7	30			18	340	5	85	
BF31 paving	32	1495	102	1575	5	10	15	155	32	520	4	60			

G = Grayware.

Table B9: Jemdet Nasr and Early Dynastic Body Sherds

Unit	Thick Ct.	Thick Wgt.	Buff Medium Ct.	Buff Medium Wgt.	Thin Ct.	Thin Wgt.	Painted Buff Ct.	Painted Buff Wgt.	Coarse Grit Ct.	Coarse Grit Wgt.	Beveled Rim Bowl Ct.	Beveled Rim Bowl Wgt.	Other Ct.	Other Wgt.	
A above 155.8, all	63	1107	414	1965	18	15	16	140	12	329					
A 155.6-155.8 all	17	493	326	2470	12	48	2	26	99	438					
A3± all	36	1340	427	3830	7	—	12	150	102	720			5	55	
A5W	26	685	366	2930	4	—	48	775	190	1365					
A5E	113	920	377	2986	34	80	63	640	181	1110					
A6S	32	1000	346	3150			93	745	206	1625					
A7N	17	685	518	2460	18	15	28	180	80	655					
A7S	32	1397	326	2530	6	5	18	132	140	930					
A8N			243	2820			31	420	116	1200					
A8S	44	1320	355	3075	22	5	22	370	46	500					
A9,10N	12	530	185	1770			15	165	96	1235					
A9,10SE	13	805	286	2600	28	15	23	520	112	910					
A9,10SW	8	420	90	1300	6	—	7	120	76	980					
A11N	5	65	49	310	3	5			19	40					
A11Center	2	20	82	882	7	—	5	—	23	150					
A11SW	23	825	191	1665	1		13	120	35	365					
A11SE			51	395	6	10	9	100	22	120					
A12N	30	745	111	755	27	12	5	—	22	120					
A12S	16	340	84	545	4	—	7	65	7	50					
A13U S	37	920	210	1590	20	—	21	170	21	200					
A13U N	39	1420	195	1995	26	—	13	125	34	385					
A13 all	77	1535	321	3162	23	—	25	145	50	430	11	85	1	—	G
A14 all	10	189	116	1182	3	—	2	20	8	85	2	5	3	20	
A15 all	27	815	201	1440	42	35	19	100	17	150	9	180			
A16 all	36	1030	214	2140	8	20	29	275	81	950	14	275			
A17S	22	940	309	2925	36	85	7	75	26	375	43	645	3	15	G
A17N	27	1080	255	1920	20	20	28	240	27	320	38	565	2	—	G
B20U&L N	26	695	189	1355	12	—	15	200	58	495					
B20U&L SW	32	880	114	600			12	250	41	310					
B20U&L SE			233	1525			9	30	79	640					
B21U&L N	40	1270	528	4530	35	35	31	260	61	358					
B21U&L S	40	1248	219	1880			30	315	74	770					
B22U N	6	305	163	1455			18	310	18	110					
B22L N	12	260	175	1680	38	5	21	100	63	485					
B22U&L S	28	1360	67	670			11	265	39	510	1	35			
B23U&M N	13	410	155	1305	6	10	15	185	29	275	3	20			
B23L N	24	1060	212	1715	38	70	35	280	64	810	8	90	2	80	
B23U&M S	17	565	78	1000	27	125	14	210	15	405			1	45	
B23L S	26	765	185	1770	42	78	24	330	39	400	7	70			
B24U N	21	455	181	1745	71	50	24	190	48	440	26	370	2	30	
B24L N	13	320	193	1785	40	52	2	40	37	535	12	90	1	—	G
B24S	19	487	150	1140	10	30	15	90	15	130	13	160	2	30	G
B25U N	6	205	195	1605	32	40	3	30	20	290	21	280	2	—	G
B25L N	54	1890	287	2345	48	125	15	165	19	255	1	40	2	—	G
B25-27S	26	770	236	2145	48	100	19	95	14	180	22	305			
B26NE	16	715	220	1870	27	60	12	55	4	55	49	679	3	15	G
B26W	8	225	86	716	11	35	7	75	12	110			3	10	G
B27NE	36	1536	199	1980	11	25	15	165	33	410	19	355	1	20	G
B27W	4	125	89	780	9	125	6	55	3	35	23	250			
AF3 vat	8	305	84	930	16	30	31	655	29	175					
AF5 vat	3	165	6	55			1	—	5	60					
AF6 oven			17	140											
AF8 vat	6	610	14	65					7	70					
AF11 bin	10	170	25	205	2	—	7	10							
AF17 oven	3	285	91	1690	5	5	3	35	62	968	7	62			
BF13 vat	2	120	27	190	6	10	3	20	5	30					
BF15 bin	6	470	51	425	7	30	8	110	8	80	2	50			
BF18 post			16	210	2	—	9	260							

G = Grayware.

Table B10: Occurrence of Polychrome Motifs.

Layer	Shoulders																	Sides								
	A	B	C	D	EF	G	H	I	J	K	L	M	N	O	P	Q	R	A	B	D	H	J	K	M	O	R
A1-2								1											1			2	2			
A3	1							1							1	1		1	1							
A5	3			1				1		1	1	1	2		2	2	2	1	1			4	1	1		1
A6	4							1				4						1	1				1	8		
A7	3		1		1			1			1	1			1			1	1					2		
A8	3						1		3			3						2	1					2	1	1
A9-10	1	2	1		2			1	4		2	1						1	1	4				1	1	
A11-12	1							1				1							1	3						
A13-16	2	1	2		4	1	1	1	2		1	2							1	1			3			
A17-18				1	1			1			1							1	1		2					
A20				2	2	1												1		2						
B19																			1				3			
B20	2	1	1	1			1	2	2									1	1	2			2			
B21	1		1	1					2		2	1	2							1	1	1	1			
B22	4	2						1	2		2	4	2	1				1	2			1	1	2		
B23	1			3			2	1	2			1							1	2		1	1	1		
B24	1	1	1	2	1				1									1		2	4		1			
B25-26							1												1	1						

APPENDIX B 329

APPENDIX C

MEASURED CERAMICS FROM TEPE FARUKHABAD

The following six tables present the continuous and discrete attributes of pottery vessel parts from the 50 percent random sample of pre-second millennium proveniences at the University of Michigan Museum of Anthropology. The attributes observed are developed from those recorded in appendices of my monograph on an Early Dynastic site in southern Iraq (Wright 1969: 128–41) and parallel those used by G. A. Johnson in his studies of Uruk ceramics on the Susiana plain (Johnson 1973: 177–97). Before detailing the specifies of each table, considerations of the reasons for undertaking such time-consuming observations and of the limitations of such measurement are warranted.

One reason for the presentation of these data is to give others the opportunity to test and refine typological characterizations made in this monograph. For example, the proposed types of jar rims are measured on a single series of attribute dimensions, e.g. rim diameter, lip thickness, rim top angle, etc. If one suspects that "flared expanded rims" and "out-turned expanded rims" are only arbitrarily distinguished, one can consider the members of the two proposed categories as points in a single space defined by several attribute dimensions and see whether there are two discrete clusters of points in this space or, in fact, only a single continuous distribution of points. Conversely, if one has another proposed categorization of jar rims, and one can express it in terms of the measured dimensions presented below, one can ascribe a sample of Farukhabad jars to these other categories without re-examination of the actual collections.

Another reason for such presentation is to allow the rigorous comparison of samples from different sites in order to demonstrate similarities and differences in time and space. For example, the comparisons of Uruk ceramics from the Susiana, Deh Luran, and Warka areas in Chapter X is an effort to assess the nearest affinities of the Deh Luran potters. Assertions about the spread and homogeneity of styles such as "Jemdet Nasr polychrome" will eventually be assessed by comparing vessel attribute statistics.

Yet another reason for such presentation is to facilitate the use of attribute variations themselves, without reference to categorical entities such as "types" or "styles" to measure change and assess propositions about past behavior. Johnson's use of attribute measurements to date vessels and to ascribe them to localized centers of manufacture exemplifies such an approach (Johnson 1973: cf. 113–29).

In spite of these and other reasons, the reader may well question the value of measuring something as irregular as a hand-made pottery vessel. Practically speaking, there are two sources of error. One is the irregularity of the vessels themselves. Rim sherds from a single vessel may be somewhat different, and even a single sherd may vary in thickness or angle. The latter difficulty can be overcome by recording a median measurement. The former difficulty is more vexing. Measurement of six elements from a single vessel by a trained observer produced differences of up to 1 degree of Munsell Color value and chroma, up to .06 cm of linear measure with vernier calipers, and up to 11 degrees with a simple protracter. Differences between items or between sample means less than these should be treated with caution, even if they are "statistically significant." Further quantitative study of such differences is needed. Another source of error is the differences of measurement between trained observers or between the same observer at different times. At present, such differences have not been quantitatively studied. However, all of the following measurements have been checked by the author to minimize such problems. The important point regarding all such problems is that conclusions should be based not upon one measurement but upon many. A number of errors should not affect the overall pattern. Now let us turn to the measurements. Note that throughout the tables '0' or '0.0' indicate the attribute could not be measured.

Most measured ceramics are identified by a

APPENDIX C

number divisible into two parts. The first three digits are the last three digits of the five digit University of Michigan Museum of Anthropology catalogue number, presented in Table A1. The last two digits are an item number within the members of a measured category from a catalogued provenience. Thus, the two measurable conical cup rims among the sherds of excavation unit X160 catalogued as UMMA 60148 are 14801 and 14802. There is also a flat base numbered 14801, and so forth. This procedure has proven clumsy, and I now number every potentially measurable item in a sample serially, but changing the Farukhabad card file and artifact numbers would be prohibitively time-consuming. The exceptions to this identification numbering procedure are the polychrome decorated jar sherds. All members of this category, rather than merely the sample remaining in Ann Arbor, have been recorded, size permitting. The last three digits of both the field catalogue number and, where assigned, the UMMA catalogue number are given in the table.

For all sherds, a body color is given using the Munsell color terminology. This is the color of the sherd just below the surface layer; unoxidized dark cores are avoided. Colors of the freshly cleaned surface and paint are often given. For all colors, 10.0 is added to "YR" hues and 20.0 is added to "Y" hues, converting hue into a continuous numerical scale. Manufacturing traces and temper inclusions are basic to the definition of wares, as discussed in Chapters II and VII, but little formal observation of such attributes is recorded here. Technical analysis of and experimentation with clays is a necessary but unfinished prelude to such observation. The exception is the recording of temper for Gray Ware jars, in which shell (1), mixed calcite and shell (2), calcite (3), mixed calcite and chert (4), and chert (5) were noted.

All bowl rims, as variously recorded in the first four tables, are measured as diagrammed on Figure 100a. Three points require discussion. First, body thickness is measured 2.0 cm below the lip regardless of vessel size or rim modification; the measurement is always taken below any rim modification if such occurs. Second, rim thickness is measured parallel to the flattened lip surface on all rims, not parallel to the bowl's mouth. Third, lip tops may be left flat, more or less perpendicular to the vessel sides (1), rounded (2), pressed in or beveled (3), usually oblique to the vessel sides (4), or folded out (5).

Beveled rim bowls present special problems of measurement because of their irregularity (Fig. 100b). Only restorable examples are presented in Table C4. Linear and angular measurements are a mean of four measures taken along four cross-sections at right angles to each other. Diameters are an average of maximum and minimum. Volume was multiply measured with dry sand.

Jar rim shape is more varied. Measurement approaches are shown in Figure 100c-d. Five points require discussion. First, neck diameter (measured with the usual concentric circle diagram) is taken on the interior of the neck, while rim diameter is taken on the exterior of the lip. Second, rim angles are reliable measures on rims with straight neck interiors such as most flat lip rims, but on flared rims, the angle is of a line tangent to the curve of the upper neck and two trained observers can differ by as much as 10 degrees (in contrast, rim top angle on flat lip jars and bowls are easily measured and two observers usually agree). Third, shoulder thickness is measured 2.0 cm below the neck-shoulder juncture, neck thickness is measured at the midpoint of that portion of the neck below rim modifications, and rim thickness is measured as on bowls. Fourth, neck height in this series of measurements is the complete height of the neck and rim together, so that the measurements for round lip and flat lip jars will be comparable. Fifth, for jars, lip form is distinguished only as flat (1), round (2), and other (9).

Bases are measured as shown on Fig. 100e-f. Base angle and base-to-constriction on conical cup bases are similar to ring angle and ring height on ring bases.

The measurement of vessel appendages and modifications present both opportunities and difficulties. Hatch strips are measured as shown on Fig. 100g. Nose lug (Fig. 100h) width is measured immediately beside the hole, even if this is not the widest point. The length of the lug is often difficult to measure because its lower end is smoothed imperceptibly into the surface of the jar shoulder. Cross-hatch bands (Fig. 100i) and horizontal incised lines (Fig. 100j) are measured flat rather than in elevation (e.g. as if the vessel were being viewed from the side). Spouts (Fig. 100k-l) are particularly difficult to measure. All diameters are averages of length and width, and base measurements are difficult to duplicate. The most commonly measured class of modification is painted designs, all of which are measured flat, as were the incised designs. An attempt was made to measure painted bands and lines at points where the full paint brush width was represented. A median width, however, was often recorded. Periodicity is a measure of the median distance between repeated elements in a design. Many design measurements are based on restorations of broken designs. The attributes of painted designs are presented on Fig. 101. The system for recording the design statements on Table C6 is thoroughly discussed in Chapter VII.

Finally, both the tables and this introduction may require further clarification. Any reader desiring either clarification or a copy of the original punch cards should contact the author.

APPENDIX C

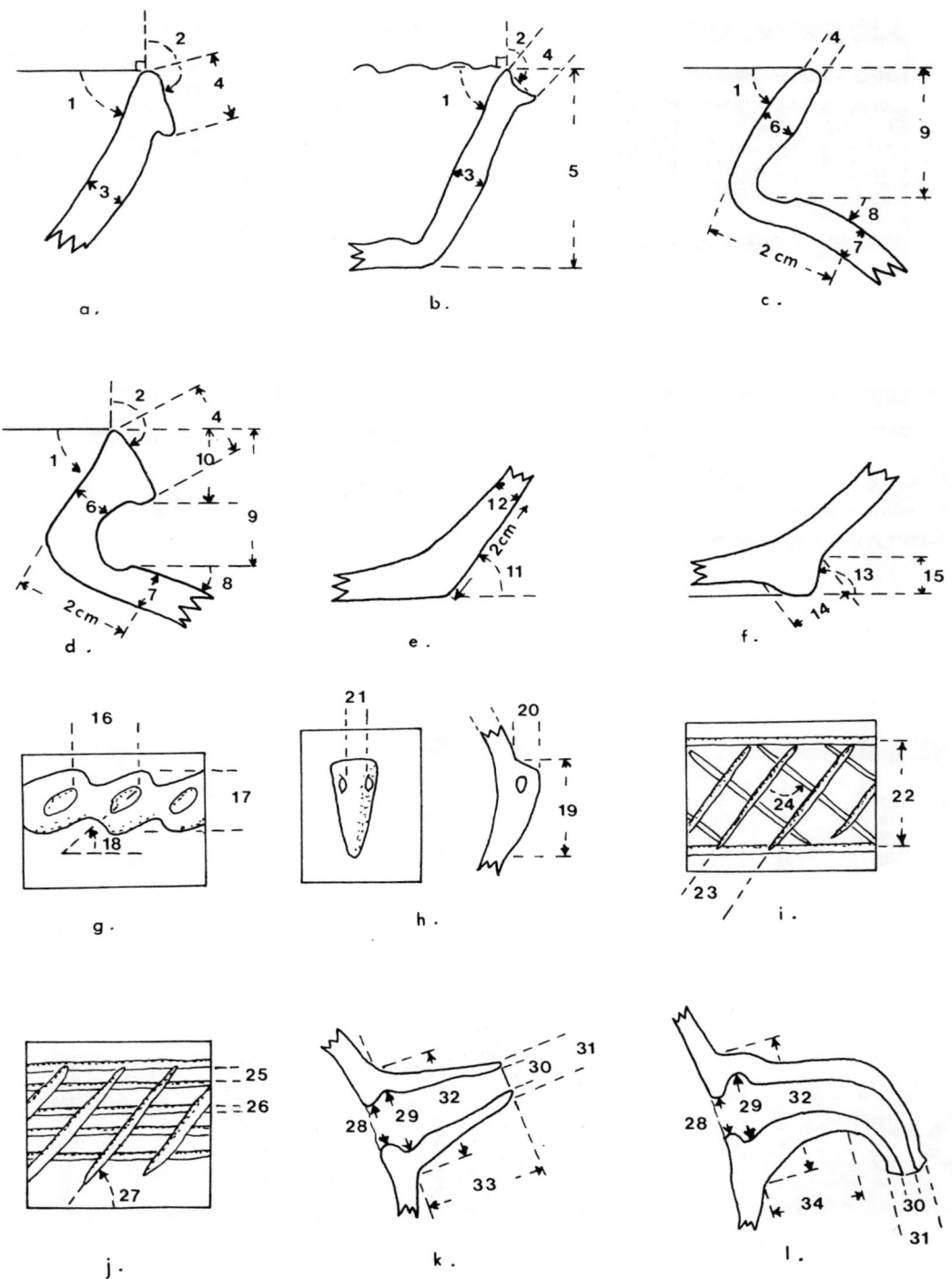

Fig. 100. Vessel part measurements. a. Flat lip bowls. b. Beveled rim bowl. c. Rand lip jars. d. Flat lip jars. e. Flat base. f. Ring base. g. Hatched strip. h. Nose lug. i. Incised cross hatched band. j. Incised horizontal and oblique lines. k. Straight spout. l. Droop spout.

1. Rim angle. 2. Rim top angle. 3. Side or wall thickness. 4. Lip thickness. 5. Exterior bowl height. 6. Rim or neck thickness. 7. Shoulder thickness. 8. Shoulder angle. 9. Neck height. 10. Rim height. 11. Side angle. 12. Tower body thickness. 13. Ring angle. 14. Ring thickness. 15. Ring height. 16. Hatch period. 17. Width strip. 18. Hatch angle. 19. Nose length. 20. Nose height. 21. Nose width at hole. 22. Band width. 23. Width between oblique lines. 24. Intersect angle. 25. Width between horizontal lines. 26. Width horizontal lines. 27. Angle oblique lines. 28. Interior hole diameter. 29. Interior base diameter. 30. Interior diameter end. 31. Exterior diameter end. 32. Exterior diameter base. 33. Length of spout. 34. Base to curve of spout.

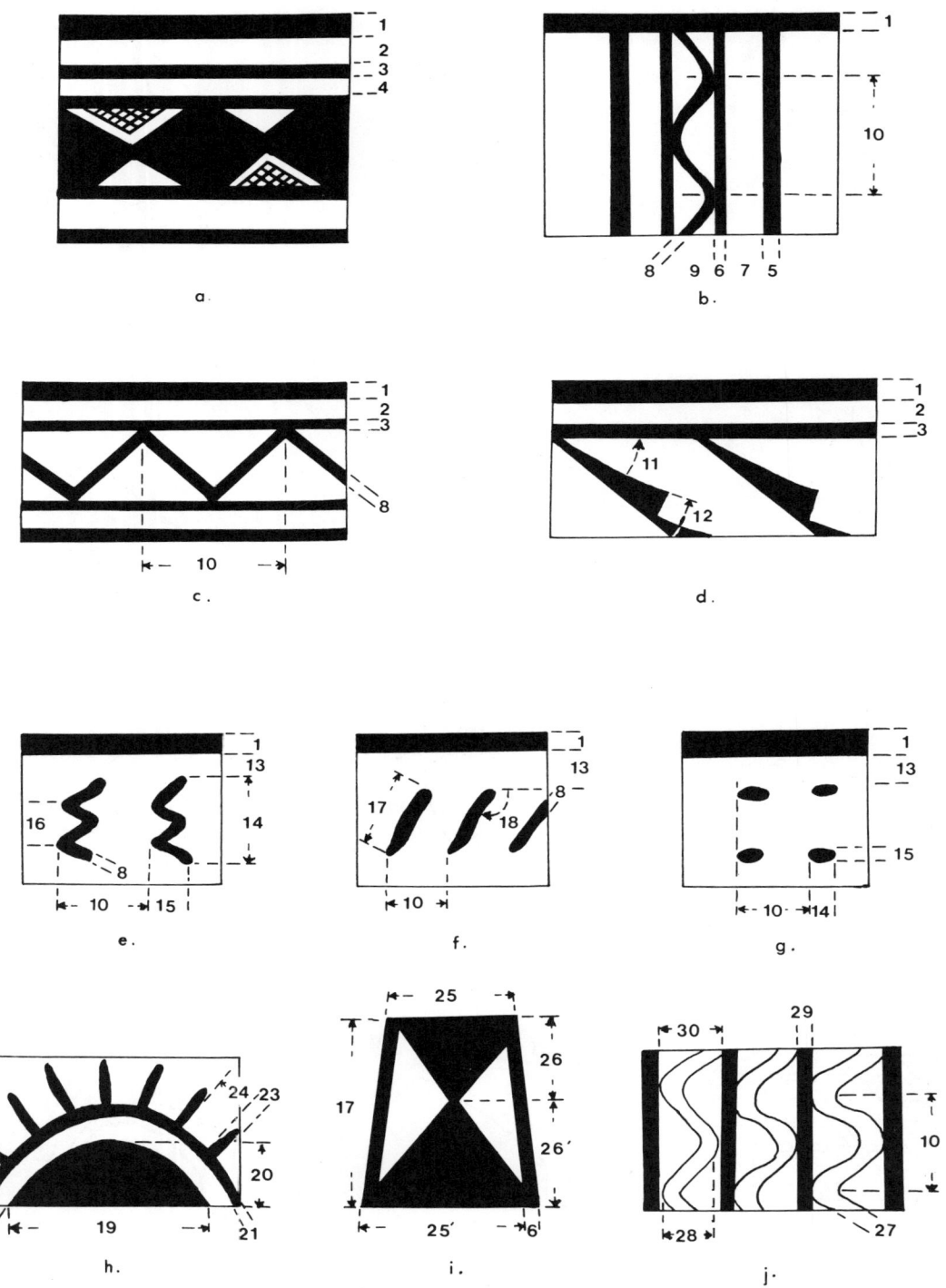

Fig. 101. Motif measurements. a. Multiple bands or diamond motifs. b. Verticle line and curved line motifs. c. Horizontal curved line motif. d. Oblique triangle or step motif. e. Sigma motif. f. Slash motif. g. Dot motif. h. Triangle and opposed triangle motifs. i. Arc and ray motif. j. Curved and straight line motifs.

1. First exterior band width. 2. First space width. 3. Second band width. 4. Second space width. 5. Inner vertical line width. 6. Outer vertical line width. 7. Inner-outer space width. 8. Motif line width. 9. Central space width. 10. Motif period. 11. Triangle space angle. 12. Triangle angle. 13. Band-to-motif width. 14. Motif height. 15. Motif width. 16. Motif left side. 17. Slash length. 18. Slash angle. 19. Arc base. 20. Arc height. 21. Line width. 22. Line space width. 23. Ray width. 24. Ray space width. 25, 25½. Average triangle base width. 26, 26½. Average triangle height. 27. Curved line (brush) width. 28. Curved line amplitude. 29. Vertical line width. 30. Vertical space width.

APPENDIX C

Table C1: Attributes of Farukh and Bayat Phase Ceramics

FARUKH-BAYAT SMALL BOWL BASES

LAYER	ARTIFACT NUMBER	BODY HUE	VAL	CHR	SURFACE HUE	VAL	CHR	BASE FORM	BASE ANGLE	BASE THICK	PAINT HUE	VAL	CHR	WIDTH LOWER	WIDTH UPPER
A23	24801	25.0	7	2	15.0	7	2	1	36	0.98	0.0	0	0	0.00	0.00
A24	24601	17.5	7	4	20.0	7	3	1	32	0.62	0.0	0	0	0.00	0.00
A24	25001	17.5	7	4	17.5	8	4	1	33	0.68	0.0	0	0	0.00	0.00
A25	25801	20.0	8	2	20.0	7	3	1	33	0.60	0.0	0	0	0.00	0.00
A26	25601	17.5	9	2	17.5	8	4	2	34	0.68	0.0	0	0	0.00	0.00
A26	26100	20.0	8	3	20.0	8	2	1	41	0.89	0.0	0	0	0.00	0.00
A26	26103	20.0	8	3	20.0	7	3	1	29	0.72	0.0	0	0	0.00	0.00
A27	26304	15.0	8	2	7.5	8	2	1	31	0.58	0.0	0	0	0.00	0.00
A34	31401	17.5	7	1	25.0	6	2	1	45	0.33	0.0	0	0	0.00	0.00
A36	32301	20.0	8	2	25.0	8	2	1	36	0.51	0.0	0	0	0.00	0.00
B36	58301	20.0	8	2	20.0	8	2	1	39	0.65	0.0	0	0	0.00	0.00
B36	58302	20.0	8	3	20.0	7	3	1	46	0.66	0.0	0	0	0.00	0.00
B36	59201	20.0	7	3	22.5	8	3	1	43	0.60	0.0	0	0	0.00	0.00
B42	64901	17.5	8	4	20.0	8	4	1	64	0.54	0.0	0	0	0.00	0.00
B42	65201	22.5	9	2	125.0	8	2	1	46	0.74	0.0	0	0	0.00	0.00
B42	65202	17.5	8	2	20.0	8	2	1	36	0.57	0.0	0	0	0.00	0.00
B42	65401	22.5	8	2	22.5	7	2	2	21	0.60	0.0	0	0	0.00	0.00
B43	66201	15.0	7	4	15.0	7	4	1	34	0.61	0.0	0	0	0.00	0.00
B44	66601	15.0	7	3	15.0	7	4	1	39	0.63	0.0	0	0	0.00	0.00
B44	67301	22.5	8	4	20.0	8	3	1	38	1.07	0.0	0	0	0.00	0.00
A23	23701	17.5	8	4	17.5	7	4	1	0	0.44	17.5	5	2	0.00	0.00
A23	24301	20.0	8	3	17.5	3	2	1	0	0.54	12.5	2	2	0.80	0.00
A23	24802	20.0	8	3	22.5	8	4	1	29	0.40	20.0	6	2	0.30	1.00
A23	24803	25.0	8	2	22.5	8	2	1	41	0.41	22.5	4	2	0.28	0.73
A23	24804	25.0	8	3	22.5	8	2	1	38	0.73	22.5	8	1	0.63	0.73
A23	24805	12.5	4	1	15.0	7	3	2	25	0.80	0.0	0	0	0.00	0.00
A24	23901	20.0	8	2	20.0	8	3	1	31	0.37	20.0	2	1	0.00	0.23
A24	24601	17.5	8	2	17.5	8	2	2	0	0.69	12.5	4	4	1.17	0.00
A24	24602	20.0	7	4	17.5	7	4	1	39	0.80	12.5	3	4	0.00	0.00
A25	25801	20.0	8	3	20.0	8	3	2	0	0.51	25.0	6	2	1.00	0.00
A25	25803	20.0	8	3	20.0	8	3	1	35	0.43	1.0	4	3	0.93	0.00
A26	25201	17.5	8	2	20.0	8	3	1	29	0.00	1.0	5	1	0.00	0.00
A26	25202	22.5	8	2	20.0	8	2	1	29	0.58	12.5	3	2	0.69	0.67
A26	25203	20.0	7	3	20.0	8	3	1	47	0.59	15.0	5	1	0.88	0.00
A26	25204	17.5	7	2	22.5	8	2	1	34	0.40	0.0	0	0	0.00	0.00
A26	25205	7.5	7	4	17.5	8	4	1	27	0.44	12.5	5	4	0.54	0.00
A26	25206	20.0	7	3	20.0	7	3	1	25	0.48	12.5	4	2	0.49	0.63
A26	25401	22.5	8	2	22.5	8	2	1	39	0.54	17.5	4	1	0.00	0.00
A26	25402	20.0	8	2	22.5	8	2	1	46	0.82	22.5	8	2	0.26	0.00
A26	26102	22.5	8	2	22.5	8	2	1	36	0.75	0.0	0	0	0.00	0.00
A26	26103	20.0	8	1	20.0	8	2	2	0	0.00	12.5	4	1	0.66	0.60
A26	26104	20.0	8	3	22.5	8	2	2	25	0.70	20.0	5	2	0.21	1.13
A26	26105	25.0	8	2	20.0	8	3	2	0	0.57	17.5	4	0	0.88	0.00
A26	26106	20.0	8	3	22.5	8	2	1	31	0.53	1.0	3	1	0.30	0.00
A26	26108	20.0	8	3	22.5	8	2	1	0	0.00	22.5	5	1	0.88	0.59
A26	26109	25.0	8	1	22.5	8	2	0	28	0.53	25.0	4	2	0.65	0.74
A27	26301	20.0	8	2	20.0	8	1	1	40	0.00	20.0	6	1	0.00	0.00
A27	26302	25.0	7	3	22.5	8	2	1	37	1.41	15.0	2	1	1.69	0.00
A27	26401	25.0	8	2	25.0	8	2	2	25	0.45	20.0	4	2	0.27	0.78
A27	26402	22.5	7	2	22.5	7	2	1	32	0.53	17.5	5	1	0.66	0.99
A27	26403	20.0	8	2	22.5	8	2	1	46	0.76	17.5	4	3	0.79	0.48
A27	26601	17.5	7	1	17.5	7	1	1	33	0.00	7.5	4	1	0.78	0.77
A28	27001	22.5	8	2	22.5	8	2	2	0	0.47	10.0	4	1	0.35	0.00
A28	27002	22.5	8	2	22.5	8	3	1	29	0.80	20.0	2	1	0.40	0.61
A28	27003	20.0	8	3	20.0	8	3	2	0	0.42	12.5	4	2	0.32	0.72
A28	27201	22.5	8	2	22.5	8	2	1	28	0.53	12.5	4	2	0.54	0.78
A28	27202	25.0	7	3	25.0	8	3	2	29	0.81	20.0	3	1	1.08	0.00
A28	27301	20.0	8	3	20.0	8	3	1	39	0.40	12.5	4	2	0.43	0.52
A28	27701	20.0	9	2	20.0	8	2	1	41	0.57	25.0	4	2	0.94	0.00
A28	27801	22.5	8	2	22.5	8	2	1	35	0.50	22.5	2	0	0.38	0.00
A29	28701	20.0	8	1	20.0	8	1	1	48	0.22	12.5	3	2	0.73	0.00
A31	30301	20.0	8	3	22.5	8	2	1	40	0.72	12.5	3	2	0.82	0.00
A32	29801	17.5	8	4	17.5	8	4	1	39	0.65	7.5	4	4	0.86	0.00
A32	30501	17.5	8	4	22.5	8	2	1	53	1.26	15.0	5	3	0.68	0.00
B36	58301	20.0	8	3	20.0	8	3	1	45	0.82	22.5	5	2	0.42	1.14
B36	59201	17.5	8	2	20.0	8	3	2	35	0.42	12.5	4	2	0.18	0.28
B37	59701	17.5	8	2	17.5	8	3	1	56	0.99	12.5	3	3	0.91	0.00
B38	60301	20.0	8	1	20.0	8	2	1	38	0.64	20.0	5	2	0.00	0.00
B39	60501	20.0	8	2	20.0	8	3	1	46	0.60	20.0	4	2	0.44	1.25
B39	60502	20.0	8	3	20.0	8	3	1	38	0.77	20.0	4	3	0.74	0.00

FARUKH-BAYAT SMALL BOWL BASES

LAYER	ARTIFACT NUMBER	BODY HUE	VAL	CHR	SURFACE HUE	VAL	CHR	BASE FORM	BASE THICK	RING DIAM	RING THK	RING ANGLE	PAINT HUE	VAL	CHR	WIDTH LOWER	WIDTH UPPER
B39	60701	22.5	8	2	22.5	8	2	1	34	0.71			12.5	3	2	0.80	0.00
B39	61301	20.0	8	2	22.5	8	2	2	25	0.76			15.0	3	1	0.35	0.76
B40	61501	20.0	8	2	20.0	8	3	2	0	0.47			12.5	4	2	0.62	0.21
B40	61502	20.0	8	3	22.5	8	2	1	28	0.39			15.0	3	2	0.40	0.00
B40	61504	17.5	7	4	20.0	8	3	2	33	0.74			20.0	2	2	0.30	0.68
B40	62007	15.0	8	2	15.0	8	2	1	59	1.20			12.5	3	2	1.31	0.00
B40	62601	25.0	8	2	25.0	8	2	1	43	0.55			1.0	4	2	0.66	0.00
B40	62602	20.0	8	3	20.0	8	3	1	42	1.03			1.0	4	3	0.00	0.00
B40	62603	22.5	8	2	22.5	8	2	1	80	0.44			12.5	3	0	0.00	0.00
B41	63001	20.0	8	3	20.0	8	3	1	28	0.68			17.5	6	2	0.57	0.52
B41	63002	20.0	8	3	20.0	8	2	1	41	0.65			17.5	5	3	0.50	0.45
B41	63003	20.0	8	3	22.5	8	2	2	0	0.54			27.5	4	0	0.48	0.34
B41	63004	15.0	7	3	15.0	7	3	2	25	0.52			1.0	4	2	0.42	0.36
B41	63005	20.0	8	2	20.0	8	3	2	0	0.49			12.5	3	0	0.00	0.52
B41	63106	20.0	8	2	22.5	8	2	1	28	0.56			20.0	2	1	0.33	0.00
B41	63301	20.0	8	3	20.0	8	3	1	41	0.60			12.5	4	0	0.47	0.54
B41	63601	20.0	8	3	20.0	8	3	2	0	0.70			12.5	3	2	0.64	0.00
B41	63602	25.0	7	2	25.0	7	2	1	0	0.54			22.5	4	2	0.00	0.00
B41	63801	20.0	8	2	25.0	8	2	1	28	0.00			20.0	3	1	0.22	0.45
B41	64001	20.0	8	3	20.0	8	3	1	47	0.00			12.5	4	2	0.27	1.08
B42	64901	22.5	8	2	22.5	8	2	1	35	0.65			12.5	4	0	1.45	0.37
B42	64902	20.0	8	3	22.5	8	2	2	0	0.82			12.5	3	0	0.53	0.52
B42	64903	17.5	8	2	20.0	8	2	1	26	0.70			15.0	2	1	0.41	0.00
B42	64904	17.5	8	2	22.5	8	2	2	21	0.60			12.5	4	0	0.00	1.51
B42	64905	12.5	6	6	12.5	6	4	2	21	1.00			7.5	4	4	0.00	0.00
B42	65001	25.0	8	3	25.0	8	2	2	21	1.60			20.0	4	3	0.61	1.18
B42	65402	20.0	7	3	22.5	8	2	2	21	0.90			17.5	4	0	0.00	0.00
B42	65601	25.0	6	3	25.0	6	3	2	31	1.15			22.5	3	0	0.44	0.43
B42	65801	20.0	8	3	20.0	8	3	2	0	0.34			20.0	6	1	0.50	0.80
B42	65802	20.0	7	2	22.5	8	2	2	0	1.27			20.0	4	2	0.50	0.00
B43	66001	25.0	8	2	25.0	8	1	1	41	0.58			22.5	4	0	0.00	0.00
B43	66002	20.0	8	3	20.0	8	3	2	0	0.41			20.0	4	1	1.07	0.59
B43	66201	20.0	8	3	20.0	8	2	1	0	0.42			20.0	6	1	0.00	0.00
B44	66303	25.0	8	2	25.0	8	2	1	34	0.95			10.0	2	1	0.00	0.00
B44	66802	20.0	8	2	25.0	8	2	0	31	0.00			20.0	5	1	1.22	0.00
B44	66803	25.0	8	2	25.0	8	2	1	40	0.00			25.0	6	3	0.32	0.42
B44	66804	17.5	7	4	20.0	7	2	1	44	1.00			17.5	5	2	0.37	0.41
B44	66901	20.0	7	2	20.0	7	3	2	54	0.00			17.5	5	1	0.24	0.50
B44	66902	20.0	7	3	17.5	8	4	1	32	0.98			20.0	5	1	0.44	0.53
B44	67102	25.0	7	2	25.0	7	2	2	25	0.83			25.0	4	1	0.40	0.72
B44	67103	20.0	7	3	20.0	8	3	1	48	0.60			17.5	3	0	0.86	0.00
B44	67301	25.0	8	2	25.0	7	2	1	30	0.95			25.0	5	1	0.74	0.00
B45	67501	20.0	8	3	20.0	8	3	1	34	0.47			5.0	5	1	0.48	0.68
B45	68301	17.5	7	4	17.5	8	4	1	33	0.77			10.0	3	3	0.50	0.90
B45	68501	20.0	7	3	20.0	8	3	1	45	0.46			10.0	3	2	0.48	0.00
B45	68901	25.0	8	3	25.0	8	3	1	48	1.07			20.0	5	3	0.46	0.99
B46	69101	22.5	7	2	25.0	8	3	1	43	0.60			17.5	4	0	0.85	0.00
B46	69102	20.0	7	3	20.0	7	3	1	36	0.78			17.5	3	2	0.93	0.00
B46	69103	17.5	7	4	17.5	7	4	1	32	0.64			10.0	4	3	0.48	0.85
B46	69104	22.5	8	2	22.5	7	2	1	30	0.69			22.5	6	1	0.64	0.00
B46	69105	22.5	7	2	22.5	8	2	1	48	0.87			22.5	3	0	0.00	0.00
B46	69301	20.0	7	3	20.0	7	3	1	35	0.45			17.5	6	0	0.75	0.95
B46	69302	20.0	8	3	20.0	8	3	1	26	0.55			17.5	6	0	0.49	1.44
B46	69303	22.5	8	2	22.5	8	2	38	31	0.65			15.0	5	4	1.38	0.00
B46	69304	25.0	7	2	25.0	7	2	1	56	0.81			0.0	0	0	0.00	0.00
B46	69306	22.5	8	2	22.5	8	2	1	38	0.84			17.5	5	0	1.24	0.00
B46	69307	25.0	8	2	25.0	8	2	1	41	0.86			22.5	3	0	1.21	0.00
B46	69308	20.0	7	2	22.5	8	2	1	32	0.72			20.0	5	1	0.57	0.00
A23	24801	15.0	7	4	15.0	7	4	1	47	0.64			15.0	5	1	0.51	0.99
A25	25804	20.0	8	3	25.0	8	3	1	26	0.48			25.0	2	2	0.00	0.40
A26	25207	25.0	7	4	25.0	7	3	2	32	0.62			20.0	2	2	1.51	0.85
A26	26101	17.5	8	2	17.5	8	2	2	24	0.59			15.0	4	3	0.84	0.00
A26	26110	25.0	7	2	25.0	8	2	2	30	0.57			22.5	3	0	0.94	0.14
B42	64937	12.5	6	6	12.5	6	6	2	39	0.39			12.5	2	4	0.00	0.00
B44	66801	20.0	8	3	20.0	8	2	1	31	0.00			20.0	3	1	0.89	0.68
A26	78401	22.5	8	2	22.5	8	2	1	70	0.89			0.0	0	0	0.00	0.00
A27	26401	20.0	8	2	25.0	8	2	1	72	0.17			0.0	0	0	0.00	0.00
A29	28901	17.5	8	3	20.0	8	3	1	63	0.45			0.0	0	0	0.00	0.00
A29	28902	20.0	8	3	20.0	8	3	2	52	1.05			0.0	0	0	0.00	0.00
A29	29201	20.0	8	2	20.0	8	3	1	65	2.05			0.0	0	0	0.00	0.00

APPENDIX C

FARUKH-BAYAT SMALL BOWL BASES

LAYER	ARTIFACT NUMBER	BODY HUE	VAL	CHR	SURFACE HUE	VAL	CHR	BASE FORM	BASE THICK	RING DIAM	RING THK	RING ANGLE	PAINT HUE	VAL	CHR	WIDTH LOWER	WIDTH UPPER
A31	30301	22.5	8	2	25.0	8	2	2	50	0.95							
A31	78701	17.5	8	3	25.0	8	2	1	70	0.48			C.0	0	0	0.00	0.00
A31	78702	25.C	8	3	25.0	8	2	1	65	0.45			C-0	0	0	0.00	0.00
A31	78901	25.0	8	2	25.0	8	3	1	65	0.48			0.0	0	0	0.00	0.00
A32	31001	25.C	8	2	25.0	8	2	2	59	0.07			C.C	0	0	0.00	0.00
A32	31002	25.0	8	1	25.0	8	2	2	44	0.45			0.0	0	0	0.00	0.0C
A36	32301	25.0	8	3	25.0	8	3	2	54	0.15			C.0	0	0	0.00	0.00
B36	58301	20.C	9	3	20.0	8	3	2	62	0.17			C.0	0	0	0.00	0.00
B40	61501	17.5	8	3	17.5	8	2	1	72	1.55			0.0	0	0	0.00	0.00
B41	63301	25.C	8	2	25.0	7	2	2	59	1.05			0.0	0	0	0.00	0.00
B42	64901	20.0	8	2	22.5	8	2	1	78	0.75							
B43	66203	17.5	8	3	20.0	8	2	2	56	0.70			C.C	0	0	0.00	0.C0
B44	66801	25.0	8	3	25.0	8	3	1	77	0.35			0.0	0	C	0.00	0.00
B44	68701	22.5	8	2	25.0	7	3	1	73	1.90			C.0	0	0	0.00	0.00
B45	67901	22.0	8	2	22.5	8	2	2	48	0.95			C.0	0	0	0.00	0.00
B45	68901	25.0	8	2	25.0	7	3	2	67	1.10			0.0	0	0	0.00	0.00
B46	69303	25.C	8	2	25.0	8	2	2	59	1.10			0.0	0	0	0.00	0.00
B46	69304	25.0	7	1	25.0	7	1	2	61	0.95			C.0	0	0	0.00	0.00

FARUKH-BAYAT RING BOWL BASES

LAYER	ARTIFACT NUMBER	BODY HUE	VAL	CHR	SURFACE HUE	VAL	CHR	BASE FORM	BASE THICK	RING DIAM	RING THK	RING ANGLE	PAINT HUE	VAL	CHR	WIDTH LOWER	WIDTH UPPER
A24	24601	20.C	8	3	20.0	8	3	1	1.10	9	1.31	84	10.0	4	1	1.14	0.00
A25	25801	20.0	8	3	20.0	8	3	1	0.80	10	1.52	90	22.5	3	2	0.77	0.00
A26	26102	25.C	8	2	25.0	8	2	1	1.00	9	1.07	68	20.0	4	2	1.10	0.00
A27	26301	20.0	8	3	25.0	8	2	1	0.83	13	0.74	69	10.0	4	2	1.09	0.00
A27	26302	17.5	8	4	17.5	8	4	1	0.64	8	1.03	75	C.0	0	0	0.00	0.00
A27	26401	17.5	8	4	20.0	8	4	1	0.89	9	1.22	58	10.0	4	2	1.10	0.00
A27	26402	17.5	7	4	17.5	8	4	1	0.93	12	1.37	88	7.5	4	2	0.91	0.00
B36	58302	20.C	8	4	20.0	8	4	1	0.66	7	0.92	65	10.0	4	4	0.40	0.C0
B39	61100	20.0	8	4	20.0	8	3	1	1.08	10	1.35	92	10.0	4	2	1.00	0.00
B4C	61501	25.0	8	2	25.0	8	3	1	0.93	10	1.51	51	22.5	4	2	1.13	0.00
B40	62001	20.0	8	3	22.5	8	4	0	0.00	7	1.C5	85	1C.0	5	2	0.57	0.00
B41	63701	12.5	6	6	15.0	8	4	1	1.10	12	1.07	89	10.0	3	4	1.10	0.00
B41	63801	12.5	6	6	12.5	6	4	0	0.00	10	0.82	88	10.0	4	4	0.84	0.00
B41	64002	25.0	8	3	25.0	8	3	1	0.60	7	0.86	110	7.5	3	4	0.53	0.00
B41	64003	20.0	8	3	22.5	8	4	1	0.61	7	1.12	104	10.0	3	4	0.46	0.00
B42	65401	12.5	6	4	12.5	8	2	1	0.92	11	C.95	92	7.5	3	4	0.63	0.00
B42	65402	12.5	6	4	20.0	8	3	1	0.83	10	1.14	93	C.0	0	0	0.00	0.00
B42	65404	12.5	6	4	22.5	8	2	1	0.94	11	1.23	90	7.5	3	4	0.48	0.00
B42	65405	12.5	6	4	20.0	8	3	1	0.89	10	1.12	75	7.5	3	4	0.54	0.00
B42	65407	12.5	6	6	20.0	8	4	1	1.58	10	1.47	76	10.0	4	3	1.16	0.C0
B42	65408	12.5	6	6	17.5	7	4	1	1.55	10	0.84	101	1C.0	4	3	1.06	0.00
B42	65601	25.C	7	3	25.0	8	3	1	0.91	11	0.93	76	12.5	3	0	0.99	0.00
B42	65802	17.5	8	2	25.0	8	2	1	0.00	10	0.82	85	12.5	5	2	0.75	0.00
B46	69101	17.5	7	4	12.5	8	2	1	1.30	18	2.15	111	10.0	4	3	1.80	0.C0
B46	69102	22.5	8	4	22.5	8	4	0	0.00	11	1.16	72	10.0	4	3	1.02	0.00
B46	69103	15.0	7	4	20.0	8	3	1	0.00	7	0.91	96	7.5	3	6	0.92	0.00
B46	69104	25.0	8	2	25.0	8	3	1	0.83	12	1.21	51	22.5	3	2	0.82	0.00
B46	69105	25.0	8	2	25.0	8	3	1	1.14	12	1.22	6C	12.5	4	2	1.05	0.00

FARUKH-BAYAT SMALL BOWL RIMS : PLAIN

LAYER	ARTIFACT NUMBER	BODY HUE	VAL	CHR	SURFACE HUE	VAL	CHR	RIM FORM	RIM DIAM	RIM ANGLE	BODY THICK
A23	23701	20.C	8	3	22.5	8	2	2	23	69	0.54
A24	24601	17.5	7	4	25.0	8	2	2	23	59	1C.80
A25	25801	17.5	8	3	22.5	8	2	2	12	67	0.62
A25	25802	20.C	8	2	22.5	8	2	2	8	66	0.65
A26	25201	20.0	8	2	22.5	8	2	2	9	64	1C.50
A26	25202	17.5	7	3	17.5	8	3	2	18	70	0.63
A26	25401	25.C	8	2	25.0	8	3	2	13	72	1C.30
A26	25402	20.0	8	3	25.0	8	2	2	12	70	1C.59
A26	25403	25.0	8	1	25.0	8	2	2	14	76	0.55
A26	25404	20.0	8	4	7.5	7	3	2	9	1	1C.43
A26	26101	25.C	7	3	25.0	8	3	2	8	62	1C.43

FARUKH-BAYAT SMALL BOWL RIMS : PLAIN

LAYER	ARTIFACT NUMBER	BODY HUE	VAL	CHR	SURFACE HUE	VAL	CHR	RIM FORM	RIM DIAM	RIM ANGLE	BODY THICK
A26	26102	15.0	6	3	15.0	7	4	2	6	65	0.55
A26	26103	17.5	6	4	15.0	7	4	2	10	57	0.41
A26	78401	22.5	8	2	22.5	8	2	2	11	80	0.49
A27	26301	20.0	8	3	22.5	8	2	2	14	62	0.72
A27	26302	22.5	8	2	25.0	8	2	2	9	58	0.63
A27	26303	20.0	7	2	20.0	8	2	2	9	82	0.49
A27	26401	25.0	8	1	25.0	8	2	2	12	64	0.51
A27	26601	22.5	8	2	25.0	8	3	2	15	70	0.50
A27	26801	17.5	7	2	20.0	7	2	2	14	71	0.55
A28	27201	22.5	8	2	22.5	8	2	2	12	72	0.48
A28	27701	20.0	8	2	22.5	8	2	2	9	85	0.55
A28	27702	20.0	8	3	20.0	8	2	2	11	80	0.33
A28	27703	20.0	6	1	22.5	8	2	2	16	70	0.54
A28	27704	22.5	7	2	25.0	7	3	2	13	67	0.54
A28	27901	20.0	7	3	22.5	8	3	2	13	1	0.44
A29	28301	22.5	8	2	25.0	8	3	2	11	73	0.30
A29	28501	25.0	8	2	25.0	8	3	2	15	74	0.63
A29	28701	22.5	7	2	25.0	8	2	2	15	77	0.50
A29	28901	20.0	8	3	22.5	8	2	2	27	68	0.66
A29	29301	22.5	8	2	22.5	8	3	2	15	70	0.40
A29	29302	20.0	7	3	22.5	8	2	2	13	65	0.69
A29	29303	22.5	7	2	25.0	8	3	2	14	66	0.41
A29	29304	20.0	8	3	22.5	8	2	2	12	57	0.45
A29	29305	20.0	8	2	22.5	8	2	2	10	65	0.37
A29	29306	20.0	8	3	22.5	8	2	2	13	58	0.34
A29	29307	20.0	8	2	22.5	8	2	2	13	65	0.40
A29	29308	22.5	8	2	20.0	8	3	2	12	65	0.44
A29	29309	22.5	8	2	22.5	8	2	2	14	73	0.36
A29	29701	20.0	6	1	20.0	7	1	2	15	60	0.37
A30	29101	20.0	7	2	22.5	8	2	2	11	81	0.33
A30	29102	20.0	7	3	25.0	7	3	2	12	64	0.36
A30	29103	25.0	6	2	25.0	6	4	2	15	60	0.28
A30	29901	20.0	7	2	20.0	8	3	2	12	69	0.40
A31	78701	17.5	8	3	25.0	8	2	2	19	80	0.60
A31	78702	25.0	8	3	25.0	8	2	2	10	80	0.42
A31	78901	25.0	8	2	25.0	8	3	2	10	75	0.44
A32	30501	22.5	8	2	25.0	8	1	2	15	61	0.33
A33	30801	25.0	7	2	25.0	7	3	2	16	47	0.34
A33	31001	25.0	7	2	25.0	7	3	2	13	67	0.36
A33	31002	22.5	7	2	25.0	8	3	2	15	70	0.35
A33	31003	22.5	8	2	25.0	8	3	2	11	66	0.24
A33	31004	20.0	7	2	22.5	8	2	2	16	63	0.46
A35	31701	22.5	7	2	25.0	7	3	2	19	76	0.40
A36	32301	17.5	7	2	20.0	8	2	2	21	81	0.75
A36	32302	17.5	8	2	20.0	8	3	2	15	73	0.30
A36	32303	25.0	8	2	25.0	7	3	2	14	79	0.36
A36	32304	20.0	7	2	25.0	7	2	2	14	83	0.35
B36	58301	22.5	7	2	25.0	7	3	2	13	52	0.45
B36	58302	15.0	8	4	22.5	8	2	2	7	73	0.87
B36	58701	20.0	8	3	20.0	8	3	2	1	73	0.79
B36	58702	20.0	8	3	20.0	8	4	2	1	76	0.79
B36	58703	17.5	6	2	25.0	7	4	2	14	61	0.38
B36	59201	17.5	8	2	17.5	8	4	2	45	80	0.87
B36	59202	25.0	8	4	22.5	8	4	2	1	76	0.33
B36	59203	17.5	7	4	17.5	8	4	2	9	76	0.47
B36	59204	12.5	6	6	20.0	8	4	2	1	74	0.70
B37	59001	15.0	7	3	20.0	8	2	2	22	53	0.84
B37	59701	15.0	7	3	20.0	8	3	2	23	50	0.87
B38	60101	22.5	8	2	22.5	8	2	2	13	61	0.32
B38	60102	20.0	8	3	22.5	8	2	2	16	72	0.25
B39	60501	22.5	8	2	22.5	8	2	2	1	1	0.33
B39	61301	22.5	8	2	22.5	8	3	2	1	1	0.33
B40	61501	17.5	7	4	20.0	8	3	2	34	46	0.83
B40	61502	22.5	8	2	22.5	7	2	2	8	67	0.49
B40	62201	20.0	7	3	20.0	8	3	2	17	74	0.58
B40	62202	20.0	7	2	22.5	8	2	2	12	58	0.47
B40	62601	20.0	8	3	25.0	8	3	2	9	81	0.47
B41	63301	22.5	8	2	20.0	8	2	2	17	88	0.43
B41	64001	20.0	8	3	20.0	8	2	2	16	78	0.70

APPENDIX C

FARUKH-BAYAT SMALL BOWL RIMS : PLAIN

LAYER	ARTIFACT NUMBER	BODY HUE	BODY VAL	BODY CHR	SURFACE HUE	SURFACE VAL	SURFACE CHR	RIM FORM	RIM DIAM	RIM ANGLE	BODY THICK
B41	64501	20.0	7	3	22.5	8	2	2	12	62	0.35
B41	64502	20.0	8	2	22.5	8	2	2	14	83	0.44
B42	65201	17.5	7	2	22.5	8	2	2	12	71	0.52
B42	65202	20.0	7	3	20.0	8	3	2	10	53	0.65
B42	65203	20.0	7	2	20.0	8	2	2	10	56	0.62
B42	65204	15.0	7	4	17.5	7	3	2	28	56	0.63
B42	65801	17.5	7	4	17.5	7	5	2	1	1	1.00
B44	66401	20.0	7	2	22.5	8	2	2	22	91	0.43
B44	66402	17.5	8	3	22.5	8	3	2	20	70	0.55
B44	66403	20.0	8	4	25.0	8	1	2	33	75	0.86
B44	66501	25.0	8	1	25.0	8	2	2	12	76	0.42
B44	66701	25.0	7	1	25.0	7	2	2	9	76	0.34
B44	66801	25.0	8	1	25.0	8	3	2	19	69	0.50
B44	66802	20.0	8	2	20.0	8	2	2	21	75	0.52
B44	66803	17.5	8	4	20.0	7	2	2	12	23	0.35
B44	66804	22.5	8	2	22.5	8	2	2	11	60	0.35
B44	66805	25.0	8	2	25.0	8	3	2	1	1	0.25
B44	67101	25.0	8	1	25.0	8	2	2	1	1	0.28
B44	67102	20.0	8	3	20.0	7	3	2	18	68	0.37
B44	67103	17.5	8	2	20.0	6	1	2	26	79	0.79
B45	68701	22.5	8	2	22.5	8	2	2	11	66	0.30
B45	68702	25.0	8	3	25.0	8	2	2	10	66	0.60
B45	68901	17.5	8	3	20.0	8	4	2	13	61	0.40
B46	69101	25.0	8	2	22.5	8	2	2	14	73	0.39
B46	69102	25.0	8	4	25.0	8	4	2	9	71	0.45
B46	69301	22.5	8	2	22.5	8	2	2	10	72	0.44
B47	69401	25.0	8	0	25.0	8	1	2	1	74	0.43

FARUKH-BAYAT SMALL BOWL RIMS : SINGLE BAND

LAYER	ARTIFACT NUMBER	BODY HUE	BODY VAL	BODY CHR	SURFACE HUE	SURFACE VAL	SURFACE CHR	RIM FORM	RIM DIAM	RIM ANGLE	RIM THICK	PAINT HUE	PAINT VAL	PAINT CHR	INT BAND	EXT BAND
A23	23701	17.5	7	4	20.0	8	3	2	11	82	0.42	12.5	2	0	0.74	0.71
A23	24801	20.0	8	3	22.5	8	2	2	9	76	0.30	22.5	3	0	0.63	0.53
A23	24802	17.5	8	2	20.0	8	2	2	26	96	0.63	22.5	3	0	0.70	0.82
A23	24804	25.0	8	1	22.5	8	2	2	10	76	0.41	22.5	3	0	0.53	0.74
A24	23901	25.0	6	6	25.0	7	2	2	10	98	0.53	22.5	3	0	0.63	0.53
A24	24101	20.0	8	3	22.5	8	2	2	19	48	0.68	10.0	3	4	2.18	0.63
A24	24102	25.0	8	3	25.0	8	1	2	10	88	0.64	12.5	3	0	0.30	1.82
A24	24103	20.0	8	4	25.0	8	2	2	15	88	0.68	22.5	3	0	0.47	0.52
A24	24601	12.5	6	4	17.5	6	4	2	16	77	0.64	12.5	6	6	0.64	0.74
A24	24602	22.5	8	2	25.0	8	3	2	15	70	0.30	17.5	3	0	0.53	0.30
A24	24604	20.0	7	4	20.0	8	4	2	14	84	0.63	12.5	2	2	0.52	0.92
A24	24605	17.5	7	4	20.0	8	3	2	16	72	0.64	20.0	0	1	0.52	0.79
A24	24606	25.0	8	3	22.5	8	2	2	9	74	0.63	22.5	3	0	0.74	0.80
A24	24607	20.0	8	3	20.0	8	2	2	11	72	0.31	12.5	3	6	0.31	0.30
A24	24608	25.0	8	2	25.0	8	2	2	25	75	0.63	22.5	3	0	0.80	0.96
A25	25802	25.0	7	4	25.0	7	3	2	14	80	0.40	15.0	3	2	0.41	0.30
A26	25201	20.0	8	1	20.0	8	3	2	20	90	0.42	20.0	2	1	1.41	0.74
A26	25401	20.0	8	2	22.5	8	2	2	12	78	0.63	22.5	3	0	0.90	0.63
A26	25601	20.0	7	2	22.5	8	2	2	12	62	0.63	22.5	3	0	0.30	0.30
A26	25602	20.0	8	2	25.0	8	2	2	18	86	0.53	22.5	3	0	0.63	0.30
A26	26101	17.5	7	4	20.0	8	2	2	11	96	0.42	15.0	3	2	0.41	0.41
A27	26301	25.0	8	2	25.0	8	2	2	16	104	0.63	15.0	3	2	0.30	0.29
A27	26302	20.0	8	3	22.5	8	2	2	14	68	0.41	10.0	2	2	0.29	0.29
A27	26303	15.0	7	4	25.0	8	1	2	17	94	0.64	10.0	3	4	0.42	0.52
A27	26304	25.0	7	3	25.0	7	4	2	13	97	0.40	15.0	3	2	0.41	0.44
A27	26305	17.5	8	2	25.0	8	3	2	18	94	0.74	20.0	4	3	0.01	0.64
A27	26306	12.5	6	4	22.5	8	2	2	13	97	0.53	10.0	3	4	0.79	0.53
A27	26307	25.0	8	2	25.0	8	2	2	14	102	0.41	22.5	3	0	1.07	0.68
A27	26401	22.5	8	2	20.0	8	2	2	18	80	0.70	22.5	3	0	1.18	2.70
A28	27001	15.0	6	4	17.5	8	4	2	11	70	0.41	10.0	3	4	0.81	0.53
A28	27002	20.0	8	2	25.0	8	2	2	11	60	0.57	22.5	3	0	0.42	0.42
A28	27003	25.0	8	1	25.0	8	2	2	11	78	0.30	22.5	2	2	0.52	0.51
A28	27701	25.0	8	3	25.0	8	2	2	14	86	0.01	12.5	2	2	0.68	0.31
A28	27901	15.0	6	4	17.5	8	4	2	6	89	0.64	10.0	2	2	0.52	0.64
A29	28901	20.0	8	2	20.0	8	3	2	12	84	0.41	10.0	3	6	0.92	0.41
A29	28902	25.0	8	3	22.5	8	0	2	20	72	0.64	22.5	3	0	1.17	0.01
A29	29301	25.0	8	3	25.0	8	3	1	25	97	1.18	17.5	3	2	0.01	0.69
A30	29101	10.0	4	6	20.0	8	1	2	22	68	0.68	10.0	3	6	0.01	0.01
A30	29103	17.5	8	2	20.0	8	3	2	22	80	0.70	10.0	3	6	0.01	1.42
A31	30301	17.5	7	4	20.0	8	3	2	15	70	0.68	10.0	2	2	4.30	0.86

FARUKH-BAYAT SMALL BOWL RIMS : SINGLE BAND

LAYER	ARTIFACT NUMBER	BODY HUE	VAL	CHR	SURFACE HUE	VAL	CHR	RIM FORM	RIM DIAM	RIM ANGLE	BODY THICK	PAINT HUE	VAL	CHR	INT BAND	EXT BAND
A36	32301	22.5	6	4	20.0	8	3	2	11	75	0.41	10.0	3	4	4.10	1.46
A36	32302	20.0	8	3	20.0	8	2	1	17	85	0.74	10.0	3	3	0.19	0.01
B36	58301	12.5	6	8	15.0	7	4	2	19	78	0.64	10.0	3	4	0.28	0.01
B36	58701	25.0	8	2	25.0	8	1	2	18	78	0.40	25.0	3	0	0.73	0.53
B36	58702	25.0	8	2	25.0	8	1	2	15	84	0.46	25.0	3	0	0.55	0.47
B36	59201	25.0	8	1	25.0	8	1	2	10	74	0.54	25.0	3	0	0.71	0.63
B36	59202	25.0	8	1	25.0	8	1	2	14	53	0.80	10.0	3	4	0.32	0.60
B39	61101	17.5	8	4	20.0	8	4	2	7	85	0.32	10.0	3	6	2.30	1.00
B39	61102	17.5	8	6	20.0	8	3	2	12	80	0.50	25.0	3	0	0.43	0.30
B39	61103	20.0	8	4	25.0	8	2	2	22	83	0.43	25.0	3	1	0.96	0.45
B39	61104	20.0	8	4	25.0	8	2	2	18	85	0.52	25.0	3	0	0.79	0.90
B40	61501	20.0	8	4	25.0	8	2	2	16	82	0.58	25.0	3	0	0.48	0.01
B40	61502	17.5	7	4	25.0	8	2	2	14	70	0.47	12.5	3	4	0.37	0.28
B40	61503	25.0	8	3	22.5	8	2	2	21	73	0.47	10.0	4	4	1.17	0.71
B40	61504	25.0	7	6	22.5	6	4	2	17	81	0.55	10.0	3	6	0.80	0.66
B40	61505	17.5	7	4	25.0	8	2	2	15	80	0.35	10.0	2	2	0.50	0.67
B40	61701	12.5	8	2	25.0	8	2	2	16	84	0.56	10.0	2	2	0.76	0.70
B40	62201	25.0	8	3	25.0	8	2	2	14	84	0.50	22.5	3	0	0.67	0.01
B40	62601	25.0	8	3	25.0	8	2	2	11	84	0.45	22.5	3	0	0.56	0.55
B40	62602	17.5	6	6	25.0	8	2	2	12	78	0.69	22.5	3	0	0.54	0.74
B41	63101	15.0	8	4	25.0	8	2	2	12	66	0.40	10.0	4	6	0.76	0.53
B41	63102	25.0	8	4	25.0	8	2	2	14	77	0.40	22.5	3	0	0.62	0.46
B41	64001	25.0	7	6	25.0	8	1	2	20	82	0.52	10.0	3	2	0.46	0.01
B42	64901	17.5	7	4	22.5	8	2	2	1	60	0.68	22.5	3	0	0.15	0.59
B42	64902	17.5	7	4	22.5	8	2	2	27	60	0.72	22.5	3	0	0.23	0.66
B42	64903	17.5	6	6	25.0	8	1	2	30	70	0.67	22.5	3	0	0.34	0.36
B42	65001	17.5	8	2	22.5	8	2	2	30	57	0.74	22.5	3	0	0.35	0.43
B42	65201	25.0	8	2	25.0	8	2	2	14	88	0.58	22.5	3	0	0.64	0.55
B42	65202	17.5	7	2	25.0	8	2	2	11	88	0.62	22.5	3	0	0.48	0.63
B42	65601	20.0	7	3	17.5	8	2	2	15	75	0.45	12.5	3	2	0.30	0.67
B42	65801	17.5	7	2	25.0	8	2	2	14	48	0.73	17.5	4	2	0.37	0.52
B43	66001	12.5	6	6	0.1	0	0	2	15	73	0.59	12.5	3	0	0.64	0.52
B43	66201	12.5	6	4	25.0	8	1	2	16	83	0.52	12.5	3	4	0.30	0.31
B44	66801	12.5	6	6	25.0	8	1	2	13	67	0.67	12.5	3	0	0.41	0.36
B44	66802	25.0	8	1	25.0	8	1	2	13	76	0.31	12.5	3	0	0.01	0.28
B44	67101	12.5	6	4	17.5	7	4	2	17	96	0.55	10.0	3	4	0.52	0.45
B44	67102	25.0	8	2	25.0	8	1	2	14	88	0.47	12.5	3	0	0.42	0.20
B44	67103	20.0	8	4	25.0	8	2	2	12	86	0.41	12.5	3	0	0.41	0.32
B44	67104	25.0	8	1	25.0	8	2	2	13	84	0.32	22.5	3	0	0.54	0.50
B44	67301	25.0	8	1	25.0	8	1	2	12	87	0.50	22.5	3	0	0.46	0.46
B45	67501	22.5	8	2	25.0	8	2	2	16	84	0.43	15.0	2	1	0.72	0.46
B45	68101	10.0	5	6	12.5	6	4	2	10	105	0.30	10.0	3	6	0.74	0.31
B45	68301	17.5	7	4	17.5	7	4	1	36	70	0.74	10.0	3	4	0.29	1.29
B45	68501	25.0	8	2	25.0	8	3	2	13	94	0.43	12.5	3	4	0.01	0.68
B45	68701	25.0	8	1	12.5	8	2	2	14	93	0.42	25.0	3	0	0.30	0.81
B46	69101	17.5	7	4	17.5	8	4	2	24	88	0.70	10.0	3	4	0.79	0.63
B46	69102	25.0	8	3	25.0	8	1	2	11	92	0.50	10.0	3	3	1.07	0.79
B46	69103	17.5	7	4	25.0	8	2	2	11	64	0.68	15.0	4	3	0.31	0.81
B46	69301	25.0	8	3	25.0	8	1	2	12	96	0.31	17.5	3	2	0.32	0.80
B46	69302	17.5	8	4	17.5	8	2	2	15	95	0.79	10.0	3	3	0.80	1.08

FARUKH-BAYAT SMALL BOWL RIMS : MULTIPLE BAND

LAYER	ARTIFACT NUMBER	BODY HUE	VAL	CHR	SURFACE HUE	VAL	CHR	RIM FORM	RIM DIAM	RIM ANGLE	BODY THICK	PAINT HUE	VAL	CHR	INT BAND	EXT BAND	1ST SPACE	2ND BAND	2ND SPACE	3RD BAND
A23	24801	25.0	7	3	20.0	8	3	2	27	85	0.01	20.0	3	2	0.45	0.59	4.85	0.59	0.00	0.00
A24	23901	25.0	8	3	25.0	7	3	2	40	83	0.50	22.5	4	2	1.50	0.73	2.68	0.00	0.00	0.00
A24	23902	22.5	8	4	25.0	8	3	2	1	104	0.80	15.0	3	2	0.81	0.52	2.50	0.90	0.00	0.00
A24	24101	22.5	8	4	22.5	8	4	2	12	87	0.40	20.0	4	2	0.41	0.50	1.19	0.26	0.00	0.00
A25	25801	17.5	7	4	1.0	3	2	2	28	84	0.01	20.0	8	3	11.38	1.05	0.40	0.00	0.00	0.00
A25	25803	17.5	6	4	20.0	7	4	2	1	84	0.56	12.5	3	4	0.46	0.41	2.37	0.50	0.00	0.00
A25	25901	20.0	8	3	25.0	8	3	2	13	91	0.41	15.0	3	2	0.63	0.31	0.42	0.28	0.00	0.00
A26	25201	20.0	8	1	22.5	7	2	2	15	87	0.01	22.5	4	0	0.80	0.59	0.59	0.19	0.00	0.00
A26	25401	20.0	8	3	20.0	8	3	2	16	80	0.01	17.5	4	0	1.13	0.42	0.40	0.30	0.00	0.00
A26	25402	25.0	8	2	25.0	8	2	2	22	82	0.33	22.5	3	0	0.70	0.49	0.06	0.28	0.00	0.00

APPENDIX C

FARUKH-BAYAT SMALL BOWL RIMS : MULTIPLE BAND

LAYER	ARTIFACT NUMBER	BODY HUE	VAL	CHR	SURFACE HUE	VAL	CHR	RIM FORM	RIM DIAM	RIM ANGLE	BODY THICK	PAINT HUE	VAL	CHR	INT BAND	EXT BAND	1ST SPACE	2ND BAND	2ND SPACE	3RD BAND
A26	26101	25.0	8	2	25.0	8	3	2	13	83	0.60	20.0	3	2	0.95	0.53	0.32	0.20	0.00	0.00
A26	26102	25.0	8	2	25.0	8	3	2	13	85	0.47	12.5	2	2	0.69	0.56	0.30	0.47	0.00	0.00
A26	26103	17.5	7	4	17.5	7	4	2	12	88	0.45	15.0	3	3	0.58	0.59	0.81	0.26	0.00	0.00
A26	26104	25.0	5	4	25.0	5	4	2	10	83	0.43	15.0	3	3	0.72	0.48	0.74	0.85	0.00	0.00
A26	26105	22.5	7	2	20.0	8	3	2	14	86	0.45	15.0	4	1	0.82	0.41	0.52	0.29	0.00	0.00
A26	26106	25.0	8	1	25.0	8	1	2	15	86	0.50	20.0	4	1	0.80	0.40	0.13	0.23	0.00	0.00
A27	26301	20.0	8	3	25.0	8	3	2	17	84	0.45	20.0	3	2	0.59	0.23	0.16	0.26	0.00	0.00
A27	26302	25.0	7	3	25.0	8	2	2	15	85	0.48	20.0	3	1	0.71	0.28	0.18	0.29	0.00	0.00
A27	26402	20.0	8	2	25.0	8	2	2	20	79	0.51	15.0	3	1	0.80	0.38	0.36	0.29	0.00	0.00
A27	26403	22.5	8	2	25.0	8	3	2	18	72	0.42	20.0	4	2	0.84	0.34	0.15	0.19	0.00	0.00
A27	26404	20.0	8	3	25.0	8	2	2	17	72	0.40	15.0	3	1	0.92	0.52	0.22	0.33	0.00	0.00
A27	26801	22.5	8	2	22.5	8	2	2	16	81	0.35	15.0	3	1	0.68	0.48	0.39	0.25	0.00	0.00
A28	27001	22.5	7	2	25.0	7	3	2	12	80	0.40	22.5	4	2	0.86	0.34	0.09	0.25	0.00	0.00
A28	27702	17.5	7	2	20.0	7	2	2	15	80	0.46	12.5	2	4	0.78	0.62	0.20	0.21	0.00	0.00
B36	58301	20.0	7	3	20.0	8	1	2	16	90	0.59	22.5	4	2	0.63	0.50	0.51	0.38	0.00	0.00
B36	58302	17.5	8	2	25.0	7	3	2	11	79	0.38	20.0	3	1	0.52	0.48	0.55	0.00	0.00	0.00
B36	58304	20.0	8	3	25.0	8	3	2	11	80	0.32	20.0	3	1	0.86	0.57	0.90	0.13	0.00	0.00
B36	59201	20.0	8	3	22.5	8	4	2	14	78	0.40	7.5	3	2	0.63	0.54	0.28	0.31	0.00	0.00
B36	59202	20.0	7	2	22.5	7	2	2	12	89	0.50	10.0	3	1	0.76	0.49	0.46	1.35	0.00	0.00
B37	59001	20.0	7	3	25.0	7	3	2	16	81	0.70	15.0	3	1	2.43	0.01	0.40	1.29	0.00	0.00
B38	60101	12.5	6	4	15.0	6	6	2	17	77	0.68	12.5	3	2	0.70	0.72	1.95	0.43	0.00	0.00
B39	60901	17.5	8	2	20.0	8	3	2	16	75	0.45	20.0	3	1	0.67	0.83	0.86	0.31	0.00	0.00
B39	61101	22.5	7	2	25.0	8	3	2	14	72	0.44	15.0	4	2	0.57	0.42	0.47	0.34	0.00	0.00
B39	61102	20.0	7	2	15.0	7	4	2	15	73	0.56	12.5	3	2	0.45	0.40	0.76	0.28	0.00	0.00
B39	61103	25.0	6	3	25.0	7	3	2	12	86	0.34	20.0	2	2	0.57	0.55	0.35	0.12	0.00	0.00
B39	61104	20.0	7	3	20.0	8	3	2	13	88	0.41	20.0	3	1	0.39	0.48	0.99	0.24	0.00	0.00
B39	61301	20.0	8	2	22.5	8	2	2	15	85	0.41	22.5	5	2	0.56	0.49	0.53	0.16	0.00	0.00
B40	61501	20.0	8	3	20.0	8	2	2	12	84	0.36	12.5	2	2	0.48	0.68	0.00	0.00	0.00	0.00
B40	61502	20.0	7	4	25.0	7	3	2	13	85	0.41	17.5	3	0	0.38	0.35	0.89	0.18	0.00	0.00
B40	61503	15.0	6	4	15.0	7	4	2	16	74	0.47		0	0	0.84	0.01	0.31	0.28	0.00	0.00
B40	61701	25.0	7	3	25.0	8	3	2	23	80	0.68	20.0	5	2	0.75	0.01	1.30	0.28	0.00	0.00
B40	62001	20.0	7	3	20.0	8	3	2	15	85	0.48	20.0	4	3	0.38	0.37	0.31	0.27	0.00	0.00
B40	62201	22.5	7	2	25.0	7	2	2	16	90	0.68	15.0	2	1	0.48	0.59	1.01	0.20	0.00	0.00
B40	62601	20.0	7	2	22.5	8	2	2	20	88	0.40		0	0	0.59	0.01	1.04	0.24	0.00	0.00
B40	62602	22.5	7	2	22.5	7	2	2	9	70	0.50	15.0	3	2	1.90	0.26	0.84	0.12	0.00	0.00
B41	63301	17.5	7	2	22.5	8	2	2	15	87	0.43		0	0	0.70	0.47	0.68	0.33	0.00	0.00
B41	63302	15.0	7	2	22.5	8	2	2	20	90	0.56	15.0	3	1	0.77	0.63	0.33	0.20	0.00	0.00
B41	63303	20.0	7	2	22.5	8	2	2	14	81	0.65	15.0	3	2	0.97	0.60	0.48	0.35	0.00	0.00
B41	64201	17.5	7	2	20.0	7	3	2	19	77	0.37	12.5	2	4	0.70	0.47	0.26	0.31	0.00	0.00
B41	64301	20.0	8	2	25.0	7	3	2	17	87	0.43	15.0	3	1	0.70	0.70	0.68	0.27	0.00	0.00
B42	64901	20.0	7	4	20.0	8	3	2	12	72	0.50	15.0	3	2	0.29	0.18	0.68	0.18	0.00	0.00
B42	65201	20.0	7	3	20.0	8	3	2	14	75	0.30	20.0	4	3	0.42	0.53	1.31	0.18	0.00	0.00
B45	68701	17.5	7	4	22.5	8	2	2	18	83	0.41	12.5	3	4	1.18	0.40	0.47	0.24	0.00	0.00
B46	69301	20.0	8	3	22.5	8	2	2	15	63	0.68	10.0	3	3	2.06	0.97	0.00	0.00	0.00	0.00
A23	24802	20.0	7	2	22.5	8	2	2	10	84	0.41	15.0	3	2	0.68	0.60	0.46	0.18	0.18	0.18
A27	26301	20.0	7	2	20.0	8	3	2	21	86	0.53	20.0	3	2	1.21	0.53	0.26	0.16	0.21	0.18
B36	58303	20.0	8	3	17.5	7	4	2	12	1	0.46	15.0	3	1	0.55	0.68	0.80	0.22	0.24	0.24
B37	59001	20.0	8	3	25.0	8	3	2	15	80	0.42	20.0	3	2	0.63	0.53	0.43	0.25	0.30	0.74
B40	62401	22.5	7	2	25.0	8	2	2	15	77	0.68	25.0	8	3	0.89	0.63	0.22	0.25	0.10	0.27
B41	63101	17.5	7	2	20.0	8	3	2	87	87	0.45	12.5	3	6	0.67	0.83	0.16	0.31	0.41	0.29
B42	64901	20.0	8	2	20.0	7	8	2	18	81	0.42	12.5	2	2	0.73	0.18	0.68	0.18	0.09	0.18
B42	64902	17.5	8	2	20.0	7	2	2	11	86	0.30	15.0	3	3	0.53	0.29	0.74	0.42	0.30	0.00
B42	65201	20.0	7	2	25.0	7	3	2	18	79	0.57	12.5	2	4	0.58	0.18	3.31	0.68	0.00	0.00
B42	65202	25.0	7	2	25.0	8	2	2	16	76	0.63	20.0	3	3	0.80	0.41	0.29	0.31	0.28	0.00
B42	65801	12.5	6	6	12.5	6	4	2	13	84	0.68	10.0	4	6	0.90	0.68	0.68	0.31	0.29	0.30
B43	66201	20.0	8	3	25.0	8	1	2	12	84	0.41	17.5	4	2	0.68	0.50	3.05	0.52	0.41	0.74
B44	66401	25.0	8	3	25.0	8	1	2	22	64	0.58	22.5	3	1	0.92	0.57	0.29	0.30	0.18	0.29
B45	68501	20.0	8	3	22.5	8	2	2	18	68	0.58	15.0	3	2	1.20	1.09	0.22	0.24	0.49	0.26
A25	25802	25.0	8	1	22.5	8	4	2	12	86	0.56	10.0	2	1	0.54	0.53	1.50	1.08	0.19	0.29
A28	27002	25.0	8	2	25.0	8	3	2	17	80	0.68	22.5	4	0	1.40	0.57	0.18	0.46	0.18	0.18
B40	62001	20.0	8	4	17.5	8	4	2	12	87	0.46	12.5	3	2	0.41	0.38	0.32	0.57	0.64	0.00
B40	62601	25.0	8	3	25.0	8	2	2	1	1	0.48	12.5	4	2	0.62	0.74	0.68	0.16	0.23	0.14
B41	63001	20.0	7	4	20.0	8	3	2	10	78	0.41	15.0	3	3	0.50	0.53	0.50	0.52	0.29	0.18
B41	63601	17.5	7	4	20.0	8	3	2	14	1	0.57	20.0	4	1	0.80	0.67	0.29	0.57	0.18	0.18
B42	65601	25.0	7	3	25.0	8	3	2	19	79	0.46	25.0	3	2	0.74	0.53	0.18	0.63	0.29	0.00
B44	66801	22.5	7	2	22.5	7	2	2	1	1	0.40	15.0	3	2	0.80	0.40	0.22	0.23	0.20	0.22

FARUKH-BAYAT SMALL BOWL RIMS : HORIZONTAL CURVED BAND

LAYER	ARTIFACT NUMBER	BODY HUE	VAL	CHR	SURFACE HUE	VAL	CHR	RIM FORM	RIM DIAM	RIM ANGLE	BODY THICK	PAINT HUE	VAL	CHR	INT BAND	EXT BAND	1ST SPACE	2ND BAND	2ND SPACE	CURVE WIDTH	CU PR
A27	11201	20.0	8	3	20.0	8	3	2	0	0	0.50	20.0	2	1	1.19	0.59	0.00	0.00	0.00	0.00	0.
A31	30301	20.0	8	3	22.5	8	2	2	16	81	0.50	15.0	3	2	0.61	0.54	0.21	0.28	0.61	0.22	0.
A36	32301	25.0	8	3	25.0	8	2	2	22	80	0.51	15.0	3	1	1.39	0.77	0.19	0.34	0.86	0.32	0.
B39	60701	20.0	7	3	25.0	8	3	2	47	81	0.53	22.5	3	0	1.26	1.34	0.31	0.33	0.91	0.26	0.
B40	61701	20.0	8	3	25.0	8	3	2	31	77	0.68	15.0	3	1	1.45	0.80	0.29	0.28	0.48	0.25	0.
B40	62202	20.0	8	3	20.0	8	3	2	12	90	0.40	112.2	3	2	0.50	0.54	1.94	0.36	0.00	0.81	0.
B41	64501	25.0	7	3	25.0	8	3	2	25	80	0.40	20.0	2	2	0.83	0.40	1.29	0.20	0.00	0.00	0.
B42	64801	17.5	7	2	20.0	8	3	2	23	89	0.60	15.0	3	1	0.15	0.32	0.34	0.29	2.44	0.25	2.
B44	67301	22.5	7	2	25.0	8	2	2	30	75	0.50	12.5	3	0	0.70	0.80	0.33	0.35	0.40	0.16	0.

FARUKH-BAYAT SMALL BOWL RIMS : VERTICAL CURVED LINE

LAYER	ARTIFACT NUMBER	BODY HUE	VAL	CHR	SURFACE HUE	VAL	CHR	RIM FORM	RIM DIAM	RIM ANGLE	BODY THICK	PAINT HUE	VAL	CHR	INT BAND	EXT BAND	OUTER VRTCL	VRTCL SPACE	INNER VRTCL	CURVE SPACE	CU WI
A25	25801	20.0	7	2	20.0	7	2	2	0	0	0.56	12.5	3	2	0.00	0.00	0.31	0.18	0.25	0.36	0.
B40	61501	20.0	7	2	20.0	7	2	2	19	83	0.53	15.0	2	2	0.43	0.30	0.18	0.37	0.24	0.32	0.
B40	62201	20.0	8	3	22.5	8	4	2	0	0	0.56	15.0	3	2	0.00	0.00	0.22	0.20	0.20	0.46	0.
B41	63101	20.0	7	2	20.0	7	2	2	0	0	0.55	7.0	7	4	0.00	0.20	0.39	0.18	0.22	0.25	0.
B41	64701	22.5	8	2	25.0	8	3	2	0	0	0.40	22.5	4	0	0.80	0.00	1.70	0.23	1.60	0.20	0.

FARUKH-BAYAT SMALL BOWL RIMS : VERTICAL LINES

LAYER	ARTIFACT NUMBER	BODY HUE	VAL	CHR	SURFACE HUE	VAL	CHR	RIM FORM	RIM DIAM	RIM ANGLE	BODY THICK	PAINT HUE	VAL	CHR	INT BAND	EXT BAND	VRTCL BAND	VRTCL SPACE
B36	58201	20.0	8	3	20.0	8	4	2	13	78	0.42	5.0	3	4	1.19	0.42	2.09	0.00
B40	63801	25.0	7	2	25.0	7	3	2	16	63	0.24	12.5	2	2	0.58	0.58	0.36	0.25
B41	64002	25.0	8	2	25.0	7	3	2	28	0	0.50	25.0	3	1	0.82	0.63	0.62	0.43
B41	64502	25.0	7	3	25.0	6	4	2	26	78	0.69	25.0	3	1	0.50	0.58	0.96	0.79
B42	64802	20.0	8	2	22.5	8	2	2	20	88	0.43	20.0	4	1	0.53	0.41	0.20	0.00

FARUKH-BAYAT SMALL BOWL RIMS : DOTS

LAYER	ARTIFACT NUMBER	BODY HUE	VAL	CHR	SURFACE HUE	VAL	CHR	RIM FORM	RIM DIAM	RIM ANGLE	BODY THICK	PAINT HUE	VAL	CHR	INT BAND	EXT BAND	BAND-DOTS	DOT PRIOD	DOT WIDTH	DOT HT
A25	25801	20.0	8	3	20.0	8	4	2	15	85	0.42	20.0	5	1	0.35	0.45	1.72	0.37	0.20	0.20
A26	25603	20.0	8	2	20.0	8	2	2	11	75	0.51	10.0	3	2	0.45	0.32	1.23	0.49	0.14	0.14
A26	26101	20.0	8	3	20.0	8	3	2	16	80	0.52	15.0	4	1	0.33	0.32	0.80	0.33	0.19	0.19
A27	26302	20.0	8	3	22.5	8	2	2	20	88	0.24	12.5	3	4	0.39	0.36	1.17	0.33	0.16	0.16
A27	26601	20.0	8	4	20.0	8	4	2	12	88	0.34	10.0	3	4	0.31	0.48	0.95	0.24	0.09	0.09
A28	27001	25.0	8	2	25.0	7	3	2	12	91	0.42	25.0	3	1	0.51	0.36	1.04	0.34	0.13	0.13
A28	27701	17.5	8	4	17.5	8	4	2	12	89	0.43	5.0	4	4	0.36	0.26	1.44	0.33	0.13	0.13
A28	27702	25.0	8	2	17.5	8	2	2	11	79	0.48	10.0	4	1	0.55	0.36	1.36	0.42	0.14	0.14
B40	61501	20.0	8	4	20.0	8	3	2	12	72	0.47	10.0	4	2	0.58	0.48	0.37	0.78	0.08	0.18
B40	62301	20.0	8	2	25.0	8	2	2	13	89	0.37	17.5	5	0	0.60	0.39	0.74	0.31	0.19	0.14
B40	62601	20.0	8	3	22.5	8	2	2	12	85	0.48	12.5	3	2	0.48	0.33	0.27	0.65	0.13	0.28
B40	62602	20.0	8	2	22.5	8	2	2	14	78	0.46	15.0	5	1	0.39	0.42	1.45	0.48	0.12	0.23
B41	63101	20.0	8	3	22.5	8	2	2	27	83	0.54	15.0	4	2	0.67	0.61	1.66	0.41	0.16	0.16
B42	65601	20.0	8	3	20.0	8	3	2	14	81	0.44	17.5	4	0	0.39	0.34	1.44	0.14	0.10	0.21
B42	65602	20.0	8	3	20.0	8	3	2	11	86	0.49	20.0	4	1	0.42	0.36	1.21	0.30	0.14	0.14
B42	65603	20.0	8	3	20.0	8	3	2	10	88	0.53	2C.0	5	1	0.27	0.43	1.17	0.25	0.13	0.13
B43	66201	22.5	8	2	22.5	8	2	2	19	81	0.37	12.5	3	2	0.44	0.45	0.94	0.32	0.21	0.14
B43	66202	22.5	8	2	22.5	8	2	2	18	88	0.34	12.5	3	2	0.36	0.31	0.71	0.26	0.11	0.11
B44	66401	17.5	8	4	17.5	8	4	2	21	87	0.38	5.0	4	1	0.35	0.37	2.16	0.44	0.17	0.17
B44	66801	20.0	8	3	20.0	8	3	2	13	88	0.48	20.0	5	1	0.42	0.36	0.55	0.27	0.11	0.11
B44	66901	20.0	8	3	22.5	8	2	2	20	83	0.74	15.0	3	1	0.35	0.65	0.86	0.43	0.16	0.17
B44	67101	17.5	8	4	20.0	8	4	2	16	83	0.54	15.0	3	1	0.43	0.26	0.60	0.40	0.09	0.24
B44	67301	20.0	8	3	20.0	8	3	2	13	81	0.35	15.0	3	1	0.53	0.29	0.39	0.21	0.09	0.16
B46	69101	20.0	8	2	25.0	7	3	2	16	88	0.31	10.0	4	2	0.16	0.39	0.60	0.39	0.24	0.21
B46	69301	25.0	8	1	25.0	8	1	2	14	84	0.42	22.5	3	0	0.31	0.49	0.64	0.28	0.24	0.24
B46	69301	22.5	8	2	22.5	7	2	2	23	72	0.32	15.0	3	1	2	0.32	0.44	0.66	0.33	0.21	0.21

APPENDIX C

FARUKH-BAYAT SMALL BOWL RIMS : SIGMAS

LAYER	ARTIFACT NUMBER	BODY HUE	VAL	CHR	SURFACE HUE	VAL	CHR	RIM FORM	RIM DIAM	RIM ANGLE	BODY THICK	PAINT HUE	VAL	CHR	INT BAND	EXT BAND	1ST SPCE	2ND BAND	BAND-SIGMA	SIGMA PRIOD	SIGMA LINE
A23	23701	25.0	8	4	25.0	8	3	2	22	95	0.78	20.0	3	1	0.83	0.76	1.74	0.64	0.45	1.57	0.20
A26	26101	20.0	7	3	20.0	8	2	2	12	0	0.40	22.5	4	0	0.14	0.09	1.75	0.00	0.55	0.43	0.16
A30	29701	17.5	7	4	17.5	7	4	2	7	98	0.41	17.5	3	0	0.14	0.07	0.86	1.03	0.05	0.57	0.30
A31	30101	20.0	8	3	22.5	8	2	2	18	84	0.34	12.5	2	2	0.39	0.47	2.19	0.69	0.78	0.70	0.15
B42	64901	20.0	7	4	20.0	8	3	2	0	0	0.27	25.0	3	2	0.57	0.52	0.82	0.38	0.14	0.54	0.16
B44	66901	20.0	7	3	25.0	8	3	2	42	90	0.56	22.5	3	0	0.61	0.75	1.57	0.12	0.26	2.74	0.15

FARUKH-BAYAT SMALL BOWL RIMS : STEPS

LAYER	ARTIFACT NUMBER	BODY HUE	VAL	CHR	SURFACE HUE	VAL	CHR	RIM FORM	RIM DIAM	RIM ANGLE	BODY THICK	PAINT HUE	VAL	CHR	INT BAND	EXT BAND	1ST SPACE	2ND BAND	STEP ANGLE	TRIAN ANGLE
A24	24601	20.0	8	3	25.0	8	2	2	14	82	0.62	112.5	2	4	0.69	0.65	0.65	0.32	35	36
A26	25601	25.0	7	3	25.0	8	3	2	17	81	0.39	117.5	4	0	0.62	0.31	0.50	0.24	34	40
A26	26101	22.5	8	4	22.5	8	4	2	15	86	0.41	112.5	2	2	0.62	0.69	0.89	0.30	16	30
A27	26301	15.0	7	3	20.0	8	3	2	18	94	0.84	112.5	2	4	1.09	0.32	0.50	0.27	0	0
A27	26302	20.0	7	2	25.0	8	2	2	13	92	0.46	115.0	2	2	0.70	0.28	0.18	0.26	30	35
A27	26601	22.5	8	2	22.5	8	2	2	11	96	0.45	122.5	3	0	0.79	0.46	0.34	0.33	29	39
A28	27001	20.0	7	2	25.0	8	2	2	14	82	0.58	120.0	5	3	0.96	0.32	0.30	0.28	0	0
A29	26801	22.5	7	2	25.0	8	2	2	12	90	0.49	115.0	2	2	0.01	0.01	0.41	0.22	22	42
A29	26802	17.5	8	2	20.0	8	1	2	14	92	0.55	115.0	3	1	0.69	0.50	0.23	0.21	21	33
A30	29601	22.5	8	4	25.0	8	3	2	14	88	0.50	117.5	3	0	0.62	0.38	0.19	0.28	15	36
A30	29701	20.0	8	3	25.0	8	3	2	16	90	0.35	115.0	3	1	0.78	0.60	0.32	0.22	32	35
A30	29702	20.0	7	2	20.0	8	3	2	14	82	0.44	120.0	4	1	1.03	0.42	0.05	0.30	15	29
B39	61201	20.0	7	3	20.0	7	3	2	10	95	0.41	120.0	3	1	0.52	0.33	0.51	0.19	45	53
B40	62001	25.0	8	3	25.0	8	2	2	10	84	0.51	125.0	4	4	0.52	0.41	0.50	0.14	25	37
B40	62601	25.0	7	3	25.0	8	2	2	13	92	0.42	115.0	3	1	0.70	0.65	1.43	0.32	31	36
B41	63301	22.5	8	4	25.0	8	2	2	14	84	0.60	7.5	5	2	1.60	0.66	0.63	0.32	30	47
B41	63302	25.0	7	3	22.5	8	3	2	13	78	0.41	120.0	5	3	0.64	0.61	0.43	0.31	30	0
B43	66201	25.0	8	2	25.0	8	2	2	12	87	0.65	125.0	3	1	0.32	0.23	0.83	0.20	52	0
B44	66401	15.0	8	4	17.5	7	4	2	14	79	0.45	112.5	3	6	0.85	0.54	0.21	0.22	17	35
B45	67501	22.5	8	2	25.0	8	2	2	13	86	0.55	115.0	3	2	0.80	0.30	0.42	0.20	24	42
B45	68301	22.5	8	2	22.5	8	2	2	12	76	0.38	122.5	3	0	0.92	0.60	0.42	0.30	19	0
B45	68901	22.5	8	2	22.5	8	2	2	15	78	0.40	122.5	3	0	0.98	0.30	0.29	0.20	0	0

FARUKH-BAYAT SMALL BOWL RIMS : SLASHES

LAYER	ARTIFACT NUMBER	BODY HUE	VAL	CHR	SURFACE HUE	VAL	CHR	RIM FORM	RIM DIAM	RIM ANGLE	BODY THICK	PAINT HUE	VAL	CHR	INT BAND	EXT BAND	1ST SPCE	2ND BAND	BAND-SLASH	SLASH PRIOD	SLASH LINE
A27	26301	17.5	8	3	20.0	8	3	2	23	95	0.67	112.5	2	2	0.75	0.46	0.24	0.39	1.93	0.19	0.28
A28	27201	20.0	8	2	22.5	8	2	2	26	86	0.45	117.5	5	1	1.23	1.01	0.30	0.29	0.59	0.13	0.17
B40	62201	20.0	8	2	20.0	8	3	2	51	85	0.45	117.5	4	1	0.69	0.21	0.25	0.22	1.02	0.35	0.21
B40	78001	15.0	7	6	20.0	8	3	2	17	70	0.36	115.0	3	1	0.73	0.50	0.73	0.42	0.19	0.69	0.12
B42	65201	25.0	8	2	20.0	7	6	2	22	87	0.53	120.0	4	1	1.31	0.47	0.19	0.16	1.20	0.38	0.12
B44	66801	17.5	8	2	20.0	8	3	2	45	84	0.65	112.5	5	1	0.98	0.55	0.25	0.31	1.26	0.35	0.11

FARUKH-BAYAT SMALL BOWL RIMS : DIAMONDS

LAYER	ARTIFACT NUMBER	BODY HUE	VAL	CHR	SURFACE HUE	VAL	CHR	RIM FORM	RIM DIAM	RIM ANGLE	BODY THICK	PAINT HUE	VAL	CHR	INT BAND	EXT BAND	1ST SPACE	2ND BAND	2ND SPACE	3RD BAND
A23	24801	20.0	7	3	22.5	8	2	2	1	1	0.61	15.0	4	1	1.03	0.74	1.55	0.13	0.27	0.57
A26	26101	20.0	7	2	22.5	8	2	2	17	83	0.44	120.0	5	1	0.64	0.50	1.52	0.07	0.13	0.16
A26	26102	15.0	7	3	20.0	8	3	2	22	1	0.01	112.5	5	2	0.70	0.17	0.23	0.14	0.00	0.00
B39	61101	22.5	7	2	25.0	8	2	2	1	1	0.59	122.5	4	0	1.07	0.63	1.21	0.08	0.24	0.36
B40	62601	20.0	8	3	22.5	8	4	2	34	86	0.61	110.0	3	3	0.98	0.61	0.38	0.25	0.19	0.30
B42	65601	22.5	8	2	22.5	8	2	2	18	86	0.45	117.5	5	0	0.87	0.40	0.12	0.19	0.16	0.18
B43	66401	20.0	8	3	20.0	8	2	2	27	87	0.50	115.0	4	1	0.74	0.36	0.42	0.20	0.17	0.24
B44	66402	20.0	7	3	22.5	8	2	2	24	66	0.57	115.0	4	1	0.97	0.50	0.19	0.33	0.24	0.28
B44	66403	22.5	8	2	25.0	8	3	2	27	68	0.83	117.5	5	0	0.99	0.42	1.22	0.31	0.00	0.00
B44	66801	22.5	8	2	25.0	8	2	2	18	89	0.52	122.5	3	0	0.81	0.40	0.27	0.19	0.20	0.19
B44	67101	20.0	7	3	20.0	8	3	2	19	85	0.41	112.5	4	2	0.86	0.42	0.25	0.30	0.17	0.35
B45	67501	17.5	8	4	17.5	8	2	2	23	71	0.60	115.0	4	1	1.18	0.53	0.29	0.29	0.20	0.30
B46	69301	22.5	8	4	25.0	8	3	2	31	80	0.70	112.5	3	2	0.95	0.46	0.11	0.30	0.13	0.23

FARUKH-BAYAT LARGE FLAT BASES

LAYER	ARTIFACT NUMBER	BODY HUE	VAL	CHR	SURFACE HUE	VAL	CHR	BASE ANGLE	BASE THICK	SIDE THICK
A23	23401	25.0	8	3	25.0	8	3	41	1.00	1.62
A23	23402	25.0	8	3	25.0	8	3	48	0.89	0.00
A23	23701	20.0	8	3	25.0	8	3	51	1.99	1.62
A23	23702	17.5	8	4	22.5	8	2	45	1.20	0.84
A23	24801	15.0	7	4	20.0	8	4	45	0.00	0.78
A23	24802	12.5	6	4	20.0	8	3	32	0.68	0.70
A23	24803	17.5	7	2	20.0	7	3	65	1.27	1.06
A23	24804	15.0	6	4	17.5	8	2	71	0.91	0.68
A23	24805	12.5	6	4	17.5	8	4	45	0.82	0.90
A23	24806	17.5	8	3	17.5	8	3	68	1.25	0.91
A25	25801	20.0	8	3	20.0	8	3	41	1.07	0.97
A26	25601	20.0	8	3	22.5	8	2	73	1.13	0.80
A26	25602	17.5	7	4	20.0	8	3	57	0.70	1.17
A26	25603	20.0	8	3	20.0	7	3	54	1.02	0.69
A26	26101	20.0	8	3	25.0	8	3	50	1.62	1.54
A26	26102	20.0	8	3	22.5	8	3	35	0.80	0.80
A27	26301	20.0	8	4	20.0	8	3	37	0.00	1.00
A27	26302	25.0	8	3	22.5	8	2	43	1.20	1.58
A27	26303	17.5	8	4	20.0	8	3	41	1.34	1.60
A27	26304	17.5	8	2	25.0	8	3	57	1.18	1.21
A27	26401	25.0	8	3	25.0	8	3	54	0.42	1.00
A27	26402	12.5	8	2	20.0	8	3	42	1.30	0.50
A27	26801	15.0	8	3	22.5	8	2	46	1.26	1.10
A28	27001	15.0	7	4	12.5	6	4	45	1.08	1.06
A28	27401	22.0	8	2	22.5	7	4	77	0.96	1.06
A29	28501	20.0	7	4	20.0	8	3	45	1.00	1.54
A30	29101	15.0	8	3	17.5	8	3	56	0.93	1.25
A30	29701	20.0	8	2	20.0	8	2	44	1.05	1.15
A35	31701	25.0	7	4	17.5	8	4	52	0.00	1.45
A35	31901	20.0	8	4	17.5	8	4	48	0.98	0.00
A36	32501	17.5	7	2	20.0	7	2	58	1.00	1.28
B36	58701	15.0	8	3	22.5	8	2	46	1.10	1.14
B37	59501	17.5	8	4	15.0	8	4	45	0.62	0.78
B38	60101	25.0	7	4	22.5	8	3	46	0.00	0.00
B39	60501	22.5	7	2	22.5	8	2	59	1.10	0.00
B39	60901	17.5	8	2	20.0	8	2	53	1.12	0.88
B39	60902	20.0	8	2	25.0	8	3	33	1.08	0.80
B39	61101	17.5	8	2	17.5	8	2	60	0.91	1.07
B39	61301	17.5	8	3	12.5	8	2	53	1.65	1.37
B40	61701	12.5	6	4	20.0	8	4	54	1.12	1.29
B40	62401	20.0	7	2	20.0	8	3	68	1.08	0.97
B40	62601	20.0	8	3	15.0	8	3	48	1.23	1.65
B40	62602	20.0	7	3	20.0	8	3	62	0.98	1.31
B40	62701	17.5	7	4	17.5	7	4	53	1.35	1.62
B40	62901	17.5	8	4	22.5	8	4	61	1.70	2.13
B41	63101	12.5	6	4	12.5	6	4	36	1.05	0.00
B41	63601	22.5	8	2	20.0	8	3	44	0.60	0.75
B41	64001	22.5	7	2	22.5	8	2	44	0.72	0.60
B42	65001	17.5	8	2	22.5	8	2	0	0.00	1.49
B42	65002	20.0	8	3	20.0	8	2	73	1.40	1.00
B42	65003	12.5	7	2	12.5	8	2	55	1.23	0.90
B42	65004	12.5	6	3	17.5	9	2	50	1.50	0.95
B42	65005	25.0	8	3	25.0	8	3	53	1.55	0.56
B42	65006	17.5	7	2	20.0	8	3	46	0.94	0.78
B42	65201	17.5	7	2	20.0	8	2	40	0.58	0.69
B42	65401	25.0	8	3	25.0	8	3	55	1.40	0.88
B42	65402	20.0	8	3	20.0	8	3	33	1.20	0.00
B42	66201	17.5	7	4	20.0	8	3	61	0.88	1.43
B43	65903	22.5	8	3	22.5	8	3	41	1.20	0.66
B44	66501	25.0	8	3	25.0	8	3	55	1.20	0.70
B44	67301	25.0	8	3	25.0	8	3	52	0.89	0.95
B44	67302	12.5	5	4	20.0	8	3	0	1.60	1.14
B44	67303	15.0	7	2	15.0	7	2	53	1.22	1.14
B45	67401	20.0	8	3	22.5	8	3	90	1.02	0.90
B45	67901	17.5	7	4	25.0	8	3	47	1.17	0.90
B45	67902	25.0	8	3	25.0	8	3	45	0.99	0.86
B46	69101	20.0	8	3	22.5	8	3	45	1.16	0.75
B46	69102	20.0	7	3	20.0	7	2	66	2.26	2.62

APPENDIX C

FARUKH-BAYAT HIGH NECK JAR RIMS

LAYER	ARTIFACT NUMBER	BODY HUE	VAL	CHR	SURFACE HUE	VAL	CHR	LIP FORM	NECK DIAM	NECK ANGLE	NECK THICK	NECK HT	SHOUL THICK	PAINT HUE	VAL	CHR	INT BAND	EXT BAND
B36	58301	15.0	7	4	12.5	6	4	2	13	115	0.85	1.82	0.95	0.0	0	0	0.00	0.00
B37	59701	20.0	8	2	25.0	8	2	2	38	68	1.03	1.05	0.84	0.0	0	0	0.00	0.00
B39	61301	25.0	8	3	25.0	8	3	2	0	0	0.00	0.00	0.70	0.0	0	0	0.00	0.00
B24	62401	17.5	7	4	17.5	8	4	2	0	0	0.00	0.47	1.05	0.0	0	0	0.00	0.00
A23	24801	12.5	6	6	20.0	8	3	2	20	54	0.86	4.80	1.82	10.0	3	4	0.10	5.20
A25	25801	15.0	7	4	20.0	8	3	2	7	35	0.55	1.20	1.05	17.5	3	2	0.58	2.10
A26	25601	15.0	6	4	20.0	8	2	1	21	65	1.80	3.40	2.70	20.0	3	1	0.00	4.10
A27	26401	20.0	7	2	22.5	8	2	3	70	70	1.05	4.32	0.00	15.0	3	2	0.13	4.32
A27	26402	12.5	6	4	12.5	6	4	1	12	65	1.96	2.60	1.10	7.5	4	6	0.52	3.20
A27	26404	12.5	6	4	12.5	6	4	2	11	119	0.90	2.70	0.00	0.0	0	0	0.00	0.00
A28	27001	22.5	7	2	20.0	7	2	2	11	90	0.40	0.80	0.82	20.0	3	1	0.28	0.87
A33	31001	20.0	7	2	20.0	7	3	0	13	60	5.26	4.95	0.00	15.0	3	1	0.00	4.95
A34	31201	20.0	7	2	22.5	8	2	2	0	0	0.00	0.00	0.98	17.5	3	2	0.00	0.00
B38	60201	17.5	7	3	15.0	7	3	1	26	70	1.53	4.50	0.00	10.0	3	3	2.00	4.50
B39	60701	15.0	7	4	17.5	7	4	2	10	70	0.50	2.50	0.00	10.0	6	3	0.19	2.50
B40	61501	22.5	8	3	25.0	8	3	2	8	40	0.60	0.70	0.60	20.0	4	1	0.31	1.34
B40	62001	22.5	8	4	25.0	8	4	2	9	60	0.69	1.50	0.90	20.0	3	2	0.55	2.30
B40	62002	20.0	7	2	22.5	8	3	2	36	125	1.66	3.50	1.96	20.0	3	1	1.12	7.42
B40	62401	17.5	7	4	17.5	8	4	3	13	60	1.20	3.90	0.00	10.0	4	3	0.23	0.00
B40	62901	20.0	8	2	22.5	8	3	3	73	45	1.50	3.20	0.00	22.5	4	1	0.26	3.60
B43	66201	17.5	7	4	15.0	7	3	2	0	0	0.94	0.00	1.10	15.0	3	2	0.00	0.00
B44	66801	20.0	7	2	22.5	7	2	1	24	55	1.50	2.70	1.40	17.5	5	2	0.40	2.95
B44	67101	25.0	7	4	17.5	7	4	3	11	70	1.05	3.95	1.10	7.5	3	0	0.18	4.65
B44	67301	20.0	8	2	22.5	8	2	2	28	65	1.08	3.20	1.34	17.5	4	2	0.00	3.81
B44	67302	20.0	7	2	22.5	8	2	2	7	75	0.58	1.35	0.00	15.0	3	1	0.00	1.55
B45	68101	20.0	7	2	20.0	7	3	2	20	60	2.12	4.50	0.00	20.0	3	1	0.00	5.08
B46	69101	15.0	6	4	20.0	8	3	2	13	75	0.68	1.90	0.90	17.5	3	2	0.52	1.78
B46	69102	20.0	7	2	22.5	8	2	2	13	60	0.72	3.40	0.00	20.0	5	3	0.69	3.42
B46	69301	25.0	6	3	25.0	7	2	1	19	75	1.43	3.20	1.70	15.0	3	1	0.62	3.95
B46	69302	15.0	7	3	15.0	7	3	1	38	90	2.53	3.35	0.00	17.5	3	2	0.00	3.45
B46	69303	20.0	7	2	20.0	8	2	2	11	0	0.82	4.33	0.00	15.0	3	1	0.00	7.43
B46	69304	20.0	7	3	25.0	8	3	2	12	70	0.70	5.35	0.00	20.0	3	1	0.60	5.35
B47	69401	17.5	6	4	20.0	7	2	2	15	0	0.79	4.38	0.00	15.0	3	2	0.00	7.44
A24	24101	12.5	6	6	15.0	8	3	3	12	60	0.79	3.85	0.96	10.0	3	6	0.00	0.52
A27	26403	12.5	6	6	12.0	9	2	0	8	70	0.94	4.20	1.94	10.0	3	4	0.00	0.70
B39	61301	12.5	5	4	22.5	5	4	0	10	60	0.64	2.15	0.75	0.0	0	0	0.00	0.00
B43	66202	20.0	7	2	20.0	8	2	2	9	65	0.80	3.75	0.00	10.0	3	4	0.63	0.59
B44	66802	20.0	8	4	20.0	8	3	3	12	50	0.85	2.89	0.93	0.0	0	0	0.00	0.00

FARUKH-BAYAT BASIN RIMS

LAYER	ARTIFACT NUMBER	BODY HUE	VAL	CHR	SURFACE HUE	VAL	CHR	RIM FORM	RIM DIAM	RIM ANGLE	RIM THICK	BODY THICK	PAINT HUE	VAL	CHR	INT BAND	EXT BAND
A23	24301	20.0	8	3	20.0	8	3	1	60	73	1.60	1.60	0.0			0.00	0.00
A23	24801	20.0	8	4	20.0	8	3	1	33	86	0.72	0.01	0.0			0.00	0.00
A23	24802	20.0	8	3	20.0	8	3	8	61	79	0.11	1.06	0.0			0.00	0.00
A24	24601	20.0	5	1	22.5	8	2	4	52	77	1.05	1.08	0.0			0.00	0.00
A24	24602	12.5	6	4	20.0	8	3	3	27	77	1.00	0.00	0.0			0.00	0.00
A24	24603	17.5	7	4	22.5	8	2	2	45	58	1.05	1.14	0.0			0.00	0.00
A25	25801	22.5	7	2	25.0	8	2	1	38	70	1.35	0.01	0.0			0.00	0.00
A25	25802	22.5	8	2	22.5	8	2	2	42	64	1.14	1.30	0.0			0.00	0.00
A26	25201	17.5	7	2	20.0	8	2	3	53	77	1.34	0.94	0.0			0.00	0.00
A26	25202	20.0	8	3	20.0	8	2	1	26	82	0.82	0.94	0.0			0.00	0.00
A26	25203	20.0	7	3	25.0	7	3	1	50	87	0.87	1.08	0.0			0.00	0.00
A26	25401	20.0	7	1	17.5	6	4	2	54	81	1.33	1.35	0.0			0.00	0.00
A26	25402	15.0	7	3	22.5	8	2	8	24	73	0.59	0.93	0.0			0.00	0.00
A26	25601	17.5	6	4	20.0	7	2	1	47	61	1.13	1.00	0.0			0.00	0.00
A26	25602	22.5	8	2	22.5	8	2	1	1	65	1.08	1.12	0.0			0.00	0.00
A26	25603	20.0	8	2	20.0	8	2	1	52	88	0.83	0.95	0.0			0.00	0.00
A26	26101	17.5	7	2	22.5	8	2	1	30	63	0.68	0.85	0.0			0.00	0.00
A26	26102	20.0	8	3	25.0	7	3	2	40	68	0.90	1.03	0.0			0.00	0.00
A26	26103	20.0	7	3	22.5	8	2	2	49	84	1.53	1.20	0.0			0.00	0.00
A26	26104	20.0	8	2	22.5	8	2	2	58	63	1.50	1.15	0.0			0.00	0.00

FARUKH-BAYAT BASIN RIMS

LAYER	ARTIFACT NUMBER	BODY HUE	VAL	CHR	SURFACE HUE	VAL	CHR	RIM FORM	RIM DIAM	RIM ANGLE	RIM THICK	BODY THICK	PAINT HUE	VAL	CHR	INT BAND	EXT BAND
A27	26301	15.0	8	2	22.5	8	2	2	49	62	1.29	1.36	0.0			0.00	0.00
A27	26302	22.5	7	2	22.5	8	2	1	64	80	1.22	1.15	0.0			0.00	0.00
A27	26303	17.5	7	2	15.0	6	3	1	1	83	0.70	0.93	0.0			0.00	0.00
A27	26401	25.0	8	3	22.5	8	2	2	31	74	1.67	0.01	0.0			0.00	0.00
A27	26402	12.5	6	4	20.0	7	3	2	1	83	1.44	1.18	0.0			0.00	0.00
A27	26403	22.5	8	2	22.5	8	2	2	49	64	1.69	1.38	0.0			0.00	0.00
A27	26404	20.0	8	2	25.0	7	3	1	39	66	0.89	0.88	0.0			0.00	0.00
A27	26405	20.0	8	3	22.5	8	2	2	50	65	1.51	1.23	0.0			0.00	0.00
A27	26406	20.0	8	2	22.5	8	2	1	43	65	1.52	0.01	0.0			0.00	0.00
A27	26407	25.0	8	2	25.0	8	3	1	53	61	1.66	1.62	0.0			0.00	0.00
A27	26408	12.5	6	4	22.5	8	2	2	51	64	0.97	1.10	0.0			0.00	0.00
A28	27701	25.0	7	3	25.0	7	3	2	45	69	1.42	0.01	0.0			0.00	0.00
A28	27702	20.0	8	2	22.5	8	2	2	46	70	1.13	0.01	0.0			0.00	0.00
A28	27703	22.5	8	2	22.5	8	2	1	47	85	0.98	0.01	0.0			0.00	0.00
A28	27704	20.0	7	3	22.5	8	2	2	46	62	1.14	1.10	0.0			0.00	0.00
A28	27705	22.5	8	2	22.5	8	2	1	51	88	0.94	0.01	0.0			0.00	0.00
A29	28501	20.0	7	3	20.0	7	3	1	58	66	1.40	1.43	0.0			0.00	0.00
A29	28502	25.0	8	3	17.5	8	2	1	45	67	1.52	1.45	0.0			0.00	0.00
A29	28503	15.0	7	3	17.5	8	2	4	53	75	0.70	1.02	0.0			0.00	0.00
A29	28504	20.0	7	3	22.5	8	2	1	1	57	1.44	1.48	0.0			0.00	0.00
A29	28901	25.0	8	2	22.5	8	2	1	51	100	1.64	1.60	0.0			0.00	0.00
A29	29301	22.5	7	2	22.5	8	2	2	42	66	0.70	1.00	0.0			0.00	0.00
A30	29701	15.0	7	2	20.0	8	2	1	54	79	1.88	1.60	0.0			0.00	0.00
A30	29901	20.0	8	2	20.0	8	2	4	47	78	0.67	0.71	0.0			0.00	0.00
A32	30501	20.0	8	2	25.0	8	2	6	39	71	0.84	1.00	0.0			0.00	0.00
B36	58701	15.0	6	6	15.0	7	4	2	32	1	1.22	1.10	0.0			0.00	0.00
B36	59201	20.0	7	2	22.5	7	2	1	1	58	0.70	0.97	0.0			0.00	0.00
B36	59202	12.5	6	4	15.0	7	3	1	1	82	1.07	1.05	0.0			0.00	0.00
B36	59203	20.0	7	3	20.0	7	2	1	47	79	1.71	1.74	0.0			0.00	0.00
B38	60101	20.0	8	3	22.5	8	2	1	1	52	1.40	1.37	0.0			0.00	0.00
B38	60102	25.0	8	2	25.0	8	2	2	60	75	2.02	1.22	0.0			0.00	0.00
B38	60103	17.5	7	2	15.0	6	4	1	48	62	1.20	1.48	0.0			0.00	0.00
B39	60501	20.0	7	2	20.0	8	2	2	1	65	0.94	0.01	0.0			0.00	0.00
B39	60502	20.0	7	3	17.5	7	4	3	27	72	1.04	1.00	0.0			0.00	0.00
B39	60601	20.0	7	2	20.0	8	3	1	47	79	0.81	0.01	0.0			0.00	0.00
B39	60701	20.0	8	3	22.5	8	2	2	58	70	1.55	1.40	0.0			0.00	0.00
B39	60902	17.5	7	2	20.0	7	2	3	32	57	1.13	0.95	0.0			0.00	0.00
B39	61201	22.5	7	2	20.0	8	2	1	14	55	0.51	0.87	0.0			0.00	0.00
B39	61301	17.5	7	2	20.0	8	3	3	58	79	0.80	0.93	0.0			0.00	0.00
B39	61302	22.5	8	2	20.0	8	3	1	19	77	0.78	0.86	0.0			0.00	0.00
B40	62001	15.0	7	4	20.0	8	2	1	25	1	1.26	1.33	0.0			0.00	0.00
B40	62002	20.0	8	4	20.0	8	3	4	36	65	1.07	1.26	0.0			0.00	0.00
B40	62601	20.0	8	3	20.0	7	4	1	50	67	1.56	1.57	0.0			0.00	0.00
B40	62602	12.5	6	4	20.0	7	3	1	20	65	0.74	0.90	0.0			0.00	0.00
B40	62603	17.5	8	3	22.5	8	2	4	29	76	1.11	0.97	0.0			0.00	0.00
B40	62604	22.5	8	2	22.5	8	4	1	28	74	0.80	0.84	0.0			0.00	0.00
B40	62605	17.5	6	4	25.0	8	3	2	63	68	2.41	1.92	0.0			0.00	0.00
B40	62606	17.5	8	2	15.0	8	2	1	49	1	0.60	0.59	0.0			0.00	0.00
B40	62607	12.5	6	4	12.5	6	4	2	47	92	1.64	1.49	0.0			0.00	0.00
B40	62608	15.0	7	4	20.0	8	3	1	21	57	0.66	0.87	0.0			0.00	0.00
B40	62609	17.5	7	4	20.0	7	3	1	24	72	0.80	0.96	0.0			0.00	0.00
B40	62610	17.5	7	4	20.0	8	3	1	23	65	0.64	0.64	0.0			0.00	0.00
B40	62611	22.5	6	4	17.5	8	4	3	55	65	1.52	1.58	0.0			0.00	0.00
B41	63001	17.5	7	3	20.0	8	2	1	1	53	1.15	0.01	0.0			0.00	0.00
B41	63601	22.5	6	3	22.5	6	4	1	51	53	1.05	0.01	0.0			0.00	0.00
B41	63602	20.0	8	3	22.5	8	2	2	43	77	1.27	1.20	0.0			0.00	0.00
B41	63603	20.0	8	3	20.0	8	3	2	37	81	1.25	1.17	0.0			0.00	0.00
B41	64501	20.0	7	2	20.0	7	4	3	28	55	0.99	1.11	0.0			0.00	0.00
B42	64901	20.0	8	3	25.0	8	1	1	41	65	1.54	1.64	0.0			0.00	0.00
B42	64902	20.0	8	3	22.5	8	2	1	51	70	1.44	1.55	0.0			0.00	0.00
B42	64903	17.5	7	4	20.0	8	3	5	48	58	1.03	1.19	0.0			0.00	0.00
B42	65001	25.0	8	3	25.0	8	3	1	33	58	1.12	1.42	0.0			0.00	0.00
B42	65401	20.0	8	4	22.5	8	4	1	43	48	1.40	1.56	0.0			0.00	0.00
B42	65402	22.5	8	3	25.0	8	2	1	44	64	1.45	1.14	0.0			0.00	0.00
B42	65403	20.0	8	3	25.0	8	4	1	49	72	1.57	1.22	0.0			0.00	0.00
B42	65404	22.5	8	2	22.5	8	2	2	31	70	1.12	1.07	0.0			0.00	0.00
B42	65405	25.0	8	3	25.0	8	3	2	52	74	2.52	1.07	0.0			0.00	0.00
B42	65406	20.0	8	2	25.0	8	3	6	1	55	1.08	1.48	0.0			0.00	0.00
B42	65407	20.0	8	3	25.0	8	3	1	40	73	1.55	1.27	0.0			0.00	0.00
B42	65408	20.0	8	3	25.0	8	3	8	1	55	1.61	1.31	0.0			0.00	0.00
B42	65409	25.0	8	3	25.0	8	3	6	1	57	1.09	1.13	0.0			0.00	0.00
B42	65410	22.5	8	2	22.5	8	2	2	48	78	1.50	1.13	0.0			0.00	0.00
B42	65801	17.5	8	2	20.0	8	3	1	33	68	0.74	0.99	0.0			0.00	0.00
B42	65802	20.0	7	3	22.5	8	2	2	45	63	1.25	1.17	0.0			0.00	0.00
B42	65803	20.0	8	2	25.0	8	1	1	43	72	1.04	1.14	0.0			0.00	0.00
B42	68701	22.5	8	4	25.0	8	2	1	30	70	0.98	0.89	0.0			0.00	0.00

APPENDIX C

FARUKH-BAYAT BASIN RIMS

LAYER	ARTIFACT NUMBER	BODY HUE	VAL	CHR	SURFACE HUE	VAL	CHR	RIM FORM	RIM DIAM	RIM ANGLE	RIM THICK	BODY THICK	PAINT HUE	VAL	CHR	INT BAND	EXT BAND
B43	66001	22.5	8	2	25.0	8	3	1	40	84	0.87	0.90	0.0			0.00	0.00
B44	66301	20.0	7	4	22.5	8	4	1	55	72	1.72	0.43	0.0			0.00	0.00
B44	66401	20.0	8	2	22.5	8	0	1	49	60	1.04	1.12	0.0			0.00	0.00
B44	66402	25.0	7	4	15.0	7	3	2	51	65	1.36	1.21	0.0			0.00	0.00
B44	66403	17.5	7	4	15.0	8	3	1	52	62	1.78	1.46	0.0			0.00	0.00
B44	66404	25.0	8	3	25.0	8	3	2	1	76	1.76	0.68	0.0			0.00	0.00
B44	66405	15.0	7	4	20.0	8	3	1	41	61	1.06	1.01	0.0			0.00	0.00
B44	66406	25.0	8	3	25.0	8	3	1	56	62	1.68	1.49	0.0			0.00	0.00
B44	66407	15.0	7	4	22.5	8	2	3	29	67	1.12	1.13	0.0			0.00	0.00
B44	66408	15.0	7	4	17.5	7	4	2	42	67	1.43	1.32	0.0			0.00	0.00
B44	66409	20.0	7	3	17.5	8	4	1	76	65	1.70	1.38	0.0			0.00	0.00
B44	66601	12.5	8	2	25.0	8	2	2	31	62	1.07	0.74	0.0			0.00	0.00
B44	66801	17.5	7	2	20.0	8	3	1	1	71	1.48	1.39	0.0			0.00	0.00
B44	66803	22.5	8	2	22.5	8	2	1	44	81	1.05	1.05	0.0			0.00	0.00
B44	66804	15.0	5	6	17.5	6	3	1	55	70	1.91	1.62	0.0			0.00	0.00
B44	66805	17.5	7	3	22.5	8	2	1	40	71	1.47	1.39	0.0			0.00	0.00
B44	66806	20.0	7	2	22.5	8	2	1	47	55	1.34	1.21	0.0			0.00	0.00
B44	66807	25.0	7	3	25.0	8	3	8	52	60	2.45	1.43	0.0			0.00	0.00
B44	66808	20.0	7	4	15.0	7	4	8	37	65	1.43	1.18	0.0			0.00	0.00
B44	66901	15.0	7	4	15.0	7	4	8	45	71	1.71	1.33	0.0			0.00	0.00
B44	67101	25.0	8	3	25.0	8	2	1	55	56	1.03	0.97	0.0			0.00	0.00
B44	67102	22.5	8	2	25.0	8	3	1	40	67	0.90	0.91	0.0			0.00	0.00
B44	67301	25.0	8	3	22.5	7	2	1	52	71	1.38	1.20	0.0			0.00	0.00
B44	67302	25.0	8	3	20.0	7	2	1	58	72	1.25	1.29	0.0			0.00	0.00
B44	67303	25.0	8	3	25.0	8	3	2	52	63	1.13	0.87	0.0			0.00	0.00
B44	67304	25.0	8	3	25.0	8	3	2	40	60	1.17	0.78	0.0			0.00	0.00
B44	67305	25.0	6	4	25.0	7	3	2	58	73	1.39	1.33	0.0			0.00	0.00
B45	67701	20.0	7	1	20.0	7	1	1	47	83	2.06	0.01	0.0			0.00	0.00
B45	68301	17.5	7	4	25.0	8	3	2	51	82	1.43	1.33	0.0			0.00	0.00
B45	68302	25.0	8	3	25.0	8	2	2	53	57	0.98	0.81	0.0			0.00	0.00
B45	68901	25.0	8	4	25.0	7	3	2	33	57	1.16	0.70	0.0			0.00	0.00
B45	68902	25.0	8	3	25.0	8	3	2	20	72	1.04	0.79	0.0			0.00	0.00
B46	69101	15.0	7	4	17.5	8	2	1	36	69	0.79	0.90	0.0			0.00	0.00
B46	69102	15.0	7	5	15.0	7	5	1	28	73	0.78	0.93	0.0			0.00	0.00
B46	69103	15.0	7	3	17.5	8	3	1	39	84	0.91	0.86	0.0			0.00	0.00
B46	69301	25.0	8	2	25.0	8	2	2	45	73	1.12	1.18	0.0			0.00	0.00
B46	69302	22.5	7	2	22.5	8	2	1	57	81	0.99	1.19	0.0			0.00	0.00
B46	69303	15.0	5	4	17.5	6	3	1	47	83	0.74	0.85	0.0			0.00	0.00
B46	69304	25.0	8	2	20.0	8	3	1	52	61	1.27	0.01	0.0			0.00	0.00
B46	69305	25.0	8	3	20.0	8	4	1	76	76	1.21	0.01	0.0			0.00	0.00
B46	69306	22.5	8	2	22.5	8	2	4	49	60	0.96	1.05	0.0			0.00	0.00
A25	25801	20.0	7	3	25.0	8	3	2	25	74	0.91	0.71	25.0	4	1	0.44	0.46
A33	30801	20.0	8	2	22.5	8	2	5	62	70	0.86	0.82	20.0	3	4	0.80	0.89
B40	62001	20.0	8	4	22.5	8	2	5	44	80	1.01	1.24	20.0	3	4	0.00	0.00
B41	63001	20.0	7	3	20.0	8	3	2	1	75	1.37	1.08	15.0	3	2	0.00	0.00
B42	64901	12.5	6	4	1.0	4	6	1	49	60	1.19	1.17	12.5	5	6	0.00	0.00
B45	67901	20.0	8	2	25.0	8	3	6	67	89	1.09	1.13	17.5	3	2	1.48	1.70

Table C2: Attributes of Uruk, Jemdet Nasr, and Early Dynastic Ceramics

SARGARAB WARE : ROUND LIP BOWL RIMS

LAYER	ARTIFACT NUMBER	BODY HUE	VAL	CHR	SURFACE HUE	VAL	CHR	LIP FORM	RIM DIAM	RIM ANGLE	BODY THICK	RIM THICK	PAINT HUE	VAL	CHR
B31	49302	17.5	8	4	12.5	8	2	2	28	49	0.71	0.74	0.0	0	0
B32	50101	17.5	7	4	10.0	6	6	2	21	45	0.59	0.35	0.0	0	0
B33	53501	25.0	8	3	25.0	8	3	2	19	60	0.51	0.63	0.0	0	0
B33	53504	20.0	8	3	15.0	6	5	2	26	80	0.40	0.45	0.0	0	0
B33	53901	25.0	8	3	25.0	8	3	2	18	70	0.50	0.46	0.0	0	0
B35	56701	25.0	8	3	25.0	8	2	2	15	75	0.31	0.41	0.0	0	0
B35	57801	12.5	6	6	20.0	7	4	2	12	55	0.46	0.39	0.0	0	0

SARGARAB WARE : INCURVED BOWL RIMS

LAYER	ARTIFACT NUMBER	BODY HUE	VAL	CHR	SURFACE HUE	VAL	CHR	LIP FORM	RIM DIAM	RIM ANGLE	BODY THICK	RIM THICK	PAINT HUE	VAL	CHR
A21	121101	20.0	7	4	25.0	8	2	2	11	106	0.62	0.40	0.0	0	0
A20	83301	22.5	6	2	22.5	8	2	2	18	105	0.66	0.59	0.0	0	0
A22	121301	22.5	7	2	22.5	8	2	2	16	111	0.71	0.54	0.0	0	0
B30	46701	20.0	8	3	15.0	8	4	2	17	84	0.82	0.72	0.0	0	0
B32	50301	20.0	4	0	20.0	8	4	2	14	55	0.57	0.43	12.5	6	4
B35	56701	15.0	6	6	22.5	8	3	2	14	99	0.85	0.60	0.0	0	0
B36	58301	12.5	7	6	15.0	7	6	2	15	114	0.70	0.60	12.5	5	6
B39	61101	15.0	7	6	22.5	8	2	2	18	120	0.60	0.64	10.0	5	5

SARGARAB WARE: INCURVED BEADED RIM BOWL RIMS WITH HATCHED STRIP

LAYER	ARTIFACT NUMBER	BODY HUE	VAL	CHR	SURFACE HUE	VAL	CHR	LIP FORM	RIM DIAM	RIM ANGLE	RM TP ANGLE	BODY THICK	RIM THICK	RIM HT	PAINT HUE	VAL	CHR
A21	21701	22.5	6	6	25.0	8	2	6	43	100	85	1.11	1.68	130	0.0	0	0
A22	121304	22.5	7	2	25.0	8	4	6	55	125	120	1.05	1.90	121	0.0	0	0
A22	121305	20.0	5	6	12.5	6	6	6	18	75	105	0.65	1.50	20	12.5	6	6
B32	49701	17.5	7	3	22.5	8	2	6	51	120	125	1.26	2.49	162	10.0	4	3
B33	53503	20.0	4	2	15.0	6	4	6	48	130	110	0.81	2.27	208	10.0	5	5
B33	53504	22.5	7	3	25.0	8	3	6	41	125	120	0.72	1.90	138	0.0	0	0
B33	53901	12.5	5	6	22.5	8	3	6	40	90	135	1.04	1.57	140	10.0	4	4
B34	55301	15.0	7	5	25.0	8	2	6	36	90	110	0.75	1.52	145	0.0	0	0
B36	58701	22.5	8	2	22.5	8	2	2	13	125	0	0.59	0.55	0	15.0	7	4
B39	60901	10.0	5	1	12.5	6	6	1	48	75	90	1.00	1.30	64	0.0	0	0

SARAGRAB WARE : HATCHED STRIPS FROM INCURVED BEADED RIM BOWLS

LAYER	ARTIFACT NUMBER	BODY HUE	VAL	CHR	SURFACE HUE	VAL	CHR	THICK SHERD	WIDTH STRIP	HT STRIP	WIDTH HATCH	PRICC HATCH	ANGLE HATCH
A21	21701	22.5	6	6	25.0	8	2	1.02	0.14	0.48	0.45	1.05	38
A21	23401	15.0	6	5	25.0	8	2	0.73	1.15	0.20	1.17	1.12	85
A22	121306	22.5	7	2	25.0	8	4	0.91	0.90	0.25	0.48	1.05	32
B32	49701	17.5	7	3	22.5	8	2	1.16	1.40	0.44	0.80	2.35	37
B33	53503	20.0	4	2	15.0	6	4	0.97	1.35	0.45	0.50	1.50	42
B33	53504	22.5	7	3	25.0	8	3	0.81	0.88	0.27	0.56	0.70	58
B33	53901	12.5	5	6	22.5	8	3	1.11	0.70	0.28	0.75	1.85	32
B34	55301	15.0	7	5	25.0	9	2	0.75	0.95	0.29	0.55	1.00	38
B36	58701	22.5	8	2	22.5	8	2	0.50	0.65	0.17	0.20	0.51	46
B39	60901	10.0	5	1	12.5	6	6	1.02	1.10	0.31	1.36	1.45	95

SARGARAB WARE : LARGE BOWLS WITH THICKENED RIMS

LAYER	ARTIFACT NUMBER	BODY HUE	VAL	CHR	SURFACE HUE	VAL	CHR	LIP FORM	RIM DIAM	RIM ANGLE	RM TP ANGLE	BODY THICK	RIM THICK	RIM HT	PAINT HUE	VAL	CHR
A20	83301	20.0	4	2	15.0	6	4	2	48	50	0	0.97	1.10	0	0.0	0	0
A20	83302	20.0	7	2	17.5	7	3	6	49	60	0	1.40	1.96	185	0.0	0	0
B33	52601	20.0	3	1	17.5	5	4	6	44	55	0	1.40	2.05	205	0.0	0	0
B34	54901	17.5	5	2	12.5	6	4	6	57	55	160	1.02	1.59	159	12.5	4	4
B34	55301	20.0	5	2	15.0	6	4	6	72	45	160	1.41	2.20	220	10.0	5	4
B34	56901	17.5	6	1	15.0	5	6	2	55	45	0	0.76	1.00	0	7.5	4	4
B34	56902	20.0	3	1	17.5	6	4	6	60	35	175	1.45	3.38	228	10.0	4	4
B34	56903	20.0	4	1	15.0	5	4	6	48	40	170	1.60	2.15	215	12.5	5	6

APPENDIX C

SARGARAB WARE : FLAT LIP BOWL RIMS

LAYER	ARTIFACT NUMBER	BODY HUE	VAL	CHR	SURFACE HUE	VAL	CHR	LIP FORM	RIM DIAM	RIM ANGLE	RM TP ANGLE	BODY THICK	RIM THICK	PAINT HUE	VAL	CHR
A21	21701	25.0	8	2	25.0	8	2	1	41	75	100	1.20	2.12	0.0	0	0
B31	49301	15.0	6	4	17.5	7	4	1	30	85	90	0.60	0.75	7.5	5	4
B32	49501	12.5	6	6	15.0	6	6	1	26	85	95	0.68	0.80	10.0	4	4
B33	53502	17.5	7	4	15.0	7	4	1	36	90	95	0.61	0.90	7.5	5	4
B34	54901	20.0	6	4	17.5	7	4	1	12	95	105	0.44	0.62	10.0	4	4
B34	55901	20.0	8	3	22.5	8	2	1	8	125	90	0.45	0.75	0.0	0	0
B35	56301	15.0	7	4	12.5	6	4	1	32	80	95	0.60	0.68	7.5	5	5

SARGARAB WARE : THICKENED ROUND LIP JARS

LAYER	ARTIFACT NUMBER	BODY HUE	VAL	CHR	SURFACE HUE	VAL	CHR	LIP FORM	NECK DIAM	RIM DIAM	RIM ANGLE	NECK THICK	RIM THICK	NECK HT	PAINT HUE	VAL	CHR
A22	121305	20.0	6	3	20.0	7	3	2	13	16	43	0.82	0.90	2.40	12.5	30	40
A22	121306	25.0	8	3	22.5	8	3	2	8	11	35	0.59	0.62	3.52	0.0	0	0
B33	51901	20.0	5	2	15.0	5	4	2	11	14	60	0.75	0.99	1.62	10.0	50	60
B33	53502	20.0	5	2	15.0	6	4	2	15	18	50	0.89	1.11	1.99	10.0	50	60
B33	53503	17.5	4	0	15.0	5	6	2	13	17	50	1.05	1.40	1.85	10.0	50	40
B34	55301	15.0	6	6	10.0	5	6	2	11	14	45	0.62	0.77	1.75	10.0	50	40
B34	55992	20.0	5	2	17.5	6	4	2	11	14	45	0.77	0.91	1.69	10.0	50	40
B35	56901	15.0	5	6	15.0	5	6	2	9	12	35	0.70	0.80	2.42	10.0	40	50
B35	57101	17.5	6	5	15.0	6	6	2	13	15	45	0.59	0.87	1.93	10.0	40	40

URUK WARE, COARSE BODY : THICKENED ROUND LIP JAR RIMS

LAYER	ARTIFACT NUMBER	BODY HUE	VAL	CHR	SURFACE HUE	VAL	CHR	LIP FORM	NECK DIAM	RIM DIAM	RIM ANGLE	NECK THICK	RIM THICK	NECK HT	PAINT HUE	VAL	CHR
A21	21201	20.0	7	3	15.0	7	4	2	14	18	60	1.10	0.96	1.41	0.0	0	0
B32	48101	17.5	6	4	12.5	6	6	2	13	16	30	0.80	0.80	1.49	0.0	0	0
B32	49701	17.5	7	4	15.0	7	4	2	11	15	35	1.52	0.90	1.60	0.0	0	0
B32	50301	20.0	7	3	20.0	8	3	2	6	7	75	0.63	0.50	1.69	0.0	0	0
B33	51401	20.0	7	3	12.5	6	4	2	14	16	45	0.83	0.80	1.70	0.0	0	0
B33	51902	22.5	8	3	22.5	8	3	2	12	14	75	0.73	0.75	1.17	0.0	0	0
B33	52601	17.5	6	4	22.5	6	4	2	12	14	50	0.95	0.89	1.54	0.0	0	0
B33	53101	20.0	8	4	22.5	8	4	2	13	16	50	0.97	1.02	1.97	0.0	0	0
B33	53505	15.0	6	4	15.0	7	6	2	14	17	65	0.92	0.96	1.70	0.0	0	0
B33	53901	15.0	7	4	15.0	7	4	2	9	12	50	0.70	0.78	1.39	7.5	50	40
B34	55302	20.0	5	2	15.0	6	4	2	15	20	65	1.20	1.64	2.80	0.0	0	0
B34	55303	17.5	7	3	15.0	7	4	2	11	15	55	1.00	0.92	1.75	0.0	0	0
B34	55304	20.0	7	2	15.0	6	3	2	10	13	45	0.76	0.76	1.50	10.0	50	40
B35	56701	17.5	7	5	20.0	6	4	2	6	8	65	0.71	0.58	1.00	0.0	0	0
B35	57301	20.0	6	4	17.5	7	4	2	14	18	30	0.90	0.74	2.53	12.5	55	60
B35	57302	20.0	6	4	17.5	7	4	2	9	12	40	0.70	0.76	0.95	10.0	50	50
B35	57303	20.0	6	2	17.5	7	4	2	10	13	30	0.77	0.61	1.54	17.5	45	20

URUK WARE , COARSE BODY : THICKENED RIM JAR RIMS WITH LIP FLATTENING

LAYER	ARTIFACT NUMBER	BODY HUE	VAL	CHR	SURFACE HUE	VAL	CHR	LIP FORM	NECK DIAM	RIM DIAM	RIM ANGLE	RM TP ANGLE	NECK THICK	RIM THICK	NECK HT	RIM HT	PAINT HUE	VAL	CHR
A20	20401	20.0	8	1	15.0	7	3	1	14	16	70	80	1.06	1.30	1.02	0.58	0.0	0	0
B27	40601	20.0	6	2	12.5	6	4	1	12	16	85	85	1.25	2.05	1.06	0.40	0.0	0	0
B33	51901	25.0	8	3	25.0	8	3	1	10	12	67	83	0.77	0.90	1.79	0.71	0.0	0	0

SARGARAB WARE : FLARED ROUND LIP JAR RIMS

LAYER	ARTIFACT NUMBER	BODY HUE	VAL	CHR	SURFACE HUE	VAL	CHR	LIP FORM	NECK DIAM	RIM DIAM	RIM ANGLE	NECK THICK	RIM THICK	NECK HT	PAINT HUE	VAL	CHR
A22	121307	25.0	8	3	25.0	8	2	2	8	11	35	0.00	0.56	3.78	0.0	0	0
B30	48402	15.0	7	4	15.0	8	4	1	8	10	51	0.60	0.52	2.61	0.0	0	0
B31	48102	17.5	8	4	20.0	8	2	2	7	10	43	0.51	0.39	2.47	0.0	0	0
B32	50801	20.0	5	2	17.5	6	5	2	10	11	55	0.51	0.31	1.75	10.0	40	40
B33	53302	20.0	7	3	25.0	8	2	2	9	13	50	0.65	0.75	2.68	0.0	0	0
B33	53504	15.0	7	5	25.0	8	3	2	9	12	50	0.51	0.63	2.70	0.0	0	0
B35	57802	22.5	8	2	22.5	8	2	2	6	8	65	0.55	0.48	1.24	0.0	0	0
B36	59202	17.5	7	6	20.0	8	3	2	7	10	50	0.56	0.73	2.95	0.0	0	0

SARGARAB WARE : FINE JAR RIMS

LAYER	ARTIFACT NUMBER	BODY HUE	BODY VAL	BODY CHR	SURFACE HUE	SURFACE VAL	SURFACE CHR	LIP FORM	NECK DIAM	RIM DIAM	RIM ANGLE	RIM THICK	NECK THICK	RIM HT	PAINT HUE	PAINT VAL	PAINT CHR
A20	77701	22.5	8	2	15.0	7	4	2	8	12	41	0.51	0.55	1.46	0.0	0	0
A21	20701	12.5	6	6	22.5	7	2	2	11	13	66	0.42	0.34	0.65	0.0	0	0
A21	20702	20.0	6	3	20.0	7	2	2	13	15	50	0.40	0.41	0.61	0.0	0	0
A21	20901	15.0	7	4	20.0	8	2	2	14	16	57	0.35	0.34	0.85	0.0	0	0
A21	21201	20.0	7	1	20.0	8	2	2	9	9	53	0.40	0.34	0.60	0.0	0	0
A20	83301	12.5	5	6	20.0	8	3	2	9	11	60	0.45	0.43	0.69	0.0	0	0
A22	121301	25.0	7	3	25.0	7	3	2	9	10	70	0.50	0.31	0.82	0.0	0	0
A22	121302	20.0	8	3	22.5	8	2	2	9	10	50	0.50	0.41	0.68	0.0	0	0
A22	121303	25.0	8	2	25.0	8	2	2	9	10	66	0.45	0.30	0.59	0.0	0	0
A22	121304	25.0	8	1	25.0	8	1	2	9	11	50	0.54	0.44	0.85	0.0	0	0
A22	121305	17.5	6	2	25.0	8	1	2	9	11	40	0.50	0.40	0.86	0.0	0	0
B32	49704	20.0	8	3	22.5	8	2	2	10	12	48	0.41	0.30	0.67	0.0	0	0
B33	51401	15.0	7	6	22.5	8	4	2	10	11	40	0.41	0.50	0.50	12.5	40	60
B33	52401	15.0	6	6	15.0	6	6	2	12	13	60	0.41	0.40	0.69	7.5	45	50
B34	53301	17.5	7	4	25.0	8	2	2	8	11	45	0.69	0.70	3.72	0.0	0	0
B33	53501	15.0	6	4	20.0	7	3	2	10	11	60	0.61	0.40	0.60	0.0	0	0
B34	54601	25.0	8	4	25.0	8	3	2	9	11	47	0.48	0.43	0.52	0.0	0	0
B34	56106	12.5	6	6	22.5	8	4	2	10	11	60	0.54	0.33	0.47	0.0	0	0
B34	55901	25.0	8	3	25.0	8	2	2	9	10	65	0.49	0.38	0.57	0.0	0	0
B36	58701	17.5	6	3	24.0	7	2	2	10	11	75	0.60	0.32	0.96	0.0	0	0
B36	58702	12.5	6	8	20.0	8	3	2	8	9	70	0.36	0.35	0.38	0.0	0	0
B36	58703	15.0	6	4	25.0	8	2	2	11	12	75	0.40	0.31	0.00	0.0	0	0
B36	59201	12.5	6	4	22.5	8	2	2	8	9	55	0.48	0.32	0.46	0.0	0	0

SARGARAB WARE : OTHER ROUND LIP JAR RIMS

LAYER	ARTIFACT NUMBER	BODY HUE	BODY VAL	BODY CHR	SURFACE HUE	SURFACE VAL	SURFACE CHR	LIP FORM	NECK DIAM	RIM DIAM	RIM ANGLE	RIM THICK	NECK THICK	RIM HT	PAINT HUE	PAINT VAL	PAINT CHR
A20	77701	20.0	6	4	17.5	7	4	2	10	11	95	0.70	0.60	2.10	0.0	0	0
A22	121307	12.5	6	3	12.5	6	4	2	13	17	55	0.97	1.03	2.60	12.5	30	40
B31	48101	17.5	7	4	20.0	8	2	1	4	5	49	0.50	0.37	1.46	0.0	0	0
B33	52201	17.5	7	4	17.5	7	4	2	3	4	65	0.24	0.22	0.40	12.5	50	50
B37	59701	15.0	7	6	15.0	7	4	2	8	10	30	0.35	0.31	0.89	10.0	50	40

SARGARAB WARE : FLARED EXPANDED LIP JAR RIMS

LAYER	ARTIFACT NUMBER	BODY HUE	BODY VAL	BODY CHR	SURFACE HUE	SURFACE VAL	SURFACE CHR	LIP FORM	NECK DIAM	RIM DIAM	RIM ANGLE	RM TP ANGLE	NECK THICK	RIM THICK	NECK HT	RIM HT	PAINT HUE	PAINT VAL	PAINT CHR
A20	83301	12.5	6	6	20.0	8	2	1	11	14	50	170	0.00	1.20	1.72	1.20	0.0	0	0
A20	83302	10.0	6	6	22.5	8	3	1	11	14	40	175	0.75	1.20	2.15	1.20	0.0	0	0
A21	20901	12.5	6	6	22.5	8	3	1	10	13	45	165	0.84	1.22	2.00	0.00	0.0	0	0
B26	41401	20.0	8	3	20.0	8	2	1	16	19	55	165	0.73	0.97	2.48	0.95	0.0	0	0
B26	41402	20.0	8	4	22.5	8	2	1	11	14	60	150	0.00	0.92	2.20	0.88	0.0	0	0
B30	46202	20.0	7	3	22.5	8	2	1	17	20	65	160	1.12	1.40	1.75	1.40	0.0	0	0
B32	58701	20.0	7	5	22.5	8	4	1	10	13	70	115	0.62	0.83	2.66	0.64	0.0	0	0
B33	52401	20.0	7	4	25.0	7	2	1	5	19	49	160	0.91	1.08	3.20	1.08	0.0	0	0
B33	53502	20.0	8	3	25.0	8	2	1	16	20	65	159	0.79	1.77	2.65	1.77	0.0	0	0
B33	53503	15.0	7	5	25.0	8	3	1	12	16	37	152	0.87	0.96	3.04	0.96	0.0	0	0
B33	53901	25.0	7	2	25.0	8	3	1	11	15	22	188	0.74	1.00	3.50	1.00	0.0	0	0
B33	54101	12.5	6	4	22.5	8	2	1	10	13	25	192	0.76	1.12	3.05	1.12	0.0	0	0
B34	55701	20.0	7	3	25.0	8	3	1	10	14	21	138	0.89	0.97	3.09	0.93	0.0	0	0
B33	78601	22.5	8	3	25.0	8	2	1	6	9	45	165	0.41	0.48	1.95	0.45	0.0	0	0
B33	78602	25.0	8	2	25.0	8	2	1	10	14	30	175	0.80	1.24	3.00	1.24	0.0	0	0
B34	56102	20.0	6	3	22.5	7	2	1	7	10	42	185	0.65	0.85	2.22	0.85	0.0	0	0
B35	57301	15.0	6	4	22.5	8	3	1	10	14	24	182	1.12	0.84	2.95	0.84	0.0	0	0
B35	57801	20.0	8	3	22.5	8	2	1	9	12	20	189	0.52	0.85	1.20	0.40	0.0	0	0
B36	58301	17.5	7	4	22.5	8	2	1	12	15	32	187	0.65	0.80	3.25	0.80	0.0	0	0
B36	58302	12.5	5	8	22.5	8	3	1	11	14	38	140	0.68	1.03	3.60	1.03	0.0	0	0

SARGARAB WARE : FLARED EXPANDED LIP JAR RIMS, RED SLIP

LAYER	ARTIFACT NUMBER	BODY HUE	BODY VAL	BODY CHR	SURFACE HUE	SURFACE VAL	SURFACE CHR	LIP FORM	NECK DIAM	RIM DIAM	RIM ANGLE	RM TP ANGLE	NECK THICK	RIM THICK	NECK HT	RIM HT	PAINT HUE	PAINT VAL	PAINT CHR
A20	20401	15.0	4	0	15.0	5	5	1	17	22	35	165	1.10	1.15	2.32	1.11	10.0	5	4
B32	49501	20.0	6	2	12.0	6	4	1	12	15	30	170	0.79	0.81	3.61	0.82	7.5	5	4
B32	49701	17.5	5	1	12.5	5	5	1	13	10	25	180	0.72	0.92	2.05	0.92	7.5	5	4
B32	50801	17.5	6	4	15.0	6	6	1	12	15	85	95	0.74	1.25	1.75	0.64	10.0	5	3
B33	53301	18.0	7	3	10.0	6	5	1	14	18	45	175	0.71	1.10	2.40	1.10	7.5	4	5
B33	53502	20.0	4	1	17.5	6	4	1	7	9	60	195	0.63	0.53	1.10	0.45	10.0	4	4
B34	55702	20.0	7	2	15.0	6	4	1	13	15	75	105	0.62	0.70	1.87	0.37	7.5	5	4

APPENDIX C

SARGARAB WARE : HIGH EXPANDED BAND RIM JAR RIMS

LAYER	ARTIFACT NUMBER	BODY HUE	BODY VAL	BODY CHR	SURFACE HUE	SURFACE VAL	SURFACE CHR	LIP FORM	NECK DIAM	RIM DIAM	RIM ANGLE	RM TP ANGLE	NECK THICK	RIM THICK	NECK HT	RIM HT	PAINT HUE	PAINT VAL	PAINT CHR
A21	23401	12.5	6	6	22.5	8	4	1	21	25	45	170	1.00	2.00	2.19	1.89	0.0	0	0
A21	23402	15.0	6	4	25.0	8	2	1	11	15	25	185	0.93	1.40	1.42	1.40	0.0	0	0

SARGARAB WARE : OTHER FLAT LIP JAR RIMS

LAYER	ARTIFACT NUMBER	BODY HUE	BODY VAL	BODY CHR	SURFACE HUE	SURFACE VAL	SURFACE CHR	LIP FORM	NECK DIAM	RIM DIAM	RIM ANGLE	RM TP ANGLE	NECK THICK	RIM THICK	NECK HT	RIM HT	PAINT HUE	PAINT VAL	PAINT CHR
B35	56701	12.5	7	7	12.5	7	8	1	11	14	45	187	0.60	0.77	2.04	0.96	0.0	0	0

SARGARAB WARE : NOSE LUGS

LAYER	ARTIFACT NUMBER	BODY HUE	BODY VAL	BODY CHR	SURFACE HUE	SURFACE VAL	SURFACE CHR	SHLDR THICK	LNGTH NOSE	WIDTH NOSE	HT NOSE	LNGTH HOLE	WIDTH HOLE
A20	82701	20.0	8	4	22.5	8	2	0.74	2.90	1.40	0.82	0.40	0.35
A22	121101	25.0	7	1	25.0	8	2	0.90	3.49	1.65	1.30	0.31	0.33
B36	58701	17.5	7	4	22.5	8	2	0.38	2.50	1.45	0.80	0.32	0.30
B33	51401	25.0	6	2	25.0	8	3	1.12	4.87	2.16	1.39	0.56	0.45

SARGARAB WARE : CROSS-HATCH INCISED BANDS

LAYER	ARTIFACT NUMBER	BODY HUE	BODY VAL	BODY CHR	SURFACE HUE	SURFACE VAL	SURFACE CHR	SHLDR THICK	BAND WIDTH	LINE WIDTH	SPACE WIDTH	ANGLE INTRS
A20	82701	20.0	7	2	20.0	8	2	0.64	1.67	0.17	0.22	89
A21	23001	20.0	8	2	20.0	8	3	0.64	1.85	0.18	0.20	82
B36	58701	15.0	6	5	22.5	8	2	0.80	0.00	0.12	0.85	110

SARGARAB WARE : STRAIGHT SPOUTS

LAYER	ARTIFACT NUMBER	BODY HUE	BODY VAL	BODY CHR	SURFACE HUE	SURFACE VAL	SURFACE CHR	IN DM HOLE	IN DM BASE	EX DM BASE	IN DM END	EX DM END	LNGTH
A21	82701	15.0	8	2	20.0	8	4	2.20	2.00	3.70	0.00	0.00	0.00
B33	53501	15.0	8	4	22.5	8	4	0.94	0.00	0.00	0.62	1.10	4.12
B42	64901	12.5	6	8	12.5	6	8	2.53	2.76	4.34	2.30	3.15	5.04
A22	121101	12.5	6	7	15.0	8	3	2.90	2.90	3.60	1.30	1.95	4.10
B33	78601	22.5	8	3	25.0	8	2	2.70	2.75	3.95	1.80	1.20	6.70
B36	59001	20.0	6	4	12.5	6	6	3.20	3.20	4.70	2.20	3.10	5.20
B42	64901	15.0	7	5	22.5	8	2	3.00	3.10	4.00	3.00	3.20	2.25

SARGARAB WARE : FLAT BASES

LAYER	ARTIFACT NUMBER	BODY HUE	BODY VAL	BODY CHR	SURFACE HUE	SURFACE VAL	SURFACE CHR	BASE DIAM	SIDE ANGLE	BASE THICK	SIDE THICK
A21	21701	25.0	8	2	25.0	8	2	14	45	0.95	0.95
A22	121301	25.0	4	0	20.0	7	2	14	45	0.84	1.00
A22	121302	20.0	4	1	25.0	6	1	14	30	0.61	0.97
A22	121303	15.0	5	4	25.0	8	3	70	29	0.67	0.58
B33	51401	25.0	8	3	25.0	8	3	7	48	0.68	0.50
B33	52601	20.0	7	3	17.5	7	3	11	40	0.70	0.90
B33	53101	17.5	6	2	22.5	7	3	6	40	0.77	0.81
B33	53501	17.5	6	4	25.0	8	3	70	39	0.57	0.38
B33	78601	25.0	8	2	25.0	8	2	12	50	1.47	0.63
B33	78602	22.5	8	3	25.0	8	2	5	45	0.40	0.65
B35	56301	25.0	7	3	25.0	7	3	60	46	0.43	0.60
B35	56701	15.0	7	4	17.5	7	3	8	40	0.46	0.33
B35	57301	17.5	6	6	15.0	6	6	85	36	0.88	0.73
B36	58301	20.0	5	1	20.0	8	3	60	46	0.82	0.68
B36	58703	17.5	6	3	24.0	7	2	4	45	0.95	0.75
B36	59001	17.5	7	4	20.0	8	3	70	38	0.61	0.58

URUK WARE : ROUND LIP BOWL RIMS

LAYER	ARTIFACT NUMBER	BODY HUE	VAL	CHR	SURFACE HUE	VAL	CHR	LIP FORM	RIM DIAM	RIM ANGLE	BODY THICK	RIM THICK	PAINT HUE	VAL	CHR
A2	07501	20.0	7	2	20.0	8	1	2	18	95	0.66	0.70	0.0	0	0
A5	08404	17.5	8	2	17.5	8	2	2	15	74	0.70	0.75	0.0	0	0
A6	09401	20.0	7	4	20.0	7	4	2	9	79	0.75	0.65	0.0	0	0
A6	09402	15.0	7	4	22.5	8	2	2	12	68	0.49	0.60	0.0	0	0
A6	09403	20.0	8	2	20.0	5	2	2	11	93	0.72	0.76	0.0	0	0
A7	10301	27.5	8	3	20.0	8	2	1	19	66	0.63	0.70	0.0	0	0
A7	10604	17.5	8	3	17.5	8	2	2	12	69	0.63	0.63	0.0	0	0
A6	10801	20.0	8	4	20.0	8	4	2	14	79	0.82	0.78	0.0	0	0
A7	11801	20.0	8	3	20.0	8	3	1	22	96	0.82	0.91	0.0	0	0
A9	12701	20.0	8	3	20.0	8	3	2	27	95	1.02	0.76	0.0	0	0
A11	13501	20.0	8	3	20.0	8	3	2	10	85	0.49	0.42	0.0	0	0
A12	15601	17.5	8	3	17.5	8	3	1	32	50	0.95	0.82	0.0	0	0
A13	14801	20.0	8	3	17.5	7	3	2	25	100	0.78	0.81	0.0	0	0
A14	16801	20.0	8	3	20.0	8	3	2	9	96	0.68	0.48	0.0	0	0
A15	17601	20.0	8	3	20.0	8	3	2	14	62	0.68	0.57	0.0	0	0
A16	17801	22.5	7	2	22.5	8	2	2	19	95	0.64	0.65	0.0	0	0
A16	17804	20.0	8	3	20.0	8	3	2	9	58	0.50	0.42	0.0	0	0
B18	81706	17.5	7	4	17.5	8	2	2	25	82	0.53	0.58	0.0	0	0
B18	81708	20.0	8	3	20.0	8	3	2	18	87	0.68	0.68	0.0	0	0
A19	18901	20.0	8	2	20.0	8	2	2	12	78	0.40	0.44	0.0	0	0
A21	20701	20.0	8	2	20.0	8	2	2	21	83	0.66	0.76	0.0	0	0
A21	20901	20.0	8	3	17.5	7	3	2	18	78	0.97	0.95	0.0	0	0
A21	21201	20.0	8	3	20.0	8	4	2	27	86	0.67	0.50	0.0	0	0
B20	34002	17.5	7	4	20.0	8	3	2	16	70	0.58	0.59	0.0	0	0
B20	34010	15.0	8	4	15.0	8	4	2	8	102	0.46	0.54	0.0	0	0
B21	35001	22.5	8	4	18.0	8	3	2	14	92	0.61	0.66	0.0	0	0
B22	35901	20.0	7	3	20.0	8	3	2	24	40	0.68	0.62	0.0	0	0
B22	35902	20.0	8	3	22.5	8	2	2	15	70	0.74	0.76	0.0	0	0
B23	36501	20.0	8	3	20.0	8	3	2	23	53	0.58	0.52	0.0	0	0
B23	37001	20.0	8	3	20.0	8	3	2	11	71	0.66	0.47	0.0	0	0
B23	37003	15.0	6	4	17.5	8	3	2	13	61	0.56	0.50	0.0	0	0
B24	37502	17.5	8	2	15.0	8	4	2	11	78	0.59	0.47	0.0	0	0
B24	38701	17.5	7	4	17.5	8	4	2	15	77	0.75	0.52	0.0	0	0
B28	43701	17.5	8	2	12.5	8	2	2	26	71	0.63	0.58	0.0	0	0
B29	45201	17.5	8	2	20.0	8	3	2	26	73	0.66	0.66	0.0	0	0
B29	45202	20.0	7	2	20.0	7	2	2	23	81	0.65	0.74	0.0	0	0
B29	45501	15.0	7	4	12.5	8	2	2	24	81	0.80	0.95	0.0	0	0
B29	45502	20.0	8	3	15.0	7	4	2	32	69	0.87	0.80	0.0	0	0
B29	45503	15.0	6	4	20.0	8	3	2	23	72	0.90	0.88	0.0	0	0
B29	45701	12.5	8	2	12.5	8	2	1	46	95	0.76	0.71	0.0	0	0
B29	45702	20.0	8	2	22.5	8	2	2	26	86	0.62	0.70	0.0	0	0
B30	45901	20.0	8	3	20.0	8	3	2	25	82	0.71	0.88	0.0	0	0
B30	46101	20.0	8	3	20.0	8	3	1	34	89	0.75	0.68	0.0	0	0
B30	46202	17.5	8	4	17.5	8	4	2	22	72	0.75	0.87	0.0	0	0
B30	46204	20.0	8	3	20.0	8	3	2	48	41	0.63	0.59	0.0	0	0
B31	47101	12.5	8	2	12.5	8	2	2	19	63	0.80	0.78	0.0	0	0
B31	47601	20.0	8	3	12.5	8	2	2	28	70	0.75	0.86	0.0	0	0
B31	48101	17.5	8	3	20.0	8	3	2	26	82	0.84	0.64	0.0	0	0
B30	48401	20.0	8	3	17.5	7	3	2	19	72	0.64	0.71	0.0	0	0
B30	48402	20.0	7	3	20.0	8	3	2	18	60	0.59	0.69	0.0	0	0
B32	48901	17.5	7	3	17.5	8	2	2	33	59	0.86	0.77	0.0	0	0
B32	49101	17.5	7	3	17.5	7	3	2	22	61	0.74	0.70	0.0	0	0
B31	49301	1.0	4	1	15.0	6	3	2	52	61	1.02	0.92	0.0	0	0
B32	49501	15.0	7	4	20.0	8	3	2	16	76	0.70	0.70	0.0	0	0
B32	49502	15.0	7	4	20.0	8	3	2	18	75	0.70	0.70	0.0	0	0
B32	49701	17.5	8	2	17.5	7	3	2	21	82	0.87	0.78	0.0	0	0
A20	77701	20.0	8	2	20.0	8	2	2	28	76	0.63	0.71	0.0	0	0
A20	83007	20.0	8	2	20.0	8	2	2	21	88	0.74	0.59	0.0	0	0
A20	83301	22.5	8	2	22.5	8	2	2	20	94	0.77	0.67	0.0	0	0
B30	121901	20.0	6	2	20.0	8	3	2	36	45	0.82	0.70	0.0	0	0
B30	121902	20.0	6	3	22.5	8	2	2	45	45	0.77	0.55	0.0	0	0

APPENDIX C

URUK WARE : CONICAL CUP RIMS

LAYER	ARTIFACT NUMBER	BODY HUE	VAL	CHR	SURFACE HUE	VAL	CHR	LIP FORM	RIM DIAM	RIM ANGLE	BODY THICK	RIM THICK	PAINT HUE	VAL	CHR
A2	07501	20.0	8	3	20.0	8	3	2	14	70	0.47	0.57	0.0	0	0
A2	07502	17.5	8	2	20.0	7	3	2	12	68	0.59	0.60	0.0	0	0
A2	07503	17.5	8	3	20.0	8	3	2	15	58	0.45	0.57	0.0	0	0
A3	07701	20.0	8	2	20.0	8	3	2	18	71	0.47	0.64	0.0	0	0
A3	07704	22.5	8	2	22.5	8	2	2	18	63	0.61	0.60	0.0	0	0
A3	07705	17.5	8	2	20.0	8	3	2	11	78	0.49	0.63	0.0	0	0
A3	07706	15.0	8	4	20.0	8	2	2	12	73	0.39	0.39	0.0	0	0
A3	07901	17.5	8	3	17.5	8	3	2	14	70	0.53	0.50	0.0	0	0
A3	07902	20.0	8	3	20.0	8	2	2	15	62	0.53	0.58	0.0	0	0
A5	08101	20.0	8	3	17.5	8	3	2	14	64	0.48	0.48	0.0	0	0
A5	08402	20.0	8	3	17.5	8	2	2	15	89	0.43	0.54	0.0	0	0
A5	08403	15.0	8	3	15.0	6	4	2	14	75	0.36	0.36	0.0	0	0
A6	09401	17.5	8	3	17.5	8	3	2	15	61	0.60	0.53	0.0	0	0
A6	09404	20.0	8	2	20.0	8	2	2	13	69	0.42	0.57	0.0	0	0
A6	09405	17.5	8	3	22.5	8	2	2	18	71	0.64	0.67	0.0	0	0
A6	09406	17.5	7	3	17.5	7	3	2	15	74	0.58	0.55	0.0	0	0
A6	09901	20.0	8	3	20.0	8	3	2	12	78	0.39	0.34	0.0	0	0
A7	10302	22.5	8	2	22.5	8	2	2	13	71	0.36	0.50	0.0	0	0
A7	10601	20.0	8	2	20.0	8	2	2	15	68	0.55	0.65	0.0	0	0
A7	10602	15.0	8	3	17.5	8	3	2	12	59	0.62	0.38	0.0	0	0
A7	10605	20.0	8	3	20.0	8	3	2	19	59	0.48	0.62	0.0	0	0
A7	10606	20.0	8	3	17.5	8	3	2	14	66	0.54	0.57	0.0	0	0
A7	10607	20.0	8	3	17.5	8	3	1	14	82	0.54	0.60	0.0	0	0
A7	10608	25.0	8	2	25.0	8	3	2	15	59	0.46	0.65	0.0	0	0
A7	10611	20.0	8	3	22.5	8	2	2	15	75	0.55	0.65	0.0	0	0
A7	10612	17.5	7	2	17.5	7	2	2	16	68	0.37	0.38	0.0	0	0
A7	10613	25.0	8	2	22.5	8	2	2	17	64	0.42	0.67	0.0	0	0
A6	10801	20.0	8	2	20.0	8	2	2	12	78	0.52	0.55	0.0	0	0
A6	10802	20.0	8	2	20.0	8	3	2	10	82	0.42	0.45	0.0	0	0
A6	10803	20.0	8	3	22.5	8	2	2	22	68	0.66	0.72	0.0	0	0
A6	11801	20.0	8	2	22.5	8	2	2	16	73	0.47	0.48	0.0	0	0
A7	12001	20.0	8	3	17.5	8	2	2	14	78	0.59	0.56	0.0	0	0
A8	12401	20.0	8	2	17.5	8	2	2	15	63	0.63	0.60	0.0	0	0
A9	12702	20.0	8	2	20.0	8	3	2	11	63	0.39	0.38	0.0	0	0
A9	12703	17.5	7	3	20.0	8	3	2	13	71	0.45	0.42	0.0	0	0
A9	12705	20.0	8	2	20.0	8	2	2	15	92	0.46	0.43	0.0	0	0
A9	12706	20.0	8	2	20.0	8	3	2	10	69	0.32	0.29	0.0	0	0
A9	12708	17.5	7	3	17.5	8	3	2	12	75	0.29	0.27	0.0	0	0
A9	12709	20.0	8	2	22.5	8	2	2	10	72	0.31	0.29	0.0	0	0
A9	12710	20.0	9	3	22.5	8	2	2	12	73	0.46	0.48	0.0	0	0
A9	13107	20.0	9	3	20.0	8	3	2	10	97	0.44	0.35	0.0	0	0
A9	13109	22.5	8	2	22.5	8	2	2	15	85	0.30	0.30	0.0	0	0
A11	13301	20.0	8	2	22.5	8	2	2	12	71	0.39	0.45	0.0	0	0
A11	13302	17.5	8	3	17.5	8	3	2	23	74	0.44	0.39	0.0	0	0
A11	13303	22.5	8	2	22.5	8	2	2	11	57	0.51	0.42	0.0	0	0
A11	13304	20.0	8	3	20.0	8	3	2	10	89	0.49	0.44	0.0	0	0
A11	13306	20.0	8	3	20.0	8	2	2	11	56	0.42	0.37	0.0	0	0
A11	13307	20.0	8	3	20.0	8	3	2	10	94	0.56	0.45	0.0	0	0
A11	13308	20.0	8	3	20.0	8	2	2	10	75	0.37	0.35	0.0	0	0
A11	13309	15.0	7	4	17.5	8	3	2	11	68	0.51	0.40	0.0	0	0
A11	13310	17.5	8	3	20.0	8	2	2	13	81	0.57	0.46	0.0	0	0
A11	13311	20.0	8	3	17.5	7	3	2	23	59	0.66	0.51	0.0	0	0
A11	13312	17.5	9	3	17.5	8	3	2	14	70	0.42	0.40	0.0	0	0
A11	13314	20.0	8	3	20.0	8	3	2	13	65	0.37	0.35	0.0	0	0
A11	13315	22.5	8	2	22.5	8	2	2	11	74	0.32	0.25	0.0	0	0
A11	13316	22.5	8	2	22.5	8	2	2	9	71	0.32	0.38	0.0	0	0
A11	13317	20.0	8	2	20.0	8	3	2	7	78	0.40	0.35	0.0	0	0
A11	13319	17.5	8	3	20.0	8	2	2	8	73	0.42	0.36	0.0	0	0
A12	122101	15.0	6	5	15.0	7	6	2	19	55	0.60	0.60	0.0	0	0
A13	14801	20.0	7	3	20.0	7	3	2	18	71	0.62	0.52	0.0	0	0
A9	12712	20.0	8	3	20.0	8	3	2	11	74	0.30	0.25	0.0	0	0
A9	12713	22.5	8	2	22.5	8	2	2	15	61	0.37	0.45	0.0	0	0
A9	12715	20.0	8	3	20.0	8	3	2	12	72	0.39	0.32	0.0	0	0
A9	12716	20.0	8	3	22.5	8	3	2	13	107	0.31	0.32	0.0	0	0
A9	13101	20.0	8	3	20.0	8	3	2	10	85	0.50	0.37	0.0	0	0
A9	13102	22.5	8	2	25.0	8	3	2	12	103	0.48	0.47	0.0	0	0
A9	13103	20.0	9	3	17.5	8	3	2	18	57	0.46	0.38	0.0	0	0
A9	13104	22.5	8	2	22.5	8	2	2	11	102	0.52	0.45	0.0	0	0
A9	13105	20.0	9	2	22.5	8	2	2	13	96	0.53	0.45	0.0	0	0
A9	13106	17.5	8	3	20.0	8	3	2	22	62	0.44	0.41	0.0	0	0

URUK WARE : CONICAL CUP RIMS

LAYER	ARTIFACT NUMBER	BODY HUE	VAL	CHR	SURFACE HUE	VAL	CHR	LIP FORM	RIM DIAM	RIM ANGLE	BODY THICK	RIM THICK	PAINT HUE	VAL	CHR
A13	14802	17.5	7	3	17.5	7	2	2	8	74	0.49	0.42	0.0	0	0
A13	15002	17.5	8	3	20.0	8	2	2	12	71	0.48	0.40	0.0	0	0
A13	15004	22.5	8	2	22.5	8	2	2	16	67	0.52	0.56	0.0	0	0
A13	15005	15.0	6	4	15.0	7	4	2	19	69	0.58	0.61	0.0	0	0
A13	15006	20.0	8	2	20.0	8	2	2	10	69	0.27	0.21	0.0	0	0
A13	15007	17.5	8	3	17.5	8	2	2	11	84	0.37	0.40	0.0	0	0
A13	15301	25.0	8	2	22.5	8	2	2	11	74	0.52	0.42	0.0	0	0
A13	15801	22.5	8	2	22.5	8	2	2	14	98	0.40	0.30	0.0	0	0
A13	16001	17.5	8	2	20.0	8	2	2	7	79	0.26	0.25	0.0	0	0
A13	16201	25.0	8	1	22.5	8	2	2	13	64	0.61	0.40	0.0	0	0
A13	16203	17.5	8	3	17.5	8	2	2	10	76	0.38	0.38	0.0	0	0
A16	17801	20.0	8	3	20.0	8	4	2	10	75	0.59	0.45	0.0	0	0
A17	18201	20.0	8	2	22.5	8	2	2	13	68	0.37	0.42	0.0	0	0
A17	18501	20.0	8	3	22.5	8	2	2	12	97	0.49	0.40	0.0	0	0
A18	19601	22.5	8	2	22.5	8	2	2	11	70	0.39	0.33	0.0	0	0
A19	18901	20.0	8	3	20.0	8	2	2	11	72	0.46	0.50	0.0	0	0
A19	18902	17.5	8	3	17.5	8	2	2	12	88	0.46	0.45	0.0	0	0
A20	77702	22.5	8	2	22.5	8	2	2	11	86	0.66	0.43	0.0	0	0
A20	77703	20.0	8	4	20.0	8	4	2	15	74	0.52	0.43	0.0	0	0
A20	77704	20.0	8	2	20.0	8	4	2	15	72	0.41	0.42	0.0	0	0
A20	83002	15.0	7	3	15.0	7	3	2	16	55	0.45	0.46	0.0	0	0
A20	83003	22.5	8	2	22.5	8	2	2	11	66	0.34	0.23	0.0	0	0
A20	83004	17.5	8	3	17.5	8	3	2	12	95	0.45	0.46	0.0	0	0
A20	83005	17.5	8	3	15.0	8	4	2	12	70	0.47	0.49	0.0	0	0
A20	83006	17.5	8	3	17.5	8	3	2	13	88	0.44	0.44	0.0	0	0
A20	83008	17.5	6	3	17.5	7	3	2	19	71	0.55	0.50	0.0	0	0
A20	83009	17.5	8	2	12.5	8	2	2	16	97	0.37	0.40	0.0	0	0
A20	83302	17.5	7	4	20.0	8	3	2	10	68	0.43	0.27	0.0	0	0
A20	83304	17.5	7	4	15.0	8	4	2	11	77	0.47	0.34	0.0	0	0
A20	83305	12.5	6	4	17.5	8	4	2	14	71	0.44	0.42	0.0	0	0
A20	83306	17.5	8	4	20.0	8	3	2	19	67	0.43	0.33	0.0	0	0
A20	83309	15.0	7	4	15.0	7	4	2	13	78	0.34	0.32	0.0	0	0
A20	83501	17.5	7	4	15.0	7	4	2	10	74	0.41	0.33	0.0	0	0
A20	83503	12.5	5	4	12.5	6	4	2	10	77	0.41	0.39	0.0	0	0
A20	83803	12.5	6	4	15.0	7	4	2	12	52	0.46	0.41	0.0	0	0
A21	20701	17.5	8	3	17.5	8	3	2	12	61	0.39	0.36	0.0	0	0
A21	20901	20.0	3	3	22.5	8	2	2	6	61	0.57	0.40	0.0	0	0
A21	121301	12.5	5	5	15.0	7	5	2	10	65	0.39	0.41	0.0	0	0
A22	22301	17.5	8	2	17.5	8	3	2	11	58	0.50	0.50	0.0	0	0
B20	34001	17.5	8	4	20.0	7	3	2	16	95	0.58	0.40	0.0	0	0
B20	34004	12.5	6	4	15.0	3	8	2	16	105	0.32	0.32	0.0	0	0
B20	34005	20.0	8	3	20.0	8	3	2	14	83	0.34	0.36	0.0	0	0
B20	34007	15.0	8	3	15.0	7	3	2	9	85	0.34	0.33	0.0	0	0
B20	34009	17.5	8	4	20.0	8	3	2	16	72	0.41	0.32	0.0	0	0
B21	34801	17.5	7	4	17.5	7	4	2	24	66	0.45	0.52	0.0	0	0
B21	35001	20.0	7	3	20.0	8	3	2	11	85	0.53	0.46	0.0	0	0
B21	35002	17.5	7	4	17.5	7	4	2	15	45	0.34	0.34	0.0	0	0
B21	35003	17.5	7	4	17.5	8	2	2	18	90	0.44	0.42	0.0	0	0
B21	35004	20.0	8	3	20.0	8	3	2	25	96	0.50	0.35	0.0	0	0
B21	35005	15.0	7	4	15.0	7	3	2	30	78	0.58	0.68	0.0	0	0
B21	35006	17.5	8	2	17.5	8	2	2	16	75	0.30	0.30	0.0	0	0
B21	35007	17.5	7	4	17.5	8	4	2	29	58	0.34	0.27	0.0	0	0
B21	35008	17.5	7	4	17.5	8	2	2	29	85	0.37	0.38	0.0	0	0
B21	35009	20.0	8	3	20.0	8	2	2	20	108	0.59	0.46	0.0	0	0
B21	35011	20.0	7	3	20.0	7	3	2	14	62	0.41	0.33	0.0	0	0
B21	35012	20.0	8	3	20.0	8	3	2	24	57	0.41	0.32	0.0	0	0
B21	35013	20.0	7	2	17.5	7	2	2	21	100	0.43	0.33	0.0	0	0
B21	35014	15.0	7	4	15.0	7	4	2	18	78	0.38	0.34	0.0	0	0
B21	35015	17.5	8	2	17.5	8	2	2	16	93	0.47	0.48	0.0	0	0
B21	35017	15.0	8	3	15.0	8	3	2	15	76	0.38	0.33	0.0	0	0
B21	35201	20.0	7	3	20.0	7	3	2	17	76	0.43	0.42	0.0	0	0
B22	35401	17.5	8	2	15.0	8	3	2	24	105	0.47	0.33	0.0	0	0
B22	35402	12.5	8	2	12.5	8	3	2	18	95	0.61	0.37	0.0	0	0
B22	35902	17.5	7	4	17.5	7	4	2	13	46	0.39	0.32	0.0	0	0
B22	35903	17.5	8	2	17.5	8	2	2	16	64	0.34	0.32	0.0	0	0
B22	35904	12.5	8	2	20.0	8	2	2	13	96	0.35	0.29	0.0	0	0
B22	36101	17.5	7	4	17.5	7	4	2	19	82	0.36	0.36	0.0	0	0
B22	36102	20.0	8	3	20.0	8	3	2	20	90	0.58	0.53	0.0	0	0
B22	36103	17.5	6	4	17.5	6	4	2	20	55	0.33	0.33	0.0	0	0
B23	36301	15.0	6	4	15.0	6	4	2	10	81	0.55	0.50	0.0	0	0

APPENDIX C

URUK WARE : CONICAL CUP RIMS

LAYER	ARTIFACT NUMBER	BODY HUE	VAL	CHR	SURFACE HUE	VAL	CHR	LIP FORM	RIM DIAM	RIM ANGLE	BODY THICK	RIM THICK	PAINT HUE	VAL	CHR
B23	36302	20.0	7	3	20.0	8	3	2	13	82	0.50	0.28	0.0	0	0
B23	36303	20.0	8	2	20.0	8	3	2	14	71	0.43	0.14	0.0	0	0
B23	36304	20.0	8	2	22.5	7	2	2	10	67	0.58	0.50	0.0	0	0
B23	36305	15.0	7	3	15.0	7	4	2	11	83	0.34	0.32	0.0	0	0
B23	36307	15.0	6	4	17.5	8	3	2	16	80	0.55	0.47	0.0	0	0
B23	36502	15.0	6	4	15.0	7	4	2	20	80	0.57	0.40	0.0	0	0
B23	36801	17.5	7	3	17.5	8	3	2	11	82	0.31	0.28	0.0	0	0
B23	36802	17.5	8	4	17.5	9	1	2	12	84	0.39	0.32	0.0	0	0
B23	36803	17.5	8	3	17.5	7	2	2	10	70	0.38	0.29	0.0	0	0
B23	36804	20.0	7	3	20.0	8	3	2	9	80	0.40	0.36	0.0	0	0
B23	36805	15.0	6	4	15.0	7	4	2	17	87	0.55	0.40	0.0	0	0
B23	37003	15.0	8	3	20.0	9	2	2	10	73	0.40	0.30	0.0	0	0
B23	37005	20.0	8	3	20.0	9	2	2	12	70	0.40	0.30	0.0	0	0
B23	37006	20.0	7	3	20.0	8	3	2	14	72	0.63	0.48	0.0	0	0
B23	37007	20.0	7	3	20.0	8	3	2	12	68	0.52	0.29	0.0	0	0
B24	37501	17.5	7	3	15.0	7	4	2	15	50	0.58	0.40	0.0	0	0
B23	37702	15.0	7	6	15.0	6	6	2	8	63	0.52	0.38	0.0	0	0
B24	38001	12.5	8	2	12.5	8	2	2	8	72	0.33	0.28	0.0	0	0
B24	38002	17.5	8	2	17.5	7	4	2	20	87	0.38	0.43	0.0	0	0
B24	38301	20.0	8	4	20.0	8	4	2	12	78	0.25	0.25	0.0	0	0
B24	38302	20.0	8	3	20.0	8	4	2	11	94	0.39	0.42	0.0	0	0
B25	39501	20.0	8	3	20.0	8	4	2	4	63	0.37	0.31	0.0	0	0
B25	40001	20.0	7	3	17.5	8	2	2	14	79	0.41	0.42	0.0	0	0
B25	40401	17.5	8	4	17.5	8	4	1	10	76	0.38	0.38	0.0	0	0
B25	40402	20.0	8	3	20.0	8	3	2	16	76	0.52	0.55	0.0	0	0
B27	40601	15.0	7	4	15.0	7	4	2	11	64	0.62	0.60	0.0	0	0
B26	41002	20.0	8	2	20.0	9	3	2	6	84	0.25	0.10	0.0	0	0
B27	41701	12.5	7	2	12.5	7	2	2	11	53	0.33	0.48	0.0	0	0
B27	42001	15.0	7	4	20.0	8	3	2	18	76	0.52	0.36	0.0	0	0
B27	42003	17.5	8	2	17.5	8	4	2	9	89	0.30	0.23	0.0	0	0
B28	42401	12.5	6	4	12.5	6	4	2	8	80	0.80	0.60	0.0	0	0
B28	43501	15.0	7	4	20.0	8	3	2	10	55	0.49	0.40	0.0	0	0
B28	43701	15.0	7	4	15.0	7	4	2	9	57	0.36	0.36	0.0	0	0
B29	44601	15.0	6	4	20.0	8	3	1	10	64	0.43	0.40	0.0	0	0
B29	45001	15.0	7	4	17.5	8	4	2	12	73	0.48	0.50	0.0	0	0
B30	46201	17.5	8	4	12.5	8	2	2	11	76	0.27	0.23	0.0	0	0
B30	46401	20.0	8	3	20.0	8	3	2	11	79	0.35	0.38	0.0	0	0
B31	46901	15.0	7	4	17.5	7	4	2	11	70	0.37	0.60	0.0	0	0
B31	47101	12.5	6	6	22.5	8	2	2	26	76	0.67	0.70	0.0	0	0
B31	48101	22.5	8	2	22.5	8	2	2	12	64	0.42	0.36	0.0	0	0
B31	48102	20.0	8	3	20.0	8	3	2	11	58	0.67	0.36	0.0	0	0
B32	48901	12.5	6	4	17.5	7	4	2	13	52	0.45	0.36	0.0	0	0
B32	48902	15.0	7	4	15.0	7	4	2	9	73	0.42	0.36	0.0	0	0
B31	49303	17.5	7	4	17.5	7	4	2	8	74	0.46	0.50	0.0	0	0
B31	49304	17.5	8	2	20.0	8	3	2	9	62	0.92	0.30	0.0	0	0
B32	49501	17.5	7	4	22.5	8	2	1	19	102	0.63	0.70	0.0	0	0
B32	49502	17.5	7	2	20.0	8	2	2	12	60	0.51	0.37	0.0	0	0
B32	49702	17.5	8	4	20.0	8	3	2	11	65	0.47	0.50	0.0	0	0
B33	53401	15.0	7	4	20.0	8	3	2	9	65	0.41	0.40	0.0	0	0
B33	53502	15.0	7	3	15.0	7	4	2	5	85	0.49	0.50	0.0	0	0
B33	53503	25.0	6	3	25.0	6	3	2	17	65	0.46	0.30	0.0	0	0

URUK WARE : CONICAL CUPS WITH WIDE CUT BASES

LAYER	ARTIFACT NUMBER	BODY HUE	VAL	CHR	SURFACE HUE	VAL	CHR	BASE DIAM	CNSTR DIAM	BASE-CNSTR	SIDE ANGLE	BASE ANGLE	BASE THICK	SIDE THICK	MISSN GROUP
A2	07501	17.5	8	3	17.5	8	3	3.06	0.00	0.00	70	0	0.15	0.59	6
A2	07502	22.5	8	2	22.5	8	2	4.80	4.55	0.42	43	112	0.45	0.78	0
A5	08402	20.0	8	3	22.5	8	2	3.78	3.70	0.80	60	105	0.90	0.59	8
A5	11801	17.5	8	3	17.5	8	2	4.90	0.00	0.00	48	0	0.90	0.71	9
A6	09401	22.5	8	2	22.5	8	2	4.86	0.00	0.00	62	0	0.25	0.79	6
A6	09402	22.5	8	2	22.5	8	2	3.60	0.00	0.00	42	0	1.00	0.59	0
A6	09403	17.5	7	3	22.5	8	2	4.50	4.40	0.38	55	95	0.77	0.74	9
A7	10301	20.0	8	3	20.0	8	3	4.35	0.00	0.00	43	0	0.95	0.90	9
A8	12401	20.0	8	3	22.5	8	2	3.85	0.00	0.00	53	0	0.90	0.45	8
A9+	12703	20.0	8	4	17.5	8	3	5.05	0.00	0.00	50	0	1.10	0.94	9
A9+	13101	17.5	8	3	22.5	8	2	4.34	0.00	0.00	58	0	0.75	0.64	9
A11	13301	22.5	8	2	22.5	8	2	3.50	3.40	0.32	65	95	0.95	0.60	7
A11	13302	22.5	8	2	22.5	8	2	4.30	0.00	0.00	50	0	1.25	0.67	8
A11	13303	17.5	7	3	22.5	8	2	2.50	0.00	0.00	52	0	0.41	0.68	7
A13	19001	20.0	8	2	17.5	8	3	4.70	4.60	0.40	75	105	0.40	0.66	5
A22	121301	20.0	7	3	20.0	8	3	2.50	0.00	0.00	60	0	0.71	1.60	0
B20	33601	20.0	8	2	20.0	8	2	4.91	0.00	0.00	56	0	0.25	0.77	8
B23	35401	12.5	6	4	12.5	6	4	3.12	0.00	0.00	57	0	0.90	0.69	7
B23	37001	15.0	7	4	15.0	7	4	4.20	4.18	0.60	58	90	0.75	0.76	8
B23	39301	15.0	7	3	20.0	8	3	4.13	0.00	0.00	67	0	0.95	0.66	7
B25	39502	20.0	7	2	15.0	7	3	3.60	0.00	0.00	65	0	0.65	0.75	8
B25	40001	20.0	7	2	20.0	7	2	3.50	3.35	0.75	53	124	0.50	0.95	7
B29	45201	20.0	7	1	17.5	8	3	3.50	0.00	0.00	60	0	0.45	0.91	6
B31	49301	20.0	8	3	17.5	8	3	4.20	4.15	0.20	57	110	0.51	0.77	8
B32	49501	20.0	7	2	17.5	7	3	3.97	3.88	0.39	67	105	0.45	0.81	6

URUK WARE : CONICAL CUPS WITH CONSTRICTED CUT BASES

LAYER	ARTIFACT NUMBER	BODY HUE	VAL	CHR	SURFACE HUE	VAL	CHR	BASE DIAM	CNSTR DIAM	BASE-CNSTR	SIDE ANGLE	BASE ANGLE	BASE THICK	SIDE THICK	MISSN GROUP
A7	12001	20.0	8	2	20.0	8	3	3.45	3.30	0.55	70	108	1.10	0.55	4
A9+	12702	20.0	8	3	20.0	8	3	3.40	3.31	0.60	75	121	0.85	0.57	4
A9+	12704	20.0	8	3	22.5	8	2	3.05	3.05	0.30	75	90	1.30	0.64	4
A16	17801	20.0	8	3	25.0	7	4	3.61	3.49	0.70	67	105	1.45	0.68	5
B21	35001	12.5	6	4	12.5	6	4	2.66	2.60	0.50	67	105	0.80	0.68	5
B23	37002	20.0	8	3	20.0	8	3	3.50	3.50	0.49	65	95	1.25	0.82	4
B23	37003	17.5	8	4	22.5	8	2	2.86	2.85	0.45	63	95	1.35	0.70	4

URUK WARE : CONICAL CUPS WITH SOLID CUT BASES

LAYER	ARTIFACT NUMBER	BODY HUE	VAL	CHR	SURFACE HUE	VAL	CHR	BASE DIAM	CNSTR DIAM	BASE-CNSTR	SIDE ANGLE	BASE ANGLE	BASE THICK	SIDE THICK	MISSN GROUP
A9+	12701	20.0	7	3	20.0	8	3	3.04	1.60	1.25	85	124	0.00	0.00	2
A11	13501	20.0	8	3	20.0	8	2	3.04	1.24	1.75	85	126	0.00	0.00	2
A17	18001	17.5	8	2	17.5	8	2	3.40	1.81	1.10	0	148	0.00	0.00	2
A19	18901	17.5	8	2	20.0	8	2	3.40	1.41	1.75	0	125	0.00	0.00	1
A19	18902	17.5	8	2	7.5	8	2	3.55	1.70	1.80	0	121	0.00	0.00	1
A19	19801	12.5	6	6	15.0	7	3	2.33	1.30	1.15	69	130	0.00	0.50	2
B19	81901	17.5	7	4	20.0	8	3	3.30	1.50	1.90	0	108	0.00	0.00	2
B23	36502	20.0	8	2	20.0	8	2	2.72	1.50	1.30	0	121	0.00	0.00	1
B23	36801	15.0	6	4	15.0	6	5	3.95	1.96	0.90	0	138	0.00	0.00	2
B23	37001	17.5	7	3	17.5	8	3	3.10	1.70	1.70	80	125	0.00	0.59	2
B24	37503	20.0	8	2	20.0	8	2	3.22	1.91	1.60	85	128	0.00	0.00	2
B24	37504	20.0	8	3	20.0	8	2	3.05	1.32	1.80	85	123	0.00	0.00	1
B24	38301	15.0	7	4	20.0	8	2	3.26	1.60	1.40	0	130	0.00	0.00	2
B24	38701	15.0	7	4	15.0	7	4	2.72	1.59	1.90	0	113	0.00	0.00	1
B25	38901	20.0	8	2	20.0	8	3	2.64	1.61	1.20	80	149	0.00	0.80	1
B25	39502	15.0	7	3	15.0	7	3	2.72	1.38	1.10	0	132	0.00	0.00	2
B26	41001	12.5	5	6	12.5	6	4	3.26	1.90	1.37	71	130	0.00	0.61	1
B27	40601	17.5	7	4	20.0	8	3	2.80	1.84	1.50	0	124	0.00	0.00	1
B26	41401	20.0	8	4	20.0	8	3	2.51	1.45	1.20	75	125	0.00	0.70	1
B27	42001	20.0	8	2	20.0	8	2	2.50	1.57	0.80	85	114	0.00	0.75	1
B28	43702	17.5	7	3	17.5	7	4	2.55	1.40	1.10	0	140	0.00	0.00	2

APPENDIX C

URUK WARE : INCURVED BOWL RIMS

LAYER	ARTIFACT NUMBER	BODY HUE	BODY VAL	BODY CHR	SURFACE HUE	SURFACE VAL	SURFACE CHR	LIP FORM	RIM DIAM	RIM ANGLE	BODY THICK	RIM THICK	PAINT HUE	PAINT VAL	PAINT CHR
A9	13101	17.5	7	4	20.0	8	3	2	11	150	0.40	0.54	0.0	0	0
B25	40201	12.5	6	4	20.0	8	2	2	11	125	0.40	0.45	0.0	0	0

URUK WARE : INCURVED BOWL RIMS WITH FLAT LIPS AND HATCHED STRIPS

LAYER	ARTIFACT NUMBER	BODY HUE	BODY VAL	BODY CHR	SURFACE HUE	SURFACE VAL	SURFACE CHR	LIP FORM	RIM DIAM	RIM ANGLE	RM TP ANGLE	BODY THICK	RIM THICK	PAINT HUE	PAINT VAL	PAINT CHR
A18	19601	25.0	7	2	25.0	8	2	1	58	40	30	1.30	1.65	0.0	0	0
B33	51401	17.5	7	5	20.0	8	2	1	42	105	80	1.29	1.99	0.0	0	0
B33	53301	17.5	7	4	25.0	8	3	1	41	110	70	0.75	1.34	0.0	0	0
B33	53507	20.0	7	2	25.0	8	3	1	52	110	85	1.10	1.45	0.0	0	0
B33	53903	20.0	7	3	25.0	8	3	1	39	110	75	1.10	1.70	0.0	0	0
B33	54101	20.0	6	3	15.0	6	6	1	45	85	90	1.10	1.33	10.0	4	4
B35	57102	15.0	6	5	12.5	6	6	1	32	35	90	0.85	2.15	7.5	4	5
B35	78601	25.0	8	3	22.5	8	4	1	29	95	70	0.93	1.16	0.0	0	0

URUK WARE : HATCHED STRIPS ON INCURVED BOWL RIMS WITH FLAT LIPS

LAYER	ARTIFACT NUMBER	BODY HUE	BODY VAL	BODY CHR	SURFACE HUE	SURFACE VAL	SURFACE CHR	THICK SHERD	WIDTH STRIP	HT STRIP	WIDTH HATCH	PRIOD HATCH	ANGLE HATCH
A18	19601	25.0	7	2	25.0	8	2	1.09	1.40	0.45	0.90	0.80	65
A21	21701	12.5	6	2	22.5	8	2	1.16	1.15	0.31	0.50	0.89	35
B33	51401	17.5	7	5	20.0	8	2	0.92	0.83	0.18	0.61	0.85	95
B33	53301	17.5	7	4	25.0	8	3	0.81	1.00	0.48	0.34	0.79	91
B33	53507	20.0	7	2	25.0	8	3	1.05	1.05	0.22	1.60	1.50	95
B33	53903	20.0	7	3	25.0	8	3	1.19	1.25	0.36	1.25	1.70	95
B33	54101	20.0	6	3	15.0	6	6	1.02	0.95	0.25	0.32	0.52	80
B35	57102	15.0	6	5	12.5	6	6	0.65	1.80	0.30	1.20	1.20	95

URUK WARE : FLAT LIP BOWL RIMS

LAYER	ARTIFACT NUMBER	BODY HUE	BODY VAL	BODY CHR	SURFACE HUE	SURFACE VAL	SURFACE CHR	LIP FORM	RIM DIAM	RIM ANGLE	RM TP ANGLE	BODY THICK	RIM THICK	PAINT HUE	PAINT VAL	PAINT CHR
A11	13501	20.0	8	3	25.0	8	3	1	21	60	90	0.65	0.64	0.0	0	0
A21	121301	20.0	5	3	12.5	5	6	1	26	95	100	1.21	2.07	0.0	0	0
B28	43301	20.0	7	1	20.0	2	3	4	28	60	160	1.14	1.39	0.0	0	0
B31	48102	20.0	7	3	17.5	7	4	1	50	80	85	1.55	2.10	7.5	5	4
B33	53504	17.5	7	3	20.0	7	3	1	10	90	100	0.40	0.31	0.0	0	0
B33	57802	17.5	8	3	22.5	8	3	1	22	80	90	0.64	0.69	0.0	0	0
B33	57803	25.0	8	2	25.0	8	2	1	21	80	135	0.42	0.53	0.0	0	0
B35	57801	25.0	8	3	25.0	8	2	1	20	85	133	0.45	0.52	0.0	0	0

URUK WARE : BEVELED LIP BOWL RIMS

LAYER	ARTIFACT NUMBER	BODY HUE	BODY VAL	BODY CHR	SURFACE HUE	SURFACE VAL	SURFACE CHR	LIP FORM	RIM DIAM	RIM ANGLE	RM TP ANGLE	BODY THICK	RIM THICK	PAINT HUE	PAINT VAL	PAINT CHR
A3	07901	17.5	8	2	17.5	8	2	4	55	65	128	1.13	1.21	0.0	0	0
B25	39501	17.5	7	4	20.0	8	3	4	33	90	104	0.85	1.70	0.0	0	0
B29	45501	15.0	7	4	17.5	8	4	4	26	70	121	0.78	1.07	0.0	0	0
B30	46401	17.5	7	6	20.0	8	3	4	24	75	150	0.73	1.65	0.0	0	0
B31	47001	20.0	7	2	15.0	8	4	4	40	87	150	0.79	1.85	0.0	0	0
B31	47101	15.0	7	4	20.0	8	2	4	42	82	120	0.79	1.83	0.0	0	0
B31	47901	17.5	7	4	20.0	8	3	4	41	70	118	1.36	2.10	0.0	0	0
B32	50001	20.0	6	3	17.5	7	4	4	35	70	125	1.21	1.82	0.0	0	0

URUK WARE : LEDGE RIM BOWL RIMS

LAYER	ARTIFACT NUMBER	BODY HUE	BODY VAL	BODY CHR	SURFACE HUE	SURFACE VAL	SURFACE CHR	LIP FORM	RIM DIAM	RIM ANGLE	RM TP ANGLE	BODY THICK	RIM THICK	PAINT HUE	PAINT VAL	PAINT CHR
A6	09401	17.5	8	4	12.5	8	2	5	31	102	121	0.62	1.70	0.0	0	0
A17	18001	17.5	7	4	12.5	8	2	5	45	70	122	0.91	1.19	0.0	0	0
A19	83001	17.5	7	4	20.0	8	3	5	32	75	95	0.91	1.28	0.0	0	0
A19	83601	15.0	7	3	15.0	7	4	5	24	92	90	0.51	0.71	0.0	0	0
A20	20401	17.5	7	4	17.5	8	3	5	34	75	105	1.03	1.10	0.0	0	0
B20	34001	15.0	7	6	20.0	8	4	5	22	90	95	1.19	0.86	0.0	0	0
B30	46201	20.0	8	1	17.5	7	4	5	50	90	95	1.74	0.84	0.0	0	0
B31	47601	17.5	7	4	15.0	8	4	5	41	78	95	1.98	1.33	0.0	0	0
B31	48101	15.0	7	4	20.0	8	4	5	30	90	105	0.78	0.67	0.0	0	0

URUK WARE : ROUND LIP JAR RIMS

LAYER	ARTIFACT NUMBER	BODY HUE	VAL	CHR	SURFACE HUE	VAL	CHR	LIP FORM	NECK DIAM	RIM DIAM	RIM ANGLE	RIM THICK	NECK THICK	RIM HT	PAINT HUE	VAL	CHR
A3	07501	12.5	6	4	20.0	8	2	1	11	15	41	0.58	0.57	1.02	0.0	0	0
A3	07701	17.5	6	4	17.5	7	4	2	8	11	54	0.61	0.68	1.21	0.0	0	0
A3	07702	20.0	7	4	12.5	6	6	2	10	13	51	0.68	0.76	1.47	0.0	0	0
A3	07703	17.5	8	2	20.0	8	3	2	10	12	80	0.48	0.57	2.70	0.0	0	0
A3	07704	22.5	8	2	22.5	8	2	2	13	14	80	0.60	0.67	2.41	0.0	0	0
A3	07901	15.0	7	2	15.0	7	3	1	7	11	65	0.54	0.63	0.91	0.0	0	0
A3	07903	17.5	7	2	15.0	7	3	2	7	9	51	0.55	0.54	2.49	0.0	0	0
A3	07904	15.0	7	2	17.5	8	2	1	8	10	47	0.52	0.53	1.19	0.0	0	0
A3	07905	17.5	7	2	15.0	7	3	1	8	12	78	0.46	0.54	3.87	0.0	0	0
A5	08101	20.0	7	3	20.0	8	1	2	9	11	47	0.50	0.51	2.16	0.0	0	0
A5	08102	20.0	8	2	20.0	8	2	2	11	13	65	0.58	0.67	1.98	0.0	0	0
A5	08103	15.0	6	4	15.0	6	4	1	12	14	80	0.38	0.33	1.81	0.0	0	0
A6	08401	17.5	8	2	20.0	8	3	2	12	13	56	0.61	0.61	2.50	0.0	0	0
A6	09401	15.0	7	3	20.0	8	2	2	6	9	53	0.81	0.74	2.30	0.0	0	0
A6	09403	20.0	7	2	20.0	8	3	2	8	11	51	0.44	0.53	2.29	0.0	0	0
A6	10801	20.0	8	2	20.0	8	2	1	6	9	43	0.41	0.58	2.40	0.0	0	0
A6	10802	17.5	8	2	22.5	8	2	2	9	11	52	0.44	0.48	2.20	0.0	0	0
A7	10601	20.0	8	3	20.0	8	3	2	10	12	80	0.66	0.82	2.49	0.0	0	0
A7	10603	22.5	8	2	20.0	7	1	2	12	16	51	0.58	0.58	1.18	0.0	0	0
A7	10604	17.5	8	4	20.0	8	3	2	9	12	61	0.41	0.46	1.76	0.0	0	0
A7	11801	15.0	6	4	15.0	7	4	2	10	13	65	0.86	0.79	2.65	0.0	0	0
A7	12001	25.0	7	2	22.5	8	2	1	11	14	41	0.78	0.71	1.74	0.0	0	0
A7	12002	17.5	8	4	20.0	8	3	1	12	15	42	0.69	0.79	1.64	0.0	0	0
A9	12701	15.0	7	2	15.0	7	4	2	0	11	75	0.60	0.68	0.00	0.0	0	0
A12	19001	20.0	5	2	12.5	6	4	1	16	21	80	1.30	1.63	2.21	0.0	0	0
A13	14801	20.0	8	2	20.0	8	3	1	8	10	75	0.59	0.47	0.00	0.0	0	0
A18	19601	15.0	7	4	17.5	8	4	2	3	5	45	0.35	0.32	1.17	0.0	0	0
A21	21201	15.0	7	4	15.0	8	4	2	14	19	40	0.00	1.09	1.58	0.0	0	0
A21	21202	20.0	8	3	25.0	8	3	2	9	10	65	0.52	0.41	1.50	0.0	0	0
B20	34001	17.5	8	2	22.5	8	2	2	10	12	77	0.75	0.89	2.54	0.0	0	0
B21	35001	15.0	7	3	20.0	8	3	2	18	21	87	0.75	0.62	1.93	0.0	0	0
B21	35002	17.5	8	2	17.5	7	2	2	8	9	70	0.60	0.50	2.75	0.0	0	0
B21	35003	15.0	7	3	17.5	8	2	2	13	18	58	0.74	0.64	2.02	0.0	0	0
B21	35004	17.5	8	4	20.0	7	4	2	10	12	92	0.66	0.69	2.40	0.0	0	0
B21	35005	15.0	8	2	20.0	8	2	2	15	18	57	0.71	0.71	1.48	0.0	0	0
B21	35006	22.5	8	2	22.5	8	2	2	11	15	36	0.50	0.46	1.98	0.0	0	0
B21	35007	15.0	7	3	17.5	8	2	2	15	21	59	0.72	0.69	2.23	0.0	0	0
B22	35901	17.5	7	4	20.0	7	4	2	7	10	45	0.68	0.77	2.43	0.0	0	0
B22	35902	15.0	8	3	17.5	8	4	2	9	11	50	0.63	0.65	2.35	0.0	0	0
B22	78501	25.0	8	1	22.5	8	1	2	5	6	70	0.31	0.25	0.54	0.0	0	0
B23	36501	17.5	8	4	20.0	8	3	2	11	14	62	0.84	0.85	2.58	0.0	0	0
B23	36801	20.0	8	3	17.5	8	2	2	16	21	70	0.69	0.65	2.63	0.0	0	0
B23	36802	12.5	6	4	20.0	6	2	1	13	15	79	0.42	0.51	0.81	15.0	40	110
B25	38901	17.5	7	2	17.5	7	4	1	7	8	23	0.35	0.38	0.89	0.0	0	0
B27	40601	20.0	6	3	12.5	6	6	2	11	14	15	0.95	0.90	1.11	0.0	0	0
B27	41701	15.0	8	3	17.5	8	4	2	11	15	54	0.83	0.79	1.80	0.0	0	0
B27	41702	20.0	8	3	17.5	8	2	1	16	21	62	1.08	0.76	5.13	0.0	0	0
B27	42001	17.5	7	2	22.5	8	2	1	14	17	55	0.70	0.67	2.36	0.0	0	0
B27	42002	20.0	8	2	22.5	8	2	1	16	19	49	0.62	0.62	2.19	0.0	0	0
B28	43701	20.0	7	2	15.0	7	3	2	16	19	46	0.96	0.91	1.55	0.0	0	0
B29	44601	12.5	6	6	15.0	7	4	2	13	17	32	0.67	0.71	1.96	0.0	0	0
B29	44602	20.0	7	2	17.5	8	2	1	14	17	71	0.76	0.79	2.14	0.0	0	0
B29	44603	12.5	6	4	22.5	8	2	2	12	16	41	0.70	0.66	1.83	0.0	0	0
B29	45001	15.0	7	2	15.0	6	2	1	18	20	96	0.45	0.49	1.03	0.0	0	0
B29	45002	12.5	6	4	15.0	7	4	2	13	16	62	0.80	0.67	1.97	0.0	0	0
B29	45201	17.5	7	4	20.0	8	2	2	11	14	68	0.71	0.72	1.71	0.0	0	0
B30	45901	22.5	8	2	15.0	8	4	2	15	18	55	0.71	0.53	1.98	0.0	0	0
B30	46203	17.5	8	3	20.0	8	3	2	10	12	80	0.85	0.80	1.51	0.0	0	0
B30	46204	20.0	7	3	15.0	8	4	2	15	18	55	0.66	0.51	1.77	0.0	0	0
B30	46301	17.5	7	4	20.0	7	1	2	10	13	33	0.68	0.56	2.24	0.0	0	0
B30	46501	20.0	8	3	17.5	7	4	2	10	12	61	0.72	0.65	2.02	0.0	0	0
B30	46702	20.0	8	2	12.5	8	2	2	23	20	48	1.09	0.90	2.10	0.0	0	0
B30	121903	20.0	6	3	22.5	8	2	2	31	35	55	1.22	1.30	2.72	0.0	0	0
B30	48401	20.0	8	2	22.5	8	2	2	10	12	67	0.54	0.52	1.70	0.0	0	0
B30	48403	20.0	8	2	22.5	7	2	2	7	10	89	0.59	0.52	1.80	0.0	0	0
B31	46801	15.0	8	3	17.5	8	2	2	9	11	71	0.57	0.55	2.08	0.0	0	0
B31	46901	22.5	8	2	20.0	7	1	2	11	14	114	0.21	0.24	1.04	0.0	0	0
B31	46902	20.0	8	3	15.0	7	4	1	7	9	64	0.51	0.42	1.74	0.0	0	0
B31	47601	15.0	7	4	12.5	8	2	2	9	10	61	0.37	0.38	2.75	0.0	0	0
B31	48101	20.0	6	2	17.5	7	2	2	14	16	75	0.45	0.52	2.85	15.0	50	15

APPENDIX C

URUK WARE : ROUND LIP JAR RIMS

LAYER	ARTIFACT NUMBER	BODY HUE	VAL	CHR	SURFACE HUE	VAL	CHR	LIP FORM	NECK DIAM	RIM DIAM	RIM ANGLE	NECK THICK	RIM THICK	NECK HT	PAINT HUE	VAL	CHR
B31	48102	15.0	6	4	12.5	6	6	2	14	17	30	0.75	0.83	1.45	0.0	0	0
B31	48402	22.5	7	2	22.5	8	2	2	10	11	75	0.45	0.41	2.30	12.5	30	20
B32	49701	12.5	6	2	12.5	6	6	1	11	13	66	0.60	0.68	1.73	0.0	0	0
B32	49702	15.0	7	3	17.5	8	4	2	8	11	78	0.64	0.62	1.61	0.0	0	0
B32	49703	17.5	7	4	22.5	8	2	2	9	10	78	0.61	0.60	1.66	0.0	0	0
B32	49705	15.0	7	4	22.5	8	2	2	9	12	50	0.61	0.64	1.69	0.0	0	0
B32	49706	20.0	8	4	22.5	8	4	2	14	16	71	0.65	0.62	1.68	0.0	0	0
B32	49707	17.5	7	4	15.0	7	3	2	11	15	45	1.11	1.00	1.75	0.0	0	0
B32	50001	17.5	7	4	20.0	8	3	2	9	10	75	0.48	0.53	2.71	0.0	0	0
B32	50801	25.0	8	2	25.0	8	3	2	6	7	45	0.41	0.38	0.70	0.0	0	0
B33	51903	22.5	8	4	22.5	8	4	2	6	7	65	0.41	0.36	1.61	0.0	0	0
B33	53504	20.0	7	3	20.0	7	3	2	20	23	70	0.70	1.00	2.40	0.0	0	0
B34	55701	20.0	7	4	15.0	6	6	2	60	70	70	0.40	0.38	1.50	12.5	50	60
B35	57501	20.0	6	2	16.0	7	4	2	14	17	45	0.89	0.79	0.71	0.0	0	0

URUK WARE : SMALL EXPANDED RIM JAR RIMS

LAYER	ARTIFACT NUMBER	BODY HUE	VAL	CHR	SURFACE HUE	VAL	CHR	LIP FORM	NECK DIAM	RIM DIAM	RIM ANGLE	RM TP ANGLE	NECK THICK	RIM THICK	NECK HT	RIM HT	PAINT HUE	VAL	CHR
A17	18001	20.0	6	2	20.0	4	1	1	13	16	40	115	0.90	0.90	1.35	0.75	0.0	0	0
A18	19601	15.0	7	4	15.0	7	4	1	10	13	60	115	0.84	1.06	1.22	0.92	0.0	0	0
A20	20402	20.0	7	3	15.0	7	3	1	9	11	65	83	0.84	0.79	1.22	0.11	0.0	0	0
B29	45702	17.5	8	2	20.0	8	3	1	13	15	80	85	0.68	0.90	1.80	0.05	0.0	0	0
B30	48402	15.0	7	6	22.5	8	4	1	9	11	75	100	0.62	0.73	1.67	0.38	0.0	0	0
B30	121701	20.0	7	4	22.5	8	2	2	12	14	85	95	0.76	0.97	1.40	0.34	0.0	0	0
B31	47601	20.0	6	1	17.5	8	2	1	11	13	75	95	1.00	1.10	1.49	0.09	0.0	0	0
B32	49101	20.0	8	3	20.0	8	3	1	20	22	100	85	0.70	0.79	1.82	0.36	0.0	0	0
B35	57101	17.5	7	3	15.0	7	4	1	9	11	65	125	0.65	0.80	1.75	0.31	0.0	0	0
B35	57801	25.0	6	3	22.5	6	3	1	6	8	75	95	0.42	0.42	1.06	0.28	0.0	0	0

URUK WARE: LARGE EXPANDED RIM JAR RIMS

LAYER	ARTIFACT NUMBER	BODY HUE	VAL	CHR	SURFACE HUE	VAL	CHR	LIP FORM	NECK DIAM	RIM DIAM	RIM ANGLE	RM TP ANGLE	NECK THICK	RIM THICK	NECK HT	RIM HT	PAINT HUE	VAL	CHR
A20	19001	15.0	7	4	20.0	6	2	1	17	21	75	105	1.01	1.68	2.25	0.45	0.0	0	0
B29	45704	20.0	8	1	17.5	7	3	1	17	29	60	130	0.95	1.54	2.20	1.15	0.0	0	0
B30	46205	17.5	7	2	17.5	8	2	1	18	22	90	85	0.96	1.51	1.90	0.32	0.0	0	0
B30	46401	15.0	7	3	20.0	8	2	1	18	22	95	115	1.05	1.60	1.95	1.01	0.0	0	0
B34	56101	25.0	8	2	22.5	8	3	1	18	22	75	135	0.97	1.52	2.18	0.94	0.0	0	0
B35	56301	15.0	7	4	25.0	8	3	1	12	15	65	110	0.00	1.38	1.90	0.51	0.0	0	0
B35	57101	15.0	7	4	20.0	8	2	1	10	15	43	140	0.72	1.31	2.10	1.20	0.0	0	0

URUK WARE: OUT-TURNED EXPANDED RIM JAR RIMS

LAYER	ARTIFACT NUMBER	BODY HUE	VAL	CHR	SURFACE HUE	VAL	CHR	LIP FORM	NECK DIAM	RIM DIAM	RIM ANGLE	RM TP ANGLE	NECK THICK	RIM THICK	NECK HT	RIM HT	PAINT HUE	VAL	CHR
A18	19301	20.0	8	2	22.5	8	2	1	10	13	70	100	0.82	1.11	1.23	0.66	0.0	0	0
B27	40601	20.0	7	3	20.0	8	3	1	15	18	85	85	0.46	1.50	1.97	0.30	0.0	0	0
B29	45001	17.5	6	2	20.0	8	2	1	19	24	65	90	0.80	1.50	2.15	0.35	0.0	0	0
B31	47101	20.0	7	3	15.0	7	4	1	13	17	55	95	0.64	0.90	1.29	0.55	0.0	0	0

URUK WARE : HIGH EXPANDED BAND RIM JAR RIMS

LAYER	ARTIFACT NUMBER	BODY HUE	VAL	CHR	SURFACE HUE	VAL	CHR	LIP FORM	NECK DIAM	RIM DIAM	RIM ANGLE	RM TP ANGLE	NECK THICK	RIM THICK	NECK HT	RIM HT	PAINT HUE	VAL	CHR
B30	46204	20.0	7	2	22.5	7	2	1	9	12	65	160	1.12	0.97	2.40	0.88	0.0	0	0
B32	49501	20.0	8	3	20.0	8	3	1	13	16	95	80	0.67	1.03	4.20	0.30	0.0	0	0

URUK WARE: LOW EXPANDED BAND RIM JAR RIMS

LAYER	ARTIFACT NUMBER	BODY HUE	VAL	CHR	SURFACE HUE	VAL	CHR	LIP FORM	NECK DIAM	RIM DIAM	RIM ANGLE	RM TP ANGLE	NECK THICK	RIM THICK	NECK HT	RIM HT	PAINT HUE	VAL	CHR
A18	18501	20.0	8	2	20.0	8	2	1	11	14	70	200	0.85	1.47	1.90	1.47	0.0	0	0
A19	20001	17.5	8	2	20.0	8	2	1	10	12	55	145	0.94	1.39	1.46	1.32	0.0	0	0
A20	83001	20.0	8	2	20.0	8	3	1	11	13	55	175	0.83	1.21	1.19	1.21	0.0	0	0
A20	83303	25.0	7	3	25.0	8	2	1	20	26	25	210	1.31	2.10	2.15	2.10	0.0	0	0
B28	42401	20.0	8	3	22.5	8	2	1	12	14	35	205	0.85	1.80	2.05	1.83	0.0	0	0
B29	45701	15.0	7	4	17.5	8	3	1	12	15	40	180	0.95	1.60	1.70	1.52	0.0	0	0
B30	21901	15.0	7	3	22.5	8	3	1	11	12	70	170	0.83	1.20	1.48	1.20	0.0	0	0
B30	21902	15.0	7	3	20.0	7	3	1	15	18	65	175	1.07	1.54	1.70	1.54	0.0	0	0
B30	45901	20.0	7	3	22.5	8	2	1	10	12	55	170	0.99	1.38	1.67	1.37	0.0	0	0
B30	46203	20.0	8	3	20.0	8	2	1	9	12	60	160	1.22	1.05	1.30	1.00	0.0	0	0
B30	46301	15.0	7	4	20.0	8	1	1	13	16	65	205	1.00	1.30	1.75	1.30	0.0	0	0
B30	46704	20.0	7	2	20.0	8	2	1	9	12	45	185	0.95	1.28	1.55	1.28	0.0	0	0
B31	47102	17.5	8	2	17.5	8	2	1	11	14	45	205	0.84	1.36	1.60	1.47	0.0	0	0
B31	47103	15.0	6	4	15.0	8	4	1	7	9	45	185	0.75	1.25	1.40	1.20	0.0	0	0
B31	48102	22.5	8	2	10.0	8	2	1	8	12	80	160	0.95	1.25	1.41	1.25	0.0	0	0
B32	50801	20.0	6	3	20.0	8	3	1	11	16	25	209	1.18	2.21	2.25	2.21	0.0	0	0
B33	52601	25.0	8	3	22.5	8	3	1	18	23	55	185	1.57	2.70	2.87	2.05	0.0	0	0

URUK WARE : FLARED EXPANDED LIP JAR RIMS

LAYER	ARTIFACT NUMBER	BODY HUE	VAL	CHR	SURFACE HUE	VAL	CHR	LIP FORM	NECK DIAM	RIM DIAM	RIM ANGLE	RM TP ANGLE	NECK THICK	RIM THICK	NECK HT	RIM HT	PAINT HUE	VAL	CHR
A3	07701	15.0	6	3	20.0	8	2	1	12	14	85	140	0.56	0.87	2.60	0.76	0.0	0	0
A6	10301	17.5	6	4	15.0	7	4	1	10	12	85	160	0.66	0.75	2.70	0.70	0.0	0	0
A13	14301	22.5	7	2	22.5	7	2	1	12	15	30	195	0.93	0.92	1.20	1.02	0.0	0	0
A13	14302	15.0	7	3	17.5	8	2	1	11	14	40	200	0.85	0.76	1.30	0.76	0.0	0	0
A20	77701	22.5	8	2	22.5	8	2	1	7	9	25	167	0.49	0.56	2.35	0.56	0.0	0	0
B21	39301	17.5	6	4	20.0	8	3	1	10	13	50	170	0.00	1.23	3.16	1.18	0.0	0	0
B23	36801	20.0	8	3	20.0	8	3	1	15	19	55	175	0.90	1.21	2.79	1.17	0.0	0	0
B23	39302	20.0	8	1	25.0	8	1	1	14	16	75	110	0.98	1.15	3.25	0.92	0.0	0	0
B25	39501	22.5	8	2	22.5	8	2	1	14	16	75	115	0.70	1.12	3.45	1.01	0.0	0	0
B26	41202	22.5	8	2	22.5	8	2	1	18	20	60	135	0.67	0.79	2.30	0.55	0.0	0	0
B27	40603	20.0	8	3	20.0	8	3	1	11	14	60	65	0.67	1.07	3.20	1.03	0.0	0	0
B30	46201	20.0	7	3	20.0	8	3	1	9	12	65	80	0.80	1.05	2.49	0.67	0.0	0	0
B31	49301	20.0	7	3	20.0	8	3	1	10	14	55	165	0.80	0.85	2.30	0.85	0.0	0	0
B33	51402	20.0	6	4	12.5	6	4	1	13	16	35	175	0.63	0.76	1.80	0.71	0.0	0	0
B33	51902	25.0	8	2	25.0	8	2	1	9	12	45	175	0.70	0.89	1.60	0.89	0.0	0	0
B34	54301	17.5	6	4	17.5	6	4	1	7	10	58	145	0.81	0.68	1.77	0.42	7.5	4	5
B34	54901	20.0	7	3	22.5	8	2	1	11	16	45	185	1.25	1.35	2.50	1.35	0.0	0	0
B35	56301	12.5	6	4	25.0	8	3	1	12	15	65	100	0.98	1.41	1.68	0.67	0.0	0	0
B36	58701	17.5	7	3	20.0	8	3	1	11	14	75	110	0.66	0.09	2.55	0.48	0.0	0	0

URUK WARE : OTHER EXPANDED RIM JAR RIMS

LAYER	ARTIFACT NUMBER	BODY HUE	VAL	CHR	SURFACE HUE	VAL	CHR	LIP FORM	NECK DIAM	RIM DIAM	RIM ANGLE	RM TP ANGLE	NECK THICK	RIM THICK	NECK HT	RIM HT	PAINT HUE	VAL	CHR
A19	18901	20.0	5	2	20.0	8	3	1	17	22	10	185	1.54	1.01	5.18	0.00	0.0	0	0
A20	82702	17.5	7	4	15.0	7	4	1	9	14	35	190	1.10	0.95	2.49	0.87	0.0	0	0
B31	48103	22.5	7	2	22.5	7	2	1	12	17	80	75	0.48	1.10	2.92	0.65	0.0	0	0
B32	49503	22.5	8	2	22.5	8	2	1	16	18	90	90	0.80	1.15	1.10	0.67	0.0	0	0

APPENDIX C

URUK WARE : LEDGE RIM JAR RIMS

LAYER	ARTIFACT NUMBER	BODY HUE	VAL	CHR	SURFACE HUE	VAL	CHR	LIP FORM	NECK DIAM	RIM DIAM	RIM ANGLE	RM TP ANGLE	NECK THICK	RIM THICK	NECK HT	RIM HT	PAINT HUE	VAL	CHR
A2	07502	20.0	8	2	20.0	8	2	1	14	18	70	110	0.56	1.33	2.53	0.94	0.0	0	0
A5	08401	20.0	7	3	20.0	7	3	1	9	12	85	115	0.40	0.58	2.60	0.42	0.0	0	0
A8	12401	22.5	8	2	22.5	8	2	1	9	11	80	130	0.45	0.81	2.24	0.70	0.0	0	0
A9	12701	17.5	8	2	17.5	8	3	1	9	11	70	95	0.46	0.70	1.65	0.50	0.0	0	0
A11	13302	17.5	7	3	17.5	8	3	1	9	12	80	115	0.58	0.92	2.36	0.66	0.0	0	0
A13	14301	20.0	7	2	20.0	7	1	1	9	13	75	105	0.93	1.49	2.77	0.90	0.0	0	0
A13	15001	15.0	6	4	20.0	7	2	1	10	13	80	108	0.80	1.27	3.31	0.74	0.0	0	0
A13	15002	15.0	6	3	15.0	7	3	1	10	14	75	118	0.72	1.38	3.26	0.72	0.0	0	0
A16	17801	20.0	7	1	20.0	8	3	1	9	11	80	115	0.37	0.91	0.65	0.54	0.0	0	0
A20	83301	22.5	8	2	22.5	8	2	1	9	12	90	95	0.68	1.51	2.20	0.57	0.0	0	0
B22	35405	20.0	8	3	22.5	7	2	1	9	11	85	95	0.42	0.85	2.05	0.55	0.0	0	0
B22	35901	20.0	8	2	20.0	8	2	1	11	13	90	95	0.72	1.18	2.80	0.55	0.0	0	0
B23	39301	17.5	7	4	17.5	7	3	1	6	7	75	95	0.40	0.80	1.80	0.60	0.0	0	0
B24	37503	17.5	8	3	17.5	8	3	1	7	9	85	95	0.32	0.62	2.28	0.50	0.0	0	0
B24	38002	20.0	8	3	20.0	8	3	1	10	12	85	115	0.46	0.94	2.10	0.75	0.0	0	0
B24	38301	17.5	8	3	22.5	8	2	1	9	10	60	115	0.47	0.76	1.52	0.60	0.0	0	0
B26	41203	20.0	8	3	20.0	8	3	1	10	13	90	115	0.69	1.18	1.95	0.85	0.0	0	0
B27	40602	15.0	6	4	17.5	8	3	1	13	16	40	130	0.56	0.94	1.90	0.85	0.0	0	0
B29	45703	20.0	7	3	17.5	7	3	1	10	13	85	100	0.65	1.29	2.25	0.75	0.0	0	0
B30	46204	20.0	7	2	22.5	7	2	1	9	12	65	160	0.59	0.97	2.40	0.88	0.0	0	0
B30	46703	20.0	8	2	22.5	8	2	1	13	16	80	115	1.35	1.30	1.20	1.00	0.0	0	0
B30	46705	17.5	8	2	20.0	8	2	1	16	18	80	95	0.65	0.75	2.05	0.41	0.0	0	0

URUK WARE : LEDGE RIMS OF JARS WITH POLYCHROME DECORATION

LAYER	ARTIFACT NUMBER	BODY HUE	VAL	CHR	SURFACE HUE	VAL	CHR	LIP FORM	NECK DIAM	RIM DIAM	RIM ANGLE	RM TP ANGLE	NECK THICK	RIM THICK	NECK HT	RIM HT	RED PAINT HUE	VAL	CHR
A5	09901	20.0	7	5	20.0	8	2	1	12	16	65	160	0.61	0.92	4.80	0.83	12.5	6	6
A7	10601	17.5	8	3	20.0	8	2	1	9	12	65	155	0.48	0.65	1.95	0.62	0.0	0	0
A8	12401	22.5	8	1	22.5	8	2	1	10	14	60	135	0.77	1.05	2.95	0.79	10.0	3	6
B20	34301	20.0	8	2	22.5	8	2	1	9	13	60	125	0.51	1.14	4.98	0.95	10.0	3	6
B22	35401	22.5	8	3	22.5	8	3	1	15	18	75	100	0.54	1.00	0.00	0.75	10.0	5	3
B22	35403	17.5	7	4	22.5	8	3	1	12	15	70	115	0.50	1.20	2.40	0.70	10.0	4	4
B23	36501	15.0	7	4	15.0	7	4	1	7	8	80	55	0.38	0.94	1.90	0.65	10.0	5	4
B27	40604	17.5	7	4	22.5	8	2	1	12	17	75	110	0.60	1.40	0.00	0.80	7.5	4	4
B33	53301	20.0	6	3	12.5	5	4	1	9	10	80	95	0.69	0.75	1.65	0.29	20.0	2	2

URUK WARE : BOTTLE NECKS

LAYER	ARTIFACT NUMBER	BODY HUE	VAL	CHR	SURFACE HUE	VAL	CHR	LIP FORM	NECK DIAM	RIM DIAM	RIM ANGLE	RM TP ANGLE	NECK THICK	RIM THICK	NECK HT	RIM HT	PAINT HUE	VAL	CHR
A19	20002	20.0	8	3	20.0	8	2	1	2	5	90	160	0.52	0.99	2.16	0.87	0.0	0	0
B24	38302	15.0	7	4	15.0	8	3	1	2	4	75	149	0.47	1.22	1.88	1.17	0.0	0	0
B29	45201	25.0	5	2	25.0	5	3	1	2	4	80	160	0.32	1.39	1.77	1.30	0.0	0	0
B29	45501	17.5	6	4	22.5	8	2	1	2	5	80	150	0.55	1.76	2.82	1.64	0.0	0	0
B30	45904	17.5	7	4	17.5	8	4	1	3	4	65	160	0.41	1.37	1.95	1.32	0.0	0	0
B30	46206	15.0	7	4	22.5	8	2	1	3	6	65	120	0.50	2.07	3.18	1.99	0.0	0	0
B30	121501	17.5	6	4	20.0	8	3	1	3	4	50	165	0.39	1.50	2.20	1.40	0.0	0	0
B32	46206	15.0	8	4	25.0	8	3	1	3	6	75	150	0.00	2.11	2.90	2.00	0.0	0	0

URUK WARE : BAND RIM JAR RIMS

LAYER	ARTIFACT NUMBER	BODY HUE	VAL	CHR	SURFACE HUE	VAL	CHR	LIP FORM	NECK DIAM	RIM DIAM	RIM ANGLE	RM TP ANGLE	NECK THICK	RIM THICK	NECK HT	RIM HT	PAINT HUE	VAL	CHR
A5	08403	15.0	7	4	17.5	8	2	1	7	9	85	155	0.48	0.95	2.64	1.01	0.0	0	0
A7	10302	15.0	7	3	15.0	7	4	1	11	13	75	190	0.59	2.11	3.15	2.15	0.0	0	0
A15	17001	17.5	8	3	17.5	8	3	1	10	13	70	170	0.74	1.05	2.10	1.05	0.0	0	0
A15	19001	20.0	3	1	15.0	7	5	1	27	31	80	120	1.06	1.40	2.42	1.38	0.0	0	0
B19	81901	20.0	8	3	20.0	8	3	1	11	13	80	175	0.65	1.25	2.00	1.25	0.0	0	0
B20	34001	20.0	8	3	22.5	8	2	1	11	13	70	80	0.60	1.50	2.00	0.52	0.0	0	0
B23	37002	20.0	8	3	17.5	7	3	1	11	13	80	175	0.65	1.30	2.82	1.30	0.0	0	0
B23	39301	20.0	8	3	20.0	8	3	1	12	10	70	60	0.50	1.00	2.68	1.00	0.0	0	0
B23	43001	20.0	8	3	20.0	8	3	1	15	19	55	175	0.60	1.42	2.50	1.35	0.0	0	0

URUK WARE : OTHER LEDGE RIM JAR RIMS

LAYER	ARTIFACT NUMBER	BODY HUE	VAL	CHR	SURFACE HUE	VAL	CHR	LIP FORM	NECK DIAM	RIM DIAM	RIM ANGLE	RM TP ANGLE	NECK THICK	RIM THICK	NECK HT	RIM HT	PAINT HUE	VAL	CHR
A7	12001	15.0	8	4	15.0	7	4	1	11	17	55	145	0.80	1.37	3.31	1.27	0.0	0	0
B22	35902	20.0	8	3	20.0	8	3	1	12	16	85	105	0.92	1.71	2.80	1.20	0.0	0	0
B31	48101	22.5	8	2	22.5	8	2	1	6	7	95	160	0.48	0.40	0.90	0.35	0.0	0	0
B33	51401	20.0	6	2	17.5	6	4	1	16	20	58	110	1.18	1.09	2.43	0.84	0.0	0	0

URUK WARE : LOCK RIM JAR RIMS

LAYER	ARTIFACT NUMBER	BODY HUE	VAL	CHR	SURFACE HUE	VAL	CHR	LIP FORM	NECK DIAM	RIM DIAM	RIM ANGLE	RM TP ANGLE	NECK THICK	RIM THICK	NECK HT	RIM HT	PAINT HUE	VAL	CHR
A20	82701	17.5	8	2	20.0	7	4	1	9	12	20	192	1.00	1.07	3.05	1.07	0.0	0	0
B21	35001	25.0	8	3	25.0	7	3	9	12	16	80	190	1.03	1.68	3.46	1.90	0.0	0	0
B23	36801	20.0	2	1	20.0	8	2	9	10	12	75	170	0.81	1.37	2.30	1.60	0.0	0	0
B25	39501	22.5	8	4	20.0	8	4	9	12	15	95	185	0.75	1.50	3.20	1.38	0.0	0	0
B26	40401	15.0	6	4	15.0	7	3	9	13	16	85	185	0.81	1.25	3.04	1.09	0.0	0	0

URUK WARE : NOSE LUGS

LAYER	ARTIFACT NUMBER	BODY HUE	VAL	CHR	SURFACE HUE	VAL	CHR	SHLDR THICK	LNGTH NOSE	WIDTH NOSE	HT NOSE	LNGTH HOLE	WIDTH HOLE
A5	08401	25.0	7	3	17.5	7	4	0.44	2.80	1.21	1.05	0.39	0.30
A18	19301	17.5	6	4	17.5	8	2	0.79	3.34	1.40	1.21	0.66	0.60
A20	77701	15.0	6	6	15.0	8	4	0.53	1.72	0.88	0.58	0.29	0.27
A20	83801	17.5	7	4	20.0	8	3	1.40	5.15	1.73	1.04	0.58	0.56
A22	22101	17.5	7	4	22.5	8	2	0.00	1.85	0.87	0.83	0.34	0.32
B22	78501	25.0	8	1	22.5	8	1	0.50	2.00	0.96	0.55	0.11	0.25
B30	48401	15.0	8	4	15.0	6	6	0.00	2.72	1.10	0.70	0.26	0.24
B32	49501	20.0	7	6	22.5	8	2	0.87	3.59	1.20	1.13	0.60	0.52
B32	50001	17.5	6	3	20.0	8	3	0.55	3.12	1.35	0.80	0.32	0.18

URUK WARE : HATCHED STRIPS ON JARS

LAYER	ARTIFACT NUMBER	BODY HUE	VAL	CHR	SURFACE HUE	VAL	CHR	THICK SHERD	WIDTH STRIP	HT STRIP	WIDTH HATCH	PRIOD HATCH	ANGLE HATCH
A2	07502	20.0	7	3	12.5	6	4	0.87	1.10	0.33	0.48	0.92	115
A3	07901	20.0	8	2	22.5	8	2	0.45	1.42	1.14	0.63	1.83	125
A3	07902	17.5	6	4	17.5	7	2	0.60	1.28	0.31	0.69	1.32	40
A6	08401	20.0	8	3	20.0	8	4	1.04	1.99	0.92	1.19	1.83	52
A6	09401	17.5	8	4	17.5	8	4	1.03	1.88	1.20	0.41	2.48	145
A6	09402	17.5	7	4	17.5	7	4	0.62	1.49	0.93	0.84	1.25	130
A6	09403	17.5	6	4	17.5	7	4	0.73	1.02	0.60	0.32	0.55	90
A6	10801	20.0	7	2	22.5	8	2	0.71	1.51	0.72	0.64	1.91	35
A6	10802	17.5	7	2	17.5	7	2	0.70	1.12	0.41	0.89	1.24	125
A6	10803	22.5	8	3	22.5	8	3	0.81	2.12	0.91	0.97	1.99	90
A7	12001	20.0	7	3	20.0	7	2	0.84	0.98	0.31	0.83	1.67	25
A8	12401	20.0	7	2	20.0	8	2	1.02	1.09	0.45	0.59	1.67	30
A9	13101	15.0	7	4	17.5	8	2	0.80	0.82	0.28	0.87	1.07	115
A11	13501	20.0	8	3	20.0	8	3	0.61	1.38	0.44	0.94	1.81	90
A11	13502	17.5	6	4	17.5	7	2	0.71	1.27	0.49	0.62	1.58	55
A13	15001	20.0	4	2	20.0	6	1	0.67	1.48	0.58	0.84	2.37	144
A17	18001	17.5	7	4	20.0	8	2	0.82	0.81	0.18	0.38	0.68	90
A18	19301	15.0	8	4	15.0	8	3	0.73	0.43	0.08	0.22	0.56	90
B20	33601	25.0	8	3	25.0	8	3	0.95	1.26	0.57	0.91	1.37	70
B23	37001	22.5	8	2	22.5	8	2	0.52	1.27	0.68	0.98	1.37	105
B23	39301	12.5	6	2	20.0	7	3	1.37	1.19	0.67	0.92	1.46	85
B23	39302	22.5	7	2	22.5	7	2	0.99	1.45	0.70	0.60	1.13	125
B28	42401	20.0	8	3	22.5	8	2	0.73	0.85	0.08	0.80	0.98	90
B30	46201	15.0	7	4	17.5	8	3	1.51	1.88	0.74	1.27	2.00	90
B31	47101	25.0	8	2	25.0	8	4	1.23	1.68	0.51	1.30	1.51	90
B31	48101	22.5	6	4	20.0	6	4	1.29	1.75	0.68	1.40	1.57	88
B31	48102	20.0	7	3	22.5	8	2	1.39	1.78	0.38	1.26	1.44	90
B34	55701	20.0	7	4	15.0	6	6	0.55	0.50	0.08	0.22	0.40	65

APPENDIX C

URUK WARE : CROSS-HATCH INCISED BANDS

LAYER	ARTIFACT NUMBER	BODY HUE	VAL	CHR	SURFACE HUE	VAL	CHR	SHLDR THICK	BAND WIDTH	LINE WIDTH	SPACE WIDTH	ANGLE INTRS
A13	15301	15.0	8	4	15.0	8	3	0.69	0.00	0.16	0.50	85
B25	39501	17.5	7	2	22.5	8	2	0.64	3.23	0.03	0.60	114
B27	41701	22.5	8	2	22.5	8	2	0.64	0.00	0.14	0.81	64
B28	44601	15.0	7	3	17.5	8	2	0.62	0.00	0.09	0.50	72
B30	46701	17.5	8	2	17.5	8	2	0.89	0.00	0.14	0.79	116
B30	48401	20.0	7	2	22.5	8	2	0.68	1.44	0.03	0.25	135
B31	47101	20.0	7	2	20.0	8	2	0.88	0.00	0.18	0.71	61
B32	49501	20.0	7	6	22.5	8	2	0.87	2.61	0.13	0.40	88
B32	49701	17.5	7	2	17.5	8	2	0.73	0.00	0.07	0.50	85
B33	53301	15.0	6	4	20.0	8	4	0.54	0.00	0.08	0.26	111
B33	53501	22.5	7	3	25.0	8	2	0.49	0.00	0.05	0.35	93

URUK WARE : INCISED HORIZONTAL LINES

LAYER	ARTIFACT NUMBER	BODY HUE	VAL	CHR	SURFACE HUE	VAL	CHR	SHLDR THICK	WIDTH HORIZ	SPACE HORIZ	NO. HORIZ	WIDTH OBLQ	ANGLE OBLQ
A17	18001	20.0	7	2	17.5	8	2	0.76	0.13	0.54	5	0.00	0
A17	18501	20.0	8	2	17.5	8	4	0.55	0.25	0.43	3	0.00	0
A19	83001	17.5	7	4	20.0	8	3	0.86	0.17	0.39	4	0.28	64
A19	83301	20.0	8	4	20.0	8	3	0.62	0.10	0.43	4	0.00	0
A20	20401	15.0	8	4	17.5	8	4	0.95	0.12	0.32	10	0.39	111
B20	77701	20.0	8	3	17.5	7	4	0.69	0.20	0.30	5	0.36	110
B27	40601	15.0	6	4	12.5	5	4	0.64	0.10	0.44	6	0.00	0
B28	43501	20.0	6	4	20.0	8	3	0.77	0.14	0.23	6	0.00	0
B28	44001	17.5	7	4	20.0	8	3	0.80	0.29	0.06	7	0.45	104
B30	121901	20.0	6	3	22.5	8	3	0.70	0.29	0.13	12	0.30	127
B31	49301	15.0	7	5	22.5	8	2	0.97	0.01	0.47	3	0.00	0

URUK WARE : STRAP HANDLES

LAYER	ARTIFACT NUMBER	BODY HUE	VAL	CHR	SURFACE HUE	VAL	CHR	STRAP WIDTH	MAX THICK
A19	83301	20.0	7	2	22.5	8	2	1.38	5.08
B23	37701	25.0	7	3	17.5	8	4	0.89	4.06
B27	41701	22.5	8	2	12.5	8	2	0.46	1.15
B28	44601	20.0	7	3	17.5	8	4	0.84	3.85
B29	45701	20.0	8	2	20.0	8	3	1.80	4.19
B31	47101	22.5	8	2	25.0	8	2	0.85	4.17
B31	47102	20.0	8	2	15.0	7	4	0.98	3.52
B32	49501	20.0	8	2	22.5	8	2	1.07	4.35
B33	53501	15.0	5	4	22.5	8	2	0.81	3.50
B35	57101	17.5	2	3	15.0	7	4	1.07	3.90
B43	66001	22.5	6	2	22.5	6	2	0.97	3.50
B38	60101	17.5	8	2	20.0	8	3	0.82	3.60

URUK WARE : STRAIGHT SPOUTS

LAYER	ARTIFACT NUMBER	BODY HUE	VAL	CHR	SURFACE HUE	VAL	CHR	IN DM HOLE	IN DM BASE	EX DM BASE	IN DM END	EX DM END	LNGTH
A7	12001	20.0	8	3	22.5	8	4	2.00	1.80	3.60	0.00	0.00	0.00
A7	12101	15.0	6	4	15.0	6	4	1.50	2.50	2.80	1.20	1.90	3.90
A21	23401	17.0	7	4	20.0	8	3	1.95	2.00	3.80	1.01	1.93	3.50
B21	35001	20.0	7	4	20.0	7	4	1.70	2.45	3.00	1.20	2.00	3.20
B23	43001	17.5	7	4	22.5	8	2	1.60	2.90	2.90	0.00	0.00	0.00
B29	44401	20.0	7	3	20.0	8	4	1.75	1.90	3.05	0.00	0.00	0.00
B30	46201	20.0	7	2	20.0	8	2	1.95	2.25	5.20	1.00	2.00	5.20
B31	49301	20.0	8	3	20.0	8	4	2.25	2.25	3.10	1.10	2.00	2.35
B32	49701	20.0	7	2	17.5	7	4	2.20	2.40	2.90	1.80	2.80	4.30
B33	51401	25.0	8	2	25.0	8	2	0.90	0.95	1.55	0.60	1.30	2.55
B33	53501	15.0	7	4	20.0	8	4	1.70	1.70	2.00	0.60	1.15	4.15
B33	57801	25.0	9	3	22.5	8	3	2.80	2.80	3.70	1.55	2.80	1.90
B34	54701	25.0	7	6	25.0	8	3	2.70	2.70	4.10	1.05	1.70	5.20
B34	55701	25.0	8	3	22.5	8	2	2.60	2.60	3.80	0.95	1.60	6.05

URUK WARE : FINE FLAT BASES

LAYER	ARTIFACT NUMBER	BODY HUE	VAL	CHR	SURFACE HUE	VAL	CHR	BASE DIAM	SIDE ANGLE	BASE THICK	SIDE THICK
A9	12701	22.5	8	2	22.5	8	2	3	68	0.25	0.36
A20	77701	22.5	8	2	22.5	8	2	3	50	0.55	0.76
A20	82701	17.5	8	2	20.0	8	4	3	60	0.52	0.52
A20	82702	17.5	8	3	17.5	8	2	3	58	0.60	0.57
A20	83301	20.0	8	2	22.5	8	2	3	60	0.75	0.74
A20	83501	17.5	8	2	22.5	8	2	3	60	0.50	0.51
A20	83801	17.5	7	2	17.5	7	2	4	62	0.49	0.67
A20	83802	20.0	5	2	17.5	7	4	3	61	0.70	0.46
A22	21901	17.5	7	5	15.0	7	4	4	55	0.35	0.31
B22	78501	25.0	9	1	22.5	8	1	5	32	0.55	0.60
B23	78301	17.5	7	4	20.0	8	3	4	54	0.35	0.44
B25	40401	15.0	8	3	20.0	7	2	3	52	0.55	0.65
B27	40601	17.5	7	3	20.0	7	2	3	65	0.45	0.34
B29	45001	17.5	7	2	20.0	8	3	3	55	0.39	0.62
B29	45002	20.0	7	3	20.0	7	3	3	59	0.74	0.59
B29	45701	20.0	8	1	20.0	8	2	3	43	0.38	0.24
B30	46201	20.0	8	2	20.0	8	3	3	52	0.48	0.30
B30	46701	17.5	8	2	20.0	8	2	4	55	0.65	0.76
B32	50801	22.5	7	3	22.5	8	3	4	30	0.72	0.52
B33	52201	20.0	8	3	15.0	7	3	4	39	0.42	0.41
B33	52601	25.0	7	3	25.0	8	3	2	53	1.00	0.39
B33	53501	25.0	8	3	25.0	6	3	7	45	0.62	0.68
B34	54601	22.5	8	3	22.5	8	3	5	48	0.60	0.61
B34	54602	25.0	8	3	22.5	8	4	6	50	0.62	0.67
B34	55901	20.0	7	4	22.5	8	3	2	43	0.45	0.45
B35	57801	25.0	8	3	22.5	8	3	5	45	0.70	0.65

URUK WARE : DROOP SPOUTS

LAYER	ARTIFACT NUMBER	BODY HUE	VAL	CHR	SURFACE HUE	VAL	CHR	IN DM HOLE	IN DM BASE	EX DM BASE	IN DM END	EX DM END	BASE-CURVE
A9	13101	20.0	8	2	20.0	8	2	0.00	0.00	0.00	0.90	1.60	0.00
B25	39101	17.5	8	4	20.0	8	4	0.00	0.00	0.00	0.85	1.65	0.00
B27	40601	17.5	7	4	22.5	8	2	2.50	2.55	4.40	0.00	0.00	2.01
B27	40602	22.5	7	2	20.0	8	4	0.00	0.00	0.00	0.80	0.90	0.00
B29	44402	17.5	8	4	20.0	8	3	0.00	0.00	0.00	0.85	1.80	0.00
B29	45701	20.0	7	2	20.0	8	3	2.15	2.90	4.15	0.80	2.15	1.71
B31	46901	17.5	8	4	20.0	8	4	0.00	0.00	0.00	0.95	1.40	0.00
B31	46902	20.0	8	3	15.0	8	2	0.00	0.00	0.00	0.72	0.92	0.00
B31	47901	17.5	7	4	22.5	8	2	2.50	2.95	4.25	0.00	0.00	2.00
B36	58701	15.0	6	5	22.5	8	2	2.70	3.10	5.40	0.81	1.85	0.00

URUK WARE : FLAT BASES

LAYER	ARTIFACT NUMBER	BODY HUE	VAL	CHR	SURFACE HUE	VAL	CHR	BASE DIAM	SIDE ANGLE	BASE THICK	SIDE THICK
A1X	07101	20.0	7	2	17.5	7	3	11	55	0.82	0.73
A1X	07102	20.0	8	2	20.0	8	2	9	52	1.09	1.26
A3	07701	20.0	5	3	20.0	7	3	4	40	0.90	0.77
A3	07702	20.0	8	2	22.5	8	2	13	39	0.49	0.52
A3	07901	20.0	7	3	17.5	8	2	4	36	0.75	0.55
A5	10301	20.0	8	3	20.0	8	2	11	46	0.56	0.84
A6	08401	20.0	8	3	22.5	8	2	14	42	0.50	0.86
A6	08402	17.5	8	3	20.0	8	4	12	44	0.77	0.71
A6	08403	20.0	8	2	20.0	8	3	14	47	0.55	0.80
A6	09401	20.0	8	2	20.0	8	3	14	48	0.68	0.73
A6	10801	17.0	8	2	15.0	8	3	8	48	0.49	0.55
A6	10802	17.5	8	3	20.0	8	3	15	31	1.20	0.95
A7	10601	20.0	8	2	22.5	8	2	7	34	0.79	0.85
A7	10602	20.0	8	3	22.5	8	2	8	65	0.60	0.80
A7	12001	17.5	8	2	20.0	8	2	9	40	0.66	0.91
A8	12401	15.0	7	3	17.5	8	2	8	48	0.72	0.78
A9X	13101	22.5	8	2	22.5	8	2	9	37	0.68	0.67
A9X	13102	20.0	8	2	20.0	8	3	11	45	0.54	0.57
A11	13301	20.0	8	2	20.0	8	2	12	51	1.14	0.85
A13	14301	15.0	8	3	17.5	8	3	14	54	1.13	0.98

APPENDIX C

URUK WARE : FLAT BASES

LAYER	ARTIFACT NUMBER	BODY HUE	VAL	CHR	SURFACE HUE	VAL	CHR	BASE DIAM	SIDE ANGLE	BASE THICK	SIDE THICK
A13	14801	17.5	8	3	17.5	8	2	14	38	1.37	1.14
A13	15301	22.5	8	2	22.5	8	2	9	38	0.60	0.76
A13	15302	22.5	6	1	22.5	7	2	13	50	1.06	0.80
A13	15801	20.0	8	2	22.5	8	2	11	40	0.79	0.60
A14	16601	17.5	8	3	20.0	8	2	12	38	0.95	0.76
A15	17601	15.0	8	4	17.5	8	3	12	36	1.24	1.03
A17	18201	20.0	8	2	20.0	8	2	11	41	0.65	0.78
A17	18202	20.0	8	3	22.5	8	2	10	48	1.02	0.91
A18	18501	20.0	8	3	22.5	8	2	9	33	0.93	0.79
A18	19601	20.0	8	3	20.0	8	3	34	50	1.84	1.71
A19	18901	20.0	8	2	20.0	8	2	5	41	1.31	0.92
A19	18902	20.0	8	3	20.0	8	3	14	60	1.62	1.47
A19	18903	20.0	8	3	17.5	8	2	7	37	0.79	0.92
A19	19801	20.0	7	2	20.0	8	2	16	46	0.92	1.11
A19	20001	20.0	7	3	17.5	7	3	8	60	0.67	0.88
A20	82701	20.0	8	2	20.0	8	3	5	37	0.74	1.22
A20	83301	20.0	8	2	20.0	8	2	9	31	0.67	1.17
A20	83303	20.0	8	2	22.5	8	2	10	40	0.54	0.64
A20	83304	20.0	8	2	17.5	7	3	8	43	0.73	0.49
A21	20701	22.5	8	2	22.5	8	2	13	48	0.82	0.86
A21	21201	20.0	8	3	20.0	8	2	11	46	0.87	0.90
A21	21202	20.0	8	2	20.0	8	2	17	46	1.02	1.18
A21	21701	20.0	8	3	20.0	8	3	11	35	0.85	0.91
A21	21702	20.0	8	3	15.0	7	4	6	33	0.57	0.50
A21	23001	20.0	8	3	22.5	8	2	24	45	1.05	1.27
A21	83305	20.0	7	3	15.0	6	4	6	50	0.50	1.55
B20	34001	20.0	8	3	20.0	8	2	8	42	0.34	0.41
B20	34002	20.0	8	3	20.0	8	3	8	45	0.51	0.67
B23	36301	17.5	7	3	20.0	8	3	7	31	0.71	0.64
B23	36302	20.0	8	3	20.0	8	3	4	22	0.37	0.43
B23	37001	20.0	8	2	20.0	8	3	7	26	1.36	1.20
B23	39301	17.5	7	4	17.5	7	3	6	35	0.30	0.54
B24	37501	20.0	8	2	20.0	8	2	7	50	0.70	1.03
B24	37503	20.0	8	2	20.0	8	3	19	40	1.03	1.00
B24	38301	20.0	8	3	20.0	8	3	11	42	0.78	1.00
B25	39501	20.0	8	2	20.0	8	2	12	38	0.75	0.83
B25	40401	20.0	7	2	20.0	8	3	17	34	0.77	0.85
B26	39701	20.0	8	3	20.0	8	3	11	45	0.97	1.47
B26	39801	15.0	7	4	20.0	8	2	5	61	1.07	1.10
B26	41001	17.5	8	2	20.0	8	3	5	38	1.46	1.00
B26	41002	22.5	8	2	22.5	8	2	26	60	1.06	0.97
B26	41201	20.0	8	3	20.0	8	3	5	38	0.87	0.68
B26	41401	20.0	8	2	20.0	8	2	18	53	1.20	1.78
B26	41402	20.0	8	3	20.0	8	3	12	48	0.89	0.63
B28	42401	15.0	6	3	20.0	8	2	7	40	1.25	1.13
B28	42402	20.0	8	2	20.0	8	3	6	40	1.06	1.30
B28	44601	20.0	8	3	20.0	8	3	7	40	1.20	0.86
B29	44401	20.0	8	3	20.0	8	2	8	48	0.80	1.02
B29	44402	20.0	8	2	17.5	7	2	6	49	0.77	1.30
B29	44403	20.0	8	3	20.0	8	2	5	54	0.97	1.12
B29	45201	22.5	8	2	22.5	8	2	13	40	1.07	1.08
B29	45202	20.0	8	3	20.0	8	2	6	36	0.96	1.17
B29	45502	20.0	8	2	15.0	7	4	5	59	1.40	1.14
B29	45701	22.5	8	2	20.0	8	3	5	43	0.52	0.73
B29	45702	20.0	8	2	15.0	7	3	19	50	1.05	1.13
B29	45703	20.0	8	2	20.0	8	3	7	51	0.55	0.79
B29	45704	20.0	8	2	20.0	8	0	15	48	1.31	0.97
B29	45705	20.0	8	2	20.0	8	3	15	40	0.65	0.67
B30	46201	20.0	8	3	20.0	8	2	6	36	0.46	0.57
B30	46203	20.0	8	2	20.0	8	3	8	30	0.80	0.78
B30	46204	20.0	8	2	22.5	8	2	11	39	1.00	1.04
B30	46401	20.0	8	3	20.0	8	2	3	44	0.76	0.60
B30	46402	20.0	8	3	20.0	8	3	8	36	0.93	1.03
B30	46403	20.0	8	3	20.0	8	3	6	34	1.03	0.97
B30	46701	20.0	8	2	20.0	8	2	21	47	1.13	1.95
B30	48401	20.0	8	3	17.5	8	2	15	35	0.80	0.94
B30	121901	15.0	6	4	22.5	8	2	9	38	0.55	0.81
B30	121902	22.5	6	2	22.5	6	2	9	35	0.35	0.79
B31	47101	20.0	8	2	20.0	8	2	7	55	0.65	0.81
B31	47102	20.0	8	3	20.0	8	3	5	61	1.25	1.10

URUK WARE : FLAT BASES

LAYER	ARTIFACT NUMBER	BODY HUE	VAL	CHR	SURFACE HUE	VAL	CHR	BASE DIAM	SIDE ANGLE	BASE THICK	SIDE THICK
B31	47601	20.0	8	3	17.5	8	2	6	34	0.45	0.94
B31	47602	20.0	8	3	20.0	8	3	7	46	1.08	1.10
B31	47901	20.0	8	2	20.0	8	3	6	50	0.39	0.61
B31	48101	17.5	8	2	20.0	8	2	9	33	0.57	0.61
B31	48102	17.5	8	2	17.5	8	2	6	36	0.85	1.42
B31	48103	20.0	7	3	17.5	7	4	12	35	1.10	2.65
B31	49301	20.0	8	3	20.0	8	3	5	40	0.40	0.57
B31	49302	20.0	8	3	20.0	8	3	9	37	0.67	0.98
B32	48901	20.0	8	2	20.0	8	2	7	47	0.60	0.57
B32	49502	25.0	8	3	22.5	8	2	4	43	0.50	0.44
B32	49701	17.5	8	2	20.0	8	2	15	59	0.87	0.75
B32	49702	20.0	8	2	20.0	8	2	4	35	0.55	0.50
B32	49703	20.0	8	2	20.0	8	3	6	42	0.56	0.69
B32	50801	20.0	7	4	25.0	8	3	7	40	0.54	0.58
B32	50802	20.0	8	4	17.5	8	4	4	37	0.51	0.60
B33	51401	17.5	7	4	17.5	7	4	8	40	0.74	0.93
B33	51901	25.0	8	3	25.0	8	3	7	29	1.08	0.41
B33	51902	15.0	7	5	15.0	7	4	3	40	0.84	0.63
B33	51903	20.0	6	4	20.0	8	3	7	38	0.63	0.80
B33	52601	20.0	8	4	17.5	8	3	9	34	0.57	0.78
B33	52602	22.5	8	4	22.5	8	3	6	38	0.84	0.61
B33	52603	22.5	6	1	22.5	6	1	8	35	0.60	1.00
B33	53101	15.0	7	6	20.0	8	3	9	36	0.70	0.73
B33	53301	17.5	8	4	20.0	8	3	6	43	0.56	0.60
B33	53302	17.5	8	4	20.0	8	3	9	42	0.70	0.75
B33	53901	17.5	6	4	15.0	6	6	8	55	0.91	1.10
B33	53902	22.5	8	4	25.0	8	4	16	36	1.45	1.46
B33	53904	20.0	7	3	22.5	8	4	11	49	0.76	0.92
B33	53905	22.5	8	4	25.0	8	3	11	38	0.66	0.82
B33	54101	22.5	7	3	22.5	8	3	7	40	0.56	0.72
B33	55301	20.0	6	3	15.0	7	5	7	43	0.95	0.79
B33	55302	17.5	8	4	15.0	7	4	8	39	1.07	0.52
B33	55303	15.0	7	4	20.0	8	3	10	48	0.98	1.17
B33	55304	15.0	7	6	20.0	8	3	6	41	0.54	0.83
B33	55305	20.0	6	3	20.0	8	3	7	34	1.02	1.23
B34	55701	20.0	7	4	15.0	6	6	5	35	0.50	0.52
B34	55901	17.5	7	4	20.0	8	1	18	56	1.15	1.04
B35	57101	20.0	7	4	20.0	8	2	11	45	0.79	0.56
B35	57102	17.5	7	3	15.0	7	4	6	40	0.37	0.63
B35	57301	20.0	6	3	15.0	6	6	8	39	1.03	0.77
B35	57802	17.5	8	3	22.5	8	3	7	40	0.75	0.70
B36	59201	17.5	7	3	17.5	7	3	10	50	0.50	0.65

URUK WARE : TURNED RING BASES

LAYER	ARTIFACT NUMBER	BODY HUE	VAL	CHR	SURFACE HUE	VAL	CHR	RING DIAM	RING ANGLE	BASE-THICK	SIDE THICK	RING THICK	RING HT
B33	53901	17.5	4	0	17.5	7	4	8.1	105	0.50	0.51	1.38	1.15
A3	07905	17.5	7	6	15.0	7	4	15.0	55	1.00	0.97	0.50	1.67
A5	09901	17.5	6	4	17.5	6	4	18.0	85	0.91	0.72	1.50	2.10
A6	07908	17.5	6	4	15.0	8	3	1.5	125	1.10	0.88	1.05	1.73
A5	79101	20.0	8	3	15.0	8	3	15.5	70	1.00	1.06	1.79	1.40
A6	09402	20.0	8	2	20.0	8	2	4.5	90	0.39	0.59	0.70	0.45
A7	10601	20.0	7	2	20.0	7	5	19.0	50	0.45	0.59	1.31	1.38
A8	12401	17.5	7	4	15.0	7	5	11.5	80	0.67	1.22	1.30	0.95
A8	12402	17.5	8	6	20.0	5	6	9.0	90	0.65	0.59	0.76	0.90
A14	16802	20.0	7	3	22.5	8	2	8.0	55	0.65	0.80	1.00	0.80
A18	19601	17.5	7	2	22.5	7	2	7.5	85	0.50	0.54	1.15	0.70
B23	36501	17.5	8	4	20.0	8	3	22.0	80	1.12	1.10	1.30	1.30
B28	35401	15.0	6	6	20.0	8	3	12.5	65	0.62	0.65	0.46	0.92
B29	44401	15.0	8	4	15.0	8	4	6.0	105	0.80	0.90	0.50	0.72
B33	57803	25.0	8	2	25.0	8	2	7.7	90	0.85	0.68	1.20	0.60
B34	54601	20.0	8	3	17.5	7	5	0.6	80	0.62	0.86	0.91	0.46
B34	56402	20.0	8	6	20.0	8	3	0.6	80	0.61	0.78	0.36	0.37

APPENDIX C

URUK WARE : PINCHED RING BASES

LAYER	ARTIFACT NUMBER	BODY HUE	VAL	CHR	SURFACE HUE	VAL	CHR	RING DIAM	RING ANGLE	BASE THICK	SIDE THICK	RING THICK	RING HT
A2	07101	20.0	7	4	20.0	7	4	8.0	85	0.40	0.70	0.90	0.70
A2	07501	20.0	8	4	20.0	8	3	9.5	90	0.89	1.00	1.00	1.05
A3	07701	22.5	7	3	22.5	7	3	6.0	115	0.35	0.59	0.75	0.60
A3	07902	15.0	7	5	17.5	8	2	9.5	105	0.98	1.09	0.90	0.50
A3	07903	22.5	7	2	20.0	7	3	10.0	80	0.88	0.71	1.10	1.20
A5	08401	20.0	6	3	15.0	5	4	5.5	85	0.90	0.74	0.85	0.57
A6	09401	20.0	7	3	17.5	7	4	8.0	100	0.39	0.75	0.85	0.55
B23	35401	15.0	6	6	20.0	5	6	12.5	115	0.69	0.73	0.81	0.80
B23	35601	17.5	8	4	22.5	8	2	9.0	85	0.75	1.05	0.87	1.05
B24	38701	15.0	7	6	15.0	7	4	9.5	80	0.90	0.72	1.00	0.90

Table C3: Attributes of Polychrome Motifs

URUK WARE : POLYCHROME JAR DECORATION - MOTIF C - VERTICAL CURVED LINES

LAYER	EXC NO	UMMA NO	SP NO	BODY HUE	VAL	CHR	SHERD THICK	SHOUL DIAM	NECK DIAM	BLACK PAINT HUE	VAL	CHR	RED PAINT HUE	VAL	CHR	CURVE WIDTH	CURVE PRIOD	CURVE AMPTD	COLOR PATRN	LOCUS MOTIF
A7	102	102	04	22.5	8	2	0.80	0	0	17.5	2	0	7.5	4	6	0.30	1.10	0.50	3	2
A9	119		01	20.0	8	4	0.80	0	0	15.0	4	1	7.5	5	4	0.10	0.95	0.34	3	2
A13	160	148	01	20.0	7	3	0.64	0	0	12.5	4	2	7.5	4	4	0.18	0.55	0.31	2	2
A16	217	178	03	17.5	7	4	0.87	0	0	15.0	4	2	5.0	4	3	0.21	2.20	0.42	2	2
A17	250		01	17.5	7	4	0.55	0	0	10.0	5	1	10.0	5	4	0.14	1.60	0.39	1	2
B21	143	346	01	17.5	8	4	1.00	40	0	10.0	4	2	10.0	5	4	0.18	0.60	0.60	2	2
B24	240	380	01	20.0	7	3	0.54	0	0	15.0	3	1	7.5	4	4	0.10	0.65	0.31	2	2

URUK WARE : POLYCHROME JAR DECORATION - MOTIF D - HORIZONTAL CURVED LINES

LAYER	EXC NO	UMMA NO	SP NO	BODY HUE	VAL	CHR	SHERD THICK	SHOUL DIAM	NECK DIAM	BLACK PAINT HUE	VAL	CHR	RED PAINT HUE	VAL	CHR	CURVE WIDTH	CURVE PRIOD	CURVE AMPTD	COLOR PATRN	LOCUS MOTIF
A1	041	79	01	20.0	7	3	0.77	0	0	0.0	0	0	10.0	4	6	0.82	1.35	1.60	2	3
A3	048		01	17.5	7	4	0.53	30	0	20.0	3	1	10.0	5	3	0.58	3.40	1.65	3	3
A6	069		01	15.0	7	6	0.75	45	0	12.5	2	0	12.5	5	6	1.10	3.30	1.90	3	3
A8	093		01	17.5	7	4	0.68	0	0	12.5	3	2	10.0	4	0	0.00	0.19	0.05	3	3
A9	120	131	02	20.0	8	3	0.89	28	0	0.0	0	0	7.5	4	4	0.35	1.90	1.00	2	3
A9	119		03	17.5	6	4	0.95	27	0	10.0	3	2	12.5	6	6	0.65	1.45	1.50	2	3
A11	125	133	01	20.0	8	3	0.94	0	0	12.5	3	2	17.5	5	6	0.35	1.40	0.80	2	3
A11	125	133	03	20.0	8	4	0.59	0	0	0.0	0	0	10.0	4	6	0.50	1.30	1.10	2	3
A11	125	133	04	20.0	8	3	0.74	38	0	10.0	3	2	10.0	4	6	0.77	1.55	1.35	2	3
A13	160	148	02	17.5	6	4	1.08	38	0	0.0	0	0	7.5	4	4	0.71	1.30	1.25	2	3
A13	160	148	03	17.5	6	4	0.79	33	0	10.0	3	2	10.0	4	6	0.28	1.70	0.80	2	3
A17	306	808	01	17.5	7	2	0.40	21	0	15.0	4	2	7.5	4	6	0.15	1.40	0.50	2	3
B19	129	819	04	20.0	7	3	0.90	40	0	0.0	0	0	7.5	4	5	0.60	2.75	1.12	2	3
B20	140	340	04	17.5	7	4	1.11	34	0	7.5	2	0	7.5	4	3	0.55	1.85	1.05	2	3
B20	131		03	17.5	8	4	0.70	24	0	10.0	4	2	7.5	5	4	0.35	1.45	0.70	2	3
B21	144		01	17.5	7	4	0.60	0	0	10.0	4	2	7.5	5	5	0.32	1.20	0.90	2	3
B22	175		01	22.5	8	2	0.62	28	0	0.0	0	0	7.5	4	6	0.36	1.20	1.10	2	3
B24	313	412	01	17.5	7	4	0.60	19	0	15.0	4	1	10.0	5	4	0.15	1.15	0.50	2	3
A17	250		02	17.5	7	4	0.86	0	0	15.0	3	1	10.0	4	4	0.22	0.85	0.60	3	2
B20	140	340	08	20.0	6	5	0.70	0	19	15.0	4	2	10.0	4	4	0.20	0.70	0.37	2	2
B23	238	377	01	12.5	6	6	0.65	0	0	12.5	3	2	10.0	5	4	0.28	0.95	0.45	2	2
B23	324	430	01	12.5	6	3	0.80	0	0	0.0	0	0	12.5	5	5	0.20	1.75	0.45	2	2
B24	244	387	01	20.0	8	3	0.81	0	0	15.0	3	2	10.0	5	3	0.15	0.90	0.55	3	2
B24	313	412	01	17.5	7	4	0.55	0	0	15.0	4	1	10.0	5	4	0.17	0.90	0.45	2	2
A17	306	808	01	17.5	7	2	0.70	0	19	15.0	4	2	7.5	4	6	0.14	1.55	0.40	2	2
A17	338	833	01	15.0	7	6	0.55	21	0	12.5	4	3	10.0	4	4	0.12	1.14	0.35	2	2

URUK WARE : POLYCHROME JAR DECORATION -MOTIF E-F- ISOCELES TRIANGLE

LAYER	EXC NO	UMMA NO	SP NO	BODY HUE	VAL	CHR	SHERD THICK	SHOUL DIAM	NECK DIAM	BLACK PAINT HUE	VAL	CHR	RED PAINT HUE	VAL	CHR	BASE TRIAN	HT TRIAN	WIDTH BORDR	FL LN WIDTH	FL SP WIDTH	COLOR PATRN	LOCUS MOTIF
A7	88		01	15.0	7	5	0.55	0	0	15.0	4	2	7.5	4	5	1.80	2.00	0.30	0.06	0.12	1	2
A9	119		03	17.5	6	4	0.93	27	0	10.0	3	2	12.5	6	6	4.05	3.95	0.25	0.20	0.25	3	2
A13	156		01	20.0	7	4	0.73	52	0	12.5	3	4	7.5	4	6	5.80	7.70	0.25	0.22	0.22	1	2
A12	208		01	20.0	8	4	1.07	30	0	15.0	4	2	7.5	4	6	4.30	5.00	0.27	0.23	0.28	1	2
A16	216	178	01	20.0	8	3	1.00	28	0	12.5	3	1	7.5	5	6	4.90	5.00	0.22	0.22	0.20	1	2
A20	306	808	01	17.5	7	2	0.71	25	0	15.0	4	2	10.0	4	4	5.50	5.20	0.60	0.10	0.25	3	2
A20	338	833	01	15.0	7	6	0.46	13	0	12.5	4	3	10.0	5	4	1.55	1.55	0.17	0.00	0.00	2	2
B24	313	412	01	17.5	7	4	0.72	19	0	15.0	4	1	12.5	6	6	5.60	4.30	0.49	0.11	0.20	3	2
B23	319	422	01	17.5	7	5	0.68	18	0	17.5	4	2	0.0	0	0	5.75	3.90	0.45	0.12	0.19	3	2

URUK WARE : POLYCHROME JAR DECORATION -MOTIF H- ARC AND RAY

LAYER	EXC NO	UMMA NO	SP NO	BODY HUE	VAL	CHR	SHERD THICK	SHOUL DIAM	NECK DIAM	BLACK PAINT HUE	VAL	CHR	RED PAINT HUE	VAL	CHR	BASE ARC	HT ARC	WIDTH LINE	WIDTH SPACE	RAY WIDTH	RAY SPACE	COLOR PATRN	LOCUS MOTIF
A8	104	124	03	20.0	8	3	0.86	0	14	0.0	0	0	12.5	5	6	15.90	2.14	0.00	0.00	0.00	0.00	2	2
A13	148	148	03	17.5	6	4	0.80	33	0	10.0	3	2	10.0	4	6	6.95	2.34	0.00	1.40	0.00	0.00	3	2
B20	133	336	01	22.5	8	3	1.07	0	13	7.5	3	2	7.5	4	6	8.00	1.50	0.55	0.90	0.20	0.25	1	2
B26	311	418	01	17.5	6	3	0.43	25	0	15.0	4	1	7.5	4	4	5.30	3.82	0.20	1.10	0.18	0.21	1	2
B23	177		01	20.0	5	4	0.60	0	0	15.0	3	1	7.5	3	6	2.50	1.25	0.50	1.00	0.09	0.10	1	2
B21	144		02	17.5	7	4	0.80	30	0	12.5	3	6	7.5	5	8	6.30	2.17	0.69	0.68	0.12	0.20	1	3
B24	244	387	02	17.5	7	4	0.60	28	0	12.5	4	4	10.0	5	4	4.80	1.35	0.45	0.60	0.20	0.18	1	3
B24	246		01	20.0	6	4	0.85	20	0	12.5	3	1	0.0	0	0	3.10	2.65	0.60	0.75	0.18	0.20	3	3
B23	236		01	22.5	8	3	0.51	25	0	12.5	4	4	7.5	4	5	4.50	2.15	0.26	1.50	0.25	0.18	3	3
B25	268		01	22.5	8	3	0.65	25	0	12.5	4	4	7.5	4	5	4.80	2.25	0.30	1.60	0.32	0.27	3	3

URUK WARE : POLYCHROME JAR DECORATION -MOTIF J- VERTICAL STRAIGHT AND CURVED LINES

LAYER	EXC NO	UMMA NO	SP NO	BODY HUE	VAL	CHR	SHERD THICK	SHOUL DIAM	NECK DIAM	BLACK PAINT HUE	VAL	CHR	RED PAINT HUE	VAL	CHR	CURVE WIDTH	CURVE PRIOD	CURVE AMPTD	STRT WIDTH	STRT SPACE	COLOR PATRN	LOCUS MOTIF
A1	40	71	01	22.5	2	3	0.60	38	0	10.0	2	0	10.0	4	4	0.25	2.05	0.55	0.90	0.70	1	3
A5	60	84	03	20.0	8	3	0.80	52	0	5.0	2	1	5.0	4	4	0.32	2.77	0.90	1.35	0.55	1	3
A5	60	84	02	20.0	7	3	0.82	38	0	5.0	2	1	5.0	5	4	0.35	1.80	0.65	0.65	0.86	1	3
A5	61		01	17.5	8	4	0.70	48	0	7.5	2	1	7.5	4	6	0.30	0.90	0.60	0.90	1.30	1	3
A6	69		03	17.5	7	5	0.57	38	0	7.5	2	1	7.5	5	5	0.40	1.75	0.75	0.60	0.72	1	3
A5	79		01	17.5	7	4	0.91	55	0	7.5	2	1	7.5	5	5	0.29	2.25	0.75	1.25	0.50	1	3
A8	104	124	06	17.5	7	4	1.19	0	0	0.0	0	0	7.5	5	4	0.22	0.75	0.63	0.24	0.69	1	2
A8	93		01	17.5	7	4	0.70	0	0	7.5	5	4	12.5	5	6	0.18	1.03	0.62	0.33	0.90	1	2
A9	120	131	04	17.5	7	4	1.13	0	18	10.0	3	2	10.0	5	5	0.11	1.12	0.46	0.40	0.55	1	2
A9	119		03	17.5	6	4	0.91	27	0	10.0	3	2	12.5	6	6	0.08	0.79	0.45	0.18	0.52	1	2
A10	121		01	22.5	8	2	0.86	48	0	12.5	3	2	7.5	4	6	0.16	0.65	0.30	0.19	0.60	1	2
A13	162		01	17.5	7	4	0.71	0	0	12.5	2	0	12.5	6	4	0.18	1.03	0.39	0.21	0.52	1	2
A16	216		02	17.5	7	4	0.58	0	12	12.5	3	3	7.5	4	6	0.19	1.63	0.74	0.32	0.51	1	2
B19	115		01	22.5	8	3	0.69	0	0	10.0	2	1	5.0	4	4	0.25	0.98	0.57	0.43	0.40	1	2
B20	131		02	20.0	8	3	0.90	27	0	10.0	3	1	7.5	4	6	0.18	0.76	0.40	0.15	0.82	1	2
B20	131		04	17.5	7	4	0.64	0	0	7.5	2	0	7.5	4	6	0.18	0.60	0.33	0.10	0.35	2	2
B21	169	352	01	17.5	8	4	0.65	0	0	15.0	4	3	10.0	5	4	0.17	1.04	0.40	0.45	0.43	1	2
B22	172		01	12.5	6	6	0.74	34	0	15.0	4	2	10.0	5	6	0.14	0.65	0.31	0.28	0.69	1	2
B23	229	320	02	17.5	7	4	0.56	0	0	12.5	3	2	10.0	4	4	0.19	1.20	0.55	0.19	0.68	1	2
B23	232	372	01	22.5	8	3	0.64	40	0	7.5	2	0	7.5	4	6	0.25	1.05	0.60	0.30	0.80	1	2
B22	171		01	20.0	8	4	0.90	0	2	10.0	3	2	10.0	4	5	0.25	1.07	0.57	0.34	0.50	1	2

URUK WARE : POLYCHROME JAR DECORATION -MOTIF K- HORIZONTAL STRAIGHT AND CURVED LINES

LAYER	EXC NO	UMMA NO	SP NO	BODY HUE	VAL	CHR	SHERD THICK	SHOUL DIAM	NECK DIAM	BLACK PAINT HUE	VAL	CHR	RED PAINT HUE	VAL	CHR	CURVE WIDTH	CURVE PRIOD	CURVE AMPTD	STRT WIDTH	STRT SPACE	COLOR PATRN	LOCUS MOTIF
A1	041	108	02	20.0	8	4	1.04	34	0	15.0	4	1	10.0	4	5	0.22	3.20	2.28	0.51	3.20	2	3
A6	086	108	01	22.5	8	2	0.72	43	0	7.5	2	1	7.5	4	6	0.46	1.60	1.75	0.60	2.37	2	3
A5	086	108	02	20.0	8	4	0.60	38	0	10.0	3	1	10.0	5	5	0.59	1.44	0.90	1.10	1.55	1	3
A6	086	108	04	17.5	7	4	0.59	30	0	10.0	3	1	10.0	4	4	0.71	2.15	1.15	1.12	1.20	1	3
A6	086	108	05	20.0	8	4	0.50	17	0	10.0	3	1	10.0	4	3	0.70	3.10	1.55	0.96	1.49	1	3
A5	069		02	20.0	8	4	0.70	0	0	27.5	2	0	7.5	4	4	0.70	1.75	1.95	0.60	2.40	2	3
A5	069		02	22.5	8	4	0.75	34	0	10.0	3	0	10.0	4	4	0.42	1.25	1.25	0.54	1.60	2	3
A6	078	94	03	20.0	6	4	0.70	0	0	0.0	0	0	10.0	5	4	0.44	1.60	1.30	0.30	1.00	2	3
A7	084		02	22.5	8	2	0.85	0	0	7.5	2	0	7.5	4	5	0.60	1.27	1.30	0.21	1.80	2	3
A8	104	124	02	22.5	8	3	0.64	27	0	15.0	4	2	7.5	4	2	0.60	2.28	1.65	0.25	1.58	2	3
A8	104	124	09	17.5	7	3	0.85	40	0	7.5	2	2	7.5	4	4	1.50	4.25	3.05	2.50	2.40	1	3
A9	120	131	03	17.5	7	4	0.55	34	0	15.0	4	2	7.5	3	6	1.05	2.35	1.90	0.45	2.55	2	3
B19	129	819	01	20.0	6	4	0.75	36	0	17.5	4	4	7.5	4	5	0.96	3.40	2.00	0.60	1.85	2	3
B19	129	819	02	17.5	7	3	0.60	31	0	17.5	4	1	7.5	4	4	1.20	1.75	1.75	0.50	2.00	2	3
B19	129	819	03	15.0	7	4	0.70	20	0	12.5	4	1	10.0	4	6	0.75	1.60	1.40	0.45	1.35	2	3
B20	140	340	01	17.5	8	4	1.11	24	0	7.5	3	2	7.5	4	4	1.60	6.30	3.00	0.75	2.40	2	3
B20	131		05	17.5	8	4	0.94	33	0	7.5	3	0	7.5	4	4	1.30	2.50	2.55	0.52	2.35	2	3
B21	167	350	02	17.5	5	4	0.80	35	0	7.5	2	0	10.0	4	4	0.85	3.40	1.70	0.48	1.82	2	3
B22	172		01	12.5	6	6	0.80	34	0	15.0	4	2	10.0	5	6	0.40	3.00	0.82	0.27	0.80	2	3

APPENDIX C

URUK WARE : POLYCHROME JAR DECORATION -MOTIF L- VERTICAL OPPOSED TRIANGLES

LAYER NO	EXC NO	UMMA NO	SP NO	BODY HUE	VAL	CHR	SHERD THICK	SHOUL DIAM	NECK DIAM	BLACK PAINT HUE	VAL	CHR	RED PAINT HUE	VAL	CHR	BASE TRIAN	HT TRIAN	WIDTH LINE	LNGTH MOTIF	COLOR PATRN	LOCUS MOTIF
A10	121		01	22.5	8	2	1.01	48	0	12.5	3	2	7.5	4	6	4.70	1.45	0.25	3.52	1	2
A16	216		01	17.5	7	4	0.51	28	0	12.5	3	3	7.5	4	6	3.70	2.67	0.20	5.36	1	2
A17	250		02	20.0	7	3	0.91	0	0	7.5	3	0	7.5	4	5	3.49	2.60	0.14	0.00	1	2
B21	169	352	01	17.5	7	4	0.69	36	0	15.0	4	3	10.0	5	4	2.48	1.55	0.14	0.00	1	2
B21	167		01	17.5	8	6	0.50	34	0	20.0	4	2	7.5	4	4	2.01	1.25	0.15	2.30	1	2
B22	172		01	12.5	6	6	0.70	0	20	15.0	4	2	10.0	5	6	3.28	1.54	0.07	3.28	1	2
B22	171		01	20.0	8	4	0.84	0	0	10.0	3	2	10.0	4	5	3.20	2.01	0.14	4.00	1	2

URUK WARE : POLYCHROME JAR DECORATION -MOTIF M- HORIZONTAL OPPOSED TRIANGLES

LAYER NO	EXC NO	UMMA NO	SP NO	BODY HUE	VAL	CHR	SHERD THICK	SHOUL DIAM	NECK DIAM	BLACK PAINT HUE	VAL	CHR	RED PAINT HUE	VAL	CHR	BASE TRIAN	HT TRIAN	WIDTH LINE	LNGTH MOTIF	COLOR PATRN	LOCUS MOTIF
A9	118	127	01	22.5	8	3	0.95	40	0	10.0	3	1	10.0	4	3	4.25	1.85	0.23	3.70	1	3
B22	172		01	12.5	6	6	0.68	34	0	15.0	4	2	10.0	5	6	2.10	1.23	0.18	2.73	1	3
B23	232	372	01	22.5	8	3	0.75	40	0	7.5	2	0	7.5	4	6	3.20	2.01	0.10	4.12	1	3
B22	121		02	17.5	6	4	0.83	35	0	10.0	4	1	10.0	4	4	3.10	1.65	0.14	3.65	1	3
A5	64		01	20.0	6	3	0.62	44	0	10.0	2	0	10.0	4	4	1.66	0.72	0.00	1.44	1	2
A6	86		07	22.5	8	2	0.65	0	0	7.5	2	0	7.5	5	6	1.10	0.90	0.14	1.75	1	2
A6	78	94	01	22.5	8	2	0.88	0	12	10.0	4	1	10.0	4	3	2.20	0.95	0.45	1.90	1	2
A10	121		01	22.5	8	2	1.09	48	0	12.5	3	2	7.5	4	6	2.15	1.11	0.33	2.38	1	2
A11	152		06	17.5	7	4	0.75	0	40	10.0	3	1	7.5	5	4	1.41	0.70	0.00	1.55	1	2
A16	216		01	20.0	8	3	0.75	28	0	12.5	3	1	15.0	4	1	2.45	1.70	0.00	3.55	3	2
B21	143	346	01	20.0	8	4	0.59	0	0	15.0	3	2	7.5	5	4	0.68	0.70	0.24	1.40	1	2
B22	171		01	20.0	8	4	1.06	0	20	10.0	3	2	10.0	4	5	1.55	1.35	0.30	2.35	1	2

Table C4: Attributes of Straw Tempered Ceramics

STRAW TEMPERED WARE : RESTORED BEVELED RIM BOWLS

LAYER	NUMBER	BODY HUE	VAL	CHR	SURFACE HUE	VAL	CHR	RIM DIAM	IN RM DIAM	BASE DIAM	IN BS DIAM	SIDE HT	INNER HT	RIM ANGLE	LIP ANGLE	SIDE THICK	VOLUME (CC)
A20	83705	20.0	7	3	17.2	6	4	22	20	10	8	5.6	5.0	47	68	1.1	800
A20	83707	17.5	7	4	17.3	6	4	18	18	9	8	5.9	5.5	46	56	1.0	650
A20	83708	17.7	7	3	17.7	7	4	20	17	7	7	5.3	5.5	56	55	1.1	550
A20	83709	17.5	7	4	17.7	7	4	21	20	8	8	5.6	5.1	49	62	1.2	790
A20	83710	19.5	6	3	17.0	6	4	21	19	8	8	5.7	5.4	50	64	1.0	720
A20	83711	20.0	6	3	16.7	7	4	20	18	9	8	5.2	5.4	53	67	1.1	700
A20	82627	20.5	8	1	20.0	8	2	19	16	8	7	5.7	5.4	58	55	1.1	600
A20	82628	20.2	6	3	17.5	7	4	20	18	8	7	5.4	5.4	54	53	1.1	550
A20	82629	20.0	6	3	16.2	6	4	31	26	11	10	8.4	8.1	55	67	1.5	1850
A20	83457	19.7	6	3	15.2	6	4	30	27	12	10	8.8	8.5	52	65	1.3	2140
A20	82967	20.0	7	3	16.0	6	4	18	18	9	8	5.3	5.5	54	59	1.1	600
B32	48905	20.0	7	4	15.0	6	4	17	17	8	7	6.6	6.0	65	64	1.1	650
B32	49702	20.0	6	3	15.0	6	4	17	16	7	6	6.6	5.6	69	44	1.1	450
B32	49706	20.0	7	3	15.0	7	4	17	17	8	7	7.2	6.6	59	62	1.1	700
B32	49801	20.0	6	3	15.0	7	5	17	17	7	7	6.9	6.1	50	61	0.9	600
B34	55314	20.0	7	3	17.0	7	4	16	15	8	7	7.6	7.0	70	71	0.9	600
B34	55315	20.0	8	3	20.0	8	3	16	16	9	7	7.7	7.4	76	57	0.9	675
B35	57118	20.0	5	3	17.5	8	3	13	13	7	6	6.4	5.7	60	54	1.0	350
B36	58701	17.5	7	4	15.0	7	4	17	15	7	7	6.2	5.9	49	37	1.1	500
B37	59701	17.5	6	4	22.5	8	2	19	18	7	6	7.0	6.4	47	45	1.0	715

STRAW TEMPERED WARE : SHALLOW PLATES

LAYER	ARTIFACT NUMBER	BODY HUE	VAL	CHR	SURFACE HUE	VAL	CHR	LIP FORM	RIM DIAM	RIM ANGLE	BODY THICK	RIM THICK	PAINT HUE	VAL	CHR
A20	77701	20.0	5	2	15.0	7	3	2	9	45	0.92	0.72	0.0	0	0
B30	48401	22.5	7	3	15.0	7	4	2	13	30	1.15	1.06	0.0	0	0
B35	56702	20.0	7	3	20.0	8	3	2	8	40	0.75	0.75	0.0	0	0
B36	59201	20.0	7	2	12.5	6	6	2	11	50	0.60	0.76	0.0	0	0

Table C5: Attributes of Grayware Jars

GRAY WARE : JAR RIMS

LAYER	ARTIFACT NUMBER	BODY HUE	VAL	CHR	SURFACE HUE	VAL	CHR	LIP FORM	NECK DIAM	RIM DIAM	RIM ANGLE	SHOUL THICK	NECK THICK	NECK HT	BURN	TEMP
A1	07101	20.0	6	1	20.0	5	1	2	15	17	65	0.86	0.57	1.50	1	1
A1	07102	20.0	6	1	20.0	5	1	2	19	21	75	0.68	0.73	2.20	1	1
A1	07104	22.5	6	2	20.0	6	3	2	12	14	65	0.80	0.68	1.31	1	3
A3	07701	20.0	6	2	20.0	5	2	2	14	16	66	0.51	0.55	1.50	2	3
A5	08401	20.0	6	2	20.0	3	0	2	18	21	45	1.00	0.54	1.17	2	3
A5	09101	15.0	5	1	20.0	5	3	2	14	16	50	0.50	0.51	2.67	0	0
A6	09401	20.0	3	1	20.0	5	2	2	15	18	65	0.51	0.65	1.95	1	1
A6	09402	20.0	6	2	20.0	6	2	1	14	16	87	0.75	0.60	2.52	1	1
A5	10301	20.0	6	2	20.0	5	1	2	19	22	75	0.42	0.57	2.04	1	4
A6	10801	20.0	7	1	20.0	6	1	2	16	20	60	0.63	0.57	2.22	1	2
A6	10802	17.5	6	4	20.0	5	1	2	11	14	70	0.44	0.51	2.58	1	1
A7	12001	15.0	5	3	20.0	5	2	2	14	16	75	0.33	0.47	1.96	1	4
A7	12003	20.0	6	1	20.0	6	1	2	11	13	60	0.49	0.56	1.39	2	2
A7	12004	20.0	6	1	15.0	2	1	2	11	13	60	0.68	0.59	1.48	2	2
A7	12005	20.0	6	2	20.0	5	1	2	11	13	65	0.48	0.42	1.21	1	2
A7	12007	17.5	6	2	20.0	3	2	2	15	17	80	0.49	0.42	1.91	1	2
A7	12008	15.0	6	4	15.0	4	2	2	13	15	60	0.79	0.50	1.59	2	3
A8	12401	20.0	6	1	20.0	6	2	2	15	17	75	0.53	0.57	1.72	1	2
A11	13301	20.0	5	1	20.0	5	1	1	15	17	80	0.80	0.41	2.72	1	3
A11	13501	17.5	6	2	20.0	5	1	2	13	14	70	0.70	0.56	2.02	2	3
A11	13502	17.5	6	2	20.0	5	1	2	12	14	81	0.62	0.65	1.62	1	2
A13	14801	15.0	5	1	15.0	5	2	2	9	11	67	0.58	0.74	1.68	2	4
A13	14802	15.0	6	4	20.0	6	2	2	17	18	60	0.82	0.64	1.39	2	3
A14	16801	20.0	5	1	12.5	5	0	2	13	16	55	0.83	0.60	1.57	2	2
A15	15301	20.0	6	2	20.0	5	1	2	13	16	78	0.94	0.70	1.89	1	3
A15	15302	20.0	5	1	20.0	6	3	2	18	21	65	1.02	1.00	3.38	2	3
A15	17001	20.0	5	1	20.0	6	3	2	17	19	85	0.72	0.84	2.70	1	3
A16	17801	20.0	5	1	20.0	5	1	2	16	19	85	0.71	0.70	3.10	2	2
A16	17802	20.0	7	2	20.0	4	1	2	10	13	70	0.70	0.74	1.72	2	3
A16	17803	22.5	7	2	20.0	6	2	1	15	19	80	0.95	0.72	2.24	2	4
A16	17804	20.0	7	2	20.0	6	1	1	10	12	90	0.55	0.52	1.72	1	2
A16	17805	20.0	5	1	20.0	5	1	1	10	12	65	0.73	0.40	1.77	1	3
A17	18501	20.0	5	0	20.0	5	1	2	14	17	80	0.89	1.15	3.12	2	3
A20	77701	20.0	4	2	17.5	7	4	2	13	16	70	0.63	0.64	1.40	1	3
B21	35101	17.5	7	3	20.0	5	1	1	10	12	80	0.46	0.56	1.13	1	3
B22	35901	20.0	6	1	20.0	2	0	2	14	15	60	0.67	0.62	1.63	1	3
B23	39301	20.0	6	2	20.0	4	1	2	14	18	55	1.01	0.73	3.67	0	0
B23	36501	20.0	6	2	20.0	5	0	2	14	16	55	0.49	0.39	1.29	1	4
B23	36801	20.0	6	3	22.5	5	2	2	11	13	75	0.61	0.74	1.95	1	4
B23	39301	20.0	5	2	20.0	5	1	1	16	19	73	0.64	0.78	2.85	2	3
B27	40601	20.0	6	2	20.0	6	2	2	11	12	55	0.55	0.53	1.42	1	3
B27	40602	20.0	5	2	20.0	5	2	2	10	12	45	0.89	0.68	1.82	2	3
B26	41201	20.0	6	3	20.0	4	1	2	14	16	80	0.80	0.85	3.20	2	3
B32	50801	20.0	4	1	20.0	4	1	1	10	14	65	1.00	1.66	2.68	3	7
B32	50802	20.0	6	2	20.0	8	3	1	14	17	70	1.30	1.58	2.50	1	9
B33	54101	20.0	4	2	20.0	4	2	2	8	10	65	0.59	0.53	1.10	1	3

APPENDIX C

Table C6: Select Design Statements for Polychrome Decoration on Jar Shoulders and Sides.

Field #	UMMA #	Vessel #	Exc./Layer	Figure	Design Statement
X040	60071	01	A1	—	1. –(–(Jrdbl)bl–)–, 2. –rd,bl(Jrdbl)bl,rd,bl
X081	60099	01	A5	—	1. bl,rd,bl(Dbl), 2. rd,bl((Nbl)bl,rd,bl(Qbl)bl,rd,bl(Abl,bl,rd,bl,Abl)bl,rd,bl(Rbl))bl,rd, bl(rd,bl(Qbl)bl,rd,bl(Nbl)bl,rd,bl(Nbl)bl,rd,bl(Qbl)bl,rd,bl(Ardbl)bl, rd,bl(Ardbl))bl,rd,bl, 3. (rd,bl,rd,bl(R+bl)bl,rd,bl,rd,...). (complete vessel)
X063	60791	01	A5	Pl. 1	1. rd(Bbl)rd,rd, 2. rd(((uniquebl)(Kbl))(Qrdbl)(bl(uniquerdbl)–))rd., 3. rd,bl(Jrdbl,M+bl,...)bl,rd(Bbl)rd. (complete vessel)
X104	60124	10	A8	—	2. rd,bl(Abl)bl, 3. rd,bl(–Ordbl,–)–
X104	60124	03	A8	—	2. (–bl,rd,bl(Hbl)–)bl, 3. (Drd)
X104	60124	07	A8	—	2. (–rd,bl(Abl)–)bl,rd, 3. bl(Ard,Mbl,–)
X118	60127	01	A9,10	Fig. 61l	2. ((–)bl,rd,bl(uniquebl)–)bl,rd, 3. bl(Ard,Mbl,...)bl,rd,bl(Drd)–
X119	—	02	A9,10	—	2. (–(Fbl)bl,rd,bl(–Brd,Lbl)–)bl, 3. (Drd)–
X119	—	03	A9,10	—	2. –((<Frdbl,...> bl,rd,bl <Frdbl,...> bl)bl,rd,bl(Jrdbl)bl,rd,bl,...)bl, 3. rd,bl(Drd)bl,rd
X121	—	01	A10	Fig. 60f	2. (–(–<Lbl,Brd> bl)rd(bl(Jblrd)bl,rd,bl <Mbl,Ard,...>–)bl, 3. rd(Drd?)–
X152	—	01	A12	—	2. –(–(Irdbl)(Mbl)rd–)bl, 3. bl(Drd)–
X156	—	01	A13	Fig. 58j	2. –(Fbl,...)bl, 3. rd,bl,rd–
X160	60148	03	A13	Fig. 59d	2. (–rd,bl(Hblrd)–)bl, 3. (Drd)–
X164	60153	01	A13,15	—	1. –rd(Abl)rd, 2. bl(Abl,Mblrd,...)bl,rd,bl(Brd,bl,uniqueblrd)–
X216	—	01	A16	Fig. 58k	2. rd,bl(Abl,Mrdbl,...)rd,bl(Fbl,...)bl, 3. rd,bl(Abl?,–)–
X251	—	01	A17	—	2. –(–bl(Ibl,Rrdbl–))rd, 3. bl(Abl)bl,rd.
X306	60830	01	A20	Fig. 58i	1. rd,bl(Abl)bl, 2. (Drd)bl(Erdbl),...), 3. bl(Drd)bl,rd.
X338	60833	01	A20	Fig. 58h	1. –(Drd), 2. bl(Fblrd,...)bl, (Drd)bl,rd.
X143	60346	01	B21	—	2. –((Pbl?)bl,rd,bl(Crd)–)bl, 3. rd,bl(Drd)–
X167	60350	04	B21	Fig. 61a	2. ((Lbl,Nrdbl,Lbl)bl,rd,bl(Jrdbl)bl,rd,bl)bl,rd, 3. bl,rd,bl(Kblrd)–
X144	—	02	B21	—	1. rd,bl(Abl)bl, 2. (Drd)bl–, 3. –(Hbl)bl,rd
X171	—	01	B22	Fig. 59g Fig. 60e	1. –rd,bl, 2. bl,rd((–)bl,rd,bl(Lbl,Brd,–)bl,rd,bl(Jrdbl)bl,rd,bl(<Mbl,Ard,...>bl, rd,bl(Obl)bl,rd,bl<Mbl,Ard,...>rd)–)bl
X172	—	01	B22	Fig. 60a	2. ((–Jrdbl)bl,rd,bl(Lbl,Brd,Lbl)bl,rd,bl,(Ibl,Rrdbl,))bl,rd,bl, 3. (Ard,Mbl,...)bl,rd,bl(Kblrd)–
X198	—	01	B23	—	2. –(–rd,bl(Hbl)–), 3. bl(Drd)–
X232	60372	01	B23	Fig. 60c	2. (–(Jrdbl)rd–)rd, 3. (Ard,Mbl,...)–
X229	60370	02	B23	—	2. (–Jrdbl,Mbl,Ard)bl,rd, 3. bl(Dbl?)–
X313	60412	01	B24	Fig. 58g	1. –(Abl)bl, 2. (Drd)bl(Frdbl,...)bl, 3. (Drd)bl,rd.

APPENDIX D

OTHER MEASURED ARTIFACTS FROM TEPE FARUKHABAD

These diverse artifacts are more commonly measured than are ceramics. A repeated justification of measurement procedure would be superfluous. In this appendix, all provenience is designated by excavation unit number; in Tables D1 and D2 a two digit item number is added. Those few items lacking an excavation number were marked with a layer designation in the field, but by error not otherwise ascribed to excavation units. All linear measures are in cm and weights are in gm except where noted. Items unweighed in Tables D3 to D10 are among those remaining in Tehran.

The chipped stone items presented in the first two tables are made from eight commonly occurring stone types: dark brown chert (1), medium to coarse gray cherts (2), fine red and green cherts (3), fine white or mottled white cherts (4), fine pink or mottled pink cherts (5), fine banded brown cherts (6), fine tan-brown and translucent tan or brown chert (7), unrecognizably burnt cherts (8), and other cherts (9). The blade tools may be from intact blades (1), proximal segments (2), distal segments (3), medial segments (4), or longitudinally broken pieces (5). They may lack bitumen (1), have an intact haft (2), have bitumen staining (3), or have remnant particles of bitumen (4). The retouched blade tools may have backing (1), natural backing (2), denticulation (3), irregular utilization (4), flat scraper retouch (5), notching (6), hafting (7), or very fine retouched (8). These may be located on the left edge (1), right edge (2), proximal end (3), or distal end (4). On sickle blades sheen may be on the top left (1), top right (2), bottom left (3), bottom right (4), top and bottom left (5), top and bottom right (6), or top and bottom right and left (7), all referent to a blade segment held with proximal end upwards. Sheen condition may be heavy (1), medium (2), light (3), or only traces (4). For all blade tools, the discrete value '9' and continuous value '.01' means that modification is absent. The core attributes given on Table D2 are similar. Few cores are blade cores (1) and most are of dark brown chert (1) or medium gray chert (2). The 'face height' is the length of the last flake or blade removed, and the length around the platform edge is the 'face perimeter.'

The attributes of celts, handstones, utilized pebbles, grinding slabs, beads, whorls, perforated items, drains, stone bowls, bone tools, bitumen items and woven items are all self-evident or discussed in Chapters IV and VIII.

APPENDIX D

Table D1: Attributes of Blade and Flake Tools

FARUKH PLAIN BLADES AND BLADE SEGMENTS

LAYER	ARTIFACT NUMBER	LN	WD	TH	WT	FACETS	MATERIAL	PART	BITUMEN
A24	44601	3.1	1.3	0.39	2.11	3	9	3	1
A26	45304	1.4	0.9	0.39	0.58	1	2	3	1
A26	45305	1.4	0.9	0.20	0.37	2	9	4	1
A26	45306	3.8	1.3	0.36	2.62	2	2	3	3
A26	48802	2.3	0.9	0.19	0.56	1	2	4	1
A26	48803	2.1	0.8	0.23	0.42	2	4	3	1
A26	48808	1.3	0.8	0.19	0.39	2	9	3	1
A26	48810	2.3	1.9	0.46	2.56	2	2	2	1
A27	49303	1.8	1.2	0.19	0.48	1	4	3	1
A27	49304	2.1	0.7	0.37	0.70	2	4	2	1
A27	49305	2.0	0.9	0.33	0.65	2	5	2	1
A27	49308	1.7	0.8	0.21	0.35	2	5	3	1
A27	50101	2.0	1.0	0.23	0.70	2	9	2	1
A28	53701	3.1	0.9	0.33	1.16	2	9	4	1
A30	61404	1.4	0.8	0.21	0.38	2	1	3	1
A31	63801	2.8	1.1	0.34	1.20	1	1	1	1
A34	67002	2.8	1.4	0.41	1.93	1	1	2	1
A35	67202	2.0	1.6	0.33	1.50	3	1	2	1
B40	63202	2.8	1.1	0.47	1.36	1	9	2	1
B40	63204	1.6	1.2	0.40	1.10	3	2	4	1
B40	63206	4.1	1.0	0.43	2.53	2	2	1	1
B40	63207	3.4	1.4	0.50	3.26	2	9	4	1
B40	63502	2.6	1.2	0.23	0.89	1	7	2	1
B40	64503	3.5	0.9	0.19	0.83	2	4	3	1
B40	64801	2.6	1.5	0.34	1.75	2	2	2	1
B40	64802	2.0	0.8	0.29	0.68	2	7	3	1
B41	68301	1.6	1.7	0.46	1.53	2	4	2	1
B42	69203	3.9	1.2	0.40	2.16	1	9	2	1
B43	70802	3.8	1.0	0.24	1.44	2	2	1	4
B43	70804	2.1	1.0	0.25	0.63	2	2	3	1
B44	71402	3.6	1.6	0.40	2.73	2	1	1	1
B44	71802	2.8	1.1	0.39	1.79	2	2	2	1
B44	71807	2.1	0.7	0.17	0.35	1	7	2	1
B44	72201	2.1	0.7	0.13	0.29	2	4	3	1
B45	73003	4.9	1.5	0.32	3.44	2	9	2	1
B45	73901	4.4	1.4	0.26	2.16	2	9	1	1
B46	75103	4.0	1.1	0.33	1.57	2	9	1	1
B46	75203	2.9	0.6	0.14	0.46	2	9	1	1
B46	75204	3.7	1.2	0.36	2.03	2	1	4	1
B47	75603	5.6	1.3	0.24	2.49	2	2	1	1
B47	75605	3.0	1.2	0.36	1.62	1	2	3	1

URUK PLAIN BLADES AND BLADE SEGMENTS

LAYER	ARTIFACT NUMBER	LN	WD	TH	WT	FACETS	MATERIAL	PART	BITUMEN
A21	30201	2.8	1.0	0.45	1.58	2	2	1	1
A21	32701	3.0	1.2	0.27	1.60	2	1	1	1
A21	32703	2.5	1.1	0.20	0.54	1	1	1	1
A21	33605	1.1	0.8	0.23	0.25	2	1	2	1
A21	33603	2.5	1.8	0.36	2.53	2	1	2	1
A21	33602	1.5	0.7	0.15	0.29	1	1	2	1
A21	33601	1.3	1.1	0.32	0.68	1	1	3	1
B	52201	8.3	1.8	0.30	4.61	3	1	1	1
B30	40102	2.1	1.0	0.55	1.31	4	1	4	1
B30	40301	2.8	0.7	0.57	1.18	4	1	1	1
B31	40403	3.3	1.4	0.51	3.10	1	2	3	1
B31	41002	4.3	3.1	0.10	14.30	1	2	2	1
B31	41201	4.2	1.1	0.56	3.63	1	2	3	1
B32	45801	3.2	1.3	0.32	1.39	1	1	1	1
B32	46301	1.7	1.3	0.44	1.35	2	1	2	1
B32	46302	3.3	1.3	0.43	1.71	1	1	1	1
B32	46501	1.3	0.9	0.27	0.27	1	4	3	1
B32	46502	6.0	2.5	0.72	10.32	1	9	1	1
B32	46804	4.2	1.3	0.69	5.14	4	1	2	1
B33	47601	2.1	0.5	0.20	0.26	1	9	3	1
B33	47602	2.4	1.2	0.30	0.97	1	9	2	1
B33	48102	5.8	1.3	0.38	2.98	2	9	1	1
B33	51102	1.5	1.1	0.49	0.91	1	1	3	1
B33	51701	2.4	1.3	0.36	1.77	2	2	2	1
B34	55701	2.7	1.3	0.50	2.70	3	2	4	1
B34	55803	3.7	1.6	0.47	3.66	2	9	2	1
B35	56603	2.8	1.1	0.20	0.95	2	1	2	1
B35	57401	1.4	0.8	0.19	0.31	2	9	4	1
B35	57901	4.2	1.5	0.26	3.04	2	2	4	1

JEMDET NASR AND EARLY DYNASTIC PLAIN BLADES AND BLADE SEGMENTS

LAYER	ARTIFACT NUMBER	LN	WD	TH	WT	FACETS	MATERIAL	PART	BITUMEN
A3	04703	2.2	1.5	0.41	1.44	1	2	2	1
A5	06001	3.1	1.3	0.33	1.61	2	1	1	1
A7	08501	3.9	1.4	0.60	4.08	2	1	1	1
A9	11801	2.2	1.8	0.80	4.08	1	1	2	1
A13	15701	3.1	1.7	0.42	2.95	1	1	1	1
A13	15702	2.2	1.2	0.17	0.53	2	1	1	1
A13	16402	1.5	1.1	0.25	0.61	1	1	2	1
A15	19601	4.0	1.2	0.27	1.97	1	1	1	1
A16	21701	3.0	1.7	0.52	1.89	1	1	3	1
A17	24801	3.9	1.8	0.47	4.50	1	2	1	1
A17	25605	2.1	1.2	0.30	1.08	2	1	2	1
A17	25607	2.7	1.1	0.35	1.41	1	9	1	1
A17	25608	3.2	0.9	0.34	1.06	1	1	1	1
A18	29301	5.5	1.0	0.32	2.10	1	3	1	1
A18	29303	1.9	1.0	0.32	0.51	2	2	2	1
B6	01401	1.4	1.3	0.33	0.86	2	2	4	1
B23	22601	3.4	1.3	0.40	2.24	2	9	3	1
B25	26501	2.5	0.8	0.25	0.60	1	1	1	1
B25	26502	3.2	1.3	0.27	21.88	2	2	2	1
B25	27701	2.3	1.3	0.22	1.68	2	1	4	1
B25	27702	2.2	2.0	0.34	2.08	2	1	2	1
B27	31601	3.8	1.4	0.42	2.92	2	1	1	1
B28	32202	1.8	1.4	0.43	1.41	2	5	4	1
B28	32301	3.3	1.3	0.44	2.79	1	1	1	1
B28	32302	2.9	1.4	0.32	1.62	1	2	1	1
B28	32304	1.3	1.3	0.30	0.58	1	1	2	1
B29	36501	2.6	0.9	0.36	1.97	1	1	2	1
B29	36502	1.6	0.9	0.29	0.56	2	9	3	1
B29	36801	2.6	1.4	0.55	2.23	1	2	4	1
B29	36903	2.8	0.7	0.23	0.55	1	1	1	1
B29	36904	2.6	0.9	0.35	0.91	1	1	1	1
B29	36905	1.5	1.8	0.50	1.58	1	2	2	1
B29	36906	1.8	1.1	0.30	0.94	2	2	3	1

FARUKH RETOUCHED BLADES AND BLADE SEGMENTS

LAYER	ARTIFACT NUMBER	LN	WD	TH	WT	FACT	MTRL	PART	RET TYPE	RET LOCN	RET LN	NOTCH WD	NOTCH DEPTH	RET TYPE	RET LOCN	RET LN	NOTCH WD	NOTCH DEPTH	BITMN COND
A20	29801	5.3	1.8	0.72	6.75	1	2	1	4	1	1.5	0.01	0.01	9	9	0.1	0.01	0.01	1
A22	37901	3.6	1.2	0.25	1.89	2	2	2	4	1	3.0	0.01	0.01	4	2	2.8	0.01	0.01	1
A23	44501	2.4	1.0	0.29	1.04	2	9	4	4	2	2.3	0.01	0.01	4	1	1.8	0.01	0.01	1
A23	44901	2.9	0.9	0.14	0.64	2	5	2	4	1	1.6	0.01	0.01	9	9	0.1	0.01	0.01	1
A24	38601	1.5	0.8	0.15	0.32	2	4	2	4	1	0.6	0.01	0.01	9	9	0.1	0.01	0.01	1
A24	38602	5.4	1.5	0.42	4.65	3	9	1	4	2	4.8	0.01	0.01	4	1	4.4	0.01	0.01	1
A24	44301	2.2	1.2	0.33	1.24	2	4	3	5	2	0.9	0.01	0.01	9	9	0.1	0.01	0.01	1
A24	44602	4.6	1.9	0.34	4.22	2	2	3	4	1	3.6	0.01	0.01	4	2	2.6	0.01	0.01	1
A26	45301	2.0	1.4	0.31	1.16	2	2	2	4	2	1.4	0.01	0.01	9	9	0.1	0.01	0.01	1
A26	45303	1.6	1.6	0.32	1.43	2	4	4	4	2	1.6	0.01	0.01	4	1	1.3	0.01	0.01	1
A26	45501	2.8	0.9	0.23	0.85	2	4	3	4	2	2.6	0.01	0.01	9	9	0.1	0.01	0.01	1
A26	48801	3.0	1.0	0.32	1.07	1	7	1	4	2	2.9	0.01	0.01	4	1	2.2	0.01	0.01	1
A26	48804	3.3	1.4	0.42	2.07	2	9	2	4	1	2.3	0.80	0.28	4	2	1.8	0.75	0.05	1
A26	48805	3.4	1.4	0.46	3.00	2	5	2	4	2	2.9	0.01	0.01	9	9	0.1	0.01	0.01	1
A26	48806	0.8	1.6	0.30	0.53	2	5	4	4	1	0.6	0.01	0.01	4	2	0.7	0.01	0.01	1
A26	48807	1.5	1.1	0.30	0.77	2	9	4	5	1	1.3	0.01	0.01	9	9	0.1	0.01	0.01	1
A26	48809	1.6	1.2	0.42	0.98	2	2	4	4	1	0.8	0.01	0.01	4	2	0.6	0.01	0.01	1
A26	48811	1.6	1.8	0.40	1.62	2	5	4	4	4	0.7	0.01	0.01	4	2	0.7	0.01	0.01	1
A27	49301	2.6	1.1	0.42	1.58	2	2	3	4	1	1.8	0.01	0.01	9	9	0.1	0.01	0.01	1
A27	49302	1.7	1.3	0.44	1.38	2	2	4	4	1	1.0	0.01	0.01	9	9	0.1	0.01	0.01	1
A27	49306	2.0	1.4	0.39	1.32	2	6	4	6	2	1.0	0.48	0.09	6	1	0.7	0.54	0.09	1
A27	49307	2.7	0.8	0.19	0.61	2	7	4	4	2	2.6	0.01	0.01	4	1	2.3	0.01	0.01	1
A27	50102	2.4	1.3	0.41	1.94	2	2	4	4	1	2.4	0.01	0.01	4	2	2.2	0.01	0.01	1
A28	53801	2.0	1.3	0.34	1.61	2	9	2	4	2	1.7	0.01	0.01	4	2	1.7	0.01	0.01	1
A28	54201	1.7	1.9	0.36	1.45	1	1	4	4	1	1.7	0.01	0.01	4	2	1.3	0.01	0.01	1
A29	58301	1.6	1.1	0.34	0.67	1	1	2	5	1	0.5	0.01	0.01	9	9	0.1	0.01	0.01	1
A29	58302	2.8	0.8	0.37	3.13	2	1	2	4	1	2.3	0.01	0.01	5	4	1.6	0.01	0.01	1
A29	60701	2.3	1.0	0.21	0.68	1	1	1	4	1	1.7	0.01	0.01	4	2	1.4	0.01	0.01	1
A29	60702	1.0	1.2	0.25	0.43	2	1	4	4	2	0.8	0.01	0.01	9	9	0.1	0.01	0.01	1
A30	58501	2.3	1.4	0.33	1.79	2	9	4	4	2	2.0	0.01	0.01	4	1	2.0	0.01	0.01	1

APPENDIX D

FARUKH RETOUCHED BLADES AND BLADE SEGMENTS

LAYER	ARTIFACT NUMBER	LN	WD	TH	WT	FACT	MTRL	PART	RET TYPE	RET LOCN	RET LN	NOTCH WD	NOTCH DEPTH	RET TYPE	RET LOCN	RET LN	NOTCH WD	NOTCH DEPTH	BIT MN COND
A30	58502	3.9	1.6	0.38	3.88	3	9	1	5	1	3.4	0.01	0.01	4	2	2.9	0.01	0.01	1
A30	61401	1.5	0.9	0.30	0.63	3	2	4	4	2	1.0	0.01	0.01	5	3	1.0	0.01	0.01	1
A30	61403	2.1	1.2	0.27	1.05	2	1	3	5	2	1.7	0.01	0.01	9	9	0.1	0.01	0.01	1
A30	61405	3.7	1.0	0.43	2.04	1	9	1	4	2	0.5	0.01	0.01	9	9	0.1	0.01	0.01	1
A31	63802	2.4	1.0	0.58	1.41	1	1	1	4	2	2.1	0.01	0.01	4	1	1.8	0.01	0.01	1
A31	63803	1.9	1.1	0.40	1.09	2	1	2	4	2	1.7	0.01	0.01	4	1	1.3	0.01	0.01	1
A34	66701	4.1	1.0	0.23	1.38	2	9	2	4	2	3.0	0.01	0.01	4	1	2.9	0.01	0.01	1
A34	66702	1.7	1.1	0.30	0.50	2	1	3	4	2	1.1	0.01	0.01	9	9	0.1	0.01	0.01	1
A34	66702	3.8	1.2	0.32	1.94	2	2	1	4	2	2.8	0.01	0.01	4	2	1.7	0.01	0.01	1
A34	66703	4.1	1.2	0.31	2.80	2	2	2	3	2	3.5	0.17	0.05	3	2	3.6	0.14	0.05	1
A34	66704	1.5	1.4	0.35	1.07	2	1	1	4	1	0.9	0.01	0.01	9	9	0.1	0.01	0.01	1
A34	67001	2.4	1.3	0.34	1.82	2	1	2	4	2	1.9	0.01	0.01	6	1	5.2	0.52	0.14	1
A35	67201	2.0	1.0	0.30	1.24	2	1	2	4	2	1.5	0.01	0.01	9	9	0.1	0.01	0.01	1
A36	69901	2.4	1.5	0.50	2.63	3	4	4	4	1	2.3	0.01	0.01	4	2	1.9	0.01	0.01	1
A36	69902	3.2	1.2	0.34	1.75	1	1	1	4	1	3.0	0.01	0.01	4	2	2.4	0.01	0.01	1
A36	69903	3.1	1.5	0.35	1.70	1	1	1	4	2	2.1	0.01	0.01	9	9	0.1	0.01	0.01	1
A36	69904	2.6	1.2	0.40	1.29	1	9	4	6	2	0.8	0.80	0.13	6	1	2.0	0.12	0.05	1
A36	70401	1.0	1.6	0.60	1.38	2	7	4	6	4	1.3	0.62	0.21	4	2	1.0	0.01	0.01	1
A36	70402	1.7	1.3	0.34	0.94	1	1	2	4	2	1.5	0.01	0.01	4	1	1.0	0.01	0.01	1
B38	61601	2.5	0.9	0.24	0.75	2	9	4	4	1	2.4	0.01	0.01	1	2	1.9	0.01	0.01	1
B40	63201	1.9	1.6	0.41	1.86	1	1	2	4	1	0.8	0.01	0.01	9	9	0.1	0.01	0.01	1
B40	63203	1.7	1.7	0.37	1.45	2	2	3	8	4	1.4	0.01	0.01	4	2	0.8	0.01	0.01	1
B40	63205	1.6	0.9	0.22	0.53	2	4	3	5	1	1.6	0.01	0.01	4	2	0.8	0.01	0.01	1
B40	63501	2.4	1.5	0.33	1.55	2	2	3	1	4	0.7	0.01	0.01	9	9	0.1	0.01	0.01	4
B40	64501	1.9	0.8	0.34	0.65	1	1	3	2	1	1.3	0.13	0.02	9	9	0.1	0.01	0.01	1
B40	64502	2.2	1.0	0.30	0.98	2	4	4	5	1	2.1	0.01	0.01	1	2	1.6	0.01	0.01	1
B40	64802	1.9	0.9	0.21	0.54	2	9	4	4	1	1.9	0.01	0.01	4	2	1.8	0.01	0.01	1
B40	64803	1.6	1.4	0.20	0.90	2	5	4	5	1	1.7	0.01	0.01	1	2	1.3	0.01	0.01	1
B40	64804	2.7	1.4	0.28	1.50	2	2	4	4	2	2.7	0.01	0.01	9	9	0.1	0.01	0.01	1
B40	64805	2.7	1.2	0.30	1.64	3	2	2	4	1	2.2	0.01	0.01	4	2	1.9	0.01	0.01	1
B40	64806	2.9	1.3	0.42	2.35	3	2	4	4	2	2.9	0.01	0.01	9	9	0.1	0.01	0.01	1
B41	65301	1.6	1.1	0.30	0.79	2	5	2	4	1	1.7	0.01	0.01	4	2	1.6	0.07	0.01	1
B41	65901	2.7	1.5	0.29	2.16	2	4	3	4	1	2.2	0.01	0.01	9	9	0.1	0.01	0.01	1
B41	67501	5.6	1.6	0.40	5.74	2	9	3	4	1	5.1	0.01	0.01	4	2	4.1	0.01	0.01	1
B41	68001	3.6	1.2	0.31	1.95	2	9	3	6	2	2.5	0.25	0.07	9	9	0.1	0.01	0.01	1
B42	69001	2.9	0.6	0.12	0.35	2	7	1	9	9	0.1	0.01	0.01	9	9	0.1	0.01	0.01	1
B42	69201	6.5	1.2	0.31	3.01	2	9	1	4	1	5.1	0.01	0.01	9	9	0.1	0.01	0.01	1
B42	69202	6.2	1.6	0.53	6.34	2	9	2	4	2	2.6	0.01	0.01	9	9	0.1	0.01	0.01	1
B42	69204	8.7	2.1	0.58	13.05	3	9	1	4	1	8.1	0.01	0.01	6	2	0.7	0.69	0.19	4
B42	69201	6.3	1.7	0.75	10.26	3	9	2	4	2	5.9	0.01	0.01	9	9	0.1	0.01	0.01	1
B42	69201	3.8	1.1	0.52	2.52	1	9	2	7	0	1.6	0.01	0.01	9	9	0.1	0.01	0.01	1
B42	69701	4.2	1.6	0.51	3.72	1	1	1	4	1	2.3	0.01	0.01	4	2	1.5	0.01	0.01	1
B42	69702	3.0	1.3	0.39	2.12	2	4	2	4	1	2.6	0.01	0.01	5	2	2.2	0.01	0.01	1
B42	69703	3.2	1.0	0.26	1.22	3	3	2	4	1	2.7	0.01	0.01	4	2	0.9	0.01	0.01	1
B43	70601	3.0	1.4	0.34	2.19	2	2	2	4	2	2.3	0.01	0.01	4	1	1.8	0.01	0.01	1
B43	70801	4.7	1.8	0.77	8.16	1	2	3	5	1	4.5	0.01	0.01	5	2	4.2	0.01	0.01	1
B43	70803	4.0	1.3	0.35	2.84	3	2	2	4	1	3.9	0.01	0.01	4	2	4.1	0.01	0.01	1
B44	71401	4.4	1.4	0.28	2.12	1	1	1	6	2	3.5	0.35	0.13	9	9	0.1	0.01	0.01	1
B44	71801	1.6	1.1	0.25	0.70	2	9	3	9	9	0.1	0.01	0.01	9	9	0.1	0.01	0.01	1
B44	71803	2.5	0.8	0.30	0.64	1	1	3	4	1	2.5	0.01	0.01	4	2	2.5	0.01	0.01	1
B44	71805	1.1	0.7	0.14	0.19	1	7	4	4	1	1.1	0.01	0.01	4	2	1.0	0.39	0.10	1
B44	71806	2.1	1.1	0.20	0.92	2	2	4	4	1	2.0	0.01	0.01	9	9	0.1	0.01	0.01	1
B45	73002	2.0	1.8	0.51	3.20	3	9	4	5	1	1.7	0.01	0.01	5	2	1.6	0.01	0.01	1
B45	73801	3.4	1.1	0.32	1.51	2	9	1	4	1	2.7	0.01	0.01	9	9	0.1	0.01	0.01	1
B45	73901	4.0	1.3	0.46	2.71	2	2	2	5	1	3.4	0.00	0.01	0	0	0.0	0.00	0.00	4
B46	75102	2.0	1.4	0.50	2.13	2	2	4	6	2	1.1	0.78	0.15	9	9	0.1	0.01	0.01	1
B46	75201	3.4	1.0	0.50	2.14	2	4	3	5	1	2.1	0.01	0.01	9	9	0.1	0.01	0.01	1
B46	75202	4.0	1.2	0.32	1.89	1	2	2	4	1	3.2	0.01	0.01	6	2	1.4	0.14	0.11	1
B46	75205	2.1	1.3	0.31	0.96	1	1	3	4	1	1.6	0.01	0.01	5	4	0.9	0.01	0.01	1
B47	75601	3.8	1.4	0.36	2.85	2	9	4	9	9	0.1	0.01	0.01	9	9	0.1	0.01	0.01	1
B47	75602	2.4	0.6	0.27	0.51	1	9	2	4	2	1.6	0.01	0.01	9	9	0.1	0.01	0.01	1
B47	75604	5.1	1.6	0.30	4.08	3	4	1	4	1	4.3	0.01	0.01	4	2	4.4	0.01	0.01	1
B47	75606	1.4	1.2	0.35	1.56	2	2	2	9	9	0.1	0.01	0.01	9	9	0.1	0.01	0.01	1

URUK RETOUCHED BLADES AND BLADE SEGMENTS

LAYER	ARTIFACT NUMBER	LN	WD	TH	WT	FACT	MTRL	PART	RET TYPE	RET LOCN	RET LN	NOTCH WD	NOTCH DEPTH	RET TYPE	RET LOCN	RET LN	NOTCH WD	NOTCH DEPTH	BITMN COND
A19	26101	2.2	1.2	0.67	2.72	1	2	4	9	9	0.1	0.01	0.01	9	9	0.1	0.01	0.01	1
A19	26102	1.3	1.1	0.43	0.84	1	1	4	4	1	0.9	0.01	0.01	4	2	0.9	0.01	0.01	1
A20	29802	3.4	1.2	0.28	1.28	1	9	1	4	1	2.2	0.01	0.01	9	9	0.1	0.01	0.01	1
A20	29803	6.0	1.7	0.71	10.11	3	9	2	5	2	6.0	0.01	0.01	4	2	5.0	0.01	0.01	1
A20	29804	8.2	1.8	0.93	12.48	2	2	1	4	1	3.8	0.01	0.01	4	2	2.9	0.01	0.01	1
A20	29805	2.8	1.2	0.48	2.15	3	2	2	7	2	1.3	0.28	0.30	6	1	3.3	0.23	0.10	1
A20	29806	2.6	1.0	0.22	0.54	2	2	4	9	9	0.1	0.01	0.01	9	9	0.1	0.01	0.01	1
A20	29807	2.2	1.1	0.28	0.79	1	1	2	4	1	1.5	0.01	0.01	4	2	1.4	0.01	0.01	1
A20	29810	0.8	1.2	0.25	0.37	1	1	4	8	1	0.7	0.01	0.01	1	2	0.6	0.01	0.01	1
A20	29811	1.2	0.9	0.21	0.43	1	1	2	4	2	1.2	0.01	0.01	9	9	0.1	0.01	0.01	1
A20	29812	1.2	0.9	0.19	0.26	2	3	4	4	1	1.2	0.01	0.01	4	2	1.2	0.01	0.01	1
A20	29813	0.2	1.2	0.35	1.11	1	1	2	4	1	1.1	0.01	0.01	9	9	0.1	0.01	0.01	1
A21	32702	3.4	1.9	0.36	3.34	2	9	2	4	1	2.5	0.01	0.01	4	2	2.5	0.01	0.01	1
A21	33001	1.7	2.1	0.86	3.56	1	1	2	5	2	1.4	0.01	0.01	9	9	0.1	0.01	0.01	1
A21	33604	2.1	1.1	0.29	0.80	2	2	3	4	1	1.6	0.01	0.01	9	9	0.1	0.01	0.01	4
A21	33606	7.3	2.0	0.92	18.78	2	2	1	4	2	5.4	0.01	0.01	3	2	1.5	0.50	0.17	1
A21	33901	1.6	1.4	0.32	1.18	1	1	3	4	1	1.3	0.01	0.01	9	9	0.1	0.01	0.01	1
A21	33902	3.7	1.5	0.32	2.50	1	2	1	4	1	3.5	0.01	0.01	4	2	3.3	0.01	0.01	1
B28	31901	1.7	1.3	0.35	1.31	2	7	4	4	2	1.8	0.01	0.01	4	1	1.4	0.01	0.01	1
B28	32101	3.0	1.4	0.43	2.75	2	9	3	8	1	3.0	0.01	0.01	4	2	2.8	0.01	0.01	1
B28	32102	2.8	1.3	0.30	1.61	2	4	2	4	1	2.3	0.01	0.01	4	2	2.1	0.01	0.01	1
B28	32103	1.7	1.1	0.29	0.89	2	4	4	4	2	1.4	0.37	0.08	9	9	0.1	0.01	0.01	1
B28	32303	3.0	1.2	0.54	2.13	1	2	2	4	2	1.6	0.01	0.01	9	9	0.1	0.01	0.01	1
B28	32305	1.8	1.3	0.30	1.04	1	1	2	4	1	1.1	0.01	0.01	4	2	1.0	0.01	0.01	1
B29	36802	3.6	1.8	0.46	3.72	2	9	4	4	2	3.1	0.01	0.01	5	1	1.2	0.01	0.01	1
B29	37301	3.2	1.3	0.45	2.51	2	4	2	4	1	1.8	0.01	0.01	9	9	0.1	0.01	0.01	1
B29	37302	4.7	2.3	0.66	8.54	1	9	1	4	2	3.2	0.01	0.01	4	1	3.1	0.01	0.01	1
B29	35901	1.3	1.2	0.28	0.68	2	2	4	4	2	1.3	0.01	0.01	9	9	0.1	0.01	0.01	1
B29	35902	0.9	1.2	0.28	0.35	1	1	6	4	1	0.6	0.01	0.01	4	2	1.0	0.01	0.01	1
B29	36501	1.4	2.0	0.33	1.77	1	1	4	5	2	0.6	0.01	0.01	4	2	1.0	0.01	0.01	1
B29	36503	2.7	1.2	0.41	1.68	2	4	3	8	2	2.4	0.08	0.03	3	1	2.4	0.40	0.10	1
B	36601	2.0	1.4	0.35	1.23	2	1	2	4	2	1.9	0.01	0.01	9	9	0.1	0.01	0.01	1
B	36602	2.0	1.2	0.36	1.14	2	1	4	4	2	1.9	0.01	0.01	6	1	0.8	0.80	0.23	1
B30	40302	3.2	1.7	0.45	3.83	2	9	3	4	1	2.7	0.01	0.01	9	9	0.1	0.01	0.01	1
B31	40402	2.6	1.6	0.47	2.85	2	1	2	4	2	2.4	0.80	0.18	9	9	0.1	0.01	0.01	1
B31	41001	2.9	1.2	0.32	1.59	2	9	2	4	1	1.8	0.01	0.01	4	2	1.5	0.01	0.01	1
B31	41202	4.9	1.4	0.55	4.32	1	2	2	4	2	3.5	0.01	0.01	9	9	0.1	0.01	0.01	1
B31	41203	4.6	1.6	0.40	3.82	2	9	3	8	2	4.2	0.01	0.01	8	1	2.7	0.01	0.01	1
B31	42001	2.3	1.0	0.25	0.61	1	9	2	4	2	2.2	0.01	0.01	4	1	2.0	0.01	0.01	1
B31	42002	2.4	1.4	0.45	1.77	1	4	2	1	2	1.6	0.01	0.01	4	1	1.6	0.01	0.01	1
B31	42003	2.5	1.4	0.30	1.49	2	2	4	4	1	2.3	0.01	0.01	4	2	1.9	0.01	0.01	1
B32	42902	3.2	1.4	0.26	1.81	3	5	3	5	2	0.9	0.01	0.01	9	9	0.1	0.01	0.01	1
B31	43201	5.2	1.7	0.87	10.01	1	1	1	5	1	4.4	0.01	0.01	9	9	0.1	0.01	0.01	4
B31	43202	3.2	1.2	0.47	2.42	2	2	2	4	1	2.3	0.01	0.01	9	9	0.1	0.01	0.01	1
B31	43203	2.7	1.9	0.47	3.04	3	1	2	6	2	0.5	0.50	0.08	9	9	0.1	0.01	0.01	1
B32	46601	2.2	1.8	0.50	2.57	1	1	2	4	2	1.3	0.01	0.01	9	9	0.1	0.01	0.01	1
B32	46602	2.3	1.1	0.38	1.21	2	2	3	6	3	0.8	0.41	0.06	6	2	0.6	0.43	0.04	1
B32	46604	4.5	1.7	0.48	4.62	1	5	2	4	1	3.2	0.01	0.01	3	2	1.8	0.09	0.15	1
B32	46605	6.6	2.2	0.62	12.89	1	1	1	4	2	4.8	0.01	0.01	4	2	3.2	0.01	0.01	1
B32	46801	11.1	3.5	1.37	66.43	1	2	1	4	2	8.3	0.01	0.01	4	1	6.9	0.01	0.01	1
B32	46802	3.0	1.4	0.42	3.05	2	2	4	4	1	2.9	0.01	0.01	1	2	2.8	0.01	0.01	1
B32	46805	3.4	0.9	0.26	1.14	2	9	4	4	1	2.5	0.01	0.01	9	9	0.1	0.01	0.01	1
B33	51001	2.9	1.1	0.25	1.16	2	4	3	4	1	2.5	0.01	0.01	9	9	0.1	0.01	0.01	1
B33	51101	4.3	1.6	0.39	3.78	1	4	4	4	2	3.9	0.01	0.01	4	1	3.7	0.01	0.01	1
B33	51201	4.7	2.1	0.34	2.32	3	1	4	4	2	2.1	0.01	0.01	4	1	1.8	0.01	0.01	1
B33	51401	3.5	1.5	0.46	2.39	1	1	1	4	1	2.1	0.01	0.01	4	2	1.5	0.01	0.01	1
B33	51402	3.4	1.5	0.30	2.20	2	2	2	1	1	2.8	0.01	0.01	9	9	0.1	0.01	0.01	1
B33	51501	9.2	1.6	0.57	8.31	1	2	1	4	2	8.6	0.01	0.01	4	1	6.2	0.01	0.01	1
B33	51503	4.1	1.3	0.43	3.80	2	9	1	4	2	3.0	0.01	0.01	9	9	0.1	0.01	0.01	1
B33	51504	4.2	0.9	0.40	1.89	1	9	2	4	1	0.9	0.01	0.01	9	9	0.1	0.01	0.01	1
B33	51505	6.3	1.6	0.43	2.82	1	2	2	4	1	2.0	0.01	0.01	1	4	1.6	0.01	0.01	4
B33	51702	3.0	0.9	0.17	0.67	2	4	4	1	1	3.0	0.01	0.01	4	2	2.3	0.01	0.01	1
B33	51703	2.4	1.1	0.26	1.41	2	7	3	5	1	0.6	0.01	0.01	9	9	0.1	0.01	0.01	1
B34	52801	1.6	1.3	0.35	1.15	2	1	4	4	1	1.4	0.01	0.01	4	2	1.3	0.01	0.01	1
B34	52802	1.7	1.3	0.29	0.97	2	2	4	4	1	1.7	0.01	0.01	9	9	0.1	0.01	0.01	1
B34	53101	3.3	1.6	0.44	2.81	1	7	2	4	1	2.1	0.01	0.01	4	2	1.7	0.01	0.01	1
B34	53301	4.6	1.6	0.41	3.89	1	1	2	4	1	3.9	0.01	0.01	4	2	3.4	0.01	0.01	1
B34	55702	2.0	1.1	0.24	1.19	3	1	3	4	2	1.2	0.01	0.01	9	9	0.1	0.01	0.01	1
B34	55801	8.5	1.3	0.45	7.18	2	2	1	4	1	8.0	0.01	0.01	4	2	7.2	0.01	0.01	1
B34	55802	7.7	1.1	0.34	3.78	2	1	1	5	1	4.3	0.01	0.01	9	9	0.1	0.01	0.01	1

APPENDIX D

URUK RETOUCHED BLADES AND BLADE SEGMENTS

LAYER	ARTIFACT NUMBER	LN	WD	TH	WT	FACT	MTRL	PART	RET TYPE	RET LOCN	RET LN	NOTCH WD	NOTCH DEPTH	RET TYPE	RET LOCN	RET LN	NOTCH WD	NOTCH DEPTH	BITMN COND
B35	56601	3.1	1.0	0.28	1.37	2	1	2	4	2	1.5	0.01	0.01	9	9	0.1	0.01	0.01	1
B35	56602	1.9	1.7	0.32	1.56	2	5	3	4	1	1.9	0.01	0.01	4	2	1.7	0.01	0.01	1
B35	56801	5.0	1.9	0.59	9.32	2	1	1	1	1	2.1	0.01	0.01	9	9	0.1	0.01	0.01	1
B35	56802	5.3	1.2	0.52	4.78	2	6	2	4	2	3.9	0.01	0.01	3	1	3.5	0.28	0.06	1
B35	56803	4.9	1.4	0.74	5.98	1	1	4	6	1	0.6	0.57	0.15	6	2	6.5	0.45	0.20	1
B35	56901	6.1	1.5	0.60	4.92	2	1	1	4	2	2.9	0.01	0.01	9	9	0.1	0.01	0.01	1
B35	57902	5.9	1.6	0.46	5.26	3	1	2	5	2	4.2	0.16	C.40	5	4	0.4	0.11	0.30	1
B36	58701	2.0	1.1	0.26	0.71	2	1	4	4	2	1.9	0.01	0.01	9	9	0.1	0.01	0.01	1
B36	58702	2.4	1.1	0.30	1.01	1	9	3	1	1	2.0	0.01	0.01	4	2	2.2	0.01	0.01	1
B36	58703	6.3	1.6	0.45	6.48	2	2	1	4	2	5.2	0.01	0.01	4	1	4.3	0.01	0.01	4
B36	58705	5.2	1.7	0.54	9.26	2	2	3	4	1	2.7	0.01	0.01	4	2	1.3	0.01	0.01	1
B36	58802	7.3	1.2	0.48	3.70	3	1	1	5	1	4.3	C.00	0.00	5	3	0.9	0.00	0.00	1
B36	59601	6.2	1.3	0.41	3.69	3	9	4	5	1	5.7	0.00	0.00	4	2	3.0	0.00	0.00	1

JEMDET NASR AND EARLY DYNASTIC RETOUCHED BLADES AND BLADE SEGMENTS

LAYER	ARTIFACT NUMBER	LN	WD	TH	WT	FACT	MTRL	PART	RET TYPE	RET LOCN	RET LN	NOTCH WD	NOTCH DEPTH	RET TYPE	RET LOCN	RET LN	NOTCH WD	NOTCH DEPTH	BITMN COND
A3	04701	8.3	1.5	0.54	8.54	1	2	1	4	1	5.2	0.15	0.03	4	2	5.1	0.06	0.02	1
A3	04702	3.0	1.0	0.33	1.09	1	1	2	4	1	1.9	0.04	C.02	4	2	1.3	0.02	0.02	1
A3	04801	4.4	1.5	0.53	4.60	1	2	2	4	2	3.2	0.14	0.03	9	9	0.1	0.01	0.01	1
A6	07801	1.8	1.2	0.30	0.76	1	1	2	4	1	1.5	0.01	0.01	4	2	1.5	0.01	0.01	1
A6	07802	2.9	1.4	0.31	1.86	2	9	2	4	1	1.9	0.01	C.01	4	2	2.0	0.01	0.01	1
A6	C8601	2.6	1.2	0.32	1.45	2	2	4	4	2	1.7	0.01	0.01	4	1	1.3	0.01	0.01	1
A7	08701	2.8	1.1	0.25	1.12	2	9	3	4	1	2.4	0.01	0.01	4	2	2.4	0.01	0.01	1
A8	10401	3.1	1.1	0.48	1.98	2	2	1	4	1	1.2	0.01	0.01	4	2	1.1	0.01	0.01	1
A9	11802	3.0	1.1	0.32	1.12	3	7	1	4	1	0.2	0.01	0.01	9	9	0.1	0.01	0.01	1
A9	11803	3.5	1.7	0.42	2.87	1	2	1	4	1	0.1	0.01	C.01	4	2	0.1	0.01	0.01	1
A9	11804	3.9	1.2	0.20	1.29	2	2	1	4	2	1.9	0.01	0.01	9	9	0.1	0.01	0.01	1
A9	12001	1.8	1.4	0.40	1.13	1	2	4	4	2	1.2	0.01	0.01	9	9	0.1	0.01	0.01	1
A11	12501	5.6	1.0	0.28	2.03	2	2	1	4	2	4.0	0.01	0.01	9	9	0.1	0.01	0.01	1
A11	12502	7.4	1.8	0.57	9.84	4	2	1	4	1	5.0	0.01	0.01	9	9	0.1	0.01	0.01	1
A11	12601	3.6	1.4	C.46	2.63	1	2	2	4	1	2.5	0.01	0.01	9	9	0.1	0.01	0.01	1
A11	12603	1.4	1.4	0.29	0.94	2	4	4	4	1	1.4	0.01	0.01	9	9	0.1	0.01	0.01	1
A12	20801	3.1	1.0	0.35	1.62	3	9	3	4	1	2.5	0.01	0.01	4	2	2.3	0.01	0.01	1
A12	20802	3.9	1.4	0.31	1.79	1	1	1	4	1	2.2	C.01	0.01	4	2	2.4	0.01	0.01	1
A13	16001	2.3	1.6	0.38	2.04	2	2	4	4	1	2.2	0.01	0.01	9	9	0.1	0.01	0.01	1
A13	16101	1.8	1.8	0.33	0.00	2	1	4	1	3	1.8	0.01	0.01	1	4	1.8	0.01	0.01	1
A13	18501	2.2	1.1	0.37	1.05	1	1	9	4	3	1	1.9	0.24	0.08	3	2	1.8	0.16	0.08	1
A15	21301	2.8	1.8	0.46	2.02	1	1	2	3	4	2	1.8	0.01	0.01	9	9	0.1	0.01	0.01	1
A15	21302	1.3	1.1	0.27	0.56	2	1	4	4	1	0.9	0.01	0.01	4	2	1.2	0.01	0.01	1
A17	24802	4.7	1.9	0.70	8.11	3	8	1	5	1	3.2	0.00	0.00	5	2	3.1	0.00	0.00	1
A17	25402	1.9	1.7	0.26	1.35	2	2	4	4	2	1.5	0.01	0.01	4	1	0.9	0.01	0.01	1
A17	25403	2.3	1.6	0.35	2.09	2	2	4	4	1	1.7	0.01	0.01	9	9	0.1	0.01	0.01	1
A17	25405	1.5	2.2	0.49	1.48	1	1	1	5	2	2.4	0.01	0.01	5	4	0.8	0.01	0.01	1
A	25406	1.1	0.8	0.27	0.37	2	4	3	4	2	1.0	0.01	0.01	5	1	0.6	0.01	0.01	1
A17	25601	1.5	1.5	0.25	1.35	2	2	4	4	2	1.1	0.01	0.01	4	1	0.5	0.01	0.01	1
A17	25602	1.9	0.9	0.26	0.56	1	1	1	4	1	0.8	0.38	0.09	9	9	0.1	0.01	0.01	1
A17	25604	3.6	2.0	0.50	6.28	2	1	4	4	1	2.2	0.01	C.01	4	2	1.3	0.01	0.01	1
A17	25609	2.3	0.9	0.40	1.07	1	9	4	9	0	0.1	0.01	0.01	9	9	0.1	0.01	0.01	1
A18	29302	2.0	0.9	0.21	0.59	2	2	1	2	1	1.9	0.01	0.01	9	9	0.1	0.01	0.01	1
A18	29304	1.6	1.2	0.25	0.61	1	9	4	4	1	1.6	0.01	0.01	9	9	0.1	0.01	0.01	1
B20	14001	1.1	1.7	0.48	1.00	1	1	4	5	1	1.2	0.01	0.01	9	9	0.1	0.01	0.01	1
B20	14002	3.1	2.4	0.50	6.37	2	2	4	4	2	2.8	0.01	C.01	1	1	2.1	0.01	0.01	1
B20	14003	1.6	2.2	0.35	1.94	2	2	4	4	1	1.1	0.01	0.01	9	9	0.1	0.01	0.01	1
B20	14004	1.8	1.1	0.39	1.00	2	9	2	4	2	1.8	0.01	0.01	9	9	0.1	0.01	0.01	1
B21	16701	2.0	1.3	0.28	1.14	2	2	4	4	1	2.3	0.01	C.01	9	9	0.1	0.01	0.01	1
B22	17601	2.2	1.6	0.39	2.30	2	4	4	5	2	1.9	0.01	0.01	4	1	1.6	0.01	0.01	1
B22	17604	3.0	1.0	0.32	1.36	2	6	4	4	1	2.7	0.75	C.14	4	2	2.8	0.00	0.00	1
B23	22401	1.9	2.1	0.52	3.32	2	9	4	1	3	1.6	0.01	0.01	4	2	1.4	0.01	0.01	1
B23	22402	1.1	0.8	0.32	0.50	2	4	5	4	2	1.4	0.01	0.01	1	1	0.9	0.01	0.01	1
B22	17602	1.8	1.5	0.3C	C.93	3	4	3	5	1	1.4	0.01	0.01	9	9	0.1	0.01	0.01	1
B24	24301	2.2	1.7	0.26	1.75	1	1	3	6	1	1.8	0.13	C.60	5	2	1.9	0.01	0.01	1
B25	26601	2.C	1.4	0.45	1.46	1	1	2	4	2	1.0	0.01	0.01	9	9	0.1	0.01	0.01	1
B25	26602	5.0	1.8	0.36	7.92	3	4	1	4	2	5.2	0.01	0.01	9	9	0.1	0.01	0.01	1
B25	27701	2.6	1.0	0.31	0.77	1	1	4	4	1	2.3	0.01	0.01	4	2	2.4	0.01	0.01	1
B26	27801	2.1	1.0	C.31	C.89	1	1	1	4	1	2.1	0.01	0.01	4	2	1.8	0.01	0.01	1
B27	28401	2.6	0.9	0.23	0.53	1	1	3	4	2	1.2	0.01	0.01	9	9	0.1	0.01	0.01	1

JEMDET NASR AND EARLY DYNASTIC RETOUCHED BLADES AND BLADE SEGMENTS

LAYER	ARTIFACT NUMBER	LN	WD	TH	WT	FACT	MTRL	PART	RET TYPE	RET LOCN	RET LN	NOTCH WD	NOTCH DEPTH	RET TYPE	RET LOCN	RET LN	NOTCH WD	NOTCH DEPTH	BITMN COND
B26	28901	6.4	1.4	0.46	5.48	2	9	3	4	2	5.1	0.01	0.01	4	1	3.8	0.01	0.01	1
B26	28902	2.8	0.8	0.30	0.79	2	9	4	5	2	2.1	0.12	0.08	5	1	2.4	0.01	0.01	1
B26	31101	2.7	1.6	0.41	2.13	2	2	3	4	1	2.2	0.01	0.01	4	2	2.1	0.01	0.01	1
B26	31102	1.9	1.6	0.43	1.80	2	9	4	4	2	1.0	0.01	0.01	1	3	1.2	0.01	0.01	1
B26	31103	5.2	1.4	0.35	3.54	2	9	1	4	1	4.8	0.01	0.01	4	2	4.4	0.01	0.01	1
B27	31702	2.3	1.3	0.28	1.49	2	9	4	4	2	1.8	0.01	0.01	4	1	2.0	0.01	0.01	1
B27	31703	2.9	1.1	0.29	1.18	1	9	3	4	1	2.8	0.01	0.01	4	2	2.4	0.01	0.01	1

MICROLITHS

LAYER	ARTIFACT NUMBER	LN	WD	TH	WT	FACT	MTRL	PART	RET TYPE	RET LOCN	RET LN	NOTCH WD	NOTCH DEPTH	RET TYPE	RET LOCN	RET LN	NOTCH WD	NOTCH DEPTH	BITMN COND
A1	04401	1.5	1.7	0.25	0.52	2	7	4	5	4	1.5	0.00	0.00	5	3	1.4	0.00	0.00	1
A5	06801	1.7	1.6	0.31	1.28	4	1	4	5	3	2.3	0.00	0.00	4	1	2.8	0.00	0.00	1
A15	21303	1.8	1.7	0.26	0.85	2	1	4	5	3	1.9	0.00	0.00	5	4	1.8	0.00	0.00	1
A17	25407	1.0	1.7	0.40	1.02	2	4	4	1	3	1.6	0.01	0.01	1	4	1.4	0.01	0.01	1
B23	22403	1.8	1.4	0.35	0.95	2	2	6	1	4	1.5	0.01	0.01	9	9	0.1	0.01	0.01	1
A30	61408	1.7	1.1	0.30	0.33	2	1	4	5	3	1.2	0.00	0.00	4	1	1.1	0.00	0.00	1
B31	40401	0.9	1.9	0.40	0.79	2	9	4	5	3	1.8	0.00	0.00	5	4	1.5	0.00	0.00	1

ENDSCRAPERS

LAYER	ARTIFACT NUMBER	LN	WD	TH	WT	FACT	MTRL	PART	RET TYPE	RET LOCN	RET LN	NOTCH WD	NOTCH DEPTH	RET TYPE	RET LOCN	RET LN	NOTCH WD	NOTCH DEPTH	BITMN COND
A11	12503	3.3	1.1	0.37	1.79	1	7	3	4	1	3.0	0.05	0.01	5	2	3.0	0.15	0.06	1
B32	46803	4.2	1.1	0.38	2.41	3	9	3	5	1	7.7	0.00	0.00	5	3	0.9	0.00	0.00	1
B33	48101	3.0	1.1	0.43	1.54	1	1	4	5	1	2.8	0.01	0.01	4	2	2.3	0.01	0.01	1
B42	69005	3.0	0.6	0.16	0.31	3	7	1	5	4	0.4	0.00	0.00	0	0	0.0	0.00	0.00	1
B46	75206	3.0	0.7	0.16	0.41	3	7	1	5	4	0.3	0.00	0.00	0	0	0.0	0.00	0.00	1

BURINS

LAYER	ARTIFACT NUMBER	LN	WD	TH	WT	FACT	MTRL	PART	RET TYPE	RET LOCN	RET LN	NOTCH WD	NOTCH DEPTH	RET TYPE	RET LOCN	RET LN	NOTCH WD	NOTCH DEPTH	BITMN COND
A23	43703	1.9	1.8	0.40	1.58	3	4	4	4	2	0.8	0.00	0.00	0	0	0.0	0.15	0.18	1
A26	45302	1.7	1.3	0.54	1.97	2	9	4	1	2	0.8	0.01	0.01	4	1	1.2	0.01	0.01	1
B32	46601	3.7	1.7	0.51	4.47	3	3	4	5	2	2.9	0.00	0.00	5	1	1.0	0.26	0.29	1

PERFORATERS AND RELATED PIECES

LAYER	ARTIFACT NUMBER	LN	WD	TH	WT	FACT	MTRL	PART	RET TYPE	RET LOCN	RET LN	NOTCH WD	NOTCH DEPTH	RET TYPE	RET LOCN	RET LN	NOTCH WD	NOTCH DEPTH	BITMN COND
A1	04003	1.6	2.5	0.27	1.18	2	1	2	5	1	1.6	0.00	0.00	5	2	1.4	0.00	0.00	1
A11	12602	4.8	0.7	0.39	1.97	2	1	3	5	1	4.7	0.14	0.04	5	2	4.4	0.13	0.05	1
A20	29801	2.7	1.0	0.26	0.41	3	9	1	5	2	2.2	0.00	0.00	5	1	1.5	0.00	0.00	1
A22	40701	3.2	1.3	0.41	2.95	2	2	1	5	2	2.3	0.00	0.00	5	1	1.8	0.00	0.00	1
A25	48501	2.8	1.0	0.36	0.79	3	9	2	5	2	2.0	0.00	0.00	5	1	2.0	0.00	0.00	1
A27	49309	1.5	1.0	0.31	0.45	0	5	5	4	1	0.5	0.00	0.00	0	0	0.0	0.00	0.00	1
A27	49310	3.5	1.1	0.24	0.92	2	5	2	5	2	3.5	0.00	0.00	5	1	3.3	0.00	0.00	1
A28	53802	4.2	1.1	0.38	1.98	3	3	3	5	1	4.1	0.00	0.00	5	2	3.3	0.00	0.00	1
A29	58303	3.3	1.9	0.50	3.12	3	1	1	5	1	3.2	0.00	0.00	5	4	1.9	0.00	0.00	1
A36	69901	2.3	1.5	0.52	2.59	4	9	3	5	1	5.3	0.00	0.00	5	3	1.1	0.00	0.00	1
B27	28402	2.7	1.6	0.83	3.68	2	1	2	5	1	5.3	0.00	0.00	6	4	0.0	0.15	0.16	1
B32	46607	2.0	1.2	0.40	1.15	3	9	3	4	1	0.7	0.00	0.00	5	4	0.9	0.00	0.00	1
B41	67601	5.4	2.2	0.75	8.56	3	1	1	5	2	5.4	0.00	0.00	5	1	4.4	0.00	0.00	1

FARUKH SICKLE BLADES

LAYER	ARTIFACT NUMBER	LN	WD	TH	WT	FACT	MTRL	PART	RET TYPE	RET LOCN	RET LN	NOTCH WD	NOTCH DEPTH	RET TYPE	RET LOCN	RET LN	NOTCH WD	NOTCH DEPTH	SHEEN LOCN	SHEEN COND
A23	44903	4.7	1.7	0.53	4.85	1	1	2	4	3	2.9	0.13	0.06	5	3	1.1	0.00	0.00	6	2
A24	44602	2.7	1.3	0.35	1.78	2	2	4	4	2	2.4	0.06	0.04	0	0	0.0	0.00	0.00	6	2
A29	54702	2.9	1.2	0.26	1.70	2	2	4	0	0	0.0	0.00	0.00	0	0	0.0	0.00	0.00	6	2
A29	58204	2.7	1.3	0.26	1.15	2	9	2	5	3	1.5	0.07	0.01	5	1	0.7	0.05	0.01	6	2
A36	69905	3.3	1.6	0.41	2.87	2	2	2	3	2	1.8	0.17	0.07	0	0	0.0	0.00	0.00	6	3
B39	62002	2.0	1.4	0.29	1.36	2	2	4	4	1	2.0	0.14	0.05	0	0	0.0	0.00	0.00	5	2
B40	64806	1.9	1.0	0.21	0.68	3	2	4	4	1	1.7	0.02	0.02	0	0	0.0	0.00	0.00	5	2
B41	68302	3.4	1.4	0.26	2.22	3	9	4	8	1	2.1	0.17	0.06	0	0	0.0	0.00	0.00	5	1
B45	73004	3.3	1.4	0.33	2.20	2	4	4	8	1	2.4	0.13	0.03	4	2	3.0	0.15	0.04	5	4
B45	73501	4.3	1.4	0.44	3.85	2	2	4	0	0	0.0	0.00	0.00	0	0	0.0	0.00	0.00	6	3

APPENDIX D

LAYER	ARTIFACT NUMBER	LN	WD	TH	WT	FACT	MTRL	PART	RET TYPE	RET LOCN	RET LN	NOTCH WD	NOTCH DEPTH	RET TYPE	RET LOCN	RET LN	NOTCH WD	NOTCH DEPTH	SHEEN LOCN	SHEEN COND
B45	73901	3.9	1.3	0.29	2.75	1	2	2	8	2	3.6	0.05	0.03	0	0	0.0	0.00	0.00	6	3
B46	75104	5.9	1.6	0.42	6.45	2	9	2	3	2	5.2	0.14	0.07	3	1	5.0	0.18	0.05	7	2
B46	75105	3.7	1.3	0.32	2.21	2	2	4	2	2	3.4	0.17	0.04	4	1	3.2	0.13	0.03	7	3
B46	75106	2.6	1.1	0.26	1.13	2	4	4	3	1	2.1	0.52	0.10	0	0	0.0	0.00	0.00	5	3
B47	75607	1.8	1.2	0.28	0.90	2	2	4	3	2	1.6	0.10	0.02	0	0	0.0	0.00	0.00	7	3
B40	63208	4.5	1.4	0.46	3.81	2	2	2	0	0	0.0	0.00	0.00	0	0	0.0	0.00	0.00	6	4

URUK SICKLE BLADES

LAYER	ARTIFACT NUMBER	LN	WD	TH	WT	FACT	MTRL	PART	RET TYPE	RET LOCN	RET LN	NOTCH WD	NOTCH DEPTH	RET TYPE	RET LOCN	RET LN	NOTCH WD	NOTCH DEPTH	SHEEN LOCN	SHEEN COND
A20	29809	4.9	1.7	0.59	7.08	2	5	4	8	2	4.8	0.08	0.09	4	1	4.8	0.03	0.02	7	2
A22	37902	1.5	1.2	0.25	0.78	3	3	4	3	1	1.5	0.09	0.07	0	0	0.0	0.00	0.00	5	2
A23	44501	3.0	1.4	0.24	1.93	2	2	4	2	2	3.0	0.00	0.00	0	0	0.0	0.00	0.00	5	3
B29	36902	1.6	1.4	0.37	1.25	2	2	4	3	1	1.6	0.10	0.02	0	0	0.0	0.00	0.00	6	3
B32	46806	1.4	1.5	0.32	0.99	2	2	4	0	0	0.0	0.00	0.00	0	0	0.0	0.00	0.00	5	3
B33	51103	3.5	1.4	0.30	2.65	2	2	4	4	2	3.0	0.20	0.03	0	0	0.0	0.00	0.00	6	2
B33	51104	3.4	1.7	0.46	3.92	2	2	4	4	2	2.8	0.12	0.02	4	1	2.6	0.14	0.05	6	2
B33	51506	2.2	1.4	0.36	1.59	1	2	4	3	1	2.0	0.05	0.03	9	2	2.2	0.09	0.02	7	3
B34	53102	2.0	1.4	0.44	1.88	2	2	4	8	2	2.0	0.20	0.08	0	0	0.0	0.00	0.00	6	3
B34	55703	3.7	1.4	0.34	2.39	2	2	4	4	2	3.0	0.17	0.06	5	4	0.9	0.08	0.02	6	3
B34	56001	3.9	1.5	0.45	3.52	2	9	4	8	1	3.5	0.28	0.07	5	2	1.1	0.12	0.06	5	3
B35	56602	2.7	2.0	0.38	3.28	3	2	4	0	0	0.0	0.00	0.00	0	0	0.0	0.00	0.00	5	4
B35	56604	2.9	1.2	0.41	1.71	1	5	4	4	2	2.4	0.00	0.00	0	0	0.0	0.00	0.00	6	3
B36	58708	2.0	1.3	0.38	1.80	2	2	4	4	1	1.9	0.04	0.02	9	2	1.8	0.02	0.02	7	2
B36	58709	2.4	1.2	0.34	1.50	1	2	4	4	1	2.3	0.18	0.05	0	0	0.0	0.00	0.00	5	3

JEMDET NASR AND EARLY DYNASTIC SICKLE BLADES

LAYER	ARTIFACT NUMBER	LN	WD	TH	WT	FACT	MTRL	PART	RET TYPE	RET LOCN	RET LN	NOTCH WD	NOTCH DEPTH	RET TYPE	RET LOCN	RET LN	NOTCH WD	NOTCH DEPTH	SHEEN LOCN	SHEEN COND
A	04002	2.3	1.4	0.38	1.95	2	9	4	3	2	2.6	0.35	0.17	3	1	1.7	0.23	0.09	7	2
A	04301	2.3	0.9	0.40	0.65	2	7	5	3	1	2.3	0.20	0.12	0	0	0.0	0.00	0.00	5	3
A	08101	4.7	1.6	0.40	14.17	2	2	4	3	1	4.1	0.15	0.09	0	0	0.0	0.00	0.00	6	3
A	08102	4.2	1.6	0.25	13.83	2	2	2	3	2	4.0	0.11	0.05	0	0	0.0	0.00	0.00	7	2
A5	06002	1.8	1.1	0.27	0.85	2	2	3	3	2	1.7	0.31	0.14	5	4	0.9	0.11	0.02	5	3
A6	07801	3.9	1.4	0.51	3.37	2	9	4	3	2	3.5	0.19	0.10	0	0	0.0	0.00	0.00	2	4
A6	07802	5.4	1.9	0.30	4.71	2	2	4	3	1	5.3	0.15	0.05	0	0	0.0	0.00	0.00	5	3
A7	08702	2.1	1.0	0.39	2.52	2	6	4	3	1	1.8	0.15	0.08	3	2	1.7	0.23	0.23	7	2
A7	08703	2.5	1.4	0.60	2.77	1	2	4	2	2	0.0	0.00	0.00	0	0	0.0	0.00	0.00	5	1
A7	08704	4.2	2.0	0.47	5.31	2	6	4	3	1	4.2	0.22	0.11	7	3	0.0	0.00	0.00	5	2
A7	10201	3.1	1.0	0.29	8.62	2	2	4	3	2	3.0	0.18	0.11	0	0	0.0	0.00	0.00	6	2
A8	10401	3.6	1.5	0.38	3.45	2	6	4	3	1	3.5	0.25	0.16	3	2	2.9	0.15	0.09	7	2
A9	11805	3.1	1.8	0.42	3.98	2	2	5	3	2	3.0	0.13	0.06	6	1	9.0	0.85	0.24	6	2
A9	11806	2.2	1.4	0.35	2.21	2	2	4	3	1	2.2	0.20	0.07	3	2	2.1	0.22	0.04	7	2
A9	11807	3.6	1.4	0.44	3.59	2	2	4	3	2	3.5	0.20	0.12	3	1	2.9	0.25	0.16	7	3
A9	11808	3.1	1.3	0.21	1.28	2	3	4	3	2	2.9	0.17	0.11	0	0	0.0	0.00	0.00	6	2
A9	11809	3.3	2.1	0.35	1.98	2	2	4	3	2	3.1	0.19	0.09	3	1	3.1	0.19	0.08	7	2
A9	11810	2.6	1.3	0.33	2.01	2	1	4	3	1	2.6	0.28	0.08	3	2	2.5	0.40	0.08	7	3
A9	11811	3.1	1.7	0.39	2.88	2	2	2	3	4	2.4	0.13	0.05	6	4	1.4	0.00	0.00	6	2
A9	11812	4.8	1.6	0.41	4.30	2	2	4	3	2	4.8	0.25	0.10	0	0	0.0	0.00	0.00	6	2
A9	12002	1.2	1.6	0.29	0.83	2	7	2	4	1	1.1	0.08	0.03	4	2	7.5	0.05	0.02	5	2
A9	12003	4.0	1.6	0.34	3.58	2	2	4	3	1	3.8	0.09	0.03	0	0	0.0	0.00	0.00	5	2
A9	12004	4.4	1.7	0.66	6.19	1	2	2	5	2	1.0	0.10	0.05	6	2	2.9	0.70	0.16	6	3
A11	12604	2.4	1.2	0.30	1.47	2	2	4	3	1	2.2	0.23	0.06	3	2	2.4	0.26	0.10	7	2
A12	20803	1.9	1.1	0.32	1.21	2	2	4	3	1	1.7	0.19	0.09	3	2	1.9	0.10	0.07	5	1
A12	20804	3.0	1.6	0.39	3.34	2	2	4	3	1	3.0	0.21	0.08	3	2	2.2	0.18	0.16	7	2
A12	20805	2.2	1.4	0.40	1.98	2	2	4	3	2	2.2	0.24	0.10	4	1	2.2	0.16	0.02	7	4
A12	20806	3.6	1.3	0.50	3.34	2	2	4	3	2	2.9	0.17	0.06	3	1	3.2	0.24	0.11	6	1
A12	20807	2.5	1.6	0.44	2.63	2	2	4	3	1	1.9	0.20	0.07	8	2	2.1	0.20	0.14	7	2
A12	20808	2.3	1.3	0.31	1.71	2	2	4	3	1	2.2	0.18	0.09	3	2	2.2	0.23	0.10	7	3
A12	20809	2.1	1.3	0.32	1.22	1	2	2	3	2	1.6	0.12	0.07	3	1	1.6	0.11	0.04	6	3
A12	20810	2.2	1.3	0.50	1.98	2	2	4	3	2	1.7	0.17	0.09	0	0	0.0	0.00	0.00	7	3
A13	25610	2.1	1.1	0.30	0.79	2	9	2	4	2	1.0	0.06	0.02	0	0	0.0	0.00	0.00	5	3
A13	26103	4.1	1.5	0.31	3.06	2	2	4	3	1	3.2	0.16	0.06	3	2	3.1	0.06	0.03	7	1
A17	25401	3.3	1.4	0.24	1.72	2	9	2	3	2	2.7	0.04	0.03	0	0	0.0	0.00	0.00	5	3
A17	25603	1.6	1.3	0.28	0.83	2	1	4	4	2	0.8	0.17	0.05	0	0	0.0	0.00	0.00	6	2
B20	14001	2.8	1.7	0.20	1.78	2	7	4	3	1	2.6	0.29	0.09	0	0	0.0	0.00	0.00	5	3
B21	16702	2.6	1.3	0.45	1.89	1	2	3	3	1	2.5	0.17	0.13	0	0	0.0	0.00	0.00	5	3
B22	17301	2.5	0.8	0.27	0.88	1	2	4	4	1	2.1	0.14	0.07	0	0	0.0	0.00	0.00	6	3
B22	20201	2.6	1.5	0.28	1.70	2	2	4	3	2	2.6	0.16	0.05	3	1	2.0	0.17	0.08	7	3
B23	22602	2.6	1.4	0.55	2.64	2	2	4	3	2	1.8	0.14	0.07	3	1	2.3	0.16	0.08	5	2
B23	22603	3.8	1.4	0.45	3.82	3	2	4	8	2	3.7	0.20	0.08	8	1	3.7	0.20	0.10	7	2
B24	23501	3.4	1.8	0.34	3.15	2	2	4	3	1	3.2	0.37	0.12	0	0	0.0	0.00	0.00	5	1
B24	23502	3.1	1.2	0.64	3.50	2	2	4	0	0	0.0	0.00	0.00	0	0	0.0	0.00	0.00	5	2
B23	23801	3.9	1.2	0.48	2.33	2	2	4	3	2	3.5	0.32	0.11	0	0	0.0	0.00	0.00	5	2
B25	26503	2.6	1.6	0.36	2.61	2	2	2	2	2	2.2	0.08	0.05	0	0	0.0	0.00	0.00	6	3
B26	31104	2.7	1.8	0.23	1.08	2	2	2	3	2	2.0	0.20	0.09	0	0	0.0	0.00	0.00	6	3
B26	31105	4.1	2.9	0.60	10.60	2	2	2	3	2	3.9	0.14	0.09	0	0	0.0	0.00	0.00	6	2

Table D2: Attributes of Blade Cores

CORES

LAYER	NUMBER	CHERT TYPE	BLADE CORE?	STAGE OF WK	FACE HT	FACE PERIM	PLTFM LNGTH	PLTFM WIDTH	PLTFM ANGLE	WEIGHT (GM)
A3	04701	1			0	3.1	7.8	4.9	0.9	74	93
A5	04901	1			7	2.3	2.8	4.0	0.0	72	35
A5	08601	1			8	1.8	5.3	2.5	0.5	66	17
A6	08602	3			6	2.1	5.3	2.5	0.3	80	27
A7	08701	1			0	2.1	4.9	3.7	0.8	75	48
A7	08702	1			7	4.4	3.2	5.2	0.7	78	195
A7	10201	1	1		0	4.1	9.0	5.0	0.5	85	143
A8	10401	1			0	1.8	5.0	3.0	0.3	70	25
A9	11801	1			7	2.7	4.0	3.6	0.7	72	28
A9	12001	1			0	4.0	4.6	3.7	0.7	70	32
A9	12002	2			7	3.6	6.0	4.0	0.0	75	32
A13	15801	1			0	2.8	3.5	1.5	0.0	74	48
A13	16001	1			8	2.4	4.0	2.5	0.0	63	41
A15	16401	1			7	3.9	3.5	2.5	0.9	86	56
A15	16402	4	1		8	2.9	2.9	0.0	0.0	0	11
A17	25401	2			7	3.2	6.1	2.6	0.2	84	68
A18	29301	1			8	2.9	3.5	3.4	0.5	75	19
A19	26101	1			8	2.1	2.3	2.3	0.8	81	14
A19	29501	1			8	1.5	2.3	2.5	0.7	68	13
A19	29502	2			7	2.9	5.8	3.6	0.6	75	78
A19	29602	1			8	2.2	3.0	2.2	0.1	75	25
A20	29801	1			8	3.1	4.6	2.8	0.8	78	33
A20	29802	1			7	4.3	3.1	2.2	0.5	78	73
A20	29803	1			0	2.2	6.7	2.4	0.5	70	75
A20	29804	1			8	3.0	3.4	1.2	0.7	67	37
A20	29805	4	1		7	4.1	6.6	0.0	0.9	0	82
A20	30201	2			6	5.4	6.8	4.1	0.6	75	93
A21	33901	2			6	3.3	3.7	2.4	0.0	80	43
A23	44901	1			0	2.3	4.8	2.6	0.2	80	38
A24	44301	1			0	1.5	5.1	2.3	0.0	82	18
A26	45501	1			0	2.3	5.0	5.2	0.3	65	101
A25	45502	1			0	2.0	2.0	2.7	0.0	72	23
A26	45503	2			0	2.7	5.5	2.3	0.4	82	37
A25	48401	1			8	2.8	3.4	2.2	0.4	67	25
A27	49301	2			7	2.4	8.5	4.0	0.5	64	70
A27	49302	8	1		7	6.1	5.2	0.0	0.0	0	91
A27	49303	1			0	4.3	3.7	4.0	0.8	85	114
A28	53901	1			0	3.3	4.8	2.1	0.9	75	47
A29	58301	1			8	2.0	3.3	1.3	0.0	68	10
A31	61401	2			8	2.3	9.0	3.5	0.0	73	16
A31	63801	1			7	2.8	3.0	2.2	0.7	75	27
A36	69901	1			8	3.1	6.9	2.7	0.1	63	34
A36	70401	1			7	3.7	4.0	2.9	0.3	70	31
A36	70402	1			8	2.5	3.8	1.3	0.4	71	12
B20	14001	1			7	5.3	6.0	3.8	0.9	61	163
B20	14002	1			0	3.9	3.6	2.4	0.9	70	92
B21	16901	1			7	2.3	4.7	3.7	0.5	77	59
B22	17601	1			0	3.5	4.7	5.0	0.5	65	141
B23	22401	2			0	4.3	8.2	4.8	0.6	90	117
B24	23501	1			0	2.7	6.0	4.5	0.9	65	80

APPENDIX D

CORES

LAYER	NUMBER	CHERT TYPE	BLADE CORE?	STAGE OF WK	FACE HT	FACE PERIM	PLTFM LNGTH	PLTFM WIDTH	PLTFM ANGLE	WEIGHT (GM)
B24	24401	1		0	3.3	4.0	2.0	0.0	80	51
B24	31301	1		0	3.0	5.7	7.5	0.9	68	250
B25	26501	1		0	3.6	5.4	2.0	0.0	76	30
B25	26601	1		7	3.7	3.5	3.8	0.3	70	90
B25	26602	1		8	2.8	2.5	3.5	0.6	68	36
B25	27701	1		0	2.2	4.5	3.4	0.4	66	59
B26	27801	1		7	3.8	2.0	3.0	0.7	78	115
B25	28301	1		7	2.7	4.6	4.2	0.7	70	47
B27	28401	1		7	2.7	6.5	3.8	0.8	77	45
B27	28402	1		0	4.5	6.1	4.0	0.5	70	259
B27	28403	1		0	3.9	5.3	1.9	0.5	78	38
B27	28404	1		7	2.8	6.0	2.4	0.0	89	53
B27	28405	1		0	4.9	3.4	4.0	0.6	72	86
B27	28406	1		7	2.7	3.6	1.9	0.5	88	43
B27	28407	1		8	2.4	3.0	2.5	0.7	65	37
B27	28408	1		7	4.2	6.5	3.3	0.2	67	250
B29	36801	1		0	2.9	6.6	3.0	0.9	65	45
B29	36901	1	1	7	3.0	10.2	2.9	0.5	70	32
B29	36902	5	1	7	3.6	5.3	1.8	0.3	45	32
B29	37301	1		7	3.6	3.7	2.0	0.9	86	52
B29	37302	2		0	3.3	4.5	2.7	0.4	84	34
B29	37303	2		0	3.1	22.1	2.5	0.0	61	141
B29	37304	2		7	4.4	3.9	2.5	0.5	75	72
B29	37305	1		7	2.2	5.7	4.3	0.7	80	48
B30	39401	1		7	3.8	5.0	3.6	0.7	71	78
B30	39603	2		7	4.3	3.8	4.0	0.6	80	191
B30	39604	1	1	0	6.4	4.7	2.0	0.5	69	66
B30	39605	2		0	1.8	7.0	5.0	0.6	75	75
B30	39606	2		7	4.1	4.2	0.0	0.0	0	135
B31	40601	1		6	2.6	4.4	1.5	0.4	78	49
B31	40602	1		7	2.1	5.0	2.5	0.7	75	15
B31	41201	1		8	3.8	1.5	1.4	0.5	77	29
B31	41202	2		7	5.9	8.9	5.6	0.8	70	210
B31	42001	1		8	2.3	3.4	2.3	0.2	73	37
B32	39601	2		7	5.0	8.0	3.6	0.9	70	131
B32	39602	2		0	3.2	5.0	4.4	0.2	80	106
B32	39603	1		7	2.7	6.0	3.6	0.7	76	56
B32	43101	1		0	3.3	4.8	2.7	0.1	82	45
B32	43102	1		6	2.7	4.0	8.5	0.0	68	74
B32	45801	1		8	2.6	3.5	3.4	0.7	60	20
B32	46201	1		8	3.9	3.4	2.5	0.4	75	42
B32	46202	2		7	5.2	4.5	2.7	0.9	88	334
B33	51101	1		0	2.7	4.4	3.7	0.2	78	53
B33	51201	1		8	1.5	3.3	1.6	0.2	77	15
B34	53101	2		8	3.6	4.5	1.4	0.4	80	22
B34	53201	1		8	3.1	5.5	3.0	0.1	76	18
B35	58801	1		0	2.9	6.4	4.0	0.4	74	79
B36	69601	2		6	3.8	0.0	4.0	0.6	0	170
B37	60001	2	1	7	5.4	5.8	2.3	0.5	65	56
B38	61601	2	1	7	6.4	4.3	1.7	0.2	76	68
B39	61901	9		6	2.8	4.1	1.8	0.8	85	27
B39	62001	2		7	4.8	8.9	4.5	0.3	82	137
B39	62601	2	1	0	6.3	4.3	1.9	0.1	82	69
B39	62602	2	1	6	6.2	4.5	1.4	0.6	75	68
B39	62603	2		0	4.5	5.8	1.6	0.7	60	75
B40	63201	2		8	5.7	3.7	1.4	0.5	71	107
B40	63501	2		7	3.5	10.3	3.5	0.5	70	523
B42	69001	9	1	7	4.0	2.9	1.1	0.0	110	18
B42	69501	2		7	3.0	3.9	1.9	0.7	74	30
B42	69701	2		7	3.7	5.2	3.2	0.6	78	42
B43	70801	1		7	4.6	3.8	3.2	0.2	85	101
B43	70802	5		7	3.7	7.6	5.4	0.8	69	82
B43	70803	9		0	6.5	5.5	6.0	0.9	74	225
B44	71801	3		6	3.1	4.6	6.0	0.6	85	166
B45	75101	2	1	6	5.0	7.0	1.6	0.3	90	46

Table D3: Attributes of Celts and Related Objects

Units	Layer	Material	Length	Width	Thickness	Weight	Comment
Celts							
—	C	calcite	14.27	5.87	1.72	181	trace asphalt
X579	B34	calcite	12.97	5.72	2.02	154	
X511	B33	calcite	8.57	4.75	1.48	84	trace asphalt
X695	B42	calcite	13.97	5.67	1.71	—	much asphalt
Wedge							
X229	B23	calcite	9.05	8.70	3.32	411	
Hoe							
X396	B30	sandstone	9.55	6.87	1.83	130	

Table D4: Attributes of Utilized Pebbles (Calcite unless noted)

Unit	Layer	Length	Width	Thickness	Weight	Comment
Ovoid Handstones						
X048	A3	10.0	10.0	6.5	1200	edge battered, scratched
X085	A7	11.0	9.5	6.5	900	edge battered, Andesite
X088	A7	12.5	12.5	7.0	1300	pecked depression on edge
X104	A8	8.0	6.0	6.0	600	edge battered
X208	A12-13	9.0	9.0	3.0	350	surface scratched
X187	A13	13.0	13.0	2.5	850	edge battered
X309	B26	11.0	11.0	4.0	1300	edge battered, scratched
X696	B42	10.5	10.5	5.5	1250	slight surface polish
—	B42	11.0	10.5	6.5	1170	one surface polished, other pecked
Oblong Stones						
X069	A6	22.0	8.0	4.0	1130	no use
X103	A8	12.0+	4.5	4.5	—	end battered
X103	A8	19.0	3.0	3.0	300	no use
X104	A8	11.5+	4.5	4.0	—	end battered, edge polished
X104	A8	13.6	6.0	5.2	770	end battered, edge polished
X151	A12	8.5+	5.3	4.6	—	edge scratched, polished
X156	A13	15.0	5.5	4.0	700	end battered, edge scratched
X157	A13	26.5	6.0	4.0	880	no use
X704	A36	18.5+	7.8	6.8	1350	no use
X100	B16	9.9+	2.8	2.8	150	no use
X140	B20	17.5	11.5	7.5	2600	edge battered
X228	B23	12.7	5.8	3.5	430	polished
X309	B26	24.5	11.0	4.5	2400	edge battered
—	B30	17.5	9.5	8.5	1950	no use
X366	B30	16.0	5.5	5.0	730	no use
X632	B40	16.1	5.1	3.5	510	edge battered, bitumen stained
X750	C23	20.5	8.8	7.5	2250	bitumen haft remnant

APPENDIX D

Table D5: Attributes of Grinding Slabs and Mortars

Unit	Layer	Material	Type	Max. Ht.	Thickness	Width	Length	Weight (kg)
X206	B22	quartzite	flat	4	4	—	—	—
X101	A7	basalt	flat	4	4	16	23	2.4
X127	A9	basalt	flat	7	7	17	—	—
—	A1-10	basalt	saddle	4	3	17	—	—
X088	A7	basalt	saddle	5	3	20	27	3.7
X309	B26	calcite	flat w/ mortar[1]	8	8	19	—	—
X282	B25	calcite	saddle	—	6	16	19	2.8
X161	A13	calcite	saddle	12	8	20	40	6.0
X309	B26	calcite	basin	11	8	25	30	9.0
X299	A20	calcite	flat	6	6	18	—	—
—	A21	calcite	flat	17	17	18	45	17.0
X519	B33	calcite	flat w/ mortar[2]	6	6	16	—	—
X596	B36	calcite	saddle	9	5	16	37	3.5
X524	B34	calcite	saddle	—	9	17	—	—
X306	A20	calcite	saddle	14	5	19	46	11.0
X524	B33	calcite	basin	14	6	15	25	6.5
X524	B33	calcite	basin	16	13	13	21	9.5
—	B28	calcite	mortar	15	4	24	—	—

[1] Mortar 6.5 cm in diameter, 2.5 cm deep
[2] Mortar 8 cm in diameter, 2 cm deep

Table D6: Attributes of Beads

Number	Layer	Material	Weight	Diameter	Length	Hole	Comment
X089	A	ceramic	—	.36	.40	.10	field measurements, bitumen coat
X102	A7	ceramic	.30	.59	1.06	.20	bitumen coat
X515	B33	ceramic	6.66	1.89	2.07	.61	polished, broken
X528	B34	ceramic	3.23	1.41	1.47	.41	polished
X529	B34	ceramic	12.94	2.04	2.50	.68 x .72	—
X564	B34	ceramic	1.61	1.32	1.08	.41	—
X564	B34	ceramic	2.26	1.51	1.00	.45	—
X044	A2	lapis lazuli	.89	.49 x .59	1.75	.20	parallelogram section
X118	A9,10	lapis lazuli	.07	.34	.33	.10	transverse scratches
X121	A10	lapis lazuli	.14	.40	.55	.11	—
X129	B19	lapis lazuli	.20	.42	.60	.11	—
X141	B20	lapis lazuli	.26	.34 x .41	.86	.16	longitudinal scratches
X207	B22	lazurite?	.33	.44	1.03	.15	—
X151	A12	carnelian	.54	.63 x .54	1.04	.11	—
X262	A17	carnelian	—	.50	.54	—	field measurements
X357	B29	carnelian	.11	.53	.18	.11	—
X153	A12	agate	4.78	1.60 x .85	2.20	.24	slightly worked
X125	A11	glazed	.18	.75 x .52	.55	.12	—
X540	A28	glazed	.93	1.39 x 1.25	.55	.46	—
X141	B20	glazed	.39	.58	1.41	.13	spiral grooves
X087	A7	calcite	5.56	2.00 x 1.78	1.38	.55	hole incomplete
X511	B33	marble	.47	.40	.95	.33	finished
X659	B41	travertine	2.25	.72	1.33	.50	hole incomplete
X467	B32	chlorite?	—	2.20	.73	—	field measurements

Table D7: Attributes of Spindle Whorls

Units	Layer	Material/Color	Max. Diam.	Thick.	Min. Hole Diam.	Weight	Notch Length	Notch Width	Notch Period	Notch Angle
Disc Whorls										
X462	B32	—	5.73	1.62	.81	20.9				
X468	B32	calcite	4.22	1.12	.64	14.1				
X466	B32	calcite	5.07	1.04	.97	38.9				
X568	B35	gypsum	4.58	1.14	.52	—				
X569	B35	—	5.03	.96	.65	—				
X569	B35	calcite	6.30	1.70	1.18	—				
X596	B36	calcite	4.86	.85	.64	30.1				
Plain Ovoid Whorls										
X485	A25	10YR 6/3	2.78	1.95	.35	10.12				
X701	A35	5YR 7/6	2.36	1.85	.49	8.67				
X481	B33	5YR 7/3	2.29	1.78	.34	6.53				
X628	B39	5YR 8/4	3.35	2.16	.57	13.71				
X630	B40	10YR 8/3	2.14	1.42	.51	4.72				
X634	B40	2.5YR 6/6	3.07	1.91	.57	15.10				
X648	B40	5YR 8/6	2.61	2.49	.52	11.55				
X698	B42	5Y 8/2	2.47	1.64	.50	6.72				
Notched Ovoid Spindle Whorls										
X213	A15	5Y 8/1	2.91	1.57	.48	8.67	.69	.15	.76	90
X342	AF23	2.5Y 8/1	2.71	1.17	.58	5.65	.53	.37	1.03	86
X342	AF23	5Y 8/2	2.98	1.33	.56	9.75	.49	.12	.58	81
X390	A21	5YR 8/4	3.57	1.57	.75	10.00	.85	.17	.90	92
X277	B25	5YR 8/4	3.34	1.84	.74	15.14	.94	.32	1.07	90
X476	B33	5Y 8/2	2.58	2.02	.48	8.56	.78	.14	.63	94
X529	B34	5Y 8/1	2.84	1.71	.53	8.85	.63	.59	.57	92
X587	B36	10YR 7/2	2.25	1.50	.46	6.42	.56	.04	.40	51
X659	B41	2.5Y 8/2	2.92	2.00	.50	11.19	.82	.18	.82	95
X693	B42	10YR 8/3	2.78	1.43	.52	10.14	.96	.26	.99	93

APPENDIX D

Table D8: Attributes of Perforated and Partially Perforated Stones

Unit	Layer	Material	Max. Diam.	Thick.	Outer Hole Diam.	Min. Hole Diam.	Est. Intact Weight	Hole Type	Edge Use
Fully Perforated Stones									
X125	A11	gypsum	12.0	5.6	2.2		1250	Cyl.Dr.	
X669	A34	calcite	14.1	6.0	4.2		1890	Bic.Pk.Pol.	Bat.
X100	B16	calcite	8.5	2.8	3.2		370	Bic.Pk.Pol.	
X176	B22	calcite	19.0	5.0	5.0		2200	Bic.Pk.	
X311	B26	calcite	14.0	5.4	4.8		1100	Bic.Pk.	
X311	B26	calcite	7.0	2.7	3.2		210	Bic.Pk.	
X396	B30	calcite	7.0	3.0	3.0		220	Bic.Pk.Pol.	
X509	B33	calcite	10.5	3.3	3.6		730	Bic.Dr.	
X511	B33	calcite	10.7	3.5	3.0		510	Bic.Pk.Pol.	
X518	B33	calcite	17.5	4.0	4.0		1420	Bic.Pk.	
X518	B33	calcite	15.0	6.3	6.1		1130	Bic.Pk.Pol.	
X596	B36	calcite	8.9	3.1	3.5		360	Bic.Pk.Pol.	
X690	B42	calcite	7.8	4.0	4.9		405	Bic.Pk.Pol.	Bat.
X688	B42	calcite	8.2	6.0	3.3		420	Bic.Dr.	Pol.
Partially Perforated Stones						Hole Depth			
X148	A11	calcite	18.5	7.0	5.5	1.5	2900	Pk.	
X660	A32	calcite	5.5	2.5	3.0	1.4	110	Pk.	
X170	B21	—	20.0	5.5	5.5	1.5	3000	—	
X207	B24	calcite	14.5	8.4	3.5	1.5	2570	Pk.	
X364	B29	calcite	11.0	6.0	4.2	2.0	800	Pk.	
X530	B34	—	13.5	4.5	.2	.1	1050	—	
X600	B37	sandstone	6.4	4.0	1.8	1.1	170	Pk.	
X696	B42	calcite	8.6	6.5	3.2	.6	760	Pk.	
	B41	—	12.5	7.0	3.5	1.5	2460	—	

Table D9: Attributes of Perforated and Partially Perforated Sherds

Unit	Layer	Material/ Color	Max. Diam.	Thick.	Outer Hole Diam.	Min. Hole Diam.	Weight	Comment
Ceramic Discs								
X086	A6	10YR 8/3	4.90	.82	1.21	.73	21.8	bichrome sherd
X184	A13	2.5YR6/8	3.79	.58	1.08	1.08	16.0	bichrome sherd
X248	A17	7.5YR7/4	4.63	1.22	.86	—	30.2	partial hole
X445	A23	—	2.21	.39	.84	—	1.7	partial hole
X484	A26	5Y 7/3	2.00	.42	.58	—	—	
X229	B23	2.5Y 8/4	3.67	.63	.82	.55	6.6	
X458	B32	5Y 8/3	3.11	.41	1.23	.55	4.6	
Cement Vat Discs								
X254	A17	gypsum	7.20	1.80	1.17	.92	75.5	
X299	A20	gypsum	6.60	1.80	2.00	—	97.6	partial hole
X203	B22	gypsum	11.20	2.80	2.13	1.72	—	
X277	B25	gypsum	8.5	2.00	1.08	.95	160.2	

Table D10: Attributes of Molded Gypsum Concrete Objects

Unit	Layer	Max. Diam.	Thick.	Outer Hole Diam.	Min. Hole Diam.	Weight	Comment
Discs							
X104	A8	9.1	2.0	—	—	150.4	
X207	BF10 B	16.8	4.8	—	—	—	
Discs with Holes							
X119	A10	14.4	1.6	1.81	1.31	—	
X121	A10	20.5	4.1	3.45	2.72	1680.0	
X131	B20	18.6	2.4	2.95	1.90	871.0	
X010	surface	14.8	2.2	2.50	1.62	487.1	
Hemispheres							
X088	A7	15.6	8.1	2.47	1.20	—	
X152	A12	19.5	12.2	1.27	—	—	

Table D11: Attributes of Ceramic Troughs and Cylinder Drains

Exc.	Layer	Inclusions	Color	Side Thick.	Side Ht.	Base Thick.	Base Width
Trough Drains							
X437	A23	sand	2.5Y 8/4	1.80	14.0+	1.61	—
X451	A26	straw	10YR 7/5	1.57	5.18	1.69	16.20
X484	A26	straw	10YR 7/6	2.00	7.8+	—	—
X316	B27	straw	10YR 8/3	1.68	13.5+	—	—
X406	B31	straw	7.5YR 6/4	1.78	—	—	—
X424	B31	straw	7.5YR 6/4	2.19	9.31	1.76	24.20
X512	B33	straw	5Y 8/3	2.31	10.34	1.84	—
X515	B3	straw	10YR 8/4	1.93	9.02	1.33	—
X299	A20	straw	5YR 7/4	1.83	8.3+	—	—
X374	A20	straw	7.5YR 7/4	1.98	9.70	1.80	—
X374	A20	straw	10YR 7/4	1.67	6.7+	1.66	—
Cylindrical Drains					Diam.		
X223	A20	sand	5YR 7/4	1.29	17		
X424	B31	sand, calcite	10YR 8/4	2.19	20		
X512	B33	straw	5YR 7/5	1.83	22		

APPENDIX D

Table D12: Attributes of Stone Vessels

Unit	Layer	Material	Form	Rim Diam.	Body Thick.	Rim Angle	Band Ht.	Surface
X043	A1-3	calcite	Cn	9.5	.95	75		Rough
X060	A5	gypsum	Cn	12.5	.90	50	—	Rough
X063	A5	gypsum	Cn	13.5	.89	60	—	Rough
X068	A5	gypsum	Hm	16.0	.82	75	—	Rough
X108	B17	calcite	Cn	17.0	.89	65	—	Smooth
X292	A18	gypsum	Cn	18.0	1.08	45	—	Smooth
X295	A19	gypsum	Cn	29.0	1.27	65	—	Smooth
X302	A21	concrete	—	38.0	1.54	40	—	Smooth
X306	AF19	gypsum	Hm	17.0	.95	80	—	Rough
X327	A21	calcite	Exc	25.0	.75	65	1.50	Polished
X108	B17	calcite	Cn	17.0	1.03	55	—	Smooth
X147	B20	gypsum	Cn	12.0	.98	55	—	Rough
X471	B32	calcite	Cn	16.0	.34	50	—	Polished
X477	B33	calcite	Exc	28.0	1.82		1.86	Smooth
X517	B33	calcite	Exc	26.0	1.15	50	1.76	Smooth
X531	B34	calcite	Exc	15.0	1.22	65	1.09	Polished
X545	—	concrete	Exc	15.0	.99	65	1.24	Smooth
X545	—	concrete	Exc	8.6	.75	70	.82	Smooth
X545	—	gypsum	Cn	9.1	.65	70		Rough
X762	C32	calcite	Exc	21.0	1.52	55	2.10	Smooth

Table D13: Attributes of Bone Tools

Unit	Layer	Length	Edge Width	Edge Thick.	Edge Angle
X085	A7	14.42	2.34	.58	25
X087	A7	11.70	1.60	.92	20
X104	A8	10.11	1.41	.34	15
X635	B40	–	–	.31	40
X694	B42	10.15+	5.50+	.48	30
X709	B43	12.00+	–	.82	–
X709	B43	10.10	5.30±	.67	30
X750	C23	7.22	.90±	.20	–

Table D14: Bitumen Waste Attributes

Layer	Rock Weight	Asphalt Count	Angular Weight	Melted Count	Flat Weight	Melted Count	Unclassified Weight	Shaped Pieces
Excavation A								
above 155.8					42.0	3		2 mat impressed (1.8), 1 sickle mount (3.8)
155.6-155.8								1 sherd impressed (20.5)
3± all			35.7	3				
5W			15.3	2			13.1	
5E	228.5	7	71.6	4			4.8	
6N	392.7	4	107.3	3	60.1	5	42.9	1 lump (25.5)
6S	14.4	1	42.1	1	204.0	14	16.4	2 sickle mounts (8.3), 1 lump (74.9)
7N	8.3	1	968.9	23			96.4	1 sherd impressed (4.1)
7S			271.4	5	2.6	1	25.2	
8S			64.0	4	18.2	2		
9-10N			2.8	1	14.8	1		
9-10SE	118.4	1	47.3	7	43.6	10	33.1	
11SW			85.7	3				1 sherd impressed (12.3)
13U S			18.9	3	33.0	2	6.9	
13U N	7.1	1						
13 all			25.1	4				
14 all			37.5	10				
16 all							4.0	3 sherd impressed (185.0)
17N			3.9	1				
18N			30.3	5			4.9	
20					12.3	3	21.9	
21U S					11.3	1		1 sherd impressed (12.8)
21U N	215.6	1						
21M Rooms B,C			13.8	1			5.3	
21M Rooms D,E			16.2	1	13.7	1	8.5	
21L					13.8	1		
22 all			11.3	3				
23 all			85.9	8	71.5	9	21.8	1 sickle mount (1.5), 1 wood impressed (1.1)
24U NE			35.6	11	44.4	2	18.5	1 reed impressed (1.6)
24U SW					6.7	1		1 sherd impressed (28.0)
24L SW					13.9	2	2.4	
24L NE			6.6	1	4.0	3	14.3	1 mat impressed (4.6)
25S					16.1	2		
26S							1.7	
27N			22.1	2			1.2	
27S					1.8	1		
28NW			8.3	1				1 sickle mount (1.1)
29U			6.3	1				
29					4.9	1		
29L			26.6	5			7.9	1 mat impressed (0.6)
29NW			3.7	1				
30-31	19.3	1	10.6	5	11.8	3	5.2	
33 all					16.2	2	0.9	
34 all	77.1	5	4.8	1	15.1	1	5.3	1 mat impressed (0.4)
36 SE F 32					9.9	3		
36 in F 32							0.7	
36 outside F 32			4.1	1	1.4	1		
Excavation B								
20U+L N					68.6	4	9.0	1 sherd impressed (28.2)
20U+L SW			23.0	1	6.0	1	3.6	
20U+L SE					43.0	2		
21U+L N	10.5	5	27.7	4	36.1	2	4.8	
21U+L S	29.4	1	2.5	1	8.2	1	8.8	1 mat impressed (15.6)
22U N	484.2	17	17.4	3	8.8	1	36.8	
22L N	670.8	13	513.9	56			135.3	
23U+M N			11.5	2	2.1	2		1 sherd impressed (10.0)
23L N			16.0	1				
24U N	402.3	62					30.2	
24L N	79.4	13	1.3	1	3.8	1		
25U N	11.9	1	6.3	1				

APPENDIX D

Table D14: (Cont.)

Layer	Rock Weight	Asphalt Count	Angular Weight	Melted Count	Flat Weight	Melted Count	Unclassified Weight	Shaped Pieces
25L N			204.7	2	30.9	17	17.2	
25-27S							1.8	
28N							6.7	
28S					119.7	2		
29U N					66.5	3		
20U S	52.5	1			30.6	1		1 mat impressed (3.5)
29L E	84.8	2			100.6	4	7.7	1 mat impressed (3.8), 1 sherd impressed (5.0)
30NE	29.9	1			16.0	3		
30W					18.0	2		
31U N	30.2	1	163.4	11	103.4	27	62.6	
31U S	83.7	2	83.7	2				
31L N	28.8	1	209.5	7	2.9	3	8.3	
31L S			11.2	2	123.6	20	55.3	1 sherd impressed (5.0)
32U N							4.5	
32U S			47.1	2			6.0	
32L N	75.5	2						1 ovoid (4.7), 1 mat impressed (18.4)
32L S			88.2	2			1.7	
33U+M SE					35.6	1	5.6	
33U+M SW							1.5	
33L N			18.4	1	33.3	4	7.1	
34U S			9.7	1	11.9	1		1 ovoid (10.3)
34L Center					4.1	3		
35U all	136.4	2						
35L all			10.8	1			2.2	
36L all			170.9	12	63.2	26	16.4	1 sherd impressed (4.2)
37 all			11.5	1			11.5	1 lump (12.5)
37U E			8.5	5				
39U W			23.9	1	8.4	2	1.3	
39M E	14.8	1	26.3	1				
39M W			20.1	3				
39L E			38.4	7			5.5	1 ball (66.7)
40U E			11.0	1	18.0	7	13.6	1 ball (12.4)
40U W			42.9	2	19.8	12	4.3	2 lumps (13.6), 1 sherd impressed (10.0)
40L E	20.3	1	79.0	5	9.1	3	8.3	1 lump (24.7), 2 mat impressed (1.5)
40L W			17.5	3			4.8	1 mat impressed (0.5)
41U NW	14.4	5	54.0	10			4.7	
41M NW			12.1	1	17.9	3	1.9	
41M SE			30.5	1				1 mat impressed (0.2)
41L NW			13.9	2				
41.1 SE			70.3	1	2.2	1	0.9	
42U NW			68.2	5	72.8	5	19.6	
42U SE							11.7	
42L N			27.3	3	53.4	4	8.9	1 sherd impressed (0.9)
42L S					4.5	2	4.2	3 mat impressed (6.6)
43N	53.2	3	26.1	6	12.5	6	10.0	2 mat impressed (9.2), 1 sherd impressed (1.6)
43S					5.1	2	7.1	
44U S	10.3	1	12.6	4				
44L SE							1.8	1 sherd impressed (1.8)
45L N					6.4	2	3.5	1 ball (16.4)
46U SW			3.9	1	4.7	1	21.6	1 ovoid (21.6)

Table D15: Attributes of Finished Bitumen Artifacts

Spheres

Units	Layers	Diameter	Weight
X628	B39	4.46	66.7
X635	B40	2.55	12.7
X745	B45	2.94	16.4

Perforated Ovoids

Units	Layers	Length	Maximum Thickness	Minimum Thickness	Weight	Comment
X469	B32	1.82+	2.14	1.44	4.70+	broken
X479	B33	6.58	3.23	1.39	34.95	reed imprint in hole
X533	B34	2.86	2.22	1.70	10.25	—
X744	B46	5.19+	2.27-	3.80-	60.05	reed imprint in hole

Table D16: Attributes of Woven Mats, Fabrics, and Lashings

Mats

Unit	Layer	Impressed Material	Weight	Width Rush	Weave	Comment
X060	A5	bitumen	9.15	.60	2o-2u	
X081	A6	bitumen	17.90	.80	2o-2u	
X082	A6	bitumen	3.65	1.20+	2o-2u	
X087	A7	bitumen	240.75	1.54	2o-2u	
X088	A7	bitumen	57.04	1.41	2o-2u)	two layers of matting
				.72	2o-2u)	
X213	A15	bitumen	3.96	1.12	2o-2u	
X444	A24	bitumen	19.46	1.40+	—	
X674	A35	bitumen	2.86	1.64	2o-2u	
X699	A36	bitumen	10.56	1.78	2o-2u	
X129	B19	bitumen	5.28	.60?	—	
X170	B21	bitumen	.72	1.15?	—	
X173	B22-23	bitumen	2.90	1.00	—	
X206	B22	bitumen	15.65	1.31	2o-2u	corner of basket?
X247	B24	bitumen	10.10	1.48	2o-2u	
X316	B27	bitumen	2.33	1.80	—	very coarse material
X370	B29	bitumen	2.93	1.80	2o-2u	
X468	B32	bitumen	18.28	.96	2o-2u	close to edge binding
X646	B41	bitumen	1.30	1.60	2o-2u	
X657	B41	bitumen	68.36	1.56	2o-2u	
X738	B45	silt-bitumen	—	.70	2o-2u	
X758	B45	bitumen	93.95	1.76+	—	

Fabrics

Unit	Layer	Impressed Material	Warp Thread	Warp Space	Weft Thread	Weft Space	Weight	Weave
X366	B29	plaster vat interior	.08	.09	.06	.06±	—	1o-1u
X338	A20	bitumen sealing	.33	—	2.6	.01	14.01	1o-1u

Lashings

Unit	Layer	Impressed Material	Thread	Strand	Twist Period	Weight
X338	A20	bitumen sealing	.45	.22	.71	14.01
X451	A24	bitumen	.51	.60	1.70	43.12*
X581	A29	bitumen	.72	.60		4.74*
X695	B42	bitumen	.45	.30		6.31**

*twisted reed lashing on reed
**cords across carved wood paneling?

APPENDIX E

FAUNAL ELEMENTS FROM TEPE FARUKHABAD

This appendix contains the data on which the contributions by Richard W. Redding in Chapter XIV and Nancy Talbot in Chapter VIII are based. The only table with confusing abbreviations, Table E4, contains an explanatory key.

Table E1: Elements of the Class Osteichthyes (The Fish) Recovered at Tepe Farukhabad

Phase	Element	Excavation Unit	Ident.
Elamite	1 unident.	B6	
	1 spine	B8 west	
	1 lf. opercular	B8 west	
Early Dynastic	1 spine	B20 F10	
	1 hyomandibular	B20 F10	Cyprinidae
	2 vertebrae	B20 se.	
	1 anal spine	B20 se.	
	1 spine	B20 se.	
	1 unident.	B20 se.	
	1 spine	A3	
	1 unident.	A5 F1	
	1 anal spine	A5 F2	
	1 opercular	A5 F2	
	2 unident.	A5 F3	
	1 spine	A5 F3	
	1 angular	A5 F3	
	1 spine	A5 east	
Jemdet Nasr	1 vertebra	A6 south	
	1 unident.	A6 south	
	1 premaxillia	A6 north	Pomadasyidae
	1 vertebra	A7 north	
	4 spines	A7 north	
	1 pharngyeal arch	A7 north	Pomadasyidae
	1 vertebrae	A7 F10	
	1 spine	A7 F10	
	1 angular	A7 F10	
	1 unident.	A7 F10	
	1 opercular	A8 south	
	1 vertebra	A8 north	Perciform, cf. Pomadasyidae
	1 anal spine	A8 north	
	1 pharngyeal arch	A8 north	Cyprinidae
	1 anal spine	A9	
	1 angular	A9	
	1 unident.	A9	
	1 dentary	B21 south	
	1 spine	B21 north	
	1 anal spine	B21 north	
	1 frontal	B21 north	
	1 anal spine	B22 lower north	
	3 pharngyeal archs	B22 lower north	Pomadasyidae
	2 unident.	B22 lower north	
	1 anal spine	B22 & 23 F10	
	1 spine	B23 F10	
	1 frontal	A12 north	Pomadasyidae
	6 vertebrae	AF13	

Table E1: Continued

Phase	Element	Excavation Unit	Ident.
	2 spines	AF13	
	1 spine	A17 lower and 18 upper	
	1 spine	B25 lower north	
	1 premaxillia	B26	Pomadasyidae
Late Uruk	9 vertebrae	A20 F19	
	3 spines	A20 F19	
	1 spine	A20 F19	*Varicorhinus* sp.
	1 spine	B29 F23	
Middle Uruk	1 spine	B32 upper south	
	1 spine	B33 F26	
	1 spine	B33 upper and middle s.w.	
	1 tooth	B33 lower	
Early Uruk	1 vertebra	B35 lower	
	1 vertebra	B36 lower and 37 upper	
Farukh	1 vertebra	B40 lower east	

Table E2: Elements of the Class Reptilia (The Reptiles) Recovered at Tepe Farukhabad

Phase	Element	Excavation Unit	Ident.
Elamite	3 carapace frags.	B4	
	1 mandible	B11 lower	Agamidae
	3 carapace frags.	B11 lower	*Trionyx euphraticus*
	1 hypoplastron	B11 lower	*Clemmys caspica*
	22 carapace frags.	B11 and 12	*T. euphraticus*
	13 carapace frags.	B12	*T. euphraticus*
	1 humerus	B12	*T. euphraticus*
	*1 marginal	B14	*C. caspica*
Early Dynastic	*1 illium	B20 north	*Agamidae
Jemdet-Nasr	1 mandible	AF3	Agamidae
	1 articular	A8 south	
	1 mandible	A9	Agamidae
Middle Uruk	1 plastron frag.	B32 upper refuse conc.	
	*5 vertebrae	B33 upper and middle center	
	*1 vertebra	B33 lower north	
Early Uruk	*1 humerus	B35 lower	
	1 vertebra	B36 lower and 37 upper	
Farukh	1 vertebra	A29	
	1 vertebra	B40 lower east	

*Considered not to be intrusive

Table E3: Elements of the Class Aves (The Birds) Recovered at Tepe Farukhabad

Phase	Element	Excavation Unit	Ident.
Elamite	1 rt. distal ulna	B7 F3	*Columba* sp.
	1 rt. ulna	B11 lower	*Falco* sp.
	1 rt. ulna	B12	
	1 rt. first phalanx of digit II	B13 lg. pit	Threskiornithidae
	1 distal tarsometatarsus	B18	
Jemdet Nasr	1 rt. tarsometatarsus	A6 south	*Egretta garzetta*
	1 unident.	A7 east	
	1 lf. distal humerus	A7 east	
	1 lf. coracoid	A7 north	Threskiornithidae
	1 lf. radius	A8	
	1 lf. ulna	B21 north	Anatidae
	1 rt. prox. humerus	B25 lower	Anatidae
Late Uruk	1 cervical vertebra	B26 east	
	1 rt. prox. humerus	A19 all	*Gallinula chloropus*
	1 rt. prox. carpometacarpus	A19 all	*Columba* sp.
	1 rt. distal tibia	B31 lower north	
Middle Uruk	1 lf. carpometacarpus	B33 lower and middle se.	*Larus* sp.
	1 unident.	B33	
	1 lf. tarsometatarsus	B34	Passerine
Farukh-Bayat	1 lf. prox. tibia	B44	*Phalacrocorax carbo*

Table E4: Identifiable Elements of the Class Mammalia (The Mammals) Recovered at Tepe Farukhabad

Key

Table E4 is a series of grids in which each identifiable mammal element is placed. At the top of each grid is the taxonomic designation of the elements in that grid. The columns in the grids are the excavation units and the rows osteologic designations. Each element is represented by a series of symbols at the appropriate intersection in the grid. The first symbol is a number representing the number of elements of a single type recovered. It is always present. This may be followed by either an L or an R. This refers to the symmetry of the element(s). The absence of either of these two symbols indicates that element(s) is medial or that it is symmetry indeterminate. The symbols P and D are utilized only with limb elements. They refer to proximal and distal respectively. The symbols U, F, and I refer to the state of fusion of the elements. They may be interpreted as unfused, fused, and fusing respectively. The symbol Foe. may replace the symbol U and should be read as foetal. The symbol Dec. is utilized with teeth that have been identified as being deciduous. Following the number of elements in the rows Mx and M^x (lower and upper molars) there may be a second number in parenthesis. This indicates the number of these elements that are third molars.

Examples: 1RPF   One, right, proximal, fused
1L   One, left
2DF   Two, distal, fused

Hyaena hyaena

	B12
Radius	1RF
Ulna	1RF
Total Num. Elems.	2
Minimum Indvs.	1

Felis sp.

	A6
Scapula	1L
Total Num. Elems.	1
Minimum Indvs.	1

Vulpes sp.

	A5 e.	A18	B18 lg.pit	B21 s.	B27 s.	B33 Up.-M. sw.	B34 F-32	B34 F-35	B45 Low. rm.D
Metatarsal				1R					
Tibia						1RDF			
Femur		2LDF							
		1LPF			1LPF				
Radius			1RPF						
Ulna	1RPU		1RF						
Humerus				1LDF					
Mandible							1R		1L
M_1								1L	1L
M_2									1L
Total Num. Elems.	1	3	2	2	1	1	1	1	3
Minimum Indvs.	1	2	1	1	1	1	1	1	1

Canis spp.

	A24 Up.ne	A28 nw.	B7 w.	B11-12	B12	B13	B34 Low.s.	B35	B35 F-35	B40 Low.w.	B46 Low.sw.
Metapodial			1D								
Metatarsal	1L						1L	1L			
							1R				
Tarsal							1L				
Tibia							1RDF				
Femus							1LPF				
Carpal							1L				
Ulna											
Scapula							1R				
Skull frag.					1L						
Mandible			1R				1R				1R
Premaxilla											
Maxilla											
PM^4		1R									1L
M^1		1R									1L
M^2		1R									1L
M_3									1		
C						1					2
Total Num. Elems.	1	3	2	0	1	1	8	1	1	1	6
Minimum Indvs.	1	1	1	0	1	1	1	→1←		1	1

Canis familiaris

	B7 w.	B11-12
Mandible	1R	1R
Maxilla		1L
Total Num. Elems.	1	2
Minimum Indvs.	1	1

Equus spp

	A5 e.	A5 w.	A5 F-3	A6 s.	A6 n.	A11 sw.	A12-13 Up.n.	A13 s.	A16 all	A16 s.	A17-19 Low.n.	A19 all	A20 F-19	A F-23
Third Phalanx												1		1
Second Phalanx														
First Phalanx													1F	1F
Metapodial			1D		1DF									
Sesamoid														
Metatarsal						1R								
Tarsal														3L 1R 1LDF 1LDU
Tibia														1RDF
Femur														
Patella														
Pelvis Fragment														
Metacarpal														
Carpal														
Radius														
Ulna														
Humerus							1RDF							
Scapula													1RDF	
Skull Fragment														1R
Atlas														
Axis										1R				
Petrous Temporal	1R								1			1		
Mandible Frag.			1R					1			1LDec.			
P²														
M³				1R										
Pˣ or Mˣ		1L												
P₂														
M₃														
Pₓ or Mₓ	1R		1R											
I														
Total Num. Elems.	2	1→←1	3	1→←1↓		1	1	1	1	1	1	1	2	10
Minimum Indvs.						1	1	1	1		1	1	1	2

Equus spp.

	A21 Up.s.	A21 m.	A21 F-25	A29± nw.	B4	B6	B7 w.	B8 w.	B10	B11 Low.	B11-12	B12	B13	B14
Third Phalanx														
Second Phalanx				1										
First Phalanx			2PF											
Metapodial		1D										1D		
Sesamoid												1		
Mctatarsal														
Tarsal						1L								
Tibia								1RD	1R					
Femur														
Patella						1D								
Pelvis Fragment				1R										
Metacarpal								1RP				2R		
Carpal										1L		1R	1RPF	
Radius	1L									1RDF				
Ulna										1RPF				
Humerus										1L			1LDF	
Scapula													1R	
Skull Fragment														
Atlas														
Axis														
Petrous Temporal													1	
Mandible Frag.													1L 1R	
P²														
M³			1R											
Pˣ or Mˣ								1R				1R	1L 1R	1R
P₂					1L			1R	1L	1L		1L		1R
M₂												1 1Dec		
Pₓ or Mₓ														
	↑	↓												
Total Num. Elems.	1	1	3	2	1	2	1	4	2	5	0	9	8	2
Minimum Indvs.	1	1	1	1	1	1	1	1	1	1	0	1	1	1

Equus spp

	B17 w.	B18	B20 sw.	B22 Low.n.	B23 Up.n.	B25 Low.n.	B25-27	B26	B27 ne.	B28 n.	B28 s.	B29 Up.s.	B29 Up.F-21	B31 Low.n.
Third Phalanx														
Second Phalanx														
First Phalanx	1	1												
Metapodial													1DF	
Sesamoid														
Metatarsal					1R									
Tarsal														
Tibia														
Femur							1RDF							
Patella														
Pelvis Fragment		1RP												
Metacarpal				1L										
Carpal									1R					
Radius														
Ulna														
Humerus										1RDF				
Scapula														
Skull Fragment														
Atlas														
Axis														
Petrous Temporal														
Mandible Frag.														
P²	1R													
M³	1R													
Pˣ or Mˣ		1R	1L											
P₂		1L 1R												
M₂		1L												
Pₓ or Mₓ							1L				1			
I						1						1		1L
Total Num. Elems.	3	6	1	1	1	1	3	0	1	1 ↔	1	1 ↔	1	1
Minimum Indvs.	1	1	1	1	1	1	1	0	1	1		1		1

397

Equus spp.

	B31 Low.s.	B31 Up.s.	B32 Low.s.	B32 Up.s.	B33 Low.s.	B33 Up.s.	B34 Low.c.	B34 Up.c.	B34 Low.s.	B34 Up.s.	B34 Up.n.	B34 below F-28	B34 F-32	B35 Low.
Third Phalanx														
Second Phalanx														
First Phalanx		1												
Metapodial													1	
Sesamoid	1D													
Metatarsal				1L										
Tarsal									2L					2L 4R
Tibia										1RDF				1LDF
Femur														
Patella														
Pelvis Fragment					1L				1L			1LDF		
Metacarpal														
Carpal														
Radius					1LDU				1RPF 1RP				1RP	
Ulna													1RDF	
Humerus									1L					
Scapula														
Skull Fragment					1L 1R									
Atlas														
Axis														
Petrous Tempora	1		1											
Mandible Frag.					5			1R						
P²														
M³														
Pˣ or Mx						1L	1L 2L 1		1L	1L 2L 1	1L			
P₂														
M₂									1L	1L				
Pₓ or Mₓ														
Total Num. Elems.	1	1	1	1	9	1	4	1	7	6	1	1	3	7
Minimum Indvs.	1	1	1	1	1	1	1	1	1	2	1	1	1	1

Equus spp.

	B35 pot group	B36 Low. all	B36 Low.se.	B36 Up.se.	B36 Up.sw.	B36 Up.nw.	B36 all	B37 all	B40 Low.e.	B44 Low.s.	B45 Up.sw.R-A	B46 Up.sw.	B47 sw.	B48±
Third Phalanx														
Second Phalanx														
First Phalanx														3F
Metapodial														
Sesamoid														
Metatarsal	1RP													
Tarsal			1L											
Tibia				1L 1R					1D		1F			
Femur					1RDF	1L								
Patella														
Pelvis Fragment														
Metacarpal														
Carpal														
Radius														
Ulna														
Humerus														1RDF
Scapula								1R						
Skull Fragment														
Atlas														
Axis														
Petrous Temporal														
Mandible Frag.														
P^2														
M^3														
P^x or M^x				1R			1L			1				1L
P_2							1R							
M_2														
P_x or M_x												1	1R	
Total Num. Elems.	1	1	1	3	1	1	2	2	1	1	1	1	1	5
Minimum Indvs.	1			1			1	1	1	1	1	1	1	1

399

Bos taurus

	A7 n.	A9-10 sw.	A11 se.	A13 s.	A16 all	A F-23	A23 all	A24 Low.n.	A25 s.	A26 n.	A35 all	A36 se.F-32	B7 w.	B11 Low.
Third Phalanx														
Second Phalanx														
First Phalanx						1F							1PF	
Metapodial														
Metatarsal														
Tarsal														
Tibia		1LPF												
Femur														
Patella														
Pelvis Fragment														
Metacarpal									1R					
Carpal														
Radius														
Ulna														
Humerus														1RPU
Scapula														
Skull Fragment														
Petrous Temporal														
Mandible Frag.														
Horn Core														
Axis														
Atlas	1L													
M^x		1R												
P^x														
M_x			1L(1)	2R	1R		1L			1R(1)				
P_x														
I											1	2		
Total Num. Elems.	1	2	1	2	1	1	1	0	1	1	1	2	1	1
Minimum Indvs.	1	1	1	1	1	1	1	0	1	1	1	1	1	1

Bos taurus

	B11-12	B12	B14	B21 s.	B24 Low.n.	B24 F-18	B25-27 s.	B27 ne.	B30 w.	B30 se.	B30 ne.	B33 Up.-M.c.	B34 Low.s.	B34 Low.c.
Third Phalanx	1	3												
Second Phalanx	1F	4												
First Phalanx	4F	6F												
Metapodial	1P 2D	2P 2D												
Metatarsal			1RP									2DF		
Tarsal	1L	2R												
Tibia									1					
Femur														
Patella														
Pelvis Fragment										1L				
Metacarpal		1LP 1RP												
Carpal	2R	1L												
Radius	1RPF	1RDF		1LDU										
Ulna	1RP	1RDF								1LDU				
Humerus	1R													
Scapula														
Skull Fragment	1R	1R			1R	1L								
Petrous Temporal														
Mandible Frag.		1R			1R	1L		1R					1	1L
Horn Core		1												
Axis														
Atlas	1L													
M^x														
P^x							2L(1)							
M_x	2R(1)	2L(1)									1R 1L			
P_x		1R												
I														
Total Num. Elems.	20	32	1	1	1	1	2	1	1	2	2	2	1	1
Minimum Indvs.	1	1	1	1	1	1	1	1	↑1	1↑	1	1	1↑	↓1

Bos taurus

	B35 Low.	B38 e.	B39 M.w.	B47 sw.
Third Phalanx				
Second Phalanx				1F
First Phalanx				
Metapodial				
Metatarsal				
Tarsal	1L	1		
Tibia				
Femur				
Patella				
Pelvis Fragment				
Metacarpal				
Carpal				
Radius				
Ulna				
Humerus				
Scapula				
Skull Fragment				
Petrous Temporal				
Mandible Frag.				
Horn Core				
Axis				
Atlas				
M^x				
P^x				
M_x	1L			
P_x			1R	1
Total Num. Elems.	2	1	1	2
Minimum Indvs.	1	1	1	1

402

Sus scrofa

	A above 155.8 cm	A3	A5 e.	A7 n.	B1-3	B5	B8 w.	B18	B20 n.	B21 n.	B22 Low n.	B24
Third Phalanx	1											
Second Phalanx	1U	3F										
First Phalanx	1U 1F											
Metapodial	1											
Metatarsal	1R 1RU	1R	1RF				1				2	
Tarsal		1LPU										
Tibia			1RDU						1L			
Femur			1RU									
Metacarpal	1R	2L										
Carpal												
Radius												
Ulna			1LPU									
Humerus			1L									
Scapula												
Skull Fragment		1								1R		
Mandible Frag.												1R
P^2				1L								
P^4				1LDec.								
M$_1$				1	1L 1R							
M$_3$												
P$_3$						1R				2L Dec.		
1												
Total Num. Elems.	8	8	5	3	2	1	1	0	1	3	2	1
Minimum Indvs.	1	1	1	1	1	1	1	0	1	1	1	1

Ovis-Capra-Gazella

	A above 155.8 cm	A3 all	A5 e.	A5 w.	A5 F-3	A6 n.	A6 s.	A7 n.	A7 s.	A7 around F-1	A8 n.	A8 s.	A8±
Third Phalanx	2 Capra 1 Ovis	1 Ovis	1 Capra 1 Ovis	1 Capra 1 Ovis	1 Capra		1 Capra					2 Capra	
Second Phalanx	1F 1	2F	2F 1I	1		1	1					2	
First Phalanx	1F	2F 1U	2F Gaz 1 2F 2U		3F	1	2		1			3	
Metapodial	1DU Ovis		1U Gaz 1F 3D			1D	1DU	3DU Capra			1	1D Capra 1	1L Ovis
Metatarsal	1		1LP 1RP	1RP 2R		1LP 2R							
Tarsal	2L 2R	2L 1R	1L		1R	3L 3R		1L				1L	
Tibia	1RPF	1LDU	1RPF	1RP	1RDF	1LPF 1RDF	1LP 1RDF		1LDF 1RD		1L Capra		
Femur	1LDU 1RDU	1RPU 1RDU 1RD	1RD			1RPF	1LPF 2RDF 1LPU 2RDU 1RD	1RPF Gaz 1LDU	1LDU	1PU	1LDU 1RPU	1LDF	
Patella													
Illium	1R							1R					
Ischium													
Pubis					1L								
Metacarpal	1RP												
Carpal	2R	1L Ovis	1R										
Radius	2LPF		1RDF 1RDU 1RP			1LPF	1LPF	1RD	1LPF		1LDU 1RDU 1RPF 1RP		1LPF 2R 1RP
Ulna	1RDU	1LD 1RD 1RD 1RDF	1RDF 1RDU	1LPF 1RPU 1RPF		1LP		1LDF 1RDF	1RP			1RDF	1R
Humerus													
Scapula	1R	1R								1R			
Atlas	1		1										
Axis													
Petrous Temporal	1L Ovis	1L Capra 1R Ovis	1R 1R Capra									1L Capra	
Skull Fragment				1L 1R		1L	1L		1R				
Horn Core	2R		2R	2L	1L	1L	1L 1R	1 Gaz					
Mandible Frag.			1L 6R(2) 1L 3L(2) 3R				1L 1R(1) 3L 3R 2L(2)	1L				1R(1)	
Sesamoid													
M^x	1L			1LDec. 2L	1LDec.				2R(1)				
P^x	1L 1												
M_x			4R 1RDec. 1	3L 1LDec. 2					2R			4L	
P_x	2L												
1	3							1					
Total Num. Elems.	35	20	55	24	8	13	34	12	12	2	8	18	6
Minimum Indvs.	3	2		3		5			2		2	2	2
Capra Min. Indvs.	1	1		1		1			1		1	1	
Ovis Min. Indvs.	1	1		1		1			1				1
Gazella Min. Indvs.													

404

Ovis-Capra-Gazella

	A9-10 n.	A9-10 se.	A9-10 sw.	A10-11	A11 n.	A11 se.	A11 sw.	A11 c.	A12 n.	A12 s.	A12-13	A13-15 Low.	A13 all	A13 Up.n.
Third Phalanx									1 Gaz			1 Ovis		
Second Phalanx	1F 1		1 Capra 2						2F	1F 1U 2U			3F 1U	1F 1U
First Phalanx		1D	1U				1D Capra	1D Ovis	1DF Gaz 1DF Ovis					1DF
Metapodial			1DF Ovis 1DU		1						1	1DU	1RP 1	1R
Metatarsal	1						2L 2R Capra			1LP 2L		1RD		
Tarsal					1L									
Tibia						1L							1P	
Femur		1LPU												
Patella														
Illium								1L		1				
Ischium									1L					
Pubis									1LP		1RP			
Metacarpal		1LP		1RP 1L					1LPF					
Carpal	1L					1R								
Radius							1RDU							
Ulna		1LDF 1LDU 1RD 1L					1LDU						1RP	1RDU
Humerus							1R			1RD			1R	1RDF
Scapula											1L			
Atlas		1L												
Axis														
Petrous Temporal														
Skull Fragment														
Horn Core														
Mandible Frag.				1L										
Sesamoid														
M^x							2R(1) 1L(1)		3R(2)					
P^x														
M$_x$		1L(1)	1R 1L(1)	1L							1L	1		1L
P$_x$														
1		1	1		1									1L
Total Num. Elems.	4	10	9	4	3	2	11	4	11	9	4	4	10	7
Minimum Indvs.		2		1			2		2		1		1	
Capra Min. Indvs.		1					1		1			1		
Ovis Min. Indvs.		1					1		1					
Gazella Min. Indvs.														

Ovis-Capra-Gazella

	A13 Up.s.	A13 F-11	A15 all	A16 all	A17 n.	A17 s.	ALow.17 Up.18	A17-19 Low.	A18 n.	A19 all	A19 oven	A19-20
Third Phalanx								1Capra				
Second Phalanx			1F			1U	1		1F 2U		1F	1
First Phalanx	2F 1U 2		1F 1D	1D	1 DF	1D Gaz			1F 1			
Metapodial												
Metatarsal												
Tarsal	1L											
Tibia			1R Ovis	1RPF	1R	1RDF		1R		1L 1RDU		
Femur					1RPU							
Patella												
Illium												
Ischium				1L				1R				
Pubis												
Metacarpal	1RP					1R						
Carpal		1RPF										
Radius								1LDU				
Ulna	1LPU			1LD					1RD			
Humerus	1LD											
Scapula												
Atlas												
Axis			1L Ovis						2			
Petrous Temporal			1R Capra									
Skull Fragment				1 Capra	1L Gaz							
Horn Core												
Mandible Frag.	1R		1R	1L	1R	1L		1L	1R	1R		
Sesamoid								1L	1R			
M^x												
P^x				2L								
M_x			1R Dec.	1					1	1		1R
P_x	2											
Total Num. Elems.	13	1	8	10	4	6	1	6	11	4	1	2
Minimum Indvs.	2		2	1	1	1	1	1	2	1	1	1
Capra Min. Indvs.			1	1				1				
Ovis Min. Indvs.			1			1						
Gazella Min. Indvs.					1							

Ovis-Capra-Gazella

	A20	A20 se.	A20 F-19	A21 Up.n.	A21 Up.s.	A21 M.	A21 M. rooms B & C	A21 Low.	A21 Low. rooms C, D & E	A21 F-25	A21 F-26	A F-23	A22 all	A22 F-24
Third Phalanx												1 Capra		1 Capra
Second Phalanx	2F				1F									1F
First Phalanx			1D				1D		1				1DU	1D
Metapodial														1D Capra
Metatarsal	1L		1R		1L Gaz						1LP		1L	1R
Tarsal											3L 1R			
Tibia											1R Ovis	1LDF		
											1RDF			
											1RPU			
											1RDU			
Femur											1RPU			1PU
Patella														
Illium			1L										1L	1L
Ischium														
Pubis													1R	
Metacarpal									1L					
Carpal												1L	1R	1LP
Radius											1RPF Gaz	1LPF		2R
												1LPU		
Ulna			1LP									1RDF		
Humerus	1RD									1R	1LD 1RDI	1L	1LD	1RDF
Scapula			1L										1LDU	
Atlas														
Axis														
Petrous Temporal														
Skull Fragment								1 Capra				1L		1L Capra
Horn Core														
Mandible Frag.												1L		1D
Sesamoid														
M^x												4L(3)		
												4R(2)		
P^x							1R	1L(1) 1R						
M_x			1R			1R						4R(2)	1L	
P_x				1										
1												1L	1L	
Total Num. Elems.	4	0	6	1	2	1	2	3	2	1	13	22	9	13
Minimum Indvs.		1					3					3	2	
Capra Min. Indvs.							1							2
Ovis Min. Indvs.							1					1		1
Gazella Min. Indvs.							1							

Ovis-Capra-Gazella

	A F-25	A22 &F-25	A23 Low.n.	A23 all	A23 brickfill of F-25	A24 Up.ne.	A24 Low.n.	A24 Low.ne.	A24 Up.sw.	A24 Low.sw.	A24 Low.	A25 n.	A25 s.	A26 n.	A26 s.
Third Phalanx	1 Capra 1			1 Gaz											
Second Phalanx	2F 1D 1					2F									
First Phalanx				1	1F 1	1			1U		1			1	1
Metapodial	1RP														
Metatarsal															
Tarsal		1R		1 1R					1R						1R
Tibia	1PU 1RD	1RDI		1LDF		1RDU			1LPU						
Femur	1R														
Patella		1L													
Ilium								1L							
Ischium				1L											
Pubis															
Metacarpal	1L			1L				1R							
Carpal												1LPF		1R	
Radius												1LP		1RPF	
Ulna				1LDF											
Humerus											1R				
Scapula															
Atlas						1									
Axis									1L Gaz 1						
Petrous Temporal				1 Gaz		1			1R Gaz		1L				
Skull Fragment															
Horn Core															1 Gaz.
Mandible Frag.															
Sesamoid															
M^x	1R	2R		5R(1) 1L		6L(3)		2R(1)		1L	3R(2)				
P^x		2R		2L 3R		1L 1L Dec. 1R 1R Dec.		1R	1R		3R	3R	1R(1)		
M_x		2L		6L(2) 1R(1)		5L(3) 3R(3)		6R(3)		1R	3R		1L(1) 2R		
P_x		1R		2L 1R	2	3L 1R		1L	1			1		1R	
1				3											
Total Num. Elems.	12	10	0	33	4	28	0	6	14	2	10	6	6	7	3
Minimum Indvs.	1	1	↑ 2	↑ 2		↑ 6						↑ 2	↑ 2	↑ 2	
Capra Min. Indvs.	1														
Ovis Min. Indvs.				1			↑ 1							↑ 1	
Gazella Min. Indvs.															

408

Ovis-Capra-Gazella

	A27 n.	A27 s.	A28 nw.	A28 se.	A28	A28 Up.	A28 Low.	A28 between F-30-31	A29±	A30 between F-30-31	A33	A34	A35 all
Third Phalanx	1 Gaz	1 Gaz											
Second Phalanx		2F		1F			1F				1F	1D	1D
First Phalanx	1 Gaz 2F	1U	1F									2 Ovis	
Metapodial			1LP										
Metatarsal	2L		1L										
Tarsal									1LDU	1L			
Tibia								1RDF			1RDU		
Femur			1L						1L				
Patella													
Illium													
Ischium													
Pubis													
Metacarpal		1R											
Carpal			1RDF						1LPF				
Radius													
Ulna													
Humerus			1L						1R	1RD			
Scapula													
Atlas									1				
Axis													
Petrous Temporal	1R Gaz												
Skull Fragment													
Horn Core			1R Gaz 1L Gaz	1			1R Gaz 1L Gaz						
Mandible Frag.													
Sesamoid					1L(1)	1L							
M^x													2(1)
P^x													
M_x												1L	3R(1)
P_x													
1		1											
Total Num. Elems.	7 ↑	6 ↓	8 ↑	2 ↓	1	1	3	1	5	2	2	4	6
Minimum Indvs.	2		1	1					1	1	1	1	1
Capra Min. Indvs.													
Ovis Min. Indvs.	↑	↓	↑	↓	↑	1	↑					1	
Gazella Min. Indvs.	1		1	1			1						

409

Ovis-Capra-Gazella

	A36 se. F-32	A36 inside F-32	A F-33	B1-3	B6	B7	B7 e.	B7 w.	B7 F-3	B8 w.	B10	B11	B11 Low.	B11 Up.	B11-12
Third Phalanx								1 Ovis							
Second Phalanx	1F 1U 2	1D		1F	1 Ovis	1F	1			2F			1	1F	1F
First Phalanx	1			1F 1		1	1F Gaz							1D Ovis	
Metapodial				1DU	1D Capra	1L			1DF Capra						
Metatarsal															
Tarsal	1R			1L 1R								2L 1R			
Tibia						1LDF			1R			1RDF	1R Ovis	1LPF 1LD	
Femur									1RD	1LDF 2U 1RDF 1RP					
Patella						1L 1R							1RDF		
Illium				1R		1L 1R									1L
Ischium						1L 1R									
Pubis															
Metacarpal									1P	1L		1RP			
Carpal															
Radius				1LPF	1LPF 1RDF 1RD	1LPF								1LPF 1LP	1D
Ulna						1LPF			1PU						1L 1R
Humerus				1L 1R					1R			1L	1RDF		1
Scapula				1											
Atlas							4			1					
Axis							1R								
Petrous Temporal		1L Ovis		1L Capra						1L Capra 1L 1R	1R Capra	1L Capra 1R	1 Ovis	2 1R	1L Capra 1L 1R
Skull Fragment										1 Capra					
Horn Core	1R														
Mandible Frag.															
Sesamoid															
M^x		1L							1R	1L 3R					4R
P^x									1R	1R					
M_x				1R	1R	2R		3R(2)		2R					
P_x	3L(1)			2R	1R	2L		2L Dec.	1L	1L 2R 1R Dec.					
										1					
Total Num. Elems.	10	2	1	15	7	16	7	6	9	25	1	9	5	10	13
Minimum Indvs.	1		1	1	2		3	1		2	1		1		2
Capra Min. Indvs.				1	1		1	1		1					1
Ovis Min. Indvs.			1		1		1						1		
Gazella Min. Indvs.							1								

410

Ovis-Capra-Gazella

	B12	B13 lg. pit	B14	B15-16	B16	B16 F-7	B17 w.	B18	B18 lg. pit	B19	B20	B20 sw.	B20 Low.n.	B20 n.
Third Phalanx														
Second Phalanx	1F Gaz	2U		1DU		1			1	1		1F 2U		1 Gaz 2 2D Capra 1D Ovis
First Phalanx														
Metapodial														
Metatarsal		1LP			1L		1R				1LPU 1LPI	1RP		1L
Tarsal	1R													
Tibia									1RDU			1L	1R	1LPI 1LDF 1LDU 1LP 1RDU
Femur					1LPF									
Patella	1L 1R								1R			1		1L
Illium	1L 2R													1R
Ischium	1L													
Pubis		1LD Capra 1RP						1LD						
Metacarpal				1RD					1L		1R			1R 1LDU 1RPF 3RP 1LDF 1RDF 1RPU
Carpal					1RPF		2RDF							
Radius	1LDI 1RD	1U		1RD				1LD	1LP 1RP 1LD			1LDF		
Ulna														
Humerus	3L 1L Gaz				1	1L			1L					
Scapula	1L Ovis 1R Ovis													
Atlas														
Axis	1	1R Capra					1L				1R		1L	1 Gaz
Petrous Temporal														
Skull Fragment														
Horn Core														
Mandible Frag.														
Sesamoid	6L(1) 3R(1)							1R	2L 1R	3L(2)				
M^x	3R					4L(2)	1R 2R	3R	3L 1L					
P^x	4L(2) 9R(2)	1L 2R	1L											
M_x	3L 4R	1R					1L 1R Dec.		1L 1	1	1R	2		
P_x														
1														
Total Num. Elems.	49	11	1	3	4	6	9	6	18	5	5	9	2	24
Minimum Indvs.	3	2	1	1	↑2	↓2		↑2				3		
Capra Min. Indvs.		1							1			1		
Ovis Min. Indvs.	1											1		
Gazella Min. Indvs.	1											1		

Ovis-Capra-Gazella

	B20± n.	B20-21	B21 s.	B21 n.	B21 Low. F-21	B22-23 Up.	B22 s.	B22 Low.n.	B22 Up.n.	B23 s.	B23 Low.s.	B23 Up.s.	B23 n.	B23 Low.n.	B23 F-15
Third Phalanx				1 Ovis			1F								
Second Phalanx				2F			1F	2F 2U	1U		2	1F		3F	
First Phalanx				1F	1	2F		2F 2U 1 Capra	1DU		1DU				1F
Metapodial		2D Capra													
Metatarsal	1L		1LP			1L 1R Ovis	1L 1R Ovis	1L Capra 2L 2R	1L		1R	1R		2L 1R Capra	
Tarsal															
Tibia				1RDU 1RDF				1LPU 1LDF			1LPU		1LDU	1RDF	
Femur	1LPU 1LDU 1RPU	1LPU		1PU 1RDU		1RDU		1RDU 1DU 1LPU 1RPU	1PU	1RPF		1D			1RP 1RDF
Patella															
Illium		1R				1									
Ischium						1L									
Pubis															
Metacarpal				1LP											
Carpal															
Radius			1LDF	1LDU 1RPF 1RP 2LDF 1RDU				1RD 1R 1RDF			1L			1LPF	
Ulna		1RD	1RP 1LDU 1RDF		1LP			1RP 1LDF 1LDI 1RPF 1RD	1LDF 1RDF 2LDF 2RDF	1RDI	1LDU	1LPU 1RPU 1RDF	1LP		
Humerus															
Scapula							1	2L							
Atlas			1	1				1							
Axis															
Petrous Temporal											1L Capra				
Skull Fragment			1R	1R											
Horn Core															
Mandible Frag.													1L		
Sesamoid															
M^x	1R		1R												
P^x															
M_x	2R		1R 3R	1L 1		1R		1R	3R		1L				1RP 1RDF
P_x												2L Dec.		1R(1)	
1	1											1		1R	
Total Num. Elems.	8	3	13	20	2	8	5	30	11	2	13	9	3	10	4
Minimum Indvs.	2	1				1		4				2			
Capra Min. Indvs.						1		1				1			
Ovis Min. Indvs.								1							
Gazella Min. Indvs.															

Ovis-Capra-Gazella

	B24 s.	B24 Low.s.	B24 Low.n.	B24 Up.n.	B24 F-18	B25 Low.	B25 Low.n.	B25 Up.n.	B25 F-15	B25-27 s.	B26	B26 s.	B26 ne.	B27 w.	B27 ne.
Third Phalanx															
Second Phalanx	1	1		2 Ovis											
First Phalanx	1F		1F	3F		1F	1	2F		2 1 Gaz			1 Capra		
Metapodial	1D Gaz			4F	1D Capra									1D Capra	
Metatarsal			1LP	1L Ovis 1R Ovis											
Tarsal															
Tibia			1L	1L 3R		1L 3R				1LDF					1L 1R
Femur				1LDU			1RPU						1PU		1L
Patella															1L
Illium	1R			1R			1R 1L 1L								
Ischium												1L			
Pubis			1LP	1RP 1R 1P	1LPF	1LP	1RPF			1LPF 1LDF 1RPF					
Metacarpal			1L												
Carpal															
Radius									1LPI 1LPF	1LDF					1LP 1RDF
Ulna															
Humerus	1RD														
Scapula															
Atlas															
Axis															
Petrous Temporal										1R			1R Capra	1R	
Skull Fragment				1L Capra 1L Ovis 1R Ovis	1R Capra										
Horn Core				1R	1L Capra										
Mandible Frag.					1L Capra										
Sesamoid			2R	2L 2R 2D 2P											
M^x				4L 4R 2L 3R	2R	1L	4L 2R 1R 3R 2R						1L	1	1L 2R
P^x			1L 1R	3L 5R(2) 2L 2R						3R			4L 5R 3L 2R 2L 1R	3R	1L
M_x							1	1L		2R 1LDec.		1L	1L 1LDec. 1R	3R	3L 4R(2) 2L
P_x											1	2			
1			1												
Total Num. Elems.	5	1	10	57	7	3	23	3	2	15	1	4	24	9	19
Minimum Indvs.			3				2			1	1	2		2	2
Capra Min. Indvs.			1									1		1	1
Ovis Min. Indvs.			1												
Gazella Min. Indvs.			1							1					

Ovis-Capra-Gazella

	B28 s.	B28 n.	B28 ash pit	B29 Up.n.	B29 Up.s.	B29 Low.e.	B29 Low.w.	B29 F-21	B30 ne.	B30 se.	B30 w.	B31 Up.n.	B31 Low.n.	B31 Up.s.	B31 Low.s.
Third Phalanx															
Second Phalanx	2F								1F 1			1 Capra	1 Capra 1		1F
First Phalanx	1F	1U 1		1 Ovis			1F		2F 1			1U Gaz	1U		1D
Metapodial		1DU		1U						1LDF	1D Capra	1DU 1	1		1DF
Metatarsal				1LPU						1LP		1LP			
Tarsal	1L Ovis			1R Ovis				1R	1L 1R	1R		1L			
Tibia		1LDF			1RDU	1LDF						1RDF	1LDF		
Femur					1LDF							1LDU 1PU		1L	
Patella															
Illium	1R			1L				1L				1			
Ischium				1R		1L 1R				1L		1L			
Pubis				1LP								1R			
Metacarpal				1L	1L	2L 1RPF 2LP									
Radius							1LP								
Ulna		1LP				1LDF 1LD									
Humerus		1RD 1LD		2L					1R	1LDF		1RDF	1RDF	1RDF	
Scapula				1									1L 1R		
Atlas						1L			1						
Axis															
Petrous Temporal	1L Capra	1L Capra								1L Capra					
Skull Fragment		1L													
Horn Core															
Mandible Frag.		1L 1R			1D	1R				1L					
Sesamoid			1												
M^x	1L 1R	3L 2R	1L	1L 3R					1L		1R				1R
P^x	2R	1L 1R		2L					1R	1R	1L			1R	1R
M_x		2L													1R
P_x	2L	1L 3R				1L 1RDec.	1R								
1												1	1		1
Total Num. Elems.	10	26	2	19	5	14	3	1	12	8	3	13	10	3	7
Minimum Indvs.		3				3				2			2		
Capra Min. Indvs.		2								1			1		
Ovis Min. Indvs.		1				1							1		

Total Num. Elems.
Minimum Indvs.
Capra Min. Indvs.
Ovis Min. Indvs.
Gazella Min. Indvs.

Ovis-Capra-Gazella

	B31± inside F-23 wall	B31 Up.n.	B31 Low.n.	B31 Up.s.	B31 Low.s.	B33 Up.n	B33 Low.n.	B33 Low.s.	B33 Up.-M. c.	B33 Up.-M. se.	B33 Up.-M. sw.	B33 F-26	B33 F-30
Third Phalanx	1F	1 Ovis											
Second Phalanx						1U	3F	1F		2F		1F	
First Phalanx					1F	1PF		2F		1F			
Metapodial		1D	1DF					1D Ovis	1DU				
Metatarsal													
Tarsal			1L Capra	1L Ovis		1L	1R Gaz			1R / 1R Capra			
Tibia		1RDF						1LDU 1RDU		1RDU 1PU			
Femur		1P 1D						1DU					
Patella													
Illium						1							
Ischium													
Pubis													
Metacarpal				1LP									1RP
Carpal													
Radius		1RDF				1RPF	1LPF Gaz	1L				1RPF	
Ulna		1L				1RPF		1RD / 1RDF Gaz		1LDF	1RDU		
Humerus										1L			
Scapula													
Atlas													
Axis													
Petrous Temporal		1L Ovis											
Skull Fragment													
Horn Core													
Mandible Frag.								1L / 1R Gaz					
Sesamoid	1R					1R	2R						
M^x					4L	1L(1)		2R	3L(2) / 1R	1LDF			
P^x	1												
M_x	1L 1R			1L	1R	2L	2R	1R	1L / 3R(2) / 2L 3R / 1R Dec.	1L 1R			
P_x						1R							
1							1						
Total Num. Elems.	6	8	2	3	6	9	11	16	15	11	1	2	1
Minimum Indvs.	1	↑	↑2	↑	↑	↑	↑	↑	↑3	↑	↑	↑	↑
Capra Min. Indvs.		↑	↑1	↑	↑	↑	↑	↑	↑1	↑	↑	↑	↑
Ovis Min. Indvs.		↑	↑1	↑	↑	↑	↑	↑	↑1	↑	↑	↑	↑
Gazella Min. Indvs.									↑1				

Ovis-Capra-Gazella

	B34 Up.n.	B34 Low.n.	B34 Up.s.	B34 Low.s.	B34 Up.c.	B34 Low.c.	B34 below F-28	B34 F-32	B34 bricks of F-31	B35 all	B35 Up.	B35 Low.	B35 pot group
Third Phalanx													
Second Phalanx	1F		1F		1F	1F				1F			
First Phalanx			1			1F				2F	1DF	1D	
Metapodial	1RP												
Metatarsal				1R			1RP	1L Ovis			1L Gaz	1R	1LDF
Tarsal					1RDF			1LDF			1RDF	1LPF	1RPF
Tibia			1RDF					1RDF			1D	1RPF	
Femur						1							
Patella													
Illium					1L	1R							
Ischium										1L			
Pubis													
Metacarpal			1LPF	1RPF							1L		
Carpal			1LP	1LDF 1L							1LDF	1RPF	
Radius			1LDF								1RD	1RDU 1LD	
Ulna								1R Gaz					
Humerus								1L 1R					
Scapula													
Atlas					1								
Axis						1L Ovis		1L Ovis					
Petrous Temporal						1R Ovis							
Skull Fragment													
Horn Core			1L										
Mandible Frag.	1L	1L	2L	1L							2L	1L	
Sesamoid	1R		1R	1L				1L 1R			1R		
M^x			2L										
P^x													
M_x													
P_x													
Total Num. Elems.	4	1	12	6	3	6	1	9		4	10	8	2
Minimum Indvs.				3							2		
Capra Min. Indvs.				2									
Ovis Min. Indvs.				1							1		
Gazella Min. Indvs.													

Ovis-Capra-Gazella

	B36 all	B36 Low.	B36 Up.ne.	B36 Up.nw.	B36 Low.se.	B36 Low.sw.	B36 Low.sw.	B37	B38	B39 Up.e.	B39 M.e.	B39 Low.e.	B39 M.w.	B39 Low.w.
Third Phalanx														
Second Phalanx						1								
First Phalanx		1PF 1F		1F	1F			1F	1F					
Metapodial				1Gaz	1DF Capra			1D Capra						
Metatarsal	1RP								1L					1L
Tarsal			1L	1L	1R		1R							
Tibia														
Femur					1RPU			1RPF					1RPF	
Patella								1R						
Illium														
Ischium														
Pubis														
Metacarpal														
Carpal														
Radius													1LPF	
Ulna														
Humerus								1RDF			1RDF			
Scapula												1L		
Atlas														
Axis														
Petrous Temporal										1L	1R			
Skull Fragment										1L				
Horn Core														
Mandible Frag.						1L		1L 1R Dec.			1R	1L	1L 1R	1L
Sesamoid												1L		
M^x		1R												
P^x		1L	1R											
M_x				1R										
P_x			2											
Total Num. Elems.	1	4	4	4	4	1	2	7	2	2	3	3	4	2
Minimum Indvs.				2				2	1			1		
Capra Min. Indvs.				1				1						
Ovis Min. Indvs.								1						
Gazella Min. Indvs.				1										

417

Ovis-Capra-Gazella

	B40 Up.e.	B40 Low.e.	B40 Up.w.	B40 Low.w.	B41 Up.nw.	B41 M.nw.	B41 Up.se.	B42 Up.nw.	B42 Low.n.	B42 Low.s.	B42 Up.se.	B43 n.	B43 s.
Third Phalanx	1F												
Second Phalanx												1	1
First Phalanx	1 Ovis												
Metapodial			1F										
Metatarsal								1D			1RP		
Tarsal		1R					1R						1L
Tibia							1RPF						1RP
Femur												1RDF	
Patella		1L											
Illium					1L								
Ischium					1L							1R	
Pubis													
Metacarpal													
Carpal			1LPF										
Radius				1LDF						1RDF			
Ulna								1RP		1RPF			
Humerus													
Scapula				1R Capra									
Atlas													
Axis													
Petrous Temporal						1R Ovis							
Skull Fragment		1R								2R			
Horn Core				1L / 1R Dec.		1R		3L 1R	1L				
Mandible Frag.													
Sesamoid													
M^x													
P^x												3L(1)	
M_x			1L 4R(2) 2L(1) 2R					1L	1L 2R(1) 2L(2) 1R	4R(2) 3R	1L	1	
P_x												1R	
1		2				2							
Total Num. Elems.	2	5	11	4	2	5	2	8	6	11	2	8	4
Minimum Indvs.	2	2			2	2	2		3		2	1	1
Capra Min. Indvs.		1				1							
Ovis Min. Indvs.		1				1							
Gazella Min. Indvs.													

Ovis-Capra-Gazella

	B44 Up.n.	B44 Low.s.	B44 Low.se.	B44 Low.nw.	B45 Up.n. rooms F & G	B45 Up.se.	B46 Up.sw.	B46 Low.sw.	B47 all	B48±
Third Phalanx										
Second Phalanx										
First Phalanx									1DF Capra	1F
Metapodial									1LP	1
Metatarsal									2L	
Tarsal			1R							
Tibia		1LPU					1LPF		1LDF	
Femur			1L							
Patella										
Illium						1L				1L
Ischium						1L				1L
Pubis			1R			1L			1L	
Metacarpal										
Carpal										
Radius		1RD					1LPF			
Ulna			1LD				1RD	1RDF		
Humerus	1LDF			1RDU 1R						
Scapula				1						
Atlas										
Axis										
Petrous Temporal										
Skull Fragment					1R Ovis					
Horn Core				1R Capra			1L Capra 1L		1R Capra 2R	
Mandible Frag.							1R		2L(1) 2R 3R	
Sesamoid										
M^x									5L(1) 6R(3)	
P^x		1L					1L 1R(1)	1L(1)		
M$_x$		1L(1)		1L(1)					2R 1R Dec. 1	1L
P$_x$				1L						
Total Num. Elems.	2	4	4	6	1	3	8	2	31	5
Minimum Indvs.	1	↑2	↑2		↑1	↑1	↑2	↑2	4	1
Capra Min. Indvs.		↑1	↑1				↑1	↑1	1	
Ovis Min. Indvs.										
Gazella Min. Indvs.										

***Tatera* sp.**

	A9-10	A22	A31 F-30	B28 s.	B30 w.	B42 Low.s.	B44 Up.n.	B45	B47
Mandible	1L 1R				1R	1R		1L 1R	
Maxilla	1L 1R	1L	1L	1L		1R	1R	1L 1R	1LF

***Mus* sp.**

	A F-11	A F-13	A F-14
Mandible		2L 3R	1L
Maxilla	1R	1R	1R

APPENDIX E

Table E5: Weights of Unidentifiable Mammal Fragments Recovered From Farukhabad Listed by Unit

Excavation Unit	Vertebrae Fragments gm	Teeth Fragments gm	Limb and Other Fragments gm
A5 above 155.8 m	29.9	12.6	314.8
A3	27.7	7.7	160.5
A5 east	31.5	19.2	373.5
A5 west	30.5	3.1	133.4
A5 fea. 3	47.4	3.0	32.9
A6 north	1.5	5.6	132.8
A6 south	14.9	11.8	36.1
A6 fea.	0.0	3.0	9.7
A7 north	3.0	0.0	107.3
A7 south	3.0	0.0	77.1
A7 fea. 1	0.0	0.0	25.9
A7 fea. 8	0.0	10.6	12.0
A8 north	1.9	0.0	71.5
A8 south	8.5	3.8	155.8
A8-below fea. 8	10.9	0.0	9.2
A9&10 north	34.6	0.0	58.1
A9&10 southeast	0.0	0.0	36.6
A9&10 southwest	5.3	1.4*	52.0
A10&11	0.0	0.0	10.9
A11 north	0.0	0.0	14.2
A11 southeast	1.5	2.2*	34.9
A11 southwest	2.7	0.0	91.9
A11 center	0.0	2.5	49.5
A12 north	0.0	0.0	49.0
A12 south	0.0	1.1*	25.1
A12&13 upper north	0.0	0.0	2.7
A13 lower & 15 upper	0.0	0.0	5.4
A13 all	2.2	11.4	75.6
A13 upper north	0.0	5.3	36.4
A13 upper south	0.0	1.3	41.9
A13 south	0.0	2.0	19.5
A13 fea. 11	0.0	2.2	5.6
A14 all	0.0	0.0	25.6
A15	1.9	0.0	93.3
A16 all	0.0	8.9*	61.3
A17 north	0.0	10.1*	71.0
A17 south	0.0	0.0	32.7
A17 lower & 18 upper	0.0	5.1	91.3
A17, 18, & 19	1.6	4.9	48.4
A18 north	2.6	4.0	139.5
A18 brick debris	0.0	0.0	10.6
A19 all	0.0	0.0	34.8
A19 upper fea. oven	0.0	0.0	5.6
A19&20	0.0	0.0	8.2
A20	0.0	4.9	105.8
A20 fea. 19	7.1	19.3*	323.1
A fea. 23	0.0	24.8	699.7
A21 upper north	0.0	0.0	23.6
A21 upper south	0.0	0.0	58.0
A21 middle room D&E	0.0	0.0	2.4
A21 middle room B&C	3.5	0.0	24.6
A21 middle	0.0	1.8	20.3
A21 middle room A	0.0	1.2	43.2
A21 lower	1.4	3.9	11.6
A21 lower room C,D,&E	0.0	0.0	9.5
A21 fea. 25, granary	0.0	0.0	2.6
A21 fea. 26	0.0	0.0	129.9
A22 all	0.0	2.7	64.0
A22 fea. 24	16.6	0.0	135.9
A22 fea. 25	0.0	4.0	91.3
A22 & fea. 25	10.7	14.7	91.8
A23 all	0.0	26.8*	402.3
A23 brick fill fea. 25	0.0	0.0	57.2

Table E 5: Continued

Excavation Unit	Vertebrae Fragments gm	Teeth Fragments gm	Limb and Other Fragments gm
A24 upper northeast	0.0	39.3	202.4
A24 upper southwest	0.0	14.2	86.4
A24 lower	0.0	6.4	22.4
A24 lower northeast	0.0	5.8	58.0
A25 north	2.1	8.9	120.4
A25 south	0.0	2.2	10.8
A26 north	0.0	9.2	199.3
A26 south	6.4	8.5	87.5
A27 north	0.0	6.9	83.0
A27 south	1.8	0.0	71.1
A28 northwest	4.9	0.0	120.2
A28 southeast	0.0	0.0	47.2
A29	0.0	0.0	15.3
A29 upper	0.0	2.6	28.4
A29 lower	31.4	0.0	64.9
A29 L-shaped room	0.0	3.1	2.8
A29 alley between fea. 30&31	0.0	5.3	41.2
A33 all	0.0	0.0	21.9
A34 all	0.0	1.0	24.7
A35 all	0.0	0.0	17.3
A36 southeast of fea. 32	0.0	8.2	119.9
A36 inside fea. 32	0.0	0.0	51.2
A37 inside fea. 30	4.3	0.0	0.0
B1-3	19.4	9.1	184.6
B4	38.8	14.0*	164.3
B6	1.0	4.9	154.6
B7	0.0	8.5	125.1
B7 east	21.1	46.8	100.2
B7 west	0.0	2.2	33.4
B7 fea. 3	0.0	10.7	141.0
B8 west	29.9	74.9	294.0
B9	0.0	4.8	54.2
B10	0.0	1.0	62.0
B11	0.0	15.4	392.1
B11 lower	3.6	70.7	270.5
B11 upper	31.9	10.4	116.5
B11&12	37.3	22.5*	509.7
B12	53.2	72.5*	1665.9
B13 large pit	15.0	25.4	740.7
B14	20.4	0.0	66.8
B15	0.0	2.3	0.0
B15&16	0.0	0.0	13.1
B16±	7.9	0.0	169.5
B16± fea. 7	1.0	0.0	40.6
B17 west	2.4	7.4*	72.6
B17 fea. 11	0.0	0.0	6.7
B18 large pit	1.9	1.7	75.5
B18	1.5	6.3*	329.1
B19	0.0	0.0	63.3
B20	4.3	2.4	48.0
B20 north	9.5	2.0	150.6
B20 lower north	0.0	3.8	7.8
B20 southeast	0.0	0.0	18.6
B20 southwest	0.0	1.9	44.4
B20 upper	0.0	0.0	9.6
B20±	0.0	13.2	150.2
B20&21	1.8	1.8	24.8
B21 north	29.8	8.0	172.9
B21 south	14.2	9.0	61.2
B21 lower fea. 12	0.0	1.8	18.6
B22 upper north	30.7	8.3	124.4
B22 lower north	57.7	4.5	250.4
B22 south	2.7	0.0	25.5

APPENDIX E

Table E 5: Continued

Excavation Unit	Vertebrae Fragments gm	Teeth Fragments gm	Limb and Other Fragments gm
B22&23 upper	15.8	0.0	70.3
B23 north	8.5	1.9	53.2
B23 lower north	6.0	1.0	71.7
B23 south	15.6	2.3	28.9
B23 upper south	1.5	0.0	32.9
B23 lower south	4.4	1.4	44.9
B23 fea. 15	0.0	0.0	4.0
B23 southeast	0.0	0.0	1.4
B24 upper north	3.3	1.4	123.1
B24 lower north	6.5	7.8*	62.7
B24 upper south	0.0	8.1	58.1
B24 lower south	0.0	0.0	29.4
B24 southeast	2.4	0.0	1.1
B24 fea. 18	0.0	1.6	52.4
B25 upper north	0.0	0.0	61.3
B25 lower north	12.0	3.2	127.1
B25 lower	0.0	0.0	1.9
B25 lower southeast	0.0	0.0	42.9
B25 fea. 15	4.5	0.0	32.5
B25-27 south	5.1	9.7*	138.7
B26	0.0	0.0	2.0
B26 northeast	0.0	4.2	172.0
B26 upper northeast	0.0	0.0	33.1
B26 south	1.5	0.0	27.7
B27 northeast	21.3	19.1	113.5
B27 west	0.0	0.0	42.3
B28 north	0.0	10.9	194.3
B28 south	8.1	1.5	45.4
B28 ash pit	32.2	0.0	22.5
B29 upper north	12.8	22.4	192.8
B29 upper south	1.2	4.5	88.1
B29 lower east	47.4	5.6	103.7
B29 lower west	0.0	0.0	25.1
B29 top fea. 20	0.0	1.2	7.4
B29 upper fea. 21	0.0	0.0	53.9
B30 northeast	31.1	22.6	199.9
B30 southeast	2.8	36.4*	197.3
B30 lower jub contents	0.0	0.0	8.8
B31 upper north	0.0	12.7	391.4
B31 lower north	17.8	27.4	285.8
B31 upper south	0.0	26.0	200.4
B31 middle south	0.0	2.4	0.0
B31 lower south	0.0	36.1*	246.5
B31± north	0.0	9.9	41.7
B32 upper	0.0	7.1	48.7
B32 upper north	0.0	21.9	167.8
B32 lower north	0.0	8.1	58.1
B32 upper south	2.6	14.8	219.9
B32 lower south	6.5	8.0	104.8
B33 upper north	45.1	9.8	257.8
B33 lower north	4.1	14.3	132.9
B33 lower south	47.6	21.9*	255.4
B33 upper & middle southeast	0.0	6.6	91.9
B33 upper & middle southwest	0.0	3.8	222.3
B33 upper & middle center	0.0	16.0	241.5
B33 upper center	0.0	0.0	67.0
B33 upper & middle southwest fea. 26	1.1	1.3	27.0
B33 upper & middle fea. 30	3.9	0.0	18.3
B33 lower fea. 28	0.0	0.0	16.8
B34 upper north	0.0	1.8	64.0
B34 lower north	3.4	2.7	27.4
B34 upper south	30.5	17.6	382.1
B34 lower south	230.9	26.5	477.4

Table E 5: Continued

Excavation Unit	Vertebrae Fragments gm	Teeth Fragments gm	Limb and Other Fragments gm
B34 upper center	1.8	1.0	63.7
B34 lower center	0.0	13.1*	83.5
B34 below fea. 28	0.0	6.1	53.1
B34 fea. 32	39.6	3.4	386.9
B34 upper brick fea. 31	0.0	0.0	16.3
B35 upper	0.0	0.0	344.9
B35 lower	10.6	16.1	193.7
B35 all	0.0	0.0	20.8
B35 pot group	0.0	0.0	18.9
B35 lower fea. 35	0.0	0.0	35.1
B36 all	0.0	1.6	52.0
B36 lower	0.0	1.1	122.1
B36 upper northeast	0.0	1.1	81.8
B36 upper southeast	0.0	2.5	67.6
B36 lower southeast	0.0	7.4*	78.4
B36 upper southwest	0.0	5.6*	93.7
B36 lower southwest	1.4	0.0	38.4
B37	0.0	5.7	104.0
B38 east	0.0	0.0	9.9
B39 middle east	0.0	0.0	3.6
B39 lower east	0.0	8.6	25.6
B39 upper west	0.0	0.0	10.1
B39 middle west	0.0	6.3	43.0
B39 lower west	0.0	0.0	17.4
B40 upper east	5.7	2.0	69.7
B40 lower east	0.0	8.1	90.8
B40 upper west	2.4	8.0	124.9
B40 lower west	4.4	1.5	35.9
B41 upper northwest	2.3	0.0	21.7
B41 middle northwest	0.0	3.0	20.7
B41 lower northwest	0.0	0.0	7.3
B41 upper southeast	0.0	2.4	21.0
B41 middle southeast	0.0	0.0	19.5
B41 lower southeast	3.2	0.0	54.1
B41 pit into B42	0.0	0.0	36.4
B42 upper northwest	0.0	4.3	204.2
B42 upper southeast	0.0	0.0	16.8
B42 lower north	0.0	14.3	65.3
B42 lower south	0.0	7.1	58.8
B43 north	0.0	2.2	50.2
B43 south	0.0	1.4	26.6
B44 upper north	4.6	0.0	35.7
B44 lower northwest	0.0	0.0	50.2
B44 lower south	0.0	0.0	30.3
B44 lower southeast	0.0	0.0	14.2
B44 lower southwest	0.0	0.0	14.8
B44 lower southwest room A&C	0.0	0.0	1.7
B44 Room G	0.0	0.0	28.1
B45 upper north room F&G	0.0	0.0	2.9
B45 upper southeast	0.0	0.0	14.8
B45 upper southwest	0.0	0.0	6.0
B45 upper southwest room A	0.0	0.0	3.8
B45 lower north	0.0	3.4	4.6
B45 lower southeast	0.0	1.3	10.1
B45 lower southwest	0.0	0.0	8.7
B45 room D	0.0	0.0	6.3
B46 upper southwest	3.6	6.5	89.7
B46 lower southwest	0.0	3.0	57.9

* Indicates mixing of equid and/or cattle with sheep-goat-gazelle teeth fragments.

APPENDIX E

Table E6: Distal Metapodial Measurements and Identifications

Excavation Unit	Inner Spool (cm)	Outer Spool (cm)	%	Genus
A3 all	1.665	1.105	66.37	Ovis
A5 east	1.625	1.178	72.49	Gazella
	1.600	1.150	71.87	Gazella
A7 north	1.782	1.005	59.76	Capra
	1.598	.912	57.07	Capra
	1.594	.960	60.23	Capra
A8 south	1.376	.778	57.27] *	Capra
	1.419	.817	57.58	Capra
A8± below F8	1.504	1.014	67.42] *	Ovis
	1.582	1.073	67.83	Ovis
A9,10 southwest	1.541	1.034	67.10	Ovis
A11 center	1.545	1.074	69.51] *	Ovis
	1.455	.974	66.94	Ovis
A11 southwest	1.400	.880	62.86	Capra
A12 north	1.555	1.000	64.31] *	Ovis
	1.482	.925	62.41	Ovis
	1.375	.926	70.18] *	Gazella
	1.369	.948	69.24	Gazella
A17 south	1.619	1.186	73.25	Gazella
A21 south	1.680	.928	55.24	Capra
A22 F24	1.792	1.035	57.76	Capra
A34 all	1.537	1.064	67.64] *	Ovis
	1.493	1.010	67.65	Ovis
	1.544	1.077	69.75] *	Ovis
	1.619	1.131	69.86	Ovis
B6	1.588	.886	55.79] *	Capra
	1.635	.880	53.82	Capra
B7 F3	1.550	.954	61.55	Capra
B11 upper	1.535	1.007	65.60	Ovis
B12	1.627	.900	55.32	Capra
	1.570	.884	56.30	Capra
B18	1.520	.835	54.93] *	Capra
	1.504	.767	50.99	Capra
B20 north	1.611	1.010	62.69] *	Capra
	1.488	.820	55.11	Capra
	1.443	.952	65.97	Ovis
B21 south	1.475	.856	58.03	Capra
B22 lower north	1.478	.870	58.86] *	Capra
	1.452	.876	60.33	Capra
	1.516	.870	57.39	Capra
B24 F18	1.450	.846	58.34] *	Capra
	1.462	.807	55.19	Capra
B24 upper north	1.564	1.060	67.77	Ovis
	1.577	1.044	66.20	Ovis
	1.505	1.058	70.30	Gazella
B24 south	1.420	1.033	72.75	Gazella
B27 west	1.515	.940	62.05	Capra
B30 west	1.527	.882	57.76	Capra
B32 lower north	1.509	.911	60.37	Unident.
	1.465	.940	64.16	Unident.
B37 all	1.925	1.136	59.01	Capra
B40 upper east	1.599	1.076	67.29	Ovis
B47 southwest	1.362	.802	58.88	Capra

* Indicates that measurements are from one unbroken element.

Table E7: Marine Molluscs from Tepe Farukhabad

Name	Known range of genus	Habitat of genus	Layer
Nerita albicilla	Gulf and North Indian Ocean	intertidal rocks and mud-covered rocks (1:272; 5:29)	A21-X331
Cypraea sp.	Gulf and North Indian Ocean	intertidal and shallow rocks (3:321; 5:39)	A6-X078
Engina medicaria	North Indian Ocean	rocky bottoms (5:47)	A11-X124
B23-X177
B27-X284
Oliva ispidula	Gulf and North Indian Ocean	intertidal sandy bottoms (2:47; 5:51)	A20-X306
Strigatella litterata	North Indian Ocean	intertidal sand and mud flats (5:52)	A17-X259
Conus tessalatus	Gulf (4:110)	—	A3-X025
B10-X046
B20-X130
B23-X225
B29-X363
B35-X579
Dentalium sp.	Gulf	beaches (1:275)	A11-X124
A15-X213
A18-X255
Cardium sp.?	Gulf (4:116)	—	B15-17-X110
Liochoncha sulcotina	Gulf	shallow sand bottoms (2:47)	B22-23-X173
Mytilus sp.?	Gulf	deep water	A6-069
B32-X469
B32-X469
Thais (purpura) *mancinella*	Gulf and North Indian Ocean	intertidal sand or mud (1:273; 2:47; 5:43)	C1-X038
B128-X106
B21-X144

TABLE REFERENCES

[1] Biggs, H.E.J.
  1958 Littoral Collecting in the Persian Gulf. *J. Conch. London* 24: 270–75. London

[2] Haas, F.
  1954 Some Marine Shells from the Persian Gulf. *Nautilus* 68(2):46–49. Philadelphia.

[3] Hornell, J.
  1949 The Study of Indian Molluscs, Part I. *J. Bombay Nat. Hist. Soc.* 48(2):303–37.

[4] Melvill, J.C.
  1928 The Marine Mollusca of the Persian Gulf, Gulf of Oman, and North Arabian Sea, as Evidenced Mainly through the Collection of Captain F.W. Townsend, 1893–1914. *Proc. Malacol. Soc. London* 18:95–117.

[5] Subrahmanyam, T.V., K.R. Karandikar, and N.N. Murti
  1952 Marine Gasteropoda of Bombay—Part II. *J. Univ. Bombay* N.S., 21B(3):26–73.

APPENDIX F

FLORAL ELEMENTS FROM TEPE FARUKHABAD

These two tables contain the data on which Chapter XIII by Naomi Miller is based. The first table presents the data on the 50 percent selection of the flotation samples available in Ann Arbor. In some cases the actual volume in liters floated is not available, and thus densities are not computable. On the second table, presence is indicated by a plus and multiple occurrences are represented by two pluses.

Table F1: Botanical Samples from Tepe Farukhabad.

Sample #	seeds/liter	seeds	legumes	grains	wheat spike-let forks	spikelet forks/liter
X067	0.40	2	1	0	0	0
X092		0	0	0	0	
X122	0.42	1	1	0	0	0
X219	1.60	5	4	0	1½	0.48
X220	1.67	10	3	0	2	0.33
X222	101.00	50½	0	48½	12½	25.00
X257I X257II	0.25	1	0	1	0	0
X286	0.96	6½	0	5½	4½	0.67
X332	12.00	37½	30	6½	1½	0.48
X332	0	0	0	0	0	0
X336		0	0	0	0	
X344	2.0	1	1	0	0	0
X496	0	0	0	0	0	0
X499	0.89	4	4	0	0	0
X665	9.11	41	33	1	18	4.00
X702I X702II		40	39	0	4	
X036		14½	13½	1	20½	—
X051		0	0	0	0	
X051I		0	0	0	0	—
X2331	0.49	2	0	0	5½	1.36
X269	16.00	64	56	6	9	2.25
X274	0	0	0	0	3	0.50
X436I		0	0	0	0	
X436II	0	0	0	0	0	0
X474	0	0	0	0	14	3.50
X520	0.58	3	1	0	1	0.19
X732	2.50	10	0	7	3½	0.87
X742	1.83	11	9	0	2½	0.42
X757	1.50	6	6	0	1½	0.37

Table F2: Carbonized remains from Tepe Farukhabad

	Boraginaceae: *Lithospermum arvense*	cf. *Aegilops*	*Aegilops* glume base	cf. *Avena*	*Hordeum*	*Hordeum* internodes	cf. *Lolium*	cf. *Phalaris*	*Triticum monococcum*	*T. monococcum/dicoccum*	*T. dicoccum*	*Triticum* spikelet forks	*T. aestivum* rachis fragments	Gramineae, indeterminate	Gramineae fragments
X067														1	
X092															+
X122															
X219			1									1½		1	
X220		1										2		6	+
X222*					40	4	1			1	7½	10½	2	1	++
X257I															+
X257II					1										+
X286					4½	1			1			4½			+
X332					4½					2		1½			+
X336															+
X344															+
X496															
X499															
X665					1							18		5	+
X702I															
X702II												4			+
X036					1							20½			+
X051															
X051II															
X233				1								5½		1	
X269	1				6							9			+
X274												3			
X436I															
X436II															
X474												14			+
X520	1							1				1			+
X732	1				2		2				5	3½			++
X742												2½		2	
X757												1½			
TOTAL	3	1	1	1	60	5	3	1	1	3	12½	102½	2	17	+

*See note on Table F1

Table F2: Continued

	Leguminosae:	cf. *Astragalus*	cf. *Coronilla*	*Hippocrepis*	cf. *Medicago*	cf. *Melilotus*	cf. *Trifolium*	*Trigonella*	cf. *Trigonella*	Leguminosae, indeterminate	Malvaceae: *Malva*	Plantaginaceae: *Plantago*	Ranunculaceae: cf. *Adonis*	Rosaceae: *Amygdalus*	Rubiaceae: *Galium*	Seeds, indeterminate	Total, identifiable seeds
X067										1							2
X092																	
X122				1													1
X219	1		1	2													5
X220	1			1		1								++			10
X222														+		c.5	50½
X257I																	
X257II																3	1
X286														1			6½
X332				23			1		2	4		1				3	37½
X336																	
X344					1												1
X496																	
X499				4													4
X665				11		17	3			2	1	1				7	41
X702I				1						4							5
X702II	2					3	14			15					1		35
X036				4		2	1	1		5½						1	14½
X051																	
X051I																	
X233																	2
X269		5		24	10		4		5	8		1				27	64
X274																1	
X436I																	
X436II																	
X474																2	
X520				1													3
X732														+		1	10
X742	2			5	1					1				+			11
X757				1			2	1		2						2	6
	6	5	1	78	12	23	25	2	7	42½	1	3	1	+	1	c.52	310

Table F3: Identified Charcoal From Tepe Farukhabad.

Phase	Tamarix	Quercus	Populus	Prunus
Transitional Elamite	X026(B7):10			X535(F6):5
Sukkalmahhu Elamite	X055(B11,12):6			
	X056(B14):1			
	X057(B12):1			
Early Dynastic	X040(A1):2	X040(A1):2		
	X042(A1):4			
	X050(A5):1			
	X065(A5):1			
	X068(A5):5			
Late Jemdet Nasr	X120(A9,10):15	X086(A6):5	X085(A7):5	
	X125(A11):1			
	X126(A11):3			
	X144(B21):5			
	X172(B22,23):5			
Early Jemdet Nasr	X246(B24):4	X315(B27):7 cf.		
Middle Uruk	X407(A21):5			
Farukh	X493(A27):1			
	X625(B39):5 cf.			
	X690(B42):5			

N.B.: Initial identification by Franklin Johnson; checked and corrected by Naomi Miller.

APPENDIX G

HUMAN OSTEOLOGICAL REMAINS FROM TEPE FARUKHABAD

By Margaret Schoeninger

Elamite Burials

Fragmentary Burial In Shaft (Feature 6, Excavation B, Layer 14 or above; X059) These are the remains of an adult. The sex is indeterminate because of the fragmentary nature of the material. The cranium is represented by fragments of the vault bones but little of the cranial base or face appears to be present. The post-cranial skeleton is represented by portions of the right upper limb. Portions of the right hand are present including: a complete second metarcarpal, the proximal half of the third metacarpal, a proximal hand phalanx (second or third), a lunate, and a capitate. In addition, there is a radius head, the central portion of the shaft of the right ulna, and the proximal portion of the right radius just distal to the radial tuberosity.

Fragmentary Infant In Jar (Excavation B, Layer 13 or above; X057) This individual was a fetus or newborn. A card in the box containing the bones reads that the infant was a "pot burial". The remaining identifiable bones are the distal end of one humerus, the proximal end of an ulna, and some rib fragments.

Flexed Adult Burial With Artifacts (Feature 7, Excavation B, Layer 15 or above; X096) This adult skeleton is very fragmentary and sex is indeterminate due to the condition of the bones. The cranium appears to be represented mainly by the vault bones with little present of the cranial base or the face. The distal portions of both left and right mandibular rami are present and an LM_3 fits into an alveolus in the jaw. In addition to this LM_3 there are also the LI_1, four premolars, RI^1, RM^1, RM^2, and RM^3. The RM^3 is completely unworn although the other teeth have considerable dentin exposure. There are contact facets on both the RM^2 and RM^3; when contacted, the M^3 sits in a rotated position. Perhaps the tooth was never in occlusion which would explain its lack of wear.

The post-cranial skeleton is represented by 1) the lower limb: central portion of the left and right femoral shafts, portions of both patellae, the central portion of the left tibial shaft including the nutrient foramen, the left and right fibular shafts broken just proximal to the distal end, the right talus, left third cuneiform, left cuboid, the distal portion of the left and right third, fourth and fifth metatarsals, and some phalanges; 2) the upper limb: the distal portion of the right humeral shaft missing the portion distal to the olecranon fossa, the central portion of the left and right ulnar shaft, left hamate, left capitate, left second metacarpal, right third metacarpal, and some phalanges.

Measurements of the teeth of this and subsequent burials are presented in Table G 1.

Extended Adult Burial (Feature 11, Excavation B, Layer 18)

(X135) This individual is an adult represented by fragments of both the cranium and the post-cranium. Sex is indeterminate because of the fragmentary nature of the material. The cranium includes pieces of vault and the left mastoid with the mandibular fossa. There is a small piece of mandible from near the symphsis and both the left and right mandibular condyles. The teeth present include left and right I_1&$_2$, left and right C_x's, left P_3, left and right lower P_4, very worn left and right lower M_1's, a worn left M_2 with a caries on the distal face, a left M_3 with the anterior one third of the tooth missing from decay, and a right upper molar, probably a right M^2 with a fairly deep patch of exposed dentin on the lingual portion.

Most of the post-cranial skeleton is from the upper limb. Present are the almost complete shaft of the left humerus with both ends missing except for a fragment including the trochlea, a three inch length of the shaft of the right humerus including the nutrient foramen and a fragment of the distal portion of the shaft, a length of radial shaft, a broken radial head, the coronoid porcess and part of the shaft of the left ulna, almost complete right hamate, two proxmial and middle hand phalanges, and a first cervical vertebra and rib fragments.

Middle Uruk Burials

Infant Burial (Feature 29, Excavation B, Layer 34)
(X534) This individual was an infant between one and two years old. The age is based on the teeth present (following Schours and Massler, 1944): left dm_1 and dm_2, left dm^1 and dm^2, the complete cap of the left M^1 and right M_1. The roots of all teeth are missing. The post cranial skeleton is represented by a part of the right scapula including the base of the spine and the superior portion of the medial border and a piece of distal humerus.
Flexed Infant Burial (Feature 34, Excavation B, Layer 34)
(X577) This individual was an infant between nine months to one year old. The age is based on the teeth present (following Schours and Massler, 1944) which include: the unerupted cap of the left dm^1, the left and right dm_1&$_2$, the complete cap of the dc_x, the complete cap and part of the root of dx^x, the incomplete enamel cap of the RM_1, erupted right di_2 and both the left and right di_2's. In addition to the teeth there are only very fragmentary pieces of rib and cranium.
Adult Burial with Artifacts (Between Excavations A and B)
(X545) These remains include small fragments of an adult cranium, vertebrae, tarsals, and some loose teeth. Sex was indeterminate. The teeth include left and right P^3&^{4}'s which have the dentin exposed, the left M^1 and left and right M^2's, all three of which have pits of dentin exposed, the left and right M^3's; there is a caries in the center of the left M^3. Of the mandibular teeth present, there are the left and right canine, worn right P_3&$_4$, left M_1 with most of the enamel surface worn away and with a large area of dentin exposed, and the left M_2 which has dentin pits exposed.
Flexed Adult Burial (Feature 35, Excavation B, Layer 34, in three different units)
(X578) These remains are of a fragmentary adult of indeterminate sex. In addition, the vertebral centra of an infant, are included with the fragments of the adult post-cranium. The infant was between one and three years based on the size of the centra and the neural arch and on the fact that the two halves of the neural arch are newly fused (Bass, 1971). Among the broken adult teeth are a left M^3, left and right M_1's which have dentin patches exposed on the surface, and RM_3. There is also an incisor (probably an upper incisor) that has a straight depression worn in it that runs medially-distally across the tooth as if something had been rubbed across its surface.
(X569) The only elements identifiable in this unit are about five foot phalanges including two distal ones from the left and right first digit, two middle phalanges, and one proximal phalanx and, in addition, the distal portion of one metatarsal.
(X592) This unit consists of two distal foot phalanges of an adult.
Flexed Adult Burial (Feature 36, Excavation B, Layer 34)
(X591) This was an adult individual represented by fragments of both the cranium and post-cranium. Sex is indeterminate due to the fragmentary nature of the material. In addition to several phalanges, there is also the distal end of the left second and right third metacrapals, and the distal end of one of the fourth metacarpals, the proximal end of the fifth metacarpal, and the right hamate. The feet are represented by the left second cuneiform, part of a cuboid, and a right fifth metatarsal. There are a couple of vertebral centra which show some lipping. Among the loose teeth there is a RM_3 with exposed dentin patches; and anterior to this tooth and cemented to it is the root of the M_2 which must have been lost due to decay. In addition there remain a RM^2 or ^{3} with a patch of exposed dentin on the lingual half and a worn premolar with part of the root destroyed by decay.

REFERENCES CITED

Bass, W. M.
    1971   *Human Osteology* Special Publications, Missouri Archaeological Society: Columbia, Missouri.
Schour, I. and M. Massler
    1944   Chart-Development of the Human Dentition. Second edition. American Dental Association; Chicago.

APPENDIX G

Table G1: Tooth Measurements From the Farukhabad Burials

Maxilla—Mesial-Distal Length

	0096 L	0096 R	0135 L	0135 R	0545 L	0545 R	0578 L	0578 R
I^1	–	7.2	–	–	–	–	–	–
I^2	–	–	–	–	–	–	–	–
C^x	–	–	–	–	–	–	–	–
P^3	–	–	–	–	–	6.6	–	–
P^4	–	–	–	–	–	6.7	–	–
M^1								
M^2	–	9.1	–	10.4	9.6	9.8	–	–
M^3	–	9.1	–	–	8.8	8.3	8.4	–

Maxilla—Buccal-Lingual Length

	0096 L	0096 R	0135 L	0135 R	0454 L	0454 R	0578 L	0578 R
I^1	–	6.2	–	–	–	–	–	–
I^2	–	–	–	–	–	–	–	–
C^x	–	–	–	–	–	–	–	–
P^3	–	–	–	–	–	9.0	–	–
P^4	–	–	–	–	–	8.4	–	–
M^1	–	–	–	–	–	–	–	–
M^2	–	10.8	–	12.0	10.5	10.4	–	–
M^3	–	9.8	–	–	9.8	9.4	8.4	9.1

Mandible—Mesial-Distal Length

	0096 L	0096 R	0135 L	0135 R	0545 L	0545 R	0578 L	0578 R
I_1	5.0	–	5.7	5.3	–	–	–	–
I_2	–	–	6.2	6.3	–	–	–	–
C_x	–	–	7.1	7.5	6.6	–	–	–
P_3	–	–	7.9	–	–	–	–	–
P_4	–	–	7.6	8.1	–	7.1	–	–
M_1	–	–	–	–	–	11.2	–	–
M_2	–	–	–	–	10.6	–	10.8	10.0
M_3	10.2	–	–	–	–	–	–	9.8

Mandible—Buccal-Lingual Length

	0096 L	0096 R	0135 L	0135 R	0545 L	0545 R	0578 L	0578 R
I_1	5.6	–	–	–	–	–	–	–
I_2	–	–	6.2	–	–	–	–	–
C_x	–	–	7.6	7.8	6.3	–	–	–
P_3	–	–	7.5	–	–	–	–	–
P_4	–	–	8.4	8.2	–	7.8	–	–
M_1	–	–	11.0	11.0	–	–	–	–
M_2	–	–	10.8	–	9.2	–	10.3	10.5
M_3	9.6	–	10.6	–	–	–	–	9.0

Table G2: Strontium Assays for Human and Animal Bone

Excavation Number	Phase	Individual	Strontium (ppm)*
Elamite Phases			
X059	Transitional	*Homo* (adult)	358.70 (3)
X096	Sukkalmahhu	*Homo* (adult)	455.32 (3)
X135	Simashki	*Homo* (adult)	395.22 (3)
——	Simashki	*Ovis/Capra* (sheep/goat)	488.40 (3)
Uruk Phases			
——	Late Uruk	*Vulpes* (fox)	597.80 (1)
X578	Middle Uruk	*Homo* (adult)	504.55 (3)
X577	Middle Uruk	*Homo* (juvenile)	517.25 (1)
X591	Middle Uruk	*Homo* (adult)	589.42 (3)
——	Middle Uruk	*Ovis/Capra* (sheep/goat)	698.90 (3)

*The figure in parentheses is the number of fragments from a single skeleton which were measured before computing a mean parts per million assay.

BONE STRONTIUM AND HUMAN DIET AT TEPE FARUKHABAD

By Antoinette B. Brown

The amount of the trace element strontium (Sr) in the bones of a vertebrate can be an indicator of the animal's relative position in its food chain. Strontium is incorporated into bone in the same manner as calcium, though it is regularly discriminated against during the process of bone deposition. It is also preferentially excreted by the body, and as little as one eighth of the strontium actually ingested is incorporated into the bone.

Strontium in the soil is metabolized by plants which form the diet of herbivores. Initially carnivores ingest less strontium since it has already been discriminated against during the growth of their herbivorous prey. It is further discriminated against before deposition in the carnivore's bones. Therefore the bones of carnivores will contain consistently less strontium than the bones of herbivores.

Unfortunately, burial of bones in the soil can alter the amount of strontium present. Control of such alterations can be achieved by comparing only material from a single context of burial and fossilization. Toos and Voorhies (1965) have demonstrated that homogenous samples from fossil biotic communities are prerequisites for meaningful analysis. Given the remains of known carnivores, known herbivores, and humans from a single site, one can estimate relative proportions of plant and animal content in the diet by comparing human bone strontium content to that of the known carnivores and herbivores from the same site.

In the laboratory process, bone was extracted with concentrated hydrochloric acid. A defect apatite substituting strontium for calcium was manufactured and used as a standard throughout the study (Brown 1973). An Elmer-Perkin 303 model atomic absorption spectrophotometer was used to assay each sample's strontium content. Results are expressed in parts per million in Table G2. Assays of skeletal remains are available rom two broad periods of time, the Uruk dating between 3600 and 3300 B.C. and the Elamite dating between 2100 and 1300 B.C. Three mammalian groups—human, fox, and sheep/goat—were assayed. Unfortunately the three groups are not represented in precisely the same layers, and fox is not available from the later period. In any event, fox is not a pure carnivore, and is thus less than ideal as a standard.

For the Elamite period, the three human individuals come from the Simashki, Sukkalmahhu, and Transitional Phases. Human strontium content is about 400 ppm, while sheep/goat is about 490 ppm. Thus the Elamite samples indicate that human diet contained relatively less vegetation and more animal content than that of a sheep or goat. The variation in human bone strontium levels may indicate a variation in diet or may simply reflect a normal range of bone strontium variation.

In the middle phase of the Uruk Period, human bone strontium content is about 500 ppm, while that of sheep/goat is about 700 ppm, indicating that during this earlier time the human diet also contained more animal matter than that of a sheep or goat. A measurement of the strontium of a fox from a Late Uruk Layer closely corresponds to that of the humans, re-enforcing the indication of relatively omnivorous diet for the site's occupants. Again, the range in human bone strontium may reflect the normal range of variation in bone strontium or some variation in diet.

The mean of the human bone strontium assays from the Elamite period is 82.6% that of the sheep/goat. The mean for the Uruk Period is 78.25% that of the sheep/goat. This indicates broadly comparable diets during these two periods at Farukhabad. The greater absolute strontium levels of the earlier samples must result from their greater relative age and consequent greater exposure to strontium bearing ground water.

In order to establish the normal range of human bone strontium variation, a sample of 50 individuals—adult men and women—from the Bussinger

Site on the Lower Peninsula of Michigan was assayed. This population was chosen because the archaeological evidence (Fitting 1970:143–191; Halsey 1976) indicates that this population consisted of hunters and gatherers who maintained no class distinctions and doubtless and basically similar diet throughout the population. This sample had a coefficient of variation of 35.9%. The human samples from the Uruk Period have a coefficient of variation of only 7.13% well within the variation established for the unstratified society. The Elamite human samples have a coefficient of variation of 23.3%, still within the range of variation established for the Bussinger population.

Thus the population appears to have been one with a fairly omnivorous diet, consistent through both periods, with only small variations of diet within the population. This is precisely what one would expect given the faunal and floral evidence for these periods discussed in Chapters XIII and XIV. One must remember, however, that this method is relatively new, and with improved techniques and larger sample sizes more complex dietary variations will no doubt be documented.

REFERENCES

Brown, Antoinette B.
    1973   Bone Strontium Content as a Dietary Indicator in Human Skeletal Populations. Doctoral Dissertation, University of Michigan, Department of Anthropology. University Microfilms, Ann Arbor.

Toots, H. and M. R. Voorhies
    1965   Strontium in Fossil Bones and Reconstruction of Food Chains. *Science* 149:854–55.

Fitting, James E.
    1970   The Archaeology of Michigan. A Guide to the Prehistory of the Great Lakes Region. The Natural History Press, Garden City, NY.

Halsey, John R.
    1976   The Bussinger Site: A Multicomponent Site in the Saginaw Valley of Michigan with a Review of Early Late Woodland Mortuary Complexes in the Northeastern Woodlands. Ph.D. dissertation, University of North Carolina, Dept. of Anthropology.

APPENDIX H

RADIOCARBON AGE DETERMINATIONS FROM TEPE FARUKHABAD

Four determinations have been made of samples from Farukhabad (Crane and Griffin 1972:191). All samples were checked for bitumen contamination with a sulphur test. The dates and a commentary on each are as follows.

M-2151: Charcoal, probably Tamarix. Excavation B, Layer 24 Feature is a bin ascribed to the Late Jemdet Nasr Phase.
    5568 half life: 3990 b.p. ± 180
                         2040 b.c.
    5730 half life: 2160 b.c.
    MASCA
    corrected: 2600 B.C.

Comment: This is several centuries younger than expected. Two explanations of the discrepancy are possible. First, erosion had truncated Feature 15 so that while its earliest mud plaster articulated with the Layer 24 upper floor, it was not actually sealed by a younger floor. Perhaps the feature was disturbed in later times and the charcoal did not date the gray ware jar (X272 Fig. 65a) and polychrome sherd (X232, Fig. 60c) found in the bin. Second, perhaps the "Jemdet Nasr Phase" of the Deh Luran Plain extended into the mid-third millennium. A second sample was submitted to clarify this issue (see M-2419).

M-2152 Charcoal, probably Tamarix. Excavation A, Layer 21 Feature 24 a hearth ascribed to the Middle Uruk Phase.
    5568 half life: 4460 b.p. ± 190
                         2510 b.c.
    5730 half life: 2650 b.c.
    MASCA
    corrected: 3210-3310 B.C.

Comment: This date was mispublished in the original publication. The MASCA correction places the date at a point where there are a range of possible dates (Ralph, Michael, and Han 1973:12). This range is a reasonable one for a relatively late Uruk sample. The hearth is sealed by the top of Layer 21. The problem in this case is the question of what is being dated. The two associated rimsherds in Feature 24 could occur in either Middle or Late Uruk assemblages. The other sherds on the floors of the Layer 24 buildings are damaged extrusive Susiana sherds and a few non-descript Uruk sherds. Also there is one fragment of a twist handle, charactertistically Late Uruk. Is this feature actually of the Late Uruk Phase, or is it Middle Uruk and is the twist handle intrusive from clearly Late Uruk Layer 20?

M-2153 Charcoal, probably Tamarix. Excavation B, Layer 45. Charcoal scattered on the floors of rooms A, L, and G of the Feature 45 building of the Early Farukh Phase.
    5568 half life: 5760 b.p. ± 200
                         3810 b.c.
    5730 half life: 3980 b.c.
    MASCA
    corrected   4600 B.C.

Comment: This sample, though aggregated from several rooms, is well-sealed and clearly associated with exclusively Farukh Phase ceramics. The date is conformable with the large series from the slightly earlier Bayat Phase reported by Hole, Flannery, and Neely (1969:332,335). Though only a single determination, it helps confirm the existing sequence.

M-2419 Charcoal, probably Tamarix. From the same locus as sample M-2151.
    5568 half life: 3800 b.p. ± 160
                         1850 b.c.
    5730 half life: 1964 b.c.
    MASCA
    corrected: 2190-2290 B.C.

Comment: This sample dates to the time of the Awan Dynasty, after polychrome pottery ceased to be made. It supports the possibility that Feature 15 was disturbed. More samples from other Jemdet Nasr Phase Loci must be analyzed.

In retrospect, it is likely that there are difficulties with the Farukhabad analyses because the archaeologist violated two simple principles. In the one case of well-sealed context with good artifactual associations, the date (M-2153) is reasonable. In the case of good context but minimum association, the date (M-2152) conforms to the later of the possible associations. In the case of uncertain context but good associations, the dates (M-2151, M-2419) are so young that disturbance of context seems likely. Other charcoal samples, and also bone samples, have been retained for future radiocarbon age determinations.

REFERENCES CITED

Crane, H.R., and J.B. Griffin
    1972   University of Michigan Radiocarbon Dates XIV. *Radiocarbon* 14:155–94.

Hole, Frank, K.V. Flannery, and J.A. Neely
    1969   Prehistory and Human Ecology of the Deh Luran Plain: An Early Village Sequence from Khuzistan, Iran. *Memoirs of the Museum of Anthropology, University of Michigan*, No. 1. Ann Arbor.

Ralph, E.K., H.N. Michael, and M.C. Han
    1973   Radiocarbon Dates and Reality. *MASCA Newsletter* 9/1:1–20.

APPENDIX I

MULTI-ELEMENT NEUTRON ACTIVATION OF OBSIDIAN SAMPLES FROM TEPE FARUKHABAD

By Arthur S. Keene

Obsidian has proven to be a significant and sensitive indicator of changing patterns of exchange, communication, and social interaction in the Near East. The transportation and trade of large quantities of obsidian by ancient peoples of the Near East can be documented from as early as 8000 B.C. to 2000 B.C. (G. A. Wright 1969). Pioneer applications of both spectrographic methods (Renfrew, Dixon, and Cann 1966) and neutron activation analysis (G. A. Wright 1969) have proved successful in ascribing archaeological artifacts to geological sources. Thee results have contributed to the formulation and testing of stimulating theoretical propositions concerning early trade (Renfrew 1969, 1977). However, the dearth of obsidian artifacts of the fifth millennium B.C. and later has necessarily forced a focus on exchange among the earlier village communities. This study presents new analyses of artifacts transported during these last centuries of the obsidian trade in the hopes that we can contribute to the answering of some of the questions raised by earlier considerations of Deh Luran obsidian (Renfrew 1969, 1977).

The reference samples from geological sources are those collected in 1970 by Prof. Richard A. Watson of Washington University and Ibrahim T. Cakmak. Their work was facilitated by Dr. Saadettin Alpan, Director-General of the Maden Tetkik Arama Enstitütü and was funded by the U.S. National Science Foundation through its support of the Turkish Prehistoric Project under the direction of Prof. Robert J. Braidwood of the University of Chicago and Prof. Halet Cambel of Istanbul University. The full provenience data on each source sample will be detailed in a separate paper. The archaeological samples from Tepe Sabz were recovered in 1963, also with support of the N.S.F., by Prof. Frank Hole of Yale University, who has kindly made them available for reanalysis. The actual analyses of geological samples, archaeological samples, and rock standards at the University of Michigan Phoenix Memorial Laboratory was supported by U.S. Atomic Energy Commission Grant No. AT(11-1)-21117. I am indebted to the program manager, John D. Jones, and to Thomas Myers for their material assistance and advice and to Dr. James Blackman of the Smithsonian Institution for his constructive critique of this brief report.

Methods

Samples were prepared and analyzed at the Phoenix Memorial Laboratory at the University of Michigan. USGS rock standards were used both to determine quantities of the various trace elements present in the specimens and to verify these determinations (cf. Meyers 1974; DeVoe and La Fleur 1969). USGS standard BCR-1 (Flanagan 1969, 1973) was used as the primary reference standard to determine the CPS:PPM ratio. USGS W-1 (Flanagan 1973) and RGM-1 (Flanagan 1974) were included in the analysis as unknowns. Their results were cross checked against published values for these standards as a measure of the accuracy of the method (cf. Table IV). (The complete standard data are reported in Table I-4). Powdered standards were sealed in quartz tubing. Solid obsidian chips were weighed, and pieces of approximately 50 mg were wrapped in 99.999 percent pure aluminum foil. Both samples and standards were irradiated for six hours on September 26, 1974 and on September 30, 1974 at a neutron flux of approximately 1.5×10^{13} neutrons per cm^2 per second.

Following irradiation the samples were allowed to decay for five days prior to counting. This was primarily to reduce the background from ^{24}Na, a short-lived but extremely abundant nuclide.

Samples were then unwrapped, weighed, placed in test tubes, and counted for 1000 seconds each in a Nuclear Data 2048 channel pulse-height analyser interfaced to an ORTEC GE (Li) gamma ray detector spectroscopy system. Samples were changed automatically and spectral data stored on magnetic tape for subsequent computer processing. The samples were recounted after two additional weeks. Second counts were for 4000 seconds each under conditions otherwise identical to the first counts.

Spectral data were reduced on a Nuclear Data ND-812 computer at the Phoenix Memorial Laboratory. After an automated search of each spectrum to determine which elements were present, a computerized integration was performed on those peaks of interest to us using the Nuclear Data ND-1085 spectrum analysis program. These integral data were then fed into a Phoenix Memorial Laboratory multi-element analysis computer program (MEA-7410) which produced the parts per billion (ppb) data for specified trace elements and the associated standard deviation values. Eighteen peaks were counted for 15 elements. Of these, 11 elements were utilized in this analysis (Table I-2).

Results

The data on standards and summary statistics on the source samples available for this study are presented in Table I-4. These summary statistics were compared for goodness of match with the total range of ppm values for each individual artifact. We can be more confidant of assignment of artifacts to the sources at Nemrut Dağ, Suphan Dağ, Kocadağ, and Gollü Tepe, for each of which we have a number of samples which exhibit a narrow range of values. In the case of other sources, where samples are few, characterization must be correspondingly less certain. Furthermore, there exist sources from which we have no samples, from some of which our unascribed archaeological specimens must have originated.

Six of the eight archaeological artifacts characterized (Table I-5) match closely the source samples from Nemrut Dağ. These include the single piece from Mehmeh Phase Tepe Sabz (5031), one of two from Bayat Phase Tepe Sabz (5029), the two pieces from Farukh Phase Farukhabad (3325, 3329), one of the two pieces from the Early Uruk Phase at Farukhabad (3327), and the single piece from the Middle Uruk Phase at Farukhabad (3326). Thus, most of the small amount of obsidian reaching Deh Luran in the fifth and fourth millennia B.C. was obtained from the volcano southwest of Lake Van in southeastern Anatolia.

One characterized artifact is from an unknown source similar to Nemrut Dağ in most respects but differing in its amounts of Thorium, Hafnium, Iron and Cobalt (3328). We must regard this Early Uruk obsidian artifact as indeterminate pending the study of more samples from the Lake Van area.

One other characterized artifact is from an unknon source similar in some respects to Central Anatolian sources and in others to sources in Soviet Armenia (5030). Some of the earlier obsidian artifacts from nearby Chogha Sefid and later artifacts from Tepe Sharafabad on the Susiana Plain, to be detailed in a subsequent paper, are also from this unknown source. If this source is also that of Renfrew's Group 1g, it is indeed a commonly utilized obsidian whose location is critical to the understanding of the obsidian trade.

Discussion

The obsidian finds from Farukhabad allow us to amplify our understanding of the end of the obsidian trade. Table I-3 is patterned after that of Renfrew (1977:300, Table 93) with revisions of the screened volumes and of the total chipped stone counts so that those from Farukhabad (see Table B-1,2) are comparable to those from Tepe Sabz (Hole, Flannery and Neely 1969:104, Table 7). Obsidian comprises only a fraction of a percent of the chipped stone pieces discarded during the fifth and early fourth millennia. The amounts are so small that one must consider the possibility that these occurrences are earlier pieces collected from the surface of long-abandoned sites such as Ali Kosh and re-utilized. This possibility can be discounted only because these latest occurrences are largely from Nemrut Dağ, in contrast to the earlier samples of mixed origins.

Renfrew (1977:310) has proposed that the marked dimunition in obsidian movement during the sixth millennium B.C. results from a shift from "down-the-line" exchange to "redistributional" exchange. If so, it follows that obsidian would be concentrated in the redistributional centers. This would mean that obsidian would be relatively more frequent in larger centers than smaller centers in any given area and in the more populous areas rather than the less populous areas. The samples reported above from Mehmeh and Bayat Phase Tepe Sabz and Farukh Phase Tepe Farukhabad indicate extremely low densities of obsidian and low ratios of obsidian to chert on small centers. Unfortunately, we have only limited samples from these centers and no samples at all from the sometime major center at Tepe Musiyan.

It may in the end be easier to assess Renfrew's proposition by comparing obsidian densities at Deh Luran sites in general with those at Susiana sites in general. Unfortunately, data from screened excavations of known volume are not common outside the Deh Luran Plain. Testing and amplification of Renfrew's proposition will require additional data.

References Cited

DeVoe, James R. and Philip D. LaFleur, eds.
    1969   Modern trends in activation analysis. National Bureau of Standards, *Special Publication*, no. 312.

Flanagan, F. J.
    1969   U.S. Geological Survey Standards II, *Geochemica et Cosmochemica Acta*. 33: 81–120.
    1973   1972 values for international geochemical reference samples, *Geochemica et Cosmochemica Acta*. 37: 1189–1200.
    1974   Descriptions and analyses of seven new USGS rock standards. U.S. Geological Survey, *Professional Paper* 340.

Hole, Frank, Kent V. Flannery, and James A. Neely
    1969   Prehistory and Human Ecology of the Deh Luran Plain. *Memoirs of the Museum of Anthropology*, University of Michigan, no. 1.

Meyers, J. Thomas
    1974   The need for standardization of results in archeological chemistry. Paper presented at the 1974 Annual meeting of the Society for American Archaeology, Washington, D.C.

Renfrew, Colin
    1969   The sources and supply of Deh Luran obsidian. In: Hole, Flannery, and Neely, *op. cit.*
    1977   The later obsidian of Deh Luran—the evidence of Chagha Sefid. In: Studies in the Archaeological History of the Deh Luran Plain, *Memoirs of the Museum of Anthropology*, University of Michigan, no. 9, Frank Hole, ed.

Renfrew, Colin, and J. E. Dixon
    1977   Obsidian in Western Asia—a review. In: Problems in Economic and Social Archaeology, I. Longworth and G. Sieveking, eds. London: Duckworth.

Renfrew, Colin, J. E. Dixon and J. R. Cann
    1966   Obsidian and early culture contact in the Near East. *Proceedings of the Prehistoric Society*, no. 32: 30–72.

Wright, Gary A.
    1969   Obsidian Analyses and Prehistoric Near Eastern Trade: 7500–3500 B.C. *Anthropological Papers of the Museum of Anthropology, University of Michigan*, no. 37.

Table 11: Obsidian Artifacts

UMMA Ob.#	Exc. No.	Provenience	Phase	Description	Length	Width	Thick.	Weight	Color
3325	X648	Ex.B Layer 40	Farukh	utilized medial blade segment	1.94	.93	.20	.48	dark green
3326	X461	Ex.B Layer 32	Middle Uruk	small end-scraper on flake or core remnant	1.82	1.60	1.78	2.10	dark green
3327	X587	Ex.B Layer 36	Early Uruk	utilized proximal blade segment	2.87	.64	.15	.40	dark green
3328	X574	Ex.B Layer 35	Early Uruk	truncated medial blade segment	1.50	.84	.18	.28	dark green
3329	X501	Ex.A Layer 27	Farukh	medial blade segment	2.20	1.05	.28	.66	dark green

APPENDIX I

Table I2: Trace Elements Used in the 1974 Obsidian Analyses

Element	First Count		Element	Second Count	
	Isotope	γ-ray Energy		Isotope	γ-ray Energy
Samarium	^{153}Sm	103 Kev	Thorium	^{233}Pa(Th)	312 Kev
Lutecium	^{177}Lu	208 Kev	Hafnium	^{181}Hf	481 Kev
Ytterbium	^{175}Yb	396 Kev	Iron	^{59}Fe	1099 Kev
Scandium	^{46}Sc	889 Kev	Colbalt	^{60}Co	1173 Kev
Sodium	^{24}Na	1368 Kev	Tantalum	^{182}Ta	1222 Kev
Lanthanum	^{140}La	1596 Kev			

Table I3: Quantitative Change of the Later Deh Luran Obsidian Industry

Site	Period	Cubic Meters	Obsidian Pieces	Total Chipped Stone	Obsidian Pieces/m^3	% Obsidian
Farukhabad	Middle Uruk	29.8	1	894	.033	.12
	Early Uruk	12.4	2	304	.161	.66
	Farukh	69.2	2	1421	.028	.14
Tepe Sabz	Bayat	52.5	6	1267	.038	.42
	Mehmeh	40.4	3	713	.074	.47

Table I4: Parts Per Million Determination for Obsidian Trace Elements from Geological Sources and Standards

Location	N	Sm	Lu	Yb	Sc	Na
Obsidian Source Samples: Means and Standard Deviations of Multiply Determined Means						
Nemrut Daǧ	7	20.26±1.86	3.03±.17	12.20±.11	.25±.06	38,857±1786
Suphan Daǧ	5	5.94±.15	.87±.21	3.28±.78	2.84±.66	29,695±972
Ergiyes Daǧ	2	4.54±.19	.84±.09	2.28±.93	1.53±.19	28,883±493
Acigöl	2	6.37±.57	1.36±.10	3.83±.21	2.08±.08	30,712±1259
Koca Daǧ	3	4.76±.10	.80±.21	2.85±.39	1.15±.33	32,065±3779
Gollü Tepe	3	4.40±.18	.62±.16	2.38±.93	1.90±.05	29,782±1219
Hasan Daǧ	2	3.54±.23	.24±.03	2.41±.56	2.44±	31,925±911
Kaleci/Bogaskoÿ	2	4.68±	.64±	3.80±	1.38±	31,795±
Tifcis/Erivan	2	5.29±	.60±	3.55±	3.42	35,467
USGS Rock Standards: Means						
BGR 1		6.60	.55	3.36	33.0	24,260
W1 (Flanagan)		3.60	.35	2.10	35.1	15,950
W1 (this study)		3.48	.49	1.88	37.9	17,240
RGM 1 (Meyers)		4.80	.43	2.85	4.50	31,200
RGM 1 (this study)		5.09	.44	3.12	4.99	32,419

Table 14: Continued

Location	La	Th	Hf	Fe	Co	Ta
Obsidian Source Samples: Means and Standard Deviations of Multiply Determined Means						
Nemrut Dağ	101.04±15.8	28.51±7.76	21.33±5.71	22,899±6761	2.29±.62	4.31±1.17
Suphan Dağ	17.46±9.2	14.52±4.46	2.61±.84	7474±2238	1.34±.64	1.19±.32
Ergiyes Dağ	22.69±0.6	21.29±2.35	2.39±.23	5097±384	.94±.30	2.27±.38
Acigöl	13.25±0.6	33.80±1.54	3.26±.20	5785±454	1.90+.67	4.19±.13
Koca Dağ	32.16±5.9	30.32±6.64	3.92±1.28	9268±3915	1.58±.80	2.88±1.00
Gollü Tepe	24.95±2.3	26.41±4.96	2.62±.30	6010±295	1.54±.31	2.97±.74
Hasan Dağ	27.88±1.3	20.20±.02	3.35±.88	8113±825	2.33±.12	2.07±.50
Kaleci/Bogaskoÿ	34.70±	37.31±	5.02±	10,823±	2.78±	3.51±
Tifcis/Erivan	37.51±	25.37±	5.37±	9827±	3.73±	5.86±
USGS Rock Standard: Means						
BGR 1	26.00	6.00	4.70	94,100	38.00	.91
W 1 (Flanagan)	9.80	2.42	2.67	77,600	47.00	.50
W 1 (this study)	12.20	n.a.	2.67	81,189	47.00	.76
RGM 1 (Meyers)	24.40	13.08	5.91	12,900	1.90	n.a.
RGM 1 (this study)	26.31	20.52	6.07	14,091	3.87	1.81

Table 15: Parts Per Million Determinations for Obsidian Trace Elements from Archaeological Sites

UMMA Sample #	Location/Phase	Sm	Lu	Yb	Sc	Na
Obsidian Artifacts From Tepe Farukhabad						
3325	Ex.B Layer 40 Farukh	21.43±.25	2.84±.43	16.39±.16	—	41,693±346
3326	Ex.B Layer 32 Middle Uruk	21.45±.31	2.73±.44	16.23±2.26	—	40,185±476
3327	Ex.B Layer 36 Early Uruk	21.31±.32	2.59±.43	15.84±2.24	—	40,603±501
3328	Ex.B Layer 35 Early Uruk	20.89±.30	2.73±.44	16.00±2.23	.23±.04	39,488±457
3329	Ex.A Layer 27 Farukh	21.19±.27	3.00±.46	16.11±2.16	—	39,702±381
Obsidian Artifacts From Tepe Sabz						
5029	Zone A Bayat	19.53±.07	3.81±.55	n.a.	.21±.01	38,676±309
5030	Zone A Bayat	5.05±.05	1.07±.18	n.a.	2.65±.03	36,330±353
5031	Zone B Mehmeh	20.05±.07	4.30±.61	n.a.	.29±.01	38,476±310

Table 15: continued

UMMA Sample	La	Th	Hf	Fe	Co	Ta
Obsidian Artifacts From Tepe Farukhabad						
3325	104.06±1.44	42.46±4.03	29.32±2.43	24,104±335	2.30±.27	8.73±6.17
3326	102.27±1.75	39.92±3.83	28.45±2.38	22,736±406	4.66±.37	8.13±5.78
3327	100.85±1.78	39.31±3.78	27.85±2.34	22,752±430	4.68±.40	9.36±6.64
3328	100.27±1.68	70.63±6.69	49.88±4.13	39,786±525	6.03±.42	13.08±9.26
3329	103.31±.53	n.a.	n.a.	n.a.	n.a.	n.a.
Obsidian Artifacts From Tepe Sabz						
5029	98.03±.53	22.64±.23	26.37±.23	20,550±175	n.a.	n.a.
5030	41.60±.46	27.48±.30	7.55±.15	13,345±185	n.a.	n.a.
5031	98.40±.52	23.40±.23	26.72±.23	20,776±175	n.a.	n.a.

Plate 2. General Views of Tepe Farukhabad. A. Farukhabad from the northwest showing men on the lower terrace on the east flank and the Jebel Hamrin beyond. B. Farukhabad from the southwest showing Excavation A on the right and Excavation B on the left (with men at work).

Plate 3. Farukh Phase Structures. A. A small building and associated features on floors, Excavation B, Layer 41, Feature 40 (see Fig. 9c). B. A large building showing buttress, Excavation A, Layer 31, Features 30–31 (see Fig. 9d).

Plate 4. Uruk Structures. A. Stone footing of small building. Excavation B, Layer 36, Feature 37 (see Fig. 36a). B. Footings of circular mud brick platforms. Excavation B, Layer 29, Features 20 and 21, (see Fig. 39b). Note the footing of a wall (Feature 22) and a drain (Feature 24) appearing where Layer 29 has been removed, and the intrusive Elamite shaft (Feature 6).

Plate 5. Details of Uruk Structures. A. Footings of small building in Excavation A, Layer 21, Features 20, 21, 22. Note retaining wall (Feature 18) and hearth (Feature 24), (see Fig. 36c). B. Side view of wall of miniature bricks in Excavation B, Layers 31 and 30, Feature 22. Note curbing at foot of stub (see Fig. 38a).

Plate 6. Jemdet Nasr Structures. A. Footing of large building with gypsum brick addition, Excavation B, Layers 24–22, Features 10C and 14 (see Fig. 38c). Layer 25 has been removed, so the associated floors, bin (Feature 15), and other features are not visible. B. Footing of large building in Excavation A, Layers 22 and 21, Feature 10B (see Fig. 38d). Rock fill visible in Elamite Shaft (Feature 6), and top of earlier gypsum brick wall (Feature 14) just emerging to right.

Plate 7. Details of Jemdet Nasr Structures. A. Space with packed mud brick floor in Excavation A, Layers 11–8. Feature 10A to left; Features 1D and 9B to right. Note gypsum plaster vat (Feature 8). The worker points to a gypsum concrete disc on the floor of Layer 10 (see Fig. 37d). B. View showing several crosscutting structures in Excavation A, Layers 14–12. To left of scale is portion of Feature 12B, Layer 15, curbed with oval stones (see Fig. 37a). Scale rests on Feature 12A, Layer 13 lower (see Fig. 37b). Above and to the right of scale is a wall stub (Feature 1E) of Layer 12 (see Fig. 37c), which incorporates a remnant of gypsum cement brick (Feature 9F) of Layer 13 upper (see Fig. 34s).

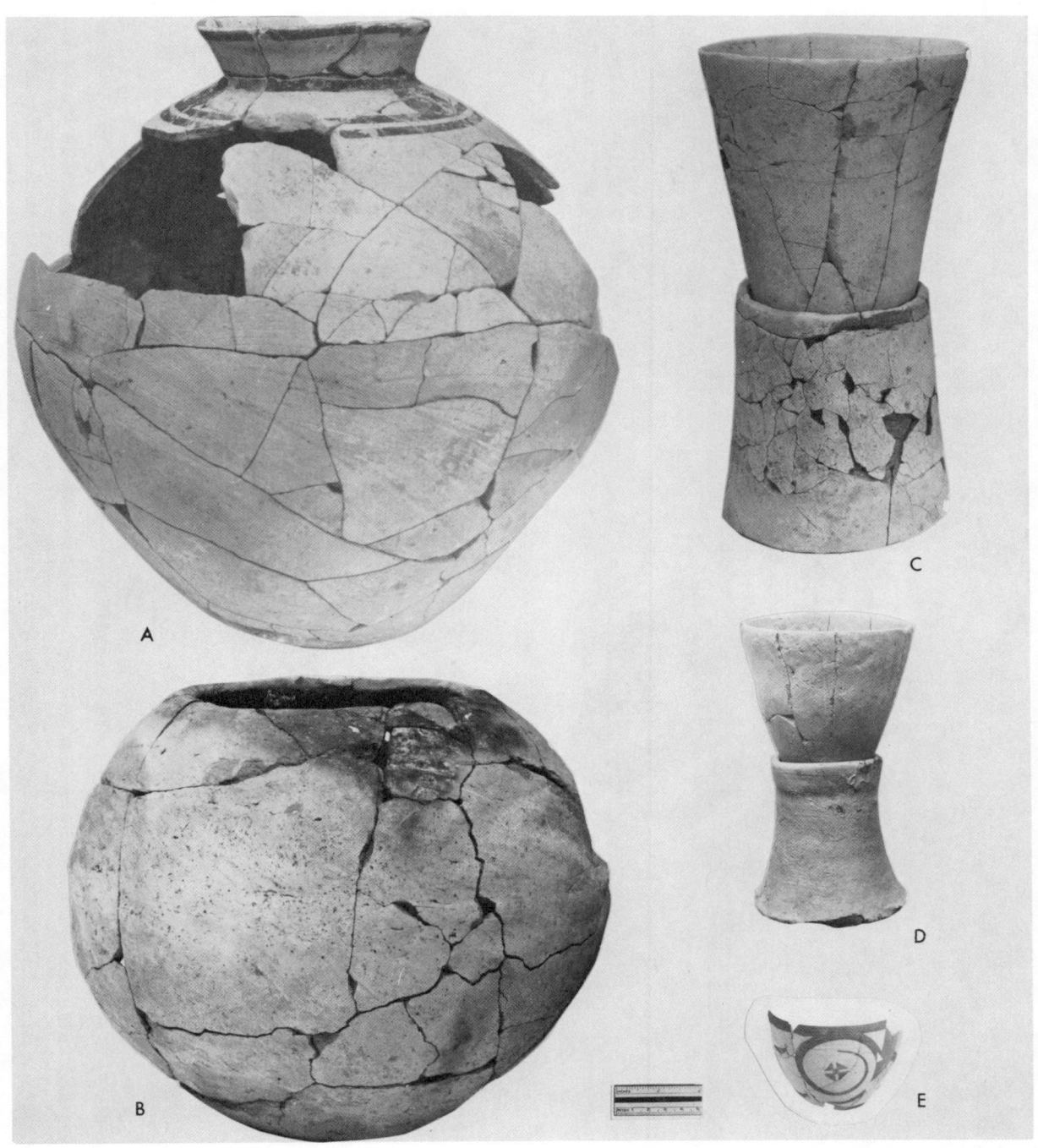

Plate 8. Farukh Phase Vessels. A. High jar of Susiana Ware, X710 (B43). B. Hole mouth jar of Khazineh Ware, X719 (B43). C. Large conical bowl (6078701) on stand (60789), X609 (A31), (see Fig. 13a, 14c). D. Small conical bowl (6078901) on stand (60778), X609 (A37) and X252 (A18) respectively (see Fig. 13b,c). E. Small bowl of Susiana Ware, X449 (60248, A23), (see Fig. 22f).

Plate 9. Other Farukh Phase Artifacts. A. Stone sphere; X675, 60639 (B47). B. Animal figurine; X389 (A, Feature 25 Fill). C. Excised slab; X384 (same). D. Stamp seal; X698 (B42).

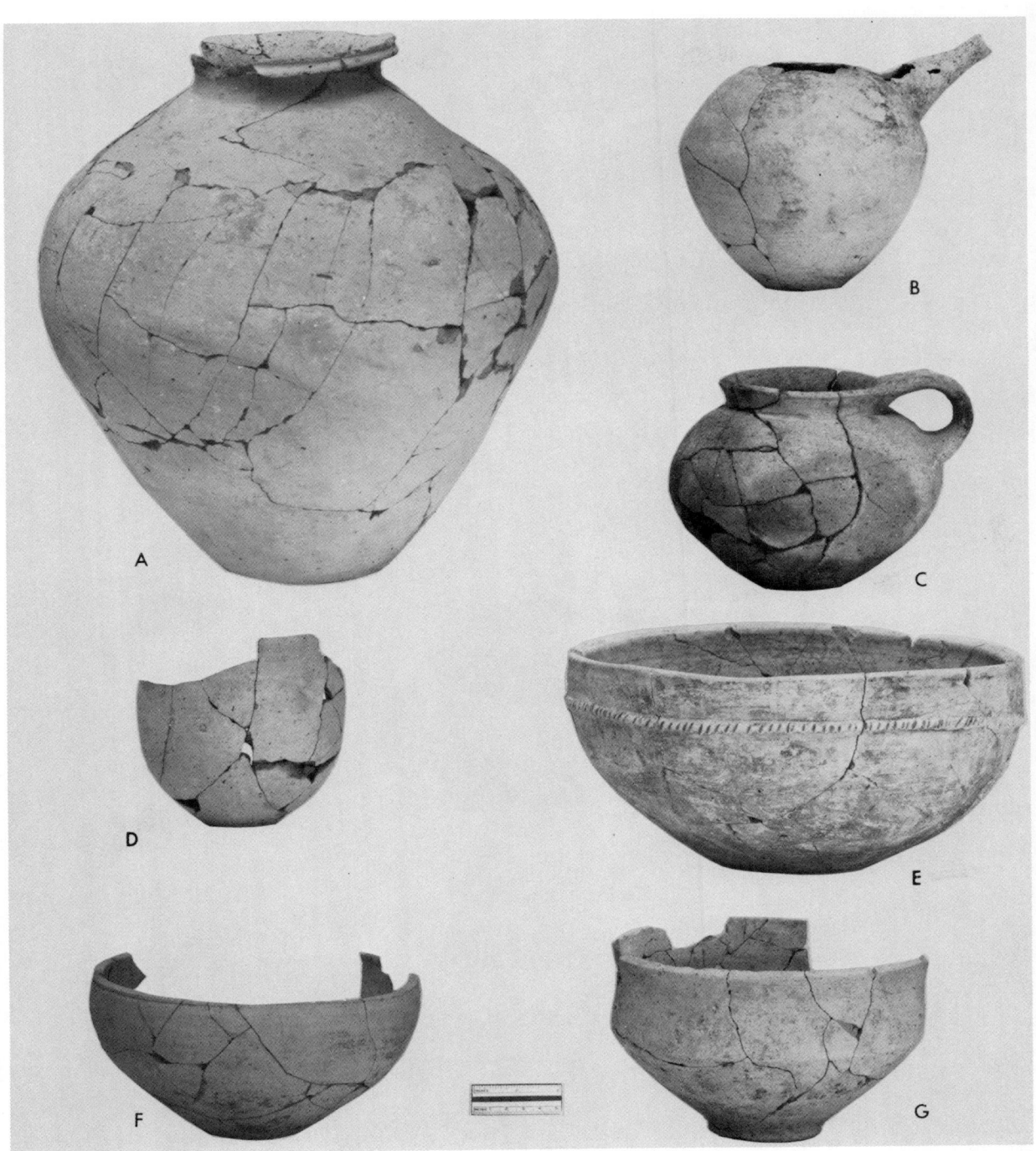

Plate 10. Early and Middle Uruk Ceramic Vessels. A. Flared expanded rim jar, Sargarab Ware; X579, 6078602 (B34), (see Fig. 40a). B. Small flared expanded rim jar, Sargarab Ware; X579, 6078601 (B34), (see Fig. 40b). C. Small expanded rim jar with strap handle, Uruk Ware; X569, 6057101 (B35), (see Fig. 50a). D. Fine jar, Sargarab Ware; X588, 6058703 (B36), (see Fig. 43a). E. Incurved flat rim bowl with red slip, Uruk Ware; X579, 60786 (B34), (see Fig. 41d). F. Flat lip bowl, Uruk Ware; X579, 6057802 (B34), (see Fig. 47a). G. Flat lip bowl with carination; X579, 6057803 (B34), (see Fig. 47b).

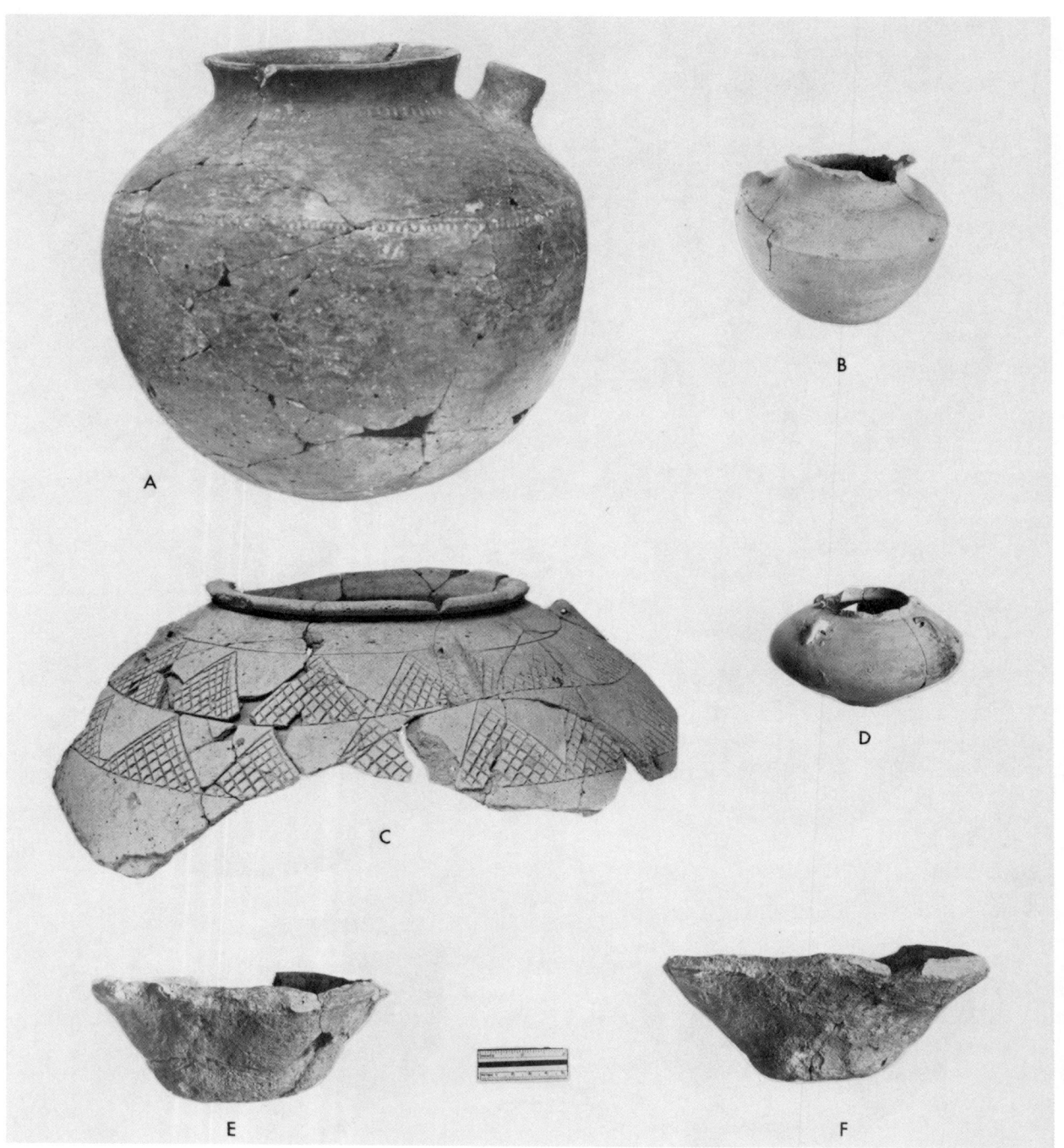

Plate 11. Late Uruk and Jemdet Nasr Ceramic Vessels. A. Grayware jar with spout; X232, 6039207 (BF15), (see Fig. 65a). B. Ledge rim jar with appendage, Uruk Ware; X272, 6039301 (BF15), (see Fig. 53a). C. Large expanded rim jar with nose lugs and cross-hatched triangles; X329 (A21). D. Small jar with lugs and fugitive painted design; X467, 60785 (B32), (see Fig. 63j). E. Beveled rim bowl; X462, 60498 (B32). F. Beveled rim bowl; X223, 60826 (AF19).

Plate 12. Grinding Tools and Drain of the Uruk and Jemdet Nasr Phases. A. Andesite hand stone, X085, 60729 (A7). B. Limestone saddle slab, X596, 60776 (B36). C. Basalt flat slab, X127, 60740 (A9). D. Limestone basin slab, X309, 60755 (B26). E. Basalt saddle slab, X088, 60729 (A7). F. Small limestone pallette with red ocher stains, X579, 60768 (B34). G. End of limestone oblong stone, X151, 60734 (A12). H. Ceramic trash drain, X424, 60759 (B31–BF24).

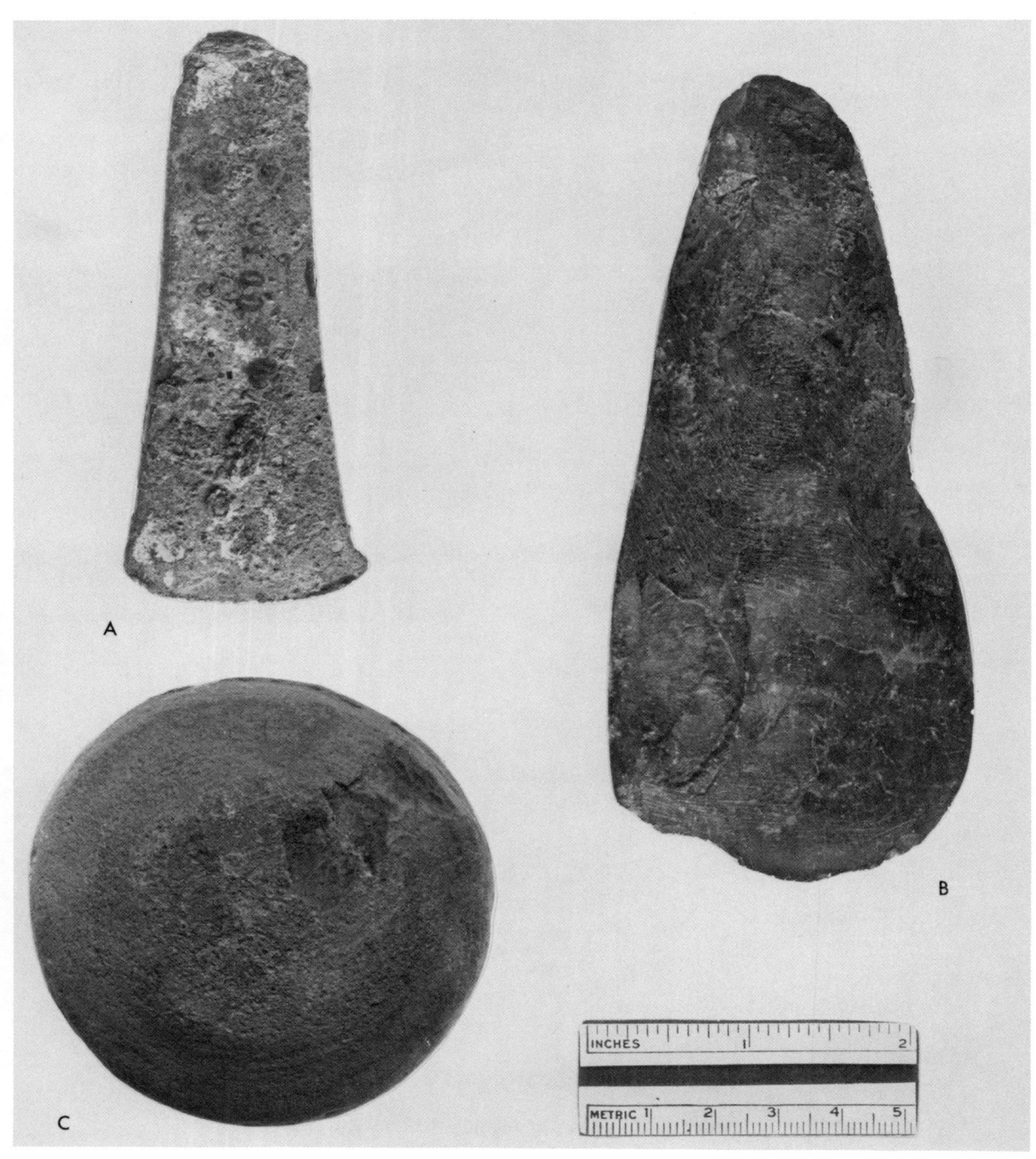

Plate 13. Celts and Grinder of Uruk and Later Phases. A. Celt of cuprous metal; X010, 60396 (surface). B. Calcite celt; X579, 60579 (B34). C. Quartzite rotary borer; X595, 60801 (B36).

Plate 14. Perforated Stones. A. Fully perforated stone of calcite; X511, 60762 (B33). B. Fully perforated stone of calcite; X518, 60764 (B33). C. Partially perforated stone of calcite; X207, 60749 (B23–22). D. Fully perforated star of gypsum; X125, 60739 (A11).

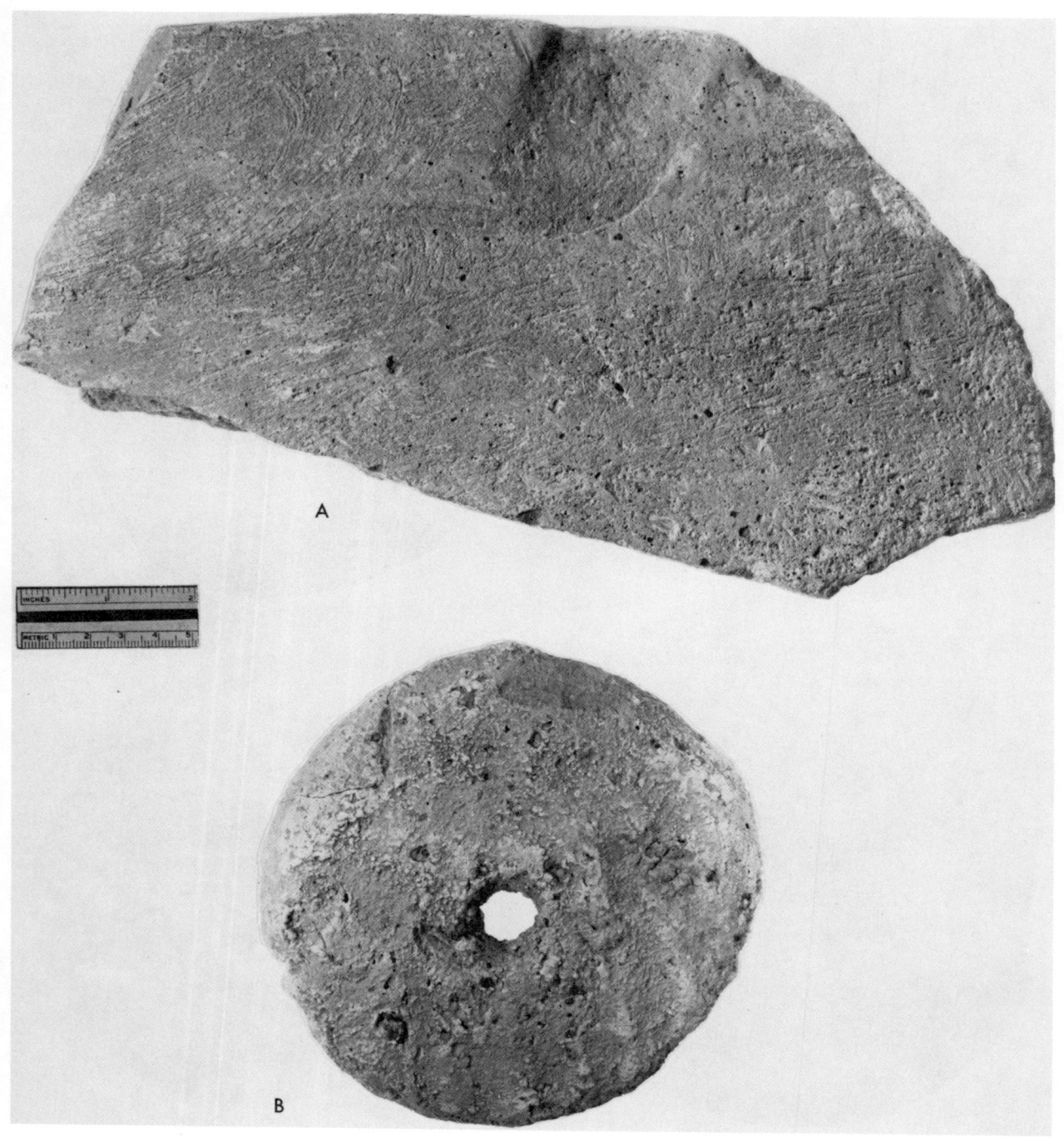

Plate 15. Concrete Artifacts. A. Vat rim; X101, 60731 (A8, AF8). B. Molded perforated disc; X010 (surface).

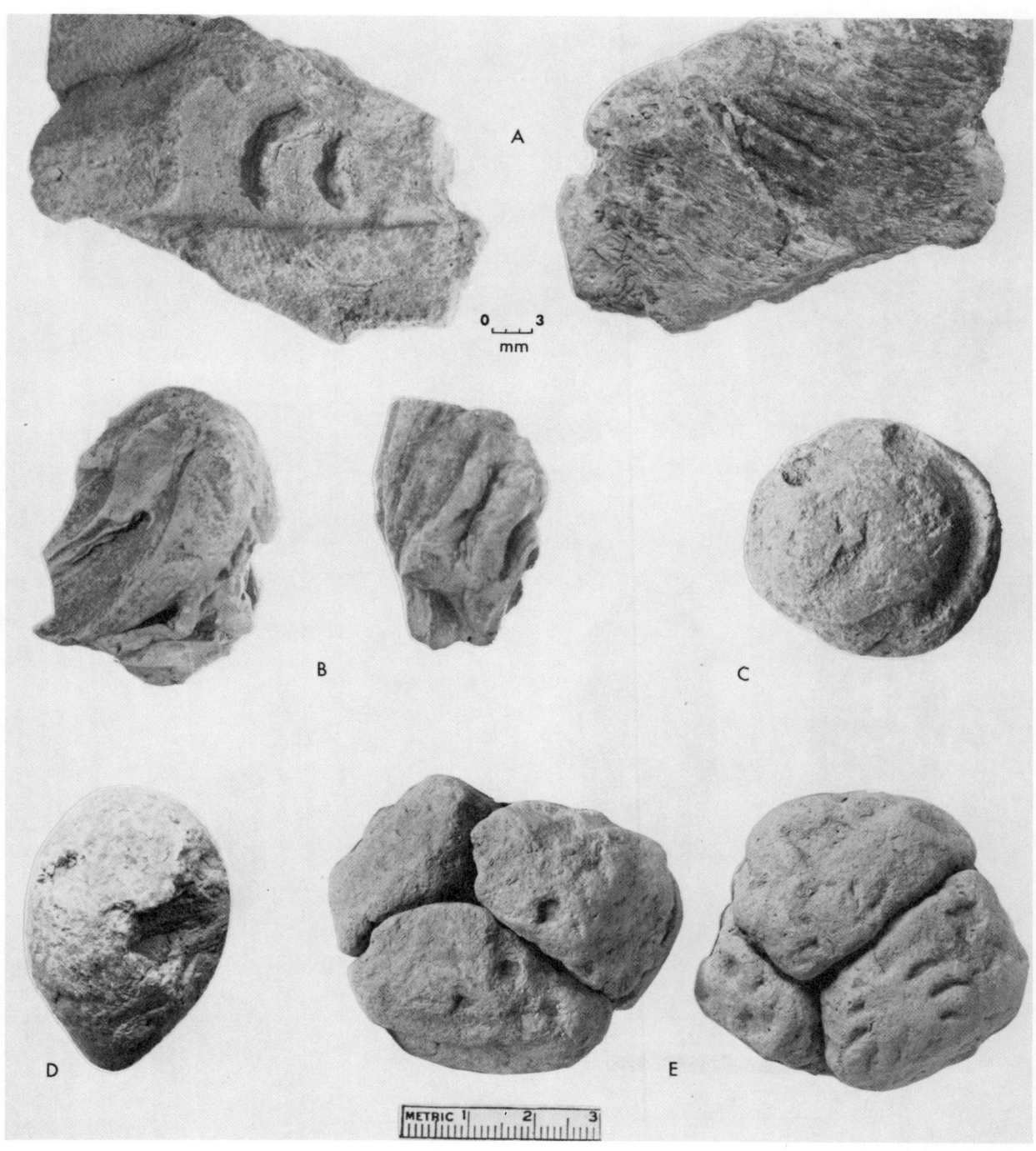

Plate 16. Unbaked Clay Artifacts. A. Cylinder seal impression; X299, 60203 (A20). Hind legs of animal to left; impression of hair or fiber on reverse to right. B. Clay smoothings with ropy texture; X490 (A25). C. Clay stopper; X341, 61211 (Excavation A, mixed zone between Feature 19 and Feature 23 pits, probably from the former). D. Clay ovoid; X338, 60833 (A20–AF19). E. Spherical bulla with seal impressions; X556 (B34). Possible numbers on left; stamp seal imprints on the right.

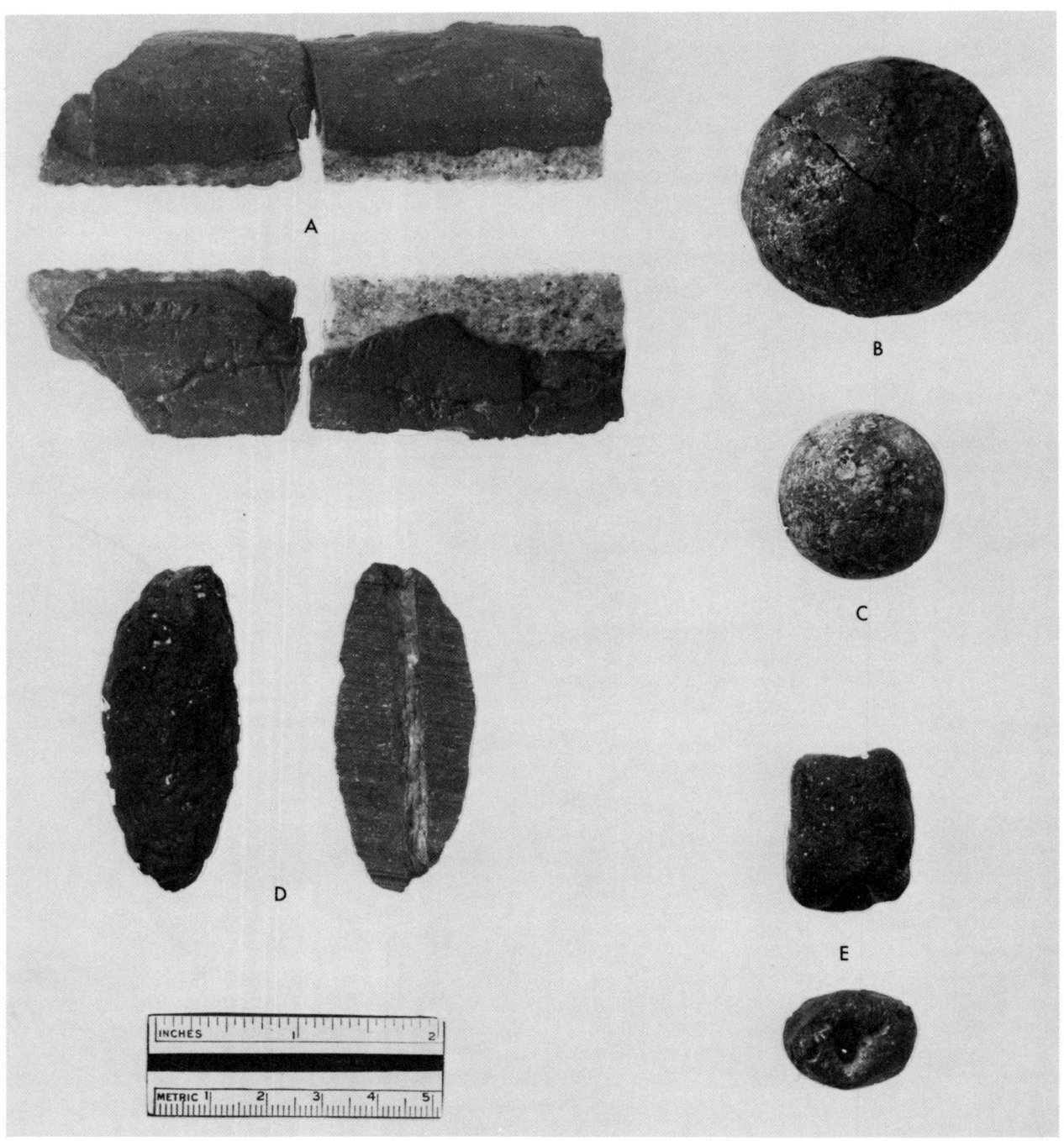

Plate 17. Bitumen Artifacts. A. Bitumen mounting for sickle blades; X081, 60101 (AF70). Above is the exterior; below is the impression of the sickle stock. B. Bitumen ball; X628 (B39). C. Bitumen ball, X533, 60555 (B34). D. Perforated ovoid, X479 (B33). Left is exterior; right is section made by sawing showing imprint of cord. E. Perforated ovoid, somewhat melted X745 (B45). Above side view; below end view.

Plate 18. Fine Stone and Bone Items. A. Alabaster ornament; X126, 60736 (A11). B. Calcite "Eye Amulet"; X173, 60357 (B22–23). C. Bone stamp seal; X567, 60798 (B35). D. Calcite bead blank; X087, 60114 (A7). E. Unfinished travertine blank; X659, 60638 (B41). F. Finished calcite bead; X511, 60528 (B33).

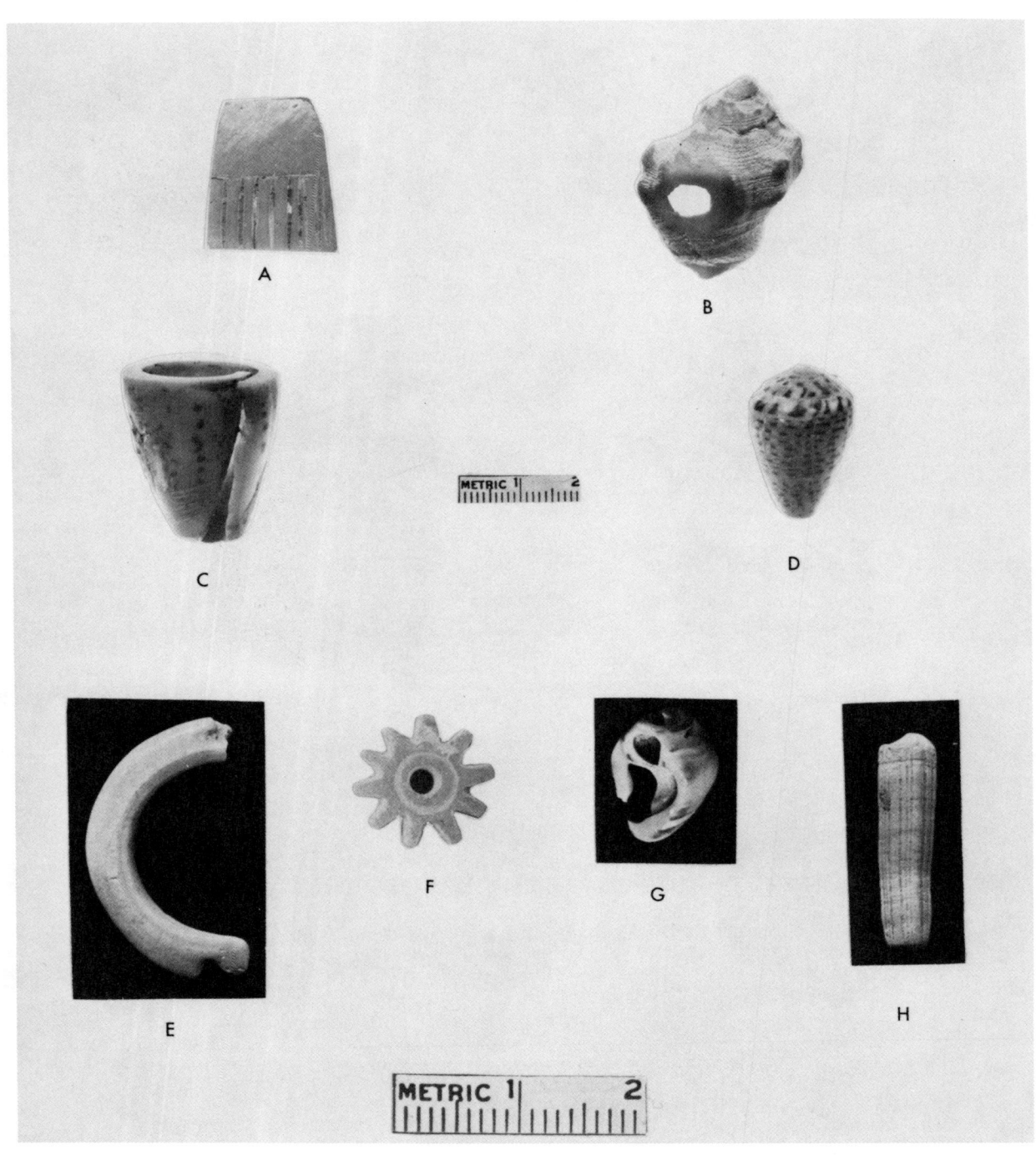

Plate 19. Marine Shell Artifacts. A. Mother-of-pearl inlay; X469, 60803 (B32). B. *Thais mancinella*; X144 (B21), note planar abrasion. C. *Canis tesselatus*; X579, 60580 (B34), note cut. D. *Canis tesselatus*; X225 (B23), intact. E. Ring cut from *Conus*; X363 (B29). F. Mother-of-pearl star; X069 (A6). G. *Engina mendicaria*; X177 (B23). H. *Dentalium* sp.; X213, 60173 (A15).

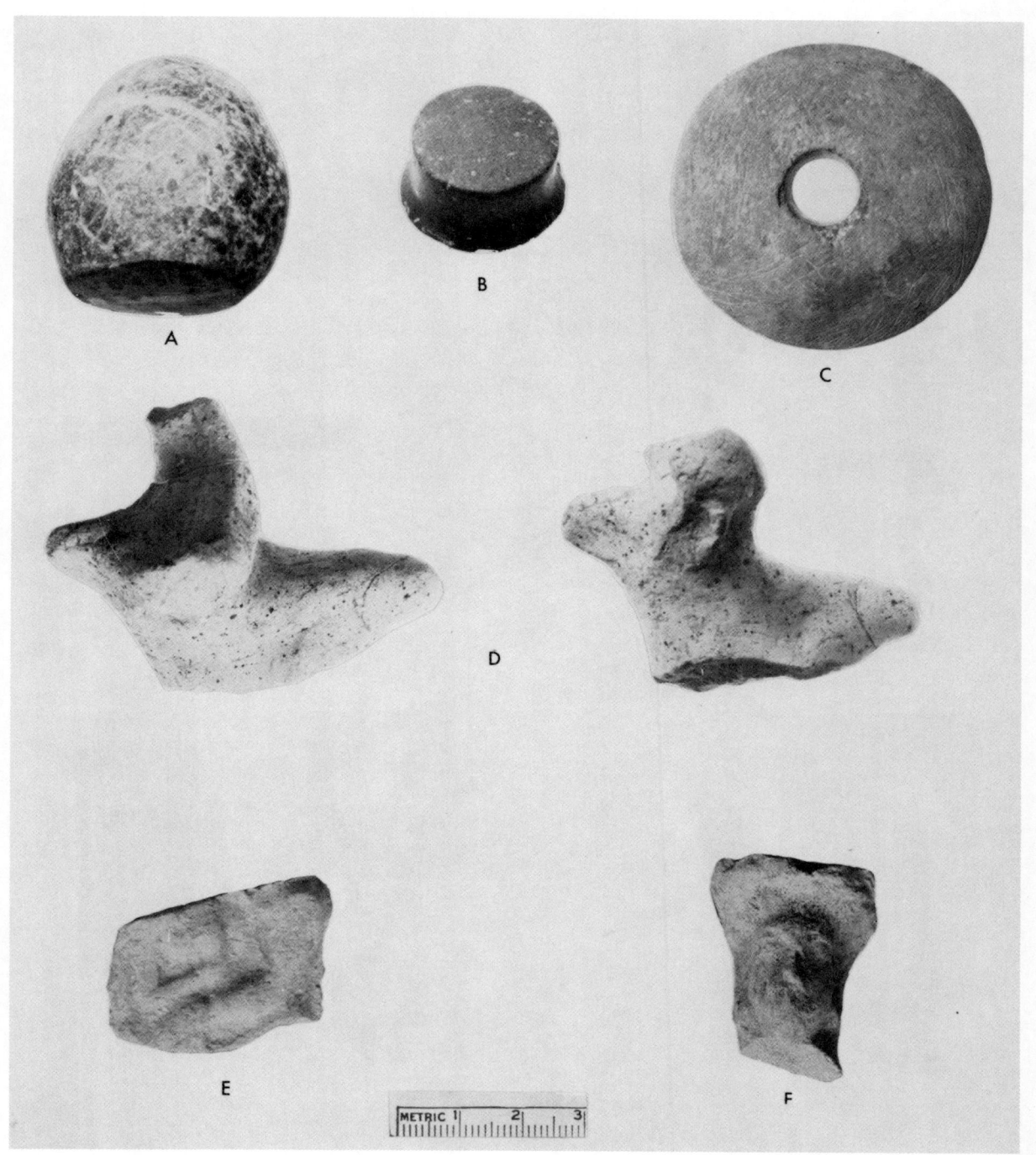

Plate 20. Fine Stone and Ceramic Items. A. Weight; X368, 60453 (B29). B. Flanged cylinder; X069 (A6). C. Stone whorl; X466, 60566 (B32). D. Animal figurine; X012 (B6). E. Figurine torso; X013 (B6). F. Figurine head; X020 (B7).

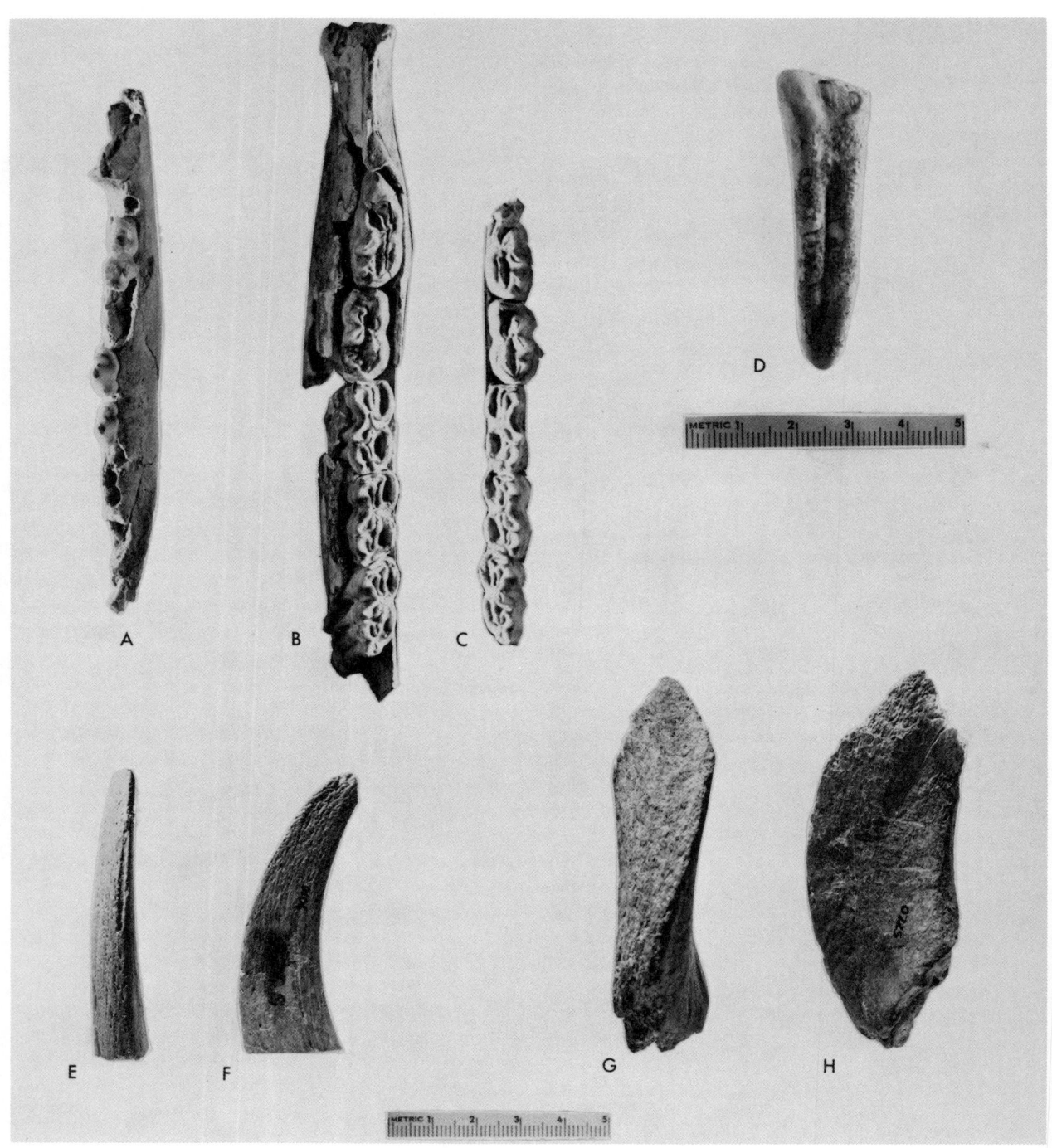

Plate 21. Select Mammalian Elements. A. Canid mandible exhibiting crowding of premolars supposedly characteristic of the dog, *Canis familaris*; X018 (B11-12). B-C. Equid mandibles, probably from a horse, *Equus equus*; X072 (B11-12). D. Equid lower incisor with anomolus wear facet on the labial surface; X072 (B11-12). E. Medially flattened goat horn core, anterior view; X106 (B18). F. Medially flattened goat horn core, medial view; X106 (B18). G. Twisted goat horn core, anterior view; X725 (B44). H. Twisted goat horn core, medial view; X725 (B44).